THE
ALL ENGLAND
LAW REPORTS
1997

Volume 1

Editor
CAROLINE VANDRIDGE-AMES LLM

London
BUTTERWORTHS

UNITED KINGDOM   Butterworths a Division of Reed Elsevier (UK) Ltd,
Halsbury House, 35 Chancery Lane, **London** WC2A 1EL
and 4 Hill Street, **Edinburgh** EH2 3JZ

AUSTRALIA   Butterworths, **Sydney, Melbourne, Brisbane, Adelaide, Perth, Canberra** and **Hobart**

CANADA   Butterworths Canada Ltd, **Toronto** and **Vancouver**

IRELAND   Butterworth (Ireland) Ltd, **Dublin**

MALAYSIA   Malayan Law Journal Sdn Bhd, **Kuala Lumpur**

NEW ZEALAND   Butterworths of New Zealand Ltd, **Wellington** and **Auckland**

SINGAPORE   Reed Elsevier (Singapore) Pte Ltd, **Singapore**

SOUTH AFRICA   Butterworths Publishers (Pty) Ltd, **Durban**

USA   Michie, **Charlottesville**, Virginia

ISBN for the complete set of volumes: 0 406 85159 X
for this volume: 0 406 894132

Printed and bound in Great Britain by William Clowes Ltd, Beccles and London

House of Lords

The Lord High Chancellor of Great Britain: Lord Mackay of Clashfern

Lords of Appeal in Ordinary

Lord Goff of Chieveley
Lord Browne-Wilkinson
Lord Mustill
Lord Slynn of Hadley
Lord Lloyd of Berwick
Lord Nolan
Lord Nicholls of Birkenhead

Lord Steyn
Lord Hoffmann
Lord Clyde
Lord Hope of Craighead
Lord Hutton of Bresagh
(appointed 6 January 1997)

Court of Appeal

The Lord High Chancellor of Great Britain

The Lord Chief Justice of England: Lord Bingham of Cornhill
(President of the Criminal Division)

The Master of the Rolls: Lord Woolf
(President of the Civil Division)

The President of the Family Division: Sir Stephen Brown

The Vice-Chancellor: Sir Richard Rashleigh Folliott Scott

Lords Justices of Appeal

Sir Martin Charles Nourse
Dame Ann Elizabeth Oldfield Butler-Sloss
Sir Murray Stuart-Smith
Sir Christopher Stephen Thomas Jonathan
    Thayer Staughton
Sir Anthony James Denys McCowan
Sir Alexander Roy Asplan Beldam
Sir Andrew Peter Leggatt
Sir Paul Joseph Morrow Kennedy
Sir David Cozens-Hardy Hirst
Sir Simon Denis Brown
Sir Anthony Howell Meurig Evans
Sir Christopher Dudley Roger Rose
Sir John Douglas Waite
Sir John Ormond Roch
Sir Peter Leslie Gibson
Sir John Stewart Hobhouse
Sir Denis Robert Maurice Henry
Sir Mark Oliver Saville

Sir Peter Julian Millett
Sir Swinton Barclay Thomas
Sir Robert Andrew Morritt
Sir Philip Howard Otton
Sir Robin Ernest Auld
    (Senior Presiding Judge for England and
    Wales)
Sir Malcolm Thomas Pill
Sir William Aldous
Sir Alan Hylton Ward
Sir Michael Hutchison
Sir Konrad Hermann Theodor Schiemann
Sir Nicholas Addison Phillips
Sir Mathew Alexander Thorpe
Sir Mark Howard Potter
Sir Henry Brooke
Sir Igor Judge
Sir George Mark Waller
Sir John Frank Mummery

High Court of Justice

The Lord High Chancellor of Great Britain
The Lord Chief Justice of England
The President of the Family Division
The Vice-Chancellor
The Senior Presiding Judge for England and Wales
The puisne judges of the High Court

Chancery Division

The Lord High Chancellor of Great Britain
The Vice-Chancellor

Sir Jeremiah LeRoy Harman
Sir Donald Keith Rattee
Sir Francis Mursell Ferris
Sir John Murray Chadwick
Sir Jonathan Frederic Parker
(Vice-Chancellor of the County Palatine
of Lancaster)
Sir John Edmund Frederic Lindsay
Dame Mary Howarth Arden
Sir Edward Christopher Evans-Lombe

Sir Robin Raphael Hayim Jacob
Sir William Anthony Blackburne
Sir Gavin Anthony Lightman
Sir Robert Walker
Sir Robert John Anderson Carnwath
Sir Colin Percy Farquharson Rimer
Sir Hugh Ian Lang Laddie
Sir Timothy Andrew Wigram Lloyd
Sir David Edmund Neuberger

Queen's Bench Division

The Lord Chief Justice of England

Sir Christopher James Saunders French
Sir Iain Charles Robert McCullough
Sir Oliver Bury Popplewell
Sir Richard Howard Tucker
Sir Patrick Neville Garland
Sir Michael John Turner
Sir John Downes Alliott
Sir Harry Henry Ognall
Sir John Arthur Dalziel Owen
Sir Francis Humphrey Potts
Sir Richard George Rougier
Sir Ian Alexander Kennedy
Sir Stuart Neill McKinnon
Sir Thomas Scott Gillespie Baker
Sir Edwin Frank Jowitt
Sir Douglas Dunlop Brown
Sir Michael Morland
Sir Roger John Buckley
Sir Anthony Brian Hidden
Sir John Michael Wright
Sir Charles Barrie Knight Mantell
Sir John Christopher Calthorpe Blofeld

Sir Peter John Cresswell
Sir Anthony Tristram Kenneth May
Sir John Grant McKenzie Laws
Dame Ann Marian Ebsworth
Sir Simon Lane Tuckey
Sir David Nicholas Ramsey Latham
Sir Christopher John Holland
Sir John William Kay
Sir Richard Herbert Curtis
Sir Stephen John Sedley
Dame Janet Hilary Smith
Sir Anthony David Colman
Sir Anthony Peter Clarke
Sir John Anthony Dyson
Sir John Thayne Forbes
Sir Michael Alexander Geddes Sachs
Sir Stephen George Mitchell
Sir Rodger Bell
Sir Michael Guy Vicat Harrison
Sir Bernard Anthony Rix
Dame Anne Heather Steel
Sir William Marcus Gage

[continued on next page]

Queen's Bench Division *(continued)*

Sir Jonathan Hugh Mance
Sir Andrew Centlivres Longmore
Sir Thomas Richard Atkin Morison
Sir Richard Joseph Buxton
Sir David Wolfe Keene
Sir Andrew David Collins
Sir Maurice Ralph Kay
Sir Frank Brian Smedley
Sir Anthony Hooper
Sir Alexander Neil Logie Butterfield

Sir George Michael Newman
Sir David Anthony Poole
Sir Martin James Moore-Bick
Sir Julian Hugh Gordon Langley
Sir Roger John Laugharne Thomas
Sir Robert Franklyn Nelson
Sir Roger Grenfell Toulson
Sir Michael John Astill
Sir Alan George Moses
Sir Timothy Edward Walker

Family Division

The President of the Family Division

Sir Anthony Barnard Hollis
Sir Edward Stephen Cazalet
Sir Robert Lionel Johnson
Dame Joyanne Winifred Bracewell
Sir Michael Bryan Connell
Sir Jan Peter Singer
Sir Nicholas Allan Roy Wilson
Sir Nicholas Peter Rathbone Wall

Sir Andrew Tristram Hammett Kirkwood
Sir Christopher Stuart-White
Dame Brenda Marjorie Hale
Sir Hugh Peter Derwyn Bennett
Sir Edward James Holman
Dame Mary Claire Hogg
Sir Christopher John Sumner

CITATION

These reports are cited thus:

[1997] 1 All ER

REFERENCES

These reports contain references to the following major works of legal reference described in the manner indicated below.

Halsbury's Laws of England

The reference 26 *Halsbury's Laws* (4th edn) para 577 refers to paragraph 577 on page 296 of volume 26 of the fourth edition of *Halsbury's Laws of England*.

The reference 7(1) *Halsbury's Laws* (4th edn reissue) para 267 refers to paragraph 267 on page 200 of reissue volume 7(1) of the fourth edition of *Halsbury's Laws of England*.

Halsbury's Statutes of England and Wales

The reference 40 *Halsbury's Statutes* (4th edn) 734 refers to page 734 of volume 40 of the fourth edition of *Halsbury's Statutes of England and Wales*.

The reference 19 *Halsbury's Statutes* (4th edn) (1994 reissue) 497 refers to page 497 of the 1994 reissue of volume 19 of the fourth edition of *Halsbury's Statutes of England and Wales*.

The Digest
(formerly The English and Empire Digest)

The reference 37(2) *Digest* (Reissue) 424, *2594* refers to case number 2594 on page 424 of the reissue of green band volume 37(2) of *The Digest*.

The reference 27(1) *Digest* (2nd reissue) 330, *2849* refers to case number 2849 on page 330 of the second reissue of green band volume 27(1) of *The Digest*.

Halsbury's Statutory Instruments

The reference 17 *Halsbury's Statutory Instruments* 305 refers to page 305 of volume 17 of the grey volumes series of *Halsbury's Statutory Instruments*.

The reference 14 *Halsbury's Statutory Instruments* (1994 reissue) 201 refers to page 201 of the 1994 reissue of volume 14 of the grey volumes series of *Halsbury's Statutory Instruments*.

Cases reported in volume 1

Digest of cases reported in volume 1

House of Lords petitions

This list, which covers the period 13 December 1996 to 20 March 1997, sets out all cases which have formed the subject of a report in the All England Law Reports in which an Appeal Committee of the House of Lords has, subsequent to the publication of that report, refused leave to appeal. Where the result of a petition for leave to appeal was known prior to the publication of the relevant report a note of that result appears at the end of the report.

Circuit Systems Ltd (in liq) v Zuken-Redac (UK) Ltd [1996] 3 All ER 748, CA. Leave to cross-appeal refused 5 March 1997 (Lord Mustill, Lord Nolan and Lord Clyde)

Mulcahy v Ministry of Defence [1996] 2 All ER 758, CA. Leave to appeal refused 17 February 1997 (Lord Browne-Wilkinson, Lord Lloyd of Berwick and Lord Steyn)

R v Crown Court at Maidstone, ex p Lever, R v Crown Court at Maidstone, ex p Connell [1995] 2 All ER 35, CA. Leave to appeal refused 17 February 1997 (Lord Browne-Wilkinson, Lord Lloyd of Berwick and Lord Steyn)

R v Secretary of State for the Home Dept, ex p Rahman [1997] 1 All ER 796, CA. Leave to appeal refused 19 March 1997 (Lord Slynn, Lord Steyn and Lord Hope)

Rock Refrigeration Ltd v Jones and another

b

COURT OF APPEAL, CIVIL DIVISION

SIMON BROWN, MORRITT AND PHILLIPS LJJ

3 SEPTEMBER, 10 OCTOBER 1996

c
Restraint of trade by agreement – Employer and employee – Restrictive covenants in contract of employment to take effect on termination of contract 'howsoever arising' or 'howsoever occasioned' – Whether unreasonable and in unlawful restraint of trade.

In 1995 the plaintiff company promoted the first defendant from general
d engineering manager to industrial sales director. The first defendant's new contract of employment contained restrictive trade covenants on his part which were variously expressed to take effect after the termination of the contract 'howsoever arising' or 'howsoever occasioned'. He later gave one month's notice, and in January 1996 left the plaintiffs' employment and went to work for the second defendants, who were their competitors. Thereafter the plaintiffs
e issued proceedings against the defendants, claiming damages for breach of covenant and injunctive relief. At an early trial of the claim for injunctive relief claim the judge held that the restrictive covenants were necessarily unreasonable and therefore in unlawful restraint of trade and unenforceable since by their terms they could apply even if the employer repudiated the contract. The
f plaintiffs appealed, contending that the covenants should be construed as not applying in the event of a repudiatory breach by the employer.

Held – Even if the restrictive covenants were capable on their true construction of applying in the event of a repudiatory breach by the employer, they were not
g on that account necessarily unreasonable and in unlawful restraint of trade, since (per Simon Brown and Morritt LJJ; Phillips LJ dubitante) where an employer repudiated a contract of employment and that repudiation was accepted by the employee, the employee was thereupon released from his obligations under the contract and restrictive covenants otherwise valid against him could not be enforced, and (per Phillips LJ) such repudiation was merely a remote possibility.
h Accordingly, the appeal would be allowed (see p 8 e, p 9 f, p 10 g j, p 13 g h, p 14 d, p 18 f and p 20 f to j, post).

General Billposting Co Ltd v Atkinson [1908–10] All ER Rep 619 applied.

Briggs v Oates [1991] 1 All ER 407, *Living Design (Home Improvements) Ltd v Davidson* [1994] IRLR 69 and *PR Consultants Scotland Ltd v Mann* [1996] IRLR 188
j considered.

D v M [1996] IRLR 192 overruled.

Notes

For restraint of trade, see 47 *Halsbury's Laws* (4th edn reissue) paras 13–39, and for cases on the subject, see 47(1) *Digest* (Reissue) 218–219, 901–910.

Cases referred to in judgments

A v B (30 March 1994, unreported), QBD.

Aramark plc v Sommerville 1995 SLT 749, Ct of Sess.

Briggs v Oates [1991] 1 All ER 407, [1990] ICR 473.

Coral (UK) Ltd v Richardson [1995] CA Transcript 1386.

D v M [1996] IRLR 192.

Dairy Crest Ltd v Pigott [1989] ICR 92, CA.

Deacons (a firm) v Bridge [1984] 2 All ER 19, [1984] AC 705, [1984] 2 WLR 837, PC.

Freeth v Burr (1874) LR 9 CP 208, [1874–80] All ER Rep 751.

General Billposting Co Ltd v Atkinson [1909] AC 118, [1908–10] All ER Rep 619, HL.

Heyman v Darwins Ltd [1942] 1 All ER 337, [1942] AC 356, HL.

Littlewoods Organisation Ltd v Harris [1978] 1 All ER 1026, [1977] 1 WLR 1472, CA.

Living Design (Home Improvements) Ltd v Davidson [1994] IRLR 69, Ct of Sess.

Lux Traffic Controls Ltd v Healey 1994 SLT 1153, Ct of Sess.

Marshall (Thomas) (Exports) Ltd v Guinle [1978] 3 All ER 193, [1979] Ch 227, [1978] 3 WLR 116.

Mersey Steel and Iron Co Ltd v Naylor Benzon & Co (1884) 9 App Cas 434, [1881–5] All ER Rep 365, HL.

Mont (J A) (UK) Ltd v Mills [1993] IRLR 172, CA.

Photo Production Ltd v Securicor Transport Ltd [1980] 1 All ER 556, [1980] AC 827, [1980] 2 WLR 283, HL.

PR Consultants Scotland Ltd v Mann [1996] IRLR 188, Ct of Sess.

Cases also cited or referred to in skeleton arguments

Business Seatings (Renovations) Ltd v Broad [1989] ICR 729.

Clarke v Newland [1991] 1 All ER 397, CA.

Dennis (W) & Sons Ltd v Tunnard Bros & Moore (1911) 56 SJ 162.

Haynes v Doman [1899] 2 Ch 13, CA.

Home Counties Dairies Ltd v Skilton [1970] 1 All ER 1227, [1970] 1 WLR 526, CA.

John Michael Design plc v Cooke [1987] 2 All ER 332, [1987] ICR 445, CA.

Lansing Linde Ltd v Kerr [1991] 1 All ER 418, [1991] 1 WLR 251, CA.

Lawrence David Ltd v Ashton [1989] ICR 123, CA.

Lucas (T) & Co Ltd v Mitchell [1972] 3 All ER 689, [1974] Ch 129, CA.

Office Angels Ltd v Rainer-Thomas [1991] IRLR 214, CA.

Plowman (G W) & Son Ltd v Ash [1964] 2 All ER 10, [1964] 1 WLR 568, CA.

Rex Stewart Jeffries Parker Ginsberg Ltd v Parker [1988] IRLR 483, CA.

Sadler v Imperial Life Assurance Co of Canada Ltd [1988] IRLR 388.

Scorer v Seymour-Johns [1966] 3 All ER 347, [1966] 1 WLR 1419, CA.

Smith (C R) Glaziers (Dunfermline) Ltd v McGuire (12 December 1986, unreported), Ct of Sess.

Spafax Ltd v Harrison, Spafax Ltd v Taylor [1980] IRLR 442, CA.

Appeal

By notice dated 31 July 1996 Rock Refrigeration Ltd (Rock) appealed from the order of Sir Michael Davies sitting as a judge of the High Court on 22 July 1996 dismissing their claims for damages and injunctive relief against Michael Anthony Jones and Seward Refrigeration Ltd, (the respondents, their former employee and his new employer) for breach of restrictive trade covenants. The facts are set out in the judgment of Simon Brown LJ.

a   *Eldred Tabachnik QC* and *Antony Sendall* (instructed by *Ashurst Morris Crisp*) for
      Rock.
      Andrew Stafford (instructed by *Eversheds*, Manchester) for the respondents.

                                                                    Cur adv vult

b   10 October 1996. The following judgments were delivered.

SIMON BROWN LJ. The question raised on this appeal is one of some
importance in the law relating to covenants in restraint of trade. Shortly stated it
is this: is a restrictive covenant which is expressly provided to take effect upon the
termination of a contract of employment 'howsoever occasioned' necessarily
c   unreasonable and thus unenforceable?

The judge below, Sir Michael Davies, held that it was, founding his decision
squarely upon Laws J's judgment in *D v M* [1996] IRLR 192. By this appeal the
erstwhile employers challenge that view.

It will readily be appreciated that this issue is one of general application whose
d   resolution cannot depend upon the precise circumstances of the present case.
The details here, indeed, are calculated rather to obscure than to illuminate the
point arising. I shall accordingly sketch in the facts only very briefly.

The appellants, Rock Refrigeration Ltd (Rock), the plaintiffs below, carry on
business in the Manchester area in connection with the sale, installation and
maintenance of refrigeration and environmental control equipment. They have
e   a number of associate companies carrying on broadly similar businesses
throughout England.

Amongst their competitors in the Manchester area is the respondent company,
Seward Refrigeration Ltd, the second defendants below. Seward Refrigeration's
managing director, Mr Brian Seward, who had formerly been managing director
f   of Rock, left in June 1993 to set up Seward Refrigeration. The other respondent,
Mr Michael Anthony Jones, was first employed by Rock in 1984. From 1985 to
1988 he had then worked for another company until rejoining Rock in October
1988, first as contracts manager, and later as general engineering manager. In
1995 he made it clear that he was not happy and that he had been approached by
another prospective employer (not Seward Refrigeration). To induce him to stay
g   Rock offered him, and he accepted, the position of industrial sales director. It was
a more responsible job and attracted a higher salary. His new contract was signed
on 27 October 1995 to come into effect on 1 January 1996.

In the event he remained in employment under this new contract for less than
a month. In December 1995 he was approached by Seward Refrigeration and was
h   offered the position of sales director with them. He accepted the offer, gave Rock
a month's notice, and during January 1996 duly left their employment.

On 26 April 1996 Rock issued the present writ, which included claims both for
damages and for injunctive relief based upon certain restrictive covenants in the
1995 contract.

j   On 10 May 1996 it was ordered that Rock's 'claim for final injunctive relief in
this action be dealt with by way of an early trial'. That trial took place in July 1996
before Sir Michael Davies and by agreement was confined to the question of the
lawfulness or otherwise of the restrictive covenants. In the event they were held
unlawful. Had they been held lawful, the further issues as to whether the
defendants or either of them had breached the covenants and, if so, what if any
damages Rock had suffered, would have had to be litigated thereafter.

The relevant covenants in the 1995 contract are these:

> '... 10. *Termination* ...
>
> 10.3 The expiration or determination of this Contract howsoever arising shall not operate to affect such of the provisions hereof as are expressed to operate or have effect thereafter and shall be without prejudice to any other accrued rights or remedies of the parties ...
>
> 11. *Prevention of Unfair Competition* ...
>
> 11.2 The Employee shall not except as authorised or required by his/her duties reveal or disclose or through any failure to exercise all due care and diligence cause any unauthorised disclosure to any person persons or company any of the trade secrets secret or confidential operations processes or dealings or any confidential information concerning the organisation business finance transactions details of its research projects (including their organisation and staff involved) list of details of customers prices or commercial relationships or affairs of the Company or any trade secrets or confidential information obtained by the Employee from any third party which may come to his knowledge. This restriction shall continue to apply after the termination of this Contract without limit in point of time but shall cease to apply to information or knowledge which may become public knowledge otherwise than by the Employees default ...
>
> 11.6 The Employee shall not while this Contract remains in force or for a period of twelve months after its termination howsoever occasioned: a) solicit or canvas or approach any person who to his/her knowledge was provided with goods or services by the Company at any time during the last year of his/her employment or was negotiating with the Company for the provision of goods or services by the Company at the date of termination provided that this sub-clause shall only be enforceable if and so long as the Company or its assigns shall carry on or continue to carry on the business of the Company or any part thereof; b) offer to any person with whom the Employee shall have dealt in the course of his/her employment goods or services which were provided to him/her by the Company during the year prior to the termination of his/her employment year or which were the subject of the negotiations at the date of that termination provided that this sub-clause shall only be enforceable if and so long as the Company or its assigns shall carry on or continue to carry on the business of the Company or any part thereof; c) accept orders from such a person for goods or services similar to or competitive with the goods or services which were provided to him/her by the Company during the last year of his/her employment or which were the subject of the negotiations at the time of that termination provided that this sub-clause shall only be enforceable if so long as the Company or its assigns shall carry on or continue to carry on the business of the Company or any part thereof ...'

That is a sufficient recitation of the facts with regard to the main issue. To set the scene for the resolution of the bare point of law now arising, I add only that the judge below found, and it is not now contested, that Rock did indeed have legitimate interests suitable for protection by way of restrictive covenants of this general nature. The question, I repeat, is whether these particular covenants are unlawful because they are declared to operate upon the determination of the contract 'howsoever arising' (cl 10.3, as applied to cl 11.2), or 'howsoever occasioned' (cl 11.6—and similarly, although no issue now arises with regard to it, cl 11.5).

In holding these covenants unenforceable Sir Michael Davies expressly agreed with and followed Laws J's judgment in *D v M*, from which he cited at length. It is essentially the correctness of that decision, therefore, which lies at the heart of this appeal and it is convenient at once to analyse the basis upon which it was
b reached.

Its starting point was the decision of the House of Lords in *General Billposting Co Ltd v Atkinson* [1909] AC 118, [1908–10] All ER Rep 619. The employers there had dismissed their employee 'in deliberate disregard of the terms of the contract' so as 'to evince an intention no longer to be bound by the contract'. In those circumstances it was held that the employee 'was thereupon justified in
c rescinding the contract and treating himself as absolved from the further performance of it on his part' so as no longer to be bound by the restrictive trade covenant which the employers were seeking to enforce. For reasons which will appear, it is worth noting that the case was decided 'on broader lines than those ... as to mutual and independent covenants' (see [1909] AC 118 at 122, [1908–10]
d All ER Rep 619 at 624).

I turn next to Scott J's decision in *Briggs v Oates* [1991] 1 All ER 407 where the question arose whether an assistant solicitor, whose contract had been brought to an end by the dissolution of the partnership which had employed him, was nevertheless bound by a restrictive provision expressed to operate once the agreement 'shall have determined for whatever reason'. Scott J (at 416–417) held
e not:

f 'I am unable to accept this submission. First, the obligation to which the defendant subjected himself under cl 8 cannot in my opinion be wholly separated from the other provisions of the agreement. The bargain between the plaintiff and Mr Rees on the one hand and the defendant on the other hand was in broad terms that, in return for a five-year employment on cl 6 remuneration terms, the defendant would, during the five-year term, discharge the duties imposed on him and after the termination of his employment observe the cl 8 restraint. The plaintiff and Mr Rees were together responsible for withholding from the defendant the benefit of
g employment for the last year of the five-year term. One year out of five is certainly not de minimis. The defendant was deprived, by a breach of contract for which the plaintiff and Mr Rees were together responsible, of the full consideration in exchange for which he accepted the cl 8 restriction. In such a case, in my opinion, he is not bound by the restriction. Secondly, and
h this is another way of putting the same point, the breach of contract for which, as I have held, the plaintiff and Mr Rees were jointly responsible was accepted by the defendant as putting an end to the contract. In such a case outstanding contractual obligations of the injured party are in law discharged together with the contract. This result does not, in my judgment, depend on the construction of the contract. But the point goes further. Suppose I am
j wrong. Suppose counsel for the plaintiff is right in submitting that under the true construction of the contract cl 8 binds the defendant regardless of whether the 1979 agreement is brought to an end by the decision of the plaintiff and Mr Rees to discontinue their partnership, or by some other wrongful dismissal of the defendant. The termination of the defendant's employment under the 1979 agreement could, on that footing, have taken

place at any time after 3 September 1979, but the defendant would still have been bound by the five-year restraint clause. It is well settled that the reasonableness of a restraint clause is to be tested by reference to the position as at the date of the contract of which it forms part. If the submissions of counsel for the plaintiff are right I would regard the cl 8 restraint as unreasonable as between the parties. A contract under which an employee could be immediately and wrongfully dismissed, but would nevertheless remain subject to an anti-competitive restraint, seems to me to be grossly unreasonable. I would not be prepared to enforce the restraint in such a contract.'

The first of those three reasons appears to rely on the 'mutuality' approach, not the approach which founded the decision of the majority of their Lordships' House in *General Billposting*. The second reason (perhaps not really on true analysis 'another way of putting the same [ie the mutuality] point') is, of course, the *General Billposting* approach.

It is the third reason, however, which is critical for present purposes since it is this which expressly underlies Laws J's decision in *D v M* [1996] IRLR 192. Indeed, Laws J described it as a principle which, albeit obiter, was 'clearly right' and which he understood and applied as follows (at 198):

'A restrictive covenant, having effect after the termination of a contract of service or for services, which on its face applies to the employer's benefit even where the termination has been induced by his own breach is necessarily unreasonable. Such a provision, if given effect, would constitute an evasion of the rule in *General Billposting* ([1909] AC 118, [1908–10] All ER Rep 619). Indeed, so far as I can see, the only purpose of inserting the material words ("for whatever reason" or "whether lawful or unlawful" or however otherwise it might be expressed) would be to secure coercive rights to the employer which would survive his own contractual misconduct. I cannot think that that would be reasonable.'

To Scott J's third reason it will be necessary to return. For the moment I observe only that it is expressly founded on the premise that reasons one and two are unsound. It begins 'Suppose I am wrong', and later continues 'If the submissions of counsel for the plaintiff are right'.

I pass now to the decision of Lord Coulsfield in the Outer House of the Court of Session in *Living Design (Home Improvements) Ltd v Davidson* [1994] IRLR 69, a decision from which Laws J drew support for his view. The relevant covenants in the *Living Design* case were to run for six months after the termination of the employee's employment 'however that comes about and whether lawful or not'. Lord Coulsfield (at 71) regarded that as 'manifestly wholly unreasonable', agreeing with Scott J's observations in *Briggs v Oates*. 'Those observations', he said, 'may have been obiter but they seem to me to be clearly correct'.

Laws J held there to be no distinction between the phrase in *D v M* 'terminated for any reason whatsoever' and the phrase just quoted from *Living Design*, noting indeed that counsel for the employers 'correctly, did not submit as much' (see [1996] IRLR 192 at 198).

Before turning to the arguments advanced on this appeal I must refer to one further Scottish case, *PR Consultants Scotland Ltd v Mann* [1996] IRLR 188, again in the Outer House of the Court of Session, a case decided before *D v M* but not in fact cited to Laws J. The covenant there was to operate for 12 months 'following *a* the termination of [the employee's] employment hereunder (howsoever caused)'. Lord Caplan said (at 191–192):

> *b* 'With regard to the argument that the reference to termination of employment "howsoever caused" is too wide, because it would countenance a situation where the employer could unlawfully dismiss his employee and then avail himself of the covenant, I find difficulty in following this. I find no difficulty with the views expressed by Lord Coulsfield and Lord Abernethy to the effect that a provision which provided for the operation of a covenant on a termination of employment however caused, be it lawfully or unlawfully on the part of the employer, would be objectionable. However, the question remains whether the particular provision being considered is as wide as this and I need not concern myself *c* with the construction that it was appropriate to place on the provisions in the *Living Design* case and [*Lux Traffic Controls Ltd v Healey* 1994 SLT 1153]. In my view the relevant provision "howsoever caused" in the present case is not apt to cover unlawful termination. There are many ways in which an employment contract can be lawfully terminated. The contract may be *d* terminated upon proper notice, the term of a contract may expire, the parties may agree that it should be terminated precipitately, or the employer may dismiss the employee if he has a legitimate reason for doing so. In all of these situations the employer will have a valid interest in applying the restrictive covenant to protect his business connection. On the other hand, there *e* would be no effective purpose in providing against a termination caused by the employer's unlawful conduct. If the employer were to dismiss his employee unlawfully then by the operation of the principle of mutuality of contractual provisions the restrictive covenant would not be available to him. In the situation considered by Lord Coulsfield in the *Living Design* case the contract (for some reason) specifically provided that the covenant should *f* cover an unlawful termination. However, in the absence of such a specific provision I do not think that it can be readily inferred that the parties intended that the contract be read so as to incorporate such a provision.'

Now to the present appeal. The main argument advanced by Mr Tabachnik QC for Rock was that Lord Caplan was right to recognise a distinction—indeed a *g* critical distinction—between, on the one hand, a covenant merely using the words 'howsoever caused', and on the other hand a provision which expressly then adds in the words 'whether lawful or not'. Whereas the latter plainly cannot be construed to exclude unlawful termination by the employer, the former can be. The covenants in the present case, he submits, just as in *PR Consultants* (and *h* indeed in *D v M*), should be construed as not applying in the event of termination by a wrongful act of the employer—or at any rate as not applying following a repudiatory breach by the employer (accepted by the employee).

In other words, the argument runs, the covenants can and should be saved by a process of construction, it being implicit in this argument that otherwise, as *j* Laws J held, they would offend the *General Billposting* principle, and thereby fall foul of the restraint of trade doctrine.

That argument, I should note, Mr Stafford for the respondents, seeks to meet by submitting that the 'howsoever caused' type of clause, even when standing alone, cannot properly be construed merely to include everything short of repudiatory breach, but not termination by repudiatory breach itself. He argues that the words 'howsoever caused' are themselves words of delimitation such as

necessarily require the court charged with their construction to look at the widest
possible circumstances in which termination may take place. The position is, he
suggests, different from when the covenant is expressed to run merely 'from
termination'; the court then *can* construe the provision to exclude termination by
wrongful act of the employer. On this approach, of course, *PR Consultants* rather
than *D v M* was the case wrongly decided on the point.

For my part, however, I believe that all these arguments proceed on a
fundamentally false footing. The law applicable to covenants and restraint of
trade simply has no relevance to the present situation. Of course covenants
which purport to subject ex-employees to greater restrictions than their erstwhile
employers can justify are unenforceable, and elementary it is too that the
legitimacy of such covenants falls to be determined as at the date they are entered
into and not by reference to the circumstances in which the employment
eventually terminates. But in my judgment the most basic premise upon which
the whole restraint of trade doctrine is founded is that, but for the doctrine's
application, the covenant in question would otherwise operate to restrain the
employee unduly. In other words the doctrine applies only where there exists an
otherwise enforceable covenant. It renders unenforceable what otherwise would
be enforceable.

The whole point about the *General Billposting* principle is that, in cases of
repudiatory breach by the employer, the employee is on that account released
from his obligations under the contract and restrictive covenants, otherwise valid
against him, accordingly cannot be enforced. Once that principle was decided, its
future application necessarily postulated that such restrictive covenants upon
their true construction would otherwise be enforceable against employees.

In short, Scott J was clearly right, not wrong, in the initial reasons he gave for
holding the restrictive covenant unenforceable against the wronged solicitor.
Thus the essential premise for his conclusion that the covenant would constitute
an unreasonable restraint of trade collapsed: a covenant which in certain
circumstances is discharged cannot be unenforceable under the restraint of trade
doctrine merely because in the self-same circumstances it would be unreasonable
to enforce it.

It further follows that in my judgment, assuming always that no relevant
distinction exists between Scots and English law with regard to mutuality or the
General Billposting principle, the Scots cases also proceed on an erroneous basis
(although not generally to an erroneous conclusion): logically it matters not
whether covenants include or exclude phrases such as 'whether lawfully or not'.
If they do, then to that extent they are merely writ in water, unenforceable under
the *General Billposting* principle.

Mr Stafford sought to argue that, despite the apparent sufficiency of the *General
Billposting* principle to meet the justice of the case when employers repudiate the
contract, there nevertheless remains a need for the restraint of trade doctrine to
strike down such clauses in their entirety. This, he submits, is so that employees
will not be unfairly influenced by them to their detriment, declining perhaps to
accept their employers' repudiatory breaches of contract lest the clauses
nevertheless operate to restrict their future opportunities. He seeks here to
invoke by analogy a dictum of my own in *J A Mont (UK) Ltd v Mills* [1993] IRLR
172 at 176, where I was endeavouring to explain why the courts should not too
readily construe restrictive covenants, ex facie too wide, as being subject to
implicit limitations:

a   'Thus would be perpetuated the long-recognised vice of ex-employees being left subject to apparently excessive restraints and yet quite unable, short of expensive litigation and at peril of substantial damages claims, to determine precisely what their rights may be.'

b   With the best will in the world, however, no expensive litigation is necessary to inform an employee that his employer's repudiatory breach of contract will absolve him from restrictive trade covenants. The point if anything seems to me rather to go the other way: on the respondent's argument it becomes necessary to construe these clauses not only to decide whether, assuming otherwise they are valid, they would operate unreasonably in restraint of trade once the employment is ended, but in addition to decide whether they appear inconsistent

c   with the rule in *General Billposting*.

Until this recent run of cases, erected upon the slender foundation of Scott J's obiter dictum in *Briggs v Oates*, this further process of construction had never been thought necessary. In my judgment it never was and is not now. That, rather than counsel's oversight down the years, explains the long line of previous

d   decisions in which covenants in restraint of trade in just the same terms as the present have been examined in the minutest detail without anyone ever suggesting that phrases like 'for any reason whatsoever' (the phrase used, for example, in the covenants examined in *Littlewoods Organisation Ltd v Harris* [1978] 1 All ER 1026, [1977] 1 WLR 1472 and *Deacons (a firm) v Bridge* [1984] 2 All ER 19, [1984] AC 705), or 'termination or cessation in any manner' (the phrase in *Dairy*

e   *Crest Ltd v Pigott* [1989] ICR 92) are themselves fatal to the enforceability of such covenants.

I would therefore hold *D v M* to have been wrongly decided.

All this, I should perhaps add, assumes: (a) that all restrictive covenants necessarily become unenforceable upon the employee's acceptance of the employer's repudiatory breach—ie that the *General Billposting* principle remains

f   wholly unaffected by the *Photo Production Ltd v Securicor Transport Ltd* [1980] 1 All ER 556, [1980] AC 827 line of authority; and (b) that any wrongful termination of the contract by the employers will necessarily involve a repudiatory breach. Clearly the plot thickens, although not to the respondents' advantage on the narrow point presently at issue, if either of those assumptions is unfounded.

g   I pass very briefly to two further arguments advanced by Mr Stafford under a respondent's notice by which he seeks to challenge the enforceability of these restrictive covenants.

The first argument centres on a further clause in the 1995 contract: '11.7 For the purpose of clauses 10.1 to 10.6 any reference to the Company shall include

h   any Associated Company.' (The reference to cll 10.1 to 10.6 is clearly in error for cll 11.1 to 11.6.)

What is said in this regard is that Mr Jones never had and was never expected to have any concern with Rock Refrigeration's associated companies so that this additional protection was unjustifiable. Let that be assumed—and certainly Rock

j   Refrigeration have never sought to enforce this aspect of the contract. Why then should this particular restriction not simply be severed? Mr Stafford submits that this would impermissibly alter the scope of cll 11.1 to 11.6, where the word 'company' is given an extended definition by cl 11.7. I disagree. Indeed, it seems to me difficult to think of a clearer case for severance: both the blue pencil test is satisfied, and so too in my judgment is the requirement that the meaning of the affected covenants are not substantially altered.

The second argument is to my mind no more substantial. It is that whereas *a* cl 11.5 (which I have not thought it necessary to set out) refers to not soliciting for employment by 'any person firm or company', cl 11.6 (one of the two clauses on which Rock *do* seek to rely) refers only to not canvassing 'any person', such person thereafter being referred to as 'his/her'. This, submits Mr Stafford, requires cl 11.6 to be construed as forbidding solely dealings with individuals. Again, I disagree. I see no reason whatever why 'person' in cl 11.6 should not be *b* construed according to its ordinary legal meaning, ie in the wider sense in which it was plainly intended to apply.

In reality, as Mr Stafford came close to acknowledging, this was a one point case. That point, for the reasons already given, I would decide in favour of Rock. I would accordingly allow this appeal. This result having been indicated to the parties at the conclusion of the argument on 3 September 1996, the respondents *c* gave fresh undertakings to comply with cl 11.2 (omitting the reference to 'trade secrets') and cl 11.6, both clauses being treated as unaffected by cl 11.7. I would now make whatever order is required to crystallise that result.

MORRITT LJ. The circumstances in which this appeal arises have been *d* described by Simon Brown LJ and I do not need to repeat them. The central question is whether, as the judge thought, the provision in cl 10.3 and repeated in cll 11.5 and 11.6 that covenants expressed to apply after the termination of the contract should so apply howsoever such termination was occasioned or arose necessarily caused those covenants to be void as unreasonable restraints of trade.

This is a point of considerable importance, for covenants in those or similar *e* terms are frequently employed in contracts of employment but have only recently been found to be invalid on this ground. Counsel for Rock have drawn to our attention no fewer than 12 reported cases decided between 1964 and 1991 in which covenants in similar terms were not alleged or found to be invalid on this ground; nine of them were decisions of the Court of Appeal and one was an *f* advice of the Privy Council.

The origin of the point is to be found in the judgment of Scott J in *Briggs v Oates* [1991] 1 All ER 407. This decision was followed by Lord Coulsfield in *Living Design (Home Improvements) Ltd v Davidson* [1994] IRLR 69, Laws J in *D v M* [1996] IRLR 192 and by Sir Michael Davies in this case.

It is not in doubt that if one party repudiates a contract and that repudiation is *g* accepted by the other the latter is discharged from all further performance of primary obligations of the contract in question in addition to acquiring a right to damages for compensation for the breach. If however the innocent party does not accept the repudiation then, although he has his remedy in damages for compensation for the breach, the contract continues to bind both parties. This *h* latter situation is comparable to that of a breach which does not go to the root of the contract and therefore does not constitute a repudiation capable of acceptance. In such a case the innocent party has his remedy in damages but remains bound to perform the contract.

These basic propositions apply to contracts of employment as they apply to *j* contracts of all other descriptions. Thus, in *General Billposting Co Ltd v Atkinson* [1909] AC 118, [1908–10] All ER Rep 619 an employee who had accepted the employer's repudiation of the contract of employment was not thereafter bound to perform or observe the restrictions on his activities after the termination of his employment contained in the contract. As the House of Lords held, he was 'justified in rescinding the contract and treating himself as absolved from the further performance of it on his part' (see [1909] AC 118 at 122, [1908–10] All ER a Rep 619 at 624). In principle, the breach of a contract of employment by the employer in consequence of which the contract of employment determined or the employment ceased must have been one which went to the root of the contract and was accepted as a repudiation by the employee. If the employer's breach was sufficiently serious to constitute a repudiation but the contract of employment remains in existence this must be because the employee decided not to accept the repudiation but to permit the contract to continue.

b It is against this background, as to which I do not believe there was or could be any dispute, that the judgment of Scott J in *Briggs v Oates* [1991] 1 All ER 407 must be read. In that case a firm of solicitors consisting of two partners agreed to employ the plaintiff, a solicitor, for five years. The contract of employment contained restrictions on his activities for a period after his employment 'shall

c have determined for whatever reasons'. Before the term of the employment had elapsed the partnership was dissolved. Scott J held that the dissolution of the partnership constituted a repudiation of the contract of employment. He then considered whether, as submitted, the restrictions contained in the contract could still be enforceable. He decided that they could not. He gave three reasons

d for that conclusion. The first was that the restriction was not separate from the employment contract. The second and third were expressed in these terms (at 417):

> 'Secondly, and this is another way of putting the same point, the breach of contract for which, as I have held, the plaintiff and Mr Rees were jointly
e responsible was accepted by the defendant as putting an end to the contract. In such a case outstanding contractual obligations of the injured party are in law discharged together with the contract. This result does not, in my judgment, depend on the construction of the contract. But the point goes further. Suppose I am wrong. Suppose counsel for the plaintiff is right in submitting that under the true construction of the contract cl 8 binds the
f defendant regardless of whether the 1979 agreement is brought to an end by the decision of the plaintiff and Mr Rees to discontinue their partnership, or by some other wrongful dismissal of the defendant. The termination of the defendant's employment under the 1979 agreement could, on that footing, have taken place at any time after 3 September 1979, but the defendant would still have been bound by the five-year restraint clause. It is well settled
g that the reasonableness of a restraint clause is to be tested by reference to the position at the date of the contract of which it forms part. If the submissions of counsel for the plaintiff are right I would regard the cl 8 restraint as unreasonable as between the parties. A contract under which an employee could be immediately and wrongfully dismissed, but would nevertheless
h remain subject to an anti-competitive restraint, seems to me to be grossly unreasonable. I would not be prepared to enforce the restraint in such a contract.'

It is clear that the second reason, and in substance the first also, was a straightforward application of the usual principles concerning the effect of the
j acceptance of a repudiation of a contract. As such Scott J was following *General Billposting Co Ltd v Atkinson* [1909] AC 118, [1908–10] All ER Rep 619. It is the third reason which has led to the decision under appeal and the other cases to which I have referred. That reason assumes that although the employment has been terminated by the wrongful act of the employer the contractual restraint on his post-employment activities still binds the employee. But in my view this assumption is contrary to the decision of the House of Lords in *General Billposting*

Co v Atkinson. If the employment has been terminated by the wrongful act of the
employer then, by definition, the employee must have accepted the repudiation　*a*
and is no longer bound by its other terms. It is true that a breach of contract by
the employer may not constitute a repudiation or if it does may not be accepted
by the employee. In either of these cases the contract of employment will
continue to bind both parties. But in such a case there is, in my view, no reason
why the restrictive clauses should be invalidated merely by reason of the breach　*b*
of contract by the employer which for one reason or another did not have the
effect of terminating the contract. Accordingly in my view the statement of
Scott J must be understood, as it appears to be, to be the rejection of the
submissions of counsel put forward on a hypothesis which did not arise in that
case and is, in my view, a legal impossibility.

The first of the two subsequent cases to which I have referred is *Living Design*　*c*
(Home Improvements) Ltd v Davidson [1994] IRLR 69. In that case the contract of
employment contained a restriction on the employee's activities 'after the
termination of her employment hereunder (however that comes about and
whether lawful or not)'. Lord Coulsfield said (at 71):

> 'In my view, a restrictive covenant which is phrased so as to operate on the　*d*
> termination of the employment of an employee, however that comes about,
> and whether lawfully or not, is manifestly wholly unreasonable. In that
> respect, I agree with the observations in *Briggs v Oates*. Those observations
> may have been obiter but they seem to me to be clearly correct.'

In my view it is clear from that passage that Lord Coulsfield considered that the　*e*
covenant was capable of operating as expressed in the case of a repudiation by the
employer and accepted by the employee for no one appears to have argued the
contrary. If the assumption were correct then I would agree with the conclusion.
But for the reasons I have given in my view the assumption is not correct. If the
contract is terminated because the employer's repudiation has been accepted by　*f*
the employee then the covenant will no longer bind the employee. Other cases
of unlawful termination would be where the employee has repudiated the
contract; in such a case it is reasonable that the covenant, if otherwise
unobjectionable, should be enforceable.

The third case is the decision of Laws J in *D v M* [1996] IRLR 192. In that case,
the restriction on the activities of the employee operated 'if this appointment　*g*
under this agreement is terminated for any reason whatsoever' and by reference
to the termination date defined as 'the date on which this agreement shall
determine irrespective of the cause or manner'. In his judgment Laws J referred
to the decision of the House of Lords in *General Billposting Co v Atkinson* as now
being settled and elementary law. He recorded the submission of the employee　*h*
that the covenants in question were 'an evasion of this principle and as such are
necessarily unreasonable'. His conclusion on this point is clearly expressed where
he said (at 198):

> 'In my judgment, upon the true construction of clause 13.5, the plaintiffs　*j*
> would be entitled to enforce the clause even though the contract's
> termination were caused by their own repudiatory breach ... A restrictive
> covenant, having effect after the termination of a contract of service or for
> services, which on its face applies to the employer's benefit even where the
> termination has been induced by his own breach is necessarily unreasonable.
> Such a provision, if given effect, would constitute an evasion of the rule in
> *General Billposting* ([1909] AC 118, [1908–10] All ER Rep 619). Indeed, so far

as I can see, the only purpose of inserting the material words ("for whatever reason" or "whether lawful or unlawful" or however otherwise it might be expressed) would be to secure coercive rights to the employer which would survive his own contractual misconduct. I cannot think that that would be reasonable.'

It does not appear to have been argued that the provision could not have that effect in law and could not therefore, whether it was an attempt or not, be an evasion of the rule in *General Billposting Co v Atkinson*. By contrast, the judge assumed that it would have effect contrary to the rule which he had earlier described as settled and elementary law.

In my view these two cases are founded on a misconception of what Scott J was holding in *Briggs v Oates*. His conclusion was grounded on the assumption that the restrictive covenant would be enforceable by the employer after the termination of the employment due to his breach without any finding to that effect. Lord Coulsfield and Laws J appear to have decided that the covenant would be so enforceable and would therefore be unreasonable. In my view the initial decision is wrong in law so that the conclusion does not follow.

That the judgment of Scott J in *Briggs v Oates* in this respect was not of general application appears to have been the view of the Court of Session in *Aramark plc v Sommerville* 1995 SLT 749 and *PR Consultants Scotland Ltd v Mann* [1996] IRLR 188, of Sachs J in *A v B* (30 March 1994, unreported) and of Balcombe LJ in *Coral (UK) Ltd v Richardson* [1995] CA Transcript 1386. In the first two of those cases the Court of Session construed phrases referring to the termination of employment 'for any reason whatever' or 'howsoever caused' so as not to extend to unlawful terminations. In the third case Sachs J said, in my view correctly:

'I am bound to say that based on authority taking account of the decision in *Living Design* and *Briggs v Oates* I cannot say for one moment that I am persuaded that the law now is as those two latter cases assert as opposed to a long line of cases to the contrary.'

In *Coral (UK) Ltd v Richardson* Balcombe LJ said that he did not consider that *Briggs v Oates* and *Living Design (Home Improvements) Ltd v Davidson* established that 'the words "for whatever reason" in a contract of this kind necessarily make it bad'.

Counsel for the employer submitted that the judge was wrong to have construed the covenant to apply to the case of the termination of the employment by reason of the employer's own repudiation. I do not see the question as depending on a point of construction. I would resolve it on the basis that the covenants, however expressed, cannot achieve the legally impossible. If the assumption of enforceability in the event of termination due to the employer's repudiation accepted by the employee is impossible then even if as a matter of language the covenant applied in those assumed circumstances the covenant cannot be unreasonable and therefore invalid as a whole on that account.

Counsel for the employee accepted that, however expressed, the post-employment restrictions were unenforceable in the event of the employment terminating because of the employer's repudiation accepted by the employee. He accepted that in those circumstances the employee would be discharged from any further performance of the contract. But he contended that the covenants were wholly invalid on the grounds of unreasonable restraint of trade because the claim, implicit in the form of covenants, to be entitled to enforce them in such circumstances, though an empty one, might have an effect on the mind of the employee in deciding whether or not to accept the employer's repudiation. I acknowledge the ingenuity of the submission but I am unable to accept it. The objection is to an unreasonable restraint on trade. The extravagant claim is unenforceable anyway without the need to resort to that objection. It is the restriction which would otherwise be valid which must be considered and its reasonableness or otherwise must be determined on its own merits.

It has been suggested that the application of the principle of *General Billposting Co Ltd v Atkinson* [1909] AC 118, [1908–10] All ER Rep 619 may enable an employee to retain for himself that which he should not when his employment has been terminated even by his acceptance of his employer's repudiation. For my part I doubt it. The employer's rights of property will remain unimpaired even if the employment terminated as a result of the employee's acceptance of his wrongful repudiation. As the employment will be at an end the employee's licence to use the company car, for example, will have come to an end too. Similar situations will arise with regard to the employer's trade secrets and papers and access to his property.

In my view, Sir Michael Davies was wrong on the central point of law argued before him and on which he based his decision. In relation to the points raised by the respondent's notice, which Sir Michael Davies did not decide, I agree with the conclusions of Simon Brown LJ and have nothing to add. In those circumstances I agree that this appeal should be allowed and that there should be an order in the terms to which Simon Brown LJ has referred.

PHILLIPS LJ. I agree that this appeal should be allowed, but I do not find the route that leads to this conclusion as clear as the other members of the court.

The principal issue

This action raises the issue of the validity of certain restrictive covenants, incorporated into the contract of employment between the appellant, Rock Refrigeration Ltd (Rock), and the respondent, Mr Michael Anthony Jones. These covenants purported to impose restraints upon Mr Jones which operated 'while this Contract remains in force or for a period of twelve months after its termination howsoever occasioned' (see cll 11.5 and 11.6). The effect of this provision was underlined by cl 10.3, which provided:

> 'The expiration or determination of this Contract howsoever arising shall not operate to affect such of the provisions hereof as are expressed to operate or have effect thereafter and shall be without prejudice to any other accrued rights or remedies of the parties.'

Before the trial judge Mr Stafford on behalf of Mr Jones successfully contended: (1) that on the true construction of these provisions the restrictive covenants purported to remain binding even in the event of the wrongful termination of Mr Jones' employment by Rock; and (2) that this feature rendered the covenants an unreasonable restraint of trade, with the consequence that they were void. For myself I have no difficulty in accepting the first proposition. The second requires a more detailed analysis.

The cardinal principle

The validity of the covenants in issue on this appeal falls to be determined according to the following principle. A restrictive covenant in a contract of employment will be void ab initio unless the restraints that it imposes are reasonable having regard to the interests of the parties and of the public. In

a practice this test of what is reasonable tends to be resolved by considering
whether or not the restrictive covenant is reasonably necessary to protect
legitimate interests of the employer in preserving goodwill and confidential
information: see *Chitty on Contracts* (27th edn, 1994) para 16-084.

It is Mr Stafford's contention, however, that a covenant cannot be reasonable
if it purports to bind the employee even after his employment has been
b terminated consequent upon the repudiation of the contract by the employer.
The starting point in considering this contention must be the decision of the
House of Lords in *General Billposting Co Ltd v Atkinson* [1909] AC 118, [1908–10] All
ER Rep 619.

The rule in General Billposting

c In *General Billposting* a manager was employed on terms that he was entitled to
12 months' notice and subject to a covenant that after termination of his
employment he would not compete with his employers within an area of a
specified radius. His employers wrongfully dismissed him without notice, and
then sought to enforce this covenant. The House of Lords held that the covenant
d did not survive the termination. The reasoning of the majority appears from the
following passage in the speech of Lord Collins ([1909] AC 118 at 122, [1908–10]
All ER Rep 619 at 624):

> 'I think the true test applicable to the facts of this case is that which was laid
> down by Lord Coleridge C.J. in *Freeth* v. *Burr* ((1874) LR 9 CP 208 at 213,
> [1874–80] All ER Rep 751 at 753), and approved in *Mersey Steel Company* v.
e > *Naylor* ((1884) 9 App Cas 434, [1881–5] All ER Rep 365) in the House of Lords,
> "That the true question is whether the acts and conduct of the party evince
> an intention no longer to be bound by the contract." I think the Court of
> Appeal had ample ground for drawing this inference from the conduct of the
> appellants here in dismissing the respondent in deliberate disregard of the
f > terms of the contract, and that the latter was thereupon justified in
> rescinding the contract and treating himself as absolved from the further
> performance of it on his part. I think the appeal should be dismissed.'

The effect of this decision, and of a number of cases which have followed it, is
summarised in *Chitty* para 16-080 as follows:
g
> 'If the party in whose favour a covenant in restraint of trade is entered into
> wrongly repudiates the agreement in which the covenant is contained, the
> covenantor is thereby discharged from his obligation. Wrongful dismissal,
> therefore, puts an end to any restrictive covenant in a contract of
> employment.'
h
It is implicit in the decision in *General Billposting*: (1) that the restrictive covenant
in that case purported to apply even after wrongful termination of the employee's
contract; and (2) that the covenant remained valid up to the moment of wrongful
termination. If Mr Stafford's submission in the present case is correct, there is no
room for the rule in *General Billposting*. If a restrictive covenant in a contract of
j employment which purports to bind even after a repudiatory termination of that
employment by the employer is necessarily void ab initio, no question can ever
arise as to whether the employee has been discharged from complying with the
covenant by the employer's repudiation.

Until recently, no suggestion has been made that covenants such as the ones in
this case are void ab initio because they purport to apply even after a repudiatory
termination. Mr Tabachnik QC, on behalf of Rock, referred us to a series of some

12 cases which proceeded on the basis that a restrictive covenant wide enough to apply even after repudiation of the contract by the employer was not rendered invalid simply on that account. Mr Stafford has, however, founded his argument on three recent decisions to which I now turn.

The recent decisions

In *Briggs v Oates* [1991] 1 All ER 407 two partners in a firm of solicitors repudiated the contract under which they employed the defendant. That contract contained a covenant which imposed restraints upon the defendant for a period after his employment 'shall have determined for whatever reasons'. Proceedings were brought by one of the partners to enforce the restrictive covenant. Scott J held that the restrictive covenant did not survive the termination of the defendant's contract of employment. His reasons appear in the following passage of his judgment (at 416–417):

'If the 1979 agreement was, as I hold, brought to an end by the breach of contract on the part of the plaintiff and Mr Rees, is the defendant nonetheless bound by the restraint provisions in cl 8? Counsel for the plaintiff argues that on the wording of cl 8 the clause applies, notwithstanding the manner in which the plaintiff's employment pursuant to the 1979 agreement might come to an end. He relied on the words "shall have determined for whatever reason". Even if the reason were the wrongful dismissal of the defendant cl 8, he submitted, would on its true construction still apply and bind. I am unable to accept this submission. First, the obligation to which the defendant subjected himself under cl 8 cannot in my opinion be wholly separated from the other provisions of the agreement. The bargain between the plaintiff and Mr Rees on the one hand and the defendant on the other hand was in broad terms that, in return for a five-year employment on cl 6 remuneration terms, the defendant would, during the five-year term, discharge the duties imposed on him and after the termination of his employment observe the cl 8 restraint. The plaintiff and Mr Rees were together responsible for withholding from the defendant the benefit of employment for the last year of the five-year term. One year out of five is certainly not de minimis. The defendant was deprived, by a breach of contract for which the plaintiff and Mr Rees were together responsible, of the full consideration in exchange for which he accepted the cl 8 restriction. In such a case, in my opinion, he is not bound by the restriction. Secondly, and this is another way of putting the same point, the breach of contract for which, as I have held, the plaintiff and Mr Rees were jointly responsible was accepted by the defendant as putting an end to the contract. In such a case outstanding contractual obligations of the injured party are in law discharged together with the contract. This result does not, in my judgment, depend on the construction of the contract. But the point goes further. Suppose I am wrong. Suppose counsel for the plaintiff is right in submitting that under the true construction of the contract cl 8 binds the defendant regardless of whether the 1979 agreement is brought to an end by the decision of the plaintiff and Mr Rees to discontinue their partnership, or by some other wrongful dismissal of the defendant. The termination of the defendant's employment under the 1979 agreement could, on that footing, have taken place at any time after 3 September 1979, but the defendant would still have been bound by the five-year restraint clause. It is well settled that the reasonableness of a restraint clause is to be tested by reference to the position

a

as at the date of the contract of which it forms part. If the submissions of counsel for the plaintiff are right I would regard the cl 8 restraint as unreasonable as between parties. A contract under which an employee could be immediately and wrongfully dismissed, but would nevertheless remain subject to an anti-competitive restraint, seems to me to be grossly unreasonable. I would not be prepared to enforce the restraint in such a contract.'

b

It is plain that the reason for Scott J's decision was that the rule in *General Billposting v Atkinson* applied. It was only on the basis that he was wrong in this conclusion that he indicated that he would hold void a clause which would otherwise have the effect of imposing restraints after wrongful termination of the defendant's employment. This expression of view was thus both hypothetical and obiter.

c

Scott J's obiter view was followed by the Court of Session in interlocutory proceedings in *Living Design (Home Improvements) Ltd v Davidson* [1994] IRLR 69. In that case the petitioners sought an interdict restraining the respondent from breach of a restrictive covenant which purported to apply for six months after the termination of her employment with them 'however that comes about and whether lawful or not'. It was common ground that the respondent's employment had been terminated by repudiation. The issue was whether the petitioners had wrongfully dismissed the respondent or whether they had been entitled to do so consequent upon her repudiation. It also seems to have been common ground that the restrictive covenant, if reasonable, would be effective notwithstanding the repudiatory termination—whether by employers or employee. In refusing the interdict, Lord Coulsfield said (at 71):

d

e

'In my view, a restrictive covenant which is phrased so as to operate on the termination of the employment of an employee, however that comes about, and whether lawfully or not, is manifestly wholly unreasonable. In that respect, I agree with the observations in *Briggs v Oates*.'

f

It is apparent, when Lord Coulsfield's judgment is read in its entirety, that he was proceeding on the premise that the covenant in that case would, had it been valid, have survived termination consequent upon the employers' repudiation.

The final decision upon which Mr Stafford relied was that of Laws J in *D v M* [1996] IRLR 192. This, also, was a case where employers sought an interlocutory injunction enforcing an employer's restrictive covenant in circumstances where the primary issue was whether the termination of employment was consequent upon repudiation by the employers or by the employee. The contract provided that the covenant should take effect upon termination of employment 'for any reason whatsoever'. In refusing an injunction Laws J gave the following reason (at 198):

g

h

'In my judgment, upon the true construction of clause 13.5, the plaintiffs would be entitled to enforce the clause even though the contract's termination were caused by their own repudiatory breach. There is no distinction to be made between the phrase "terminated for any reason whatsoever", which therein appears, and the phrase "termination ... however that comes about and whether lawful or not" which was the expression used in *Living Design*. Miss McNeill, correctly, did not submit as much. She accepted that to succeed on this part of the case she would have to persuade me that *Living Design* was erroneous, as were the relevant remarks of Scott J in *Briggs*. Neither of these decisions is binding upon me,

j

and the observations of Scott J were obiter. But in my judgment the principle
enunciated in those decisions is clearly right. A restrictive covenant, having
effect after the termination of a contract of service or for services, which on
its face applies to the employer's benefit even where the termination has
been induced by his own breach is necessarily unreasonable. Such a
provision, if given effect, would constitute an evasion of the rule in *General
Billposting* ([1909] AC 118, [1908–10] All ER Rep 619). Indeed, so far as I can
see, the only purpose of inserting the material words ("for whatever reason"
or "whether lawful or unlawful" or however otherwise it might be
expressed) would be to secure coercive rights to the employer which would
survive his own contractual misconduct. I cannot think that that would be
reasonable.'

Laws J appears to have proceeded upon the basis that it was at least possible that
the covenant could evade the rule in *General Billposting v Atkinson*.

Before us Mr Stafford did not seek to contend that a restrictive covenant,
however drafted, could survive the termination of the employment consequent
upon the employer's repudiation. He conceded that a covenant which purported
to have this effect agreed to something which was impossible in law. His
argument was that it was mischievous for an employer to incorporate within a
contract of employment a covenant which purported to bind in circumstances
where this was a legal impossibility, and that this mischief alone justified
declaring such a covenant void.

In my judgment, once Mr Stafford rejected the premise underlying the
relevant parts of the three recent judgments upon which he relied, he cut away
any support that they could afford to his case. If a covenant, otherwise
reasonable, purports to remain binding in circumstances where the law will
inevitably strike it down, I can see no justification for holding that it is, on that
account, in unlawful restraint of trade. Thus if Mr Stafford is correct to concede
that the rule in *General Billposting* is of universal application, he cannot
successfully support the decision of Sir Michael Davies. This is the short and
simple route which leads to the conclusion that this appeal should be allowed.

The alternative route

In the course of argument I expressed reservations as to whether the rule in
General Billposting was consistent with more recent developments of the law of
contract. When considering this case since the conclusion of argument, my
reservations have grown. I have concluded that the rule in *General Billposting*
accords neither with current legal principle nor with the requirements of business
efficacy. It must be open to question whether this court can legitimately
distinguish *General Billposting*. This is not a point I need decide, for whether or
not the rule in *General Billposting* remains applicable, does not in my judgment
affect the result of this appeal. I think it right, however, to express the
reservations that I have about basing a general rule on the result in that case and
to explain why it is that those reservations do not affect the result of this appeal.

Problems with the rule in General Billposting

In *General Billposting* the majority of the House of Lords held that the manager,
having been wrongfully dismissed, was 'justified in rescinding the contract and
treating himself as absolved from the further performance of it on his part'. Since
1909 the law in relation to the discharge of contractual obligations by acceptance
of a repudiation has been developed and clarified. In *Heyman v Darwins Ltd* [1942]

a 1 All ER 337 at 360, [1942] AC 356 at 399 Lord Porter observed: 'Strictly speaking, to say that, upon acceptance of the renunciation of a contract, the contract is rescinded is incorrect.' In that case the House of Lords held that an arbitration clause remained binding after the acceptance of a repudiation. Lord Macmillan explained why this was ([1942] 1 All ER 337 at 347, [1942] AC 356 at 374):

b 'The contract is not put out of existence, though all further performance of the obligations undertaken by each party in favour of the other may cease. It survives for the purpose of measuring the claims arising out of the breach, and the arbitration clause survives for determining the mode of their settlement. The purposes of the contract have failed, but the arbitration clause is not one of the purposes of the contract.'

c The theory that the contract was abrogated upon acceptance of a repudiation, or a fundamental breach, was finally laid to rest by the decision of the House of Lords in *Photo Production Ltd v Securicor Transport Ltd* [1980] 1 All ER 556 at 567, [1980] AC 827 at 849, where Lord Diplock summarised the effect of accepting a repudiation as follows:

d '(a) there is substituted by implication of law for the primary obligations of the party in default which remain unperformed a secondary obligation to pay money compensation to the other party for the loss sustained by him in consequence of their non-performance in the future and (b) the unperformed obligations of the other party are discharged.'

e There is no difficulty in applying these words to the reciprocal positive obligations that arise under a contract of employment: to provide services on the part of the employee and to provide the consideration for those services on the part of the employer. But I consider that there are real difficulties in applying those words to the negative obligations that are placed on an employee by a
f restrictive covenant in relation to the period after his employment has ceased. I can best demonstrate this difficulty by taking as an example the situation where the employee commits serious misconduct which warrants his dismissal. If the employer exercises his right of summary dismissal, is it to be suggested that he thereby discharges the employee from his obligation to observe negative
g restrictions imposed either expressly or impliedly under his contract of employment, such as the duty not to disclose confidential information? This would seem to follow if one applies the principles underlying *General Billposting* to such obligations, yet such a result borders on the absurd. The absurdity becomes more marked if one accepts the theory that either employer, by
h summary dismissal, or employee by leaving without notice, can unilaterally terminate by repudiation the primary mutual obligations that arise under a contract of employment: see the discussion in *Thomas Marshall (Exports) Ltd v Guinle* [1978] 3 All ER 193 esp at 205, [1979] Ch 227 esp at 242–243; and cf *Chitty* para 37-134.

j The considerations to which I have just referred demonstrate the practical problems that *General Billposting* can pose for the employer faced with an employee who repudiates the contract. But that case also poses practical problems for the employer who repudiates the contract. I do not accept that it is unreasonable for an employer to seek to impose restraints on his employee that will subsist, even should the employment come to an end as a consequence of a repudiation by the employer. On the contrary, it seems to me commercially desirable that it should be possible to achieve this end, for the following reasons.

Where an employer discloses to an employee confidential information, or otherwise puts the employee in a position to harm the employer's goodwill, it will usually be reasonable to impose negative restraints sufficient to protect those legitimate interests of the employer. Contracts of employment are now subject to complex statutory regulation, much of it designed to protect the employee. Cases of deliberate wrongful dismissal of employees, or repudiatory breach of the duties owed to them, are much less common than bona fide disputes as to whether or not there has been unfair or constructive dismissal. Employees who have been unfairly dismissed are entitled to statutory compensation. It does not seem to me necessarily fair or reasonable that an employer who is held liable to pay such compensation should also be at risk of losing the protection that is reasonably necessary to safeguard his confidential information or goodwill.

Can General Billposting be distinguished?

In my judgment negative restraints agreed to apply after the termination of employment should not be equated with the primary obligations that are discharged when a contract of employment is terminated consequent upon repudiation. The consideration for such restraints is in reality not the obligation to give the appropriate notice of termination of the employee's services, but the granting of employment that affords access to confidential information and goodwill. Such restraints are not 'one of the purposes of the contract' (*Heyman v Darwins*): they are ancillary to those purposes. But for *General Billposting* I can see no principle of law which precludes the parties from validly agreeing to restraints that will subsist, even if the employment is brought to an end by repudiation. I think it at least arguable that, having regard to the subsequent development of this area of the law, not every restrictive covenant will be discharged upon a repudiatory termination of the employment. However, for the reasons which follow, it is not necessary to resolve this issue.

Are the present covenants reasonable?

If, contrary to Mr Stafford's concession, the restrictive covenants would, if valid, have survived had Mr Jones been wrongfully dismissed by Rock, does this feature render them unreasonable and consequently void as being in unlawful restraint of trade? I am in no doubt that the answer to this question is no. I have already explained my general approach to this question, but it is always necessary to look at the facts of the particular case. Mr Jones had been employed by Rock for some eight years. Under the terms of his new contract he was entitled to three months' notice or £7,500 salary in lieu. I do not consider that the remote possibility that Rock might terminate his employment in circumstances where they repudiated their obligation to comply with those terms rendered unreasonable covenants which purported to apply even if that contingency occurred.

For these reasons, whichever route is adopted, it leads to the conclusion that the decision reached by Sir Michael Davies on the principal issue should be reversed.

I agree with Simon Brown LJ for the reasons which he has given, that the subsidiary arguments advanced in support of the order of the trial judge are without merit.

Appeal allowed.

Paul Magrath Esq   Barrister.

a

Cheltenham and Gloucester plc v Krausz and another

COURT OF APPEAL, CIVIL DIVISION
BUTLER-SLOSS, MILLETT AND PHILLIPS LJJ

b 10, 22 OCTOBER 1996

Mortgage – Order for possession of mortgaged property – Suspension of execution of order – Mortgagor negotiating sale of property – Mortgagee refusing consent since proceeds of sale not sufficient to discharge mortgage debt – Mortgagor applying to
c *county court for suspension of possession order pending determination of High Court application for sale of property under s 91(2) of the Law of Property Act 1925 – Whether county court having jurisdiction to suspend possession order – Administration of Justice Act 1970, s 36 – Administration of Justice Act 1973, s 8.*

In January 1987 the defendants obtained £58,300 from the plaintiff building
d society which was secured by a mortgage on their home. The defendants defaulted on their repayment obligations and on 25 July 1991 the plaintiff obtained an order for possession. Following the issue of a warrant for possession, the defendants negotiated a sale of the property for £65,000. However, the plaintiff refused to agree to the sale on the ground that a higher price could be obtained. In June 1995, by which time the mortgage debt amounted to some
e £83,000, the defendants applied to the county court for an order suspending the warrant for possession on the ground that they had found a purchaser and gave notice of their intention to apply to the High Court for an order for sale pursuant to s 91(2)[a] of the Law of Property Act 1925. The district judge dismissed their application. The county court judge allowed the defendants' appeal and ordered
f a stay of execution of the warrant for possession pending determination of the application under s 91(2). The plaintiff appealed.

Held – Where the proceeds of sale were likely to discharge the mortgage debt, s 36[b] of the Administration of Justice Act 1970 (as amended by s 8[c] of the
g Administration of Justice Act 1973) conferred on the court the power to suspend a warrant for possession of mortgaged property in order to enable the mortgagor to make an application for sale under s 91 of the 1925 Act; however, it did not so empower the court where the mortgage debt would not be fully discharged, in the absence of other funds being available to the mortgagor to make up the shortfall. In those circumstances the mortgagee's rights were of primary
h importance and it was incumbent on the mortgagors to seek from the High Court any relief which that court was empowered to give before the possession warrant took effect. It followed that the county court judge had had no jurisdiction to suspend the warrant for possession in order to enable the mortgagors to apply to the High Court for an order for sale of the property under s 91(2) of the 1925 Act
j in circumstances where the proceeds of sale would be insufficient to discharge the mortgage debt. The appeal would accordingly be allowed (see p 29 *c* and p 30 *d e g h*, post).

---

a   Section 91, so far as material, is at out at p 24 *h* to p 25 *a*, post
b   Section 36 is set out at p 27 *j* to p 28 *c*, post
c   Section 8 is set out at p 28 *e* to *j*, post

Royal Trust Co of Canada v Markham [1975] 3 All ER 433 and *National and Provincial Building Society v Lloyd* [1996] 1 All ER 630 applied.
a

Notes

For court's powers to suspend an order for possession, see 32 *Halsbury's Laws* (4th edn) para 836, and for cases on the subject, see 35 *Digest* (Reissue) 257, 258–259, 2130, 2132–2134.
b

For the Law of Property Act 1925, s 91, see 37 *Halsbury's Statutes* (4th edn) 205.

For the Administration of Justice Act 1970, s 36, see ibid 397.

For the Administration of Justice Act 1973, s 8, see ibid 432.

Cases referred to in judgments
c

Barrett v Halifax Building Society (1995) 28 HLR 634.

Birmingham Citizens Permanent Building Society v Caunt [1962] 1 All ER 163, [1962] Ch 883, [1962] 2 WLR 323.

Connelly v DPP [1964] 2 All ER 401, [1964] AC 1254, [1964] 2 WLR 1145, HL.

Halifax Building Society v Clark [1973] 2 All ER 33, [1973] Ch 307, [1973] 2 WLR 1. *d*

National and Provincial Building Society v Lloyd [1996] 1 All ER 630, CA.

Palk v Mortgage Services Funding plc [1993] 2 All ER 481, [1993] Ch 330, [1993] 2 WLR 415, CA.

Royal Trust Co of Canada v Markham [1975] 3 All ER 433, [1975] 1 WLR 1416, CA.

Union Bank of London v Ingram (1882) 20 Ch D 463, CA.
e

Cases also cited or referred to in skeleton arguments

Cuckmere Brick Co Ltd v Mutual Finance Ltd [1971] 2 All ER 633, [1971] Ch 949, CA.

First Middlesbrough Trading and Mortgage Co Ltd v Cunningham (1974) 28 P & CR 69, CA.
f

Fourmaids Ltd v Dudley Marshall (Properties) Ltd [1957] 2 All ER 35, [1957] Ch 317.

Stewart Chartering Ltd v C & O Managements SA, The Venus Destiny [1980] 1 All ER 718, [1980] 1 WLR 460.

Target Home Loans Ltd v Clothier [1994] 1 All ER 439, CA.
g

Appeal

By notice dated 19 October 1995 the mortgagees, Cheltenham and Gloucester plc, appealed with leave from the decision of Judge Green QC in Shoreditch County Court on 9 June 1995 whereby he allowed the appeal of the defendant mortgagors, Aaron Krausz and Rebecca Josephine Krausz, from the decision of *h* District Judge Silverdale and ordered a stay of execution of a warrant for possession of the property known as 8 Springhill, Clapton, London, E5, pending determination of the mortgagors' application for an order for sale pursuant to s 91(2) of the Law of Property Act 1925. The facts are set out in the judgment of Phillips LJ.
j

Kathryn Purkis (instructed by *Church Adams Tatham & Co*) for the mortgagees.

Howard Smith (instructed by *Bude Nathan Iwanier*) for the second defendant.

The first defendant did not appear.

Cur adv vult

22 October 1996. The following judgments were delivered.

a

PHILLIPS LJ (giving the first judgment at the invitation of Butler-Sloss LJ). This appeal raises an important issue as to the extent of the jurisdiction of the court to suspend a warrant for possession of a dwelling house.

b THE FACTS

On 30 January 1987 the Guardian Building Society, whose rights the plaintiffs, Cheltenham and Gloucester plc, have inherited, lent to the defendants, Aaron Krausz and Rebecca Josephine Krausz (the mortgagors), £58,300, secured by a mortgage on their home, 8 Springhill, Clapton, London, E5 (the property). I shall refer to the plaintiffs and to their predecessors in title as 'the mortgagees'. On 12 *c* February 1990 a possession action was commenced by the mortgagees against the mortgagors, who had defaulted on their repayment obligations. On 25 July 1991 an order for possession was made. On four occasions, warrants for possession were issued. On each occasion an accommodation was reached between the mortgagors and the mortgagees, under which the warrant was discharged. On *d* each occasion the terms of that accommodation were breached by the mortgagors and a fresh warrant was issued. The fifth warrant fell due to execution on 12 June 1995.

On 23 February 1995 the mortgagors obtained a written valuation of their home from a firm of chartered surveyors, who reported:

e   'Although the area could be considered reasonably popular, this particular house is in such a poor state of repair needing a substantial amount of money spent on it, that we are of the opinion that its current value is no more than £65,000 ... We ought to point out that should the property be offered at auction, we doubt whether it would reach that level.'

f The mortgagors then contacted the MYA Charitable Trust. This trust purchases properties from owners who are facing dispossession and then lets the properties to them. The trust offered to buy 8 Springhill from the mortgagors for £65,000 on this basis. The mortgagees were not prepared to agree to this sale. They considered that the property had a value of about £90,000, based on what has been described as a 'drive-by' valuation.

g On 7 April 1995 the mortgagors informed the mortgagees that they intended to apply for an order that the property be sold, pursuant to s 91(2) of the Law of Property Act 1925, and requested the mortgagees to agree to this application being made to the county court. On 18 April 1995 the mortgagees refused their consent. On 9 June the mortgagors applied to District Judge Silverdale for:

h   '(1) An Order suspending the Warrant for Possession on the grounds that the Defendants have found a purchaser for their property and will apply to the High Court of Justice for an Order pursuant to Section 91(2) of the [1925 Act].'

j By this time arrears had grown to the extent that the total mortgage debt amounted to some £83,000. The district judge dismissed their application. The same afternoon they appealed to Judge Green QC on short notice. He allowed their appeal and ordered a stay of execution of the warrant for possession pending an application which the mortgagors undertook to make promptly to the High Court under s 91(2) of the 1925 Act. Against that order the mortgagees now appeal, with the leave of this court. The appeal is resisted solely by the second

defendant. Mr Krausz has been declared bankrupt and his trustee makes no claim
to any interest in the property.   *a*

There were two issues before Judge Green. The first was whether he had
jurisdiction to suspend the warrant for possession. The second was, if he had
such jurisdiction, whether in his discretion he should exercise it. Before us the
primary argument advanced by the mortgagees was that the judge had no
jurisdiction to suspend the warrant. Alternatively, the mortgagees have sought   *b*
to challenge the manner in which the judge exercised his discretion. So far as the
latter issue is concerned the judge was anxious to evaluate the strength of the
mortgagors' contention, supported by their valuation, that the market value of
the property was £65,000. He offered the mortgagees a short adjournment to
enable them to obtain a valuation in support of their contention that the property
had a higher value. They declined this offer. In these circumstances the judge   *c*
concluded that it was appropriate, if he had the jurisdiction, to suspend the
warrant for possession pending the determination of an application by the
mortgagors under s 91(2). He went on to decide, not without some reservations,
that he had jurisdiction to take this course.

On 31 August 1995 the mortgagors issued an originating summons in the   *d*
Chancery court claiming an order that the property be sold to the trust, pursuant
to the power of the court conferred by s 91(2). Directions were given on 15
November 1995 as a result of which the action was transferred to the Shoreditch
County Court on 20 March 1996. That court has not yet provided a hearing date,
perhaps because the result of this appeal has been awaited.

On 26 June 1995 the mortgagees obtained a valuation of the property for the   *e*
purposes of the s 91 proceedings. On the day of the hearing of this appeal the
mortgagees sought leave to adduce this by way of further evidence. We refused
their application. It did not seem to us that the mortgagees, having declined the
opportunity to place such evidence before the judge, could properly seek to
improve their case by putting it before us at the very last moment.

With this introduction I turn to consider the principal issue raised by this   *f*
appeal, the question of jurisdiction.

THE LAW

This appeal requires consideration of the inter-relationship of two areas of the
law relating to the mortgage of a dwelling house: (1) the circumstances in which   *g*
the mortgagor is entitled to an order for the sale of the mortgaged property; and
(2) the circumstances in which the court has jurisdiction to suspend entry into
possession of the dwelling house by the mortgagee.

Mortgagor's right of sale   *h*
Section 91 of the 1925 Act provides as follows:

'(1) Any person entitled to redeem mortgaged property may have a
judgment or order for sale instead of for redemption in an action brought by
him either for redemption alone, or for sale alone, or for sale or redemption
in the alternative.   *j*

(2) In any action, whether for foreclosure, or for redemption, or for sale,
or for the raising and payment in any manner of mortgage money, the court,
on the request of the mortgagee, or of any person interested either in the
mortgage money or in the right of redemption, and, notwithstanding that—
(a) any other person dissents; or (b) the mortgagee or any person so
interested does not appear in the action; and without allowing any time for

a   redemption or for payment of any mortgage money, may direct a sale of the mortgaged property, on such terms as it thinks fit, including the deposit in court of a reasonable sum fixed by the court to meet the expenses of sale and to secure performance of the terms ...'

The origin and history of these provisions are described by Nicholls V-C in *Palk v Mortgage Services Funding plc* [1993] 2 All ER 481 at 484, [1993] Ch 330 at 335.

b   Nicholls V-C also cited the statement of Jessel MR in *Union Bank of London v Ingram* (1882) 20 Ch D 463 at 464 about the essentially identical provisions of s 25(2) of the Conveyancing and Law of Property Act 1881:

c   'The Act is a remedial Act, one effect of it being to allow a mortgagor whose property is worth more than the mortgage-money, but who cannot raise it, to obtain a sale and get the benefit of the surplus.'

Until *Palk's* case it was the practice of the Chancery court only to entertain an application for sale by the mortgagor if the proceeds of sale were expected to be sufficient to discharge the entirety of the mortgage debt. In such circumstances

d   the mortgagor might initiate proceedings by bringing an action for sale under s 91(1), or, if the mortgagee sought to foreclose, the mortgagor could apply for an order for sale in place of foreclosure. The practice thus reflected the heading to s 91: Sale of mortgaged property in action for redemption or foreclosure.

Palk's case established, for the first time, that the court has power under s 91(2) to make an order for sale on the application of a mortgagor, notwithstanding that

e   the proceeds of sale will be insufficient to discharge the mortgage debt. In *Palk's* case the mortgagees had obtained an order for possession with the intention, not of proceeding to sell the property but of waiting in the hope that the market might improve. The mortgagor was anxious that the property should be sold so that the proceeds would reduce the mortgage debt, on which interest was

f   accruing at an alarming rate. The Court of Appeal held that, as the mortgagees could buy the property themselves if they wished to speculate on an increase in its value, in the interests of fairness the property should be sold.

In *Palk's* case the mortgagor had initially applied for an order for sale to the Eastbourne County Court. It is not clear on what basis that court entertained the claim, for the jurisdiction of the county court to make an order for sale is limited

g   to cases where the value of the property does not exceed £30,000. It also appears from the judgment in the Court of Appeal that the mortgagees obtained an order for possession, which was suspended pending the result of their application. It is not clear which court made the order for possession, or which court suspended that order. What does seem clear is that no challenge was made of the

h   jurisdiction to suspend the possession order.

In *Palk's* case the issue was simply whether or not the property should be sold. No issue arose as to the terms on which it should be sold. As to that matter, s 91(2) empowers the court to direct a sale 'on such terms as it thinks fit'. In cases before *Palk*, where the proceeds of sale were likely to exceed the mortgage debt,

j   the court was prepared to entrust the sale to the mortgagor on the basis that the mortgagor had a keener interest than the mortgagee in obtaining the best price. We have not been referred to any case, however, where there was a contest between the mortgagee and the mortgagor as to who should have conduct of the sale.

Barrett v Halifax Building Society (1995) 28 HLR 634 marks the next development in this area of the law, and one which demonstrates the importance of the present

appeal. In that case the plaintiffs had mortgaged their home and then defaulted
on their repayment obligations. The situation was one of negative equity—the
mortgage debt substantially exceeded the value of their home. On 6 August 1992
the mortgagees obtained a possession order, with a view to exercising their
power of sale. There were numerous suspensions of this order to give the
plaintiffs a chance to discharge the instalment arrears. What then occurred was
explained by the judge as follows (at 636):

> 'On 6 March 1995 there was a further suspension of the order for the
> purpose of leaving [the] mortgagors in possession of the property themselves
> to find a buyer notwithstanding that there was a deficit over the sum secured
> so that the property would be on the market, lived in and without it
> becoming known to the market that it was subject to a forced sale, thereby
> increasing the realisations available to discharge at least part of the amount
> due.'

The plaintiffs then applied to the Chancery court for an order for sale pursuant to
s 91 of the 1925 Act. By the time that their action came on for hearing they had
negotiated a sale of the property, subject to contract. They sought an order that
they be permitted to proceed with that sale and to remain in possession until
completion. The judge summarised the evidence on which they relied as follows
(at 637):

> 'The evidence of the plaintiffs, including the expert evidence of a valuer, is
> that it is a recognised feature of today's property market that where a
> mortgagee obtains possession of property and sells in the exercise of its
> power of sale it is able to obtain a price which is usually not as good as the
> price which might have been obtained by the mortgagor had the mortgagor
> remained in possession and the fact of the forced sale not become apparent.
> It is also the plaintiffs' evidence that if the mortgagee building society were
> to take over the sale or were now to obtain possession and proceed to sell
> itself there would be likely to be a delay of some months at least before a
> fresh purchaser could be found and a sale completed.'

The mortgagees resisted the order sought. They did not contend that they
would be able to obtain a better price, but urged that if the sale went ahead it
would break their established policy not to permit borrowers with negative
equity themselves to conduct the sale of their property without also at the same
time making proposals for the repayment of any resulting deficit. The judge held
that this was not a material circumstance which he ought to take into account
when exercising his discretion. He held (at 640):

> 'I am left, therefore, with a case [in] which, on the evidence before me,
> there is no discernible advantage to the building society in refusing to allow
> this sale to complete, whereas there is an obvious advantage to the
> mortgagors to complete their proposed sale at what is accepted as the best
> price that is likely to be obtainable in the current market.'

He proceeded to grant the plaintiffs the order that they sought.

Just as in *Palk's* case the report does not suggest that in *Barrett's* case any
challenge was made by the mortgagees to the order suspending possession
pending the plaintiffs' application to the Chancery court.

The consequences of the procedure followed in *Barrett's* case appear to me to
be far reaching. In any case in which there is negative equity, it will be open to

a the mortgagor to resist an order for possession on the ground that he wishes to obtain a better price by remaining in possession and selling the property himself. In not every case will the primary motive for such an application be the wish to obtain a better price than that which the mortgagee is likely to obtain on a forced sale. Often the mortgagor will be anxious to postpone for as long as possible the evil day when he has to leave his home. This court has ample experience of

b hopeless applications for leave to appeal against possession orders designed to achieve just that end. There will be a danger, if the mortgagee does not obtain possession, that the mortgagor will delay the realisation of the property by seeking too high a price, or deliberately procrastinating on completion. At present there is a simple procedure for seeking possession in the county court and the issue tends to be whether there are arrears and whether the mortgagor is

c likely to be able to discharge these in a reasonable time. If possession is to be suspended whenever this appears reasonable in order to give mortgagors the opportunity to sell the property themselves, the courts are going to have to enter into an area of difficult factual inquiry in order to decide in the individual case whether or not this course will be to the common benefit of mortgagor and

d mortgagee. Furthermore, there will be obvious practical difficulties for mortgagees in monitoring the negotiations of mortgagors who are permitted time to market their properties.

For these reasons, it seems to me that the procedure followed and the decision reached in *Barrett's* case tend fundamentally to undermine the value of the mortgagee's entitlement to possession.

e Having touched on the implications of the issue raised in this case I turn to consider whether, in law, the county court has jurisdiction to suspend possession in such circumstances.

Suspension of possession

f The right of a mortgagee to enter into possession of the mortgaged property was one which the common law protected strictly. The position was accurately stated in *Birmingham Citizens Permanent Building Society v Caunt* [1962] 1 All ER 163 at 182, [1962] Ch 883 at 912 by Russell J:

g 'Accordingly, in my judgment, where, as here, the legal mortgagee under an instalment mortgage under which, by reason of default, the whole money has become payable, is entitled to possession, the court has no jurisdiction to decline to make the order or to adjourn the hearing, whether on terms of keeping up payments or paying arrears, if the mortgagee cannot be persuaded to agree to this course. The *sole exception* to this is that the

h application may be adjourned for a short time to afford to the mortgagor a chance of paying off the mortgagee in full or otherwise satisfying him; but this should not be done if there is no reasonable prospect of this occurring. When I say the sole exception, I do not, of course, intend to exclude adjournments which in the ordinary course of procedure may be desirable in circumstances such as temporary inability of a party to attend, and so forth.'

j (My emphasis.)

The rigours of the common law in this respect were mitigated by s 36 of the Administration of Justice Act 1970, which provided:

'(1) Where the mortgagee under a mortgage of land which consists of or includes a dwelling-house brings an action in which he claims possession of

the mortgaged property, not being an action for foreclosure in which a claim
for possession of the mortgaged property is also made, the court may
exercise any of the powers conferred on it by subsection (2) below if it
appears to the court that in the event of its exercising the power the
mortgagor is likely to be able within a reasonable period to pay any sums due
under the mortgage or to remedy a default consisting of a breach of any
other obligation arising under or by virtue of the mortgage.

(2) The court—(a) may adjourn the proceedings, or (b) on giving
judgment, or making an order, for delivery of possession of the mortgaged
property, or at any time before the execution of such judgment or order,
may—(i) stay or suspend execution of the judgment or order, or (ii) postpone
the date for delivery of possession, for such period or periods as the court
thinks reasonable.'

It seems likely that the draughtsman of this section intended to confer on the
court power to suspend possession where the mortgagor was in a position to pay
arrears of instalments within a reasonable period. He overlooked the fact that
most mortgages provide for the principal to become immediately payable if
instalments are in arrears. It was held in *Halifax Building Society v Clark* [1973] 2
All ER 33, [1973] Ch 307, that in that event, the court was only given power to
suspend if it appeared that the mortgagor would be able within a reasonable time
to repay the total mortgage debt. To reverse the effect of this decision s 36 was
amended by s 8(1) of the Administration of Justice Act 1973, which provided:

'**8.** *Extension of powers of court in action by mortgagee of dwelling-house.*—
(1) Where by a mortgage of land which consists of or includes a
dwelling-house, or by any agreement between the mortgagee under such a
mortgage and the mortgagor, the mortgagor is entitled or is to be permitted
to pay the principal sum secured by instalments or otherwise to defer
payment of it in whole or in part, but provision is also made for earlier
payment in the event of any default by the mortgagor or of a demand by the
mortgagee or otherwise, then for purposes of section 36 of the
Administration of Justice Act 1970 (under which a court has power to delay
giving a mortgagee possession of the mortgaged property so as to allow the
mortgagor a reasonable time to pay any sums due under the mortgage) a
court may treat as due under the mortgage on account of the principal sum
secured and of interest on it only such amounts as the mortgagor would have
expected to be required to pay if there had been no such provision for earlier
payment.

(2) A court shall not exercise by virtue of subsection (1) above the powers
conferred by section 36 of the Administration of Justice Act 1970 unless it
appears to the court not only that the mortgagor is likely to be able within a
reasonable period to pay any amounts regarded (in accordance with
subsection (1) above) as due on account of the principal sum secured,
together with the interest on those amounts, but also that he is likely to be
able by the end of that period to pay any further amounts that he would have
expected to be required to pay by then on account of that sum and of interest
on it if there had been no such provision as is referred to in subsection (1)
above for earlier payment.'

The effect of s 36, as amended, on the power to suspend possession is as
follows: (1) the power can be exercised to enable the mortgagor to pay off

a instalment arrears due under the mortgage agreement from sources other than the sale of the mortgaged property, but (2) if the mortgagor intends to sell the mortgaged property to provide the source of payment, the court must be satisfied that the proceeds will be sufficient to discharge the entirety of the mortgage debt (see *Royal Trust Co of Canada v Markham* [1975] 3 All ER 433, [1975] 1 WLR 1416 and *National and Provincial Building Society v Lloyd* [1996] 1 All ER 630).

b Before the decision in *Palk* it seemed that s 36 of the 1970 Act and s 91 of the 1925 Act were complementary. An application under s 91 would only be contemplated where the proceeds of sale were expected to exceed the mortgage debt. In these circumstances s 36 gave the court the power to suspend possession in order to enable an application for sale under s 91 to be made. It is, however, quite clear that s 36 does not empower the court to suspend possession in order c to permit the mortgagor to sell the mortgaged premises where the proceeds of sale will not suffice to discharge the mortgage debt, unless of course other funds will be available to the mortgagor to make up the shortfall.

A mortgagor seeking relief in the circumstances of *Palk*'s case is thus unable to invoke any statutory power to suspend the mortgagee's right to enter into d possession.

For the mortgagors, Mr Smith argued that the provisions of s 36 did not define exclusively the jurisdiction of the court to suspend possession. The section was accurately headed 'Additional powers of court in action by mortgagee for possession of dwelling-house'. The court enjoyed in addition a power to suspend possession as part of its inherent jurisdiction. He referred us to the general e statement or principle, albeit in a criminal context, of Lord Morris of Borth-y-Gest in *Connelly v DPP* [1964] 2 All ER 401 at 409, [1964] AC 1254 at 1301:

> 'There can be no doubt that a court which is endowed with a particular jurisdiction has powers which are necessary to enable it to act effectively within such jurisdiction. I would regard them as powers which are inherent f in its jurisdiction. A court must enjoy such powers in order to enforce its rules of practice and to suppress any abuses of its process and to defeat any attempted thwarting of its process.'

Mr Smith elaborated his argument as follows:

g   'On an application by a mortgagor for sale under s 91 of the 1925 Act the court has power to order that the mortgagor be entrusted with the sale and that he remain in possession while effecting the sale (see *Barrett*). Should the mortgagee attempt to frustrate such an order by entering into possession, the court seized of the s 91 application must have an inherent power to h restrain him from doing so. In these circumstances, the county court must also have an inherent power to suspend an order or warrant for possession, at least for such short period as is necessary to enable the mortgagor to make a s 91 application.'

In my judgment this argument breaks down at a number of stages.

j   In *Royal Trust Co of Canada v Markham* Sir John Pennycuick, when delivering the leading judgment of this court, cited with approval the passage from the judgment of Russell J in *Caunt*'s case which I have myself cited above. He then said ([1975] 3 All ER 433 at 436–437, [1975] 1 WLR 1416 at 1420):

> 'A characteristic instance in which that sole exception is applicable is where the mortgagor has entered or is about to enter into a contract for the sale of

the property at a price which will enable the mortgage to be paid off in full ... So, as the law stood before 1970, the mortgagee had a right, subject only to that one exception mentioned by Russell J, to possession, and it was not in the power of the court to refuse him possession.'

Megaw LJ added ([1975] 3 All ER 433 at 440, [1975] 1 WLR 1416 at 1423–1424):

'There was, as I think is clear, no power, before the enactment of s 36 of the Administration of Justice Act 1970, for a court to grant a stay or suspension of execution of an order for possession in a mortgagees' action, such as the present one, based on default in payment or breach of other obligations. Therefore, if there be such power to suspend or stay the execution of the order for possession, it can come only from the provisions of s 36 of the 1970 Act as amended by s 8 of the Administration of Justice Act 1973.'

In my judgment, the very specific delimitation of the power given by s 36 makes it clear that the legislature did not intend that the court should have any wider jurisdiction to curtail the mortgagee's right to possession. That right enables the mortgagee to exercise his power of sale in the manner he chooses and in the confidence that he can offer a purchaser vacant possession. Section 36 circumscribes that right where the proceeds of sale are likely to discharge the mortgage debt. It does not do so where the mortgage debt will not be fully discharged, and it is in those circumstances that the mortgagee's rights are of particular importance.

I recognise the principle of the inherent jurisdiction of the court, as explained by Lord Morris in *Connelly v DPP*, but I question whether that principle can justify the court in exercising its power to order a sale of mortgaged property under s 91 in circumstances where the mortgagee is seeking to enter into possession in order to sell property in which there is negative equity and where the sole object with which the mortgagor seeks that order is to prevent the mortgagee exercising his right to possession so that the mortgagor can negotiate his own sale while in possession.

Even if one assumes that the Chancery court has power to order sale of mortgaged property on terms that displace the mortgagee's right to possession, I do not consider that it follows from this that the county court, as part of its inherent jurisdiction, can properly suspend an order or warrant for possession in order to enable a mortgagor to apply to the High Court for an order under s 91. It seems to me incumbent on the mortgagor to seek from the High Court any relief which that court is empowered to give before the possession warrant takes effect.

In the present case the judge purported in 1995 to suspend a warrant for possession that was properly issued pursuant to an order for possession made in 1991. For the reasons I have given, I consider that he had no jurisdiction to make such an order and this appeal should be allowed.

MILLETT LJ. I have had the advantage of reading in draft the judgment of Phillips LJ with which I am in full agreement.

Palk v Mortgage Services Funding plc [1993] 2 All ER 481, [1993] Ch 330 was a case in which the mortgagee had no wish to realise its security in the foreseeable future, whether by sale or foreclosure. It established that in such a case the mortgagor might obtain an order for sale even though the proceeds of sale would *a* be insufficient to discharge the mortgage debt. It does not support the making of such an order where the mortgagee is taking active steps to obtain possession and enforce its security by sale. Still less does it support the giving of the conduct of the sale to the mortgagor in a case where there is negative equity, so that it is the mortgagee who is likely to have the greater incentive to obtain the best price and the quickest sale.

b Both these steps were taken in *Barrett v Halifax Building Society* (1995) 28 HLR 634. I have serious doubt whether that case was rightly decided. In fairness to the judge it should be said that it does not appear to have been argued as a matter of principle; the mortgagor's application was resisted on purely pragmatic grounds, and somewhat feeble ones at that.

For the reasons given by Phillips LJ, I agree that this appeal should be allowed.

c **BUTLER-SLOSS LJ.** I agree with both judgments and that this appeal should be allowed.

Appeal allowed.

d
                                        Paul Magrath Esq   Barrister.

Re Hayward (deceased)

a

CHANCERY DIVISION
RATTEE J
27, 28 MARCH 1996

b

Insolvency – Jurisdiction – Trustee in bankruptcy – Vesting of property in trustee – Bankrupt owning half-share in property in Spain – Bankrupt dying intestate and widow declaring in Spain that she was person entitled to bankrupt's interests under intestacy – Widow transferring half-share to other joint owner for consideration – Trustee claiming bankrupt's half share in Spanish property – Whether proceedings relating to succession or bankruptcy – Whether bankruptcy court in England having jurisdiction to determine trustee's claim – Civil Jurisdiction and Judgments Act 1982, Sch 1, art 1.

c

Conflict of laws – Jurisdiction –Title to foreign immovables – Exclusive jurisdiction of court where immovable property situated – Bankrupt jointly owning property in Spain dying intestate – Widow claiming half interest and transferring it to other joint owner for consideration – Joint owner becoming sole registered proprietor in Spanish property register – Trustee in bankruptcy claiming entitlement to bankrupt's half-share and rectification of Spanish property register – Whether proceedings having as object rights in rem in immovable property in Spain – Whether proceedings having as object validity of entries in public registers – Whether English court having jurisdiction – Civil Jurisdiction and Judgments Act 1982, Sch 1, art 16.

d

e

In 1986 the first respondent and H jointly purchased a villa in Spain, the title to which was registered in the Minorcan property register as being held by them 'in indivisible halves'. H was subsequently declared bankrupt and his assets vested in his trustee in bankruptcy. He died intestate, and thereafter his widow, the second respondent, declared in Spain that she was the person entitled to H's interests under his intestacy and purported to transfer his half-interest in the villa to the first respondent in consideration for the release of a debt owed by her to him in respect of moneys which he had spent in maintaining the villa. On completion of the purported transfer, the first respondent became sole registered proprietor of the villa. In 1994 the trustee in bankruptcy instituted proceedings in the county court claiming declarations, inter alia, that H's half-interest in the villa formed part of his bankruptcy estate and vested in the trustee on his appointment as trustee in bankruptcy and that any purported transfers to or by his widow were void. He also sought an order that both respondents should immediately take steps to rectify the Minorcan property register to show that the villa was held in the joint names of the first respondent and the trustee. The first respondent applied to strike out the trustee's application on the principal ground that the court had no jurisdiction to entertain the proceedings because the matter had been expressly removed from the English court by the provisions of the Convention on Jurisdiction and the Enforcement of Judgments in Civil and Commercial Matters 1968 (set out in Sch 1 to the Civil Jurisdiction and Judgments Act 1982). The judge upheld that contention and struck out the trustee's application holding that, by virtue of art 16[a], the Spanish court had exclusive jurisdiction in relation to the trustee's claim by reason of the fact that the

f

g

h

j

---

a   Article 16, as amended, so far as material, is set out at p 36 j to p 37 a, post

a proceedings were either proceedings which had as their object 'rights in rem in immovable property' or were proceedings which had as their object 'the validity of entries in public registers'. The trustee appealed, contending (i) that art 1[b] of the convention excluded the application of the convention because the trustee's application related to matters of succession and bankruptcy within the meaning of that article, and (ii) that in any event the proceedings did not fall within art 16 *b* of the convention.

Held – (1) The application of the convention to the proceedings was not precluded by art 1 because: (a) the basis of the trustee's claim was that the bankrupt had been entitled to a half-share of the villa and that, on his appointment as trustee, he had taken over the bankrupt's entitlement thereto, *c* which raised no question of succession; and (b) although the claim which the trustee sought to assert depended on the bankruptcy of H, the nature of the claim was not a matter of bankruptcy, in the sense that any question of bankruptcy was the principal subject matter of the proceedings, but was essentially a claim by the trustee to recover from a third party assets said to belong to the bankrupt's estate *d* and therefore to be vested in the trustee, which was analogous to a claim made by a liquidator of a company to recover the company's debts, and such relief could be obtained from the court outside the bankruptcy jurisdiction (see p 40 *j* to p 41 *e j* and p 42 *b*, post); *Gourdain v Nadler* Case 133/78 [1979] ECR 733 distinguished.

e (2) The trustee's claim was a claim in proceedings which had as their object a right in rem in immovable property, since it was a claim to legal ownership of one-half of the villa. Moreover, since the trustee claimed that the property register in Minorca required rectification by reason of the fact that it showed void transactions, the proceedings also had as their object the validity of entries in a public register. Accordingly, as art 16 of the convention conferred exclusive *f* jurisdiction on the courts of Spain in which the relevant property and registers were situated, the English court had no jurisdiction to entertain the trustee's application and it should be struck out. The appeal would therefore be dismissed (see p 43 *e* to p 44 *b*, post).

g **Notes**
For the Convention on Jurisdiction and the Enforcement of Judgments in Civil and Commercial Matters, see 1(1) *Halsbury's Laws* (4th edn reissue) paras 358–361 and 8(1) *Halsbury's Laws* (4th edn reissue) paras 768–773.

For the Civil Jurisdiction and Judgments Act 1982, Sch 1, arts 1, 16, see 11 *h* *Halsbury's Statutes* (4th edn) (1991 reissue) 1133, 1143.

As from 1 December 1991 Sch 1 to the 1982 Act was substituted by the Civil Jurisdiction and Judgments Act 1982 (Amendment) Order 1990, SI 1990/2591, art 12(1), Sch 1.

j **Cases referred to in judgment**
Gourdain v Nadler Case 133/78 [1979] ECR 733.
Scherer v Counting Instruments Ltd [1986] 2 All ER 529, [1986] 1 WLR 615, CA.
Webb v Webb Case C-294/92 [1994] 3 All ER 911, [1994] QB 696, [1994] 3 WLR 801, [1994] ECR I-1717, ECJ.

b   Article 1, as amended, is set out at p 36 *f* to *h*, post

Cases also cited or referred to in skeleton arguments

Deschamps v Miller [1908] 1 Ch 856.

Spiliada Maritime Corp v Cansulex Ltd, The Spiliada [1986] 3 All ER 843, [1987] AC 460, HL.

Appeal

The applicant, John Stefan Wheatley, the trustee in bankruptcy of Malcolm William Hayward, deceased, appealed from the order of Judge Geddes sitting in the Walsall County Court in bankruptcy dated 20 December 1995 striking out, on the application of the first respondent, John Gerald Hulse, the trustee's application dated 4 October 1994, whereby he sought to establish his title to a half-share in a villa in Minorca, Spain which had been jointly owned by the deceased and the first respondent in whose name the villa was currently registered in the relevant property register in Minorca, on the ground that the court had no jurisdiction to entertain it. The first respondent cross-appealed from the judge's refusal to make an order for costs in his favour following his successful application. The second respondent, Molly Hayward, was the widow of the deceased. The facts are set out in the judgment.

Kevin Hegarty (instructed by *Edge & Ellison*, Birmingham) for the trustee.
Isabel Hitching (instructed by *Sydney W Smith & Co*, Wednesbury) for the first respondent.
The second respondent did not appear.

RATTEE J. I have before me two appeals, that is to say an appeal and a cross-appeal, from decisions of Judge Geddes given in the Walsall County Court in bankruptcy on 20 and 21 December 1995. The proceedings in which the judge determined the application were themselves commenced by an ordinary application issued on 4 October 1994 by the trustee in bankruptcy of one Malcolm William Hayward, now deceased. The ordinary application, made purportedly under ss 363 and 366 of the Insolvency Act 1986, according to the title to the proceedings, sought various heads of relief designed to establish the trustee's title to a half-share in a villa in Minorca, Spain, which I shall refer to simply as 'the villa'.

The judge struck out the ordinary application on the grounds that the court had no jurisdiction to entertain it by reason of the provisions of the Convention on Jurisdiction and the Enforcement of Judgments in Civil and Commercial Matters made applicable in English Law by the Civil Jurisdiction and Judgments Act 1982. The application to strike out was made by the first respondent to the ordinary application, who himself is the person in whose name the villa is currently registered in the relevant property register in Minorca. Although the judge struck out the ordinary application in accordance with the submissions of the first respondent made to him, he declined to make any order for costs of the application.

The trustee appeals against the substantive decision to strike out the ordinary application. The first respondent appeals against the judge's failure to make an order for costs to follow the event, that is to say an order for costs in favour of the first respondent. I should say that the second respondent to the ordinary application, who in fact is the deceased bankrupt's widow, did not, as I understand it, appear below and she has not appeared before me, although I have seen a letter written by her solicitors to the effect that she wishes her costs to be provided for in the event of the trustee's appeal failing before me.

a The relevant background facts can be fairly shortly stated and have been helpfully set out by Judge Geddes in his judgment. On 1 October 1986 the villa was purchased by the deceased, Mr Hayward, and the first respondent, Mr Hulse, by contribution between them in equal shares of the purchase price. The title to the villa was, in consequence, registered in the Minorcan property register as being held by them 'by indivisible halves', as it is put in a translation of the entries b in the register which I have seen.

Mr Hayward was made bankrupt by an order of 5 June 1987. On 21 June 1987 the trustee was appointed as his trustee in bankruptcy. Accordingly, prima facie, on the appointment of the trustee, the assets of Mr Hayward, the bankrupt, vested in him under the provisions of the 1986 Act. On 9 December 1987 Mr Hayward died intestate. In March 1992, according to the judgment, Mrs c Hayward, the second respondent, and I quote from the judgment: 'declared in Spain that she was the person entitled to Mr Hayward's interests under his intestacy.' She then transferred, or purported to transfer, her late husband's half-interest in the villa to Mr Hulse in consideration, as she understood the matter, for the release of a debt owed by her to Mr Hulse in respect of moneys which he had spent on the maintenance of the villa. On completion of the d purported transfer by Mrs Hayward to Mr Hulse, Mr Hulse became sole registered proprietor of the villa in the appropriate land register in Minorca.

The essence of the present proceedings, or rather the proceedings which were struck out by the judge in the county court, namely the proceedings begun by the originating application, was an attempt by the trustee to establish and protect, e and indeed perfect, what he alleged was his entitlement as trustee in the bankruptcy of Mr Hayward to what had been Mr Hayward's half-share in the villa. By the ordinary application, various heads of relief designed for that purpose were claimed by the trustee. The relief sought can be summarised as follows: (1) a declaration that the interest of Mr Hayward in the villa formed part f of his 'bankruptcy estate' and vested in the trustee on his appointment as trustee in bankruptcy; (2) a declaration that, on the death of Mr Hayward on 9 December 1987, he had no interest in the villa capable of being passed to any person entitled to benefit under his intestacy and that, in particular, he had no interest in the villa at the date of his death capable of being passed to his widow, the second respondent; (3) a declaration that the purported transfer of Mr Hayward's estate g or interest in the villa to his widow is void (I take it that what is there intended to be referred to by 'the transfer of Mr Hayward's interest to his widow' is the widow's purported inheritance of that interest under the law of intestacy. I am not conscious, from the papers I have seen, of there being any suggestion that there was any other transfer of Mr Hayward's interest to her); (4) a declaration h that the first respondent, Mr Hulse, was aware of the bankruptcy order made in respect of Mr Hayward prior to December 1991; (5) a declaration that Mr Hulse was aware prior to December 1991 that the trustee claimed that he was entitled to Mr Hayward's interest in the villa as trustee in bankruptcy; (6) a declaration that the purported transfer of an interest in the villa from Mr Hayward, the second respondent, to Mr Hulse, the first respondent, is void; (7) an injunction j restraining Mr Hulse dealing with the villa without the trustee's consent; (8) an inquiry and declaration as to the extent of Mr Hulse's interest in the villa; (9) an order that both respondents should immediately take steps to rectify the Spanish register of the villa to acknowledge that 'the purported transfer (a) of the interest of Mr Hayward in the villa to Molly Hayward and (b) of the interest thereby purportedly acquired by the second respondent to the first respondent are void' (the rectification sought was to the effect that the register should show that the villa is held in the joint names of the first respondent, Mr Hulse, and the trustee); (10) an order that the villa should be sold in England with the trustee to have conduct of the sale, the proceeds to be divided between him and Mr Hulse in accordance with the declaration sought under (8).

The ordinary application sought further ancillary relief, which is not relevant for present purposes. The ordinary application was supplemented by points of claim delivered by the trustee, which underwent certain amendments and, as amended, set out the trustee's claim that he became entitled on his appointment as trustee in bankruptcy to Mr Hayward's half-share in the villa and that, in effect, nothing that has happened since was effective to impinge upon that entitlement. The first respondent put in a defence, which again in due course was amended, in which, in particular, it was denied that any entitlement to the villa or any share in it had vested in the trustee.

As I have already indicated, the first respondent, Mr Hulse, launched an application to strike out the originating application. The defence which he delivered expressly made plain that it was without prejudice to his argument that the application should be struck out in limine. The basis on which it was sought to strike out the originating application was that, in effect, by virtue of the fact that the matter in issue was ownership of foreign land, the English court had no jurisdiction to deal with the matter. However, the principal ground on which that contention was put forward was that jurisdiction to deal with the matter had been expressly removed from the English court, even if it would otherwise have had it, by the provisions of the convention, to which I have referred. The terms of that convention are set out in Sch 1 to the Civil Jurisdiction and Judgments Act 1982. I should refer to some of its provisions. Article 1, as amended, provides:

> 'This Convention shall apply in civil and commercial matters whatever the nature of the court or tribunal. It shall not extend, in particular, to revenue, customs or administrative matters. The Convention shall not apply to—
> 1. The status or legal capacity of natural persons, rights in property arising out of a matrimonial relationship, wills and succession.
> 2. Bankruptcy, proceedings relating to the winding-up of insolvent companies or other legal persons, judicial arrangements, compositions and analogous proceedings.
> 3. Social security.
> 4. Arbitration.'

Article 2 provides:

> 'Subject to the provisions of this Convention, persons domiciled in a Contracting State [which both this country and Spain are] shall, whatever their nationality, be sued in the courts of that State. Persons who are not nationals of the State in which they are domiciled shall be governed by the rules of jurisdiction applicable to nationals of that State.'

Article 16 of the convention is in these terms, so far as material:

> 'The following courts shall have exclusive jurisdiction, regardless of domicile:
> 1.(a) In proceedings which have as their object rights *in rem* in immovable property or tenancies of immovable property, the courts of the Contracting State in which the property is situated ...

a **3.** In proceedings which have as their object the validity of entries in public registers, the courts of the Contracting State in which the register is kept ...'

Judge Geddes held that the convention did apply to the proceedings commenced by the trustee's ordinary application and that the convention's application was not excluded by the provisions of art 1, which I have read. He

b further held that, by virtue of art 16, the courts of Spain had exclusive jurisdiction in relation to the subject matter of the originating application, that is to say the trustee's claim to a half-share in the villa, by reason of the fact that the proceedings were either proceedings which had as their object rights in rem in immovable property or were proceedings which had as their object the validity

c of entries in public registers.

The trustee's contention, both before the judge and before this court, was to the effect that art 1, on its true construction, does exclude the application of the convention to the proceedings begun by the originating application, because, within the meaning of that article, the proceedings relate both to matters of succession and to matters of bankruptcy. They relate to matters of succession

d because the title, or alleged title, of the first respondent to the half-share in the villa originally owned by the bankrupt depends upon Mrs Hayward, the second respondent, having succeeded to that share on the bankrupt's death.

The proceedings relate to matters of bankruptcy, submitted the trustee, because the title which he seeks to assert is one he only has as trustee in

e bankruptcy and, therefore, which arises only by virtue of Mr Hayward's bankruptcy. Moreover, submitted the trustee, the proceedings are brought under the provisions of the 1986 Act in the bankruptcy court. On either basis, submitted the trustee, the other provisions of the convention do not, having regard to the terms of art 1, apply to the relevant proceedings.

For the first respondent it was submitted by Miss Hitching that that is not so.

f The argument put very clearly by her in a very helpful skeleton argument sets the submissions out in summary. It was submitted that the subject matter of the proceedings begun by the trustee is neither succession nor bankruptcy within the true meaning of those words in art 1 of the convention.

In support of that submission, Miss Hitching relied on the judgment of the

g Court of Justice of the European Communities in *Gourdain v Nadler* Case 133/78 [1979] ECR 733, to which I should refer. The proceedings were proceedings under a particular provision of French law in which a liquidator sought to make the manager of the company whose affairs he was liquidating personally liable for the company's debts. The court was asked to consider the question of whether

h the relevant proceedings were proceedings to which the convention applied or proceedings to which the convention's application was ousted by virtue of the provisions of art 1, which I have read. In the course of its judgment, the court said (at 743 (para 3)):

j 'As Article 1 serves to indicate the scope of the Convention it is necessary, in order to ensure, as far as possible, that the rights and obligations which derive from it for the Contracting States and the persons to whom it applies are equal and uniform, that the terms of that provision should not be interpreted as a mere reference to the internal law of one or other of the States concerned. By providing that the Convention shall apply "whatever the nature of the court or tribunal" the first paragraph of Article 1 shows that the concept of "civil and commercial matters" cannot be interpreted solely in the light of the division of jurisdiction between the various types of courts existing in certain states. The concepts used in Article 1 must be regarded as independent concepts which must be interpreted by reference, first, to the objectives and scheme of the Convention and, secondly, to the general principles which stem from the corpus of the national legal systems.'

In that passage, as Miss Hitching submitted, it is clear that the Court of Justice was deciding that in interpreting the provisions of art 1 of the convention and, in particular, in interpreting its references to succession and bankruptcy, one must, so far as possible, treat the concepts of succession and bankruptcy as independent concepts of European law, having similar effect throughout the contracting states, parties to the convention, and not dependent on particular provisions of a particular contracting state's national law.

In *Gourdain v Nadler* the court went on, immediately following the passage I have just read, to deal with the concept of bankruptcy in a passage which I think is helpful for present purposes and which I shall read:

'As far as concerns bankruptcy, proceedings relating to the winding-up of insolvent companies or other legal persons, judicial arrangements, compositions and analogous proceedings, according to the various laws of the Contracting Parties relating to debtors who have declared themselves unable to meet their liabilities, insolvency or the collapse of the debtor's creditworthiness, which involve the intervention of the courts culminating in the compulsory "liquidation des biens" in the interest of the general body of creditors of the person, firm or company, or at least in supervision by the courts, it is necessary, if decisions relating to bankruptcy and winding-up are to be excluded from the scope of the Convention, that they must derive directly from the bankruptcy or winding-up and be closely connected with the proceedings for the "liquidation des biens" or the "règlement judiciaire". In order to answer the question referred to the Court by the national court it is therefore necessary to ascertain whether the legal foundation of an application such as that provided for in Article 99 of the French Law [the article under which the proceedings in that case were brought] is based on the law relating to bankruptcy and winding-up as interpreted for the purposes of the Convention. The application under Article 99, called an application to make good a deficiency in the assets, for which special provision is made in a law on bankruptcy and winding-up is made only to the court which made the order for the "règlement judiciaire" or the "liquidation des biens". It is only the "syndic"—apart from the court which can make the order of its own motion—who can make this application on behalf of and in the interest of the general body of creditors with a view to the partial reimbursement of the creditors by respecting the principle that they rank equally and by taking account of any preferential rights lawfully acquired.' (See [1979] ECR 733 at 744 (paras 4–5).)

As I understand it, the reference to the 'syndic' is a reference to somebody in the position of a liquidator or trustee as in the present case. The judgment went on (at 744–745 (paras 5–6)):

'In this application, which derogates from the general rules of the law of liability, the *de jure* or *de facto* managers of the company are presumed to be liable and they can only discharge this burden by proving that they managed the affairs of the company with all the requisite energy and diligence.

a   The period of limitation of three years for the application runs from the date when the final list of claims is drawn up and is suspended for the duration of any scheme of arrangement which may have been entered into and begins to run again if such a scheme is terminated or declared void.

If the application directed against the manager of the company succeeds it is the general body of creditors which benefits, some assets being added to
b   the funds to which they are entitled, as happens where the "syndic"' establishes a claim which benefits the general body of creditors.

Furthermore, the court may order the "règlement judiciaire" or the "liquidation des biens" of those managers who have been made responsible for part or all of the liabilities of a legal person and who do not discharge the said liabilities, without having to verify whether the said managers are
c   businessmen and whether they are unable to meet their liabilities.

It is quite apparent from all these findings that the legal foundation of Article 99, the object of which, in the event of the winding-up of a commercial company, is to go beyond the legal person and proceed against its managers and their property is based solely on the provisions of the law
d   of bankruptcy and winding-up as interpreted for the purpose of the Convention.'

Thus, submitted Miss Hitching, it is plain from the comments made by the Court of Justice in that case that a matter is not one of bankruptcy from which the application of the convention is excluded by art 1 merely because some question of bankruptcy law may arise incidentally in the course of the relevant
e   proceedings. In *Gourdain v Nadler* itself, the court, in the last paragraph of the passage I have just cited, stressed the fact that the relief available to the liquidator against the allegedly defaulting company manager in that case was relief which was available only by virtue of the relevant insolvency law of France.

Miss Hitching further drew my attention to s 3 of the 1982 Act, which applies
f   the convention in English law and which provides:

'(1) Any question as to the meaning or effect of any provision of the Brussels Conventions shall, if not referred to the European Court in accordance with the 1971 Protocol, be determined in accordance with the principles laid down by and any relevant decision of the European Court ...
g   (3) Without prejudice to the generality of subsection (1), the following reports (which are reproduced in the Official Journal of the Communities), namely—(a) the reports by Mr. P. Jenard on the 1968 Convention and the 1971 Protocol; and (b) the report by Professor Peter Schlosser on the Accession Convention; and (c) the report by Professor Demetrios I.
h   Evrigenis and Professor K. D. Kerameus on the 1982 Accession Convention; and (d) the report by Mr. Martinho de Almeida Cruz, Mr. Manuel Desantes Real and Mr. P. Jenard on the 1989 Accession Convention, may be considered in ascertaining the meaning or effect of any provision of the Brussels Conventions and shall be given such weight as is appropriate in the
j   circumstances.'

In the light of that provision, Miss Hitching referred me to passages in the report of Mr Jenard referred to in sub-s (3). In the course of that report, the author, Mr Jenard, said (OJ 1979 C 59, pp 10, 12):

'However, matters falling outside the scope of the Convention do so only if they constitute the principal subject matter of the proceedings. They are

thus not excluded when they come before the court as a subsidiary matter
either in the main proceedings or in preliminary proceedings ... Proceedings
relating to a bankruptcy are not necessarily excluded from the Convention.
Only proceedings arising directly from the bankruptcy and hence falling
within the scope of the Bankruptcy Convention of the European Economic
Community are excluded from the scope of the Convention.'

As Miss Hitching pointed out, that passage assumed that there was going to be
a Bankruptcy Convention of the EEC which, she told me, never came into being.

In *Dicey and Morris on the Conflict of Laws* (12th edn, 1993) vol 1, pp 277–278
(Rule 22) in commenting on the convention and, in particular art 1 of it, the
authors say:

'*Wills and succession.* Matters relating to wills and succession were
excluded because it was thought that the divergence in laws, especially in the
relevant rules of private international law, among the original 1968
Convention Contracting States was so great that it would be premature to
include them before the rules of private international law had been unified.
The expression "wills and succession" covers all claims to testate or intestate
succession, including disputes as to validity or interpretation of wills setting
up trusts; but disputes concerning the relations of the trustee with persons
other than beneficiaries may come within the scope of the Conventions.

Bankruptcy, etc. This exclusion extends to bankruptcy, proceedings relating
to the winding-up of insolvent companies or other legal persons, judicial
arrangements, compositions and analogous proceedings. Bankruptcy was
excluded because of the great disparities in national practice between the
original 1968 Convention Contracting States, because of its proximity to
public law, and because a draft Bankruptcy Convention was being
considered by the Community. In *Gourdain* v. *Nadler* (Case 133/78 [1979]
ECR 733 at 744) the European Court held that for proceedings to be excluded
on the basis that they concern bankruptcy, etc., it was necessary that they
must derive directly from the bankruptcy or winding-up and be closely
connected with the bankruptcy proceedings. Thus a claim by an English
liquidator against the directors of a company for fraudulent trading under
section 630 of the Companies Act 1985 would be outside the scope of the
Conventions. But an action by a liquidator to recover debts due to an
insolvent company would not be excluded, since the claim in no sense relates
to bankruptcy.'

For my part, I cannot see that the claim made by the originating application by
the trustee can properly be said to raise any question of succession. Mr Hegarty
for the trustee submitted that it does, on the basis that the first respondent's claim
himself to be entitled to the half-share in the villa which is claimed by the trustee
depends upon a claim that the second respondent succeeded to that share on the
death of the bankrupt.

However, it seems to me that the trustee's claim in these proceedings raised no
issue of succession. Succession was in no sense the principal subject matter of the
proceedings. The trustee's claim was simply on the basis that the bankrupt had
been entitled to a half-share of the villa and that, on his appointment as trustee,
the trustee had taken over the bankrupt's entitlement thereto. That in no sense,
in my judgment, raises any question of succession.

a So far as the reference in art 1 of the convention to bankruptcy is concerned, Mr Hegarty for the trustee forcefully and attractively argued that the claim made by the originating application is a matter of bankruptcy, because that claim depends essentially on the bankruptcy of the late Mr Hayward. Only by virtue of that bankruptcy does the trustee have the claim which he seeks to assert in the proceedings.

b That, of course, is perfectly true. But for the bankruptcy, the trustee himself would have no claim such as he seeks to establish in the proceedings. However, the nature of the claim made by the trustee in the proceedings, in my judgment, is not a matter of bankruptcy in the sense that any question of bankruptcy is the principal subject matter of the proceedings. The claim made in the proceedings is essentially a claim by the trustee to recover from a third party, Mr Hulse, assets

c said to belong to the bankrupt's estate and, therefore, to be vested in the trustee. It is very like a claim made by a liquidator of a company to recover the company's debts, such as was contemplated in the passage from *Dicey and Morris*, which I have just quoted, in which the editors, in my judgment rightly, suggest that such a claim is not taken outside the provisions of the convention by art 1.

d Unlike the situation in *Gourdain v Nadler*, the relief sought by the trustee in the present case by his originating application cannot be said, in my judgment, to be relief available to the trustee only in the bankruptcy jurisdiction and in accordance with bankruptcy law. The issue between the parties in the proceedings started by the originating application is no aspect of bankruptcy law, but is the effect under Spanish law as the lex situs of the villa, of the fact that,

e rightly or wrongly, the first respondent, Mr Hulse, is at present the sole registered proprietor of the whole of the villa.

It is true that in the present case, as Mr Hegarty rightly stressed, the relief the trustee sought was sought in the bankruptcy court in the context of proceedings relating to Mr Hayward's bankruptcy, and was purportedly sought, according to

f Mr Hegarty's submissions, under the provisions of s 367 of the 1986 Act:

> '(1) If it appears to the court, on consideration of any evidence obtained under Section 366 or this section, that any person has in his possession any property comprised in the bankrupt's estate, the court may, on the application of the official receiver or the trustee of the bankrupt's estate,
>
> *g* order that person to deliver the whole or any part of the property to the official receiver or the trustee at such time, in such manner and on such terms as the court thinks fit ...'

On the face of it, it seems to me at least doubtful whether the court has jurisdiction to grant the relief sought by the originating application and, in

h particular, orders for the rectification of the Minorcan property register under s 367 of the Act. However, in my judgment, it matters not whether such orders could be made under that section. For it is plain that the relief sought is not (as was the relief in *Gourdain v Nadler*) relief of a type which can only be obtained from the court under the provisions of some law relating to bankruptcy or insolvency. The trustee, if he has a good claim, as he alleges, could clearly pursue

j that claim in an action against Mr Hulse quite outside the bankruptcy jurisdiction.

The only connection between these proceedings and bankruptcy, it seems to me, is that the title sought to be established by the trustee depends, as a first step, on the fact that, as trustee in bankruptcy, under the English statute, the trustee is entitled to whatever property was vested in Mr Hulse at the date of the bankruptcy. That does not, in my judgment, make bankruptcy the principal subject matter of the proceedings so as to bring the application within the excluding terms of art 1 of the convention, construed in the light of the comments to which I have referred, made by the Court of Justice in *Gourdain v Nadler* and by Mr Jenard in the report on the convention which I am told by s 3(3) of the 1982 Act I have to take into account when construing the convention.

Accordingly, in my judgment, Judge Geddes was entirely correct in his conclusion that the application of the convention to the proceedings begun by the trustee's originating application was not precluded by the provisions of art 1 of the convention. The proceedings concerned are not either succession or bankruptcy proceedings within the meaning of that article.

It therefore becomes necessary to consider the alternative grounds of appeal relied upon by Mr Hegarty, namely that even if the provisions of art 1 do not oust the application of the other provisions of the convention in this case, none the less, the judge in the county court was wrong to decide that, by virtue of the provisions of art 16 of the convention, exclusive jurisdiction in respect of the trustee's claims is given to the Spanish court, so that this court has no jurisdiction to entertain the trustee's application.

As appears from paras 1 and 3 of art 16, which I have already read, exclusive jurisdiction in the courts of Minorca (I suppose, more properly, the courts of Spain) can exist either on the footing that the trustee's proceedings are proceedings which have, as their object, rights in rem in immovable property situated in Spain, or on the basis that they are proceedings which have, as their object, the validity of entries in public registers.

Mr Hegarty sought valiantly to argue on behalf of the trustee that his proceedings fell within neither of those paragraphs of art 16. So far as the first paragraph is concerned, he submitted that the trustee's proceedings did not have, as their object, rights in rem in immovable property because what they sought were orders in personam against the respondents to cause the Spanish property register to be rectified by showing the trustee as proprietor of one-half of the villa. Alternatively, Mr Hegarty sought, as I understood his submission, to argue that the trustee had some personal claim or claim in personam against Mr Hulse by reason of the fact that Mr Hulse had purported to take a transfer of the bankrupt's half-share in the villa from Mrs Hayward and to register himself as the sole proprietor of the villa in circumstances in which he knew perfectly well that the trustee himself was claiming Mr Hayward's half-share as trustee in bankruptcy.

So far as para 3 of art 16 is concerned, Mr Hegarty denied that the proceedings had, as their object, the validity of entries in the Minorcan land registry. He said he was not, in his proceedings, challenging the validity of the register, but merely seeking a declaration in the first place that he was entitled to a half-share in the villa and, consequent upon that, orders against the respondents to compel them to cause the necessary amending entries to be made in the register so as to show the trustee's half-share in the villa.

On this part of the case, Miss Hitching contended that, indeed, what the trustee was claiming in his proceedings was the clearest possible right in rem. For that proposition she relied on a passage from the report of Professor Schlosser referred to in s 3(3) of the 1982 Act, in which he refers to ownership as being 'the most comprehensive right in rem' (see OJ 1979 C 59, pp 120–121, para 166).

A little earlier in that paragraph he had commented on the essential differences between rights in personam and rights in rem where he said:

a   'The concept of a right in rem—as distinct from a right in personam—is
common to the legal systems of the original member states of the E.E.C.,
even though the distinction does not appear everywhere with the same
clarity. A right in personam can only be claimed against a particular person;
thus only the purchaser is obliged to pay the purchase price and only the
lessor of an article is obliged to permit its use. A right in rem, on the other
b   hand, is available against the whole world. The most important legal
consequence flowing from the nature of a right in rem is that its owner is
entitled to demand that the thing in which it exists be given up by anyone not
enjoying a prior right.'

I was referred to a decision of the Court of Justice of the European
c   Communities in *Webb v Webb* Case C-294/92 [1994] 3 All ER 911, [1994] ECR
I-1717, where, on a reference from the Court of Appeal, the Court of Justice
decided that a claim by a plaintiff based on an allegation that a defendant held
land as trustee for the plaintiff and for relief against the defendant accordingly was
a claim, not to a right in rem, but to a right in personam. It was pointed out in
the decision that in that case the plaintiff concerned did not claim that he already
d   enjoyed legal ownership of the property concerned. His claim was based on the
proposition that he was entitled as cestui que trust to enforce a trust of the
property against the defendant.

In the present case, submitted Miss Hitching for the first respondent, what is
claimed by the trustee is not a right in personam in relation to the villa but the
e   very right of ownership to one-half of it, which, apparently under Spanish law,
judging by the entries on the register that I have seen, can exist as what we would
regard as a legal and not only (as under our system) an equitable interest in the
villa. The trustee's claim, submitted Miss Hitching, was of the very essence of a
claim to a right in rem, in that it was a claim to ownership itself of one-half of the
f   villa.

In my judgment, that submission is sound. Although English law does not
perhaps recognise quite the same distinction between rights in personam and
rights in rem as explained by Professor Schlosser in the report to which I have
referred, it seems to me clear that, within the meaning of art 16 of the convention,
construed even apart from Professor Schlosser's report, let alone in the light of it,
g   it is difficult to contemplate any right more clearly a right in rem than a right to
legal ownership such as is claimed by the trustee in the present case.

Accordingly, in my judgment, the trustee's claim by the originating application
was a claim in proceedings which, within the meaning of para 1 of art 16, had as
their 'object' (I think by that must be meant subject matter) a right in rem in
h   immovable property, namely the villa.

In the light of that conclusion, it is really unnecessary to decide whether the
claim also fell within para 3 of art 16, as being made in proceedings which had as
their object the validity of entries in public registers. It seems to me that, given
the trustee's claim as formulated in the points of claim, to the effect that the
j   register of land held in Minorca required rectification by reason of the fact that it
showed what the trustee said were void transactions, indeed the proceedings
brought by the trustee were proceedings which had as their object (or subject
matter) the validity of entries in a public register. There is no doubt, as I
understand the proceedings, that the whole purpose of them, from the trustee's
point of view, was to get the Minorcan property register rectified so as to show
him as the owner of half the property because, without that, he was facing

difficulties, if not an impossibility, of effectively dealing with the half- share which he claimed to be entitled to as part of the bankrupt's estate.

Thus, in my judgment, the judge in the county court was entirely right in the conclusions he reached and in his overall conclusion that, given that the convention applied to the proceedings brought by the trustee's originating application, and given that art 16 of the convention conferred exclusive jurisdiction on the courts of Spain, being the country in which the relevant property is situated and the relevant registers are situated, the English court had no jurisdiction to entertain the trustee's application and that it should accordingly be struck out. For those reasons, I dismiss the trustee's appeal.

So far as the first respondent's cross-appeal is concerned, that arises in this way. Although the first respondent won before the judge in the county court in the sense that he was successful in his application to strike out the trustee's ordinary application, the judge declined to make any order for costs in favour of the first respondent. There is no transcript of any reasons given by the judge for that conclusion, but it has apparently been agreed between counsel, for the purposes of this appeal, that his reasons are accurately set out in ground 2 of the grounds of appeal specified in the first respondent's notice of appeal before this court, where he says:

'The reason given by the learned judge for refusing the first respondent his costs of the ordinary application was that, so the learned judge held, the first respondent had in his defence put in issue a point of English bankruptcy law which was not really an issue in the proceedings but which, had it been in issue, would or could arguably have made the proceedings a matter principally concerned with bankruptcy which would have been outside the scope of the Brussels Convention.'

I fail to see the reality of that point taken by the judge. As I understand the first respondent's defence, he denied that the bankrupt's title to half the villa vested in the trustee. Neither before the judge below nor before this court has the first respondent made any submission to the effect that, quite apart from the application of Spanish law, as the lex situs, the trustee was not entitled to whatever property rights were vested in the bankrupt at the date of the bankruptcy order. It is quite clear that the first respondent's case is based on the proposition that Spanish Law, in relation to registration of title to property, has the effect, in the events which have happened, that the trustee is not now entitled to any interest in the villa.

On this cross-appeal, Mr Hegarty for the trustee relied on a reference in the judge's judgment to the fact that, before the judge, it was conceded on behalf of the first respondent that he took no point on the application of the provisions of the English Insolvency Act 1986 vesting the bankrupt's estate in the trustee, as opposed to the point that any effect which those provisions might otherwise have had in relation to the villa were ousted by the relevant provisions of Spanish law in the events which have happened. Mr Hegarty sought to justify the judge's conclusion on costs on the basis that the judge made it plain in his judgment that he reached the conclusion he did, namely that the convention applied to the trustee's proceedings, on the basis, at least in part, of the first respondent's concession that he was not arguing any point on the provisions of the 1986 Act itself. Therefore, Mr Hegarty submitted, the judge was perfectly entitled to say that, since the first respondent had not made any such concession clear in his a pleading, he ought not to have his costs of the successful application to strike out the trustee's claim.

Of course the question of costs is in the discretion of the judge. Miss Hitching on behalf of the first respondent rightly referred me to what was said by the Court of Appeal in relation to the exercise of a judge's discretion on costs in *Scherer v Counting Instruments Ltd* [1986] 2 All ER 529, [1986] 1 WLR 615, where the court
b stated what, if I may say so, is fairly obvious, namely that a judge's discretion on costs must be exercised judicially, and that a judge cannot penalise a party in costs except on the basis of some relevant consideration.

Miss Hitching submitted that, in the present case, it is apparent that the judge did not properly exercise his discretion in relation to the first respondent's costs of the application before him. That application succeeded. Prima facie, costs
c would be expected to follow the event, yet the judge declined to let costs follow the event on the grounds, so far as appears from the agreed statement in the notice of appeal, that somehow the first respondent had encouraged the trustee's resistance to the application to strike out his originating application by appearing in the first respondent's defence to put some question of English bankruptcy law
d in issue.

With great respect to the judge, I think he did err fundamentally in purporting to exercise the discretion in the way in which he did. The question before him was whether the trustee's application amounted to bankruptcy or succession proceedings within the meaning of art 1 of the convention. Even if it had been right that the first respondent in his defence raised some question of bankruptcy
e law, it is not obvious to me that that would have the effect of converting the trustee's claim into something which it otherwise was not.

Be that as it may, in my judgment, on a fair reading of the defence in this case, it did not put in issue any question of bankruptcy law. It simply denied that the trustee had title to the relevant half-share of the villa, which is a denial which is
f still maintained by the first respondent on the footing (albeit that this footing was not spelt out perhaps as clearly as one might have ideally liked in the defence) that Spanish law, being the relevant lex situs relating to the registration of title to Spanish property, has the effect that Mr Hulse's registered title defeats any title that the trustee might otherwise have.

g To say that that denial in the defence could somehow be treated as having encouraged the trustee's persistence in resisting the application to strike out the originating application seems to me, with all due respect to the judge, to have been misconceived.

Accordingly, in my judgment, the only reason given by the judge for the decision he reached on costs was not a reason relevant to the issue of costs. The
h judge gave no valid reason for costs not following the event. Accordingly, I allow the cross-appeal and vary the judge's order by providing that the costs of the application to the judge should be paid by the trustee.

Appeal dismissed. Cross-appeal allowed.

j
                                                    Mary Rose Plummer   Barrister.

Banco Exterior Internacional SA v Thomas and another

a

COURT OF APPEAL, CIVIL DIVISION

SIR RICHARD SCOTT V-C, ROCH AND POTTER LJJ

b

4, 5, 31 JULY 1996

Equity – Undue influence – Presumption of undue influence – Close friends – Woman executing guarantee and legal charge in favour of bank as security for indebtedness of close male friend in return for regular income payments – Bank requiring woman to obtain independent legal advice – Woman ignoring solicitor's advice not to proceed and executing security – Solicitor informing bank of his advice to woman – Bank bringing action to enforce guarantee – Whether entry into security procured by undue influence – Whether bank fixed with constructive notice of undue influence.

c

In 1984 Mrs D, who was living in straitened financial circumstances, agreed to a *d* suggestion from a close personal friend, M, that he would pay her a regular income, if she would guarantee his borrowing and provide her house as security for an expansion of his secondhand car business. On approaching M's bank to effect the transaction, the bank required Mrs D to obtain independent legal advice about the nature and effect of the proposed transaction, and she duly consulted the solicitor nominated by the bank. Thereupon, Mrs D executed a guarantee *e* and a legal charge whereby she guaranteed M's liability to the bank up to a limit of £75,000 plus interest and costs and charged her residence as security for his indebtedness. In order to complete the transaction, the deeds to the property had to be obtained from Mrs D's former solicitor, F, who advised her strongly against entering the transaction and informed the bank of his views by telephone. F also *f* informed the bank by letter that, despite his strong advice to the contrary, Mrs D had decided to proceed. Thereafter, M's indebtedness to the bank increased to over £108,000, whereupon the bank made a formal demand on Mrs D for payment under the guarantee, and commenced proceedings against her for recovery. Following Mrs D's death, her executors continued as defendants, and with the bank's agreement the property was sold. The executors contended that *g* Mrs D had been induced to provide the security by M's undue influence; that the bank had notice of that undue influence and, accordingly, it was not entitled to enforce its security. The judge held that a presumption of undue influence arose in the circumstances and that, while the bank did not have actual or constructive notice of that undue influence when the guarantee and legal charge were signed, *h* it was put on notice thereof by F's telephone communication and so could not enforce its security in respect of overdrawings by M after that date. The bank appealed, contending that undue influence had not been established and that F's telephone communication had not put it on notice of any undue influence. The executors challenged the judge's conclusion that the bank did not have *j* constructive notice of any undue influence prior to the signing of the guarantee and legal charge.

Held – Since a bank had no business inquiring into the personal relationship between those with whom it had dealings or as to their personal motives for wanting to help one another, it was not the bank's business to ask itself why a   Mrs D was willing to stand surety for M's indebtedness but merely to ensure that she knew what she was doing and wanted to do it, which she did, having received independent legal advice about the nature and effect of the transaction. Accordingly, the bank did not have constructive notice of any undue influence when the guarantee and legal charge were signed. Neither, having regard to the content, had F's telephone communication to the bank put the bank on notice of

b   any such undue influence. Moreover, in the circumstances, the presumption of undue influence had been rebutted and the evidence did not justify a finding that Mrs D had lacked a free and full will when she signed the documents. It followed that the bank was entitled to enforce the guarantee and legal charge and to be paid £75,000 with interest out of the proceeds of sale of the property, and the appeal would therefore be allowed (see p 55 *b* to *e j* to p 56 *b h* to p 57 *e*, post).

c   *Barclays Bank plc v O'Brien* [1993] 4 All ER 417 considered.

Notes

For the avoidance of a guarantee procured by duress or undue influence, see 20 *Halsbury's Laws* (4th edn reissue) paras 133–138, and for cases on the subject, see

d   26(1) *Digest* (2nd reissue) 93–95, *302–309*.

Cases referred to in judgments

Allcard v Skinner (1887) 36 Ch D 145, [1886–90] All ER Rep 90, CA.
Barclays Bank plc v O'Brien [1993] 4 All ER 417, [1994] 1 AC 180, [1993] 3 WLR 786, HL.

e   *Zamet v Hyman* [1961] 3 All ER 933, [1961] 1 WLR 1442, CA.

Cases also cited or referred to in skeleton arguments

Abbey National Building Society v Cann [1990] 1 All ER 1085, [1991] 1 AC 56, HL.
Bailey v Barnes [1894] 1 Ch 25, CA.

f   *Banco Exterior Internacional v Mann* [1995] 1 All ER 936, CA.
Bank of Baroda v Rayarel [1995] 2 FLR 376, CA.
Blackwood v London Chartered Bank of Australia (1874) LR 5 PC 92.
Bradford Banking Co Ltd v Henry Briggs, Son & Co Ltd (1886) 12 App Cas 29, HL.
Chaplin & Co Ltd v Brammall [1908] 1 KB 233, CA.
CIBC Mortgages plc v Pitt (1993) Times, 7 April, [1993] CA Transcript 580; *rvsd*

g   [1993] 4 All ER 433, [1994] 1 AC 200, HL.
Cooke v Wilton (1860) 29 Beav 100, 54 ER 564.
Coomber, Re, Coomber v Coomber [1911] 1 Ch 723, CA.
Deeley v Lloyds Bank Ltd [1912] AC 756, HL.
Hodgson v Marks [1971] 2 All ER 684, [1971] Ch 892, CA.

h   *Hopkinson v Rolt* (1861) 9 HL Cas 514, 11 ER 829.
Inche Noriah v Shaik Allie Bin Omar [1929] AC 127, PC.
Macmillan Inc v Bishopsgate Investment plc Trust (No 3) [1995] 3 All ER 747, [1995] 1 WLR 978.
Massey v Midland Bank plc [1995] 1 All ER 929, CA.

j   *Midland Bank plc v Serter* [1995] 1 FLR 1034, CA.
Motor Oil Hellas (Corinth) Refineries SA v Shipping Corp of India, The Kanchenjunga [1990] 1 Lloyd's Rep 391, HL.
O'Sullivan v Management Agency and Music Ltd [1985] 3 All ER 351, [1985] QB 428, CA.
Peyman v Lanjani [1984] 3 All ER 703, [1985] Ch 457, CA.
Scholefield v Templer (1859) 4 De G & J 429, 45 ER 166.

Spence v Crawford [1939] 3 All ER 271, HL.

TSB Bank plc v Camfield [1995] 1 All ER 951, [1995] 1 WLR 430, CA.   *a*

Appeal

By notice dated 18 January 1995 the plaintiff, Banco Exterior Internacional SA (formerly Banco Exterior-UK) (the bank), appealed from the judgment of Mr Recorder Ross Martyn given on 2 November 1994 in the Mayor's and City of *b* London Court whereby he found that the bank was not entitled to enforce a guarantee and legal charge in respect of overdrawings against the defendant executors, Edward Hugh Gwyn Thomas and John Edward Barry, of the guarantor, Mrs Patricia Dempsey, since the guarantee had been procured by undue influence of which the bank had notice. The facts are set out in the *c* judgment of Sir Richard Scott V-C.

Hazel Williamson QC and *Thomas Jefferies* (instructed by *Eversheds*, Norwich) for the bank.

Charles Falconer QC and *Marcus Smith* (instructed by *Keene Marsland*) for the *d* executors.

Cur adv vult

31 July 1996. The following judgments were delivered.

e

SIR RICHARD SCOTT V-C. This is an appeal from the judgment of Mr Recorder Ross Martyn given on 2 November 1994 in the Mayor's and City of London Court.

The plaintiff in the action, and appellant before us, is Banco Exterior Internacional SA (the bank). The point at issue is whether or to what extent the *f* bank was entitled to rely on and enforce, first, a guarantee dated 12 February 1985 under which Mrs Patricia Dempsey guaranteed the liability to the bank of a Mr John Patrick Mulchay (up to a limit of £75,000 plus interest and costs) and, second, a legal charge signed by Mrs Dempsey on the same date, 12 January 1985, but dated 7 June 1985, whereby she charged her residence, 4 Arran Mews, Crosslands Avenue, Ealing, as security for the payment to the bank of Mr *g* Mulchay's indebtedness.

The bank's action to enforce the guarantee and the legal charge was commenced against Mrs Dempsey by originating summons dated 28 October 1988. Mrs Dempsey died, however, on 15 August 1992 before the action had been brought to trial. An order to carry on against her executors, Edward Hugh *h* Gwyn Thomas and John Edward Barry, was made on 5 January 1993. They, therefore, were the defendants when the trial took place and are the respondents before us. Following Mrs Dempsey's death, 4 Arran Mews was, by agreement between the bank and the executors, sold. The bank's claim under the legal charge became, therefore, transferred to the proceeds of sale.

j

The executors' defence to the bank's action is, very summarily stated, as follows: (1) Mrs Dempsey was induced by Mr Mulchay's undue influence to agree to provide security (in the form of the guarantee and the legal charge) for the overdraft facility that the bank was willing (if it obtained the security) to allow him; (2) the bank was, in the circumstances of the case, on notice of that undue influence; and (3) the bank, accordingly, was not entitled to enforce its security.

The judge held that the undue influence had been proved. He held that the
a bank did not, at the time the guarantee and legal charge were signed, have notice,
actual or constructive, of the undue influence. However, he went on to hold that
certain events that took place in April 1988, some three months after the
guarantee and the legal charge had been signed, did put the bank on notice of the
undue influence. He held that the bank could not rely on the guarantee and legal
b charge in respect of overdrawings by Mr Mulchay after April 1988. For reasons
that I will later explain he thought, however, that the bank was entitled to £30,000
out of the proceeds of sale.

In this appeal the bank has challenged the judge's conclusion that undue
influence had been established and has challenged his conclusion that the events
of April 1988 put the bank on notice of any undue influence. The executors have
c served a respondents' notice challenging the judge's conclusion that prior to the
signing of the documents the bank did not have constructive notice of undue
influence and challenging the decision regarding the £30,000.

Accordingly, it is necessary for me to describe the facts of the case with some
care.
d Mrs Dempsey was, in 1985, 46 years old. Her partner of many years, Mr
Dempsey, had died in 1982. Prior to his death she had carried on a small retail
business, a dress shop, in premises owned by Mr Dempsey and adjacent to those
in which he carried on his own business. Mr Dempsey died without having made
testamentary provision for Mrs Dempsey. The residence they occupied was in
e their joint names and passed to Mrs Dempsey by virtue of survivorship but,
thereapart, none of his estate passed to her. Her straitened financial
circumstances obliged her to cease carrying on the dress shop business. She sold
the residence and with the proceeds purchased a smaller residence, namely 4
Arran Mews. The capital left over after the purchase of 4 Arran Mews provided
her with a small income.
f Mrs Dempsey's difficulties brought about by the death of her long-standing
partner were added to by the discovery in 1983 that she was suffering from
cancer. This cancer was the cause of her death in 1992.

In 1983 Mrs Dempsey met Mr Mulchay. He was some six years younger than
she was. They became friendly. The judge recorded, and I should do so as well,
g that although a relationship of close friendship developed between them, their
relationship was neither a romantic nor a sexual one.

Mr Mulchay was in business as a dealer in secondhand motor cars. By
November 1984 he had been a customer of the bank for about a year and was
allowed an overdraft of up to £4,000. He had in mind plans to expand his car
h dealing activities but for that purpose required additional capital. The bank made
it clear to Mr Mulchay that additional overdraft facilities would require suitable
security to be provided. So Mr Mulchay suggested to Mrs Dempsey that if she
would guarantee his borrowing and provide her house as security, he, in return,
would pay her a regular income. The evidence regarding this arrangement,
j which was never recorded in writing, left unclear the exact terms that were
agreed. It was certainly agreed that a regular sum should be paid, but it is not
clear whether it would be £500 per calendar month or £125 per week. In his
evidence Mr Mulchay referred on occasion to £150 per week. There was also
some agreement under which Mr Mulchay would pay various household and
other bills for Mrs Dempsey. The judge found that—

'the regular payment was to be of the order of £500 a month, and ... any payment of bills were recoverable by Mr Mulchay from Mrs Dempsey, so far as they had not been debited against the regular payments ...'

The arrangement between Mr Mulchay and Mrs Dempsey having been agreed upon, the bank agreed to allow Mr Mulchay an overdraft of £70,000 supported by Mrs Dempsey's guarantee (limited to £75,000) and by a legal charge of 4 Arran Mews securing Mr Mulchay's indebtedness (up to the same limit). The bank's records show that they placed a value of £120,000 on 4 Arran Mews. Very shortly before 12 February 1985, Mrs Dempsey and Mr Mulchay visited the bank and discussed the proposed transaction with Mr Guirao, the manager of the bank's Spitalfield branch at which Mr Mulchay kept his account. Mrs Dempsey was not a customer of the bank. Mr Guirao told Mrs Dempsey that she would have to go to a solicitor independent of the bank for the solicitor to explain to her the nature and effect of the guarantee and legal charge that it was proposed she should sign.

The bank had a standing practice that a third party proposing to provide security in support of a loan by the bank to a customer would be required to go to an independent solicitor to be advised about the nature and effect of the proposed transaction. This very sensible practice preceded the decision of the House of Lords in *Barclays Bank plc v O'Brien* [1993] 4 All ER 417, [1994] 1 AC 180. The wisdom of the practice was indorsed by the judgments in that case. The bank's Spitalfield branch had an arrangement with a local solicitor, Mr David Bishop, that it would refer to him individuals who did not have solicitors of their own to whom they would prefer to go. So Mr Guirao referred Mrs Dempsey to Mr Bishop. Mr Guirao was not told about the collateral arrangement under which Mr Mulchay was to pay a regular income to Mrs Dempsey. Of that the bank knew nothing.

On 12 February 1985 Mrs Dempsey visited Mr Bishop at his office. Mr Mulchay accompanied her. Mr Bishop could not recall whether Mr Mulchay had been present while he advised Mrs Dempsey but he said, in evidence, that his 'normal practice ... would be not to have anybody else in the room, other than the person signing'. Mrs Dempsey had with her the guarantee and legal charge that she was being asked to sign. She signed both documents in the presence of Mr Bishop. Mr Bishop witnessed her signature and on each document added the words:

'In the presence of the undersigned who prior to the execution hereof explained the nature and effect of this Guarantee which Mrs Dempsey appeared to fully understand.'

Mr Bishop, when questioned about the occasion, understandably could not recall any details, but there is no reason to doubt that Mr Bishop did advise Mrs Dempsey as to the 'nature and effect' of the two documents or to doubt that Mrs Dempsey fully understood his advice. Mr Bishop did not, on the other hand, give Mrs Dempsey any advice as to the wisdom of her agreeing to provide the requested security. He did not seek to discover why she was willing to do so. He was not told and knew nothing about the collateral arrangement for Mr Mulchay to pay a regular income to Mrs Dempsey.

The guarantee signed by Mrs Dempsey was in an unexceptional form, common for bank guarantees. It was expressed to be 'in consideration of the Bank making or continuing advances or otherwise giving credit or affording banking facilities or other financial accommodation ...' to Mr Mulchay. It provided that Mrs Dempsey would 'on demand in writing made to the Guarantor pay or discharge to the Bank all liabilities of the Debtor to the Bank whether present or in future ...' together also with interest, banking charges and other costs and expenses, but subject to the following proviso:

> 'Provided always that ... the aggregate amount for which the Guarantor shall be liable under the guarantee shall not exceed the sum of £75,000 ... together with interest thereon or on such part or parts of the total balance remaining unpaid by the Debtor (not exceeding in aggregate the net amount specified above) as may be due from the date of the Debtor's default, until payment thereof ...'

Mr Mulchay was not a party to and did not sign the guarantee. An issue of construction arises as to the date from which the interest referred to in the proviso should run. As the proviso stands it seems arguable that interest would run on the £75,000 before the date on which demand for payment by the guarantor was first made. We do not need to decide the issue, however, for Miss Williamson QC, counsel for the bank, has told us that the bank does not claim interest on the £75,000 from any earlier date than the date of the demand on Mrs Dempsey for payment.

The legal charge was expressed to be made between Mr Mulchay, Mrs Dempsey and the bank. It was not, however, signed by Mr Mulchay. It contained a covenant by 'the Borrower' (ie Mr Mulchay) to pay on demand any indebtedness of his to the bank and expressed 'the Estate Owner' (ie Mrs Dempsey) to charge 4 Arran Mews 'with payment to the bank of all principal money liabilities interest and other money hereby covenanted to be paid by the Borrower'. The legal charge appears, therefore, to secure the repayment of the whole of Mr Mulchay's indebtedness to the bank.

Miss Williamson has accepted that the indebtedness of Mr Mulchay secured by the legal charge should have been subject to the same £75,000 limitation as was expressed in the guarantee. If it were necessary the legal charge could be rectified accordingly. But since both sides agree that, assuming the legal charge is enforceable, it should be given only the limited effect intended by the parties, a formal order for rectification is not necessary. This feature of the legal charge might, however, be thought to cast somewhat of a cloud over the advice given by Mr Bishop to Mrs Dempsey as to the effect of the legal charge. It was not, however, a point that was put to Mr Bishop in the course of his evidence and I do not think it has any importance in deciding the issues that arise on this appeal.

On 12 February 1985, the day on which Mrs Dempsey signed the two documents, Mr Mulchay's account with the bank was already overdrawn by about £25,000. A note dated 18 February 1985 records the receipt by the bank of the two documents duly signed and witnessed and that the bank was awaiting receipt of the deeds to 4 Arran Mews.

The deeds to 4 Arran Mews were in the custody of a Mr Frere-Smith, a solicitor who had acted for Mr Dempsey, and also for Mrs Dempsey, in the past. It was necessary for Mrs Dempsey to ask him to forward the deeds to the bank. In order to do so she had a meeting with Mr Frere-Smith, in the course of which she informed Mr Frere-Smith of her arrangement with Mr Mulchay under which he was to pay her a regular income. Mr Frere-Smith thought that the arrangement, under which Mrs Dempsey provided capital assets as security for Mr Mulchay's indebtedness in exchange for a regular income to be paid to her by him, was a highly improvident one for her to be entering into. He advised in very strong terms against it. He recorded his advice in an attendance note dated 4 March 1985 in the following terms:

> 'I advised you as strongly as I could against your proposal to mortgage your property to the Bank of Bilbao for the benefit of a man who will in return pay you £125 a week (Mrs Dempsey was clearly in a very emotionally upset state).'

In his evidence Mr Frere-Smith described his view of the arrangement thus:

> 'I smelt a rat straight away because I thought it sounded a very familiar story, that widows and elderly women and the very naive fall for: you produce capital and I will pay you something each week.'

When asked how the matter was left, he said: 'I am afraid I thought she probably was not going to accept my advice ... I was subsequently asked to send the papers to his solicitors.'

Having spoken to Mrs Dempsey, Mr Frere-Smith communicated by telephone with the bank. Since it is this telephone call (it may be there were two calls) that the judge relied on as fixing the bank with notice of undue influence, it is necessary to pay careful attention to the content of the call or calls.

Mr Frere-Smith's evidence-in-chief contained these passages:

> '*Q.* Can you remember the import of your conversation with the bank? *A.* I know the impression I formed at the time, because I hoped that the bank would stop her from doing this.
>
> *Q.* What was the impression you formed? *A.* I know what the response was, the bank simply took an entirely different view to the view I had taken ... they were not prepared to stop her doing anything ...
>
> *Q.* Can you recall whether you made that [ie Mr Frere-Smith's view that Mrs Dempsey was a vulnerable person being taken advantage of] clear to the bank? *A.* I cannot honestly say at this stage because I have not seen the files ... all I can say is that the bank were not prepared to take the line which I hoped they would take, and they appeared to go along with the proposal of Mrs Dempsey.'

Later the judge took up the questioning:

> '*The Recorder* ... I was not entirely clear whether you gave evidence that you actually had a telephone conversation with the bank? ... *A.* To the best of my recollection I did, but I could not say that I definitely did.
>
> *Q.* How many such conversations ...? *A.* It would not be many, probably two.
>
> *Q.* ... who did you speak to? *A.* It would be the person who was dealing with the transaction.
>
> *Q.* ... what did you say to him? *A.* I think I said, because I cannot be certain about this—the tenor of what I would have said would have been that I did not think that the proposal should be accepted by the bank, bearing in mind Mrs Dempsey's position, financially and otherwise.'

The telephone communications between Mr Frere-Smith and the bank probably took place on 5 March. On 6 March 1985 Mrs Dempsey signed an authority for Mr Frere-Smith to deliver to the bank the deeds of 4 Arran Mews. This authority was lodged with the bank. The bank forwarded it to Mr Frere-Smith under cover of a letter referring to 'our telephone conversations of *a* yesterday'. The judge found that the authority had been prepared in the bank. Mr Frere-Smith responded on 12 March by saying that he would take Mrs Dempsey's instructions. He plainly did so for, by letter to the bank dated 11 April 1985, he said that Mrs Dempsey, despite his strong advice to the contrary, had decided to proceed, but only on the basis that a limit of £30,000 should be placed on the indebtedness of Mr Mulchay secured by the legal charge. The bank had *b* no record of having received this letter, but the judge expressed himself as satisfied on the balance of probabilities that the bank had received it. In the event, Mr Mulchay's liability to the bank was already well in excess of the proposed £30,000 limit. By 1 March he was over £35,000 overdrawn, by 1 April over £67,000 overdrawn and by 11 April the figure stood at over £76,000. The legal charge was dated 7 June 1985. The evidence does not disclose any obvious reason *c* for the delay in the dating of the document. However, the delay is, in my view, immaterial. Both the guarantee and the legal charge were, in my opinion, prima facie effective from the time they were lodged, duly signed, with the bank. That was done on, or very shortly after, 12 February.

Mr Mulchay's indebtedness to the bank continued to increase. By February *d* 1986 it stood at over £90,000 and by 24 November 1986 at over £108,000. In 1987 there were letters from the bank to Mr Mulchay pressing for repayment and, in August, at a meeting at the Spitalfields branch between Mrs Dempsey and bank officials, the situation regarding Mr Mulchay's indebtedness and her liabilities under the guarantee and legal charge were discussed. On 4 January 1988 the bank made a formal demand on Mrs Dempsey for payment under the guarantee. In *e* December 1988, the action was commenced.

I should record also that Mr Mulchay's payments of income to Mrs Dempsey and his payment of her bills did not continue beyond 1986 or 1987. The relevant evidence was given by Mr Mulchay:

f '*Q.* How long did you go on making payments to her? *A.* Up to 1986, something like that, 1987.

Q. 1986/1987? *A.* Yes ... I paid—first of all I paid her money every week, her £125 or £150. She got that every week. And I paid other bills of hers, Yes ...

Q. Then what happened in 1986 or 1987? *A.* I think the bills came to *g* £40,000 or something that I paid, and then I said 'Look we cannot keep up the same arrangement as this' but I did pay other bills for her after that, I did not pay weekly money any more but I still paid some of her bills.

Q. So you sort of stopped the arrangement? *A.* Yes ... what stopped in 1986/1987 was the weekly money.

Q. And you had paid out about £40,000 in total? *A.* Yes.
h *The Recorder* ... you say £40,000 in total. Is that £40,000 including the £125 or £150 per week? *A.* No, Sir.'

It seems from this evidence that the total amount paid by Mr Mulchay to Mrs Dempsey may have been something approaching £50,000.

j In presenting the executors' case, Mr Falconer QC has placed very great reliance on a passage from the opinion of Lord Browne-Wilkinson in *Barclays Bank plc v O'Brien* [1993] 4 All ER 417 at 428, [1994] 1 AC 180 at 195, where he said:

'A wife who has been induced to stand as a surety for her husband's debts by his undue influence, misrepresentation or some other legal wrong has an equity as against him to set aside that transaction.'

In *O'Brien's* case itself the husband was joint owner with his wife of the mortgaged property. So the second mortgage, whereby the matrimonial home *a* was charged with repayment of the husband's indebtedness to the bank, was a transaction to which the husband, the wife and the bank were all parties. An analysis under which that transaction could have been set aside by the wife against the husband on account of misrepresentation and by the wife against the bank if the bank had constructive notice of that misrepresentation presents no *b* conceptual difficulty. What would have been the situation, however, if the husband had not been a party to the legal charge? If the *O'Brien* facts had been identical, save that the wife had been the sole owner of the matrimonial home, would the result have been any different? I do not think that any sensible system of jurisprudence could justify a difference in result that depended on whether the debtor (the husband) happened to be a party to the transaction between the *c* surety (the wife) and the lender (the bank). In such a case, if the lender had constructive (or actual) notice of the misrepresentation or undue influence by the borrower that had led the surety to contract with the bank, the surety would surely be able to set aside the contract.

In the present case, Mr Mulchay was not a party to the guarantee nor, although *d* named as a party, did he sign the legal charge. The bank knew, of course, that Mrs Dempsey had agreed to stand as surety for Mr Mulchay and to provide her house, 4 Arran Mews, as security, but it did not know, actually or constructively, or have any interest in knowing, on what, if any, terms Mrs Dempsey had agreed with Mr Mulchay to do so. In a case such as the present it does not seem to me *e* to make any sense to ask whether Mrs Dempsey had an equity as against Mr Mulchay to set aside the transaction she had entered into with the bank. The question to my mind is simply whether the bank had any actual or constructive notice that she had entered into the transaction with the bank under undue influence exerted by Mr Mulchay.

f

The case depends, of course, on the requisite undue influence being established. The judge dealt with this part of the case by asking himself, first, whether there was a presumption of undue influence. He found that there was. The bank has challenged this finding. There is, to my mind, some substance to their challenge. Mrs Dempsey was advised by Mr Bishop as to the 'nature and effect' of the transaction. Mr Bishop was satisfied that she understood it. After *g* receiving Mr Bishop's advice, she continued with it. Later, she received very strong and positive advice from Mr Frere-Smith against the transaction. She rejected Mr Frere-Smith's advice and decided to continue with the transaction. She took no step, having received that advice, to have the transaction set aside. It is not alleged, and the evidence does not justify the conclusion, that Mrs *h* Dempsey lacked the capacity to contract with the bank. Yet, that is the conclusion towards which Mr Falconer's submissions seem, to me, to tend. I would accept that the arrangement made between Mrs Dempsey and Mr Mulchay was one that any adviser would advise strongly against. But the purpose of advisers is to advise. The recipient of the advice does not have to accept it. He *j* or she can decide, fully informed by the advice that has been received, whether or not to proceed with the allegedly ill-advised and improvident transaction. In the present case, Mrs Dempsey may well have been attracted by the offer of £500 per month (or £125 per week). She was of full age. She suffered from no mental infirmity. And she had had the nature and effect of the transaction with the bank explained to her by an independent solicitor.

The so-called 'presumption' of undue influence does no more than to require

a that, in the absence of any rebutting evidence, a conclusion of undue influence should be reached. The classic rebutting evidence would be evidence that advice had been given by an independent solicitor. Mr Bishop was such a solicitor. Having received his advice Mrs Dempsey signed the two documents. It cannot be said that when she did so she lacked a full understanding of their nature and

b effect. In my judgment, there was, at the foot of Mrs Dempsey's meeting with Mr Bishop, no further part to be played by the presumption and I would hold that the presumption was rebutted. Mr Falconer argued that her signing of the two documents showed that she was so fully under the influence of Mr Mulchay that Mr Bishop's advice made no difference. This argument is circuitous and, if accepted, would turn what is only a presumption of undue influence into an

c irrebuttable conclusion. In my judgment, the evidence did not justify a finding that, when she signed the documents, Mrs Dempsey lacked a free and full will and informed understanding of what she was doing (see *Allcard v Skinner* (1887) 36 Ch D 145, [1886–90] All ER Rep 90 and *Zamet v Hyman* [1961] 3 All ER 933, [1961] 1 WLR 1442, both of which were referred to by the judge).

d In any event, the judge was, in my opinion, correct in rejecting the assertion that, at the time the two documents were signed, the bank had constructive notice of undue influence. The bank knew no more of Mrs Dempsey's affairs and relationship with Mr Mulchay than that she was prepared to stand surety for his indebtedness to the bank. It was not the bank's business to ask itself why she was willing to do this. It was the bank's business to make sure that she knew what she

e was doing. So the bank required her to go to an independent solicitor to be advised about the 'nature and effect' of the transaction and in whose presence she could, if so advised, sign the documents. Mrs Dempsey did so. The signed documents were returned to the bank with Mr Bishop's confirmation indorsed thereon that she had had the documents explained to her and understood them.

f That put an end, in my opinion, to any question of constructive notice of any vitiating element undermining Mrs Dempsey's apparent consent to the transaction.

In any case in which constructive notice of some alleged impropriety is relied on, it is relevant to ask what inquiries ought to have been made or what steps ought to have been taken by the person said to have been affected by the

g constructive notice. The answers to these questions will sometimes show the unreasonableness of the constructive notice charge. So here. Mr Falconer submitted that the bank should have made inquiries of Mr Mulchay and Mrs Dempsey as to the nature of their relationship and as to the nature of the arrangement between them under which Mrs Dempsey had agreed to stand

h surety for Mr Mulchay's indebtedness. These inquiries, he said, would or should have revealed four things: (i) that Mrs Dempsey had no assets other than her house; (ii) that she had no source of income other than Mr Mulchay; (iii) that she was a friend of Mr Mulchay and that he assisted her in a number of ways; and (iv) that the arrangement was, as Mrs Dempsey saw it, a way of relieving her financial

j predicament.

The bank would thus, Mr Falconer submitted, have been alerted to the possible existence of undue influence. These submissions are, in my opinion, unacceptable for a number of reasons. First, the inquiries that it is suggested the bank should have made would have constituted unwarrantable impertinence on the bank's part. A bank has no business inquiring into the personal relationship between those with whom it has business dealings or as to their personal motives for wanting to help one another. A bank is not to be treated as a branch of the social services agencies. Second, if these impertinent inquiries had been made, and if answers on the lines suggested had been elicited, the answers, far from suggesting undue influence, would have revealed that Mrs Dempsey might have had a very firm and clearly thought-out reason for entering into the arrangement, namely, that she wanted extra income and was prepared to take a risk with her capital in order to achieve it. The critical point, however, to my mind is that the bank was engaging in a business transaction and had no reason to do more than to ensure that Mrs Dempsey knew what she was doing and wanted to do it.

I now come to Mr Frere-Smith's involvement. As to this, the judge referred to Mr Frere-Smith's telephone conversations with the bank and then continued as follows:

'In my view, the bank must be treated from the time of those telephone conversations, or a reasonable time thereafter (to allow it to consider its position), as having notice that Mrs Dempsey might have an equity to set aside the guarantee and legal charge. My reasoning is this. A lender has taken a guarantee and legal charge as security. A short time thereafter it has at least two telephone conversations with a solicitor who had been consulted by the guarantor. That solicitor expresses himself forcefully in the terms I have found Mr Frere-Smith did express himself. If that is not enough to give the notice, I ask rhetorically, what would be, short of some document?'

In this passage, in my opinion, the judge fell into error. What was it of which it is said the bank had notice? The 'equity' could not be a right to set the legal charge and guarantee aside, for those transactions had already been entered into in circumstances that were not, as the judge had correctly found, impeachable by Mrs Dempsey. Was it an equity to prevent the bank from making any further advances to Mr Mulchay that would be secured by the guarantee and legal charge? This, I think, is what the judge must have had in mind. But Mrs Dempsey had had full and firm advice from Mr Frere-Smith as to the inadvisability and improvidence of the transaction, but had none the less decided to proceed. This decision was evidenced by her signing on 6 March 1988 the authority to deliver up the title deeds and by her leaving that authority with the bank. Those acts constituted, in my opinion, an unequivocal decision, made after receiving Mr Frere-Smith's advice, to proceed with the transaction. Mrs Dempsey was not bound to accept Mr Frere-Smith's advice and she did not do so. It was not for the bank to decline to allow her to proceed.

In any event, Mr Frere-Smith's evidence of what he said to the bank official to whom he spoke on the telephone did not, in my judgment, come within a mile of putting the bank on notice that Mrs Dempsey was a victim of undue influence. If the strong views expressed by Mr Frere-Smith had come from a lay friend, it might, at most, be said that the bank should have advised Mrs Dempsey to consult a solicitor about her position. But Mr Frere-Smith was a solicitor. He had advised her. And she had decided to proceed.

In my judgment, the telephone communication between Mr Frere-Smith and the bank did not put the bank on notice of any equity or any continuing impropriety that might affect the validity of the bank's security.

I would, accordingly, allow the bank's appeal. The bank was, in my judgment, entitled to enforce the guarantee and legal charge that Mrs Dempsey had granted. In the circumstances the bank is entitled to be paid out of the net proceeds of sale a   of 4 Arran Mews (and the accumulated interest thereon) the sum of £75,000 together with interest thereon calculated from 4 January 1988.

ROCH LJ. I agree. I would wish to reserve the question whether the principles in *Barclays Bank plc v O'Brien* [1993] 4 All ER 417, [1994] 1 AC 180 can apply where there is no transaction between the person said to be the subject of the undue influence or misrepresentation and the person said to have applied the undue

b   influence or to have made the misrepresentation, for another case.

In the present case, it suffices that Mrs Dempsey was advised on the legal consequences to her of entering into the guarantee and the legal charge. She had those transactions explained to her. Mrs Dempsey received strong advice on the wisdom or rather lack of wisdom of the steps she proposed to take from another

c   solicitor, yet still went ahead with the two transactions.

Mrs Dempsey was not a customer of the bank, who had no knowledge of her financial affairs at the time the guarantee and the legal charge were signed by her. There was no obligation on the bank to inquire into her affairs, either financial or personal. I agree with Sir Richard Scott V-C that any such inquiry would have

d   been an impertinence on the bank's part.

There was no actual or constructive notice on the bank's part of any equity in Mrs Dempsey. I too would allow the plaintiff's appeal and make the orders proposed by Sir Richard Scott V-C.

POTTER LJ. I also agree.

e   *Appeal allowed.*

Celia Fox   Barrister.

Re P-B (a minor) (child cases: hearings in open court)

COURT OF APPEAL, CIVIL DIVISION

BUTLER-SLOSS, PETER GIBSON AND THORPE LJJ

16 MAY, 20 JUNE 1996

Family proceedings – Orders in family proceedings – Residence order – Procedure – Application for residence order to be heard in open court – Judge refusing application on grounds of lack of jurisdiction – Whether judge fettering discretion to conduct trial in open court – Whether exercise of discretion should always be in favour of hearings in open court – Family Proceedings Rules 1991, r 4.16(7).

The court has a discretion under r 4.16(7)[a] of the Family Proceedings Rules 1991 to hear all or part of a case brought under the Children Act 1989 in public, but it is not bound to do so by considerations of open justice or freedom of expression. However, in view of the existing practice of hearing such cases in private, it is unlikely that the court will, other than rarely, hear the evidence relating to the welfare of a child in public (see p 59 h, p 60 c, p 61 b to d j to p 62 a g j and p 63 b f g, post).

Notes

For nature of family proceedings, see 5(2) *Halsbury's Laws* (4th edn reissue) paras 746–749.

For the Family Proceedings Rules 1991, r 4.16, see 12 *Halsbury's Statutory Instruments* (1995 reissue) 89.

Cases referred to in judgments

L (a minor) (police investigation: privilege), Re [1996] 2 All ER 78, [1996] 2 WLR 395, HL.

Oxfordshire CC v M [1994] 2 All ER 269, [1994] Fam 151, [1994] 2 WLR 393, CA.

Scott v Scott [1913] AC 417, [1911–13] All ER Rep 1, HL.

Cases also cited or referred to in skeleton arguments

A-G v Leveller Magazine Ltd [1979] 1 All ER 745, [1979] AC 440, HL.

Agricultural Industries Ltd, Re [1952] 1 All ER 1188, CA.

G (adult patient: publicity), Re [1996] 1 FCR 413.

R v Cambridge and Huntingdon Health Committee, ex p B (1995) Times, 15 March, [1995] CA Transcript 210.

Appeal

By notice dated 29 March 1996 the father of a child, P-B, appealed with leave from the decision of Judge Goldstein sitting in Bow County Court on 14 March 1996 whereby he held that the father's application for a residence order under the Children Act 1989 should not be heard in open court. The facts are set out in the judgment of Butler-Sloss LJ.

The father appeared in person.

Janet Plange (instructed by *Lucas & Ball*) for the mother.

Harry Turcan (instructed by the *Official Solicitor*) as amicus curiae.

Cur adv vult

---

a   Rule 4.16, so far as material, is set out at p 59 j, post

a 20 June 1996. The following judgments were delivered.

BUTLER-SLOSS LJ. Dr P, the appellant, is the father of a small boy aged 5, born on 20 November 1990, in respect of whom he has made an application for a residence order. He raised before the judge a preliminary issue which is the subject of the appeal to this court. He acts for himself and has made it clear that
b this is a matter which he intends to place before the European Court of Human Rights.

None of the facts relating to the family are relevant, save that there are cross-applications for a residence order which raise issues described by the judge as typical and run-of-the-mill. The appellant has not suggested that there are any unusual features. It was due to be heard, with a two day estimate, on 14 March
c 1996. On that day, the appellant father, who appeared in person before Judge Goldstein, asked for the whole case, evidence and judgment, to be in open court. A Mr G, a member of the public, had previously been joined as an intervenor in the proceedings and he supported the father's application. The mother and the Official Solicitor did not object, although the Official Solicitor was concerned at the possibility of the identity of the child being revealed during the hearing. In a
d long and careful judgment the judge decided that all the proceedings should be heard in private and gave the father leave to appeal to this court on this preliminary issue.

In his judgment the judge set out in some detail the father's arguments and concluded:

e 'I can only read, and I do so read and interpret r 4.16(7) of the Family Proceedings Rules 1991, which is the rule to which reference has been made, as being a direction—a rule of court—that hearings of family cases shall be heard and shall continue to be heard in chambers. Like the Earl of Halsbury, I would want chapter and verse as to what should be put before the judge
f before he otherwise directs a hearing of a case in open court. I am not prepared in the course of this judgment to give myself any guidelines as to the sort of case that might be ... I do not feel that I have any power, even if I wished to do so—which I do not—to hear this particular case in open court. I think I would be breaking the law, in the sense that I would be interpreting in a perverse manner the rules of court laid down under the Children Act
g 1989. Therefore, despite all the arguments to the contrary—and again I commend the way in which they were presented to me—I feel I have no alternative but to direct that the hearing of this case shall be in camera.'

The appellant criticises the judge's decision on two main grounds, that he
h fettered his discretion by indicating that he had no option but to hear the case in private and secondly his exercise of discretion was flawed since, if he had exercised it correctly, the only conclusion to which he could come was to hear the entire case in open court.

When the Children Act 1989 came into force in October 1991 there were new rules of procedure for the High Court and the county court contained in the
j Family Proceedings Rules 1991, SI 1991/1247. Rule 4.16 governs hearings and r 4.16(7) states:

'Unless the court otherwise directs, a hearing of, or directions appointment in, proceedings to which this Part applies shall be in chambers.'

The appellant does not suggest that r 4.16(7) is ultra vires the 1989 Act. Consequently the circuit judge hearing the residence applications in the Bow

County Court must apply para (7). What is its effect? To my mind the words are clear and simple. The appellant, however, suggests to us that the default position, as he describes it, if no application is made to hear the case in public, is to hear it in chambers but that the judge ought to exercise his discretion in each case to come to the inevitable conclusion that all cases should be heard in public. He set out a number of arguments in support of hearing child cases in public, including: the right of the public to know what is going on, criticism of secret justice, the dangers of hearing cases in private without the scrutiny of the public and the press, the inability of litigants in person to get experience in conducting child cases, or to find out what the judge is like. He suggested they were rotten laws and a rotten use of discretion.

In support of his arguments he has relied upon a line of cases which set out the importance of open justice in the courts and in particular upon the decision in *Scott v Scott* [1913] AC 417, [1911–13] All ER Rep 1. In that case the House of Lords considered the jurisdiction to hear a nullity suit in camera. The principle of the open administration of justice was clearly and trenchantly asserted in the speeches, (see eg [1913] AC 417 at 476ff, [1911–13] All ER Rep 1 at 29ff per Lord Shaw of Dunfermline). Viscount Haldane LC said:

'While the broad principle is that the Courts of this country must, as between parties, administer justice in public, this principle is subject to apparent exceptions, such as those to which I have referred. But the exceptions are themselves the outcome of a yet more fundamental principle that the chief object of Courts of justice must be to secure that justice is done. In the two cases of wards of Court and of lunatics the Court is really sitting primarily to guard the interests of the ward or the lunatic. Its jurisdiction is in this respect parental and administrative, and the disposal of controverted questions is an incident only in the jurisdiction. It may often be necessary, in order to attain its primary object, that the Court should exclude the public. The broad principle which ordinarily governs it therefore yields to the paramount duty, which is the care of the ward or the lunatic.' (See [1913] AC 417 at 437, [1911–13] All ER Rep 1 at 9.)

The appellant recognised the long-established procedure in wardship and sought to distinguish the hearing of wardship cases in private from all other children cases. He is not, in my view, able to sustain that distinction. The paramount duty expressed by Viscount Haldane LC is now found in s 1 of the 1989 Act in words very similar to the previous Guardianship of Minors Acts, that 'the welfare of the child shall be the court's paramount consideration'. Further, both Sir Stephen Brown P in *Oxfordshire CC v M* [1994] 2 All ER 269, [1994] Fam 151 and Lord Jauncey of Tullichettle in *Re L (a minor) (police investigation: privilege)* [1996] 2 All ER 78, [1996] 2 WLR 395 referred to the non-adversarial character of Children Act proceedings which are akin to wardship proceedings.

The appellant relied also upon the views of several members of the judiciary given in lectures or articles in support of hearing children cases in open court, principally Lord Denning MR and Booth J. However, to my knowledge, there is no judgment to the effect that a court should always or even regularly hear family cases in public. The practice in children cases has been and is to the contrary despite the views of some judges which are irrelevant to the decision we have to make as to the meaning and proper application of para (7).

He provided us, most helpfully, with information about the procedures in the courts of other countries hearing children cases. Mr Turcan, on behalf of the Official Solicitor as amicus curiae, equally helpfully, added to the information.

a   There is a wide divergence of practice. I do not propose to set out a list of what we have been told. Suffice it to say that the practice extends from the entire proceedings in private to the entire proceedings in public with some other countries hearing evidence in private but judgment in open court or the discretion of the court to hear part or the whole case in private. Consequently, even if this court was free to do so, we would not be able to draw helpful
b   guidance from the diversity of approach in other jurisdictions.

The appellant has also addressed us upon the European Convention for the Protection of Human Rights and Fundamental Freedoms (Rome, 4 November 1950; TS 71 (1953); Cmd 8969) and has suggested that family proceedings in the English jurisdiction are in conflict with arts 6 and 10 of the convention. The United Kingdom is a signatory to the convention, but its articles have not been
c   incorporated as such in to English law. Article 6(1) provides for the public hearing and the public pronouncement of judgment of cases, but with the proviso of exclusion of the press and the public from all or part of the trial 'in the interests of morals, public order or national security in a democratic society, where the interests of juveniles or the protection of the private life of the parties so require'.
d   The right of freedom of expression contained in art 10(1) is subject to formalities, conditions, restrictions or penalties which may be imposed by the member states under art 10(2). It would seem to me that the present procedures in family proceedings are in accordance with the spirit of the convention.

The long-established practice in the English High Court and county court hearing applications for custody/access (now called residence/contact) or
e   wardship has been and remains to hear the whole of the evidence in private. In the High Court, which hears the more difficult cases and those which create public interest, judgment will often be given in public either in part or in whole where the court believes there to be a public interest in the case or to give guidance to practitioners.

f   Appeals in the Court of Appeal are almost invariably heard in public, but oral evidence is almost never given and the appeal is conducted on the documents and written and oral argument. The documents placed before the Court of Appeal include a transcript or agreed note of the judgment of the court appealed and frequently some or all the transcripts of the proceedings. It is the practice for the Court of Appeal to give a direction for non-identification of the child in child
g   appeals exercising the High Court's inherent jurisdiction to protect the child.

In the magistrates' courts the procedure has varied in the past according to whether the cases before 1991 were public or private law cases. Family proceedings now heard in the magistrates' courts are bound by s 97 of the 1989 Act amending s 69 of the Magistrates' Courts Act 1980, and by r 16(7) of the
h   Family Proceedings Courts (Children Act 1989) Rules 1991, SI 1991/1395. In general the public is not admitted to family proceedings in the magistrates court, but the press often are admitted.

The differences in procedures of the various courts in child cases, in relation to admission of the public, of the press and the right to report proceedings have been
j   usefully set out in a consultation paper, Review of Access to and Reporting of Family Proceedings, provided by the Lord Chancellor's Department in August 1993. In that consultation paper the main arguments for and against opening all or part of child proceedings to the public are set out. The arguments in support of opening the proceedings to the public have been redeployed by the appellant to this court.

Despite the arguments advanced by Dr P, it is abundantly clear that the courts are bound by para (7) to hear child cases generally in private. That was obviously the intention of the Rules Committee and it follows the long-established practice in the hearing of child cases. Paragraph (7) allows for all or part of the case to be heard in public. In the light of the long-established practice it is unlikely that judges will, other than rarely, hear the evidence relating to the welfare of a child in public. The judgment is in a somewhat different position and it may be that the practice of giving judgment in private is partly due to the parties not asking for it to be heard in public and partly because in the county court, where the vast majority of children cases are heard, it is less likely that there will be issues of public interest. Where issues of public interest do arise it would seem entirely appropriate to give judgment in open court providing, where desirable in the interests of the child, appropriate directions are given to avoid identification. If the case raises issues of principle or of law, the judgments are increasingly provided to the law reporters and are published in the large number of law reports which report family cases. But the majority of cases are of no interest to any one beyond the parties and their families.

In answer, therefore, to the appellant's first criticism of the judge that he fettered his discretion, the judge undoubtedly used language which might by reading the judgment in a narrow way be said to restrict him to hearing the case in camera. The judge was, however, recognising that the existing practice of hearing the case in private was restated in para (7) unless there were unusual features to the case. This was a run-of-the-mill case and the general practice would seem appropriate to this case. In my judgment, the judge ought not to be criticised for a cautious view of the exercise of his discretion.

Mr Turcan provided us with helpful information about the Family Court of Australia which has moved from private to public hearings of child cases. That change of procedure followed wide consultation and was embodied in statutory form. The Australian example, together with the consultation exercise which the Lord Chancellor's Department has initiated, point to the desirability of moving carefully and thoughtfully towards any change of procedure which may affect the welfare of the child.

In answer to the appellant's second point that the exercise of discretion should always be in favour of hearings in open court, it would seem to me that he is directing his arguments to the wrong forum. The wording of para (7) is clear. The exercise of discretion remains in the hands of the trial judge and it is a matter for the judge in each case to exercise that discretion if called upon to do so. In the absence of an application to hear the case in open court and unusual circumstances, the normal position would remain, as recognised by the wording of the sub-paragraph, that the evidence would be heard in private.

I would dismiss this appeal by Dr P.

Mr G, although an intervenor in the court below, has not appealed nor sought to intervene in this appeal as a respondent, and is not a party to the appeal.

PETER GIBSON LJ. There can be no doubt but that r 4.16(7) of the Family Proceedings Rules 1991, SI 1991/1247, leaves the court with a discretion whether to direct that the hearing should be in public. But by providing that unless the court otherwise directs the hearing *shall* be in chambers, the framers of the rules have clearly indicated the policy that was intended to apply normally, namely that the hearing should not be in public. In other words, it requires a special direction to be made for the hearing to be in public. The judge's language in saying that he had no power to hear the case in open court is unfortunate in that it has given rise to the suggestion by Dr P that the judge was fettering his discretion. But like Butler-Sloss LJ I think that that is too narrow a reading of the a judge's words. What he appears to me to be saying is that in the case before him, which he described as 'a typical case heard by Family Hearing Centres ... up and down the land on a daily basis', there was nothing, other than the fact that Dr P was challenging the practice and procedure of the court, to take the case out of the norm, and that in such a case it was inappropriate to direct the hearing to be in public. I see nothing wrong in that.

b   It follows that I cannot accept Dr P's submission that the only way that the court can properly exercise its discretion is to direct that the hearing be in public. That was said to be because of the principle requiring the administration of justice to be conducted publicly which was established by *Scott v Scott* [1913] AC 417, [1911–13] All ER Rep 1. But all the members of the House of Lords in the case recognised that there were exceptions to that principle, and wardship cases were

c specifically mentioned as constituting one such exception by Viscount Haldane LC, the Earl of Halsbury, Lord Atkinson and Lord Shaw (see [1913] AC 417 at 437, 441, 462, 483, [1911–13] All ER Rep 1 at 9, 11, 22–23, 33). I accept the Official Solicitor's submission that for this purpose proceedings under the 1989 Act are analogous to wardship proceedings. Dr P's submission seems to me to be flying in the face of the language of the rule.

d   As for Dr P's reliance on art 6(1) of the European Convention for the Protection of Human Rights and Fundamental Freedoms (Rome, 4 November 1950; TS 71 (1953); Cmd 8969), that convention has not yet been incorporated into English law. Further that article itself recognises that the right to a public trial is qualified where the interests of juveniles or the protection of the private

e life of the parties so require. In agreement with Butler-Sloss LJ, I do not regard the present practice as inconsistent with art 6. It is a future question whether judgment should be given in open court. Under English law it need not be so given. But the court has power to give judgment publicly and in exercising its discretion it can take into account the provision of art 6(1) that judgment should

f be pronounced publicly, though, if so pronounced, it should be done in such a way as to avoid detriment to the child.

    For these and the reasons given by Butler-Sloss LJ I would dismiss this appeal.

THORPE LJ. I agree that this appeal should be dismissed and I agree with both judgments.

g   Amongst the arguments for open court hearings advanced by Dr P in his skeleton argument at para 4(ii) appear the following:

> 'The reasonable right of a Litigant in Person to check out the judicial process in advance and in particular the judge who will try his case; the right of a LIP to a friend in court; the dangers of a LIP being taken advantage of in
h the secrecy of chambers; judges mis-stating the Law and not following proper procedure and even denying [a] LIP right of audience; uncritical reliance by judges on experts; the right of the public to scrutinise the validity and [premises] of expert evidence, the scientific, social, or psychological theory behind it; disgraceful orders about Contact and the way Contact
j orders are not enforced.'

Dr P is a member of the association, Families Need Fathers, and a paper prepared for the East London Branch of that association which is amongst the court papers shows a number of the points in the quotation from the skeleton argument reproduced in the paper. I assume that the convictions which Dr P holds are shared by other members of the association. But is this a widespread concern in society?

It is important to emphasise that matters of practice and procedure in the family justice system are the subject of constant inter-disciplinary review. The jurisdiction is divided into 51 care centres, at each one of which the designated judge of the care centre presides over an inter-disciplinary business committee. Each of the following disciplines sends a representative to the business committee: social services, the police, guardians ad litem, the medical practitioners, the legal practitioners, the courts' administrators. These local business committees report to the National Children Act Advisory Committee chaired by a judge of the Family Division of the High Court. Were there any general concerns at the current practice of chambers sittings then it is probable, if not certain, that they would have found expression through this appropriate channel. In addition, at each care centre there was established a service committee with an even wider representation. Service committees have now evolved into Children Act forums. Again any public dissatisfaction with current practice may there be expressed. These forums report to the annual Children Act inter-disciplinary conference held on each of the circuits throughout the jurisdiction. Again there has not to my knowledge been any dissatisfaction expressed at current practice through this appropriate channel.

For the appellant it can be said that there is no particular rational basis for the differing terminology of r 4.16(7) of the Family Proceedings Rules 1991, SI 1991/1247, and r 16(7) of the Family Proceedings Courts (Children Act 1989) Rules 1991, SI 1991/1395. Furthermore, it can be said that neither rule makes any significant contribution to regulating practice since both practitioners and courts function on a more rigid and unexpressed rule that cases brought under the Children Act 1989 are invariably heard in chambers, even if judgment is subsequently given in open court. So it can be said that there is an opportunity and perhaps a need for the rationalisation and restatement of the rules governing procedure at least to reflect the reality of what is done.

Whether there is a need for change in the current practice, is, of course, a much more complex question. The Lord Chancellor's Department initiated a consultation exercise in 1993. In November 1993 the Official Solicitor submitted a detailed response which has been provided to this court. Shortly thereafter the judges of the Family Division also responded. No doubt the department received submissions from many other sources. The department has not as yet published any analysis of those responses nor made any other public statement. No doubt that indicates the complexity of the issues and the diversity of the submissions on those issues. But I entirely share Butler-Sloss LJ's view that if there is to be a change in practice it should be preceded by the most careful consideration of the outcome of consultation and should be achieved by the legislative processes that alone can introduce uniformity throughout the family justice system.

Appeal dismissed. Leave to appeal to the House of Lords refused.

19 December 1996. The Appeal Committee of the House of Lords (Lord Lloyd of Berwick, Lord Nicholls of Birkenhead and Lord Hope of Craighead) refused leave to appeal.

Paul Magrath Esq   Barrister.

a
Re T and another (minors) (termination of contact: discharge of order)

COURT OF APPEAL, CIVIL DIVISION

SIMON BROWN LJ AND HOLMAN J

b
5, 21 NOVEMBER 1996

Child – Care – Parental contact – Refusal to allow contact – Local authority seeking in long term to place children in adoptive placements with no parental contact – Court making order granting local authority leave to terminate parental contact – Mother
c *applying to discharge order on ground that care plan had changed – Whether order justified in the circumstances – Whether correct approach to discharge of order followed – Children Act 1989, s 34(4)(9).*

In December 1994, on the application of the local authority, the court made care
d orders in respect of two children, S and B, on the ground that they had suffered significant harm due to lack of care from their parents; it also made an order under s 34(4)[a] of the Children Act 1989 granting the local authority leave to terminate contact between the parents and the children because of the children's need to settle. At that time the long term care plan in relation to the children was adoption with no parental contact and for S to have a pre-adoptive placement and
e B to undergo a therapeutic residential placement. In April 1996 the mother applied under s 34(9)[b] of the 1989 Act to discharge the s 34(4) order on the ground that the care plan had changed, since the local authority was then considering the possibility of a therapeutic residential setting for S instead of adoption, and there was no adoption placement in sight for B and therefore it was no longer
f appropriate to leave to the local authority the decision when contact with the mother should cease. The judge, who had made the original orders, dismissed the mother's application, holding that she had failed to show that there was such a change in the circumstances to justify reversing the decision. The mother appealed to the Court of Appeal, contending that the judge should have discharged the s 34(4) order, since it should not have been made in the first place,
g as the local authority's plans at that stage were not sufficiently advanced to justify such an order, which would only be appropriate (i) where otherwise the local authority's imminent plans would be thwarted, (ii) if the nature and quality of contact was such that it was not in the child's interests for it to continue, or (iii) if the person named in the order could not be found.

h
Held – The court would only make an order under s 34(9) of the 1989 Act discharging an earlier s 34(4) order if there had been some material change in circumstances since the making of the order, taking account of the fact that such an order would only be justified if the probable need to terminate contact was foreseeable and not too remote and not if there was a realistic possibility of the
j child being rehabilitated with the person named in the order, or if it had been

---

a   Section 34(4), so far as material, provides: 'On an application made by the authority ... the court may make an order authorising the authority to refuse to allow contact between the child and any person ... named in the order.'
b   Section 34(9), so far as material, provides: 'The court may vary or discharge any order made under this section on the application of ... the person named in the order.'

made merely against the possibility of a change in the circumstances making such action desirable. In reaching its decision, the court should consider, with the child's welfare in mind as the paramount consideration (save only in the very limited circumstances provided for by s 91(17)^c when the court's leave was required), the extent to which the circumstances had changed and, bearing those changes in mind, the extent to which it would be appropriate to reinvestigate the central question of whether contact should be terminated. In the instant case, the s 34(4) order was justified because of the need to prepare the children for adoption and the possible need to end contact during therapy. There were no grounds for discharging the order in relation to B as his care plan had not changed but had substantially advanced with the therapy. S's situation, however, was totally different as adoption was no longer being considered and it was unclear when or if the proposed therapeutic residential placement would begin. Accordingly, the appeal would be allowed only in so far as it related to S (see p 73 d e, p 74 d e, p 75 d g, p 76 b c g h, p 77 a b h and p 78 f post).

Dicta of Butler-Sloss LJ in Re B (minors) (contact) [1994] 2 FLR 1 at 5 and in Re L (sexual abuse: standard of proof) [1996] 1 FLR 116 at 124 applied.

Notes

For parental contact with children in care, see 5(2) Halsbury's Laws (4th edn reissue) paras 790–791.

For the Children Act 1989, s 34, see 6 Halsbury's Statutes (4th edn) (1992 reissue) 437.

Cases referred to in judgments

A and ors (minors) (residence order), Re [1992] 3 All ER 872, [1992] Fam 182, [1992] 3 WLR 422, CA.

B (minors) (care: contact: local authority's plans), Re [1993] 1 FLR 543, CA.

B (minors) (contact), Re [1994] 2 FLR 1, CA.

B and anor (minors) (termination of contact: paramount consideration), Re [1993] 3 All ER 524, [1993] Fam 301, [1993] 3 WLR 63, CA.

E (a minor) (care order: contact), Re [1994] 1 FLR 146, CA.

L (sexual abuse: standard of proof), Re [1996] 1 FLR 116, CA.

W v Ealing London BC [1993] 2 FLR 788, CA.

Cases also cited or referred to in skeleton arguments

A v Liverpool City Council [1981] 2 All ER 385, [1982] AC 363, HL.

G v G [1985] 2 All ER 225, [1985] 1 WLR 647, HL.

H v H (residence order: leave to remove from jurisdiction) [1995] 1 FLR 529, CA.

W (a minor) (secure accommodation order), Re [1993] 1 FLR 692.

Appeal

By notice dated 14 May 1996 the mother of four children appealed from the decision of Judge Michael Baker in the Chichester County Court on 10 April 1996 whereby he dismissed her application under s 34(9) of the Children Act 1989 in respect of the two middle children, S and B, to discharge an order made by him on 16 December 1994 when making care orders in respect of all four children, giving the local authority leave under s 34(4) of the 1989 Act to terminate contact

c   Section 91, so far as material, is set out at p 74 c, post a between the parents and the three eldest children. The facts are set out in the judgment of Simon Brown LJ.

Roderic Wood QC and Diane Barnett (instructed by Williams Macdougall & Campbell, Worthing) for the mother.
Michael Liebrecht (instructed by Donna Newbury, Chichester) for the local
b authority.
Stephen Cobb (instructed by Bennett Griffin & Partners, Worthing) for the guardian ad litem.

Cur adv vult

c 21 November 1996. The following judgments were delivered.

SIMON BROWN LJ. This is a mother's appeal with the leave of the judge below against the order of Judge Michael Baker in the Chichester County Court on 10 April 1996 refusing her application to discharge a s 34(4) order which he had earlier made on 16 December 1994 when making care orders in respect of all four
d of her children.

The appeal is confined to consideration of the middle two children only: S, born on 14 December 1985, who is now therefore ten years old, and B, born on 21 January 1989, now seven.

The chequered history of this family appears in the greatest possible detail
e from the papers before the court. It makes, alas, sorry reading indeed. Suffice it for present purposes to pick up the story on 16 December 1993 when interim care orders were made for the three elder children and an interim supervision order was made for the youngest child, J. It was at this time too that S moved to foster parents, the Fs.

f On 3 September 1994 B too moved to the Fs. The move did not work out, however. Put shortly, both boys told of sexual misbehaviour including buggery between the three elder children. In October 1994 B was moved to new foster parents, and was excluded from school.

On 18 November 1994 the first respondent local authority applied for care orders and for leave to terminate contact between the parents, then still together,
g and the three elder children under the provisions of s 34(4) of the Children Act 1989. Those applications were the subject of a five-day hearing before Judge Baker in December 1994. The information before the court on that occasion was, so far as concerned S and B, essentially this. The local authority plan for S was that he be placed in the long term for adoption with no parental contact, a
h pre-adoptive placement to be identified at an early stage. The plan for B too was for an adoptive placement in the long term with no parental contact, but with an initial residential placement for at least a year with intensive therapy. As to parental contact prior to placement, the local authority planned a reduction. Mother had previously been enjoying two hours' supervised contact twice per
j week with each child. This was planned to be reduced to one visit each two weeks for a month, then one visit per month for two months, then, if necessary, one visit each two months until the children were ready for their respective placements and a final contact.

So far as the guardian ad litem was concerned, she recognised that S had a good understanding of his natural family but thought it probable that adoption would be in his best interests; she found it difficult to be sure about a future adoptive

family placement for B until he had received therapy and his behaviour had
become acceptable. She said:

'I have carefully considered the Applications to refuse contact in respect of
[S and B] ... This has not been an easy decision to make at this stage. I am
satisfied that the Local Authority will continue with their plans as presented,
but situations do change and it may be more beneficial in the future for some
form of contact to continue. However, it may well become necessary to stop
contact during any therapy that is undertaken, or indeed if there are
problems with contact. The reviews will monitor this ... I therefore also
support the Applications for Permission to Refuse Contact in respect of [S
and B] ...'

In giving judgment, Judge Baker said:

'In respect of S, he has been with foster parents for some time. Fortunately
... he appears to have settled well. He is less disturbed than A [the eldest
child] or B but clearly, from the history, he has gone through a traumatic
childhood and what is of great cause for concern are the disclosures of
buggery and that he learnt it from watching his parents. He also told the
guardian ad litem that things had happened at home which he could not tell
... S had indicated that he was concerned about his own safety and the
incident on the pier is no doubt indelible on his mind. [This was a reference
to an incident in December 1993 when S suffered a broken heel by jumping
off Worthing Pier.] I am satisfied that he has suffered significant harm due
to the care, or lack of it, from his parents. I therefore make a care order. In
respect of B, he is a very disturbed child. [The social worker] said that he was
so badly behaved she had difficulty in assessing him. He has alleged physical
and sexual abuse by his brothers, and sexual abuse by his mother. He has
been excluded from school and is now at a special school. I am satisfied that
he has suffered significant harm due to the care, or lack of it, from his parents.
I therefore make a care order ... In respect of contact matters, the local
authority and the guardian ad litem argue that to enable the children to settle
it is important for the local authority to be given the right to terminate
contact, if it is thought necessary. That places a great responsibility on the
local authority. The parents say that it is not necessary to do that but it is
right to maintain a link with the parents. It is a difficult decision but the
weight of evidence is in favour of the local authority. The alternative would
be for the local authority to come back at the time when contact, it is
thought, should be terminated. There should be flexibility about contact,
particularly when the children are undergoing therapy, and it is not practical
for the local authority to keep coming back to court. I put my trust in the
local authority to deal with it appropriately. Therefore the local authority
have leave to terminate contact between the parents and S [and] B ...'

It is necessary now to indicate something of what happened to the children
between December 1994 and April 1996 when the matter returned before Judge
Baker upon the mother's application made on 22 August 1995. This application,
one should note, was put in terms that Mrs T 'wish[ed] to increase the present
level of contact to S and B'. As, however, Judge Baker observed at the outset of
his judgment on 10 April 1996, the application had by then been amended to seek
revocation of the s 34(4) order made in December 1994. I should further indicate
that in March 1995 Mr and Mrs T had separated, Mr T having reached the view

that the children should be given a new start in life without contact with him and,
a   indeed, that the mother's application too should be opposed. Father played no
part in this appeal.

On 20 January 1995 B had been placed in a small specialist residential children's
home where he remains to this day. Following the making of the December 1994
care order, B had had two fortnightly sessions of contact with his mother, and
b   thereafter supervised contact for one hour a month at a family centre. As to S, he
had continued to live with the Fs until January 1996 when he moved to a new
foster placement, the Js. It is convenient to note at this stage that as recently as
11 October 1996, S moved from the Js to yet further foster parents. S, like B, had
two fortnightly sessions of contact following the making of the care order and
then joined B in the monthly contact session. In April 1996 S was requesting
c   more contact.

What, then, was the revised care plan for each child in April 1996? So far as S
was concerned, although adoption had been approved by the local authority
adoption panel on 11 July 1995, no suitable permanent placement had been
found. Consideration was being given to finding him a therapeutic residential
d   setting. The local authority were continuing to talk of 'appropriate contact
arrangements' for S, and their reports were directed to countering mother's
application for increased and unsupervised contact. As to B, the local authority
had on 9 February 1996 stated:

e   'Contact has been maintained at its present level for [B's] benefit and to
give him a sense of continuity and reassurance during a period of his life
when he is in transition and when he does not yet have new parental
relationships to which he can commit himself. I think that four weekly
contact is adequate for this purpose: more frequent contact will confuse and
unsettle [B], and an increase in frequency at this point would give him a very
misleading message about the future and one which I think he would find
f   disturbing. Our eventual aim will be to terminate contact when we are
closer to planning a move to a permanent family. It is impossible at this
moment to predict precisely when this stage will be reached. Before contact
is terminated it may well be helpful to reduce its frequency. Quite apart
from the progress of the adoption plan it may also become necessary to
g   reduce the frequency of or to terminate [B's] contact in order to meet his
developing emotional and therapeutic needs.'

By the date of the hearing, we are told, the local authority had in fact suspended
contact between mother and B with a view to final termination.

The guardian ad litem concluded her report of 1 April 1996 thus:

h   'It remains essential for the Local Authority to have the ability to alter the
contact arrangements according to the needs of the children and if necessary
to terminate contact. I cannot support this Application by Mrs [T].'

Although the matter was listed before Judge Baker for a two-day hearing, with
j   witnesses in attendance, as an application by mother for increased contact to S
and B (and, indeed, J), mother withdrew her application in relation to J and, as
stated, amended her application relating to S and B to one seeking the discharge
of the s 34(4) order made 16 months previously.

What appears to have been argued on mother's behalf was essentially that the
local authority's care plan for both boys had changed and that it was no longer
appropriate to leave to the local authority the decision as to when contact with

mother should cease. So far as S was concerned, the local authority was reconsidering the whole question of his adoption and wondering whether perhaps there should be instead a therapeutic residential placement, as in B's case. As for B himself, he was still at the residential children's home with no adoption placement in sight.

Faced with this argument, the judge had first to decide what should be his approach to an application for the discharge of a s 34(4) order. The authority from which he appears to have derived most assistance was *Re B and anor (minors) (termination of contact: paramount consideration)* [1993] 3 All ER 524, [1993] Fam 301, and in particular this passage from Butler-Sloss LJ's judgment:

'... [the local authority's] plan has to be given the greatest possible consideration by the court and it is only in the unusual case that a parent will be able to convince the court, the onus being firmly on the parent, that there has been such a change of circumstances as to require further investigation and reconsideration of the local authority plan.' (See ([1993] 3 All ER 524 at 532, [1993] Fam 301 at 312.)

Directing himself in accordance with that approach the judge then considered the position of each child. As to B, he said:

'He is undergoing, or about to undergo ... an intensive therapeutic programme. Whereas there is little evidence, medical evidence particularly, to support this view ... the social worker indicates in his report that it may be necessary to reduce the frequency of, or to terminate, B's contact with his mother in order to meet his needs. That is quite apart from the consideration of adoption in the long term ... it would not, in my view, be appropriate to remove the local authority's powers to terminate simply because no adoption placement is yet available. For all I know a placement may be found quite soon. In that event the local authority would have to return to court to apply again if mother's application today was successful. I said in my judgment in December 1994 that I was prepared to rely on the ... good sense and integrity of the local authority, advised as they always are in these matters by experts. I still am. If there are no plans for placement in the immediate future then, subject to the other consideration to which I have referred relating to B's therapy, I am sure that the local authority will continue contact. This is not, as has been suggested by [mother's counsel] ... an abrogation of the court's powers to regulate contact—it is an exercise of those powers by the court to vest in the local authority the right to make decisions in the best interests of the child and I agree with [counsel for the guardian ad litem], that to remove the right to refuse contact with the local authority and thus to require them to afford reasonable contact with the mother might very well put the local authority in a difficult position in regard to B's therapeutic programme and adversely affect that programme. I am not prepared to risk that.'

So far as S was concerned, the judge said that the fresh possibility of—

'some kind of therapeutic residential placement ... does not, in my view, constitute such a fundamental change as to require reconsideration of the local authority's care plan. The local authority still needs to regulate and monitor contact and, if necessary, to terminate it ...'

By way of overall summary, the judge said:

> 'The position is that in December 1994 I carefully considered the question of whether this was an appropriate case for authorising the local authority to terminate contact and I decided that it was. The onus is now on the mother to satisfy me that there has been such a change in the circumstances that I should reverse that decision. I am not so persuaded and, therefore, I refuse the application.'

In the event, no evidence was called and the hearing lasted less than a day.

Mr Roderic Wood QC, counsel appearing for mother on this appeal, seeks to criticise the judge's approach in a number of ways. Firstly, he submits that the s 34(4) order should never have been made in the first place: the local authority's care plans at that stage, he argues, were not sufficiently advanced to justify such an order. In the result, he contends, the judge ought certainly to have revoked it when the opportunity arose upon mother's application sixteen months later.

The immediate, and to my mind insuperable, difficulty faced by this argument is, of course, that it seeks to undermine the April 1996 decision by way of a challenge to the underlying order which was itself never appealed. For my part, I think it right to approach the 1996 decision—that presently under appeal—on the footing that the original s 34(4) order was properly made. In any event, for reasons I shall explain later, I think the 1994 decision justifiable.

How, then, should the judge have approached the application to discharge that order? That is the novel question raised by this appeal, a question not apparently the subject of earlier authority.

Clearly, the correct starting point for the determination of this question must be a consideration of the circumstances in which it is appropriate to make a s 34(4) order in the first place.

As to this, Mr Wood invited us to give general guidance and more particularly an indorsement of his submission that a s 34(4) order will only ever be appropriate in three particular situations: '(i) Where not to make such an order would thwart the local authority plans for the care and upbringing of the child made pursuant to the provisions of the care plan approved by the Court on the making of the care order, and where those plans are imminently to be put into effect. (ii) [Where the] nature and quality of the contact is such that it is not in the interests of the child for it to continue. (iii) Where the relevant named person in the order cannot be found.' For my part, I would resolutely decline both limbs of this invitation. As to general guidance, one must note this passage from the judgment of Sir Stephen Brown P in Re E (a minor) (care order: contact) [1994] 1 FLR 146 at 153:

> 'The court has been very strongly pressed by Mr Harris in particular to give what he termed "guidance" on s 34 of the Children Act 1989. I do not consider it appropriate to say more than that this case endorses the approach indicated by Butler-Sloss LJ in the case of Re B emphasising that contact must not be allowed to destabilise or endanger the arrangements for the child.'

Where the President himself has feared to tread it would be foolish indeed for us to rush in.

As for Mr Wood's tripartite proposition, that too I would reject as unhelpfully rigid and restrictive. What is meant by 'imminently' in (i)? The form of (ii) suggests that the requirement for a final termination of contact there is even more immediate than 'imminent'. As for (iii), it would be necessary to read into

that the further postulate that if such person were suddenly to appear it would be
necessary to prevent contact with the child.   *a*

Perhaps the greatest help on this part of the case is to be found in
Butler-Sloss LJ's judgment in *Re L (sexual abuse: standard of proof)* [1996] 1 FLR 116.
Not, however, from the first of the two passages on which Mr Wood sought to
rely, namely:

b

'The effect of the Children Act is to set aside the former powers of the court
in wardship and to remove from the court any continuing control over
children after the making of a care order unless or until a further application
was made to the court. On the making of a further application, such as for
residence or contact to the child, the powers of the court and the exercise of
discretion under s 1 are restored for the duration of the application. If the *c*
care order remains in place, other than by control over contact by virtue of
the provisions of s 34, the court has no further part to play in the future
welfare of the child: see *Re B (Minors) (Care: Contact: Local Authority's Plans)*
([1993] 1 FLR 543 at 548). This interchange between the judicial control of
children, the subject of applications, and the local authority responsibility for
children placed in care under the Children Act, is a difficult and sensitive *d*
area. The point at which the court withdraws from further control over the
child and passes the responsibility to the local authority is a matter of the
exercise of discretion by the court and will vary with each set of
circumstances. But at some point, if a care order is made by the court, it
must hand over the future arrangements for the child to the local authority. *e*
That is not abdication of responsibility by the court; it is acting in accordance
with the intention of the legislation. The Children Act provides for many of
the most important decisions, including whether to place a child for
adoption, to be made by the local authority and therefore there is nothing
untoward in the judge leaving the ultimate decision in the hands of the local *f*
authority with whom the child is placed.' (See [1996] 1 FLR 116 at 124–125.)

That passage appears in the part of the judgment dealing with, and indeed
upholding, the judge's decision there to make a final care order as opposed to a
series of interim care orders. There may be some broad analogy between the
court's position when deciding respectively whether or not to make a final care *g*
order and whether or not to make a s 34(4) order: each decision in its different
way alters the balance between the court and the local authority in the control of
the child. The above passage, however, in no way helps identify the point at
which, or the circumstances in which, a s 34(4) order should be made.

Rather, the helpful passage in *Re L* is the following under the heading 'Contact': *h*

'The guardian ad litem asked for an order to be made under s 34(4),
authorising the local authority to refuse to allow contact between the
children and the family, although the local authority did not seek such an
order. The judge said: "It seems to me on balance I ought to accede to Mr
Tolson's submission because, as I see it, it can do no harm if the county *j*
council do not wish to terminate contact and on the other hand if there
should arise an occasion where, for whatever reason, whether it be the
destructive behaviour of the children or whatever, their professionals come
to the conclusion that contact ought to be refused then it can be done
without further application to the court, because I cannot foresee that there
would be any evidence before the court on that occasion which the guardian

a   has not put forward today, so I am prepared to make that order." The order
giving leave to terminate contact was contrary to the local authority's
present intentions and to the indications made by the judge as to the
possibility of rehabilitation. Section 34(1) requires a local authority to allow
the child in care reasonable contact with his parents unless by s 34(4) the
court authorises termination of such contact. A s 34(4) order in our view is
b   appropriate where there is no likelihood of rehabilitation and the child is, for
instance, to be placed for adoption or with foster-parents without continuing
contact with the natural family. In the context of this case it was surprising
that a s 34(4) order should be made and to do so to save a further application
to the court if the circumstances should change had the effect of handing
over to the local authority the residual responsibility still vested in the court.
c   It was premature to make an order which was not to be implemented in the
foreseeable future.' (See [1996] 1 FLR 116 at 126–127.)

With the aid of that passage one reaches this position: a s 34(4) order should not
be made: (1) whilst there remains a realistic possibility of rehabilitation of the
child with the person in question; or (2) merely against the possibility that
d   circumstances may change in such a way as to make termination of contact
desirable. For an order to be justified, a probable need to terminate contact must
be foreseeable and not too remote. Beyond that it seems to me impossible to go.

I may say that on that approach I, for my part, would regard the orders made
here by Judge Baker in December 1994 as having been justifiable given in
e   particular that there appeared not merely the need to prepare the boys for
long-term closed adoption but also the possible need to end contact during
therapy, at any rate in B's case. The position here was certainly very different to
that in Re L and the plans more advanced. And there was, of course, no possibility
of rehabilitating either child with mother, as, indeed, she herself has now come
to accept.

f   Given that the above is the correct approach to the making of a s 34(4) order in
the first place, in what circumstances should it be discharged? More particularly,
what, if any, inhibitions are there upon a person's entitlement to seek such
discharge?

In answering this question it is necessary first to note the following features of
g   the s 34 scheme.

(1) All applications under s 34 must be decided by reference to s 1(1) and the
welfare checklist in s 1(3)—see s 1(4)(b) (s 34 being in Pt IV of the Act).

(2) Prima facie, a child in local authority care should be allowed reasonable
contact with, amongst others, his parents (s 34(1)). The local authority's
h   obligations, indeed, go further: para 15(1) of Sch 2 to the Act provides:

> 'Where a child is being looked after by a local authority, the authority shall,
> unless it is not reasonably practicable or consistent with his welfare,
> endeavour to promote contact between the child and—(a) his parents ...'

j   A child in local authority care is by definition 'being looked after' by them (see
ss 105(4) and 22(1)).

(3) How much or little contact is 'reasonable' must be for the local authority
to decide subject to any order of the court—and the local authority's duty under
Sch 2 to 'promote' (ie encourage and facilitate) contact arises only if and in so far
as they perceive this to be consistent with the child's welfare. Bearing in mind,
however, that even in cases of urgent necessity s 34(6) permits only refusal of

contact for up to seven days, it may be thought that reasonable contact should *a*
not ordinarily be unduly restricted unless by agreement or pursuant to court
order—for which, of course, the local authority itself may apply under s 34(2).

(4) Under s 34(3) a 'named person', including a parent, can apply for contact,
or increased contact, at any time. Logically, however, if a s 34(4) order is in
place—whether or not the local authority has then actually made use of it to
refuse contact—any such application would need to be coupled with an *b*
application under s 34(9) for the discharge of the s 34(4) order.

(5) The only express statutory restriction upon the making of any kind of s 34
application is that provided by s 91(17) of the Act:

> 'Where—(a) a person has made an application for an order under section
> 34; (b) the application has been refused; and (c) a period of less than six *c*
> months has elapsed since the refusal,—that person may not make a further
> application for such an order with respect to the same child, unless he has
> obtained the leave of the court.'

With those considerations in mind, I turn now to consider what should be the
court's general approach to a s 34(9) application for the discharge of a s 34(4) *d*
order.

Clearly, such an application must be considered by the court, and considered
indeed with the child's welfare in mind as the paramount consideration—save
only in the very limited circumstances provided for by s 91(17) when the court's
leave is required. *e*

That said, it is plain that there must be demonstrable some material change of
circumstance between the making of the s 34(4) order and the application to
discharge it: the courts are obviously entitled to screen out what are essentially
no more than disguised appeals against the original orders.

How much help, then, is to be derived from the passage which I have already *f*
cited from Butler-Sloss LJ's judgment in *Re B*—the passage relied upon by the
judge below? To my mind, in this context very little. In the first place one must
bear in mind the very different situation which the court was there considering:
a particular category of care case in which a parent applies for contact with a view
to rehabilitation. Butler-Sloss LJ was not speaking in the context of an existing
s 34(4) order, let alone an application to discharge such an order. Secondly, the *g*
formulation in any event appears, perhaps unavoidably, to beg more questions
than it raises: 'such a change of circumstances as to require further investigation
and reconsideration'. How much change is 'such a change', and what precisely
is encompassed within a requirement for 'further investigation and
reconsideration' (in that case, of the local authority plan, in this case of the *h*
desirability of the local authority retaining their s 34(4) authorisation to terminate
contact)? This second question seems to me of equal importance to the first. As
Butler-Sloss LJ said in *Re B (minors) (contact)* [1994] 2 FLR 1 at 5:

> '[Counsel] argued that … a judge is obliged to hold a full hearing,
> permitting the parties to call oral evidence and cross-examine any witness *j*
> they may choose. In my view a judge in family cases has a much broader
> discretion both under the Children Act 1989 and previously to conduct the
> case as is most appropriate for the issues involved and the evidence available
> (see the judgment of Sir Stephen Brown P in *W v Ealing London BC* ([1993] 2
> FLR 788 at 794)). There is a spectrum of procedure for family cases from the
> ex parte application on minimal evidence to the full and detailed

a investigations on oral evidence which may be prolonged. Where on that spectrum a judge decides a particular application should be placed is a matter for his discretion. Applications for residence orders or for committal to the care of a local authority or revocation of a care order are likely to be decided on full oral evidence, but not invariably. Such is not the case on contact applications which may be and are heard sometimes with and sometimes

b without oral evidence or with a limited amount of oral evidence.'

The judgment in the *Ealing* case had cited a dictum of Balcombe LJ in *Re A and ors (minors) (residence order)* [1992] 3 All ER 872 at 880, [1992] Fam 182 at 194— '... this is not ordinary civil litigation: it concerns children'—and Sir Stephen Brown P continued thus:

c
'In our judgment that is a salutary observation and it would be unwise in this jurisdiction to seek to restrict the discretion of the court by imposing a rigid formula upon the conduct of proceedings.' (See [1993] 2 FLR 788 at 794.)

d Applying these considerations to an application to discharge a s 34(4) order, I conclude that the court should initially have two main interlocking considerations in mind: first, the extent to which circumstances have changed from when the order was originally made; and second, bearing those changes in mind, the extent to which it now seems appropriate to reinvestigate the central question. The court should ask itself: where on the 'spectrum of procedure'

e should this particular application be placed? Clearly, the greater the apparent change in circumstances, the more intensively will the court be prepared to reconsider the desirability of leaving the s 34(4) order in place.

I would not myself speak in terms of the onus being on the applicant. But it should certainly be borne in mind that there are clear implications in all this not

f merely for the best use of court time but more importantly for the welfare of the children themselves. Children are often aware of the court's processes and troubled by the uncertainty and disruption engendered. Nor should the courts be expected to welcome applications which essentially seek to reopen already decided questions.

g Let me now return to consider the present appeal on its own facts. As stated, so far as B was concerned, by April 1996 contact had in fact ceased. True, he remained at the children's home with no adoption placement in sight, but plainly the care plan for him had not changed and, indeed, realistically it was substantially further advanced than when the s 34(4) order had first been made. In those circumstances, there could, in my judgment, be no sound basis whatever

h for suddenly discharging that order; quite the reverse. The only basis for arguing the contrary would be if mother's real case was that she wanted to prevent the local authority from terminating contact and needed the s 34(4) order discharged to achieve that—if, in short, her real case was under s 34(3) to which the s 34(9) application was ancillary. It is apparent that was not how Judge Baker

j understood the case being advanced at the hearing. For my part, however, even if mother's application to maintain contact with B had remained four-square before the court, I entertain no doubt that the judge would have dismissed it, and dismissed it moreover without thinking it necessary to hear oral evidence in the case. Nor do I think he could have been faulted in such an approach. The basic fact here is that the local authority now have B in their care. The responsibility for him is properly and essentially theirs. That is so not least whilst he is undergoing therapy as at present. I think the judge was well entitled to leave the question of B's contact, as expressly he did, to the 'good sense and integrity of the local authority, advised ... by experts'. I would dismiss the appeal so far as it concerns B.

I turn to S with regard to whom a very different situation arises. It was different already by the date of the hearing before Judge Baker. It has become more so since. As stated, already by April 1996 the local authority were reconsidering the whole question of S's adoption. As matters now stand, however, we are told not only that no longer is an adoption placement being sought but that funds are presently unavailable even for a therapeutic residential placement. Only now are S's needs for therapy being assessed and it is unclear when, if at all, therapy will begin. In these circumstances the local authority themselves express—

'the view that it is no longer likely that circumstances which will warrant a refusal of contact will prevail in the foreseeable future in relation to [S]. Accordingly the first respondent would accede to the discharge of the grant of leave to refuse contact between the appellant and [S].'

The guardian ad litem argues a different view and invites us to leave the s 34(4) order in place. True, submits Mr Cobb, there is no longer a plan for S's long-term adoption. But a countervailing consideration has now come into play, namely the real possibility that S's therapeutic needs will quite soon make it desirable to end contact in his case too.

I, for my part, would unhesitatingly reject the guardian ad litem's invitation and would discharge the s 34(4) order in S's case, leaving it to the local authority to reapply for a further such order if and when they find they actually need it. In these circumstances, I think it unnecessary to reach any view upon the justifiability or otherwise of Judge Baker's decision, on the facts before him, to leave the s 34(4) order in place in S's case. Suffice it to say, that the argument for its discharge was clearly stronger in his case, even on the facts as then known, than in B's.

In the result, I would allow this appeal to the extent of discharging the s 34(4) order in S's case but not otherwise.

HOLMAN J.

The law

I agree with all that Simon Brown LJ has said as to the proper approach of the court on an application under s 34(9) of the Children Act 1989 to discharge an earlier order under s 34(4), and summarise my views as follows.

(1) It is not appropriate on such an application to reinvestigate whether the original order was appropriately made in the circumstances prevailing when it was made. Indeed, the court must be astute to see that the application made under s 34(9) is a bona fide application to discharge, and not a disguised attempt to appeal, the earlier order. To this extent, but only to this extent, there is an onus on the applicant to show, as a threshold test, that there has been some change of circumstances such that the application is a genuine application made in the light of those changed circumstances. There is no greater threshold test since the discretion in s 34(9) is unqualified and there is no statutory restriction on the right to apply unless s 91(17) applies. The inquiry at this stage should not be elaborate and, indeed, one would often expect the point to be conceded.

a (2) Once that threshold is passed, the duty of the court is to apply the tests in s 1(1), (2), (3) and (5) of the 1989 Act. I agree with Simon Brown LJ that we should not attempt to lay down any guidance save to say that it could not be right to make an order under s 34(4), nor subsequently to leave one in place, unless at the time the court is considering, or reconsidering the matter: (a) there is no realistic possibility of rehabilitation of the child with the person in question; and (b) a

b probable need to terminate contact is foreseeable and not too remote.

(3) A judge hearing an application to discharge is entitled to, and indeed must, consider where on the 'spectrum of procedure' described by Butler-Sloss LJ in *Re B (minors) (contact)* [1994] 2 FLR 1 at 5 the particular application should be placed. If that question arises at an interlocutory hearing, then the sort of considerations referred to by Butler-Sloss LJ are likely to be relevant (see [1994] 2 FLR 1 at 6).

c (4) Like Simon Brown LJ, I doubt whether it is helpful to speak in terms of onus once the threshold to which I have referred in para (1) above is passed. *If,* exceptionally, the court considers at the conclusion of the inquiry that the factors are so evenly balanced as not to come down one side or the other on the question of discharge, then I, for my part, would consider that the order should be

d discharged. If an order under s 34(4) cannot be justified, it should not remain in force.

(5) Clearly, orders under s 34(3) and (4) cannot logically co-exist (unless, unusually, there is an order for contact for a limited period under s 34(3) coupled with an order under s 34(4) to take effect at the end of that period). But I see no reason why an application under s 34(3) cannot be considered together with an

e application under s 34(9) for the discharge of an order under s 34(4), at any rate once the threshold referred to in para (1) above is passed. Once the threshold is passed, the issues under s 34(3) and s 34(4) need to be considered together and in the round. If the court concludes that there should be a positive order for contact under s 34(3), then, save in the unusual situation mentioned above, it will logically discharge the s 34(4) order. But the s 34(4) order does not have to be got

f out of the way before the court can consider s 34(3).

The facts of this case

I now turn to the facts of the present case. So far as S is concerned, the local authority themselves now effectively ask that the s 34(4) order be discharged

g since they recognise that a probable need to terminate contact in the foreseeable future no longer exists. Like Simon Brown LJ, I am not persuaded that the arguments of the guardian ad litem should prevail, and it would be ridiculous if the local authority now had to make a fresh application to a judge for the discharge of the s 34(4) order. I would allow the appeal and discharge the order

h in relation to S.

I have found the position of B much more difficult. By her application under s 34(3) dated 22 August 1995, the mother herself clearly asked for a definition of (and she hoped an increase in) her contact. At the hearing, this was orally amended to an application simply for the discharge of the s 34(4) order and I must, therefore, assume that this reflected the mother's then-position; although

j I have an uneasy feeling that it more reflected some confusion as to the proper legal approach to the situation as I have endeavoured to explain it at para (5) above.

In passages which Simon Brown LJ has quoted, the judge himself approached the question as one of onus rather than as an application of the tests in s 1 of the 1989 Act. In my judgment, he erred in doing so. Further, the judge said:

'If there are no plans for placement in the immediate future then, subject
to the other consideration to which I have referred relating to B's therapy, I
am sure that the local authority will continue contact.'

That passage does not lie easily with the fact that by the date of the hearing the
local authority had in fact already terminated the contact, in reliance upon the
s 34(4) order. However we were assured by the bar, including counsel for the
mother, that the judge was well aware that contact had indeed already been
terminated.

The two pre-requisites to which I have referred in para (2) above were
certainly satisfied in that (a) the mother herself had accepted that there was no
prospect of B returning to live with her; and (b) contact had in fact been
terminated. The essence of the judge's decision is, I think:

'I agree with [counsel for the guardian ad litem] that to remove the right to
refuse contact from the local authority and thus to require them to afford
reasonable contact to mother might very well put the local authority in a
difficult position in regard to B's therapeutic programme and adversely affect
that programme. I am not prepared to risk that.'

That was a conclusion based on welfare and I agree with Simon Brown LJ that
even if the judge had approached the application on the correct legal basis, and
even if the mother's application under s 34(3) for a definition of contact had
remained four-square before the court, the conclusion of the judge would have
been the same. Further, it is a conclusion which he was entitled to reach on the
evidence.

I do have misgivings that the mother's original application for contact did not
receive the direct consideration that it was entitled to. But I am not persuaded
that the wrong result has been reached for B. So I, too, would dismiss the appeal
in so far as it concerns B.

Appeal allowed in part.

Paul Magrath Esq   Barrister.

Robertson v Banham & Co (a firm)

COURT OF APPEAL, CIVIL DIVISION

16, 31 OCTOBER 1996

ROCH LJ AND CONNELL J

Writ – Service on partnership – Service of writ on partner – Service by insertion of writ through letter box at 'usual or last known address' of partner – Whether service may be effected by insertion of writ through letter box at firm's address – Whether good service only constituted by insertion through letter box at partner's place of residence – RSC Ord 10, r 1(2)(b), Ord 81, r 3(1)(a).

In January 1994 the plaintiff commenced an action against the defendant firm of solicitors for breach of contract and negligence in respect of their handling of an earlier action against another firm of solicitors. On 14 January she put an envelope containing the writ, the statement of claim and the form of acknowledgment of service, together with a covering letter addressed to the defendant solicitor who had handled her affairs, through the letter box at the practising address of that solicitor. At that point the plaintiff did not know that the defendant partnership had been dissolved before the commencement of the action and that the solicitor who had advised her was part of a new partnership. On 26 January the defendants acknowledged service of the writ and statement of claim and on 18 February the plaintiff signed judgment in default of defence. The master granted the defendants' subsequent application to set aside the judgment and ordered them to pay the plaintiff's costs, holding that the judgment of 18 February had been regularly obtained since the writ suing partners in the name of the firm had been duly served on one of the partners on 14 January by virtue of RSC Ord 81, r 1(3)(a)[a] and Ord 10, r 1(2)(b)[b], and under Ord 18, rr 2 and 5 a defence should have been served within 28 days thereafter. On appeal, the deputy judge held that the default judgment had been irregularly obtained on the ground that the writ was not duly served until the defendants entered an appearance on 26 January, and so they had until 23 February to serve a defence, and he awarded costs in favour of the defendants. The plaintiff appealed.

Held – Where partners were sued in the name of a firm, the writ would be deemed to have been duly served on the firm for the purposes of RSC Ord 81, r 3(1)(a) and Ord 10, r 1(2)(b) if it was inserted through the letter box at the 'usual or last known address' of one or more of the partners. Since the purpose of the Rules of the Supreme Court as to service was that the originating process should be brought to the attention of the defendant so that he had knowledge of the existence of proceedings against him, the 'usual or last known address' of a partner for the purposes of Ord 10, r 1(2)(b) was not confined to his place of residence but included the address at which he practised his profession or his business address. It followed that the writ had been duly served on one of the partners in the defendant firm on 14 January and therefore the default judgment had been regularly obtained. The appeal would accordingly be allowed and the

---

a   Rule 1(3), so far as material, provides: 'Where … partners are served in the name of a firm, the writ may … be served—(a) on any one or more of the partners …'

b   Rule 1, so far as material, is set out at p 83 *j* to p 84 *b*, post

master's order as to costs would be restored (see p 82 *g h*, p 83 *c g h*, p 85 *g* to *j* and p 90 *a d h* to p 91 *a*, post).

Barclays Bank of Swaziland Ltd v Hahn [1989] 2 All ER 398 and *Forward v West Sussex CC* [1995] 4 All ER 207 applied.

Dictum of Leggatt LJ in *Marsden v Kingswell Watts (a firm)* [1992] 2 All ER 239 at 242 not followed.

Notes

For service of a writ on a partnership sued in the firm name, see 35 *Halsbury's Laws* (4th edn reissue) para 82.

Cases referred to in judgments

Austin Rover Group Ltd v Crouch Butler Savage Associates (a firm) [1986] 3 All ER 50, [1986] 1 WLR 1102, CA.

Barclays Bank of Swaziland Ltd v Hahn [1989] 2 All ER 398, [1989] 1 WLR 506, HL; affg [1989] 1 All ER 193, [1989] 1 WLR 13, CA.

Forward v West Sussex CC [1995] 4 All ER 207, [1995] 1 WLR 1469, CA.

Hodgson v Hart DC [1986] 1 All ER 400, [1986] 1 WLR 317, CA.

Marsden v Kingswell Watts (a firm) [1992] 2 All ER 239, CA.

Morecambe and Heysham Borough v Warwick (1958) 9 P & CR 307, DC.

Price v West London Investment Building Society [1964] 2 All ER 318, [1964] 1 WLR 616, CA.

R v Braithwaite [1918] 2 KB 319, [1918–19] All ER Rep 1145, CA.

R v Southend Magistrates' Court, ex p Kingsway Furniture (West Thurrock) Ltd [1996] CA Transcript 705.

Stylo Shoes Ltd v Prices Tailors Ltd [1959] 3 All ER 901, [1960] Ch 396, [1960] 2 WLR 8.

Young v Bristol Aeroplane Co Ltd [1944] 2 All ER 293, [1944] KB 718, CA; affd [1946] 1 All ER 98, [1946] AC 163, HL.

Cases also cited or referred to in skeleton arguments

Abu Dhabi Helicopters Ltd v International Aerodio plc [1986] 1 All ER 395, [1986] 1 WLR 312, CA.

Leal v Dunlop Bio-Processes International Ltd [1984] 2 All ER 207, [1984] 1 WLR 874, CA.

Sheldon v Brown Bayley's Steelworks Ltd [1953] 2 All ER 894, [1953] 2 QB 393, CA.

Sompertex Ltd v Philadelphia Chewing Gum Corp [1968] 3 All ER 26, CA.

Appeal

By notice dated 5 July 1995 the plaintiff, Felicity Robertson, appealed with leave from the decision of Douglas Day QC, sitting as a deputy judge of the High Court, given on 11 November 1994, allowing an appeal by the defendants, Banham & Co (a firm), from a decision of Master Rose given on 5 October 1994 granting the defendants' application to set aside the judgment entered by the plaintiff against them in default of defence but ordering the defendants to pay the plaintiff's costs of that application. The facts are set out in the judgment of Roch LJ.

Robert Denman (instructed by *Palmer Hart*, Bristol) for the plaintiff.
Patrick Lawrence (instructed by *Wansbroughs Willey Hargrave*, Bristol) for the defendants.

Cur adv vult

a 31 October 1996. The following judgments were delivered.

ROCH LJ. This is an appeal from the decision of Mr Douglas Day QC sitting as a deputy judge of the High Court given on 11 November 1994. A month earlier on 5 October 1994 Master Rose had ordered that a judgment obtained by the plaintiff, Mrs Robertson, against the defendants, two solicitors who were

b formerly in partnership, in default of a defence be set aside. The master had also ordered that the plaintiff's costs including the costs of entering judgment were to be paid by the defendants forthwith. There was to be a legal aid taxation direction of the plaintiff's costs. The master gave directions for the subsequent conduct of the action.

In reaching the decision on which those orders were based, the master

c determined that the default judgment which the plaintiff had obtained on 18 February 1994 had been obtained regularly. The defendants appealed that finding and the costs order made in the plaintiff's favour based upon that finding.

The deputy judge on 11 November 1994 held that the default judgment of 18 February 1994 had been obtained irregularly and he varied the orders made by

d Master Rose by ordering that the defendants were to have their costs of having the default judgment set aside as from the date of their application to do so, that is to say from 5 September 1994, including the costs before the master and before the deputy judge, but that that order was not to be enforced without leave of the court. The deputy judge directed a legal aid taxation of the plaintiff's costs and gave the plaintiff leave to appeal.

e The background of this case is that the plaintiff started an action against two solicitors, Ian Southward and George Banham, by writ on 13 January 1994. The writ described those two solicitors as 'Banham & Co (a firm)'. The writ was accompanied by a statement of claim and a form of acknowledgment of service. Mr Southward and Mr Banham had practised as solicitor-partners under the style

f Banham & Co at 28A The Cheese Market, Salisbury.

On 14 January 1994 at approximately 5.45 am, the plaintiff put the envelope containing the writ, the statement of claim and the form of acknowledgment of service together with a covering letter, the envelope and letter being addressed to 'Ian Southward', through the letter box of the premises of the Griffiths Banham Partnership at Griffin House, Salisbury. Later that morning the

g envelope and its contents came to the attention of Mr Southward, and before the morning was over Mr Southward had informed his professional negligence insurers that he had received that writ and statement of claim.

Unbeknown to the plaintiff, as at 13 and 14 January 1994, the firm of Banham & Co had been dissolved, Mr Banham going into retirement and Mr Southward

h with a Mr R L Griffiths forming the Griffiths Banham Partnership. The name Banham was kept because Mr Banham was to act as a consultant. Banham & Co had been dissolved on 4 January 1994.

It was Mr Southward who had dealt with the plaintiff's affairs when she was a client of Banham & Co.

j The statement of claim alleged breach of contract and negligence on the part of Banham & Co, which had caused the plaintiff loss and damage. In the statement of claim the plaintiff claimed damages to be assessed and interest. The alleged breaches of contract and negligence related to the defendants' handling of an action brought by Mrs Robertson against another firm of solicitors whom she had retained prior to her going to Banham & Co.

On 18 February 1994 the plaintiff signed judgment in default of defence.

On 26 January 1994 the defendants acknowledged service of the writ and statement of claim. That acknowledgment indicated that the defendants intended to contest the action.

The issue at the hearings before the master and before the deputy judge was: was the judgment of 18 February 1994 regularly obtained by the plaintiff? If the writ was duly served on Mr Southward on 14 January 1994, then that judgment was regularly obtained as a judgment in default of defence. If the writ was not duly served until Mr Southward entered an appearance on 26 January 1994, when, by virtue of that appearance to the writ being entered service of the writ was deemed to have taken place on that day (see RSC Ord 10, r 1(5)), then the judgment in default was irregular. In that situation, the defendants would have had until 23 February 1994 to serve a defence and the entering of judgment by the plaintiff on 18 February would have been five days premature.

The grounds of appeal are first, that the judgment obtained was regular because service of the writ by delivering it through the letter box of the practising address of one of the partners of the defendant firm was due service. Therefore, service occurred either on 21 January 1994, deemed service, or on 14 January 1994, the date on which the plaintiff could prove that the writ had come to the actual knowledge and attention of Mr Southward. The alternative ground of appeal is that the defendants submitted to the jurisdiction of the court because they did not make any application under Ord 12, r 8 and they are consequently prevented from alleging that the writ was not duly served. By not applying to the court to set aside service of the writ or alternatively to make a declaration that it had not been duly served, the defendants waived the irregularity in service. The third ground of appeal, which was not pursued before us, was that even if the judgment in default of 18 February 1994 was irregular, a proper exercise of the deputy judge's discretion would have been to make a costs order in the plaintiff's favour.

It was common ground that a defence is to be served before the expiration of 14 days from the time limited for acknowledging service (Ord 18, r 2) and that the time for acknowledging service is 14 days after service of the writ, including the day of service (Ord 12, r 5). Consequently for the judgment of 18 February 1994 to be regular, due service of the writ must have occurred on or before 21 January 1994.

The first submission made by Mr Denman, on behalf of the plaintiff, is that the plaintiff duly served the defendants by placing the envelope addressed to Mr Southward through the letter box of Griffin House, which was his usual and, to her, last known address. The plaintiff could prove that the copy had reached Mr Southward on that day. Consequently service of the writ had been duly effected on 14 January 1994, pursuant to the Rules of the Supreme Court.

But for the decision of this court in *Marsden v Kingswell Watts (a firm)* [1992] 2 All ER 239, I would without hesitation accept that submission made on behalf of the plaintiff. Mr Lawrence, for the defendants, in a powerful argument, submitted that the decision in that case was correct, or alternatively it was a decision of the Court of Appeal and binding on us as it did not fall within any of the exceptions to the principle that the Court of Appeal is bound to follow its own decisions as stated by the court in *Young v Bristol Aeroplane Co Ltd* [1944] 2 All ER 293, [1944] KB 718. I propose to set out the reasons why I would accept the first submission made by Mr Denman, absent the decision in *Marsden's* case, and then go on to consider the question whether this court is bound by that decision.

a Order 81, r 1 allows persons alleged to be liable as partners to be sued in the name of the firm of which they were partners when the cause of action accrued. Service of originating process where partners are sued in the name of the firm is governed by Ord 81, r 3, unless the partnership has, to the knowledge of the plaintiff, been dissolved before an action against the firm is begun (Ord 81, r 3(3)).

b In this case, it was agreed that on 13 and 14 January 1994 the plaintiff did not know of the dissolution of Banham & Co, on 4 January 1994, although the plaintiff clearly knew that Mr Southward had moved from 28A The Cheese Market, Salisbury to Griffin House.

Order 81, r 3 enables a writ suing partners in the name of the firm to be served in three ways so as to be deemed due service on the firm, that is to say on all the partners whether or not any member of the firm is out of the jurisdiction. As I

c understand Ord 81, r 3, it is not concerned with a writ suing one or more partners where those partners are named as defendants as opposed to being sued in the name of the firm. The first method is by service on any one or more of the partners. As *The Supreme Court Practice 1997* vol 1, para 81/3/2 points out, this may be personal service on the partner or in accordance with Ord 10, r 1(2). The

d second method is service at the principal place of business of the partnership within the jurisdiction on any person having at the time of service the control or management of the partnership business there (Ord 81, r 3(1)(b)). This is service on all the partners although the person served may not be a partner. Putting it through the letter box at the principal place of business of the partnership will not satisfy this part of the rule. The third method is by ordinary first class post to the

e firm at the firm's principal place of business within the jurisdiction.

Order 81, r 3(2) is helpful in construing the rules in that it shows that when service is on the firm by first class post to its principal place of business, the date of service is deemed, unless the contrary is shown, to be the seventh day after the date on which the copy writ was sent to the firm, and that an affidavit of service

f has to contain a statement of opinion by the deponent that the copy of the writ sent by first class post to the firm's principal address will have come to the knowledge either of a partner or of a person having the control or management of the partnership business at its principal place of business. Those provisions do not apply to service under Ord 81, r 3(1)(b) because service takes place at the moment when the person having control or management of the partnership

g business at its principal place of business receives the copy writ.

In this case, the plaintiff relied upon Ord 81, r 3(1)(a) claiming that the writ had been properly served on one of the partners, Mr Southward, on 14 January. That in turn raised the question whether the events of 14 January constituted due service on Mr Southward under Ord 10, r 1. Here the plaintiff relied upon Ord

h 10, r 1(2)(b). That rule so far as is relevant reads:

> 'A writ for service on a defendant within the jurisdiction may, instead of being served personally on him, be served … (b) if there is a letter box for that address, by inserting through the letter box a copy of the writ enclosed in a sealed envelope addressed to the defendant …'

j
'That address' refers to the defendant's 'usual or last known address' (see Ord 10, r 1(2)(a)).

Under Ord 10, r 1(3) it is provided:

> 'Where a writ is served in accordance with paragraph (2)—(a) the date of service shall, unless the contrary is shown, be deemed to be the seventh day

'... after the date on which the copy was ... inserted through the letter box for
the address in question; (b) any affidavit proving due service of the writ must
contain a statement to the effect that—(i) in the opinion of the deponent ...
the copy of the writ ... inserted through the letter box for the address in
question, will have come to the knowledge of the defendant within seven
days thereafter ...'

Certain matters are established by decisions of this court in respect of those
rules. First, that 'last known address' means the defendants' last address known
to the plaintiff (see *Forward v West Sussex CC* [1995] 4 All ER 207, [1995] 1 WLR
1469). That authority also establishes that the two alternatives to personal service
provided in para (2) of Ord 10, r 1 are 'allowed because they found a good
working presumption (rebuttable, but still a good working presumption) that
they will bring the proceedings to the notice of the defendant' (see [1995] 4 All ER
207 at 214, [1995] 1 WLR 1469 at 1477 per Bingham MR).

It is therefore open to the defendants to show that the copy writ never came to
their notice (see *Forward's* case) and it is open for the plaintiff to establish that the
copy writ came to the defendants' notice prior to the seventh day after service by
post or insertion through the letter box (see *Hodgson v Hart DC* [1986] 1 All ER
400, [1986] 1 WLR 317).

The issue remains whether service on Mr Southward at Griffin House, the
address at which, in January 1994, he was practising as a solicitor, was service at
'his usual or last known address'? In answering that question, in my opinion, a
court should start from the position that the purpose of the rules is that service
should take place when the originating process is brought to the notice of the
defendant. That was the approach of the House of Lords in *Barclays Bank of
Swaziland Ltd v Hahn* [1989] 2 All ER 398, [1989] 1 WLR 506. In that case the bank
issued a writ against the defendant, who, with his wife lived in various parts of
the world. The defendant came within the jurisdiction from time to time when
he lived with his wife in a flat rented by his wife. At about 1530 hrs on 14 April
1987, believing that the defendant was at that flat or would be there on that day,
the bank inserted a copy of the writ in a sealed envelope through the letter box.
It is to be observed that this was a residential as opposed to a business address.
The defendant arrived in this country at 1727 hrs, to be met by the caretaker of
the flat, who warned him of the envelope that had been put through the letter
box. As a consequence, the defendant did not go to the flat, spending the night
in a hotel and returning to Switzerland the following day. The bank claimed that
there had been good service under Ord 10, r 1(2)(b) in that they had complied
with that rule and could show that the copy writ had come to the defendant's
attention on that day. The defendant maintained that as he had not gone to the
flat nor had he physically received the copy of the writ, there had not been due
service of the writ upon him. The Court of Appeal ([1989] 1 All ER 193, [1989] 1
WLR 13) upheld the bank's case ruling that the words 'within the jurisdiction' in
Ord 10, r 1(2) described the writ and its service and not the defendant and
consequently the defendant had been duly served. The House of Lords upheld
the decision of the Court of Appeal but for different reasons, accepting the
defendant's proposition that he had to be within the jurisdiction at the time when
the writ was served. In his speech, with which the other members of their
Lordships' House agreed, Lord Brightman said ([1989] 2 All ER 398 at 402, [1989]
1 WLR 506 at 511):

'My Lords, I entirely applaud the common sense of the decision of the Court of Appeal, but I prefer to reach the same destination by another route. I think that the clue to the problem is to be found in para (3)(a) of Ord 10, r 1. This provides, inter alia, that the date of service is to be the seventh day after the date on which the copy writ was inserted through the letter box for the address in question "unless the contrary is shown". It follows from the exception that there may be circumstances where the date of service is not the date of letter-box insertion. I therefore ask myself: in what circumstances might a plaintiff or defendant be able to show that the seventh day after the date of insertion through the letter box was not the date of service; do such circumstances exist in the present case; and, if so, what date of service takes the place of the deemed date of service? My Lords, in the case of letter-box service I can think of nothing which is capable of giving content to the expression "unless the contrary is shown" save that it refers to the defendant's knowledge of the existence of the writ, nor was the appellant's counsel able to suggest any other solution. Indeed, it is the obvious solution because the purpose of serving a writ is to give the defendant knowledge of the existence of proceedings against him; that is exactly what a defendant acquires when a writ is served on him personally; and it is exactly what I would expect the procedural rules would require when service is impersonal and not personal. So I answer the first question which I have posed by saying that a plaintiff or a defendant may displace the deemed date of service by proving that the defendant acquired knowledge of the writ at some other date.'

Lord Brightman then went on to point out that it was clear, despite the defendant's denial, that the defendant had known what was in the envelope which he had been told had been put through the letter box of his wife's flat on that afternoon.

With the principle that the purpose of the rules is that the originating process should be brought to the attention of the defendant in mind, what is meant by 'his usual or last known address'? Is that phrase to be confined to residential addresses? Free of authority I have no doubt that it should not be so confined. First, examination of other parts of the rules such as Ord 6, r 5, makes it clear that where the draftsman of the rules wishes to confine the address to a party's place of residence he does so in express terms; and that the same is true where the draftsman intends to refer to a business address. Second, in the case of a professional person the address known to the erstwhile client who wishes to sue the professional person will be the address at which he practises his profession. A professional person may be careful to ensure that clients do not know his home address, not wishing to be troubled with work at his home and, in some cases, not wishing to be troubled or to have members of his family troubled by difficult clients at his home. As Connell J observed during argument, if a professional man is being sued in his professional capacity, then his address last known to the plaintiff will inevitably be his business address. It will also be his usual address as a professional man. Service by post or by insertion through a letter box at such an address causes no unfairness because it is always open to him to prove that the originating process did not come to his attention.

Next there are a number of authorities which support a purposive construction of the rules, albeit that those authorities are not authorities on Ord 10, r 1. I bear

in mind the observation of Bingham MR in *Forward's* case [1995] 4 All ER 207 at
214, [1995] 1 WLR 1469 at 1477:

> 'But none of these authorities [the authorities to which that court was
> referred in that case] concerns Ord 10, r 1 as it now reads or formerly read,
> and where (as here) the court is required to construe a detailed statutory
> code it is in our view dangerous to seek to apply statements made with
> reference to different statutory codes. That might be necessary if the
> statutory code in question were not clear.'

Those authorities start with *R v Braithwaite* [1918] 2 KB 319, [1918–19] All ER
Rep 1145. The issue in this case was whether a summons for non-payment of a
general district rate issued under s 256 of the Public Health Act 1875 was properly
served. Section 267 of that Act provided:

> 'Notices orders and any other documents required or authorised to be
> served under this Act may be served by delivering the same to or at the
> residence of the person to whom they are respectively addressed ...'

Section 1 of the Summary Jurisdiction Act 1848 provided:

> '... every such summons shall be served ... upon the person to whom it is
> so directed, by delivering the same to the party personally, or by leaving the
> same with some person for him at his last or most usual place of abode ...'

The summons was served, not by leaving it at the ratepayer's dwelling house,
but by leaving it at the house where the ratepayer carried on his practice as a
solicitor. This court held that for the purposes of the service of such a summons
the ratepayer's place of business was to be treated as his 'residence' within the
meaning of s 267, although he did not sleep there; and that service of such a
summons at his place of business under s 267 was good. In the course of his
judgment Warrington LJ said ([1918] 2 KB 319 at 328, [1918–19] All ER 1145 at
1148):

> 'Then can it be served at the place of business? Independently of authority,
> I should say Yes. Such an expression as residence, which has no technical
> meaning, may properly be construed having regard to the objects of the Act
> in which it is found ... The only possible object in the case of the statute in
> question is that the documents mentioned may be brought to the knowledge
> of the defaulter. For this purpose I can see no reason why a man's private
> house or lodging should be selected as the place of service exclusively of his
> place of business. In fact, seeing that the section authorizes service by post,
> I should say that there was much more chance of the documents getting by
> accident into the fire or the waste-paper basket at the private house or
> lodging than at his business premises where part of the routine of the day is
> to open and read all letters.'

Scrutton LJ said ([1918] 2 KB 319 at 331–332, [1918–19] All ER Rep 1145 at 1150):

> 'What, then, is the purpose of the provision by which a summons need not
> be personally served, but may be left at the "place of residence"? Obviously
> that it shall get to the person summoned by being left at a place where it is
> likely to reach him. His place of business will usually be at least as suitable a
> place for that purpose as the place where he sleeps; frequently more so, as
> more care is usually taken of business than of private documents. On

a principle, therefore, I see no reason why the place of business should not be the place of residence for the purposes of serving this summons ...'

Then Scrutton LJ went on to set out authorities to that effect.

This case was followed in *Morecambe and Heysham Borough v Warwick* (1958) 9 P & CR 307, a case which involved the service of an enforcement notice under the Town and Country Planning Act 1947. This was a decision of the Divisional Court. In a short judgment Lord Goddard CJ said (at 308):

b

'R v. *Braithwaite and others* is clear authority for the proposition that when it comes to the point of the service of notices, and service is required to be at the last place of abode, service at the last place of business is good service. In my opinion it is perfectly clear that the notice is served if it is left at the business address of the person to be served.'

c

In *Stylo Shoes Ltd v Prices Tailors Ltd* [1959] 3 All ER 901, [1960] Ch 396, a case involving the service of a notice to quit under the Landlord and Tenant Act 1927, s 23(1) of which allowed for such a notice to be served 'either personally, or by leaving it for him [that is the tenant] at his last known place of abode', Wynn-Parry J held, in a case where the tenant company sought a declaration that the landlord's notice had not been properly served because it had been sent to the tenant company's principal place of business in Huddersfield after the tenant company had transferred its principal place of business to Leeds, arguing that their former principal place of business in Huddersfield was not 'their last known place of abode', that there had been valid service. In the case of a limited company 'place of abode' meant 'place of business'. It is true that Wynn-Parry J considered that s 23(1) of the 1927 Act was permissive and that although there were certain modes of service set out in the subsection they were not to be regarded as being exhaustive (see [1959] 3 All ER 901 at 905–906, [1960] Ch 396 at 405–406). The importance of that decision is that it is another instance of a court adopting a purposive approach to the construction of a statutory provision governing service of process.

d

e

f

The final authority is another Court of Appeal decision, *Price v West London Investment Building Society* [1964] 2 All ER 318, [1964] 1 WLR 616. This was another case under the Landlord and Tenant Act 1954. Again it was a landlord's notice terminating a business tenancy. The notice was sent to the business premises, was received and signed for by an employee of the tenant but owing to an oversight the tenant himself did not receive the notice until six days after its delivery. The issue was whether the counternotice served by the tenant was within time. The counternotice was within time if time ran from the date on which the tenant himself received notice but was out of time if it ran from the date six days earlier when the notice was delivered to the business premises. Again the question of service was governed by the terms of s 23(1) of the 1927 Act as applied by s 66(4) of 1954 Act. The argument for the tenant was that the business premises were not his 'place of abode' and therefore service was not effected until the notice was received by him personally. This court consisting of Willmer, Danckwerts and Diplock LJJ held that a phrase such as 'place of abode' had to be construed with reference to the subject matter with which it was concerned in each case. As Pt II of the 1954 Act was concerned solely with business premises, its sensible and natural meaning was not the residence of the tenant but his business address. It was thus plainly the intention of the 1954 Act to include a tenant's business address and not to confine 'place of abode' to his

g

h

j

personal residence. In this case, *R v Braithwaite, Morecambe and Heysham Borough v Warwick* and the *Stylo Shoes Ltd* case were considered and followed, Danckwerts LJ describing them as 'a formidable lot of authorities showing that the phrases "residence" or "last known place of abode" may very well include a business address, if the context is appropriate' (see [1964] 2 All ER 318 at 321–322, [1964] 1 WLR 616 at 622). Danckwerts LJ did go on to observe that it was not always appropriate so to construe the phrase 'place of abode'.

These authorities were cited with approval by this court in *R v Southend Magistrates' Court, ex p Kingsway Furniture (West Thurrock) Ltd* [1996] CA Transcript 705, which concerned the service of a summons on a company for non-payment of rates.

Here the case is stronger because the phrase is 'usual or last known address'. When a solicitor is being sued as a solicitor, his usual address as a solicitor must be the address at which he practises. That will probably be the only address known to the person who wishes to serve the writ. That will be the address at which he is most likely to receive the writ. That, in my judgment, is the ordinary and natural meaning of those words. The rules could have used the words 'his place of residence' or 'residential address'. A person can have, as Mr Lawrence conceded, more than one 'usual address'.

Since the conclusion of submissions in this case, the industry of Mr Lawrence has brought to our attention a further authority in this court, namely that of *Austin Rover Group Ltd v Crouch Butler Savage Associates (a firm)* [1986] 3 All ER 50, [1986] 1 WLR 1102. There the plaintiffs wished to sue the defendants, a firm of architects, and the question was whether a writ addressed to the firm at what had been the firm's principal place of business and posted first class, which was then redirected to the firm's new premises in Wheeleys Road, Birmingham and received there by one of the partners, Mr Cliff, had been duly served. This court considered the terms of Ord 81, r 3(1)(c) and Ord 10, r 1(2)(a), although the interpretation of Ord 10, r 1(2)(a) was not necessary to the decision reached by the court. However, May LJ observed ([1986] 3 All ER 50 at 56, [1986] 1 WLR 1102 at 1111):

'I would if it were necessary be prepared to hold that the new address in Wheeleys Road, Birmingham was, within the rule, Mr Cliff's usual address at that time.'

This authority was not cited to the court in *Marsden's* case.

In *Marsden's* case the defendants were a firm of solicitors who had acted for the plaintiffs when they bought a plot of land. The plaintiffs issued a writ in the name of the firm and on 19 June 1989, the last day for service of the writ before its expiry, the plaintiffs caused a copy to be put through the letter box at the address of the defendant firm by a process server. The district registrar and the judge on appeal from the district registrar struck out the writ as not having been duly served during the period of its validity. Parker LJ in his judgment, agreeing with Leggatt LJ, decided the matter by reference to Ord 10, r 1(3)(a) that the date of service shall be deemed to be the seventh day after the date on which the copy was inserted through the letter box unless the contrary is shown. Here service of the writ would only have occurred within the period of validity of the writ if the plaintiffs could have established that the writ had come to the attention of a partner in the firm on 19 June. The plaintiffs could not prove that, the evidence indicating that the insertion through the letter box had occurred after close of

a business. That was the second ground on which Leggatt LJ held that the service
was bad (see [1992] 2 All ER 239 at 243–244). The district judge and the judge in
that case had made these findings: first, that the documents were placed in the
letter box of the defendant firm on 19 June after the close of business on that day
and second, that the documents were found on 20 June by the relevant partner of
the defendant firm. The argument before this court on behalf of the Marsdens
b was that because they could show that the relevant partner had received the copy
writ within the seven-day period, the deeming provision in Ord 10, r 1(3)(a) had
no application and the moment of service became the moment when the
envelope had been inserted through the letter box. This court rejected that
submission holding that the moment of service was when the copy writ came to
the attention of the relevant partner. In the course of his judgment Leggatt LJ
c said (at 242):

  'Mr Engleman accepts, I think, that no service by insertion of the copy writ
  through the letter box was possible on the firm as such, but he argues that
  service by that means could properly be effected upon any partner, or at any
  rate any partner normally working at that address, because it would
d constitute the usual or last known address of such a partner. I do not agree.
  In order to constitute service on a firm under Ord 81, r 3(1)(a) the service on
  a partner must be such as would constitute service on him under Ord 10, r 1
  if he were a personal defendant. If service by post or by insertion through
  the letter box is chosen it must be effected at "his usual or last known
e address". In my judgment that means at the place where he lives or he was
  last known to have lived. It does not mean at the address of the partnership,
  otherwise Ord 81, r 3 would have been so worded as to allow for insertion of
  a copy writ through the letter box "at the principal place of business of the
  partnership within the jurisdiction". The mode of service attempted was in
  my judgment therefore bad.'
f
I respectfully disagree with this interpretation of the rules. I do so with
considerable hesitation considering the composition of the court in Marsden's
case.
    Order 81, r 3(1)(a) contemplates, as The Supreme Court Practice 1997 vol 1, para
g 81/3/2 accepts, that service on any one or more partners under Ord 10, r 1 of a
writ naming the partnership by its business name is to be deemed due service on
all the partners although some are out of the jurisdiction. Order 81, r 3(1)(b) is
not concerned with service on a partner or with delivery of the copy writ to a
partner, still less with placing an envelope through the letter box of a partner's
h usual or last known address. It is concerned with delivery of the copy writ to the
person having the management or control of the partnership business at its
principal place of business. The terms of that rule cannot shed any light on the
meaning of 'usual or last known address' in Ord 10, r 1(2). The terms of an order
which is concerned with partners cannot control the interpretation of a rule
which effects service on persons who are not partners. There was no need for
j Ord 81, r 3(1)(b) to have been so 'worded as to allow for insertion of a copy writ
through the letter box "at the principal place of business of the partnership within
the jurisdiction"'. Order 81, r 3(1)(b) was not concerned with service on a
partner; it was concerned with service on the firm by giving the copy writ to a
person who managed or controlled the partnership business at its principal place
of business. That rule is quite separate from service on 'one or more partners'. It

is an additional method of service to those set out in Ord 10, r 1. It is not intended
to limit or cut down the methods of service under Ord 10, r 1. Consequently, in
my judgment, it does not follow from the wording of Ord 81, r 3(1)(b) that the
words in Ord 10, r 1(2) 'usual or last known address' must be confined to a
partner's place of residence.

Are we bound by the decision of this court in *Marsden's* case? In my judgment,
we are not. That case had to be decided against the appellants on the ground set
out at the end of the judgment of Leggatt LJ and in the short judgment of
Parker LJ which concerned the interpretation of Ord 10, r 1(3)(a) and was not
concerned with the meaning of Ord 10, r 1(2). The observations of Leggatt LJ on
the interpretation of the phrase 'his usual or last known address' were not
necessary to the decision in that case. Those observations were made in an
extempore judgment, following argument in which Leggatt LJ had not been
referred to the authorities which I have endeavoured to summarise in this
judgment or to the speech of Lord Brightman in *Barclays Bank of Swaziland Ltd v
Hahn*.

Consequently, in my judgment this appeal succeeds on the first submission
made by Mr Denman.

The second submission made by Mr Denman on behalf of the plaintiff would
not have lead me to allow this appeal. It was to the effect that assuming service
on Mr Southward was irregular, the defendants had nevertheless waived the
irregularity by failing to make application under Ord 12, r 8(1) for an order setting
aside the writ or service of the writ or a declaration that the writ had not been
duly served. Order 12 deals with acknowledgment of service of a writ or an
originating summons. Order 12, r 7 provides that acknowledgment by a
defendant of service of a writ shall not be treated as a waiver by him of any
irregularity in the writ or service of the writ. Order 12, r 8(7) reads:

> 'Except where the defendant makes an application in accordance with
> paragraph (1) the acknowledgment by a defendant of service of a writ shall,
> unless the acknowledgment is withdrawn by leave of the Court under Order
> 21, rule 1, be treated as a submission by the defendant to the jurisdiction of
> the Court in the proceedings.'

In those circumstances, the writ is deemed to be duly served on the date on
which the defendant acknowledged service by virtue of Ord 10, r 1(5). The rule
is not concerned with deemed service but with deemed due service. As Mr
Lawrence submitted, that rule is expressly premised on the writ having not been
duly served. The word 'so' is important because it stresses that it is regular
service which is deemed to occur on the date on which a defendant acknowledges
service.

I accept the submissions of Mr Lawrence on this ground of appeal and had it
stood alone this appeal would have failed.

I would therefore allow the appeal and restore the orders of the master in
relation to costs.

CONNELL J. I agree. Order 10, r 1(2)(b) provides for service on a defendant via
a letter box at his usual or last known address. When considering the situation
between a lay client and solicitor it is in the highest degree unlikely that the lay
client will know where the solicitor lives; it is most likely that he will know the
solicitor's professional address. Given that a main purpose of the Rules of the
Supreme Court as to service is to give the defendant knowledge of the existence

a of proceedings against him, it would in my view be a strange result if the rules as to service were to be so designed as to make that main purpose more difficult to achieve by requiring service at an address which the plaintiff is unlikely to know rather than easier to achieve by permitting service at an address which the plaintiff is likely to know. For the reasons given by Roch LJ, I would allow this appeal and restore the decision of the master as to costs.

b

Appeal allowed. Leave to appeal to the House of Lords refused.

Paul Magrath Esq   Barrister.

MRS Environmental Services Ltd v Marsh and another

a

COURT OF APPEAL, CIVIL DIVISION
NEILL, MILLETT AND PHILLIPS LJJ
27 JUNE, 9 JULY 1996

b

Unfair dismissal – Right not to be unfairly dismissed – Restriction of right when employee not continuously employed for period of two years – Dismissal in connection with transfer of undertaking – Employees continuously employed for period of less than two years – Whether employees entitled to claim compensation for unfair dismissal – Employment Protection (Consolidation) Act 1978, ss 54, 64 – Transfer of Undertakings (Protection of Employment) Regulations 1981, reg 8(1) – Council Directive (EEC) 77/187, art 4(1).

c

On 11 November 1991 the respondents commenced employment with a local authority in the local authority's street cleansing undertaking. On 31 March 1993 the local authority purported to dismiss them and the following day contracted out street cleansing work to the appellant company. That action constituted the transfer of an undertaking to the company within the meaning of the Transfer of Undertakings (Protection of Employment) Regulations 1981. The respondents claimed compensation for unfair dismissal pursuant to s 67 of the Employment Protection (Consolidation) Act 1978 and their claim was upheld by the industrial tribunal. The Employment Appeal Tribunal dismissed an appeal by the company, which thereafter appealed to the Court of Appeal, contending that although s 54[a] of the 1978 Act conferred a general right not to be unfairly dismissed, the respondents were excluded from that right under s 64[b] of the Act as they had not been continuously employed for a period of two years. The respondents contended that they were not so excluded from the right not to be unfairly dismissed by virtue of art 4(1)[c] of Council Directive (EEC) 77/187 and reg 8(1)[d] of the 1981 regulations, which provided that when an employee was dismissed for reasons connected with the transfer of an undertaking the employee 'shall be treated for the purposes of Part V of the 1978 Act ... as unfairly dismissed'.

d

e

f

g

Held – Regulation 8 of the 1981 regulations did not confer a free-standing right not to be unfairly dismissed by reason of the transfer of an undertaking; by amending Pt V of the 1978 Act, reg 8 conferred that right on those who enjoyed the right not to be unfairly dismissed by virtue of s 54 of the 1978 Act and not on the category of employee excluded by s 64(1), which exclusion was permitted by art 4(1) of Council Directive (EEC) 77/187. Since the respondents fell into the excluded category as they had not been continuously employed for a period of two years, it followed that they were not entitled to compensation for unfair dismissal. The appeal would therefore be allowed (see p 102 *b c f* to *h* and p 103 *c*, post).

h

j

Milligan v Securicor Cleaning Ltd [1995] ICR 867 overruled.

---

a   Section 54 is set out at p 95 *c d*, post
b   Section 64, so far as material, is set out at p 95 *g h*, post
c   Article 4(1), so far as material, is set out at p 96 *g h*, post
d   Regulation 8(1) is set out at p 98 *b*, post

Notes

a For the right not to be unfairly dismissed and the qualifying period of employment, see 16 *Halsbury's Laws* (4th edn reissue) paras 313–314.

For unfair dismissal because of a transfer of undertaking, see ibid para 354, and for cases on the subject, see 20(2) *Digest* (2nd reissue) 103–104, *2195–2197*.

For employees' rights under Community law on transfers of undertakings, see
b 52 *Halsbury's Laws* (4th edn) para 21·20.

For the Employment Protection (Consolidation) Act 1978, ss 54, 64, 67, see 16 *Halsbury's Statutes* (4th edn) (1990 reissue) 276, 290.

For the Transfer of Undertakings (Protection of Employment) Regulations 1981, reg 8, see 7 *Halsbury's Statutory Instruments* (1993 reissue) 239.

c **Cases referred to in judgments**

Abels v Administrative Board of the Bedrijfsvereniging voor de Metaalindustrie en de Electrotecnische Industrie Case 135/83 [1985] ECR 469.

d'Urso v Ercole Marelli Elettromeccanica Generale SpA Case C-362/89 [1991] ECR I-4105.

d *EC Commission v Belgium* Case 237/84 [1986] ECR 1247.

Foreningen af Arbejdsledere i Danmark v Daddy's Dance Hall A/S Case 324/86 [1988] ECR 739.

Foreningen af Arbejdsledere i Danmark v A/S Danmols Inventar (in liq) Case 105/84 [1985] ECR 2639.

Litster v Forth Dry Dock and Engineering Co Ltd [1989] 1 All ER 1134, [1990] 1 AC
e 546, [1989] 2 WLR 634, HL.

Milligan v Securicor Cleaning Ltd [1995] ICR 867, EAT.

R v Secretary of State for Trade and Industry, ex p Unison [1996] IRLR 438, DC.

Rask v ISS Kantineservice A/S Case C-209/91 [1992] ECR I-5755.

Reaney v Kanda Jean Products Ltd [1978] IRLR 427.

f

Cases also cited or referred to in skeleton arguments

Brasserie du Pêcheur SA v Germany, R v Secretary of State for Transport, ex p Factortame Ltd Joined cases C-46/93 and C-48/93 [1996] All ER (EC) 301, ECJ.

EC Commission v Belgium Case 215/83 [1985] ECR 1039.

g *EC Commission v UK* Case C-382/92 [1994] ECR I-2435.

EC Commission v UK Case C-383/92 [1994] ECR I-2479.

Johnston v Chief Constable of the Royal Ulster Constabulary Case 222/84 [1986] 3 All ER 135, [1987] QB 129, ECJ.

Lemm v Mitchell [1912] AC 400, PC.

Macer v Abafast Ltd [1990] ICR 234, EAT.
h
Marshall v Southampton and South West Hampshire Area Health Authority (Teaching) Case 152/84 [1986] 2 All ER 584, [1986] QB 401, ECJ.

Melluish (Inspector of Taxes) v BMI (No 3) Ltd [1995] 4 All ER 453, [1996] AC 454, HL.

NV Algemene Transport—en Expeditie Onderneming van Gend & Loos v Nederlandse administratie der belastingen Case 26/62 [1963] ECR 1.

j *Pepper (Inspector of Taxes) v Hart* [1993] 1 All ER 42, [1993] AC 593, HL.

Pickstone v Freemans plc [1988] 2 All ER 803, [1989] AC 66, HL.

Polydor Ltd v Harlequin Record Shop Ltd [1980] 1 CMLR 669.

R v Secretary of State for Employment, ex p Seymour-Smith [1996] All ER (EC) 1, CA.

Three Rivers DC v Bank of England [1995] 4 All ER 312, [1996] QB 292, CA.

Three Rivers DC v Bank of England (No 2) [1996] 2 All ER 363.

Wilson v St Helens BC [1996] ICR 711, EAT.

Appeal

By notice dated 3 January 1996 the employer, MRS Environmental Services Ltd, appealed with leave from the decision of the Employment Appeal Tribunal made on 1 December 1995 affirming the decision of an industrial tribunal sitting at Stratford made on 2 August 1995, which held that it had jurisdiction to entertain the complaints of unfair dismissal made by the employees, Charles Marsh and Darren Harvey, notwithstanding that they had not completed two years of continuous service with the employer, because the reason for their dismissal was connected with a transfer of undertaking. The facts are set out in the judgment of Phillips LJ.

Bob Hepple QC and *Barry Cotter* (instructed by *Barnett Alexander Chart*) for the appellants.
Brian Langstaff QC and *Jennifer Eady* (instructed by *Thompsons*) for the respondents.

Cur adv vult

9 July 1996. The following judgments were delivered.

PHILLIPS LJ (giving the first judgment at the invitation of Neill LJ). Mr Marsh and Mr Harvey, who are respondents to this appeal, took up employment with Castle Point Borough Council on 11 November 1991. They were employed in the commercial services department's street cleansing undertaking. On 31 March 1993 the council purported to dismiss them. On the following day the council contracted out street cleansing work to the appellants, MRS Environmental Services Ltd. It is common ground that this constituted the transfer of an undertaking within the Transfer of Undertakings (Protection of Employment) Regulations 1981, SI 1981/1794.

The issue raised on this appeal is whether under the provisions of those regulations and the Employment Protection (Consolidation) Act 1978, as interpreted in the light of Council Directive (EEC) 77/187 (the acquired rights directive), the respondents are entitled to claim compensation for unfair dismissal. The appellants accept that, by virtue of the provisions of the 1981 regulations, any claim for unfair dismissal lies against them. Two industrial tribunals and the Employment Appeal Tribunal have held that the respondents are entitled to compensation for unfair dismissal. In so holding, they followed the decision of the Employment Appeal Tribunal in *Milligan v Securicor Cleaning Ltd* [1995] ICR 867. The Employment Appeal Tribunal gave the appellants leave to appeal in order to enable them to challenge that decision, and they must succeed in so doing if they are to succeed on this appeal.

The respondents have no common law right to damages for unfair dismissal. Nor do they contend that the acquired rights directive has direct effect so as to enable them to base their claim for compensation on that directive. Their claim is based upon the provisions of the 1981 regulations and the 1978 Act and depends upon the true interpretation of those provisions. The respondents contend, and contend rightly, that those provisions must be interpreted in a purposive manner so as to make them accord with the acquired rights directive, in so far as this can be achieved.

I propose to approach the issue in this case in the following manner. First, I shall consider the relevant provisions of domestic legislation in respect of a compensation for dismissal. Next, I shall consider the acquired rights directive. Finally, I shall consider the 1981 regulations and the other relevant provisions of domestic law in the light of that directive.

DOMESTIC LEGISLATION BEFORE THE ACQUIRED RIGHTS DIRECTIVE

Prior to 1971 an employee had no protection against being dismissed, other than any that might be afforded by the terms of his contract of employment. This
b position was altered by provisions of the Industrial Relations Act 1971, which were re-enacted with amendments in the Trade Union and Labour Relations Act 1974 and consolidated in Pt V of the 1978 Act. That Act has been much amended. The relevant provisions, as embodied in the 1978 Act in its original form, were as follows:

c   '**54.** *Right of employee not to be unfairly dismissed.*—(1) In every employment to which this section applies every employee shall have the right not to be unfairly dismissed by his employer.

(2) This section applies to every employment except in so far as its application is excluded by or under any provision of this Part or by section
d   141 to 149.'

Sections 55 to 63 come under the heading 'Meaning of unfair dismissal'. Section 55 deals with the meaning of 'dismissal'. Section 57 makes general provisions relating to the fairness of dismissal, the effect of which is that a dismissal will be unfair unless it is reasonably made for a substantial reason which
e justifies dismissal. Section 58 makes specific provisions whereby dismissal is to be 'regarded as having been unfair' if it is attributable to specified reasons relating to trade union membership. Such reasons constitute 'inadmissible reasons'. Section 59 makes specific provisions whereby dismissal is to be 'regarded as unfair' if, in the circumstances specified, the reason for it has been redundancy. Section 60(1)
f provides: 'An employee shall be treated for the purposes of this Part as unfairly dismissed if the reason or principal reason for her dismissal is that she is pregnant ...'

Section 64 excludes from those who enjoy the general right not to be unfairly dismissed, certain categories of employee. In particular, it provides:

g   '(1) Subject to subsection (3), section 54 does not apply to the dismissal of an employee from any employment if the employee—(a) was not continuously employed for a period of not less than twenty-six weeks ending with the effective date of termination ...'

But s 64(3) makes an exception to this exclusion:

h   'Subsection (1) shall not apply to the dismissal of an employee if it is shown that the reason (or, if more than one, the principal reason) for the dismissal was an inadmissible reason.'

A further exclusion is made by s 141, which falls outside Pt V of the Act:

j   '*Employment outside Great Britain* ... (2) Sections 8 and 53 and Parts II, III, V and VII do not apply to employment where under his contract of employment the employee ordinarily works outside Great Britain ...'

Section 67 sets out the procedure for claiming remedies for unfair dismissal. It begins: '(1) A complaint may be presented to an industrial tribunal against an employer by any person (in this Part referred to as the complainant) that he was

unfairly dismissed by the employer.' Section 68 provides for the remedies that
may be awarded, which include an award of compensation.

THE ACQUIRED RIGHTS DIRECTIVE

The preamble to this directive includes the following explanation of its
purpose:

'... Whereas economic trends are bringing in their wake, at both national
and Community level, changes in the structure of undertakings, through
transfers of undertakings, businesses or parts of businesses to other
employers as a result of legal transfers or mergers; Whereas it is necessary to
provide for the protection of employees in the event of a change of
employer, in particular, to ensure that their rights are safeguarded; Whereas
differences still remain in the Member States as regards the extent of the
protection of employees in this respect and these differences should be
reduced; Whereas these differences can have a direct effect on the
functioning of the common market; Whereas it is therefore necessary to
promote the approximation of laws in this field ...'

The material provisions of the directive are as follows:

'Article 1

1. This Directive shall apply to the transfer of an undertaking, business or
part of a business to another employer as a result of a legal transfer or
merger ...

SECTION II

Safeguarding of employees' rights

Article 3

1. The transferor's rights and obligations arising from a contract of
employment or from an employment relationship existing on the date of a
transfer within the meaning of Article 1(1) shall, by reason of such transfer,
be transferred to the transferee ...

Article 4

1. The transfer of an undertaking, business or part of a business shall not
in itself constitute grounds for dismissal by the transferor or the transferee.
This provision shall not stand in the way of dismissals that may take place for
economic, technical or organisational reasons entailing changes in the
workforce. Member States may provide that the first subparagraph shall not
apply to certain specific categories of employees who are not covered by the
laws or practice of the Member States in respect of protection against
dismissal ...'

Mr Langstaff QC was at odds with Mr Hepple QC, who appeared for the
appellant, as to the effect of art 4 of this directive. Mr Langstaff submitted that
art 4 imposes an absolute prohibition upon dismissing an employee by reason of
the transfer of an undertaking, even where the terms of the contract of
employment and the provisions of the employment law of the member state of
the employer give the employer an independent right to dismiss him, with or
without notice.

a Mr Hepple submitted that art 4 is ancillary to art 3. It ensures that where, in the absence of a transfer, the employee is protected from dismissal, transfer does not deprive him of that protection. On transfer, his contract of employment is transferred to the transferee and he enjoys precisely the same protection against dismissal by the transferee as he had previously enjoyed under his employment with the transferor.

b We were referred to what, I suspect, must be most, if not all, of the relevant decisions of the European Court on this directive (see *Foreningen af Arbejdsledere i Danmark v Daddy's Dance Hall A/S* Case 324/86 [1988] ECR 739, *Foreningen af Arbejdsledere i Danmark v A/S Danmols Inventar (in liq)* Case 105/84 [1985] ECR 2639, *Rask v ISS Kantineservice A/S* Case C-209/91 [1992] ECR I-5755, *EC Commission v Belgium* Case 237/84 [1986] ECR 1247, *Abels v Administrative Board of* c *the Bedrijfsvereniging voor de Metaalindustrie en de Electrotecnische Industrie* Case 135/83 [1985] ECR 469 and *d'Urso v Ercole Marelli Elettromeccanica Generale SpA* Case C-362/89 [1991] ECR I-4105).

These decisions all involved situations where the employees remained employed by the undertakings in question, notwithstanding the transfers of those d undertakings. They support the following statement of the scheme of the directive made by the court in *EC Commission v Belgium* Case 237/84 [1986] ECR 1247 at 1255 (paras 12 and 13):

e '12. It is clear both from the wording of Article 4(1) and from the scheme of the directive that the provision in question is designed to ensure that employees' rights are maintained by extending the protection against dismissal by the employer afforded by national law to cover the case in which a change in employer occurs upon the transfer of an undertaking.

13. Consequently, that provision applies to any situation in which employees affected by a transfer enjoy some, albeit limited, protection f against dismissal under national law, with the result that, under the directive, that protection may not be taken away from them or curtailed solely because of the transfer.'

This accords with Mr Hepple's submission as to the effect of the directive. It seems to me that the directive is primarily intended to prevent either the g operation of law, or the act of transferor or transferee bringing contracts of employment to an end by reason of the transfer of an undertaking in circumstances where, absent the transfer, there would be no right to do so. The employees are to be protected from being constrained to accept fresh employment with the transferee on less advantageous terms, or from seeing their h jobs filled by others prepared to accept such terms (see *Litster v Forth Dry Dock and Engineering Co Ltd* [1989] 1 All ER 1134, [1990] 1 AC 546). I do not find it necessary, however, to reach a final view on this point and thus to resolve the difference between Mr Langstaff and Mr Hepple for, even if Mr Langstaff is correct, he has accepted that the result for which Mr Hepple contends in this case does not require a construction of our domestic legislation which is at odds with j the directive. To that legislation, I now return.

TRANSFER OF UNDERTAKINGS
The relevant provisions of the 1981 regulations, which were plainly intended to comply with arts 3 and 5 of the acquired rights directive, are the following:

'**5.**—(1) ... A relevant transfer shall not operate so as to terminate the
contract of employment of any person employed by the transferor in the
undertaking or part transferred but any such contract which would
otherwise have been terminated by the transfer shall have effect after the
transfer as if originally made between the person so employed and the
transferee ...

Dismissal of employee because of relevant transfer

8.—(1) Where either before or after a relevant transfer, any employee of
the transferor or transferee is dismissed, that employee shall be treated for
the purposes of Part V of the 1978 Act and Articles 20 to 41 of the 1976 Order
(unfair dismissal) as unfairly dismissed if the transfer or a reason connected
with it is the reason or principal reason for his dismissal ...'

The following provision is also material:

'*Exclusion of employment abroad or as dock worker*

13.—(1) Regulations 8, 10 and 11 of these Regulations do not apply to
employment where under his contract of employment the employee
ordinarily works outside the United Kingdom ...'

THE RIVAL CONTENTIONS

Appellants' contention

Mr Hepple submitted that reg 8 of the 1981 regulations is a typical piece of
legislation by reference. It has to be read with Pt V of the 1978 Act. The effect of
reg 8 is to alter that Act by adding to the provisions that define ' unfair dismissal',
that is, the provisions of ss 55 to 63. But reg 8 does not, and does not purport to,
confer any right to complain of unfair dismissal. The source of that right remains
s 54 of the 1978 Act, and those categories of people who are excluded from that
right remain excluded. The respondents fall into an excluded category under
s 64. This is because, by the time the respondents were dismissed, the period of
26 weeks in s 64 had been increased, by amendment, to two years (see the Unfair
Dismissal (Variation of Qualifying Period) Order 1985, SI 1985/782). Thus the
industrial tribunal, and the Employment Appeal Tribunal, should have ruled that
they had no right to compensation for unfair dismissal. In support of his
submission, Mr Hepple relied upon the observations of the Divisional Court in *R
v Secretary of State for Trade and Industry, ex p Unison* [1996] IRLR 438. This case
raised, inter alia, the question of whether it was lawful under Community law to
increase to two years the period of employment required to be performed, in
order to avoid exclusion from protection against unfair dismissal. In ruling that
this did not offend against Community law, Otton LJ observed (at 447):

'Paragraph 2 of Article 4(1) permits or envisages derogation by Member
States in respect of "certain specific categories of employees" from
protection against dismissal, i e to exclude certain specific categories from the
benefits and protection of the Directive.'

After setting out s 54 of the 1978 Act, Otton LJ continued:

'Thus there is a right not to be unfairly dismissed under s.54 and a right to
complain against unfair dismissal. However, the s.54 right is cut down,
diminished or derogated from by s.64(1) which under a subheading to part V
is headed "Exclusion of s.54": "(1) Section 54 does not apply to the dismissal

of an employee from any employment if the employee—(a) was not continuously employed for a period of not less than two years ending with the effective date of termination, or (b) attained the following age on or before the effective date of termination, that is to say ... the age of 65." Paragraph 2 of Article 4, on a proper construction, permits Member States to derogate from the protection provided under the first paragraph in respect of certain specific categories. There can be little argument that a statutory provision in our domestic law which exempts from the right not to be unfairly dismissed those who have less than two years' service or who are over the age of 65 is a legitimate exercise of the right to derogation. In so stating, I have in mind that when the Commission laid complaints against the UK government, they did not suggest that either of the specific categories of employees was not a legitimate exemption or exclusion. The TUPE Regulations 1981 were expressed to "implement Council Directive 77/187". Article 3(1) was transposed into reg. 5 (as amended by s.33(1) Trade Union Reform and Employment Rights Act 1993); Article 4(1) was transposed into reg. 8—"Dismissal of employee because of relevant transfer": "Where either before or after a relevant transfer the employee of the transferor or transferee is dismissed, that employee shall be treated for the purposes of part V of the 1978 Act ... as unfairly dismissed if the transfer or a reason connected with it is the reason or principal reason for his dismissal." Thus the express reference to part V of the 1978 Act ensures that a person who is dismissed as a result of a transfer shall be treated as unfairly dismissed. In other words, any employee, ie who has a right or is deemed to have a right. If there was no right under s.64 because of a valid exclusion from the right under s.54, there was no protection under the Regulations. Thus the effect is to exempt certain specific categories of employees.'

While not overruling it, Otton LJ dissented from the conclusion of the Employment Appeal Tribunal in *Milligan v Securicor Cleaning Ltd* [1995] ICR 867.

Respondents' contention

Mr Langstaff repeated before us the argument that he had successfully deployed in *Milligan's* case. That argument can best be summarised by reference to the judgment of Mummery J in that case (at 873–874):

'The starting point is article 4 of Directive (77/187/E.E.C.) which provides that the transfer of an undertaking *shall not in itself* constitute grounds for dismissal. In other words, an employee has a right not to be dismissed by reason of a transfer and to have his rights—whether contractual or statutory—safeguarded in the event of a transfer. That provision, in mandatory form, protects the position of the employee on a transfer. The purpose is to protect the employee against adverse effects in member states by reason of a change in the identity of the employer. The employee's position is preserved, not improved or diminished, on the occurrence of an event (the transfer) outside his control. It is a more limited right than a general right not to be unfairly dismissed. It is only a right that *the transfer itself* should make no difference to the continuity of his employment. The right is subject to the second sentence of the first paragraph of article 4(1) which states that the provision does not stand in the way of dismissals that may take place "for economic, technical or organisational reasons entailing

changes in the workforce." The second paragraph of article 4(1) envisages
that, prior to Council Directive (77/187/E.E.C.), certain employees were a
not protected against dismissal either by the laws or practice of member
states. The provision assumes that the prohibition against dismissal by
reason of a transfer in the first paragraph will have effect despite the fact that
in member states certain employees were not protected against dismissal. In
other words, Mr. Langstaff argued, the dismissal of an employee by reason b
of a transfer is prohibited, even though that employee would have had no
rights in domestic law to prevent dismissal for any other reason. Any law
within a member state denying or restricting the right to claim for dismissal
by reason of a transfer is subject to the prohibition in the first paragraph of
the article. By way of an exemption to the first paragraph of article 4(1) a
member state has a discretion to provide that it shall not apply "to certain c
specific categories of employees." Thus, if the member state wishes to make
an exemption, provision that the first paragraph shall not apply must be
made in relation to "certain specific categories of employees." The
provisions in the domestic law of a member state must specifically identify
the category of employee or employees removed from protection of the d
prohibition and make it clear that the Directive does not apply to them.
Regulation 8(1) of the Transfer of Undertakings (Protection of Employment)
Regulations does not in terms exempt any specific category of employees
from the operation of article 4 of Directive (77/187/E.E.C.) or of the
Regulations. Regulation 8(4) does make an exemption in respect to a certain
specific category of employees, namely, those whose dismissal is required by e
reason of the application of the Aliens Restriction (Amendment) Act 1919
(now repealed). There is no comparable provision in the Regulations in
relation to employees with less than two years' service. Mr. Langstaff
identified the crucial question as being whether the words in regulation
8(1)—"that employee shall be *treated* for the purposes of Part V of the 1978 f
Act ... as unfairly dismissed"—have the effect of excluding employees with
less than two years' qualifying service from protection. He submitted that
those words do not have that effect and, in the context of the Directive, were
not intended to have that effect. The Directive requires not simply a
provision which can be construed so as to confer an exemption. It requires
a provision enacted for that particular purpose. We agree with his argument g
that the language of regulation 8(1) was not employed for the purpose of
excluding or exempting specific categories of employees from protection:
compare the language of regulation 8(4). The purpose of regulation 8(1) was
to make it clear what right was being conferred, to clarify what is meant by
the statutory concept "unfair dismissal" as applied to an employee dismissed h
before or after a relevant transfer. The transfer was not to constitute a
ground for dismissal. The structure and language of regulation 8(1) was not
apt to confer an exemption on a specific category, such as employees with
less than two years' qualifying service. The language was couched as a
deeming provision, treating dismissal by reason of a transfer as unfair
dismissal, so as to lead to the consequences of such dismissal identified in j
Part V of the Act of 1978, regardless of whether the dismissal is actionable as
unfair under those provisions.' (Mummery J's emphasis.)

Implicit in this passage, and in Mr Langstaff's argument, is the premise that the
phrase 'shall be treated for the purposes of Part V of the 1978 Act ... as unfairly

a dismissed' confers a right not to be unfairly dismissed. Mr Langstaff repeated this submission before us. The word 'treated', he contended, carried with it the inference that the employees would receive treatment—that treatment being entitlement to those remedies provided for by s 68 that could be claimed before an industrial tribunal under s 67 of the Act.

b CONCLUSIONS

It is, I believe, logical to consider the scheme and effect of the relevant provisions of Pt V of the 1978 Act in its original form, before turning to reg 8 of the 1981 regulations.

Section 67, if read in isolation, suggests that anyone who has been unfairly dismissed is entitled to complain to an industrial tribunal. When read in the
c context of the other provisions of Pt V, it is apparent that this is not the case. It seems to me clear, if s 54 is to have any effect at all, that those entitled to complain of unfair dismissal are those upon whom s 54 confers the right not to be unfairly dismissed. Thus, in relation to any complaint, two separate requirements have to be satisfied before a complaint can be made: (i) the complainant was unfairly
d dismissed, within the provisions of ss 55 to 63; and (ii) the complainant had a right not to be unfairly dismissed under s 54(1) and subject to the exclusions provided for by s 54(2).

Thus, those who had been employed for less than the period specified in s 64(1) had no right to complain, unless dismissed for an 'inadmissible reason', ie one
e relating to trade union membership.

These are conclusions that I reached on initially considering the relevant provisions. I then found, however, a commentary that challenged them in a respect which is highly material.

Sections 58 and 59 of the 1978 Act derive from the Trade Union and Labour
f Relations Act 1974. Section 60 reproduces, virtually verbatim, s 34 of the Employment Protection Act 1975. The phraseology used in ss 58 and 59, whereby the dismissal is to be 'regarded as unfair' contrasts with that of s 60, which speaks of a complainant being 'treated as unfairly dismissed'. My initial reaction was that this difference in phraseology simply reflected the different sources of the relevant provisions, but that each had the same effect. This view
g was not, however, shared by the editors of *Current Law Statutes Annotated*. They commented in relation to s 60:

'Dismissal on grounds of pregnancy is unfair and such a dismissed employee when claiming to an industrial tribunal *is to be treated* without
h more as unfairly dismissed. *Cf.* the provisions of s. 58(1) and s. 59, where dismissal is to be regarded as unfair. Unlike the case of these provisions, the tribunal is here not to have regard to otherwise relevant factors in providing a remedy to the dismissed employee (e.g. it seems likely that the qualifications specified in s. 64(1) should not apply; but opinion is divided on
j this question and an industrial tribunal has held, without the point having apparently been argued, that the 26-week qualification does apply—*Reaney v. Kanda Jean Products Ltd.* ([1978] IRLR 427)). It is submitted that the complainant is to be treated as unfairly dismissed regardless of those provisions (though subject to the remainder of this section).' (See [1978] CLS 44/60; editors' emphasis.)

This commentary merits careful consideration for the phraseology of s 60 is the same as that adopted in reg 8 of the 1981 regulations and Mr Langstaff's submissions in relation to the latter mirror the commentary on the former.

Having given the matter further consideration, I remain of the conclusion that s 60 of the 1978 Act gives rise to no free-standing right to complain of unfair dismissal, without reference to the provisions of ss 54 and 64. So to find would run counter to the clear scheme of this part of the Act. Sections 57, 58, 59 and 60 provide for different circumstances in which a dismissal will be unfair, but none of those sections confers a right not to be unfairly dismissed. No significance is to be attached to the difference between dismissal which is 'regarded' as unfair (ss 58 and 59) and dismissal which is 'treated' as unfair (s 60). The difference in language is attributable to the fact that the 1978 Act consolidates provisions from different statutes.

This conclusion is supported by the fact that s 64 contained its own exception in respect of 'inadmissible' reasons—namely those relating to trade union membership (s 58). Had it been the draftsman's intention that the right not to be unfairly dismissed by reason of pregnancy should not be subject to the exclusion in s 64(1), the obvious way of achieving this would have been to provide that, in the case of a s 60 dismissal, pregnancy was an inadmissible reason. Indeed, just such a method was subsequently adopted to achieve this end—see amendments made by s 24(3) of the Trade Union Reform and Employment Rights Act 1993. A note to 16(S) *Halsbury's Statutes* (4th edn) (1990 reissue) 404 accurately comments in relation to these amendments that they provide—

'for all employees, irrespective of their length of service or the number of hours worked, a right not to be dismissed on the grounds of pregnancy or childbirth, thereby implementing EEC Council Dir 92/85 on the rights of pregnant women.'

That was not the case under the unamended provisions.

Having reached this conclusion, I consider that precisely the same effect must be given to the identical phraseology that has been adopted in reg 8 of the 1981 regulations. That regulation did not confer a free-standing right not to be unfairly dismissed by reason of the transfer of an undertaking. By amending Pt V of the 1978 Act, it conferred this right on those who enjoyed the right not to be unfairly dismissed by virtue of s 54 of that Act and not on that category excluded by s 64(1). That exclusion was permitted by art 4(1) of the directive and the respondents fall into the excluded category.

For these reasons, I consider that both *Milligan v Securicor Cleaning Ltd* [1995] ICR 867 and this case were wrongly decided and that the appeal should be allowed.

POSTSCRIPT

In 1995 the following paragraph was added to reg 8 of the 1981 regulations by way of amendment:

'(5) Paragraph (1) above shall not apply in relation to a dismissal of an employee if—(a) the application of s 54 of the 1978 Act to the dismissal of the employee is excluded by or under any provision of Part V or sections 141 to 149 of the 1978 Act or of sections 237 or 238 of the Trade Union and Labour Relations (Consolidation) Act 1992 ...' (See the Collective Redundancies and a Transfer of Undertakings (Protection of Employment) (Amendment) Regulations, SI 1995/2587.)

This amendment was designed to reverse the effect of the decision in *Milligan*. If the conclusion I have reached is correct, the amendment was unnecessary. The reference to s 141 of the 1978 Act was doubly unnecessary, for the draftsman had already, in what must have been an excess of caution, made it clear by reg 13, that
b reg 8 did not apply to employees falling within s 141. All that this goes to show is, that in legislation as complex and as frequently amended as that which this court has had to consider, the existence of provisions which duplicate one another should not occasion too much surprise.

c **MILLETT LJ.** I agree.

NEILL LJ. I also agree.

Appeal allowed.

d   Paul Magrath Esq   Barrister.

Chaggar and another v Chaggar

a

COURT OF APPEAL, CIVIL DIVISION
ALDOUS AND PHILLIPS LJJ
23 MAY, 1 JULY 1996

b

Legal aid – Order for costs – Award of costs against assisted person – Enforcement of order – Costs to be paid out of proceeds of sale of dwelling house – Whether proceeds of sale forming disposable capital of assisted person – Legal Aid Act 1988, s 17.

In proceedings brought by the plaintiff to establish the beneficial interests of the   *c*
parties in a freehold property the trial judge made an order declaring that the first
and second defendants held the property on trust for the plaintiff and first
defendant as tenants in common in equal shares. The judge further ordered that
a deed of transfer, by which the property had been transferred out of the joint
names of the plaintiff and the first defendant and into the joint names of the first
and second defendants, should be cancelled and that the defendants should pay   *d*
the plaintiff's costs, such costs not to be enforced without further order of the
court. All the parties were legally aided. The defendants subsequently applied
for an order for sale of the property. The plaintiff did not oppose that application
but applied for an order entitling him to enforce the order for costs made by the
trial judge against the first defendant's half share in the proceeds of sale. The   *e*
judge granted leave to enforce the costs order to the extent of the first defendant's
half share on the basis that a fund representing the proceeds of sale of a former
dwelling house was not within the restriction in s 17(3)[a] of the Legal Aid Act 1988,
which provided that a legally assisted person's dwelling house could not be
subject to execution or any corresponding process to enforce an order for costs.
The judge also held that, in circumstances where both parties were legally aided,   *f*
it would not be a fair result if proceeds recovered by a successful plaintiff would
be lost to him by virtue of the statutory charge conferred on the Legal Aid Board
by s 16(6)[b] of the 1988 Act, while the defendant's share would be available to him
to assist in the purchase of a new dwelling house. The defendants appealed,
contending that the available proceeds resulted from the sale of their home and
that their half share would be used to purchase another dwelling house and   *g*
consequently the judge's considerations of fairness were inappropriate as an
unfair result for the plaintiff was a direct consequence of the legal aid scheme as
set up by Parliament.

Held – When deciding the liability of an assisted party for costs under s 17 of the   *h*
1988 Act, the court had to take into account all the circumstances, including the
general purpose of the Act. Moreover, the potential for an 'unfair' result for the
successful plaintiff (ie that a party who sued an assisted party normally was left to
pay his own costs even if he won) was built into the Act and had to be taken by
the court as the position from which to begin its consideration. Since the   *j*
dwelling house of an assisted party should not be sold to pay his costs, the court
would not order costs to be paid out of the proceeds of sale of a property, which
prima facie formed part of the assisted party's disposable capital, if the proceeds

---

a   Section 17 is set out at p 107 *g* to *j*, post
b   Section 16, so far as material, is set out at p 107 *d e*, post

a of sale were needed to purchase a dwelling house of acceptable type. In the instant case, however, as the defendants had obtained a mortgage and were able to purchase a new house without the need of the half share of the proceeds of sale, such proceeds were part of the defendants' disposable capital and could be applied to satisfy the order for costs without offending the purpose of the 1988 Act. The appeal would accordingly be dismissed (see p 110 c to p 111 d, post).

b Decision of Chadwick J [1995] 4 All ER 795 affirmed.

Notes

For costs awarded against an assisted person, see 27(2) *Halsbury's Laws* (4th edn reissue) paras 2002–2003, and for cases on the subject, see 37(3) *Digest* (Reissue) 353–357, 5064–5082.

c For the Legal Aid Act 1988, ss 16, 17, see 24 *Halsbury's Statutes* (4th edn) (1989 reissue) 28, 30.

Case referred to in judgments

Parr v Smith [1995] 2 All ER 1031, CA.

d **Appeal**

The defendants, Avtar Singh Chaggar and his wife, Maria Chaggar, appealed from the decision of Chadwick J ([1995] 4 All ER 795) made on 5 April 1995 in the Chancery Division of the High Court at Birmingham whereby he ordered in favour of the plaintiff, Jaswir Singh Chaggar, the first defendant's brother, that

e leave be given to enforce an order for costs against the defendants, who were legally aided, albeit that the fund from which the costs would be paid would come from proceeds of the sale of a house in which the defendants resided. The facts are set out in the judgment of Aldous LJ.

f *David Stockill* (instructed by *Willcox Lane Clutterbuck*, Birmingham) for the defendants.
James Corbett (instructed by *Willson Hawley & Co*, Nuneaton) for the plaintiff.

Cur adv vult

g 1 July 1996. The following judgments were delivered.

ALDOUS LJ. This application and appeal arise from an order giving leave to enforce an order for costs against a legally assisted person in circumstances where the fund from which the costs would be paid would come from proceeds of the sale of a house in which the legally assisted person resided.

h The plaintiff, Mr Jaswir Singh Chaggar, is the brother of the first defendant, Mr Avtar Singh Chaggar. The second defendant is the wife of the first defendant.

In 1982 the plaintiff and the first defendant purchased 56 Oak Farm Close, Walmley, Sutton Coldfield for £23,500 with the aid of a mortgage of £22,080. The title was registered at the Land Registry on 17 August 1982. Although the

j property was owned jointly by the plaintiff and the first defendant it was occupied by the defendants, first by themselves, and then with their children.

In 1986 the defendants became the registered proprietors of the property. This was achieved by production of a transfer dated 10 April 1986 signed by the first defendant and seemingly signed by the plaintiff. The plaintiff became aware of the transfer and claimed that his signature on the transfer was a forgery. That led to proceedings which came before Judge Micklem, sitting as a deputy judge of the

High Court. He gave judgment on 1 November 1994 and concluded that the
signature was a forgery. In so doing, he rejected the defendants' case that the   *a*
signature had either been made by the plaintiff's late mother or by the plaintiff in
a suspicious form so as to enable him to claim, if necessary, that it was not his
signature. The judge found that the plaintiff and the first defendant were
unsatisfactory witnesses and did not find it necessary to establish what was the
reason behind the savage family row which existed. The judge therefore made a   *b*
declaration in the plaintiff's favour, ordered a rectification of the register, and as
both parties were legally aided, ordered that the defendants should pay the
plaintiff's taxed costs, but that the order for costs should not be enforced without
further order. He refused to order that the property should be sold because that
had not been specifically sought in the pleadings and no evidence had been
directed to that issue.   *c*

After the judgment of Judge Micklem, the defendants attempted to purchase
the plaintiff's half share in the property, but in November 1994 solicitors acting
for the plaintiff made it clear that any arrangement for the purchase of the
plaintiff's half share by the defendants would have to include provision for
payment by the defendants of the plaintiff's costs of the action. That was not   *d*
acceptable to the defendants and the defendants decided that the best way to
proceed was to place the property on the market at an asking price of £65,000. An
offer of £63,500 was received and the defendants applied to the court for an order
for sale at that price. Originally that was resisted by the plaintiff, but was
subsequently accepted. Thus the parties were agreed that the property should be
sold at the price offered, but there remained the dispute as to payment of costs.   *e*
Therefore, the plaintiff issued a notice of motion seeking an order that he should
have leave to enforce the costs order made in the action against the proceeds of
sale of the property.

The first defendant in his affidavit of 24 March 1995 set out the reasons why the
costs order should not be enforced. He said that it was the defendants' intention   *f*
to use the half share of the proceeds of sale to buy a new house and therefore, by
analogy with the exemption in s 17 of the Legal Aid Act 1988, the sum received
should be exempt from any order for costs. It was the defendants' case that with
the half share of the proceeds of sale they would just, but only just, afford the
purchase of a new house.

As I have said, the plaintiff did not oppose the sale as that would, after   *g*
repayment of the mortgage and sale costs, provide a fund of about £31,000 of
which he would be entitled to £15,500. That did not satisfy his bill of costs which
after trial amounted to about £28,000 and no doubt by now have exceeded the
net proceeds of sale of the property.

By the time that the dispute between the parties came before Chadwick J, the   *h*
only real issue between the parties was whether the costs order should be
enforced against the net proceeds of sale of the property. The judge concluded
that the Legal Aid Board might want to be represented and adjourned the hearing
for a short time to enable them to be informed of the application that was to be
made. They decided not to appear and the application came back before him in   *j*
April 1995. By that time, the defendants had arranged a mortgage for their
proposed new house so that it became possible for them to purchase it without
the use of the half share of the proceeds of sale of 56 Oak Farm Close. Chadwick J
([1995] 4 All ER 795) gave judgment on 5 April 1995. He ordered that the plaintiff
should be at liberty to enforce the order for costs made by Judge Micklem and
that the defendants' liability for costs should be limited to the half share of the

a proceeds of sale. He also made an order for the sale of the property, the proceeds of sale being paid into an account in the name of the defendants' solicitors to be held by them and paid out to satisfy the costs order.

The defendants sought leave to appeal which was refused by the judge. They applied to Peter Gibson LJ. He also refused leave on the ground that it would not be proper for this court to interfere with the judge's discretion. The defendants b renewed their application for leave to the court. That application came before us as an application for leave to appeal with the appeal to follow if leave were given. That was, I believe, the right course to adopt as I have come to the conclusion that leave to appeal should be granted because the issue raised relates to an important matter of practice which is proper to be reviewed by this court.

c *The statutory background*

Both the plaintiff and the defendants were legally assisted in the action, but their obligations to the Legal Aid Board after trial are different. Section 16 of the 1988 Act provides for reimbursement of the board by contributions out of sums or property recovered. Subsection (6) is as follows:

d 'Except so far as regulations otherwise provide—(a) any sums remaining unpaid on account of a person's contribution in respect of the sums payable by the Board in respect of any proceedings, and (b) a sum equal to any deficiency by reason of his total contribution being less than the liability of the Board on his account, shall be a first charge for the benefit of the Board e on any property which is recovered or preserved for him in the proceedings ...'

That subsection applied to the plaintiff as he recovered or preserved his half share of the property. As costs of £28,000 had been expended, all his share of the sale had to be paid to the Legal Aid Board.

f Section 16(6) did not apply to the defendants as they did not recover or preserve any property. Section 17 applied to them. It places a limit on the liability of assisted parties to pay costs. Section 17 is in this form:

'(1) The liability of a legally assisted party under an order for costs made against him with respect to any proceedings shall not exceed the amount (if g any) which is a reasonable one for him to pay having regard to all the circumstances, including the financial resources of all the parties and their conduct in connection with the dispute.

(2) Regulations will make provision as to the court, tribunal or person by whom that amount is to be determined and the extent to which any h determination of that amount is to be final.

(3) None of the following, namely, a legally assisted person's dwelling house, clothes, household furniture and the tools and implements of his trade shall—(a) be taken into account in assessing his financial resources for the purposes of this section, or (b) be subject to execution or any corresponding process in any part of the United Kingdom to enforce the j order, except so far as regulations may prescribe.'

The procedure laid down requires the court to determine the amount of an assisted person's liability for costs pursuant to s 17(1) of the Act and reg 124 of the Civil Legal Aid (General) Regulations 1989, SI 1989/339, requires the court to determine the amount of an assisted person's liability for costs before such costs can be recovered. Regulation 126 makes it clear that when carrying out that determination certain assets, such as a dwelling house, have to be excluded from consideration. Regulation 127 allows the assessment of liability to be deferred, and reg 129 governs the order that can be made.

In the present case Judge Micklem ordered that the defendants should pay the plaintiff's costs, but the order should not be enforced without further order of the court. That was an order made under reg 129(b).

The parties agree that if the defendants had purchased the plaintiff's half share in the property and continued to live in it, the court had no power to order that the defendants should pay any part of the plaintiff's costs. The reason being that the house, being the defendants' dwelling house, was excluded from consideration when assessing the amount of the defendants' liability to pay, and without it the defendants did not have sufficient assets to enable the court to make an appropriate order for payment. That was, I suspect, the reason why the plaintiff refused to agree to the proposal of the defendants that they should purchase his share. However, that is not what happened. The property was to be sold with the defendants intending to use their share of the proceeds to help purchase a new dwelling house for themselves and their children. Thus, two issues came before the judge for decision. First, did he have jurisdiction, when assessing the liability of the defendants, to take into account the proceeds of sale of the property; and second, if he had, whether it was reasonable that they should pay their share of the proceeds to the plaintiff in compliance with the order for costs that had been made.

The judge concluded that he had jurisdiction. He said ([1995] 4 All ER 795 at 799):

'In my view a fund representing the proceeds of sale of a former dwelling house is not within the restriction in s 17(3)—a fortiori when the fund represents a share of the proceeds of sale—and, accordingly, there is jurisdiction to make an order which leads to enforcement of costs against such a fund. The question is whether, in all the circumstances, such an order ought to be made as a matter of discretion.'

To come to that conclusion the judge drew support from *Parr v Smith* [1995] 2 All ER 1031. In that case, a successful plaintiff had obtained charging orders over property owned by assisted parties to cover damages, costs during a period when the parties were not assisted and also during the period when they were. A number of issues arose, one of which required the court to decide whether the charging orders had been properly made. The court held that the charge in respect of the post-legally assisted period was not properly made and therefore it could not be enforced, even though at the time of enforcement the property had been sold. Bingham MR said (at 1040):

'The judge did not authorise enforcement of the charge for the Parrs' post-legal aid costs by sale of the Smiths' house but against the proceeds of sale of the house. If I am right that the judge was not entitled to impose, or should not have imposed, a charging order to enforce payment of these costs it must follow that this part of the order cannot stand. It may be that if the house is sold and if a fund then arises, the Parrs may then be entitled to return to the judge and seek a variation of his costs order under reg 130 so as to permit enforcement against the fund. But they would have to persuade the judge that it was fair in all the circumstances to permit enforcement against the fund when the house itself had been immune, or else to identify a part of

a   the fund which was not attributable to the house. I express no view on their
           prospects of success.'

Bingham MR did not decide that when, as in this case, a dwelling house is sold
with a view to the funds being rolled over into a new dwelling house, the court
had power to take into account the sale proceeds when assessing liability for
payment of costs by an assisted person. Certainly, he did not decide to the
b   contrary.

Before this court Mr Stockill, who appeared for the defendants, did not submit
that the judge was wrong to conclude that he had jurisdiction in the
circumstances of this case. I believe that he was right not to make that
submission. Both s 17 and reg 126 are specific as to what assets are to be omitted
c   from account. The proceeds of a sale of a dwelling house may or may not be used
to purchase a new dwelling house, and at the point in time when they are held as
cash, form part of a person's disposable capital. Therefore it is necessary for them
to be taken into account in determining the amount of an assisted person's
liability for costs.

d   The judge went on to decide as a matter of discretion whether the order for
costs should be enforced against the defendants' half share of the proceeds of sale.
First, he considered the consequences of refusing the order sought. Having
reminded himself of s 16(6) of the 1988 Act, he rightly concluded that the
plaintiff's half share would be swallowed up by his requirement to reimburse the
Board. He said ([1995] 4 All ER 795 at 800):

e
           'Accordingly, if the plaintiff is not enabled to enforce his order for costs
           against the first defendant, the result of this litigation will be that the
           plaintiff's share, which he has recovered in successful litigation, will be lost
           to him by virtue of the statutory charge; while the first defendant's share will
           be available to the defendants to assist them in the purchase of their new
f   dwelling house. That is not a result which I can regard as fair.'

The defendants submitted that that conclusion was inappropriate as the result
which the judge concluded was unfair was a result laid down in the 1988 Act and
was an inevitable consequence of the way that the legal aid scheme is set up. A
plaintiff who succeeds against a legally aided defendant has to pay, except in
g   exceptional circumstances, his costs from the proceeds of his success. The result,
referred to by the judge, was the direct consequence of the legal aid scheme set
up by Parliament and should not be held to be unfair. In any case, the 'unfairness'
was clear at the time Judge Micklem made his order and nothing that has
happened since has made it any more 'unfair'.

h   The judge went on, as he was required to do, to consider the financial
resources of the parties, the conduct of the parties and all the circumstances of the
case. The defendants criticised his analysis because they submitted that he failed
to take account of the fact that the defendants were prepared to purchase the
plaintiff's share, that it was by no means certain that the court would order sale
j   of the property under s 30 of the Law of Property Act 1925, and also because he
did not pay sufficient attention to the fact that the order would not benefit the
plaintiff to any significant extent as all or most of the proceeds of sale would be
paid to the Board; whereas if no order was made, half of the proceeds would be
available to the defendants to pay for a new house.

It is true that the judge did not specifically refer to those matters, but for my
part, that omission is not of sufficient weight to vitiate his conclusion.

The defendants also submitted that the judge paid insufficient weight to the
fact that the proceeds of sale came from the defendants' dwelling house and that
their share was going to be used to purchase another dwelling house at a price
that they could just afford. In so doing, he had not paid sufficient attention to the
intention of Parliament as set out in the scheme provided for in the 1988 Act.
Further, he had wrongly concluded that he should take into account that 'the
interest in enforcing the order for costs is the public interest reflected through the
Legal Aid Board' (see [1995] 4 All ER 795 at 801). Their interest was, it was said,
limited to the amount recovered or preserved by the plaintiff, namely £15,500.
That, they would recover without enforcing any order for costs against the
defendants.

The judge seems to have been heavily influenced by what he regarded as
'unfair' which in reality was the result of the legislation. A party who sues an
assisted party normally is left to pay his costs even if he wins. That may seem to
be unfair, but it is the result of the legislation and must be taken by the courts as
an appropriate result. It may seem unfair that a plaintiff can win an action and
that all his winnings go to his costs, but that is the scheme of the 1988 Act and that
would be appreciated before litigation was commenced. No doubt it is a feature
to be taken into account, but it must be seen in the context of the legislation as a
whole. I do not believe that the judge had that in mind, and therefore conclude
that it would be right for this court to consider the matter afresh.

The task of the court is set out in s 17: it is to decide the assisted parties' liability
for costs. Those costs must not exceed that which it is reasonable for the party to
pay in all the circumstances. Thus, all the circumstances have to be taken into
account, but particular reference has to be paid to the financial resources of both
parties taking into account reg 126. In essence, the court should consider the
parties disposable income and disposable capital excluding the assets referred to
in the regulations. The court must also take into account the conduct of the
parties in connection with the dispute. That means the conduct leading up to the
proceedings and the way that the proceedings have been conducted.

A 'relevant circumstance' is the general purpose of the 1988 Act. The court
must not shut its eyes to the result when a successful plaintiff finds that the fruits
of his success are swallowed up by his costs, but that should not be taken in every
case as pointing to a need to make the defendant liable to pay costs. That was not
the intention of Parliament. The potential of an 'unfair' result is built into the Act
and that must be taken by the court as the position from which to start.

The Act also makes it clear that, when deciding liability for costs, the dwelling
house of the assisted person cannot be taken into account. When a house is sold
the proceeds form part of a party's disposable capital and therefore can be taken
into account. However, the court must bear in mind that the dwelling house of
an assisted party should not be sold to pay his costs. That being so, it would not
be right to order costs to be paid out of the proceeds of sale, if the proceeds of sale
were needed to purchase a dwelling house of acceptable type. Each case will
depend upon the particular facts. For instance, the court might conclude that the
purpose of the Act was not being achieved if the house being sold was worth a lot
of money.

Upon the evidence before the judge at the first hearing, I would have refused
the order sought, as it appeared that the first defendant's half share of the
proceeds of sale was needed to finance a new dwelling house. However, that was
not the position at the second hearing. By that time, the judge had been told that
the defendants had obtained a mortgage and were able to purchase a new house

a without the need of the half share of the proceeds of sale. That is what happened. Thus the £15,500 could properly be taken as a capital asset which was not needed to buy a dwelling house. It was therefore part of the defendants' disposable capital which could be applied to satisfy the order for costs without offending the purpose of the Act. That I believe to be determinative of this appeal. As the judge demonstrated in his judgment, the general circumstances of the case, including *b* the conduct of the parties, did not suggest that the plaintiff should not recover his costs.

Upon the facts before him the judge came to the right conclusion. The defendants had available to them £15,500, being the proceeds of the sale of the property, and the judge had to decide whether it was reasonable that that money should be applied to pay the costs of the action which they had lost or should be *c* used by them to better their standard of living. In those circumstances, I believe it was appropriate to make the defendants pay costs. For those reasons, I would dismiss this appeal.

PHILLIPS LJ. I agree.

d *Appeal dismissed.*

L I Zysman Esq   Barrister.

R v Ireland

COURT OF APPEAL, CRIMINAL DIVISION

SWINTON THOMAS LJ, TUCKER AND DOUGLAS BROWN JJ

22 APRIL, 14 MAY 1996

Criminal law – Assault – Assault occasioning actual bodily harm – Psychiatric injury – Defendant making repeated silent telephone calls to victims – Victims suffering psychological damage as a result of calls – Whether silent telephone calls capable of constituting assault – Offences against the Person Act 1861, s 47.

The defendant admitted making a large number of telephone calls to three woman and remaining silent when they answered. He was charged with three counts of assault occasioning actual bodily harm under s 47[a] of the Offences against the Person Act 1861, to which he pleaded guilty. At the trial psychiatric evidence was given that each of the victims had suffered significant psychological symptoms as a result of the repeated telephone calls. Those symptoms included palpitations, difficulty in breathing, cold sweats, inability to sleep, anxiety, tearfulness, headaches and stress. The defendant was convicted and sentenced to three years' imprisonment. He appealed against his conviction, contending, inter alia, that the judge had erred in accepting the guilty pleas, since the facts relied on did not disclose an assault for the purposes of s 47 of the 1861 Act.

Held – The making of a telephone call followed by silence, or a series of telephone calls, was capable of amounting to an assault for the purposes of s 47 of the 1861 Act. The relevant act consisted in the making of the call and it did not matter whether words or silence ensued, since calls of that nature were likely to cause the victims to apprehend immediate and unlawful violence. Moreover, it was not necessary that there should be an immediate proximity between defendant and victim: fear could be readily instilled over the telephone. In the instant case, the telephone calls had clearly made the victims apprehensive and caused them psychological damage and it was inherent in the defendant's pleas of guilty that he had so intended and consequently there was sufficient evidence on which to determine that the defendant had committed an assault. It followed that the guilty pleas had been correctly accepted and the appeal would accordingly be dismissed (see p 114 *g* to *j*, p 115 *f g* and p 118 *d e g j*, post).

Barton v Armstrong [1969] 2 NSWR 451, *R v Savage, R v Parmenter* [1991] 4 All ER 698 and *R v Chan-Fook* [1994] 2 All ER 552 applied.

Smith v Chief Superintendent, Woking Police Station (1983) 76 Cr App R 234 considered.

Notes

For assault occasioning actual bodily harm, see 11(1) *Halsbury's Laws* (4th edn reissue) para 490, and for cases on the subject, see 14(2) *Digest* (2nd reissue) 147, 6600–6603.

---

a   Section 47, so far as material, provides: 'Whosoever shall be convicted upon an indictment of any assault occasioning actual bodily harm shall be liable ... [to imprisonment for not more than five years].'

For the Offences against the Person Act 1861, s 47, see 12 *Halsbury's Statutes* (4th edn) (1994 reissue) 105.

Cases referred to in judgment

Barton v Armstrong [1969] 2 NSWR 451, NSW SC.
Fagan v Metropolitan Police Comr [1968] 3 All ER 442, [1969] 1 QB 439, [1968] 3 WLR 1120, DC.
R v Chan-Fook [1994] 2 All ER 552, [1994] 1 WLR 689, CA.
R v Johnson [1996] Crim LR 828, CA.
R v Savage, R v Parmenter [1991] 4 All ER 698, [1992] 1 AC 699, [1991] 2 WLR 408, HL.
Smith v Chief Superintendent, Woking Police Station (1983) 76 Cr App R 234, DC.
Tuberville v Savage (1669) 1 Mod Rep 3, 86 ER 684.

Cases also cited or referred to in skeleton arguments

Ansell v Thomas [1974] Crim LR 31, CA.
Chiltern DC v Hodgetts [1983] 1 All ER 1057, [1983] 2 AC 120, HL.
DPP v Merriman [1972] 3 All ER 42, [1973] AC 584, HL.
Dullaghan v Hillen [1957] Ir Jur Rep 10, Ir Circuit Ct.
Jemmison v Priddle [1972] 1 All ER 539, [1972] 1 QB 489, DC.
Logdon v DPP [1976] Crim LR 121, DC.
R v Byrne [1968] 3 CCC 179, BC CA.
R v Clarence (1888) 22 QBD 23, [1886–90] All ER Rep 133.
R v Gelder (15 December 1994, unreported), CA.
R v Hanson (1849) 2 Car & Kir 912, 175 ER 383.
R v Kimber [1983] 3 All ER 316, [1983] 1 WLR 1118, CA.
R v Knight (1988) 35 A Crim R 314, NSW CCA.
R v Mansfield Justices, ex p Sharkey [1985] 1 All ER 193, [1985] QB 613, DC.
R v Meade and Belt (1823) 1 Lew CC 184, 168 ER 1006.
R v Salisbury [1976] VR 452, Vic Full Ct.
R v Venna [1975] 3 All ER 788, [1976] QB 421, CA.
R v Walkden (1845) 1 Cox CC 282.
R v Wilson (Clarence), R v Jenkins (Edward John) [1983] 3 All ER 448, [1984] AC 242, HL.
Read v Coker (1853) 13 CB 850, 138 ER 1437.
Stephens v Myers (1830) 4 C & P 349, 172 ER 735.

Appeal against conviction

Robert Matthew Ireland appealed with leave against his conviction in the Crown Court at Newport on three counts of assault occasioning actual bodily harm contrary to s 47 of the Offences against the Person Act 1861 before Judge Prosser QC on 10 March 1995 on the ground that the convictions should be set aside as unsafe or unsatisfactory and/or on the ground that the judge erred in accepting his guilty pleas since the facts relied on did not disclose an assault for the purposes of s 47 of the 1861 Act. The facts are set out in the judgment of the court.

Philip Richards (assigned by the *Registrar of Criminal Appeals*) for the appellant.
Christopher Llewellyn-Jones QC and *Roger Griffiths* (instructed by the Crown Prosecution Service, Gwent) for the Crown.

Cur adv vult

14 May 1996. The following judgment of the court was delivered.

SWINTON THOMAS LJ. On 6 February 1995, in the Crown Court at Newport (Gwent) before Judge Prosser QC, the appellant pleaded guilty to three counts of assault occasioning actual bodily harm. On 10 March 1995 he was sentenced to serve three years' imprisonment on each count concurrently. He appeals against his conviction and his sentence with leave.

The appellant pleaded guilty to counts 2, 3 and 5 in the indictment and not guilty to counts 1 and 4. Those pleas were accepted.

Count 2 charged the appellant with assault occasioning actual bodily harm, contrary to s 47 of the Offences against the Person Act 1861. The particulars of the offence charged him that on a day between 1 June 1994 and 11 September 1994 he assaulted Patricia Ann Hannam, thereby occasioning her actual bodily harm. Count 3 was in similar terms, charging him that on a day between 1 June 1994 and 11 September 1994 he assaulted Sarah Jane Williams, thereby occasioning her actual bodily harm. Count 5 charged him that on a day between 1 June 1994 and 11 September 1994 he assaulted Susan Young, thereby occasioning her actual bodily harm.

The charges arose as a result of the appellant making a large number of unwanted telephone calls to the three women. The telephone calls occurred very frequently between the dates set out in the counts in the indictment. When the women answered the telephone there was silence. The calls lasted sometimes for a minute or so, and sometimes for several minutes. On occasions there were repeated calls over a relatively short period. For example, one complainant said that she received no less than 14 telephone calls within an hour on 9 September 1994. The other complainants had similar experiences. Each of the complainants was examined by a psychiatrist, who said in his witness statement that the result of the repeated telephone calls was that each of them suffered significant psychological symptoms. For example, one of the complainants suffered from palpitations, difficulty in breathing and cold sweats of an intensity which made it difficult for her to leave her home or to answer the telephone. Another of the complainants suffered anxiety, inability to sleep, tearfulness, headaches, tingling in her fingers, dizziness and a constant feeling of being on edge. The third complainant suffered from stress, inability to sleep, and a skin condition brought about by her nervousness.

The issue that arises on this appeal is whether a telephone call, followed by silence, can constitute an assault for the purposes of s 47 of the Offences against the Person Act 1861. Leave to appeal was granted in order that the court could consider whether the facts spoken to in the witness statements disclosed an offence. The Crown conceded that if they did not, then the appellant should be permitted to change his plea and the convictions should be quashed.

It is submitted by Mr Philip Richards, on behalf of the appellant, that the making of a telephone call, followed by silence, or a series of telephone calls, followed by silence, does not constitute an assault for the purposes of s 47 of the 1861 Act.

An assault is any act by which a person intentionally or recklessly causes another to apprehend immediate and unlawful violence. This definition, which is to be found in *Archbold's Criminal Pleading, Evidence and Practice* (1996) para 19-166, has received judicial approval in a number of cases, most recently in *R v Savage, R v Parmenter* [1991] 4 All ER 698 at 711, [1992] 1 AC 699 at 740. Mr Richards submits that the facts relied upon by the prosecution do not disclose an a apprehension on the part of the victims of immediate unlawful violence. He submits that violence cannot include psychological harm. He goes on to submit that before a defendant can be convicted of an offence under s 47, the Crown must prove: (1) that the accused has completed the relevant act; (2) that that act must have caused the victim to apprehend immediate and unlawful violence; (3) the accused must have either intended the victim to apprehend violence or to

b have foreseen the risk that the victim might apprehend violence; and (4) that the act has caused actual bodily harm.

Mr Richards then submits that in this case there was no relevant act, that before there can be an apprehension of immediate and unlawful violence there must be physical proximity between the defendant and the victim, which is absent when the act consists of a telephone call, and that the facts complained of

c could not result in an apprehension of immediate violence.

It was held in *R v Chan-Fook* [1994] 2 All ER 552, [1994] 1 WLR 689 that 'actual bodily harm' may include injury to any part of the body, including internal organs, the nervous system and the brain. It is capable of including psychiatric injury, but not mere emotion such as fear, distress or panic. In the present case

d there was abundant evidence that the victims have suffered psychiatric damage, and this was conceded before Judge Prosser and by the appellant in this appeal. In *R v Chan-Fook* [1994] 2 All ER 552 at 557, [1994] 1 WLR 689 at 694 Hobhouse LJ said:

e 'Similarly an injury can be caused to someone by injuring their health; an assault may have the consequence of infecting the victim with a disease or causing the victim to become ill. The injury may be internal and may not be accompanied by any external injury.'

Mr Richards submits that because a person has sustained physical injury as a

f consequence of the act of the appellant, it does not follow that the act caused the victim to apprehend immediate and unlawful violence. In our judgment, if the Crown can prove that the victims have sustained actual bodily harm, in this case psychological harm, and that the accused must have intended the victims to sustain such harm, or have been reckless as to whether they did sustain such harm, and that harm resulted from an act or acts of the appellant, namely

g telephone calls followed by silence, it is open to the jury to find that he has committed an assault. As to immediacy, by using the telephone the appellant put himself in immediate contact with the victims, and when the victims lifted the telephone they were placed in immediate fear and suffered the consequences to which we have referred.

h Our attention was drawn to a number of cases concerning the definition of assault, some of them of some antiquity. It is of importance that an assault does not necessarily include a battery, and the distinction is important in this case. It has been recognised for many centuries that putting a person in fear may amount to an assault. The early cases pre-date the invention of the telephone. We must

j apply the law to conditions as they are in the twentieth century. In *Tuberville v Savage* (1669) 1 Mod Rep 3, 86 ER 684 T laid his hand upon his sword saying, 'If it were not assize-time, I would not take such language'. It was held that the act could have amounted to an assault but for 'the declaration ... that he would not assault him, the Judges being in town'. Pointing an imitation or toy gun at the victim, dangerous driving and kidnapping have all been held to be capable of amounting to an assault.

In *Fagan v Metropolitan Police Comr* [1968] 3 All ER 442 at 445, [1969] 1 QB 439 at 445, James J, in a judgment in which Lord Parker CJ agreed, drew the distinction between an assault and a battery and said:

'For an assault to be committed, both the elements of actus reus and mens rea must be present at the same time. The "actus reus" is the action causing the effect on the victim's mind ... The "mens rea" is the intention to cause that effect.'

Smith v Chief Superintendent, Woking Police Station (1983) 76 Cr App R 234 is an important case for the purpose of this appeal. The defendant was charged under s 4 of the Vagrancy Act 1824, which provides: '... every person being found ... in any enclosed ... garden ... for any unlawful purpose ... shall be deemed a rogue and a vagabond ...'

The defendant entered the grounds of a private house and looked through the windows of the house occupied by the victim. She was terrified. The justices were of the opinion that the defendant had deliberately frightened the victim, and that that constituted an assault, and accordingly they found him guilty of the offence charged, i e being in an enclosed garden for an unlawful purpose, namely to assault the victim thereby causing her fear and shock. It was held that the defendant intended to frighten the victim and that she was frightened. Mr Richards endeavoured to distinguish that case from the present case by saying that it could not be proved that the victims in this case had any fear of some act of immediate violence.

In *Smith*'s case it was contended by the defendant that an assault was the doing of an act which intentionally or recklessly caused another to apprehend immediate and unlawful violence; that the evidence was that the victim had not been caused to have such apprehension; and that there was no evidence upon which the justices could say that the defendant had intended she should so apprehend.

In his judgment Kerr LJ said (at 237–238):

'The question of law is: "whether there was evidence upon which the magistrates' court could conclude that the purpose of the defendant was to assault [Miss M] and consequently 'an unlawful purpose' within the meaning of the Vagrancy Act 1824" ... In the present case, on the findings which I have summarised, there was quite clearly an intention to cause fear, an intention to frighten, and that intention produced the intended effect as the result of what the defendant did, in that it did frighten and indeed terrify Miss [M] to the extent that she screamed. It is not a case where she was merely startled or surprised or ashamed to be seen in her nightclothes; she was terrified as the result of what the defendant deliberately did, knowing and either intending or being reckless as to whether it would cause that fear in her. Ultimately, as it seems to me, the only point taken by Mr. Denny which requires some consideration is whether there was a sufficient apprehension, within the definition which I have read, of immediate and unlawful violence. He takes the point that there is no finding here that what Miss [M] was terrified of was some violence, and indeed some violence which can be described as immediate. However, as it seems to me, Mr. Greenbourne is right when he submits, really in the form of a question: "What else, other than some form of immediate violence, could Miss [M] have been terrified about?" ... In the present case the defendant intended to frighten Miss [M] *a*   and Miss [M] was frightened. As it seems to me, there is no need for a finding that what she was frightened of, which she probably could not analyse at that moment, was some innominate terror of some potential violence. It was clearly a situation where the basis of the fear which was instilled in her was that she did not know what the defendant was going to do next, but that, whatever he might be going to do next, and sufficiently immediately for the *b*   purposes of the offence, was something of a violent nature.'

Clearly the facts of *Smith*'s case bear some similarity to the present case. The appellant did not touch the victim. He stood outside her window causing her to be terrified. She was frightened of some potential violence. The distinctions which can be drawn are the physical proximity of the appellant to the victim and *c*   the fact that her fear must have been a fear of some direct injury to her body as opposed to psychological injury. Since *R v Chan-Fook* the last distinction is irrelevant.

Barton v Armstrong [1969] 2 NSWR 451, was a civil action in the Supreme Court of New South Wales. The action was based in part on an allegation of assault. Assaults were alleged to have been committed by telephone. Taylor J said *d*   (at 455):

'Mr. Staff's first and second propositions can, I think, be best dealt with together. They are the ones upon which he most strongly relied. There are, undoubtedly, many authorities which show that mere words do not constitute an assault, however insulting or even menacing they may be, and *e*   that the intention to do violence must be expressed in acts ... Whatever the reason may be, it is clear from the many authorities cited on this subject that mere words themselves are not sufficient to constitute an assault and that the threatening act must put the victim in immediate fear or apprehension of violence. For these reasons Mr. Staff contended that all threats over the *f*   telephone could not in law be capable of constituting an assault. I am not persuaded that threats uttered over the telephone are to be properly categorized as mere words. I think it is a matter of the circumstances. To telephone a person in the early hours of the morning, not once but on many occasions, and to threaten him, not in a conversational tone but in an atmosphere of drama and suspense, is a matter that a jury could say was well *g*   calculated to not only instil fear into his mind but to constitute threatening acts, as distinct from mere words. If, when threats in this manner are conveyed over the telephone, the recipient has been led to believe that he is being followed, kept under surveillance by persons hired to do him physical harm to the extent of killing him, then why is this not something to put him *h*   in fear or apprehension of immediate violence? In the age in which we live threats may be made and communicated by persons remote from the person threatened. Physical violence and death can be produced by acts done at a distance by people who are out of sight and by agents hired for that purpose. I do not think that these, if they result in apprehension of physical violence *j*   in the mind of a reasonable person, are outside the protection afforded by the civil and criminal law as to assault. How immediate does the fear of physical violence have to be? In my opinion the answer is it depends on the circumstances. Some threats are not capable of arousing apprehension of violence in the mind of a reasonable person unless there is an immediate prospect of the threat being carried out. Others, I believe, can create the apprehension even if it is made clear that the violence may occur in the future, at times unspecified and uncertain. Being able to immediately carry out the threat is but one way of creating the fear of apprehension, but not the only way. There are other ways, more subtle and perhaps more effective. Threats which put a reasonable person in fear of physical violence have always been abhorrent to the law as an interference with personal freedom and integrity, and the right of a person to be free from the fear of insult. If the threat produces the fear of apprehension of physical violence then I am of opinion that the law is breached, although the victim does not know when that physical violence may be effected.'

Accordingly, Taylor J held that threats made over the telephone were capable of amounting to an assault. In the present case there were no threats but merely silence. In the circumstances in which these constant telephone calls were made to the victims, followed by silence, they were, in our judgment, just as capable of being terrifying to the victims as if actual threats had been made.

We agree with the reasoning of Taylor J in *Barton v Armstrong* and, in particular, with his proposition that whether a particular act, or particular acts, amount to an assault is a question of fact which will depend upon the circumstances.

In our judgment, the making of a telephone call followed by silence, or a series of telephone calls, is capable of amounting to a relevant act for the purposes of s 47. The act consists in the making of the telephone call, and it does not matter whether words or silence ensue. There is no doubt that the telephone calls made the victims apprehensive. Equally, there is no doubt that they caused them psychological damage. In our judgment, once the fear and the damage are established, then when a telephone call is made by the appellant and the victim lifts the telephone and then knows that the man is telephoning them yet again, they will be apprehensive of suffering the very psychological damage from which they did suffer, namely palpitations, difficulty in breathing, cold sweats, anxiety, inability to sleep, dizziness, stress, and the like. As in *Smith's* case, these victims would not know what the appellant was going to do next. In most cases an assault is likely to involve direct physical violence to the body. However, the fact that the violence is inflicted indirectly, causing psychological harm, does not render the act to be any less an act of violence. Nor, in our judgment, is it necessary that there should be an immediate proximity between defendant and victim. Fear can be instilled as readily over the telephone as it can through the window. In our judgment repetitious telephone calls of this nature are likely to cause the victims to apprehend immediate and unlawful violence. That the appellant so intended was inherent in his pleas of guilty.

Academic writers have indicated that judges should not stretch the ambit of specific crimes beyond their proper limits in order to punish behaviour which members of the public would consider ought to be punished (see, for example, Glanville Williams *Criminal Law, The General Part* (2nd edn, 1961) p 176). We are very mindful of that admonition, but, in this case, and in the case in which Tucker J has just given judgment, *R v Johnson* [1996] Crim LR 828 we are satisfied that the conduct complained of falls squarely within the recognised definition of the offence.

For those reasons this appeal against conviction is dismissed.

Appeal dismissed.

N P Metcalfe Esq   Barrister.

R v Wilson

a

COURT OF APPEAL, CRIMINAL DIVISION
EVANS LJ, SCOTT-BAKER AND SEDLEY JJ
9, 25 JULY 1996

b

Insurance – Illegality – Restriction on carrying on insurance business – Insurance business carried on without authority of Secretary of State – Defendant purporting to sell debt collecting and debt indemnity services on behalf of a limited company – Neither defendant nor company authorised to sell such insurance – Defendant convicted of carrying on insurance business without authorisation – Circumstances in which an individual could be guilty of offence charged – Whether necessary to have concluded contract to be 'carrying on insurance business' – Insurance Companies Act 1982, ss 2, 14.

c

The defendant approached two traders, A and D, giving them brochures and other documents which purported to be issued by a company, DIS (UK) Ltd, which offered debt collecting and debt indemnity services. A gained the impression that the defendant was a director of that company, although none of the documents actually named the directors. A then signed what purported to be a debt collecting agreement and wrote three cheques in favour of 'DIS' totalling £3,500, on the understanding that that was the premium for insurance cover for a business of his size. Two weeks later he received a letter which contained an offer of indemnity cover and thanked him for the interest he had shown. The printed letterhead gave the name and address of DIS (UK) Ltd but it was signed by the defendant as 'Senior Sales Executive (UK) Division'. When a customer later defaulted A never received any payment in respect of its debt. In the second case, D wrote a cheque in respect of an agency agreement in favour of DIS (UK) Ltd, but before payment 'Ltd' was erased, it was not clear by whom. The defendant gave D a business card describing himself as 'Senior executive consultant' for DIS Ltd. Neither the defendant nor any company under the name DIS (UK) Ltd was authorised under the Insurance Companies Act 1982 to sell such insurance. The defendant was subsequently charged and convicted of carrying on insurance business without authority, contrary to ss 2[a] and 14[b] of the 1982 Act. He appealed against conviction, contending, inter alia, (i) that he could not be guilty of the offence charged under ss 2 and 14 of the 1982 Act unless DIS (UK) Ltd was either non-existent or a sham company, neither of which had been proved, and (ii) that contracts of insurance had not actually been entered into with the traders so that the attempts which he had made to solicit insurance business did not amount to carrying on insurance business for the purposes of s 2 of the Act.

d

e

f

g

h

Held – The appeal would be dismissed for the following reasons—
(1) A person breached s 2 of the 1982 Act if he sold insurance business on his own account without authorisation. If, however, he did so on behalf of an unauthorised company, so that any contracts of insurance which he made were with the company rather than himself, then the company was guilty of the offence and he was only guilty of aiding and abetting that offence if he knew that

j

---

a   Section 2, so far as material, is set out at p 121 *c*, post
b   Section 14, so far as material, provides: '(1) A person who carries on business in contravention of this Part of this Act shall be guilty of an offence ...'

the company was unauthorised. In the instant case, there was no evidence or
finding as to whether the company for which the defendant claimed to have been   *a*
acting existed, nor as to the defendant's state of knowledge of its affairs.
However, since the defendant had conspicuously failed to sign any of the letters
or other documents on behalf of the company, and he was nowhere described in
writing as a director of that or any other company, the jury could not fail to
conclude that the business which the defendant was carrying on was his own,   *b*
which was a proper basis for his conviction under s 2 (see p 123 *f g j* to p 124 *a e f h*,
and p 127 *b*, post).

(2) Since the statutory definitions of 'insurance business' and 'contracts of
insurance' contained in ss 95 and 96 of the 1982 Act both referred to 'effecting'
insurance contracts and were not exclusive for the purposes of s 2(1) of the 1982
Act, to 'carry on any insurance business' included not only the conclusion of a   *c*
contract but also the processes of pre-contract negotiation which began not later
than the issue of an invitation to treat and soliciting such business. It followed
that a person who sought insurance business on the basis of a document such as
the brochure issued in the instant case and who held himself out as having
authority both to make insurance contracts and to receive premiums on behalf of   *d*
an insurer did carry on insurance business for the purposes of s 2 (see p 125 *f g*,
p 126 *e* to *g* and p 127 *b*, post).

Notes

For the meaning of insurance business and statutory restrictions on carrying on
insurance business, see 25 *Halsbury's Laws* (4th edn reissue) paras 18, 19.   *e*

For the Insurance Companies Act 1982, ss 2, 14, see 22 *Halsbury's Statutes* (4th
edn) (1995 reissue) 230, 324.

Cases referred to in judgment

A-G's Reference (No 1 of 1995) [1996] 4 All ER 21, [1996] 1 WLR 970, CA.   *f*
Bedford Insurance Co Ltd v Instituto de Resseguros do Brasil [1984] 3 All ER 766, [1985]
    QB 966, [1984] 3 WLR 726.
Phoenix General Insurance Co of Greece SA v Administratia Asigurarilor de Stat [1987]
    2 All ER 152, [1988] QB 216, [1987] 2 WLR 512, QBD and CA.
R v Boal [1992] 3 All ER 177, [1992] QB 591, [1992] 2 WLR 890, CA.
United General Commercial Insurance Corp Ltd, Re [1927] 2 Ch 51.   *g*

Case also cited

Huckerby v Elliott [1970] 1 All ER 189, DC.

Appeal against conviction

Rupert George Wilson appealed with leave against his conviction in the Crown   *h*
Court at Birmingham on 17 January 1996, before Judge Peter Crawford QC and
a jury, of carrying on an insurance business without authority, contrary to ss 2
and 14 of the Insurance Companies Act 1982, for which he was sentenced to 100
hours of community service and was disqualified under the Company Directors
Disqualification Act 1986 from holding office as a company director for five years.   *j*
The facts are set out in the judgment of the court.

Mark Eades (assigned by the *Registrar of Criminal Appeals*) for the appellant.
David Seconde (instructed by *Faber & Co*, Birmingham, agents for the *Solicitor to
    the Department of Trade and Industry*) for the Crown.

Cur adv vult

a   25 July 1996. The following judgment of the court was delivered.

EVANS LJ. The appellant, who is aged 54, was convicted on 17 January 1996
after trial in the Crown Court at Birmingham before the Recorder of Birmingham
(Judge Peter Crawford QC) and a jury on a charge of carrying on an insurance
business without authority, contrary to ss 2 and 14 of the Insurance Companies

b   Act 1982. He was sentenced to 100 hours of community service and was
disqualified for five years from holding office as a company director, under the
Company Directors Disqualification Act 1986. He now appeals against his
conviction by leave of the single judge.
        The issues raised by the appeal are questions of law. Section 14(1) makes any
person who carries on business in contravention of Pt I of the 1982 Act guilty of

c   a criminal offence, and so we can concentrate on s 2(1), which reads:

        'Subject to the following provisions of this section, no person shall carry on
        any insurance business in the United Kingdom unless authorised to do so [by
        the Secretary of State].'

d   None of the exceptions is relevant. The questions of law are: (1) in what
circumstances can an individual be guilty of the offence of carrying on an
insurance business in contravention of s 2(1); and (2) does a person carry on
insurance business for the purposes of s 2(1) unless he enters or purports to enter
into contracts of insurance? The reason for the second question is that the
appellant denies having concluded any agreement with the principal prosecution

e   witness, Mr Ahmed, and he contends that the attempts which he made to obtain
business from Mr Ahmed and from a second complainant, Mr Stephen Dutton,
do not amount to carrying on an insurance business within the Act.
        It is important to note that no charge was brought under s 91, which is
expressly concerned with the conduct of individuals. It reads:

f   '*Criminal liability of directors.*—(1) Where an offence under this Act
        committed by a body corporate is proved to have been committed with the
        consent or connivance of, or to be attributable to any neglect on the part of,
        any director, chief executive, manager, secretary or other similar officer of
        the body corporate or any person who was purporting to act in any such
        capacity, he, as well as the body corporate, shall be guilty of that offence and

g   liable to be proceeded against and punished accordingly ...'

        The offence created by s 91(1) is ancillary to an offence committed by a body
corporate, and when it applies the individual is guilty of 'that offence'; it is
essentially parasitic. The present appeal is concerned with a different question: in

h   what circumstances does an individual, as distinct from a body corporate,
commit an offence under s 2?
        We begin with the evidence in this case. Mr Ahmed is the proprietor of a
textile business in Rochdale. In November 1989 he saw an advertisement in a
trade journal which was something to do with debt indemnity, in other words,

j   insurance cover against bad debts. Soon afterwards he received a visit from two
men, the appellant and another called Goodman. They gave him a brochure and
other documents which purported to be issued by a company, Debt Indemnity
Service UK Ltd (DIS (UK) Ltd). Mr Ahmed gained the impression that the
appellant was a director of that company, but he could not remember whether
that was an assumption he made or was because the appellant introduced himself
as such. None of the documents said who the directors were. They explained
that the company offered two kinds of services: collecting debts as agents for their

customers, and the debt indemnity service. On 10 November the same two men returned to the office. On this occasion, Mr Ahmed signed what purports to be a debt collecting agreement and he made out three cheques in favour of 'DIS.' totalling £3,500. These were for £2,500 (a cheque dated 10 November), £500 (postdated 10 December) and £500 (postdated 10 January 1990). Mr Ahmed understood that that was the premium for insurance cover for a business of his size, with £500,000 turnover. Just two weeks later he received a letter dated 23 November which contained an offer of indemnity cover and thanked him for the interest he had shown. The printed letter-heading gave the name and address of DIS (UK) Ltd but it was signed 'R G Wilson Senior Sales Executive (UK) Division'. Later, a customer defaulted but Mr Ahmed never received any payment in respect of its debt. At about the same time, the appellant tried to enlist Mr Ahmed as an agent for the company himself.

Mr Stephen Dutton gave evidence that the appellant called on him and offered him the same debt collection and debt indemnity service, leaving the same brochure as Mr Ahmed had received. Mr Dutton made out a cheque in respect of an agency agreement. This was in favour of 'Debt Indemnity Service (UK) Ltd' in the sum of £805, but before payment 'Ltd' was erased, it is not clear by whom. The appellant gave Mr Dutton a business card describing him as 'Senior executive consultant' for DIS Ltd.

The prosecution case was that there was clear evidence of the appellant offering insurance cover and in Mr Ahmed's case of selling him insurance cover. They contended that he was carrying on insurance business and of course he was not authorised to do so by the Secretary of State.

Mr Eades, for the defence, submitted that the appellant could not commit the offence charged under ss 2 and 14 of the Act unless DIS (UK) Ltd on whose behalf he purported to act was either non-existent or a sham company, neither of which had been proved. So, he submitted, there was a fatal flaw in the prosecution case. If DIS (UK) Ltd was a registered company, then it, as the appellant's principal, being unauthorised by the Secretary of State, committed an offence under ss 2 and 14, and the appellant as an individual could only be guilty, if at all, under s 91, which was not charged. He also submitted that no offence could be committed under ss 2 and 14 unless it was proved that a contract of insurance was actually entered into.

The Recorder of Birmingham rejected this submission. He ruled that there was evidence that the appellant had solicited insurance business and that it was a question for the jury whether he had carried on the business. It was irrelevant whether the appellant was acting as an individual on his own account or whether he was a director of a limited company or of a larger concern. Mr Eades then disclosed to the judge that the appellant accepted that 'he was engaged in the selling of insurance by way of getting indemnity to customers' on behalf of the company but denied that he had 'a more prominent or central role'. The judge said that it was open to the jury to find that he was carrying on an insurance business.

> 'He represented himself to be a person in authority in the business. He solicited custom, but it would be open to the defendant, I suppose, to adduce evidence before the jury that he was merely a cog. Merely somebody who did what he was told.'

a The judge in his summing up directed the jury accordingly. The question was whether the defendant was carrying on insurance business:

> 'What this means is that this defendant took an active and significant part in insurance business. If he was just a cog, if he was just somebody who did what he was told, if he had no independent input or no significant independent input, then it would not be fair to say that he was carrying on
b an insurance business.'

It was irrelevant whether the business was carried on by a limited company, or by a partnership, or by a simple individual.

During their retirement the jury asked for further clarification of carrying on an insurance business, and after hearing submissions by counsel the judge
c repeated the direction he had given. It was for the jury to decide whether the defendant played an active and significant part in an insurance business. After a short further retirement, the jury returned their unanimous guilty verdict.

It is apparent from this short history of the proceedings that the jury was directed to, and did, decide two issues only. First, did the appellant offer
d insurance to the prosecution witnesses? This he did not challenge. Secondly, if he was acting or purporting to act on behalf of DIS (UK) Ltd, did he play a significant and active part in that business, as opposed to being a mere cog in its machinery? The jury rejected his evidence that he was a commission agent who did not play a significant part and that the business was the company's, not his.

e Because of the judge's rulings, both the existence of the company and the appellant's knowledge of whether it existed, or not, were regarded as irrelevant. They were not the subject of evidence and they were not left as issues for the jury to decide.

In our judgment, the scope of s 2 is different from what the judge held it to be. Our starting point is the same as his: what did the defendant do? If he was selling
f insurance business (as distinct, for example, from an office secretary or other employee who has no contact with customers) and was doing so on his own account then clearly he was acting in contravention of s 2. But if he was doing so on behalf of a company, and was authorised to do so, so that any contracts of insurance which he made were with the company rather than himself, then different considerations would arise, and the existence of the company might not
g be irrelevant, as the judge held that it was. Moreover, the individual agent could not be found guilty of aiding and abetting an offence committed by the company unless he knew that the company was unauthorised by the Secretary of State, and the judge ruled that the appellant's state of knowledge was irrelevant also.

h Mr Eades submits that a bona fide agent or commission agent for a genuine insurance company, who concludes business on behalf of the company and who does not know that the company is unauthorised under the Act, does not commit any offence under s 2 although the company does. The business is the company's, not his.

That however is not this case. The present case is an intermediate situation.
j There is no evidence and no finding as to whether the company for which the appellant claimed to have been acting was a genuine company, nor as to the appellant's state of knowledge of its affairs. He was convicted of an offence under ss 2 and 14 on the basis that he did himself solicit insurance business, and although he may have purported to act on behalf of DIS (UK) Ltd, there was no evidence whether that company existed or not, although it was agreed that no

such company was authorised under the Act. The question we have to decide is whether he was rightly convicted on the basis of those facts.

In our judgment, he was, and the correct analysis is as follows. The jury found that the appellant was playing an active and significant part in selling insurance, and he did this in contravention of s 2, whether he was acting on his own behalf or on behalf of a genuine company, which was unauthorised under the Act. If there was such a company and his dealings were solely on behalf of the company, then we can assume that he would not incur any personal liability towards third parties and he committed no offence under s 2 although the company would do so; as stated above, we need not decide whether that is correct or not. But if the company was a figment of his imagination, or if he had no authority to act on its behalf, then he would incur personal liability towards third parties and in our judgment he would commit the offence under s 2. That would be because the business that he carried on, whatever it consisted of, could only be his.

So the question becomes one of the burden of proof. The prosecution did not prove that there was no company registered as DIS (UK) Ltd; was the charge nevertheless made out? It is clear, in our judgment, that what is called the evidential burden shifts to the defendant in these circumstances. If it is proved that he was carrying on a business, either his own or someone else's, then it is for him to assert that it was not his and to produce some evidence to that effect. We can assume that the burden of proving that an offence was committed remains on the prosecution, but this does not require the prosecution to negative a possibility which is not established by the evidence (cf *Blackstone's Criminal Practice* (6th edn, 1996) pp 1801–1810).

Here, the appellant may have claimed that he was a director of DIS (UK) Ltd in conversation with Mr Ahmed. He produced an elaborate and detailed brochure of the services offered by a company of that name, and letters were written by him and by others under the company's letterhead. But he, and they, conspicuously failed to sign any of the letters or other documents on behalf of the company, and he was nowhere described in writing as a director of that or any other company. (In one letter dated 11 January 1990 (not to Mr Ahmed or Mr Dutton) under the company's letterhead, the appellant signed as 'Managing Director' but the text of the letter referred simply to 'DIS UK Div' avoiding any reference to the limited company.) The cheques he obtained from Mr Ahmed were made to out 'DIS' and not to the alleged company. Mr Dutton's cheque was made out to DIS (UK) Ltd but 'Ltd' was later erased, clearly by the appellant who received it or at his request.

The quality of this evidence was not such, in our judgment, as to require the prosecution to prove formally that no such company as DIS (UK) Ltd existed or that it did not carry on a bone fide insurance business. Conversely, on the whole of the evidence the jury could not fail to be sure that the business which the appellant was carrying on was his own. This in our view was a proper basis for his conviction of an offence under s 2.

As will be apparent, we are not persuaded that the law requires the jury to distinguish between playing an active and significant part, as distinct from being a mere 'cog' in the business, when the question is whether or not the individual defendant was carrying on business on his own behalf. That may be relevant when the issue is whether the acts of an individual should be attributed to a company for the purpose of establishing that the company committed an offence, but not in our judgment when the individual rather than the company is charged.

a   It may also be relevant when considering the application of s 91 (cf *R v Boal* [1992] 3 All ER 177, [1992] QB 591 and *A-G's Reference (No 1 of 1995)* [1996] 4 All ER 21, [1996] 1 WLR 970).

       Nevertheless, even if the jury's finding was strictly irrelevant, it does put beyond doubt the fact that the appellant was playing an active and significant part in a business which was not authorised under the Act.

b   The second issue is whether an offence can be committed under ss 2 and 14 before any insurance contract is entered into, even by the (unauthorised) insurer. Mr Eades submits that there is no contravention of s 2 unless and until a contract is made. He accepts that pre-contract there might be conduct which constitutes an attempt to commit the offence, but that was not the charge brought here. He relies both on the wording of the Act and on the following authorities.

c   In *Bedford Insurance Co Ltd v Instituto de Resseguros do Brasil* [1984] 3 All ER 766 at 772, [1985] QB 966 at 982 Parker J said:

        '... what is aimed at and what is prohibited is both the making and performance of any contract of insurance of a relevant class *by way of business*. Thus a company opening business premises for the purpose of carrying on
d   insurance business would commit an offence when in the course of that business and without authorisation from the Secretary of State it entered into the very first contract of insurance of a relevant class.' (Parker J's emphasis.)

e   In *Phoenix General Insurance Co of Greece SA v Administratia Asigurarilor de Stat* [1987] 2 All ER 152 at 176, [1988] QB 216 at 274 Kerr LJ agreed with this and another passage, where Parker J said: 'It is thus both the contracts themselves and the performance of them at which the statute is directed' (see [1984] 3 All ER 766 at 772, [1985] QB 966 at 981).

       There is no definition in the Act of 'carrying on business' and the descriptions
f   of different classes of business all begin with the words 'effecting and carrying out contracts' (see Schs 1 and 2). The same words are found in the interpretation section, s 95: 'For the purposes of this Act "insurance business" includes—(a) the effecting and carrying out ... of contracts ...' and s 96(1) defines 'contract of insurance' as including 'any contract the effecting of which constitutes the carrying on of insurance business by virtue of section 95 above'.
g   The judge directed the jury as follows:

        'You may think that it does not really matter whether the prosecution establish one instance or two instances of selling insurance, if you are satisfied that insurance was being sold. Indeed, it would not stop somebody
h   carrying on an insurance business even if he was not very good at it and had not managed to sell any policies at all. The crime is not carrying on a successful or busy insurance business, the crime is carrying on an insurance business.'

       In *Bedford Insurance Co* and *Phoenix Insurance* the principal question was whether
j   a contract of insurance made by an unauthorised insurer was both illegal and void. The Act makes it necessary to consider whether the relevant class of business was authorised or not (see ss 1 and 2). An insurance company may carry on more than one class of business, and it is only the unauthorised class of business which gives rise to criminal liability under the Act. In that context, it is understandable that the contravention of s 2 should be measured in terms of the

first unauthorised contract of the relevant kind. Parker J preceded the passage quoted above with the following ([1984] 3 All ER 766 at 772, [1985] QB 966 at 982):

> 'This ... indicates that if, for example, a person was lawfully carrying on business of some class other than marine business pursuant to an authorisation for that class it would be sufficient to constitute a contravention of the Act if he were then to enter into a single contract of marine insurance.'

Neither Parker J nor Kerr LJ had in mind, in our judgment, the issue which arises here. Any contract of insurance must be preceded by negotiations, if only the formal steps of offer and acceptance, and the reference to 'making' an unauthorised contract can scarcely have been intended to exclude these necessary preliminary steps from the process of 'carrying on an insurance business', which if unauthorised is what the Act forbids. If an insurance company opened an office where its employees and agents actively sought business of a relevant and unauthorised kind, then it would be artificial and unreal to say that no such business was carried on there until the moment when the first such contract was concluded (the contract would be illegal and void, in any event, and therefore the legal significance of concluding the agreement would merely be that the carrying on of business had begun). It would be equally unrealistic to hold that sales activities thereafter did count as carrying on the business regardless of whether any further agreements resulted from them.

The statutory definitions speak of 'effecting and carrying out' insurance contracts of the relevant kinds (see s 1(2) and Schs 1 and 2). We would hold simply that 'effecting' includes the processes of negotiation which begins not later than the issue of what the law regards as an invitation to treat. A person who seeks insurance business on the basis of a document such as the brochure issued in the name of DIS (UK) Ltd in the present case and who holds himself out as having authority both to make insurance contracts and to receive premiums on behalf of an insurer does 'carry on [an] insurance business', in our judgment, for the purposes of s 2. We would also hold, if necessary, that the statutory definitions are not exclusive and that 'carrying on [an] insurance business' clearly does include soliciting such business, as the appellant did in the present case.

A related question might be whether an insurer was carrying on business in this country when contracts were negotiated here but formally concluded by signature abroad. If carrying on an insurance business consisted solely of the formal 'making' of the contracts then no offence would be committed under s 2, even though all the other business of the insurer, including receiving applications and premiums and handling claims, was in fact conducted in this country. In *Re United General Commercial Insurance Corp Ltd* [1927] 2 Ch 51 at 56 the contracts were made and policies were issued in London and so this question did not arise, but in his description of the insurer's business Lord Hanworth MR included not only 'the act of issuing policies', but he added 'Any negotiation in reference to them as to the terms or conditions or as to losses claimed for under them must be determined at the head office'. This supports the view we have expressed above.

If, contrary to this view, there is no carrying on of business unless and until a contract is made, then the appellant is entitled to say that there is no such finding by the jury in the present case: but when Mr Ahmed gave evidence that he made *a* an agreement with the appellant and parted with cheques for £3,500 on the strength of that agreement, we do not think that they could properly have made any other finding.

Conclusion

b For these reasons, although we have differed from the judge's interpretation of ss 2 and 14 of the Act, we conclude that the jury's verdict was correct on the basis of the facts which they found proved. The appeal must be dismissed.

Appeal dismissed.

Carolyn Toulmin   Barrister.

Practice Note

a

QUEEN'S BENCH DIVISION
LORD BINGHAM OF CORNHILL CJ, SACHS AND TOULSON JJ
6 DECEMBER 1996

b

Practice – Crown Office list – Judicial review – Application for leave to apply for judicial review – Documents to be lodged – Relevant legislative provisions and statutory instruments.

LORD BINGHAM OF CORNHILL CJ gave the following direction at the sitting of the court. On lodging an application for leave to apply for judicial review the *c* applicant's solicitor must lodge, in addition to the material required to be lodged by the practice direction ([1994] 4 All ER 671, [1994] 1 WLR 1551), a paginated indexed bundle of the *relevant* legislative provisions and statutory instruments required for the proper consideration of the application.

An applicant who acts in person should comply with this direction so far as he / *d* she is able. In any event, an applicant acting in person should list the legislative provisions and statutory instruments upon which he / she relies.

Dilys Tausz　　Barrister.

O'Hara v Chief Constable of the Royal Ulster Constabulary

a

HOUSE OF LORDS

b

LORD GOFF OF CHIEVELEY, LORD MUSTILL, LORD STEYN, LORD HOFFMANN AND LORD HOPE OF CRAIGHEAD

2 OCTOBER, 12 DECEMBER 1996

c

Arrest – Arrest without warrant – Terrorist – Suspicion of being a terrorist – Constable arresting person on suspicion of being a terrorist following briefing – Constable acting on instructions of superior officer – Whether arresting officer having reasonable grounds for suspicion – Whether arresting officer's own state of mind only relevant consideration in deciding whether reasonable grounds – Whether superior officer's instructions capable of amounting to reasonable grounds – Prevention of Terrorism (Temporary Provisions) Act 1984, s 12(1)(b).

d

The appellant was arrested by a police officer in connection with a murder under s 12(1)(b)[a] of the Prevention of Terrorism (Temporary Provisions) Act 1984 on suspicion of being a terrorist. The appellant was eventually released two weeks later without being charged with any offence and he subsequently brought an action for damages against the chief constable for, inter alia, wrongful arrest. At the trial, the officer gave evidence that prior to going to the appellant's house he had attended a briefing given by his superior officer at which he was told that the appellant had been involved in the murder and told to arrest him. The judge accepted that the officer had suspected the appellant of having been concerned in terrorist acts and that his suspicion was based on the briefing and held that the arrest was lawful on the basis that, although the evidence was scanty, in the circumstances the officer had had reasonable grounds for suspecting the appellant to be a person who had been concerned in the commission, preparation or instigation of acts of terrorism within the meaning of s 12(1)(b) of the 1984 Act. The Court of Appeal in Northern Ireland upheld that decision, on the grounds that the information given to the officer at the briefing had been sufficient to constitute the required state of mind of an arresting officer under s 12(1)(b). The appellant appealed to the House of Lords, contending that s 12(1)(b) of the 1984 Act required that the reasonable grounds on which the arresting officer based his suspicion should exist in fact and that that objective test required proof of something more than just what was in the officer's mind. The chief constable contended that the order to arrest the appellant given to the officer by his superior officer was by itself sufficient to afford him a reasonable suspicion.

e

f

g

h

Held – When determining whether an arresting officer had reasonable grounds for his suspicion under s 12(1) of the 1984 Act, the court was not required to look beyond what was in the officer's mind, since it was the grounds which were in his mind at the time which were relevant. Furthermore, the officer's suspicion did not need to be based on his own observations but could be based on what he had been told, or on information which had been given to him anonymously, and it was not necessary for him to prove what was known to his informant or that any

j

---

a   Section 12(1) is set out at p 136 c, post

of the facts on which he based his suspicion were in fact true. Whether such
information provided reasonable grounds for the officer's suspicion depended on   *a*
its source and context, viewed in the light of the whole surrounding
circumstances. However, the mere fact that an arresting officer had been
instructed by a superior officer to effect the arrest was not capable of amounting
to reasonable grounds for the necessary suspicion. Accordingly, although the
matters which were disclosed at the briefing to the officer were scanty, the trial   *b*
judge had been entitled to weigh up that evidence in the light of the surrounding
circumstances and, having regard to the source of that information, to draw
inferences as to what a reasonable man would make of it. It followed that neither
the trial judge nor the Court of Appeal had misdirected themselves as to the test
to be applied and the appeal would therefore be dismissed (see p 131 *d e j* to
p 132 *a*, p 134 *j*, p 135 *e f*, p 138 *j* to p 139 *d* and p 143 *e f*, post).   *c*

Notes
For a constable's power to arrest a suspected terrorist, see 11(1) *Halsbury's Laws*
(4th edn reissue) para 118.
    As from 22 March 1989 the Prevention of Terrorism (Temporary Provisions)   *d*
Act 1984, s 12, was replaced by the Prevention of Terrorism (Temporary
Provisions) Act 1989, s 14. For s 14 of the 1989 Act, see 12 *Halsbury's Statutes* (4th
edn) (1994 reissue) 1332.

Cases referred to in opinions
Brady v Chief Constable of the Royal Ulster Constabulary (15 February 1991,   *e*
    unreported), NI QBD.
Castorina v Chief Constable of Surrey (1988) Times, 15 June, [1988] CA Transcript
    499.
Copeland v McPherson 1970 SLT 87, HC of Just.
Dallison v Caffery [1964] 2 All ER 610, [1965] 1 QB 348, [1964] 3 WLR 385, CA.   *f*
Dryburgh v Galt 1981 JC 69, HC of Just.
Emergency Powers Bill 1976 (Article 26 of the Constitution), Re [1977] IR 159, Ir SC.
Fox v UK (1990) 13 EHRR 157, ECt HR.
Hanna v Chief Constable, Royal Ulster Constabulary [1986] NI 103, NI QBD.
Holgate-Mohammed v Duke [1984] 1 All ER 1054, [1984] AC 437, [1984] 2 WLR 660,
    HL.   *g*
Liversidge v Anderson [1941] 3 All ER 338, [1942] AC 206, HL.
Lynch, Ex p [1980] NI 126, NI QBD.
McKee v Chief Constable for Northern Ireland [1985] 1 All ER 1, [1984] 1 WLR 1358,
    HL.
R v Chief Constable of the Devon and Cornwall Constabulary, ex p Central Electricity   *h*
    Generating Board [1981] 3 All ER 826, [1982] QB 458, [1981] 3 WLR 967, CA.
Shaaban Bin Hussien v Chong Fook Kam [1969] 3 All ER 1626, [1970] AC 942, [1970]
    2 WLR 441, PC.
Wheeler v Whiting (1840) 9 C & P 262, 173 ER 828, NP.

j
Appeal
The plaintiff, Gerard O'Hara, appealed with leave of the Appeal Committee of
the House of Lords from the decision of the Court of Appeal in Northern Ireland
(Kelly LJ, Pringle and Higgins JJ) on 6 May 1994 dismissing his appeal against a
decision of McCollum J sitting in the Queen's Bench Division of the High Court
of Justice in Northern Ireland on 14 September 1990 whereby he dismissed the

a plaintiff's claim for damages for unlawful arrest against the defendant, the Chief Constable of the Royal Ulster Constabulary. The facts are set out in the opinion of Lord Hope of Craighead.

Hugh P Kennedy QC and *Barry MacDonald* (both of the Northern Ireland Bar) (instructed by *B M Birnberg & Co*, agents for *Denis E Mullan*, Londonderry) for
b the plaintiff.
Patrick Coghlin QC and *Piers Grant* (both of the Northern Ireland bar) (instructed by the *Treasury Solicitor*, agent for the *Crown Solicitor*, Belfast) for the chief constable.

c Their Lordships took time for consideration.

12 December 1996. The following opinions were delivered.

LORD GOFF OF CHIEVELEY. My Lords, I have had the opportunity of reading in draft the speeches to be delivered by my noble and learned friends
d Lord Steyn and Lord Hope of Craighead. For the reasons which they give I, too, would dismiss the appeal.

LORD MUSTILL. My Lords, I have had the opportunity of reading in draft the speeches to be delivered by my noble and learned friends Lord Steyn and Lord Hope of Craighead. I agree with both, and would dismiss the appeal.
e

LORD STEYN. My Lords, I gratefully adopt the account of the background to this appeal given by my noble and learned friend Lord Hope of Craighead. The appeal can be decided on narrow grounds. The arrest was prima facie unlawful. At trial the respondent, the chief constable, sought to justify the arrest under
f s 12(1) of the Prevention of Terrorism (Temporary Provisions) Act 1984. So far as it is material, s 12(1) provides:

'... a constable may arrest without warrant a person whom he has reasonable grounds for suspecting to be ... (b) a person who is or has been concerned in the commission, preparation or instigation of acts of terrorism
g to which this Part of this Act applies ...'

The constable made the arrest in connection with a murder which was undoubtedly an act of terrorism within the meaning of s 12(1) of the 1984 Act. It was common ground that subjectively the constable had the necessary suspicion. The question was whether the constable objectively had reasonable grounds for
h suspecting that the plaintiff was concerned in the murder. The constable said in evidence that his reasonable grounds for suspecting the plaintiff were based on a briefing by a superior officer. He was told that the plaintiff had been involved in the murder. The constable said that the superior officer ordered him to arrest the plaintiff. He did so. Counsel for the plaintiff, Mr Kennedy QC, took the tactical
j decision not to cross-examine the constable about the details of the briefing. The trial judge described the evidence as scanty. But he inferred that the briefing afforded reasonable grounds for the necessary suspicion. In other words, the judge inferred that some further details must have been given in the briefing. The legal burden was on the chief constable to prove the existence of reasonable grounds for suspicion. Nevertheless, I am persuaded that the judge was entitled on the sparse materials before him to infer the existence of reasonable grounds

for suspicion. On this basis the Court of Appeal in Northern Ireland was entitled to dismiss the appeal. That means that the appeal before your Lordships' House *a* must also fail on narrow and purely factual grounds.

Plainly, leave to appeal was granted by the Appeal Committee because it was thought that the appeal raised an issue of general public importance. It was far from clear from the printed cases of the plaintiff and chief constable what the issue of principle was. But during his oral submissions Mr Coghlin QC, on behalf *b* of the chief constable, raised an issue of principle. He submitted that the order to arrest given by the superior officer to the arresting officer in this case was by itself sufficient to afford the constable a reasonable suspicion within the meaning of s 12(1). This point is of continuing relevance in relation to the Prevention of Terrorism (Temporary Provisions) Act 1989, which contains a provision in identical terms to s 12(1)(b) of the 1984 Act. But the point is also of wider *c* importance. In the past many statutes have vested powers in constables to arrest where the constable suspects on reasonable grounds that a person has committed an offence or is committing an offence (see *Moriarty's Police Law* (24th edn, 1981) p 19ff and the Report of the Royal Commission on Criminal Procedure, *The Investigation and Prosecution of Criminal Offences in England and Wales: The Law and* *d* *Procedure* (Cmnd 8092-1 (1981)) pp 135–138, App 9.2). An important modern example of such a power is to be found in s 24(6) of the Police and Criminal Evidence Act 1984. Some of the older specific powers also remain. Moreover, the point is of considerable practical importance since orders to arrest are no doubt routinely given by superior officers to constables. It is therefore necessary to examine the point in some detail. *e*

Counsel for the chief constable relied on the decision of the House of Lords *McKee v Chief Constable for Northern Ireland* [1985] 1 All ER 1, [1984] 1 WLR 1358 in support of his submission on the point of principle. The issue was the lawfulness of the arrest of a suspected terrorist. The matter was governed by s 11(1) of the Northern Ireland (Emergency Provisions) Act 1978. It provides: 'Any constable *f* may arrest without warrant any person whom he suspects of being a terrorist.'

Applying that provision Lord Roskill, speaking for all their Lordships observed ([1985] 1 All ER 1 at 4, [1984] 1 WLR 1358 at 1361):

> 'On the true construction of s 11(1) of the statute, what matters is the state of mind of the arresting officer and of no one else. That state of mind can *g* legitimately be derived from the instruction given to the arresting officer by his superior officer. The arresting officer is not bound and indeed may well not be entitled to question those instructions or to ask on what information they are founded.'

The statutory provision under consideration in *McKee's* case did not require that *h* an arresting officer must have reasonable grounds for suspicion. Moreover, the legislation was in much wider terms inasmuch as it authorised arrest for the purpose of internment. That statute was repealed in 1987 and your Lordships are concerned with a quite different statutory provision. In these circumstances, Lord Roskill's observations throw no light on the proper construction of s 12(1) *j* of the 1984 Act, which in terms provides that the power to arrest under it only arises where the constable has reasonable grounds for the necessary suspicion. Contrary to Mr Coghlin's submission, I would hold that it is misuse of precedent to transpose Lord Roskill's observations made in the context of the subjective requirement of a genuine belief to the objective requirement of the existence of reasonable grounds. *McKee's* case is irrelevant on the point of principle under

consideration in this case. On the other hand, the decision of the House of Lords
in *Holgate-Mohammed v Duke* [1984] 1 All ER 1054, [1984] AC 437 is of assistance.
The House had to consider the issue whether an arrest was lawful in the context
of a statutory provision which authorised arrest when a constable suspected on
reasonable grounds that an arrestable offence had been committed. Lord
Diplock made the following general observations ([1984] 1 All ER 1054 at 1059,
[1984] AC 437 at 445):

> 'My Lords, there is inevitably the potentiality of conflict between the
> public interest in preserving the liberty of the individual and the public
> interest in the detection of crime and the bringing to justice of those who
> commit it. The members of the organised police forces of the country have,
> since the mid-nineteenth century, been charged with the duty of taking the
> first steps to promote the latter public interest by inquiring into suspected
> offences with a view to identifying the perpetrators of them and of obtaining
> sufficient evidence admissible in a court of law against the persons they
> suspect of being the perpetrators as would justify charging them with the
> relevant offence before a magistrates' court with a view to their committal
> for trial for it. The compromise which English common and statutory law
> has evolved for the accommodation of the two rival public interests while
> these first steps are being taken by the police is twofold. (1) No person may
> be arrested without warrant (ie without the intervention of a judicial
> process) unless the constable arresting him has reasonable cause to suspect
> him to be guilty of an arrestable offence ... (2) A suspect so arrested and
> detained in custody must be brought before a magistrates' court as soon as
> practicable ...'

Lord Diplock made those observations in the context of statutes containing
provisions such as s 12(1). He said that the arrest can only be justified if the
constable arresting the alleged suspect has reasonable grounds to suspect him to
be guilty of an arrestable offence. The arresting officer is held accountable. That
is the compromise between the values of individual liberty and public order.

Section 12(1) authorises an arrest without warrant only where the constable
'has reasonable grounds for' suspicion. An arrest is therefore not lawful if the
arresting officer honestly but erroneously believes that he has reasonable
grounds for arrest but there are unknown to him in fact in existence reasonable
grounds for the necessary suspicion, e g because another officer has information
pointing to the guilt of the suspect. It would be difficult without doing violence
to the wording of the statute to read it in any other way.

A strong argument can be made that in arresting a suspect without warrant a
constable ought to be able to rely on information in the possession of another
officer and not communicated to him (see Feldman *The Law Relating to Entry,
Search and Seizure* (1986) pp 204–205). Arguably that ought as a matter of policy
to provide him with a defence to a claim for wrongful arrest. Such considerations
may possibly explain why art 5(1) of the European Convention for the Protection
of Human Rights and Fundamental Freedoms (Rome, 4 November 1950; TS 71
(1953); Cmd 8969) contains a more flexible provision. It reads as follows:

> 'Everyone has the right to liberty and security of person. No one shall be
> deprived of his liberty save in the following cases and in accordance with a
> procedure prescribed by law ... (c) the lawful arrest or detention of a person
> effected for the purpose of bringing him before the competent legal

authority on reasonable suspicion of having committed an offence or when it is reasonably considered necessary to prevent his committing an offence or fleeing after having done so ...'

It is clear from the drafting technique employed in art 5(1)(c), and in particular the use of the passive tense, that it contemplates a broader test of whether a reasonable suspicion exists and does not confine it to matters present in the mind of the arresting officer. That is also the effect of the judgment of the European Court of Human Rights in *Fox v UK* (1990) 13 EHRR 157 at 167–169 (paras 33–35). But s 12(1), and similar provisions, cannot be approached in this way: they categorise as reasonable grounds for suspicion only matters present in the mind of the constable. Feldman *Civil Liberties and Human Rights in England and Wales* (1993) p 199 lucidly explained the difference between two classes of statutes:

'Where reasonable grounds for suspicion are required in order to justify the arrest of someone who turns out to be innocent, the [Police and Criminal Evidence Act 1984] requires that the constable personally has reasonable grounds for the suspicion, and it would seem to follow that he is not protected if, knowing nothing of the case, he acts on orders from another officer who, perhaps, does have such grounds. On the other hand, under statutes which require only the objective existence of reasonable grounds for suspicion, it is possible that the officer need neither have the reasonable grounds nor himself suspect anything; he can simply follow orders.'

Section 12(1) is undeniably a statutory provision in the first category. The rationale for the principle in such cases is that in framing such statutory provisions Parliament has proceeded on the long-standing constitutional theory of the independence and accountability of the individual constable (see Marshall and Loveday 'The Police Independence and Accountability' in Jowell and Oliver *The Changing Constitution* (3rd edn, 1994) p 295ff and Ryan and Williams 'Police Discretion' [1986] PL 285 at 305). This case must therefore be approached on the basis that under s 12(1) the only relevant matters are those present in the mind of the arresting officer.

Certain general propositions about the powers of constables under a section such as s 12(1) can now be summarised. (1) In order to have a reasonable suspicion the constable need not have evidence amounting to a prima facie case. Ex hypothesi one is considering a preliminary stage of the investigation and information from an informer or a tip-off from a member of the public may be enough (see *Shaaban Bin Hussien v Chong Fook Kam* [1969] 3 All ER 1626 at 1631, [1970] AC 942 at 949). (2) Hearsay information may therefore afford a constable reasonable grounds to arrest. Such information may come from other officers (see *Hussien's* case). (3) The information which causes the constable to be suspicious of the individual must be in existence to the knowledge of the police officer at the time he makes the arrest. (4) The executive discretion to arrest or not as Lord Diplock described it in *Holgate-Mohammed v Duke* [1984] 1 All ER 1054 at 1059, [1984] AC 437 at 446, vests in the constable, who is engaged on the decision to arrest or not, and not in his superior officers.

Given the independent responsibility and accountability of a constable under a provision such as s 12(1) of the 1984 Act, it seems to follow that the mere fact that an arresting officer has been instructed by a superior officer to effect the arrest is not capable of amounting to reasonable grounds for the necessary suspicion within the meaning of s 12(1). It is accepted, and rightly accepted, that a mere

a request to arrest without any further information by an equal ranking officer, or a junior officer, is incapable of amounting to reasonable grounds for the necessary suspicion. How can the badge of the superior officer, and the fact that he gave an order, make a difference? In respect of a statute vesting an independent discretion in the particular constable, and requiring him personally to have reasonable grounds for suspicion, it would be surprising if seniority made **b** a difference. It would be contrary to the principle underlying s 12(1) which makes a constable individually responsible for the arrest and accountable in law. In *R v Chief Constable of the Devon and Cornwall Constabulary, ex p Central Electricity Generating Board* [1981] 3 All ER 826 at 835, [1982] QB 458 at 474 Lawton LJ touched on this point. He observed:

c   '... [chief constables] cannot give an officer under command an order to do acts which can only lawfully be done if the officer himself with reasonable cause suspects that a breach of the peace has occurred or is imminently likely to occur or an arrestable offence has been committed.'

Such an order to arrest cannot without some further information being given **d** to the constable be sufficient to afford the constable reasonable grounds for the necessary suspicion. That seems to me to be the legal position in respect of a provision such as s 12(1). For these reasons, I regard the submission of counsel for the chief constable as unsound in law. In practice, it follows that a constable must be given some basis for a request to arrest somebody under a provision such as s 12(1), e g a report from an informer.

e   Subject to these observations, I agree that the appeal ought to be dismissed.

LORD HOFFMANN. My Lords, I have had the advantage of reading in draft the speeches prepared by my noble and learned friends Lord Steyn and Lord Hope of Craighead. I agree with both and I, too, would dismiss the appeal.

f

LORD HOPE OF CRAIGHEAD. My Lords, at about 6.15 a m on 28 December 1985 police officers entered the plaintiff's house at 72 Duncreggan Road, Londonderry and conducted a search of the premises. At the conclusion of the search, at about 8.05 a m, they arrested the plaintiff under s 12(1)(b) of the Prevention of Terrorism (Temporary Provisions) Act 1984. They took him to **g** Castlereagh Police Office, where the police questioned him in a series of interviews. On 29 December 1985 an order was made by the Secretary of State under s 12(4) of the 1984 Act extending the period of 48 hours provided by that subsection by five days. On 13 January 1986 the plaintiff was released without being charged either then or subsequently with any offence. Later that year he **h** brought an action for damages against the chief constable for various tortious acts said to have been committed against him by the police officers, including wrongful arrest, assault and unlawful confiscation of documents.

On 14 September 1990, following a trial which took place on 16 and 17 January 1989, the trial judge, McCollum J, in a reserved judgment dismissed all the **j** plaintiff's claims except his claim for the unlawful confiscation of documents. He ordered the documents to be returned to the plaintiff and that a sum of £100 be paid to him as compensation for their confiscation. He was not satisfied on balance of probabilities that the plaintiff had been assaulted during his detention at Castlereagh Police Office. No appeal has been taken against his decision on either of these points. In regard to the claim for wrongful arrest, the trial judge held that the plaintiff's arrest had been lawful. This was because he was satisfied

on the evidence of Det Con Stewart, who was the arresting officer, that he was
entitled to arrest the plaintiff without warrant under s 12(1)(b) of the 1984 Act   *a*
because he had reasonable grounds for suspecting the plaintiff to be a person who
had been concerned in the commission, preparation or instigation of acts of
terrorism. On 6 May 1994 the Court of Appeal (Kelly LJ, Pringle and Higgins JJ)
upheld the decision of the trial judge and dismissed the appeal. The plaintiff has
now appealed with leave to this House.   *b*

The 1984 Act expired on 21 March 1989 and has been replaced by the
Prevention of Terrorism (Temporary Provisions) Act 1989. Section 12(1) of the
1984 Act—see now s 14(1) of the 1989 Act—is in these terms:

> 'Subject to subsection (2) below, a constable may arrest without warrant a
> person whom he has reasonable grounds for suspecting to be—(a) a person   *c*
> guilty of an offence under section 1, 9 or 10 above; (b) a person who is or has
> been concerned in the commission, preparation or instigation of acts of
> terrorism to which this Part of this Act applies; (c) a person subject to an
> exclusion order.'

d

Det Con Stewart said in his evidence that at 5.30 am on 28 December 1985 he
attended a briefing at Strand Road Police Station. The purpose of the briefing was
to mount an operation to search houses and to arrest a number of people in
connection with the murder of Mr Kurt Koenig about two months previously. It
was common ground that the murder of Kurt Koenig, which had been
committed in Londonderry in November 1985, was an act of terrorism within the   *e*
meaning of s 12(1) of the 1984 Act. The briefing was conducted by Insp Brown
and it was attended by a number of other police officers. The purpose of the
search was to look for weapons or other evidence. Det Con Stewart went with a
search party to 72 Duncreggan Road to carry out a search there, to arrest the
plaintiff and to convey him to Castlereagh Police Office. He said that his   *f*
reasonable grounds for suspecting that the plaintiff was involved in the murder
were based on the briefing which he had received, in the course of which he was
told that the plaintiff had been involved in the murder and was also told to arrest
him. When he arrested the plaintiff under s 12(1)(b) of the 1984 Act, he told him
that he suspected him of having been concerned in the commission, preparation
or instigation of acts of terrorism. In cross-examination he said that he had no   *g*
other basis for the suspicion apart from what he had been told at the briefing, and
that he did not specify any particular offence when he was arresting the plaintiff.
Neither party sought to elicit from him the details of the information which the
briefing officer had disclosed to him and the briefing officer, Insp Brown, did not
give evidence.   *h*

The trial judge noted that the burden of proving that the arrest was lawful was
on the chief constable. He found on the evidence that burden had been satisfied,
for the reasons expressed in the following passage of his judgment:

> 'I would not wish to lay down the proposition that reasonable suspicion   *j*
> could in all circumstances be based on the opinion of another officer
> expressed without any supporting allegations of fact. But it does seem to me
> that a briefing officially given by a superior officer would give reasonable
> grounds for suspicion of the matters stated therein. The fact that I have such
> scanty evidence of the matters disclosed to Det Con Stewart means that I am
> only just satisfied of the legality of the arrest, but I am fortified in my view by

a the lack of detailed challenge in cross-examination as to the nature of the information given to him.'

The judgment of the Court of Appeal was delivered by Kelly LJ, who said that, although the information given at the briefing to the arresting officer was 'scanty', to use the words of the trial judge, it was sufficient to constitute the required state of mind of an arresting officer under s 12(1)(b) of the 1984 Act.

b My Lords, it is important to observe that the position of the arresting officer was not simply that he had been told to arrest the plaintiff. Nor was it that he had simply been told that the plaintiff had been concerned in the commission, preparation or instigation of acts of terrorism. His position, as stated by him in evidence, was that he suspected the plaintiff of having been concerned in such c acts, and that his suspicion was based on the briefing which had been given to him by his superior officer. The trial judge accepted the arresting officer's evidence on both points. The question is whether he was entitled also to hold that the arresting officer had reasonable grounds for this suspicion, as the only evidence about these grounds was what the arresting officer himself said about them in the witness box.

d The plaintiff maintains that s 12(1)(b) requires proof not only that the arresting officer had the suspicion which that subsection requires but also that the reasonable grounds on which he based his suspicion existed in fact. It is said that, in order to prove that the alleged grounds were reasonable in the objective sense, the chief constable must prove that reasonable grounds for the suspicion did e exist, not only that the arresting officer had knowledge of them at the time of the arrest. As he developed these arguments, however, Mr Kennedy QC accepted that it was not necessary for a prima facie case to be established, nor was it necessary for the evidence about the grounds for the suspicion to disclose the sources of that evidence. He accepted that the police were entitled to proceed upon hearsay evidence, and that evidence which could give rise to a reasonable f suspicion might turn out later to be wrong. But he said that it was necessary nevertheless for the court to be given some evidence, in addition to that of the arresting officer, to enable it to hold that reasonable grounds existed. The objective test required proof of something more than what was in the mind of the arresting officer.

g Mr Kennedy based his submissions on Lord Atkin's well-known observation in his dissenting speech in *Liversidge v Anderson* [1941] 3 All ER 338 at 362, [1942] AC 206 at 245 that one of the pillars of liberty in English law is the principle that 'every imprisonment is prima facie unlawful, and that it is for a person directing imprisonment to justify his act'. He referred also to *Dallison v Caffery* [1964] 2 All h ER 610 at 619, [1965] 1 QB 348 at 370, where Diplock LJ said:

'Since arrest involves trespass to the person and any trespass to the person is prima facie tortious, the onus lies on the arrestor to justify the trespass by establishing reasonable and probable cause for the arrest.'

j He described the powers given by s 12 of the 1984 Act as unique, especially in view of the length of time the suspect could be detained in custody after his arrest. He drew our attention to the fact that in *Ex p Lynch* [1980] NI 126 at 132–133 Lord Lowry LCJ described the observations of the Supreme Court of Ireland when considering a reference by the President of Ireland in *Re Emergency Powers Bill 1976 (Article 26 of the Constitution)* [1977] IR 159 as an impeccable statement of the rules which ought to be applied both in interpreting the meaning of emergency

legislation which abridges the liberty of the subject and in judging the validity of
acts purporting to be done under its authority.   What O'Higgins CJ said, under   *a*
reference to the powers to be given by s 2 of that Bill, was this (at 173):

> 'A statutory provision of this nature which makes such inroads upon the
> liberty of the person must be strictly construed. Any arrest sought to be
> justified by the section must be in strict conformity with it. No such arrest   *b*
> may be justified by importing into the section incidents or characteristics of
> an arrest which are not expressly or by necessary implication authorised by
> the section.'

It is plain that s 12(1) of the 1984 Act makes provision for the circumstances in
which a person may be deprived of his liberty. But I do not accept Mr Kennedy's
suggestion that it is a unique provision, notwithstanding the power in sub-s (4)   *c*
which enables the period of detention to be extended by five days after the initial
period of 48 hours. Powers of arrest or detention which may be exercised where
a constable has reasonable grounds for suspecting that a person is committing or
has committed an offence are far from unique in our legislation. Section 24(6) of
the Police and Criminal Evidence Act 1984, for example, provides that where a   *d*
constable has reasonable grounds for suspecting that an arrestable offence has
been committed, he may arrest without a warrant anyone whom he has
reasonable grounds for suspecting to be guilty of the offence. A similar provision
is to be found in s 14(1) of the Criminal Procedure (Scotland) Act 1995, which
provides that where a constable has reasonable grounds for suspecting that a
person has committed or is committing an offence punishable by imprisonment,   *e*
the constable may detain that person for questioning at a police station.

Provisions to the same effect have been part of our law for more than half a
century (see e g s 10(2) of the Children and Young Persons Act 1933 and s 7(3) of
the Public Order Act 1936).   Other familiar examples of similar legislation
affecting the liberty of the person are to be found in s 23(2)(a) of the Misuse of   *f*
Drugs Act 1971, which enables a constable to search any person whom he has
reasonable grounds for suspecting to be in possession of a controlled drug and to
detain him for the purpose of searching him, and s 6(1) of the Road Traffic Act
1988, which enables any constable to require a person whom he has reasonable
cause to suspect of driving or attempting to drive a motor vehicle with alcohol in
his body to provide a specimen of breath for a breath test and, in the   *g*
circumstances provided for by sub-s (5), without warrant to arrest him. It is now
commonplace for Parliament to enable powers which may interfere with the
liberty of the person to be exercised without warrant where the person who
exercises these powers has reasonable grounds for suspecting that the person
against whom they are to be exercised has committed or is committing an   *h*
offence. The protection of the subject lies in the nature of the test which has to
be applied in order to determine whether the requirement that there be
reasonable grounds for the suspicion is satisfied.

My Lords, the test which s 12(1) of the 1984 Act has laid down is a simple but
practical one. It relates entirely to what is in the mind of the arresting officer   *j*
when the power is exercised. In part it is a subjective test, because he must have
formed a genuine suspicion in his own mind that the person has been concerned
in acts of terrorism. In part also it is an objective one, because there must also be
reasonable grounds for the suspicion which he has formed. But the application
of the objective test does not require the court to look beyond what was in the
mind of the arresting officer. It is the grounds which were in his mind at the time

a which must be found to be reasonable grounds for the suspicion which he has formed. All that the objective test requires is that these grounds be examined objectively and that they be judged at the time when the power was exercised. This means that the point does not depend on whether the arresting officer himself thought at that time that they were reasonable. The question is whether a reasonable man would be of that opinion, having regard to the information

b which was in the mind of the arresting officer. It is the arresting officer's own account of the information which he had which matters, not what was observed by or known to anyone else. The information acted on by the arresting officer need not be based on his own observations, as he is entitled to form a suspicion based on what he has been told. His reasonable suspicion may be based on information which has been given to him anonymously or it may be based on

c information, perhaps in the course of an emergency, which turns out later to be wrong. As it is the information which is in his mind alone which is relevant however, it is not necessary to go on to prove what was known to his informant or that any facts on which he based his suspicion were in fact true. The question whether it provided reasonable grounds for the suspicion depends on the source

d of his information and its context, seen in the light of the whole surrounding circumstances.

This approach to the wording of s 12(1) of the 1984 Act is consistent with authority. In *Dallison v Caffery* [1964] 2 All ER 610, [1965] 1 QB 348, which preceded the enactment of s 2(4) of the Criminal Law Act 1967, the arrest had been effected in the exercise of the common law power. Diplock LJ's description

e of the test to be applied does, however, provide a useful starting point for the examination of the power which has been given by the statute. What he said was ([1964] 2 All ER 610 at 619, [1965] 1 QB 348 at 371):

> 'The test whether there was reasonable and probable cause for the arrest
> f   or prosecution is an objective one, namely, whether a reasonable man,
> assumed to know the law and possessed of the information which in fact was
> possessed by the defendant, would believe that there was reasonable and
> probable cause.'

In *McKee v Chief Constable for Northern Ireland* [1985] 1 All ER 1, [1984] 1 WLR
g 1358 the appellant had been arrested by the constable under s 11 of the Northern Ireland (Emergency Provisions) Act 1978. That section provided, not that the constable had to have reasonable grounds for suspecting, but simply that: 'Any constable may arrest without warrant any person whom he suspects of being a terrorist.' It was held that the suspicion had to be honestly held, but that it need not be a reasonable suspicion. Section 11 of that Act was, of course, subsequently

h repealed and replaced by s 12 of the 1984 Act, which requires that the suspicion be based on reasonable grounds. Nevertheless, I believe that despite the difference in wording, Lord Roskill's words when he emphasised that what matters is what was in the mind of the arresting officer, remain relevant:

> j   'On the true construction of s 11(1) of the [Emergency Powers Act 1978],
> what matters is the state of mind of the arresting officer and of no one else.
> That state of mind can legitimately be derived from the instruction given to
> the arresting officer by his superior officer. The arresting officer is not bound
> and indeed may well not be entitled to question those instructions or to ask
> on what information they are founded. It is, in my view, not legitimate in
> the light of the trial judge's findings as to Pc Graham's state of mind at the

time of the arrest to seek to go behind that finding and deduce from Det Con
Moody's evidence as to questioning which took place some time after the   *a*
arrest what Sgt Jackson's state of mind may have been when he gave Pc
Graham his instructions. It is Pc Graham's state of mind that matters and
that alone.' (See [1985] 1 All ER 1 at 4, [1984] 1 WLR 1358 at 1361–1362.)

In *Hanna v Chief Constable, Royal Ulster Constabulary* [1986] NI 103 at 108
Carswell J said: *b*

'It was argued that because a person who wrongfully directs another to
arrest a third is liable in tort to the arrested person for damages, it follows
that the existence and reasonableness of the suspicion of the senior officer
who gave orders to the arrestor to arrest the plaintiff must be relevant. This
is in my view a non sequitur. It is of course correct that if A orders B   *c*
(whether B be a policeman or not) to arrest C, it is an imprisonment by A as
well as B, and if it is unjustified C can sue A for false imprisonment: see such
cases as *Wheeler v Whiting* ((1840) 9 C & P 262, 173 ER 828). I do not consider
that it follows that one has to consider in the context of arrests under
section 12 of the 1984 Act the mind of anyone but the actual arrestor. In my   *d*
view the wording of section 12(1) is intended to refer only to the arrestor
himself, and it is his suspicion alone which is material, and not that of any
person by whom he was given instructions.'

He said that he was satisfied that in considering the existence of a reasonable
suspicion he should look solely at the evidence relating to the mind of the   *e*
arresting officer (see [1986] NI 103 at 109).

He returned to the same point in *Brady v Chief Constable of the Royal Ulster
Constabulary* (15 February 1991, unreported). In that case, the plaintiff who had
been arrested in Londonderry on the same day as the plaintiff in the present case
had also claimed damages for unlawful arrest and false imprisonment. The
arresting officer said that he had attended a briefing by a police superintendent in   *f*
which he was instructed to arrest the plaintiff at his home address and that the
reason for his arrest was that he had been involved in the murder of Kurt Koenig.
Detailed evidence was given in that case by senior CID officers about their
possession of information about the part which the plaintiff was believed to have
taken in the murder. Carswell J made this comment on the evidence: *g*

'If it were material, I should hold that each reasonably suspected that [the
plaintiff] had been involved in planning the murder. Since it is the arresting
officer's suspicion which alone is relevant, however, I consider that the belief
of those other officers does not operate to strengthen or weaken the
genuineness or reasonableness of the former's suspicion except in so far as it   *h*
may tend to confirm or contradict his account of what he was told at the
briefing. Constable McGonigle was told by a senior officer at an arrest
briefing that the plaintiff had been involved in Koenig's murder. I accept that
the constable believed what he was told and I hold that he entertained a
genuine suspicion that the plaintiff had played some part in the murder. I   *j*
also hold that it was reasonable for Constable McGonigle to form that
suspicion in the circumstances. An arrest operation had been planned, in
which a number of persons were to be arrested. A senior officer held a
briefing session for the uniformed officers who were to carry out the arrests,
in the course of which he told them the reasons for arresting each person.
When he told Constable McGonigle that the plaintiff was to be arrested

a   because he was involved in Koenig's murder, it was in my opinion reasonable for the constable to accept that and to suspect the plaintiff of being concerned in a terrorist murder.'

The same approach has been taken in the context of other statutory powers where the question has been raised whether the constable who exercised the power had reasonable grounds to suspect that an offence had been committed.

b   In *Castorina v Chief Constable of Surrey* (1988) Times, 15 June, which was concerned with s 2(4) of the Criminal Law Act 1967, Sir Frederick Lawton said:

'Suspicion by itself, however, will not justify an arrest. There must be a factual basis for it of a kind which a court would adjudge to be reasonable. The facts may be within the arresting constable's own knowledge or have

c   been reported to him. When there is an issue in a trial as to whether a constable had reasonable cause, his claim to have had knowledge or to have received reports on which he relied may be challenged. It is within this context that there may be an evidential issue as to what he believed to be the facts, but it will be for the court to adjudge what were the facts which made

d   him suspect that the person he arrested was guilty of the offence which he was investigating.'

In *Dryburgh v Galt* 1981 JC 69 at 72, in a case which was concerned with the question whether police officers had reasonable cause to suspect that the appellant had alcohol in his body while he was driving, having received an

e   anonymous telephone message to that effect, the Lord Justice Clerk (Wheatley) said:

'Suffice it to say that the fact that the information on which the police officer formed his suspicion turns out to be ill-founded does not in itself necessarily establish that the police officer's suspicion was unfounded. The

f   circumstances known to the police officer at the time he formed his suspicion constitute the criterion, not the facts as subsequently ascertained. The circumstances may be either what the police officer has himself observed or the information which he has received.'

g   *Copeland v McPherson* 1970 SLT 87 shows how the question whether the constable had reasonable cause to suspect may arise in a case where the exercise of the power is the result of co-operation between several police officers. The respondent in that case was driving along a road when he was stopped by two plain clothes police officers. They noticed a smell of alcohol on his breath, so they sent for uniformed police officers and breath sampling equipment for the

h   carrying out of a roadside breath test. The respondent refused to provide a sample of his breath when he was required to do so by the uniformed officers. He was removed to a police station where he again refused to provide a breath sample. He was charged with offences under s 2(3) of the Road Safety Act 1967. He was acquitted by the sheriff on the ground that the uniformed police officers

j   had not seen the respondent driving or attempting to drive before they required him to submit to the breath test. On appeal by the prosecutor it was held that the uniformed police officers had reasonable cause to suspect the respondent of having alcohol in his body and that, as it was conceded that the respondent at the time was a person who came within the category of a person driving a motor vehicle, they were acting within their powers when they required the respondent to provide a sample of his breath. Lord Cameron rejected the respondent's

contention that reasonable cause could not exist in any case in which the
uniformed police officers did not themselves see the person suspected himself   a
driving or attempting to drive the motor car. He pointed out that to hold
otherwise would involve that a uniformed constable could never act in such a
case on information received, however compelling and reliable in quality and
source. He went on to say (at 90):

> 'The issue then becomes purely one of fact: the findings in the case, in my   b
> opinion, clearly support the conclusion that the uniformed police officers
> who were called to the scene at the request of their plain clothes colleagues
> had such reasonable cause. No doubt the "reasonable cause" must have
> arisen in the mind of the officer before he makes the statutory request of a
> person in the necessary category but when, as here, uniformed officers are   c
> called on by plain clothes colleagues to attend on a driver whose conduct has
> led to such a call and for so obvious a reason as is found in this case, I think
> that in such circumstances the uniformed officers have in fact very
> reasonable cause for suspicion that the driver has alcohol in his body.'

Many other examples may be cited of cases where the action of the constable   d
who exercises a statutory power of arrest or of search is a member of a team of
police officers, or where his action is the culmination of various steps taken by
other police officers, perhaps over a long period and perhaps also involving
officers from other police forces. For obvious practical reasons police officers
must be able to rely upon each other in taking decisions as to whom to arrest or
where to search and in what circumstances. The statutory power does not   e
require that the constable who exercises the power must be in possession of all
the information which has led to a decision, perhaps taken by others, that the
time has come for it to be exercised. What it does require is that the constable
who exercises the power must first have equipped himself with sufficient
information so that he has reasonable cause to suspect before the power is   f
exercised.

I should add that I see no conflict in principle between the approach which has
been taken in these cases and the judgment of the European Court of Human
Rights in *Fox v UK* (1990) 13 EHRR 157 to which we were referred by Mr
Kennedy. The applicants had been detained without warrant under s 11 of the
Northern Ireland (Emergency Provisions) Act 1978. As has already been noted,   g
this section provided for the arrest without warrant of any person whom a
constable suspected of being a terrorist. It was held that as the constable's
suspicion had not been shown to be reasonable, the United Kingdom were in
breach of art 5(1) of the European Convention for the Protection of Human
Rights and Fundamental Freedoms (Rome, 4 November 1950; TS 71 (1953); Cmd   h
8969), which provides:

> 'Everyone has the right to liberty and security of person. No one shall be
> deprived of his liberty save in the following cases and in accordance with a
> procedure prescribed by law ... c. the lawful arrest or detention of a person
> effected for the purpose of bringing him before the competent legal   j
> authority on reasonable suspicion of having committed an offence ...'

In that case the arrest and detention of the applicants was based on a suspicion
which was bona fide or genuine (see 13 EHRR 157 at 169 (para 35)). But the court
held that the government had not provided sufficient material to support the
conclusion that the suspicion was reasonable, and that its explanations did not

a meet the minimum standard set by art 5(1)(c) for judging the reasonableness of a suspicion for the arrest of an individual. As to what these requirements are, they are to be found in the following passage in the judgment (13 EHRR 157 at 167 (para 32)):

b '32. The "reasonableness" of the suspicion on which an arrest must be based forms an essential part of the safeguard against arbitrary arrest and detention which is laid down in Article 5(1)c. The Court agrees with the Commission and the Government that having a "reasonable suspicion" presupposes the existence of facts or information which would satisfy an objective observer that the person concerned may have committed the offence. What may be regarded as "reasonable" will however depend upon
c all the circumstances.'

What Parliament has enacted in s 12(1)(b) of the 1984 Act, as in the other statutes to which I have referred, is that the reasonable suspicion has to be in the mind of the arresting officer. So it is the facts known by or the information given to the officer who effects the arrest or detention to which the mind of the
d independent observer must be applied. It is this objective test, applying the criterion of what may be regarded as reasonable, which provides the safeguard against arbitrary arrest and detention. The arrest and detention will be unlawful unless this criterion is satisfied.

My Lords, in this case the evidence about the matters which were disclosed at the briefing session to the arresting officer was indeed scanty. But, as Mr
e Coghlin QC pointed out, the trial judge was entitled to weigh up that evidence in the light of the surrounding circumstances and, having regard to the source of that information, to draw inferences as to what a reasonable man, in the position of the independent observer, would make of it. I do not think that either the trial judge or the Court of Appeal misdirected themselves as to the test to be applied.
f I would dismiss this appeal.

Appeal dismissed.

Celia Fox   Barrister.

Credit Lyonnais Bank Nederland NV v Burch

COURT OF APPEAL, CIVIL DIVISION

NOURSE, MILLETT AND SWINTON THOMAS LJJ

1 MAY, 20 JUNE 1996

Equity – Undue influence – Presumption of undue influence – Employer and employee – Employer requesting junior employee to mortgage flat as security for increase in company's bank overdraft – Bank requiring unlimited all moneys guarantee – Employee not told of amount of overdraft – Bank advising employee to take independent legal advice – Employee not doing so – Company going into liquidation – Bank suing for possession of employee's home – Whether guarantee procured by employer's undue influence – Whether relationship of trust and confidence between employer and employee – Whether presumption of undue influence arising – Whether bank rebutting presumption – Whether advice to seek independent legal advice sufficient to exonerate bank.

The defendant was employed in a junior capacity at a modest wage by a tour operating company which wished to increase its bank overdraft limit from £250,000 to £270,000. P, the main shareholder and alter ego of the company, asked the defendant to provide the security required by the bank for the increased overdraft by giving a second charge over her flat and an unlimited all moneys guarantee. The flat was valued at £100,000 and the defendant's equity was £70,000. The defendant signed the mortgage document in P's presence at the offices of the bank's solicitors. At no time was the defendant informed either by P or the bank of the company's indebtedness to the bank or the extent of the overdraft facility being granted. The bank's solicitors wrote to the defendant pointing out that the guarantee was unlimited both in time and amount and advising her to seek independent legal advice before entering into the transaction but she did not do so. The company later went into liquidation and when the bank was unable to recoup from P the full amount owing on the overdraft, it demanded payment of the amount outstanding, some £60,000, from the defendant and when the defendant failed to pay it, issued proceedings in the county court for possession of the defendant's flat. The county court judge found that there was a relationship of trust and confidence between P and the defendant which gave rise to a presumption of undue influence which had not been rebutted and dismissed the action and set aside the bank's charge over her property. The bank appealed to the Court of Appeal, contending that it had discharged its duty to the defendant by urging her to seek independent legal advice and that it was not responsible for the consequences of her choosing not to do so.

Held – The transaction was so manifestly disadvantageous to the defendant, in that without knowing the extent of the liability involved she had committed herself to a liability far beyond her means and risked the loss of her home and personal bankruptcy to help a company in which she had no financial interest and of which she was only a junior employee, that the presumption of undue influence on the part of P was irresistible. The bank had not taken reasonable steps to avoid being fixed with constructive notice of that undue influence, since neither the potential extent of her liability had been explained to her nor had she a received independent advice. It was not sufficient for the bank's solicitors to tell her that the guarantee was unlimited both in time and amount since without being informed of the amount of the company's indebtedness to the bank or the extent of the overdraft facility being granted she was in no position to assess the significance of the guarantee being unlimited. Nor was it sufficient for the bank's solicitors to advise her to seek independent legal advice since, in the

b circumstances, the bank was required to ensure that she obtained independent legal advice. The bank was aware that the relationship between P and the defendant was that of employer and employee and should have been aware that it was capable of developing into a relationship of trust and confidence with the attendant risk of abuse. The fact that the defendant chose not to seek independent legal advice should have alerted the bank to the possibility that the

c defendant was acting under the undue influence of P. Accordingly, the transaction had properly been set aside. The appeal would therefore be dismissed (see p 151 h to p 152 j, p 154 e to h, p 155 e, p 156 j to p 157 a e to h and p 158 b f to j, post).

Barclays Bank plc v O'Brien [1993] 4 All ER 417 applied.

d Per Millett LJ. Taking independent legal advice is neither always necessary nor always sufficient to rebut the presumption of undue influence. As between the complainant and the alleged wrongdoer, the presumption cannot be rebutted merely by evidence that the complainant understood what he or she was doing and intended to do it; but only by showing that the complainant was either free from any undue influence on his part or had been placed, by the receipt of

e independent advice, in an equivalent position. That involves showing that the complainant was advised as to the propriety of the transaction by an adviser fully informed of all the material facts. It is not sufficient that the complainant received independent advice unless she has acted on that advice and the solicitor must not be content to satisfy himself that his client understands the transaction and wishes

f to carry it out. His duty is to satisfy himself that the transaction is one which his client could sensibly enter into if free from improper influence; and if he is not so satisfied, to advise her not to enter into it, and to refuse to act further for her if she persists. He must advise his client that she is under no obligation to enter into the transaction at all and, if she still wishes to do so, that she is not necessarily bound to accept the terms of any document which has been put before her but

g (where this is appropriate) that he should ascertain on her behalf whether less onerous terms might be obtained (see p 155 j to p 156 h, post).

Notes

h For the avoidance of a guarantee procured by undue influence, see 20 *Halsbury's Laws* (4th edn reissue) paras 133–139, and for cases on the subject, see 26(1) *Digest* (2nd reissue) 95–99, 312–325.

Cases referred to in judgments

j *Alec Lobb (Garages) Ltd v Total Oil GB Ltd* [1983] 1 All ER 944, [1983] 1 WLR 87; *rvsd in part* [1985] 1 All ER 303, [1985] 1 WLR 13, CA.

Avon Finance Co Ltd v Bridger (1979) [1985] 2 All ER 281, CA.

Aylesford (Earl) v Morris (1873) LR 8 Ch App 484, [1861–73] All ER Rep 300.

Backhouse v Backhouse [1978] 1 All ER 1158, [1978] 1 WLR 243.

Bank of Credit and Commerce International SA v Aboody [1992] 4 All ER 955, [1990] 1 QB 923, [1989] 2 WLR 759, CA.

Barclays Bank plc v O'Brien [1993] 4 All ER 417, [1994] 1 AC 180, [1993] 3 WLR 786,
HL.
Bester v Perpetual Trustee Co Ltd [1970] 3 NSWLR 30, NSW SC.
Brusewitz v Brown (1922) 42 NZLR 1106, NZ SC.
Cresswell v Potter [1978] 1 WLR 255n.
Fry v Lane, re Fry, Whittet v Bush (1889) 40 Ch D 312, [1886–90] All ER Rep 1084.
Huguenin v Baseley (1807) 14 Ves 273, [1803–13] All ER Rep 1, 33 ER 526, LC.
Lloyds Bank Ltd v Bundy [1974] 3 All ER 757, [1975] QB 326, [1974] 3 WLR 501, CA.
Multiservice Bookbinding Ltd v Marden [1978] 2 All ER 489, [1979] Ch 84, [1978] 2
WLR 535.
Permanent Trustee Co of New South Wales Ltd v Bridgewater [1936] 3 All ER 501, PC.
Powell v Powell [1900] 1 Ch 243.

Cases also cited or referred to in skeleton arguments
Bainbrigge v Browne (1881) 18 Ch D 188.
Bank Melli Iran v Samadi-Rad [1995] 1 FCR 465; *rvsd* [1995] 3 FCR 735, CA.
Chaplin & Co Ltd v Brammall [1908] 1 KB 233, CA.
Craig (decd), Re, Meneces v Middleton [1970] 2 All ER 390, [1971] Ch 95.
Horry v Tate & Lyle Refineries Ltd [1982] 2 Lloyd's Rep 416.
Massey v Midland Bank plc [1995] 1 All ER 929, CA.
O'Sullivan v Management Agency and Music Ltd [1985] 3 All ER 351, [1985] QB 428,
CA.
Turnbull & Co v Duval [1902] AC 429, PC.

Appeal
By notice dated 11 December 1995, the plaintiff bank, Credit Lyonnais Bank
Nederland NV, appealed from the decision of Mr Recorder Harrod at Willesden
County Court on 14 November 1995, setting aside a deed of mortgage and
guarantee entered into between the bank and the defendant, Helen Burch, and
dismissing the bank's application for possession of the mortgaged property. The
facts are set out in the judgment of Nourse LJ.

Kathryn Purkis (instructed by *Blake Lapthorn*, Fareham) for the bank.
Yvonne Green (instructed by *Beauchamps*) for Miss Burch.

Cur adv vult

20 June 1996. The following judgments were delivered.

NOURSE LJ. This is a case in which it is sought to set aside a mortgage of
residential property given as security for another's debt on the ground that it was
procured by the undue influence of the debtor over the mortgagor of which the
mortgagee had notice. Thus, although the relationship between the debtor and
the mortgagor was not that of persons living together but employer and
employee, it may broadly be said to fall under *Barclays Bank plc v O'Brien* [1993] 4
All ER 417, [1994] 1 AC 180. At the same time, the terms of the mortgage were
so harsh and unconscionable as to make it hardly necessary for a court of equity
to rely on that decision as a basis for avoiding the transaction.
    It is convenient to start by stating those of the facts, as agreed or found by Mr
Recorder Harrod in the court below, which are no longer in dispute. I can do so
mainly in the recorder's own words. In 1982 the defendant, Helen Burch, then

a aged 18, began to work for companies controlled by an Italian national called Andrea Pelosi. He was ten years older than she and she trusted him. She knew him to be a successful businessman and visited his substantial house in Gerrards Cross and his large villa in Italy. Her links with him were close. In addition to working for him during the day, she did baby-sitting at his home in the evenings and visited the family at weekends and for holidays in Italy. By the summer of 1990 Miss Burch was working for a company called A P International Travel Ltd (API), which carried on Mr Pelosi's tour operating business. It was a very demanding job and she was deeply involved in it. At that time, she had almost no life apart from her work and was often there until 10 pm.

In 1985 Miss Burch, with the assistance of a mortgage from the Halifax Building Society, had acquired a lease for 125 years from 25 March 1970 at an annual ground rent of £25 rising to £45, of a second floor one-bedroomed flat and garage at 8 Cornerways, Sudbury Court Road, Wembley, Middlesex. In about June 1990, API being in financial difficulties, Mr Pelosi asked Miss Burch to put up her property as collateral security for its overdraft with the plaintiff, Credit Lyonnais Bank Nederland NV (the bank). She agreed to do so.

In evidence before the recorder was an internal memorandum of the bank from Mr David Herod, the manager of its London office, to Mr D Jones, in which it was stated that API required a facility of £270,000 as opposed to the £250,000 they were then working to. Mr Herod added that the bank was offered additional security in the form of a charge on Miss Burch's property, which was valued at £100,000 but was subject to a first mortgage of £30,000.

On 5 July 1990 the bank wrote to Messrs Belmont & Lowe, solicitors, informing them that Miss Burch had agreed to grant a second legal charge over the property to secure the borrowing of API and asking them to act for it on its behalf in connection with the transaction. Enclosed with the letter was the bank's standard form of third party legal mortgage. The letter stated: 'Miss Burch should, of course, be advised to take independent legal advice.'

On 9 July Belmont & Lowe replied, accepting the instructions. The recorder thought that they had probably been suggested by Mr Pelosi to the bank because they had offices in London EC1, close to his own place of business.

Also on 9 July Mr Martyn Whaley, a partner in Belmont & Lowe, wrote to Miss Burch at 8 Cornerways, informing her that they had been instructed by the bank in relation to the second legal charge over her home. He said:

'Strictly speaking our instructions are to act for the bank. We must advise you that you should take separate legal advice upon the documentation you will be asked to sign and the underlying reasons behind the request and of course the potential risks you may face ... Finally although I am acting for the bank I feel I must mention to you the fact that the document that you are being asked to sign is unlimited both in amount and in time. Is this actually what has been agreed?'

On 16 July Mr Whaley telephoned Miss Burch and told her that he was unable to proceed until he received the title deeds from the Halifax Building Society. On the same day he wrote to her, referring to that conversation and his letter of 9 July. He said:

'Could I please ask you to let me have written confirmation that notwithstanding what I have said in my letter of 9th July you still wish to proceed in this matter and that you will be taking separate legal advice on the

documentation involved. I do not want to labour the point but you should
be aware that the document you are being asked to sign is unlimited both in   *a*
time and in amount and there is no provision or agreement so far as I am
aware relating to you being released by the bank at any time in the near
future. I look forward to hearing from you.'

On 17 July Mr Whaley wrote to Mr Pelosi, asking for £50 on account of search   *b*
fees as quickly as possible. On 18 July Mr Pelosi replied, enclosing a cheque for
£50 as requested. The letter ended:

'I would like to thank you for your kind co-operation, and I would be
grateful if you could do your utmost to expedite the completion of this
matter.'   *c*

That letter was typed or printed on headed writing paper showing Mr Pelosi's
business address in London EC1.

Also on 18 July Miss Burch signed a typed or printed letter addressed to Mr
Whaley, bearing her own address at 8 Cornerways. Although the recorder made
no finding on the point, this letter appears to have been typed or printed on the   *d*
same instrument as Mr Pelosi's letter of the same date. It reads:

'Thank you for your letter of 16 July, the contents of which I have noted.
With reference to your letter of 9 July, I would like to confirm that I am fully
aware of the implication of offering my property as a collateral for the
increased overdraft facilities made available by CL Bank Nederland to AP   *e*
International Travel Ltd. I also understand that such guarantee is unlimited
both in time and amount, and I wish to offer such guarantee on this basis. I
further understand from your recent conversation with Mr Pelosi that there
is no objections to myself signing the necessary documents prior to the
completion of your searches, and to this effect I would be grateful if you   *f*
could call me on Tel 071 278 5319, to arrange a suitable time for me to come
to your office.'

The recorder found that Miss Burch had discussed Mr Whaley's letters to her of
9 and 16 July with Mr Pelosi and that he either prepared her reply of 18 July for
her or told her the effect of what he wanted her to say.   *g*

On Friday, 20 July Miss Burch went with Mr Pelosi to Belmont & Lowe's
offices nearby and executed the legal charge. On Monday, 23 July Mr Whaley
wrote to Miss Burch:

'RE: A P INTERNATIONAL TRAVEL LIMITED I refer to our meeting last week. I   *h*
have now spoken to CL Bank Nederland in relation to the Charge and they
have confirmed what I told you and that is to say that the Charge is both
unlimited in time and in amount. The Charge is to back a facility granted to
AP International Travel Limited which is reviewed yearly.'

The transaction was completed on 3 August, the legal charge being dated   *j*
accordingly. By 10 August Belmont & Lowe's fees had been duly paid, either by
API or by Mr Pelosi himself. On 12 October 1990 Belmont & Lowe wrote to the
Halifax Building Society informing them that registration of the legal charge had
been completed.

The legal charge, which was executed in the standard form sent by the bank to
Belmont & Lowe on 5 July, was made between Miss Burch as mortgagor of the

a   one part and the bank as mortgagee of the other part. The obligations assumed
by Miss Burch were onerous in the extreme. The first part of cl 2 provides:

'[Miss Burch] HEREBY COVENANTS with the Bank to pay satisfy and
discharge to the Bank on demand all such sums of money and liabilities
whether certain or contingent which are now or at any time hereafter may
be due owing or incurred by [API] to the Bank or for which [API] may be or
b   become liable on any current or other account or in any manner whatever
and whether alone or jointly with any other or others in partnership or
otherwise and in whatever names style or firm and whether as principal
surety or otherwise anywhere upon any account or in respect of bills of
exchange cheques notes or other instruments drawn endorsed or accepted
c   by [API] or for any other reason whatsoever together with interest to the
date of repayment commission banking charges legal and other costs charges
and expenses ...'

Clause 3 provides for the bank's costs, charges and expenses to be charged on the
mortgaged property. By cl 4 Miss Burch charged the property by way of legal
d   mortgage with the payment to the bank of the principal money, liabilities,
interest and other moneys thereby covenanted to be paid by her.

API's financial difficulties were not resolved and in due course it went into
liquidation. By August 1992 Mr Pelosi's house in Gerrards Cross had been sold
and he had gone to live in Italy. From the beginning of June 1993 the bank
unsuccessfully pressed him to make firm proposals for the repayment of API's
e   residual debt, which then stood in the region of £56,000. On 18 April 1994 it made
a formal demand on Miss Burch under the legal charge in the sum of £60,249·12.
That was followed by a solicitor's letter on 29 June and a visit by Miss Burch to
the bank on 5 July, at which Mr Herod recorded her as remaining very loyal to
Mr Pelosi and confident that the bank would be repaid.

f   In early September she went to Italy to see what could be done. She came back
with a letter from Mr Pelosi to Mr Herod brimming with charm and airy
promises and a cheque for £700. The bank required Mr Pelosi thereafter to make
monthly payments of £750, but none were made.

On 21 April 1994 the bank issued proceedings for possession and payment
against Miss Burch in the Willesden County Court. By that time it had closed its
g   London office and was acting through the agency of Hampshire Trust plc. On 25
September 1995 Miss Burch put in a defence and counterclaim, in which she
alleged that she was induced to enter into the legal charge as a result of a
misrepresentation made by Mr Pelosi, further or alternatively, by the undue
influence he had exerted over her. She further alleged that the bank, further or
h   alternatively, its agents, Belmont & Lowe, were on notice, actual or constructive,
of the misrepresentation and undue influence. She denied the bank's right to
possession of the property and counterclaimed for a declaration that the legal
charge was unenforceable against her.

The action came for trial before Mr Recorder Harrod on 12 November 1995.
j   On the following day he gave judgment for Miss Burch and made an order
dismissing the bank's application and setting the legal charge aside. He gave Miss
Burch her costs on scale 2 and granted the bank leave to appeal to this court.

The recorder heard evidence from Miss Burch and Mr Whaley. Neither Mr
Herod nor any other officer or employee of the bank gave evidence. Indeed, the
two affidavits put in on behalf of the bank were sworn by an employee of
Hampshire Trust plc, who had no first hand knowledge of the events of June and

July 1990 and gave no second hand evidence of them either. When tendered for
cross-examination he merely confirmed that he had no first hand knowledge. Mr
Pelosi did not give evidence.

The recorder found that Mr Pelosi had explained to Miss Burch before 26 June
1990 that API was in financial difficulties, that it needed to extend its overdraft
with the bank by £20,000 and that, if he could not provide collateral security for
the extension, API would fail and Miss Burch would be out of a job. He was,
however, satisfied that Mr Pelosi did not tell Miss Burch the extent of API's
borrowing. In other words, he did not tell her that the current borrowings were
at least £163,000, that the limit already stood at £250,000 and that the proposal
was to extend it to £270,000. The recorder also found that, in order to reassure
Miss Burch, Mr Pelosi told her that his own house in England and his villa in Italy
could be sold to pay off all the debts but that the bank would not lend up to 100%
of their value. He told Miss Burch that in consequence, her mortgage would not
be called on.

Having made those findings, the recorder rejected the case based on
misrepresentation. It has not been sought to revive it in this court. Turning to
the case based on undue influence, the recorder found without hesitation that
there existed between Mr Pelosi and Miss Burch such a relationship of trust and
confidence as to raise a presumption of undue influence. He said that if she had
been seeking to set aside the legal charge as against API, she would certainly have
succeeded. As between Miss Burch and the bank, he found that the bank knew
that she was only an employee of API and, further, that the transaction was
manifestly to her disadvantage. It knew that Mr Pelosi was putting forward, as
the provider of collateral security for a possible debt of £270,000, an employee of
his company who had no interest in it as shareholder or director. He held that
that was notice of facts which put the bank on inquiry. I respectfully agree.

Applying *Barclays Bank plc v O'Brien* [1993] 4 All ER 417, [1994] 1 AC 180, the
recorder then considered whether the bank had taken reasonable steps to satisfy
itself that Miss Burch's agreement to stand surety had been properly obtained.
He answered that question in the negative. Having observed that Miss Burch had
been told repeatedly that the mortgage was unlimited in time and amount, he
said:

'Was this enough? I do not think so. What the defendant was not told was
that the guarantee would cover the borrowing of the company, whatever
facilities might later be given it, and, more important, she was not told what
the proposed facilities were. It would have been very simple to inform the
solicitors and ask them to pass onto the defendant that the company's facility
was £250,000 and that this was to be increased to £270,000. Those figures
would have been required by any competent adviser advising the defendant
about the wisdom of the transaction and without them it was impossible for
her to give an informed consent to the transaction.'

In that passage the recorder identified, although without pejorative comment,
the truly astonishing feature of this case. Under the terms of the legal charge,
Miss Burch was required not simply to pledge her home as security for the
£20,000 extension; she was required to pledge it without limit. Worse than that,
she was required to enter into a personal covenant guaranteeing not simply
repayment of the additional £20,000, nor even repayment up to the new limit of
£270,000; she was required to guarantee without limit repayment of all API's
borrowings from the bank, present and future and of whatever kind, together

with interest, commission, charges, legal and other costs, charges and expenses.
All that was required as the price of extending the limit by no more than £20,000
and, be it remembered, of someone who was a mere employee of API, to whom
the only detriment in API's collapse would have been the loss of her job. It could
not have helped the bank to say that it used its standard form. A mortgagee who
uses such a form without regard to its impact on the individual case acts at his
peril.

On that state of facts it must, I think, have been very well arguable that Miss
Burch could, directly against the bank, have had the legal charge set aside as an
unconscionable bargain. Equity's jurisdiction to relieve against such
transactions, although more rarely exercised in modern times, is at least as
venerable as its jurisdiction to relieve against those procured by undue influence.
In *Fry v Lane, re Fry, Whittet v Bush* (1889) 40 Ch D 312 at 322, [1886–90] All ER Rep
1084 at 1089, where sales of reversionary interests at considerable undervalues by
poor and ignorant persons were set aside, Kay J, having reviewed the earlier
authorities, said:

> 'The result of the decisions is that where a purchase is made from a poor
> and ignorant man at a considerable undervalue, the vendor having no
> independent advice, a Court of Equity will set aside the transaction. This will
> be done even in the case of property in possession, and *a fortiori* if the interest
> be reversionary. The circumstances of poverty and ignorance of the vendor,
> and absence of independent advice, throw upon the purchaser, when the
> transaction is impeached, the onus of proving, in Lord *Selborne*'s words, that
> the purchase was "fair, just, and reasonable".'

Lord Selborne LC's words will be found in *Earl of Aylesford v Morris* (1873) LR 8
Ch App 484 at 491, [1861–73] All ER Rep 300 at 303. The decision of Megarry J in
Cresswell v Potter [1978] 1 WLR 255 at 257 where he suggested that the modern
equivalent of 'poor and ignorant' might be 'a member of the lower income group
… less highly educated', demonstrates that the jurisdiction is in good heart and
capable of adaptation to different transactions entered into in changing
circumstances. See also the interesting judgment of Balcombe J in *Backhouse v
Backhouse* [1978] 1 All ER 1158 at 1165–6, [1978] 1 WLR 243 at 250–252, where he
suggested that these cases may come under the general heading which Lord
Denning MR referred to in *Lloyds Bank Ltd v Bundy* [1974] 3 All ER 757 at 765,
[1975] QB 326 at 339 as 'inequality of bargaining power'.

A case based on an unconscionable bargain not having been made below, a
decision of this court cannot be rested on that ground. But the unconscionability
of the transaction remains of direct materiality to the case based on undue
influence. Since it was so manifestly disadvantageous to Miss Burch, the bank
could not be said to have taken reasonable steps to avoid being fixed with
constructive notice of Mr Pelosi's undue influence over her when neither the
potential extent of her liability had been explained to her nor had she received
independent advice.

As to the first of those requirements, I agree with the recorder that it was not
enough for Miss Burch to be told repeatedly that the mortgage was unlimited in
time and amount. She could not assess the significance of that without being told
of the extent of API's current borrowings and the current limit. She might have
thought that the limit was only being extended from £10,000 to £30,000. Had she
known that API's failure could have exposed her, on the figures then current, to

the loss of her home and a personal debt of £200,000 on top, her reaction would have been very different.

As to the second requirement, it was not enough for Miss Burch to be advised to take independent legal advice. It was at the least necessary that she should receive such advice. That is because the first thing an independent solicitor would have done, on looking at cl 2 of the draft legal charge, was to inquire as to the extent of API's current borrowings and the current limit and, on receiving the answers, to advise Miss Burch that she should not on any account enter into a transaction in that form.

In her valiant argument on behalf of the bank, Miss Purkis, in addition to disputing the recorder's decision in regard to the matters already discussed, attacked his finding that there existed between Mr Pelosi and Miss Burch such a relationship of trust and confidence as to raise a presumption of undue influence. There was ample evidence on which that finding could be made. Indeed, the recorder's findings as to how Miss Burch's letter of 18 July came to be written suggests that this could have been treated as a case of actual undue influence. In any event, that part of his decision is as unassailable as any other. This is as clear a case for the setting aside of a transaction as against a mortgagee as it is possible to think of. The appeal is hopeless and must be dismissed.

MILLETT LJ. This transaction cannot possibly stand.

This is sufficiently demonstrated by a recital of the principal facts. Mr Pelosi was the alter ego of his company. The company ran a small business and had an overdraft facility with its bank. The overdraft was operating within an agreed limit of £250,000. Mr Pelosi asked the bank to increase the limit of the facility to £270,000. The bank agreed but required additional security to be provided. So far the story is familiar, even commonplace. What follows, I hope, is not.

Mr Pelosi provided the bank with an unlimited all moneys guarantee given by Miss Burch at his request. She was a junior employee of the company employed at a modest wage. She was not a director of the company or shareholder in it. Her guarantee was supported by a second charge on her home, a small flat of suitably modest value, which was valued at £100,000 and was subject to a mortgage of £30,000. She understood that the guarantee and charge were unlimited in time and amount, but she had not taken independent legal advice.

No court of equity could allow such a transaction to stand. The facts which I have recited are sufficient to entitle Miss Burch to have the transaction set aside as against Mr Pelosi and the company. Every one of those facts was known to the bank when it accepted the security. The bank must accordingly be taken to have had notice of Miss Burch's equity, and must submit to the transaction being set aside against it also.

An eighteenth century Lord Chancellor would have contented himself with saying as much. It is an extreme case. The transaction was not merely to the manifest disadvantage of Miss Burch; it was one which, in the traditional phrase, 'shocks the conscience of the court'. Miss Burch committed herself to a personal liability far beyond her slender means, risking the loss of her home and personal bankruptcy, and obtained nothing in return beyond a relatively small and possibly temporary increase in the overdraft facility available to her employer, a company in which she had no financial interest. The transaction gives rise to grave suspicion. It cries aloud for an explanation.

Miss Burch did not seek to have the transaction set aside as a harsh and unconscionable bargain. To do so she would have had to show not only that the terms of the transaction were harsh or oppressive, but that 'one of the parties to

a it has imposed the objectionable terms in a morally reprehensible manner, that is
   to say, in a way which affects his conscience' (see *Multiservice Bookbinding Ltd v
   Marden* [1978] 2 All ER 489 at 502, [1979] Ch 84 at 110 per Browne-Wilkinson J
   and *Alec Lobb (Garages) Ltd v Total Oil GB Ltd* [1983] 1 All ER 944 at 961, [1983] 1
   WLR 87 at 95, where I pointed out that there must be some impropriety, both in
   the conduct of the stronger party and in the terms of the transaction itself, but
b added that 'the former may often be inferred from the latter in the absence of an
   innocent explanation').

      In the present case, the bank did not obtain the guarantee directly from Miss
   Burch. It was provided to the bank by Mr Pelosi, who obtained it from Miss
   Burch by the exercise of undue influence. In such a context, the two equitable
   jurisdictions to set aside harsh and unconscionable bargains and to set aside
c transactions obtained by undue influence have many similarities. In either case
   it is necessary to show that the conscience of the party who seeks to uphold the
   transaction was affected by notice, actual or constructive, of the impropriety by
   which it was obtained by the intermediary, and in either case the court may in a
   proper case infer the presence of the impropriety from the terms of the
d transaction itself.

      In saying this I do not dissent from the observations of Sir John Salmond in
   Brusewitz v Brown (1922) 42 NZLR 1106 at 1109–1110, where he said:

      'The mere fact that a transaction is based on an inadequate consideration
      or is otherwise improvident, unreasonable, or unjust is not in itself any
e   ground on which this Court can set it aside as invalid. Nor is such a
      circumstance in itself even a sufficient ground for a presumption that the
      transaction was the result of fraud, misrepresentation, mistake, or undue
      influence, so as to place the burden of supporting the transaction upon the
      person who profits by it. The law in general leaves every man at liberty to
f   make such bargains as he pleases, and to dispose of his own property as he
      chooses. However improvident, unreasonable, or unjust such bargains or
      dispositions may be, they are binding on every party to them unless he can
      prove affirmatively the existence of one of the recognised invalidating
      circumstances, such as fraud or undue influence.'

g But Sir John Salmond proceeded to describe an important exception:

      'Where there is not merely an absence or inadequacy of consideration for
      the transfer of property, but there also exists between the grantor and the
      grantee some special relation of confidence, control, domination, influence
h   or other form of superiority, such as to render reasonable a presumption that
      the transaction was procured by the grantee by some unconscientious use of
      his power over the grantor, the law will make that presumption ... The
      commonest and most important instances of this presumption are those
      cases in which the relation between the parties is some recognised legal
      relationship of confidence, such as that existing between solicitor and client
j   and between trustee and beneficiary. The rule, however, is not limited to
      any exclusive and defined list of recognised legal relations. It is quite general
      in its application. The question in each case is ... did there exist between [the
      parties] such a relation of superiority on the one side and inferiority on the
      other (whatever the source or nature of that superiority or inferiority may
      be), and therefore such an opportunity and temptation for the
      unconscientious abuse of the power and influence so possessed by the

superior party, as to justify the legal presumption that such an abuse actually took place and that the transaction was procured thereby?'   *a*

This is an early description of the threefold classification adopted by the Court of Appeal in *Bank of Credit and Commerce International SA v Aboody* [1992] 4 All ER 955 at 964, [1990] 1 QB 923 at 953, which was approved by the House of Lords in *Barclays Bank plc v O'Brien* [1993] 4 All ER 417 at 423, [1994] 1 AC 180 at 189. This   *b* classifies cases of undue influence in three categories: class 1 where the complainant proves affirmatively that she was induced to enter into the transaction by the exercise of undue influence upon her; class 2a where she need prove, in the first instance, only the existence of a relationship between her and the wrongdoer of a kind which is sufficient in law to give rise to a rebuttable presumption that any transaction between them which is favourable to the   *c* wrongdoer has been obtained by the exercise of undue influence; and class 2b where she must prove the existence in fact of a relationship between her and the wrongdoer which, although not of a kind which falls within class 2a, was one under which the complainant was accustomed to repose trust and confidence in the wrongdoer, in which case the same rebuttable presumption arises. The   *d* difference between class 2a and class 2b is that in the former case there is an irrebuttable presumption of law that the relationship is one of trust and confidence; in the latter this must be proved as a fact. (I refer throughout for convenience to the complainant as a woman and the wrongdoer as a man, because that is the present case; but it is not of course always the case.)

In the present case, the only relationship between Mr Pelosi (and his company)   *e* on the one hand and Miss Burch on the other which has been proved (and of which the bank had any knowledge) was that of employer and junior employee. That is not a relationship within class 2a. At the same time, it is clearly one which is capable of developing into a relationship of trust and confidence with the attendant risk of abuse, particularly in the case of a small business where the   *f* parties are accustomed to work closely together.

Accordingly, it was for Miss Burch to prove that the relationship between her and Mr Pelosi had developed into a relationship of trust and confidence. Whether it had done so or not was a question of fact. While she had to prove this affirmatively, she did not have to prove it as a primary fact by direct evidence. It   *g* was sufficient for her to prove facts from which the existence of a relationship of trust and confidence could be inferred. In the present case, the excessively onerous nature of the transaction into which she was persuaded to enter, coupled with the fact that she did so at the request of, and after discussion with Mr Pelosi, is in my judgment, quite enough to justify the inference, which is really   *h* irresistible, that the relationship of employer and employee had ripened into something more and that there had come into existence between them a relationship of trust and confidence which he improperly exploited for his own benefit.

I do not accept the bank's submission that this conclusion is inconsistent with   . the authorities. I repeat that the mere fact that a transaction is improvident or   *j* manifestly disadvantageous to one party is not sufficient by itself to give rise to a presumption that it has been obtained by the exercise of undue influence; but where it is obtained by a party between whom and the complainant there is a relationship like that of employer and junior employee which is easily capable of developing into a relationship of trust and confidence, the nature of the transaction may be sufficient to justify the inference that such a development has *a*   taken place; and where the transaction is so extravagantly improvident that it is virtually inexplicable on any other basis, the inference will be readily drawn.

The bank submitted that in the absence of evidence that there was a sexual or emotional tie between Mr Pelosi and Miss Burch the facts were insufficient to justify the recorder's finding that there was a relationship of confidence between them; and that, in the absence of evidence that the bank was aware of such a tie *b*   between Mr Pelosi and Miss Burch, the facts known to the bank were insufficient to fix it with notice of the existence of a relationship of trust and confidence between them. I do not accept this. The presence of a sexual or emotional tie would at least make the transaction explicable. A wife might well consider (and be properly advised) that it was in her interest to provide a (suitably limited) guarantee of her husband's business borrowings and to charge it on her interest *c*   in the matrimonial home, even if she had no legal interest in the company which owned the business. Her livelihood and that of her family would no doubt depend on the success of the business; and a refusal to entertain her husband's importunity might put at risk the marital relationship as well as the continued prosperity of herself and her family. Similar considerations would no doubt *d*   influence a cohabitee and her adviser.

But Miss Burch had no such incentive to induce her to enter into the transaction. No competent solicitor could possibly have advised her to enter into it. He would be bound to warn her against it in the strongest possible terms, and to have refrained from acting for her further if she had persisted in it against his advice (see *Powell v Powell* [1900] 1 Ch 243 at 247).

e   The bank had actual notice of the facts from which the existence of a relationship of trust and confidence between Mr Pelosi and Miss Burch could be inferred. It knew that they were respectively employer and junior employee working in a small business, and should have 'appreciated that the possibility of influence exist[ed]' (see *Avon Finance Co Ltd v Bridger* (1979) [1985] 2 All ER 281 at *f*   288 per Brandon LJ). It also knew that Miss Burch was neither a shareholder nor a director of the company and, so far as it knew, had no incentive to enter into the transaction, which was entirely for his benefit and to her detriment. This was sufficient to put the bank on inquiry. It probably appreciated this, or it would not have encouraged Miss Burch to take legal advice.

The bank submitted that it had discharged its duty to Miss Burch by urging her *g*   to obtain independent legal advice. This does not accurately reflect the legal position. The bank owed no duty to Miss Burch. If it urged Miss Burch to take independent legal advice, this was for its own protection. If it had not had cause to suspect that Miss Burch's agreement to enter into the transaction might have been improperly obtained, it would have had no need to encourage her to take *h*   legal advice. Since it did have cause to suspect it, it could not avoid the consequences unless two conditions were satisfied: (i) it must have taken reasonable steps to allay any such suspicion; and (ii) the result of the steps which it took must be such as would reasonably allay any such suspicion.

The bank urged Miss Burch to obtain independent legal advice. In a letter obviously written at the instance of Mr Pelosi and after consultation with him, *j*   she declined to do so. The bank had taken all reasonable steps open to it to allay any suspicion it might have had that Miss Burch's agreement to the transaction had been procured by the exercise of undue influence on the part of Mr Pelosi. But what followed could not reasonably have allayed any such suspicion; on the contrary, it should have confirmed it.

That is sufficient to dispose of this appeal, but I should not be taken to accept that it would necessarily have made any difference even if Miss Burch had entered into the transaction after taking independent legal advice. Such advice is neither always necessary nor always sufficient. It is not a panacea. The result does not depend mechanically on the presence or absence of legal advice. I think that there has been some misunderstanding of the role which the obtaining of independent legal advice plays in these cases.

It is first necessary to consider the position as between the complainant and the alleged wrongdoer. The alleged wrongdoer may seek to rebut the presumption that the transaction was obtained by undue influence by showing that the complainant had the benefit of independent legal advice before entering into it. It is well established that in such a case the court will examine the advice which was actually given. It is not sufficient that the solicitor has satisfied himself that the complainant understands the legal effect of the transaction and intends to enter into it. That may be a protection against mistake or misrepresentation; it is no protection against undue influence. As Lord Eldon LC said in *Huguenin v Baseley* (1807) 14 Ves 273 at 300, [1803–13] All ER Rep 1 at 13: 'The question is, not, whether she knew what she was doing, had done, or proposed to do, but how the intention was produced ...'

Accordingly, the presumption cannot be rebutted by evidence that the complainant understood what she was doing and intended to do it. The alleged wrongdoer can rebut the presumption only by showing that the complainant was either free from any undue influence on his part or had been placed, by the receipt of independent advice, in an equivalent position. That involves showing that she was advised as to the propriety of the transaction by an adviser fully informed of all the material facts (see *Powell v Powell, Brusewitz v Brown, Permanent Trustee Co of New South Wales Ltd v Bridgewater* [1936] 3 All ER 501 at 507 and *Bester v Perpetual Trustee Co Ltd* [1970] 3 NSWLR 30 at 35–36).

Some of those cases were concerned with the equity to set aside a harsh and unconscionable bargain rather than one obtained by the exercise of undue influence, but the role of the independent adviser, while not identical, is not dissimilar. The solicitor may not be concerned to protect the complainant against herself, but he is concerned to protect her from the influence of the wrongdoer. The cases show that it is not sufficient that she should have received independent advice unless she has acted on that advice. If this were not so, the same influence that produced her desire to enter into the transaction would cause her to disregard any advice not to do so. They also show that the solicitor must not be content to satisfy himself that his client understands the transaction and wishes to carry it out. His duty is to satisfy himself that the transaction is one which his client could sensibly enter into if free from improper influence; and if he is not so satisfied to advise her not to enter into it, and to refuse to act further for her if she persists. He must advise his client that she is under no obligation to enter into the transaction at all and, if she still wishes to do so, that she is not necessarily bound to accept the terms of any document which has been put before her but (where this is appropriate) that he should ascertain on her behalf whether less onerous terms might be obtained.

It is next necessary to consider the position of the third party who has been put on enquiry of the possible existence of some impropriety and who wishes to avoid being fixed with constructive notice. One means of doing so is to ensure that the complainant obtains competent and independent legal advice before entering into the transaction. If she does so, and enters into the transaction nonetheless, the third party will usually escape the consequences of notice. This is because he is normally entitled to assume that the solicitor has discharged his a duty and that the complainant has followed his advice. But he cannot make any such assumption if he knows or ought to know that it is false.

In the present case, the bank did not have actual notice of the exercise of undue influence, or even of the existence of a relationship of trust and confidence between Miss Burch and Mr Pelosi. It did not know for a fact that Miss Burch had no incentive to enter into the transaction. For all the bank knew, for example,
b the parties might be intending to set up home together and live off the profits of the company's business. It did not, therefore, know (as was the case) that no competent solicitor could possibly advise Miss Burch to guarantee the company's overdraft.

But it must have known that no competent solicitor could advise her to enter into a guarantee in the terms she did. He would be bound to inquire, of the bank
c if necessary, of the reason why it required additional security. Having discovered that it was to enable the limit of the company's overdraft to be increased from £250,000 to £270,000, he would be bound to advise Miss Burch that an unlimited guarantee was unnecessary and inappropriate for this purpose, and that, if she felt that she must accommodate Mr Pelosi's wishes, she should offer a limited
d guarantee with a limit of £20,000 or (better still) a guarantee of the company's liability in excess of £250,000 with a maximum of £270,000. The terms of Miss Burch's letters indicate that if she had been given appropriate advice of the alternatives which were legally available, she would have chosen one which was less onerous to her while still meeting the bank's ostensible requirements.

I do not, therefore, accept that a bank, in circumstances where it ought to
e appreciate the possibility that undue influence has been exercised, can escape the consequences by putting forward an unnecessarily onerous form of guarantee and relying on the failure of the guarantor's solicitor to advise her of the possibility of offering a guarantee on less onerous terms and more appropriate to the situation.

f In the present case, the bank accepted an unlimited guarantee of her employer's indebtedness obtained by the employer from a junior employee with no incentive to give it; and who had, at the instance of her employer, declined to obtain legal advice, was known to be concerned at the unlimited nature of the obligation which she was undertaking, and was almost certainly unaware of the alternatives open to her. In my opinion, the transaction must be set aside and the
g appeal must be dismissed.

SWINTON THOMAS LJ. I have had the advantage of reading the judgment of Nourse LJ. I agree with it and gratefully adopt his recitation of the material facts.

In considering the issues as to whether there was a relationship of trust and
h confidence giving rise to a presumption of undue influence between Miss Burch and Mr Pelosi; whether the bank had express or constructive notice of that relationship; and whether the bank had discharged its duty towards Miss Burch, it is necessary to consider the material facts in the round. In my judgment, the important facts were these. (1) Miss Burch was a young woman in her twenties.
j (2) She was an employee of the company API. (There was no suggestion of any emotional relationship between her and Mr Pelosi.) (3) She was a relevantly junior employee, a booking clerk, earning £12,000 to £14,000 per annum. (4) She lived in a flat valued at £100,000 with a mortgage of £30,000, and consequently an equity of £70,000. (5) She was being asked to enter into a charge whereby she made herself liable to discharge the liability of the company to the bank in the sum of £270,000, and mortgaged her home to the bank. (6) At the time that she entered into the charge, the indebtedness of the company to the bank was at least

£163,000 and was likely to rise to £270,000 as the company required an increase in their bank overdraft facility from £250,000 to £270,000. (7) Miss Burch was not at any time told of the company's current indebtedness to the bank, or the extent of the overdraft facility being granted.

I have no hesitation in upholding the recorder's finding that there was, on the facts of this case, a relationship of trust and confidence as between Mr Pelosi and Miss Burch giving rise to a presumption of undue influence, and there was no evidence to rebut that presumption.

I accept the submission made by Miss Purkis, on behalf of the bank, that the courts must be cautious in their application of the principles set out by Lord Browne-Wilkinson in his speech in *Barclays Bank plc v O'Brien* [1993] 4 All ER 417 at 423, [1994] 1 AC 180 at 189. If they are not, then banks, in their turn, will become over-cautious in granting overdraft facilities to the detriment of their customers. Certainly, in many cases, no presumption will arise in the case of an employer/employee relationship.

However, in this case, the facts speak for themselves and, in my judgment, any neutral bystander, looking at the facts without evidence in rebuttal, would have no difficulty in drawing the overwhelming inference that there was undue influence by Mr Pelosi on his young employee.

As to notice, Mr Herod, the manager of the relevant branch of the bank, who arranged the overdraft facilities knew all the facts set out above except, perhaps, (3). Even as to those facts, he certainly would have known that Miss Burch was a relatively junior employee, and that she could not have been earning a very large salary. On the basis of those facts, it would have been well open to the recorder to find that Mr Herod had actual knowledge of the relationship of trust and confidence. I would have thought that it would cause a bank manager to raise his eyebrows more than a little when he was engaged in entering into a contract with a young employee which involved guaranteeing her employer's indebtedness in the sum of £270,000, and mortgaging her home to the bank. Be that as it may, there can be no doubt that the facts known to Mr Herod were amply sufficient to put him on inquiry as to whether or not there was a relationship of trust and confidence, as in *Avon Finance Co Ltd v Bridger* (1979) [1985] 2 All ER 281.

The third issue is whether the bank discharged its duty to Miss Burch. It is true that the bank, by letters dated 9 and 16 July 1990, advised Miss Burch that the charge was unlimited in time and amount and advised her that she should take independent legal advice. What the bank failed to tell her, and undoubtedly should have told her, was the extent of the company's present indebtedness and, even more important, that she was exposing herself to a potential liability of £270,000 which would, of course, involve the loss of her home. Furthermore, I have no doubt that in these circumstances they should have insisted that she took independent legal advice before entering into the charge. If she had taken advice, an independent solicitor would certainly have advised her as strongly as he could that she should in no circumstances enter into the mortgage.

For these reasons, and for the reasons given by Nourse and Millett LJJ, I too would dismiss this appeal.

Appeal dismissed.

L I Zysman Esq   Barrister.

a
R v Central Criminal Court, ex parte Abu-Wardeh

QUEEN'S BENCH DIVISION

b
AULD LJ AND SACHS J

20 MAY, 6 JUNE 1996

Criminal law – Committal – Remand in custody – Custody time limits – Applicant charged with co-defendants with conspiracy to cause explosions and remanded in custody – Trial date postponed – Recorder extending custody time limit until new trial
c
date because no other suitable judge available before then, protection of the public might be at risk and desirability of all defendants being tried together – Whether those reasons constituting 'good and sufficient cause' to grant extension – Prosecution of Offences Act 1985, s 22(3) – Prosecution of Offences (Custody Time Limits) Regulations 1987, reg 5.

d
On 8 September 1995 the applicant was committed in custody for trial at the Central Criminal Court before a High Court judge, together with three co-defendants, charged with conspiracy to cause explosions and associated offences following the discovery in May 1995 of a cache of arms and primed bombs. After an initial postponement, the trial date was eventually fixed for 1 October 1996, the judge originally designated to try the case having withdrawn
e
and the judge assigned in his place being unable to start the trial before then. Thereafter, the Recorder of London extended the custody time limit (prescribed by reg 5[a] of the Prosecution of Offences (Custody Time Limits) Regulations 1987) until 1 October under s 22(3)[b] of the Prosecution of Offences Act 1985, on the grounds that (i) no other suitable judge was available to try the case before
f
October, (ii) the circumstances of the case were such that the protection of the public might be at risk if the applicant and co-defendants were released on bail, and (iii) it was desirable that all four defendants should be tried together. The applicant applied for judicial review of the recorder's decision, contending that none of the reasons relied on by the recorder amounted to 'good and sufficient cause' within s 22(3) of the 1985 Act.

g
Held – For the purposes of s 22(3) of the 1985 Act, 'good ... cause' consisted of some good reason for the sought postponement of the trial carrying with it the need to extend the custody time limit. Since many defendants facing serious charges were remanded in custody for the protection of others, Parliament could
h
not have intended that the original reason for custody could in itself be a good cause for extending the custody time limit. It followed that protection of the public could not in itself be a 'good and sufficient cause' for doing so. However, the unavailability of a judge or court to try a defendant in custody could in law amount to a 'good and sufficient cause', as could also the interest of justice that
j
jointly charged defendants be tried together. Accordingly, as the recorder had

---

a   Regulation 5, so far as material, provides: '... the maximum period of custody between the preferment of the bill and the accused's arraignment shall be 112 days ...'

b   Section 22(3), so far as material, provides: 'The appropriate court may, at any time before the expiry of a time limit imposed by the regulations, extend, or further extend, that limit if it is satisfied—(a) that there is good and sufficient cause for doing so ...'

taken into account all the relevant circumstances, his conclusion that there was
'good and sufficient cause' to justify extending the custody time limit to 1   *a*
October could not be held to be perverse. The application would therefore be
dismissed (see p 164 *b c h*, p 165 *e*, p 166 *e* to p 167 *c g* and p 168 *a*, post).

R v Norwich Crown Court, ex p Cox (1992) 97 Cr App R 145 and R v Maidstone
Crown Court, ex p Schulz (1992) 157 JP 601 followed

R v Luton Crown Court, ex p Neaves [1992] Crim LR 721 not followed.   *b*

Notes

For custody time limits in the Crown Court, see 11(2) Halsbury's Laws (4th edn
reissue) para 853.

For the Prosecution of Offences Act 1985, s 22, see 12 Halsbury's Statutes (4th   *c*
edn) (1994 reissue) 964.

Cases referred to in judgments

Associated Provincial Picture Houses Ltd v Wednesbury Corp [1947] 2 All ER 680,
    [1948] 1 KB 223, CA.
R v Crown Court at Maidstone, ex p Freeman (25 October 1994, unreported), DC.   *d*
R v Crown Court at Maidstone, ex p Hollstein [1995] 3 All ER 503, DC.
R v Governor of Winchester Prison, ex p Roddie [1991] 2 All ER 931, [1991] 1 WLR
    303, DC.
R v Luton Crown Court, ex p Neaves [1992] Crim LR 721, DC.
R v Maidstone Crown Court, ex p Schulz (1992) 157 JP 601, DC.   *e*
R v Norwich Crown Court, ex p Cox (1992) 97 Cr App R 145, DC.
R v Norwich Crown Court, ex p Stiller (1992) 156 JP 624, DC.

Cases also cited or referred to in skeleton arguments

R v Crown Court at Norwich, ex p Parker (1992) 96 Cr App R 68, DC.   *f*
R v Sheffield Justices, ex p Turner [1991] 1 All ER 858, [1991] 2 QB 472, DC.

Application for judicial review

Mahmoud Abu-Wardeh applied, with leave granted on 3 April 1996, for judicial
review by way of an order of certiorari of the decision of the Recorder of London *g*
at the Central Criminal Court on 19 February 1996 whereby he, inter alia,
extended the custody time limit applicable in the applicant's case until 1 October
1996 and for a declaration that the applicant's detention from the date of that
decision was unlawful. The facts are set out in the judgment of Auld LJ.

                                                                            h
Rock Tansey QC and Simon Pentol (instructed by Kaim Todner) for the applicant.
David Calvert-Smith and William Boyce (instructed by the Crown Prosecution Service)
    for the respondent.

                                                      Cur adv vult

                                                                            j

6 June 1996. The following judgments were delivered.

AULD LJ. The applicant, Mahmoud Abu-Wardeh, stands charged with three
others, Nadia Zekra, Samar Alami and Jawad Botmeh, at the Central Criminal
Court with conspiring to cause explosions and associated offences. Two of the

a associated offences were bomb attacks in July 1994 against the Israeli Embassy in London and against the Jewish Philanthropic Association's premises in Finchley.

The applicant's three co-defendants were arrested and charged with offences relating to the two explosions, and in May 1995 they were committed on bail to the Central Criminal Court for trial on those charges. Shortly after their committal the police found a cache of arms and primed bombs at a storage depot.

b There was evidence to connect the applicant, Alami and Botmeh with that cache. In June 1995 the police arrested the applicant for the conspiracy, the two July 1994 bombings and for unlawful possession of the arms and explosives, and re-arrested Alami and Botmeh for the latter matters.

By that time, the trial of Zekra, who was still on bail, Alami and Botmeh, who were now in custody, had been fixed to start at the Central Criminal Court on 2

c January 1996. Because of its importance it was listed for trial by a High Court judge and Scott Baker J was designated by Kennedy LJ, on behalf of the Lord Chief Justice, to try it. On 8 September 1995 the applicant was committed in custody for joint trial with them, and on 5 October the Recorder of London ordered that the trial of all four should start on the fixed date of 2 January 1996.

d That date was just within the custody time limit of 112 days from the latest committal of joint defendants to arraignment imposed by reg 5 of the Prosecution of Offences (Custody Time Limits) Regulations 1987, SI 1987/299. However, on 7 December 1995, Scott Baker J, on an application on behalf of Alami and the applicant for postponement of the start of trial, re-fixed it for 19

e February 1996, a date which suited the applicant but which was not as long as Alami had wanted. And, under s 22(3) of the Prosecution of Offences Act 1985, the judge extended the custody time limit to that date. He had such power under the section on being satisfied, as he was, 'that there [was] good and sufficient cause for doing so' and 'that the prosecution [had] acted with all due expedition'.

In mid-January 1996 Scott Baker J had to withdraw from the case because he

f had just realised that he and one of the prosecution witnesses were acquaintances. Kennedy LJ then assigned Garland J to try the case.

On 26 January 1996 Garland J heard applications on behalf of the prosecution, Alami and Botmeh to break the fixture for 19 February. The prosecution sought a delay of two to three weeks for the convenience of its leading counsel, and

g Alami and Botmeh sought a delay of about four to five months, that is until about the beginning of June, in order to enable them properly to prepare their defences. The applicant opposed any adjournment. Garland J, because of his judicial commitments, had already consulted with Kennedy LJ, who had in turn consulted with the Lord Chief Justice, and informed counsel that he could not,

h in any event, start the trial before the beginning of October. He said that they had decided that it would be inappropriate to assign the case to a third High Court judge and indicated that, in any event, no other judge of sufficient seniority was available to try it before October. He did, however, offer to rearrange his holiday so that he could start the trial at the beginning of September, but all counsel in the case indicated that that was not convenient.

j He, therefore, adjourned the trial to 1 October.

The prosecution, on 5 February, notified the defendants' representatives in writing of its intention to apply for a further extension of the custody limit to 1 October. On 19 February counsel on its behalf made that application to the Recorder of London; counsel on behalf of the applicant, Alami and Botmeh opposed it. The only issue before the recorder was whether there was 'good and

sufficient cause' for extending the limit; there was no suggestion that the *a*
prosecution had not acted with all due expedition. In a short, extemporary
ruling, the recorder found that there was good and sufficient cause for doing so
for three reasons: first, he was satisfied that there was no other suitable judge
available to try it before October; second, the circumstances of the case, in
particular, the discovery in May 1995 of the cache of arms and primed bombs,
were such that the protection of the public might well be at risk if the applicant, *b*
Alami and Botmeh were released on bail; and third, it was desirable that the four
defendants should be tried together and that counsel on behalf of Alami had
indicated that, because of Alami's illness, she could not be ready for trial before
May or June.

The recorder ordered that the limit be extended to the start of the trial on 1
October or, if he was incorrect on both his first two reasons, to 28 June when, as *c*
he directed, the arraignment of all four defendants and the plea and directions
hearing would take place.

The applicant, Alami and Botmeh remain in custody, and the applicant now
applies, with leave, for judicial review of the recorder's decision so extending the
custody time limit.   *d*

Mr Tansey QC, on his behalf, prefaced his challenge to the recorder's order by
observing that the effect of it is that the applicant would spend a further 224 days
in custody before trial, double the statutory time limit of 112 days, making a total
of 389 days in all. So long a period, he submitted, is contrary to the whole
purpose of the 1985 Act and supporting regulations, which is to shorten the *e*
period during which a defendant in custody has to await trial.

Mr Tansey submitted that none of the reasons for extension relied upon by the
recorder amounted to 'good and sufficient cause' within s 22(3) of the Act. I deal
first with the competing arguments on the first two reasons.

Mr Tansey submitted that, whilst it was no doubt necessary for this serious
matter to be tried by a senior High Court judge, its assignment to a judge who, *f*
because of his other judicial commitments, could not try it before the autumn
could not, in the circumstances, be a 'good and sufficient cause'. He accepted
that unavailability of a judge might be capable of so qualifying in certain
circumstances, say when a trial date is fixed for the near future, but not for so
long a period as over seven months.   *g*

As to protection of the public, Mr Tansey submitted that it is not capable of
amounting to 'good and sufficient cause', for, if that had been the intention, the
custody time limit would not have been applied to all offences other than treason
(see reg 5(2)(a) of the 1987 regulations).

Mr Boyce, on behalf of the respondent, argued that unavailability of a judge to *h*
try the matter is capable in law of amounting to 'good and sufficient cause' and
that it was not *Wednesbury* unreasonable of the recorder to so regard it in the
circumstances of this case, and to grant so long an extension (see *Associated
Provincial Picture Houses Ltd v Wednesbury Corp* [1947] 2 All ER 680, [1948] 1 KB
223). As to protection of the public, he maintained that it too was capable of so
qualifying. He argued that this case, concerning as it does the bombing of *j*
buildings and failure to disclose the existence of a cache of primed bombs
intended for further atrocities, justified the recorder's ruling.

The use in the statutory formula of the two adjectives 'good' and 'sufficient'
must, in my view, have some purpose other than mere emphasis. 'Good ...
cause' must mean some cause for the extension of time sought, not the

a corresponding need to keep the defendant in custody. 'Sufficient' means what it says, and requires a court when considering a 'good ... cause' to evaluate its strength. Thus, in *R v Governor of Winchester Prison, ex p Roddie* [1991] 2 All ER 931, [1991] 1 WLR 303, while the court was of the view that it was undesirable to define 'good ... cause' and that it should be left to the good sense of the tribunal, it held that the seriousness of the offence or the fact that only a short
b extension is sought could not be 'good ... cause'. Lloyd LJ, with whom Tudor Evans J agreed, said ([1991] 2 All ER 931 at 934, [1991] 1 WLR 303 at 306):

'... Parliament has provided the same time limit for all offences, other than treason, whether the offence be a serious one or not. Obviously the more serious the charge, the more important it is for the police to get on with
c preparing the case. But is it good cause in itself? Good cause in s 22(3) means what it says. It will usually consist of some good reason why the case is not ready to be put before the magistrates for a decision whether to commit or not. It need not, as I see it, be anything exceptional. But it must be good cause ... It must be left to the good sense of magistrates in each case as it comes before them. But the seriousness of the offence is not in my view in
d itself a good cause in law. Nor can it be a good cause that the extension is only for a short period.'

In *R v Luton Crown Court, ex p Neaves* [1992] Crim LR 721, a case of alleged rape where the delay arose from lack of a judge to try the case, Mann LJ took a different view of the formula 'good and sufficient'. Whilst agreeing with Lloyd
e LJ that the courts should not attempt to define the words, he was not then prepared to accept that the word 'good' limited in any way the categories of cause that could qualify. He said, after referring to the passage from Lloyd LJ's judgment that I have just cited:

f 'I also resist the temptation to be definitive. I do, however, observe that the language "good and sufficient cause" is unconstrained. By that I mean it is not constrained as to causes which are of a particular nature.'

From that starting point he went on to hold, as I shall mention again, that there was nothing in the language of the statute to compel him to exclude the
g protection of the public as a good and sufficient cause for an extension of the custody time limit and that it would offend common sense if it did.

However, shortly afterwards, in *R v Norwich Crown Court, ex p Cox* (1992) 97 Cr App R 145 at 151, where the cause for the sought extension of only 20 days was the unavailability of a court and judge to try the case, Mann LJ acknowledged
h that there were some matters that could be identified as being not capable of constituting 'sufficient cause', two of them being the seriousness of the offence and the shortness of the time sought as stated by Lloyd LJ in *Ex p Roddie*.

Of the recorder's first two reasons for extending the custody time limit, I consider first the need to protect the public. Mr Tansey submitted that, in general, protection of the public, like the seriousness of the offence charged,
j cannot amount to a 'good and sufficient cause'. He sought to distinguish *Ex p Neaves*, in which, as I have said, the prosecution sought an extension of time because of unavailability of a judge to try it. The judge granted the application, justifying his decision on the ground that the complainant of rape was in danger of serious bodily harm from the defendant. The defendant applied for judicial review on the ground that protection of the complainant or the public was not

capable of being a 'good and sufficient cause'. The Divisional Court, consisting *a*
of Mann LJ and French J, dismissed the application, holding, as I have mentioned,
that there was nothing in the language of s 22(3) to constrain its application in
that way and that it would offend common sense if it did. Mr Tansey's suggested
distinction was that in that case there was a readily identifiable threat to a
particular individual, the complainant, whereas here the threat relied on is a
matter of supposition and is unparticularised. *b*

In my view, as all serious charges save treason are subject to the custody time
limits, and as many defendants facing serious charges are remanded in custody
for the protection of others, Parliament cannot have intended that that original
reason for custody could in itself be a good cause for extending the custody time
limit. To amount to 'good ... cause' there must be some good reason for the
sought postponement of the trial carrying with it the need to extend the custody *c*
time limit. I am reassured in that conclusion by the following characteristically
perceptive commentary of Professor D J Birch to the short report of *Ex p Neaves*
[1992] Crim LR 721 at 722–723:

> 'The court's power to extend a custody time limit for "good and sufficient *d*
> cause" has been considered on a number of occasions but ... the focus has
> been upon the reason why the case is not ready for trial rather than upon the
> consequences of granting the accused automatic bail. Thus in ... *ex parte
> Roddie* ... for example, it was held that the seriousness of the offence and the
> fact that the delay was minimal were not of themselves reasons for
> extending the limit. More recently, in ... *ex parte Stiller* ... it was held that *e*
> the unavailability of a courtroom and judge to try the case did not justify an
> extension. In both cases, attention was drawn to the risk that the protection
> afforded to the accused by the time limits would be negated if understaffing
> and pressure of work were to be regarded as good cause for extension. A
> similar argument may be constructed against the reasoning in the present *f*
> case, which permits the extension of a custody time limit on the ground that
> the accused is dangerous. Just as Parliament has laid down the same time
> limit for all offences, serious or not, so the limit is the same however
> dangerous the offender ... the prosecutor should come to court prepared to
> say why the case has not been proceeded with in time, rather than why the
> accused should not be released.' *g*

I, therefore, respectfully disagree with the court's view in *Ex p Neaves* that
protection of the public can in itself be a 'good and sufficient cause' for extending
the custody time limit. I add that, if I am wrong about that, no one could criticise
the recorder for regarding the circumstances of this case as justifying some
extension for that reason. The distinction that Mr Tansey sought to draw *h*
between *Ex p Neaves* and this case based on the difference between an identifiable
danger to a particular person and a general danger to the public is immaterial.

The first of the recorder's reasons, the unavailability of a judge or court to try
a defendant in custody, is more difficult. It has been considered by this court in
a number of cases. In *R v Norwich Crown Court, ex p Stiller* (1992) 156 JP 624 Rose *j*
J, giving the judgment of the court, left open the question whether such
unavailability could so qualify as a matter of law, but held that, in the
circumstances, an extension of 56 days where there was no clear indication when
the trial could proceed did not, in any event, satisfy the test. He cited *Ex p Roddie*
[1991] 2 All ER 931 at 934–935, [1991] 1 WLR 303 at 306, which also concerned

a the question whether the prosecution had acted with due diligence when it was delayed by staff shortage, and referred to the following passage from the judgment of Lloyd LJ, with which Tudor Evans J agreed:

'The purpose of laying down specific time limits for custody ... was to prompt the prosecution to move with expedition, and to avoid the accused
b being kept in custody for an excessive period at any stage. Parliament having willed that very desirable end, must also, as it seems to me, will the means.'

Rose J then continued:

c 'With those observations we respectfully agree ... It may be (but we express no final view) that the lack of immediate facilities for trial is capable of amounting to a good and sufficient reason when, on an application to extend custody time limits, a trial date in the near future can be specified. But that is not this case. Neither on November 14 nor before us has there been any clear indication as to when, if ever, there will be a court and Judge
d available for the trial. To hold that, in such circumstances, there is good and sufficient reason for an extension is, in our view, totally to negate the protection against long periods of pre-trial incarceration which the custody time limits are intended to afford.' (See (1992) 156 JP 624 at 627.)

In at least three subsequent cases the court was clearly of the view that
e unavailability of a judge or courtroom is capable in law of amounting to 'good and sufficient cause'. The first is Ex p Cox, to which I have referred, in which both Mann LJ and Leonard J so held, deciding on the facts that the 20 days sought met the test. However, they did so on different bases. Mann LJ, as I have mentioned, acknowledged that there were some matters, such as seriousness of the offence
f and the shortness of the extension sought, that could not qualify, but said that he—

'[could] see no reason why the lack of a court and a judge is not capable in law of being a good and sufficient cause for the purpose of section 22(3). Whether in any particular case it should be so regarded must depend upon
g the facts of that instant case including, in particular, whether a trial date has been specified.' (See (1992) 97 Cr App R 145 at 151.)

Leonard J, on the other hand, appears to have proceeded on the basis of Mann LJ's original approach to such question in Ex p Neaves, namely that there is no category of cause which is legally outside the definition and that the test was one
h of reasonableness. He said (97 Cr App R 145 at 150):

'I have come to the conclusion that ... the proper approach in cases of this kind is for each set of circumstances to be considered independently. If one is able to find good and reasonable cause in the circumstances of a particular case, the fact that there is no particular category into which the good and
j reasonable cause can be put is immaterial. The sole question is whether the court, in coming to its conclusion, has acted reasonably or not.'

In R v Maidstone Crown Court, ex p Schulz (1992) 157 JP 601 Beldam LJ, with whom Tudor Evans J agreed, appears to have accepted that difficulty in listing a case could amount to 'good and sufficient cause', but held that an extension of 14 days merely in the hope that an earlier date might be found was not in the circumstances 'good and sufficient cause'.

In *R v Crown Court at Maidstone, ex p Freeman* (25 October 1994, unreported) the court, consisting of Rose LJ and Potts J followed *Ex p Cox* in holding that difficulties in listing a trial are capable of amounting to 'good and sufficient cause'. They held on the facts that an extension of over four months to a fixed trial date, a longer period than that in *Ex p Stiller* but where there was no fixed trial date, was not *Wednesbury* unreasonable. Rose LJ, no doubt with that comparison in mind, observed that the decision—

'[was] not authority for the proposition that, if a date is fixed for trial five months or so after the expiry of the initial custody time limits, good and sufficient cause is shown. It is no such authority for two reasons in particular. First, this court is not exercising its own discretion as to whether good and sufficient cause is shown, but is merely reviewing the judge's exercise of discretion. Whether or not this court would have exercised its discretion in the same way is immaterial. Secondly, as cannot be too clearly emphasised, all cases in relation to custody time limits have different facts and the circumstances in each case merit separate consideration. It is not, for example, in my judgment, profitable to compare, in isolation from the other circumstances of the case, the number of days spent in custody in one case with the number of days spent in custody in another case.'

There is no provision comparable to s 22(3)(b) requiring, in addition to a good and sufficient cause, that the judges or the Court Service should provide a trial judge with all due expedition. My first instinct, before considering the above authorities, was that it could defeat the whole purpose of the provision, which is to secure speedy trial of those in custody, if lack of judges or courtrooms could, in conjunction with the oft occurring need to protect the public, amount to good cause. It seemed to me that the observation of Lloyd LJ in *Ex p Roddie* [1991] 2 All ER 931 at 935, [1991] 1 WLR 303 at 306, in relation to the duty of the prosecution to proceed with all due expedition, that Parliament having willed the speedy trial of defendants in custody 'must also ... will the means', might also apply to the provision of a judge or a courtroom to try the case.

After much hesitation, I have come to the view that there is no indication in s 22(3), considered alone or in its statutory context, that the words 'good ... cause' should be construed in any stricter sense than that the suggested cause must be a reason for postponement of the trial and, for that reason, an extension of the custody time limit. In applications based on unavailability of a judge or courtroom, as on any other cause, the judge has another means of ensuring that it does not subvert the statutory purpose of speedy trial for those in custody. It is to examine the circumstances rigorously to determine whether the cause is also 'sufficient' for any extension and, if so, for the length of extension sought. As the authorities to which I have referred make plain, each case must be decided by the judge hearing the application on its own facts. On such an issue, the issue of sufficiency, I consider that the judge is entitled to have regard to the nature of the case and any particular limitations that that may impose on the status and seniority of the judge to try it and to the difficulty of making such a judge available. He must decide in the circumstances whether any such difficulty is a sufficient cause for an extension and, if so, for one of the length sought. The function of this court on an appeal from such decision is, of course, much *a*   narrower, namely whether on the material before him the judge's decision was perverse.

In my view, this very experienced judge considered all the relevant circumstances with great care. He bore in mind: the importance of the case; that it was necessary for it to be tried by a senior High Court judge; the exceptional and unforeseeable circumstance of the late re-assignment of the case to

b   Garland J; his unavailability and the unavailability of any other suitable judge to try the case before the autumn; and the parties' rejection of Garland J's offer to cancel his holiday and start the case at the beginning of September. In addition, the history of the matter showed that various of the defendants and their legal representatives at different stages sought postponements to suit their own

c   requirements. In all those exceptional circumstances, I could not say that the recorder was perverse in finding that there was 'good and sufficient cause' to justify extending the custody time limit to 1 October 1996.

Finally, there is the recorder's third reason that all four defendants should be tried together and that that could not take place much before June in any event because of Alami's unreadiness for arraignment before then, leading him to fix

d   28 June 1996 as an alternative to 1 October.

Mr Tansey said that the practical effect of that order is to keep the applicant in custody until 1 October 1996 because, under the 1987 regulations, arraignment removes their protection. He submitted that the order was wrong: because the recorder, from remarks that he made in the course of argument, clearly saw no

e   point in it; because the desirability of trying all four defendants together was not a good and sufficient cause for extending the applicant's otherwise permissible time in custody; and because such an arraignment was merely a device to overcome the applicant's statutory protection, it being known that all defendants intended to plead not guilty (see e g *R v Crown Court at Maidstone, ex p Hollstein*

f   [1995] 3 All ER 503).

Mr Boyce's answer was that the interest of justice that jointly charged defendants be tried together is capable of being a good and sufficient cause for extension of the custody time limit of one or more of them. He submitted that, given the recorder's acceptance of the desirability of trying these four defendants

g   together and of Alami's unreadiness to be arraigned and for a plea and direction hearing before June, he was entitled to regard those matters together as good and sufficient cause to extend the applicant's custody time limit to at least that date.

In my judgment, Mr Boyce is right. The combined causes here go to the reason for postponement of the start of the trial and hence are capable of

h   amounting to 'good cause' for extension of the custody time limit of the applicant. On the material before the recorder, I can see no basis for suggesting that he was perverse in his view that the four defendants should be tried together or that Alami, because of her ill-health, would not be ready to give proper instructions to her advisers to enable her to prepare for trial before May or June. In those circumstances, his direction that all four defendants should be arraigned

j   at a plea and directions hearing at the end of June seems to me entirely reasonable. In a case of such importance, I would expect there to be such a plea and directions hearing well before the start of the trial; there is certainly no material before the court to suggest that the directed arraignment was merely a device to overcome the protection given to the applicant by the custody time limit.

Accordingly, while I would reject the validity of the recorder's second reason *a*
for extending the time limit, I can see no basis for saying that his first and third
rulings were wrong in law or perverse. I would, therefore, dismiss the
application.

SACHS J. I agree.

b

Application dismissed.

Dilys Tausz   Barrister.

a

State Bank of India v Sood and others

COURT OF APPEAL, CIVIL DIVISION

HIRST, PETER GIBSON AND PILL LJJ

3, 4, 30 OCTOBER 1996

b

Land registration – Overriding interest – Rights of person in actual occupation of land – Trustees for sale mortgaging land to bank as security for discharge on demand of present and future liabilities – No capital money being advanced by mortgagee contemporaneously with the mortgage – Trustees failing to satisfy demand for payment – Possession sought by mortgagee – Whether beneficiaries under trust for sale in actual occupation having overriding interests – Whether equitable interests of beneficiaries overreached by mortgage – Whether capital money required to be advanced contemporaneously with conveyance for overreaching to occur – Law of Property Act 1925, s 2(1)(ii) – Land Registration Act 1925, s 70(1)(g).

c

d In 1983 the first and second defendants, who were the registered proprietors and trustees for sale of a property, charged the property by way of legal mortgage to a bank as security for the discharge on demand of all present and future liabilities on any account. In 1989 the bank assigned the benefit of the legal charge to the plaintiff. In 1993 the plaintiff claimed that it was owed over £1m and when its demands were not satisfied it commenced proceedings against the first and second defendants seeking possession of the property. The third to seventh defendants claimed to be beneficiaries under the trust for sale and in the defence asserted that their equitable interests, coupled with their actual occupation of the property, gave them overriding interests under s 70(1)(g)[a] of the Land Registration Act 1925 which were binding on the plaintiff. The plaintiff applied to strike out that part of the defence on the grounds that it disclosed no reasonable defence or was frivolous and vexatious or otherwise an abuse of the process of the court, contending that any such equitable interests had been overreached by the legal charge under s 2(1)(ii)[b] of the Law of Property Act 1925. The deputy district judge granted the application but the judge allowed an appeal by the defendants, holding that the equitable interests had not been overreached under s 2(1)(ii) of the Law of Property Act 1925, because no capital money had arisen contemporaneously with the disposition of the legal estate. The plaintiff appealed.

e

f

g

Held – On its true construction s 2(1)(ii) of the Law of Property Act 1925 only required compliance with the statutory requirements respecting capital money if capital money arose on a conveyance and such capital money did not have to arise for equitable interests to be overreached under the section. It followed that the interests of the third to seventh defendants had been overreached and attached to the equity of redemption and therefore they did not have overriding interests under s 70(1)(g) of the Land Registration Act 1925. Accordingly the appeal would be allowed and that part of the defence struck out (see p 178 *g*, p 180 *b c g h*, p 181 *e* to *g* and p 182 *j*, post).

h

j

City of London Building Society v Flegg [1987] 3 All ER 435 applied.

---

a   Section 70(1), so far as material, is set out at p 175 *e f*, post
b   Section 2(1) is set out at p 173 *b* to *e*, post

Notes

For overriding interests in relation to registered land, see 26 *Halsbury's Laws* (4th edn) paras 987–991, and for cases on the subject, see 39(1) *Digest* (Reissue) 145–153, 1597–1622.

For the power to overreach equitable interests in land, see 39 *Halsbury's Laws* (4th edn) paras 590–595.

For the Law of Property Act 1925, s 2, see 37 *Halsbury's Statutes* (4th edn) 80.

For the Land Registration Act 1925, s 70, see ibid 578.

Cases referred to in judgments

Bristol's (Marquis of) Settled Estates, Re [1893] 3 Ch 161.

Carl-Zeiss-Stiftung v Herbert Smith & Co (a firm) [1968] 2 All ER 1002, [1969] 1 Ch 93, [1968] 3 WLR 281, CA.

City of London Building Society v Flegg [1987] 3 All ER 435, [1988] AC 54, [1987] 2 WLR 1266, HL; *rvsg* [1986] 1 All ER 989, [1986] Ch 605, [1986] 2 WLR 616, CA.

Everett v Ribbands [1952] 1 All ER 823, [1952] 2 QB 198, CA.

Tilling v Whiteman [1979] 1 All ER 737, [1980] AC 1, [1979] 2 WLR 401, HL.

Williams & Glyn's Bank Ltd v Boland, Williams & Glyn's Bank Ltd v Brown [1980] 2 All ER 408, [1981] AC 487, [1980] 3 WLR 138, HL; *affg* [1979] 2 All ER 697, [1979] Ch 312, [1979] 2 WLR 550, CA.

Williams & Humbert Ltd v W & H Trade Marks (Jersey) Ltd, Rumasa SA v Multinvest (UK) Ltd [1986] 1 All ER 129, [1986] AC 368, [1986] 2 WLR 24, HL.

Cases also cited or referred to in skeleton arguments

Abbey National Building Society v Cann [1990] 1 All ER 1085, [1991] 1 AC 56, HL.

Lonrho plc v Fayed [1991] 3 All ER 303, [1992] 1 AC 448, HL.

Appeal

By notice dated 10 May 1995 the plaintiff, State Bank of India, appealed with leave of Ward LJ from the decision of Judge Willis, sitting in the Croydon County Court on 13 April 1995, whereby he allowed an appeal by the first defendant, Sardul Singh Sood, and the third to seventh defendants, Parmjit Singh Sood, Daman Sood, Raksha Sood, Kamaljit Singh Sood and Renu Sood, from the order of Deputy District Judge Fink on 31 October 1994, striking out parts of their defence on the ground that they disclosed no reasonable defence or were frivolous and vexatious or otherwise constituted an abuse of the process of the court. Following the death of the fifth defendant, the first defendant as his personal representative was substituted as a respondent to the appeal. The facts are set out in the judgment of Peter Gibson LJ.

Grant Crawford (instructed by *Royds Treadwell*) for the plaintiff.

Peter Havey (instructed by *Vijay Sharma*) for the first, third and fourth defendants.

Andrew Williams (instructed by *Dickinson Parker Hill & Son*, Ormskirk) for the seventh defendant.

The sixth defendant did not appear.

Cur adv vult

30 October 1996. The following judgments were delivered.

PETER GIBSON LJ (giving the first judgment at the invitation of Hirst LJ). This is an appeal, brought with the leave of Ward LJ, from the order of Judge Willis in the Croydon County Court. It raises a question of importance for conveyancers, for creditors the debts owed to whom are secured on property and for persons *a* with only equitable interests in registered land. The question can be formulated in this way: where two trustees for sale hold registered land for themselves and other beneficiaries and mortgage the land as security for existing and future liabilities of themselves and other persons, are the equitable interests of the beneficiaries overreached, notwithstanding that no money was advanced by the mortgagee to or at the direction of the trustees contemporaneously with the *b* mortgage? The judge in effect answered that question in the negative.

The question arises in the following circumstances. On 23 February 1978 the freehold property, 19 Landseer Road, Sutton, Surrey, was transferred to the first and second defendants, who were registered shortly thereafter as, and have remained, the proprietors of the property. On 13 December 1983 the first and *c* second defendants executed a deed of legal charge which was a second legal charge on the property. By that deed, they charged the property by way of legal mortgage as security to Punjab National Bank for the discharge on demand of all present and future liabilities of them jointly and severally and of Sobel Textiles (UK) Ltd (Sobel) on any account and all other present, future, actual and contingent liabilities of them jointly and severally and of Sobel to the Punjab *d* National Bank, as well as costs, charges and expenses in relation to the charge, and interest. The statutory power of sale was to be exercisable at any time after demand. On 4 December 1989 the Punjab National Bank assigned the benefit of the legal charge to the plaintiff, the State Bank of India. It claims in the statement of claim that it is owed over £1m by the first and second defendants under the *e* legal charge. This is made up of the liabilities of (1) Sobel, (2) the second defendant as a partner in a firm called SMC Video, (3) the first and second defendants as guarantors of the debts of Kohli & Sood Ltd, and (4) the second defendant as guarantor of the debts of Sood Properties Ltd. In April 1992 and January 1993 it demanded payment from the first and second defendants respectively and, when the demands were not satisfied, it commenced *f* proceedings by originating summons under RSC Ord 88 against those defendants on 20 September 1993, seeking possession of the property.

A bankruptcy order had been made against the second defendant on 5 March 1992. The Official Receiver, in whom the property of the bankrupt vested, indicated that he did not oppose the relief sought by the plaintiff. But the third to *g* seventh defendants were added as parties by orders of the court in March and May 1994. The court ordered that the proceedings continue as though they commenced by writ and a statement of claim was served on 11 May 1994. On 7 June 1994 a single defence was served by the first and the third to seventh defendants. A number of grounds of defence were pleaded, including allegations *h* that the third to seventh defendants or some of them have beneficial interests in the property. Those interests are said to have arisen (1) by a written agreement or agreements dated 23 February 1978 and 20 June 1979 respectively, in which the first and second defendants declared that they held the property in trust for themselves and the third and sixth defendants in equal shares, (2) by resulting trust in favour of the third to seventh defendants, or (3) by constructive trust in *j* favour of the fourth, fifth and seventh defendants. It is further pleaded that the property was the main residence of all the defendants between 1978 and 1989 and that in December 1983 all the defendants were in actual possession of the property. By 'possession' the pleader probably meant occupation, as it is claimed that the third to seventh defendants' beneficial interests in respect of the property are overriding interests and that on that basis the plaintiff is not entitled to possession of the property.

The action was transferred to the county court where the plaintiff on 10 *a* August 1994 applied to strike out those parts of the defence which related to the allegation that the third to seventh defendants had beneficial interests in respect of the property. That application was made pursuant to CCR Ord 13, r 5 and under the inherent jurisdiction of the court on the grounds that those pleadings disclosed no reasonable defence to the plaintiff's claim or were frivolous and vexatious or otherwise an abuse of the process of the court. The application was *b* supported by an affidavit which in effect verifies the statement of claim, shows that interest has accrued since September 1993 and exhibits the entries in the register relating to the property and the legal charge. Deputy District Judge Fink acceded to the application, but on appeal by those defendants, the judge allowed the appeal. The plaintiff, represented by Mr Crawford, now appeals. Since the hearing before the judge the fifth defendant has died and the first defendant as his *c* personal representative has been substituted as a respondent to the plaintiff's appeal. The first defendant in that capacity and the third and the fourth defendants appear by Mr Havey. The sixth defendant does not appear but surprisingly the seventh defendant has separate counsel, Mr Williams, although it is hard to see any difference in interest from that of Mr Havey's clients on this *d* appeal.

It is not in dispute that on the facts assumed to be true the first and second defendants have at all material times been trustees of the legal estate in the property, holding it on trust for sale and the net proceeds of sale and the net rents and profits until sale for themselves and the third to seventh defendants or some *e* of them as tenants in common. The interests of the third to seventh defendants have therefore always been limited as a matter of legal theory to rights not in the property itself but in the proceeds of sale and the rents and profits until sale, though until sale the entitlement to share in the rents and profits carries with it the right, together with the other tenants in common, to occupy the property. But that right is not independent of the entitlement to share in the rents and *f* profits until sale. The register shows no restriction on the registered proprietors' powers of disposition nor is there any entry in the register relating to the third to seventh defendants' claimed interests and no caution against dealing has been registered.

Before I turn to the statutory provisions, I would make a few general *g* observations on overreaching. As is explained by Charles Harpum in his illuminating article, 'Overreaching, Trustees' Powers and the Reform of the 1925 Legislation' [1990] CLJ 277, overreaching is the process whereby existing interests are subordinated to a later interest or estate created pursuant to a trust or power. Mr Harpum arrived at that statement of the true nature of overreaching by a *h* consideration of the effect of the exercise of powers of disposition in a settlement, referring to *Sugden on Powers* (8th edn, 1861) pp 482, 483. He argued cogently that a transaction made by a person within the dispositive powers conferred upon him will overreach equitable interests in the property the subject of the disposition, but ultra vires dispositions will not, and the transferee with notice will take the property subject to those interests. Mr Harpum expressed the view that the *j* exercise intra vires of a power of disposition which does not give rise to any capital money, such as an exchange of land, overreaches just as much as a transaction which does. There is every reason to think that the draftsman of the 1925 property legislation fully appreciated the true nature of overreaching. A principal objective of the 1925 property legislation was to simplify conveyancing and the proof of title to land. To this end equitable interests were to be kept off a   the title to the legal estate and could be overreached on a conveyance to a purchaser who took free of them.

The statutory provision governing overreaching is s 2 of the Law of Property Act 1925, which provides:

b   '(1) A conveyance to a purchaser of a legal estate in land shall overreach any equitable interest or power affecting that estate, whether or not he has notice thereof, if—(i) the conveyance is made under the powers conferred by the Settled Land Act, 1925, or any additional powers conferred by a settlement, and the equitable interest or power is capable of being overreached thereby, and the statutory requirements respecting the payment of capital money arising under the settlement are complied with; c   (ii) the conveyance is made by trustees for sale and the equitable interest or power is at the date of the conveyance capable of being overreached by such trustees under the provisions of subsection (2) of this section or independently of that subsection, and the statutory requirements respecting the payment of capital money arising under a disposition upon trust for sale d   are complied with; (iii) the conveyance is made by a mortgagee or personal representative in the exercise of his paramount powers, and the equitable interest or power is capable of being overreached by such conveyance, and any capital money arising from the transaction is paid to the mortgagee or personal representative; (iv) the conveyance is made under an order of the court and the equitable interest or power is bound by such order, and any e   capital money arising from the transaction is paid into, or in accordance with the order of, the court.'

The opening words of s 2(1) and para (ii) are the provisions most material to the appeal. The term 'conveyance' is given a wide meaning in s 205(1)(ii). It f   includes 'a mortgage, charge, lease, assent, vesting declaration, vesting instrument, disclaimer, release and every other assurance of property or of an interest therein by any instrument, except a will ...' Plainly, therefore, the legal charge is such a conveyance. The term 'purchaser' is defined as meaning, for the relevant part of the Act, 'a person who acquires an interest in or charge on property for ... money's worth; and in reference to a legal estate includes a g   chargee by way of legal mortgage ...' (s 205(1)(xxi)). Although the legal charge does not expressly state the consideration passing to the first and second defendants, Mr Havey and Mr Williams rightly do not suggest that the Punjab National Bank was not a purchaser. It is not in issue that the first and second defendants are trustees for sale.

h   The term 'capital money' is by s 205(1)(xxvi) to have the same meaning as in the Settled Land Act 1925. That Act contains no definition of 'capital money' simpliciter, but there is a definition of 'capital money arising under this Act' in s 117(1)(ii), viz 'capital money arising under the powers and provisions of this Act or the Acts replaced by this Act, and receivable for the trusts and purposes of the settlement and includes securities representing capital money'. It is far from clear j   precisely how this definition was intended to assist with the meaning of 'capital money' in the Law of Property Act 1925. By s 28(1) of that Act trustees for sale have all the powers of a tenant for life in relation to land and to the proceeds of sale. Thus, they have the power of the tenant for life to raise money by mortgage for the limited purposes specified in s 71(1) of the Settled Land Act 1925, including money raised for the discharge of an incumbrance. But I do not think that 'capital money' in the Law of Property Act 1925 can be confined to money arising under the Settled Land Act powers and provisions. Take an express trust for sale. The proceeds of sale received when the trust was executed would not be capital money arising under the powers and provisions of the Settled Land Act 1925, but would plainly be capital money for the purposes of the Law of Property Act 1925. I do not think that the exact significance of 'capital money' matters for the purposes of the present case as I am prepared to assume that, in respect of at least some of the indebtedness secured under the legal charge, capital money did not arise under the disposition, and also that some capital money may have done subsequently to the execution of the legal charge.

There is no dispute that the equitable interests of the third to seventh defendants were at the date of the legal charge capable of being overreached. That condition of s 2(1)(ii) was therefore satisfied. Most of the argument has turned on the final condition of that paragraph relating to compliance with the statutory requirements respecting the payment of capital money, and I shall shortly return to this.

Trustees for sale have a duty under s 26(3) of the Law of Property Act 1925 to consult, so far as practicable, the persons beneficially interested in possession in the rents and profits of the land until sale and to give effect to their wishes, but a purchaser is not to be concerned to see that the provisions of that subsection have been complied with. Section 27(1) provides that a purchaser of a legal estate from trustees for sale is not to be concerned with the trusts affecting the proceeds of sale of land subject to a trust for sale or affecting the rents and profits of the land until sale.

Section 27(2) (as amended by s 7 of the Law of Property (Amendment) Act 1926) provides (so far as material):

'... the proceeds of sale or other capital money shall not be paid to or applied by the direction of fewer than two persons as trustees for sale, except when the trustee is a trust corporation ...'

It is common ground that this provision contains the statutory requirements regulating the payment of capital money which are referred to in s 2(1)(ii).

The Land Registration Act 1925 contains provisions plainly intended to fit with, and not to be in derogation of, the Law of Property Act 1925. One sees that immediately from the definition section. In s 3(xi) of the Land Registration Act 'Legal Estates' are defined as meaning 'the estates interests and charges in or over land subsisting or created at law and which are by the Law of Property Act 1925, authorised to subsist or to be created at law'; in contrast 'Equitable interests' are defined as 'all the other interests and charges in or over land or in the proceeds of sale thereof ...' 'Minor interests' are defined as—

'the interests not capable of being disposed of or created by registered dispositions and capable of being overridden (whether or not a purchaser has notice thereof) by the proprietors unless protected as provided by this Act, and all rights and interests which are not registered or protected on the register and are not overriding interests, and include—(a) in the case of land held on trust for sale, all interests and powers which are under the Law of Property Act 1925, capable of being overridden by the trustees for sale, whether or not such interests and powers are so protected ...' (See s 3(xv).)

'Overriding interests' mean 'all the incumbrances, interests, rights, and powers not entered on the register but subject to which registered dispositions are by this Act to take effect ...' (s 3(xvi)).

By s 2 of the Land Registration Act a proprietor can only be registered in respect of estates capable of subsisting as legal estates; all other interests in registered land (except, so far as material, overriding interests) are to take effect in equity as minor interests. By s 74 neither the registrar nor any person dealing with a registered estate or charge is to be affected with notice of a trust, express, implied or constructive.

Section 18 (in the case of freeholds, including dispositions by way of charge: s 18(4)), s 21 (in the case of leaseholds) and s 25 empower the registered proprietor of any registered land to charge the registered land. As is stated in Ruoff and Roper *Registered Conveyancing* para 32-05:

'In registered conveyancing it is fundamental that any registered proprietor can exercise all or any powers of disposition unless some entry on the register exists to curtail or remove these powers ... In order to deprive registered proprietors of full powers of mortgaging or leasing, for example, there would have to be a restriction on the register expressly preventing them from exercising those powers.'

Section 20 prescribes the effect of registration of dispositions of freeholds registered with an absolute title. Such a disposition for valuable consideration confers on the transferee the legal estate expressed to be created in the land dealt with subject to the overriding interests, if any, affecting the estate transferred or created but free from all other estates and interests.

By s 70 of the Land Registration Act:

'(1) All registered land shall, unless under the provisions of this Act the contrary is expressed on the register, be deemed to be subject to such of the following overriding interests as may be for the time being subsisting in reference thereto, and such interests shall not be treated as incumbrances within the meaning of this Act, (that is to say) ... (g) The rights of every person in actual occupation of the land or in receipt of the rents and profits thereof, save where enquiry is made of such person and the rights are not disclosed ...'

The case of the third to seventh defendants has always been that their beneficial interests in respect of the property, being registered land, coupled with their actual occupation of the property, give them overriding interests within s 70(1)(g) which subsisted at the time of the legal charge. They say that their interests were not overreached by the legal charge because no capital money arose thereunder contemporaneously therewith and that accordingly their interests bound the plaintiff and take priority over its interests under the legal charge. The plaintiff's case has always been that the equitable interests of the third to seventh defendants were overreached by the legal charge, there being no statutory requirement that capital money should arise contemporaneously with the disposition.

The first point I should deal with is a procedural objection taken by Mr Havey. He pointed out that there will be a trial even if the plaintiff's application were to succeed, and he submitted that it was inappropriate for the court to entertain an application to strike out on the basis of hypothetical and disputed facts when a difficult and important point of law is involved. If he had been able to point to facts which might be found at the trial and which would provide the third to seventh defendants with a good defence to the plaintiff's claim, then he would be entitled to the dismissal of this appeal. But he did not put his submission that high. It is therefore a matter for the discretion of this court.

I accept that a novel and important point of law is raised by this appeal. Lending institutions regularly take security from businessmen in the form of a legal charge on property (which very frequently means that the matrimonial home is charged) to secure existing and future indebtedness, and very commonly that property will be registered land held by two registered proprietors on trust for sale with no restriction registered in respect of their power to transfer or mortgage that property. It was not suggested that it had ever been the practice of mortgagees to make enquiries of occupiers of the property as to any claimed rights. Yet if the third to seventh defendants are right, that is what the mortgagees must do if they are not to take subject to the beneficial interests of the occupiers.

It is remarkable that the point of law taken by those defendants does not appear to have arisen before in any reported case. We were taken by counsel to only two cases, both in the Court of Appeal and the House of Lords: *Williams & Glyn's Bank Ltd v Boland, Williams & Glyn's Bank Ltd v Brown* [1979] 2 All ER 697, [1979] Ch 312; *affd* [1980] 2 All ER 408, [1981] AC 487 and *City of London Building Society v Flegg* [1986] 1 All ER 989, [1986] Ch 605; *rvsd* [1987] 3 All ER 435, [1988] AC 54. In *Boland's* case it was common ground between the parties that there was no overreaching. Money was raised on mortgage of registered land and paid to a single trustee holding the land on trust for sale, and it was held that the rights of beneficiaries who were in occupation, and of whom no inquiries had been made, were not mere minor interests but overriding interests within s 70(1)(g) and so binding on the mortgagee. In the present case, as in *Flegg*, the registered proprietors were two in number. But in *Flegg* it was held that where money was raised on mortgage of registered land to discharge an existing incumbrance (and so in exercise of the power conferred by s 28(1) of the Law of Property Act 1925 by reference to s 71(1)(i) of the Settled Land Act 1925) and paid to two trustees for sale, the rights of occupying beneficiaries were overreached. In the present case the legal charge was not entered into to raise money for the discharge of an existing incumbrance nor was any money raised contemporaneously with the legal charge. No less surprising is the fact that counsel were not able to point to a single textbook for assistance nor to any other academic writing, though the court drew counsel's attention to Mr Harpum's article to which I have already referred.

As for the hypothetical and disputed facts, on a striking out application like this we must make every possible assumption in favour of the third to seventh defendants. Thus, we must assume that their pleaded factual averments are true and that those defendants or some of them have at all material times had beneficial interests and were in occupation of the property when the legal charge was executed. In conformity with the practice in the High Court, it is not appropriate to look at the affidavit evidence in support of the application to strike out on the ground specified in Ord 13, r 5(1)(a), viz that the relevant pleadings disclose no reasonable defence, but we are entitled to look at that evidence, which is not challenged, for the purposes of the application to strike out on the other grounds relied on by the plaintiff. We can also take account of the admissions by the defendants. We must assume, in the absence of evidence or admissions to the contrary, that no money was raised under the legal charge contemporaneously with it. The wording of the legal charge suggests that at the date of its execution then existing liabilities owed to the Punjab National Bank were thereby secured (see the references to 'all present ... indebtedness ... [and] all other liabilities ... present ...') and we must assume that there may have been such liabilities. It is plain that liabilities within the legal charge accrued after its execution, if only because of the evidence of accruing interest, and it appears that the argument before the judge proceeded on the basis that advances were made after the legal charge was executed. There is no suggestion that the plaintiff made any inquiry of the third to seventh defendants in occupation of the property such as would defeat what would otherwise be overriding interests. Finally, I should record that Mr Havey and Mr Williams accept that the first and second defendants were acting intra vires as trustees for sale in entering into the legal charge.

I would not wish to give encouragement to striking out applications based on a novel and important point of law when so many facts have to be assumed. But in all the circumstances, I do not think that the dismissal of the appeal on the procedural objection taken by Mr Havey would be justified. This appeal having come before the court, there would be a waste of time and costs if we were to decline to arrive at a decision on the substantial point underlying this appeal, nor for the reasons which I am about to give would it be satisfactory to leave the judge's ruling on the law standing.

The crucial issue is the true construction of the final condition of s 2(1)(ii) of the Law of Property Act 1925 relating to compliance with statutory requirements respecting the payment of capital money. There is no dispute that if capital money does arise under a conveyance by trustees for sale to a purchaser it must be paid to or applied as s 27(2) of that Act dictates. But for overreaching to occur, does capital money have to arise on and contemporaneously with the conveyance?

Willis J appears to have assumed that there could be no overreaching if no capital money arose.

He said:

> '...we have to look to see whether capital money was paid [to] or applied by the direction of the two trustees. If it was, then the defendants have no defence; if it was not, then the bank cannot overreach as they have an arguable defence on the evidence'.

Mr Havey and Mr Williams submitted that was indeed the position and they said that the arising of capital money on the conveyance was the assumption on which s 2(1)(ii) was drafted. Mr Crawford's initial submission accorded with that view, but he sought to escape the consequences by contending that capital money arose whenever the Punjab National Bank advanced money, even if before the legal charge was executed. However, I cannot accept that what was done prior to the legal charge has any relevance to the condition that 'the statutory requirements respecting the payment of capital money arising under a disposition upon trust for sale are complied with'. Nor can I accept Mr Crawford's further submission that the debt existing at the date of the legal charge was not materially different from the secured debt which existed at the date of the mortgage in *Flegg* and was discharged in that case out of the money raised. The circumstances are wholly different.

Mr Crawford, however, had recourse to a further submission, adopting a point suggested by the court, that the relevant condition in s 2(1)(ii) should be construed as applying only to those cases where there was capital money arising under a disposition upon trust for sale, the statutory requirements of s 27(2) being simply irrelevant to a transaction under which no capital money arises. There are several types of conveyance to a purchaser (within the statutory meanings of those terms) other than a charge to secure existing and future debt which do not give rise to capital money, for example, an exchange or a lease not at a premium.

Why should the legislature have intended to exclude such conveyances from having an overreaching effect? It is interesting to note that the precursor of s 2(1), viz s 3(2) of the Law of Property Act 1922, used as one of the conditions for overreaching to occur the formula: 'If any capital money arises from the transaction ... the requirements of this Act respecting the payment of capital money arising under a trust for sale ... are complied with.' However, the form of s 3(2) differed in a number of respects from s 2(1) of the 1925 Act and it may not be safe to infer that the later provision was intended to re-enact the substance of the earlier provision. But it points to the relevant condition of s 2(1) being worded in surprisingly oblique fashion if what was intended was that capital money must arise so that the statutory requirements can be complied with. Mr Havey drew attention to the word 'any' in connection with 'capital money' in s 2(1)(iii) and (iv) and suggested that its omission from the reference to 'capital money' in s 2(1)(i) and (ii) was significant. But the structure of those paragraphs is quite different from s 2(1)(iii) and (iv) and the draftsman could not have achieved the effect of s 3(2) of the 1922 Act by adding 'any' before 'capital money' in s 2(1)(i) or (ii).

The relevant condition in s 2(1)(ii) is the same as that in s 2(1)(i). The overreaching powers conferred by the Settled Land Act 1925 include power to convey by an exchange or lease as well as by a mortgage or charge where capital money may not arise (see s 72 of that Act). The statutory requirements governing capital money (to be paid to or applied by the direction of not less than two individuals or a trust corporation: ss 94, 95 of that Act) can only apply to those conveyances giving rise to capital money. The same interpretation must apply to the condition in s 2(1)(i) as it does to the conveyancing condition in s 2(1)(ii).

A more substantial argument of policy advanced on behalf of the third to seventh defendants is that if overreaching occurs where no capital money arises, the beneficiaries' interests may be reduced by the conveyance leaving nothing to which the interests can attach by way of replacement save the equity of redemption, and that may be or become valueless. I see considerable force in this point, but I am not persuaded that it suffices to defeat what I see to be the policy of the legislation, to allow valid dispositions to overreach equitable interests. In my judgment, on its true construction s 2(1)(ii) only requires compliance with the statutory requirements respecting the payment of capital money if capital money arises. Accordingly, I would hold that capital money did not have to arise under the conveyance.

The judge further said:

'I consider that overreaching must take place at the time of the execution. I think that the plaintiff does not object to that in principle, but says that the defendants' right simply attaches to the equity of redemption; but I do not think one can have a condition of overreaching on moneys which may or may not be drawn down later. For overreaching to take effect all parts of s 27(2) must be complied with; it is a two stage process which requires, first, the existence of either proceeds of sale or capital moneys and, secondly, those are either to be paid to the two trustees or applied at their discretion. The plaintiff says it does not matter—because there was a general direction for application in the charge—if it comes into existence or is applied at a subsequent time. I think that is wrong; it is necessary for the moneys to be in existence at the time of the charge so that those moneys can either be received or applied at the trustees' directions.'

a The judge found assistance for that conclusion in *Re Marquis of Bristol's Settled Estates* [1893] 3 Ch 161, in which Kekewich J reached the unsurprising conclusion that the discretion conferred on the court by s 15 of the Trustee Act 1890, to direct or authorise capital money to be applied, could not be exercised nunc pro tunc when the capital money was not yet in hand. With respect to the judge, that decision is no help to the construction of s 2(1)(ii), nor did Mr Havey or Mr
b Williams seek to argue before us that it was relevant.

The judge also considered that certain words of Lord Oliver in *Flegg*'s case [1987] 3 All ER 435 at 453, [1988] AC 54 at 90 were of assistance to the third to seventh defendants. Lord Oliver said:

c 'If, then, one asks what were the subsisting rights of the respondents [the occupying beneficiaries] referable to their occupation, the answer must, in my judgment, be that they were rights which, vis-à-vis the appellants [the mortgagee], were, eo instanti with the creation of the charge, overreached and therefore subsisted only in relation to the equity of redemption.'

d What is said in that passage is precisely what the plaintiff says occurred in the present case. It is not suggested that the overreaching can be undone by subsequent events.

Both Mr Havey and Mr Williams supported the judge's conclusion that some capital money must arise contemporaneously with the conveyance for there to be overreaching. They said that if a conveyance provided only for deferred
e payment, that would not suffice. They further submitted that provided some capital money arose contemporaneously with the conveyance and s 27(2) was complied with, overreaching would occur even though other money was subsequently advanced under the conveyance. Thus, if a £1m facility was secured by a mortgage and in the course of time was fully drawn on but at the
f time of the mortgage only £100 was advanced, there would nevertheless be overreaching in respect of the whole £1m thereby secured, whereas if the £100 had not been advanced at the time of the mortgage, there would have been no overreaching. I do not believe that the statutory language supports a requirement producing such a surprising and illogical result. Mr Havey drew our attention to a large number of provisions in the Settled Land Act 1925 which, he
g said, showed that money arising from a transaction must be received or applied at the same time as the transaction. I cannot agree, though I of course accept that to be paid or applied, capital money must be in hand. If and to the extent that capital money arises after the conveyance, s 27(2) must be complied with for the mortgagee to obtain a good receipt. If it is not, for example if an advance is made
h after a mortgage has been executed but under a facility provided for by the mortgage but is not paid to or at the direction of two or more trustees or a trust corporation, that would not affect the overreaching which would have occurred on the mortgage.

I take the following statement in *Snell's Equity* (29th edn, 1990) p 63 to be
j correct:

'A conveyance to a purchaser of a legal estate for money or money's worth will overreach ... any equitable interest or power affecting the estate whether or not the purchaser has notice of it, if the conveyance is made ... (ii) by trustees for sale ... provided that the ... equitable interest or power is one of those which are capable of being overreached by the conveyance, and that *any* capital money arising from the transaction is paid [in case] ... (ii) to

the trustees, who must be at least two in number, or a trust corporation ...'   *a*
(My emphasis.)

The correct analysis of the position in the present case is that on the execution
of the legal charge, the interests of the third to seventh defendants were
overreached and attached to the equity of redemption. The legal estate in the
property was by the legal charge made subject to the rights thereunder of the   *b*
Punjab National Bank which were subsequently assigned to the plaintiff,
including the right to sell the property. The value of the equity of redemption on
the execution of the legal charge would reflect the then existing liabilities thereby
secured. That value would be further reduced as further liabilities arose and were
secured under the legal charge. In the light of *Flegg*, it follows from the
overreaching that s 70(1)(g) does not avail the third to seventh defendants and   *c*
that their defence on this point cannot succeed and should be struck out. On the
assumption that they were not consulted about the legal charge by the first and
second defendants, it may be that they have the right to obtain redress against the
trustees.

Much though I value the principle of overreaching as having aided the   *d*
simplification of conveyancing, I cannot pretend that I regard the resulting
position in the present case as entirely satisfactory. The safeguard for
beneficiaries under the existing legislation is largely limited to having two
trustees or a trust corporation where capital money falls to be received. But that
is no safeguard at all, as this case has shown, when no capital money is received
on and contemporaneously with the conveyance. Further, even when it is   *e*
received by two trustees as in *Flegg*, it might be thought that beneficiaries in
occupation are insufficiently protected. Hence, the recommendation for reform
in the Law Commission's report, *Transfer of Land, Overreaching: Beneficiaries in
Occupation* (1989) (Law Com No 188), that a conveyance should not overreach
the interest of a sui juris beneficiary in occupation unless he gives his consent. Mr *f*
Harpum in the article to which reference has been made proposed an alternative
reform, limiting the power of trustees to mortgage. Whether the legislature will
reform the law remains to be seen. I should add for completeness that we were
assured by counsel that the recent Trusts of Land and Appointment of Trustees
Act 1996 was of no assistance and we have not considered its effect.

Despite the dissatisfaction with the existing law which I have voiced, for the *g*
reasons which I have given I would allow this appeal and strike out the passages
in the defence identified by the plaintiff in its summons of 10 August 1994.

PILL LJ. I agree. The preliminary point now at issue turns upon the construction
of s 2(1)(ii) of the Law of Property Act 1925 and whether, for overreaching to   *h*
occur, capital money has to arise on and contemporaneously with the
conveyance. On this issue, I address the questions raised on the effect of the
presence or absence of the word 'any' in the statutory provisions.

Peter Gibson LJ has set out s 2(1) of the Law of Property Act 1925 in his
judgment. Section 2(1)(ii) provides that a conveyance to a purchaser of a legal   *j*
estate in land shall overreach any equitable interest or power affecting that estate,
whether or not he has notice thereof, if—

'the conveyance is made by trustees for sale and the equitable interest or
power is at the date of the conveyance capable of being overreached by such
trustees under the provisions of subsection (2) of this section or
independently of that subsection, and the statutory requirements respecting

a   the payment of capital money arising under a disposition upon trust for sale are complied with ...'

The paragraph does not expressly require the payment of capital money as a prerequisite of overreaching but does provide that the statutory requirements respecting the payment of capital money arising are complied with. The defendants submit that because it is necessary to comply with statutory

b   requirements respecting the payment of capital money arising under a disposition upon trusts for sale, it follows that overreaching can occur only if capital money does arise. The words 'if any' do not appear after 'capital money' in para (ii) (or in para (i)), as they would if capital money were not a prerequisite. By contrast, it is submitted, the word 'any' appears before 'capital money' in paras

c   (iii) and (iv) of sub-s (1). Reference was also made to the presence of the word 'any' in s 3(2) of the Law of Property Act 1922, the precursor of s 2(1)(ii). The subsection provides that overreaching shall not occur unless:

> '(ii) If *any* capital money arises from the transaction, the same is paid into court, or the requirements of this Act respecting the payment of capital
d   > money arising under a trust for sale or a settlement, are complied with.'

I agree with the conclusion of Peter Gibson LJ and see no merit in the submission based upon the presence of the word 'any' in the other provisions mentioned and its absence in para (ii). The second limb of para (ii) is concerned (as is that of para (i)) to ensure compliance with statutory requirements and the

e   requirements concerned are those 'respecting the payment of capital money'. The words 'capital money arising' serve to identify the relevant statutory requirements and the sentence would read oddly if the word 'any' appeared in this context. The requirements arise only if capital money arises; it does not follow that there is no overreaching unless capital money does arise. If capital

f   money does not arise, compliance does not arise.

In paras (iii) and (iv) of s 2(1), the expression 'capital money arising' is not linked with 'statutory requirements' and the word 'any' can appear before 'capital money' without doing offence to the language of that paragraph. The presence of the word 'any' demonstrates the statutory intention and I regard its presence in paras (iii) and (iv) as an indication that s 2(1) as a whole does not require the

g   payment of capital money contemporaneously with the conveyance if overreaching is to occur. No logical reason for a distinction between the situations contemplated in paras (i) and (ii) on the one hand and those in (iii) and (iv) on the other was suggested.

As to the 1922 Act, the form of drafting adopted in s 3(2) was quite different
h   from that in s 2(1) of the 1925 Act. The subsection was negative in form and precluded overreaching except in the circumstances set out. The words 'if any' before 'capital money' in para (ii) did establish beyond any doubt that overreaching could occur without capital money arising from the transaction. However, the words 'if any' fall naturally into the text in the context of that

j   subsection as drafted. I cannot accept that their absence in s 2(1)(ii) of the 1925 Act, which was a consolidating Act, demonstrates any changed or different legislative intention between the 1922 and 1925 Acts. I cannot read into the provisions of the 1925 Act, an assumption that, for overreaching to occur, capital money must arise on and contemporaneously with the conveyance. Indeed, the appropriate construction is that it need not arise.

Counsel for the defendants accept that, even in a case such as the present where large sums of money are involved, a nominal payment of capital at the time of the conveyance would enable the mortgagee to overreach. Such a system *a* would render the protection of the equitable interests of the beneficiaries, for which the defendants contend, largely illusory in the event. Had Parliament intended to protect those interests by requiring the contemporaneous payment of capital money if overreaching is to occur, I would have expected express and stringent provision.

b

Procedure

The request to resolve the point of law identified by Peter Gibson LJ in the first paragraph of his judgment comes before the court by way of the plaintiff's application to the district judge to strike out those paragraphs of the defence which depend upon the point being resolved in the plaintiffs' favour. The *c* application was made under CCR Ord 13, r 5, which follows RSC Ord 18, r 19(1).

This is already the second appeal, the present appeal being from the decision of the county court judge on appeal from the district judge. While I agree that it would not have been appropriate in the circumstances for this court to accede to Mr Havey's procedural objection to the point being heard before this court, I too would not wish to give encouragement to striking out applications being made *d* in circumstances such as these where, as Peter Gibson LJ has put it, a novel and important point of law is involved. The first objection is that the court has had to assume the existence of facts. The second is that there are many other issues in the case, both of fact and of law, which will have to be resolved in the county court whatever the outcome of the appeal on point of law to this court. Judges to whom applications are made should keep in mind the words of Lord Mackay *e* of Clashfern in *Williams & Humbert Ltd v W & H Trade Marks (Jersey) Ltd, Rumasa SA v Multinvest (UK) Ltd* [1986] 1 All ER 129 at 143, [1986] AC 368 at 441:

'If on an application to strike out it appears that a prolonged and serious argument will be necessary there must, at the least, be a serious risk that the court time, effort and expense devoted to it will be lost since the pleading in *f* question may not be struck out and the whole matter will require to be considered anew at the trial. This consideration, as well as the context in which Ord 18, r 19 occurs and the authorities upon it, justifies a general rule that the judge should decline to proceed with the argument unless he not only considers it likely that he may reach the conclusion that the pleading *g* should be struck out, but also is satisfied that striking out will obviate the necessity for a trial or will so substantially cut down or simplify the trial as to make the risk of proceeding with the hearing sufficiently worth while.'

Had the application been, as it could have been to seek the same result, for the *h* trial of the point as a preliminary issue, similar considerations should apply (see *Everett v Ribbands* [1952] 1 All ER 823 at 827, [1952] 2 QB 198 at 206 per Romer LJ and *Carl-Zeiss-Stiftung v Herbert Smith & Co (a firm)* [1968] 2 All ER 1002 at 1004, [1969] 1 Ch 93 at 98 per Lord Denning MR, where the appropriate test is stated). Preliminary points of law, stated Lord Scarman in *Tilling v Whiteman* [1979] 1 All ER 737 at 744, [1980] AC 1 at 25, 'are too often treacherous short cuts'. *j*

HIRST LJ. I agree with both judgments.

Appeal allowed. Leave to appeal to the House of Lords refused.

Paul Magrath Esq　Barrister.

a

Fairpo v Humberside County Council

QUEEN'S BENCH DIVISION (CROWN OFFICE LIST)

LAWS J

9, 10, 16 JULY 1996

b

Education – Local education authority – Statutory duty to provide special education – Authority declining to make statement of special educational needs in respect of child with learning difficulties – Child subject of care order in favour of local authority – Foster parent appealing to Special Educational Needs Tribunal – Whether foster parent having right to appeal as 'parent' to High Court against decision of Special Educational Needs Tribunal – Education Act 1944, s 114(1D) – Tribunals and Inquiries Act 1992, s 11(1) – Education Act 1993, s 169.

c

A local education authority made an assessment of a boy, D, who suffered from defective vision, learning difficulties and communication problems, but declined to make a statement as to his special educational needs under the provisions of the Education Act 1993. D's foster mother (the appellant), with whom he had been placed in December 1989 by the authority, in whose favour a care order had been made, appealed to the Special Educational Needs Tribunal under s 169[a] of the 1993 Act, which provided for such an appeal by a 'parent', the definition of which, set out in s 114(1D)[b] of the Education Act 1944, was incorporated into the 1993 Act and included, unless the context otherwise required, (a) a person who was not a parent but had parental responsibility for a child, or (b) who had care of him. The tribunal dismissed the appeal holding that although D had special educational needs, sufficient provision could be made for him within the resources of the school he was attending, and the appellant appealed, out of time, to the High Court under s 11(1)[c] of the Tribunals and Inquiries Act 1992. The authority contended that the appellant did not have locus standi to bring the appeal on the ground that she was not a 'parent' and so not a proper 'party' to the proceedings before the tribunal.

d

e

f

Held – For the purposes of s 11(1) of the 1992 Act, a 'party' to proceedings before a tribunal was a person who was properly before the tribunal according to the terms of any legislation which prescribed who might be the parties before that tribunal. In the instant case, although the appellant did not have parental responsibility for D, since she was involved in his full-time care on a settled basis, and the statutory context did not require a different construction, she had care of him within the meaning of s 114(1D)(b) of the 1944 Act. It followed that the appellant was a 'parent' enjoying the right of appeal to the tribunal and so a proper 'party' to the proceedings before the tribunal who was entitled to appeal to the High Court under s 11(1) of the 1992 Act (see p 186 *h j*, p 188 *j*, p 190 *j*, p 191 *g* and p 192 *d*, post).

g

h

j

Notes

For children with special educational needs and the extent of the local authority's duty, see 15 *Halsbury's Laws* (4th edn reissue) paras 126–132.

---

a   Section 169, so far as material, is set out p 185 *d e*, post
b   Section 114(1D), so far as material, is set out p 187 *a*, post
c   Section 11(1), so far as material, is set out p 186 *e*, post

For the Education Act 1944, s 114, see 15 *Halsbury's Statutes* (4th edn) (1994 reissue)187.

For the Tribunal and Inquiries Act 1992, s 11, see 10 *Halsbury's Statutes* (4th edn) (1995 reissue) 479.

For the Education Act 1993, s 169, see 15 *Halsbury's Statutes* (4th edn) (1994 reissue) 963.

Cases referred to in judgment

R v Telford Juvenile Court, ex p E (a minor) [1989] 2 FLR 101.

S (a minor) v Special Educational Needs Tribunal [1996] 2 All ER 286, [1996] 1 WLR 382, CA; *affg* [1996] 1 All ER 171, [1995] 1 WLR 1627.

Z (a minor) (freedom of publication), Re [1995] 4 All ER 961, [1996] 2 WLR 88, CA.

Case referred to in skeleton argument

S v Walsall Metropolitan BC [1985] 3 All ER 294, [1985] 1 WLR 1150, CA.

Appeal

By notice dated 23 October 1995 a local authority foster parent Jean Fairpo appealed against a decision of the Special Educational Needs Tribunal made on 26 April 1995 whereby the tribunal upheld the decision of Humberside County Council (whose activities were transferred to Kingston-upon-Hull City Council during the course of the proceedings) declining to make and maintain a statement of special education needs in favour of D, the appellant's foster child, pursuant to s 168 of the Education Act 1993. The facts are set out in the judgment.

Paul Greaney (instructed by *Langleys*, York) for the appellant.

Roger McCarthy QC (instructed by *Lynne Bird*, Kingston-upon-Hull) for the respondent council.

Cur adv vult

16 July 1996. The following judgment was delivered.

LAWS J. This is a statutory appeal, brought under the Tribunals and Inquiries Act 1992 as amended, against a decision of the Special Educational Needs Tribunal made on 26 April 1995. Such an appeal is available on a point of law only.

The appellant is a foster parent employed by Humberside County Council (whose activities have now been transferred to Kingston-upon-Hull City Council) (the respondent). She is a 'local authority foster parent' within the meaning of s 23(3) of the Children Act 1989. A little boy, D, who was born on 9 April 1988, was placed with her by the authority. D is the subject of a care order to the respondent under s 31 of the 1989 Act. The appellant has, as I understand it, looked after him since 31 December 1989, at first for four short periods until he was some 20 months old and thereafter continuously. Unfortunately, he suffers from defective vision, learning difficulties, and communication problems. An assessment was carried out and the respondent, as the relevant local education authority, obtained a series of experts' reports upon him which are summarised in the applicant's affidavit. At length, however, the respondent declined to make a statutory statement in respect of D under s 168(1) of the Education Act 1993, which provides:

a

'If, in the light of an assessment under section 167 of this Act of any child's educational needs and of any representations made by the child's parent in pursuance of Schedule 10 to this Act, it is necessary for the local education authority to determine the special educational provision which any learning difficulty he may have calls for, the authority shall make and maintain a statement of his special educational needs.'

b

Under the statute various consequences flow from the making of a statement, but for present purposes it is unnecessary to go into them.

Certain experts, and the appellant, made representations to the respondent questioning the decision not to make a statement, but it was confirmed in a letter to the appellant from the respondent's director of education dated 25 November 1994. In her affidavit before me the appellant says she was shocked and surprised by this decision; and it is plain that she entertains a very powerful belief that a statement should have been made. She brought an appeal against the decision to the Special Educational Needs Tribunal. Such an appeal is available (and only available) under s 169 of the 1993 Act. Subsections (1) and (2) provide:

c

d

'(1) If, after making an assessment under section 167 of this Act of the educational needs of any child for whom no statement is maintained under section 168 of this Act, the local education authority do not propose to make such a statement, they shall give notice in writing of their decision, and of the effect of subsection (2) below, to the child's parent.

e

(2) In such a case, the child's parent may appeal to the Tribunal against the decision.'

The respondent's letter of 25 November 1994 had notified the appellant that she was entitled to appeal to the tribunal.

The tribunal held that D indeed had special educational needs, but that sufficient provision could be made for him within the resources of the school he was attending. It accordingly dismissed the appeal. Its decision was communicated to the appellant by a letter which she received on 3 May 1995. An appeal to this court under the 1992 Act should have been brought within 28 days. It was not, and one of the issues I must decide is whether to extend time under RSC Ord 3, r 5.

f

g

What in fact happened was this. After receiving notice of the tribunal's decision the appellant consulted a solicitor who unfortunately fell ill, so that some time passed without anything being done. The appellant consulted her present solicitors in July 1995. After obtaining legal aid, they made an application for leave to apply for judicial review, naming as respondent not the local authority but the tribunal. On 31 July 1995 Popplewell J granted leave. But the tribunal applied to set the leave aside, and on 11 October 1995 the same judge set aside the leave he had granted, accepting the tribunal's argument that the challenge should have been brought by statutory appeal and not by way of judicial review. He also accepted a submission that the tribunal was not a proper respondent.

h

j

On 23 October 1995 a notice of motion to launch a statutory appeal under the 1992 Act was served, but time again went by and the case was not listed until 9 July 1996 when it came before me. It is said that over a long period the papers were lost in the Crown Office, but in any event there is no basis on which any blame can be attached to the appellant as regards any delay after 23 October 1995.

On 9 July 1996 I heard brief submissions upon the question whether I should extend time for appealing under RSC Ord 3, r 5. It seemed to me, however, and counsel agreed, that it would be inappropriate to determine that question *a* without first hearing argument upon another issue raised by the respondent council: an issue which although (like the time point) logically prior to any consideration of the merits of the appeal, is of some substance and perhaps of some general importance in the context of the statutory regimes relating to the education and care of children. It arises in this way. Mr McCarthy QC, for the respondent, submits that the appellant had no legal right to appeal to the tribunal; *b* only a 'parent' (I use quotation marks advisedly) enjoys such a right, and the appellant is not and was not within the meaning of the term 'parent' as it is defined for the purposes of the 1993 Act. If that is right, he submits further that she has no locus before me, since an appeal under the 1992 Act may only be brought by a 'party' to the proceedings below, and 'party' must mean a proper party having regard to the statutory measures relating to locus before the tribunal *c* whose decision is sought to be appealed. Mr Greaney, for the appellant, accepts that only a 'parent' may appeal to the tribunal under s 169 of the 1993 Act; having regard to sub-s (2), that is plainly right. The tribunal has no general jurisdiction, but only that which is conferred by the subsection (and by other express provisions, irrelevant for present purposes). However, Mr Greaney submits not *d* only that his client fell within the statutory definition of 'parent' but also that, even if she did not, she is nevertheless a proper party before me under the terms of the 1992 Act.

It is convenient first to deal with this latter point, as to the sense to be attributed to 'party' in the 1992 Act. Section 11(1) simply provides: '... if any party to *e* proceedings before any tribunal specified ... is dissatisfied in point of law with a decision of the tribunal he may ... appeal ...' In an obvious sense, of course, the appellant was plainly a party to the appeal before the Special Educational Needs Tribunal: she brought the appeal. But if in point of law she had no legal right whatever to do so, I do not consider that she can be regarded as a 'party' within the meaning of s 11(1). To hold otherwise would be to validate the proceedings *f* before the tribunal, which ex hypothesi would have been invalid. It is, I think, not without significance that in regulating the powers of this court upon a statutory appeal Ord 55, r 7 provides that the court may receive further evidence (para (2)), draw inferences of fact (para (3)), and make any decision which ought to have been made by the tribunal, make any further order as the case may *g* require, or remit the matter for redetermination (para (5)): the premise of the whole scheme is that the proceedings below were properly constituted in the first place. In these circumstances, it seems to me plain that a 'party' entitled to appeal to this court under the 1992 Act must be a person who was properly before the tribunal below according to the terms of any legislation which prescribes who may be the parties before that tribunal. I derive support for this view from a *h* decision of Latham J in *S (a minor) v Special Educational Needs Tribunal* [1996] 1 All ER 171, [1995] 1 WLR 1627 in which he held that only a parent on the one hand or the local education authority on the other may bring an appeal to the High Court under s 11(1) against a decision of the Special Educational Needs Tribunal. An appeal against Latham J's decision was dismissed by the Court of Appeal *j* ([1996] 2 All ER 286, [1996] 1 WLR 382). Accordingly, I reject Mr Greaney's argument that even if his client was not entitled to appeal to the tribunal, nevertheless she is entitled to appeal here. The real question is whether she had any legal right to go to the tribunal under s 169 of the 1993 Act.

That depends on whether she fell within the statutory definition of 'parent', which comes into the 1993 Act by a somewhat circuitous route. Paragraph 10 of a Sch 13 to the Children Act 1989 added a new subsection (sub-s (1D)) to s 114 of the Education Act 1944. Section 114(1D) provides:

'In this Act, unless the context otherwise requires, "parent", in relation to a child or young person, includes any person—(a) who is not a parent of his but who has parental responsibility for him, or (b) who has care of him ...'

b It is plain from the words which follow that (save for irrelevant purposes which are specified) a parent within this definition need not be a natural person, and so may include a local authority. The definition is incorporated into the 1993 Act by s 305(3) of that Act, which provides that it is to be construed as one with the 1944 Act.

c Mr Greaney's case, of course, is that his client falls within s 114(1D)(b). Mr McCarthy accepts, as obviously he must, that as a matter of ordinary language a long term full time foster mother plainly 'has care' of the child who is placed with her. It follows that he must persuade me that in the subsection Parliament intended to attribute some other sense to the phrase. He also accepts that there is nowhere a statutory definition of the expression 'has care': indeed, it is itself d part of the statutory definition of 'parent'. He has therefore to argue that Parliament has *by implication* displaced the ordinary meaning of the expression 'has care'. On the face of it, it is an uphill task.

Mr McCarthy approaches it by two alternative routes. The first depends on the sense to be given to the words 'unless the context otherwise requires' in the subsection. The argument was developed as follows. The respondent has e parental responsibility for the child, by virtue of the care order in its favour. Section 33(3) of the 1989 Act provides:

'While a care order is in force with respect to a child, the local authority designated by the order shall—(a) have parental responsibility for the child; and (b) have the power ... to determine the extent to which a parent or f guardian of the child may meet his parental responsibility for him.'

'Parent' here means natural parent. 'Parental responsibility' is a term of art under the Act. Section 3(1) defines it as meaning 'all the rights, duties, powers, responsibilities and authority which by law a parent has in relation to the child and his property'. Under the Act the natural mother always (so far as relevant for g present purposes) has parental responsibility; the natural father only if he was married to the mother at the time of the child's birth (s 2(1)) or if he acquires it under s 4, which I need not set out. 'Parental responsibility' includes the duty to arrange for the child's education (see *Re Z (a minor) (freedom of publication)* [1995] 4 All ER 961 at 980, [1996] 2 WLR 88 at 107). Moreover, a parent has a pivotal h role in relation to many functions provided for by the Education Acts, such as choice of school, consultation over schooling and over closure of a school, and so forth. Mr McCarthy says the phrase 'unless the context otherwise requires' is intended to exclude the s 114(1D) definition from cases where on the facts the definition's application would, as his skeleton argument puts it, be j 'inappropriate'.

Mr McCarthy submits that a foster mother in the applicant's position does not have parental responsibility under the 1989 Act. So far as it goes, that is right. Moreover, a local authority foster parent has no express rights under the Act or the Foster Placement (Children) Regulations 1991, SI 1991/910, to make decisions as to the child's schooling. Essentially, as I understand it, Mr McCarthy's argument is that in those circumstances the application of

s 114(1D)(b) to a person (not being a natural parent or the local authority) who
'has care' of the child in the ordinary language sense is always inappropriate
where there exists another person, be it local authority or natural parent, who is
actively exercising parental responsibility. The reason is that unacceptable
conflicts might otherwise arise. In the present case, D's natural parents are on the
evidence playing no part whatever in his upbringing. But it might not be so; and
Mr McCarthy says that where the natural parent takes an active interest in the
child's education even though the child is fostered, Parliament must have
intended that the wishes of the natural parent, who has parental responsibility, as
regards the child's education should prevail over those of what he calls a
'non-parent'. So, by inference, it is submitted that in such a case the 'non-parent'
cannot have been intended to be included in the s 114(1D) definition for the
purposes of rights of appeal under s 169 of the 1993 Act or, I assume, for any other
purposes.

Likewise it is said that where a local authority has and exercises parental
responsibility, its views as to the child's education must necessarily prevail over
those of a 'non-parent' carer; not least, perhaps, because where the non-parent is
(as here) a local authority foster parent, the local authority has the power to
terminate the placement if that is judged appropriate (see reg 7 of the 1991
regulations). But the submission is in essence the same: the authority has
parental responsibility, the foster parent does not, and the former's views must
prevail. So in such a case the foster parent is taken out of the definition of 'parent'
because 'the context otherwise requires'.

On Mr McCarthy's own approach there might be a conflict between a natural
parent and the local authority. But Mr McCarthy says that such a potential for
conflict has been specifically resolved by s 33(3)(b) of the 1989 Act, which I have
set out. He submits that by virtue of that provision the local authority is
empowered to prohibit a natural parent from mounting an appeal under s 169. I
doubt whether that proposition is correct. Section 33(3)(b) clearly allows a local
authority to whom a care order has been made to restrict the extent to which a
natural parent may perform the functions described in s 3(1) of the 1989 Act. But
I am not persuaded that the right of appeal under s 169 of the 1993 Act is within
the collection of rights and other functions referred to in s 3(1), which I take to be
rights and functions directly to control and regulate the child's upbringing,
conferred by the general law. An appeal under s 169 is not on the face of it within
any such category. The parent asks the tribunal in effect to reconsider a
determination by a local education authority about the child's education. In
doing so he or she is not, as it seems to me, making a decision which *itself directly*
affects the child's education, and is not I think exercising a function conferred on
him by the general law concerning the relationship between children and parents
as it is described in s 3(1). In addition one would expect Parliament to use clear
words if it intended to permit a local authority to deprive a parent of what
otherwise is his plain statutory right of appeal to the tribunal.

But whether or not that view of s 33(3)(b) is right, there are, in my judgment,
fatal objections to this limb of Mr McCarthy's argument. A major pillar in the
argument's structure consists in the proposition that under the whole scheme of
the 1989 Act no situation can arise in which a person not being the child's natural
parent can possess parental responsibility while a care order to the local authority
is in force. It is beyond contest that in the events which have happened the
appellant does not have parental responsibility (and a care order is of course in
force). So far as it goes Mr McCarthy's proposition is true (see the statutory
citations set out below). However, it does not grapple with another

a proposition—not, I should say at once, addressed by counsel before me—which is that a local authority foster parent may in certain circumstances acquire parental responsibility so as to displace a care order in favour of the authority and thereby discharge the authority's parental responsibility.

Section 8(1) of the 1989 Act defines a 'residence order' as meaning 'an order settling the arrangements to be made as to the person with whom a child is to
b live'. Mr McCarthy accepts that a residence order may be made in favour of someone who is not a natural parent. Section 12(2) provides that in such a case, the person in whose favour the residence order is made shall have parental responsibility while the residence order remains in force. But s 91(2) provides: 'The making of a care order with respect to a child who is the subject of any section 8 order [which, of course, includes a residence order] discharges that
c order.' So plainly the making of the care order in such circumstances would also bring to an end the parental responsibility of the person to whom the s 8 order had been made. Hence, Mr McCarthy's proposition that parental responsibility cannot at once subsist both in a 'non-natural' parent and the local authority. However, s 9(1) and (3) provides:

d
'(1) No court shall make any section 8 order, other than a residence order, with respect to a child who is in the care of the local authority ...

(3) A person who is, or was at any time within the last six months, a local authority foster parent of a child may not apply for leave to apply for a section 8 order with respect to a child unless—(a) he has the consent of the
e authority; (b) he is a relative of the child; or (c) the child has lived with him for at least three years preceding the application.'

See also s 10(5), which provides in part:

'The following persons are entitled to apply for a residence or contact
f order with respect to a child ... (b) any person with whom the child has lived for a period of at least three years ...'

Then s 91(1) provides: 'The making of a residence order with respect to a child who is the subject of a care order discharges the care order.'

g The result of this collection of provisions is, as I have indicated, that while parental responsibility cannot subsist in a 'non-natural' parent and the local authority at the same time, it is not always the case that it will subsist in the latter: a local authority foster parent, or indeed another de facto carer, having (in effect) had the care of the child for at least three years may by the making of a residence order acquire parental responsibility in place of the authority. This appellant has
h not in fact applied for a residence order. I do not of course suggest that had she done so such an order would have been made, nor is anything I say intended to encourage her to make any such application. My purpose in referring to these provisions is only to indicate that as a matter of construction, quite aside from the facts of the present case, the status or at least the potential status of a long term
j local authority foster parent is not as secondary or subordinate as Mr McCarthy's argument would imply, and to that extent the force of the argument is, in my judgment, accordingly weakened.

Moreover, it is of some interest to notice that the same formula as is used in s 114(1D) of the 1944 Act appears in s 3(5) of the 1989 Act, which provides:

'A person who—(a) does not have parental responsibility for a particular child, but (b) has care of the child, may (subject to the provisions of this Act) do what is reasonable in all the circumstances of the case for the purpose of safeguarding or promoting the child's welfare.'

The subsection's application is plainly not limited to circumstances where no other person (or local authority) is actively exercising parental responsibility. That being so, its inclusion in the statute also seems to me to undermine the force of Mr McCarthy's contention that the active exercise of parental responsibility by another must be taken to displace a person in the appellant's position from the s 114(1D)(b) definition. Indeed there might, I think, be cases where the operation of s 3(5) could give rise to possible conflicts of the kind which Mr McCarthy says the statute is drafted to avoid.

More important, perhaps, is the fact, accepted by Mr McCarthy, that in the event that there is neither a natural parent nor a local authority nor anyone else having parental responsibility on the scene, a de facto carer *would* fall within the s 114(1D) definition. It follows that his reliance on the expression 'unless the context otherwise requires' would require me to interpret the notion of 'context' as meaning something altogether different from the 'context' of any particular statutory provision: in a word, it would depend on the facts of the case whether the statutory definition applied or not. The definition would sometimes apply, sometimes not, according to shifting circumstances. I cannot think that that is right. In truth, the whole of the first limb of Mr McCarthy's argument upon analysis is to the effect that there are good policy reasons for excluding a person such as the applicant from the definition of 'parent' in any situation where there is another party possessing and concerned to exercise statutory parental responsibility. Whether or not such good policy reasons exist (and I shall have a little more to say about that in discussing the second limb of the argument), I am concerned to construe s 114(1D), and I am unable to see how the words 'unless the context otherwise requires' can be said to incorporate such reasons into the statute. In my judgment, the expression naturally refers to a statutory context in which the word 'parent' appears: and its effect is that if the terms of any provision containing the word 'parent' were such that as a matter of language, and the general sense of the provision in question, the word must bear a meaning different from that prescribed in s 114(1D), then pro tanto the statutory definition is disapplied. In fact, Mr Greaney was unable to point to an instance in the relevant statutes where that would be the case. I have not myself trawled through the whole of the statutory provisions to which the s 114(1D) definition potentially applies, but even if there is no such instance I do not consider that the fact assists Mr McCarthy. A phrase such as 'unless the context otherwise requires' may be included by the draftsman out of caution. Even if upon its natural construction it has no discernible particular application it cannot, in my judgment, then be accorded a meaning which is at once at variance with its natural sense and apt, in the name of a policy nowhere expressly stated, to create an uncertain regime in which the existence of apparently firm appeal rights depends upon various and shifting facts. It is also, I think, not without significance that the draftsman of the 1989 Act was at pains to make clear by express words both the nature and the reach of the functions which parental responsibility confers, the circumstances in which it is acquired and those in which it is lost. Had it been intended to disapply the s 114(1D)(b) definition from a person such as the appellant whenever parental responsibility was being actively exercised by another, whether natural parent or local authority, one would have expected the 1993 Act to say so.

a   For all these reasons, I am unable to accept Mr McCarthy's first line of
argument. The second line was to the effect that even without resort to the
phrase 'unless the context otherwise requires' the term 'parent' as defined in
s 114(1D) cannot include a person in the applicant's position. In large measure
his submissions were the same as those advanced under the first limb. His
conspicuously clear skeleton argument asserts:

b   'As a foster parent the appellant has no right in law to care for [D], has no
    rights in relation to him and is not entitled in law to exercise parental
    responsibility. She has no rights in law to decide on the child's schooling.
    The local authority has complete discretion to remove the child from the
    foster parent if it thinks it appropriate to do so.'

c   Quite a bludgeon, on the face of it; but it does not in my judgment address the
statutory definition. Section 114(1D)(b) is not qualified so as to require that the
person having care of the child should possess such 'rights'. Mr McCarthy's
second argument is, I think, yet more difficult than his first, for it must proceed
on the premise that the s 114(1D)(b) definition is generally applicable: there is no
d   escape from the statutory words such as he claims exists by virtue of the
expression 'unless the context otherwise requires'. As a matter of law I would
incline to accept that even absent such a phrase there might in theory be a case
where a statutory definition, on its face generally applicable, might nevertheless
fall to be disapplied because it makes no sense in the context of a particular
statutory provision. But that is not the position here. Mr McCarthy's argument
e   is not to the effect that no sense can be made of s 169 of the 1993 Act if the
statutory definition applies. It is that the definition must be read narrowly, so as
to exclude a person not having parental responsibility when there is someone else
exercising it. But once it is accepted that in their natural sense the words of
s 114(1D) are apt to apply to a person in the appellant's position, I cannot think it
f   legitimate to displace their ordinary meaning by appeal to any such proposition.
Just as with the first limb of Mr McCarthy's argument, there is no basis for reading
the policy concerns which he articulates into the statutory definition. He says
that if Mr Greaney is correct 'then all temporary carers however short term
would have a similar right [of appeal]'. But I doubt whether the position is as
stark as Mr McCarthy asserts. Quite obviously s 114(1D)(b) does not apply to a
g   nanny or baby-sitter; and in fairness I do not suppose that that is what Mr
McCarthy means. Without wishing to commit the solecism of re-defining the
statutory definition, I apprehend that the reference in the subsection must be to
someone involved in the full-time care of the child on a settled basis. I
acknowledge that that is itself a formulation without hard edges, but it seems to
h   me to represent the thrust of what Parliament intended and to conform to the
ordinary meaning of the words used.
    On that footing the potential for conflict upon which Mr McCarthy places so
much emphasis may be modest in practice, at least vis-à-vis the child's natural
parents. As regards a local authority having parental responsibility, it is by no
j   means obvious to me, having regard to the whole of the statutory background,
that where the authority disagrees with the foster parent about a matter touching
the child's education (which is capable of resolution by the Special Educational
Needs Tribunal) it is undesirable that the foster parent should be allowed to test
the issue before the tribunal. It is a consequence of Mr McCarthy's argument that
in a case such as this (where the natural parents play no active part) the only
proper appellant to the tribunal is the authority itself—against its own decision.
No doubt the authority wears two hats, one as local education authority and the

other as recipient of the care order thus having parental responsibility; and no
doubt it seeks to fulfil both roles conscientiously in the child's best interests. But
I do not think that Mr McCarthy has demonstrated that the provisions of the 1989
and 1993 Acts to which he has drawn attention indicate any intention on the part
of Parliament that the foster mother should not be entitled to go to the tribunal.

Mr Greaney sought to place some reliance on provisions contained in the 1933
and 1969 Children and Young Persons Acts relating to the concept of 'guardian',
and on *R v Telford Juvenile Court, ex p E (a minor)* [1989] 2 FLR 101. However with
respect, I do not consider that these materials carry the matter further forward,
not least once it is accepted that on the face of it the natural and ordinary meaning
of the words in s 114(1D)(b) are apt to apply to the appellant. He also canvassed
a submission in his skeleton argument to the effect that the respondent is
estopped from denying that his client is a 'parent' because no such point was
taken before the tribunal (and indeed the respondent appears to have treated the
appellant as a person with appeal rights). But he effectively conceded that since
the issue goes to the jurisdiction of the tribunal (and, given the view I have taken
of the term 'party' in the 1992 Act, the jurisdiction of this court), no such
argument could confer the status of 'parent' on the appellant were I to hold that
it is not conferred by s 114(1D).

In the event, however, that is not my finding, and for all the reasons I have
given I accept that the appellant was indeed a 'parent' enjoying the right of appeal
to the tribunal.

There remains for consideration the question whether I should extend time for
appealing under Ord 3, r 5. Mr McCarthy says that D's educational circumstances
will inevitably have moved on since the tribunal considered the matter. A fresh
decision has been taken to the effect that no formal reassessment needs to be
made under the 1993 Act, nor therefore a statutory statement. This decision itself
attracts new appeal rights. Mr Greaney says that if I were to entertain this appeal
and decide to remit the matter to the tribunal for rehearing, it could receive fresh
evidence about the up-to-date position; and I understand that that is conceded. If
the appeal before me were purely historic and its resolution could have no
discernible effects on D's education, I would certainly refuse to extend time since
to do so would merely be to invite a sterile debate. However, that is not the
position.

I have come to the conclusion that I should extend time. The first solicitor's
illness was a misfortune; so was the long delay in which the papers were or may
have been lost in the Crown Office. Popplewell J, on what was admittedly a
misconceived application for leave to move for judicial review, considered there
was enough in the merits to grant leave. There is force in Mr Greaney's
submission that further delay is likely to be caused if his client is required to start
the appeal process afresh.

Unfortunately, however, I cannot proceed at once to determine the appeal
since as I understand it there is a difficulty with the papers which may require Mr
Greaney to seek an adjournment, which will be opposed. That is not a matter I
have yet looked into; the parties agreed that I should first determine the issues
which are the subject of this judgment.

Locus standi of the appellant to appeal affirmed.

Dilys Tausz   Barrister.

Sidhu and others v British Airways plc
Abnett (known as Sykes) v British Airways plc

HOUSE OF LORDS

LORD BROWNE-WILKINSON, LORD JAUNCEY OF TULLICHETTLE, LORD MUSTILL, LORD STEYN AND LORD HOPE OF CRAIGHEAD

14, 15, 16 OCTOBER, 12 DECEMBER 1996

Carriage by air – Carriage of passengers – International carriage – Passengers sustaining damage when aircraft landed in war zone for refuelling – Cause of action not within scope of Warsaw Convention – Whether convention providing exclusive cause of action and sole remedy – Whether passenger having common law remedy – Carriage by Air Act 1961, Sch 1.

The appellants (the three plaintiffs and the pursuer) were passengers on a scheduled international flight operated by the respondent airline (BA) which left London on 1 August 1990 for Malaysia via Kuwait. On 2 August the aircraft landed in Kuwait for refuelling several hours after Iraqi forces had begun to invade Kuwait at the commencement of the Gulf War. While the passengers were in the airport terminal, the airport was attacked by Iraqi forces who took them prisoner and later removed them to Baghdad. The appellants were released several weeks later and returned to the United Kingdom. On 30 July 1993, which was outside the two-year time limit allowed by art 29 of the Warsaw Convention, as set out in Sch 1 to the Carriage by Air Act 1961, for bringing an action for damages but inside the three-year time limit prescribed for common law negligence, the plaintiffs brought an action against BA in the county court claiming damages for personal injury alleging that by reason of BA's negligence in landing the aircraft in Kuwait after hostilities had started they had suffered physical and psychological damage and they also claimed for lost baggage. The judge dismissed their claim on the ground that the plaintiffs' sole remedy was under the convention and that any rights they might have had against BA were extinguished by virtue of art 29 of the convention since they had not issued proceedings within the two-year time limit. The Court of Appeal upheld the decision and the plaintiffs appealed to the House of Lords. The pursuer brought her action in the Court of Session in Scotland claiming, inter alia, damages at common law for breach of an implied condition of the contract that BA would take reasonable care for her safety. The Lord Ordinary held that the convention excluded recourse to any common law remedy and dismissed her action. The pursuer reclaimed but the Inner House of the Court of Session dismissed her reclaiming motion and she appealed to the House of Lords.

Held – Having regard to the objects and structure of the convention, which was to achieve a uniform international code in those areas with which it dealt, including the liability of the international carrier, which could be applied by all the High Contracting Parties without reference to the rules of their own domestic law, Sch 1 provided the exclusive cause of action and sole remedy for a passenger who claimed for loss, injury and damage sustained in the course of, or arising out of, international carriage by air notwithstanding that that might leave claimants without a remedy. Accordingly, where the convention did not provide

a remedy, no remedy was available. The appeals would therefore be dismissed
(see p 195 *j*, p 212 *d e* and p 213 *b* to *d*, post).

　　Grein v Imperial Airways Ltd [1936] 2 All ER 1258 and *Gatewhite Ltd v Iberia Lineas
Aereas de España SA* [1989] 1 All ER 944 considered.

Notes

For legislation governing carriage by air and application of common law rules,
see 2 *Halsbury's Laws* (4th edn reissue) paras 1528–1530.

　　For the Carriage by Air Act 1961, Sch 1, see 4 *Halsbury's Statutes* (4th edn) (1987
reissue) 28. As from a date to be appointed under s 7(2) of the Carriage by Air and
Road Act 1979, Sch 1 to the 1961 Act is substituted by s 1(1) of and Sch 1 to the
1979 Act (4 *Halsbury's Statutes* (4th edn) (1987 reissue) 70, 74).

Cases referred to in opinions

Abramson v Japan Airlines Co Ltd (1984) 739 F 2d 130, US Ct of Apps (3rd Cir).
Air France v Saks (1985) 470 US 392, 18 Avi Cas 18,538, US SC.
Boehringer-Mannheim Diagnostics Inc v Pan American Airways Inc (1984) 737 F 2d
　　456, 18 Avi Cas 18,090, US Ct of Apps (5th Cir).
Eastern Airlines Inc v Floyd (1991) 499 US 530, US SC.
Finkelstein v Trans World Airlines Inc (1978) 15 Avi Cas 17,379, NY SC.
Fischer v Northwest Airlines Inc (1985) 623 F Supp 1064, US District Ct (ND Illinois
　　ED).
Fothergill v Monarch Airlines Ltd [1980] 2 All ER 696, [1981] AC 251, [1980] 3 WLR
　　209, HL.
Gatewhite Ltd v Iberia Lineas Aereas de España SA [1989] 1 All ER 944, [1990] 1 QB
　　326, [1989] 3 WLR 1080.
Grein v Imperial Airways Ltd [1936] 2 All ER 1258, [1937] 1 KB 50, CA.
Ismail A Mohamed v British Airways plc (8 November 1995, unreported), Tribunal
　　de Grande Instance de Paris.
Metz v KLM Royal Dutch Airlines (1979) 15 Avi Cas 17,843, US District Ct (Mass).
Saloom v British Airways plc (22 February 1993, unreported), US District Ct (SD
　　Cal).
T v Secretary of State for the Home Dept [1996] 2 All ER 865, [1996] AC 742, [1996] 2
　　WLR 766, HL.
Tasman Pulp and Paper Co Ltd v Brambles J B O'Loghlen Ltd [1981] 2 NZLR 225, NZ
　　HC.
Walker v Eastern Airlines Inc (1991) 23 Avi Cas 17,904, US District Ct (SD NY).

Appeals

Sidhu and ors v British Airways plc

The plaintiffs, Karan Sidhu, Harjinder Sidhu and Ravinder Sidhu, appealed with
leave of the Appeal Committee of the House of Lords given on 13 July 1995 from
the decision of the Court of Appeal (Leggatt, Swinton Thomas and Otton LJJ) on
27 January 1995 dismissing their appeal from the order of Judge Marcus Edwards
sitting at Brentford Count Court on 28 February 1994 whereby he dismissed their
claims against the respondent, British Airways plc, for damages for negligence
arising from their detention on 2 August 1990, while in transit on a British
Airways flight at Kuwait Airport, by Iraqi forces who had invaded Kuwait, on the
ground that their claim had been extinguished by virtue of art 29 of the Warsaw
Convention (as set out in Sch 1 to the Carriage by Air Act 1961). The facts are set
out in the opinion of Lord Hope of Craighead.

a
Abnett (known as Sykes) v British Airways plc

The pursuer, Judith Helen Abnett (known as Sykes), appealed from interlocutors of an Extra Division of the Inner House of the Court of Session in Scotland (Lord Allanbridge, Lord Mayfield and Lord Clyde) (1996 SLT 529) on 28 April 1995 and 19 May 1995 (expenses of the action) refusing a reclaiming motion by the pursuer from an interlocutor of the Lord Ordinary (Lord Marnoch) dated 20 December

b
1993 dismissing her action against the defender and respondent, British Airways plc, for, inter alia, breach of contract on the ground that her claim had been excluded by the Warsaw Convention (as set out in Sch 1 to the Carriage by Air Act 1961). The facts are set out in the opinion of Lord Hope of Craighead.

c
Clive Nicholls QC and *Tim Kerr* (instructed by *Raja & Partners*, Southall) for the plaintiffs.

Robert Webb QC and *Philip Shepherd* (instructed by *Beaumont & Son*) for the respondent.

Colin McEachran QC and *Peter Macdonald* (both of the Scottish Bar) (instructed by *Pattinson & Brewer*, agents for *Drummond Miller WS*, Edinburgh, for *Frank*

d
Lefevre Practice, Aberdeen) for the pursuer.

Derek Emslie QC and *Marian Gilmore* (both of the Scottish Bar) (instructed by *Beaumont & Son*, agents for *Shepherd & Wedderburn WS*, Edinburgh) for the respondent.

e
Their Lordships took time for consideration.

12 December 1996. The following opinions were delivered.

LORD BROWNE-WILKINSON. My Lords, for the reasons given in the speech

f
to be delivered by my noble and learned friend Lord Hope of Craighead, which I have read in draft and with which I agree, I would dismiss both these appeals.

LORD JAUNCEY OF TULLICHETTLE. My Lords, for the reasons given in the speech to be delivered by my noble and learned friend Lord Hope of Craighead, which I have read in draft and with which I agree, I, too, would dismiss both these

g
appeals.

LORD MUSTILL. My Lords, for the reasons given in the speech to be delivered by my noble and learned friend Lord Hope of Craighead, which I have read in draft and with which I agree, I, too, would dismiss both these appeals.

h
LORD STEYN. My Lords, for the reasons given in the speech to be delivered by my noble and learned friend Lord Hope of Craighead, which I have read in draft and with which I agree, I would dismiss both these appeals.

j
LORD HOPE OF CRAIGHEAD. My Lords, the question in these two appeals is whether the Warsaw Convention 1929 as amended at The Hague in 1955, as set out in Sch 1 to the Carriage by Air Act 1961, provides the exclusive cause of action and sole remedy for a passenger who claims against the carrier for loss, injury and damage sustained in the course of, or arising out of, international carriage by air.

In both cases claims were made against the respondent, British Airways plc, by passengers who had been travelling on a scheduled international flight from the

United Kingdom to Malaysia via Kuwait. The flight left London Heathrow for Kuala Lumpur on 1 August 1990. It landed in Kuwait for refuelling on 2 August 1990, about five hours after Iraqi forces had begun to invade Kuwait at the commencement of what became known as the Gulf War. The passengers and crew were all taken prisoner by the Iraqis. They were detained initially at Kuwait Airport, then at Kuwait City and thereafter in Baghdad. The appellants, who were subsequently released and returned to the United Kingdom, claimed damages against the respondent for the consequences of their captivity. Their claims for personal injury were made at common law, as it was accepted that they had no remedy in this regard under art 17 of the convention.

Mrs Judith Helen Abnett, to whom I shall refer as 'the pursuer', raised her action in the Court of Session in Scotland. She was resident in England where the respondent's principal place of business is situated, and she had purchased her ticket there. But the respondent also has a place of business in Edinburgh, which the pursuer contended was sufficient to confer jurisdiction on the Scottish courts at common law. She based her claim on art 19 of the convention under which the carrier is liable for damage occasioned by delay and, alternatively, at common law for breach of an implied condition of the contract that the respondent would take reasonable care for her safety. When the case came before the Lord Ordinary, Lord Marnoch, for debate on the procedure roll he was invited to dismiss the action on various grounds. One of these was that the Scottish courts had no jurisdiction, having regard to art 28 of the convention. After a careful review of the wording of that article and of various authorities which were cited to him from the United States of America, France and Nigeria, he held that the Scottish courts did have jurisdiction and no appeal has been taken against his decision on this point. He also held that the pursuer's case for damage occasioned by delay under art 19 of the convention was irrelevant, and that the convention excluded recourse to any common law remedy by a passenger who suffered injury in the course of or arising out of an international flight. On 20 December 1993 he repelled the respondent's plea in law to the jurisdiction of the Court of Session, but he sustained its second and third pleas in law and dismissed the action as irrelevant (see 1996 SLT 529 at 531–538). The pursuer reclaimed on the single question as to whether her claim at common law had been excluded by the convention. On 28 April 1995 an Extra Division of the Inner House of the Court of Session (Lord Allanbridge, Lord Mayfield and Lord Clyde), who had the advantage of the judgment of the Court of Appeal in the English action which supported the view which had been taken by Lord Marnoch, refused her reclaiming motion (see 1996 SLT 529 at 538–547). The pursuer has now appealed from this decision to your Lordships' House.

Miss Karan Sidhu, Miss Harjinder Sidhu and Mr Ravinder Sidhu, to whom I shall refer as 'the plaintiffs,' raised their action in the Brentford County Court. In their particulars of claim they alleged that the loss and damage which they had suffered was caused by the respondent's negligence. Their proceedings were issued on 30 July 1993, which was outside the two-year time limit allowed by art 29 of the convention but inside the three-year time limit which was otherwise applicable. No claim was made by them under any of the provisions of the convention. The respondent applied for an order that their action be dismissed as it was time-barred by art 29. When its application came before Judge Marcus Edwards, it also submitted that the convention provided the exclusive remedy in respect of claims for damages arising out of international carriage by air of persons and baggage for reward. On 28 February 1994 the judge, who was

a   referred to Lord Marnoch's decision in the pursuer's case, held for the same
reasons as those given by Lord Marnoch that the plaintiffs had no rights save
under the convention. He also held that their right to damages, if any, was
extinguished by art 29 of the convention two years after 2 August 1990, and he
dismissed their claims.   On 27 January 1995 the Court of Appeal (Leggatt,
Swinton Thomas and Otton LJJ), dismissed the plaintiffs' appeal against the order
b   which had been made by Judge Marcus Edwards. The plaintiffs' appeal to this
House from the order made by the Court of Appeal was heard together with the
pursuer's appeal against the interlocutor of the Extra Division of the Court of
Session.

THE FACTS

c   The pursuer and the plaintiffs were all fare paying passengers on the same
flight, BA 149, which left London Heathrow for Kuala Lumpur at about 6.15 pm
on 1 August 1990. The flight was scheduled to travel to Kuala Lumpur by way of
Kuwait and Madras. It was due to arrive at Kuwait in the early hours of the
following day, 2 August 1990. According to the pursuer's pleadings in the
d   Scottish action, relations between Iraq and Kuwait had been deteriorating for
some days prior to the departure of the flight from Heathrow. She avers that the
respondent knew or ought to have known that the passengers would be at severe
risk if the aircraft were to land in Kuwait after hostilities had been commenced
against Kuwait by Iraq. The same point is made by the plaintiffs in their
particulars of claim, where they refer to the respondent's negligence in landing
e   their aeroplane in Kuwait when they knew or ought to have known of the hostile
situation between Iraq and Kuwait and the possibility that war might break out
and Kuwait be invaded by Iraq. In the event, the invasion of Kuwait by Iraq
began at about 11.15 pm on 1 August 1990. About four hours later, at about 3 am
on 2 August 1990, the respondent's aircraft landed at Kuwait airport for
f   refuelling. The passengers disembarked into the transit lounge at the airport
terminal. While they were in the terminal the airport was attacked by Iraqi
aircraft and taken over by Iraqi soldiers. The airport was closed, and the
passengers and crew of flight BA 149 were detained by the Iraqis and later
removed to Baghdad.

g   The pursuer avers that she was detained by Iraqi forces for a period of about a
month. She claims to have suffered psychological injury due to the stress
resulting from her captivity and the pain of separation from her family. She also
claims that she was off work on a number of occasions as a result of the
psychological consequences. She claims damages of £100,000 on the ground that
the respondent was in breach of an implied condition of her contract with it that
h   it would take reasonable care for the safety of its passengers, in respect that it
allowed its aircraft to land at Kuwait when it knew or ought to have known that
the passengers were exposed to risk due to the invasion. Her alternative claim for
damages caused by delay under art 19 of the convention was, as I have said, held
by Lord Marnoch to be irrelevant and no further issue arises on that point. She
j   made no claim against the respondent under art 17 of the convention.

    The plaintiffs state that they were detained by the Iraqi forces until about 21
August 1990. In their particulars of injuries they allege that they suffered physical
and psychological injuries. These included mental injury comprising stress and
anxiety and possible permanent psychological damage as a result, and bodily
injury comprising loss of weight, eczema and excessive menstrual bleeding.
They also claim for loss of baggage amounting to £2,562·93 as special damages.

Their action has been based entirely on negligence at common law. The
negligence relied on in their particulars falls under three heads: landing its aircraft
in Kuwait when the respondent knew or ought to have known of the hostile
situation between Kuwait and Iraq and the possibility that war might break out
and Kuwait be invaded; flying its aircraft into a war zone or war situation; and
failing to divert its aircraft to a safer airport for refuelling when it knew or ought
to have known that Kuwait airport was at risk of being attacked or invaded. They
make no claim against the respondent under art 17 of the convention.

THE ISSUE

Although there are some differences of detail between the two actions—the
pursuer claims only for psychological injury, while the plaintiffs claim also for
bodily injury and loss of baggage, and the pursuer's claim is for breach of contract
while the plaintiffs' claim is in negligence—the issue of law which arises in both
of these appeals is the same. It is whether the Warsaw Convention as amended
at The Hague in 1955 provides the exclusive cause of action and remedy in
respect of claims for loss, injury and damage sustained in the course of, or arising
out of, international carriage by air. If the answer to that question is in the
affirmative, it is accepted that the claims which have been brought in each case
for damages at common law for personal injury must be dismissed. It is not
disputed that the plaintiffs' claim for loss of baggage must be dismissed also, on
the additional ground that it was brought outwith the period of two years
referred to in art 29 of the convention after which the right to damages under the
convention is extinguished. It is common ground, for reasons to which I shall
return later, that neither the pursuer nor the plaintiffs have any claim against the
respondent under art 17 of the convention in respect of their personal injuries.

THE PROVISIONS OF THE CONVENTION

I shall have something to say later about the background to the convention. At
this stage it is necessary to identify the statutory provisions which are relevant to
this case. These are to be found in the Carriage by Air Act 1961, by which effect
was given to the convention concerning international carriage by air known as
'The Warsaw Convention as amended at The Hague, 1955', so that it might have
the force of law in the United Kingdom in relation to any carriage by air to which
the convention applied, and the rules contained in the convention were enabled
to be applied, with or without modification, in other cases and in particular to
non-international carriage by air not governed by the convention. Force of law
to the convention in regard to international carriage by air is given by s 1(1) of the
Act read together with Sch 1, in which the provisions of the convention are set
out. Part I of the schedule sets out the English text of the convention, and Pt II
sets out the French text. Section 1(2) provides that, if there is an inconsistency
between the text in English in Pt I of Sch 1 and the text in French in Pt II of that
schedule, the text in French shall prevail.

The headnote to the English text in Pt I of Sch 1 describes the convention as
being 'for the Unification of Certain Rules relating to International Carriage by
Air'. There then follow five chapters, headed respectively: Ch I, 'Scope—
Definitions'; Ch II, 'Documents of Carriage'; Ch III, 'Liability of the Carrier'; Ch
IV, 'Provisions Relating to Combined Carriage'; and Ch V, 'General and Final
Provisions'.

In Ch I, art 1(1) is in these terms:

a   'This Convention applies to all international carriage of persons, baggage or cargo performed by aircraft for reward. It applies equally to gratuitous carriage by aircraft performed by an air transport undertaking.'

Article 1(2) of this chapter contains a definition of the expression 'international carriage' which need not be quoted, as it is common ground that the present case is concerned with international carriage by air because the place of departure and

b   the place of destination were both situated within the territories of High Contracting Parties.

Among the documents of carriage for which rules are provided by Ch II is the passenger ticket. Article 3(1) of section 1 of this chapter is in these terms:

c   'In respect of the carriage of passengers a ticket shall be delivered containing (a) an indication of the places of departure and destination; (b) if the places of departure and destination are within the territory of a single High Contracting Party, one or more agreed stopping places being within the territory of another State, an indication of at least one such stopping place; (c) a notice to the effect that, if the passenger's journey involves an

d   ultimate destination or stop in a country other than the country of departure, the Warsaw Convention may be applicable and that the Convention governs and in most cases limits the liability of carriers for death or personal injury and in respect of loss of or damage to baggage.'

The only other chapter which contains provisions relevant to this case is Ch III,
e   which is headed 'Liability of the Carrier'. The articles comprised in this chapter are those numbered from 17 to 30, of which the following is a brief summary. Article 17 is concerned with the carrier's liability for death or injury suffered by a passenger. Article 18 is concerned with the carrier's liability for destruction or loss of or damage to registered baggage or cargo. Article 19 provides that the
f   carrier is liable for damage occasioned by delay in the carriage by air of passengers, baggage or cargo. These provisions must be read together with art 24, which provides that, in the cases covered by these articles, any action for damages, however founded, can only be brought subject to the conditions and limits set out in the convention. Article 20 provides:

g   'The carrier is not liable if he proves that he and his servants or agents have taken all necessary measures to avoid the damage or that it was impossible for him or them to take such measures.'

Article 21 deals with cases where the damage was caused or contributed to by the injured person's negligence. Article 22 makes provision for the limitation of the
h   liability of the carrier for each passenger and for registered baggage and cargo, and art 23 provides: '(1) Any provision tending to relieve the carrier of liability or to fix a lower limit than that which is laid down in this Convention shall be null and void ...'; art 25 provides that these limits of liability shall not apply if the damage results from an act or omission of the carrier, his servants or agents done
j   with intent to cause damage or recklessly. Articles 25, 25A, 26 and 27 contain various ancillary provisions. Article 28, which deals with jurisdiction, restricts the places where an action for damages may be brought, and provides that 'questions of procedure shall be governed by the law of the court seised of the case'. Article 29 provides that the right to damages shall be extinguished if the action is not brought within two years. Lastly, art 30 deals with the case where the carriage is to be performed by various successive carriers.

As I shall require to examine the wording of arts 17, 18, 23 and 24 more closely at a later stage, it is convenient now to set out the full terms of these articles. They are as follows:

'Article 17

The carrier is liable for damage sustained in the event of the death or wounding of a passenger or any other bodily injury suffered by a passenger, if the accident which caused the damage so sustained took place on board the aircraft or in the course of any of the operations of embarking or disembarking.

Article 18

(1) The carrier is liable for damage sustained in the event of the destruction or loss of, or of damage to, any registered baggage or any cargo, if the occurrence which caused the damage so sustained took place during the carriage by air.

(2) The carriage by air within the meaning of the preceding paragraph comprises the period during which the baggage or cargo is in charge of the carrier, whether in an aerodrome or on board an aircraft, or, in the case of a landing outside an aerodrome, in any place whatsoever.

(3) The period of the carriage by air does not extend to any carriage by land, by sea or by river performed outside an aerodrome. If, however, such a carriage takes place in the performance of a contract for carriage by air, for the purpose of loading, delivery or transshipment, any damage is presumed, subject to proof to the contrary, to have been the result of an event which took place during the carriage by air.

Article 23

(1) Any provision tending to relieve the carrier of liability or to fix a lower limit than that which is laid down in this Convention shall be null and void, but the nullity of any such provision does not involve the nullity of the whole contract, which shall remain subject to the provisions of this Convention.

(2) Paragraph (1) of this Article shall not apply to provisions governing loss or damage resulting from the inherent defect, quality or vice of the cargo carried.

Article 24

(1) In the cases covered by Articles 18 and 19 any action for damages, however founded, can only be brought subject to the conditions and limits set out in this Convention.

(2) In the cases covered by Article 17 the provisions of the preceding paragraph also apply, without prejudice to the questions as to who are the persons who have the right to bring suit and what are their respective rights.'

THE COMPETING ARGUMENTS

The issue between the parties is confined to a single but important point which depends for its answer on the interpretation of the convention. Much of the background is common ground. As both cases are being dealt with on a preliminary issue of law, the facts have not been investigated. The respondent made it clear that it was not to be taken as admitting that all the allegations which *a* have been made against it are true. But it was content that the issue of law should be dealt with on the pursuer's pleadings in the Scottish action and on the particulars of claim in the English action. For their part, the pursuer and the plaintiffs accept that their claims against the respondent arise out of international carriage by air. Their apprehension by the Iraqis took place in the terminal at Kuwait, but they accept that they were still in the course of international carriage *b* by air at that point because they were still in transit to their ultimate destination in Malaysia. The breaches of duty which they allege all relate to decisions taken while the aircraft was in the air between London and Kuwait. It is, however, also common ground between the parties that neither the pursuer nor the plaintiffs have a claim against the respondent under art 17 of the convention.

c I do not think that it is necessary to explore the reasons why the view has been taken that art 17 does not provide a remedy in this case. It is sufficient to say that two particular reasons were given for this view in the course of the hearing before the Inner House in the Court of Session. First, it was said that no 'accident' causing the damage took place on board the aircraft. Secondly, it was said that the injury sustained by the pursuer—the stress resulting from her captivity and *d* the pain of separation from her family, absence from work and loss of income due to the psychological consequences of the captivity—did not fall within the scope of 'bodily injury' for the purposes of art 17. In the English action, the plaintiffs conceded in the Court of Appeal that no accident causing damage took place on board the aircraft or in the course of disembarkation. In their case, bodily injury *e* is alleged, but it was submitted on their behalf that liability for damage to the person under art 17 only arises in the event of any bodily injury suffered by a passenger and that psychological damage, which was the principal basis for their claim, probably did not come within that category. It was suggested to your Lordships in the course of the argument that the phrase 'bodily injury' in art 17 ought now to be construed as including psychological damage, especially if it *f* were shown to have a physiological basis by medical evidence. But that point does not arise for decision in this case and it was not fully argued. I prefer to express no opinion upon it.

It should be recorded also that all parties were agreed that, if a passenger had a claim under art 17 against the carrier, there was no concurrent common law *g* remedy. It is common ground, therefore, that a passenger who has a claim for bodily injury caused by an accident which took place on board the aircraft, or in the course of any of the operations of embarking or disembarking, cannot maintain a separate claim at common law for any loss, injury or damage not covered by art 17 of the convention. That seems to follow inevitably from the *h* provisions of art 24(2), which declares that in the cases covered by art 17 any action of damages, however founded, can only be brought subject to the conditions and limits set by the convention.

So the stark issue which is before us in this appeal is whether a passenger who has sustained damage in the course of international carriage by air due to the fault of the carrier, but who has no claim against the carrier under art 17 of the *j* convention, is left without a remedy.

THE APPROACH TO CONSTRUCTION

I now turn to the material which we were invited to consider in reaching our decision as to how we should decide this issue. Some of this material is plainly relevant, some of it plainly is not and some of it will require consideration and

analysis in order to decide whether it is of any assistance to us in this case. The
following catalogue provides the starting point.

(i) *The Carriage by Air Act 1961*

Mr Robert Webb QC, for the respondent, took us through various provisions
in the statute which he said could be relied on as indicating that the intention was
that the convention should provide the exclusive remedy. Similar arguments
were considered in the courts below. For my part, I do not think that the wording
of the statute can assist us one way or the other. What we are concerned with in
this case is the meaning to be given to the convention. This must depend upon
the wording and structure of the convention itself. All that needs to be taken
from the Act for present purposes is that, in terms of s 1(1), the convention as set
out in Sch 1 to the Act has the force of law in the United Kingdom in relation to
any carriage by air to which the convention applies; and that, in terms of s 1(2), if
there is any inconsistency between the text in English in Pt I of Sch 1 and the text
in French in Pt II of that schedule, the text in French shall prevail.

(ii) *The English text of the convention*

This plainly is the primary source to which we must turn for a solution to the
point raised in this case. It may be convenient, however, to record at this point
that all parties were agreed, as they were in the courts below, that the convention
should receive a purposive construction. This point was fully explored in
Fothergill v Monarch Airlines Ltd [1980] 2 All ER 696, [1981] AC 251, where the
question at issue arose under art 26(2) of the convention. It does not need to be
elaborated upon in this case. It is now well established that a purposive approach
should be taken to the interpretation of international conventions which the
force of law in this country. As Lord Diplock said, one must give a purposive
construction to the convention looked at as a whole (see [1980] 2 All ER 696 at
704, [1981] AC 251 at 279). The observations of Greene LJ in *Grein v Imperial
Airways Ltd* [1936] 2 All ER 1258 at 1277–1278, [1937] 1 KB 50 at 74–76, to which
I shall return later, are to the same effect.

(iii) *The travaux préparatoires*

Here again the parties were in agreement. Reference was made in the courts
below to the negotiating history of the convention, and in particular to the
minutes of the International Conference on Private Aeronautical Law at Warsaw
from 4 to 12 October 1929. We also were referred to various passages from these
minutes in the course of the argument. The question whether it is legitimate to
resort to material of this kind was discussed in *Fothergill v Monarch Airlines Ltd*, and
it is unnecessary to go over this ground again. It is sufficient to say that cautious
use may be made of this material, the availability to the public of which is not in
doubt. But it will only be helpful if, after proper analysis, it clearly points to a
definite intention on the part of the delegates as to how the point at issue should
be resolved.

(iv) *Decisions by the courts of the United Kingdom*

The only cases to which we were referred as having any possible bearing on
the issue which we have to decide in this case were *Grein v Imperial Airways Ltd*
[1936] 2 All ER 1258, [1937] 1 KB 50 and *Gatewhite Ltd v Iberia Lineas Aereas de
España SA* [1989] 1 All ER 944, [1990] 1 QB 326. The issue which was raised in
Grein v Imperial Airways Ltd was a different one from that which arises here. It was

a whether a passenger who met his death while travelling by aeroplane on a return ticket between London and Antwerp, Belgium not being a High Contracting Party, was engaged on 'international carriage' within the meaning of the convention. But Greene LJ, made some observations about the approach to be taken to the construction of the convention which are helpful in the present case (see [1936] 2 All ER 1258 at 1277–1278, [1937] 1 KB 50 at 74–76). The *Gatewhite*

b case arose out of a contract for the carriage of goods by air. The question was whether the owner of goods not named as the consignor or consignee on the air waybill was entitled to sue the carrier for damages to the goods while in transit. I shall return to this case later in order to see what help it can give to us in the present case.

c (v) *Decisions by foreign courts*

Much of the discussion in the Court of Session, both in the Outer House before the Lord Ordinary, Lord Marnoch, and in the Extra Division, was taken up with an examination of decisions of various courts in the United States. We were referred to the cases mentioned in the courts below and to several other cases

d from the same source. We were also referred to a recent decision in the Tribunal de Grande Instance de Paris arising out of the same incident as the claims which are being made in the present case (see *Ismail A Mohamed v British Airways plc* (8 November 1995, unreported)). Parties were agreed that we might have regard to this material for such assistance as it might give. Clearly, much must depend upon the status of each court and of the extent to which the point at issue has

e been subjected to careful analysis. Material of this kind, where it is found to be of the appropriate standing and quality, may be of some help in pointing towards an interpretation of the convention which has received general acceptance in other countries. But the value of the material will be reduced if the decisions conflict with each other or if no clear line of approach appears from them after

f they have been analysed.

(vi) *European Convention on Human Rights*

Mr Clive Nicholls QC, for the plaintiffs, submitted that it would be inconsistent with the obligations of the United Kingdom under various articles of the European Convention on Human Rights (Convention for the Protection of

g Human Rights and Fundamental Freedoms (Rome, 4 November 1950; TS 71 (1953); Cmd 8969)) if a construction were to be placed on art 17 of the Warsaw Convention which excluded the claim which they were seeking to make in this case. Your Lordships had no hesitation in rejecting that argument. The provisions of the 1950 Convention have no bearing on the interpretation of

h international conventions such as the Warsaw Convention on carriage by air (and there are many other examples), which are concerned with commerce between countries and which seek, by a process of compromise, to achieve uniformity across international frontiers in the application of trade law.

It must also be observed that, while some parties to the Warsaw Convention

j are parties to the 1950 Convention, some, notably the United States of America, are not. We cannot assume that the principles expressed in the 1950 Convention are common to all those countries who are parties to the Warsaw Convention. Thus, we would risk introducing an element of distortion into the debate, in conflict with the broad aim of uniformity of interpretation between states, if we were to rely on the 1950 Convention as an aid to the construction of the Warsaw Convention in the present case. In *T v Secretary of State for the Home Dept* [1996] 2

All ER 865 at 891, [1996] AC 742 at 779, Lord Lloyd of Berwick said that in a case
concerning an international convention it was obviously desirable that decisions   *a*
in different jurisdictions should, so far as possible, be kept in line with each other.
As *Dicey and Morris on the Conflict of Laws* (12th edn, 1993), p 9, observe:

> 'The purpose of an international convention is to harmonise the laws of all
> contracting states on the particular topic dealt with by the convention. It is
> therefore very important that the interpretation of the convention should be   *b*
> the same, so far as possible, in all contracting states.'

(vii) *Analysis of this material*
It follows from what I have just said that no analysis is required of the 1961 Act
or of the 1950 Convention. I turn therefore immediately to the Warsaw   *c*
Convention itself, which is the primary source to which we must look for a
solution to the question we have to decide.

(a) The English text of the convention
I can confine myself to the English text, because all parties were agreed that,   *d*
except in one respect with which I can deal briefly, there was for present purposes
no material difference between it and the French text.

The convention describes itself as a 'Convention for the Unification of Certain
Rules relating to International Carriage by Air'. The phrase 'Unification of
Certain Rules' tells us two things. The first, the aim of the convention is to unify
the rules to which it applies. If this aim is to be achieved, exceptions to these rules   *e*
should not be permitted, except where the convention itself provides for them.
Second, the convention is concerned with certain rules only, not with all the rules
relating to international carriage by air. It does not purport to provide a code
which is comprehensive of all the issues that may arise. It is a partial
harmonisation, directed to the particular issues with which it deals.   *f*

These issues are identified in the principal chapter headings, which are those to
Chs II, III and IV: 'Documents of Carriage', 'Liability of the Carrier' and
'Provisions Relating to Combined Carriage'. Nothing is said in this convention
about the liability of passengers to the carrier, for example. Nor is anything said
about the carrier's obligations of insurance, and in particular about compulsory
insurance against third party risks. It is clear from the content and structure of   *g*
the convention that it is a partial harmonisation only of the rules relating to
international carriage by air. That is sufficient to give content to the phrase
'Certain Rules'. I do not find in that phrase an indication that, in regard to the
issues with which the convention does purport to deal, its provisions were
intended to be other than comprehensive.   *h*

The principal search for indications of an intention one way or the other about
exclusivity of provision in regard to the carrier's liability must be conducted
within the provisions of Ch III. But before I come to this chapter, there are two
provisions in the earlier chapters which are worth noting as being of some value.
First, art 1(1) states that the convention applies to 'all international carriage of
persons, baggage or cargo performed by aircraft for reward'. The word 'all' is   *j*
important, simply because it is so all-embracing. It indicates that the framers of
the convention were looking to solutions, no doubt by a process of adjustment
and compromise, which could be regarded as acceptable for universal application
in all cases. The other provision is art 3(1)(c), which requires that the ticket to be
delivered to the passenger must contain among other things—

a
'a notice to the effect that, if the passenger's journey involves an ultimate destination or stop in a country other than the country of departure, the Warsaw Convention may be applicable and that the Convention governs and in most cases limits the liability of carriers for death or personal injury and in respect of loss of or damage to baggage.'

b
This provision was relied on to some extent by Lord Clyde (see 1996 SLT 529 at 545). He said that the words used here would seem quite absolute, the qualification that the limits apply 'in most cases' presumably covering such exceptions as are contained in art 25, which deals with cases where the carrier, his servants or agents have caused intentional damage or acted recklessly. It is here that the French text may be important. The relevant part of the provision is
c
stated there in these terms:

'(c) … leur transport peut être régi par la Convention de Varsovie qui, en général, limite la responsabilité du transporteur en cas de mort ou de lésion corporelle, ainsi qu'en cas de perte ou d'avarie des bagages.'

d
The word 'governs' which is to be found in the English text is an accurate translation of the word 'régi' in the French text. But the English version does not follow the French wording precisely—the phrase 'peut être régi' is not, as such, reproduced. So, on balance, I am inclined not to attach significance to this provision, which in any event is dealing only with the wording of a notice on the passenger's ticket and not with the substance of the rules about the carrier's
e
liability.

Turning to Ch III itself, the chapter heading expresses its subject matter in the words 'Liability of the Carrier'. In contrast to the title to the convention itself, which uses the expression 'Certain Rules', we find here a phrase which is unqualified. My understanding of the purpose of this chapter therefore, from
f
what we have seen so far, is that it is designed to set out all the rules relating to the liability of the carrier which are to be applicable to all international carriage of persons, baggage or cargo by air to which the convention applies.

Chapter III begins by setting out the three primary rules. These are the rules relating to the carriage of passengers, to the carriage of registered baggage or cargo and to delay in the carriage by air of passengers, baggage or cargo. While
g
art 19 is unqualified—it states simply that the carrier is liable for damage occasioned by delay in the carriage by air—the other two articles are qualified, because the liability which they create applies only in the events described and only if certain other conditions are satisfied (see arts 20 and 21). This, however, is not in itself a reason for regarding these provisions as non-exclusive remedies.
h
One has to look further into the details of the chapter in order to grasp the whole context in which these carefully defined liabilities have been devised.

Articles 20 and 21 enable the carrier to avoid liability in whole or in part. They contain nothing of significance for present purposes. Article 22, however, is important, because it limits the liability of the carrier. It does so in terms which
j
enable the limitation of liability to be applied generally to all cases where the carrier is liable in the carriage of persons and of registered baggage and cargo. Article 22(1) begins simply with the words 'In the carriage of persons'; art 22(2)(a) begins with the words 'In the carriage of registered baggage and of cargo'. The intention which emerges from these words is that, unless he agrees otherwise by special contract, for which provision is made elsewhere in the article, the carrier can be assured that his liability to each passenger and for each package will not

exceed the sums stated in the article. This has obvious implications for insurance by the carrier and for the cost of his undertaking as a whole. Article 22(4) makes provision for the award, in addition, of the whole or part of the costs of the litigation. But this is subject to the ability of the carrier to limit his liability for costs by an offer in writing to the plaintiff. The effect of these rules would, I think, be severely distorted if they could not be applied generally to all cases in which a claim is made against the carrier.

Articles 23 and 24 also are provisions which seem to have been designed to apply generally, and to indicate that the possibility of exceptions to the rules laid down in Ch III was not being contemplated. Article 23 states that any provision tending to relieve the carrier of liability or to fix a lower limit than that which is laid down in the convention shall be null and void. It then goes on to state that the nullity of any such provision does not involve the nullity of the whole contract, which is to remain subject to the provisions of the convention. The generality of effect is to be found in the opening words, since the article applies to 'any provision' which tends to relieve the carrier of liability or to fix a lower limit than that laid down by the convention. I think that the purpose of this provision is clear. It is to protect the passenger or other person dealing with the carrier against provisions of the kind which it describes. Contracting out of liability in contracts of carriage is, of course, now widely regulated by statute. But no doubt in the early 1920s, when what became the Warsaw Convention was being negotiated, carriers engaged in international carriage by air were free to contract on whatever terms they cared to select, controlled only by the demands of the marketplace in which they were operating. To surrender freedom of contract on this issue was an important concession on the part of carriers, which made sense only in the context of the entire set of rules by which their conduct was to be regulated.

The counterpart of what was plainly a compromise is to be found in the following article, art 24. This article provides that in the cases covered by arts 18 and 19 and by art 17 respectively (these cases are dealt with separately in two different paragraphs) 'any action for damages, however founded, can only be brought subject to the conditions and limits set' by the convention. It should be noted in passing that para (2) of the article states that this rule is to apply to the cases covered by art 17 'without prejudice to the questions as to who are the persons who have the right to bring suit and what are their respective rights'. As Professor Rene H Mankiewicz has pointed out in his article, 'The Judicial Diversification of Uniform Private Law Conventions—The Warsaw Convention's Days in Court' (1972) 21 ICLQ 718 at 741, no one could expect states to be prepared to amend their laws relating to these questions, which are basic to the laws of tort and contract and therefore of a wide-reaching significance, for the sole purpose of unifying and accommodating all matters relating to the law of the air carrier's liability.

The structure of these two provisions seems to me, therefore, to be this. On the one hand, the carrier surrenders his freedom to exclude or to limit his liability. On the other hand, the passenger or other party to the contract is restricted in the claims which he can bring in an action for damages by the conditions and limits set out in the convention. The idea that an action for damages may be brought by a passenger against the carrier outside the convention in the cases covered by art 17, which is the issue in the present case, seems to be entirely contrary to the system which these two articles were designed to create.

The reference in the opening words of art 24(2) to 'the cases covered by Article 17' does, of course, invite the question whether art 17 was intended to cover only those cases for which the carrier is liable in damages under that article. The answer to that question may indeed be said to lie at the heart of this case. In my opinion, the answer to it is to be found not by an exact analysis of the particular words used but by a consideration of the whole purpose of the article. In its context, the purpose seems to me to be to prescribe the circumstances, that is to say the only circumstances, in which a carrier will be liable in damages to the passenger for claims arising out of his international carriage by air.

The phrase 'the cases covered by Article 17' extends therefore to all claims made by the passenger against the carrier arising out of international carriage by air, other than claims for damage to his registered baggage which must be dealt with under art 18 and claims for delay which must be dealt with under art 19. The words 'however founded' which appear in art 24(1), and are applied to passenger's claims by art 24(2), support this approach. The intention seems to be to provide a secure regime, within which the restriction on the carrier's freedom of contract is to operate. Benefits are given to the passenger in return, but only in clearly defined circumstances to which the limits of liability set out by the convention are to apply. To permit exceptions, whereby a passenger could sue outwith the convention for losses sustained in the course of international carriage by air, would distort the whole system, even in cases for which the convention did not create any liability on the part of the carrier. Thus, the purpose is to ensure that, in all questions relating to the carrier's liability, it is the provisions of the convention which apply and that the passenger does not have access to any other remedies, whether under the common law or otherwise, which may be available within the particular country where he chooses to raise his action. The carrier does not need to make provision for the risk of being subjected to such remedies, because the whole matter is regulated by the convention.

Only two other articles may be mentioned in this analysis: arts 28 and 29. These restrict the places in which 'an action for damages' must be brought, and provide that 'the right to damages' shall be extinguished if an action is not brought within two years. Here again, it seems that a balance has been struck in the interests of uniformity of treatment and of certainty. I see no sign in the generality with which these provisions have been expressed of a recognition that there may be some actions for damages arising from the international carriage of passengers by air which are not subject to these rules. It would be largely destructive of the system which this chapter seems to have been designed to lay down if a passenger were to be able, for example, to maintain a claim of damages for non-bodily injury, for loss of or damage to the personal possessions which he had with him inside the aircraft or for economic loss, outside the conditions and limits set by the convention while maintaining a claim under the convention for the bodily injury. No doubt it was for this reason that it was conceded that, if he had a claim under art 17, the passenger would not be able to maintain any other claim against the carrier arising out of the same incident. But it seems to me that, by parity of reasoning, the same approach must be taken to cases arising out of international carriage by air where he has no claim under art 17 at all.

(b) The travaux préparatoires

We were shown a copy, in the English translation, of the minutes of the Second International Conference on Private Aeronautical Law, 4 to 12 October 1929 at Warsaw. Attached to these minutes are copies of the documents

submitted to the conference. These comprise (a) a preliminary draft of the *a*
convention prepared by the International Technical Committee of Legal
Aeronautical Experts (CITEJA), together with a report on the preliminary draft
by Mr Henri De Vos in name of the committee and (b) proposals of amendments
submitted to the Warsaw Conference by a preparatory committee and by various
delegations to the conference. The first conference had been held in Paris in 1925,
so the material which was before the conference in Warsaw in 1929 was the *b*
product of four years work by the committee.

I do not think that it would be profitable for me to attempt to summarise this
material. There are various passages in the minutes where the delegates are
recorded as expressing views about the object of the convention. For example,
Sir Alfred Dennis, on behalf of Great Britain, said that the object of the *c*
convention was to ensure uniformity of law (p 85), and he said that what became
art 24(1) touched the very substance of the convention because it excluded resort
to the common law (p 213). Similar observations are attributed to the Soviet
delegate, Mr Sabanin (p 40) and to the French delegate, Mr Ripert (p 47). Mr De
Vos referred to various questions relating to the carrier's liability as being
connected to each other, as they constituted 'the parts of a whole which is the *d*
system of liability' (p 49). But these are mere straws in the wind which emerged
during several days of detailed discussion to which many delegates contributed.
I do not find a sufficiently clear and consistent expression of views here about the
objects of the convention on the point which is at issue in this case to enable me
to say that the answer to the problem is to be found in the minutes. The most *e*
that can be said is that I have not found anything in these minutes or in the
accompanying material which contradicts the impression which I have already
formed on reading the convention.

There is one particular point arising from the minutes however on which I
think I should comment. It relates to the phrase 'Certain Rules' in the title to the *f*
convention. The title in the preliminary draft did not contain this phrase. In their
proposals, however, the delegates from Czechoslovakia had proposed an
amendment to ch IV of the draft to the effect that there should be inserted in it
an article which would have provided that, in the absence of a stipulation in the
convention, the provisions of laws and national rules relating to carriage in each
state should be applicable. The effect of that amendment, if introduced, would *g*
have been to enable the common law to apply when liability could not be
established under the convention. There was a brief discussion of this
amendment during the sixth session of the conference on 9 October (see p 176 of
the minutes). When the proposal was drawn to the attention of the delegates, the
head of the Italian delegation, Mr Giannini, said that, following a suggestion *h*
made by the German delegation, they were going to propose adopting as a title
for the convention the words 'Convention relating to certain rules for the
unification of private aeronautical law'. He added that, given that this title
indicated the special character of the convention, the Czechoslovak delegation no
longer insisted on its amendment. The Czechoslovak proposal was then *j*
withdrawn without further discussion. A proposal by the Yugoslav delegation
that the Berne Convention (the Convention of the International Union for the
Protection of Literary and Artistic Work 1886, (binding between France and the
United Kingdom since 10 July 1974), as revised at Paris on 24 July (Paris, 24 July
1971; TS9 (1975); Cmnd 5844)) should be applied for cases not provided for by the
convention was also withdrawn.

a   Mr Nicholls suggested that the meaning to be given to the words 'Certain Rules' in the title should reflect the text of the withdrawn Czechoslovakian amendment. In my opinion, however, the circumstances in which the Czechoslovak delegation agreed to withdraw their proposal are not sufficiently explored in the minutes to enable us to take that meaning from these words. Nor, indeed, is it sufficiently clear what the scope was of the amendment which that
b   delegation had originally proposed. In an earlier discussion (noted at p 85 of the minutes), both the British and the Soviet delegates had expressed concern at the insertion of a clause which would have opened gaps in the convention, as its object was to ensure uniformity. It may be that all the Czechoslovak delegates were seeking to do was to insert a clause in order to clarify the position in regard to chapters of law relating to international carriage by air with which the
c   convention was not attempting to deal. Their agreement to the substitution of the words 'Certain Rules' in the title can easily be explained if that was the only purpose which their amendment was intended to serve.

(c) Decisions by the courts in the United Kingdom

d   As I said earlier, the only United Kingdom cases to which we were referred were *Grein v Imperial Airways Ltd* [1936] 2 All ER 1258 at 1277–1278, [1937] 1 KB 50 at 74–76, in which Greene LJ made certain observations about the approach to construction of the convention, and *Gatewhite Ltd v Iberia Lineas Aereas de España SA* [1989] 1 All ER 944, [1990] 1 QB 326, in which Gatehouse J held that, in the
e   absence of express provision in the convention excluding the owner's right of action, the owner of goods damaged or lost by a carrier was entitled to sue in his own name in accordance with the lex fori and accordingly, that the plaintiffs were entitled to damages to be assessed at common law.

In *Grein v Imperial Airways Ltd* [1936] 2 All ER 1258 at 1277–1278, [1937] 1 KB 50
f   at 74–76, Greene LJ made observations about the general objects of the convention, the desirability of an international code for air carriage, and the need to approach the convention with a proper appreciation that it was one of the main objects of the convention to secure the removal of various difficulties which might otherwise have arisen by means of a uniform international code. These observations are helpful as they support the approach which I have taken in my
g   reading of the convention. But there is nothing in the facts of the case or the particular decision arrived at which is relevant to the issue in this case.

In *Gatewhite Ltd v Iberia Lineas Aereas de España SA* the defendants had argued that, as that was a case of international carriage of cargo by air, it was governed by the convention and that the plaintiffs had no claim under it as only the
h   consignor or the consignee had a right of action against the carrier. The judge rejected this argument. He said that it was remarkable that nowhere did the convention expressly exclude the right of the owner of goods to sue the carrier for damage to or loss of the goods and that the limitation of this right to consignor or consignee alone arose, if at all, by implication (see [1989] 1 All ER 944 at 948,
j   [1990] 1 QB 326 at 331). Having examined various decisions from other jurisdictions which were directed to this issue, he was attracted by the reasoning in *Tasman Pulp and Paper Co Ltd v Brambles J B O'Loghlen Ltd* [1981] 2 NZLR 225. It seemed to him that, as the convention did not expressly deal with the position by excluding the owner's right of action, although it could so easily have done so, the lex fori could fill the gap (see [1989] 1 All ER 944 at 950, [1990] 1 QB 326 at 334).

Lord Marnoch in the Outer House of the Court of Session was able to distinguish the *Gatewhite* case on the ground that it was dealing with a quite separate aspect of the convention (see 1996 SLT 529 at 537). Lord Clyde in the Inner House said that the area of title to sue was one in which the convention was not necessarily exhaustive (see 1996 SLT 529 at 546). This decision, however, does not sit easily with the idea that the object of the convention, in the areas with which it deals, was to provide uniformity of application internationally. As Shawcross and Beaumont *Air Law* (4th edn reissue) vol 1 (Issue 64, October 1996) para VII (188) have observed, the rule in civil law countries is that only a party to a contract of carriage, or a principal for whom he was acting, is regarded as the appropriate plaintiff. In common law countries the proper plaintiff is the owner of the goods, whose right to sue depends on his interest in the goods, not on the fact that he may also be a party to the contract. It would seem to be more consistent with the purpose of the convention to regard it as providing a uniform rule about who can sue for goods which are lost or damaged during carriage by air, with the result that the owner who is not a party to the contract has no right to sue in his own name.

We were not asked to review the *Gatewhite* case in detail however, and as the point was not fully argued, I would not wish to cast further doubt on the decision which Gatehouse J reached. It is sufficient for present purposes to say that I am not persuaded that we should apply his reasoning to the question which is before us here, which is not concerned with the question of standing or title to sue but with the question whether a person who has an undoubted title to sue under the convention can pursue a claim outside the convention where the convention itself does not provide him with a remedy.

(d) Decisions by the foreign courts

Much of the discussion in both the Outer House and the Inner House in the Court of Session was taken up with a detailed examination of various cases on this topic from the United States of America. All the judges in that court were of the view however that, in the end, no clear guidance was available from this source to enable them to rely on this material in reaching their decision in the present case. Lord Marnoch observed (1996 SLT 529 at 536), that the Supreme Court had on two occasions in recent times found it either unnecessary or inappropriate to consider the question whether the convention provided an exclusive cause of action for injuries sustained during international air transportation (see *Air France v Saks* (1985) 470 US 392 and *Eastern Airlines Inc v Floyd* (1991) 499 US 530). The result of his review was that there was no clear or very consistent line of reasoning in these cases to guide him in this area of international air law. Lord Mayfield said that it was impossible to draw any clear conclusion as to the state of US law and Lord Clyde expressed the same view having observed earlier that it was pointless and perhaps impertinent to subject all these cases to critical analysis (see 1996 SLT 529 at 544, 547). Lord Allanbridge was able to find support in some of the cases for the view which he had already reached on his examination of the convention. But in the end he agreed with the observations of Leggatt LJ in *Sidhu v British Airways plc* in the Court of Appeal ([1995] CA Transcript 107) that, in view of the conflicting nature of these authorities and the fact that the Supreme Court had twice refrained from addressing the present problem, it was necessary to reach a conclusion in this case without any definite aid from the United States (see 1996 SLT 529 at 542). As Leggatt LJ said in his judgment, it appears that the point is not settled in the United States as between a   circuits and even in some instances within the same circuit. From his consideration of the cases cited to him he was not prepared to say where the preponderance of current opinion lies in the United States.

I do not think that I can usefully add much to these observations. One could, of course, attempt to prepare an analysis of the various cases which were cited to us in order to show why *Metz v KLM Royal Dutch Airlines* (1979) 15 Avi Cas 17,843,
b   *Abramson v Japan Airlines Co Ltd* (1984) 739 F 2d 130, *Fischer v Northwest Airlines Inc* (1985) 623 F Supp 1064 and *Walker v Eastern Airlines Inc* (1991) 23 Avi Cas 17,904, which favour the position of the pursuer and the plaintiffs in this case, should be rejected in the light of the contrary view expressed in *Finkelstein v Trans World Airlines Inc* (1978) 15 Avi Cas 17,379 and *Saloom v British Airways plc* (22 February 1993, unreported). *Saloom's* case is of particular interest, as the claims which the
c   court held were governed exclusively by the convention and could not be made out on the facts arose out of the same incident as that with which we are concerned in this case. There are dicta in some other cases, notably *Boehringer-Mannheim Diagnostics Inc v Pan American Airways Inc* (1984) 737 F 2d 456, which support the general view that the convention provides the sole cause
d   of action where a passenger seeks to establish a claim against an air carrier and is the exclusive remedy. But, as Lord Clyde pointed out, these general observations are of little value unless they are based on a clear and precise understanding of what matters are governed by the convention (see 1996 SLT 529 at 547). I am not confident, with great respect to the many American judges who have participated in this debate, that that has always been the case. I believe that it would be
e   unwise to attempt to reconcile all these dicta, or to try to subject each of the various decisions to analysis in order to extract from them a view which one could be confident would be regarded as authoritative.

In any event, as Mr Webb pointed out, the United States is only one jurisdiction among many. Although the volume of litigation in that country on
f   aviation matters is substantial and the jurisprudence which has been developed is an important source of information on aviation law generally, views formed there cannot be assumed to be the same as those formed in other jurisdictions which are party to the convention. Some of the cases in the United States may also be influenced by the question whether the claim for damages was properly to be litigated in the state courts rather than the federal courts. Lord Diplock in
g   *Fothergill v Monarch Airlines Ltd* [1980] 2 All ER 696 at 708, [1981] AC 251 at 284 drew attention to the factors on which the persuasive value of the decisions of a foreign court must depend. These include the reputation and status of the court, and the extent to which the decision is binding upon courts of co-ordinate and inferior jurisdiction in that country. As matters have developed it will ultimately
h   be for the Supreme Court of the United States of America to offer guidance to the American judges on this issue, and at this stage I do not think that we should attempt to enter into the difficult debate as to how the balance of view is likely to be resolved when the matter is dealt with by that court.

As for the French case to which we were referred, I think that it also must be
j   regarded as being of no persuasive value in the present case. In *Ismail A Mohamed v British Airways plc* (8 November 1995, unreported) 65 passengers and their close relatives, who were all French nationals, claimed damages from British Airways for the consequences of the same events as those which have given rise to the claims which are before us in these appeals. The Tribunal de Grande Instance de Paris reached the view on the facts that the damages claimed were not linked with disembarkation operations as such, and that they could not be linked to

those risks inherent in aerial navigation as provided by the Warsaw Convention. In these circumstances the court felt free to determine the law applicable, on the view that the consequential damages claimed were not covered by the field of application of the convention. French law was applied, and the plaintiffs were found entitled to damages unrestricted by the limits set by art 22 of the convention.

That, however, was a decision at first instance, and we were told that it is now under appeal. The copy of the judgment with which we have been provided, in an English translation, does not contain a close analysis of the convention, nor is there any reference to previous decisions on the issue in the French courts or elsewhere. The reasons given do not disclose a detailed examination of the issues raised by the defence. It is reasonably clear, however, that the case proceeded upon a different view from that which has been taken in the present case, where it is conceded that the claims can properly be regarded as arising out of international carriage of passengers by air.

CONCLUSION
I believe that the answer to the question raised in the present case is to be found in the objects and structure of the convention. The language used and the subject matter with which it deals demonstrate that what was sought to be achieved was a uniform international code, which could be applied by the courts of all the High Contracting Parties without reference to the rules of their own domestic law. The convention does not purport to deal with all matters relating to contracts of international carriage by air. But in those areas with which it deals—and the liability of the carrier is one of them—the code is intended to be uniform and to be exclusive also of any resort to the rules of domestic law.

An answer to the question which leaves claimants without a remedy is not at first sight attractive. It is tempting to give way to the argument that where there is a wrong there must be a remedy. That indeed is the foundation upon which much of our own common law has been built up. The broad principles which provide the foundation for the law of delict in Scotland and of torts in the English common law have been developed upon these lines. No system of law can attempt to compensate persons for all losses in whatever circumstances. But the assumption is that, where a breach of duty has caused loss, a remedy in damages ought to be available.

Alongside these principles, however, there lies another great principle, which is that of freedom of contract. Any person is free, unless restrained by statute, to enter into a contract with another on the basis that his liability in damages is excluded or limited if he is in breach of contract. Exclusion and limitation clauses are a common feature of commercial contracts, and contracts of carriage are no exception. It is against that background, rather than a desire to provide remedies to enable all losses to be compensated, that the convention must be judged. It was not designed to provide remedies against the carrier to enable all losses to be compensated. It was designed instead to define those situations in which compensation was to be available. So it set out the limits of liability and the conditions under which claims to establish that liability, if disputed, were to be made. A balance was struck, in the interests of certainty and uniformity.

All the obvious cases in which the carrier ought to accept liability were provided for. But, as one of the French delegates to the Warsaw Convention, Mr Ripert, observed (minutes, p 73) when the definition of the period of carriage was being discussed, there are an infinite variety of cases not all of which can be put *a*   in the same formula. No doubt the domestic courts will try, as carefully as they may, to apply the wording of art 17 to the facts to enable the passenger to obtain a remedy under the convention. But it is conceded in this case that no such remedy is available. The conclusion must be therefore that any remedy is excluded by the convention, as the set of uniform rules does not provide for it. The domestic courts are not free to provide a remedy according to their own law,

b   because to do this would be to undermine the convention. It would lead to the setting alongside the convention of an entirely different set of rules which would distort the operation of the whole scheme.

    The convention is, of course, tightly drawn on these matters. This has been done in the interests of the carrier, whose exposure to these liabilities without the freedom to contract out of them was a principal consequence of the system

c   which it laid down. Were remedies outside the convention to become available, it would encourage litigation in other cases to restrict its application still further in the hope of obtaining a better remedy, against which the carrier would have no protection under the contract. I am in no doubt that the convention was designed to eliminate these difficulties. I see no escape from the conclusion that,

d   where the convention has not provided a remedy, no remedy is available.

    For these reasons, I would dismiss both appeals.

Appeals dismissed.

Mary Rose Plummer   Barrister.

Seifert v Pensions Ombudsman and others

Lynch and another v Pensions Ombudsman and another

a

b

QUEEN'S BENCH DIVISION (CROWN OFFICE LIST)

LIGHTMAN J

25 JUNE, 30 JULY 1996

Pension – Pension scheme – Maladministration of pension scheme – Jurisdiction of Pensions Ombudsman – Exercise of jurisdiction of Pensions Ombudsman – Maladministration by Pensions Ombudsman – Necessity for statutory procedure to be followed – Necessity for the rules of natural justice to be applied – Pension Schemes Act 1993, ss 149(1), 151.

c

The appellants, L, H and S, were the trustees of S Ltd's pension scheme, although S was not a member of the scheme. Clause 21 of the trust deed provided that the trustees should be entitled to all the indemnities conferred on trustees by law and that a trustee should not be liable for any acts or omissions not due to his own wilful neglect or default. In December 1991 K, a director and employee of S Ltd who had reached the age of 60, was made redundant; it was agreed, however, that for pension purposes he should be treated as having taken early retirement under the scheme. The assurer of the scheme, G plc, subsequently advised that it was under-funded and that K's share of the assets would be 63% of the pension to which he was entitled. His final pension arrangements were still under negotiation when the scheme was formally wound up on 30 June 1992, following which S Ltd went into administrative receivership. In October 1992 G plc calculated that the scheme's funds in fact covered 83% of its liabilities. Thereafter, K complained to the Pensions Ombudsman pursuant to the provisions of the Pension Schemes Act 1993 of maladministration by the appellants. In particular, he complained that he had only been offered 63% of his entitlement when there were sufficient funds to pay 83%; and he claimed payment of that 83% and of the loss of two and a half years' pension to date. The ombudsman sent copies of K's complaint to the trustees but he did not disclose to them a letter dated 4 August 1995 from K alleging, inter alia, that the trustees were culpably responsible for the deficit in the pension scheme funds and had failed to carry out their fiduciary duties. The ombudsman upheld K's complaint, holding in para 31 of his determination that the appellants had denied responsibility for a benefit which had effectively been consented to and that their lack of interest and concern was inconsistent with their fiduciary position. He further directed that K should receive his full pension with effect from the date when his employment terminated, to be funded by a reduction in the benefits of L and H over whom he was to take priority, and that the appellants should pay K compensation of £1,200. The appellants appealed.

d

e

f

g

h

j

Held – The appeals would be allowed for the following reasons—

(1) Where a complaint was made to the Pensions Ombudsman the ombudsman had to comply with the procedure in s 149(1)[a] of the 1993 Act and

_____

a   Section 149(1) is set out at p 219 *h*, post

a with the principles of natural justice. Those principles required that he should (i) make clear to the respondents the specific allegations made in the complaint and (ii) disclose to them all potentially relevant information obtained by him, in particular all evidence and representations received by him from the complainant. It followed that the ombudsman was obliged to disclose K's letter of 4 August 1995 to the trustees as soon as it was received and his failure to do so *b* rendered the determination fundamentally flawed (see p 222 *g* to p 223 *b*, post).

(2) It was not open to the ombudsman to make a determination in respect of allegations not made in the complaint. However, the finding in para 31 of the determination was not of the allegation made in the complaint, nor were the directions appropriate to the complaint. Moreover, the relief granted was not the relief claimed, since K had only sought payment of 83% of his pension *c* entitlement (see p 223 *e* and p 224 *d*, post).

(3) Although the ombudsman had jurisdiction to award compensation for maladministration, the penalties imposed on L and H were a form of award of compensation for breach of trust or maladministration which was incompatible with cl 21 of the pension scheme trust deed, which constituted part of the terms *d* on which a trustee accepted his appointment and provided protection in respect of his conduct as a trustee, even after he ceased to be such (see p 225 *e* to *g*, post).

(4) Section 151[b] of the 1993 Act required the ombudsman to give reasons which, in clear and unambiguous terms, explained the line of reasoning which led him to make his finding and give his directions. In the instant case, however, the *e* determination fell well below the standard required (see p 226 *e f*, post).

(5) In any event there was no substance in K's complaint since the figure of 83% was merely an estimate and all K could be entitled to was the percentage of his entitlement arrived at when the final figure was arrived at. Nor was there any substance in para 31 of the determination, since the appellants had quite properly *f* refused to pay K his full entitlement because of the deficit in the scheme assets, which it was their duty to do in view of their overriding obligation to act fairly between all members of the scheme and in accordance with its rules (see p 224 *f* and p 225 *b*, post).

Notes

g For occupational pension schemes generally, see 33 *Halsbury's Laws* (4th edn) para 973.

Cases referred to in judgment

Duffield v Pensions Ombudsman (1996) Times, 30 April.
h *Miller v Stapleton* [1996] 2 All ER 449.
Westminster City Council v Haywood [1996] 2 All ER 467, [1996] 3 WLR 563.

Cases also cited or referred to in skeleton arguments

Armitage v Nurse (28 June 1995, unreported), Ch D.
j *Bartlett v Barclays Bank Trust Co Ltd (No 2)* [1980] 2 All ER 92, [1980] Ch 515.
Chapman, Re, Cocks v Chapman [1896] 2 Ch 763, [1895–9] All ER Rep 1104, CA.
City Equitable Fire Insurance Co Ltd, Re [1925] Ch 407, [1924] All ER Rep 485, CA.

---

b   Section 151, so far as material, provides: 'Where the Pensions Ombudsman has conducted an investigation ... he shall send a written statement of his determination ... and any such statement shall contain the reasons for his determination ...'

Dias, The, Palamisto General Enterprises SA v Ocean Marine Insurance Co Ltd [1972] 2
All ER 1112, [1972] 2 QB 625, CA.

Galoo Ltd (in liq) v Bright Grahame Murray (a firm) [1995] 1 All ER 16, [1994] 1 WLR
1360, CA.

Leeds City Brewery Ltd's Debenture Stock Trust Deed, Re, Leeds City Brewery Ltd v Platts
[1925] Ch 532, CA.

Lloyd v McMahon [1987] 1 All ER 1118, [1987] AC 625, HL.

Providence Capitol Trustees Ltd v Ayres (7 June 1996, unreported), Ch D.

R v Comr for Local Administration, ex p Eastleigh BC [1988] 3 All ER 151, [1988] QB
855, CA.

Raineri v Miles (Wiejski and anor, third parties) [1980] 2 All ER 145, [1981] AC 1050,
HL.

Shiloh Spinners Ltd v Harding [1973] 1 All ER 90, [1973] AC 691, HL.

Target Holdings Ltd v Redferns (a firm) [1995] 3 All ER 785, [1996] AC 421, HL.

Vickery, Re, Vickery v Stephens [1931] 1 Ch 572, [1931] All ER Rep 562.

Wild v Pensions Ombudsman (2 April 1996, unreported), QBD.

Wilkins v Hogg (1861) 31 LJ Ch 41.

Wilson v Law Debenture Trust Corp plc [1992] 2 All ER 337.

Appeals

John Seifert, Anthony Lynch and Philip Helm, the former trustees of the pension
scheme of Seifert Ltd, and Fairmount Trustee Services Ltd appealed from a
determination of the Pensions Ombudsman, Julian Farrand QC, dated 5
December 1995 whereby he upheld complaints by Erdogan Kural, a former
director and employee of Seifert Ltd and a member of its pension scheme, of
maladministration by them. The facts are set out in the judgment.

David Rees (instructed by *Jacobsens*) for Mr Seifert.
Paul Newman (instructed by *Halls*) for Mr Lynch and Mr Helm.
Josephine Hayes (instructed by *Sacker & Partners*) for Fairmount Trustee Services
Ltd.
Mr Kural appeared in person.

Cur adv vult

30 July 1996. The following judgment was delivered.

LIGHTMAN J.

I. INTRODUCTION

The Social Security Act 1990, s 12(1) and Sch 3, now consolidated in ss 145 to
152 of the Pension Schemes Act 1993, created the office and jurisdiction of the
Pensions Ombudsman (the ombudsman). His statutory function under the Act
(as extended by the Personal and Occupational Pension Schemes (Pensions
Ombudsman) Regulations 1991, SI 1991/588) is (a) to investigate written
complaints made to him of injustice in consequence of maladministration in
connection with any act or omission of the trustees or managers of, and of
employers in relation to, an occupational pension scheme or personal pension
scheme; and (b) to investigate and determine any dispute of fact or law. The
ombudsman investigated and on 5 December 1995 made a determination (the
determination) upholding a complaint by Mr Kural of maladministration by Mr
Lynch, Mr Helm and Mr Seifert (the appellants), the three trustees of the Seifert
Group Pension and Life Assurance Scheme (the scheme). On these two appeals

a from the determination, one by Mr Lynch and Mr Helm, and the other by Mr Seifert, the appellants contend that the determination is vitiated, not merely by errors of law, but also by 'maladministration' by the ombudsman i e the unjust way he reached that decision. In my view both complaints are well made out. I think that the determination is also objectionable for the failure, contrary to s 151 of the Act, to set out the reasons in language which is clear and meaningful i e for b unintelligibility.

II. SPECIAL PROCEDURE IN THIS CASE

Neither Mr Kural nor the ombudsman was represented by counsel at the hearing of this appeal on 25 June 1996. Mr Kural attended in person and the ombudsman attended by a solicitor. Neither made any representations, though c invited to do so. Prior to the hearing the ombudsman sent to the court a letter dated 21 June 1996 (the June letter) seeking to assist on the issues raised on the appeal. With the June letter was enclosed an important letter from Mr Kural to the ombudsman dated 4 August 1995 (Mr Kural's letter), which had not previously been disclosed to any of the other parties. In the circumstances at the d hearing, I thought it right to give leave to the appellants to raise as an additional ground on the appeal the failure of the ombudsman to disclose Mr Kural's letter before he made his provisional determination (the PD) or the determination. I also myself at the hearing raised the question whether the determination was objectionable on the grounds of unintelligibility. As the ombudsman was not represented at the hearing by counsel and in the light of the importance of the e issue relating to Mr Kural's letter, I resolved, after preparing a provisional draft of this judgment, to send a copy to the ombudsman and all the other parties and to give the ombudsman an opportunity to make representations in writing and the parties thereafter, the opportunity to make their comments in writing on his representations. I made it clear to all that (to save costs) there would be no f further hearing unless the ombudsman or a party gave sufficient reason why there should be one.

The ombudsman made his representations by letter dated 10 July 1996 (the July letter). His representations were not confined to the effect of non-disclosure of Mr Kural's letter, but included (amongst others) the issue of unintelligibility; and the parties (including Mr Kural) made their comments in writing on these g representations. No application has been made for a further hearing. I accordingly give judgment today confident that the parties (and in particular the ombudsman) have been given a fair opportunity to say what they wish on the various grounds on which this appeal is being decided.

h III. FACTS

Mr Kural was a director as well as for 27 years an employee of Seifert Ltd (Seifert), a company providing architectural services. He attained his 60th birthday on 23 May 1991. Seifert as the principal employer had its own final salary pension and life assurance scheme, namely the scheme of which the appellants j until 18 August 1992 were the trustees. The assurer was Guardian Assurance plc (Guardian). The members of the scheme who were entitled to deferred benefits under it included Mr Lynch, Mr Helm and Mr Kural. These three (together with Mr Seifert) were directors of Seifert. Mr Helm was the finance director. The scheme included as cl 21 of the definitive deed dated 12 August 1971 a provision to the following effect:

'WITHOUT prejudice to the powers and discretions vested in the Trustees by the other provisions hereof the Trustees shall be entitled to all the indemnities conferred on trustees by law and shall not be liable for acting on the advice of the Auditor or the Actuary appointed hereunder or on any other professional advice nor shall any Trustee be liable for any acts or omissions not due to his own wilful neglect or default.'

During 1991, Seifert (as all the directors, including Mr Kural, well knew) fell into severe financial difficulties, and for this reason by letter dated 9 December 1991, Mr Kural was given notice expiring on 8 June 1992. He was made redundant, but it was agreed that for pension purposes he should be treated as having taken early retirement under the scheme. Under the rules, Mr Kural was in these circumstances entitled to elect whether to take an early retirement pension in lieu of a preserved pension.

On 17 February 1992 Seifert provided Mr Kural with a quotation prepared by Guardian for the retirement benefits to which he was entitled under the scheme. The quotation was either an annual personal pension of £17,327·40 or a tax free lump sum payment of £29,240·86 and a reduced annual personal pension of £14,676·36. In either case, there was to be a widow's annual pension of £8,663·76. The quotation included the following note:

'Note that the assumed outgo exceeds the amount reserved for this member under the scheme. If the date by which the scheme's long-term liabilities are fully funded is not to be deferred, an extra contribution of £75,300 will be needed. This could be covered by a single premium payment.'

This payment of £75,300 could not be made by Seifert: its bankers would not have allowed it and the directors knew that such a payment by Seifert might be open to challenge as a wrongful preference.

On 7 April 1992 Mr Kural wrote to Mr Helm as Seifert's finance director (inter alia) asking for confirmation of the details in the quotation on the basis of his taking the maximum lump sum payment and that Guardian would pay the £14,676·36 by monthly instalments into his bank account. Certain discussions thereafter proceeded (to which Mr Kural was not a party) regarding a switch of pension arrangements from final salary to money purchase. In the course of considering these proposals, Guardian on 18 May 1992 wrote to Mr Helm to the effect that the scheme was under funded on a discontinuance basis and that on a current funding position £132,803 (which was 63% of the pension to which Mr Kural was entitled under the scheme) fairly represented Mr Kural's share of the assets of the scheme, whilst £260,467·43 would be required to secure the proposed early retirement pension to which Mr Kural was entitled under the scheme.

On 28 May 1992 Mr Helm sent Mr Kural a memorandum dated 20 May 1992 to the effect that the trustees would make available to him the sum of £132,800 and were currently seeking quotations in respect of the benefits which this sum would purchase. On 3 June 1992, Mr Helm sent Mr Kural these quotations. On offer was an annual pension of £10,901·52 or a lump sum of £29,240·86 and a reduced annual pension of £8,481·12. In both cases, there was a widow's annual pension of one half of Mr Kural's pension. On 8 June 1992 Mr Kural's notice expired. Mr Kural's final pension arrangements were still under negotiation and accordingly he was not in receipt of a pension when on 30 June 1992, the scheme

a formally went into wind up. On 8 July Seifert went into administrative
receivership. On 18 August 1992, pursuant to s 57C of the Social Security
Pensions Act 1975 (now s 119 of the 1993 Act), the administrative receivers
appointed Fairmount Trustee Services Ltd (Fairmount) as independent trustee to
act in winding up the scheme. On 14 October Mr Seifert and Mr Lynch retired as
trustees of the scheme. On 8 October 1992 Guardian made a valuation of the
b scheme assets (the 1992 valuation) in which they calculated (without making any
of a number of provisions which they said required to be made) that the scheme
funds only covered 83% of its liabilities. This deficit brought into play rule 16.3
of the scheme under which (in short) the assets of the scheme had first to be
applied in ensuring existing pensioners continued to receive their pensions and
only the balance of the assets was available to provide benefits for all other
c members at their normal retirement date (and that included Mr Kural, as well as
Mr Lynch and Mr Helm).

On 24 February 1993 Fairmount wrote to Mr Kural informing him (1) that
there was a shortfall in the assets of the scheme, that there was in this regard a
claim against Seifert, but that it was unlikely that the receivers would have
d surplus assets to pay into the scheme; and (2) as to the effect of rule 16.3. On 19
October 1995, after making the necessary provisions referred to in their valuation
dated 8 October 1992 (but not provision for the costs of these proceedings),
Guardian calculated the current funded position to be 71·6%.

On 22 January 1995 Mr Kural wrote to the ombudsman making his complaint
of maladministration, at that stage against Guardian only, and seeking his
e intervention to obtain a satisfactory settlement from Guardian. This complaint,
and the complaint repeated in his subsequent letters dated 31 January and 28
March 1995, (a letter to Ms Herbert, an OPAS adviser) and as extended by a letter
dated 15 June 1995 so as to include Seifert and the appellants amongst those
against whom he made his complaint, was that the premium offered in June 1992
f was only £132,800, which was 63% of his entitlement, when (as stated in
Guardian's letter dated 8 October 1992), funds were available to pay 83% of his
entitlement. His claim was for payment of a premium equal to 83% of his
entitlement and of the loss of two and a half years' pension to date.

On 22 June 1995 the ombudsman wrote to the appellants setting out the
complaints procedure, which included a provision requiring the ombudsman to
g provide to the appellants, as persons against whom complaints were made, the
opportunity to comment on the allegations in the complaint. This provision
reflects s 149(1) of the 1993 Act:

'Where the Pensions Ombudsman proposes to conduct an investigation
h into a complaint made or dispute referred under this Part, he shall give—(a)
the trustees and managers of [and employers in relation to] the scheme
concerned, and (b) any other person against whom allegations are made in
the complaint or reference, an opportunity to comment on any allegations
contained in the complaint or reference.'

j The ombudsman supplied the appellants with copies of the correspondence to
which I have referred, and invited their answers to the complaint made. The
appellants did answer.

The ombudsman then sent copies of the appellants' answers to Mr Kural. Mr
Kural in his reply, namely Mr Kural's letter, did not confine himself to responding
to the answers, but made far-reaching and damaging further complaints and
allegations. These included that (1) all decisions at Seifert were made by five

executive shareholders and Mr Helm: Mr Kural was a salaried director and not
included in the decision-making body; (2) the appellants as trustees were
responsible for the deficit in scheme funds by reason of their culpable failure to
secure further contributions to the funds of the scheme from Seifert and to
transfer the funds from Guardian to another assurer; (3) Seifert, if unable to fulfil
its financial obligations under the scheme, was breaking the law by continuing
trading and the appellants (as well as being trustees) 'also being employers, were
fully aware of the situation and they also failed to carry out their fiduciary duties';
and (4) in a number of respects Mr Helm was telling untruths. As I have already
said, the ombudsman never disclosed the existence of Mr Kural's letter or its
contents to any of the appellants.

On 12 October 1995 the ombudsman communicated his PD to the appellants.
In the PD, the ombudsman upheld the complaint against Seifert for unreasonably
denying Mr Kural the benefits to which he was entitled and declined to uphold
the complaint against Guardian. As regards the appellants he said:

'23. I further uphold the complaint against the [appellants], who denied
responsibility for a benefit which, in my judgment, had effectively been
consented to. They were all senior officers of the Employer and as such it is,
for present purposes, impossible to disentangle their knowledge and actions
as trustees from their knowledge and actions in the former capacity. The
Finance Director, who dealt directly with the matter, clearly bears the
greatest responsibility, but the other trustees must be taken to have been
aware of the events and I find their lack of interest and concern to be
inconsistent with their fiduciary position.'

His directions were as follows:

'25. Within one month of the date of this Determination the Independent
Trustee and the remaining Individual Trustee (the "Present Trustees") are to
obtain the Complainant's decision in writing as to the form in which he
wishes to take his early retirement benefits, based on the Assurer's February
1992 quotation.

26. Within two months of the date of this Determination the Present
Trustees are to commence payment of the benefits required by the
Complainant with effect from 8 June 1992.

27. Interest is to be paid on benefits paid late, calculated on a daily basis at
the Statutory Rate of Interest (as prescribed under the Supreme Court Act
1981) from time to time applying.

28. On any tax free cash sum elected by the Complainant interest is to be
calculated from 8 June 1992 to the date of payment. On instalments of
pension paid in arrears, interest is to be calculated from the due date of each
instalment to the date of payment.

29. The deferred benefit rights of the two Individual Trustees who are
members of the Scheme are to be reduced to the extent needed to fully fund
the Complainant's benefits, the reduction being the same percentage in each
case and based on the value, not the amount, of their benefit rights.

30. Within one month of the date of this Determination the Finance
Director is to pay the Complainant £900 and the other two Individual
Trustees £300 each in order adequately to compensate him for the upset and
inconvenience constituting injustice sustained by him from the
maladministration.'

a The appellants thereupon made representations to the ombudsman in respect of the PD. It is sufficient to refer to four of them: (1) the finding did not represent or reflect Mr Kural's complaint made in the correspondence made available to the appellants; (2) the entitlement of the appellants under cl 21 to exoneration from liability for any breach of trust and an indemnity in respect of the compensation directed was ignored; (3) the responsibility for non-payment to Mr Kural of his full entitlement lay with Seifert in failing fully to fund the scheme, and not the appellants; and (4) implementation of his directions would afford to Mr Kural a priority to which he was not entitled under the terms of the scheme at the expense of other members.

The representations did not elicit any disclosure of Mr Kural's letter, but on 5 December 1995 the ombudsman made the determination which (save in two respects) was to the same effect as the PD culminating in para 31, which is in the same terms as para 23 of the PD. There was a minor adjustment to the direction in para 29 of the PD to add the words 'but adjusted so far as necessary between the two of them to ensure that their GMP rights are not prejudiced'. And there were added paragraphs dealing with certain of the representations made. The relevant paragraphs read as follows:

'22. A number of arguments were put to me in response to my provisional Determination. The first of these was that the complaint investigated is that it was impliedly represented to the Complainant that the Employer would pay the sum of £75,300 referred to in paragraph 4 and that this complaint was never made and cannot be made out from correspondence. Reference to the Complainant's letter of 22 January 1995 discloses at the top of the second page the pension he was told he would receive. Later paragraphs reveal the much lower pension he was expected to settle for. My investigation dealt with the basic issue of this apparent reduction ...

26. It was then argued that I would be incorrect to attribute personal responsibility to the Individual Trustees and that true responsibility actually lay with the Employer for failing to fund the benefits. Obviously one of the likely causes of the deficiency in the Scheme was inadequate funding by the Employer but there may have been other contributory factors. The Complainant received a quotation for the early retirement benefits to which he was entitled under the rules of the Scheme but the Individual Trustees sought to reduce those benefits. The Individual Trustees were also directors of the Employer and in my view they allowed their knowledge of the Employer's financial state to influence their decisions about the Complainant's benefit rights from the Scheme.

27. It was next argued that the implementation of my directions would constitute a breach of Section 23 of the Pension Schemes Act 1993, which is concerned with priorities on wind up. I do not accept this argument. Had there been no maladministration, the Complainant would have retired in June 1992, before the Scheme's winding up date, with the benefits to which he was entitled under the rules. Since maladministration has occurred, the appropriate steps to be directed as redress must be to return the Complainant to the position he should have been in but for the maladministration. There is therefore no question of interference with winding up priorities and consequently no breach under Section 23 of the Act.'

The effect of the ombudsman's direction was to treat Mr Kural as in receipt of the full pension to which he was entitled under the terms of the scheme on 8 June

1992, and afford him the priority to which receipt would have entitled him at the
expense of Mr Helm and Mr Lynch. The effect of his direction regarding the
entitlement of Mr Helm and Mr Lynch is that Mr Helm's entitlement to
£17,023·81 is reduced by £12,413·76, so that, after an under-funding reduction of
£4,272·98, he is only entitled to an annual pension of £337·09; and that Mr Lynch's
entitlement to £29,231·05 is reduced by £16,527·24, so that, after an
under-funding reduction of £7,336·99, he is only entitled to £5,366·82. The effect
of his direction as to payment of the compensation is that by virtue of cl 21 this
payment is borne by the scheme's assets which are already in deficit.

IV. DECISION

(1) *Compliance with statutory procedure and the rules of natural justice*
On 21 June 1996, in the June letter, to assist the court, the ombudsman wrote
to the court setting out his observations on the issues in the appeal. In the course
of his letter he wrote: 'In order that the complete picture is given to the court, I
also attach a copy of Mr Kural's [letter] ... received by my office on 7 August
1995.' Mr Kural's letter is indeed necessary to obtain a complete picture. Its
significance lies in the fact that it is the missing link between on the one hand the
letters disclosed to the appellants and on the other the PD and the determination.
It explains how and why the PD and determination focus, not on the subject
matter of the complaint as revealed to the appellants, but the matters taken up by
the ombudsman. For example, the terms (and indeed language) of complaint 3
in Mr Kural's letter are reflected in para 23 of the PD and the corresponding para
31 as well as para 26 of the determination. Mr Rees, counsel for Mr Seifert,
submitted that the determination cannot stand, having regard to the failure of the
ombudsman to disclose Mr Kural's letter or its contents earlier to the appellants.
Section 151 of the Act provides that the ombudsman must send to the parties
a written statement of the determination, including the reasons for the
determination, and he is given power to 'direct the trustees or managers of the
scheme concerned [or the employers] to take, or refrain from taking, such steps
as he may specify'.
The determination and any direction given by him are final and binding,
subject only to an appeal to the High Court on a point of law only. They have
the force of a county court judgment. A determination by the ombudsman can
damage or destroy reputations, as well as impose financial penalties. In these
circumstances, (a) it is mandatory that the ombudsman comply with the
statutory procedure contained in s 149(1) designed to ensure fairness; and (b)
further the ombudsman must comply with the principles of natural justice (see
Duffield v Pensions Ombudsman (1996) Times, 30 April). These require of him: (i)
that he make quite clear to the appellants the specific allegations made in the
complaint and to be investigated and of any amendment of the allegations for
which he gives leave. It is not open to the ombudsman to make a determination
save in respect of the allegations in the complaint (or any authorised amendment)
of which he has given notice to the appellants. It is highly desirable that the
ombudsman, rather than merely transmitting copies of his correspondence with
the complainant, (save in simple and obvious cases) expresses in his own words
in plain and simple language what he perceives to be the substance of the
allegation. This will limit the risk of misunderstanding; and (ii) he disclose to the
respondents all potentially relevant information obtained by him in exercise of
the power conferred by s 149(4), and most particularly all evidence and
representations received by him from the complainant. The respondents must

a   know at least the gist of what he has learnt, so as to enable them to have a fair
crack of the whip and a fair opportunity to provide any answer they may have.
Whilst the procedure before the ombudsman is intended to be quick, inexpensive
and informal, these are the minimum requirements for fairness and accordingly
for a decision that can be allowed to stand.

b   In my view, the ombudsman was obliged to disclose Mr Kural's letter as soon
as it was received and in any event whilst the investigation was still at a formative
stage and before the PD. His failure to disclose it even after the PD and prior to
the determination, renders the determination fundamentally flawed.

In the July letter the ombudsman accepted that the non-disclosure was a
serious mistake of which he personally had never been aware. He went on
however to explain the decision of his office not to disclose Mr Kural's letter as—

c
'apparently unduly influenced by the statement by Mr Seifert's solicitor in
a letter dated 25 July 1995: "We cannot justify further expenditure to our
clients by examining further documents just in case something is disclosed in
them."'

d   Nothing in Mr Seifert's solicitor's letter could have given any grounds for belief
that Mr Seifert (leave aside the other appellants) would not have wished to see Mr
Kural's letter. I find this explanation more disturbing than reassuring. The
ombudsman, however, does go on to say that he has taken administrative steps
to prevent such mistakes occurring in the future.

e   (2) *Errors of law*

(a) The complaint
In my view, the finding in para 31 of the determination is not of the allegation
made in the complaint nor are the directions appropriate to the complaint made.

f   The complaint was that there were sufficient scheme funds to pay 83% of Mr
Kural's entitlement, but that he had only been offered 63%. This is the crux of
Mr Kural's complaint in his recent comments in writing. He says that the
valuation of the fund in Guardian's letter dated 18 May 1992 was wrong, the true
value was as set out in the 1992 valuation, and that the appellants were in breach
of fiduciary duty in putting forward to him for consideration the quotations based

g   on 63% rather than 83% of his entitlement as representing his share of the assets
of the scheme. The finding by the ombudsman in this regard is practically
unintelligible. If it amounts to anything, it appears to amount to a finding which
accepts the criticism in Mr Kural's letter that the appellants, as directors of Seifert,
should at all times have known of the shortfall, but showed a lack of interest and

h   concern in this regard and failed to ensure that it was made good. The
determination is regretfully permeated by a failure to distinguish between the
duties of the appellants as directors to Seifert (and not Mr Kural), of Seifert as his
employer to Mr Kural, and of the appellants as trustees to Mr Kural. It is not
permissible to roll up these various duties and find a breach by the appellants of
some generalised fiduciary duty to Mr Kural.

j   The primary objection taken by the appellants to the findings in the PD (that
they did not reflect the complaint) is totally ignored in the determination.
Paragraph 22 of the determination merely deals with a secondary objection to the
PD made by the appellants in case the primary objection failed. The June letter
to the court is scarcely more helpful on this issue: it says nothing, though it goes
on to say:

'In particular I stress that it is the way in which a decision is reached and
not the content of the decision itself which amounts to maladministration ...
I considered that the way in which matters had been handled as opposed to
the contents of the decisions themselves amounted to maladministration.'

But the subject matter of the complaint as made was the decision to offer less
than 83%, when 83% was available for this purpose, and the complaint as found
appears to have been the existence of the deficit in the fund for which the
appellants were to be held responsible. In the July letter, the ombudsman goes
further and says that his understanding of the complaint was that, if Mr Kural's
case had been handled properly by the appellants, he would have retired before
the wind up date and would then have been classed as an existing pensioner
enjoying a priority entitling him to the continuing receipt of his full pension
entitlement. I find this understanding somewhat surprising. It is in my view a
quite untenable understanding which finds no expression or support in the
correspondence, the PD, the determination or the evidence, and only underlines
the importance (to which I have already made reference) of the ombudsman
stating in writing to all parties exactly what is his understanding of the complaint
he is investigating.

Not content with upholding a complaint that was not made, the relief granted
was not the relief claimed, ie payment of 83% of Mr Kural's entitlement, but
100%. There can be no possible basis for the grant of this relief against the
appellants. The determination must be set aside for both these reasons.

(b) Substance of complaint

There is no substance in the complaint made by Mr Kural: the figure of 83%
was merely an estimate and, whether it was a correct estimate or not, all Mr Kural
can be entitled to is the percentage of his entitlement arrived at when the final
figure (after making all appropriate provisions) is arrived at. His loss is
attributable to the shortfall in the scheme funds aggravated by the unfortuitous
happening that he was not in receipt of his pension at the date of wind up.

Nor is there any substance in paras 26, 27 or 31 of the determination.
Paragraph 26 (so far as it is intelligible) appears to criticise the appellants in respect
of the lack of full funding of the scheme. Leaving aside the fact that this was not
an issue raised by the complaint and accordingly not to be addressed by the
appellants, the appellants were not guarantors of the sufficiency of the scheme's
assets to pay Mr Kural his entitlement, nor could they consistently with the trusts
and their obligations to other members, pay Mr Kural more than his fair share of
his entitlement at the expense of other members of the scheme. Further ,there is
no reason (let alone evidence) to support the suggestion that there was anything
effective which the appellants could have done about the deficit. There is no
evidence that Seifert could, at any time when the appellants were aware of the
deficit, have made it good. As regards para 27, under the rules, (as the
ombudsman accepted), since Mr Kural was not yet in receipt of a pension, he was
not entitled to any priority, and no act of the appellants (let alone an act of
maladministration) was the occasion for the fact he was not in receipt of a
pension. Receipt of a pension on his part was delayed beyond the date of wind
up by a combination of the shortfall and protracted considerations as to the form
which Mr Kural's pension should take. In the circumstances, Mr Kural, Mr Lynch
and Mr Helm ranked equally in terms of priority in respect of provision for their
pensions out of the available scheme funds. The interference with the established

a priorities between Mr Kural on the one hand and Mr Lynch and Mr Helm on the other, effected by the ombudsman's direction that Mr Kural be given priority at their expense (a priority to which he was not entitled under the rules), is objectionable. As regards para 31, the appellants have, as it seems to me, quite properly refused to pay Mr Kural his full entitlement because, and only because, of the deficit in the scheme assets, and in view of the deficit it was their duty to do so, since their overriding obligation was to act fairly between all members of the scheme and in accordance with its rules.

b

(c) Clause 21

Quite remarkably, the ombudsman has in both the PD and the determination totally ignored cl 21 which (save in case of wilful default) exonerates the appellants from any liability for breach of trust and entitles them to an indemnity in respect of any compensation ordered to be paid. The ombudsman in the July letter pointed out that the representations to him referred to the exoneration clause in an earlier trust deed ,which is differently, but not materially differently, worded. I am not clear whether the ombudsman did so because he thought there was any significance in this error by the appellants: he has not pointed to any and I can see none. The ombudsman also points out that there is no English authority as to whether former trustees, rather than the current trustees, are able to rely on such a clause. If there was no authority, there now is such authority. Clause 21 and clauses to like effect constitute part of the terms on which a trustee accepts his appointment and provide protection in respect of his conduct as a trustee. If his acts whilst a trustee cannot give rise to liability because of cl 21, they cannot subsequently do so merely because he ceases to be a trustee. (I may add that if the ombudsman in his report had wished to take some such point and draw such a distinction between existing and retired trustees in the application of cl 21, I would expect some reference to it in the determination: again there is none.) There has never been any suggestion of wilful default nor could there be. The penalties imposed on Mr Lynch and Mr Helm, in the form of postponement of their interests under the scheme until after full satisfaction of Mr Kural's entitlement, is a form of award of compensation for breach of trust or maladministration which is totally incompatible with cl 21 and is accordingly objectionable on that ground also.

There is authority at first instance binding me to hold that the ombudsman has jurisdiction to award compensation for maladministration, but it is a jurisdiction to be exercised with great caution. The remedy for injustice awarded by the ombudsman must be appropriate and proportional, and not such as to risk creating some new injustice (see *Westminster City Council v Haywood* [1996] 2 All ER 467 at 480, [1996] 3 WLR 563 at 576). Regard in particular must be had to the identity of the person on whom the cost will ultimately fall. If, by reason of a provision to the effect of cl 21, it will fall on the scheme fund and accordingly other (innocent and unrepresented) beneficiaries, that is a fact to be borne in mind; and if it will fall on a trust fund that is already in deficit, that is a matter of the highest importance, for it will mean that it will be a cost borne by beneficiaries already penalised by the deficit. 'Robbing Peter to pay Paul' (to use the graphic language of Carnwath J in *Miller v Stapleton* [1996] 2 All ER 449 at 466) in this way only solves one injustice by creating another. The determination makes no reference to these considerations, and the ombudsman must be taken to have given no, or no proper, weight to these relevant considerations and the determination is objectionable on this ground also.

It is to be noted that in the June letter, the ombudsman now accepts that by
reason of cl 21, the determination should not impose personal liabilities on
trustees entitled to the benefit of exoneration clauses.

(d) Disproportionate liability

The ombudsman has not drawn any distinction between the relevant
culpability of the appellants in respect of the alleged acts complained of, but has
directed that the 'losses' suffered by Mr Kural should be borne by Mr Lynch and
Mr Helm alone out of their interests under the scheme, and Mr Seifert has been
required to contribute nothing. It is plain that the incidence is determined by the
fortuitous circumstance that Mr Lynch and Mr Helm are members of the scheme,
and Mr Seifert is not. The ombudsman has sought to justify this course in the July
letter as an application of the rule of equity that, where a trustee who is also a
beneficiary commits a breach of trust, his beneficial interest may be impounded
to make good his breach of trust (see *Snell's Principles of Equity* (29th edn, 1990)
p 289). But the rule of equity merely provides the trust with a form of security: it
does not require, let alone justify, the exculpation or exoneration from liability
for breach of trust of the co-trustees who do not have a beneficial interest. The
ombudsman has plainly misdirected himself in law in giving this direction.

(e) Unintelligibility

Section 151 requires the ombudsman to give reasons, and this means give
reasons which in clear and unambiguous terms explain the line of reasoning
which leads him to make his finding and give his directions. The determination
is not to be minutely examined as though it were a statute. Nor should the
examination be unduly legalistic. If its meaning can fairly and properly be
extracted from the language used, it may not matter that such language is
ill-adapted or chosen to express that meaning. But it is to be borne in mind that
the ombudsman is a lawyer and his determinations have the effect and
consequences of county court judgments, and a sensible meaning must be
expected and required. The determination in this case falls well below the
standard required to convey in a meaningful way the ombudsman's thought
processes, and is objectionable on this ground also.

The ombudsman in the July letter expresses the hope that the court will
appreciate that 'my role is often not straightforward and involves taking decisions
and drafting determinations which involve subjective considerations.' Beyond
the fact that the ombudsman has to exercise his own judgment in accordance
with law in making decisions and determinations, I do not understand what place
there is for 'subjective considerations'. Whilst the difficulty of his role is fully
appreciated, the standard of his determinations must be maintained if justice is to
be done and to be seen to be done by those who fall within his jurisdiction.

V. SUMMARY

I regretfully reach the conclusion that the ombudsman has gone seriously
astray, not merely in the contents of the determination, but also in the way his
investigation was handled and the decision reached and expressed. I accordingly
allow the appeal and discharge the directions made by the ombudsman. I do so
with considerable sympathy for Mr Kural, whose hopes and expectations raised
by the determination must now be dashed. There can be no doubt that he is the
victim of an injustice: he is not to receive the pension benefits to which he is
entitled. But that is the consequence of the default on the part of Seifert in

a   properly and sufficiently funding the scheme, the insolvency of Seifert and the unforeseen accident of timing that he was not yet in receipt of his pension when the wind up commenced. It is not the consequence of any maladministration by the appellants.

This is not necessarily the end of the matter. I have a discretionary jurisdiction under RSC Ord 55, r 6(3) to remit this matter to the ombudsman for

b   reconsideration. After anxious consideration, I have reached the conclusion that there can be no justification for making any such order, for two reasons: (1) as a matter of law it would not be open to the ombudsman on such a remit to make any direction in favour of Mr Kural against the appellants for the reasons set out in this judgment, not least because of cl 21; and (2) it would not be just to subject the appellants to a further hearing.

c   The deficiencies in respect of the determination have occasioned the scheme funds (already substantially in deficit) the additional heavy burden of costs of this appeal. In the circumstances, I have given the appellants leave to apply for an order that the ombudsman pay the costs of this appeal.

d   *Appeals allowed.*

Dilys Tausz   Barrister.

R v Secretary of State for the Home Department, ex parte Fayed and another

COURT OF APPEAL, CIVIL DIVISION

LORD WOOLF MR, KENNEDY AND PHILLIPS LJJ

17 OCTOBER, 13 NOVEMBER 1996

Alien – British nationality – Acquisition – Naturalisation – Applications made by persons of full age and capacity – Secretary of State having discretion whether to grant or refuse applications – Statutory provision expressly exempting Secretary of State from obligation to give reasons and providing that decision was not to be subject to appeal or review – Secretary of State refusing applications without giving reasons – Whether statutory provision relieving minister of obligation to be fair – Whether natural justice requiring that applicants should be given opportunity to meet case against them before decisions made – British Nationality Act 1981, ss 6, 44(2), Sch 1.

The applicants were two brothers who were born in Egypt but had lived and worked in the United Kingdom for many years where they had substantial business interests and a high public profile. Both had been granted leave to remain indefinitely. One brother was married to a British citizen, the other to a citizen of Finland, and both had children who were British citizens. Eventually the brothers applied for naturalisation as British citizens under s 6(1) and (2) respectively of the British Nationality Act 1981, and although they satisfied the requirements of Sch 1 to the Act, their applications were refused without any reasons being given. A news release made by the Home Secretary prior to his decisions indicated that their applications were regarded as being 'especially difficult or sensitive' but the applicants were not informed as to the matters which had given rise to the difficulties and reservations about their applications. The applicants applied for judicial review by way of orders of certiorari to quash the decisions on the grounds that there had been a breach of the rules of natural justice and that the Home Secretary was required to give reasons. The judge dismissed their applications, holding that since s 44(2) of the 1981 Act did not require the Home Secretary to assign any reasons for the grant or refusal of any application involving the exercise of discretion, the failure to give the applicants an opportunity to deal with matters considered to be adverse to their applications was not unlawful. The applicants appealed.

Held (Kennedy LJ dissenting) – Although the Home Secretary was not required to give reasons for refusing an application for British citizenship, by virtue of s 44(2) of the 1981 Act, where the decision involved the exercise of discretion, he was required to exercise that discretion reasonably and accordingly was not relieved of the obligation to be fair in arriving at his decision. During the process of reaching a decision, the Home Secretary was therefore required to give the applicant sufficient information as to the subject matter of his concern in such terms as to enable him to make such representations as he could and, where that would involve disclosing matters not in the public interest, to indicate that that was the position so that the applicant could challenge the justification for the refusal before the courts. It followed that since the applicants had not enjoyed the fairness to which they were entitled, justice had not been seen to be done. The

a appeal would therefore be allowed and the Home Secretary's decisions would be quashed so that they could be retaken in a fair manner (see p 230 *d* to *f*, p 238 *c*, p 239 *b*, p 241 *b c g h*, p 242 *b c*, p 252 *b* and p 253 *e h*, post).
A-G v Ryan [1980] AC 718 applied.

Notes

b For the obligation to give reasons for decisions, and natural justice and fairness generally, see 1(1) *Halsbury's Laws* (4th edn reissue), paras 83,84.
For the British Nationality Act 1981, ss 6, 44, Sch 1, see 31 *Halsbury's Statutes* (4th edn) (1994 reissue) 135, 168, 181.

Cases referred to in judgments

c *A-G v Ryan* [1980] AC 718, [1980] 2 WLR 143, PC.
Anisminic Ltd v Foreign Compensation Commission [1969] 1 All ER 208, [1969] 2 AC 147, [1969] 2 WLR 163, HL.
Armah v Government of Ghana [1966] 3 All ER 177, [1968] AC 192, [1966] 3 WLR 828, HL.

d *Cooper v Wandsworth Board of Works* (1863) 14 CBNS 180, 143 ER 414.
Doody v Secretary of State for the Home Dept [1993] 3 All ER 92, [1994] 1 AC 531, [1993] 3 WLR 154, HL.
Francis v Yiewsley and West Drayton UDC [1957] 1 All ER 825, [1957] 2 QB 136, [1957] 2 WLR 627; affd [1957] 3 All ER 529, [1958] 1 QB 478, [1957] 3 WLR 919, CA.

e *Pyx Granite Co Ltd v Ministry of Housing and Local Government* [1959] 3 All ER 1, [1960] AC 260, [1959] 3 WLR 346, HL.
R v City of London Corp, ex p Matson (1995) 8 Admin LR 49, CA.
R v Civil Service Appeal Board, ex p Cunningham [1991] 4 All ER 310, CA.
R v Gaming Board for GB, ex p Benaim [1970] 2 All ER 528, [1970] 2 QB 417, [1970]

f 2 WLR 1009, CA.
R v Secretary of State for the Home Dept, ex p Mehta [1992] Imm AR 512.
Ridge v Baldwin [1963] 2 All ER 66, [1964] AC 40, [1963] 2 WLR 935, HL.
Spackman v Plumstead District Board of Works (1885) 10 App Cas 229, HL.

Cases also cited or referred to in skeleton arguments

g *R v Birmingham City Council, ex p Ferrero Ltd* [1993] 1 All ER 530, CA.
R v Chief Constable of Thames Valley Police, ex p Cotton [1990] IRLR 344, CA.
R v Higher Education Funding Council, ex p Institute of Dental Surgery [1994] 1 All ER 651, [1994] 1 WLR 242, DC.
R v Lancashire CC, ex p Huddleston [1986] 2 All ER 941, CA.

h *R v Parole Board, ex p Wilson* [1992] 2 All ER 576, [1992] QB 740, CA.
R v Secretary of State for the Home Dept, ex p Moon (1 November 1995, unreported), QBD.
Wiseman v Borneman [1969] 3 All ER 275, [1971] AC 297, HL.

j **Appeal**
The applicants, Mohamed Abdel Moneim Ali Fayed and Ali Fayed appealed, with leave from the order of Judge J hearing the Crown Office list made on 26 February 1996 dismissing their applications brought pursuant to the leave of Popplewell J given on 12 May 1995 for judicial review by way of: (i) an order of certiorari to quash the decisions of the respondent, the Secretary of State for the Home Department, communicated to the applicants in two letters dated 23

February 1995 from the Immigration and Nationality Division of the Home
Office, refusing their applications for naturalisation as British citizens under s 6(1)   a
and (2) respectively of the British Nationality Act 1981; (ii) a declaration that the
decisions were unlawful, void and of no effect; and (iii) an order of mandamus
requiring the Secretary of State to reconsider the decisions according to law. The
facts are set out in the judgment of Lord Woolf MR.

b

Michael Beloff QC and *Rabinder Singh* (instructed by *D J Freeman*) for the first
applicant.
Michael Beloff QC and *Mark Shaw* (instructed by *Palmer Cowen*) for the second
applicant.
Stephen Richards and *Stuart Catchpole* (instructed by the *Treasury Solicitor*) for the   c
Secretary of State.

Cur adv vult

13 November 1996. The following judgments were delivered.

d
LORD WOOLF MR. This appeal raises issues which concern the relationships
between the legislature, the executive and the courts. This is because of the
terms of s 44(2) of the British Nationality Act 1981. Section 44(2) lays down that
in the case of decisions to which the section applies the Home Secretary is not
'required to assign any reason for the grant or refusal of any application under'
the Act and the decisions 'shall not be subject to appeal to, or review in, any   e
court'.
   Normally any decision taken by a minister under a discretion conferred on him
by Parliament which affects a member of the public is required to be exercised in
a manner which is fair or, as used to be said, in accordance with the rules of
natural justice. This is a long-established principle confirmed by a series of cases
in the House of Lords, a recent example of which is *Doody v Secretary of State for*   f
the Home Dept [1993] 3 All ER 92, [1994] 1 AC 531. In that case, in a speech with
which all the members of the House agreed, Lord Mustill summarised the
principle in these terms:

   'What does fairness require in the present case? My Lords, I think it   g
   unnecessary to refer by name to, or to quote from, any of the often-cited
   authorities in which the courts have explained what is essentially an intuitive
   judgment. They are far too well known. From them, I derive the following.
   (1) Where an Act of Parliament confers an administrative power there is a
   presumption that it will be exercised in a manner which is fair in all the
   circumstances. (2) The standards of fairness are not immutable. They may   h
   change with the passage of time, both in the general and in their application
   to decisions of a particular type. (3) The principles of fairness are not to be
   applied by rote identically in every situation. What fairness demands is
   dependent on the context of the decision, and this is to be taken into account
   in all its aspects. (4) An essential feature of the context is the statute which   j
   creates the discretion, as regards both its language and the shape of the legal
   and administrative system within which the decision is taken. (5) Fairness
   will very often require that a person who may be adversely affected by the
   decision will have an opportunity to make representations on his own behalf
   either before the decision is taken with a view to producing a favourable
   result, or after it is taken, with a view to procuring its modification, or both.

a (6) Since the person affected usually cannot make worthwhile representations without knowing what factors may weigh against his interests fairness will very often require that he is informed of the gist of the case which he has to answer.' (See [1993] 3 All ER 92 at 106, [1994] 1 AC 531 at 560.)

b It is also a principle of our administrative law that when a decision is taken in a manner which breaches the requirement that it should be taken fairly, in the absence of any alternative satisfactory remedy, the member of the public who has been unfairly treated is entitled to a remedy from the High Court on an application for judicial review. In providing a remedy the court is ensuring that decisions of the executive are taken in the manner required by Parliament. This c principle was reflected in a statement made by Viscount Simonds in *Pyx Granite Co Ltd v Ministry of Housing and Local Government* [1959] 3 All ER 1 at 6, [1960] AC 260 at 286, when he said:

d 'It is a principle not by any means to be whittled down that the subject's recourse to Her Majesty's courts for the determination of his rights is not to be excluded except by clear words. That is, as McNAIR, J., called it in *Francis v. Yiewsley & West Drayton U.D.C.* ([1957] 2 QB 136 at 148) a "fundamental rule" from which I would not for my part sanction any departure.'

This statement was made before the distinction between public and private law rights had been developed but is equally applicable today to the situations where e the courts grant a public law remedy.

The language of s 44(2) obviously could alter the usual position and in order to determine this appeal it is necessary to decide the extent to which the section relieves the minister from the normal obligation to act fairly and interferes with the ability of the court to play its usual role of protecting members of the public who have been unfairly treated.

f THE FACTS

Although these appeals raise issues of principle the facts are not unimportant in determining the issues. My task in reciting the facts is made immeasurably easier by my ability to rely heavily on the extremely concise and clear summary of those facts contained in the judgment of Judge J, who dismissed the g applications which are the subject of this appeal.

The applicants are two brothers, Mr Mohamed Fayed (Mohamed) and Mr Ali Fayed (Ali). Both were born in Egypt; Mohamed in 1933 and Ali in 1943. Mohamed has lived permanently in this country since 1964. He was granted leave to remain indefinitely. Ali started to live permanently in this country in the h late 1960s and was granted indefinite leave to remain in 1977. Mohamed is married to a citizen of Finland, but he has dependent children who are British citizens. Ali is married to a British citizen and his three children are also British citizens. As well as making their homes here the Fayeds have substantial business interests in the United Kingdom.

j Both are resident here for tax purposes and are fulfilling their fiscal obligations. Their financial contributions to the commercial life of this country are significant. In addition both brothers have made generous contributions to UK charities. Their careers both before and after they arrived in this country have, however, been the subject of controversy and considerable media interest.

On 29 January 1993 Ali submitted an application for naturalisation as a British citizen under the 1981 Act and this was followed by an application by Mohamed on 15 February 1994. The applications were made on forms provided for this purpose which request very limited information. On 23 February 1995, in separate letters, both applications were refused.

During the lengthy period when the applications were under consideration they were merely two out of the 42,000 outstanding applications for British citizenship. The judge therefore was right in stating in his judgment that—

'as well as raising questions of moment to the applicants personally, the present case involves consideration of issues of general significance in relation to procedures currently adopted by the Secretary of State to enforce and implement the 1981 Act and the very large number of applications by citizens of other countries for naturalisation here.'

Because Ali was married to a British citizen, his application was governed by s 6(2) of the Act while Mohamed's was made under s 6(1) of the Act. I will refer to s 6 later but the difference in the two brothers' positions is of no significance to the outcome of their appeals.

Ali's application showed that he had been absent from the United Kingdom for a few more than the maximum 90 days allowed in the year prior to submission of his application. However, by letter of 10 May 1995 it is confirmed on behalf of the Home Office that Ali's failure to meet the residence requirement was not the reason for refusal of his application.

In March 1993 the then Home Secretary informed one of Ali's referees that inquiries (the nature of which have not been revealed) were under way and in August 1993 the Home Office requested further documentation including his marriage certificate and confirmation of his tax position.

On 6 December 1993 the head of the Nationality Division confirmed to those representing Ali the receipt of all documentation requested and gave what proved to be an optimistic forecast, that a decision would be made in 'up to two months' and that a report was going shortly to the Secretary of State. After consideration by officials Ali's application was passed to a junior minister at the Home Office, Mr Charles Wardle. Subsequently Mohamed's application was also considered by Mr Wardle. In April 1994 the Home Secretary himself suggested that further inquiries should be made and following a ministerial reshuffle in July 1994 Mr Nicholas Baker replaced Mr Wardle as minister responsible for making the decisions. This appeared in a news release of 24 October 1994 made by the Secretary of State in which he set out his own involvement with the applications. The release also indicated that the applications by the brothers were regarded as being 'especially difficult or sensitive'. No further inquiries or investigations were made of or directed to either of the applicants.

After questions in the House of Commons during the autumn of 1994, in November 1994 Ali's solicitors offered to meet the minister to discuss the application because they were concerned about the delay. They were also concerned that his application might, in some unspecified way, be adversely affected unless it was treated on its own merits. An assurance was given with regard to Ali's concerns but the offer of a meeting was rejected. Discussions were described as 'unnecessary'.

Neither of the brothers has ever been informed what were the aspects of their applications which have given rise to the difficulties or reservations about their applications. Without information as to this it would in practice be impossible for them to try and volunteer information which would support the applications a which they have made or any fresh applications which they might want to make in the future.

The letters communicating the decision to refuse the applications were dated 23 February 1995 and were, as the judge said, 'terse in the extreme'. They merely informed each of the Fayeds that 'after careful consideration your application has been refused'. No reasons were given for the decisions so applications were made

b to the Home Office for reasons for the refusals but they were declined. In March 1995 the applications for leave to apply for judicial review were made. Leave was granted by Popplewell J. Judge J dismissed the applications for judicial review on 26 February 1996.

THE STATUTORY FRAMEWORK

c The first section to which it is necessary to refer is s 6. This section distinguishes between the two categories of application, those by an applicant who is not married to a British citizen and those by an applicant who is. Section 6 is in these terms:

d   '(1) If, on an application for naturalisation as a British citizen made by a person of full age and capacity, the Secretary of State is satisfied that the applicant fulfils the requirements of Schedule 1 for naturalisation as such a citizen under this subsection, he may, if he thinks fit, grant to him a certificate of naturalisation as such a citizen.

e   (2) If, on an application for naturalisation as a British citizen made by a person of full age and capacity who on the date of the application is married to a British citizen, the Secretary of State is satisfied that the applicant fulfils the requirements of Schedule 1 for naturalisation as such a citizen under this subsection, he may, if he thinks fit, grant to him a certificate of naturalisation as such a citizen.'

f Schedule 1, which is referred to in s 6, is in the following terms:

      '1.—(1) Subject to paragraph 2, the requirements for naturalisation as a British citizen under section 6(1) are, in the case of any person who applies for it—(a) the requirements specified in sub-paragraph (2) of this paragraph, or the alternative requirement specified in sub-paragraph (3) of this

g   paragraph and (b) that he is of good character; and (c) that he has a sufficient knowledge of the English, Welsh or Scottish Gaelic language; and (d) that either—(i) his intentions are such that, in the event of a certificate of naturalisation as a British citizen being granted to him, his home or (if he has more than one) his principal home will be in the United Kingdom; or (ii) he intends, in the event of such a certificate being granted to him, to enter into,

h   or continue in, Crown service under the government of the United Kingdom, or service under an international organisation of which the United Kingdom or Her Majesty's government therein is a member, or service in the employment of a company or association established in the United Kingdom.

j   (2) The requirements referred to in sub-paragraph (1)(a) of this paragraph are—(a) that the applicant was in the United Kingdom at the beginning of the period of five years ending with the date of the application, and that the number of days on which he was absent from the United Kingdom in that period does not exceed 450 ; and (b) that the number of days on which he was absent from the United Kingdom in the period of twelve months so ending does not exceed 90; and (c) that he was not at any time in the period of twelve

months so ending subject under the immigration laws to any restriction on
the period for which he might remain in the United Kingdom; and (d) that *a*
he was not at any time in the period of five years so ending in the United
Kingdom in breach of the immigration laws.

(3) The alternative requirement referred to in sub-paragraph (1)(a) of this
paragraph is that on the date of the application he is serving outside the
United Kingdom in Crown service under the government of the United *b*
Kingdom.

2. If in the special circumstances of any particular case the Secretary of
State thinks fit, he may for the purposes of paragraph 1 do all or any of the
following things, namely—(a) treat the applicant as fulfilling the
requirement specified in paragraph 1(2)(a) or paragraph 1(2)(b), or both, *c*
although the number of days on which he was absent from the United
Kingdom in the period there mentioned exceeds the number there
mentioned; (b) treat the applicant as having been in the United Kingdom for
the whole or any part of any period during which he would otherwise fall to
be treated under paragraph 9(1) as having been absent; (c) disregard any such
restriction as is mentioned in paragraph 1(2)(c), not being a restriction to *d*
which the applicant was subject on the date of the application; (d) treat the
applicant as fulfilling the requirement specified in paragraph 1(2)(d) although
he was in the United Kingdom in breach of the immigration laws in the
period there mentioned; (e) waive the need to fulfil the requirement
specified in paragraph 1(1)(c) if he considers that because of the applicant's
age or physical or mental condition it would be unreasonable to expect him *e*
to fulfil it …'

It will be noted that, unlike the position as to the other express requirements in
para 1(1), the Secretary of State has no express power to dispense with the
requirement as to good character under para 2. *f*

Paragraphs 3 and 4 apply to applications under s 6(2). There are no distinctions
which are relevant to the issues in this appeal but in general the requirements are
less onerous than those contained in para 1.

The next section to which it is necessary to refer is s 44, which as its sidenote
indicates relates to 'Decisions involving exercise of discretion' and provides as *g*
follows:

'(1) Any decision vested by or under this Act in the Secretary of State, a
Governor or a Lieutenant-Governor shall be exercised without regard to the
race, colour or religion of any person who may be affected by its exercise.

(2) The Secretary of State, a Governor or a Lieutenant-Governor, as the *h*
case may be, shall not be required to assign any reason for the grant or refusal
of any application under this Act the decision on which is at his discretion;
and the decision of the Secretary of State or a Governor or
Lieutenant-Governor on any such application shall not be subject to appeal
to, or review in, any court. *j*

(3) Nothing in this section affects the jurisdiction of any court to entertain
proceedings of any description concerning the rights of any person under
any provision of this Act.'

Although the Secretary of State has no discretion to grant an application of a
person who is not of good character I still regard a decision refused on this ground

a as one to which s 44(2) applies. Mr Beloff QC, who appeared on behalf of the Fayeds, accepted that this was the position.

There are other provisions of the 1981 Act which give a person who fulfils certain conditions an entitlement to be registered as a British citizen and s 44(2) accordingly does not then apply. It is unclear whether in such cases this is because the decision does not involve the exercise of a discretion or because the b applicant has 'rights' or both. However, this is of no significance. A different example of a provision of the Act which certainly concerns rights is provided by s 40. This section sets out the procedure which has to be followed by the Secretary of State if he wishes to deprive a naturalised citizen of his British citizenship. Section 40(6) requires the Secretary of State to give a person in this situation notice in writing informing him of 'the ground or grounds on which it c is proposed' to make the order and 'his right to an inquiry under this section'.

An examination of the provisions of the Act to which reference has been made discloses at least three different statutory situations: those where the minister is expressly exempt from being *required* to give reasons, those where the minister is neither required to give nor exempt from being required to give reasons and d those to which s 40(6) applies where a more structured procedure is involved.

Jurisdiction

Both before Judge J and this court, the Secretary of State accepted that s 44(2) does not prevent the court exercising its jurisdiction to review a decision on the traditional grounds available on an application for judicial review. Although this e is not therefore in issue, the reason why the jurisdiction is accepted is of some assistance in determining the questions which are in issue.

The starting point is the decision of the House of Lords in *Anisminic Ltd v Foreign Compensation Commission* [1969] 1 All ER 208, [1969] 2 AC 147, where it was held that a provision in legislation that 'the determination by the commission f of any application made to them under this Act shall not be called in question in any court of law' did not protect a determination which was made as a result of a mistake of law. Such a decision was not protected by the provision because it was a nullity in the sense that it was liable to be quashed by the court. However, it is not only the misinterpretation of legislation which would produce this result, it is any other error which would justify the intervention of the court on judicial g review including a breach of the requirements of fairness. This is made clear by a much-quoted passage from Lord Reid's speech, where he said ([1969] 1 All ER 208 at 213, [1969] 2 AC 147 at 171):

'It has sometimes been said that it is only where a tribunal acts without h jurisdiction that its decision is a nullity. But in such cases the word "jurisdiction" has been used in a very wide sense, and I have come to the conclusion that it is better not to use the term except in the narrow and original sense of the tribunal being entitled to enter on the enquiry in question. But there are many cases where, although the tribunal had j jurisdiction to enter on the enquiry, it has done or failed to do something in the course of the enquiry which is of such a nature that its decision is a nullity. It may have given its decision in bad faith. It may have made a decision which it had no power to make. It may have failed in the course of the enquiry to comply with the requirements of natural justice. It may in perfect good faith have misconstrued the provisions giving it power to act so that it failed to deal with the question remitted to it and decided some question which was not remitted to it. It may have refused to take into account something which it was required to take into account. Or it may have based its decision on some matter which, under the provisions setting it up, it had no right to take into account. I do not intend this list to be exhaustive. But if it decides a question remitted to it for decision without committing any of these errors it is as much entitled to decide that question wrongly as it is to decide it rightly. I understand that some confusion has been caused by my having said in *Armah* v. *Government of Ghana* ([1966] 3 All ER 177 at 187, [1968] AC 192 at 234) that, if a tribunal has jurisdiction to go right it has jurisdiction to go wrong. So it has if one uses "jurisdiction" in the narrow original sense. If it is entitled to enter on the enquiry and does not do any of those things which I have mentioned in the course of the proceedings, then its decision is equally valid whether it is right or wrong subject only to the power of the court in certain circumstances to correct any error of law.'

The same approach was subsequently adopted in a number of cases but for present purposes it suffices to refer to *A-G v Ryan* [1980] AC 718, a decision of the Privy Council which I regard as being of the greatest importance to the outcome of this case. *Ryan's* case involved an application to be registered as a citizen of the Bahamas. Article 5 of the Constitution of the Bahamas provided:

'... (2) Any person who ... possesses Bahamian status under the provisions of the Immigration Act 1967 and is an ordinary resident in The Bahama Islands, shall be entitled, upon making application ... to be registered as a citizen of The Bahamas ...
(4) Any application for registration under paragraph (2) of this article shall be subject to such exceptions or qualifications as may be prescribed [under an Act of Parliament] in the interests of national security or public policy.'

The proviso to s 7 of the Bahamas Nationality Act 1973 entitled the Minister of Home Affairs to refuse an application for registration on specified grounds in paras (a) to (e) or 'for any other sufficient reason of public policy'. Section 16 of the Act provided:

'The Minister shall not be required to assign any reason for the grant or refusal of any application ... under this Act ... and the decision of the Minister ... shall not be subject to appeal or review in any court.'

Section 16 is clearly an equivalent provision to s 44(2). However Lord Diplock, in giving the judgment of the Board in relation to s 16, said (at 730):

'It is by now well-established law that to come within the prohibition of appeal or review by an ouster clause of this type, the decision must be one which the decision-making authority, under this Act the Minister, had jurisdiction to make. If in purporting to make it he has gone outside his jurisdiction, it is ultra vires and is not a "decision" under the Act. The Supreme Court, in the exercise of its supervisory jurisdiction over inferior tribunals, which include executive authorities exercising quasi-judicial powers, may, in appropriate proceedings, either set it aside or declare it to be a nullity: *Anisminic Ltd.* v. *Foreign Compensation Commission* ([1969] 1 All ER 208, [1969] 2 AC 147). It has long been settled law that a decision affecting legal rights of an individual which is arrived at by a procedure which offends against the principles of natural justice is outside the jurisdiction of the a decision-making authority. As Lord Selborne said as long ago as 1885 in *Spackman* v. *Plumstead District Board of Works* (10 App Cas 229 at 240): "There would be no decision within the meaning of the statute if there were anything ... done contrary to the essence of justice." See also *Ridge* v. *Baldwin* ([1963] 2 All ER 66, [1964] AC 40). Their Lordships, in agreement with all the judges in the court below, would therefore conclude that the

b ouster clause in section 16 of The Bahamas Nationality Act 1973 does not prevent the court from enquiring into the validity of the Minister's decision on the ground that it was made without jurisdiction and is ultra vires.'

The reference by Lord Diplock to natural justice should be noted. *Ryan's* case was decided and reported before the 1981 Act was passed, and it is appropriate to

c draw the inference that Parliament was not, in enacting s 44(2), intending by the ouster provision contained in that section to exclude the ability of the court to review a decision of the Secretary of State on the grounds, for example, that he had not complied with any requirement of fairness which the Act imposed upon him or the express prohibition against discrimination in s 44(1) when considering applications for naturalisation. That this is correct is not in issue.

d Having dealt with the question of jurisdiction, it is possible to proceed to consider the matters which are in issue on this appeal. This can be done under three heads: (a) would there be any requirement of fairness in the absence of s 44(2) and if so was it breached? (the fairness issue); (b) if so, what is the effect of the provision of s 44(2) which provides that the Secretary of State is not required

e to give reasons? (the s 44(2) issue); and (c) was the Secretary of State despite s 44(2) required to give the Fayeds reasons? (the reasons issue).

THE FAIRNESS ISSUE

It is obvious that the refusal of their applications has damaging implications for the Fayeds. This is a matter which is for them, because of their high public

f profile, of particular significance. The damage is the greater because it is not in dispute that they comply with the formal requirements other than that of good character, the relevance of which to the refusal is not known.

Apart from the damaging effect on their reputations of having their applications refused, the refusals have deprived them of the benefits of citizenship. The benefits are substantial. Besides the intangible benefit of being

g a citizen of a country which is their and their families' home, there are the tangible benefits which include freedom from immigration control, citizenship of the European Union and the rights which accompany that citizenship—the right to vote and the right to stand in Parliamentary elections. The decisions of the minister are therefore classically ones which but for s 44(2) would involve an

h obligation on the minister making the decision to give the Fayeds an opportunity to be heard before that decision was reached.

The fact that the Secretary of State may refuse an application because he is not satisfied that the applicant fulfils the rather nebulous requirement of good character or 'if he thinks fit' underlines the need for an obligation of fairness.

j Except where non-compliance with a formal requirement, other than that of good character, is being relied on, unless the applicant knows the areas of concern which could result in the application being refused in many cases, and especially this case, it will be impossible for him to make out his case. The result could be grossly unfair. The decision maker may rely on matters as to which the applicant would have been able to persuade him to take a different view. It would be a situation in which the approach of this court in *R v Gaming Board for GB, ex p*

Benaim [1970] 2 All ER 528 at 533–534, [1970] 2 QB 417 at 430–431 would apply. Lord Mustill's remarks in his speech in *Doody v Secretary of State for the Home Dept* [1993] 3 All ER 92 at 106, [1994] 1 AC 531 at 560 would also apply. It is not necessary to refer to the many other authorities to the same effect which could be relied on in support of this conclusion.

This is therefore a case where, ignoring s 44(2), the courts would intervene to achieve fairness for the Fayeds by requiring the minister to identify the areas which were causing them such difficulty in reaching their decision. I did not understand Mr Richards really to contend otherwise on behalf of the Secretary of State.

THE S 44 ISSUE

I have already explained that the fact that s 44 provides that the decision is not to be subject to appeal or review does not affect the obligation of the Secretary of State to be fair or to interfere with the power of the court to ensure that requirements of fairness are met. That this power has no application to this case depends alone on the argument that to comply with what would be the normal requirement to inform the Fayeds of the case which they had to meet would be inconsistent with the express prohibition contained in s 44(2) on the Secretary of State being *required to assign any reason for the grant of refusal of any application under this Act.* This prohibition, it is submitted, impliedly excludes the requirement to give the Fayeds and other applicants in the same position the notice which fairness dictates they need to make an application. It is contended that unless this is the situation the intention of Parliament expressed in s 44(2) would be frustrated. I cannot accept that this can possibly be the position. It is wholly inconsistent with the principles of administrative law to which I have referred.

My reasons for this conclusion can be summarised as follows.

(A) The suggestion that notice need not be given although this would be unfair involves attributing to Parliament an intention that it has not expressly stated that a minister should be able to act unfairly in deciding that a person lawfully in this country should be refused citizenship without the courts being able to do anything about it. This involves attributing to the protection which s 44(2) gives in relation to reasons far greater status than that to which it is entitled. English law has long attached the greatest importance to the need for fairness to be observed prior to the exercise of a statutory discretion. However, English law, at least until recently, has not been so sensitive to the need for reasons to be given for a decision after it has been reached. So to exclude the need for fairness before a decision is reached because it might give an indication of what the reasons for the decision could be is to reverse the actual position. It involves frustrating the achievement of the more important objective of fairness in reaching a decision in an attempt to protect a lesser objective of possibly disclosing what will be the reasons for the decision.

(B) It would be surprising if it was the implied intention of Parliament that the lack of a requirement to give reasons should have the effect of avoiding the requirement to give notice of a possible ground for refusing an application since the minister can voluntarily both give notice and reasons if he chooses to do so. In other words, it is difficult to attach much weight to a prohibition the minister is free to ignore. It cannot be based on an objection of principle to the giving of reasons.

(C) In many situations the giving of notice of areas of concern will do no more than identify possible rather than the actual reasons. Thus as long as the minister seeks representations for more than one area of concern the applicant in the absence of reasons will not know whether any particular area of concern played any part in the decision to refuse the application.

(D) As the minister has a discretion to give the applicant notice of an area of concern, that discretion must itself be exercised reasonably. If not to give notice would result in unfairness then the discretion can only reasonably be exercised by giving notice. It is already the practice of the minister to inform the applicant if one of the preconditions which are discretionary bars to success are not fulfilled. If this is the practice, it is by no means obvious that there is any logical reason for not taking the same course in the areas where the Secretary of State has an even wider discretion when the identity of the issues will be less ascertainable by the applicant.

(E) If the Secretary of State is correct in his contention, the effect of the restriction on the obligation to give reasons is far reaching indeed. In any readily identifiable situation it will totally exclude the court's power of review. It would apply for example if the Secretary of State was guilty of discrimination contrary to s 44(1). On an application for judicial review there is usually no discovery because discovery should be unnecessary because it is the obligation of the respondent public body in its evidence to make frank disclosure to the court of the decision making process (see *R v Civil Service Appeal Board, ex p Cunningham* [1991] 4 All ER 310). If it does not, then usually this would be a reason for the court ordering discovery. However, if the giving of notice cannot be required, then for the same reasons it is said the respondent cannot be required to exercise the usual 'cards up approach' and what is more discovery cannot be required either since this would be open to the same objection that it could result in the identification of reasons. In practice therefore what the express prohibition on an appeal and review in s 44(2) does not achieve is achieved by the exclusion of a requirement to give reasons. *Anisminic Ltd v Foreign Compensation Commission* [1969] 1 All ER 208, [1969] 2 AC 147 and Viscount Simonds' statement of principle in *Pyx Granite Co Ltd v Ministry of Housing and Local Government* [1959] 3 All ER 1 at 6, [1960] AC 260 at 286 on the Secretary of State's approach are therefore bypassed.

(F) As to Mr Richard's reliance on s 40(6) and an argument that where Parliament requires fairness it says so: the reason for s 40(6) is explained by the fact that s 40(6) involves an *inquiry*. A procedure which includes an inquiry requires an express provision. The wording of s 40(6) is therefore of no assistance in deciding the issue here.

(G) The judgment of the Privy Council in *A-G v Ryan* is highly persuasive authority in favour of the Secretary of State not being relieved of his obligation to be fair by s 44(2). The language of s 16 which I have already cited is indistinguishable from that of s 44(2). Yet Lord Diplock in giving the judgment of the Board said ([1980] AC 718 at 727):

'Their Lordships agree with the judges of the Supreme Court (as did the Court of Appeal) that as an applicant for registration as a citizen of The Bahamas under article 5(2) of the Constitution, the respondent was entitled to a fair hearing in accordance with the principles of natural justice before his application was rejected by the Minister. By virtue of sections 7 and 8 of The Bahamas Nationality Act 1973, the Minister was a person having legal authority to determine a question affecting the rights of individuals. This being so it is a necessary implication that he is required to observe the principles of natural justice when exercising that authority; and, if he fails to do so, his purported decision is a nullity. In view of the citations of so many cases in the judgments below, their Lordships upon this branch of the law do not find it necessary to do more than to refer to *Ridge* v. *Baldwin* ([1963] 2 All ER 66, [1964] AC 40) and particularly to the speech of Lord Reid ([1963] 2 All ER 66 at 77–78, [1964] AC 40 at 74–76).'

There was an issue in *A-G v Ryan* involving the constitution but this was dealt with as a separate issue by Lord Diplock and does not affect the significance of the relevant passage of the judgment to which I have referred. Judge J distinguished *A-G v Ryan* because, as he pointed out correctly, in that case once the applicant was able to satisfy the statutory criteria the applicant had a right to be registered as a citizen while here, in addition to the statutory criteria, the Secretary of State also has a wide discretion to refuse an application, so the Fayeds were not basing their application on a right but seeking the grant of a privilege.

However, *A-G v Ryan* cannot be distinguished on this ground. The days when it used to be said that a person seeking a privilege is not entitled to be heard are long gone. In *R v Gaming Board for GB, ex p Benaim* [1970] 2 All ER 528, [1970] 2 QB 417 it was argued that as the applicants for a gaming licence were seeking a privilege there was no obligation to be fair but this court (which included Lord Wilberforce as a member) rejected that contention. Lord Denning MR in his judgment (with which the other members of the court agreed) did however accept, as would still be the position today, 36 years later, that the fact that the applicant did not have an entitlement could affect the content of what was required in order to be fair. Thus, in that case it was held there was no obligation to give a reasoned decision. None the less, it was still the position, according to Lord Denning MR, that—

'the board have a duty to act fairly. They must give the applicant an opportunity of satisfying them of the matters specified in Sch 2, para 4(5) [of the Gaming Act 1968]. They must let him know what their impressions are so that he can disabuse them ...' (See [1970] 2 All ER 528 at 534, [1970] 2 QB 417 at 430.)

and later Lord Denning MR added ([1970] 2 All ER 528 at 534, [1970] 2 QB 417 at 431):

'But, without disclosing every detail ... the board ought in every case to be able to give to the applicant sufficient indication of the objections raised against him such as to enable him to answer them. That is only fair. And the board must at all costs be fair. If they are not, these courts will not hesitate to interfere.'

In addition Mr Richards accepted that the mere fact that this is a 'privilege' case did not preclude the application of the rules of natural justice. This is not, however, the only reason why it is wrong to try and distinguish *A-G v Ryan* on this ground. What is primarily in issue on this appeal is not the content of the duty to be fair but whether that duty is excluded by s 44(2) and Lord Diplock, as one would expect in relation to the legislation which he was considering, dealt with this as a separate issue.

Mr Richards did, however, still seek to rely on the distinction between the statutory contexts for distinguishing *A-G v Ryan* and also drew attention to the fact that his argument was not advanced before the Privy Council and finally a submitted that the approach of Lord Diplock should be rejected. This I am not prepared to do. I am relieved to think that the protection of an applicant for citizenship is no less in this country than it is in the Bahamas.

It remains for me to deal with the practical consequences of applying the *Ryan* approach. It does not require the Secretary of State to do more than to identify the subject of his concern in such terms as to enable the applicant to make such b submissions as he can. In some situations even to do this could involve disclosing matters which it is not in the public interest to disclose, for example for national security or diplomatic reasons. If this is the position then the Secretary of State would be relieved from disclosure and it would suffice if he merely indicated that this was the position to the applicant who, if he wished to do so, could challenge the justification for the refusal before the courts. The courts are well capable of c determining public interest issues of this sort in a way which balances the interests of the individual against the public interests of the state.

I appreciate that there is also anxiety as to the administrative burden involved in giving notice of areas of concern. Administrative convenience cannot justify unfairness but I would emphasise that my remarks are limited to cases where an d applicant would be in real difficulty in doing himself justice unless the area of concern is identified by notice. In many cases which are less complex than that of the Fayeds the issues may be obvious. If this is the position, notice may well be superfluous because what the applicant needs to establish will be clear. If this is the position, notice may well not be required. However, in the case of the Fayeds this is not the position because the extensive range of circumstances e which could cause the Secretary of State concern mean that it is impractical for them to identify the target at which their representations should be aimed.

THE REASONS ISSUE

Mr Beloff argued that this is a case in which despite s 44(2) the minister is f required to give reasons. As I have indicated, the minister is not prohibited by the section from giving reasons. On the contrary, he has a clear discretion to give reasons. So, Mr Beloff argues, in a case like this which cries out for reasons the discretion can only lawfully be exercised by giving reasons.

I have already indicated that at common law there is no universal obligation to give reasons but despite this I would certainly regard this as a case where reasons g should be given but for s 44(2). However, in the light of the *express* prohibition on requiring the Secretary of State to give reasons I would not myself regard this as a case where the need for reasons is so essential that fairness cannot be achieved without reasons as long as an applicant has been given sufficient information as to the subject matter of the decision to enable him to make such h submissions as he wishes. I therefore reject Mr Beloff's argument.

THE RESULT

The Home Office wrote to the Fayeds' solicitors on 16 March 1995 giving an assurance—

j   'that very careful consideration was given to all the representations put forward ... and that further dialogue or opportunity to make further comments was not considered necessary for the purpose of reaching a properly informed decision.'

This is not, however, an answer to these applications. The problem with the assurance, though no doubt sincerely given, is that it was given without knowing what information could have been provided if there had been compliance with the requirements of fairness so the Fayeds were aware of the targets they had to address.

It is true that until the areas of concern are identified so that it can be ascertained whether the Fayeds would be in a position to make further representations it will not be possible to say whether an injustice has occurred. However, justice must not only be done but be seen to be done and it has not been seen to be done in relation to the application of the Fayeds. They have not had the fairness to which they are entitled and the rule of law must be upheld. This being so the Secretary of State is not entitled to take advantage of his own error and contend that the Fayeds have failed to show they have been prejudiced. It follows that the Secretary of State's decisions must be quashed so they can be retaken in a manner which is fair. This is the concern of the courts, Parliament not having excluded the obligation to be fair. They are not concerned with the merits of the decision which should then be made. That is the concern of the Secretary of State.

This decision does not involve any criticism of the Secretary of State or his department. Until this court decided otherwise it was perfectly reasonable to take a different view of the procedural requirements on an application for naturalisation being made.

KENNEDY LJ.

(1) *Factual background*

The details of these two applications for naturalisation are relatively unimportant. Suffice to say that Mr Ali Fayed is married to a British citizen. Mr Mohamed Fayed's wife is a citizen of Finland. Both men have children who are British citizens, and both men have lived and worked here for many years. In due course each applied for naturalisation, and after an extraordinarily long delay each application was refused, no reasons being given.

(2) *Legal background*

Mr Beloff QC, for the appellants, submits that for each appellant the application for naturalisation was an important matter. Each sought from the Secretary of State for the Home Department an administrative decision in his favour, and to that end filled in a standard form which asked only for basic information and the identity of one or two referees. All that information was provided, and, Mr Beloff submits, natural justice required that if either application was to be refused the applicant should have some opportunity to deal with those matters which troubled the Secretary of State before the decision was made. Ideally the applicants should both have had that opportunity and reasons for the subsequent decision. If reasons had been given it might not have mattered so much that before the decisions were made the applicants had no opportunity to meet any case there may have been against them, because if the reasons disclosed any error on the part of the Secretary of State the applicants would have been able to press for a reconsideration of the relevant decision, but, if no reasons were to be given, it was all the more important that each applicant, before the final decision was made, had an opportunity to deal with those matters which resulted in the Secretary of State being minded to refuse.

The argument which I have just summarised is entirely in accordance with the approach frequently adopted by the English courts in recent years to a administrative decisions having an important effect upon the lives of individuals, and many authorities can be cited to support that general proposition. For example, in R v Gaming Board for GB, ex p Benaim [1970] 2 All ER 528 at 534, [1970] 2 QB 417 at 431 Lord Denning MR said, in relation to the application for a gaming licence:

b '... without disclosing every detail, I should have thought that the board ought in every case to be able to give to the applicant sufficient indication of the objections raised against him such as to enable him to answer them. That is only fair. And the board must at all costs be fair. If they are not, these courts will not hesitate to interfere.'

c In that case it was not thought necessary for the Gaming Board when it made its decision to give reasons. Conversely, in R v City of London Corp, ex p Matson (1995) 8 Admin LR 49 the unsuccessful candidate for the office of alderman was held entitled to reasons, but was not able to demonstrate procedural unfairness although he was never informed of the case, if any, against him. As Neill LJ said in that case (at 62):

d 'It is common ground that the law does not at present recognize a general duty to give reasons for an administrative decision: see Lord Mustill in Doody ([1993] 3 All ER 92 at 110, [1994] 1 AC 531 at 564). But such a duty may be implied in appropriate circumstances. These circumstances will include the nature of the adjudicating process.'

e

(3) Statutory framework

It has been common ground before us that each case does have to be considered against the background of the statutory provisions relevant to the f application under consideration, and in the present case that means that it is necessary to look at the provisions of the British Nationality Act 1981 and subordinate legislation.

Part I of the Act deals with British citizenship and, as Mr Richards for the Secretary of State has pointed out, at an early stage it is possible to see a distinction being drawn between those entitled to citizenship, such as children of g a British citizen born abroad (s 3(2)) and other children who the Secretary of State 'may, if he thinks fit' cause to be registered as British citizens (s 3(1)). Section 6 deals with applications for naturalisation by adults such as the present appellants. The section distinguishes between applicants who are married to British citizens (s 6(2)) and those who are not (s 6(1)). Consequently the application of Mr Ali h Fayed fell to be considered under s 6(2), and that of Mr Mohamed Fayed under s 6(1) but for present purposes nothing turns on that distinction. When considering any application under s 6 the Secretary of State must be satisfied that the applicant fulfils the requirements of Sch 1. Those requirements differ to some extent, depending upon whether the applicant is or is not married to a British j citizen, but again for present purposes nothing turns on that distinction. Broadly speaking what the schedule requires of an applicant (other than those in Crown service) is: (1) a period of pre-application residence in the United Kingdom; (2) compliance with immigration laws; (3) good character; (4) linguistic proficiency (not applicable to those married to British citizens); (5) an intention to make his principal home in the United Kingdom (again not applicable to those married to British citizens).

Paragraph 2 of the schedule enables the Secretary of State to waive certain of those requirements but he cannot waive the requirement of good character. Even if the requirements of Sch 1 are satisfied the Secretary of State is under no obligation to grant a certificate of naturalisation. He may do so if he thinks fit. There is nothing in the Act or in the schedule to suggest that if the Secretary of State is minded to refuse he should make that fact known to the applicant before reaching a conclusion, but if the Secretary of State does grant registration or a certificate of naturalisation, and later becomes satisfied that the registration or the certificate was obtained by means of fraud, false representation or the concealment of any material fact s 40(1) provides that he may then deprive the citizen of his British citizenship. In that event s 40(6) provides:

'Before making an order under this section the Secretary of State shall give the person against whom the order is proposed to be made notice in writing informing him of the ground or grounds on which it is proposed to be made and of his right to an inquiry under this section.'

Section 40(7) provides the mechanism for referring the matter to a committee of inquiry, which operates under the British Citizenship (Deprivation) Rules 1982, SI 1982/988, and all of that, Mr Richards submits, can usefully be contrasted with s 6 which makes no mention of any such procedure. Mr Richards submits that s 40(6) if applied to s 6 really sets out in terms Mr Beloff's case. He is contending that an applicant for naturalisation whose application it is proposed to refuse should receive 'notice in writing informing him of the ground or grounds on which it is proposed [to refuse]'. But if Parliament intended that course to be followed in relation to s 6 as well as in relation to s 40 why, Mr Richards asks rhetorically, did it not say so?

That brings me to s 44 headed 'Decisions involving exercise of discretion'. As I have pointed out, strictly speaking not all decisions under s 6 fall into that category. If, for example, an applicant is not of good character, he fails to satisfy a requirement of Sch 1 which the Secretary of State cannot waive and therefore his application must be refused. Nevertheless counsel before us are agreed, and I accept, that for the purposes of s 44 any decision under s 6 is a discretionary decision, including a refusal because the Secretary of State is not satisfied that an applicant meets a mandatory requirement of Sch 1. That is because s 44 must be read in the context of the Act as a whole, which is permeated by the distinction to which I have already referred between those entitled to citizenship as of right and those who (like all applicants whose claims fall to be considered under s 6) can only obtain it if a discretion is exercised in their favour. Section 44(1) requires that there be no discrimination on grounds of race, colour or religion, and s 44(2), so far as material, provides:

'The Secretary of State ... shall not be required to assign any reason for the grant or refusal of any application under this Act the decision on which is at his discretion; and the decision of the Secretary of State ... on any such application shall not be subject to appeal to, or review in, any court.'

Before Judge J and before us it was accepted that the final words of the subsection do not deprive the High Court or this court of all judicial review jurisdiction. The court cannot reconsider the merits of a decision, but it can consider if a decision was made ultra vires (see *Anisminic Ltd v Foreign Compensation Commission* [1969] 1 All ER 208, [1969] 2 AC 147 and *R v Secretary of State for the Home Dept, ex p Mehta* [1992] Imm AR 512). But what about the opening words of this subsection?

a Clearly, as it seems to me, they give to the Secretary of State the discretion not to assign any reason for the grant or refusal of any s 6 application, and I simply cannot accept Mr Beloff's submission that the discretion is one that in the circumstances could only be exercised one way, namely in favour of giving reasons.

b (4) *Natural justice*

But Mr Beloff's more attractive submission is that, because even in 1981 (when the statutory provisions were re-enacted) in a situation like this, and especially if reasons were not going to be given for the decision itself, natural justice was held normally to require the decision-maker to give the applicant an opportunity to meet any case there might be against him; and because neither in s 44(2) nor c elsewhere does this particular statute expressly remove that requirement, it must remain. Attractive though that argument is, I am unable to accept it. The plain intention of Parliament was to relieve the Secretary of State of the burden of giving reasons, in any case involving the exercise of discretion, to which burden but for the words of s 44(2) he would in my judgment be subject. If the Secretary d of State must nevertheless canvass with the applicant a matter or matters which in his view weigh against the grant of citizenship that, in every case where there is ultimately a refusal, means that the reason or reasons for refusal will have had to be disclosed. If, as may often be the case, the Secretary of State has only been troubled about one matter, then the unsuccessful applicant will be in no doubt as to the reason for refusal and the Secretary of State will in reality have been e required to assign a reason for the refusal, which is precisely what s 44(2) says should not occur. Even if at the consultation stage the Secretary of State indicates that he is troubled by more than one matter the situation will be much the same. The applicant's further submission may meet some of the Secretary of State's concerns, so that when the decision is made if no reasons are given the applicant f will not know which matters continued to be of concern, but in reality at the consultation stage the Secretary of State will have been required to identify, albeit as it turned out, inter alia, the reason or reasons for his refusal. Mr Beloff rightly points out that the wording of s 44(2) relates to the decision-making stage of the process, and not to any earlier stage, but as Judge J said: 'Although the principle of audi alterem partem and the provision of the reasons for the decision are g distinct, they are closely related and derive from the concept of fairness.' I agree, and indeed I go further. In my judgment the relationship is such that Parliament cannot have overlooked it. Undoubtedly the words of the statute do impinge upon what without them fairness would require, but not, as it seems to me, to a particularly surprising extent. As Mr Beloff conceded, there will no doubt be h many occasions on which the Secretary of State, for good reason, would prefer not to explain why he is minded to refuse or is in fact refusing citizenship. In his second affidavit Mr Rawsthorne on behalf of the Secretary of State said:

'It is the practice to give reasons where refusal is based solely on failure to meet the residence, language or full capacity requirements; and not to give j reasons where refusal is based, in whole or in part, on matters of judgment relating to for example, the good character requirement or the applicant's future intentions or where security matters are involved.'

During the hearing of the appeal the possibility was canvassed of an applicant being believed to be involved in crime abroad but the situation being such that if that information were to be revealed by the Secretary of State it might endanger sources of information. Consideration was also given to the situation where the grant of citizenship to an applicant might jeopardise relations with another sovereign state. Those are but two examples of situations in which the advantage of the Secretary of State not being required to give reasons or even to explain why he was minded to refuse is obvious. And when considering those examples it is important to bear in mind that the applicants for citizenship with whom we are concerned and to whom s 44(2) applies seek a privilege not a right. I accept that if my understanding as to the effect of s 44(2) is correct such an applicant is at a disadvantage when compared with many others who seek an administrative decision, but his position is not unique. Not all decision-makers are required either to identify to those they are minded to find against the points which trouble them, or to give reasons for their decisions, as can be seen daily in any magistrates' court.

(5) A-G v Ryan

I come now to the authority which Mr Beloff put in the forefront of his case, *A-G v Ryan* [1980] AC 718. By art 5(2) of the Constitution of the Bahamas any person who on 9 July 1973 possessed Bahamian status and who is ordinarily resident in the Bahama Islands 'shall be entitled, upon making application before July 10, 1974 to be registered as a citizen of The Bahamas'. By the proviso to s 7 of the Bahamas Nationality Act 1973 the Minister for Home Affairs may refuse an application for registration on specified grounds or 'for any other sufficient reason of public policy'. Section 16 of the same Act, as far as material, provided:

'The Minister shall not be required to assign any reason for the grant or refusal of any application ... under this Act ... and the decision of the Minister ... shall not be subject to appeal or review in any court.'

The applicant in that case applied for citizenship and was refused without reasons being given, so the case has obvious similarities when compared with the cases with which we are concerned, but: (1) the prime issue before the Privy Council was whether the concluding words of the proviso to s 7 of the 1973 Act were ultra vires the constitution; (2) counsel for the Attorney General conceded that if, as was held, they were ultra vires, the applicant, who was trying to exercise a right not asking for a privilege, was entitled to relief, because he had not been given an opportunity to meet the case against him.

The Privy Council therefore never had to consider as a contentious issue whether s 16 of the 1973 Act in any way restricted the applicant's right to know the case against him, which is the point at issue in the present case. I am therefore unable to derive any particular assistance from that case.

(6) *Conclusion*

In my judgment these appeals turn in the end on a question of construction. How can this court properly give effect to the words of s 44(2) of the 1981 Act? In order to give effect to those words it seems to me that the Secretary of State when called upon to exercise his discretion must be relieved not only of any obligation to give reasons at the time of or immediately after he makes his decision, but also of any duty to indicate to an applicant at any earlier stage why he is minded to refuse. As Mr Richards points out, if Parliament intended otherwise, why is there not to be found in s 44(2) some provision equivalent to that in s 40(6)? I would therefore dismiss these appeals.

PHILLIPS LJ. 'And it's greatly to his credit that he is an Englishman!' When

a W S Gilbert wrote those words the sun never set upon the British Empire, but British nationality remains a keen aspiration of many who have made this country their home. The British Nationality Act 1981 sets out circumstances in which someone who has settled in Great Britain can reasonably hope that he will be granted British nationality. Schedule 1 to the Act sets out 'Requirements for

b naturalisation'. These include a minimum period of past residence in the United Kingdom, compliance with the immigration laws, an intention to make the United Kingdom one's principal home (where the applicant is not married to a British citizen) and good character. Some of these requirements can be waived. Section 6 of the Act provides that where the Secretary of State (the minister) is satisfied that the applicant fulfils these requirements 'he may, if he thinks fit' grant

c him a certificate of naturalisation as a British citizen. We have been told that the majority of those who satisfy the residential requirements have their applications granted.

Mr Mohamed Fayed and Mr Ali Fayed, but for one minor matter which the minister has waived, satisfy the residential requirements. Mr Mohamed Fayed

d says that he wishes to make the United Kingdom his principal home, and there would seem no reason why the minister should doubt this intention. Mr Ali Fayed is married to a British citizen. Both have applied for naturalisation as British citizens and both have had their applications refused. Neither while their applications were under consideration, nor when they were refused, were they given any indication of what, if any, adverse factors opposed the grant of the

e privilege which they sought. They have applied for judicial review of these decisions. Each contends that the minister has failed to comply with the requirements of natural justice in that the procedure has been unfair in two respects. (i) The minister failed to inform him of the matters which were causing him concern when considering his application, thereby depriving him of the

f opportunity to make representations in respect of them. I shall describe this complaint as 'failure to give disclosure'. (ii) The minister failed to give reasons for his decision.

The minister contends that the requirements of natural justice did not require him either to give disclosure or to give reasons. He further contends that s 44(2) of the 1981 Act precludes each of those obligations. That section provides:

g

'The Secretary of State ... shall not be required to assign any reason for the grant or refusal of any application under this Act the decision on which is at his discretion; and the decision of the Secretary of State ...... shall not be subject to appeal to, or review in, any court.'

h Judge J accepted the latter contention. He held:

'Although the principle audi alterem partem and the provision of the reasons for the decision are distinct, they are closely related and derive from the concept of fairness. Nothing in s 44(2) or in any other part of the

j legislation expressly permits the Secretary of State to be unfair to non-citizens and it would be astonishing if it did. In reality, however, the principle of fairness contended for in these cases means that as part of the continuing process of considering applications, if the Secretary of State forms a preliminary conclusion adverse to applicants he should notify them in sufficiently detailed terms to provide them with a proper opportunity to be heard notwithstanding the unequivocal language that he cannot be required

to give any "reasons". If the opportunity to be heard is to have any value in
practice the Secretary of State would be required to assign or identify the
reasons for any adverse decision in advance. In my judgment, the imposition
of such an obligation under the principle of fairness would be inconsistent
with the language and effect of s 44(2) of the 1981 Act. Accordingly, the
failure to give the applicants an opportunity to deal with matters considered
by the Secretary of State to be adverse to their applications was not unlawful.
The course he took was permitted by statute.'

Accordingly, he dismissed the Fayeds' applications. They now appeal against his
decision.

In my judgment the appropriate approach to this case is one that Mr Richards
for the minister urged us not to take. I propose first to consider what obligations
the requirements of natural justice would have imposed on the minister in the
absence of s 44(2) and then to turn to consider the extent to which, if at all, these
are excluded by that section.

THE DUTY OF DISCLOSURE

Mr Beloff QC, for the appellants, submitted that natural justice demands that
an applicant under s 6, and each of the appellants in particular, be informed of the
nature of the case against his application and given a reasonable opportunity of
answering it. Of the many cases that discuss the duty of disclosure, three are of
particular relevance.

The nearest case to the present is the decision of the Privy Council in *A-G v
Ryan* [1980] AC 718. That case concerned an application to be registered as a
citizen of the Bahamas. The applicant was entitled to registration unless the
minister was satisfied of one of a number of matters, each one of which would
reflect discredit upon the applicant. In reviewing the decision of the Supreme
Court of the Bahamas, Lord Diplock said (at 726–727):

'(1) *Applicability of the principles of natural justice*　In the Supreme Court
both judges were of the opinion that the respondent had a constitutional
right to a fair hearing in accordance with the principles of natural justice
before his application to be registered as a citizen was rejected by the
Minister; and that a failure to accord him this rendered the Minister's
decision a nullity. This means that he was at least entitled to be informed of
the nature of the case against acceptance of his application and to be given a
reasonable opportunity of answering it. It does not mean that there must
necessarily be an oral hearing conducted in accordance with procedures
appropriate to trials in a court of law. What is an appropriate and fair
procedure is very much a matter for the Minister to determine in his
discretion having regard to the kind of things which he is required to take
into consideration—in the instant case, the various matters referred to in the
proviso to section 7 of The Bahamas Nationality Act 1973. Their Lordships,
however, need not go further into this, on which ample authority is cited in
the judgments of the courts below, since it is now conceded that neither at
his interview with Mr. Walkine nor on any other occasion was the
respondent given any indication of the grounds upon which the Minister
contemplated rejecting his application for registration; so, cadit quaestio, he
was given no opportunity of answering them. Their Lordships agree with
the judges of the Supreme Court (as did the Court of Appeal) that as an
applicant for registration as a citizen of The Bahamas under article 5(2) of the

a   Constitution, the respondent was entitled to a fair hearing in accordance
with the principles of natural justice before his application was rejected by
the Minister. By virtue of sections 7 and 8 of The Bahamas Nationality Act
1973, the Minister was a person having legal authority to determine a
question affecting the rights of individuals. This being so it is a necessary
implication that he is required to observe the principles of natural justice
b   when exercising that authority; and, if he fails to do so, his purported
decision is a nullity. In view of the citations of so many cases in the
judgments below, their Lordships upon this branch of the law do not find it
necessary to do more than to refer to *Ridge* v. *Baldwin* ([1963] 2 All ER 66,
[1964] AC 40) and particularly to the speech of Lord Reid ([1963] 2 All ER 66
at 77–78, [1964] AC 40 at 74–76).'

c
Ryan's case differs from the present case in that in *A-G v Ryan* the decision of the
minister deprived the applicant of the *right* to registration. Under s 6 the
applicant has no more than the *hope* of a grant of naturalisation in the discretion
of the Secretary of State.

In *R v Gaming Board for GB, ex p Benaim* [1970] 2 All ER 528, [1970] 2 QB 417 the
d   applicants, the proprietors of Crockford's, renewed an application to the Court of
Appeal against the refusal of the Gaming Board to grant a certificate of consent
to entitle them to apply for a gaming licence. The relevant provision of Sch 2 to
the Gaming Act 1968 provided:

e   '4 … (5) … in determining whether to issue to an applicant a certificate
consenting to his applying for the grant of a licence under this Act in respect
of any premises, the Board shall have regard only to the question whether,
in their opinion, the applicant is likely to be capable of, and diligent in,
securing that the provisions of this Act and of any regulations made under it
will be complied with, that gaming on those premises will be fairly and
f   properly conducted, and that the premises will be conducted without
disorder or disturbance.

(6) For the purposes of sub-paragraph (5) of this paragraph the Board shall
in particular take into consideration the character, reputation and financial
standing—(a) of the applicant …'

g   At issue was the extent of the duty of the Gaming Board to disclose to the
applicants the case against them. As to the nature of Crockford's interest, Lord
Denning MR described it thus ([1970] 2 All ER 528 at 532–533, [1970] 2 QB 417
at 429):

'Counsel for the applicants criticised that outline procedure severely. He
h   spoke as if Crockford's were being deprived of a right of property or of a right
to make a living … Counsel for the applicants put his case, I think, too high.
It is an error to regard Crockford's as having any right of which they are
being deprived. They have not had in the past, and they have not now, any
right to play these games of chance—roulette, chemin-de-fer, baccarat and
the like—for their own profit. What they are really seeking is a privilege—
j   almost, I might say, a franchise—to carry on gaming for profit, a thing never
hitherto allowed in this country. It is for them to show that they are fit to be
trusted with it. If counsel for the applicants went too far on his side, I think
counsel for the board went too far on the other. He submitted that the board
are free to grant or refuse a certificate as they please. They are not bound,
he says, to obey the rules of natural justice any more than any other

executive body, such as, I suppose, the Board of Trade, which grants
industrial development certificates, or the Television Authority, which *a*
awards television programme contracts. I cannot accept this view. I think
the board are bound to observe the rules of natural justice. The question is:
what are those rules?'

Lord Denning MR answered that question as follows ([1970] 2 All ER 528 at 534,
[1970] 2 QB 417 at 430–431): *b*

'… the board have a duty to act fairly. They must give the applicant an
opportunity of satisfying them of the matters specified in Sch 2, para 4(5).
They must let him know what their impressions are so that he can disabuse
them. But I do not think that they need quote chapter and verse against him
as if they were dismissing him from an office (*Ridge v Baldwin* [1963] 2 All ER *c*
66, [1964] AC 40), or depriving him of his property, as in *Cooper v Wandsworth
Board of Works* ((1863) 14 CBNS 180, 143 ER 414). After all, they are not
charging him with doing anything wrong. They are simply enquiring as to
his capability and diligence and are having regard to his character, reputation
and financial standing. They are there to protect the public interest, to see *d*
that persons running the gaming clubs are fit to be trusted. Seeing the evils
that have led to this legislation, the board can, and should, investigate the
credentials of those who make application to them. They can, and should,
receive information from the police in this country or abroad, who know
something of them. They can, and should, receive information from any
other reliable source. Much of it will be confidential. But that does not mean *e*
that the applicants are not to be given a chance of answering it. They must
be given the chance, subject to this qualification: I do not think they need tell
the applicant the source of their information, if that would put their
informant in peril or otherwise be contrary to the public interest … If the
board were bound to disclose their sources of information, no one would *f*
"tell" on those clubs, for fear of reprisals. Likewise with the details of the
information. If the board were bound to disclose every detail, that might
itself give the informer away and put him in peril. But, without disclosing
every detail, I should have thought that the board ought in every case to be
able to give to the applicant sufficient indication of the objections raised
against him such as to enable him to answer them. That is only fair. And the *g*
board must at all costs be fair. If they are not, these courts will not hesitate
to interfere.'

That decision demonstrates two matters: (1) the duty to disclose the case that is
adverse to an applicant for the exercise of a discretion does not depend upon the *h*
pre-existence of any right in the applicant; (2) the nature and degree of disclosure
required depends upon the particular circumstances.

These two decisions assist in the application to the facts of the present case of
the general principles summarised by Lord Mustill in *Doody v Secretary of State for
the Home Dept* [1993] 3 All ER 92 at 106, [1994] 1 AC 531 at 560:
j
'(1) Where an Act of Parliament confers an administrative power there is
a presumption that it will be exercised in a manner which is fair in all the
circumstances. (2) The standards of fairness are not immutable. They may
change with the passage of time, both in the general and in their application
to decisions of a particular type. (3) The principles of fairness are not to be
applied by rote identically in every situation. What fairness demands is

a dependent on the context of the decision, and this is to be taken into account in all its aspects. (4) An essential feature of the context is the statute which creates the discretion, as regards both its language and the shape of the legal and administrative system within which the decision is taken. (5) Fairness will very often require that a person who may be adversely affected by the decision will have an opportunity to make representations on his own behalf

b either before the decision is taken with a view to producing a favourable result, or after it is taken, with a view to procuring its modification, or both. (6) Since the person affected usually cannot make worthwhile representations without knowing what factors may weigh against his interests fairness will very often require that he is informed of the gist of the case which he has to answer.'

c In the light of these authorities I am satisfied that, in the absence of s 44, an applicant under s 6 would be entitled to be informed of the nature of matters adverse to his application so as to be afforded a reasonable opportunity to deal with them. An applicant for citizenship has not at risk any vested right. In that respect this case differs from *A-G v Ryan*. The right for which he applies is,

d however, a right of great importance. It carries with it the rights of freedom of movement and establishment enjoyed by members of the European Community. It exempts from visa requirements in many parts of the world. It carries a right to vote. It is a legitimate aspiration for one who has established his home in this country, the more so if he has children here who have British nationality and if his wife is a British national.

e There is another side to the coin. The refusal of British nationality to one who has, apparently, satisfied all the technical requirements of s 6 is likely to carry the natural implication, both in this country and abroad, that he has attributes of background, character or conduct that are disreputable.

I consider that these factors give the appellants stronger grounds for urging a

f duty of disclosure than existed in the *Gaming Board* case. The refusal of the benefits of naturalisation and the adverse inferences that will be drawn from such refusal are so serious that, as a matter of natural justice, an applicant should not be visited with them without a fair chance to meet the adverse case that threatens this result.

g THE DUTY TO GIVE REASONS

Whether or not the requirements of natural justice impart an obligation to give reasons is often a difficult question of administrative law, the more so because the courts have been increasingly ready to find that such a duty exists: see De Smith Woolf and Jowell *Judicial Review of Administrative Action* (5th edn, 1995) pp 457–

h 465, paras 9-039 to 9-048. In this case, when considering procedural fairness, the extent of the duty of disclosure and the duty to give reasons are interrelated.

For the reasons that I have given in relation to the duty of disclosure, I consider that, absent s 44(2), the minister would be under a duty to give reasons for refusing an application for naturalisation under s 6 of the 1981 Act.

j THE EFFECT OF S 44(2)

The duty to give reasons

The provision that the minister 'shall not be required to assign any reason for the grant or refusal' of an application is clear and unambiguous. Mr Beloff argued that these words relate only to the minister's 'statutory duty' to give reasons and do not impinge on a parallel duty to give reasons, which exists at common law.

This seems to me to be sophistry of a high order. The duty of ministers of the Crown to act fairly in the performance of their administrative duties, which in appropriate circumstances imports a duty to give reasons, is a fundamental principle of our common law. Where the minister is performing statutory duties, it may be correct to state that the duty to give reasons, if it exists, arises in consequence of an implication in the course of statutory interpretation, but the implication falls to be made because of the common law principle. I reject the suggestion that there co-exist common law and statutory duties to give reasons, and that s 44(2) applies only to the latter. I am in no doubt that the express words of the statute preclude the obligation on the minister, that would otherwise exist, to give reasons for his decision.

The duty of disclosure

Mr Richards's submission, which Judge J accepted, was that a duty of disclosure would 'frustrate the operation of s 44(2) and the legislative purpose of protecting the respondent from any requirement to disclose his reasons'.

Section 44(2) has its origins in s 26 of the British Nationality Act 1948, which was in almost identical terms. In 1948 it might well have been thought, having particular regard to the exclusion of 'appeal to or review in any court' that the intention and effect of the subsection was to render the decision of the minister non-justiciable. By 1981, when the current statute was enacted, such a view was no longer tenable in the light of the decision in *Anisminic Ltd v Foreign Compensation Commission* [1969] 1 All ER 208, [1969] 2 AC 147. The relevant statutory provisions in *A-G v Ryan* [1980] AC 718 contained an identical 'ouster clause' to that in the present case, but the Privy Council, applying the *Anisminic* case, held that it did not apply to a decision made without jurisdiction and that:

'It has long been settled law that a decision affecting the legal rights of an individual which is arrived at by a procedure which offends against the principles of natural justice is outside the jurisdiction of the decision making authority.' (See [1980] AC 718 at 730.)

In these circumstances Mr Richards rightly conceded that the minister's decisions were justiciable. He attached no significance in the present context to the provision purporting to preclude review or appeal. In these circumstances I consider that it would be wrong, as I was initially inclined to do, to approach the provision that the minister is not required to assign reasons for his decision as being designed to render his decision non-justiciable. That provision relieves the minister of the disadvantages attendant on the duty to give reasons that are identified in *De Smith Woolf and Jowell* para 9-045, namely:

'... the possibility that reasons, especially if published, will unduly increase "legalisation" and the formal nature of the decision making process, place burdens upon decision makers that will occasion administrative delays, and encourage the disappointed to pore over the reasons in the hope of detecting some shortcoming for which to seek redress in the courts. In addition, a reluctance to give reasons perhaps because they may occasion harm (by, for example, causing personal distress, revealing confidences, or endangering national security) could discourage the making of difficult or controversial decisions or result in the production of anodyne, uninformative and standard reasons.'

The removal of these disadvantages provides explanation enough for the existence of the provision.

a   Mr Richards' argument seeks to give greater effect to the words of the provision than their natural meaning bears. He submits, in effect, that they mean 'the minister is entitled to conceal the reasons for his decision'. It is only this construction which renders it possible to argue that disclosure at the interim stage of the decision-making process will frustrate the object of the provision. Disclosure of matters of concern to the minister at that stage will by no means
b   remove all the benefits that flow from being relieved of the obligation to give reasons for his ultimate decision, even if it may enable applicants, on occasion, to make a fair guess at what they are.

    Even if the duty of disclosure were to remove essentially all the benefits of the relief from the obligation to give reasons, I would not be prepared to hold that the latter implicitly overrides the former. This is because I consider that the duty
c   of disclosure is a more significant element in the fairness of the procedure than the duty to give reasons. The duty of disclosure is calculated to ensure that the process by which the minister reaches his decision is fair. It enables the party affected to address the matters which are significant and thus helps to ensure that the minister reaches his decision having regard to all the relevant material. The
d   duty to give reasons is calculated to enable the party affected to see that the minister has acted fairly in reaching his decision. While this can have a salutary effect on the process of reaching the decision, it does not have such a direct effect as the duty of disclosure.

    For these reasons I cannot accept that the express relief from the duty to give reasons for his decision implicitly relieves the minister from the duty of disclosure
e   during the process of reaching that decision.

    Mr Richards drew our attention to the provisions of s 40 of the 1981 Act. These include a specific procedure to be followed before a British citizen can be deprived of his citizenship. He has to be informed of the grounds upon which such action is proposed and is entitled to apply for an inquiry before a committee,
f   chaired by a person having judicial experience. Mr Richards suggested that this exemplified the kind of procedure for which provision would have been made had the legislature intended there to be a duty of disclosure in favour of applicants for naturalisation.

    It is much more serious to be deprived of citizenship than to fail to be granted it, as is evidenced by the grounds of misconduct specified in s 40 that must be
g   established before one can suffer the former fate. For this reason I was not persuaded that the existence of express provisions for precise and formal steps before a citizen is deprived of his citizenship carries the implication that no steps at all by way of disclosure have to be taken in respect of applications for citizenship.
h   For these reasons I have concluded that this appeal should be allowed and concur in the order proposed by Lord Woolf MR.

    Appeal allowed. Decisions of Secretary of State quashed.

j   Mary Rose Plummer   Barrister.

Country and Metropolitan Homes Surrey Ltd v Topclaim Ltd

CHANCERY DIVISION

TIMOTHY LLOYD QC SITTING AS A DEPUTY JUDGE OF THE HIGH COURT

15 MARCH, 2 APRIL 1996

Sale of land – Notice to complete – Validity – Party giving notice ready and willing to fulfil own outstanding obligations – Notice by vendor – Vendor not deducing title on date set for completion – Vendor eventually deducing title on day notice to complete issued – Contract requiring ten working days' notice to complete – Vendor giving one working day to complete from date of notice – Purchaser not in breach – Purchaser not complying with notice – Vendor rescinding contract – Whether notice to complete ineffective under contract and general law – Whether vendor in breach of contract – Standard Conditions of Sale (2nd edn), condition 6.8.

Sale of land – Deposit – Forfeiture – Purchaser's failure to complete – Vendor rescinding contract and forfeiting deposit – Contract excluding court's discretion to order repayment of deposit – Vendor in breach of contract – Whether purchaser entitled to return of deposit – Law of Property Act 1925, s 49(2).

In March 1995 the vendor, C Ltd, agreed to sell registered land to the purchaser, T Ltd. The contract incorporated condition 6.8 of the Standard Conditions of Sale (2nd edn), which provided that, at any time on or after the completion date a party who was ready, able and willing to complete could serve the other party with a notice to complete within ten working days; and on receipt of such a notice a buyer who had paid a deposit of less than 10% of the purchase price had to pay a further deposit equal to the balance of that 10%. The contract also expressly excluded the application of s 49(2)[a] of the Law of Property Act 1925, which gave the court a discretion to order the repayment of a deposit in any action for its return. Contracts were exchanged with a completion date of 20 April, in respect of which time was expressly provided to be of the essence. C Ltd was not however in a position to deduce title as a registered proprietor in accordance with the provisions of the contract until the following day. On 4 May C Ltd received the land certificate showing it as the registered proprietor of the property and on the same day it sent T Ltd a notice to complete by 9 May, which allowed only one working day to complete. Completion did not take place on the agreed date, and on 11 May C Ltd wrote to T Ltd, stating that the contract was at an end and that the 5% deposit paid had been forfeited, and demanding payment of the outstanding 5% of the deposit in accordance with the conditions of sale. T Ltd decided to treat the contract as repudiated by the vendor and called for the return of the deposit with interest. The property was subsequently sold to a third party and C Ltd issued proceedings against T Ltd claiming damages for breach of contract and payment of the 5% balance of the deposit. The master refused C Ltd's claim and granted T Ltd summary judgment on its counterclaim for the return of the deposit already paid and damages to be assessed. C Ltd appealed.

---

a   Section 49(2) is set out at p 257 *b*, post

a **Held** – (1) Condition 6.8 of the Standard Conditions of Sale was intended to be exhaustive and set out in full the rights and obligations of the parties regarding a notice to complete following failure to complete on the agreed date. In the circumstances, the notice served by C Ltd was ineffective because it failed to allow ten working days for completion as required under condition 6.8. In any event, under the general law, C Ltd could not have served such a notice on 4 May: b C Ltd was itself in default for failing to obtain title by the original completion date and therefore it could not subsequently serve a valid notice to complete on a purchaser which was not in default on the date of the notice; moreover, when C Ltd purported to rescind the contract following T Ltd's failure to complete on 9 May, it was C Ltd that was in breach of contract, not T Ltd (see p 261 a to h, post); *Rightside Properties Ltd v Gray* [1974] 2 All ER 1169 applied.

c (2) The discretion conferred on the court by s 49(2) of the 1925 Act enabled a purchaser who was in default to recover his deposit if the justice of the case so required. The contractual exclusion of the application of s 49(2) could not enable a vendor in default to claim forfeiture of the purchaser's deposit regardless of the circumstances, nor did it alter the ordinary position at law, namely that the fate of the deposit, in a situation in which the contract was not completed, depended d on which party was at fault. In the instant case, the vendor, C Ltd, was in breach and accordingly T Ltd was entitled to the return of the deposit with interest. The appeal would therefore be dismissed (see p 262 b to f, post); dictum of Gerald Godfrey QC in *Dimsdale Developments (South East) Ltd v De Haan* (1983) 47 P & CR 1 at 11 applied.

e

Notes

For notice to complete, see 42 *Halsbury's Laws* (4th edn) para 127, and for cases on the subject, see 40 *Digest* (Reissue) 189–194, *1384–1407*.

For the Law of Property Act 1925, s 49, see 37 *Halsbury's Statutes* (4th edn) 147.

f

Cases referred to in judgment
Behzadi v Shaftesbury Hotels Ltd [1991] 2 All ER 477, [1992] Ch 1, [1991] 2 WLR 1251, CA.
Dimsdale Developments (South East) Ltd v De Haan (1983) 47 P & CR 1.
Rightside Properties Ltd v Gray [1974] 2 All ER 1169, [1975] Ch 72, [1974] 3 WLR
g 484.

Cases also cited or referred to in skeleton arguments
Ajit v Sammy [1967] 1 AC 255, [1996] 3 WLR 983, PC.
Buckland v Farmer & Moody (a firm) [1978] 3 All ER 929, [1979] 1 WLR 221, CA.
h *Cole v Rose* [1978] 3 All ER 1121.
Lock v Bell [1931] 1 Ch 35, [1930] All ER Rep 635.
Luck v White (1973) 26 P & CR 89.
Ramdass Bidaisee v Dorinda Yusidai Sampath (1995) 46 WIR 461, PC.
Woods v Mackenzie Hill Ltd [1975] 2 All ER 170, [1975] 1 WLR 613.

j **Appeal**
By notice dated 11 January 1996 the vendor, Country and Metropolitan Homes Surrey Ltd, appealed from the decision of Master Winegarten on 5 January 1996 whereby he dismissed the plaintiff's claim against the purchaser, Topclaim Ltd, for damages for breach of contract for sale and purchase of the property known as Units 12 to 17, Verdley Place, Fernhurst, Chichester, West Sussex, and ordered

that summary judgment be given for the purchaser on its counterclaim that the vendor pay the sum of £22,500, being the balance of the deposit under the contract. The appeal was heard and judgment was given in chambers. The case is reported with the leave of Timothy Lloyd QC. The facts are set out in the judgment.

Edward Cousins (instructed by *Mishcon de Reya*) for the vendor.
Isaac Jacob (instructed by *Brooke Martin & Co*) for the purchaser.

Cur adv vult

2 April 1996. The following judgment was delivered.

TIMOTHY LLOYD QC. The parties to this action and counterclaim are the vendor, as plaintiff, and the purchaser, as defendant, under a contract for the sale of land at Verdley Place, Fernhurst, Chichester, dated 9 March 1995 which was due for completion on 20 April 1995. The contract was not completed on that date, or at all, and in May 1995 the vendor resold to a different purchaser. On 19 May the vendor issued these proceedings claiming damages for breach of contract, and payment of the sum of £22,500, to bring the deposit up to 10%, and interest. On 30 June the purchaser served a defence and counterclaim, seeking the return of the £22,500 that had been paid by way of deposit, together with interest and damages. In November the purchaser sought summary judgment on the counterclaim and the vendor responded by seeking summary judgment in the action. Both these summonses came before Master Winegarten on 5 January. He considered that the purchaser's claim was plainly justified and the vendor's claim clearly unsustainable and he accordingly granted the relief sought to the purchaser. The vendor now appeals.

The owner of the property comprised in the contract was Zeneca plc. The vendor had agreed to buy some of Zeneca's land under a contract which, it seems, was (or came to be) due for completion on 20 April 1995. Early in 1995 negotiations began between the vendor and the purchaser for the purchaser to buy part of what the vendor was buying from Zeneca. The contract was to be conditional on a number of matters including the grant of planning permission and listed building consent, and an approval from the National Trust. The vendor and its solicitors pressed the purchaser and its solicitors hard to secure the exchange of contracts. Early in March, as part of the pressure, they agreed to reduce the price from £470,000 to £450,000 and to reduce the deposit from 10% to 5%. Contracts were eventually exchanged on 9 March with the completion date of 20 April, in respect of which time was expressly provided to be of the essence. The purchase price was £450,000 and on the date of the agreement, the purchaser paid 5% of that price to the vendor's solicitors to be held by them as stakeholders. By cl 8.1 it was recorded that title to the property to be conveyed, and to the property to be retained by the vendor, and to certain other land, no doubt that which was to be retained by Zeneca, was registered with absolute title under a particular title number and 'title shall be deduced in accordance with the Land Registration Act 1925, section 110'. It was also provided by cl 8.2 that the property would be transferred to the purchaser by virtue of the transfer, a draft of which was annexed to the contract and identified the vendor, being the party making the transfer, as the plaintiff in this action. By cl 12.1, the Standard Conditions of Sale (2nd edn) were to apply to the agreement so far as they were a applicable to a sale by private treaty and were not inconsistent with the terms of the agreement, but subject to certain variations. The one variation that I need to mention is that by cl 12.1.6, s 49(2) of the Law of Property Act 1925 was not to apply. That subsection provides:

> 'Where the court refuses to grant specific performance of a contract, or in any action for the return of a deposit, the court may, if it thinks fit, order the
b repayment of any deposit.'

The one provision I should cite from the Standard Conditions is condition 6.8, which, so far as is material, is as follows:

> '**6.8** *Notice to complete*
c 6.8.1 At any time on or after completion date, a party who is ready able and willing to complete may give the other a notice to complete ...
> 6.8.3 The parties are to complete the contract within ten working days of giving a notice to complete, excluding the day on which the notice is given. For this purpose, time is of the essence of the contract.
> 6.8.4 On receipt of a notice to complete: (a) if the buyer paid no deposit,
d he is forthwith to pay a deposit of 10 per cent (b) if the buyer paid a deposit of less than 10 per cent, he is forthwith to pay a further deposit equal to the balance of that 10 per cent.'

On 10 March the purchaser's solicitors wrote to the vendor's solicitors confirming exchange on the previous day and saying: 'I am also enclosing basic
e requisitions on title although we shall at completion have to agree the mechanics of registration as discussed.' On 19 April the vendor's solicitors sent an engrossment of the transfer to the purchaser's solicitors for execution by their client, with a view to completion the following day. In response, the purchaser's solicitors said that they did not believe completion could take place on the
f following day and mentioned a number of respects in which they contended the vendor had not yet complied with the provisions of the contract so as to make it unconditional. A spate of correspondence followed in the course of which, on 20 April, the purchaser's solicitors contended that the vendor was not in a position to deduce title in accordance with s 110(5) of the Land Registration Act 1925 and saying that the purchaser required the vendor to become registered as a
g precondition of completion. Section 110(5) provides, so far as material:

> 'Where the vendor is not himself registered as proprietor of the land ... he shall, at the request of the purchaser and at his own expense ... procure the registration of himself as proprietor of the land ...'

h In the event, completion did not take place on 20 April either of the contract at issue in this litigation or of the prior contract on the part of the vendor to buy land from Zeneca. That contract was completed by a transfer on 21 April. On 25 April the vendor applied to be registered as proprietor under that transfer at HM Land Registry and on 4 May the vendor's solicitors received the land certificate
j showing their client's registration as proprietor as of 25 April, and office copies of the entries on the register.

In the meantime, although the purchaser's solicitors had indicated that they might receive instructions to call for the return of the deposit on the ground that the vendor was not in a position to proceed to completion on the contractual completion date, the purchaser had not in fact sought to terminate the contract and had pursued various matters in correspondence with a view to it eventually

being completed. On 4 May the vendor's solicitors sent to the purchaser's
solicitors a letter with which they enclosed office copy entries as of 3 May   *a*
showing the vendor as the registered proprietor of the property, and said: 'Please
note that we require your client to complete the contract by 1 pm on Tuesday, 9
May. Time is of the essence.'

It should be noted that 4 May was a Thursday and Monday, 8 May was a bank
holiday. There was, therefore, one whole working day between the date of that   *b*
letter and the proposed completion date. (There is an issue whether the letter
was delivered on 4 or 5 May. In favour of the vendor for present purposes, I will
assume that it was delivered on the earlier day.) On the morning of 9 May the
vendor's solicitors sent a further letter stating: 'As you know our client is now in
a position to forfeit your client's 5% deposit and sue for the balance unless
completion takes place by 1 pm today.' On 11 May the vendor's solicitors wrote   *c*
to the purchaser's solicitors stating that the contract was at an end and that the
5% deposit had been forfeited, and requiring the purchaser to forward the
outstanding 5% deposit in accordance with condition 6.8.4(b) of the Standard
Conditions of Sale. In response, on 12 May the purchaser's solicitors
communicated their client's decision to treat the agreement of 9 March as   *d*
repudiated, and called for the return of the deposit with interest. In reply, on the
same day, the vendor's solicitors wrote a letter which is of some interest in the
light of the contentions put forward in these proceedings. Reiterating that the
contract was at an end and that the deposit had been forfeited and stating that the
question of the repudiation therefore did not arise, the writer sought to place on
record the circumstances that led to the contract being rescinded by the vendor.   *e*
He stated that title was deduced in accordance with s 110(5) of the Land
Registration Act 1925 on 4 May and that on that day the vendor required
completion on the following Tuesday, and that time was, as before, of the
essence. That notice was not complied with and as a result the contract was
rescinded. He asserted that the vendor was always willing to complete and that   *f*
it was the purchaser who refused to complete originally, essentially because its
funding was not in place. The writer then made the comment that the purchaser
had the right to rescind the contract but deliberately chose not to do so. That
right, however, disappeared, he said, 'the moment my client deduced title. Your
client has no claim for damages for the simple reason that it was your client who
refused to complete'. These proceedings then followed.   *g*

In the statement of claim the vendor alleges, as was the fact, that the purchase
was not completed on 20 April 1995, that by the letter of 4 May the vendor gave
notice to the purchaser to complete the purchase by 1 pm on 9 May, time to be
of the essence, which was a reasonable time, and that in breach of the agreement
the purchaser failed and neglected to complete the purchase on that day or at all.   *h*
By para 9 of the counterclaim it is asserted, among other things, that in the
circumstances it was a term of the contract or a request pursuant to s 110(5) of
the Land Registration Act 1925 that the vendor be registered as proprietor of the
land to be transferred prior to completion. By para 14 it is alleged, as was the case,
that on 20 April the vendor had not completed its purchase from Zeneca and had   *j*
not procured its own registration as registered proprietor. It was further asserted
that following receipt of the office copy entries enclosed with the letter of 4 May,
the purchaser was entitled to raise requisitions on title and, further, that even if
the vendor had then or at any later stage been in a position to serve a notice to
complete no such notice could have been for a period of less than ten working
days. By the reply and defence to counterclaim, para 9 of the counterclaim was

admitted. However, Mr Cousins, on behalf of the vendor, in his submissions before me made it clear that he did not accept that the vendor was bound to procure its own registration as proprietor before completion and that if the case went further he would seek leave to amend the reply and defence to counterclaim accordingly. In these circumstances, I was prepared to hear submissions from him inconsistent with the admission in the pleadings in relation to s 110(5).

Mr Cousins' submissions were essentially threefold. First, he said that the vendor's only obligation was to prove its entitlement to be registered as proprietor of the property and that the purchaser's insistence on the vendor procuring its own registration as proprietor before completion was itself a breach of the contract. Secondly, in circumstances in which time was of the essence of the original completion date, 20 April, the contract had not then been completed but the parties continued to treat with a view to eventual completion, it was open to the vendor to serve a short notice as it did by its letter of 4 May so as to make time of the essence of the new completion date of 9 May and to entitle the vendor to rescind the contract on the purchaser failing to complete on that date. He said that the contractual provision incorporated by condition 6.8 of the Standard Conditions of Sale did not exclude the party's right to serve a notice to complete under the general law. Thirdly, and separately, he contended that the exclusion of s 49(2) of the Law of Property Act 1925 by cl 12.1.6 meant that the court had no power to order the return of the deposit to the purchaser in any circumstances and that effectively the deposit was an irrecoverable deposit in all circumstances.

By contrast Mr Jacob, for the purchaser, contended, first, that the vendor was in no position to complete on any footing on 20 April since it did not obtain a transfer from its vendor until the following day; that, in circumstances where the transfer had to be made by the vendor to the purchaser in accordance with the contract, s 110(5) could only require the vendor to procure its registration before completion; that if, for the purposes of argument, the vendor was in a position to serve a notice to complete on 4 May, it could only have been a notice to complete under condition 6.8, that is to say a notice of ten working days; and that even if the condition was not inconsistent with an ability to serve a notice under the general law, the vendor could not have served a valid notice under the general law on 4 May. Lastly, in relation to the deposit he contended that the exclusion of s 49(2) only excluded, or purported to exclude, the court's power to relieve against forfeiture, and that in circumstances in which the vendor was clearly in default the purchaser was entitled to repayment of the deposit at law, not by reason of any relief against forfeiture.

I do not consider that I need to or should decide any issue as to the scope and effect of s 110(5) of the Land Registration Act 1925, because on 20 April the vendor was not able to complete on any footing. Not only had the vendor not shown title on that date, in whatever way it was bound to do, it had not obtained any sort of title. It had not then taken a transfer from Zeneca and was therefore not even entitled to be registered, still less actually registered, as proprietor. Accordingly, I approach the case on the footing that, in any event, the vendor was in default on 20 April and the purchaser could have rescinded the contract immediately.

The next question is, in those circumstances, whether the vendor was entitled to serve notice on 4 May, making 9 May a new completion date with time of the essence. It seems to me plain that it was not so entitled. In *Rightside Properties Ltd v Gray* [1974] 2 All ER 1169, [1975] Ch 72 Walton J had to consider a contract which the purchaser did not complete on the day fixed for completion, where the vendor then served a notice purportedly under condition 9 of the Statutory Conditions of Sale, which entitled the vendor to give to the purchaser in default at least 21 days' notice in writing. The notice was held to be bad under the condition because it specified a date 21 days from the date of the notice rather than from the date of receipt of the notice. The vendor sought to amend to claim in the alternative that the notice was given under the general law, not under the condition, that it was a reasonable period of notice and that, accordingly, it had the same effect as the contractual notice. In fact, because the judge would have insisted on allowing the purchaser an adjournment and the vendor was not willing to accept that, the application for an amendment of the pleadings was withdrawn but the judge made it clear that he thought the point would certainly have been a bad one for a number of reasons. He said ([1974] 2 All ER 1169 at 1177–1178, [1975] Ch 72 at 81):

'... the submission of counsel for [the defendant] involves the proposition that in spite of the terms of condition 9 it was nevertheless open to [the defendant] to serve, under the general law, a notice having the like effect to a notice under condition 9, but of shorter length. This appears to me a totally astonishing proposition, and one which only has to be stated at length to be seen to be wrong.'

There was also cited to me a decision of Mr Gerald Godfrey QC sitting as a deputy judge of the High Court in *Dimsdale Developments (South East) Ltd v De Haan* (1983) 47 P & CR 1. In that case, the contract incorporated the National Conditions of Sale (19th edn), which provided for a 28-day notice to complete by either party being ready and willing to fulfil his own outstanding obligations under the contract. The purchaser sent a notice, not expressly referring to the National Conditions of Sale, requiring completion within 28 days 'from the date hereof' and it was submitted on behalf of the vendor that this was too short, by analogy with the decision in *Rightside Properties Ltd v Gray*. The judge held that the notice was not too short in any event but also said that even if it had been too short to comply with the National Conditions he would have been prepared to hold it valid as an ordinary notice to complete under the general law which was not served unreasonably soon nor was it unreasonably short. He said (at 9–10):

'For my part I do not think a provision such as condition 22, providing for a special notice to complete, is intended or operative to exclude the right of a party to chance his arm on the well known uncertainties of the general law, which require him to make a guess as to what the court will consider a decent interval between the contractual date for completion and the date of service of the notice, and another guess as to what it would consider a reasonable period for completion to be specified by the notice itself. Condition 22 expressly saves to the aggrieved party "any other right or remedy available to him".'

He therefore distinguished *Rightside Properties Ltd v Gray*.

In the present case, the admirably succinct and clear Standard Conditions of Sale do not contain words comparable to those cited from the National Conditions of Sale saving other rights and remedies, although for completeness I note that, in a different context, in conditions 7.5 and 7.6, dealing respectively with the buyer's and the seller's failure to comply with a notice to complete, it is provided that the seller or the buyer, as the case may be, 'retains his other rights

and remedies'. It seems to me that standard condition 6.8 is intended to be
exhaustive, and to set out in full the rights and obligations of the parties as regards
notice to complete following failure to complete on the date fixed for
completion. In this respect, it seems to me, that the case is much closer to
Rightside Properties v Gray, where it seems that the statutory conditions did not
have any such saving phrase, than it is to *Dimsdale Developments (South East) Ltd v
De Haan*, where the reservation of other remedies allowed the argument that a
provision as to notice to complete was not exhaustive. I do not think that
condition 6.8 can fairly be read as merely an addition to whatever other rights the
parties might have to do the same sort of thing in the same circumstances under
the general law. I note further that the vendor was clearly proceeding, or
believed that it was proceeding, under condition 6.8 since from before the expiry
of the notice, and consistently thereafter, it asserted that failure to comply with
the notice would oblige the purchaser to pay the additional £22,500 to bring the
deposit up to 10% which is expressly provided for by condition 6.8.4. There is no
other provision in the contract that would entitle the vendor to insist on that.

Furthermore, even if the contract were not read as excluding the ability to
serve a notice to complete under the general law, the letter of 4 May 1995 could
not have sufficed as a valid notice of that kind. It is no longer the law that a party
wishing to serve such a notice must wait until the other party has been guilty of
unreasonable delay after the date fixed for completion (see *Behzadi v Shaftesbury
Hotels Ltd* [1991] 2 All ER 477, [1992] Ch 1, in which the Court of Appeal held that
such a notice could be served as soon as the party on whom the notice was to be
served was in default). But it seems a surprising proposition that a vendor who
has not deduced title by the date fixed for completion can by the same letter
thereafter both deduce title and fix a new date for completion, of which time is of
the essence. The purchaser would in the ordinary way be entitled to time to raise
requisitions on title before he could be treated as having accepted the vendor's
title. Even apart from that, he could certainly not be treated as being in default
on the very day on which the vendor first deduces his title. It seems highly
questionable whether the notice would have been of sufficient length, but that
question does not arise.

Accordingly, I hold that the letter of 4 May was not effective to make 9 May the
new date for completion of which time was of the essence, primarily because it
was not open to the vendor to serve a notice under the general law rather than
one complying with standard condition 6.8, and alternatively because a notice
under the general law could not be served on that day since the purchaser was
not, on any basis, in default on 4 May. Thus, when the vendor purported to
rescind following the purchaser's failure to complete on that date, it was the
vendor that was in breach of contract and repudiated the contract rather than the
purchaser.

I now turn to the issue on s 49(2) of the Law of Property Act 1925. By that
subsection:

> 'Where the court refuses to grant specific performance of a contract, or in
> any action for the return of a deposit, the court may, if it thinks fit, order the
> repayment of any deposit.'

It is a startling proposition that, by excluding that section in relation to the
contract, the purchaser has prevented itself from obtaining repayment of the
deposit even if the vendor has been flagrantly in breach of the contract and the
purchaser has not. It also seems curious, in relation to that submission, that

under the contract in this case the vendor's solicitors hold the deposit as
stakeholder, since that clearly implies that there could be circumstances in which
they would have to pay the deposit back to the purchaser rather than account for
it to their client the vendor.

The answer to this contention is to be found in the judgment of
Mr Godfrey QC in *Dimsdale Developments (South East) Ltd v De Haan* (1983) 47 P &
CR 1. He held that the vendor's notice to complete was validly served but,
despite that, the purchaser sought the return of the deposit under s 49(2). He
therefore had to consider the ambit of the subsection in the light of a number of
decided cases. Before doing that he made the following observations of general
relevance (at 11):

> 'It is to be observed that a purchaser has no need to pray this subsection in
> aid where it is not he but the vendor who is the defaulter. The subsection is
> needed only to enable a purchaser who is himself in default to recover his
> deposit.'

He then went on to consider circumstances in which the court might conclude
that even though the purchaser was in default, the justice of the case might
require that the deposit be repaid to the purchaser. It is that jurisdiction which,
it seems to me, is excluded by the special condition in this contract. The contract
does not alter the ordinary position at law namely that the fate of the deposit, in
a situation in which the contract is not completed, depends on which party's fault
it is that the contract is not completed. In the present position, as I have held, it
was clearly that of the vendor and the purchaser is therefore entitled to the return
of the deposit, with interest, regardless of the subsection.

Accordingly, in my judgment, the master was entirely right in the order he
made and I propose to dismiss the appeal.

Appeal dismissed.

Celia Fox   Barrister.

Re M (a minor) (care orders: jurisdiction)

FAMILY DIVISION

HALE J

22 OCTOBER, 6 NOVEMBER 1996

Family proceedings – Jurisdiction – Child formerly resident in Scotland taken to England – Care proceedings in England – Local authority plan to return child to care of grandmother in Scotland – Whether English courts having jurisdiction – Children Act 1989, Pts IV and V – Family Law Act 1986, Pt I.

T was born in 1993 to unmarried parents who were habitually resident in Scotland. In November 1995 the family moved to the south of England and shortly after their arrival the local social services department was contacted about concerns for T's welfare. On 27 November an emergency protection order was made in the local family proceedings court and the following day the local authority applied for a care order. After a contested hearing on 12 December an interim care order was made and subsequent orders were made in the usual way without opposition. Thereafter both parents returned to Scotland, and the case was transferred to the High Court. In March 1996 the local authority was granted approval, under para 19 of Sch 2 to the Children Act 1989, to arrange for T to live in Scotland with his paternal grandparents. The care plan was that T should live with his grandparents and have contact with his parents; however, for a variety of reasons, including the mother's drug addiction and the fact that the father was then in prison, it was not felt that there was a stable and safe environment into which the local authority could consider such a return. The issue arose as to the jurisdiction of the English courts to make orders in respect of that plan and it was assumed that both the mother and T had retained their habitual residence in Scotland.

Held – Although Pt I of the Family Law Act 1986 governed the jurisdiction of the court to entertain private law proceedings under the 1989 Act, it did not apply to public law proceedings under Pts IV and V of that Act. However, there was nothing in either Act to cast doubt on the proposition that the courts in England and Wales had jurisdiction to make orders under Pt IV of the 1989 Act in relation to children who were present in the jurisdiction, irrespective of whether or not they were habitually resident either abroad or in another part of the United Kingdom. The purpose of the court's jurisdiction was to protect children from harm and what applied to Pt IV applied a fortiori to the emergency protection measures contained in Pt V of the 1989 Act. That jurisdiction was not therefore limited by the habitual residence of the child and provided that the child was present in the jurisdiction when the application was made, the court had power to make an order. Accordingly the presence in England of T at the date of the first application was sufficient to give the court jurisdiction to make the emergency protection and interim care orders already made and to continue to entertain the application (see p 265 *f*, p 266 *b*, p 267 *e* to *g j*, p 268 *c d* and p 270 *d e*, post).

Re R (care orders: jurisdiction) [1995] 1 FLR 711 considered.

Notes

For the Family Law Act 1986, Pt I, see 6 *Halsbury's Statutes* (4th edn) (1992 reissue) 326.

For the Children Act 1989, Pts IV, V, see ibid 431, 448.

Cases referred to in judgment

B and anor (minors) (termination of contact: paramount consideration), Re [1993] 3 All ER 524, [1993] Fam 301, [1993] 3 WLR 63, CA.

P (G E) (an infant), Re [1964] 3 All ER 977, [1965] Ch 568, [1965] 2 WLR 1, CA.

R (care orders: jurisdiction), Re [1995] 1 FLR 711.

Applications

The local authority applied for care and supervision orders in respect of a child, T, who had been habitually resident in Scotland but was staying with his parents in England, in respect of whom an emergency protection order and interim care orders had been made in England. The local authority had been granted approval for T to live in Scotland with his grandparents. The question arose as to the jurisdiction of the court to make orders in such circumstances. The applications were heard and judgment was given in chambers. The case is reported by permission of Hale J. The facts are set out in the judgment.

Martin Blount (instructed by *Alan Belshire & Co*, Bournemouth) for the local authority.

John Ker-Reid (instructed by *David Hurley Associates*, Bournemouth) for the mother.

Gordon Bebb (instructed by *Cyril Clark & Son*, Bournemouth) for the father.

Heather Pope (instructed by *Turners*, Bournemouth) for the guardian ad litem.

Cur adv vult

6 November 1996. The following judgment was delivered.

HALE J. This case raises an important question as to the basis or bases upon which the courts in England and Wales have jurisdiction to entertain applications for care supervision and emergency protection orders under Pts IV and V of the Children Act 1989. Somewhat surprisingly, in view of its importance and the frequency with which children travel across national boundaries these days, there is, so far as the parties are aware, only one reported case which is directly concerned with jurisdiction in care cases under the 1989 Act, the decision of Singer J in *Re R (care orders: jurisdiction)* [1995] 1 FLR 711. That case, however, concerned jurisdiction as between England and Wales and countries outside the United Kingdom. This case concerns the possibly more common question of jurisdiction as between England and Wales and another part of the United Kingdom.

It arises in this way. T was born on 28 September 1993 in Scotland to unmarried parents, who were undoubtedly habitually resident there at the time. However on 6 November 1995, and in something of an emergency, they came south to Bournemouth. There is a dispute between the parties as to how long the mother intended to stay here, and therefore whether she remained habitually resident in Scotland, or whether she became habitually resident in England, or whether she had abandoned her habitual residence in Scotland but not yet

a   acquired one in England. For the sake of this judgment, however, I am prepared
to assume that she retained her habitual residence in Scotland. If she did so, then
T did so too.

Very shortly after their arrival in Bournemouth the social services department
were contacted about concerns for T's welfare. On 21 November the police child
protection unit contacted the social services department following complaints
b   that the father had assaulted T. T was medically examined the next day and
bruising noted. On 24 November the police took him into police protection and
on 27 November an emergency protection order was made in the local family
proceedings court. On 28 November the local authority applied for a care order
and on 12 December (after a contested hearing) an interim care order was made.
Subsequent orders have been made without opposition in the usual way. The
c   case has now been transferred to the High Court.

Both parents subsequently returned to Scotland. The father is currently in
prison, due to be released in 1997. The mother is living in the home in which they
all lived before coming to England. In March 1996 the local authority were
granted approval, under para 19 of Sch 2 to the Children Act 1989, to arrange for
d   T to live in Scotland with his paternal grandparents. The care plan was that he
should live with them and have contact with his parents; but, for a variety of
reasons, including the mother's drug addiction, 'it is not felt that there is a stable
and safe environment whereby we could consider a rehabilitation plan for T to
return living with his mother or father at this time'. That, as I understand it, is
still the plan and is accepted by all parties. It remains to be decided whether that
e   plan can and should be the subject of orders made in the English courts.

If these were private law proceedings under the Children Act 1989, whether
between the parents themselves or the parents and grandparents, jurisdiction
would be governed by Pt I of the Family Law Act 1986. The orders to which Pt I
applies are defined in s 1. Section 1(1)(a) refers to 'a section 8 order made by a
f   court in England and Wales under the Children Act 1989, other than an order
varying or discharging such an order'. By virtue of s 2(2), a court in England and
Wales does not have jurisdiction to make such an order unless the condition in
s 3 is satisfied. The condition laid down in s 3(1) is that on the relevant date the
child concerned '(a) is habitually resident in England and Wales, or (b) is present
in England and Wales and is not habitually resident in any part of the United
g   Kingdom or a specified dependent territory'. Section 7(c) defines the relevant
date as either the date of the application, or, if there is no application, the date on
which the court is considering whether to make the order.

Hence, if T was still habitually resident in Scotland in November 1995, then,
even though he was present in England at the time, the family proceedings court
h   would not have been able to make an order under s 8 of the Children Act relating
to him. The only private law orders available in England and Wales would have
been those referred to in s 1(1)(d) of the 1986 Act:

j   'an order made by a court in England and Wales in the exercise of the
inherent jurisdiction of the High Court with respect to children—(i) so far as
it gives care of a child to any person or provides for contact with, or the
education of, a child; but (ii) excluding an order varying or revoking such an
order ...'

Section 2(3)(b) provides an additional basis of jurisdiction to make such orders,
that—

'the child concerned is present in England and Wales on the relevant date and the court considers that the immediate exercise of its powers is necessary for his protection.'

It is, however, common ground that the 1986 Act does not apply to public law proceedings under Pts IV or V of the 1989 Act. This is clear from the provisions of the Act itself. Different drafting techniques have been employed in defining the orders covered in each part of the United Kingdom. As already seen, in relation to England and Wales, this is done in s 1(1)(a) and (d) (referred to above) by defining the precise orders covered. A similar technique is employed in s 1(1)(c) and (e) in relation to Northern Ireland. In relation to Scotland, it is done in s 1(1)(b) by referring to any orders 'with respect to the custody, care or control of a child, access to a child or the education or upbringing of a child' but then excluding a variety of orders which might otherwise fall within this definition, including orders made in the equivalent of care proceedings, under Pts II and III of the Social Work (Scotland) Act 1968.

The exclusion of public law proceedings was clearly intended. Part I of the 1986 Act stems directly from a joint report of the English and Scottish Law Commissions, *Custody of Children—Jurisdiction and Enforcement within the United Kingdom* (Cmnd 9419 (1985)). Paragraph 1.28 of the report explains that public law orders are excluded for the reasons given in paras 3.4 to 3.6; the main reasons given in para 3.5 are that orders conferring responsibilities upon public authorities are 'different in kind' from custody proceedings; and that 'the structure of existing child care law, including the jurisdictional rules and enforcement machinery, differs substantially from the structure of the law applying in custody proceedings, and could not easily be assimilated even if that course were to prove on further examination to be desirable'. It is worth bearing in mind that there was not the same need to introduce a scheme for reciprocal enforcement in care cases as machinery already existed, and still exists, for the recovery of children in care (or its equivalent) who are taken from one part of the United Kingdom to another (see, for example, s 50(13) of the 1989 Act). Lastly, the whole object of the 1986 Act scheme, as explained in para 1.9 of the report, is to provide for the different systems of law in the United Kingdom 'to accept common rules of custody jurisdiction and mutually to recognise and enforce custody orders made in accordance with those rules'. As reciprocity of recognition and enforcement was the main objective, it would be nonsense if public law orders were covered in one country but not in another.

But if the 1986 Act does not apply, what does? In *Re R (care orders: jurisdiction)* [1995] 1 FLR 711 the child was undoubtedly present in England and Wales when care proceedings were begun; but she and her mother had come to this country some years before from Jamaica with only limited permission to stay; the mother was already subject to a deportation notice and the child was also at risk of deportation; there was therefore a question mark over whether the child was habitually resident here.

After pointing out (at 712) that the 1989 Act itself 'gives no direct clue' to the jurisdictional question and that the 1986 Act deals only with the private law, Singer J observes that 'there are many points of contact' between the private and the public law parts of the 1989 Act. This seems to him—

'to indicate strong policy reasons why the group of children in relation to whom local authorities can make application under Part IV should be no less

a   extensive than the group of children in relation to whom private individuals
    can make applications under s 8.' (See [1995] 1 FLR 711 at 713.)

Later on, after examining the provision relating to the choice of local authority to
be designated under a care order, and deciding that it does not assist directly, he
repeats the view that—

b   'there could be great practical disadvantages in a situation where a different
           basis of jurisdiction applied as between Part II and Part IV. It seems to me
           that the ability of local authorities to intervene and bring the court's
           attention to cases of children in need, allegedly so much in need as to require
           the authority of the court to be given to the local authority under a Part IV
c   order for their protection, is such that the widest possible approach should
           be adopted and in no way a restrictive approach chosen which might cause
           difficulties and lead to a frustration of the object of the Act, which is to
           provide the best solution to children's difficulties that concerned adults,
           courts and local authorities can provide.' (See [1995] 1 FLR 711 at 714.)

d   He concludes as follows (at 714):

           'I therefore take the view that the jurisdictional basis for an application
           under Part IV is effectively the same as that in relation to s 8 orders
           established by the Family Law Act 1986. I hold that for the court to have
           jurisdiction ... the child ... should be either habitually resident in England
e   and Wales, which I take to mean the same as "ordinarily resident in England
           and Wales" or that that child should be present in England and Wales at the
           relevant time, which it seems to me is the time when the application to the
           court is made.'

f   Accordingly, as the child in question was undoubtedly present when the
    application was made, he held that there was jurisdiction to entertain the
    application.
        With that conclusion I respectfully entirely agree. But it is forcefully argued on
    behalf of both parents in this case that, by holding that jurisdiction in care cases
    was 'effectively the same' as that in private law cases, Singer J must have intended
g   to include within that, not only the two positive bases of jurisdiction which he
    mentioned, but also the exclusionary rule in s 3(1) of the 1986 Act relating to
    children who, although present here, are habitually resident elsewhere in the
    United Kingdom. He does, after all, refer to it earlier when paraphrasing the 1986
    Act provisions and so might be taken to have had it in his mind when reaching his
h   conclusion (see [1995] 1 FLR 711 at 713).
        I certainly do not read his judgment in that way. The ratio decidendi of the
    case is undoubtedly far more limited: that there is jurisdiction in public law cases
    in respect of children who are present here even if they are or may be habitually
    resident outside the United Kingdom. All his other observations are, strictly,
j   obiter dicta, even including the holding that there is an alternative basis of
    jurisdiction over children who are habitually resident here. But the whole tenor
    of his reasoning is in favour of there being as wide a jurisdiction as possible to
    protect children from harm, a jurisdiction at least as extensive as that in private
    law cases. He does not address himself to the implications which would flow
    from importing the whole of the Family Law Act scheme into public law cases,
    for the very good reason that it did not arise in his case.

Bearing in mind the complexity of the issues which had to be resolved before
the enactment of the Family Law Act scheme in private law cases and the length
of time it took to resolve them, it would be surprising indeed if a judge hearing a
quite different case were taken to have meant to incorporate it wholesale into
that quite different context. There is no discussion, for example, of the
implications in public law of the primacy given by ss 2(1), 2(2), 2A and 3(2) of the
1986 Act to the courts having jurisdiction over matrimonial proceedings between
the parties. Hence I cannot read the decision or observations in Re R [1995] 1 FLR
711 as any authority, persuasive or otherwise, for the proposition being advanced
on behalf of the parents in this case.

It is authority, albeit only persuasive upon me, for the proposition that
jurisdiction in care cases can be founded on the child's presence here. With that
proposition I also entirely agree. As Singer J pointed out, local authorities must
be able to draw to the court's attention children whom they believe to be in need
of its protection. If they have reason to believe that a child in their area is
suffering or is likely to suffer significant harm unless action is taken to protect
him, they should be free to seek that protection without having to consider
complicated issues of where the child may be habitually resident at the time.

Furthermore, although there is no other authority on jurisdiction under Pts IV
and V of the 1989 Act, some guidance may be obtained from the law governing
the proceedings which they were designed to replace. These were principally
care proceedings under s 1 of the Children and Young Persons Act 1969. I know
of no reported case dealing expressly with the question of jurisdiction under that
Act, but there was a clear indication within the statute itself. Section 1(1)
provided: 'Any local authority, constable or authorised person who reasonably
believes that there are grounds for making an order under this section in respect
of a child or young person may ... bring him before a juvenile court.' This
obviously envisaged that the child should be physically brought before the court.
Provision was made in s 2(9) to exempt children under five from this requirement
in certain circumstances. This is but one indication that jurisdiction under that
statute was assumed on the ground of the child's presence.

If the child had to be brought before the court, it is difficult to see how
jurisdiction under the 1969 Act could be assumed on the basis of habitual
residence. Sections 25 and 26 of that Act, together with s 75 of the Social Work
(Scotland) Act 1968, made provision to enable the transfer of children admitted
to care in one part of the United Kingdom to the equivalent in another part if it
appeared that his parent or guardian 'resides or will reside' there. (Similar
provision is now made under s 101 of the Children Act 1989 and s 33 of the
Children (Scotland) Act 1995, when it comes into force.) This again is a clear
indication that jurisdiction was assumed on the basis of presence, but that the
child could then be sent to the country where his parents lived, no doubt so that
he could be near them.

However, the public law provisions of the 1989 Act do not depend upon
bringing the child before the court, so that there is now room for jurisdiction to
be assumed on an another basis as well as presence. The 1989 Act was intended,
as Butler-Sloss LJ observed in Re B and anor (minors) (termination of contact:
paramount consideration) [1993] 3 All ER 524 at 531, [1993] Fam 301 at 310, 'to
incorporate the best of the wardship jurisdiction within the statutory
framework'. The leading modern case on jurisdiction in wardship is Re P (G E)
(an infant) [1964] 3 All ER 977, [1965] Ch 568. At that stage, as Lord Denning MR
explains, it was quite clear on the authorities that the Court of Chancery had

jurisdiction over children who were British subjects even though they were out of the country; it was also clear that there was jurisdiction over a child who was physically present here (see [1964] 3 All ER 977 at 980, [1965] Ch 568 at 582); but the child in question was not a British subject and had been removed to Israel by his father. The Court of Appeal unanimously held that jurisdiction could be assumed on the basis of ordinary residence. This might give some indication that it is open to the courts in England and Wales to base their jurisdiction in care cases on the child's ordinary or habitual residence here even if he is not physically present at the time of the first application.

However, it is not necessary for me to decide that point for the purpose of this case, any more than it was necessary for Singer J to do so in *Re R (care orders: jurisdiction)* [1995] 1 FLR 711. There may be other authority and arguments to the contrary which have not been drawn to our attention. But there is certainly no authority drawn to my attention to suggest that before the 1989 Act the courts here would hold that they were unable to exercise their powers to protect children from harm simply because the child was habitually resident elsewhere, whether abroad or in another part of the United Kingdom.

What difference could the 1989 Act have made to that? There is one highly significant difference between that Act and its predecessors. Before the 1989 Act was passed, it was possible in exceptional circumstances for the courts hearing private law applications either to commit the child to care or to make a supervision order. It was not possible for the courts hearing care proceedings to make what were then custody orders instead. Under the 1989 Act, the full range of private law orders is available, as an alternative to a care order, in every case. Hence it is strongly argued on behalf of the parents in this case that it would be absurd if the court hearing an application for a care order had jurisdiction to make the care order but did not, because of the provisions of the 1986 Act, have jurisdiction to make a residence order instead. The court would thereby be deprived of the full range of powers enabling it to give effect to the paramount consideration of the child's welfare .

It is, of course, sometimes the case that the court hearing a care case considers that it will be better for the child to order that he lives with a particular individual. However, if the court is unable to make such an order because the child is habitually resident in Scotland, there are several courses available. The local authority may be willing to place the child with that individual in any event or pending an application to the court which does have jurisdiction. If that individual lives outside England and Wales, the local authority may be given approval to send the child to live with them, as happened in this case. If the local authority do not share the court's view as to what will be best for the child, the case may be transferred to the High Court for the High Court to exercise the jurisdiction conferred upon it by s 2(3) of the 1986 Act.

The inconvenience which these courses would involve is, in my view, nothing like as great as the inconvenience which would be caused if local authorities and courts here were inhibited in using their powers to protect children by jurisdictional rules which are not only extremely complex but may also require complicated issues of fact to be determined first.

It might be suggested that the local authority would have the option of seeking to persuade the High Court to employ its emergency jurisdiction under s 2(3) of the 1986 Act. As a sidenote I should point out that if this is to be seriously considered as a solution to the problem, the orders encompassed by s 1(1)(d) of the 1986 Act (set out above) would have to include orders providing for the child

to be cared for by a local authority. This is quite contrary to the interpretation
put upon that provision (again obiter) by Singer J in *Re R* [1995] 1 FLR 711 at 712,   *a*
when he said: '"Person" in this context, it seems clear to me, means a human
individual rather than a corporation such as a local authority …' Counsel for the
parents, it seems to me, are seeking to have me read into Singer J's judgment that
which he did not say while ignoring that which he undoubtedly did say.

But in any event this solution will not work. In order to persuade the High   *b*
Court to exercise its inherent jurisdiction, the authority would have first to seek
leave under s 100(3) of the 1989 Act. More importantly, they would also have to
think up some alternative way of providing for the child, because s 100(2) of the
1989 Act states in clear terms that no court shall exercise the inherent jurisdiction
of the High Court so as to require a child to be placed in the care of a local
authority or to be accommodated by or on behalf of a local authority. There is   *c*
therefore nothing that the local authority could effectively do to provide for a
child who might be at very serious risk indeed.

I conclude, therefore, that there is nothing in either the 1986 Act or the 1989
Act to cast doubt on the proposition that the courts in England and Wales have
jurisdiction to make orders under Pt IV of the 1989 Act in relation to children   *d*
who are present here, irrespective of whether or not they are habitually resident
either abroad or in another part of the United Kingdom. What applies to Pt IV
must apply a fortiori to the measures of emergency protection contained in Pt V.
I hold, therefore, that T's presence here at the date of the applications was
sufficient to give the court jurisdiction to make the emergency protection and
interim care orders made so far and to continue to entertain the application for a   *e*
care order. It is accordingly unnecessary for me to determine whether or not he
was still habitually resident in Scotland in November 1995.

But even if the court has jurisdiction, it has been urged upon me that this is not
the convenient forum for the case to be decided. It is said that T is now living in
Scotland with his grandparents, his father is in prison until next year, and his   *f*
mother is content for things to remain as they are, so that there is no need for any
proceedings at all. If there is a need, the reporter can bring the case before the
children's hearing under the Social Work (Scotland) Act 1968 (or the Children
(Scotland) Act 1995 once the replacement provisions come into force).
Alternatively the grandparents could apply for the Scottish equivalent of a
residence order, presumably under s 11 of the Children (Scotland) Act 1995,   *g*
which came into force on 1 November 1996. This, it is said, would be much more
convenient than proceedings in England, as all the relevant parties are now living
in Scotland.

That submission has some attraction. But it also has serious drawbacks. The
guardian ad litem in the English proceedings is quite clear that an order is needed   *h*
for T's protection. Who can say whether the mother might change her mind or
what will happen when the father comes out of prison? The grandparents are
more than willing to look after T by arrangement with the local authority but
they do not wish to set themselves up in opposition to their son. They would not
want to bring proceedings in Scotland. The local authority have been in touch   *j*
with the relevant social work department in Scotland. I am told that the social
worker there has discussed it with the reporter, who has drafted grounds for
referral to the children's hearing but takes the view that it would be better for the
care case to be tried in England. This is because the evidence which would be
needed to establish the threshold criteria for a care order in English law, or the
grounds for referral in Scottish law, is mainly available here: the incident which

a led to the proceedings took place here, as did the events which are alleged to have led to the mother's two older children from an earlier relationship going to live with their father. The views of the Scottish authorities in this case must carry great weight with the court. Where there is concurrent jurisdiction to protect children, it is to be hoped that the authorities in each country would try to act in harmony rather b than in competition with one another. Moreover, the situation which arises in this case is quite different from that in many cases where the courts in two countries may have jurisdiction. Usually, the parties before the court in this country are the same as the parties who are or would be before the foreign court. If the case does not proceed here it can proceed there. In this case, the applicant local authority and the guardian ad litem could not bring proceedings in Scotland c and the parents would have no reason at all to do so. This makes it all the more important for the courts in this country to retain jurisdiction at least until the courts (in which concept I include the children's hearing) in Scotland decide to assume it. Hence unless and until a conflict arises between the courts (or other judicial authorities) here and in Scotland which the court is asked to resolve, I d hold that the English courts have and should retain jurisdiction in T's case.

Orders accordingly.

Carolyn Toulmin   Barrister.

G v G (periodical payments)

a

COURT OF APPEAL, CIVIL DIVISION

WARD AND POTTER LJJ

18, 30 JULY 1996

b

Divorce – Financial provision – Variation of order – Jurisdiction – Periodical payments order to continue until happening of certain events or until further order – Whether court having jurisdiction to vary order after happening of events – Matrimonial Causes Act 1973, ss 23(1), 31.

c

The husband and wife married in 1968 and had a son and daughter. In 1989, following the dissolution of the marriage, the court by consent ordered the husband under s 23(1)[a] of the Matrimonial Causes Act 1973 to pay the wife periodical payments of £14,000 pa until the wife remarried, cohabited for six months or until the daughter attained the age of 18, whichever occurred sooner, 'or until further order'. The order did not expressly provide that it should d automatically stand dismissed on the occurrence of the events specified, nor was it expressed to be subject to a direction under s 28(1A)[b] of the 1973 Act, the effect of which was to bar any application to extend the order. In December 1994, one month after the daughter had turned 18, the wife applied to the court to vary the periodical payments order by extending the payments to herself and for separate e payments to the daughter while she remained in full-time education. The district judge varied the order for payments to the wife, but dismissed the claim for payments to the daughter. The husband appealed, contending that the court did not in the circumstances have jurisdiction to vary or extend the order under s 31 of the 1973 Act, and the wife cross-appealed seeking more generous payments to herself, for those to be backdated, and for payments to the daughter. The judge f allowed the husband's appeal on his undertaking to pay the daughter £270 per month until she ceased full-time education; he also dismissed the wife's cross-appeal, but ordered the husband to pay her periodical payments for the benefit of the daughter. The wife appealed to the Court of Appeal. The husband cross-appealed, contending, inter alia, that s 23(1)(d) of the 1973 Act only g permitted the making of one order for payments to or for the benefit of a child, so that the undertaking he had been required to give by the judge could not stand with an order for payments to the wife for the benefit of the daughter.

Held – (1) Where the term of a periodical payments order was expressed to h expire on the happening of certain events the order ceased to have effect once those events had occurred and there was no longer any order capable of variation under s 31 of the 1973 Act. The inclusion of the words 'or until further order' in the order did not serve to continue the order's existence after the happening of the specified events such that it was capable of resuscitation by an application to vary at any time, but meant merely 'until further order in the meantime'. It j followed that the court did not have jurisdiction to vary the original order after the daughter had attained the age of 18. The wife's appeal would accordingly be

---

a   Section 23(1), so far as material, is set out at p 279 *d e*, post
b   Section 28(1A), so far as material, is set out at p 280 *a*, post

a dismissed (see p 280 *c d*, p 282 *j*, p 283 *j* to p 284 *c* and p 286 *c e*, post); *Minton v Minton* [1979] 1 All ER 79 and *T v T (financial provision)* [1988] 1 FLR 480 followed; *Jessel v Jessel* [1979] 3 All ER 645 not followed.

(2) Under s 23(1) of the 1973 Act the court had power to make an order for periodical payments to a child and to a parent for the benefit of the child, since the section provided that the court could make 'any one or more' of the orders specified, and those words were wide enough to mean not only the orders
b provided for in each paragraph, but any one or more orders within a paragraph. The cross-appeal would accordingly be dismissed (see p 284 *g h* and p 286 *c e*, post).

Notes
c For periodical payments orders on divorce and variation of such orders, see 13 *Halsbury's Laws* (4th edn) paras 1076–1095, 1168.

For the Matrimonial Causes Act 1973, ss 23, 31, see 27 *Halsbury's Statutes* (4th edn) (1992 reissue) 757, 776.

d **Cases referred to in judgments**
Bennett v Bennett (1934) 103 LJP 38.
Dipper v Dipper [1980] 2 All ER 722, [1981] Fam 31, [1980] 3 WLR 626, CA.
Hall v Hall [1915] P 105, CA.
Jessel v Jessel [1979] 3 All ER 645, [1979] 1 WLR 1148, CA.
L v L [1961] 3 All ER 834, [1962] P 101, [1961] 3 WLR 1182, CA.
e *Minton v Minton* [1979] 1 All ER 79, [1979] AC 593, [1979] 2 WLR 31, HL.
Richardson v Richardson [1993] 4 All ER 673, [1994] 1 WLR 186.
T v T (financial provision) [1988] 1 FLR 480.
Thompson v Thompson [1985] 2 All ER 243, [1986] Fam 38, [1985] 3 WLR 17, CA.
Turk v Turk, Dufty v Dufty [1931] P 116, [1931] All ER Rep 505.

f **Cases also cited or referred to in skeleton arguments**
A v A (a minor) (financial provision) [1994] 1 FLR 657.
Blease, Ex p, re Blinkhorn (1884) 14 QBD 123, DC.
Elgindata Ltd, Re (No 2) [1993] 1 All ER 232, [1992] 1 WLR 1207, CA.
G v G [1985] 2 All ER 225, [1985] 1 WLR 647, HL.
g *Gojkovic v Gojkovic (No 2)* [1992] 1 All ER 267, [1992] Fam 40, CA.
Gupta v Klito (1989) Times, 23 November, [1989] CA Transcript 1063.
Haroutunian v Jennings [1980] FLR 62, DC.
Lipkin Gorman (a firm) v Karpnale Ltd [1992] 4 All ER 331, [1989] 1 WLR 1340, CA;
  rvsd in part [1992] 4 All ER 512, [1991] 2 AC 548, HL.
h *Shead, Ex p, re Mundy* (1885) 15 QBD 338, CA.
Speight, Re, ex p Brooks (1884) 13 QBD 42.

Appeal and cross-appeal
By notice dated 28 March 1996 the wife appealed with leave from the order of
j Hale J made on 29 February 1996 dismissing her application to vary an order for periodical payments by the husband, which had been granted by District Judge Cushing on 7 November 1995. The husband cross-appealed against the judge's order requiring him to give an undertaking to make periodical payments to the daughter of the marriage while she was in full-time education. The facts are set out in the judgment of Ward LJ.

Maureen Mullally and *Seamus Kearney* (instructed by *Barrett & Thomson*, Slough) for the wife.

Mark Evans QC and *Fiona Elder* (instructed by *Allan Janes*, High Wycombe) for the husband.

Cur adv vult

30 July 1996. The following judgments were delivered.

WARD LJ. To enable periodical payments to be made only for such term as would be sufficient to allow the recipient to adjust without undue hardship to the termination of her financial dependence on the other party is a worthy purpose of a matrimonial law which strives to enhance self-respect and self-sufficiency after divorce. 'Look on the bright side' is an essential rubric for the good divorce lawyer, but not at the expense of looking out for potential lethal traps inherent in orders for a limited term of periodical payments. This unfortunate case signposts certain pitfalls of which the profession should make itself aware.

Even though the marriage of the petitioner and the respondent has long been dissolved, I shall for the sake of convenience still refer to the parties merely as husband and wife. They married in 1968. The wife practised her profession as a speech therapist until Jonathan was born in 1974. Camilla was born on 14 November 1976. In 1982 the wife began part-time employment as an elocution, speech and drama teacher and, although she did see some children with remedial problems, she was not in clinical practice. That work ceased in 1987. For his part, the husband had improved himself steadily throughout the marriage. There were periods when he undertook training or retraining partly sponsored by his employers but partly maintained by the wife's efforts. The family were dislocated from time to time in the course of the husband's employment. He was made redundant in 1987 and departed to America in December 1987 to make a new career for himself. In that he was successful. In July 1988 the wife returned to work, this time with estate agents, and she was so employed when, on 17 October 1989, the claims for ancillary relief were disposed of by order made by consent. The agreed arrangement effected a deferred clean break. The material elements of it were that the wife was to have conveyed to her the matrimonial home free of mortgage together with the collateral insurance policies that secured the charge. He paid her a modest lump sum of £5,000. He undertook to provide private health insurance for the petitioner and the children. He was to pay each of the children £2,500 pa 'until such children shall attain the age of 18 years or cease full-time education whichever shall be the later or until further order'. The order for periodical payments for the petitioner was expressed in these terms:

'The respondent do pay or cause to be paid to the Petitioner as from the First day of July 1988 periodical payments at the rate of £14,000 per annum payable monthly in advance until the Petitioner shall re-marry, cohabit with a man for a period of six months or periods totalling six months, or until the child of the family [Camilla] shall attain the age 18 years whichever shall be due sooner or until further Order.'

The order further provided that 'claims against each other of a capital nature do stand dismissed'.

a The first pitfall to which I draw attention is whether or not it was truly appropriate to limit the petitioner's entitlement to periodical payments for five years, or at all. That question has not been before us but the level of sympathy, if any, which may be felt for the wife is none the less shaped by its answer. This was, very broadly, a 20-year marriage with the wife making the fullest contribution. At the time of the order each of the parties was 43 years old. The

b wife had shown her willingness to work. I have little doubt she wished to assert her independence. I have little doubt she was more than willing to be financially, as well as emotionally, free of her husband. The question remains, however, whether or not it was ever appropriate in 1989 to say with confidence and with certainty that she could achieve the goal of independence in five years, or at all. At the time of the order Jonathan was 15 and Camilla nearly 13. They could be

c expected to live full and busy lives. Many demands were yet to be made on the time of their mother. She had not practised her profession for 15 years. She had sacrificed it for the sake of the family. She had probably forever been condemned to a weaker financial position than the bread-winning husband. If it was possible to re-enter her profession, it needed retraining, time out, and money. She could

d not, on her earnings as a receptionist, maintain herself to a standard appropriate to that which she had enjoyed. She had high hopes and, I dare say, dogged determination to succeed. I venture to think, however, that no one then looking into the crystal ball of her life would confidently have predicted any certainty of achievement of those laudable aspirations. Those agreeing and those making these term orders have a duty pursuant to s 25(2) of the Matrimonial Causes Act

e 1973 to consider whether the payee can adjust without undue hardship to the termination of dependence on the payer. Events have proved this wife is not able to do so. Whether or not that ought to have been apparent in 1989 may be open to question but I am not in a position to answer it.

Another pitfall relates to the drafting of the periodical payments order. Firstly,

f it did not provide, as the Solicitors' Family Law Association precedents prudently provide, for the order to stand dismissed upon the happening of the event. Whether or not it was strictly necessary so to provide is perhaps doubtful for reasons I shall give shortly. However, inclusion of such a term would have made this appeal impossible to argue on the wife's behalf. Secondly, it did not provide whether or not the parties intended s 28(1A) of the 1973 Act to apply. That

g provides:

'Where a periodical payments ... order in favour of a party to a marriage is made on or after the grant of a decree of divorce ... the court may direct that that party shall not be entitled to apply under section 31 below for the

h extension of the term specified in the order.'

Thorpe J explained the importance of the point in *Richardson v Richardson* [1993] 4 All ER 673 at 682, [1994] 1 WLR 186 at 194–195:

j 'In my experience it is generally understood, certainly among the specialist Bar in London, that if the respondent has won in negotiation the exclusion of the applicant's right to apply within the agreed term for its extension then a s 28(1A) direction must be included in the consent order. By contrast, if the applicant has preserved in negotiation her right to apply for an extension, that right does not have to be expressed in the order. It is sufficient to ensure that the s 28(1A) direction is not included.'

As I understand the husband's case, he was under the impression that the former position prevailed; yet there was no s 28(1A) direction.

When Jonathan reached 18, payments to him ceased. I understand he did not immediately become independent. As Camilla's eighteenth birthday loomed, the petitioner became anxious about her future. Her casual employment at the estate agents had been brought to end, and she began to work for a network marketing company selling jewellery but with little expectation of earning more than a couple of thousand pounds per annum. In May 1994 the husband put the wife on notice that he was not prepared to support her beyond November 1994. She apparently called upon him to continue the payments under the order. She instructed solicitors and I do not know what, if any, advice they then gave her. She could not afford them in any event. Camilla reached adulthood on 14 November 1994. No more money was forthcoming from the husband. On 1 December 1994 the wife applied 'to vary the maintenance paid to Camilla who is still in full time education' and 'to extend maintenance paid to myself for the time my daughter is still in full time education or I remarry or cohabit for a period of six months'.

That was resisted. There were affidavits, questionnaires, bundles over 1,000 pages long, interim orders and finally on 7 November 1995 a hearing before District Judge Cushing, who varied the order so that the husband was to pay the wife £17,000 p a from 1 November 1995 to 31 July 1996, just under £12,000 p a for the following year, reducing to £7,248 to 31 July 1998 and thereafter nominal payments of 5p p a during their joint lives or until she should remarry, cohabit for six months or further order. The claim for periodical payments for Camilla was dismissed.

That order pleased neither party. The husband appealed originally only against the imposition of the nominal order which, of course, had the intended effect of keeping her claims alive. She wished for more generous provision to be made for her and for it to be backdated. She wished an order for Camilla to be maintained. Two days before the hearing fixed before the High Court judge to hear that appeal, the husband gave notice of his intention to seek to amend his appeal in order to raise, for the first time, whether or not the court had any jurisdiction to make any order in the wife's favour.

That appeal was heard by Hale J. In her judgment of 29 February 1996 she said:

'The wife's application to vary the original order was made on 14 December 1994, one month after Camilla had reached her eighteenth birthday and, according to the husband, his liability under the 1989 order had come to an end. This is an extremely unattractive argument because of its apparent technicality, a technicality which must be mystifying to a person in the wife's position who was at the time acting in person. The technicality was not raised at any time in the course of these proceedings, specifically not in July 1995 when the husband agreed to an interim order or in November 1995 when District Judge Cushing made the order under appeal. It was first raised on Monday of this week. Furthermore, the wife's application was made only one month after the previous term had expired and the wife had drawn the problem to the attention of the husband's solicitors in August 1994. Thus, he was not taken by surprise. Counsel on behalf of the husband [not Mr Evans QC who now appears for him] disarmingly says that he did not raise the point in the court below because he did not think as much of it then as he does now. He confesses that he does not consider that the a position which has been reached on the authorities is right in principle. But of course any view of the justice of the individual case or of the merits of the existing law in policy terms cannot affect me if I am bound by statute and authority to hold that I have no jurisdiction, and that the district judge had no jurisdiction to make the order under appeal.'

I agree with all of those sentiments. The judge duly and properly examined the
b law, in particular *T v T (financial provision)* [1988] 1 FLR 480, a decision of Butler-Sloss J. Hale J felt obliged to accede to the husband's application. She said:

'I therefore reach the conclusion that I cannot distinguish *T v T* from this case or bring myself to disagree with it. It does seem particularly hard on the facts of this particular case, in view of the circumstances in which the point
c was raised and in view of the husband's acknowledgment, that some extension to the order is indeed justified on the particular circumstances of this case. One has, however, to acknowledge that hard cases make bad law. Once applications became possible outside the time limit, it would be impossible to distinguish which should go ahead and which should not. The
d variation exercise under s 31 is a quite different exercise from the full financial and property settlement which is made on or after the divorce and is governed by the principles in s 25 of the Act. Capital provision cannot be varied. Therefore, just as in some cases it may be unjust to take away continuing periodical payments when this cannot be compensated for by capital provision, similarly it may be unjust to continue periodical payments
e when one cannot take away concluded capital provision which has already been made. I reach that conclusion with considerable regret, and were any higher court to feel that it could reach a different conclusion, I for one would bear it with considerable fortitude.'

Again, I agree with every word. However, I regret that I feel unable to accept the
f invitation implicit in the final sentence quoted.

Hale J then dealt with Camilla and said:

'It is fairly clear that [the district judge] felt that in the circumstances where the wife was to continue to have some provision for her own needs, which provision would include the maintenance of the household, it was not
g appropriate for there to be any increase in the provision for Camilla. But the conclusion that I have reached in relation to the periodical payments for the wife clearly alters that situation drastically.'

Camilla had begun a university course, which would continue until 1999. The
h judge held, rightly, that she was entitled to be maintained at a level appropriate to a university student who was the child of someone in her parents' circumstances; and these include just as much the father's circumstances as those of her mother. Taking into account her grant, the father was paying her £3,500 directly, and proposed to continue to do so. The judge held, and again I agree, that that was quite insufficient to maintain her at the appropriate level given her
j particular circumstances and her special medical needs. The judge found:

'... she needs a home, she needs the use of a car, she needs feeding during vacations and the like. I see no reason why it should be assumed that Camilla should support herself from obtaining employment other than the sort of employment which might contribute towards her studies, her well-being and her growing up. Such employment would not necessarily be forthcoming and it would not necessarily earn her very much by way of an income.'

The judge then referred to the wife's very modest income as against 'well over £100,000 pa gross and at least £6,300 net per month' earned by the husband. She held:

> '... it seems to me that the financial contribution which [the wife] can be expected to make towards the maintenance of Camilla over the duration of Camilla's university course is simply the provision of the bricks and mortar, either in the existing matrimonial home or in any replacement home that could be provided; and that even that is expecting a lot because if there were no Camilla to provide for then the wife would be able to buy herself a small flat anywhere that appealed to her and that would release at least more capital for her to re-establish herself in the labour market. The husband, certainly in income terms, is a wealthy man and could reasonably be expected to meet his daughter's financial needs throughout her university course ... [He] can be expected to contribute the whole of the reasonable expenditure in keeping a home going for Camilla for the period of her university course.'

She then dealt with the assessment of the claims. She said:

> 'This is an extremely difficult sum to do because it is difficult to disentangle the various strands in the household expenditure. It is argued on behalf of the mother that the £14,000 provided for in the original order would be the appropriate figure for the rest of the university course. That seems to me to be too much because at least some of that must be attributable to the mother's own needs, quite apart from the needs of Jonathan, who cannot be included as yet in this equation because, although he does not have employment, he is not in education and does not otherwise have special needs which would justify a maintenance order for him. The husband offers, in effect, £10,000 for two years of Camilla's course and £5,000 thereafter until she ends her university career. To mind, there is no particular logic about a taper in this case. The case for providing a home for Camilla exists throughout her course. On any view the wife will not be able to earn very much during that period and on any view her contribution is made through the continuing provision of the bricks and mortar. On the other hand, the £10,000 would be perhaps a generous amount whereas the £5,000 would be too little. It is accepted by the husband that any sum should be backdated to Camilla's eighteenth birthday, giving of course credit for the sums which have already been paid. For the purpose of this calculation, I leave out altogether what is paid under the order for Camilla and the direct payments to Camilla which the father is now making. Doing the best I can, I consider that the sums offered by the husband are the appropriate ones to order with that degree of backdating.'

In the result the judge made an order which having recorded the husband's undertaking 'to continue to pay or cause to be paid periodical payments to [Camilla] until she shall cease full time education, at the rate of £270 per month', allowed the husband's appeal, dismissed the wife's cross-appeal in respect of her claim and made the staged periodical payments I have already recited. She also condemned the husband to pay the wife's costs on an indemnity basis.

a Once again there are cross-appeals by the wife against the dismissal of her claim for periodical payments and by the husband in respect of Camilla's order and in respect of costs.

Variation of a term of periodical payments

b Mrs Mullally submits that although the happening of the event of Camilla's birthday ended the husband's liability to pay under the order, the order itself, in the absence of provision for its dismissal, remained extant but in suspense pending the making of a further order which was itself an eventuality for which the order catered. Mr Evans QC for the husband submits that if the words 'or further order' have any meaning at all, they mean only 'until further order in the meantime' and that if application for variation is not made before the happening *c* of the last event, being Camilla's birthday, the order ceases to have effect and there is nothing left which is capable of being varied.

The statutory framework in the 1973 Act as amended by the Matrimonial and Family Proceedings Act 1984, is as follows:

d '... **23.** *Financial provision orders in connection with divorce proceedings, etc.*— (1) On granting a decree of divorce ... the court may make any one or more of the following orders, that is to say—(a) an order that either party to the marriage shall make to the other such periodical payments, *for such term*, as may be specified in that order ... (d) an order that a party to the marriage shall make to such person as may be specified in the order for the benefit of *e* a child of the family, or to such child, such periodical payments, for such term as may be so specified ...

(4) The power of the court ... to make an order in favour of a child of the family shall be exercisable from time to time ...

25A. *Exercise of court's powers in favour of a party to the marriage on decree of *f* divorce or a nullity of marriage.*—(1) Where ... the court decides to exercise its powers under section 23(1)(a) ... it shall be the duty of the court to consider whether it would be appropriate so to exercise those powers that the financial obligations of each party towards the other will be terminated as soon after the grant of the decree as the court considers just and reasonable.

(2) Where the court decides ... to make a periodical payments ... order ... *g* the court *shall* in particular consider whether it would be appropriate to require those payments to be made ... *only for such term* as would in the opinion of the court be *sufficient to enable the party* in whose favour the order is made *to adjust without undue hardship* to the termination of his or her financial dependence on the other party.

h (3) Where ... an application is made ... for a periodical payments ... order ... then, if the court considers that no continuing obligation should be imposed on either party to make or secure periodical payments in favour of the other, the court may dismiss the application with a direction that the applicant shall not be entitled to make any further application in relation to *j* that marriage for an order under section 23(1)(a) ... above ...

28. *Duration of continuing financial provision orders in favour of party to marriage, and effect of remarriage.*—(1) Subject ... to the provisions of sections 25A(2) above and 31(7) below, *the term* to be specified in a periodical payments ... order ... *shall be such term as the court thinks fit*, except that *the term shall not ... extend* beyond the following limits, that is to say—(a) in the case of a periodical payments order, the term ... shall be so defined as not to

extend beyond the death of either of the parties to the marriage or ... the
remarriage of the party in whose favour the order is made ...   *a*

(1A) ... the court may direct that the party shall not be entitled to apply
under section 31 below for the *extension of the term* specified in the order ...

31. *Variation, discharge, etc, of certain orders for financial relief.*—(1) Where
the court has made an order to which this section applies, then, subject to the
provisions of this section and section 28(1A) above, the court shall have   *b*
power to vary or to discharge the order or to suspend any provision thereof
temporarily and to revive the operation of any provision so suspended.

(2)   This section applies to the following orders that is to say ... (b) any
periodical payments order ...'

It is to be observed that whereas the power to make a periodical payments order   *c*
in respect of the child can be exercised from time to time, only one periodical
payments order can be made in favour of a party to the marriage. When the term
is defined by s 28(1)(a) not to extend beyond death of either spouse or remarriage,
then the order ceases on the happening of that event and cannot be revived. No
one would contest that proposition. There would, therefore, have to be very
good reason for giving different treatment to a term specified by the court so as,   *d*
in that case, to permit the kiss of life to be given to it after the obligations to pay
under it had ceased to have effect. To give consistent meaning to the Act, one
would be constrained to find there no longer is an order which is capable of
variation. On that view of the law, that is the end of this appeal.

A review of the authorities leads to the same conclusion. The leading case is   *e*
Minton v Minton [1979] 1 All ER 79, [1979] AC 593. There, the periodical payments
order was expressed to be 'at the rate of 5p per year until the matrimonial home
is conveyed to her, such payments to cease on completion of the conveyance'. It
was held that *L v L* [1961] 3 All ER 834, [1962] P 101 was correctly decided. There,
the wife had agreed to accept a lump sum in full satisfaction of her present and
future rights to maintenance and the order provided by consent that 'the   *f*
petitioner's application for maintenance be dismissed'. Lord Scarman said ([1979]
1 All ER 79 at 87–88, [1979] AC 593 at 608):

'Had Parliament, when re-enacting s 1 of the [Matrimonial Causes
(Property and Maintenance) Act 1958], wished to overrule *L v L*, it could have
added to sub-s (1) the words "from time to time". When Parliament wished   *g*
to make it clear that no previous dismissal of an application *or discharge or
termination of an order* could displace the court's power to make maintenance
orders in favour of children, it added, by sub-s (4), the words "from time to
time" to the words "at any time thereafter" which it had used in sub-s (1). No
plainer indication could be given of the intention of Parliament. For these   *h*
reasons I conclude that s 23(1) of the 1973 Act does not empower the court
to make a second or subsequent maintenance order after the earlier
application has been dismissed. Counsel for the wife, however, submits that
present is not a case of dismissal: an order was made which included
periodical payments and a property transfer order ... Thus he seeks to draw   *j*
a distinction between a dismissal and an order. I agree with him that on its
proper construction the consent order in this case is more than a dismissal.
It contains an express provision for a limited period of maintenance (the
nominal order until conveyance) and a provision for the transfer of the
home. The short answer to the point, however, is that upon the true
construction of s 23(1) the court does not have the jurisdiction. Once an

a application has been dealt with upon its merits, the court has no future jurisdiction save where there is a continuing order capable of variation or discharge under s 31 of the 1973 Act ... The court having made an order giving effect to a comprehensive settlement of all financial and property issues as between spouses, it would be a strange application of the principle of the clean break if, notwithstanding the order, the court could make a
b future order on a subsequent application made by the wife after the husband had complied with all his obligations ... I would not deny the court power, where it thinks just, to achieve finality as between spouses (children are a different matter) unless compelled to do so by clear enactment. Your Lordships are under no such compulsion; on the contrary, s 23(1) is perfectly clear: it permits the court to achieve finality, if it thinks it appropriate,
c practical and just.' (My emphasis.)

It should be observed that *Minton v Minton* does not narrowly refer only to cases where the claim for periodical payments was *dismissed*. The speech ranges much wider. In fact, the order there did not stand dismissed: it simply ceased. Lord Scarman therefore spoke of dismissal or discharge or termination as displacing
d the court's power. He referred to finality where the husband had complied with all his obligations. Thus it seems that a provision that on the happening of the specified event the periodical payments order should stand dismissed, as the Solicitors' Family Law Association recommend, is a counsel of caution rather than necessity.

e *Jessel v Jessel* [1979] 3 All ER 645, [1979] 1 WLR 1148 was a different case. There the periodical payments ran until the petitioner should remarry 'or until further order at the rate of £2,000 per annum less tax to be reduced to £1,200 less tax should the respondent cease to be a Member of Parliament'. Mrs Mullally relies heavily on a passage in the judgment of Lord Denning MR, where he says ([1979]
f 3 All ER 645 at 648, [1979] 1 WLR 1148 at 1153):

'Those words "or until further order" are of much importance. There are many cases to show this. I need not go through them all. I will just mention their names: *Hall v Hall* [1915] P 105, *Turk v Turk* [1931] P 116, [1931] All ER Rep 505 and *Bennett v Bennett* (1934) 103 LJP 38. It is plain as can be that the
g words "or until further order" keep the position alive so that an application can be made at any time for a further order to vary the periodical payments upwards or downwards as the situation changes in regard to them.'

Browne LJ also said ([1979] 3 All ER 645 at 649, [1979] 1 WLR 1148 at 1155):

h 'I entirely agree with Lord Denning MR that this not a genuinely final order, or a once and for all order. It provided for continuing periodical payments to continue indefinitely unless certain events happened, one of which was until further order.'

j Mrs Mullally relies upon those words as support for the submission that a further order is itself a further event contemplated by the order until the happening of which the order continues in effect. Mr Evans has, however, taken us to the authorities to which Lord Denning MR referred. These show that the power to vary given by s 190(2) of the Supreme Court of Judicature (Consolidation) Act 1925 was limited in that the court was able to order in addition to or instead of the amounts ordered such sum as was reasonable, provided only that the

husband's means had either decreased or increased, but not for any other reason.
In *Bennett v Bennett* (1934) 103 LJP 38 at 40 Merriman P held:

'Consideration of the matter, as dealt with so far in HALL *v.* HALL and TURK *v.* TURK; DUFTY *v.* DUFTY, have left me in no doubt whatever that it is now the practice of the Court, founded on authority, to regard the introduction of the words "until further order" in the original order made for maintenance as enabling the Court, when the matter comes up for review, to have regard to all the statutory factors available for consideration in the first instance, and in my view the whole point of the decision in TURK *v.* TURK; DUFTY *v.* DUFTY is that where those words are inserted the Court is not limited in its jurisdiction—to withhold such review—by the proviso in section 190, sub-section 2. I am not in this judgment to be taken as expressing any doubt on what I understand to be the decision in TURK *v.* TURK; DUFTY *v.* DUFTY— that in order to found the jurisdiction to review where the words "until further order" appear in the original order it is not necessary to find that the husband's means have diminished. Jurisdiction can be founded on any of the statutory grounds on which the original order could be made.'

If that was the original purpose of the words 'until further order', they are now superfluous because the purpose sought to be attained by them is plainly achieved by the wide words of s 31 which require the court to have regard to the whole range of circumstances of the case including any changes in any of the matters to which the court was required to have regard under s 25 when making the order to which the application relates.

Before the passage of the 1984 Act, it had been established in *Dipper v Dipper* [1980] 2 All ER 722, [1981] Fam 31 that claims could not be dismissed without consent. In that case Ormrod LJ said:

'There are essentially four ways of dealing with applications for periodical payments: first, to make a substantive order; secondly, to make a nominal order, the purpose of which is to enable the party obtaining it to take advantage of the variation section without undue difficulty; the third alternative is to adjourn the application generally if the court does not wish to make any order at that time; the fourth is to dismiss the application, provided the consent of the applicant is forthcoming.' (See [1980] 2 All ER 722 at 732, [1981] Fam 31 at 47.)

In *Thompson v Thompson* [1985] 2 All ER 243, [1986] Fam 38 a property adjustment order was made whereby the property was to held on trust for sale but not to be sold until a specified event 'or further order'. It was held that the court had jurisdiction to entertain an application for a sale before the prescribed event provided the object was to give effect to the spirit and construction of the original order, there being no power to vary to produce a different substantive result from that originally contemplated. Oliver LJ said ([1985] 2 All ER 243 at 249, [1986] Fam 38 at 47):

'The words "further order" are, in my judgment, unless there is some clear context to the contract, to be construed as "further order in the mean time", and the longhand version of the order in the instant case would postpone the sale "until (a) the youngest child of the family ... reaches the age of seventeen years or finishes further education (whichever is the later) or (b) such earlier

a date as may be specified in any order made before the expiry of the period
referred to in (a) above".'

Those words were adopted by Butler-Sloss J as equally applicable to an order for
periodical payments: see *T v T (financial provision)* [1988] 1 FLR 480. The facts of
that case are on all fours with the matter before us. There a periodical payments
order had been made in favour of the wife which was expressed to take effect
b 'until such date as [the wife] shall remarry, and until [the husband] retires from
John Lewis Partnership, or further order'. After the husband had retired, the wife
made an application for a variation of the order. Butler-Sloss J held (at 483):

'Since no application was made to vary prior to [the husband's retirement],
and the order for £20 came to an end, there was no order, not even an
c nominal order, upon which to hang an application to vary. In my judgment,
counsel for the wife's argument that the application was in limbo and could
be revived upon a variation application is fallacious. The original application
had been adjudicated upon, the variation application had not been made, and
application in limbo does not come within the four categories of *Dipper* v
d *Dipper* and is, in my judgment, unknown to family law. The court, therefore,
has no jurisdiction to entertain the variation application. I agree with the
conclusions of the senior registrar and his reasons. The appeal is dismissed.'

Hale J reached the same conclusion and found herself unable to depart from
T v T. She approached the matter in this way:
e
'It is therefore argued on behalf of the wife with some force that the plain
meaning of the words "until further order" must be given their effect and
that plain meaning is that a further order could be made at any time. Orders
do from time to time contain otiose words so as to clarify the meaning for
the parties and for everyone else. The words do have the advantage of
f dispelling any suggestion that the parties contemplated that there should be
no applications to vary, even though these could not be excluded. Against
that, there would have been nothing easier than to put in a clause based on
s 28(1A), which was not done in this case. This means the parties must have
contemplated that there could be an application for extension of the period.
g But it does not follow from that that they must have contemplated that the
application could be made at any time, even after the order had ended.
Although it will not appear so to the wife, or indeed perhaps to the husband,
from the point of view of that argument, whether it be one month or several
months thereafter, makes no difference.'

h She found the conclusion particularly hard on the facts of this particular case, in
view of the circumstances in which the point was raised and in view of the
husband's acknowledgement, that some extension to the order is indeed justified
on the particular circumstances of this case. I agree and had I thought it possible
to grant the wife relief, I would have been anxious to do so. I have concluded,
j however, that such a course in not open to this court. The speech of Lord
Scarman makes it clear that the order comes to an end not only when it expressly
stands dismissed but also when it 'ceases' or is 'discharged' or 'after the husband
(has) complied with all his obligations'. In those events there is no 'continuing
order capable of variation or discharge under section 31 of the Act'. This view
accords with the statutory language. Section 23 enables an order to be made 'for
such term as may be specified in the order'. Section 25A(2) enables the court to

require the periodical payments to be made 'only for such term' as is sufficient to enable adjustment to be made without undue hardship to the termination of financial dependence on the other party. Section 28 deals with 'duration of continuing financial provision orders' and provides 'the term ... shall be such term as the court thinks fit' subject to the statutory limits of death or remarriage. Consistency demands that when the term specified in the order, of whatever kind it may be, expires, the order expires with it. The words 'or further order' must be given their usual meaning and it is not possible to construe out of those words the meaning that only the obligation to pay comes to an end leaving the order comatose but capable of being kissed back to life by an application to vary. As Hale J pointed out, if that submission was correct, then an application to vary could be made years after the event. That would so fly in the face of the spirit of a clean break, even a deferred clean break, as to be unacceptable.

Practitioners should, therefore, note that unless there is a specific direction in the order under s 28(1A), the order can be extended beyond the term only provided that the application is made before the term expires. Although no argument has been addressed to us, I incline to the view that it is essential not only that application be made but that an order be made before the expiration of the term. There is no reason why the district judge of the day may not make an interim order of nominal periodical payments to preserve the position pending inter partes argument. Further, given the draconian effect of all relief being lost if the term is not extended before it expires and given the real possibility that years after the order had been made, a wife being without legal advice might overlook the urgency of a variation application, then if it is not a s 28(1A) case, it may be advisable specifically to provide for nominal periodical payments to be made after the expiration of any term provided for so as to give a peg on which to hang any late variation application.

I now turn to the husband's cross-appeal against the order made in respect of Camilla. The first submission is that the judge was wrong to require an undertaking to be given 'to continue to pay or cause to be paid periodical payments to the child' as well as ordering periodical payments to be made to the mother for the benefit of the child. The submission is that because the undertaking has the same effect as the order, there were in effect two orders for periodical payments being made when s 23(1)(d) permits the making of only one such order either to the child or to someone for the benefit of the child.

I am not prepared to give such a narrow construction to the Act. The court has power to make 'any one or more of the following orders'. In my view those words are wide enough to mean not only the orders provided in (a) to (f) but any one or more of the orders within a sub-paragraph. It is not uncommon for older children, and especially undergraduate children, to operate their own bank account and to manage an allowance provided for them. That is money which should be paid to them. It may be wholly appropriate that children learn from having personal control over a modest allowance, but it is not appropriate that there should be a relationship between parent and child which requires a parent to have to go, almost cap in hand, to the child for a contribution towards the cost of maintaining the home and all that goes with it for the benefit of the child. This is what happened in this case, and it proved embarrassing for both mother and daughter. Management of the household budget should be left to the adult. That dichotomy is properly reflected in the orders made by the judge. I reject the submission that there was no jurisdiction to make them. As Mrs Mullally pointed out, it is now common practice to make orders for payment partly to the child (or a the parent for the child) and directly to a fee paying school. There is in my judgment power to make an order to the child as well as to the parent for the child.

Mr Evans further complains of the judge's approach in deciding how much to order by way of periodical payments. He cannot criticise the way she directed herself that each parent should contribute to the child's needs as best they can;
b nor can he object to the finding of the mother's limited needs. The judge rightly found that the husband, certainly in income terms, is a wealthy man who could reasonably be expected to meet his daughter's financial needs throughout her university course. The judge's finding that the husband can be expected to contribute the whole of the reasonable expenditure on keeping a home going for Camilla for the period of that course cannot be challenged.

c The criticism is, however, that the judge erred in taking as her starting point the £14,000 provided for in the original order and endeavouring to allocate it between the mother and daughter. That criticism, it seems to me, is misplaced. The husband was offering to maintain his daughter. The judge asked counsel how much he was suggesting would be a proper contribution bearing in mind the
d allowance he was making to her. His suggestion was £10,000 for two years and £5,000 thereafter. The judge did not find it a logical response and commented that on the one hand £10,000 would be too much but on the other £5,000 too little. Since the order provides for a four-year term, the mathematics suggest that the average of £7,500 which the judge achieved is probably about right. The judgment was: 'Doing the best I can, I consider that sums offered by the husband
e are the appropriate ones to order with that degree of backdating.'

In the light of the information volunteered by the husband, there was material before the judge justifying the order she made. It does not lie in the husband's mouth now to complain in this court that he or his counsel were put under some kind of unfair pressure by the judge in asking them to state what they were
f willing to pay. The case had always been presented as one where he had the means to pay whatever was expected of him. Given his answer and the broad range of figures before the court, there was, in the particular circumstances of this case, no need for a minute breakdown of the household expenditure and the complaint that the judge was plainly wrong in arriving at the conclusion she did is not made out.

g The husband also appeals against the order for costs made against him. The judge held:

'I have already indicated, but I will repeat, that this seems to me to be a case in which it is entirely appropriate to order the husband to pay all the costs.
h The point on which he has succeeded is a point that was only raised on Monday of this week and it could have been raised at any time in the course of these proceedings. The remainder of the argument in this case has not taken up sufficient time or energy for it to be appropriate for me to order that conclusion.'

j Mr Evans submits that there was no good reason given why costs should not follow the event. Costs are, however, in the discretion of the court. Here the point was not only taken very, very late in the day but the husband had in the meantime submitted to orders made by consent providing for periodical payments to the wife. His original appeal to the judge was limited to that part of the district judge's order which made a nominal order in the wife's favour to preserve her position for the future. But that was not the end of it. There was a major issue about periodical payments to or for the child. On that issue the wife won, and won handsomely. The judge was entitled to take the view that the greater victory was obtained by the wife. It was, in my judgment, within the bounds of the proper exercise of discretion to make an order for costs in the wife's favour.

The judge did, however, go further. She ordered costs to paid on an indemnity basis. That had not been sought and Mrs Mullally does not resist an appeal against that part of the order. I say no more about it. To that extent only the husband's cross-appeal succeeds.

In the result I would dismiss the wife's appeal and uphold the order dismissing her claim for periodical payments. Save that I would substitute an order for the wife's costs to be taxed on a standard basis, not on a indemnity basis, I would dismiss the husband's cross-appeal.

I would add this. We were presented with a cardboard carton of six arch-lever files containing about 1,200 pages of material totally irrelevant on this appeal, including bank statements and the myriad of other financial documents which burdened the district judge's inquiry. Such copying represented a total waste. It would seem to be a breach of the practice statement and practice direction dated 26 July 1995 which direct solicitors how to prepare bundles for the Court of Appeal (see [1995] 3 All ER 847, [1995] 1 WLR 1188 and [1995] 3 All ER 850, [1995] 1 WLR 1191). It is now time that practitioners take note of *The Supreme Court Practice 1997* vol 1, paras 59/9/16 to 59/9/18 and the taxing master's powers to disallow costs of unnecessary copying. I shall invite him to consider such a course in this case.

POTTER LJ. I agree.

Appeal and cross-appeal dismissed.

Paul Magrath Esq   Barrister.

Practice Direction

a

HIGH COURT OF JUSTICE

Practice – Injunction – Interlocutory injunction – Standard forms of order – Provision
b *of draft on disk.*

1. The standard forms of order made on interlocutory applications for injunctions have been agreed for use in both the Chancery Division and the Queen's Bench Division.
2. Attached to this practice direction are the standard forms of the following
c orders:

    Annex 1—Injunction before the issue of a writ of summons.
    Annex 2—Order for injunction.
    Annex 3—Order containing undertaking instead of an injunction.
    Annex 4—Adjournment of application for an injunction.
d   Annex 5—Application for an injunction treated as trial of the action.

3. All such orders made in the Chancery motions court or by the Queen's Bench judge in chambers should in future, in the absence of good reason to the contrary, now follow these forms.
4. Whenever possible a draft should be provided and a disk containing the
e draft should also be available to the court. This will enable the associate or officer attending the judge to incorporate any amendments made by the judge and to arrange for the immediate sealing and entry of the order. The current word processing system used in the High Court is WordPerfect 5.1 for DOS.
5. This practice direction is issued with the concurrence of the Vice-
f Chancellor.

                              LORD BINGHAM OF CORNHILL CJ
28 October 1996   SIR RICHARD SCOTT V-C.

Note. Copies of the standard forms may be obtained from Room TM 5.10,
g Royal Courts of Justice, Strand, London WC2A 2LL. Telephone: 0171-936 6827/7393.

Practice Direction

HIGH COURT OF JUSTICE

Practice – Injunction – Mareva injunction – Standard forms of order – Revision of forms.

Practice – Discovery – Anton Piller order – Standard forms of order – Revision of forms.

With the concurrence of the President of the Family Division and the Vice-Chancellor, the standard forms attached to the practice direction issued by Lord Taylor of Gosforth CJ on 28 July 1994 (see [1994] 4 All ER 52, [1994] 1 WLR 1233) have been revised. The new forms of orders attached to this practice direction will supersede those issued on 28 July 1994 with immediate effect.

This practice direction applies to all divisions of the High Court.

LORD BINGHAM OF CORNHILL CJ
SIR STEPHEN BROWN P
SIR RICHARD SCOTT V-C.

28 October 1996

Note. Copies of the standard forms may be obtained from Room TM 5.10, Royal Courts of Justice, Strand, London WC2A 2LL. Telephone: 0171-936 6827/7393.

Farah v Commissioner of Police of the Metropolis

COURT OF APPEAL, CIVIL DIVISION

PETER GIBSON, OTTON AND HUTCHISON LJJ

25, 26 JULY, 9 OCTOBER 1996

Race relations – Unlawful discrimination – Provision of goods, facilities or services – Services – Whether police providing services in assisting or protecting members of the public – Whether commissioner of police vicariously liable for actions of officers – Whether officers authorised agents of commissioner – Race Relations Act 1976, ss 20, 32(2), 53.

In January 1995 the plaintiff, a citizen of Somalia, commenced proceedings against the Commissioner of Police, claiming damages for false imprisonment, assault and battery and malicious prosecution. She alleged that in July 1994 she was attacked by some white teenagers and summoned police assistance by a 999 call but that the police, instead of helping her and seeking to detain her attackers, arrested, detained and charged her with assault, although she was subsequently acquitted on no evidence being offered against her. She claimed that the police officers' conduct amounted to unlawful racial discrimination under s 20[a] of the Race Relations Act 1976, and that the commissioner was vicariously liable for the conduct of the officers under s 32(2)[b] of the 1976 Act. The commissioner applied to strike out the allegations of racial discrimination as disclosing no cause of action but the judge held that the claim was not unarguable and dismissed the application. The commissioner appealed to the Court of Appeal, contending that s 20 of the 1976 Act did not apply to police officers performing the duties of their office since they were not providing services, and that s 32(2) of the Act did not apply to him since such officers were exercising an original authority.

Held – (1) For the purposes of s 20 of the 1976 Act, those parts of a police officer's duties involving assistance to or protection of members of the public entailed the provision of services to the public, and fell in particular within s 20(2)(g). Accordingly, since the Act did not specifically except the police from its provisions and there was no basis in the circumstances for entertaining public policy considerations, it followed that it was unlawful for a police officer to discriminate against a person seeking to obtain such services (see p 299 *j* to p 300 *c e* to *h*, p 304 *e j*, p 305 *c* and p 306 *j*, post); *Savjani v IRC* [1981] 1 All ER 1121 applied.

(2) By virtue of s 53[c] of the 1976 Act, however, claims based on vicarious liability could only be maintained to the extent permitted by the Act and therefore the commissioner's vicarious liability for torts committed by constables under his direction and control under s 48[d] of the Police Act 1964 was excluded. Accordingly, since police officers were not agents of the commissioner but public servants and officers of the Crown exercising an original authority, the plaintiff's

---

a   Section 20 is set out at p 292 *j* to p 293 *b*, post
b   Section 32(2) is set out at p 293 *e*, post
c   Section 53, so far as material, is set out at p 293 *f*, post
d   Section 48, so far as material, is set out at p 293 *j*, post

claim for racial discrimination was not maintainable against the commissioner under s 32(2) of the 1976 Act. The appeal would therefore be allowed (see p 301 *e* to p 302 *b j* to p 303 *e j*, p 304 *a* to *e*, p 305 *h j* and p 306 *a* to *d j*, post); *Fisher v Oldham Corp* [1930] All ER Rep 96 applied; *Hawkins v Bepey* [1980] 1 All ER 797 distinguished.

Notes
For racial discrimination in relation to the provision of services, see 4(2) *Halsbury's Laws* (4th edn reissue) para 171, and for cases on the subject, see 7(2) *Digest* (2nd reissue) 205–206, 996–999.

For the Police Act 1964, s 48, see 33 *Halsbury's Statutes* (4th edn) (1993 reissue) 706.

For the Race Relations Act 1976, ss 20, 32, 53, see 6 *Halsbury's Statutes* (4th edn) (1992 reissue) 848, 856, 871.

Cases referred to in judgments
Alexandrou v Oxford [1993] 4 All ER 328, CA.
Amin v Entry Clearance Officer, Bombay [1983] 2 All ER 864, [1983] 2 AC 818, [1983] 3 WLR 258, HL.
Calveley v Chief Constable of the Merseyside Police [1989] 1 All ER 1025, [1989] AC 1228, [1989] 2 WLR 624, HL.
Enever v R (1906) 3 CLR 969, Aust HC.
Fisher v Oldham Corp [1930] 2 KB 364, [1930] All ER Rep 96.
Hawkins v Bepey [1980] 1 All ER 797, [1980] 1 WLR 419, DC.
Hill v Chief Constable of West Yorkshire [1988] 2 All ER 238, [1989] AC 53, [1988] 2 WLR 1049, HL.
Kassam v Immigration Appeal Tribunal [1980] 2 All ER 330, [1980] 1 WLR 1037, CA.
Lonrho plc v Tebbit [1991] 4 All ER 973; *affd* [1992] 4 All ER 280, CA.
Marrinan v Vibart [1962] 3 All ER 380, [1963] 1 QB 528, [1962] 3 WLR 912, CA; *affg* [1962] 1 All ER 869, [1963] 1 QB 234, [1962] 2 WLR 1224.
Savjani v IRC [1981] 1 All ER 1121, [1981] QB 458, [1981] 2 WLR 636, CA.

Cases also cited or referred to in skeleton arguments
Alexander v Home Office [1988] 2 All ER 118, [1988] 1 WLR 968, CA.
Applin v Race Relations Board [1974] 2 All ER 73, [1975] AC 259, HL.
Lewis v Cattle [1938] 2 All ER 368, [1938] 2 KB 454, DC.
R v Chief Constable of the Devon and Cornwall Constabulary, ex p Central Electricity Generating Board [1981] 3 All ER 826, [1982] QB 458, CA.
R v Metropolitan Police Comr, ex p Blackburn [1968] 1 All ER 763, [1968] 2 QB 118, CA.
Silcott v Comr of Police of the Metropolis (1996) Times, 9 July, [1996] CA Transcript 562.
Swinney v Chief Constable of the Northumbria Police [1996] 3 All ER 449, [1996] 3 WLR 968, CA.
Tejani v Superintendent Registrar for the District of Peterborough [1986] IRLR 502, CA.
Vince v Chief Constable of the Dorset Police [1992] 3 All ER 98, [1992] 1 WLR 47; *rvsd in part* [1993] 2 All ER 321, [1993] 1 WLR 415, CA.
Williams & Humbert Ltd v W & H Trademarks (Jersey) Ltd [1986] 1 All ER 129, [1986] AC 368, HL.

Appeal
By notice dated 7 May 1996 the defendant, the Commissioner of Police of the Metropolis, appealed with leave granted by the Court of Appeal (Beldam LJ and

Wall J) on 30 April 1996 from the order of Judge Harris made on 21 December 1995 in the Central London County Court whereby he dismissed the defendant's application dated 29 August 1995 to strike out those parts of the summons and particulars of claim of the plaintiff, Zeinab Farah, in which she claimed damages for unlawful racial discrimination under the Race Relations Act 1976. The facts are set out in the judgment of Hutchison LJ.

b
Robert Seabrook QC and Duncan MacLeod (instructed by the Solicitor, Metropolitan Police) for the defendant.
Andrew Nicol QC and Heather Williams (instructed by Deighton Guedalla) for the plaintiff.

c   Cur adv vult

9 October 1996. The following judgments were delivered.

HUTCHISON LJ (giving the first judgment at the invitation of Peter Gibson LJ).
d This is an appeal by the defendant from the order of Judge Harris in the Central London County Court on 21 December 1995 refusing to strike out part of the plaintiff's statement of claim.

The action arises out of an occurrence on 17 July 1994. The case pleaded by the plaintiff, who is a citizen of Somalia and a refugee and who was aged 17 at the time, is that on that date she and her 10-year-old cousin were attacked near their e home by some white teenagers, who set a dog on her and injured her. By a 999 call she summoned police assistance, but the police officers who came in response, instead of helping her and seeking to detain her attackers, arrested her without cause, detained her for a time, and charged her with affray, common assault and causing unnecessary suffering to a dog. She was released on bail the same day. On 12 January 1995 she appeared to answer the charges and, no f evidence being offered, was acquitted.

The plaintiff's claim against the Commissioner of Police of the Metropolis in proceedings begun on 13 January 1995, is for damages, including aggravated and exemplary damages, for, inter alia, false imprisonment, assault and battery, and malicious prosecution. These claims, denied by the defendant in his defence, are g accepted as disclosing causes of action.

However, the plaintiff also included in her particulars of claim an allegation that the conduct of the attending police officers amounted to unlawful racial discrimination, and it was this that the defendant sought to strike out. It is necessary to outline the way this claim is pleaded, and in doing so I refer to the h amended particulars of claim (Judge Harris, having dismissed the defendant's application to strike out, allowed an amendment sought by the plaintiff). What the plaintiff alleges is this.

She says that the defendant was the employer of the officers and that, by virtue of s 32 of the Race Relations Act 1976, he is liable for anything done in the course of their employment. This allegation is not, however (subject to a qualification j which will appear from what I say later), now pursued. Alternatively (this is the amendment) she says they were acting as the defendant's authorised agents within the meaning of s 32(2) of the 1976 Act. She contends that the defendant is vicariously liable for the conduct of the officers. She puts her claim on the basis that she was a person seeking to obtain the use of services from a person concerned with the provision of services to the public within the terms of s 20 of the 1976 Act, and that the officers deliberately omitted to provide her with the services she sought or with services of a like quality or in like manner or on the like terms to those normally provided by the officers to other members of the public. She particularises, in support of this assertion, the acts or omissions of which she says the officers were guilty as follows: (a) officers in the employment of the defendant failed to react, alternatively chose to ignore her call for assistance by way of an emergency telephone call to the police emergency service before the attendance of the said officers; (b) the said officers at the scene of her detention and involved with the interview of the plaintiff failed to investigate her account of events both at the scene of her apprehension and thereafter; (c) the defendant and the officers in his employment failed to afford the protection accorded victims of crime in like manner to the plaintiff as to white members of the public.

Then in para 12(iv) the plaintiff says that the officers brought the criminal proceedings against her on racial grounds and so treated her less favourably than they would treat other persons.

All of this was sought to be struck out as disclosing no cause of action.

Judge Harris correctly approached the matter on the basis that for the purpose of deciding such a striking out claim he should consider the pleading and only accede to the application to strike out if he was satisfied that the impugned parts of the pleading disclosed no cause of action. He rightly accepted that if the pleading was arguably good the matter must be left for trial—the remedy of striking out was available only in a plain and obvious case.

Having considered each of the arguments advanced by the defendant the judge felt unable to say that the 1976 Act claim was unarguable and dismissed the application. I now consider the arguments as they have been presented before us on the appeal from the judge's order.

I begin by referring to those provisions of the 1976 Act and the Police Act 1964 which are material. Part I of the 1976 Act defines discrimination and it is necessary to cite only s 1(1)(a), which reads:

'A person discriminates against another in any circumstances relevant for the purposes of any provision of this Act if—(a) on racial grounds he treats that other less favourably than he treats or would treat other persons ...'

Part II of the 1976 Act deals with discrimination in the employment field. Section 16 headed 'Police' provides in sub-s (1):

'For the purposes of this Part, the holding of the office of constable shall be treated as employment—(a) by the chief officer of police as respects any act done by him in relation to a constable or that office; (b) by the police authority as respects any act done by them in relation to a constable or that office.'

Part III of the 1976 Act deals with discrimination in other fields, and in that part is to be found s 20, relating to discrimination in the provision of goods, facilities or services. Its material provisions are as follows:

'(1) It is unlawful for any person concerned with the provision (for payment or not) of goods, facilities or services to the public or a section of the public to discriminate against a person who seeks to obtain or use those goods, facilities or services—(a) by refusing or deliberately omitting to provide him with any of them; or (b) by refusing or deliberately omitting to provide him with goods, facilities or services of the like quality, in the like manner and on the like terms as are normal in the first-mentioned person's case in relation to other members of the public or (where the person so seeking belongs to a section of the public) to other members of that section.

(2) The following are examples of the facilities and services mentioned in subsection (1)—(a) access to and use of any place which members of the public are permitted to enter; (b) accommodation in a hotel, boarding house or other similar establishment; (c) facilities by way of banking or insurance or for grants, loans, credit or finance; (d) facilities for education; (e) facilities for entertainment, recreation or refreshment; (f) facilities for transport or travel; (g) the services of any profession or trade, or any local or other public authority.'

In Pt IV of the 1976 Act, dealing with other unlawful acts, is s 32, which has the sidenote 'Liability of employers and principals'; it provides:

'(1) Anything done by a person in the course of his employment shall be treated for the purposes of this Act (except as regards offences thereunder) as done by his employer as well as by him, whether or not it was done with the employer's knowledge or approval.

(2) Anything done by a person as agent for another person with the authority (whether express or implied, and whether precedent or subsequent) of that other person shall be treated for the purposes of this Act (except as regards offences thereunder) as done by that other person as well as by him ...'

Part VI of the 1976 Act contains general exceptions from Pts II to IV (for example, by s 41 acts done under statutory authority and by s 42 acts safeguarding national security).

Part VIII of the 1976 Act relates to enforcement. Section 53(1) reads:

'Except as provided by this Act no proceedings, whether civil or criminal, shall lie against any person in respect of an act by reason that the act is unlawful by virtue of a provision of this Act.'

Section 57, which has the sidenote 'Claims under Part III', provides, as material:

'(1) A claim by any person ("the claimant") that another person ("the respondent")—(a) has committed an act of discrimination against the claimant which is unlawful by virtue of Part III; or (b) is by virtue of section 32 or 33 to be treated as having committed such an act of discrimination against the claimant, may be made the subject of civil proceedings in like manner as any other claim in tort ...'

Section 48(1) of the 1964 Act provides as follows:

'The chief officer of police for any police area shall be liable in respect of torts committed by constables under his direction and control in the performance or purported performance of their functions in like manner as a master is liable in respect of torts committed by his servants in the course of their employment, and accordingly shall in respect of any such tort be treated for all purposes as a joint tortfeasor.'

There are in my view two important issues which have to be determined in this case. The first is whether a police officer comes within s 20 of the 1976 Act. The second is whether, if he does, the chief officer of police for the area in which

he serves is answerable in law for any breaches of the 1976 Act which the police
officer has committed. The first of these issues is obviously of fundamental and
general importance; the second, while its resolution in the appellant's favour
might be fatal to the plaintiff's claim under the 1976 Act in this case, is unlikely to
preclude such claims being advanced in other cases. This is because, if we were
to decide the first issue against the appellant and the second in his favour, any
future plaintiff alleging racial discrimination against the police would join the
officer or officers said to be the actual offenders. (It would not be possible for the
present plaintiff to do that as the 6 months period within which proceedings are
to be brought has long since expired—see s 68(2)—unless she can persuade the
court to consider the claim out of time under s 68(6)). I ventured to suggest
during the argument that such an outcome, while disposing of the claim in the
instant case, would be for the commissioner a Pyrrhic victory, and I remain of
that view. The provisions of s 48 of the 1964 Act are, it seems to me, beneficial
to both plaintiffs and the police, for reasons which are too obvious to need
elaboration; and if the police are susceptible to a claim under the 1976 Act, it
would be unfortunate if that, like other tortious claims, could not be brought
against the commissioner. However, such considerations are only of relevance if
the first and crucial issue is decided against the appellant *and* if there is any room
for doubt as to the interpretation of the statutory provisions bearing on the
matter of the commissioner's vicarious liability. It is to the first of those questions
that I now turn.

Mr Seabrook QC invites us first to consider the scheme of the 1976 Act. He
makes the following points.

(a) It is implicit in s 16(1) (and indeed s 48 of the 1964 Act) that there is no
relationship of employer/employee between the chief officer and constables.
This is common ground—it is, as Mr Nicol QC for the plaintiff concedes,
well-established that police constables are office-holders not employees.

(b) Section 53, which is in specific and restrictive terms, prevents proceedings
for breach of the provisions of the 1976 Act unless authorised by the 1976 Act
itself. Section 57 provides the only authorisation on which the plaintiff in this case
can rely. The commissioner is not alleged to have personally committed any act
of discrimination and can only be vicariously liable for the constables' acts if they
were acting as his agents with his authority—see s 32(2): but, says Mr Seabrook,
s 32 has no application to the commissioner. The constables were not acting as
agents or with the authority of the commissioner, but were exercising an original
authority by virtue of their office. Section 48 does not avail the plaintiff because
s 53 prohibits one from looking outside the provisions of the 1976 Act.

Mr Seabrook also submits that the constables themselves are not within the
enforcement provisions of the 1976 Act. If, he says, those provisions do not
extend to the commissioner, it is inconceivable that they should extend to the
constables. He submits that the omission to make special provision, such as for
example is made in relation to Pt II of the 1976 Act by s 16, indicates that it was
never intended that individual constables should be caught by s 20.

As a matter of construction, Mr Seabrook submits, s 20 does not apply to police
officers performing the duties of their office—they are not providing services.
The acts alleged against them all entail the exercise of discretion and judgment.
What they were engaged on, from the moment the 999 call was received, was the
exercise of their powers of investigation, detection and the bringing of offenders
to justice.

In this connection Mr Seabrook referred us to a number of authorities. The first was *Kassam v Immigration Appeal Tribunal* [1980] 2 All ER 330, [1980] 1 WLR 1037. In that case a question arose as to whether a complaint of discrimination contrary to the Sex Discrimination Act 1975 was maintainable in respect of a provision of the Statement of Immigration Rules for Control on Entry: Commonwealth Citizens (HC Paper (1972–73) no 79) which required the wife or child of a male student who had been given leave of entry to study to be admitted for the period for which the husband had been authorised to enter but contained no corresponding provision in respect of the husband of a female student. Section 29 of that Act is in terms essentially similar to those of s 20 of the 1976 Act. It was held that the Secretary of State was not a person concerned with the provision of facilities to a section of the public. Stephenson LJ said ([1980] 2 All ER 330 at 334–335, [1980] 1 WLR 1037 at 1042–1043):

'I am of the opinion that the Secretary of State is not a person concerned with the provisions of facilities to a section of the public. Subsections (1) and (2) of s 29 repeat mutatis mutandis s 2(1) and (2) of the Race Relations Act 1968 (now repealed and re-enacted in s 20(1) and (2) of the 1976 Act) and so are not free from judicial interpretation. But read in their natural and ordinary meaning they are not aimed at and do not hit the Secretary of State concerned with giving leave to enter or remain in the exercise of his powers under the [Immigration Act 1971]. The kind of facilities with which the sections of the 1975 and 1968 Acts are concerned is of the same order as goods and services, and though it may not always be easy to say whether a particular person (or body of persons) is a person concerned with the provision of any of those three things to the public or a section of the public and although a minister of the Crown or a government department might be such a person (for instance, in former days the Postmaster General, as Sir David Cairns suggested in argument), I am clearly of the opinion that the Secretary of State in acting under the Immigration Act and rules is not such a person, and he cannot be held to have unlawfully discriminated against the appellant by refusing to give him leave to remain here while his wife was a student, or by refusing to interpret or alter para 22 of the statement of immigration rules which is relevant to this appeal. He is operating in a field outside the fields in which Parliament has forbidden sex discrimination.'

Ackner LJ agreeing, said ([1980] 2 All ER 330 at 335, [1980] 1 WLR 1037 at 1043):

'In my judgment when the Secretary of State is exercising his discretion in relation to powers granted to him by the Immigration Act 1971, he is not providing a "facility" within the meaning of s 29 of the Act. The word "facilities" in that section is flanked on one side by the word "goods" and on the other by the word "services". This suggests to my mind that the word "facilities" is not to be given a wholly unrestricted meaning but must be limited or confined to facilities that are akin to goods or services. Subsection (2) of s 29 provides examples of the facilities and services mentioned in subsection (1). These examples support the view which I have expressed above.'

Kassam's case was distinguished in *Savjani v IRC* [1981] 1 All ER 1121, [1981] QB 458, a case which gave rise to the question whether the Inland Revenue were concerned with the provision of services under s 20 of the 1976 Act. This court

held that they were and in the course of his judgment Lord Denning MR said
([1981] 1 All ER 1121 at 1125, [1981] QB 458 at 466):

> 'I would only mention *Kassam v Immigration Appeal Tribunal* [1980] 2 All ER
> 330, [1980] 1 WLR 1037, which was before another division of this court. In
> that case discrimination was alleged against the immigration authorities.
> The court held that, in dealing with people coming in under the immigration
> rules, the immigration authorities were not providing "services" within the
> meaning of the Sex Discrimination Act 1975. This case is very different. The
> Revenue are providing "services" in regard to relief from tax or repayment
> of tax. Those services come within the provisions of the Act. If there is
> discrimination in the carrying out of those services, it is unlawful.'

Templeman LJ said ([1981] 1 All ER 1121 at 1125–1126, [1981] QB 458 at 466–468):

> 'The Race Relations Act 1976 undoubtedly poses and is continually posing
> a large number of administrative difficulties both for the Crown and for large
> organisations; and in the present instance the Inland Revenue are to be
> treated with sympathy rather than criticism. Undoubtedly their task will be
> made more difficult by the Act if it applies to them. On the other hand, the
> Act was brought in to remedy very great evil. It is expressed in very wide
> terms, and I should be very slow to find that the effect of something which
> is humiliatingly discriminatory in racial matters falls outside the ambit of the
> Act. Nevertheless, of course, one must look at the Act and construe its
> provisions ... As counsel submitted on behalf of the commissioners, the
> board and the inspector are performing duties, those duties laid on them by
> the Act which I have mentioned, but, in my judgment, it does not necessarily
> follow that the board and the inspector are not voluntarily or in order to
> carry out their duty also performing services for the taxpayer. The duty is to
> collect the right amount of revenue; but, in my judgment, there is a service
> to the taxpayer provided by the board and the inspector by the provision,
> dissemination and implementation of regulations which will enable the
> taxpayer to know that he is entitled to a deduction or a repayment, which
> will entitle him to know how he is to satisfy the inspector or the board if he
> is so entitled, and which will enable him to obtain the actual deduction or
> repayment which Parliament said he is to have. For present purposes, in my
> judgment, the inspector and the board provide the inestimable services of
> enabling a taxpayer to obtain that relief which Parliament intended he
> should be able to obtain as a matter of right subject only to proof ... Counsel
> for the commissioners submitted that the Race Relations Act 1976 does not
> apply to the Inland Revenue at all, but he naturally and wisely recoiled from
> the suggestion that the inspector of taxes might decline to interview a
> taxpayer if the taxpayer were coloured. He made forcibly the submission
> that, when the board decides for sensible reasons that a higher standard of
> proof is required from taxpayers who come from the Indian subcontinent,
> the board are not providing a service to that taxpayer; they are carrying out
> their duty to the Crown. As I have already indicated, it does not seem to me
> that the two concepts are mutually exclusive. The board and the inspectors
> perform their duty and carry out a service and, in my judgment, it is a service
> within the meaning of s 20 of the Race Relations Act 1976.'

Both these cases were considered by the House of Lords in *Amin v Entry Clearance
Officer, Bombay* [1983] 2 All ER 864, [1983] 2 AC 818, where an issue was whether

a the grant of special vouchers under the special voucher scheme introduced by
para 38 of the statement of immigration rules came within s 29 of the Sex
Discrimination Act 1975. It was held by the majority that it did not. The
contention that *Kassam's* case was wrongly decided was rejected by the majority.
In the course of his speech Lord Fraser said ([1983] 2 All ER 864 at 872–873, [1983]
2 AC 818 at 834):

b   'My Lords, I accept that the examples in s 29(2) are not exhaustive, but they
    are, in my opinion, useful pointers to aid in the construction of sub-s (1).
    Section 29 as a whole seems to me to apply to the direct provision of facilities
    or services, and not to the mere grant of permission to use facilities. That is
    in accordance with the words of sub-s (1) and it is reinforced by some of the
c   examples in sub-s (2) ... The example in para (g) seems to me to be
    contemplating things such as medical services, or library facilities, which can
    be directly provided by local or other public authorities. So, in *Savjani v IRC*
    ... Templeman LJ took the view that the Inland Revenue performed two
    separate functions: first a duty of collecting revenue and, second a service of
    providing taxpayers with information. [Lord Fraser quotes the second of the
d   passages I have cited from the judgment of Templeman LJ, save for the last
    sentence.] In so far as that passage states the ground of the Court of Appeal's
    decision in that case, I agree with it. If Lord Denning MR intended to base
    his decision on wider grounds (see [1981] 1 All ER 1121 at 1124-1125, [1981]
    QB 458 at 465-466), I would respectfully disagree with him. In the present
e   case the entry clearance officer in Bombay was in my opinion not providing
    a service for would-be immigrants; rather he was performing his duty of
    controlling them. Counsel for the appellant sought to draw support for his
    contention from s 85(1) of the 1975 Act, which provides: "This Act applies—
    (a) to an act done by or for purposes of a Minister of the Crown or
    government department, or (b) to an act done on behalf of the Crown by a
f   statutory body, or a person holding a statutory office, as it applies to an act
    done by a private person." That section puts an act done on behalf of the
    Crown on a par with an act done by a private person, and it does not in terms
    restrict the comparison to an act *of the same kind* done by a private person.
    But in my opinion it applies only to acts done on behalf of the Crown which
    are of a kind similar to acts that might be done by a private person. It does
g   not mean that the Act is to apply to any act of any kind done on behalf of the
    Crown by a person holding statutory office. There must be acts (which
    include deliberate omissions: see s 82(1)) done in the course of formulating
    or carrying out government policy which are quite different in kind from any
    act that would ever be done by a private person, and to which the 1975 Act
h   does not apply.' (Lord Fraser's emphasis.)

Mr Seabrook places particular reliance on Lord Fraser's concluding words in this
citation. However, he was there dealing with an argument that s 85 of the Sex
Discrimination Act 1975 (the equivalent of s 75 of the 1976 Act) provided support
for the argument based on s 29 (s 20). I shall consider in a moment what is the
j significance of s 75 of the 1976 Act but before doing so I should say that in my
view the most important feature of Lord Fraser's speech in the context of the
present case is his approval of the passage in Templeman LJ's judgment in
Savjani's case.
    Section 75 of the 1976 Act has the sidenote 'Application to Crown etc' and its
material provisions are as follows:

'(1) This Act applies—(a) to an act done by or for purposes of a Minister of the Crown or government department; or (b) to an act done on behalf of the Crown by a statutory body, or a person holding a statutory office, as it applies to an act done by a private person.

(2) Pts II and IV apply to—(a) service for purposes of a Minister of the Crown or government department, other than service of a person holding a statutory office; or (b) service on behalf of the Crown for purposes of a person holding a statutory office or purposes of a statutory body; or (c) service in the armed forces, as they apply to employment by a private person, and shall so apply as if references to a contract of employment included references to the terms of service.

(3) Subsections (1) and (2) have effect subject to section 16 ...'

Mr Seabrook relies on the passage from Lord Fraser's speech cited above as authority that the relevant act must be similar to an act done by a private person—and certainly that is what Lord Fraser says, though it might be argued that his observations are obiter. Mr Nicol, while not accepting that what Lord Fraser said is applicable to the present case, argues that the assistance and protection that the plaintiff sought from the police were similar to acts which might have been performed by a private person—for example a security firm— and that accordingly Lord Fraser's test is satisfied in this case.

Mr Nicol also submits that it is arguable that s 75 applies to police constables since theirs is a service on behalf of the Crown for the purposes of a person holding statutory office or of a statutory body, and that s 32 (included in Pt IV to which s 75(2) refers) applies to constables' service as it applies to employment by a private person and as if reference to contracts of employment included reference to their terms of service. Acknowledging that this is, as he puts it, 'a somewhat strained construction', Mr Nicol points out that unless the police are within s 75(2) (and, he might have added, s 75(1)) s 75(3) makes no sense. Mr Seabrook's response to this is that Pt III of the 1976 Act is not referred to in s 75(2). Mr Nicol in turn suggests that the explanation for this omission is that Pt III of the 1976 Act is not concerned with employment.

These arguments are not easy to resolve and the statutory provisions are by no means clear. However my conclusion is that it is arguable that the limited service for which the plaintiff looked to the police comes within Lord Fraser's test. As to Mr Nicol's second submission, I agree that it is strained and I consider that the most that can be said is that s 75(3) shows that s 75(1) and (2) might easily apply to the police, not that they do so apply.

Mr Seabrook, in further support of his contention that it is plain that s 20 has no application to a police officer performing his duties, advanced a powerful argument based on considerations of public policy. He submitted that the law has consistently recognised the need to protect those involved in the investigation, preparation for and giving of evidence in criminal and civil proceedings from susceptibility to actions for damages because of the danger that this would impede or inhibit the effectiveness of legal process. It is, he suggested, unthinkable that Parliament would, incidentally as it were, have infringed such well-established interests. In support of this submission he referred us to a number of authorities, including *Marrinan v Vibart* [1962] 1 All ER 869, [1963] 1 QB 234; *affd* [1962] 3 All ER 380, [1963] 1 QB 528 (a case which reaffirmed the absolute immunity of a witness from any form of civil action in respect of his evidence in judicial proceedings and any acts done in the preparation of that a evidence), *Hill v Chief Constable of West Yorkshire* [1988] 2 All ER 238, [1989] AC 53 (where it was held that there was no general duty of care owed by the police to individual members of the public in respect of the detention and apprehension of criminals), *Calveley v Chief Constable of the Merseyside Police* [1989] 1 All ER 1025, [1989] AC 1228 (where it was held that officers investigating allegations against other police officers owed no duty of care to the subjects of the investigation on

b the grounds, inter alia, that it would be contrary to public policy to recognise such a duty) and *Alexandrou v Oxford* [1993] 4 All ER 328 (where it was held that it would not be in the public interest to impose on the police a duty of care towards the shopkeeper where they had attended as a result of but (it was said) negligently investigated a burglar alarm call). These and other cases to which Mr Seabrook referred us do, of course, exemplify a well-established strand of public policy, the

c reasons for which are readily understandable. As Lord Bridge said in *Calveley's* case [1989] 1 All ER 1025 at 1030, [1989] AC 1228 at 1238:

> 'Where no action for malicious prosecution would lie, it would be strange indeed if an acquitted defendant could recover damages for negligent investigation. Finally, all other considerations apart, it would plainly be
>
d > contrary to public policy, in my opinion, to prejudice the fearless and efficient discharge by police officers of their vitally important public duty of investigating crime by requiring them to act under the shadow of a potential action for damages for negligence by the suspect.'

e Mr Seabrook, however, readily conceded that it was open to Parliament to legislate in a manner which impinged upon such public policy immunity. The value of these authorities, concerned as they are with whether in given circumstances a common law duty of care should be held to exist, lies in the assistance they may afford in interpreting statutory provisions, the effect of which is ambiguous or otherwise unclear. They certainly do not preclude the

f acceptance of the plaintiff's contentions, if the words of the statute are clear.

The same may be said of Mr Seabrook's submission based on what I will call inconvenience, expense and difficulty. He points to the provisions of Pt VII of the 1976 Act relating to the administration of questionnaires, to the need for extensive discovery, to the necessity for the judge in the county court to sit with assessors and related matters. I do not find it necessary to make specific reference

g to the relevant provisions, since I accept Mr Nicol's submission that such considerations cannot be decisive of the question whether on its proper construction the 1976 Act applies to some aspects of police activities. For the same reason I do not propose to rehearse Mr Nicol's submissions in support of his contention that the problems are much less formidable than the appellant

h suggests they are. This case turns not on such considerations but upon the proper construction of the 1976 Act in the light of the directly relevant authorities.

In my view Mr Nicol is correct when he argues that, prima facie, s 20 is wide enough to apply to at least some of the acts undertaken by police officers in the performance of the duties of their office. The crucial words—to be interpreted of

j course in the light of the examples given, but not on the basis that the examples are definitive of the circumstances to which the section can apply—are 'any person concerned with the provision (for payment or not) of ... services to the public'.

I accept Mr Nicol's contention that these words are entirely apt to cover those parts of a police officer's duties involving assistance to or protection of members of the public. Mr Nicol emphasised that it is in regard to that aspect of the

officers' duties that the claim in the present case is advanced—it is not suggested
that pursuing and arresting or charging alleged criminals is the provision of a   *a*
service. What is said is that the service sought by the plaintiff was that of
protection and that she did not, because of her race, obtain the protection that
others would have been afforded. It seems to me that that is no less the provision
of a service than is the giving of directions or other information to a member of
the public who seeks them.   *b*

Turning to the examples in sub-s (2) I find nothing expressly or impliedly to
exclude police officers; and in my view they can properly be regarded as falling
within para (g)—'the services of any profession or trade, or any local or other
public authority'.

Furthermore, I find in *Savjani's* case support for the conclusion that the police,
in some aspects of their activities, fall within the 1976 Act. The passage in   *c*
Templeman LJ's judgment approved in *Amin's* case shows that there is no reason
why a person performing a public duty may not also be providing a service, and
strongly supports the plaintiff's arguments. The first paragraph of his judgment
helpfully states and contrasts some of the conflicting policy considerations and
emphasises the necessity, notwithstanding those matters, to construe the Act.   *d*
The last of the paragraphs I have cited from his judgment could easily be adapted
to pose an example in as stark terms but concerning a member of the public and
police officers.

Finally, I do not find in the other provisions of the 1976 Act relied upon by Mr
Seabrook anything to indicate that the prima facie clear words of s 20 should not
apply to police officers. In my view Mr Nicol is correct to contend that s 16   *e*
certainly does not have that effect, since it is explicable on the simple basis that,
since police officers are not employed but hold their office under the Crown,
some such provision was necessary if they were to be afforded the protection of
Pt II, concerned as it is with discrimination in the employment field. I am,
moreover, impressed by Mr Nicol's argument that of more significance is the fact   *f*
that, whereas Pt V of the 1976 Act contains specified exceptions to its provisions,
some of which are clearly based on public policy grounds, there is no such specific
exception of the police.

Taking the view I do on construction, I do not consider that there is any basis
for entertaining Mr Seabrook's policy arguments. I would observe, however,
that (as the judgment of Templeman LJ recognises) there are in any event   *g*
powerful arguments on each side of the public policy issue and I do not find the
spectre of claims of racial discrimination against the police, with the
inconvenience and expense that that may involve, to be more disturbing than the
prospect that a member of the public who, seeking assistance in dire need, has
been the subject of racial discrimination, should be without remedy.   *h*

The question that remains to be considered is whether, under the provisions
of ss 53 and 57 of the 1976 Act, such a claim can prima facie be advanced by an
individual plaintiff against the police officers allegedly guilty of discrimination (it
will be recalled that I am not here considering the question of vicarious liability
which arises in this case by reason of the fact that only the commissioner has been *j*
made a defendant). This depends on whether a claim of discrimination by a
member of the public against a police officer falls within s 57(1). In my view it
plainly does, for reasons too obvious to require further discussion.

Before turning to the issue of vicarious liability I wish to say that in this case I
am doubtful, as judges have been in many others involving striking out, of the
wisdom of deciding questions of the sort we have been asked to determine at this

a stage, before the facts have been established. Mr Nicol referred us to *Lonrho plc v Tebbit* [1991] 4 All ER 973, where Browne-Wilkinson V-C emphasised the virtues of deciding difficult questions of law in a new and developing field on the basis of the true facts once they are ascertained. It is true that the racial discrimination claim in the present case would probably, if allowed to proceed, increase the cost and difficulty of the hearing or hearings. Against that, however, are the

b considerations (i) that its determination now, on the basis of assumed and rather generally pleaded facts which have not even been the subject of a request for particulars, would not dispose entirely of the claim even if the decision were adverse to the plaintiff; and (ii) that it might turn out, when the facts were investigated, that no basis for this contentious claim existed. It would in my view have been better for the difficult questions to which this application and appeal

c give rise to be decided in the light of established facts rather than on the basis of the assumed truth of the pleaded facts.

The judge found the issue of vicarious liability the most difficult of those he had to decide, and I agree that it raises difficult problems.

If one begins with s 48 of the 1964 Act, and considers it apart altogether from

d the restrictive provisions of the 1976 Act or any provisions of that Act which might be invoked as establishing vicarious liability on the part of the commissioner, the position is plain beyond argument—the commissioner is answerable for the actions of the officers. This is because:

(1) Section 48 expressly provides that the chief officer of police is liable for torts committed by constables under his direction and control in the performance

e or purported performance of their duties as though they were committed by his servants in the course of their employment; and that he shall be treated for all purposes as a joint tortfeasor.

(2) An act of racial discrimination within s 20 is a statutory tort. If there were any doubt as to that it would be dispelled by the concluding words of s 57(1), 'in

f like manner as any other claim in tort'.

It follows that, if the appellant's argument that the commissioner is not vicariously liable in respect of this claim is to succeed it must be on the basis (1) that there is in the 1976 Act some provision which precludes the plaintiff's relying on s 48 of the 1964 Act; and (2) that there is not in the 1976 Act any other provision which, on the assumed facts of this case, justifies a claim based on

g vicarious liability of the commissioner.

There is no doubt that the words of s 53(1) of the 1976 Act are prima facie very restrictive. If the prohibition is considered in isolation from the introductory qualification, it is that 'no proceedings, whether civil or criminal, shall lie against any person in respect of an act by reason that the act is unlawful by virtue of a

h provision of this Act'.

Is this a prohibition affecting both types of claim and identity of parties, or only the former? It seems to me inescapable that as a matter of strict construction it applies to both. It would have been perfectly possible to frame the prohibition in terms which did not have that effect (for example by saying 'no proceedings ...

j shall be brought in respect of an act etc').

I cannot accept Mr Nicol's contention that the section is not expressed in clear language.

If (relying on the introductory words to s 53) one turns to s 57(1) there is in my view support for this construction. That subsection draws a distinction between the respondent who has himself committed an act of discrimination and someone who by virtue of s 32 or s 33 is to be treated as having committed such an act. If

the s 53 prohibition were one which did not operate to exclude claims against
persons vicariously liable for the acts of the respondent, the reference to ss 32 and   *a*
33 would be unnecessary. Thus, to take an example removed from the facts of
this case, it is in my view plain that a claim cannot be brought by virtue of s 57
against an employer in respect of his servant's discriminatory act save in reliance
on s 32(1) (or s 33). Ordinary vicarious liability *apart* from the 1976 Act does not
suffice; it is only to the extent that the 1976 Act permits vicarious liability claims   *b*
that they can be maintained.

Part of Mr Nicol's argument involved the assertion that it cannot have been the
intention of Parliament to exclude the normal adjectival or parasitic operation of
associated legislation such as the Police Act: so he seeks to draw a distinction
between ordinary vicarious liability—ie that arising simply as an incident of
relationship or authority conferred—and vicarious liability imposed (as in s 48) by   *c*
statute. The Police Act was, he says, part of the legislative background against
which the 1976 Act was passed. In advancing this argument he places particular
emphasis on the concluding words of s 48 of the Police Act, 'and accordingly shall
in respect of any such tort be treated for all purposes as a joint tortfeasor'.

However, since the term joint tortfeasor embraces the agent who commits a   *d*
tort on behalf of his principal and the employer liable in respect of his employee's
torts, I cannot accept that there is any valid distinction in scope between the
common law relationship of principal and agent and this statutory relationship.

A further variation of the argument is that s 48 characterises the imposed
relationship in terms not of principal and agent but of master and servant, and it
is in terms of that assumed relationship that they are for all purposes to be treated   *e*
as joint tortfeasors. Accordingly, says Mr Nicol, there is, by virtue of the deemed
relationship a basis for saying that the commissioner falls within s 32(1). The
difficulty about this is that the commissioner and the police officer are *not*
employer and employee, since deeming or treating persons as being in a
relationship is, so far from clothing them with that relationship, rather an   *f*
acknowledgment that they are not in that relationship. They do not therefore fall
within s 32(1).

Then Mr Nicol submits that the relationship is in any event one of agency and
that s 32(2) applies. He points to the fact that by virtue of s 4 of the Metropolitan
Police Act 1829 the commissioner has the direction and control of the force for
his area (compare the equivalent provisions in s 5(1) of the 1964 Act). He also   *g*
relies on case law which recognises that a chief officer commands the officers of
his force. This is common ground.

However, Mr Seabrook, contesting the notion that a constable is to be
regarded as the agent of the chief officer of police, relies on the decision in *Fisher
v Oldham Corp* [1930] 2 KB 364, [1930] All ER Rep 96. The question at issue in that   *h*
case was whether the police appointed by the watch committee, in effecting an
unlawful arrest, were acting as the servants or agents of the corporation so as to
render it liable to an action for false imprisonment. It was held that they were
not, and in the course of his judgment McCardie J said ([1930] 2 KB 364 at 371,
[1930] All ER Rep 96 at 101):   *j*

> 'Prima facie ... a police constable is not the servant of the borough. He is
> a servant of the State, a ministerial officer of the central power, though
> subject, in some respects, to local supervision and local regulation.'

Later he cited with approval a passage from the judgment of the High Court of
Australia in *Enever v R* (1906) 3 CLR 969 at 975, 977 in which Griffith CJ said:

a 'At common law the office of constable or peace officer was regarded as a
   public office, and the holder of it as being, in some sense, a servant of the
   Crown. Now, the powers of a constable, qua peace officer, whether
   conferred by common or statute law, are exercised by him by virtue of his
   office, and cannot be exercised on the responsibility of any person but
   himself ... A constable, therefore, when acting as a peace officer, is not
b exercising a delegated authority, but an original authority, and the general
   law of agency has no application.'

   McCardie J concluded his judgment thus ([1930] 2 KB 364 at 377–388, [1930] All
   ER Rep 96 at 104):

c 'The police, in effecting that arrest and detention, were not acting as the
   servants or agents of the defendants. They were fulfilling their duties as
   public servants and officers of the Crown sworn to "preserve the peace by
   day and by night, to prevent robberies and other felonies and
   misdemeanours and to apprehend offenders against the peace." If the local
   authorities are to be liable in such a case as this for the acts of the police with
d respect to felons and misdemeanours, then it would indeed be a serious
   matter and it would entitle them to demand that they ought to secure a full
   measure of control over the arrest and prosecution of all offenders. To give
   any such control would, in my view, involve a grave and most dangerous
   constitutional change. For the reasons given, there must be judgment for
e the defendant.'

   This case is commonly relied upon for the proposition that no relationship of
   principal and agent exists. However, Mr Nicol referred us to a passage in Clayton
   and Tomlinson *Civil Actions Against the Police* (1992) p 39, which argues as follows:

f 'It is submitted, however, that police officers must now be regarded as
   agents of their chief officer. The contrary dicta in *Fisher* v. *Oldham* are,
   strictly, *obiter* as the case was directly concerned only with the relationship of
   master and servant. In any event, the position has now, arguably, been
   altered by the effect of section 5 of the Police Act 1964 which places a police
   force under the direction and control of the chief constable. Such direction
g and control suggests a subordination of the original authority of individual
   constables to that of the chief constable. This contention is supported by the
   case of *Hawkins* v. *Bepey* in which it was held that a police officer instituting
   a prosecution was, in effect, doing so "on behalf of" his chief constable.'

h *Hawkins v Bepey* [1980] 1 All ER 797, [1980] 1 WLR 419, however, was a case of
   express authority, where a police officer had under instructions issued by the
   chief constable laid information on behalf of the police force. On his death a
   question arose as to whether the proceedings had lapsed. The court held that the
   real prosecutor was the chief constable or the force under his direction and
   control and that the proceedings had not lapsed. Bearing in mind the rather
j special facts and the fact that Watkins J in his judgment expressly held that the
   officer, in carrying out the instructions of the chief constable whose orders he had
   to obey, was acting in a representative capacity, I do not consider that this
   decision is in conflict with *Fisher's* case.
     In my view there is no valid ground for contending that the officers in the
   instant case were acting as the agents of the commissioner.

As some of the observations I have already made must have shown, I should *a*
like to be able to hold that there exists here the necessary vicarious liability to
entitle the plaintiff to maintain against the commissioner the action for racial
discrimination which, on the basis of the facts pleaded in the particulars of claim,
and for present purposes assumed to be true, I have accepted that she would have
been entitled to pursue against the officers themselves. But however the
argument is put, I can find no valid ground for holding that such a claim is *b*
maintainable against the commissioner. On this part of the case, moreover, it
cannot be and is not suggested that further elucidation of the facts might disclose
circumstances (such as existed in *Bepey*) establishing express authorisation.

Accordingly, while holding that a claim for racial discrimination under s 20 is,
in certain circumstances, maintainable against the police, I would allow this
appeal on the second ground because the claim against the commissioner is *c*
defeated by the prohibition in s 53. That part of the claim must accordingly, in
my view be struck out. I should add that, had I taken a different view on the
vicarious liability point, I should nevertheless have favoured striking our the
concluding sentence of the passage I have quoted from para 12(iv) of the
particulars of claim, which in my view clearly goes beyond anything that could *d*
fall within s 20. Moreover it also overlaps an existing claim in the action.

OTTON LJ. I have had the advantage of reading in draft the judgment of
Hutchison LJ. I agree with his analysis, reasoning and conclusions. I only wish
to add a few observations by way of emphasis.

Like Templeman LJ in *Savjani v IRC* [1981] 1 All ER 1121, [1981] QB 458, I *e*
should be slow to find that the effect of something which is humiliatingly
discriminatory in racial matters falls outside the ambit of the 1976 Act. I accept
that the police officers perform duties in order to prevent and detect crime and to
bring offenders to justice. They are also vested with powers to enable them to
perform those duties. While performing duties and exercising powers they also *f*
provide services in providing protection to the victims of crimes of violence.

Thus applying Templeman LJ's reasoning with regard to the position of the
police, the two concepts are not mutually exclusive. In *Kassam v Immigration
Appeal Tribunal* [1980] 2 All ER 330, [1980] 1 WLR 1037 the entry clearance officer
in Bombay was not providing a facility to intending immigrants when he
performed the act complained of; he was solely performing his duty of *g*
controlling them. Ackner LJ in *Kassam* [1980] 2 All ER 330 at 335, [1980] 1 WLR
1037 at 1043–1044, considered that the—

> 'word "facilities" ... is flanked on one side by the word "goods" and on the
> other by the word "services". This suggests to my mind that the word *h*
> "facilities" is not to be given a wholly unrestricted meaning but must be
> limited or confined to facilities that are akin to goods or services.'

In my view the provision of services of protection are akin to the provision of
facilities (if not goods). Given the dual role of a policeman I can see no reason
why he is not performing those services within s 20. *j*

I am unable to accept the submissions of Mr Robert Seabrook QC that public
policy requires that Pt III of the 1976 Act should not apply to the police at all, not
even when they are providing a service. He (like counsel in *Savjani's* case)
naturally and wisely shied away from the suggestion that a policeman might with
impunity decline to investigate a complaint or to protect a person from violence
on account of his or her colour. If an ambulance person and police officer

a attended at a scene of a road accident and they deliberately withheld medical services on the ground of a victim's race it would be illogical for the former to be guilty of an act of discrimination and for the latter to be immune from suit, criminal or civil.

In my judgment, if it was the intention of the Parliament to provide such immunity it would have expressly said so. In such a sensitive area as relations
b between the ethnic minorities and the police it would be to my mind surprising that Parliament would have countenanced such an exclusion from the ambit of the 1976 Act or allowed immunity to be inferred by the courts as a matter of construction. Moreover, Pt VI of the 1976 Act contains specific exceptions to its provisions, reflecting in some instances public policy (see s 42). It is significantly silent on an exception for the police, and more so for individual police officers.
c To my mind the examples of facilities and services in s 20(2) (and in particular at (g)) are wide enough to accommodate (and so not exclude) the services of protection for individuals.

Similarly I cannot accept that such an immunity can be properly brought in by a sidewind on the interpretation of s 75(1) contended for by Mr Seabrook. Lord
d Fraser in *Amin v Entry Clearance Officer, Bombay* [1983] 2 All ER 864 at 872–873, [1983] 2 AC 818 at 834–835, drew a distinction between acts done on behalf of the Crown which are of a kind similar to acts that might be done by a private person and acts done by a person holding statutory office in the course of formulating or carrying out government policy, the latter being quite different in kind from any act that would ever be done by a private person. The assertion in the pleading is
e that officers failed to react to the plaintiff's emergency telephone call, to investigate her account at the scene, and to afford her protection—all on account of her colour.

These acts (or services) which the plaintiff sought from the police were, to my mind, acts which might have been done by a private person. The second
f category envisaged by Lord Fraser covers those acts which a private person would never do, and would normally only ever be performed by the police, e g gaining forcible entry into a suspected drugs warehouse. Here the officers would be carrying out government policy to which the 1976 Act would not apply. Moreover, they would be performing duties in order to prevent and detect crime and exercising their powers to enable them to perform those duties.
g On this analysis I do not consider it necessary to address Mr Nicol QC's more complex argument based on s 75(2).

I would therefore find against the appellant on the first issue.

I am unable to accept the respondent's submissions on the second issue. I am not persuaded that the chief officer of police for an area which he serves is
h vicariously liable for an act of discrimination by one of his officers who on racial grounds has treated a person less favourably than he treated or would have treated other persons. It is engrained in the law of the Constitution that police constables are office holders; there is no relationship of employer and employee. In order to provide a remedy to a police officer who is discriminated against in
j the field of employment (in Pt II) the 1976 Act has a special provision in s 16. Section 53 has the effect of restricting proceedings for breach unless authorised by the 1976 Act. The sole authorisation is found in s 57. The combined effect of these two sections, in my view, is to exclude the plaintiff from the benefit of s 48 of the Police Act 1964.

Thus the plaintiff can only succeed against the commissioner if she can establish either that he personally committed the alleged act of discrimination (which is not alleged) or that he is vicariously liable under s 32(1) or (2). Subsection (1) expressly provides that: 'Anything done by a person in the course of his employment shall be treated ... as done by his employer ...' This provision cannot be applied to the commissioner as he is not an employer and the police constable is not an employee (except as a 'deemed employee' under Part II only). By sub-s (2) 'Anything done by a person as agent for another person with the authority (whether express or implied ...) of that other person shall be treated ... as done by that other person'.

In my view the concept of principal and agent is inimical to the status of a police constable. McCardie J in *Fisher v Oldham Corp* [1930] 2 KB 364 at 372, [1930] All ER Rep 96 at 101 cited with approval the statement of Griffith CJ in *Enever v R* (1906) 3 CLR 969 at 975, 977:

'Now, the powers of a constable, qua peace officer ... are exercised by him by virtue of his office, and cannot be exercised on the responsibility of any person but himself ... A constable, therefore, when acting as a peace officer, is not exercising a delegated authority, but an original authority, and the general law of agency has no application.'

I am prepared to accept that these observations may be strictly obiter as the case was concerned only with the relationship of master and servant. However, with respect to the authors of Clayton and Tomlinson *Civil Actions Against the Police* (1992), I do not share their view that the effect of s 5 of the 1964 Act which places a police force under 'the direction and control of the chief constable' (or commissioner) has the effect of changing the special status of a police constable or of subordinating his original authority to that of the chief constable. In reaching this conclusion I have considered *Hawkins v Bepey* [1980] 1 All ER 797, [1980] 1 WLR 419, which to my mind is primarily concerned with express authority, that the police officer originally instructed was acting in a representative capacity, and that there was a continuing authority which did not lapse on his death.

In my judgment the plaintiff in the present case could only bring herself within s 32(2) if she were able to prove that a police constable acted as he allegedly did on the express, or implied authority of a superior officer. In which case the act precedent or subsequent would then be treated as done by that superior officer as well as by the constable. She does not allege this.

I too consider it unsatisfactory that the court should be asked to determine such fundamental issues on the basis of the vague and unparticularised allegations in the particulars of claim rather than within a matrix of specific and detailed findings of fact. However, I am unable to say that for this reason the amendment (with some judicious redrafting) should not be allowed as on its fact it is arguable for the reasons given.

Accordingly, I would dismiss the appeal on the first issue and allow the appeal on the second issue with the result that the amendment should be struck out in its entirety.

PETER GIBSON LJ. I agree with both judgments.

Appeal allowed. Leave to appeal to the House of Lords granted.

Paul Magrath Esq   Barrister.

a

R v Camden London Borough Council, ex parte Martin

QUEEN'S BENCH DIVISION (CROWN OFFICE LIST)
SEDLEY J

b   3, 25 OCTOBER 1996

Solicitor – Payment of costs by solicitor personally – Costs incurred unreasonably or improperly – Application for leave to apply for judicial review withdrawn at hearing attended by prospective respondent – Whether wasted costs order appropriate – Whether prospective respondent a 'party' to proceedings – Whether court having jurisdiction to make wasted costs order in favour of prospective respondent – Supreme Court Act 1981, ss 51, 151.

c

The applicant applied for leave to apply for judicial review of, inter alia, the local authority's decision refusing her appeal against the suitability of premises which
d   it had offered her pursuant to its obligations under Pt III of the Housing Act 1985 and its further decision refusing to reconsider her appeal in the light of evidence which she had presented. On the eve of the adjourned hearing counsel advised that the application should be withdrawn. At the hearing, which the local authority attended, the judge gave the applicant leave to withdraw and, on the
e   local authority's application, directed a further hearing to determine whether the case was an appropriate one for a wasted costs order under s 51(6) of the Supreme Court Act 1981 against the applicant's solicitors. The issue arose whether the local authority was a 'party' to the proceedings within s 51(7)[a] of the Act, as defined in s 151[b].

f   **Held** – For the purposes of ss 51(6), (7) and 151 of the 1981 Act, the term 'party' was not an open-ended category and was limited to a person who had been served with notice of or had intervened in proceedings by virtue of rules of court or other statutory provision. It followed that the court had no power to make a wasted costs order in favour of or against a person who, as a prospective respondent, elected to oppose an ex parte application for leave to apply for
g   judicial review, since that person was not a 'party' within the meaning of ss 51(6), (7) and 151 of the 1981 Act. The modern practice of the court in regularly hearing and sometimes inviting the participation of such persons could not make it otherwise; only legislation or a rule change could do so. The application for a wasted costs order against the applicant's solicitors would be accordingly
h   dismissed for want of jurisdiction (see p 311 *d g h* and p 313 *c d*, post).

Notes

For the jurisdiction of the court to order costs against a legal representative personally, see 44(1) *Halsbury's Laws* (4th edn reissue) paras 167–174, and for cases
j   on solicitors' liability for costs in misconduct in contentious matters, see 44 *Digest* (Reissue) 430–435, 4668–4723.

For the Supreme Court Act 1981, ss 51, 151, see 11 *Halsbury's Statutes* (4th edn) (1991 reissue) 1019, 1071.

---

a   Section 51, so far as material, is set out at p 311 *b c*, post
b   Section 151, so far as material, is set out at p 311 *d*, post

Cases referred to in judgment

Davy-Chiesman v Davy-Chiesman [1984] 1 All ER 321, [1984] Fam 48, [1984] 2 WLR 291, CA.

Hunter & Partners v Wellings & Partners [1987] FSR 83, CA.

Pickwick International Inc (GB) Ltd v Multiple Sound Distributors Ltd [1972] 3 All ER 384, [1972] 1 WLR 1213.

R v Hackney London Borough, ex p Rowe [1996] COD 155.

R v Kensington and Chelsea Royal Borough, ex p Ghebregiogis (1994) 27 HLR 602.

R v PIA, ex p Lucas Fettes Ltd [1995] OPLR 187.

R v Secretary of State for the Home Dept, ex p Begum [1990] COD 107, CA.

Ridehalgh v Horsfield [1994] 3 All ER 848, [1994] Ch 205, [1994] 3 WLR 462, CA.

Cases also cited or referred to in skeleton arguments

R v Kensington and Chelsea Royal London BC, ex p Hammell [1989] 1 All ER 1202, [1989] QB 518, CA.

R v Wycombe DC, ex p Hazeltine (1993) 25 HLR 313, CA.

Application

On 15 May 1996 before Latham J Margaret (aka Margarita) Martin withdrew her application for leave to apply for judicial review of (i) the continuing failure of Camden London Borough Council to secure that accommodation within the meaning of s 65(2) of the Housing Act 1985 became available to her; (ii) the council's decision of 30 September 1995 refusing her appeal against the suitability of premises which it had offered her; and (iii) its further decision of 22 November 1995 refusing to reconsider her appeal against the suitability of the premises in the light of evidence which she had presented. Thereupon, on an application being made by the council, the judge directed a further hearing to determine whether the case was an appropriate one for a wasted costs order to be made against the applicant's solicitors under s 51(6) of the Supreme Court Act 1981. The facts are set out in the judgment.

Gillian Carrington (instructed by *Amanda Kelly*) for the council.
Declan O'Mahoney (instructed by *The Luper Partnership*) for the applicant's solicitors.

Cur adv vult

25 October 1996. The following judgment was delivered.

SEDLEY J. This is an application by the respondent local authority, Camden London Borough Council, following the withdrawal of an application for judicial review, for a wasted costs order against the applicant's solicitors, the Luper Partnership.

History

The applicant, Margarita Martin, had at all relevant times an accepted entitlement to permanent housing under Pt III of the Housing Act 1985. She turned down a number of offers of permanent accommodation, including finally the tenancy of a third or fourth floor flat, 18 Rochester Court, NW1. The council considered that its offer had been a proper and reasonable one and that its duties were at an end. The applicant, who considered her refusal to be reasonable, went to solicitors—Messrs Hodge Jones & Allen—who on 24 August 1995, before the *a* time for acceptance had expired, wrote to the district housing office to explain the applicant's objections. These were, at that stage, that the lift was frequently out of order and that her daughter, Leanne, was phobic about lifts because of a asthma attack she had suffered in one sometime before. These solicitors asked for a medical reassessment and a reconsideration of the case.

b There had been, earlier in August, a successful appeal by the applicant on the ground that she had been offered a fourth floor flat but had already refused such an offer on medical grounds. (There was a dispute, which it is agreed is immaterial, whether the flat was in truth on the fourth or the third floor of Rochester Court.) A fresh appeal panel considered the representations made by Hodge Jones & Allen but maintained the view that the offer was suitable. In particular, the panel had before it a report, originating with the estate manager, *c* that the lifts at Rochester Court were reliable. It had no medical evidence before it to confirm the daughter's phobia. A fresh deadline for acceptance was set and subsequently extended, but it finally expired on 27 October 1995, the applicant still not having accepted the flat. It has now been let to somebody else.

Two or three weeks later, on 15 November 1995, the Luper Partnership came *d* on the scene, asking for reconsideration of the appeal. The letter said:

e 'We ... understand that you have taken advise [sic] from the estate manager who has indicated that the flat has a reliable lift service. We have evidence that this advise is incorrect. We enclose herewith copies [of] two letters from persons who we are instructed reside in the block which we believe show that the advise which the Council received in this matter was incorrect. Accordingly we would ask that the homeless persons unit or the housing dept reconsider the matter in light of this new evidence.'

The letter went on to say that the solicitors had legal aid for judicial review but would wait for seven days to give the council a chance to reconsider. The letter *f* enclosed two short statements, one from an identified resident, who, however, did not date it, saying: 'The lifts on Rochester Court very [rarely] work', and one, dated 16 October 1995, from an unidentifiable resident saying 'The lift in Rochester Court NW1 constantly breaks down & is widely used as a urinal'.

The local authority replied a week later that it was not prepared to review the decision to reject the applicant's appeal. The borough's solicitor set out the *g* history of appeals in August and September 1995. The letter did not go as far as the affidavit sworn by the district rehousing manager, Jacqui Frost, in the present application, which by para 37 contends that the two statements about the lift would have made no difference since the appeal panel could have continued to prefer the estate manager's statement to the contrary. The real point was that *h* Camden had closed the file after giving a succession of opportunities to the applicant to demonstrate the unsuitability of the offer made to her, and were not prepared to reopen it on the basis of the two short statements sent by the Luper Partnership.

On 13 December 1995 an application for leave to apply for judicial review was *j* lodged in the Crown Office. It challenged (a) the continuing refusal of accommodation; (b) the adverse decision on appeal at the end of September; and (c) the refusal to reconsider the appeal in November. No application had been made, before issuing the proceedings, for access to the housing file pursuant to the statutory right accorded by s 106(5) of the 1985 Act. Nor, when Camden learnt of the proceedings and asked for a set of the papers, did the Luper Partnership oblige by sending a set. They sedulously refused until, almost on the

eve of the leave hearing before Judge J on 23 February 1996, the council obtained
a set of papers from the St Pancras Housing Association (its property managers)
and put in the affidavit of Jacqui Frost to which I have referred. Exhibited to it
was a bundle described in the affidavit as comprising 'copies of documents which
related to the applicant's appeal'. An opportunity given during the hearing before
me to verify it by affidavit as representing the contents of the housing file, bar
those covered by legal professional privilege, was duly taken.

When the matter came before Judge J on 26 February 1996, Mr O'Mahoney,
for the applicant, sought and obtained an adjournment in order to consider
whether the daughter's phobia of lifts might furnish a further or alternative
ground of challenge. A psychiatric report was obtained and submitted to
Camden, whose appeal panel met in order to consider it, assisted by their own
medical assessment officer. They concluded that, while her phobia made her
unable to use a lift, she was not so asthmatic that she could not use the stairs, with
the result that there was no need to reopen or replicate the offer. Mr Avadis, a
partner in the Luper Partnership, deposes that counsel advised that the
application should proceed.

Accordingly, the daughter's medical records were obtained from the hospital.
Reading them on the eve of the adjourned hearing the applicant's counsel
realised that the case was hopeless, partly because the notes showed that the
daughter had described herself as being only mildly asthmatic but mainly because
they showed that she was not living with her mother at all but with her boyfriend.
There is a difference of recollection between solicitor and counsel as to the
eventual basis of counsel's adverse advice, but it is sufficient that the decision to
withdraw was made and, in my view, justifiably made. In other words, neither
the original grounds on which the matter had come before Judge J nor the ground
subsequently explored was capable of succeeding.

The application

Upon withdrawal before Latham J on 15 May 1996 there were no means by
which Camden could expect to recover its costs against a legally aided applicant
with a nil contribution. Nor was there a prospect under the existing legislation of
recovering costs against the legal aid fund. There remained the question which
Latham J stood over with directions and which I now have to decide, whether the
case is an appropriate one for a wasted costs order. Camden's application is
directed against the Luper Partnership, the solicitors, and not against counsel
who advised them. This has created problems because both the solicitor's
affidavit (in which Mr O'Mahoney tells me he had a hand) and Mr O'Mahoney's
own statement to me from the bar have gallantly sought to draw Camden's fire
away from the solicitor and towards counsel.

On this application I am therefore concerned only to decide whether there was
any improper, unreasonable or negligent conduct on the part of the Luper
Partnership which directly caused a quantifiable waste of costs on Camden's part
(see *Ridehalgh v Horsfield* [1994] 3 All ER 848, [1994] Ch 205). Part of a solicitor's
duty is to exercise at least a measure of independent judgment in relation to
advice received from counsel (see *Davy-Chiesman v Davy-Chiesman* [1984] 1 All ER
321, [1984] Fam 48). A solicitor is also, in my judgment, under an obligation (a)
to consider evidential material produced by the other side before sending it to
counsel; and (b) to ensure that counsel deals timeously with the papers and to
withdraw and reassign instructions which are not treated with proper expedition.

Jurisdiction

a   I became concerned, after reserving my judgment, at a preliminary problem on which I have sought counsel's further submissions: as an uninvited prospective respondent, was Camden at any stage a 'party' within s 51(7) of the Supreme Court Act 1981, which governs my present powers? Section 51 includes these provisions:

b   '... (6) In any proceedings mentioned in subsection (1), the court may disallow, or (as the case may be) order the legal or other representative concerned to meet, the whole of any wasted costs or such part of them as may be determined in accordance with rules of court.
          (7) In subsection (6), "wasted costs" means any costs incurred by a party—
c   (a) as a result of any improper, unreasonable or negligent act or omission on the part of any legal or other representative or any employee of such a representative; or (b) which, in the light of any such act or omission occurring after they were incurred, the court considers it is unreasonable to expect that party to pay.'

d   Section 151 provides:

          '... "party", in relation to any proceedings, includes any person who pursuant to or by virtue of rules of court or any other statutory provision has been served with notice of, or has intervened in, those proceedings ...'

e   RSC Ord 53, r 3(2) provides: 'An application for leave must be made *ex parte* to a Judge ...'
      Mr O'Mahoney submits that neither limb of s 151 describes Camden's position: the council not only had not been but could not have been served with notice under rules of court or statute, since the only material provision—Ord 53, r 3(2)—excludes the possibility by requiring leave applications to be made ex
f   parte. Any notice of a leave application will be outside the rules, whether given out of courtesy or self-interest or because the court has required it. By parity of reasoning, Camden cannot rank as a person intervening under rules of court or statute: if they intervene, they do so by leave of the court notwithstanding the present rules.
      Miss Carrington submits, first, that the definition in s 151 is not exhaustive but
g   expansive. It omits, for example, applicants or plaintiffs, who must on any view be parties. This I accept, but I do not accept that 'party' is therefore an open-ended category. The purpose of the s 151 definition is to enlarge the category of those who are obviously parties (plaintiffs, defendants, applicants for judicial review, persons served as directly affected under Ord 53, r 5(3)) to
h   embrace those whose position might otherwise be debatable (trustees, mortgagees; persons intervening as 'proper ... to be heard' under Ord 53, r 9(1)). But this enlarged category is still confined by the explicit boundary of statutory provision relied on by Mr O'Mahoney, and Camden in these proceedings plainly stands outside it.
j   Next, Miss Carrington submits that practice has created a de facto category of respondent, known for many years in civil actions, especially in the Chancery Division, through the development of the 'opposed ex parte' application. Such an uninvited respondent may be heard under Ord 29, r 1. The court can award it costs if it was present at either the express or the tacit invitation of the applicant (see *Pickwick International Inc (GB) Ltd v Multiple Sound Distributors Ltd* [1972] 3 All ER 384, [1972] 1 WLR 1213), and it can appeal as if from an inter partes decision

(see *Hunter & Partners v Wellings & Partners* [1987] FSR 83).   This development, reflecting as it does the preference of any court for hearing both sides if it realistically can and the reasonableness of a potential party's wish not to be condemned unheard, has been possible at least in part because Ord 29 contains no provision equivalent to Ord 53, r 3(2): it is always for the court in civil proceedings to decide whether an applicant may proceed ex parte, and Ord 29, r 1(2) makes it plain that ex parte hearings are the exception, not the rule.

Courts of judicial review, responding to much the same imperatives, have found it a practical necessity to escape the trammels of Ord 53, r 3(2).   The Court of Appeal in *R v Secretary of State for the Home Dept, ex p Begum* [1990] COD 107 expressly sanctioned inter partes procedure where the application for leave itself raises doubts which the putative respondent can help to resolve—to the extent, at least, of allowing the court to invite the latter to make representations.   In other cases, where the application for leave is accompanied by a prayer for interlocutory relief, notice given to the intended respondent for the latter purpose gives it in practice locus to oppose the grant of leave.   This is now a common scenario in the Crown Office list.   In addition, an intended respondent may learn (sometimes by regularly watching the lists) of an impending leave application and will turn up uninvited to oppose the grant of leave.   I do not myself know of a case where such an intervener has been refused a hearing.

In all such cases, however, an important safeguard for applicants is lost.   The point of the requirement that leave applications must be made ex parte was to afford applicants a simple and inexpensive way of finding out whether they had a worthwhile case.   As Sir Harry Woolf (as he then was) said in his 1989 Hamlyn Lectures *Protection of the Public—A New Challenge* ((1990) p 21), 'it enables a litigant expeditiously and cheaply to obtain the view of a High Court judge on the merits of his application'.   It was also, ironically, to protect putative respondents from the expense and trouble of opposing a case which might have nothing in it.   It is the explosion of judicial review since the mid-1970s which has presented the court with a flow of applications of widely varying quality and merit but also of increasing sophistication.   If leave is obtained, research has shown that there is a 50% chance that the application will not reach a full hearing (see Sunkin, Bridges and Mészáros *Judicial Review in Perspective* (1996)); and while the full range of reasons for this is the subject of continuing research, attrition and surrender must account for some cases.   So the court has good reason in many instances—the present case would have been one had it been pursued—for hearing a putative respondent before deciding whether to grant leave, in spite of the complications it introduces into what was intended to be a simple procedure.

In accordance with its practice of hearing intended respondents, the court has been prepared to award them costs where their opposition has succeeded (see *R v PIA, ex p Lucas Fettes Ltd* [1995] OPLR 187).   It has also been prepared to award costs in the mirror-image class of case where an intended respondent, by ignoring a letter before action, has forced an applicant to apply for leave and has then, before the grant of leave, conceded the issue (see *R v Kensington and Chelsea Royal Borough, ex p Ghebregiogis* (1994) 27 HLR 602).   Such awards of costs are permitted by the catholic provisions of s 51(1)(2) and (3) of 1981 Act:

> '(1) Subject to the provisions of this or any other enactment and to rules of court, the costs of and incidental to all proceedings in—(a) the civil division of the Court of Appeal; (b) the High Court; and (c) any county court, shall be in the discretion of the court.

a
(2) Without prejudice to any general power to make rules of court, such rules may make provision for regulating matters relating to the costs of those proceedings including, in particular, prescribing scales of costs to be paid to legal or other representatives.

(3) The court shall have full power to determine by whom and to what extent the costs are to be paid.'

b
These provisions, unlike those governing wasted costs, are not predicated on the involvement of a 'party'. In *R v Hackney London Borough, ex p Rowe* [1996] COD 155 it is true that I entertained and rejected an application for a wasted costs order in a situation similar to that in *Ex p Ghebregiogis*; but the problem of jurisdiction was not canvassed.

c
In my judgment, there is no power in the court to make a wasted costs order in favour of (or, by parity of reasoning, against) a person who elects to oppose an ex parte application for leave to apply for judicial review. Such a person is not a party within the meaning of ss 51(6), (7) and 151 of the 1981 Act. The modern practice of the court in regularly hearing and sometimes inviting the participation of such persons cannot make it otherwise; only legislation or a rule change can do so.

d
Accordingly, I would dismiss this application by Camden for a wasted costs order for want of jurisdiction.

In case, however, I am held to have erred in doing so, I will set out the findings I would otherwise have arrived at. [His Lordship then considered the merits and concluded:]

e
What I find happened is that, on 14 May 1996, the day before the application was due to come back before Latham J, the Luper Partnership telephoned Camden to offer to withdraw, but because Camden would not undertake in return not to seek an order for payment of wasted costs, both parties attended before Latham J who gave the applicant leave to withdraw and made provision for the canvassing of the present issue on wasted costs.

f
In my judgment, the second hearing could and should have been abandoned without the need of attendance at court. Had counsel attended to the papers in the early part of May, as the solicitors should have insisted he did, his consequent advice would have enabled the application to be withdrawn without further expense, whether or not an application for wasted costs caused by the handling of the first hearing was thereafter to be pursued by Camden. Indeed, even if one accepts the late reappraisal of the case, there was no need for the parties to attend: the Crown Office should have been notified on 14 May that the application was being withdrawn, and there should have been no difficulty in securing a consensual order in much the same form as Latham J adopted for the trial of the present issue. If, contrary to this view, attendance was going to be necessary for directions on the wasted costs application whatever the state of the substantive leave application, the costs of the attendance before Latham J would fall for disposal as costs in the wasted costs application.

g

h

j
Conclusion

If I had jurisdiction, therefore, I would conclude that the costs incurred by Camden in attending on two occasions to oppose the grant of leave were incurred as a result of unreasonable and negligent acts and omissions on the part of the Luper Partnership. I would have ordered these solicitors to meet the costs incurred by Camden in attending on 23 February 1996 before Judge J and on 15

May 1996 before Latham J. In the event, however, the application fails for want of jurisdiction.

Because of my view of, on the one hand, the merits and, on the other, my jurisdiction, I propose to make no order for costs save (what I have no power to refuse) a legal aid taxation of the applicant's costs. As arranged with counsel at the conclusion of the hearing, there will be liberty to apply within 14 days if either side opposes the making of an order to this effect. There will also be liberty to apply in relation to any other consequential matter which the parties are not able within 14 days of the date of my handing down this judgment to agree.

For these reasons, which have been set out in writing and communicated to the parties, and which are now available to the press and the public, this application for a wasted costs order fails.

Application dismissed.

Dilys Tausz   Barrister.

Ferguson v Davies

a

COURT OF APPEAL, CIVIL DIVISION
EVANS, HENRY AND ALDOUS LJJ
9 OCTOBER, 21 NOVEMBER 1996

b

Accord and satisfaction – Acceptance of lesser sum – Cheque – Defendant sending cheque to plaintiff with letter stating it to be in full settlement – Defendant admitting on court form that cheque amount was due but asserting that remainder of claim had been paid – Plaintiff cashing cheque for part of debt but giving notice of continuing action – No consideration given to plaintiff in addition to cheque – Whether letter and court form constituting offer of settlement or admission of liability – Whether plaintiff's cashing of cheque constituting accord and satisfaction of claim.

c

In February 1992 the plaintiff sold a quantity of specialist records, tapes and discs to the defendant, who dealt in such items. The parties agreed that the defendant *d* would provide records in return to the value of £600 by a certain date, failing which he would pay to the plaintiff the cash value of the individual items to a total of £1,700. The defendant did not comply with the time limit; he only delivered records to the value of £143·50 and made a single payment of £5 to the plaintiff. Thereafter, the plaintiff brought proceedings in the county court against the defendant, limiting his claim to £486·50. On 17 February 1993 the defendant *e* wrote to the plaintiff enclosing a cheque for £150 as full payment. He also completed a county court form of defence and counterclaim in which he indicated that he admitted £150 of the claim but otherwise disputed the claim, stating that he had paid the plaintiff £450 and had sent him a cheque for the remaining £150; in addition, he wrote to the court stating that the cheque was in *f* settlement of the plaintiff's account and that he did not dispute that he owed the plaintiff money, merely the total amount claimed. The plaintiff cashed the cheque but informed the defendant that he was continuing with the action until he received full payment of his claim, which had been increased to £1,745·79. The judge dismissed the plaintiff's claim. He held that while a further £1,400 was due from the defendant and the plaintiff had not intended in presenting the cheque to *g* accept the £150 in full settlement, his doing so had nevertheless compromised his claim by a binding accord and satisfaction. The plaintiff appealed.

Held – The appeal would be allowed for the following reasons—

(1) (Per Henry and Aldous LJJ) Acceptance by a plaintiff from a defendant of a *h* lesser sum than the amount claimed did not constitute accord and satisfaction so as to compromise the action between them unless the plaintiff received some additional benefit by way of consideration. In the instant case, the judge had erred in law in that he had not considered the legal significance of the fact that the defendant had unequivocally admitted liability for the amount of the cheque on *j* completing and sending the county court form to the court and had therefore given no consideration in law for the accord suggested. Nor had the judge paid regard to the scheme of the County Court Rules governing cases where an admission was coupled with an assertion that the remainder of the claim had been paid. It followed that the judge had been wrong to conclude that cashing the cheque constituted a clear and unequivocal acceptance by the plaintiff that no further sum was due and a binding accord, since there was no consideration for

the term the defendant had sought to impose in his letter to the plaintiff once the
admission had been made (see p 323 *e* to 324 *d*, post); *D & C Builders Ltd v Rees*   *a*
[1965] 3 All ER 837 applied.

(2) (Per Evans and Aldous LJJ) Taking into account the whole of the
circumstances and documents, the defendant's entries in the county court form
were to the effect that £150 was admittedly due, and was being paid, leaving the
balance in dispute. The plaintiff was entitled to understand the defendant's offer   *b*
in that sense, and it followed that his acceptance of the cheque did not give rise
to an agreement that he would forego the balance of his claim and therefore there
had been no binding accord (see p 324 *d* and p 326 *c d*, post).

Notes

For discharge of contractual promises by accord and satisfaction, see 9 *Halsbury's*   *c*
Laws (4th edn) paras 585–593, and for cases on the subject, see 12(2) *Digest* (2nd
reissue) 361–402, 6942–7305.

Cases referred to in judgments

Caldwell v Sumpters (a firm) [1972] 1 All ER 567, [1972] Ch 478, [1972] 2 WLR 412,   *d*
  CA.
D & C Builders Ltd v Rees [1965] 3 All ER 837, [1966] 2 QB 617, [1966] 2 WLR 288,
  CA.
Foakes v Beer (1884) 9 App Cas 605, [1881–5] All ER Rep 106, HL.
Goddard & Son v O'Brien (1882) 9 QBD 37.
Newton Moor Construction Ltd v Charlton [1981] CA Transcript 555.   *e*
Pinnel's Case (1602) 5 Co Rep 117a, [1558–1774] All ER Rep 612, 77 ER 237.
Rush & Tompkins Ltd v Greater London Council [1988] 3 All ER 737, [1989] AC 1280,
  [1988] 3 WLR 939, HL.
Stour Valley Builders v Stuart [1992] CA Transcript 1281.
Tiney Engineering Ltd v Amods Knitting Machinery Ltd [1986] BTLC 324, CA.   *f*

Cases also cited or referred to in skeleton arguments

Auriema Ltd v Haigh & Ringrose Ltd [1988] Const LJ 200.
Bell v Galynsk [1974] 2 Lloyd's Rep 13, CA.
Budget Rent a Car Ltd v Goodman [1991] 2 NZLR 715, NZ HC.
Cooper v Parker (1855) 15 CB 822, 139 ER 650.   *g*
Cumber v Wane (1721) 1 Stra 426, 93 ER 613.
Merkuria Foreign Trade Corp v Dateline Electric Co Ltd [1979] CA Transcript 413.
Selectmove Ltd, Re [1995] 2 All ER 531, CA.
Sibree v Tripp (1846) 15 M & W 23, 153 ER 745.
Warren's Trusts, Re (1884) 26 Ch D 208.   *h*

Appeal

By notice dated 30 June 1995 the plaintiff, Michael Ferguson, appealed from the
decision of Judge Crane in the Northampton County Court on 19 July 1994
whereby he dismissed the plaintiff's claim against the defendant, Steven Clive
Davies, for money due under a contract. The facts are set out in the judgment of   *j*
Henry LJ.

The plaintiff appeared in person.
Terry Lynch (instructed by *J Garrard & Allen*, Olney) for the defendant.

Cur adv vult

a 21 November 1996. The following judgments were delivered.

HENRY LJ (giving the first judgment at the invitation of Evans LJ). This is an appeal from the order of Judge Crane dismissing the plaintiff's claim for money due to him under a contract on the basis that that claim had been compromised by a binding accord and satisfaction. Before the judge and before us the plaintiff
b acted in person, but his case has lost nothing in clarity because of that.

Matters arose in this way. The plaintiff wished to dispose of some specialist records, tapes and discs to the defendant, who dealt in such items. His prime interest was in obtaining other specialist items in return, to which end he gave the defendant lists of the records etc that he was looking for. In default of providing such goods to an agreed value of £600 by a certain time by way of payment, it was
c agreed that the buyer was obliged to pay cash at the valuation of the individual items delivered by the plaintiff to the defendant, to a total of some £1,700. In fact, as the judge was to find, the defendant only delivered goods to the value of £143·50 and made a single payment of £5·00. So, as the judge was to find, when the plaintiff delivered his particulars of claim there was due to him under the
d contract approximately £1,550.

For reasons which are not clear to me but do not matter, the plaintiff originally limited his claim to £486·50. It may be that part of his motive was to get the matter within the small claims jurisdiction. His claim as set out on the county court's N1 default summons was for 'Unpaid for goods/breach of contract + disbursements'. His particulars of claim read:

e   'On 24th February 1992 a quantity of records were sold to Mr Davies for £600·00. It was agreed that Mr Davies should supply £600·00 worth of records to myself at the wholesale price, within a set period. No goods were supplied within this period but a delivery of £143·50 of records and a £5·00 cash payment was made after the agreed period of payment. No further
f   goods (or cash) have been received despite repeated attempts via phone, letter (most recent 30.4.92) and in person.'

The judge was to find that the plaintiff was right that no further goods nor cash had been received from the defendant.

Form N1 had certain instructions to the defendant on it:

g   'What to do about this summons   You can
       • dispute the claim
       • make a claim against the plaintiff
       • admit the claim in full and offer to pay
h   • pay the total amount shown above
       • admit only part of the claim ...'

Enclosed with form N1 is form N9B 'Form of defence and counterclaim to accompany Form N1'. That form is addressed to the defendant. The introductory instructions to him read (so far as is relevant):

j   'When to fill in this form
          • Only fill in this form if you wish to dispute all or part of the claim and/ or make a claim against the plaintiff (counterclaim).'

Instructions are then given as to how to fill in the form, and then:

       'Where to send this form

• Send or take this form immediately to the court office at the address
shown above.   *a*
• If you admit part of the claim and you are asking for time to pay, you will
also need to fill in the blue admission form (N9A) and send both reply forms
to the court.'

The next relevant paragraph is: *b*

'What happens next
• If you complete box 3 on this form, the court will ask the plaintiff to
confirm that he has received payment. If he tells the court that you have not
paid, the court will tell you what you should do.'

Box 3 is the box you complete when you dispute the claim because you have   *c*
already paid it. That concludes the introduction. There then follows: '1 How
much of the claim do you dispute?' This gives two options to be chosen by
ticking a box. The defendant originally ticked the box for: 'I dispute the full
amount claimed' but he crossed this tick out and initialled the erasure. He ticked
the second box opposite: 'I admit the amount of' and he then inserted '£150'. The   *d*
form then continues:

'If you dispute only part of the claim you must either:
• pay the amount admitted to the person named at [his address] ... Then
send this defence to the court. or
• complete the blue admission form and send it to the court with this   *e*
defence. *Tick whichever applies* ... I paid the amount admitted on ... or I
enclose the completed form of admission ...'

The defendant ticked neither of those boxes, nor did he enclose the completed
form of admission, probably because he was not asking for time to pay (see the
introductory instructions).   *f*
Box 2 then dealt with arbitrations under the small claims procedure and box 3
asked the question: 'Do you dispute this claim because you have already paid it?
Tick whichever applies ... No [That was not ticked] ... Yes I paid £450·00 to the
plaintiff over this period ...' There then follows a box where the defendant gave
details of where and how he said he paid the sums, totalling £450 (on which, as
we have seen, he was disbelieved by the judge) and then he added 'Cheque for   *g*
£150·00 sent 17.2.93 to Mr. Ferguson'. That was the amount he had admitted was
due (see box 1).
The judge was to find that the plaintiff's presentation of that cheque
compromised the action by a binding accord and satisfaction, and the question for
us was whether he was right to do so.   *h*
On that day the defendant wrote two letters. First, to the plaintiff:

'Please find enclosed a cheque for £150·00 as a full payment on the County
Court Summons ... As the document sent to the court details I dispute the
total and have listed the reasons. I hope that this will now resolve the
matter.'   *j*

To the court he wrote:

'Further to the enclosed documents I am enclosing a cheque for the sum of
£150·00 in settlement of Mr Ferguson's account. I do not dispute the fact that
I owe him money however dispute the total amount he is claiming.'

He then makes allegations as to cash and stock payments and other matters and concludes: 'I hope that this will now resolve the matter, however should you need to contact me please note the change of address.'

Both letters made clear what was manifest on the face of form N9B: namely first, that he was admitting that £150 was due in any event; and second, that he denied the balance of the claim (then £450) was due, because he asserted he had paid it. The judge was to find that a further approximate £1,400 was in fact due from him: £1,550 in total.

As the paragraph on form N9B 'What happens next' (already quoted) makes clear, as the defendant had completed box 3, the court would then (under CCR 1981, Ord 9, r 2(7)(b)) request the plaintiff to confirm in writing that he wished the proceedings to continue. Form N236 should be sent to him for this purpose— see appellant's bundle, p 69: 'Not included in the Bundle of Documents in the Court Below'. That says:

> 'The defendant states that he has paid the money you are claiming (see enclosed form N9B). If you disagree and wish to proceed, sign and return this form to the court as soon as possible.'

The court notes read that form N236 was returned, marked not known at the address. But the form does not appear to have been re-sent, probably because the court knew that the plaintiff intended to proceed because he had attended at court to find out whether or not he could cash the cheque, had seen the documents received from the defendant and had concluded that he could safely accept the cheque on account.

So the plaintiff presented the cheque (the date for this is not known), the cheque was cleared (again on a date unknown) and after the cheque had been cleared he wrote to the defendant on 7 March 1993 as follows:

> 'Thank you for your letter and cheque recieved [sic] recently. With regard to your letter sent direct to myself and the letter recieved [sic] by the courts, I was disappointed, but unfortunately not surprised by its contents. It will come as no surprise to yourself that I am continuing with the action until full payment is received. You will therefore be receiving, in the near future a date from the courts concerning a hearing over this action. To be honest it annoys me that this matter and its conclusion has been further delayed. Due to this I am contacting my solicitor over this action plus discussing the possibility of taking out an action as per the contract signed by yourself. As you may recal [sic] the contract if enforced could increase your debt to me to in excess of £1500·00 plus legal fees ... I hope the above "refreshes" your memory with regard to the lengths I have taken in resolving this matter to your conveniance [sic], and honour your outstanding liability. I look forward to hearing from you by return.'

There was no reply to that letter, and the plaintiff returned to court and got leave to amend his claim upwards to claim £1,745·79. When the amended defence was put in, the claim for accord and satisfaction was made. But no order was made that that should be tried as a preliminary point.

As has been indicated, the judge found for the plaintiff on the contractual issues: namely that a further £1,400 was due from the defendant. But he held that presentation of the £150 cheque compromised the claim, and so the action failed.

The judge was not referred to any of the authorities in this difficult area of the law, but correctly put the question:

> '... if, immediately after that cheque was paid in and cleared, a bystander who knew the facts and looked objectively at what had passed between the parties, would that objective bystander have ... interpreted what had happened, as a firm offer to settle the matter and a firm acceptance of the [offer].'

The judge accepted that, in presenting the cheque, 'the plaintiff did not intend in fact to accept it in full settlement'. That conclusion was inevitable having regard to both the plaintiff's unchallenged evidence, and the court forms. The court forms catered for the defendant admitting a sum and immediately paying it, and for the defendant admitting a sum but asking for time to pay. They did not provide for an admission only on terms that that admission was in full and final settlement. That does not seem to me to be an unintentional omission, but a correct legal analysis of the effect of an admission in the pleadings: my reasons for this will follow.

But the judge found that the plaintiff's intention was not determinative:

> '... but this is a classic situation in the law of contract where two parties in fact intend different things and that is why the court, in judging contracts, has to look at what the parties said and did, rather than at their private intentions and I am bound to point out the fact that ... the plaintiff, later wrote the letter of 7th March, could not revive his right of action, if in fact objectively he had already compromised it.'

He then went on to find:

> '... in the circumstances, against the background of the amount then being claimed and in dispute, the paying in, followed by the clearance of the cheque, was a clear and unequivocal acceptance and it follows from that that the plaintiff agreed to a compromise of this matter, as I find, and it therefore follows that no further sums were due from the defendant to the plaintiff and for those reasons I dismiss the plaintiff's claim.'

The plaintiff then sought leave to appeal, and the matter then came before the full court (Simon Brown and Millett LJJ). The court gave leave on the basis enunciated by Millett LJ. He said:

> '... I would give leave to appeal on the sole question whether the judge was correct in his finding that the action was settled by payment of £150 and acceptance of the payment. It appears to me there may be two principles in play. In the first place, the law does not normally permit a party to retain a payment and repudiate the terms on which payment was made. In the case of documents, the principle is stated in terms in *Caldwell v Sumpters (a firm)* [1972] 1 All ER 567 at 570, [1972] Ch 478 at 495 ... A party who accepted a cheque and paid it into his own bank account and then repudiated the terms on which it was offered would be approbating and reprobating, or, as is sometimes said, blowing hot and cold, which is something which the law does not permit. That principle supports the defendant. However, in the present case, there may be a second principle in play. That is that a plaintiff is entitled to judgment on admissions and, if the admission is to part only of the claim, to continue the action for the balance. When the defendant sent

a the cheque to the county court, he accompanied it with a document in which he formally admitted that the amount of £150 was due. If the money was tendered as a sum which was admittedly due, there was no reason why the plaintiff should not have paid it into his own bank account and continued with the action for the disputed balance. There may be a conflict, between the terms on which the defendant wrote to the court admitting that £150 was

b due and the terms of the letter that he wrote to the plaintiff in which he said it was a "full payment". It may not be difficult to resolve any such conflict and decide which is the governing principle in the present case. I would give leave to appeal so that the time issue can be resolved.'

I find that passage illuminating. And it is striking to see that in a short closing
c speech, the plaintiff himself took the point. He said:

'I went to the court downstairs and spoke to ... a member of staff at the window and requested whether I could cash this cheque but pursue the cash afterward. At this point in time the person in question informed me that the
d defendant had also contacted the court, this being ... form N9B. I received a copy of this and took it away with me before I cashed the cheque ... Now my interpretation of the instructions as laid down here was that the defendant had indicated that he admitted the amount of £150. It went on to explain that the defendant should forward this cheque under no particular circumstances to the plaintiff and, in receiving that, there was no
e consequences in cashing that cheque. I mean, why should the court inform a defendant who is acknowledging a part payment to send a cheque to a plaintiff which surely would lead to a person in my position to believe there was no problem with me cashing that cheque ... I was told there was no problem if I cashed it as long as I informed the defendant that this was not accepted in full payment ... I read the document N9B referring to how much
f of the claim do you dispute. Now my interpretation of the defendant ticking the box "I admit the amount of £150" and gives two options. I cannot understand why the court would instruct a defendant to forward a part payment to a plaintiff if [when] that plaintiff accepts that cheque it would be regarded as full payment and that the case will not continue. I felt that I was
g perfectly entitled to cash that cheque as long as I pursued the matter.'

It is clear both from the transcript of the submissions and internally from the judge's judgment, that he did not address his mind to the fact that the sending of the cheque for £150 was an unqualified admission of liability, nor to the
h significance of such an admission. He refers to the defendant's letter to the plaintiff as 'plainly an offer to settle the matter' and while he indicates that he is looking at 'the whole circumstances of the "offer"' and he expressly refers to the plaintiff's sight of 'the other documents sent by the defendant ... not only of the letter to him but of the documents sent to the court', he nowhere considers the significance of the sending of the cheque as an unequivocal and formal admission
j of indebtedness, which it was.

Nor does the judge consider the effect on the objective bystander of the scheme of the rules, namely that as box 3 had been completed, asserting that nothing further was due (ie that he had paid the amount remaining in dispute after his admission), and as the case was continuing despite the cashing of the cheque, that would be because (see Ord 9, r 7(b) and form N236) the plaintiff had

indicated to the court that, in the words of the rule, he 'wished the proceedings
to continue'.

An open admission of money due is something quite different from an offer of
a sum in compromise. One obvious difference is made clear by Lord Griffiths in
his speech in *Rush & Tompkins Ltd v Greater London Council* [1988] 3 All ER 737 at
740, [1989] AC 1280 at 1299–1300:

> 'The [without prejudice] rule applies to exclude all negotiations genuinely
> aimed at settlement whether oral or in writing from being given in evidence
> ... the application of the rule is not dependent on the use of the phrase
> "without prejudice" and if it is clear from the surrounding circumstances that
> the parties were seeking to compromise the action, evidence of the content
> of those negotiations will, as a general rule, not be admissible at the trial and
> cannot be used to establish an admission or partial admission.'

It is manifest that the formal admission on the court form was not made
without prejudice as part of an offer to compromise, but was properly before the
court on the question of liability. Not only did the judge find that that £150 (and
in fact much more) was due, but the defendant at trial never at any time
contended either that it was not due nor that he believed it was not due. The
point is put attractively by David Foskett QC in *The Law and Practice of Compromise*
(4th edn, 1996) p 6:

> 'In other cases a fair analysis of the discussions between the parties may
> reveal that, whatever other specific differences lie between them, certain
> matters are not in dispute and may even be admitted. *These undisputed and
> admitted matters cannot thereafter be invested with any contentious character in
> order to found an argument that they have been the subject of compromise.* This
> situation arises not infrequently where a sum of money is in truth paid "on
> account" of some (yet to be determined) final figure and an attempt is then
> made to suggest that it was tendered or paid "in full and final settlement" of
> an alleged dispute.' (My emphasis.)

He gives by way of illustration *Newton Moor Construction Ltd v Charlton* [1981]
CA Transcript 555. That was a building case, where the plaintiff builder
submitted a bill for £18,612. The defendant's solicitor wrote on 25 October 1979
saying that he was prepared to pay £8,847, setting out in detail how that sum was
arrived at. He then concluded:

> 'In these circumstances [the defendant] has handed to me for despatch to
> you a cheque for £8,847 in full and final settlement of your account
> concerning the work ... If you are not prepared to accept this payment we
> have instructions to accept service of any proceedings concerning the same.
> Will you please acknowledge receipt of this letter and cheque.'

The cheque was received by the builder, paid into the builder's account and met
on 30 October. On 30 October the builder's solicitors wrote acknowledging the
letter and said: 'With regard to the cheque for £8,847 our clients are accepting this
cheque in part payment.' When the builders sued for the balance of the bill, they
were met by the defence that there had been an accord and satisfaction by
acceptance of the cheque sent in full and final settlement. The leading judgment
was given by Sir David Cairns. First, he found that the letter of 25 October was
an admission that £8,847 was due. He then concluded:

a   '[It] was in effect an admission by the defendant that this amount was due, and, accordingly, there was no consideration for any agreement that could be said to be implied from the letter of 25 October, the cheque and the acceptance of the cheque. There was no consideration because the admission was complete and binding once made, and that was past consideration by the time that the accord was completed by presentation of

b   the cheque.'

Neither of the other members of the court referred to that principle (they based their judgment on the fact that, in all the circumstances, the trial judge was right to find that there was no accord and satisfaction). But I agree with that passage, and, in my judgment, it applies in this case. The admission that £150 was due was

c   complete and binding once form N9B was completed and sent to the court.

Another example of the same point is in *Tiney Engineering Ltd v Amods Knitting Machinery Ltd* [1986] BTLC 324. The plaintiff was entitled to commission from the defendants on sale of certain machines. He submitted an invoice for 10% of the price. The defendants' representative amended that invoice to 5%

d   commission, added the words 'accepted in full and final settlement', and the plaintiff's representative then initialled those words and was paid the £3,000 immediately. The plaintiff sued for the balance of the 10% commission, it was found at trial that that had been the agreement between the parties, and the accord and satisfaction argument was defeated on the basis that in those circumstances there was no consideration for the agreement to accept the lesser

e   sum, and the plaintiff was entitled to the balance.

Parker LJ (with whom Sir David Cairns agreed) said (at 325):

f   'When a debtor offers to pay only that which he admits he is already due to pay, that is not something which can amount to good consideration for the creditor abandoning the rest, save possibly in certain special circumstances. That it can be no good consideration in ordinary circumstances is plain if only from *D & C Builders Ltd v Rees* [1965] 3 All ER 837, [1966] 2 QB 617.'

In the *D & C Builders'* case the court found, in the words of Danckwerts LJ:

g   '*Foakes v. Beer* ((1884) 9 App Cas 605, [1881–5] All ER Rep 106) applying the decision in *Pinnel's Case* ((1602) 5 Co Rep 117a, [1558–1774] All ER Rep 612), settled definitely the rule of law that payment of a lesser sum than the amount of a debt due cannot be a satisfaction of the debt, unless there is some benefit to the creditor added so there is an accord and satisfaction.'

h   (See [1965] 3 All ER 837 at 841, [1966] 2 QB 617 at 626.)

To like effect, Winn LJ said:

j   'In my judgment this court should now decline to follow the decision in *Goddard* v. *O'Brien* ((1882) 9 QBD 37) and should hold that where a debtor's own cheque for a lesser amount that he indisputably owes to his creditor is accepted by the creditor in full satisfaction of the debt, the creditor is to be regarded, in any case where he has not required the payment to be made by cheque rather than in cash, as having received the cheque merely as a conditional payment of part of what he was entitled to receive: he is free in law, if not in good commercial conscience, to insist on payment of the

balance of the amount due to him from the debtor.' (See [1965] 3 All ER 837
at 846, [1966] 2 QB 617 at 632–633.)

a

In my judgment, the judge here erred in law in that he did not consider the
legal significance of the fact that the defendant had unequivocally admitted
liability for the sum paid by cheque, and was not giving the plaintiff any
additional benefit on top of that. Therefore, there was in law no consideration
for the accord suggested. Nor did the judge pay regard to the scheme of the
County Court Rules governing cases where an admission is coupled with an
assertion that the remainder of the claim has been paid. Against that background,
I believe that, on the facts of this case, it was wrong in law for the judge to
conclude that cashing the cheque sent as a result of a formal and unqualified
admission on the pleadings constituted 'a clear and unequivocal acceptance that
no further sum was due' because of a side letter seeking to impose a term for
which there was no consideration once the admission had been made. Had he
directed himself properly, he would inevitably have come to the decision that
there was no binding accord, and so in my judgment, this appeal should be
allowed.

b

c

d

ALDOUS LJ. I agree with the judgments of both Evans and Henry LJJ.

EVANS LJ. The contract terms were unusual. The plaintiff sold his stock of
specialist records, tapes and discs to the defendant against the latter's promise to
provide him with similar goods up to a value of £600. But if that promise was not
performed by a certain date, then the defendant was to pay up to £1,745 in cash,
by reference to a valuation of the items which the plaintiff sold to him. I assume
that the different amounts represent wholesale and retail values respectively.
The contract was in writing.

e

Having received, as he said, only goods worth £143·50 and £5 in cash, the
plaintiff issued proceedings claiming the balance of £600 plus 'expenses' of £35, a
total of £486·50.

f

The defendant completed form N9B as his defence. His intention was to say
that he admitted that £150 was due and that he was willing to pay that sum.
Understandably, perhaps, he was uncertain how he should complete the form.
He ticked, in error, the box referring to 'I dispute the full amount claimed', then
deleted this and ticked instead 'I admit the amount of £150'. He did not comply
with the instructions which followed, which were introduced by 'If you dispute
only part of the claim', but he moved on to section 3, which is headed 'Do you
dispute this claim because you have already paid it?' He completed this section
so that it read 'Yes I paid £450·00 to the plaintiff over this period' and explained
this in the following words:

g

h

'We had an arrangement for Mr. Ferguson to collect the balance on a
Thursday when I traded at Milton Keynes market. He received £150 (3 x £50)
but failed to make any further appointments despite attempts to clarify our
arrangements. A total of approx £450·00. Cheque for £150·00 sent 17.2.93 to
Mr. Ferguson.'

j

That was the date on which the form was signed.

On the same day, the defendant wrote to the court saying that he enclosed the
cheque for £150 'in settlement of Mr Ferguson's account', adding: 'I do not
dispute the fact that I owe him money however dispute the total amount he is

claiming.' He then referred to other transactions which it seems, in the light of the evidence which he gave at the trial, were the reasons why he said that the plaintiff had received money or money's worth up to £450, and he concluded: 'I hope that this will now resolve the matter.'

To the plaintiff he wrote:

> 'Please find enclosed a cheque for £150·00 as a full payment on the County Court Summons ... As the document sent to the court details I dispute the total and have listed the reasons. I hope that this will now resolve the matter.'

The plaintiff paid in the cheque at his own bank and when it had been cleared he replied to the defendant's letter on 7 March:

> 'Thank you for your letter and cheque recieved [sic] recently. With regard to your letter sent direct to myself and the letter recieved [sic] by the court, I was disappointed, but unfortunately not surprised by its contents. It will come as no surprise to yourself to find that I am continuing with the action until full payment is received.'

He then applied for and was given leave to amend the particulars of claim so as to increase the claim to the balance of £1,745, after giving further credit for the £150 payment received. The judge found that he was entitled to recover substantially the whole of this sum, apart from the accord and satisfaction defence which has been the only issue raised on this appeal.

Although the judge was not referred to any of the authorities relating to this issue, he directed himself correctly that the question whether there was an 'accord' was essentially a question of fact and that he should apply an objective test in interpreting what the parties said and did, rather than 'to look at what was intended in fact by either the defendant or the plaintiff, because it is quite apparent they intended different things'.

Although it is correct to describe this as a question of fact, it must also be remembered that the interpretation of letters and other documents is a matter for the court and in that sense it is a question of law (see *Stour Valley Builders v Stuart* [1992] CA Transcript 1281 per Lloyd LJ). As the judge said, the whole of the circumstances including the written terms have to be taken into account.

The judge having directed himself correctly as a matter of law, and having reached the clear conclusion that the necessary accord did exist, in my view, this court should be slow to alter his finding, unless there are clear and substantial grounds for doing so.

One of the reasons he gave was that 'One also has to look at what the sum then in dispute was.' I agree. This is certainly a material factor. He continued:

> 'The claim was based on £600. The payment of the cheque did not bring the total payment on the defendant's account up to £600, but it brought it up to something over £500 ...'

The plaintiff criticises this part of the judgment in particular, because he disputed the defendant's version and he succeeded on these issues at the trial. So the judge may have overestimated the chances of the plaintiff having been prepared to accept 'the defendant's account' at the time. This is a point of some weight, but it would not be sufficient, in my view, to displace the judge's finding, if it stood alone.

I have come reluctantly to the conclusion, however, that the question whether there was an 'accord' in the present case depends almost entirely on the correct interpretation of the defendant's letters, to the plaintiff and to the court, and of the defence which he submitted on form N9B and which the plaintiff saw at the court offices. The question is whether those documents contained an unequivocal offer by the defendant to pay a further £150 only upon the basis that, if he accepted it, the plaintiff would withdraw the balance of his claim. That has to be distinguished from and contrasted with an admission that £150 was due and the balance of the claim remained in dispute.

In my judgment, the documents cannot be interpreted in the former, unequivocal, sense. The defendant's letter to the plaintiff offered the cheque 'in full payment', but the whole of the circumstances and all the documents have to be taken into account. The defendant's entries in form N9B were to the effect that £150 was admittedly due, and was being paid, leaving the balance in dispute. The plaintiff was entitled to understand the defendant's offer in this sense, and it follows that his acceptance of the cheque did not give rise to an agreement that he would forego the balance of his claim.

I would allow the appeal on this ground alone, and I express no view as to whether, if the accord on which the defendant relies was established, the agreement would fail as a contract for want of consideration as required by law.

Henry LJ's judgment contains a detailed analysis of form N9B which shows that it does not provide for a defendant who is willing to make a specified payment in full and final satisfaction of the claim, without a formal admission that part of the sum claimed is due. Maybe it is more convenient that the form should not contain this alternative, although if it had done so the present dispute would have been less likely to arise. This can perhaps be considered by the appropriate authorities as part of the current review of county court procedures.

Appeal allowed.

Paul Magrath Esq   Barrister.

R v Secretary of State for the Home Department, ex parte Venables
R v Secretary of State for the Home Department, ex parte Thompson

COURT OF APPEAL, CIVIL DIVISION
LORD WOOLF MR, HOBHOUSE AND MORRITT LJJ
1, 2, 3, 30 JULY 1996

Prison – Release on licence – Mandatory sentence – Detention during Her Majesty's pleasure – Children aged ten convicted of murder – Tariff period – Secretary of State fixing tariff period by applying policy adopted for adults sentenced to mandatory life sentences – Whether policy appropriate – Children and Young Persons Act 1933, s 53(1) – Criminal Justice Act 1991, ss 35, 51(1).

Prison – Release on licence – Mandatory sentence – Detention during Her Majesty's pleasure – Children aged ten convicted of murder – Tariff period – Secretary of State deciding tariff period – Secretary of State not disclosing all material taken into account in fixing tariff – Whether decision procedurally fair.

The applicants, two ten-year-old boys of average intelligence with no mental abnormality, were sentenced to be detained during Her Majesty's pleasure under s 53(1)[a] of the Children and Young Persons Act 1933 following their conviction for the murder of a two-year-old child. The Secretary of State later informed them by letter of his decision to fix a tariff of 15 years as the minimum period which they should serve to satisfy the requirements of retribution and deterrence; and in doing so, he did not follow the recommendations of eight and ten years made respectively by the trial judge and the Lord Chief Justice. The letters stated that, in fixing the tariff, the Secretary of State had had regard to the circumstances of the offence and age of the applicants, the recommendations of the judiciary, the representations made on their behalf and the extent to which the case could be compared with other cases, and also to the public concern about the case as evidenced by petitions and other correspondence. The letters purported to inform the applicants of the substance of the judicial recommendations and fairly summarised the judges' recommendations, but did not include the trial judge's summary of the facts and the view he had taken of them. Moreover, the Secretary of State reached his decision to increase the penal period to 15 years without having seen any of the trial papers or having read the judge's summing up. The applicants applied for judicial review by way of orders of certiorari to quash the decisions on the tariff, submitting that they were reached unfairly and in breach of the rules of natural justice. The Divisional Court granted the relief sought, and the Secretary of State appealed to the Court of Appeal. The issues which arose were: (i) whether, as the Divisional Court had held, the Secretary of State had acted unlawfully in applying to the applicants, being persons detained during Her Majesty's pleasure, the same policy as he applied in the case of adults serving mandatory life sentences; and (ii) whether his

---

a   Section 53, so far as material, is set out at p 340 *a* to *e*, post

decision as to the application of that policy was reached in a manner which was *a*
procedurally unfair and should therefore be quashed.

Held – (1) (Lord Woolf MR dissenting) Where a young offender was sentenced
to detention during Her Majesty's pleasure under s 53(1) of the 1933 Act or to
detention for life under s 53(2), he remained subject to that sentence for the
remainder of his natural life, and he was therefore in the same position as an adult   *b*
offender sentenced to life imprisonment under the Murder (Abolition of Death
Penalty) Act 1965, although he would be detained under different conditions.
Accordingly, by virtue of ss 43^b and 51(1)^c of the Criminal Justice Act 1991, a
young offender's release on licence was governed by s 35^d of that Act, which dealt
with the position of mandatory life prisoners; and the breadth of the Secretary of
State's discretion under s 35, which included fixing tariffs to indicate the part of   *c*
the sentence required for punishment and deterrence, was the same in both
classes of case. It followed that the Secretary of State had not acted unlawfully in
applying to the applicants the same policy as he applied to persons serving
mandatory life sentences (see p 358 *f g*, p 359 *b e*, p 362 *f* to *j*, p 363 *b*, p 374 *e f*,
p 375 *b* and p 376 *j* to p 377 *a*, post).   *d*
    (2) However, in applying that policy and fixing the tariff, the Secretary of State
had departed from the requisite standard of fairness, since he had not made full
disclosure of the material before him on which he would exercise his discretion
to fix the tariff to be served, and he had failed to take into account all relevant
considerations and (Morritt LJ dissenting) had wrongly taken into account
irrelevant material derived from public petitions and via the media. Accordingly,   *e*
the decisions he had reached were vitiated by unfairness and the appeal would
therefore be dismissed (see p 350 *g h*, p 351 *a* to *d*, p 352 *a c*, p 365 *e f*, p 366 *j*, p 367
c j, p 368 *e* to *g*, p 370 *f*, p 371 *a*, p 377 *h j* and p 378 *d* to *f*, post); *Doody v Secretary
of State for the Home Dept* [1993] 3 All ER 92 applied.

f

Notes
For Home Secretary's power to release on licence prisoners serving life
sentences, see 37 *Halsbury's Laws* (4th edn) para 1190.
    For detention during her Majesty's pleasure, see 11(2) *Halsbury's Laws* (4th edn
reissue) paras 1269, 1270.   *g*
    For the Children and Young Persons Act 1933, s 53, see 6 *Halsbury's Statutes*
(4th edn) (1992 reissue) 55.
    For the Criminal Justice Act 1991, ss 35, 51, see 34(S) *Halsbury's Statutes* (4th
edn) 13, 25.

Cases referred to in judgments   *h*
C v DPP [1995] 2 All ER 43, [1996] AC 1, [1995] 2 WLR 383, HL.
Doody v Secretary of State for the Home Dept [1993] 3 All ER 92, [1994] 1 AC 531,
    [1993] 3 WLR 154, HL.
Findlay v Secretary of State for the Home Dept [1984] 3 All ER 801, [1985] AC 318,
    [1984] 3 WLR 1159, HL.   *j*
Hussain v UK (1996) 22 EHRR 1, ECt HR.

---

b   Section 43 is set out at p 341 *c d*, post
c   Section 51(1), so far as material, is set out at p 341 *e*, post
d   Section 35, so far as material, is set out at p 335 *e f*, post

a *Kanda v Government of Malaya* [1962] AC 322, [1962] 2 WLR 1153, PC.

R v Abbott [1963] 1 All ER 738, [1964] 1 QB 489, [1963] 2 WLR 1011, CCA.

R v Civil Service Appeal Board, ex p Cunningham [1991] 4 All ER 310, CA.

R v Collins (1994) 16 Cr App R (S) 156, CA.

R v Fairhurst [1987] 1 All ER 46, [1986] 1 WLR 1374, CA.

R v Ford (1976) 62 Cr App R 303, CA.

b *R v Forshaw* (1984) 6 Cr App R (S) 413, CA.

R v Secretary of State for the Home Dept, ex p Causabon-Vincent (1996) Times, 19 July, DC.

R v Secretary of State for the Home Dept, ex p Handscomb (1988) 86 Cr App R 59, DC.

R v Secretary of State for the Home Dept, ex p Riaz, R v Secretary of State for the Home Dept, ex p Raja (8 December 1994, unreported), DC.

c *R v Secretary of State for the Home Dept, ex p Singh (Prem)* (1993) Times, 27 April, DC.

R v Secretary of State for the Home Dept, ex p T [1994] 1 All ER 794, [1994] QB 378, [1994] 2 WLR 190, DC; *rvsd in part sub nom R v Secretary of State for the Home Dept, ex p Hickey (No 1), R v Secretary of State for the Home Dept, ex p H, F, B and W* [1995] 1 All ER 479, [1995] QB 43, [1994] 3 WLR 1110, CA.

d *Singh v UK* Case 56/1994/503/585 (1996) 1 BHRC 119, ECt HR.

Thynne v UK (1990) 13 EHRR 666, ECt HR.

Cases also cited or referred to in skeleton arguments

Brind v Secretary of State for the Home Dept [1991] 1 All ER 720, [1991] 1 AC 696, HL.

e *Chandler v DPP* [1962] 3 All ER 142, [1964] AC 763, HL.

R v Parole Board, ex p Bradley [1990] 3 All ER 828, [1991] 1 WLR 134, DC.

R v Secretary of State for the Home Dept, ex p Benson (1988) Times, 21 November, DC.

R v Secretary of State for the Home Dept, ex p Chapman (1994) Times, 25 October, DC.

f *R v Secretary of State for the Home Dept, ex p Dowd* (17 October 1994, unreported), DC.

R v Secretary of State for the Home Dept, ex p McCartney (1994) Times, 25 May, [1994] CA Transcript 667.

R v Secretary of State for the Home Dept, ex p Pierson [1996] 1 All ER 837, [1996] 3 WLR 547, CA.

g *R v Secretary of State for the Home Dept, ex p Walsh* (1991) Times, 18 December, DC.

R v Storey [1973] 3 All ER 562, [1973] 1 WLR 1045, CA.

State v O'Brien [1973] IR 50, Ir SC.

Wynne v UK (1994) 19 EHRR 333, ECt HR.

h **Appeals**

The Secretary of State for the Home Department appealed with leave from the decision of the Queen's Bench Divisional Court (Pill LJ and Newman J) ((1996) Times, 7 May) on 2 May 1996 granting the applications of the respondents, Jon Venables and Robert Thompson, for judicial review by way of orders of certiorari *j* to quash two decisions of the Secretary of State contained in letters dated 22 July 1994 setting out the period which would in the normal way elapse before they would be considered for release from detention during Her Majesty's pleasure following their conviction for murder on 24 November 1993 after a trial before Morland J and a jury at the Crown Court at Preston. The facts are set out in the judgment of Lord Woolf MR.

David Pannick QC and *Mark Shaw* (instructed by the *Treasury Solicitor*) for the
Home Secretary.

Edward Fitzgerald QC and *Ben Emmerson* (instructed by *John Howell & Co*, Sheffield)
for Venables.

Brian Higgs QC and *Julian Nutter* (instructed by *Paul Rooney & Co*, Liverpool) for
Thompson.

Cur adv vult

30 July 1996. The following judgments were delivered.

LORD WOOLF MR. This is an appeal from a decision of the Queen's Bench
Divisional Court (Pill LJ and Newman J) ((1996) Times, 7 May) of 2 May 1996.
The Divisional Court quashed two decisions of the Home Secretary contained in
letters dated 22 July 1994 written to Jon Venables and Robert Thompson (the
applicants). The decisions were in the same terms. They set the period which
would in the normal way elapse before the applicants were considered for release
by the Home Secretary from detention during Her Majesty's pleasure. This
sentence followed their conviction for murder on 24 November 1993 after a trial
before Morland J and a jury at the Crown Court at Preston.

The circumstances of the murder were exceptionally horrific and for this
reason attracted a vast amount of media attention. They were exceptional
because of the treatment of the victim, James Bulger, who was only two years old
at the time. They were also exceptional because at the time of the offence both
Venables and Thompson were ten years of age.

The period which is to elapse before the applicants would be considered for
release was set by the Home Secretary at 15 years. This was to meet the
requirements of retribution and deterrence and is known as 'the tariff' or 'penal
element'. I emphasise that the 15-year period was not fixed by the Home
Secretary as the period which the applicants are actually to spend in detention.
That period can be substantially longer. Fifteen years is the minimum period
which will normally elapse prior to release. It is a period fixed by the Home
Secretary to enable his department and the applicants to know when the first
review should take place. This review will commence three years before the
expiry of the tariff to enable the Home Secretary to decide by the time it expires
whether it is appropriate to release the applicants from detention on licence. This
is necessary as the duration of Her Majesty's pleasure is unspecified.

The Divisional Court was only entitled to interfere with the decision of the
Home Secretary if his determination of the tariff would mean that he had or
would exercise his discretion to release in a way which was not in accordance
with the law as laid down by Parliament. The Divisional Court did not reach its
decision because it would have fixed a different period as to the tariff. It did so
because it considered that, as a result of the tariff being fixed at a period as long
as 15 years in the case of the applicants, *the Home Secretary was preventing himself
from exercising the discretion to release the applicants conferred on him by Parliament as
the law by statute required.* I emphasise this to make clear that the issues which the
Divisional Court and this court are required to adjudicate are not as to sentencing
policy.

The Home Secretary's case in a nutshell is that Parliament has given him
exactly the same breadth of discretion in the case of children and young persons
who are sentenced for murder as he has in relation to adults who are sentenced

to life imprisonment. Therefore, he is exercising that discretion perfectly lawfully as long as he complies with the guidance given by the House of Lords as to the extent and nature of his discretion in the case of adults in *Doody v Secretary of State for the Home Dept* [1993] 3 All ER 92, [1994] 1 AC 531. The Divisional Court did not accept that this is the position. The kernel of Pill LJ's reasoning (with whose judgment Newman J agreed) appears in the following passage which comes towards the end of his judgment:

'The justification for a tariff in the case of a mandatory life prisoner is that the true and judicially imposed tariff is life and that stating a term of years by way of a tariff is a form of remission which the Secretary of State is entitled to grant. The nature of detention during Her Majesty's pleasure does not permit of such an approach. There is no judicially imposed tariff from which to remit. However, the essence of the requirement upon the Secretary of State with respect to a child or a young person detained during Her Majesty's pleasure is to keep the need for detention under regular review.'

Mr Edward Fitzgerald QC appeared both before the Divisional Court and this court on behalf of Venables. His argument is adopted by Mr Brian Higgs QC, who appears for Thompson. Mr Fitzgerald goes further than the Divisional Court in his criticism of the approach adopted by the Divisional Court. His case can be summarised as follows.

(1) The sentence of detention during Her Majesty's pleasure does not order detention for life as the punishment merited by the crime of murder; rather it authorises indeterminate detention only for as long as is necessary to meet objectives that are either wholly or predominantly reformatory and preventative.

(2) At least in the case of a ten-year old offender the only legitimate objective of detention during Her Majesty's pleasure is not retribution or deterrence but the reformation of the offender and the protection of society.

(3) As an alternative to (1) and (2), if it is permissible for the Home Secretary to have regard to retribution and deterrence, it is wrong to determine the date of the review by reference to those objectives alone and so as to exclude for the period of the tariff a periodic review of the wider merits of continuing detention, including the way in which the offender progresses and matures as time passes.

(4) As an alternative to (3), if it is legitimate to fix a tariff at the outset to reflect punishment and deterrence, it is not appropriate to take into account in the case of a child or a young person the views of the public as to the period of detention, which is appropriate or to adopt an approach which is greatly in excess of that which is adopted by the judiciary.

(5) The Secretary of State had come to his decision unfairly because he did not make full disclosure of the material on which he relied and did not have sufficient information as to the applicants' background to entitle him to come to the decision which he did.

In order to determine the issues which Mr Fitzgerald's contentions raise, it is necessary to look with some care at the relevant statutory provisions. In doing so it is convenient to commence with the historical development of the powers of imprisonment for life of adults and then turn to the comparable powers in relation to children and young persons.

The position as to adults
The statutory provisions relating to adults currently make a distinction between sentences for a fixed period (determinative sentences) and sentences for

life imprisonment (indeterminative sentences). They also make a distinction between sentences for life, which are discretionary, and those which are mandatory, that is to say prescribed by law.

In the case of determinative sentences in relation to adults, there is a long tradition of prisoners obtaining remission for good behaviour. The way the provisions operate is to give a defendant automatic credit for a fixed proportion of his sentence so that he is entitled to early release unless that remission is forfeited either in whole or in part because of bad conduct.

Discretionary unlike the mandatory life sentence for murder can be imposed for different reasons. Either because the offence is so serious that it is the only appropriate sentence, or because a lesser fixed-term sentence would amount to appropriate punishment but there is also a risk of repetition or mental instability so that an indeterminate period of imprisonment is required to protect the public from the risk of further offences. A prisoner sentenced in this way will only be released after he has served the period required as a punishment (the tariff period) when it is also safe for him to be released.

In the case of both categories of life imprisonment, life only very rarely in practice means life. In both cases the prisoner can be released on licence. If the terms of the licence are not observed, and in particular, if the defendant commits a further offence, he is liable to be recalled.

The first statute to which it is necessary to refer is the Homicide Act 1957. It created a category of non-capital murder for which there was a prescribed mandatory sentence of imprisonment for life. This was followed by the Murder (Abolition of Death Penalty) Act 1965, which made imprisonment for life mandatory for all murders. It also gave the trial judge a power to recommend to the Home Secretary the minimum period which should elapse before the release of the prisoner on licence. In addition the prisoner convicted of murder could not be released on licence unless the Home Secretary had previously consulted the Lord Chief Justice and the trial judge if available. The involvement of the judiciary at that stage was to avoid the Home Secretary being too lenient.

The Criminal Justice Act 1967 established the Parole Board. I set out s 61 because it applies to children or young persons sentenced to detention during Her Majesty's pleasure the same provisions as to their release as apply to adults. The section is in these terms:

'(1) The Secretary of State may, if recommended to do so by the Parole Board, release on licence a person serving a sentence of imprisonment for life or custody for life or a person detained under section 53 of the Children and Young Persons Act 1933 (young offenders convicted of grave crimes), but shall not do so in the case of a person sentenced to imprisonment for life or custody for life or to detention during Her Majesty's pleasure or for life except after consultation with the Lord Chief Justice of England together with the trial judge if available ...'

The next step in the history was a Parliamentary statement involving a radically different approach by the then Home Secretary the Rt Hon Leon Brittan QC made on 30 November 1983. The relevant parts of the statement begin as follows (49 HC Official Report (6th series) written answers col 506):

'*Life Sentence Prisoners*   The release of life sentence prisoners is at the discretion of the Home Secretary, subject to a favourable recommendation

a by the Parole Board and to consultation with the Lord Chief Justice and, if he
is available, the trial judge.'

The statement adds that in future, because of public concern about violent crime,
serious murderers can normally expect to serve at least 20 years in custody. The
statement goes on to indicate that the Home Secretary would continue to look to
the judiciary for advice on the time to be served 'to satisfy the requirements of
b retribution and deterrence and to the Parole Board for advice on risk'. It also
indicates that the first review by a local review committee would take place three
years before the expiry of the period necessary to meet the requirements of
retribution and deterrence so that this would give sufficient time for preparation
for release if the Parole Board recommended it, 'having considered risk'.

c   The following two paragraphs then follow (cols *507–508*):

'These new procedures will separate consideration of the requirements of
retribution and deterrence from consideration of risk to the public, which
always has been, and will continue to be, the pre-eminent factor determining
release ... They will enable the prison and other staff responsible for
d   considering and reporting on life sentences cases, the local review
committees and the Parole Board, to concentrate on risk. The judiciary will
properly advise on retribution and deterrence. But the ultimate discretion
whether to refuse will remain with me ...

When a date for a first, or subsequent, formal review is set for several years
ahead, the Home Office will review the case on the basis of reports of the
e   kind now prepared for formal reviews, at regular, and in any event not
longer than three-year, intervals. Moreover, governors will be told to report
at once any exceptional development requiring action. These procedures
will ensure that I can consider any special circumstances or exceptional
progress which might justify changing the review date. But except where a
f   prisoner has committed an offence for which he has received a further
custodial sentence, first formal review date will not be put back. In any
event, Ministers will review every case when a life sentence prisoner has
been detained for 10 years.'

I draw particular attention to the final paragraphs of the statement because they
g do indicate that although consideration by the Parole Board would normally be
deferred until after the tariff period had expired, the Home Secretary was mindful
of the importance of monitoring progress and that it would be possible to depart
from the normal procedure if this was appropriate: (a) if there are any special
circumstances, (b) if there is exceptional progress by the prisoner, (c) after ten
h years.

This was very much in accordance with the well-known principles of
administrative law which permit the adoption of a standard policy as long as the
policy includes an appropriate provision enabling a departure from the policy in
special circumstances. In the absence of such a provision the policy can amount
to an unlawful fettering of the discretion given by the statute.
j
At least from this time on it was clearly established that, in relation to both
prisoners subject to mandatory and discretionary life sentences, there was a
distinction between the penal or tariff element of the sentence for which the
advice of the judiciary would be sought as to the appropriate period for
deterrence and retribution and the risk element of the sentence, for which their
advice would not be obtained.

The 1983 parliamentary statement was followed by a parliamentary statement
by the then Home Secretary, the Rt Hon Douglas Hurd, on 23 July 1987 (see 120
HC Official Report (6th series) written answers cols 346–347). This followed the
decision of the Divisional Court in a case concerning discretionary life sentences,
R v Secretary of State for the Home Dept, ex p Handscomb (1988) 86 Cr App R 59. It
primarily dealt with discretionary life sentences. I will refer to it because the
Home Secretary sets out fully the procedure with regard to those sentences and
then applies the same procedure to mandatory sentences. The relevant
paragraphs read:

> 'Following the consultation with the Lord Chief Justice it has been agreed
> that the most satisfactory way of obtaining the judicial view is to ask the trial
> judge to write to me, through him, in every case where a discretionary life
> sentence is passed giving his view on the period necessary to meet the
> requirements of retribution and deterrence. This view will be related to the
> determinate sentence that would have been passed but for the element of
> mental instability and/or public risk which led the judge to pass a life
> sentence and will also take account of the notional period of the sentence
> which the prisoner might expect to have been remitted for good behaviour
> had a determinate sentence been passed. The date of the first formal review
> by the Parole Board machinery will then be fixed in accordance with the
> judicial view on the requirements of retribution and deterrence; and the
> review will, as before, normally take place three years before the expiry of
> that period ...
>
> Although the issues before the Divisional Court related only to prisoners
> serving discretionary life sentences. I have decided that the date of the first
> formal review of the cases of prisoners serving mandatory life sentences
> should also be fixed as soon as practicable after conviction and sentence. The
> procedure under which the views of the trial judge and the Lord Chief Justice
> about the requirements of retribution and deterrence are obtained will be
> the same as that proposed for discretionary life sentence cases ...'

It will be observed that apparently at this stage the tariff was fixed in accordance
with the judicial view.

The next step in the history to which it is necessary to refer is a decision of the
European Court of Human Rights in *Thynne v UK* (1990) 13 EHRR 666. In this
case, the European Court of Human Rights, in relation to discretionary life
sentences, held that once the prisoner had served the penal element of his
sentence, he was entitled to have the remaining period of his detention under
judicial control. This did not apply to mandatory life sentences because in their
case the punishment for the offence of murder was considered to require life
imprisonment which was not necessarily the case with discretionary life
sentences where the sentence could be imposed because of the mental instability
or the risk of further offending on the part of the defendant.

To give effect to this decision of the European Court of Human Rights, the
Criminal Justice Act 1991 was passed. This Act did not only deal with the position
of the prisoner serving discretionary life sentences; it also divided determinate
sentences into short-term and long-term; four years being the dividing line
between them. Short-term prisoners were to be released after they had served
one half of their sentence and long-term prisoners had to be released after serving
two-thirds of their sentence (see s 33 of the 1991 Act).

a   In addition the Secretary of State had a discretion under s 35(1) of the 1991 Act
to release a long-term prisoner after he had served one half of his sentence if
recommended to do so by the board.
The position as to discretionary life prisoners was dealt with by s 34 of the 1991
Act. The section gave a power to the court which sentenced such an offender to
specify the penal part of the sentence and in doing so to take into account the
b   seriousness of the offences involved and the provisions of the Act dealing with
early release of long-term prisoners to which I have already referred. The reason
why it is necessary to take into account the early release provisions is that if they
were not taken into account the penal element of the sentence in the case of a
discretionary life prisoner would be longer than the period which would actually
be served by a prisoner serving an equivalent determinate sentence. Section 34
c   gives the responsibility for determining when, after the penal element of the
sentence has been served, the risk to the public no longer requires the prisoner to
remain in custody to the Parole Board. Once this is the situation, the board has
power to direct the prisoner's release and it is then the duty of the Secretary of
State to release him on licence. Furthermore, once the penal period of the
d   sentence has expired, the prisoner has the right to require the Secretary of State
to refer the case to the board. In this way the decision of the European Court of
Human Rights that the executive should not determine these matters is
honoured.
Section 35(2) and (3) of the 1991 Act deals with the position of mandatory life
prisoners in the following terms:
e

'(2) If recommended to do so by the Board, the Secretary of State may,
after consultation with the Lord Chief Justice together with the trial judge if
available, release on licence a life prisoner who is not a discretionary life
prisoner.

f   (3) The Board shall not make a recommendation under subsection (2)
above unless the Secretary of State referred the particular case, or the class of
case to which that case belongs, to the Board for its advice.'

Section 35 maintains the Home Secretary's discretion in relation to mandatory
life sentences. However, that the provisions of the Act were influenced by
g   *Thynne's* case was made clear by the Minister of State, the Rt Hon Mrs Angela
Rumbold, in a statement to the House of Commons on 16 July 1991 (see 195 HC
Official Report (6th series) cols *311–312*). Having referred to discretionary
sentences, the minister said:

h   'The nature of the mandatory sentence is different. The element of risk is
not the decisive factor in handing down a life sentence. According to the
judicial process, the offender has committed a crime of such gravity that he
forfeits his liberty to the state for the rest of his days. If necessary, he can be
detained for life without the necessity of a subsequent judicial intervention.
The presumption is, therefore, that the offender should remain in custody
j   until and unless the Home Secretary concludes that the public interest would
be better served by the prisoner's release than by his continued detention. In
exercising his continued discretion in that respect, the Home Secretary must
take account not just of the question of risk, but how society as a whole
would view the prisoner's release at that juncture. The Home Secretary
takes account of the judicial recommendation but the final decision is his.'

The minister's references to the offender forfeiting his liberty for the rest of his life and the presumption in the case of mandatory sentences of life imprisonment should be noted because on the approach of the Divisional Court they would not apply in the case of those sentenced to be detained during Her Majesty's pleasure. This statement is also relevant to comments which I have to make about the fact that in this case the Home Secretary has taken into account, in deciding on a tariff of 15 years, the demands of the public contained in petitions and other documents that a long period should be fixed. The minister in the above statement appears to be saying that the public's perception is relevant at the 'juncture' when the Home Secretary is considering release and not when fixing the penal period.

Doody's case [1993] 3 All ER 92, [1994] 1 AC 531 followed. It was concerned with the Secretary of State's discretion in relation to mandatory life sentences for adults. It did not deal expressly with sentences of detention during Her Majesty's pleasure. Lord Mustill in his speech, with which the other members of the House agreed, adopted the following approach to a number of issues which are relevant to this appeal. (1) The Secretary of State's decision relating to the release of life prisoners can only be interfered with by the court on an application for judicial review if it can be shown that it has been reached by a faulty process in one of the ways amenable to judicial review. (2) The Secretary of State is not obliged to adopt the judicial view as to the appropriate tariff period in relation to mandatory life sentences, although if he departed from it he is required to give reasons for doing so. (3) The Secretary of State before fixing the tariff is required to afford the prisoner the opportunity of submitting in writing representations as to the tariff period. To enable a prisoner to do this he should inform the prisoner of the period recommended by the judiciary and of any other opinion expressed by the judiciary which is relevant to the Secretary of State's decision as to the appropriate penal period but not as to the risk element. The general approach of Lord Mustill is apparent from these two short passages from his speech ([1993] 3 All ER 92 at 106, 111, [1994] 1 AC 531 at 560, 565):

> 'Since the person affected usually cannot make worthwhile representations without knowing what factors may weigh against his interests fairness will very often require that he is informed of the gist of the case which he has to answer ... I think it important that there should be an effective means of detecting the kind of error which would entitle the court to intervene, and in practice I regard it as necessary for this purpose that the reasoning of the Home Secretary should be disclosed.'

The relationship between the judiciary and the Secretary of State is made particularly clear by the following passage in Lord Mustill's speech ([1993] 3 All ER 92 at 104–105, [1994] 1 AC 531 at 558–559):

> '... I question the proposition that the judges are specially qualified to assess the penal element of a mandatory life sentence; I emphasise mandatory, because there are grounds for saying that in fixing the penal element of the discretionary sentence ... the judge is simply pronouncing the tariff sentence which he would have imposed but for the element of risk, and that this is the kind of function in which the judiciary has unrivalled experience. But the position as to mandatory sentences is very different. Until Mr Brittan completely changed the rules in 1983 the idea of a separate determinate penal element co-existing with the life sentence would have been meaningless. It is true that for the past ten years the judges have been

a   asked to advise upon it, and it may be that some consistent judicial practice now exists. Nevertheless, it is the Home Secretary who decides, and who has developed (with his predecessors) his own ministerial ideas on what the public interest demands. I can see no reason why the anomalous task of fixing a "tariff" penal element for an offence in respect of which the true tariff sentence is life imprisonment is one for which the Home Secretary and his
b   junior ministers, informed by his officials about the existing departmental practice, are any less experienced and capable than are the judges. In any event, however even if the respondents' argument is correct so far, it must in my opinion fail because Parliament has not by statute conferred on the judges any role, even as advisers, at the time when the penal element of a mandatory sentence is fixed. But for the fact that the Home Secretary
c   decided, when formulating the new scheme to retain in a modified shape the existing practice of inviting the opinion of the judges, they would never enter the picture at all. The Secretary of State is compelled, or at least entitled, to have regard to broader considerations of a public character than those which apply to an ordinary sentencing function. It is he, and not the judges, who is entrusted with the task of deciding upon the prisoner's release, and it is he
d   who has decided, within the general powers conferred upon him by the statute, to divide his task into two stages. It is not, and could not be, suggested that he acted unlawfully in this respect and I can see no ground whatever for suggesting that by doing so he deprived himself entirely of his discretion at the first stage, and delivered it into the hands of the judges.'

e   *Doody's* case was followed in turn by a further statement in Parliament by the present Home Secretary, the Rt Hon Michael Howard, on 27 July 1993 (see 229 HC Official Report (6th series) written answers cols 863–865). Having referred to the previous statements, Mr Howard continued in these terms (cols 863–864):

f   'Under those procedures, shortly after a person has received a mandatory life sentence, the Secretary of State invites the judiciary to give their views on the period to be served to satisfy the requirements of retribution and deterrence. The judiciary's views presently comprise the advice of the trial judge and the Lord Chief Justice. Their advice is one factor among others which the Secretary of State considers before he sets the date for the first
g   review by the Parole Board of the case for releasing the prisoner on licence. This review is timed to take place three years before the expiry of the minimum period which the Secretary of State considers necessary to satisfy the requirements of retribution and deterrence or, where that period is 20 years or more, 17 years after sentence. At present, a prisoner is not told the
h   contents of the judicial recommendation, nor the length of the period which the Secretary of State has determined to be the minimum necessary to satisfy the requirements of retribution and deterrence. However, where the period so determined is less than 20 years, the prisoner can deduce its length by adding three years to the date which he is given for his first review; and
j   where it is 20 years, he can deduce its length from the terms of the notice informing him that his first review will take place 17 years after sentence. But where the period is more than 20 years, the prisoner is not able to establish its total length. The House of Lords judgment requires me to inform the prisoner of the recommendations made by the judiciary as to the period necessary to satisfy the requirements of retribution and deterrence and of the substance of any opinions expressed by the judiciary which are

relevant to my decision as to the appropriate minimum period to be served to satisfy those requirements. In addition, I am required to afford the prisoner the opportunity to submit written representations. Although I am not required to adopt the judicial advice, I must give reasons where I or a Minister acting under my authority decides to depart from it. I propose to give effect to this judgment by informing all persons who are now serving a mandatory life sentence and any persons who may subsequently be so sentenced, as soon as is reasonably practicable, of the substance of the judicial recommendations which were made in their case as to the period to be served by them in order to satisfy the requirements of retribution and deterrence. I am consulting the Lord Chief Justice about the precise way in which this will be done. In addition, I have decided to disclose to both existing and future mandatory life sentence prisoners the Secretary of State's decision, taken after consideration of the judicial advice, on the appropriate period in question. In accordance with the judgment, reasons will be given to the prisoner for any departure from the judicial view. As the judgment makes clear, successive Secretaries of State have been, and I continue to be, willing to consider any written representations by prisoners as to the minimum period to be served by them to satisfy the requirements of retribution and deterrence. In future, prisoners will be afforded the opportunity to submit such written representations at the beginning of the sentence and before I have formed a view as to the minimum period for retribution and deterrence. I take this opportunity to emphasise that the view which I or a Minister acting under my authority takes, at the beginning of a mandatory life sentence, of the period necessary to satisfy the requirements of retribution and deterrence is an initial view of the minimum period necessary to satisfy those requirements. It therefore remains possible for me, or a future Secretary of State, exceptionally to revise that view of the minimum period, either by reducing it, or by increasing it where I, or a successor in my office, concludes that, putting aside questions of risk, the minimum requirements of retribution and deterrence will not have been satisfied at the expiry of the period which had previously been determined.'

The Secretary of State went on to say that if he was to increase the minimum period, it would give the prisoner an opportunity to make representations. The Secretary of State then refuted the suggestion which had been made by Lord Mustill in his speech that there was an illogicality involved in the statement made by the Rt Hon Mrs Angela Rumbold by saying that he wholly indorsed the latter's description of the way in which he currently exercised his discretion and intended to do so in future. The Secretary of State concluded in these words (col 865):

'Accordingly, before any such prisoner is released on licence, I will consider not only (a) whether the period served by the prisoner is adequate to satisfy the requirements of retribution and deterrence and (b) whether it is safe to release the prisoner, but also (c) the public acceptability of early release. This means that I will exercise my discretion to release only if I am satisfied that to do so will not threaten the maintenance of public confidence in the system of criminal justice. Everything that I have said about the practice of the Secretary of State in relation to mandatory life sentence prisoners applies equally to persons who are, or will be, detained during Her Majesty's pleasure under section 53(1) of the Children and Young Persons

Act 1933, as well as to persons who have been, or will be, sentenced to custody for life under section 8 of the Criminal Justice Act 1982.'

There are a number of comments which it is relevant to make about this statement. First, and most importantly, the final paragraph of the statement was the first direct intimation of the approach of the Secretary of State to children who were detained during Her Majesty's pleasure. This makes it clear that the policy is to treat them, even if they are only ten years of age, in the same way as adults sentenced to mandatory life sentences. That this should be the first statement to deal with this is surprising since this is what had happened in practice since Mr Brittan's statement. Second, the references in Mr Brittan's statement, to which I drew attention, suggesting a degree of flexibility are no longer present except perhaps in cases where the penal element is 20 years or more. At least after 17 years there will always be a review irrespective of the longer length of the tariff. It is however to be noted that the Home Secretary refers to an 'initial view' of the minimum period. Third, the element of preserving the public's confidence in the system in determining the date of release is being kept separate from the element of punishment and deterrence.

Children and young persons convicted of murder

Having considered how the position developed in relation to adult prisoners, it is now possible to turn to the position as to children and young persons, concentrating in particular on those sentenced to be detained during Her Majesty's pleasure. The relevant ages have varied but that of a child can be taken as being 10 to 14 and that of a young person 14 to 18.

The concept of detention during Her Majesty's pleasure has a very considerable history. Mr Fitzgerald relies upon that history as indicating that it is inappropriate to treat those detained in this way in the same way as if they had been sentenced to life imprisonment. Mr Fitzgerald refers to the use of the phrase in relation to disposal under the Criminal Lunatics Act 1800 and later Acts on the same subject. If a person was found to be insane by a jury lawfully empanelled for that purpose, they were to be 'kept in strict custody ... until his Majesty's pleasure shall be known' (s 2). It was also provided that—

'in all cases of insanity so found it shall be lawful for his Majesty to give such order for the safe custody of such person so found to be insane, during his pleasure, in such place and in such manner as to his Majesty shall seem fit.'

This language was adopted when Parliament decided by s 103 of the Children Act 1908 to abolish sentences of death in relation to children and young persons. Section 103 provides:

'Sentence of death shall not be pronounced on or recorded against a child or young person, but in lieu thereof the court shall sentence the child or young person to be detained during His Majesty's pleasure, and, if so sentenced, he shall, notwithstanding anything in the other provisions of this Act, be liable to be detained in such place and under such conditions as the Secretary of State may direct, and whilst so detained shall be deemed to be in legal custody.'

The language of s 53 of the Children and Young Persons Act 1933 reflects the
provisions of the 1908 Act. The terms of s 53 of the 1933 Act at the material times
were as follows:

'(1) A person convicted of an offence who appears to the court to have
been under the age of eighteen years at the time the offence was committed
shall not, if he is convicted of murder, be sentenced to imprisonment for life,
nor shall sentence of death be pronounced on or recorded against any such
person; but in lieu thereof the court shall (notwithstanding anything in this
or any other Act) sentence him to be detained during Her Majesty's pleasure,
and if so sentenced he shall be liable to be detained in such place and under
such conditions as the Secretary of State may direct.

(2) Where—(a) a child or young person is convicted on indictment of any
offence punishable in the case of an adult with imprisonment for fourteen
years or more, not being an offence the sentence for which is fixed by law; or
(b) a child is convicted of manslaughter, and the court is of opinion that none
of the other methods in which the case may legally be dealt with is suitable,
the court may sentence the offender to be detained for such period not
exceeding the maximum term of imprisonment with which the offence is
punishable in the case of an adult as may be specified in the sentence; and
where such a sentence has been passed the child or young person shall,
during that period, be liable to be detained in such place and on such
conditions as the Secretary of State may direct.

(3) A person detained pursuant to the directions of the Secretary of State
under this section shall, while so detained, be deemed to be in legal custody.'

Section 53(1) makes it clear beyond doubt that a sentence of detention during Her
Majesty's pleasure is not the same as a sentence of imprisonment for life. It is a
sentence 'in lieu of' such a sentence. The section does not provide any express
guidance as to what Parliament intends as to the duration of such a sentence. It
leaves that to the Home Secretary to determine on behalf of Her Majesty.
However, the important point for our purposes is that it only continues so long
as that is Her Majesty's, that is in practice the Home Secretary's, pleasure. Under
s 53(2) the court can also sentence a child or young person to a sentence of
detention for life since such a 'period' includes life for the purposes of that section
(see *R v Abbott* [1963] 1 All ER 738, [1964] 1 QB 489). Such a period of detention
would, however, be a discretionary sentence. In addition it would, in practice, be
a sentence which it would be inappropriate to regard as involving, as does a
mandatory life sentence, the implication that a young offender has forfeited any
expectation of release.

Mr Pannick QC on behalf of the Home Secretary draws a parallel between the
discretionary sentences of detention for life and life imprisonment and between
the mandatory sentences of detention during Her Majesty's pleasure and life
imprisonment. He submits the two discretionary sentences are treated in the
same manner by the legislation and the same approach should be adopted as to
the two mandatory sentences. He draws attention to the fact that in the case of
both mandatory sentences after release the offender remains on licence for life.

Mr Pannick argues that the correctness of the Home Secretary's approach is
confirmed by s 35(2) and (3) of the Criminal Justice Act 1991 when read with the
relevant parts of ss 43 and 51 of the same Act. These provisions he submits make
it clear that the duration of the two sentences are, from a practical point of view,
indistinguishable. The terms of s 35(2) and (3) are as follows:

a '(2) If recommended to do so by the Board, the Secretary of State may after consultation with the Lord Chief Justice together with the trial judge if available, release on licence a life prisoner who is not a discretionary life prisoner.

(3) The Board shall not make a recommendation under subsection (2) above unless the Secretary of State has referred the particular case, or the *b* class of case to which the case belongs, to the Board for its advice.'

Section 43 assimilates the position of adult prisoners and children and young persons sentenced to detention by providing:

'*Young offenders.*—(1) Subject to subsections (4) and (5) below, this Part *c* applies to persons serving sentences of detention in a young offender institution, or determinate sentences of detention under section 53 of the 1933 Act, as it applies to persons serving equivalent sentences of imprisonment.

(2) Subject to subsection (5) below, this Part applies to persons serving— (a) sentences of detention during Her Majesty's pleasure or for life under *d* section 53 of the 1933 Act; or (b) sentences of custody for life under section 8 of the 1982 Act [ie the Criminal Justice Act 1982], as it applies to persons serving sentences of imprisonment for life.'

Section 51 contains interpretation provisions in respect of Pt II of the 1991 Act. The section includes a provision which provides that, 'in this Part ... "life *e* prisoner" has the meaning given by section 34(7) above (as extended by section 43(2) above)'. Section 51(1) also includes a definition of a 'discretionary life prisoner' as having 'the meaning given by section 34 above (as extended by section 43(2) above)'. Section 43(2) does provide a further link between the provisions in the Act dealing with young offenders and those dealing with adult *f* prisoners.

I accept there is a clear relationship between the provisions as to adults and those which relate to young offenders but it does not follow from this that the symmetry is necessarily exact so that the only difference between the mandatory sentences is the conditions in which the two age groups are to be housed while in custody. The provisions of ss 43 and 51 of the 1991 Act are only for the purpose *g* of Pt II of the Act. This means the statutory source of the Home Secretary's discretion to order the release is the same in the case of both classes of offenders but it does not mean that the sentences from which they are being released are necessarily the same.

Mr Fitzgerald is therefore right in saying that Her Majesty's pleasure remains *h* a separate and different sentence from that of a mandatory life sentence. It is a sentence which still has something of the flavour of its use in connection with so-called lunatics, of retaining the individual in detention so long as there is reason to do so. In the case of an adult murderer, as the sentence is one for life, it is explicit from the sentence itself that the subject of the sentence is to forfeit for *j* the period of life any right to be released. The terms of the sentence itself provide the justification for the continued imprisonment. It can be said, as the Minister of State did, that there is a presumption of continued incarceration. In the case of a sentence of detention during Her Majesty's pleasure there is no such explicit or implicit consequence to be derived from the language of the sentence. As one would expect of a sentence relating to a child or young person, the sentence is more merciful. The subject of the sentence is not by its language deprived of all

expectation of release. There can still be an expectation of release, not on a
predetermined date, but when the Home Secretary determines that there is no   a
reason for the detention to continue. The distinction is no more than that which
flows from the fact that in the case of one sentence the *discretion is to bring custody
to an end* despite the fact that the sentence is for life, while in the case of the other
sentence *there is a discretion to continue custody* which may result in custody lasting
even for life. The distinction between the discretions remains, even though in   b
both cases on release the release is conditional for life and conditional on
compliance with the conditions of the licence.

The distinction which I draw between the two mandatory sentences expresses
in my own words the distinction which was recognised by Evans LJ in *R v
Secretary of State for the Home Dept, ex p Singh (Prem)* (1993) Times, 27 April and by
both the Commission and the European Court of Human Rights in *Hussain v UK*   c
(1996) 22 EHRR 1. A different view from that of Evans LJ was taken by Kennedy
LJ in *R v Secretary of State for the Home Dept, ex p T* [1994] 1 All ER 794, [1994] QB
378, but that can be explained by the fact that the case only concerned the release
provisions under the 1991 Act when the statutory provisions themselves make it
clear the same statutory provisions are to apply to both sentences.   d

I therefore accept that in many situations the distinction may not have any
practical implications and the difference between the two mandatory sentences
will be reduced normally to that as to the conditions in which the sentence is
served. None the less, the distinction to which I have referred remains and
should be remembered by the Home Secretary since it can affect the way the   e
Home Secretary is required to exercise his discretion.

The 1991 Act was at least in part intended to bring our law into line with the
jurisprudence of the European Court of Human Rights. The consequence of this
analysis of the sentence of detention during Her Majesty's pleasure means that
Parliament has not done so. The same is, however, probably true if Mr Pannick's
arguments are correct. Further, it would be wrong on the basis of this general   f
intention to change the underlying nature of the sentence of young offenders so
it becomes materially more punitive by a sidewind.

There are two other statutory provisions to which I need to make reference.
The first is s 44 of the Children and Young Persons Act 1933. In sub-s (1) it
provides: g

'Every court in dealing with a child or young person who is brought before
it, either as an offender or otherwise, shall have regard to the welfare of the
child or young person and shall in a proper case take steps for removing him
from undesirable surroundings, and for securing that proper provision is
made for his education and training.'   h

Although this section is referring expressly to courts and not to the Home
Secretary, if he chooses to adopt a practice which involves his performing the
same role as a court then the section is clearly of relevance as indicating the
importance that Parliament attaches to the welfare of children and young   j
persons. Under the other statutory provision, s 50 of the 1933 Act, a child under
the age of ten years cannot be guilty of any offence. Mr Fitzgerald attaches
importance to this because of the applicants' age at the time of the crime. On the
other hand, a child between the ages of 10 and 14 can only be found guilty if he
appreciates what he has done is seriously wrong and the applicants were found
guilty.

The facts

a   The applicants were born in August 1982. The murder was committed in February 1993 when they were ten and a half. At the trial in November 1993 no defence of diminished responsibility was advanced and the psychiatric evidence given was called by the prosecution to establish that the applicants were capable of knowing the difference between right and wrong.

b   After they were convicted, because the sentence was mandatory under s 53(1) of the 1933 Act, no psychiatric or social inquiry reports were adduced for the purposes of mitigation. However, the trial judge made a report to the Home Secretary dated 29 November 1993. The report was in the standard form. It summarised the facts of the offence and pointed out that the applicants did not give evidence and indicated that both boys were of average intelligence with no

c   mental abnormality. The judge referred to two detailed reports which he had. One in the case of Thompson obtained by his solicitor and the other in the case of Venables obtained by the Crown. The judge indicated:

> 'Very great care will have to be taken before either defendant is allowed out into the general community. Much psychotherapeutic, psychological
d   > and educational investigation assistance will be required. Not only must they be fully rehabilitated and no longer a danger to others but there is a very real risk of revenge attacks upon them from others.'

In answer to the question as to the trial judge's view on the actual length of detention necessary to meet the requirements of retribution and general
e   deterrence for the offence, the judge said:

> 'If the defendants had been adults I would have said that the actual length of detention necessary to meet the requirements of retribution and general deterrence should have been 18 years.'

f   The judge then briefly described the background of the boys, and continued:

> 'In my judgment the appropriate actual length of detention necessary to meet the requirement of retribution and general deterrence for murder, taking into account all its appalling circumstances and the age of the defendants when it was committed, is eight years (subject to my comments
g   > ... above) ... eight years is "very, very many years" for a 10 or 11 year old. They are now children. In eight years time they will be young men.'

The Lord Chief Justice commented:

> 'I have well in mind the trial judge is in a better position than I to assess
h   > these two boys and their crime, also I agree that a much lesser tariff should apply than in the case of an adult. I think the minimum period for punishment and deterrence should be ten years.'

The doctors who were responsible for the report on Thompson were concerned for his future and wrote to the Home Secretary and the Secretary of State for
j   Health indicating their reasons for concern and stated:

> 'Unfortunately the adversarial nature of the criminal proceedings meant that the bulk of our assessment, including our clinical hypothesis about the possible motivation for this crime, was never seen by the jury, read by the judge or reported in the press.'

They indicated that they felt that there was an urgent need for further psychiatric examination and assessment. The Home Secretary replied on 20 December 1993 indicating that a clear sentence plan would be drawn up for Thompson based on a full assessment which would include a full psychiatric assessment.

At the beginning of January 1994 each of the applicants was informed of the substance of the recommendations as to the tariff made by the judge and the Lord Chief Justice. In February 1994 representations as to the tariff were made by lawyers on behalf of Venables and in March 1994 by lawyers on behalf of Thompson. I was concerned that those lawyers who make the representations might be without any right to legal aid for this purpose and therefore without any entitlement to payment. That would be an unsatisfactory situation. However, as a result, inquiries were made at the request of the court (for which we are grateful); it appears that the position was improved from 1 May 1996 and that legal aid is now available under an extension of the green form scheme.

On 16 June 1994 a letter was written to each of the applicants by Mr Newton on behalf of the Home Secretary. The letter referred to reports in the media about representations made to the Home Office by members of the Bulger family and other members of the public. It indicated that a petition had been received from about 250,000 members of the public indicating that the applicant should not be released in any circumstances and should be detained for life. The letter also mentioned some 4,400 letters from members of the public in support of the family. In addition there was reference to a member of Parliament who had submitted a petition at the request of relatives of the Bulger family signed by nearly 6,000 people indicating that the minimum sentence should be 25 years and to 21,000 coupons published by the Sun newspaper which had been received in support of a whole life tariff. In addition there had been various letters and small petitions over a thousand of which were in favour of a whole life tariff and only 33 of which agreed with the judiciary or suggested a lower tariff.

The Home Secretary's decision letters stated that the Home Secretary—

'had regard to the circumstances of the offence, the recommendations received from the judiciary, the representations made on your behalf and the extent to which this case could be compared with other cases. *He also had regard to the public concern about this case which was evidenced by the petitions and other correspondence* [to which I have just referred] and to the need to maintain the public confidence in the system of criminal justice. The Secretary of State takes fully into account the fact that you were only 10 years old when the offence was committed. He further acknowledges that a much lesser tariff should apply than in the case of an adult.' (My emphasis.)

The letter indicates that, like the trial judge, he was not able to reach any conclusion with regard to the relative responsibility of the applicants. The letter then sets out the views of the trial judge and the Lord Chief Justice, and continues by stating:

'The Secretary of State had regard to these views. He takes the view that this was an exceptionally cruel and sadistic offence against a very young and defenceless victim committed over a period of several hours. The Secretary of State believes that if the offence had been committed by an adult then the appropriate tariff would have been in the region of 25 years and not 18 years as suggested by the trial judge. For these reasons and bearing in mind your age when the offence was committed the Secretary of State has decided to fix a a tariff of 15 years in your case. The Secretary of State is satisfied that such a tariff is consistent with tariffs fixed in other cases.'

The letter concludes by stating that the Secretary of State is prepared to consider any further representations which you or your representatives might wish to make about the length of the tariff and, in the light of such fresh representations, to reduce the tariff if appropriate.

b On 12 October 1994 further representations were made on behalf of Venables by a letter of that date. The letter indicated that judicial review would be sought on behalf of Venables. It added that the procedure adopted in fixing the period was unfair and that Venables had not been adequately informed of the information before the judiciary and the Home Secretary when they made their

c decision. The letter therefore asked the Secretary of State to reconsider the whole matter and for this purpose to consult the judiciary afresh. The letter pointed out that the psychiatric report before the judge had been limited and there had been no detailed mitigation. Similar representations were made in relation to Thompson also in a letter of 12 October 1994. By letters dated 24 January 1995 written on behalf of the Home Secretary, he indicated that he could

d not see that there was any reason to depart from his previous decision.

In an affidavit Mr Newton, who is the author of the letters written on behalf of the Home Secretary, indicates that the Secretary of State when he made his decision had only a medical report on Thompson which he did not regard as containing information which assisted him. Mr Newton drew attention to the

e fact that the report stated that it is not possible on the basis of the information currently available to reach a reliable conclusion about Thompson's state of mind at the time of the alleged offence. The affidavit also refers to the criticisms which were made of the Secretary of State reaching a decision when fresh information may come to light in the future relating to the offences or the state of mind of the applicant, in particular psychiatric reports, and then states:

f
'The Secretary of State is always prepared to consider such fresh information and to reduce the tariff if appropriate. This applies equally to any social enquiry or psychiatric reports commissioned by the applicants and containing information *relevant to the length of tariff*.' (My emphasis.)

g Mr Newton also made clear, as is accepted by Mr Pannick on behalf of the Home Secretary, that the Secretary of State would only be influenced by fresh information which comes to light which is *'relevant to the circumstances of the offence, or the applicants state of mind when the offences were committed'*. Other changes in circumstances are not regarded as being relevant. The reason for this

h approach, as I understand it, is that the Home Secretary regards subsequent events, such as changes in the character and personality of the offender, as irrelevant when determining the appropriate tariff. This approach means that if a detainee's character changes beyond recognition for the better this cannot bring forward the first review date. Again, it means that if an offender while in detention acted in a conspicuously brave manner this would not be regarded as

j relevant to changing the tariff. Mr Pannick suggests that could constitute a compassionate ground for release under the special power contained in s 36 of the 1991 Act. I am not sure about this but, in any event, this approach substantially limits the scope of the suggestions made in the statement and by Mr Newton in his evidence and in letters that the Secretary of State's decision is not 'immutable' and his statement that:

'The Secretary of State has had regard to the need for rehabilitation of the applicants. But on the facts of these cases, and in the light of the gravity of the offences and the need for punishment for them, he does not consider that the aim for rehabilitation can override the need for 15 years detention as punishment. Moreover the fixing of a tariff of 15 years *does not preclude the need for periodic monitoring of rehabilitation of the applicants.*' (My emphasis.)

While there is excellent monitoring and a care plan designed to achieve the best outcome which is possible for the applicants despite their circumstances, the results of this enlightened approach is apparently not to affect the operation of the tariff or the date of the first review.

Later in the affidavit Mr Newton states:

'The Secretary of State did not seek to apply a mathematical formula. He selected that tariff which he thought was appropriate as punishment in the light of the gravity of the offence and all of the circumstances of this case, having particular regard to the age of the applicants.'

The affidavit also makes clear that in fixing the tariff the Secretary of State has had regard to public opinion and to public concern about the particular cases.

After the fixing of the tariff, a full psychiatric report was obtained in January 1995 on Venables. This indicated that he was making excellent response to the therapeutic work and current family support that he was receiving. It also indicated 'there would be major concern for [Venables] to have to progress through young offender institutions to prison' which is what is likely to happen if the present tariff is maintained. Similar comments are made in a further psychiatric report obtained on behalf of Venables by a distinguished professor of child psychiatry at the University of London. He regards the tariff as long as 15 years as likely to have a damaging effect on the ability of a child of the age of the applicants to think constructively about preparing for the adult life. He also considers the adverse consequences of Venables being transferred either to a young offenders institution or to prison.

In response to questions by the parties it is stated on behalf of the Home Secretary that, in the case of detainees under 14 years of age, 15 years is the longest tariff imposed. However, there was one case of a tariff of 14 years set for a murderer aged 12. In that case, the judge had recommended a tariff of 12 years and the Lord Chief Justice had recommended 14 years.

Having set out the background material necessarily at some length, I return to the issues. In doing so it is convenient to have in mind that the criticisms which are made of the decisions of the Home Secretary can be conveniently assessed under three heads. (1) The tariff policy which the Home Secretary has adopted is unlawful in the case of young offenders because it conflicts with statutory discretion which he is given to release young offenders (the lawfulness of the policy). (2) If the tariff policy is lawful it has been applied too inflexibly so that it unlawfully fetters this discretion (the application of the policy). (3) In applying the policy and fixing the tariff in the case of the applicants: (a) irrelevant material in the form of petitions and other documents calling for a long tariff period was unfairly or irrationally taken into account; or (b) information which should have been disclosed to the applicants was not disclosed; or (c) information which should have been obtained was not obtained or taken into account (the fairness of the decision).

The lawfulness of the policy

a   In the case of adult offenders who are found guilty of murder, the decision in *Doody v Secretary of State for the Home Dept* [1993] 3 All ER 92, [1994] 1 AC 531 makes it clear that the policy is lawful. Mr Fitzgerald's primary submission for saying that the policy cannot be applied to young offenders is based on the statutory description of the sentence and its history. He submits that either

b   punishment should play no part in the sentence or only a limited role, and therefore, a policy relying substantially on a period representing punishment and deterrence is inappropriate.

I do not agree that punishment and deterrence necessarily have a limited role to play in the case of the detention of a young offender for murder during Her Majesty's pleasure. Even without the sidenote to s 53 of the 1933 Act, which

c   reads 'Punishment of certain grave crimes', the sentence clearly involves a punitive element. The sentence, after all, was originally introduced as a substitute for capital punishment. The idea that there should be no room for punishment for murder when there is clearly provision for punishment for lesser offences would make nonsense of the legislation. The sentence was originally

d   introduced as a substitute for capital punishment. The weight to be given to the need for punishment in the case of any particular offender, as against other legitimate considerations, is a matter for the Home Secretary to determine when deciding, in the exercise of his discretion, when a particular individual young offender should be released. As long as the Home Secretary exercises his discretion in a manner which accords with the requirements of the law, the

e   courts cannot interfere with the significance which he attaches to the need for punishment. The policy cannot therefore be faulted for the importance it attaches to the need for punishment.

Obviously an allowance must be made for the age of the offender when determining the tariff since the more mature the offender the less excuse for

f   offending. But this can be and is allowed for when fixing the tariff in accordance with the policy. The need for rehabilitation is also a relevant consideration. This can in part be catered for in the regime provided for the offender while in detention and it can also influence the decision as to when to release when punishment no longer requires continued detention.

Again, the fact that the mandatory sentence of detention for young offenders

g   has the distinction from the mandatory sentence of life imprisonment which I have described does not mean that the same tariff based approach cannot be deployed in relation to both. The distinction between the sentences can be accommodated in the application of the policy. This involves paying greater attention to the need for flexibility when circumstances require. In addition, if

h   the sentence does not involve the presumption to which the minister of state referred, there should be a greater readiness to depart from the two-stage policy. This is especially so in the case of a very young offender if otherwise there could be an inappropriate result. There appears to me no reason why the policy should not cater for this, though under the next head it is necessary to consider the

j   relevance of the absence of any recognition in the evidence of the Home Secretary of this requirement.

The application of the policy

The Home Secretary's discretion as to release is very wide. It is the type of discretion which calls out for the development of a policy as to the way it will in general be exercised. This should assist in providing consistency and certainty

which are highly desirable in an area involving the administration of justice
where fairness is particularly important.   *a*

Furthermore, in general I cannot see any legal objection to the Home
Secretary applying the two-limb approach as modified and developed from time
to time, which was regarded as unobjectionable in *Doody's* case in relation to
adults, to young offenders as happened from 1983 although this was not
mentioned to Parliament until a later date. This is because it allows a young   *b*
offender to know the period during which he is unlikely to be released and when
he should prepare himself to put forward representations. The objection which
is most often made by those subject to an indeterminate sentence is its
uncertainty. They need a target date. It is also sensible from the administrators
point of view. It avoids conducting reviews which will serve no purpose, at times
when there is no question of the offender being released from custody, which will   *c*
only give rise to unjustified expectations on the part of the detainee. In addition
it identifies the penal element which, perfectly properly, the young offender can
normally be expected to serve by way of punishment.

Just as in exercising his discretion in an individual case the Home Secretary is
required to exercise his discretion in the manner which accords with the law so   *d*
he must also do so in determining his policy. If the position was otherwise the
existence of policy would enable the discretion to be exercised in a way which
would not be permissible in the absence of the policy. This means that the policy
must not be so inflexible that it cannot accommodate the range of different
situations to which it will have to apply. Here, in the case of young offenders
from the child just over the age of criminal responsibility to the 17-year-old.   *e*

In addition, the policy must not be so rigid that it does not allow for the
exceptional case which requires a departure from the policy, otherwise it could
result in fettering of the discretion which would be unlawful.

The reason for the significance of the unlawful fettering of discretion is
accurately described by Professor Sir William Wade in *Administrative Law* (7th   *f*
edn, 1994) p 360 under the heading 'Over-Rigid Policies':

> 'It is a fundamental rule for the exercise of discretionary power that
> discretion must be brought to bear on every case: each one must be
> considered on its merits and decided as the public interest requires at the   *g*
> time.'

When the 1993 statement is compared with that of 1983 it is apparent that the
policy of 1993 is more rigid. In the case of young offenders, to put off the
commencement of a general review of their position theoretically as long as 15 years
appears to be totally unreasonable. Even, in the case of offenders of the age of   *h*
the applicants, to put it off for 12 years appears to me to be unacceptable and
contrary to the proper exercise of the discretion. If the tariff was fixed at a figure
as high as this but there was to be a general reconsideration during the period of
the tariff I would take a different view. The policy would then allow for the
changes of circumstances which will inevitably occur in the case of young   *j*
offenders as they grow up to be taken into account. The inconvenience that this
would cause would be limited because of the monitoring that already takes place.
How it could work is indicated in the policy statement of 1983.

Exceptional progress may be what is required for a departure from the tariff
but where it occurs it cannot be excluded as irrelevant without fettering the
discretion unlawfully in the case of applicants of this age. On Mr Newton's

a evidence this fettering now would, or at least could, occur because of the restriction on what is regarded as relevant when reconsidering the tariff.

The need for reconsideration is especially important if limited information is available to the Home Secretary at the time when he reaches his decision on tariff. The absence of full reports is understandable because to meet the views expressed in R v Secretary of State for the Home Dept, ex p Handscomb (1988) 86 Cr
b App R 59 the tariff is fixed expeditiously. However, when a decision is taken on limited material this makes reconsideration all the more important. After what period the reconsideration should take place is a matter for the Home Secretary but it cannot be postponed altogether for as long as 12 years for no good reason in the case of offenders of the age of these applicants. Mr Fitzgerald in argument referred to five years and I would find this acceptable, but I emphasise each case
c turns on its own circumstances and the nature of the new material which becomes available.

The position of adults is different. Their circumstances do not change to the same extent as those of children. A child of ten by the time he reaches the age of 15 may have changed beyond recognition. I do not say that progress will entitle
d the younger offender to a review let alone release. All that is required is a willingness to reconsider the date of review if there is material available to the Home Secretary indicating that this is desirable. The statute gives the Home Secretary a discretion which allows him to exercise his power of release at any time. He cannot decline to consider exercising a discretion which he has throughout the period of the detention irrespective of the circumstances of an
e exceptional case. The tariff policy is perfectly permissible as an aid to the exercise of this discretion but it cannot excuse an unwillingness to depart from the policy.

The explanation for the Home Secretary adopting this approach to the policy could be a misapprehension as to the legal position to which it applies. His approach appears to be that there is no distinction between the mandatory
f sentences in the case of a child or young person detained during Her Majesty's pleasure and an adult whereas, as I have indicated above, there is a distinction. The likelihood of the misapprehension is confirmed by Mr Newton's evidence which is totally lacking in any acknowledgement of such a distinction.

The failure to recognise the distinction between the two sentences may also be the explanation for Mr Newton's approach to fresh evidence which comes into
g existence after the tariff has been determined.

The difference between the judicial figures and that of the Home Secretary in this particular case as to the tariff is so different as to raise a doubt as to whether there is a difference of approach as to what the tariff covers. Unless the tariff is to bear some relationship to what punishment the judiciary would impose, what is
h the purpose of consulting them? This is underlined when it is remembered that the tariff is a net figure, taking into account the right to remission, so the true difference is greater than appears from comparing 8 or 10 with 15. However, I do not consider it is open for a court to interfere on this ground alone for the reasons indicated by Lord Mustill in Doody's case once it is accepted that
j punishment is part of the sentence.

The scale of the tariff selected in the case of the applicants is still of significance. It is another feature which highlights the exceptional nature of the position of the applicants. To the fact that at the time of their offence they were just over the age of criminal responsibility and the nature of their offence there has to be added the fact that the tariff considered appropriate was longer than had ever been selected for offenders of their age. Even the nearest example was less for an offender two years older and two years is a substantial difference at this age. When the limited evidence which was available about the applicants is also taken into account, together with the public interest in the tariff figures which was quite out of proportion to the significance of the tariff, there was an almost irresistible case for considering whether the tariff approach should not exceptionally be departed from. On the evidence this was not considered. It should have been. A departure from the tariff would allow the development of these young offenders to be considered. It would allow the full information to be obtained. It would avoid the Home Secretary publicly being in significant disagreement with the judiciary which could only tend to undermine the public confidence in the criminal justice system. It appears that either the ability to depart from the policy was not appreciated or, if it was appreciated, not considered.

In deciding whether consideration should have been given to departing from the policy in this case it is helpful to ask two questions. The first is whether, if there was no policy, would it be sensible to have come to this decision. To this question, I unhesitantly say No. In addition to the features I have already identified which are disadvantages which follow from the application of the policy, there is the crushing nature of the inevitable penal element of the sentence which puts off reconsideration for the same period as would a determinative sentence of 27 years. (I am taking into account the Home Secretary's discretion to consider release after half the sentence and deducting three years. I appreciate there would in any event be a review after 17 years.) Fifteen years is 150% of the applicants' life so far. It is necessary to consider what effect this has on the rehabilitation which is part of any sentence. How do the applicants and those whose task it is to be responsible for them cope with this? It is inconsistent with the very flexibility which must have been intended by Parliament in giving such a wide and untrammelled discretion to the Home Secretary.

The other question is, does the existence of the policy justify not at least considering departing from the policy? Again the answer I give is No. If there is ever going to be a justification for departing from the policy, cases with the features of these cases must be at the top of the list justifying departure. As will be apparent from what I have to say under the third head, the application of the policy is going to produce injustice.

The fairness of the decision

Here it is clear that the Home Secretary took into account the petitions and other documents presented to him urging the fixing of a higher tariff than that fixed by the judiciary. This could well provide part of the explanation for striking difference in the figures of the judiciary and the Home Secretary for the penal element. This I regard as being a departure from the standards of fairness the exercise of a discretion of this sort requires. I also regard this as the taking into account material which is not relevant at that stage but, if it is ever relevant, is relevant to the question of release after the tariff period has been served.

The fixing of a tariff involves determining the appropriate punishment within the scale of punishments which the Home Secretary applies generally. Those punishments should, as the Home Secretary advocates, take into account the need to ensure that the public has confidence in the criminal justice system if they are to be made public as happened in this case. I also accept that the Home Secretary is entitled to have his own scale which differs from that of the judges and that he is free to consider that the particular case requires particularly heavy a punishment. However, notwithstanding the width of his discretion, he cannot apply his own policy unfairly or irrationally.

To take into account the petitions etc is unfair because it is material which has come into existence in a way which it is impossible for the applicants to test or match. The petition may or may not have been conducted fairly. We do not know. We do not know how many people would have been prepared to sign the

b petition if they had been told that the tariff's only purpose is to put off the date when the Home Secretary can consider the question of release at which time the Home Secretary would be able to take into account current public feeling. We also do not know what would be the response to a petition and public campaign on behalf of the applicants.

In addition, to take into account public feeling of this nature for the purpose of

c increasing the tariff means that, if the mood of the public were to change prior to the tariff being served, a longer sentence than would otherwise be necessary would be served. This cannot be right and no doubt explains why the policy hitherto was to treat the attitude of the public as something separate from the tariff. To include it in the tariff could result in double accounting. The scale of

d punishment would in any event take into account the need for the public to have confidence in the scale. Unless care was exercised, to take into account the public clamour for a heavy penal element in a particular case could result in the influence of the same factor being repeated.

While the Home Secretary is not confined in his consideration of the tariff to the material a court would regard as relevant, he should least bear in mind when

e performing a role similar to that of the courts how the courts perform that role. A court would regard it as quite improper for this type of material to be put before a court. I do not believe any prosecutor would seek to do this. Indeed to run a campaign designed to increase the punishment in a particular case could amount to an interference with the due administration of justice. This being the

f position as to the courts, I find it difficult to see the justification for the Home Secretary taking a different view. I certainly do not consider that Lord Mustill had this type of material in contemplation when he referred to the need to maintain the public's confidence in the justice system.

The material which the Home Secretary should have before him when fixing the tariff has to be judged against the extent to which the tariff is capable of being

g reconsidered and the length of the tariff in the particular case. If it is not an initial view which will in due course be fully reviewed and the period is as long as 15 years in the case of children of this age then I can only describe the approach in these cases as perfunctory and as falling far below the standards that a court would adopt if contemplating sentencing a child for a period of 15 years'

h detention. A court would require full social and psychiatric reports.

Mr Pannick submits that what has happened, which is to sentence these children on a short summary of the views of the trial judge, is not unfair as demonstrated by the fact that the Lord Chief Justice was prepared to act on the same material. While this a proper point for an advocate to make, it is without

j substance. If the Lord Chief Justice's figure was to be the decision I have no doubt that he would not perform the role in this way. The Home Secretary is well aware that the Lord Chief Justice can, in practice, provide only a bird's-eye view as to tariff, primarily to achieve consistency. He personally has to consider well over 200 new cases each year in addition to those which come back for the purposes of review. He is entitled to expect the Home Secretary to obtain any additional information which is needed and to ensure that the detainee has a

proper opportunity to make any necessary representations as would happen if the
matter comes before a court.   a

That brings me to the final point. In this case there should have been full
disclosure of the nature of all the material before the Home Secretary which was
to be taken into account. The applicants needed to know what was not available
to him. Mr Fitzgerald submitted that it was assumed there would be available the
full reports which were absent. For these to be considered after the decision has   b
been reached is not same as for them to be taken into account before the decision
is reached. There is natural reluctance in the case of any administrative decision
to change it in the absence of very clear evidence and the applicants were entitled
to a proper decision taken on the relevant material.

                                                                                         c
The remedy

In view of the conclusions to which I have come, the proper course is for this
appeal to be dismissed so the decisions can be taken again. This will involve first
deciding whether there should be a tariff in these cases. If it is decided that there
should be a tariff it will be necessary to decide that tariff and whether there should
be the possibility of review at some stage prior to the expiry of the tariff period   d
and, if so, what steps should be taken to make that possibility a reality.

What I have said earlier in this judgment indicates that there is real need for
reconsideration of how we are administering cases which will inevitably result in
young children being detained for long periods in detention. The history of the
statements made to Parliament suggests that the policy in relation to child   e
murderers may have been adopted as an afterthought to that in the case of adults
without the detailed consideration required. Why otherwise the delay in
referring to it for ten years? Approximately 90 years ago an enlightened
Parliament recognised that a flexible sentence of detention is what is required in
these cases with a very wide discretion being given to the person Parliament   f
thought best suited to oversee that discretion so that the most appropriate
decision as to release could be taken in the public interest. The subsequent
statutes have not altered the nature of the discretion. Yet by a series of policy
decisions that flexibility has in relation to these cases all but disappeared. This
does not accord with what Parliament has laid down. Nor does it result in this
case in a just result.   g

HOBHOUSE LJ. Both these appeals raise the same questions. The points for
decision can be grouped under three headings. The first is whether there is any
element of punishment involved in a sentence under s 53(1) of the Children and
Young Persons Act 1933. The Divisional Court ((1996) Times, 7 May) held that   h
there was. The second heading is whether the Secretary of State is entitled to
adopt the same approach to the exercise of his discretion whether or not to
release a defendant detained under s 53(1) as for a defendant who, as an adult, has
been convicted of murder and mandatorily sentenced to life imprisonment under
s 1 of the Murder (Abolition of Death Penalty) Act 1965. The answer to this   j
question depends upon whether the court accepts that a sentence under s 53(1) is
a life sentence and the view it takes of the provisions of the Criminal Justice Act
1991. The Divisional Court held that the Secretary of State was not so entitled
and quashed the decisions. The third heading, which the Divisional Court did not
have to consider, concerns the decision-making process—whether the procedure
was faulty and whether it involved any irrationality.

a   The applications for judicial review relate to the decision letters of the
Secretary of State dated 22 July 1994 in which he informed each defendant of his
'decision on the period to be served in your case to meet the requirements of
retribution and deterrence'. The letters conclude:

'For these reasons, and bearing in mind your age when the offence was
committed, the Secretary of State has decided to fix a tariff of fifteen years in
b   your case. The Secretary of State is satisfied that such a tariff is consistent
with tariffs fixed in other cases. The Secretary of State is prepared to consider
any fresh representations which you or your representatives might wish to
make about the length of the tariff and, in the light of such fresh
representations, to reduce the tariff if appropriate.'

c   In writing these letters the Secretary of State was following the policy and
procedure which he had outlined in his parliamentary answer of 27 July 1993 (see
229 HC Official Report (6th series) written answers cols 863–865) after the
decision of the House of Lords in *Doody v Secretary of State for the Home Dept* [1993]
3 All ER 92, [1994] 1 AC 531. That parliamentary answer was primarily
d   concerned with adults who had been convicted of murder and had received a
mandatory sentence of life imprisonment. The answer concluded with these
words (col 865):

'Everything that I have said about the practice of the Secretary of State in
relation to mandatory life sentence prisoners applies equally to the persons
e   who are, or will be, detained during Her Majesty's Pleasure under section
53(1) of the Children and Young Persons Act 1933, as well as to persons who
have been, or will be, sentenced to custody for life under section 8 of the
Criminal Justice Act 1982.'

f   I. INTRODUCTION
Before turning to the specific points raised for decision on these appeals, it is
desirable to put them in their factual and legal context.

The trial and its aftermath
The murder of James Bulger was a truly horrific crime. This was because it
g   involved the abduction of a two-year-old child from a shopping centre, taking
him over a period of about two hours whilst he was showing increasing distress
to the place where he was killed, and there subjecting him to a sadistic and brutal
attack until he was dead. The perpetrators were two boys, themselves, aged no
more than ten years old. It was the conclusion of the trial judge, Morland J, that
h   the abduction was carried out for the purpose of killing the victim and the two
boys had earlier made two unsuccessful attempts to abduct other children.
Why this crime provoked an extreme public reaction can be easily understood.
The crime itself threatened the security of all mothers of young children. The
crime was exceptionally cruel. The crime offended against the assumptions made
j   by most members of the public about the criminal capabilities of pre-adolescent
boys. The killing itself attracted enormous publicity as did the ensuing trial and
the sentencing process. As the two defendants had been found guilty by the jury,
the judge had only one sentence open to him: that each defendant be detained
under s 53(1) during Her Majesty's pleasure. Since this was a mandatory sentence
no submissions about the sentence were heard and no further reports called for
or made.

The trial judge sentenced the defendants on 24 November 1993. In his *a* sentencing remarks he described the defendants' killing of James Bulger as 'an act of unparalleled evil and barbarity'; James Bulger was 'battered to death without mercy'; 'your conduct was both cunning and very wicked'. He told them that they would be 'detained for very, very many years'. After he had passed sentence he made some broader comments which commenced:

'How it came about that two mentally normal boys aged ten, of average *b* intelligence committed this terrible crime is very hard to comprehend.'

It therefore came as something of a surprise to many members of the general public when they read in their newspapers (from what source the affidavits do not say) that the judge had recommended to the Secretary of State a period of detention of no more than eight years; they did not feel that that was 'very very *c* many years'. They might be released before they were 20. A press campaign ensued in which extreme views were expressed, including that the defendants should remain in custody for the rest of their natural lives. The family of James Bulger made representations. A petition with 250,000 signatures was presented. Several hundred thousand letters were received by the Home Department. *d*

The situation in which the Secretary of State and his advisers found themselves was wholly exceptional. A climate of opinion had been built up in which it was very difficult to make an adequate decision on what was required for retribution and deterrence. The situation had become overlaid by a range of public pressures which lost sight of the two defendants as immature individuals and got bound up with when, many years later, it might become publicly acceptable to release the *e* murderers of James Bulger from custody on licence. It also lost sight of the fact that the practical significance of any statement by the Secretary of State would simply be to the date upon which the Parole Board would first be allowed to express a view about the defendants (s 35(3) of the 1991 Act). It appears that there was no specific attempt to obtain or marshall whatever 'mitigation' evidence *f* might be available or to evaluate the maturity or immaturity of the defendants' personalities; they were still only 11 years old. This is the context in which the letters of 22 July 1993 came to be written.

The pragmatic development of English law

It is essential to the understanding of the area of law and practice raised for *g* consideration by these appeals to appreciate that its development has not proceeded from predetermined principles. It has rather been pragmatic and empirical. Contributions have been successively made by the legislature, by the Home Department and by the judges and, in addition, by the European Court of Human Rights at Strasbourg under the European Convention for the Protection *h* of Human Rights and Fundamental Freedoms (Rome, 4 November 1950; TS 71 (1953); Cmd 8969). The history has been set out in a number of places. It suffices to refer the reader to the speech of Lord Mustill in *Doody's* case [1993] 3 All ER 92 at 99–103, [1994] 1 AC 531 at 551–556. Important though they are, I will not in this judgment trace again the stages by which the present position has been *j* reached. I will concentrate upon the 1933 and 1991 Acts, their effect and the principles they embody.

Sentences and custody

In English criminal practice, sentencing has to take place as soon after conviction as is practicable. The power to defer sentence is circumscribed and *a* rarely exercised. The sentencing judge may have to adjourn for pre-sentence reports (see s 3(1) of the 1991 Act). It may take some time to obtain these but, subject to that need, he will proceed to sentence straight away. The sentence has to take into account not only the seriousness of the crime and the need to deter but also the personal circumstances of the offender and the mitigation available to him, for example, his attitude to his offence (s 28(1) of the 1991 Act). The

b sentence is a sentence passed on an individual and has to be justified for that individual as well as for the crime.

The sentence is passed having regard to the state of affairs existing at the time sentence is passed. In principle, things which occur subsequently are irrelevant to the propriety of that sentence. They fall within the control of those responsible for the custodial regime of the offender. Where the offender is eligible for early

c release, they will be taken into account as relevant to the decision whether to allow early release. But, apart from this, the requisite service of a custodial sentence can only be reduced as an exercise in Executive mercy, now incorporated in various statutory provisions: see e g s 28 of the Prisons Act 1952 and s 36 of the 1991 Act. This is the way in which the system accommodates the

d exceptional release from custody of those not eligible for early release. Later eventualities are not the concern of the sentencing judge and are not relevant to retribution and deterrence.

In the theory of penology, there have been recurrent arguments in favour of indeterminate sentences: thus, it has at times been suggested that the courts should not be concerned at all with sentence and that the disposal of offenders

e should be left to experts in the field of the treatment of criminals giving them the power to decide in the light of the response of the offender to the treatments they have chosen how long he should be detained in custody. However, such policies have as a general rule proved unacceptable and unworkable in practice. The sentencing of those convicted of crimes has to be and to be seen to be the

f imposition of a punishment, not merely a prescription for a social disease. Save in special situations, they fail to meet the needs of the offender and the criminal justice system. They give rise to serious feelings of grievance and injustice in the offender as well as the public. Offenders have a need, in their own interest as well as in the interests of justice, to know what their punishment is to be. In relation to indeterminate as well as determinate sentences it is widely accepted that it

g assists an offender and his rehabilitation that he should know, either at the time sentence is passed or, if not, as soon as possible thereafter, what his punishment is. This policy has been recognised in legislation and parliamentary answers as well as by the courts.

However, there is superimposed upon this system an essentially executive

h system for the early release of offenders from custody. For reasons which lie beyond the scope of this judgment it has been a consistent feature of penal policy to retain and use a power to release those in custody before the end of their sentence. Over the years the rules have varied, as has their administration. In Pt II of the 1991 Act, for determinate sentences, they have been formalised in

j ss 33 and 35(1), with consequential provisions for licences and recall in ss 37 to 40.

For indeterminate sentences, in the present context life sentences, that is to say sentences which apply for the remainder of the natural life of the offender, any release is by definition early release. Therefore such release is in principle a matter for the exercise of an executive discretion. However, there has grown up a distinction between discretionary and mandatory life sentences. This has come about partly as a result of the abolition of the death penalty for murder and its replacement by a mandatory life sentence and partly by an express recognition that discretionary life sentences are only justified in two circumstances. One is where the offences are so serious that in the judgment of the sentencer the determinate period to be served in custody should be as long as the remaining life of the offender. The other is where it is necessary to protect the public from serious harm from the offender and in the opinion of the sentencing judge that the offender should not be released until that risk has been eliminated or acceptably reduced (see ss 2 and 34 of the 1991 Act). The sentencing judge therefore now states, at the time that he sentences an offender to a discretionary life sentence, how long a determinate sentence he would have passed, whether life or a lesser period of years (see ss 2 and 34 of the 1991 Act and *Practice Note* [1993] 1 All ER 747, [1993] 1 WLR 223). Further, by s 34 of the 1991 Act, the procedure for the release of discretionary life prisoners has been further formalised so as to remove any element of Executive discretion and make it depend wholly upon the assessment of the sentencing judge and the direction of the Parole Board.

This exercise makes use of the concept of assessing the period of custody required for punishment, or retribution and deterrence. This is the equivalent of the sentence that would have been passed under Pt I of the 1991 Act (see ss 2, 3 and 28). But the period is the period of actual custody that would have to be served taking into account the provisions for early release applicable to determinate sentences (see the cross-reference to ss 33(2) and 35(1) in s 34(2)(b)). It will be thus between one half and two-thirds of the equivalent determinate sentence.

It is this principle which has been adopted by successive Home Secretaries in relation to mandatory life sentences. The 1991 Act has preserved the discretion of the Secretary of State to decide whether or not to release any person who has received a mandatory life sentence. Section 35(2) requires that he shall only do so after the release of the offender has been recommended by the Parole Board and after he has consulted the Lord Chief Justice; these are restrictions on his power to release. Where he has an unqualified statutory discretion is in deciding whether to refer any case to the Parole Board (see s 35(3)). However, Home Secretaries have taken the view that they should formalise the discretion to refer. In doing so they have undoubtedly been influenced by the view expressed by judges and others that those sentenced need to know when their cases will first be considered by the Parole Board (see *R v Secretary of State for the Home Dept, ex p Handscomb* (1988) 86 Cr App R 59 at 79). It is to this that the decision relates. But, as with discretionary life sentences, the Secretaries of State have adopted as their criterion the period of custody required for retribution and deterrence. This is logical because it corresponds to the period which should be served before the question of early release should arise. Any reference before that should be premature. But the criterion introduces an element of assessment directly analogous to the judicial exercise of sentencing. It is also an exercise which, for the reasons previously referred to, is undertaken by the Secretary of State shortly after conviction, its purpose being to provide certainty for the offender so he can come to terms with his future.

It will be appreciated that this policy raises three problems. The first is that the Secretary of State, having been given a general discretion which it is his duty to exercise, cannot by his own statements preclude himself from exercising it. Thus the policy has to include an element of flexibility and to recognise that whatever may be said he is still retaining a residual discretion. Secondly, there is a potential illogicality in saying at one and the same time that the punishment for murder is custody for the remainder of the offender's natural life and at the same time recognising that some shorter period may meet the requirements of retribution and deterrence. This conflict was commented upon by Lord Mustill in *Doody*'s case [1993] 3 All ER 92 at 102, [1994] 1 AC 531 at 557 but in the parliamentary answer of 27 July 1993 the Home Secretary reaffirmed the principle of the mandatory sentence for life. At no time is there a right to be released. Thirdly, the criterion adopted by the Secretary of State has drawn him into an exercise directly comparable to that performed under our constitution by judges. What are the implications of this was the subject of *Doody*'s case and is in my judgment central to the decision of these appeals.

With this introduction, I now turn to the questions arising under the 1933 Act.

II. THE CHILDREN AND YOUNG PERSONS ACT 1933

There are two points which arise under s 53 of the Children and Young Persons Act 1933: whether it includes any provision for punishment and whether the order under s 53(1) is a life sentence. The two points are interlinked and it is not convenient to discuss them separately even though the Divisional Court decided the first against the defendants and the second in their favour.

English law, in common with other developed legal systems, has rules which govern the attribution of criminal responsibility to those who have not achieved adulthood. As is observed in the report published by *Justice*, 'Children and Homicide' (February 1996), different countries have different rules. The rules of English law have recently been reconsidered by the House of Lords in *C v DPP* [1995] 2 All ER 43, [1996] AC 1. A child under the age of ten is not criminally responsible for his acts. Between 10 and 14, he is only criminally responsible if the prosecution prove that at the time of doing the act the child knew that what he was doing was seriously wrong. After a child reaches the age of 14 he has full criminal responsibility in English law although his age may be relevant in other respects.

These defendants being aged between 10 and 14 the prosecution had to discharge the appropriate burden of proof at the trial. The defendants were convicted because they were proved to have had a sufficient understanding to be held responsible for their acts and they therefore fell to be convicted of the crime which they had committed. There are those who do not wish to accept this conclusion; but it was the verdict of the jury after hearing the evidence and being properly directed on the law.

The question of passing sentence upon an offender only arises once he has been convicted. These defendants fell to be sentenced because they had been found criminally responsible and convicted of murder. This situation is to be contrasted with that of those who are suffering from mental incapacity or madness. Those who are unfit to plead are not convicted and no finding of guilt is made against them. Those who raise the defence of insanity at their trial are entitled to be acquitted. Such persons are still liable to be detained. Historically this was the context in which persons were ordered to be detained during Her Majesty's pleasure. They were persons who were required to be detained for their own safety and the safety of the public. They were not convicts.

Despite the fact that the phrase 'during Her Majesty's pleasure' suggests some power of the sovereign falling outside the scope of the ordinary law and not regulated by statute, that impression had become obsolete by the end of the last century. It was an expression used to refer to orders for detention which were

not subject to any time limit other than, by implication, the natural life of the
person subject to the order and which required the exercise of discretionary
powers by those having responsibility for such detention. The power of release
was the subject of and defined by express statutory provision. It was no longer
implicit in the use of the phrase itself. Any release was pursuant to a statutory
provision permitting such release. Thus we will see in all the relevant Acts
express provisions governing the release of the detainee.

The use of the expression 'detained during Her Majesty's pleasure' in the
Children Act 1908 and the 1933 Act has led to some confusion. As previously
explained, the premise upon which any offender, child or adult falls to be
sentenced is that he has committed a crime for which he is criminally responsible.
Such responsibility being established, punishment will always be a legitimate
element in such a sentence; normally it will be the only or primary element.
There is nothing in the 1908 Act nor the 1933 Act which negatives the power of
the sentencing court to pass a punitive sentence. Indeed, the drafting of those
Acts contemplates that more lenient disposals will be inadequate as punishment.
Section 104 of the 1908 Act states:

> 'Where a child or young person is convicted on indictment of an attempt
> to murder or of manslaughter, or of wounding with intent to do grievous
> bodily harm, and the court is of the opinion that no *punishment* which under
> the provisions of this Act it is authorised to inflict is sufficient, a court may
> sentence the offender to be detained for such a period as may be specified in
> the sentence ...'

This is specifically a provision for punishment. It is absurd to read s 103 of the
same Act dealing with those convicted of murder rather than attempted murder
or manslaughter as saying that they are not to be punished. Yet that was the
primary submission of Mr Fitzgerald QC in the present cases. The conclusion
that s 53 of the 1933 Act provides for punishment is clear from its wording
whether or not one has regard to the sidenote.

It is also clear that the order for detention under s 53 covers either the whole
of the natural life of the offender in the case of his conviction for murder or the
period specified by the court under s 53(2) in the case of some lesser offence
which may be life or some lesser period of years (see *R v Abbott* [1963] 1 All ER
738, [1964] 1 QB 489). Under s 53(1) (like s 103 of the 1908 Act before it) the order
continues to apply for the remainder of the life of the offender. Under s 53(2) (like
s 104 of the 1908 Act) the order continues for the duration of the period stated by
the sentencing judge, either a term of years or the remainder of the offender's life.
This has been recognised by later legislation which refers to detention of young
offenders 'for life' (see s 61(1) of the Criminal Justice Act 1967 and s 43(2)(a) of the
Criminal Justice Act 1991). Here again the argument of Mr Fitzgerald encounters
an absurdity. Why should the sentence passed on a murderer under s 53(1) not
be a life sentence when for lesser offences an offender can be given a life sentence
under s 53(2)? It must also be remembered that the 1908 and 1933 Acts applied to
17-year-olds as well as to 10-year-olds and in this respect made no distinction
between them.

The discretionary element in relation to the *duration* of the young offender's
actual custody enters by way of giving the Secretary of State a statutory power to
release on licence. This power was originally contained in s 105 of the 1908 Act
and can be traced through s 53(4) of the 1933 Act and s 61(1) of the Criminal
Justice Act 1967 to s 35 of the 1991 Act. It is a power which permits the Secretary

a of State at any time during the operation of the order to release the offender on licence, conditionally or unconditionally. But the licence is always liable to be revoked and the offender must in that event return to custody. The power to release is premised upon the fact that the offender is subject to an order for his detention. Release does not discharge the order. Thus, where the offender has been sentenced to detention during Her Majesty's pleasure under s 53(1) or to

b detention for life under s 53(2), he remains subject to that sentence for the remainder of his natural life. In this respect the offender is in the same position as an offender sentenced to life imprisonment under the Murder (Abolition of Death Penalty) Act 1965. He has received a life sentence. Release on licence does not alter the status of the offender.

The fact that a convicted murderer, whatever his age, is made subject to a
c mandatory life sentence in the relevant Acts in contrast to the range of sentences available for those convicted of lesser, though also grave, offences is attributable to the special position given by English law and culture (in common with very many other legal systems and cultures) to those who have deliberately and unjustifiably taken the lives of others. Whether or not this approach is still right

d is the subject of ongoing debate but it is a matter for Parliament not the courts; the courts have to work within the existing law.

The submissions of Mr Fitzgerald in the present case and the assumptions made by others about the purpose and effect of the 1908 and 1933 Acts overlook what is the special and most important part of these sentencing provisions. It has consistently been the policy of English law that juvenile offenders should be

e detained under different conditions and in different institutions from adult prisoners. Paragraphs 698 and 699 of the *Report of the Royal Commission on Capital Punishment* (Cmd 8932 (1953)) are of interest in this connection. Discussing the distinction between the sentences of 'imprisonment for life' and 'detention during Her Majesty's pleasure', the report says:

f
> 'This difference of terminology does not make any difference to the actual duration of the sentence ... the distinction between detention and imprisonment is a real one, for it may sometimes be desirable that a young offender should serve his sentence, or part of it, in a Borstal Institution, or even in an Approved School, and not in a prison.'

g In English law the critical age governing whether an offender may be sent to prison is considered to be 21; and there are further graduated provisions regarding custodial sentences for ages down to 15. Those in custody who have not reached the age of 21 are not described as being prisoners or as being in prison, a distinction preserved by, inter alia, s 1(5) of the 1965 Act (see also ss 1A

h to 1C of the Criminal Justice Act 1982). They are detainees and, for example, for those between the ages of 14 and 20 the place of their detention under these provisions of the 1982 Act is a young offenders' institution not a prison. That these distinctions are sometimes more apparent than real as regards those over 16 is not due to a lack of statutory intention. At younger ages and for those of the age of these defendants, the distinctions have real importance and practical effect,

j e g *R v Collins* (1994) 16 Cr App R (S) 156; see now, also, the Criminal Justice and Public Order Act 1994.

Under s 53, whether it be under sub-s (1) or sub-s (2), the Secretary of State is required to decide both where and under what conditions the offender shall be detained. As is illustrated by the present cases, this duty is conscientiously and carefully discharged by those responsible for deciding upon the care plan for the offender. The present defendants have, pursuant to expert advice, been provided with a custodial regime which has full regard to their age and immaturity and reflects their needs, including the need for rehabilitation, and this will continue until they reach an age when this is no longer necessary. The purpose of s 53 and its related provisions is not to excuse the offender from punishment but to ensure that the custodial punishment is served in appropriate conditions which will assist his rehabilitation and not, so far as is possible, expose him to further corruption. It is this feature, not the date of release (which is separately provided for), which is the hallmark of the sentence of detention under ss 103 or 104 of the 1908 Act and s 53(1) or (2) of the 1933 Act.

The correct understanding of the 1908 and 1933 Acts is clear and it is regrettable that different views should have achieved currency both here and abroad. They provide for punishment. In respect of convicted murderers, ss 103 and 53(1) require the passing of a life sentence. I do not agree with what has been said by Evans LJ in *R v Secretary of State for the Home Dept, ex p Singh (Prem)* (1993) Times, 27 April, followed by Pill LJ in the present case. I also do not agree with the similar view expressed by Lord Woolf MR in his judgment (p 341 g to p 342 a, ante), which I have read in draft. I have gained the impression from the submissions of Mr Pannick QC for the Secretary of State that he is not eager to emphasise the character of the sentence under s 53(1) as a life sentence, no doubt because it gives rise to arguments under art 3 of the European Convention on Human Rights and art 37 of the United Nations Convention on the Rights of the Child (New York, 20 November 1989; TS 44 (1992); Cm 1976): see *Singh v UK* Case 56/1994/503/585 (1996) 1 BHRC 119 (paras 62ff). However, its adoption is central to the last paragraph of the parliamentary answer and the drafting of the 1991 Act and it represents the correct understanding of s 53(1).

The correct view of the powers of punishment under s 53 is implicit in a number of cases of which I will cite only two. The first is *R v Ford* (1976) 62 Cr App R 303, where, under s 53(2), deterrent sentences had been passed on young offenders for gang robberies and thefts. Scarman LJ, giving the judgment of the court, said (at 307):

> 'If one is confronted with circumstances of such gravity that a general deterrent sentence is necessary, then it appears to us plain that the Court may well be of the opinion that no other method other than a long period of detention is suitable.'

Whilst rehabilitation is a relevant consideration it does not apply to the exclusion of the need to deter by punishment.

In *R v Forshaw* (1984) 6 Cr App R (S) 413, which concerned an appellant aged 15 who had pleaded guilty to manslaughter and had been sentenced to five years' detention under s 53(2), Lord Lane CJ, delivering the judgment of the court, said (at 415):

> 'It is important that punishment should be inflicted upon people who commit crimes of this sort. It is important from this young man's point of view that he should expiate his offence. It is important to remind others of the dangers of carrying knives, let alone the danger of taking them from their sheaths and using them. It is important that the public's requirement that offenders should be made to suffer for their misdeeds should be satisfied. If that requirement is not satisfied, then people are apt to take matters into their own hands.'

a These wise words identify a number of the factors which lead to the need to pass a sentence which punishes the responsible young offender who has committed a serious crime despite his age. If those convicted are not punished the criminal law and the criminal justice system will cease to carry confidence and fail to serve the purpose of fulfilling the need to demonstrate that those who commit crimes are punished. If they are not punished by the law, members of the public may b unlawfully and disproportionately take that task upon themselves: punishment may thus in this respect also protect the offender. It is often necessary to punish in order to deter others who might be inclined to offend. Punishment may also often be an important part of the rehabilitation of an offender. It can puzzle an offender as much as it puzzles the general public if he does not receive the appropriate punishment. Punishment enables him to expiate his crime and assists c his rehabilitation. This factor is as important for the young as for the older, but repentant, offender.

III. THE CRIMINAL JUSTICE ACT 1991

The Criminal Justice Act 1991 made radical changes to various aspects of the d criminal law of this country. Part I of the Act restructured in a comprehensive fashion the powers of courts to deal with offenders. Part II made radical changes in the scheme for early release of prisoners. Part III included provisions relating to children and young persons.

In Pt I, s 2 provides that, where a court passes a custodial sentence other than one fixed by law, the length of the sentence must be commensurate with the e seriousness of the relevant offence or offences, save where the relevant offence was a violent or sexual offence in which case the court should pass such sentence as in its opinion is necessary to protect the public from serious harm from the offender. In such a case, the court is required to state that this is what it is doing and give its reasons. Thus, the Act like others before it recognises the role of f custodial sentences in providing protection to the public from those likely to re-offend and it expressly distinguishes between this part of the custodial sentence and that required to reflect the seriousness of the offence or offences for which the offender was being sentenced. An example of a sentence containing a protective element is a discretionary life sentence. In Pt II of the Act, s 34 introduced a scheme for those sentenced to a discretionary sentence of life g imprisonment. The judge identifies and states the penal element in the sentence, that is to say the part of the sentence which relates to the seriousness of the offence, either a period of years or the natural life of the offender. It is this which Lord Taylor CJ in his *Practice Note* [1993] 1 All ER 747, [1993] 1 WLR 223 referred to as 'the period of detention imposed for punishment and deterrence, taking into h account the seriousness of the offence'. Section 34 goes on to provide that once that period has been served, the question of the release of the offender shall be determined by the Parole Board if it is satisfied that it is no longer necessary for the protection of the public that the offender should be confined (see also s 32(6)).

The release of those who have been sentenced to a mandatory sentence of life j imprisonment is covered by s 35(2) and (3). It gives the Secretary of State a discretion to release such an offender on licence. But, as previously observed, it limits his discretion. He is precluded from releasing such an offender unless he has received a recommendation to do so from the Parole Board and even then he may not do so unless he has first consulted with the Lord Chief Justice together with the trial judge if available. Further, the Parole Board is precluded from making any such recommendation unless the case of the offender has been referred by the Secretary of State to the board for its advice. Thus, the Secretary of State is given an unqualified discretion which operates at two stages. The first is when he decides to refer the case to the Parole Board. The second is when, after having received a recommendation to release (pursuant to a referral) and having consulted the Lord Chief Justice, he exercises his discretion to release the offender. (Compare s 34 where he has no discretion.)

By his parliamentary answer of 27 July 1993, the Secretary of State has undertaken to exercise his discretionary powers under s 35 following certain principles. Thus, he has recognised in relation to mandatory life sentences the same distinction between the punitive element and the risk element. In doing so he was continuing the practice adopted by the Rt Hon Leon Brittan in 1983 (see 49 HC Official Report (6th series) written answers cols 506–508). In his speech in *Doody's* case [1993] 3 All ER 92 at 99–102, [1994] 1 AC 531 at 551–557 Lord Mustill commented upon the inconsistency between the principle that the crime of murder required that the offender should forfeit his right to liberty for the remainder of his natural life and the idea that custody for some limited period of years would suffice to meet the penal element in the sentence. The parliamentary answer was made in response to what had been said in *Doody's* case. The Secretary of State did not accept the inconsistency and said both that he would continue the previous procedure of taking the judges' advice and giving his decision on the minimum period to be served 'to satisfy the requirements of retribution and deterrence', and that a person convicted of murder 'has committed a crime of such gravity that he forfeits his liberty to the state for the rest of his days'. The Secretary of State thus chose to preserve the principle of the sentence for life. He has not qualified the full breadth of his statutory discretion not to release any such person. He has simply preserved, as part of the procedure which he chooses to follow in deciding when to refer a case to the Parole Board, an assessment of the period of custody which will meet the requirements of retribution and deterrence.

I have elaborated the effect of Pts I and II of the 1991 Act to demonstrate that they include a code for both sentencing and the release of offenders. In Pt II, under the heading 'Special cases', s 43 makes provision for young offenders. Section 43(2) expressly provides that Pt II shall apply to persons serving sentences of detention during Her Majesty's pleasure or for life under s 53 of the 1933 Act as it applies to those serving sentences of imprisonment for life. Section 43(3) states that references to 'life prisoners' in Pt II of the Act and to 'prison' or 'imprisonment' shall be construed accordingly, that is to say the references to prisoners include young offender detainees and to life imprisonment include detention under s 53(1) or (2) during Her Majesty's pleasure or for life. Further, s 51(1) defines the term 'life prisoner' by reference (inter alia) to s 43(2) and, therefore, as including young offenders sentenced to detention during Her Majesty's pleasure. The statutory intention is clear and is not open to argument. Young offenders sentenced under s 53(1) of the 1933 Act to be detained during Her Majesty's pleasure are governed, as regards their release, by s 35 of the 1991 Act. The breadth of the Secretary of State's discretion is the same in both classes of case. The Secretary of State was entitled in his answer of 27 July 1993 to confirm that what he had said 'in relation to mandatory life sentence prisoners applies equally to persons who are, or will be, detained during Her Majesty's pleasure under section 53(1) of the Children and Young Persons Act of 1933 ...'

Mr Fitzgerald's argument that the Secretary of State does not have the same statutory discretion in respect of young offenders detained during Her Majesty's

a   pleasure under s 53(1) as he does in respect of mandatory life prisoners is contrary
to the terms of the Act.   Whatever room for argument may or may not have
existed at earlier stages of the legislative history under different Acts, the matter
is now concluded by the express and unambiguous provisions of the 1991 Act.
The arguments and material upon which Mr Fitzgerald sought to rely in aid of
the construction of a statute which was ambiguous do not assist him: the statute
b   is unambiguous.   In any event, they did not lead to the conclusion for which he
was arguing.
       In my judgment, the conclusion of the Divisional Court cannot be supported.
However, it is still necessary to consider whether these applications for judicial
review should succeed on some other ground.

c   IV. THE DECISION-MAKING PROCESS: FAULTY PROCEDURE
       This is the aspect of the case which causes me anxiety.   But it is necessary first
to identify what is the permissible role of the court in relation to the procedure
which the Secretary of State has followed.   The governing authority is the
decision of the House of Lords in *Doody v Secretary of State for the Home Dept* [1993]
d   3 All ER 92, [1994] 1 AC 531.   One of the questions there considered was whether
the Secretary of State by his practice of consulting the judges about the
requirements of retribution and deterrence had surrendered any part of his broad
general discretion under the 1991 Act.   Lord Mustill concluded that he had not
([1993] 3 All ER 92 at 105, [1994] 1 AC 531 at 558–559):

e   'Nevertheless, it is the Home Secretary who decides, and who has
developed (with his predecessors) his own ministerial ideas on what the
public interest demands.   I can see no reason why the anomalous task of
fixing a "tariff" penal element for an offence in respect of which the true tariff
sentence is life imprisonment is one for which the Home Secretary and his
junior ministers, informed by his officials about the existing departmental
f   practice, are any less experienced and capable than are the judges.   In any
event, however, even if the respondent's argument is correct so far, it must
in my opinion fail because Parliament has not by statute conferred on the
judges any role, even as advisers, at the time when the penal element of a
mandatory sentence is fixed.   But for the fact that the Home Secretary
decided, when formulating the new scheme, to retain in a modified shape
g   the existing practice of inviting the opinion of the judges, they would never
enter the picture at all.   The Secretary of State is compelled, or at least
entitled, to have regard to broader considerations of a public character than
those which apply to an ordinary sentencing function.   It is he, and not the
judges, who is entrusted with the task of deciding upon the prisoner's
h   release, and it is he who has decided, within the general powers conferred
upon him by the statute, to divide his task into two stages.   It is not, and could
not be suggested that he acted unlawfully in this respect and I can see no
ground whatever for suggesting that by doing so he deprived himself entirely
of his discretion at the first stage, and delivered it into hands of the judges.'

j   The House of Lords therefore decided that, despite the fact that the Secretary of
State was undertaking an exercise which was directly analogous to the judicial
determination of a sentence and separating it from his discretionary decision to
release a life prisoner, nevertheless his unqualified discretion was preserved.
       However, the House of Lords had also to deal with the requirement to follow
proper procedures and held that the fact that the Secretary of State's discretion

was not qualified did not relieve him from the obligation to be fair in the
procedures which he followed. Thus, the House of Lords declared ([1993] 3 All
ER 92 at 112–113, [1994] 1 AC 531 at 567–568):

> '(1) The Secretary of State is required to afford to a prisoner serving a
> mandatory life sentence the opportunity to submit in writing
> representations as to the period he should serve for the purposes of
> retribution and deterrence before the Secretary of State sets the date for the
> first review of the prisoner's sentence. (2) Before giving the prisoner the
> opportunity to make such representations, the Secretary of State is required
> to inform him of the period recommended by the judiciary as to the period
> he should serve for the purposes of retribution and deterrence, and of any
> other opinion expressed by the judiciary which is relevant to the Secretary of
> State's decision as to the appropriate period to be served for these purposes.
> (3) The Secretary of State is obliged to give reasons for departing from the
> period recommended by the judiciary as the period to which he should serve
> for the purposes of retribution and deterrence.'

Lord Mustill expressly contemplated that the decision of the House gave scope,
albeit limited, for the judicial review of decisions of the Secretary of State upon
the requirements of retribution and deterrence for individual mandatory life
prisoners:

> 'Only if it can be shown that the decision may have been arrived at through
> a faulty process, in one of the ways now so familiar to practitioners of judicial
> review, will they have any serious prospect of persuading the court to grant
> relief.' (See [1993] 3 All ER 92 at 111, [1994] 1 AC 531 at 566.)

An example of the exercise of the jurisdiction to review the decision of the Home
Secretary on the grounds of procedural unfairness is provided by *R v Secretary of
State for the Home Dept, ex p Riaz, R v Secretary of State for the Home Dept, ex p Raja*
(8 December 1994, unreported).

In his speech, Lord Mustill explained why he considered that proper
procedures were necessary ([1993] 3 All ER 92 at 107, 109, 111, [1994] 1 AC 531 at
561, 563–565):

> 'The decision is simply to fix the penal element. On occasions this will
> involve a divergence from the judges; on others, not. In each case the
> requirements of fairness and rationality are the same. So also are the familiar
> requirements that the decision-maker should take into account all relevant
> considerations, amongst which are the opinions of the judges; that he should
> not take into account irrelevant considerations; and that his decision should
> be rational ... I would simply ask whether a life prisoner whose future
> depends vitally on the decision of the Home Secretary as to the penal
> element and who has the right to make representations upon it should know
> what factors the Home Secretary will take into account. In my view he does
> possess this right, for without it there is a risk that some supposed fact which
> he could controvert, some opinion which he could challenge, some policy
> which he could argue against, might wrongly go unanswered ... I think it
> clear that the prisoner needs to know the substance of the judges' advice,
> comprising not only the term of years which they recommended as the penal
> element, but also their reasons: for the prisoner cannot rationalise his
> objections to the penal element without knowing how it was rationalised by

the judges themselves ... the requirement is only that the prisoners shall learn the gist of what the judges have said ... It is not, as I understand it, questioned that the decision of the Home Secretary on the penal element is susceptible to judicial review. To mount an effective attack on the decision, given no more material than the facts of the offence and length of the penal element, the prisoner has virtually no means of ascertaining whether this is an instance where the decision-making process has gone astray. I think it important that there be an effective means of detecting the kind of error which would entitle the court to intervene, and in practice I regard it as necessary for this purpose that the reasoning of the Home Secretary should be disclosed. If there is any difference between the penal element recommended by the judges and actually imposed by the Home Secretary, this reasoning is bound to include, either explicitly or implicitly, a reason why the Home Secretary has taken a different view.'

Lord Mustill cited two cases in relation to the need to act fairly and give reasons: *Kanda v Government of Malaya* [1962] AC 322, [1962] 2 WLR 1153 and *R v Civil Service Appeal Board, ex p Cunningham* [1991] 4 All ER 310. Neither of these cases concerned life prisoners, nor the exercise of a discretion that is as wide as that of the Secretary of State under s 35. It is implicit in what Lord Mustill said that if, having regard to the circumstances including the breadth of the discretion, the reasons given by the Secretary of State are not rational, judicial review would be available and the decision would be liable to be quashed.

In my judgment, an unsatisfactory state of affairs is disclosed by the documents and procedures followed in the present case. As I stressed at the outset, this is an exceptional case. The Secretary of State was having to approach the exercise of his discretion in extremely difficult circumstances and the full glare of inflamed public opinion. He was dealing with defendants who at the time of the offence were only just past the threshold of criminal responsibility. In the event, the Home Secretary adopted the exceptional course of increasing the period to be served to meet the requirements of retribution and deterrence so as nearly to double the assessment of the trial judge and so as to arrive at a figure 50% higher than that considered appropriate by the Lord Chief Justice. The decision was his, but, as stated by Lord Mustill, it means that the procedures he followed before arriving at that conclusion merit close consideration.

Morland J sentenced the defendants on 24 November 1993. His confidential report to the Secretary of State was dated 29 November 1993. It included in para 5 a summary of the evidence in the case and his conclusions as to what 'in all probability' had happened. It concluded with his view that he could not determine the relative culpability of the two defendants. In para 6, he summarised the defences which had been run by the defendants referring also to certain of the answers they gave in interview. In para 7, he dealt with the very limited psychiatric evidence which was called at the trial. In para 10, he made his recommendation on the actual length of detention necessary to meet the requirements of retribution and general deterrence. He said:

'If the defendants had been adults, I would have said that the actual length of detention necessary to meet the requirements of retribution and general deterrence would have been 18 years ... [In the next three sentences the judge briefly refers to serious defects in the backgrounds from which the defendants came.] In my judgment the appropriate actual length of detention necessary to meet the requirement of retribution and general

deterrence for the murder taking into account all these appalling
circumstances and the age of the defendants when it was committed is eigḥt
years ... eight years is "very very many years" for a 10 or 11 year old. They
are now children. In eight years time they will be young men.'

The Lord Chief Justice on 4 December 1993, whilst recognising that the trial
judge was in a better position than he to assess the two boys and their crime and
agreeing that a much lesser tariff should apply than in the case of an adult,
considered that the minimum period for punishment and deterrence should be
ten years.

It will be appreciated that the trial judge's report did not solely involve the
making of a recommendation. It properly included the trial judge's own
assessment of the salient features of the case and of the effect of the evidence
which he had heard during the trial. On 7 January 1994 letters were written on
behalf of the Secretary of State to, nominally, the defendants. The letters
purported to inform the defendants, pursuant to the decision in *Doody's* case, 'of
the substance of the judicial recommendations which were made in your case'.
The letters fairly summarised the judge's recommendations, giving the gist of
para 10 and quoting the Lord Chief Justice's remarks in full. It also stated that the
trial judge had not felt able to determine the relative culpability of the two
defendants. But it did not include the trial judge's summary of the facts and the
view that he had taken of them.

The position was therefore that, although those representing the defendants
would be well aware of the evidence given at the trial and the submissions made
to the judge and jury at the trial, they would not be aware of how the trial judge
had summarised them, which features he had chosen to include or stress, nor
what comments he had made or what inferences he had drawn. We have been
told, and this is in accordance with the affidavit evidence, that the Home
Secretary reached his decision to increase the penal period to 15 years without
having seen any of the trial papers or having read the judge's summing up. It
appears that the Home Secretary, for his information about the offences and their
seriousness and the level of premeditation and responsibility of the defendants
was entirely dependant upon the judge's summary.

This is a remarkable situation for two reasons. First, this is case in which the
Secretary of State was considering increasing the period recommended by a very
substantial margin. This, he is of course entitled to do in an appropriate case. But
if he was going to do so it is essential that he should be fully informed of all the
material facts and circumstances. Otherwise he cannot know whether, to quote
Lord Mustill, he has taken into account 'all relevant circumstances'. The Court
of Appeal on a reference by the Attorney General seeking the increase of a
sentence would certainly not reach a decision without fully considering the actual
facts and circumstances of the case before it—and having the assistance of
submissions upon those facts. On the face of it, the Secretary of State was
reaching an important decision concerning the custody of these defendants
without, in the special circumstances of this case, feeling obliged to inform
himself fully of all the relevant circumstances. Similarly, he appears to have made
no inquiries about the degree of the responsibility of these ten-year-olds. There
are gradations of responsibility (see e g s 22 of the Homicide Act 1957). The
Secretary of State appears to have had no material upon which to form a view as
to the level of the personal responsibility which should be ascribed to these
defendants on account of their age, immaturity and personal circumstances nor
is it possible to tell from the letters what in fact his view was.

a This leads me to the second comment. The defendants and their representatives were never informed at this stage of the terms in which the judge had summarised the facts of the case and what inferences he had drawn notwithstanding that it was this very information which was to form the basis for the Secretary of State's decision. Any short summary, however impartial and fair (as was the summary of Morland J), has inevitably to be selective and include the summary writer's perceptions of the effect of the evidence. In the present case b what the judge had chosen to say was material. For instance, it was the prosecution case at the trial, accepted by the judge, that there was a considerable element of premeditation and that the crime had not been spontaneous or adventitious. It had been the case of one of the defendants, not accepted by the judge, that the killing had not been part of the original plan and had only come c about later. I do not consider that, in the circumstances of this case, the information which the defendants and their representatives were given prior to 22 July 1994 was adequate to enable them to make full representations nor did it comply with the guidance given by Lord Mustill in *Doody's* case.

Under the same heading, one of the defendants has a further ground of d complaint. In the interval between the time the defendants were sentenced and July 1994, the Secretary of State received an apparently unsolicited report from a psychiatrist who had been advising those representing that defendant. It bore upon the view to be taken of the seriousness of the defendant's offence. Until after these proceedings were started, his representatives were wholly unaware of the existence of this additional report or what it said and had no opportunity to e comment upon or respond to it. In my judgment, this should not have occurred.

The next aspect which causes me concern is the treatment by the Secretary of State of material supplied to him through the media which was of a *quality* which no person exercising an assessment of what was required for retribution and deterrence would properly take into account and which was only properly f relevant to a different question. This is not to say that the Secretary of State cannot properly take into account the need to uphold public confidence in the criminal justice system. Both Lord Lane CJ and Lord Mustill have said, as is obvious, that this is an element in a proper sentencing process. Lord Scarman in *Findlay v Secretary of State for the Home Dept* [1984] 3 All ER 801 at 826, [1985] AC 318 at 333 said:

g
'Deterrence, retribution and public confidence in the system are factors of importance. The Parole Board, through its judicial and other members, can offer advice on these aspects of the question. But neither the board nor the judiciary can be as close, or as sensitive, to public opinion as a minister responsible to Parliament and the electorate. He has to judge the public h acceptability of early release and to determine the policies needed to maintain public confidence in the system of criminal justice.'

Similarly, the Secretary of State is not as narrowly constrained as would be a judge in what he can take into account (see e g *R v Secretary of State for the Home Dept, ex p Causabon-Vincent* (1996) Times, 19 July). But it appears that the j Secretary of State was in the present case prepared to take into account a large amount of material which in effect amounted to taking a hopelessly unscientific poll from members of the public without any satisfactory checks or without any confidence as to the factual or legal basis upon which the responses were made. If the Secretary of State is choosing to assume the role of deciding the period necessary for these defendants for retribution and deterrence, he should not only disregard but be seen to disregard material of this kind.

On 16 June 1994 letters were sent on behalf of the Secretary of State to those representing the defendants informing them of the petitions which he had received and the quantities of newspaper coupons and other correspondence. The letters enumerated them as if they were the results of a poll. The defendants and those representing them were thus informed of the attempts that had been made by members of the public to influence his decision and that there were those who were urging the Secretary of State to adopt life as a tariff or a period as long as 25 years. What causes serious anxiety is that the Secretary of State has at no stage either by affidavit or in the decision or other letters stated that he gave this material no weight. The most it could properly do was indicate that he must consider his decision particularly carefully, conscious of a need to justify his decision, whether he was going to accept the judicial recommendations or depart from them.

The quality of this material was such that it should not be given any weight at all in the assessment of the period required for retribution and deterrence. It might relate to another aspect of the discretion of the Secretary of State—whether ultimately to licence the release of the defendants having regard to the public acceptability of such release; but this is a decision which will not, on any view, have to be taken for many years to come, by which time a different climate of public opinion may or may not prevail. I am concerned that the Secretary of State may have elided the one with the other.

The procedure followed by the Secretary of State in making the decisions communicated in his letters on 22 July 1994 was, in my judgment, unsatisfactory for the following reasons.

(1) He did not sufficiently inform those representing the defendants of the factual basis, including the inferences of fact, upon which he was going to exercise his discretion so as to give those representing the defendants an adequate opportunity to controvert supposed facts or challenge opinions expressed upon them. (And see further below.)

(2) The Secretary of State failed to exclude, and did not state he was excluding, material of a quality inappropriate to be taken into account in reaching the relevant decision and further he did not exclude the use of that material in relation to a question to which it was irrelevant.

(3) The Secretary of State, in view of the fact that he was minded substantially to increase the assessment of the judges, did not adequately inform himself of the full facts and circumstances of the case and did not consider whether his decision was premature or inappropriate having regard to the exceptional character of the case.

One can add to these criticisms of the procedure one's concern at the apparent absence of state provision for those who will be affected by the Secretary of State's decision to obtain legal aid at the stage of evaluating the relevant material and responding to it in the manner visualised by Lord Mustill. They would have that assistance on an appeal against sentence (where such an appeal is available) and, after the Secretary of State has made his decision, on a subsequent application for judicial review (as has now occurred). But they have no assistance at the critical stage before the Secretary of State makes his decision.

It has also been suggested on behalf of the defendants that the decision was on its face irrational. I do not accept this criticism. It was based upon the comment that the Secretary of State made about the trial judge's view that 18 years would have been an adequate period in respect of adult offenders who had committed the same offence. Speaking for myself, I am not surprised that the Secretary of State took the view that for a murder such as this, which was premeditated, brutal

a   and sadistic and derived from a course of conduct which was persisted in over a
period of hours, if committed by two adults, a longer period than 18 years would
have been required for retribution and deterrence. The Secretary of State
referred to his own view that a period of 25 years would be required. His view
was not unreasonable.

b   It was submitted on behalf of the defendants that, on this basis, 15 years was
out of line with the guidance contained in decisions of the Court of Appeal
(Criminal Division) for the reduction in the length of sentences to take account
of the extreme youth of the offender. There is more force in this submission but
it does not show that the assessment of 15 years in these cases is necessarily
wrong nor does it show that it was manifestly unreasonable. The Secretary of
c   State has expressly stated in his decision letters that he has taken into account the
age of the defendants and his reference to the respective periods of 25 and 15
years shows that he clearly has done so. His decision was not on its face
disproportionate for this terrible crime.

However, taking into account the age of the defendants also involves taking
into account their immaturity and the fact that at the age of ten, although
d   criminally responsible, their degree of responsibility may be reduced. It is not
clear what account the Secretary of State took of this consideration nor that he
took any steps to inform himself of the relevant facts. Nor is there any indication
that the Secretary of State considered whether in the exceptional circumstances
of this case, he should not have exercised his discretion to refrain from giving a
e   specific decision in the form that he did until he was better informed and the true
level of responsibility of the defendants had been better assessed.

This links in with another difficulty. Essentially, the Secretary of State is
seeking to determine a *minimum* period. It is in effect the minimum period that
is to elapse before he refers the case to the Parole Board for their
recommendation. On any view this will not be for some considerable time. It
f   leaves open whether his decision was not in principle unsound and premature in
an exceptional case such as this. Applying what he said in the parliamentary
answer, he has applied a rigid criterion. He does not appear to have considered
whether in the exercise of his overriding discretion, which he is under an
obligation to retain, he should not have exceptionally chosen to adopt a more
g   flexible approach better able to accommodate the extremely unusual features of
this case and suitable to the unsatisfactory character and incompleteness of the
material on which he was having to base his decision.

The Secretary of State has been able to refer in his evidence to another
apparently not dissimilar case (of which we have only very limited details) in
h   which the Secretary of State accepted the Lord Chief Justice's recommendation
of 14 years for an offender who was 12 years old at the time of the commission of
the crime. The Secretary of State was therefore able to say in his letter of 22 July
1994 that he was satisfied that 15 years in the instant case was 'consistent with
tariffs fixed in other cases'. But here again there is an element of procedural
unfairness. The Secretary of State is treating as important the decisions of
j   Secretaries of State in other cases. It is right that he should do so. But those
decisions, let alone the actual facts upon which they were based, are not a matter
of general knowledge nor are they readily available to those representing other
offenders. So here again the Secretary of State is basing his decision on material
of which the defendants have no prior knowledge and upon which, and the use
of which, they have no opportunity to comment. Applying what Lord Mustill has
said, this is not acceptable.

A final criticism of the Secretary of State's decision was based upon s 44 of the
1933 Act. This provides: *a*

> 'Every court in dealing with a child or young person who is brought before
> it, either as an offender or otherwise, shall have regard to the welfare of the
> child or young person and shall in a proper case take steps for removing him
> from undesirable surroundings, and for securing that proper provision is
> made for his education and training.'   *b*

It is submitted that although this statutory provision does not as such apply to the
Secretary of State's exercise of his discretion under s 35 of the 1991 Act, it should
nevertheless be a factor in his decision and his reasons should disclose how he has
taken it into account.

In my judgment, s 44 does not assist the defendants' case. First, it is primarily   *c*
directed to factors such as the place and conditions of detention. In that respect,
the undisputed evidence is that the Secretary of State and those acting on his
behalf have given effect to such principles both conscientiously and effectively.
Secondly, in so far as it affects any question of the duration of the custody of the
defendants, it is academic. On any view of the period during which these   *d*
defendants must be detained to meet the requirements of retribution and
deterrence, they must be detained until they reach 18—indeed, save on the trial
judge's view, until after they are 21. This being so, s 44 has no application to the
question with which we are concerned.

V. CONCLUSION   *e*
In view of my decision under the second head relating to the construction and
effect of the 1933 and 1991 Acts, I consider that the reasoning of the Divisional
Court cannot stand. In so far as Lord Woolf MR has based his decision on the
same view of s 53(1), I must respectfully dissent. Accordingly, unless the decision
of the Secretary of State is to be quashed on some other ground, the defendants'   *f*
motions must be dismissed. However, I have concluded that faulty procedures
were followed in taking the decisions recorded in the decision letters in July 1994
and they raise the concern that the Secretary of State failed to have regard to the
full extent of his discretion. In these circumstances, I consider that the decisions
should be quashed and, in the result, the appeals dismissed.

I recognise that the Secretary of State and those advising him were faced with   *g*
a difficult question. On his behalf, it has also been said repeatedly that his was an
initial view and that he is willing to review his decision in the light of any new
evidence affecting retribution and deterrence, an approach which is appropriate
once it has been decided that those are the criteria to apply. There are, therefore,
forceful arguments in leaving matters to such a review. It can also be reasonably   *h*
urged that since these proceedings have been launched, the defendants'
representatives have seen much additional material, for example, the full reports
of the judges, and have had the opportunity to make extensive further
submissions, apparently without having caused the Secretary of State to change
his mind. But one cannot be confident that the present decisions, if allowed to
stand, will not in practice lead to a postponement of further consideration—this   *j*
was after all one of the purposes of the procedures referred to in the
parliamentary answers—nor can one be confident that any further review will
not be infected by the faulty procedures which preceded the decisions of July
1994.

I am satisfied that in these exceptional cases, the just and appropriate order for
the court to make is one which requires the Secretary of State to make his

a decisions afresh and to give his reasons for his new decisions. Whether or not he comes to the same conclusions as before is for the Secretary of State to decide. But the procedures followed in the making of the original decisions were so seriously flawed and lacking in fairness and are so open to criticism, that I have concluded that it is not safe to allow them to stand. The Secretary of State must, in accordance with the law as stated by Lord Mustill, adopt fair procedures, *b* inform himself of and take into account the relevant circumstances, exclude what is irrelevant and, here, have regard to his full statutory discretion. The passage of time since July 1994 and the more appropriate climate may well assist a better decision-making process.

In conclusion, I would add that there are clearly cogent arguments in favour of the reconsideration by the legislature and the executive of the present state of the *c* law and practice concerning the treatment of those subject to mandatory sentences, especially young offenders, and the fulfilment by the UK government of its obligations under international conventions. The submissions of Mr Pannick before us on behalf of the Secretary of State accepted as much. It is also clear that such reconsideration is becoming increasingly urgent.

d **MORRITT LJ.** The circumstances in which these appeals arise have been fully described in the judgments of Lord Woolf MR and Hobhouse LJ and I do not need to repeat them. The questions to be answered are: (1) whether, as the Divisional Court held, the Secretary of State acted unlawfully in applying to the respondents, being persons sentenced to be detained during Her Majesty's *e* pleasure, the same policy as he applies in the case of persons serving mandatory life sentences; and if so (2) whether his decision as to the application of that policy to the respondents was reached in a manner which was procedurally unfair so as to be liable to be quashed on that account.

Counsel for the respondents submitted that the resolution of the first question *f* depends on three issues which he helpfully analysed. The first is whether the sentence to detention during Her Majesty's pleasure is solely preventive and reformatory. The second is whether if retribution and deterrence is a legitimate objective of such a sentence the tariff period for that purpose and hence the date of the first review may be set at the outset of the sentence by reference to those objectives alone. The third is whether, even if retribution and deterrence is a *g* legitimate objective and if the tariff may be determined at the outset, it should be fixed so as to be for the shortest possible duration and so as to balance the requirements of retribution against the welfare of the child. It seems to me that those issues depend on the legislative history and treatment of the sentence of detention during Her Majesty's pleasure on a child or young person and the *h* extent of the relevant statutory powers conferred on the Secretary of State.

Detention during Her Majesty's pleasure originated in the prerogative treatment of those found unfit to plead to a criminal charge due to insanity. By the end of the nineteenth century it had become largely statutory. It was introduced in respect of children and young persons by the Children Act 1908. Section 103 provided that sentence of death should not be pronounced or *j* recorded against a child or young person—

'but in lieu thereof the court shall sentence the child or young person to be detained during His Majesty's pleasure, and, if so sentenced, he shall, notwithstanding anything in the other provisions of this Act, be liable to be detained in such place and under such conditions as the Secretary of State may direct, and whilst so detained shall be deemed to be in lawful custody.'

Section 104 contained power to impose such a sentence in the case of a child or young person who was convicted of an attempt to murder, of manslaughter or wounding with intent to do grievous bodily harm if the court considered that the punishment otherwise authorised by the Act was insufficient. By s 105 the Secretary of State was empowered 'at any time' to discharge the child or young person so sentenced on a revocable licence in such form as the Secretary of State might determine. It is common ground that the express statutory power to release on licence overrode any prerogative or other power to release implicit in the description of the sentence. Accordingly, no implication as to the nature or duration of the sentence can be made from its description. It was (and is) a sentence for life subject to release on a revocable licence at the discretion of the Secretary of State.

Those provisions were repealed and re-enacted in s 53 of the Children and Young Persons Act 1933. The provisions of sub-s (1) of that section were amended by the Murder (Abolition of Death Penalty) Act 1965 and the express power to release contained in sub-s (4) was repealed by the Criminal Justice Act 1967 so that the power to release children and young offenders serving such a sentence might be assimilated into the general arrangements for the creation of the Parole Board and the release of prisoners on licence introduced by the latter Act. Section 53 of the 1933 Act as so amended and in force at the times relevant to this case provided:

'(1) A person convicted of an offence who appears to the court to have been under the age of eighteen years at the time the offence was committed shall not, if he is convicted of murder, be sentenced to imprisonment for life, nor shall sentence of death be pronounced on or recorded against any such person; but in lieu thereof the court shall (notwithstanding anything in this or any other Act) sentence him to be detained during Her Majesty's pleasure, and if so sentenced he shall be liable to be detained in such place and under such conditions as the Secretary of State may direct.

(2) Where—(a) a child or young person is convicted on indictment of any offence punishable in the case of an adult with imprisonment for fourteen years or more, not being an offence the sentence for which is fixed by law; or (b) a child convicted of manslaughter, and the court is of opinion that none of the other methods in which the case may legally be dealt with is suitable, the court may sentence the offender to be detained for such period not exceeding the maximum term of imprisonment with which the offence is punishable in the case of an adult as may be specified in the sentence; and where such a sentence has been passed the child or young person shall, during that period ... be liable to be detained in such place and on such conditions as the Secretary of State may direct.'

The 1967 Act authorised the establishment of the Parole Board. Section 60 empowered the Secretary of State if recommended so to do by the board to release on licence persons serving sentences of imprisonment other than for life and s 61 entitled him to do so in the case of a person serving a sentence of imprisonment for life or a person detained under s 53 of the 1933 Act if recommended by the board and after consultation with the Lord Chief Justice and the trial judge if available. These provisions were amended and re-enacted in the Criminal Justice Act 1991. The latter Act contains the provisions relevant to the actions of the Secretary of State in this case.

The material provisions of the 1991 Act are the following:

'**34.** *Duty to release discretionary life prisoners.*—(1) A life prisoner is a
discretionary life prisoner for the purposes of this Part if—(a) his sentence
was imposed for a violent or sexual offence the sentence for which is not
fixed by law; and (b) the court by which he was sentenced for that offence
ordered that this section should apply to him as soon as he had served a part
of his sentence specified in the order.

(2) A part of a sentence so specified shall be such part as the court
considers appropriate taking into account—(a) the seriousness of the offence,
or the combination of the offence and other offences associated with it; and
(b) the provisions of this section as compared with section 33(2) above and
section 35(1) below.

(3) As soon as, in the case of a discretionary life prisoner—(a) he has served
the part of his sentence specified in the order ("the relevant part"); and (b) the
Board has directed his release under this section, it shall be the duty of the
Secretary of State to release him on licence ...

35. *Power to release long-term and life prisoners.*—(1) After a long-term
prisoner has served one-half of his sentence, the Secretary of State may, if
recommended to do so by the Board, release him on licence.

(2) If recommended to do so by the Board, the Secretary of State may,
after consultation with the Lord Chief Justice together with the trial judge if
available, release on licence a life prisoner who is not a discretionary life
prisoner.

(3) The Board shall not make a recommendation under subsection (2)
above unless the Secretary of State has referred the particular case, or the
class of case to which that case belongs, to the Board for its advice.

43. *Young offenders.*—(1) Subject to subsections (4) and (5) below, this Part
applies to persons serving sentences of detention in a young offender
institution, or determinate sentences of detention under section 53 of the
1933 Act, as it applies to persons serving equivalent sentences of
imprisonment.

(2) Subject to subsection (5) below, this Part applies to persons serving—
(a) sentences of detention during Her Majesty's pleasure or for life under
section 53 of the 1933 Act; or (b) sentences of custody for life under section
8 of the 1982 Act, as it applies to persons serving sentences of imprisonment
for life ...

51. *Interpretation of Part II.*—(1) In this Part ... "life prisoner" has the
meaning given by section 34(7) above (as extended by section 43(2)
above) ...'

In my view, the current legislation and its provenance clearly demonstrates a
number of material propositions. It shows that whatever Parliament might have
considered to be the purposes of a sentence on a child of detention during Her
Majesty's pleasure when enacting the Children Act 1908, by 1991 Parliament
intended that it should include purposes of retribution and deterrence. The
terms of s 53(2) of the 1933 Act clearly envisage that the punishment of such
persons is one of the purposes of sentences for the crimes to which it applies. This
was emphasised by Lord Lane CJ in *R v Forshaw* (1984) 6 Cr App R (S) 413 at 415
and further exemplified in *R v Fairhurst* [1987] 1 All ER 46, [1986] 1 WLR 1374. It
would be surprising if punishment was one of the purposes of the sentence for the
lesser offences to which s 53(2) applies but not for the graver offence for which
s 53(1) makes provision. Moreover, if punishment was not one of the purposes,
it is hard to see what was the point of requiring the Secretary of State to consult

the Lord Chief Justice and the trial judge under s 35(2) of the 1991 Act as well as
requiring the recommendation of the Parole Board before a release on licence. *a*
Section 43(2) of the 1991 Act equates a child serving a sentence of detention
during Her Majesty's pleasure with the mandatory life prisoner for whom the
sentence is, in part, intended to be punishment; further, as the relevant provisions
apply to a young person of 17 as well as to one of 10, it is unlikely that Parliament
could have intended that punishment should not have been a purpose of the *b*
sentence. Accordingly, I would resolve the first issue formulated by counsel for
the respondents in the negative. In my view, Parliament did not intend that a
sentence of detention during Her Majesty's pleasure imposed on a child or young
person should be solely preventive and reformatory. In consequence, I would
dismiss the cross-appeal.

The determination of the second issue as formulated by counsel for the *c*
respondents depends on the nature and extent of the discretion conferred on the
Secretary of State by s 35(2) of the Criminal Justice Act 1991. In considering that
point, it is necessary to have regard to the position of the discretionary life
prisoners for whom s 34(1) makes provision. In their case, the section
contemplates that the part of their life sentence, which was discretionary anyway, *d*
as the judge at trial may have specified as appropriate to the offence should be
served before any question of release on licence is normally considered. That
part is what the judge considered was required for the purposes of punishment
and deterrence (see *Practice Note* [1993] 1 All ER 747, [1993] 1 WLR 223). It seems
to me to be plain that s 35(2), which confers the relevant power on the Secretary
of State in wide terms, cannot have been intended to preclude the Secretary of *e*
State adopting and applying a comparable policy in the case of a life prisoner, as
defined, who is not a discretionary life prisoner. The statutory definition of that
person includes a young offender serving a sentence of detention during Her
Majesty's pleasure under s 53(1) of the 1933 Act. As I have already indicated, I do
not think that the description of the sentence of detention during Her Majesty's *f*
pleasure carries any inference that its nature or duration is different to the life
sentences passed on adult offenders who the Act treats as the same.

A number of objections to this conclusion were raised by counsel for the
respondents. It was submitted that the imposition of a tariff for the purpose of
punishment and deterrence, thereby postponing the time at which the Parole
Board would consider a release, would frustrate the reformative nature of the *g*
sentence by precluding any earlier consideration of the offender's progress. But,
for the reasons I have already given, the sentence is not wholly reformative and
in the case of the lesser offences for which s 34 provides, Parliament has clearly
enacted just such a scheme. Arising from the same objection it was contended
that the statutory power did not authorise the Secretary of State to fix the earliest *h*
time at which the Parole Board might consider a release on licence without
regard to the progress towards rehabilitation made by the offender and whether
it would be safe to release him on licence. But this objection falls with the first
and for similar reasons. The regime envisaged by s 34 for those detained for lesser
offences requires the offender to serve the part specified by the judge as requisite *j*
for the purposes of punishment and deterrence before any question of his release
is considered by the Parole Board and therefore by the Secretary of State.

In the affidavit sworn on behalf of the Secretary of State by Mr Newton, he
points out that the respondents are undergoing an in-depth psychiatric
assessment and that any fresh information which comes to light will be
considered by the Secretary of State. However, this assurance is qualified by the
condition that such fresh information is relevant to the circumstances of the

a offences or the respondents' state of mind when they were committed and, therefore, to the length of the tariff. This attitude is confirmed by the concluding passage of the decision letters. Thus, the Secretary of State does not accept any obligation to consider fresh information relevant to the progress towards rehabilitation which either respondent may show as a part of the normal process of maturation. The concern of the respondents is wholly understandable; but, in b agreement with Hobhouse LJ, I am unable to accept that the Secretary of State is not legally entitled to adopt the policy and take the view he has. Accordingly, I would resolve the second issue as formulated by counsel for the respondents in the affirmative.

The nature of the discretion conferred on the Secretary of State was considered c by the House of Lords in *Doody v Secretary of State for the Home Dept* [1993] 3 All ER 92, [1994] 1 AC 531. That case concerned an adult who had been convicted of murder and the provisions of s 61(1) of the Criminal Justice Act 1967 which was re-enacted in the same terms in s 35(2) of the 1991 Act. The issues included the questions whether the prisoners were entitled to be told what the recommendations as to the length of the tariff given by the trial judge and of the d Lord Chief had been and their reasons and whether the Secretary of State was entitled to depart from those recommendations and, if so, whether he should give his reasons for doing so.

Lord Mustill, with whom the other members of the Appellate Committee agreed, specifically decided that the Secretary of State was entitled to depart from e the recommendations of the judges. He said ([1993] 3 All ER 92 at 104–105, [1994] 1 AC 531 at 558–559):

'Until Mr Brittan completely changed the rules in 1983 the idea of a separate determinate penal element coexisting with the life sentence would f have been meaningless. It is true that for the past ten years the judges have been asked to advise upon it, and it may be that some consistent judicial practice now exists. Nevertheless, it is the Home Secretary who decides, and who has developed (with his predecessors) his own ministerial ideas on what the public interest demands. I can see no reason why the anomalous task of fixing a "tariff" penal element for an offence in respect of which the true tariff g sentence is life imprisonment is one for which the Home Secretary and his junior ministers, informed by his officials about the existing departmental practice, are any less experienced and capable than are the judges. In any event, however, even if the respondents' argument is correct so far, it must in my opinion fail because Parliament has not by statute conferred on the h judges any role, even as advisers, at the time when the penal element of a mandatory sentence is fixed. But for the fact that the Home Secretary decided when formulating the new scheme, to retain in a modified shape the existing practice of inviting the opinion of the judges, they would never enter the picture at all. The Secretary of State is compelled, or at least entitled, to have regard to broader considerations of a public character than those which j apply to an ordinary sentencing function. It is he, and not the judges, who is entrusted with the task of deciding upon the prisoner's release, and it is he who has decided, within the general powers conferred upon him by the statute, to divide his task into two stages. It is not, and could not be, suggested that he acted unlawfully in this respect and I can see no ground whatever for suggesting that by doing so he deprived himself entirely of his discretion at the first stage, and delivered it into the hands of the judges. If

the decision in *Ex p Handscomb* (1987) 86 Cr App R 59 is to a contrary effect,   a
then with due respect to a very experienced court, I must disagree.

It seems to me that a number of the submissions made on behalf of the
respondents are inconsistent with the nature of the discretion Parliament has
conferred on the Secretary of State as described by Lord Mustill. First, it was
suggested that because that case concerned an adult convicted of murder and   b
sentenced to imprisonment for life the observations of Lord Mustill were
inapplicable to the case of a young offender sentenced to be detained during Her
Majesty's pleasure. I do not agree. The provisions of the 1991 Act which I have
quoted earlier show that Parliament intended the regime it laid down to apply to
both adults and young offenders and that that regime included tariffs to indicate
the part of the sentence required for punishment and deterrence. It follows that,   c
contrary to the submission made on behalf of the respondents, the Secretary of
State is entitled to depart from the recommendations of the judges.

Then it was suggested that the Secretary of State was not entitled to take
account of the 'broader considerations of a public character' constituted by public
concern or, more specifically, public concern as demonstrated by the petitions   d
submitted to the Secretary of State in this case and described in the judgment of
Lord Woolf MR. But, in my view, the decision of the House of Lords shows that
he is; and in relation to both stages, that is fixing the tariff and deciding whether
or not to release after the tariff has been served. It is true that the material in this
case is open to the criticisms made by Lord Woolf MR and Hobhouse LJ. But
public concern is not necessarily either logical, fully informed or free from   e
prejudice. It is the fact that the concern is public that gives it significance; what
weight, if any, to attach to it is a matter for the Secretary of State. Accordingly,
however alien such a consideration may be to a judge sentencing an offender it is
not one which, in my view, the Secretary of State is legally precluded from taking
into account.   f

Then it was contended that the Secretary of State was not entitled to fix the
tariff at 15 years and wrongly disregarded the need for rehabilitation and the
shortest possible tariff. But it is not suggested that the decision of the Secretary
of State was perverse in either of these respects. It must be inherent in the
Secretary of State's ability not to adopt the judicial recommendations that he may   g
increase the tariff above what the judges had thought appropriate.

Reliance was also placed on s 44(1) of 1933 Act, which has been quoted by Lord
Woolf MR. But, as it seems to me, that subsection is dealing with courts and not
the Secretary of State and the conditions of detention rather than its duration. In
any event, it was not disputed that the Secretary of State has, as Lord Woolf MR
has pointed out, put in place an excellent monitoring and care plan designed to   h
achieve the best outcome for the respondents despite their circumstances.

In the light of all these matters, I conclude that the third issue as formulated by
counsel for the respondents should be answered in the negative. Their case
depended, as their counsel accepted, on placing a sentence of detention during
Her Majesty's pleasure in a wholly separate category from that of mandatory life   j
prisoners and imposing fetters on the discretion of the Secretary of State in
relation to the former which do not exist in the case of the latter. This was the
basis of the decision of the Divisional Court. For the reasons I have endeavoured
to explain, I think that such a case is inconsistent with the intention of Parliament
as expressed in the legislation to which I have referred. Accordingly, I agree with
Hobhouse LJ on this issue and respectfully disagree with Lord Woolf MR and the

a Divisional Court. I would answer the first question I referred to at the beginning of this judgment in the negative.

In these circumstances, the question of procedural unfairness, which the Divisional Court did not deal with as on the view they took on the first question it did not arise, must now be resolved. The complaint of the respondents is that there was inadequate disclosure to them or their advisers of the material which

b would be considered by the Secretary of State when he decided the tariff to be served and that the Secretary of State reached his decision without considering all relevant matters.

The extent of the disclosure required was one of the issues considered by the House of Lords in *Doody's* case. This was considered by Lord Mustill, where he said ([1993] 3 All ER 92 at 109–110, [1994] 1 AC 531 at 564):

c
> 'In the present instance, the opinion of the judges (or opinions, if the Lord Chief Justice differs from the charge judge) are weighed in the balance when the Secretary of State makes his decision. Beyond the fact that the opinion is not invariably decisive (as witness the statistics previously cited) there is no means of knowing how it figures in the Home Secretary's reasoning. That it
> *d* does so figure is quite plain from the statements by successive ministers from which I have quoted. This being so, I think it clear that the prisoner needs to know the substance of the judges' advice, comprising not only the term of years which they recommended as the penal element, but also their reasons: for the prisoner cannot rationalise his objections to the penal element without knowing how it was rationalised by the judges themselves. This
> *e* does not mean that the document(s) in which the judges state their opinion need be disclosed in their entirety. Those parts of the judges' opinions which are concerned with matters other than the penal element (for example any observation by the judges on risk) need not be disclosed in any form, and even in respect of the relevant material the requirement is only that the
> *f* prisoner shall learn the gist of what the judges have said. This will not necessarily involve verbatim quotation from the advice, although this may often be convenient. If the Home Secretary's duty is approached in this way I doubt whether the fact that in the past the advice has been given in documents intended to be confidential will often prove to be troublesome;
> *g* and in the few cases where problems do arise it may well be that, upon request, the judges are prepared to waive the confidentiality of the documents.'

The first complaint of the respondents is that the Secretary of State did not disclose the full text of the trial judge's letter, in particular that part of it which *h* contained his summary of the facts. In my view, there is substance in this complaint. The judge's summary went further than merely to set out the relevant facts as demonstrated at the trial. As the judgment of Hobhouse LJ demonstrates, he made important inferences of his own which would not have been apparent from the parts of the letter which were disclosed to the respondents. The respondents had no opportunity to refute or comment on those inferences.

j
Then it is submitted that the respondents were not warned that the Secretary of State might set a tariff higher than that recommended by the trial judge and the Lord Chief Justice. I do not regard this complaint as having any substance. It is inherent in the nature of the discretion conferred on the Secretary of State by s 35(2) and the statements of policy made by the Secretary of State from time to time that the tariff may be increased. But, in addition, it must have been apparent

to the respondents and their advisers that a longer tariff than the judges had recommended was likely to be considered. In the letter from Mr Newton, writing on behalf of the Secretary of State on 16 June, it was specifically stated that 'if he [the Secretary of State] decides to set a period different from that recommended by the judiciary (the details of which have already been sent to you) you will also be informed [of] the reason why he has done so'. The letter went on to give details of representations made to the Home Office most of which sought the imposition of a tariff longer than that recommended by the judges.

The respondents submitted that the Secretary of State failed to take account of all relevant considerations in that he made his decision without having more than the form as completed by the trial judge and the comments thereon of the Lord Chief Justice. It is suggested that he should have had all the trial papers and such psychiatric and pre-sentencing reports as would have been available had the trial judge been passing a determinate sentence on an adult. It was suggested on behalf of the Secretary of State that there was nothing in this point because the Lord Chief Justice was able to make his recommendation on the same information in this respect as the Secretary of State had. I do not think that that is a sufficient answer for we are not concerned with the advice tendered by the Lord Chief Justice.

In my view, there is substance in this complaint too. The wider the discretion conferred on the Secretary of State the more important it must be that he has all relevant material to enable him properly to exercise it. The fact is that in this case the Secretary of State did not ensure that he was at least in possession of such material as would be available to a judge sentencing an offender to a determinate term a good deal shorter than the tariff period he had in mind. I do not suggest that the parallel is exact but, in my view, it cannot be right that the Secretary of State should exercise this very wide and onerous discretion with less.

For these reasons I agree with both Lord Woolf MR and Hobhouse LJ that the decision of the Secretary of State should be quashed on the grounds that the manner in which it was reached was procedurally unfair. This will enable the Secretary of State to reconsider the matter having obtained all relevant information, having disclosed all material matters to the respondents and having considered any representations they may wish to make in the light of such all such information and other matters.

No doubt in the course of that reconsideration he will reflect on whether the policy should be applied at all to persons of the age of the respondents at the time they committed the dreadful offences of which they were convicted. If the policy is to be applied it is to be expected that he will have in mind many of the other matters raised in the course of argument on this appeal including the weight, if any, to be attached to public concern evidenced by the petitions and other correspondence Lord Woolf MR has described, in the light of the possibility of the double counting to which he has referred and the inherent weaknesses in such petitions and correspondence to which Hobhouse LJ has drawn attention. In my view the decision, in the light of all those matters, is entrusted by Parliament to the Secretary of State alone subject only to the requirement that he reaches his decision in a manner which is procedurally fair.

Appeals dismissed. Leave to appeal and to cross-appeal to the House of Lords granted.

Mary Rose Plummer   Barrister.

Practice Note

QUEEN'S BENCH DIVISION (COMMERCIAL COURT)
COLMAN J
13 JANUARY 1997

Practice – Queen's Bench Division – Commercial Court – Arbitration – Procedure – Arbitration Act 1996 – Rules of the Supreme Court (Amendment) 1996.

COLMAN J made the following statement at the sitting of the court. Although it will be widely known that the Arbitration Act 1996 comes into effect on 31 January 1997, it may well not yet be appreciated by the profession that, in order to give effect to the new Act, an entirely new Ord 73 of the Rules of the Supreme Court is to come into force on the same day (see the Rules of the Supreme Court (Amendment) 1996, SI 1996/3219, r 5).

There will apply to arbitrations governed by the new Act substantially different procedures to those which now apply. In general, the new Act will apply to all arbitrations commenced on or after 31 January 1997. Part I of the new Ord 73 sets out the new procedures which are to apply to those arbitrations. The new Act and Pt I of the order will also apply to applications to the court made on or after 31 January in respect of arbitrations yet to be commenced at the time of the application.

For arbitrations commenced before 31 January 1997 the new Act will not apply and for applications to the court in respect of such arbitrations and for applications made before that date in respect of arbitrations yet to be commenced and also in respect of arbitrations commenced on or after 31 January, the applicable procedure will be almost identical to that now in force but will be subject to very minor alterations. That procedure is set out in Pt II of the new order.

Part III of the new order relates to enforcement of arbitration awards and introduces a procedural regime of universal application regardless of the date when the arbitration was commenced.

Amongst the most important procedural changes introduced by the new Ord 73 is that providing for a new multi-purpose form of originating process and of subsidiary process in existing proceedings to be known as an 'arbitration application'.

The form is to be used for all applications in respect of arbitrations to which the 1996 Act applies except enforcement and including applications to stay judicial proceedings, to determine issues as to jurisdiction, to enforce peremptory orders, to make orders in support of arbitral proceedings, to challenge awards on the grounds of want of jurisdiction or serious irregularity and to appeals on a question of law arising out of an award.

In conjunction with the introduction of the new uniform process for arbitration applications Ord 73, r 13 introduces a comprehensive series of directions relating to such applications which will apply automatically unless the court otherwise orders. The judges of the Commercial Court will require strict compliance with these directions except with leave of the court. Parties who do not comply will be at risk as to the dates of their hearings being vacated and/or as to adverse costs orders.

Applications for leave to appeal on a question of law arising out of an award will be determined without a hearing unless the court considers that one is required as provided by s 69(5) of the 1996 Act. Apart from the substantive hearing of appeals and of preliminary points of law, all arbitration applications will be heard in chambers unless the court orders that the hearing be in open court.

The time limit for applications challenging an award is extended from 21 to 28 days. The court may without a hearing extend that time limit upon application.

An important change in service of arbitration applications on overseas parties to arbitrations is introduced by Ord 73, r 7(2). Where an overseas party has been represented by an English solicitor who was authorised to accept service of notices or documents in the arbitration and has not determined that solicitor's authority to act in the arbitration, the arbitration application can be served on that solicitor and it will be unnecessary to obtain leave to serve the party outside the jurisdiction.

The Commercial Court will continue to have primary responsibility for the administration and monitoring of the supervisory jurisdiction over arbitrations and awards under the 1996 Act. Although such applications can be made not only in the Commercial Court but also in the mercantile courts and the Central London County Court Business List, the decision whether to retain the application or to transfer it to the Commercial Court or to some other court is to be taken by the mercantile or business list judge, as the case may be, but in consultation with the judge in charge of the Commercial List.

In giving effect to the 1996 Act and to the new Ord 73, the judges of the Commercial Court will endeavour as far as possible to achieve consistency in matters of construction both of the Act and of the new Ord 73. In order to facilitate consistency of approach, arrangements have been made for decisions on matters of construction and application to be circulated between the judges immediately they are given. Investigations are in progress as to the feasibility of the wider circulation of these decisions to the rest of the profession without the delay ordinarily entailed in awaiting published reports. Since most of the judgments on arbitration applications are likely to be given in chambers, it is hoped that all parties will co-operate in facilitating publication of those judgments which are concerned with matters of construction or application of the 1996 Act and the new Ord 73.

It is impossible to envisage in advance every problem that may arise in relation to the operation of the new Act by the new Ord 73. In the course of the next few months there will be developing experience of the working of the new regime. Members of the profession who identify particular problems in the working of the new Ord 73 are strongly encouraged to bring them to the attention of the judge in charge of the Commercial Court List to enable the judges to carry out their function of monitoring the effective working of the Act and the new Ord 73.

K Mydeen Esq   Barrister.

Practice Direction

a

QUEEN'S BENCH DIVISION

Practice – Queen's Bench Division – Liverpool and Manchester – Mercantile lists –
b Telephone summonses – When appropriate – Procedure.

This practice direction is issued by the presiding judges of the Northern Circuit
with the approval of the Lord Chief Justice.

Telephone summonses in the Liverpool and Manchester Mercantile Lists
c   1. From 2 September 1996 summonses in these lists may be heard by
telephone if they comply with the following conditions: (a) the solicitor for at
least one of the parties is based in an office more than ten miles from Manchester
Crown Court; (b) the hearing of the summons is expected to last 20 minutes or
less; (c) all parties have consented to the summons being heard by telephone; (d)
d no party is acting in person.
   2. For the purpose of this practice direction, 'summons' (a) includes the
hearing of a plaintiff's objection to transfer of an action to the Royal Courts of
Justice or to another district registry under RSC Ord 4, r 5(3); (b) does not include
a pre-trial review, for which personal attendance by a solicitor or counsel fully
acquainted with the action will remain necessary.
e   3. Before consenting to the hearing of a summons by telephone, any party
upon whom it is served should consider whether he wishes to have a summons
heard in the same action which should logically, or which can conveniently, be
heard at the same time and, if so, whether both summonses can be heard within
20 minutes.
f   4. No party to a telephone summons may attend in person.
   5. The procedure for setting up a telephone summons will be as follows.
(a) The solicitor intending to issue the summons (the initiating solicitor) must
first give notice of the terms of the summons and a copy of this practice direction
to the other party or parties and obtain their consent to a telephone hearing.
(b) The summons(es) must be marked prominently 'Telephone Summons'. The
g date and time of hearing will be inserted by the registry staff when the summons
is issued. (c) An agreed paginated bundle must be lodged at the Manchester
District Registry at least two working days before the hearing. It must contain
copies of the summons(es), all pleadings served to date, all affidavits relied upon,
any authorities relied upon, a draft of the order sought and all skeleton
h arguments. The bundle must be marked prominently on the front with the title
of the action (including the setting down number if the action has been set down)
and the words 'Telephone Summons'. Responsibility for agreeing, preparing and
lodging such bundle, and for ensuring that all parties have the bundle, lies with
the initiating solicitor. (d) The initiating solicitor, or counsel on his behalf, will
j arrange the telephone conference by the British Telecom conference call 'call
out' system for precisely the time fixed by the court. The operator will need to
be told the telephone numbers of all those participating in the conference call and
the sequence in which they are to be called, and it will be the responsibility of the
initiating solicitor to ascertain from the solicitors for all other parties whether
they have instructed counsel and, if so the identity of counsel, and whether the
solicitor and counsel will be on the same or different telephone numbers. That

sequence will be (1) the initiating solicitor and (if on a different number) his counsel; (2) the solicitor (and counsel) for all other parties; (3) the judge. The *a* judge's telephone number is 0161 833 3393. This is a line dedicated to telephone summonses. Neither the judge nor the court staff can be reached on this number for any other purpose. British Telecom will, if asked when the conference call is booked, record the conference on tape. The initiating solicitor must arrange for the conference to be recorded and must send the tape to the court. (e) Each *b* advocate will remain on the line after being called by the operator setting up the conference call—which may be two or three minutes before the time fixed for the summons. (f) When the judge has been connected the initiating solicitor (or his counsel) will introduce the parties in the usual way.

6. If the use of a 'speakerphone' by any party causes any difficulty for the judge or any other party in hearing what is said the judge may forthwith require the *c* advocate for that party to use a hand-held telephone.

7. The telephone charges debited to the account of the person initiating the conference call are to be treated as part of the costs of the summons for the purpose of taxation.

Note. This procedure is experimental. The requirements in para 1(a) and (b) *d* may be changed in the light of experience.

5 July 1996   FORBES J.

Practice Note

CHANCERY DIVISION
JACOB J
19 NOVEMBER 1996

Practice – Patents Court – Procedure – Draft orders – Experiments for litigation purposes – Assessment of costs – Notices to admit facts – Applications for interlocutory injunctions – RSC Ord 104, rr 10, 11(1)(a), 12.

JACOB J gave the following direction at the sitting of the court.

Orders following judgment

1. Where a judgment is made available in draft before being given in open court and it is desired to ask the court for an order when judgment is given, the parties should, in advance of that occasion, exchange drafts of the desired consequential order. It is highly undesirable that one party should spring a proposal on the other for the first time when judgment is given.

Experiments not part of normal research

2. The position of the admission at trial of evidence of experiments conducted for litigious purposes but not specifically for the case in hand requires clarification. RSC Ord 104, r 12 refers to establishing 'any fact by experimental proof'. This includes experiments done in other jurisdictions or any other experiments not done as part of normal research. In future the standard form of order made on the summons for directions (itself subject to variation for any particular case) should read as follows:

'Where a party desires to establish any fact by experimental proof, *including an experiment conducted for the purposes of litigation or otherwise not being an experiment conducted in the normal course of research*, he shall … [usual appropriate provisions as to service of a notice of experiments].'

Experiments done for litigation but not disclosed

3. The Intellectual Property Court Users' Committee has discussed the question of experiments conducted by a party for the purposes of litigation but not disclosed or adduced by it following the judgments in *Honeywell Ltd v Appliance Components Ltd* (22 February 1996, unreported), Jacob J and *Electrolux Northern Ltd v Black & Decker* (1996) Times, 6 May, Laddie J. As a result, it is proposed that in future it should be a requirement that an expert's report should include the statement 'I know of no experiment which is inconsistent with my evidence'. Further, practitioners are reminded that it would be contrary to their duty to the court to allow any expert evidence to be given inconsistent with an experiment of which they, but not the expert, have knowledge.

Immediate assessment of costs

4. In appropriate cases the Patents Court will adopt a more vigorous approach to costs. In particular, it will be willing to consider application for immediate assessment by the judge who has just tried the case rather than remit the matter for taxation. Such an assessment may be done on the basis of the actual detailed

bills sent to clients. Without in any way limiting the court's discretion as to when it will exercise this power, it may in particular be exercised in a case where the delays caused by a taxation of costs may themselves give rise to injustice.

Notices to admit facts in an application for a declaration of non-infringement

5. Under Ord 104, r 11(1)(a), a list of documents in an application for a declaration of non-infringement of a patent must be served by each party within 21 days after service of the notice of admissions under r 10(2), or within 21 days after the close of pleadings. However, Ord 104, r 10 does not expressly cover notices to admit facts and notices of admissions in an application for a declaration of non-infringement of a patent. A rule change will be proposed shortly to broaden the ambit of r 10. In the meantime, the parties to any action for a declaration of non-infringement of a patent are encouraged, where appropriate, to serve notices to admit facts within the period provided in Ord 104, r 10(1).

Applications for interlocutory injunctions: trial dates

6. When an application for an interlocutory injunction is made the plaintiff should, where practicable, make prior inquiries and investigations as to the estimated length of trial and possible trial dates.

Celia Fox   Barrister.

Olotu v Home Office and another

COURT OF APPEAL, CIVIL DIVISION

LORD BINGHAM OF CORNHILL CJ, AULD AND MUMMERY LJJ

13, 29 NOVEMBER 1996

Criminal law – Committal – Remand in custody – Custody time limits – Plaintiff charged with criminal offences and remanded in custody – Plaintiff released 81 days after expiry of custody time limit – Plaintiff claiming damages for false imprisonment against Home Office – Whether plaintiff falsely imprisoned – Whether prison governor should have released plaintiff following expiry of custody time limit – Prosecution of Offences (Custody Time Limits) Regulations 1987, reg 5(3)(a).

Damages – Breach of statutory duty – Breach by public authority – Failure of Crown Prosecution Service to bring plaintiff to court before expiry of custody time limit to apply for bail – Statutory duty on Crown Prosecution Service to ensure plaintiff did not spend longer in custody than permitted by custody time limit – Whether Crown Prosecution Service's failure giving rise to private law action for damages – Prosecution of Offences Act 1985, s 22 – Prosecution of Offences (Custody Time Limits) Regulations 1987, reg 6(1).

The plaintiff was arrested and charged with various criminal offences and subsequently committed in custody for trial in the Crown Court. The warrant of commitment directing the governor of the prison to which she was sent to keep her in custody until she was delivered to the Crown Court 'in due course of law'. The plaintiff was later released, 81 days after the expiry of her custody time limit as prescribed under s 22[a] of the Prosecution of Offences Act 1985 and reg 5 (3)(a)[b] of the Prosecution of Offences (Custody Time Limits) Regulations 1987. Thereafter, she brought proceedings against the Home Office, as the department with responsiblity for the prison governor in whose custody she had been, claiming damages for false imprisonment; she also sued the Crown Prosecution Service, claiming damages for breach of its statutory duty under reg 6(1)[c] of the 1987 regulations to bring her before the court before the expiry of the custody time limit so that she might be admitted to bail. The defendants applied to the court under RSC Ord 18, r 19 for the plaintiff's claims to be struck out on the ground that they disclosed no reasonable cause of action. The deputy judge (i) struck out the claim against the Home Office on the ground that the expiry of the custody time limit entitled the plaintiff to an order for release on bail by the court, not to release by the governor, but (ii) allowed the claim to proceed against the Crown Prosecution Service because it was not obviously unsustainable. The plaintiff and the Crown Prosecution Service appealed to the Court of Appeal.

Held – (1) Once the custody time limit had expired, the plaintiff was unlawfully detained and an order for her release could have been obtained either from the Crown Court or the Divisional Court. However, it did not follow that in the absence of any such order the prison governor was guilty of falsely imprisoning

a Section 22, so far as material, is set out at p 388 c to g, post
b Regulation 5(3)(a) is set out at p 389 a, post
c Regulation 6(1) is set out at p 389 b to c, post

the plaintiff: in view of the direction to him in the warrant and the fact that the plaintiff was in the custody of the Crown Court and only an order of the court could end that period of custody, he was neither entitled nor bound to release her. It followed that the claim for damages against the Home Office was unsustainable and accordingly the plaintiff's appeal would be dismissed (see p 391 j to 392 a j, p 394 c f to j and p 396 b, post).

(2) The object of s 22 of the 1985 Act and reg 6 of the 1987 regulations was to expedite the prosecution of criminal offences where defendants were remanded in custody to await trial, and (if such expedition were lacking) to ensure that defendants did not languish in prison for excessive periods. However, if the Crown Prosecution Service failed to perform its duty under reg 6 of ensuring that a defendant did not spend longer in custody than permitted by the relevant custody time limit, a defendant could apply for release on bail or habeas corpus and mandamus; it could not therefore have been the intention of the Secretary of State to confer a private law right of action for damages in such circumstances, nor was there anything in s 22 of the 1985 Act to suggest that Parliament intended to give the Secretary of State power to do so. It followed that the plaintiff's claim against the Crown Prosecution Service was also unsustainable and, accordingly, the Crown Prosecution Service's appeal would be allowed (see p 393 g to p 394 d f and p 395 h to p 396 b, post); Elguzouli-Daf v Comr of Police of the Metropolis, McBrearty v Ministry of Defence [1995] 1 All ER 833 applied.

Notes

For custody time limits in magistrates' courts and Crown Courts, see 11(2) Halsbury's Laws (4th edn) paras 852–853.

For the Prosecution of Offences Act 1985, s 22, see 12 Halsbury's Statutes (4th edn) (1994 reissue) 964.

Cases referred to in judgments

Elguzouli-Daf v Comr of Police of the Metropolis, McBrearty v Ministry of Defence [1995] 1 All ER 833, [1995] QB 335, [1995] 2 WLR 173, CA.

Hague v Deputy Governor of Parkhurst Prison, Weldon v Home Office [1991] 3 All ER 733, [1992] 1 AC 58, [1991] 3 WLR 340, HL.

Henderson v Preston (1888) 21 QBD 362, CA.

Moone v Rose (1869) LR 4 QB 486.

R v Crown Court at Maidstone, ex p Clark, R v Governor of Elmley Prison, ex p Clark [1995] 3 All ER 513, [1995] 1 WLR 831, DC.

X and ors (minors) v Bedfordshire CC, M (a minor) v Newham London BC, E (a minor) v Dorset CC [1995] 3 All ER 353, [1995] 2 AC 633, [1995] 3 WLR 152, HL.

Cases also cited or referred to in skeleton arguments

Cobbett v Grey (1849) 4 Exch 729, 154 ER 1409.

Derbyshire CC v Times Newspapers Ltd [1993] 1 All ER 1011, [1993] AC 534, HL.

Garland v British Rail Engineering Ltd Case 12/81 [1982] 2 All ER 402, [1983] 2 AC 751, ECJ and HL.

Hadkinson v Hadkinson [1952] 2 All ER 567, [1952] P 285, CA.

R v Crown Court at Leeds, ex p Hussain [1995] 3 All ER 527, [1995] 1 WLR 1329, DC.

R v Governor of Winchester Prison, ex p Roddie [1991] 2 All ER 931, [1991] 1 WLR 303, DC.

a   R v Secretary of State for the Home Dept, ex p Muboyayi [1991] 4 All ER 72, [1992] QB
     244, CA.
     R v Sheffield Justices, ex p Turner [1991] 1 All ER 858, [1991] 2 QB 472, DC.
     R v Oldham Justices, ex p Cawley [1996] 1 All ER 464, [1996] 2 WLR 681, DC.

Appeals

b   The plaintiff, Jeanette Ann Olotu, appealed with leave from the decision of
     Miss Barbara Dohmann QC, sitting as a deputy judge of the High Court on
     29 April 1996, striking out her claim for damages against the Home Office for
     false imprisonment as disclosing no reasonable cause of action. The Crown
     Prosecution Service also appealed with leave from the deputy judge's refusal to
     strike out the plaintiff's claim for damages against it for breach of its statutory
c   duty under reg 6(1) of the Prosecution of Offences (Custody Time Limits)
     Regulations 1987 to bring her before the court before the expiry of the custody
     time limit so that she might be admitted to bail. The facts are set out in the
     judgment of Lord Bingham CJ.

d   *Nicholas Blake QC* and *Tim Owen* (instructed by *Bobbetts Mackan*, Bristol) for the
     plaintiff.
     Stephen Richards (instructed by the *Treasury Solicitor*) for the defendants.

                                                                    Cur adv vult

     29 November 1996. The following judgments were delivered.

e
     LORD BINGHAM OF CORNHILL CJ. The plaintiff in this action was arrested
     on 6 February 1994, charged with criminal offences the following day and on 25
     April 1994 committed in custody by the magistrates' court for trial in the Crown
     Court. She was held at HM Prison Pucklechurch from the date of committal until
     her release on 3 November 1994, a period of 193 days. She contends that the last
f   81 days of this period of detention were unlawful, being in excess of the time limit
     of 112 days between committal and arraignment prescribed by reg 5(3)(a) of the
     Prosecution of Offences (Custody Time Limits) Regulations 1987, SI 1987/299, as
     amended. She also contends that the Crown Prosecution Service (the CPS)
     wrongfully failed, in breach of the duty imposed on them by reg 6(1) of those
     regulations, to bring her before the court so that she might be admitted to bail.
g   In November 1995 the plaintiff issued proceedings. She sued the Home Office,
     as the department responsible for prisons, claiming damages (including
     exemplary damages) for false imprisonment. She sued the CPS claiming damages
     (including exemplary damages) for breach of statutory duty. Both defendants
     applied to strike out the claim against them under RSC Ord 18, r 19 as disclosing
h   no reasonable cause of action.
     On 29 April 1996 Miss Barbara Dohmann QC, sitting as a deputy judge of the
     High Court in the Queen's Bench Division, ordered that the plaintiff's claim
     against the Home Office be struck out, but she dismissed the application to strike
     out made by the CPS. The plaintiff appeals against the first of these orders, the
j   CPS against the second, in each case with the leave of the deputy judge. The
     question for us is whether, on the facts stated, the plaintiff's claim against each
     defendant is so obviously unsustainable in law as to make it proper to strike out
     the claim at this preliminary stage. The plaintiff's claims against the two
     defendants are independent of each other, and do not stand or fall together. No
     separate issue arises at this stage on the plaintiff's claims to exemplary damages.

The relevant statutory provisions
    Section 6(3) and (4) of the Magistrates' Courts Act 1980 provides:

> '(3) Subject to section 4 of the Bail Act 1976 and section 41 below, the
> court may commit a person for trial—(a) in custody, that is to say, by
> committing him to custody there to be safely kept until delivered in due
> course of law ...
>   (4) Where the court has committed a person to custody in accordance
> with paragraph (a) of subsection (3) above, then, if that person is in custody
> for no other cause, the court may, at any time before his first appearance
> before the Crown Court, grant him bail in accordance with the Bail Act 1976
> subject to a duty to appear before the Crown Court for trial.'

The Prosecution of Offences Act 1985 provides, in s 22(1), as follows:

> 'The Secretary of State may by regulations make provision, with respect to
> any specified preliminary stage of proceedings for an offence, as to the
> maximum period—(a) to be allowed to the prosecution to complete that
> stage; (b) during which the accused may, while awaiting completion of that
> stage, be—(i) in the custody of a magistrates' court; or (ii) in the custody of
> the Crown Court; in relation to that offence.'

Subsection (2) specified some matters to which the regulations might in
particular apply. These included the procedure to be followed in criminal
proceedings in consequence of any other provision of the regulations. Subsection
(3) provided:

> 'The appropriate court may, at any time before the expiry of a time limit
> imposed by the regulations, extend, or further extend, that limit if it is
> satisfied—(a) that there is good and sufficient cause for doing so; and (b) that
> the prosecution has acted with all due expedition.'

Subsection (11) contained a number of definitions. Where an accused has been
committed for trial, 'the appropriate court' in sub-s (3) means the Crown Court.
The 'custody of the Crown Court' includes custody to which a person has been
committed in pursuance of s 6 of the 1980 Act. 'Custody time limit' is defined to
mean a time limit imposed by regulations made under sub-s (1)(b) of s 22 or,
where any such limit has been extended by a court under sub-s (3), the limit as so
extended. 'Preliminary stage', in relation to any proceedings, is defined so as not
to include any stage of the proceedings after the accused has been arraigned in the
Crown Court.
    The Secretary of State exercised his power to make regulations under s 22(1)(b)
of the 1985 Act by making the 1987 regulations, which were amended in 1988,
1989 (twice) and 1991. The following provisions of these regulations are relevant
for present purposes.
    Regulation 5, so far as material, provides:

> '(2) Where—(a) a person accused of an indictable offence other than
> treason is committed to the Crown Court for trial ... the maximum period
> during which he may be in the custody of the Crown Court in relation to that
> offence, or any other offence included in the indictment preferred against
> him, while awaiting the preliminary stage of the proceedings specified in the
> following provisions of this Regulation shall be as stated in those provisions.

(3) The maximum period of custody—(a) between the time when the accused is committed for trial and his arraignment ... shall, subject to the following provisions of this Regulation, be 112 days.'

Regulation 6, so far as relevant, provides:

'(1) Subject to the following provisions of this Regulation where an accused who is in custody pending trial in the Crown Court has the benefit of a custody time limit under Regulation 5 above the prosecution shall—(a) not less than 5 days before the expiry of the time limit give notice in writing to the appropriate officer of the Crown Court and to the accused or his representative stating whether or not it intends to ask the Crown Court to impose conditions on the grant of bail in respect of the accused and, if it intends to do so, the nature of the conditions to be sought; and (b) make arrangements for the accused to be brought before the Crown Court within the period of 2 days preceding the expiry of the time limit ...

(3) The prosecution need not comply with paragraph (1)(a) above if it has given notice under Regulation 7(2) below of its intention to make an application under section 22(3) of the 1985 Act.

(4) On receiving notice under paragraph (1)(a) above stating that the prosecution intends to ask the Crown Court to impose conditions on the grant of bail, the accused or his representative shall—(a) give notice in writing to the appropriate officer of the Crown Court and to the prosecution that the accused wishes to be represented at the hearing of the application; or (b) give notice in writing to the appropriate officer and to the prosecution stating that the accused does not oppose the application; or (c) give to the appropriate officer, for the consideration of the Crown Court, a written statement of the accused's reasons for opposing the application, at the same time sending a copy of the statement to the prosecution ...

(6) The Crown Court, on being notified that an accused who is in custody pending trial there has the benefit of a custody time limit under Regulation 5 above and that the time limit is about to expire, shall grant him bail in accordance with the Bail Act 1976, as from the expiry of the time limit, subject to a duty to appear before the Crown Court for trial.'

Regulation 7, so far as relevant, provides:

'(1) An application to a court for the extension or further extension of a custody time limit under section 22(3) of the 1985 Act may be made orally or in writing.

(2) Subject to paragraphs (3) and (4) below the prosecution shall—(a) not less than 5 days before making such an application in the Crown Court; and (b) not less than 2 days before making such an application in a magistrates' court, give notice in writing to the accused or his representative and to the proper officer of the court stating that it intends to make such an application.'

Regulation 8 provides that the Bail Act 1976 shall apply subject to certain modifications in cases to which a custody time limit applies.

Section 1(6) of the 1976 Act provides: 'Bail in criminal proceedings shall be granted (and in particular shall be granted unconditionally or conditionally) in accordance with this Act.' Where a custody time limit has expired, s 3 of the 1976 Act has effect as if sub-ss (4) and (5), dealing with sureties and security for the surrender of the defendant, were omitted. In that situation, sub-s (6) provides:

'He [a person granted bail in criminal proceedings] may be required (but only by a court) to comply, after release on bail or later, with such requirements as appear to the court to be necessary to secure that—(a) he surrenders to custody...'

Where a custody time limit has expired, s 4 of the 1976 Act has effect as if it reads:

'(1) A person to whom this section applies shall be granted bail ...
(2) This section applies to a person who is accused of an offence when— (a) he appears or is brought before a magistrates' court or the Crown Court in the course of or in connection with proceedings for the offence, or (b) he applies to a court for bail in connection with the proceedings.'

The effect of these provisions was succinctly summarised by Glidewell LJ in *R v Crown Court at Maidstone, ex p Clark, R v Governor of Elmley Prison, ex p Clark* [1995] 3 All ER 513 at 516, [1995] 1 WLR 831 at 834, when he said:

'Put shortly, the effect of those provisions is that, if a custody time limit, either the original 112 days or any period extended as a result of an order of the court, expires before arraignment in the Crown Court, then the relevant defendant is automatically entitled to bail. The courts' only powers thereafter are to impose conditions on the grant of that bail. The power of the Crown to apply to the Crown Court to extend the time limit can only be exercised by that court if it is satisfied of the two requirements in s 22(3) of the 1985 Act: good and sufficient cause and that the prosecution has acted with all due expedition.'

The warrant of commitment

The warrant committing the plaintiff for trial at the Crown Court at Bristol was only produced during the hearing before us, and as a result it was neither pleaded nor seen by the deputy judge. It was, however, agreed between the parties that for the purposes of this hearing we should treat this warrant as part of the factual material before us.

The warrant was headed with the name of the magistrates' court and gave the date, the name of the accused and the offence of which she was accused. It recorded the decision of the magistrates to commit the plaintiff for trial at the Crown Court at Bristol. It then continued:

'DIRECTION: You, the constables of the Avon and Somerset Constabulary, are hereby commanded to convey the accused to PUCKLECHURCH and there deliver the accused to the Governor thereof, together with this warrant; and you, the Governor, to receive into your custody and (unless the accused is released on bail in the meantime) keep the accused until the accused is delivered in due course of law. The custody time limit which applies to these proceedings is due to expire on 15th August 1994.'

This wording, a variation of the standard terms of Form 18 in Sch 2 to the Magistrates' Courts (Forms) Rules 1981, SI 1981/553, followed a Home Office recommendation in Circular 18/1987. It was common ground between the parties to the appeals that the words 'delivered in due course of law' were to be understood as referring to delivery to the Crown Court.

The claim against the Home Office

The deputy judge struck out the plaintiff's claim against the Home Office on the ground that expiry of the time limit entitled the plaintiff to an order for release on bail by the court, not to release by the governor. Mr Nicholas Blake QC, for the plaintiff, criticised that ruling. His argument was simple and attractive. By s 22(1) of the 1985 Act the Secretary of State had power to make regulations as to the maximum period during which an accused person might be held in the custody of the Crown Court. The Secretary of State had exercised that power by making the 1987 regulations. He had fixed 112 days as the maximum period during which an accused could be so held after committal and before arraignment. The magistrates' court could not lawfully commit the plaintiff to prison for any longer period. Unless that period was duly extended, or within that period or any extended period the plaintiff was arraigned, there was no lawful power to detain her and the magistrates' court could not confer such power. In the present case, the maximum period for which the plaintiff could lawfully be held in custody had expired, and had not been extended. It followed that the plaintiff was thereafter detained unlawfully. She accordingly had a claim for damages for false imprisonment against the party responsible for her detention, ie the Home Office as the party responsible for the governor of the prison in whose custody she had been. Reliance was placed on a summary of the law in 45 *Halsbury's Laws* (4th edn) para 1329:

> 'The governor of a prison is protected in obeying a warrant of commitment, valid on the face of it, addressed to him, and is not liable to an action for false imprisonment if he detains a person in pursuance of the warrant. However, he is liable if he … keeps a prisoner in custody without a sufficient warrant of commitment or for a longer time than is lawful.'

Mr Stephen Richards, for the Home Office, supported the decision of the deputy judge. He submitted that the duty of the governor was to obey the order of the court. Following the committal of the plaintiff under s 6 of the Magistrates' Courts Act 1980, the plaintiff was (as was clear from s 22(1)(b)(ii) of the 1985 Act and reg 5(2)(a) of the 1987 regulations) to be regarded as in the custody of the Crown Court. The governor's duty, under s 6(3)(a) of the 1980 Act and according to the direction given to him in the warrant, was to hold the plaintiff until she should be delivered to the Crown Court in due course of law. He was never at any material time called upon to deliver the plaintiff to the Crown Court in due course of law, and could not lawfully take it upon himself to release the plaintiff. She, in any event, had no right to be released after 112 days; her right was to be released on bail by order of the court. Although alerted by the terms of the warrant to the date upon which the custody time limit was to expire, the governor had no independent role in making any application to the court, nor any authority to release the plaintiff without an order of the court.

In my judgment, the submission of Mr Richards is essentially correct. The plaintiff was in the custody of the Crown Court. Only by order of the court could that period of custody be brought to an end. Once the custody time limit had expired without extension, the Crown Court would have been obliged to order the release of the plaintiff, but such release would have been on bail and the Crown Court could have imposed terms with which the plaintiff would have been obliged to comply after release. Once the custody time limit had expired, the plaintiff was in my view unlawfully detained, and an order which would have led to her release could have been obtained either from the Crown Court or from the Divisional Court; but it does not follow that in the absence of any such order the governor was guilty of falsely imprisoning the plaintiff and in my view he was neither entitled nor bound to release her.

Mr Blake addressed a supporting argument based on the following provisions of art 5 of the European Convention for the Protection of Human Rights and Fundamental Freedoms (Rome, 4 November 1950; TS 71 (1953); Cmd 8969):

'(1) Everyone has the right to liberty and security of person. No one shall be deprived of his liberty save in the following cases and in accordance with a procedure prescribed by law ... (c) the lawful arrest or detention of a person effected for the purpose of bringing him before the competent legal authority on reasonable suspicion of having committed an offence or when it is reasonably considered necessary to prevent his committing an offence or fleeing after having done so ...

(3) Everyone arrested or detained in accordance with the provisions of paragraph 1(c) of this Article shall be brought promptly before a judge or other officer authorised by law to exercise judicial power and shall be entitled to trial within a reasonable time or to release pending trial. Release may be conditioned by guarantees to appear for trial.

(4) Everyone who is deprived of his liberty by arrest or detention shall be entitled to take proceedings by which the lawfulness of his detention shall be decided speedily by a court and his release ordered if the detention is not lawful.

(5) Everyone who has been the victim of arrest or detention in contravention of the provisions of this Article shall have an enforceable right to compensation.'

If, under the statutory provisions, the right of the plaintiff to be compensated for her unlawful detention was in any way doubtful, Mr Blake submitted that those provisions should be interpreted so as to give effect to the obligation of the United Kingdom under the convention.

Mr Richards resisted this argument. He submitted that there was in this case no ambiguity, no obscurity and no absurdity in the statutory provisions, and there was accordingly no ground upon which recourse could be had to the convention. Even if the convention did apply, Mr Richards submitted that the plaintiff could show no breach of it. She had been lawfully detained for a purpose recognised in art 5(1)(c). She enjoyed the right to trial within a reasonable time or to release pending trial under art 5(3), and there was accordingly no breach on the part of the United Kingdom in that respect. Since there was no detention in contravention of the provisions of art 5 the plaintiff could not lay claim to an enforceable right to compensation.

I can see no answer to Mr Richards' submission. If it is permissible to have recourse to the convention (which in the present case I doubt), I feel bound to conclude that the excessive detention of which the plaintiff complains arose not from the failure of the United Kingdom to afford her the rights to which she was entitled under the convention but from her failure (for whatever reason) to exercise those rights.

In my judgment, the deputy judge was right to strike out the plaintiff's claim against the Home Office, since it was unsustainable in law and the outcome could not be affected by any evidence which might be called.

The claim against the CPS

The deputy judge felt some doubt whether this claim also should not be struck out, but concluded that the claim was not so obviously unsustainable as to make that a proper course. The CPS argue that she was wrong not to strike out this claim also.

Regulation 6 of the 1987 regulations makes it clear that the CPS must bring an accused person before the Crown Court shortly before expiry of a custody time limit, and it may be relieved from complying with that duty only by direction of the Crown Court. The regulation places the onus for performance of this duty squarely on the CPS, which in practice should be well-placed to discharge it. In the present case, for whatever reason, the CPS wholly failed to perform that duty, with the result that the plaintiff spent much longer in prison on remand than she should have done.

The issue is whether the statutory duty imposed on the CPS is a public law duty only, or whether it gives rise to a private law right enforceable by a person injured by breach of such duty and so entitled to recover compensation.

Although novel in the present context, this is a familiar question and there was no issue between the parties as to the principles to be applied. They are to be found in *Hague v Deputy Governor of Parkhurst Prison, Weldon v Home Office* [1991] 3 All ER 733 at 741–742, 747 and 750–752, [1992] 1 AC 58 at 159–161, 167 and 170–173 and *X and ors (minors) v Bedfordshire CC, M (a minor) v Newham London BC, E (a minor) v Dorset CC* [1995] 3 All ER 353 at 364–365, [1995] 2 AC 633 at 731–732. We must study the relevant provisions of the statute and the regulations in order to determine whether Parliament and the Secretary of State intended that anyone injured by failure of the CPS to perform its statutory duty should enjoy a private law right of action sounding in damages. In seeking to understand the intention of Parliament and the Secretary of State, regard must be paid to the object and scope of the provisions, the class (if any) intended to be protected by them, and the means of redress open to a member of such a class if the statutory duty is not performed.

The object of these provisions plainly was to achieve a greater measure of expedition in the prosecution of criminal offences where defendants were remanded in custody to await trial, and (if such expedition were lacking) to ensure that defendants did not languish in prison for excessive periods awaiting trial. The protection of prospective defendants was thus an object of the provisions. When Parliament enacted s 22 of the 1985 Act, it must have expected that custody time limits which the Secretary of State was authorised to set by regulations would be realistic and achievable and would accordingly be achieved (if necessary being extended by order of the court).

It was the 1985 Act which established the CPS, which was intended to be an efficient and highly professional prosecuting service. While the power conferred on the Secretary of State by s 22 was expressed in very broad terms, there is nothing to suggest that Parliament intended to give him power to create new private law rights of action. Regulation 6 of the 1987 regulations makes it plain that the duty of ensuring that a defendant does not spend longer in custody than permitted by any relevant custody time limit is laid on the CPS. It was no doubt assumed, as it was plainly intended, that the CPS would perform its duty. If for any reason it did not, a defendant injured by its failure was doubtless expected to apply for release on bail at once, such application being assured of success.

There is nothing in the 1985 Act or in the 1987 regulations to suggest that either Parliament or the Secretary of State foresaw the present, very unhappy, conjunction of events: failure to arraign the plaintiff before expiry of 112 days; failure by the CPS to perform its duty under reg 6; and failure by the plaintiff to seek release. It cannot, in my opinion, have been intended to confer a private law right of action for damages in such circumstances. Support for this view is to be found in *Elguzouli-Daf v Comr of Police of the Metropolis, McBrearty v Ministry of Defence* [1995] 1 All ER 833, [1995] QB 335.

On this issue I take a different view from that taken, with some hesitation, by the deputy judge. It seems to me plain that these provisions were not intended to confer any private law right on a party injured by the failure of the CPS to perform its duty, and I accordingly conclude that the plaintiff's claim against the CPS must be struck out.

In the result, therefore, I would dismiss the appeal of the plaintiff against the striking out of her claim against the Home Office and would allow the appeal of the CPS against the refusal to strike out the claim against it.

We are not in possession of the full facts concerning this matter, and must accordingly refrain from comment which may be unsound. We do not, for instance, know what if any steps were taken to alert the plaintiff to her rights on remand in custody, or whether she was at that time legally represented. It would, however, be a matter of acute concern if it were the case that the plaintiff had through no fault of her own spent an excessive time in prison on remand, and had no right to compensation for this injury. It may be that there are parties other than the Home Office and the CPS from whom the plaintiff may be entitled to redress. If not, and unless she is the author of her own misfortune, it would seem to me highly unjust if she were denied any compensation for what would, on this hypothesis, be an undoubted injury.

I have had the opportunity of reading in draft the judgment of Mummery LJ, and I fully agree with it.

AULD LJ. I have read in draft the judgments of Lord Bingham CJ and Mummery LJ and I agree with them.

MUMMERY LJ. The governor of Pucklechurch Prison was directed by the Bristol Magistrates' Court in the warrant of commitment:

'... to receive into your custody and (unless the accused is released on bail in the meantime) keep the accused until the accused is delivered in due course of law.'

It was within the jurisdiction of the Bristol Magistrates' Court to give that direction. The governor was bound to comply with the direction unless and until a court gave a contrary direction; eg an order releasing the plaintiff on bail pending the outcome of the trial in the Crown Court. The valid warrant of commitment provides a conclusive answer to the plaintiff's claim of false imprisonment against the Home Office.

The effect of the statutory custody time limit referred to in the warrant was that the Crown Prosecution Service (the CPS) was under a duty to serve a notice in writing under reg 6(1)(a) of the Prosecution of Offences (Custody Time Limits) Regulations 1987, SI 1987/299, not less than five days before the expiry of the time limit and to make arrangements for the plaintiff to be brought before the

Crown Court within the period of two days preceding the expiry of the time limit. Neither the 1987 regulations nor the provisions of the Prosecution of Offences Act 1985 absolved the governor of the prison from his duty to comply with the court's direction in the warrant or varied that duty or conferred on him a power to discharge the plaintiff from custody immediately on or after the expiration of the custody time limit, in the absence of a court order made on the application of the CPS or of the plaintiff.

This case is in contrast to *Moone v Rose* (1869) LR 4 QB 486, where the keeper of a gaol was held liable for the false imprisonment of a person committed to prison for contempt of court. The keeper of the gaol failed to comply with an express imperative statutory duty to discharge that person out of his custody after the expiration of a fixed period ('30 days from the time of his being actually in custody'). He was not, therefore, able to rely on a court direction of the kind given in this case and in *Henderson v Preston* (1888) 21 QBD 362 at 366–367.

There is no dispute that reg 6 imposed specific statutory duties on the CPS, that it failed to perform them and that the plaintiff remained in custody 81 days longer than the custody time limit. This court does not know: (a) why the CPS failed to apply for an extension or to serve the relevant notices or to bring the plaintiff before the Crown Court; or (b) why the plaintiff did not, after mid-August 1994, bring the matter before the Crown Court on an application for bail or before the High Court for judicial review. As this is an application to strike out the plaintiff's claim as disclosing no reasonable cause of action, this court is confined to the facts pleaded in the plaintiff's statement of claim. There has been no application by counsel for the plaintiff to amend the statement of claim.

In those circumstances, the only question for this court is whether, assuming the facts pleaded in the statement of claim to be true, the plaintiff has a reasonably arguable claim in law for damages for breach of statutory duty. There is no allegation of malice, of misfeasance in a public office, or of negligence, on the part of the CPS. The claim is starkly pleaded as one of strict liability for damages for breach of a duty imposed by statute.

It is a question of available remedies. The plaintiff was undoubtedly entitled to remedies in the criminal proceedings (bail) and in judicial review proceedings. The issue is whether she is entitled to an additional remedy against the CPS by way of a civil law claim for damages. It is common ground that it is not enough for the plaintiff simply to show that she has suffered damage in consequence of a breach of duty imposed by statute. The court must be satisfied that, on the true construction of the relevant statutory provisions, a right of action for damages has been created by Parliament. This question is answered by the application of well-established principles stated by Lord Bingham CJ.

As this case concerns the liberty of the subject, it requires the fullest and most anxious consideration. I am, however, unable to accept Mr Blake's submission that a claim in damages lies against the CPS for breach of statutory duty. The statute and the regulations are silent on damages. There are strong indicators against the implied creation of a statutory tort of strict liability in a case such as this: the availability to the plaintiff of other remedies both in the criminal proceedings (bail) and in public law proceedings (habeas corpus and mandamus); the absence of any indication in s 22 of the 1985 Act that the Secretary of State had power to make regulations conferring a private right of action on accused persons; and considerations of the kind relied on by the Court of Appeal in *Elguzouli-Daf v Comr of Police of the Metropolis, McBrearty v Ministry of Defence*

[1995] 1 All ER 833, [1995] QB 335 in concluding that, in the absence of voluntary
assumption of responsibility to a particular defendant in criminal proceedings,
there is no general duty of care owed by the CPS at common law in the conduct
of its prosecution of a defendant and that the CPS is immune from actions for
negligence. As the claims for damages are plainly not maintainable in law, the
plaintiff's proceedings should be struck out in their entirety.

*Plaintiff's appeal dismissed; Crown Prosecution Service's appeal allowed. Leave to
appeal to the House of Lords refused.*

L I Zysman Esq   Barrister.

R v Secretary of State for the Home Department and another, ex parte Hargreaves and others

COURT OF APPEAL, CIVIL DIVISION

HIRST, PETER GIBSON AND PILL LJJ

24, 25 OCTOBER, 20 NOVEMBER 1996

Prison – Release on licence – Home leave – Secretary of State deciding to implement new scheme governing eligibility of prisoners to apply for home leave – Prisoners entitled to apply for home leave after serving one-third of sentence under old scheme but only after having served half their sentence under new scheme – New scheme deferring applicants' earliest date for eligibility by substantial period – Whether inmate compact signed by applicants at beginning of sentence giving rise to legitimate expectation overriding new scheme – Whether decision to apply new policy lawful – Test to be applied.

The three applicants were category C prisoners serving sentences of six, seven and eight years respectively. On admission to prison in 1994 each applicant had been issued with a notice informing him that he could apply for home leave after serving one-third of his sentence. The notice made it clear that the information contained therein applied from 1 October 1992 and that home leave was a privilege. At the same time the applicants each signed an inmate compact under which the prison promised, inter alia, to consider them for home leave when they became eligible and required them to be of good behaviour. In 1995 changes to the system of temporary release of prisoners were introduced under which prisoners were entitled to apply for home leave only when they had served half their sentence, with the aim of improving public safety and increasing public confidence in the administration of justice. As a result of the new rules the earliest date for eligibility of the applicants for home leave was deferred by a substantial period. The applicants applied for judicial review of the Secretary of State's decision to implement the new scheme and the order of the prison governor applying the scheme to them, contending that the change of policy was unlawful because it frustrated a legitimate expectation as to the eligibility for home leave, which had arisen under the former rules of eligibility and was created when the applicants entered into a compact with the prison governor under the former rules. The Divisional Court dismissed their applications, holding, inter alia, that they had failed to establish any clear and unambiguous representation that they would be eligible for home leave after having served one-third of their sentence. The applicants appealed to the Court of Appeal. The issues arose as to (i) the scope of a legitimate expectation when there has been a change of policy (ii) what approach the court should adopt to a decision by the Secretary of State on a matter of substance and (iii) whether there had been any breach of the right to respect for private and family life set out in art 8 of the European Convention for the Protection of Human Rights and Fundamental Rights and Freedoms.

Held – The appeal would be dismissed for the following reasons—

(1) The inmate compact signed by the applicants did not give rise to a legitimate expectation of being considered eligible for home leave after serving one-third of their sentence which could be enforced by judicial review, since the

unfettered discretion conferred on the Secretary of State by statute to change
policy could not be thus restricted. The most a prisoner could legitimately expect
was that his case would be examined individually in the light of whatever policy
the Secretary of State saw fit lawfully to adopt. In any event, the notice and the
compact did not contain a clear and unambiguous representation as to timing of
home leave and therefore did not constitute a proper foundation for the
legitimate expectation for which the applicants contended (see p 409 *j* to 411 *a*,
p 413 *j* to 414 *b*, 415 *a* to *c*, 416 *e g* and p 417 *b*, post); *Findlay v Secretary of State for
the Home Dept* [1984] 3 All ER 801 and dictum of Lord Diplock in *Hughes v Dept of
Health and Social Security, Coy v Dept of Health and Social Security, Jarnell v Dept of the
Environment* [1985] AC 776 at 788 applied.

(2) Since the deferment of eligibility for home leave was a matter of substance
and not of procedure, the court was not required to conduct a balancing exercise
based on fairness and proportionality when deciding the lawfulness of the change
of policy; rather, the correct test was whether the decision to change the policy
was unreasonable in the *Wednesbury* sense (see p 411 *c* to *f* h *j*, p 412 *h j*, p 415 *a b*,
p 416 *b* to *e h* and p 417 *b*, post); *Associated Provincial Picture Houses Ltd v
Wednesbury Corp* [1947] 2 All ER 680 applied; dictum of Sedley J in *R v Ministry of
Agriculture Fisheries and Food, ex p Hamble (Offshore) Fisheries Ltd* [1995] 2 All ER 714
at 731, 735 overruled.

(3) There was no infringement of the principles contained in art 8 of the
convention because the fundamental interference with regard to family life was
brought about by the lawful sentences of the court. Moreover, in applying the
exceptions stipulated in art 8, it was clear that the considerations of public
confidence and public safety advanced by the Secretary of State fell within their
scope and also met the common law criteria that a pressing social need had to be
shown and that the restrictions should be no more than was proportionate to the
legitimate aim pursued (see p 413 *e f*, p 415 *a b*, p 416 *e* and p 417 *b*, post); dictum
of Lord Keith in *Derbyshire CC v Times Newspapers Ltd* [1993] 1 All ER 1011 at 1020
applied.

(4) In the circumstances the Secretary of State had not acted unreasonably in
restricting home leave to prisoners who had served half their sentence; and in
reaching his decision to change the policy he had clearly taken into account all the
relevant considerations (see p 414 *c* to *e g h*, p 415 *a b*, p 416 *e* and p 417 *b*, post).

Notes

For the Secretary of State's powers and jurisdiction with respect to prisons and
his powers to release prisoners on licence, see 37 *Halsbury's Laws* (4th edn)
paras 1105, 1189–1190.

Cases referred to in judgments

Associated Provincial Picture Houses Ltd v Wednesbury Corp [1947] 2 All ER 680,
[1948] 1 KB 223, CA.
Brind v Secretary of State for the Home Dept [1991] 1 All ER 720, [1991] 1 AC 696,
[1991] 2 WLR 588, HL.
Council of Civil Service Unions v Minister for the Civil Service [1984] 3 All ER 935,
[1985] AC 374, [1984] 3 WLR 1174, HL.
Derbyshire CC v Times Newspapers Ltd [1993] 1 All ER 1011, [1993] AC 534, [1993] 2
WLR 449, HL.
Findlay v Secretary of State for the Home Dept [1984] 3 All ER 801, [1985] AC 318,
[1984] 3 WLR 1159, HL.

a *Hughes v Dept of Health and Social Security, Coy v Dept of Health and Social Security, Jarnell v Dept of the Environment* [1985] AC 776, [1985] 2 WLR 866, HL.

McCotter v UK (1993) 15 EHRR CD98, E Com HR.

R v Board of Inland Revenue, ex p MFK Underwriting Agencies Ltd [1990] 1 All ER 91, [1990] 1 WLR 1545, DC.

R v Devon CC, ex p Baker, R v Durham CC, ex p Curtis [1995] 1 All ER 73, CA.

b *R v Ministry of Agriculture Fisheries and Food, ex p Hamble (Offshore) Fisheries Ltd* [1995] 2 All ER 714.

R v Panel on Take-overs and Mergers, ex p Guinness plc [1989] 1 All ER 509, [1990] 1 QB 146, [1989] 2 WLR 863, CA.

X v UK (1982) 30 DR 113, E Com HR.

c **Cases also cited or referred to in skeleton arguments**

A-G v Guardian Newspapers Ltd (No 2) [1988] 3 All ER 545, [1990] 1 AC 109, HL.

Bugdaycay v Secretary of State for the Home Dept [1987] 1 All ER 940, [1987] AC 514, HL.

KD (a minor) (ward: termination of access), Re [1988] 1 All ER 577, [1988] AC 806, HL.

d *Liverpool Taxi Owners' Association, Re* [1972] 2 All ER 589, sub nom *R v Liverpool Corp, ex p Liverpool Taxi Fleet Operators' Association* [1972] 2 QB 299, CA.

O'Reilly v Mackman [1982] 3 All ER 1124, [1983] 2 AC 237, HL.

Preston v IRC [1985] 2 All ER 327, [1985] AC 835, HL.

R v Governors of Haberdashers' Aske's Hatcham College Trust, ex p Tyrell (10 October 1994, unreported), QBD.

e *R v IRC, ex p Unilever plc* [1996] STC 681.

R v Lord Chancellor, ex p Hibbit & Saunders (a firm) (1993) Times, 12 March, DC.

R v Mid Glamorgan Family Health Services Authority, ex p Martin [1995] 1 All ER 356, [1995] 1 WLR 110, CA.

f *R v Ministry of Defence, ex p Smith* [1996] 1 All ER 257, [1996] QB 517, CA.

R v Secretary of State for Health, ex p US Tobacco International Inc [1992] 1 All ER 212, [1992] QB 353, DC.

R v Secretary of State for the Home Dept, ex p Khan [1985] 1 All ER 40, [1984] 1 WLR 1337, CA.

R v Secretary of State for the Home Dept, ex p McQuillan [1995] 4 All ER 400.

g *R v Secretary of State for the Home Dept, ex p Ruddock* [1987] 2 All ER 518, [1987] 1 WLR 1482.

R v Secretary of State for Transport, ex p Richmond upon Thames London BC [1994] 1 All ER 577, [1994] 1 WLR 74.

Rantzen v Mirror Group Newspapers (1986) Ltd [1993] 4 All ER 975, [1994] QB 670, *h* CA.

W v Egdell [1990] 1 All ER 835, [1990] Ch 359, CA.

Appeal

The applicants, Craig Hargeaves, Kevin Briggs and Brendan Green, appealed *j* with the leave of Hobhouse LJ granted on 4 March 1996 from the decision of the Queen's Bench Divisional Court (Kennedy LJ and McCullough J) ([1996] COD 168) on 25 July 1995 dismissing their applications for judicial review by way of orders of certiorari to quash the decision of the first respondent, the Secretary of State for the Home Department, to implement a new prison home leave scheme under r 6 of the Prison Rules 1964, SI 1964/388, as substituted by the Prison (Amendment) Rules 1995, SI 1995/983, and the order of the second respondent, the Governor of HM Prison Risley, which applied the new scheme to each of the applicants. The facts are set out in the judgment of Hirst LJ.

Patrick Elias QC and *Terence Gallivan* (instructed by *Reece Davis Wood Wild & Co*, Birmingham) for the applicants.
Michael Beloff QC and *Steven Kovats* (instructed by the *Treasury Solicitor*) for the respondents.

Cur adv vult

20 November 1996. The following judgments were delivered.

HIRST LJ.

Introduction
    This is an appeal from the decision of the Divisional Court (Kennedy LJ and McCullough J) ([1996] COD 168) to dismiss the applications by the appellants, Craig Hargreaves, Kevin Briggs and Brendan Green (the applicants), for judicial review of two related decisions, namely: (i) a decision by the Secretary of State of the Home Department to implement a new scheme governing the eligibility of prisoners to apply for home leave; and (ii) the order of the Governor of HM Prison Risley which applied the new scheme to each of the applicants.
    At all material times the three applicants were category C prisoners serving their sentences at Risley.
    Prior to the implementation of the new system, they would have been entitled to apply for home leave after serving one-third of their sentence. Under the new scheme they were entitled to apply only after having served half their sentence. Each applicant's case in a nutshell is that as a result of the new policy, which deferred his earliest date for eligibility by a substantial period, he was adversely affected in that he had been deprived of the legitimate expectation that he would be considered eligible for home leave after he had served one-third of his sentence; each relied on the terms of a notice received from the prison authorities at the time when he began to serve his sentence and also on the terms of the compact which he entered into with the prison governor at the same time. The new rules did contain some transitional provisions, but the applicants did not benefit from these: essentially their case is that if these changes were to have been made they should have been implemented in such a way as to protect their legitimate expectations, and honour the terms of the compact.

The statutory background
    Section 47(1) and (5) of the Prison Act 1952, under the heading 'Rules for the management of prisons', provides:

    '(1) The Secretary of State may make rules for the regulation and management of prisons, remand centres, detention centres and youth custody centres respectively, and for the classification, treatment, employment, discipline and control of persons required to be detained therein ...
    (5) Rules made under this Section may provide for the temporary release of persons detained in a prison, remand centre, youth custody centre, or detention centre, not being persons committed in custody for trial before the

a Crown Court or recommitted to be sentenced or otherwise dealt with by the Crown Court or remanded in custody by any court.'

Rule 6 of the Prison Rules 1964, SI 1964/388, under the heading 'Temporary release', provided:

b '(1) A prisoner to whom this Rule applies may be temporarily released for any period or periods and subject to any conditions.

(2) A prisoner may be temporarily released under this Rule for any special purpose or to enable him to engage in employment, to receive instruction or training or to assist him in his transition from prison life to freedom.

(3) A prisoner released under this Rule may be recalled to prison at any time whether the conditions of his release have been broken or not.

c (4) This Rule applies to prisoners other than persons committed in custody for trial or to be sentenced or otherwise dealt with before or by the Crown Court or remanded in custody by any court.'

The change was introduced by the Prison (Amendment) Rules 1995, SI 1995/983, which by r 2 substituted for the previous rule the following under the same
d heading 'Temporary release':

'**6.**—(1) The Secretary of State may, in accordance with the other provisions of this rule, release temporarily a prisoner to whom this rule applies.

(2) A prisoner may be released under this rule for any period or periods
e and subject to any conditions.

(3) A prisoner may only be released under this rule ... (h) to assist him in maintaining family ties or in his transition from prison life to freedom ...

(4) A prisoner shall not be released under this rule unless the Secretary of State is satisfied that there would not be an unacceptable risk of his
f committing offences whilst released or otherwise of his failing to comply with any condition upon which he is released.

(5) The Secretary of State shall not release under this rule a prisoner serving a sentence of imprisonment if, having regard to: (a) the period or proportion of his sentence which the prisoner has served; and (b) the frequency with which the prisoner has been granted temporary release
g under this rule, the Secretary of State is of the opinion that the release of the prisoner would be likely to undermine public confidence in the administration of justice ...'

These changes were introduced as a result of the recommendations of a Prison Service Working Group which was set up by the Secretary of State as a result of
h problems which had come to his attention arising out of the operation of home leave, namely absconding and the commission of offences by some prisoners while on home leave, which had attracted considerable publicity, to the detriment of public confidence in the criminal justice system.

j *The prisoners' individual circumstances*

On 18 February 1994 Hargreaves was sentenced to imprisonment for six years for assault with intent to rob and motoring offences; on 17 June 1994 Briggs was sentenced to seven years' imprisonment for conspiracy to supply cannabis, and on 14 July 1994 Green was sentenced to eight years' imprisonment for a like offence.

As a result of the new rules, Hargreaves' earliest date for application was deferred from 12 April 1995 to 12 April 1996, Briggs' from 7 July 1995 to 2 September 1996 and Green's from 26 November 1995 to 26 February 1997.

The notice to prisoners and the compact

On admission to HM Prison Risley each applicant was issued with a Notice to Prisoners (the notice) entitled 'Home leave', which provided:

'You may be eligible to ask for Home Leave. The following information applies from 1 October 1992: Short home leave is 2 days excluding travel time. Long home leave is 5 days excluding travel time. You can ask for home leave only if you are in one of these groups ... Category C (or equivalent) sentenced to 2 years of more. You can apply for short home leave after serving one-third of the total term of sentenced imprisonment, and at 6-monthly intervals after that. You can apply for long home leave 2 months before your release date ...

REMEMBER: Home leave is a privilege for sentenced prisoners under Prison Rule 6. Its purpose is to help restore self-confidence by placing trust in you under conditions of freedom, and to help you to re-adjust to life outside prison by giving you the opportunity to maintain links with family and friends. Long home leave offers in addition the chance to contact prospective employers and make firm plans for release.'

At the same time each applicant was invited to sign and did sign a compact. Such compacts were the subject matter of a recommendation of Lord Woolf's 1991 report (see *Report of an Inquiry into Prison Disturbances April 1990* (Cm 1456)), and were current in 61 prison institutions by mid-1994.

The inmate compact offered by HM Prison Risley, and signed by each applicant and by a representative of the governor, provided, inter alia, as follows:

'THE PRISON PROMISES TO PROVIDE

A. STANDARD REQUIREMENTS ... Throughcare, and the involvement of your family in your resettlement plans if you wish, including consideration for Home Leave when you become eligible ...

B. OPTIONAL ENHANCEMENTS ... The opportunity to apply for temporary release or for home leave over and above the minimum facility (e g CJA Home Leave as stated in Notice to Prisoners 37/93) ...'

There followed a number of matters to which the prisoner was expected to commit himself, such as treating staff with respect, and never using violence.

The parliamentary statement

On 18 November 1994 the Home Secretary announced in Parliament the proposed changes relating to temporary release of prisoners as follows, so far as relevant:

'... I have been conducting a thorough review of the system of leave from prisons. In too many cases, the system has been abused. I have come to the conclusion that it needs to be tightened up. I can announce to the House today changes in the system that are likely to lead to a reduction of about 40 per cent. in the amount of leave granted. I have placed full details of the new arrangements in the Library. The new system will have a number of important features. First, with immediate effect, a much more rigorous risk a assessment will be carried out before any temporary release is permitted. The safety of the public must be paramount. Secondly, there will be no automatic right to temporary release, which will be permitted only in certain carefully prescribed circumstances: first, leave on specified compassionate grounds; secondly, leave towards the end of a sentence to assist prisoners in reintegrating into the community; and finally leave for training, education or

b work experience designed to help in prisoner rehabilitation. That form of leave will not be available to the most dangerous prisoners—those in category A or B prisons—and will be considered only when suitable courses are not available within the prison. My longer-term objective will be to restrict releases in that category to an absolute minimum by providing more facilities inside prison. Thirdly, I am very disturbed by the number of

c occasions on which prisoners abscond when on temporary release. I have therefore decided to introduce a new offence designed to make breaches of licence while on temporary prison leave a criminal offence for the first time. Prison governors will have an overriding duty, in considering any release, not only to ensure the safety of the public but to maintain public confidence in the prison system. The necessary training for the full introduction of the

d new arrangements will be completed early next year. I intend to review the new system by the end of next year to see whether any further changes are needed.' (See 250 HC Official Report (6th series) col 244.)

A similar statement was made on 23 May 1995 by Baroness Blatch, the Minister
e of State, Home Office, in the House of Lords as follows:

'A working group was established in June 1993 to review the operation of the home leave and temporary release schemes. It included representatives from the police and probation services, as well as from a broad range of penal

f affairs groups. Those groups included Victim Support, the Prison Reform Trust and the Federation of Prisoner Family Support Groups. The working group recognised that, since the report of Lord Justice Woolf some two years earlier, the profile of home leave and temporary release had changed significantly. There had been public concern about the operation of both schemes following a number of serious failures where prisoners had

g committed serious and violent offences, including murder and armed robbery, while released temporarily. In addition, the working group recognised the concerns of victims that prisoners were being granted temporary release only a short time after being sentenced. The noble Lord, Lord Rodgers of Quarry Bank, asked whether the Government had

h abandoned the principles of the Woolf Report. Again, I say to the noble Lord that the Government recognise—as, indeed, did Lord Justice Woolf in his report—the benefits that the temporary release of prisoners can provide. However, it is important that it should be within a clear framework, with the necessary safeguards in place to ensure public safety. The working group established in response to the Woolf Report recommended just such a

j scheme, which we have now implemented. The report of the working group was presented to my right honourable friend the Home Secretary in October last year. The report included 47 recommendations. They took full account of the needs of both the public and prisoners and their families, the need to maintain good order and security in prisons and, most importantly, public safety. It was in the light of that report that my right honourable

friend made his announcement last November about the new system of
release on temporary licence. That came into effect on 25th April. The *a*
Government believe that there are important benefits to be gained in
releasing suitable prisoners for short periods as part of the process of
preparing for their eventual return to the community. Evidence shows that
prisoners who have a job to go to, a secure family environment and skills
developed by training or education are less likely to re-offend than those *b*
released "cold" into the community. Testing prisoners in controlled and
monitored circumstances therefore contributes to public safety. The
benefits of releasing prisoners for short periods in that way must, however,
be weighed against any potential threat that prisoners who have been
temporarily released may pose to the public and against the need to preserve
public confidence that prisoners who have been sentenced to a term of *c*
imprisonment will not be released back on to the streets shortly after they
have been sentenced. The new scheme of release on temporary licence is
more sharply focused than its predecessors. Prisoners will in future be
released only for precisely defined and specific purposes. Prisoners will
continue to be eligible to be temporarily released for justifiable purposes *d*
such as education and training leading to a recognised qualification where
that cannot be provided in prison. Any such release would be allowed only
where programmed into a prisoner's sentence plan and specifically designed
to help the prisoner to lead a law-abiding and useful life upon release. It is
unacceptable, however, for prisoners to be released for purposes which are
purely social or recreational. That will no longer be allowed. The new *e*
system will also continue to allow prisoners to be considered for temporary
release in urgent and compelling compassionate circumstances or towards
the end of their time in custody to maintain their family ties or re-establish
links with the community in preparation for their return to the community.
One of the primary purposes of the new scheme must be to ensure that the *f*
public are not placed at any risk by the unacceptable release of prisoners who
pose a threat to public safety. The new scheme includes a mandatory and
stringent risk assessment carried out in collaboration with the Police and
Probation Services. Prison governors have a duty, in considering any
release, not only to ensure the safety of the public but also to maintain public
confidence in the administration of justice. Prisoners should not be released *g*
too early after sentencing, nor too frequently. To do so would undermine
the purpose of imprisonment. Under the new scheme therefore, prisoners
will have to serve longer in prison before applications for release on licence
will be considered.' (See 564 HL Official Report (5th series) cols 1027–1028.)

h

The evidence

Affidavits were sworn on behalf of the Secretary of State by Irving Noyes Jones,
who is a higher executive officer in the Directorate of Programmes Policy Group,
Prison Service Headquarters, and by Audrey Wickington, a grade 7 administrator
in the same directorate. Mr Jones testified as follows: *j*

'The Secretary of State became concerned that the system was being
abused and that it needed to be tightened up. He considered that steps
needed to be taken to restore public confidence in the penal system ... The
Secretary of State was aware that his proposed changes would lead to

a
deferment of the date at which some serving prisoners became eligible for consideration for resettlement licence. The Secretary of State considered what, if any, transitional provision should be made. He decided that prisoners who had already successfully completed a period of home leave and who were within 12 months of their parole eligibility date should continue to be eligible to apply for temporary release on a resettlement

b
licence. However, bearing in mind the reasons which had prompted the changes, he decided that other existing prisoners sentenced on or after 1 October 1992 who were serving determinate sentences of four years or more should be fully subject to the new criteria.'

Audrey Wickington testified as follows:

c
'... 6. As part of its remit, the Working Group considered the eligibility criteria for prisoners being granted home leave. The Working Group noted that eligibility was based on sentence length and the personal security classification of prisoners. They also noted that for certain classes of prisoner who had been sentenced before the implementation of the Criminal Justice

d
Act 1991, their eligibility to be considered for home leave was linked to their parole eligibility date. They concluded that this was an important goal for prisoners serving longer sentences and a fundamental aspect of sentence planning.   7.   The Working Group also noted that following the implementation of the Criminal Justice Act 1991 there had been introduced new Home Leave Eligibility Dates ("HLEDs") for those prisoners sentenced

e
on or after 1 October 1992. The Working Group recognised that this had led to the system becoming increasingly complicated to operate and that there had been a number of serious home leave failures which had given rise to public concern. 8. The Working Group concluded that it was imperative to devise a simple set of fair but firm criteria covering release on temporary

f
licence which would lead to better decision making and more confidence that issues of public safety were properly addressed.   Recognising the principles introduced by the Criminal Justice Act 1991 for the sentencing of offenders, the Working Group concluded that the criteria for determining the eligibility for the grant of resettlement licence needed to differ for

g
determinate offenders sentenced to four years or more from those given shorter sentences of imprisonment. The Working Group also concluded that release on resettlement licence should remain linked to the prisoner's parole eligibility date and for prisoners serving four years or more should not take place before one-half of a prisoner's sentence expiry date. 9. The unanimous recommendations of the Working Group were submitted in a

h
Report to the Secretary of State for the Home Department in October 1994. On the basis of the considerations set out in that Report, the Home Secretary accepted the Working Group's recommendation that for determinate sentence prisoners serving four years or more any period of release on resettlement licence should be not earlier than one half of the sentence

j
expiry date. This coincides with the parole eligibility date set by the Criminal Justice Act 1991. 10. In November 1994 the Home Secretary announced to Parliament new arrangements, based on the recommendations made in the Working Group's report, for the release of prisoners on temporary licence to replace the existing home leave and temporary release schemes. The purpose of the new arrangements was to improve public safety and increase

public confidence in the administration of justice by ensuring that prisoners
were released on temporary licence for precisely defined and specific
purposes, justifiable as part of their rehabilitative process ... 13. The Home
Secretary also considered the effect which the new arrangements would
have on the eligibility of existing prisoners to be granted release on
temporary licence. He concluded that it would be appropriate to make
transitional arrangements for certain classes and categories of prisoners
where this would not compromise public safety and the need to maintain
public confidence in the administration of justice. 14. Accordingly, the
Home Secretary concluded that those prisoners sentenced to four years or
more before the implementation of the Criminal Justice Act 1991 should be
allowed to retain their eligibility for resettlement licence at the point at
which they would become eligible for release on parole licence. Similarly,
the Home Secretary concluded that any prisoners sentenced on or after 1
October 1992 who had been through a risk assessment and had successfully
completed a period of home leave should continue to remain eligible for
resettlement licence if they were within 12 months of their parole eligibility
date. 15. However, the Home Secretary though mindful of the expectations
of other existing prisoners, concluded that the public interest which
prompted the change of policy outweighed extending the transitional
arrangements to them. The Home Secretary also took the view that it
would be inconsistent with the purpose of the new policy to require the new
tighter arrangements to apply to only those prisoners sentenced after the
new system had come into effect. The public disquiet about the number of
serious home leave failures and the release of prisoners too early and too
frequently in sentence had been in relation to the existing prison population.
There were no grounds for believing that only those prisoners sentenced
after the implementation of the new system posed a greater degree of risk to
public safety ...'

On behalf of the applicants, affidavits were sworn by Mr Paul Francis
Cavadino, chairman of the Penal Affairs Consortium, and Mr Stephen Shaw,
director of the Prison Reform Trust.

Mr Cavadino testified as follows:

'... 4. The respondents argue that there was "an overriding public interest"
which required the reduction in home leave opportunities to be applied
retrospectively to existing prisoners. Two specific arguments are advanced
in this connection.

(a) *Public safety*

5. First, the respondents argue that: "There had been a number of serious
home leave failures which had given rise to public concern". (This is true,
and is a reference to a small number of cases in which serious offences of
violence or sexual offences were committed by prisoners on home leave). It
is therefore argued that there was a need for criteria which would produce
"more confidence that issues of public safety were being addressed".
However, before April 1995 this concern had already been specifically
addressed by rigorous "risk assessment" procedures which had been
developed in response to concern about home leave failures. Circular
instruction 43/92 contained detailed guidance for governors on risk
assessment for prisoners being considered for home leave. This advised

governors on specific issues which they should consider when assessing the level of risk, relating to the prisoner's criminal history, home circumstances, the attitude of the local community, behaviour on any previous home leaves and temporary releases, behaviour in prison, and other specific areas of concern. A subsequent instruction issued in November 1994 (70/1994) set out revised criteria which governors should consider before granting temporary release. This tightened up the risk assessment procedure by more explicit and rigorous criteria (eg requiring governors to assess whether the prisoner has "tackled his offending behaviour in a positive and successful way", for example by participating in programmes designed to change offending behaviour); by instructing governors to contact the relevant police force well in advance and to take into account any views they expressed; by specifying that the probation service should also be involved in the assessment; and by providing that the views of known victims should be sought in the case of violent or sexual offenders. 6. Tight risk assessment is the most logical response to concern about the commission of serious offences against the person by prisoners on home leave: this would not normally involve restricting home leave opportunities for non-violent offenders. The further restrictions of April 1995, which excluded the applicants from consideration for home leave, were changes in the point in the sentence at which they would become eligible for consideration. These latter changes rule out the possibility of home leave for the applicants until a later point in the sentence whether or not they would have passed the risk assessment and have been judged safe for release. Unlike the earlier changes in risk assessment, therefore, the changes of April 1995 do not directly relate to public safety.

(b) *Public disquiet about too early or too frequent home leave*

7. Secondly, the respondents argue that the changes were needed because of "public disquiet about ... the release of prisoners too early and too frequently in sentence". This is an additional and separate point, as it refers to a suggested public feeling that prisoners should not receive temporary release early or frequently even if they do not threaten public safety. However, this particular concern had not normally been expressed in relation to home leave for long term prisoners serving sentences of four years or more, who under the previous rules had to serve one-third of their sentences before becoming eligible for home leave. It arose in most cases in connection with media publicity for a small number of high profile cases in which the use of temporary release other than home leave, at an earlier point in the sentence than home leave as such could be used, had resulted in prisoners being temporarily released after very short periods of weeks or months in custody. I personally favour opportunities for family contact by means of temporary release from an early stage in the sentence. However, this issue has no direct bearing on the separate issue of whether the home leave eligibility of longer term prisoners should arise after one-third or one-half of the sentence. 8. Therefore, neither of the two specific arguments advanced for "an overriding public interest" are valid arguments for altering the point of eligibility for home leave retrospectively from one-third to one-half of the sentence in the case of the applicants or other prisoners in their position. 9. Moreover, any argument for an "overriding public interest" is even weaker when the respondents' arguments are set against the

following countervailing considerations which also relate to the public interest: (i) The reduction of opportunities for family contact increases the risk of break-up of families during a sentence. This is relevant to the public interest in two respects. The first is society's interest in promoting the stability of families. The second is that family break-up can increase the likelihood of reoffending: the report of the Prison Service working group on home leave referred to research in the USA which has suggested that a prisoner without family support is six times more likely to reoffend in the first year after release than one who has maintained close family ties. (ii) The longer the period of time without home leave, the greater the likelihood of institutionalisation of the prisoner. (iii) More frequent opportunities for home leave and family contact reduce tension in prisons and provide a powerful incentive for good behaviour by prisoners. (iv) The applicants and others in their position had signed prison compacts promising to provide *inter alia* consideration for home leave at the then applicable date of eligibility. It is in the public interest that a service which seeks to alter offenders' attitudes and behaviour in the direction of probity, honesty and honourable dealing should itself be seen to honour its promises. 10. In my view, therefore, the respondents' arguments of "overriding public interest" are weak, and certainly insufficient to outweigh the legitimate expectations of the prisoners concerned.'

Mr Stephen Shaw, director of the Prison Reform Trust, testified to like effect.

There was also a considerable body of evidence, not only from the applicants themselves, but also from others in the form of letters, which demonstrated (as is not in any way in dispute) the severely traumatic effect upon the applicants and upon other prisoners in the same predicament of the change of policy, which was promulgated in a notice to prisoners dated 20 April 1995.

The Divisional Court judgment

The Divisional Court decided that the applicants had failed to establish any clear and unambiguous representation that they would be eligible for home leave after having served one-third of their sentence, and that their legitimate expectation was no more than that their applications would be decided by reference to the criteria current at the time the application was made. In reaching this conclusion they placed strong reliance on the principles laid down by the House of Lords in *Findlay v Secretary of State for the Home Dept* [1984] 3 All ER 801, [1985] AC 318. They rejected a submission that, while giving a margin of appreciation to the Secretary of State, the court should conduct a balancing exercise based on considerations of fairness and proportionality, and that the proper test is not one based upon the *Wednesbury* principle (see *Associated Provincial Picture Houses Ltd v Wednesbury Corp* [1947] 2 All ER 680 [1948] 1 KB 223) but upon whether the Secretary of State had succeeded in showing sufficient countervailing considerations of public interest to justify his failure to give the applicants the benefit of the transitional provisions. Finally, they held that there was no reason to conclude that what had been done in the present case was in breach of the principles contained in art 8 of the European Convention for the Protection of Human Rights and Fundamental Freedoms (Rome, 4 November 1950; TS 71 (1953); Cmd 8969).

The issues

a   The questions we have to decide are therefore: (1) what is the meaning of the notice and of the compact; (2) what as a matter of principle in the light of *Findlay's* case is the general scope of a legitimate expectation when, in circumstances like the present, there is a change of policy; (3) what approach should the court adopt as a matter of principle to a decision by the Secretary of State on a matter of

b   substance such as the present one. Should it be by reference to the *Wednesbury* test, or by means of the proposed balancing exercise; (4) was there any departure here from the principles contained in art 8.

Since questions (2), (3) and (4) all raise matters of general principle, while question (1) relates simply and solely to the facts of the present case, I shall deal with the former first.

c
The general scope of legitimate expectation when there has been a change of policy

In *Findlay's* case the Home Secretary had decided in 1983 to change the policy for release of prisoners on parole in relation to certain classes of serious offenders, viz for drug traffickers and violent offenders sentenced to more than five years

d   imprisonment, by deferment of parole until the final months of their sentence, and for certain categories of murderers by deferment until they had served at least 20 years of their life sentence. Four prisoners, two of whom were serving long determinate sentences, and two of whom were lifers, sought judicial review of the decision on a number of grounds, the relevant one for present purposes being that they had been deprived of their legitimate expectations. They were

e   represented by Mr Stephen Sedley QC. Their applications failed, and Lord Scarman (with whom the other members of the Appellate Committee agreed) stated ([1984] 3 All ER 801 at 829–830, [1985] AC 318 at 337–338):

'Legitimate expectation. In the cases of Findlay and Matthews, both of whom received determinate sentences, counsel for the applicants did not

f   suggest that the statute gave rise to any greater expectation than that their cases would be considered on their becoming eligible for parole. Their cases have been considered and will continue to be considered under the new policy. Unless, therefore, the policy is unlawful (which I have held it is not), this argument avails them nothing. The cases, however, of Hogben and

g   Honeyman, each of whom is serving a life sentence, raise issues other than the lawfulness of the policy and I defer my consideration of them until a later stage ... I turn now to the special point taken on behalf of Hogben and Honeyman, namely that it was unlawful to apply the new policy to them. The post-sentence history of these two applicants, each of whom is serving a life sentence, I have already summarised. They had good reason under the

h   practice which prevailed before the adoption of the new policy to expect release much earlier than became likely after its adoption. The doctrine of legitimate expectation has an important place in the developing law of judicial review. It is, however, not necessary to explore the doctrine in this case, it is enough merely to note that a legitimate expectation can provide a

j   sufficient interest to enable one who cannot point to the existence of a substantive right to obtain the leave of the court to apply for judicial review. These two applicants obtained leave. But their submission goes further. It is said that the refusal to except them from the new policy was an unlawful act on the part of the Secretary of State in that his decision frustrated their expectation. But what was their *legitimate* expectation? Given the substance

and purpose of the legislative provisions governing parole, the most that a
convicted prisoner can legitimately expect is that his case will be examined
individually in the light of whatever policy the Secretary of State sees fit to
adopt, provided always that the adopted policy is a lawful exercise of the
discretion conferred upon him by the statute. Any other view would entail
the conclusion that the unfettered discretion conferred by the statute upon
the minister can in some cases be restricted so as to hamper, or even to
prevent, changes of policy. Bearing in mind the complexity of the issues
which the Secretary of State has to consider and the importance of the public
interest in the administration of parole, I cannot think that Parliament
intended the discretion to be restricted in this way.' (Lord Scarman's
emphasis.)

Mr Elias submitted that *Findlay's* case is distinguishable on the footing that it
was concerned not with when but with whether the prisoners should be granted
parole, in other words that it dealt with eligibility for parole and not with timing;
and that in any event the second passage quoted above was referable only to the
two lifers and not of general application.

I am unable to accept these submissions for a number of reasons. First, it is
clear that timing, and the very severe impact of the deferment of parole on the
prisoners' morale, was in the forefront of Mr Sedley's argument (see [1985] AC
318 at 324, 325). Secondly, when considering eligibility for parole, timing is
inevitably one of the main criteria, and was in fact the very criterion which was
changed under the new policy adopted in 1983. Thirdly, the second passage in
Lord Scarman's speech with its reference to 'the most that *a convicted prisoner* can
legitimately expect' (my emphasis) is clearly of general application to all the
prisoners affected by the 1983 change of policy including of course a number on
determinate sentences.

On this interpretation, the present case (deferment of the earliest date of
eligibility for making an application for home leave) and *Findlay's* case (deferment
of the earliest date of eligibility for parole) are in my judgment indistinguishable,
and consequently I think that Mr Beloff was right in his submission that *Findlay's*
case is dispositive of the present appeal, irrespective of the answer to the question
of the construction of the notice and the compact.

This conclusion is strongly reinforced by the following passage from the
leading speech of Lord Diplock in *Hughes v Dept of Health and Social Security, Coy v
Dept of Health and Social Security, Jarnell v Dept of the Environment* [1985] AC 776 at
788, which concerned a change of policy as to the retirement dates of certain
classes of civil servant:

'But this remains the case only so long as the departmental circular
announcing that administrative policy to the employees affected by it
remains in force. Administrative policies may change with changing
circumstances, including changes in the political complexion of
governments. The liberty to make such changes is something that is
inherent in our constitutional form of government. When a change in
administrative policy takes place and is communicated in a departmental
circular to, among others, those employees in the category whose age at
which they would be compulsorily retired was stated in a previous circular
to be a higher age than 60 years, any reasonable expectations that may have
been aroused in them by any previous circular are destroyed and are

a replaced by such other reasonable expectations as to the earliest date at which they can be compelled to retire if the administrative policy announced in the new circular is applied to them.'

The proper approach for the court to the Secretary of State's decision

b Mr Elias's argument in support of the balancing exercise to be conducted by the court was based entirely on the decision of Sedley J in *R v Ministry of Agriculture Fisheries and Food, ex p Hamble (Offshore) Fisheries Ltd* [1995] 2 All ER 714. The case concerned the judicial review of a decision of the minister (whereby he declared a moratorium on the permitted transfer of certain fishing licences), and was eventually resolved in the minister's favour. However, in the

c course of his judgment Sedley J (at 731) propounded a test which Mr Elias submits was correct, viz:

'These considerations, I think, bring one closer to some conceptual understanding of what makes an expectation legitimate. Legitimacy in this sense is not an absolute. It is a function of expectations induced by

d government and of policy considerations which militate against their fulfilment. The balance must in the first instance be for the policy-maker to strike; but if the outcome is challenged by way of judicial review, I do not consider that the court's criterion is the bare rationality of the policy-maker's conclusion. While policy is for the policy-maker alone, the fairness of his or her decision not to accommodate reasonable expectations which the policy

e will thwart remains the court's concern (as of course does the lawfulness of the policy). To postulate this is not to place the judge in the seat of the minister. As the foregoing citations explain, it is the court's task to recognise the constitutional importance of ministerial freedom to formulate and to reformulate policy; but it is equally the court's duty to protect the interests

f of those individuals whose expectation of different treatment has a legitimacy which in fairness outtops the policy choice which threatens to frustrate it.'

Later he asked the rhetorical question whether the minister's decision was fair, and proceeded (at 735):

g 'This, as I have held, while initially a question for the minister is ultimately a question for the court. But, in answering the question, the minister's policy objectives and reasoning form as important an element of the forensic exercise as do the potency and reasonableness of the applicant's expectations.'

h Sedley J cited a number of authorities, but they all dealt with alleged procedural irregularities on the part of a minister, on which, as is common ground, it is appropriate for the court to conduct an inquiry into the fairness of the procedure followed. But in no previous case has this been extended to decisions on matters of substance such as the present case, and indeed a

j distinction has frequently been drawn between the two, as for example in *R v Panel on Take-overs and Mergers, ex p Guinness plc* [1989] 1 All ER 509, [1990] 1 QB 146, which concerned the judicial review of a procedural ruling by the take-over panel not to adjourn certain proceedings affecting Guinness.

Lloyd LJ stated ([1989] 1 All ER 509 at 531, [1990] 1 QB 146 at 183):

'In the first place the question whether we are entitled to intervene at all is not to be answered, as counsel for the panel argued, by reference to *Wednesbury* unreasonableness (see *Associated Provincial Picture Houses Ltd v Wednesbury Corp* [1947] 2 All ER 680, [1948] 1 KB 223). It is not a question whether, in the language of Lord Diplock, quoted by Watkins LJ in the Divisional Court, the decision to hold the hearing on 2 September was: "so outrageous in its defiance of logic or of accepted moral standards that no sensible person who had applied his mind to the question to be decided could have arrived at it" (see *Council of Civil Service Unions v Minister for the Civil Service* [1984] 3 All ER 935 at 951, [1985] AC 374 at 410). Rather, the question has to be decided in accordance with the principles of fair procedure which have been developed over the years, and of which the courts are the author and sole judge. These principles, which apply as well to administrative as judicial tribunals, are known compendiously (if misleadingly) as the rules of natural justice. Counsel for the panel argued that the correct test is *Wednesbury* unreasonableness, because there could, he said, be no criticism of the way in which the panel reached its decision on 25 August. It is the substance of that decision, viz the decision not to adjourn the hearing fixed for 2 September, which is in issue. I cannot accept that argument. It confuses substance and procedure. If a tribunal adopts a procedure which is unfair, then the court may, in the exercise of its discretion, seldom withheld, quash the resulting decision by applying the rules of natural justice.'

The importance of preserving this distinction is demonstrated by another passage in Lord Scarman's speech in *Findlay's* case [1984] 3 All ER 801 at 826, [1985] AC 318 at 333:

'But the Secretary of State has clearly to consider other aspects of the early release of a prisoner serving a sentence of imprisonment. Deterrence, retribution and public confidence in the system are factors of importance. The Parole Board, through its judicial and other members, can offer advice on these aspects of the question. But neither the board nor the judiciary can be as close, or as sensitive, to public opinion as a minister responsible to Parliament and to the electorate. He has to judge the public acceptability of early release and to determine the policies needed to maintain public confidence in the system of criminal justice. This must be why Parliament saw as necessary the duality of the parole system: without the advice and recommendation of a body capable of assessing the risk of early release the Secretary of State was not to act; but, having received such advice and recommendation, he was to authorise early release only if he himself was satisfied that it was in the public interest that he should.'

Mr Beloff characterised Sedley J's approach as heresy, and in my judgment he was right to do so. On matters of substance (as contrasted with procedure) *Wednesbury* provides the correct test. If follows that while Sedley J's actual decision in the *Hamble* case stands, his ratio in so far as he propounds a balancing exercise to be undertaken by the court should in my judgment be overruled.

Article 8

I am prepared to accept, as did the Divisional Court, that although not part of English domestic law the provisions of the Convention for the Protection of Human Rights and Fundamental Freedoms can assist in the elucidation of common law or in the interpretation of a statute (see *Brind v Secretary of State for the Home Dept* [1991] 1 All ER 720, [1991] 1 AC 696).

Article 8 provides:

> 1. Everyone has the right to respect for his private and family life, his home and his correspondence.
> 2. There shall be no interference by a public authority with the exercise of this right except such as is in accordance with the law and is necessary in a democratic society in the interests of national security, public safety or the economic well-being of the country, for the prevention of disorder or crime, for the protection of health or morals, or for the protection of the rights and freedoms of others.'

Mr Gallivan submitted that a serving prisoner has a right to respect for his family and private life, albeit one necessarily circumscribed by the fact of confinement and the limitations necessarily inherent therein.

He cited two decisions of the European Commission: *X v UK* (1982) 30 DR 113 and *McCotter v UK* (1993) 15 EHRR CD98. However, although both those cases concerned prisoners in detention, neither throws any light on the present case, and in both the Commission ruled that the application was manifestly ill-founded.

In my judgment the fundamental interference with respect to family life in the present case is brought about by the lawful sentences of the court. Of course home visits are an important feature, but it must be borne in mind that there is no suggestion that any applicant was cut off from his family altogether, since prison visits continued as usual.

Moreover, in applying the exceptions which art 8 stipulates, it is to my mind quite clear that the considerations of public confidence and public safety, which are advanced by the Secretary of State, fall within their scope, and are properly to be regarded as meeting the criteria laid down by Lord Keith of Kinkel that a pressing social need must be shown, and that the restrictions should be no more than is proportionate to the legitimate aim pursued (see *Derbyshire CC v Times Newspapers Ltd* [1993] 1 All ER 1011 at 1020, [1993] AC 534 at 550).

There was thus in my view no infringement of the principles contained in art 8.

Construction of the notice and the compact

It is common ground that a representation can only be relied upon as the basis for a legitimate expectation if it is clear and unambiguous (see *R v Board of Inland Revenue, ex p MFK Underwriting Agencies Ltd* [1990] 1 All ER 91, [1990] 1 WLR 1545 and *R v Devon CC, ex p Baker*, *R v Durham CC, ex p Curtis* [1995] 1 All ER 73). It is also not in dispute that the document must be interpreted through the eyes of an ordinary prisoner.

The heading to the notice made it clear that the information which followed applied from '1 October 1992'. This to my mind indicated that there had been a change at that date, which would certainly, at the very least, leave open the possibility that the ensuing information as to entitlement to apply for home leave might change again. It is also made clear under the word 'REMEMBER' that home leave is a privilege.

The compact, in its first relevant passage, makes it clear that consideration for home leave is available 'when you become eligible', and contains no representation as to timing. The reference to temporary release or home leave in the 'Optional Enhancements' refers back to the notice, to which I have already referred.

Taken as a whole, these two documents in my judgment do not contain a clear and unambiguous representation as to timing, and therefore are not a proper foundation for the legitimate expectation for which the applicants contend. It is, nevertheless, most unsatisfactory that documents of such importance to prisoners should be other than completely clear and unambiguous, and I trust that in future great care will be taken to ensure that all references to home leave (and indeed to any other privilege) in such documents state unequivocally and in plain language that eligibility for such privileges will be subject to the regime currently in force at the time of the application.

Conclusion

I proceed finally to evaluate the decision of the Secretary of State in accordance with the correct test. It is not suggested that his decision was in any way tainted with illegality. Nor could it be reasonably be suggested that it was irrational, let alone perverse, seeing that the Prison (Amendment) Rules 1995 expressly provided in r 6(4) and (5) that a prisoner shall not be released unless the Secretary of State is satisfied that there would not be an unacceptable risk of his committing offences while released, or if the Secretary of State is of the opinion that the release of the prisoner would be likely to undermine public confidence in the administration of justice, ie the two main considerations advanced both by the Secretary of State in the House of Commons and Baroness Blatch in the House of Lords, and confirmed by the affidavit evidence of the Home Office witnesses.

The applicants' witnesses suggest that the first reason is unsound, seeing that public safety is already secured by the new risk assessment system; I reject this criticism, since, while of course that system is very important, the deferment of the earliest date for home leave is a further safeguard, in that it extends the period during which the prisoner is not at large with the opportunity to commit further offences and may also tend to reassure the public. The applicants' witnesses also contend that the public anxiety about prisoners reoffending while on home leave (to which Baroness Blatch expressly referred) was not directed against this particular class of prisoner, but to my mind that is far too fine a distinction.

Finally, it is necessary to assess whether the Secretary of State took account of the relevant considerations, or omitted any. In my judgment he cannot be faulted on this account. I have already considered the two main factors behind his decision, namely public safety and the restoration the public confidence in the administration of justice. It is also plain from the evidence that he took into account the specific factors affecting the present applicants (namely the deferment of their earliest possible date for home leave during the currency of their sentences, the precise terms of the appropriate transitional arrangements, and the inevitable distress which the change in policy would cause), together with the general benefits provided by home leave.

Mr Elias submitted that he disregarded the compact, and it is true to say that there is no specific mention of the compact either in the Parliamentary statements or in the evidence. However, as the Divisional Court held, such arrangements were widespread in the prison service, and must have been very well known to the Secretary of State when he was considering the position of those already sentenced, so that it goes without saying that he must have had the compact in mind.

It follows that his decision is invulnerable under the *Wednesbury* test. For all these reasons I would dismiss this appeal.

PETER GIBSON LJ. I have had the advantage of seeing in draft the judgments of Hirst and Pill LJJ. I am in entire agreement with them and there is nothing which I would wish to add.

PILL LJ. Central to the submissions of Mr Elias on behalf of the applicants is the submission that the Secretary of State's (the respondent) change of policy as to home leave was unlawful because it frustrated a legitimate expectation which had arisen under the former rules of eligibility. A legitimate expectation was created when the applicants entered into a compact with the prison governor of HM Prison Risley under the former rules. It cannot be the law, Mr Elias submits, that a legitimate expectation can never stand against a change of policy. The question, he submits, is whether the respondent has justified to the court his view that there is a public policy consideration which takes priority over the legitimate expectation created by the compact.

Mr Elias makes the further submission that, in answering that question, the court, analysing the situation as a whole, must decide whether the respondent has acted fairly. Is it fair that the claimed public interest takes priority?

Hirst LJ has referred to the compact. It was signed by the applicants and on behalf of the governor under the words 'We agree to the terms and conditions of this compact'. Under the heading 'The prison promises to provide' is stated, inter alia, 'consideration for Home Leave when you become eligible'. The compact was signed after service on the applicants of a notice to prisoners, which stated: 'You can apply for short home leave after serving one-third of the total term of sentenced imprisonment …' The effect of the subsequent change of policy was that the applicants could apply for home leave only when they had served one-half of their sentences.

In the compact under the heading 'The prison expects you to commit yourself' was a list of 19 requirements. These included aspects of good behaviour, general exhortations to offer support to other prisoners and be an example to others and requirements:

> '—To refrain from the use of threats or threats of violence and to fully support the declared aim of the establishment to provide a "violence free environment."
> —To treat the whole prison environment with care, including the maintenance of your cell to a high level of cleanliness and tidiness.'

I mention these requirements as examples of the comprehensive code of good behaviour contemplated.

Under the heading 'If the prison breaches the compact' opportunities are provided to make complaints to authorities within and without the prison service. It is also stated that the prisoner may 'seek judicial review of administrative action if your legitimate expectations under this compact have unreasonably been denied'. I agree with Mr Elias that, having regard to its form and substance, the document is not one to be treated lightly in the context of the present application.

I also agree with Mr Elias to the extent that the court must analyse the situation as a whole. There must first be a fact-finding exercise as to the representations made to the promisee on behalf of the respondent and their impact on the promisee. It must then be considered whether an expectation was created and, if so, whether it is one which the law regards as a legitimate expectation which cannot be defeated by the change of policy. That will depend on all the circumstances, including the nature of the expectation, the change of policy involved and any justification given for that change in the light of the expectation claimed to exist.

Where I cannot agree with Mr Elias is in his submission that the court can take and act upon an overall view of the fairness of the respondent's decision of substance. The court can quash the decision only if, in relation to the expectation and in all the circumstances, the decision to apply the new policy in the particular case was unreasonable in the *Wednesbury* sense (see *Associated Provincial Picture Houses Ltd v Wednesbury Corp* [1947] 2 All ER 680, [1948] 1 KB 223). The claim to a broader power to judge the fairness of a decision of substance, which I understand Sedley J to be making in *R v Ministry of Agriculture Fisheries and Food, ex p Hamble (Offshore) Fisheries Ltd* [1995] 2 All ER 714, is in my view wrong in principle.

As well as the governor's notice and the compact, the court must bear in mind the context of the respondent's decision, a decision which was of importance in an area where he bears grave responsibilities and which is a matter of great public concern, namely penal policy. I agree with Hirst LJ that, notwithstanding the notice and compact, these appeals must fail. The underlying reason was stated by Lord Scarman in *Findlay v Secretary of State for the Home Dept* [1984] 3 All ER 801 at 830, [1985] AC 318 at 338:

> 'But what was their *legitimate* expectation? Given the substance and purpose of the legislative provisions governing parole, the most that a convicted prisoner can legitimately expect is that his case will be examined individually in the light of whatever policy the Secretary of State sees fit to adopt provided always that the adopted policy is a lawful exercise of the discretion conferred upon him by the statute.' (Lord Scarman's emphasis.)

In this context, even if the applicants established that, when they signed the compact, they were misled by the contents of the notice and compact they could have no legitimate expectation which defeats the respondent's new policy upon home leave and its application to them.

Hirst LJ has set out the circumstances in which the respondent took the decisions complained of and the evidence before the court. In my judgment, and I apply the *Wednesbury* tests, the respondent did not take into account matters he ought not to have taken into account or neglect to take into account matters which he ought to have taken into account. He has not come to a conclusion so unreasonable that no reasonable Secretary of State could have come to it. He was entitled to treat the governor's notice and the compact as being of insufficient weight to deter him from taking the relevant decisions affecting the applicants.

I also wish to state my agreement with the view expressed by Hirst LJ as to the care which should be taken in the drafting of a document such as the compact. The issue of charters, whether for patients or passengers or others, has become commonplace as an activity of public bodies. This compact was different from most charters in that it stated not only what the prison promised to provide but what the prison expected from the prisoner in return. Mr Beloff confined his submission to one that the compact was adequate in point of law and he has *a* succeeded. I would however express the hope that care is taken to state what will be provided for the prisoner in as precise terms as possible, to quote the words in para 12.120 of the report of Woolf LJ and Judge Tumin on *Prison Disturbances April 1990* (Cm 1456 (1991)). Section 12 of the report, paras 120 to 129, recommends that prisoners should be offered the opportunity to enter into a compact such as that now under consideration. In the respect identified by

b Hirst LJ, this compact falls short of the aspirations there expressed.

I would dismiss this appeal.

Appeal dismissed.

Mary Rose Plummer   Barrister.

Metalloy Supplies Ltd (in liq) v MA (UK) Ltd

COURT OF APPEAL, CIVIL DIVISION

BUTLER-SLOSS, MILLETT AND WALLER LJJ

2, 7 OCTOBER 1996

Costs – Order for costs – Payment of costs by non-party – Circumstances in which non-party may be ordered to pay costs of proceedings – Liquidator initiating proceedings on behalf of insolvent company against defendants – Defendants obtaining order for security for costs and thereby forcing liquidator to discontinue action – Whether liquidator personally liable for defendants' costs – Whether liquidator acting improperly.

The liquidator of the plaintiff company initiated proceedings on its behalf against the defendants for payment for goods sold and delivered. Subsequently the defendants served their defence and counterclaim and indicated that they would be seeking an order for security for costs, since they believed the plaintiff had insufficient funds to cover the costs of a trial. The district judge dismissed their application for security on the grounds that the plaintiff's claim would thereby be stifled. The judge reversed the decision on appeal and ordered security of £10,000 to be paid into court within 28 days, whereupon the liquidator was forced to discontinue the action. Thereafter the defendants applied for an order that the liquidator personally pay the defendants' costs of the action, on the grounds that he had known that the plaintiff had insufficient funds to cover the cost of the trial, but had still instructed its solicitors to proceed with the action. The district judge dismissed the application but on the defendants' appeal, the judge held that since the liquidator had known from the date the defence was served that the defendants had an arguable defence and that the plaintiff had insufficient funds to cover the defendants' costs if they should win, it had thereafter become unreasonable for him to continue to manage the action, and he was therefore personally liable to pay the defendants' costs from that date. The liquidator appealed.

Held – Although the court had jurisdiction to order a liquidator as a non-party to proceedings brought by the insolvent company to pay costs personally, it would only exercise that jurisdiction in exceptional circumstances where there had been impropriety on the part of the liquidator, particularly in view of the fact that the normal remedy of obtaining an order for security for costs was available to the defendant. The caution necessary in all cases where an attempt was made to render a non-party liable for costs would be the greater in the case of a liquidator having regard to public policy considerations. Since the judge, in failing to consider the question of impropriety, had exercised his discretion on a wrong basis, the court would exercise its discretion afresh. In the circumstances, there was nothing improper in the liquidator's conduct and accordingly the appeal would be allowed (see p 423 *a d* to *h* to p 424 *b e* to *j* and p 425 *b* to *h*, post).

Notes

For jurisdiction to award costs, see 37 *Halsbury's Laws* (4th edn) para 713, and for cases on the subject, see 37(3) *Digest* (Reissue) 230–233, 4273–4289.

Cases referred to in judgments

a *Eastglen Ltd v Grafton* (12 March 1996, unreported), Ch D.
Knight v FP Special Assets (1992) 174 CLR 178, Aust HC.
Symphony Group plc v Hodgson [1993] 4 All ER 143, [1994] QB 179, [1993] 3 WLR 830, CA.
Taylor v Pace Developments Ltd [1991] BCC 406, CA.
b *Wilson Lovatt & Sons Ltd, Re* [1977] 1 All ER 274.

Cases also cited or referred to in skeleton arguments

Aiden Shipping Co Ltd v Interbulk Ltd, The Vimeira [1986] 2 All ER 409, [1986] AC 965, HL.
Aquila Design (GRP Products) Ltd v Cornhill Insurance plc [1988] BCLC 134, CA.
c *Cooper v Maxwell* [1992] CA Transcript 273.
Fairfax (John) & Sons Pty Ltd v E C De Witt & Co (Australia) Pty Ltd [1957] 3 All ER 410, [1958] 1 QB 323, CA.
Hoddle v CCF Construction Ltd [1992] 2 All ER 550.
Land and Property Trust Co plc, Re [1991] 3 All ER 409, [1991] 1 WLR 601, CA.
MC Bacon Ltd, Re (No 2) [1991] Ch 127, [1990] BCLC 607.
d *McFarlane v EE Caledonia Ltd (No 2)* [1995] 1 WLR 366, [1995] 1 Lloyd's Rep 535.
Mathais v Yetts (1882) 46 LT 497, CA.
Mills' Estate, Re, ex p Comrs of Works and Public Buildings (1886) 34 Ch D 24, CA.
Mobbs v Vandenbrand (1864) 33 LJQB 177.
R v Greene (1843) 4 QB 646, 114 ER 1042.
e *Ram Coomar Coondoo v Chunder Canto Mookerjee* (1876) 2 App Cas 186, PC.
Sturmer and Town of Breaverton, Re (1912) 25 OLR 566, Ont Div Ct.
Tajik Air Ltd, Re [1996] 1 BCLC 317.

Appeal

By notice dated 15 June 1995 the liquidator of the plaintiff company, Metalloy
f Supplies Ltd, appealed from the decision of Judge Hutton, sitting as a judge of the
High Court on 19 May 1995, whereby he allowed in part an appeal by the
defendant, MA (UK) Ltd, from the order of District Judge Peters on 17 March
1995, and ordered the liquidator personally to pay the defendant's costs, incurred
in an action brought by the plaintiff for payment for goods sold and received, after
g 30 March 1994. The facts are set out in the judgment of Waller LJ.

Terence Mowschenson QC and *Michael Rollason* (instructed by *Hartley Linfoot &
Whitlam,* Sheffield) for the plaintiff.
Peter Irvin (instructed by *Richmonds,* Doncaster) for the defendants.

Cur adv vult

h

7 October 1996. The following judgments were delivered.

WALLER LJ (giving the first judgment at the invitation of Butler-Sloss LJ). This
is an appeal from Judge Hutton sitting as a judge of the High Court, who ordered
j the liquidator of the plaintiff company, Metalloy Supplies Ltd, to pay certain of
the costs of an action personally, allowing in so doing an appeal from an order of
District Judge Peters in so far as he had refused to so order.
The plaintiff has at all material times been a company in liquidation, the
liquidator having been appointed on 11 January 1991. A writ was issued by the
plaintiffs on 2 September 1993 claiming the remainder of the price of certain
goods. Originally judgment was entered in default. An application to set that

judgment aside was initially refused by District Judge Lambert on 28 October 1993; but on 14 February 1994 Gage J allowed an appeal from that order, giving the defendants, MA (UK) Ltd, leave to defend and counterclaim on the basis of alleged deficiencies in the goods on condition that they paid into court £10,000. The defendants served a defence and counterclaim on 30 March 1994 and at the same time indicated in correspondence that they would seek an order for security for costs. A summons seeking security was issued on 14 May 1994 supported by an affidavit which asserted inter alia: (1) that costs of £9,000 had already been incurred by the defendants in setting aside the default judgment; (2) that the total costs including the trial of the defendant were estimated at £24,000; and (3) that it was believed that the liquidator had only £12,500 available.

The affidavit sought an order for security and there was no suggestion in it that a costs order would be sought against the liquidator personally or that he was acting in any way improperly, irresponsibly or unreasonably.

An affidavit was sworn by Jeremy Nuttall, a solicitor acting for the plaintiff, in response dated 7 July 1994. It resisted any order for security. It urged points which went to the merits of the plaintiff's claim in the action; it suggested that the estimates for costs put forward by the defendants were excessive; and it exhibited the plaintiff's latest statement of affairs and stated that the liquidator estimated that, after deduction of relevant fees, funds of approximately £5,000 were currently available. It further asserted that on that basis the action would be stifled by any substantial security order.

There was a further interlocutory skirmish in that on 6 July 1994 the security for costs summons was adjourned by District Judge Smythe, who made a costs order against the defendants which resulted in an appeal on which the defendants were successful. This resulted in further costs being expended and it was in that context that the defendants' solicitor wrote a letter of 15 September 1994 to the solicitors acting for the plaintiff saying (and I summarise): (1) that in the light of the fact that further costs had been incurred since the liquidator said he had £5,000, that sum would be likely to have been exhausted; (2) that such funds as the liquidator had should not be dissipated having regard to the costs orders made in the defendants' favour; (3) that an order for security was absolutely necessary; and (4) that if by chance an order for security was not made, it would be their intention to apply for a costs order against *your firm* for the future cost of preparation of the action (my emphasis).

That letter was exhibited to a further affidavit of Rose Egarr supporting the application for security for costs, which came on before District Judge Peters on 21 September 1994. The district judge in fact dismissed the application for security for costs. According to the note of his judgment he took the view that the letter of 15 September 1994 put the matter too strongly in favour of the defendants; he took the view that the original transaction between the plaintiff company and the defendants was a strange transaction and needed investigation, and that an order for security would stifle the plaintiff's claim.

His order was however reversed on appeal when on 24 October 1994 Judge Harrison-Hall ordered security of £10,000 to be paid into court within 28 days, and the action to be stayed meanwhile.

The plaintiff failed to put up security within 28 days, and on 21 February 1995 the defendants issued a summons applying to dismiss the action with costs to be paid by the liquidator personally. That summons was supported by a further affidavit from Rose Egarr, in which she referred to the letter of 15 September 1994 and to the concerns raised therein in relation to costs, and said that particularly as the liquidator had via his solicitors had notice of the defendants' concerns but clearly must have instructed them to proceed, that the liquidator should be personally liable for the cost of the action (without, it should be noticed, any limitation of time).

An affidavit from the liquidator, dated 17 March 1995, stated that in the liquidator's experience the application to render him personally liable was without precedent; he confirmed that the action had been funded by the plaintiff company's assets; and that the action had not been supported by funds from his firm, nor by funds from the creditors secured or unsecured.

The matter came once again before District Judge Peters on 17 March 1995. It was accepted that the action should be dismissed, and the only matter argued was whether a costs order should be made against the liquidator personally. It is clear that the relevant authorities were cited to the district judge, and he is recorded as recognising that he had jurisdiction to make the order sought, but was of the view, following the guidelines in *Symphony Group plc v Hodgson* [1993] 4 All ER 143, [1994] QB 179, that he would be breaking new ground if he were to make an order against the liquidator personally, and he said indeed that this approach would be highly exceptional.

The matter then came on appeal to Judge Hutton sitting as a judge of the High Court and was heard on 19 May 1995. There was clearly extensive argument before him and again full citation of authority. He concluded: (1) that the district judge had formed the view that he would be breaking new ground to order a liquidator to pay costs personally, even if it were otherwise right to make him do so, and that thus the district judge had exercised his discretion on a wrong basis; (2) that there was jurisdiction to order a liquidator to pay the costs personally; and (3) that the liquidator was right to initiate the action but that there came a stage when he should have changed his mind; that stage was identified by the judge in the following words—

> 'There came a time, as was pointed out to me by Mr Irvin for the appellant, when it was quite clear that the defendant had an arguable defence to the action brought against him and was counterclaiming and was pursuing vigorously his defence and counterclaim. At that stage it appears that the company in liquidation had insufficient funds to cover the costs of the defendant if the defendant should win and the plaintiff lose. In those circumstances, I find that it was unreasonable for the liquidator to continue, as he did, to manage this action before subsequently discontinuing and that, for a period he should be ordered to pay the defendants' costs when judgment was finally given in their favour from the time when it became unreasonable for the liquidator to continue. Having heard submissions from Mr Irvin I place that as 30 March 1994. In the exercise of my discretion, therefore, I order that the liquidator, personally, pay the defendants' costs of the action from and after that date.'

It should be noted: (1) that the first occasion when any notice was given to the liquidator that it would be contended that he might be liable for the costs personally was in February 1995; (2) that the first occasion when any suggestion was made that someone other than the plaintiff company might be liable to pay costs was in September 1994, and on that occasion the suggestion was that the solicitors would be liable, but for *the future costs if the application for security failed*; and (3) that the only grounds relied on in the affidavit in support of the application for rendering the liquidator personally liable were that the liquidator must have been aware of the concerns expressed by the defendants' solicitors as to costs and still given instructions to proceed. No impropriety was alleged, and indeed the assertion is hardly an assertion of acting irresponsibly, or unreasonably, or outside the norm for the conduct of litigation by a liquidator on behalf of an insolvent company who would always be aware of the concerns that the opposing party would have as to the difficulty there may be in recovering costs *if* the opposing party were to be successful in the action.

As Lloyd LJ said in *Taylor v Pace Developments Ltd* [1991] BCC 406 at 408: 'There is only one immutable rule in relation to costs, and that is that there are no immutable rules.' But that said, it is clear from the authorities: (1) an order for the payment of costs by a non-party will always be exceptional and the judge should treat an application with considerable caution (see *Symphony Group plc v Hodgson* [1993] 4 All ER 143 at 152, [1994] QB 179 at 192 per Balcombe LJ); (2) different considerations apply depending on whether the non-party can be said to be funding the action, or likely to obtain some financial benefit from the result of the action, or whether the non-party simply has some management of the action, but even in the maintaining or financial benefit cases as Lindsay J said in *Eastglen Ltd v Grafton* (12 March 1996, unreported)—

'*Taylor v Pace Developments Ltd* ... illustrates the propositions that the bona fides of the proceedings and of the non-party's support for them are an important feature of the s 51 [of the Supreme Court Act 1981] discretion, that support of unsuccessful proceedings and a likelihood of personal gain by the supporter, whilst factors to be borne in mind will not of themselves necessarily lead to liability in the supporter but that only in exceptional cases will a non-party be liable';

and (3) the position seems clearer still where the non-party's role is simply having some management of the action. As Balcombe LJ put it in *Symphony Group plc v Hodgson* [1993] 4 All ER 143 at 151–152, [1994] QB 179 at 191–192, such costs are ordered against such a person where he or she 'improperly' prosecutes or defends proceedings; and he refers to cases relating to directors of insolvent companies, and points out that in fact in none of those cases was an order actually made.

We were not shown any case where a liquidator had, prior to the order of the judge in this case, been ordered as a non-party to pay costs personally as distinct from the case where the liquidator brings the proceedings in his own name as for example in *Re Wilson Lovatt & Sons Ltd* [1977] 1 All ER 274. We were referred to an Australian case, *Knight v FP Special Assets* (1992) 174 CLR 178, where the High Court of Australia was concerned with whether the Supreme Court of Queensland had jurisdiction to order a non-party, in that case receivers, to pay the costs. They held by a majority that the jurisdiction was there. Three of the judges, Mason CJ, Deane and Gaudron JJ, also approved a principle to the following effect, that in relation to ordering costs where the party to the litigation is a man of straw, against a non-party who has played an active role in the management of the litigation and where the non-party or someone for whom he acts has an interest 'if the interests of justice so requires' a costs order should be made (see (1992) 174 CLR 178 at 193, 205). But Dawson J (at 204) suggested that the question whether it was right to make the order in the particular case had not in fact been argued, but commented that he would have thought that obtaining an order for security for costs would ordinarily be the appropriate remedy. McHugh J (at 217), who was against there being jurisdiction at all, clearly also thought that the appropriate remedy was to obtain an order for security for costs.

a I would myself prefer the approach that ordinarily in the case where a plaintiff is an insolvent company an order for security for costs should be the appropriate remedy.

However there may, in any event, be a distinction between the position of receivers and the position of a liquidator. There is a further passage in the judgment of Lindsay J in *Eastglen Ltd v Grafton* which refers to the public interest
b in liquidators being able to perform their duties. His statement is made in the context of not discouraging creditors from assisting the liquidator, it being a creditor who was the non-party being attacked in that case, but the public interest in relation to liquidators also demands that they should not be exposed to personal liability for costs simply where they act for insolvent companies. Certainly, as it seems to me, the primary remedy of a defendant facing a company
c in liquidation should be security for costs, and I can perhaps summarise my view on the authorities so far as the proper approach to the question whether a liquidator should be made personally liable for costs in the following way.

I think (as the judge decided and, as I read the notes, the district judge also decided) that there is jurisdiction to order a liquidator as a non-party to pay the
d costs personally; but it will only be in exceptional cases that the jurisdiction will be exercised, and impropriety will be a necessary ingredient, particularly having regard to the fact that the normal remedy of obtaining an order for security for costs is available; the caution necessary in all cases where an attempt is being made to render a non-party liable for costs will be the greater in the case of a liquidator having regard to the public policy considerations.
e The judge, as I see it, went wrong in the following respects. First, there is no indication that he considered that this was an exceptional case or that he had in mind the need for caution, particularly considering the public policy considerations. Second, he applied a test of 'unreasonable' and did not consider whether there had been any impropriety in the conduct of the liquidator. Third,
f he considered that it was unreasonable to continue litigation when there were insufficient funds to cover the costs of the *defendants* if they should win. But the remedy of security for costs, if that can be justified, is available to cover that precise situation. If by chance an application for security fails, then a fortiori, it cannot be unreasonable for a liquidator to continue with an action in which he, bona fide, believes there is some prospect of recovery, whether by trial or
g settlement prior to trial. Fourthly, the judge did not appear to take any account of the lack of warning that the liquidator had in relation to the seeking of a costs order against him personally.

Accordingly it seems to me that the judge exercised his discretion on a wrong basis, and this court is thus entitled to exercise its discretion afresh.
h The position of the liquidator in this case appears to me to be very similar to that encountered by liquidators in many cases. The company has what appears to be a debt due for goods sold and delivered. There are not sufficient funds to enable the company to pay the costs of the opposing party if a trial had to be fought and it was lost; indeed there may not be funds to fight a trial at all, if that
j is necessary. But there are sufficient funds to launch the action, and to put in pleadings, and if no application for security were made or if such an application could be successfully resisted the funds may be sufficient to be able to keep the action going so as to be able to recover some part of the debt by settlement prior to a full trial.

Mr Irvin argued that once the liquidator realised that he had not sufficient funds to pay the plaintiff's own costs of taking the matter to trial, it was unreasonable or irresponsible of the liquidator to continue with the action. That is not in fact in my view an allegation of impropriety at all in the sense required to lay the foundation for an application against a liquidator to pay costs personally as a non-party; but in any event I do not, for my part, think that it was unreasonable because the liquidator must have hoped, in the context of this action where leave to defend had only been given on the basis of a substantial payment in, that if he could keep the action going some recovery might be made. Mr Irvin suggested that this would be encouraging some sort of blackmail, but it seems to me that that starts from the assumption that the defendants are really bound to win on the merits and should not be forced to settle because of the impecuniosity of the plaintiff company. In fact, the pressure or blackmail is two-sided in a case of this kind. The defendants, it may be said by the plaintiff company, are able by counterclaiming and fighting interlocutory battles to exhaust the resources of the liquidator so that ultimately the plaintiff company must discontinue. No court can tell where the merits of these respective arguments lie prior to a trial, and to brand one or other as unreasonable or as acting improperly could only be justified if the action or defence were not being conducted bona fide in the sense of being reasonably arguable. One distinction should, in any event, be borne in mind in considering the position of the two sides and who has leverage over whom. Where a plaintiff company is insolvent, the defendant does have the remedy to apply for security for costs. It is not, however, unreasonable for that plaintiff to resist that order and leave it to the court to decide whether it is appropriate for the court to make the order in the particular case.

What happened in this case was that the action was commenced and no one attacks the bona fides of that commencement. No one has suggested that the liquidator should have appreciated that the action had become a hopeless one on the merits. All that happened was that having successfully resisted an order for security for costs, on appeal the plaintiff company was ordered to provide security. That in fact forced the liquidator to discontinue. There was nothing exceptional in his conduct; there was nothing improper in his conduct; and no one in fact warned him that they were going to suggest otherwise. In my view the appeal should be allowed and the order of District Judge Peters restored.

MILLETT LJ. It is not an abuse of the process of the court or in any way improper or unreasonable for an impecunious plaintiff to bring proceedings which are otherwise proper and bona fide while lacking the means to pay the defendant's costs if they should fail. Litigants do it every day, with or without legal aid. If the plaintiff is an individual, the defendant's only recourse is to threaten the plaintiff with bankruptcy. If the plaintiff is a limited company, the defendant may apply for security for costs and have the proceedings dismissed if the plaintiff fails to provide whatever security is ordered.

The court has a discretion to make a costs order against a non-party. Such an order is, however, exceptional, since it is rarely appropriate. It may be made in a wide variety of circumstances where the third party is considered to be the real party interested in the outcome of the suit. It may also be made where the third party has been responsible for bringing the proceedings and they have been brought in bad faith or for an ulterior purpose or there is some other conduct on his part which makes it just and reasonable to make the order against him. It is not, however, sufficient to render a director liable for costs that he was a director of the company and caused it to bring or defend proceedings which he funded and which ultimately failed. Where such proceedings are brought bona fide and for the benefit of the company, the company is the real plaintiff. If in such a case an order for costs could be made against a director in the absence of some impropriety or bad faith on his part, the doctrine of the separate liability of the company would be eroded and the principle that such orders should be exceptional would be nullified.

The position of a liquidator is a fortiori. Where a limited company is in insolvent liquidation, the liquidator is under a statutory duty to collect in its assets. This may require him to bring proceedings. If he does so in his own name, he is personally liable for the costs in the ordinary way, though he may be entitled to an indemnity out of the assets of the company. If he brings the proceedings in the name of the company, the company is the real plaintiff and he is not. He is under no obligation to the defendant to protect his interests by ensuring that he has sufficient funds in hand to pay their costs as well as his own if the proceedings fail. It may be commercially unwise to institute proceedings without the means to provide any security for costs which may be ordered, since this will only lead to the dismissal of the proceedings; but it is not improper to do so. Nor (if he considers only the interests of the company, as he is entitled to do) is it necessarily unreasonable. The defendant may offer to settle; he may not apply for security; and if he does the court may not order it to be given, particularly if such an order would stifle a meritorious claim.

In the present case the only respects in which the liquidator is alleged to have acted unreasonably is in continuing the proceedings after the date on which the defendant asked for security for costs and in resisting the defendant's application for security. It is submitted that the liquidator ought to have thrown in the towel as soon as the defendant asked for security because (i) he knew that he would be unable to provide any security which might be ordered, and (ii) he had insufficient funds in hand to pursue the case to trial if security was not ordered. But the first is a ground on which the court may properly refuse to order security; while the second made it all the more important to the liquidator to defeat the application and obtain some bargaining power with a view to a settlement. It is obviously risky for a plaintiff to begin proceedings which he cannot afford to finish, but it is not unreasonable, still less improper, for him to do so.

In my judgment, the judge's order in the present case is not only inconsistent with the principles on which non-party orders for costs are made but would invalidate the assumptions on which the jurisdiction to order security for costs against a limited company is predicated. I agree that the appeal should be allowed.

BUTLER-SLOSS LJ. I agree.

Appeal allowed.

Paul Magrath Esq   Barrister.

R v Secretary of State for the Home Department, ex parte Naughton

QUEEN'S BENCH DIVISION

SIMON BROWN LJ AND POPPLEWELL J

29 AUGUST, 4 SEPTEMBER 1996

Sentence – Reduction – Period spent in custody – Consecutive sentences – Defendant remanded in custody in respect of two separate offences – Defendant sentenced at trial to 18 months' imprisonment on each offence – Whether time spent on remand should be deducted from each sentence or from total sentence when calculating release date – Criminal Justice Act 1967, ss 67(1), 104(2).

The applicant was arrested on 26 September 1994 on a charge of possession of drugs. He was remanded in custody and not admitted to bail until 106 days later on 9 January 1995. During that period he served 25 days' imprisonment between 18 November and 12 December 1994 for other offences for which he had been sentenced to a short period of imprisonment. On 23 March 1995, while on bail, he was arrested for burglary and again remanded in custody. On 17 November 1995 he was sentenced at the Crown Court to 18 months' imprisonment on each of the offences of drug possession and burglary, the sentences to run consecutively, making a total of 36 months' imprisonment. The applicant considered that, in accordance with prison service guidelines, which provided that remand time applicable to any of the consecutive sentences imposed at the same trial were to be added together to reduce the total sentence, the period of 239 days between 23 March and 17 November 1995 when the applicant was in custody on remand for both offences should be taken into account in respect of each offence, and not just once, when calculating the applicant's release date and that he should have been released on 24 December 1995. The Home Secretary, taking the view that the prison service guidelines were misconceived, exercised his statutory powers to cancel them. Under s 67(1)[a] of the Criminal Justice Act 1967 the 'length of any sentence of imprisonment imposed on an offender' was to be reduced by any relevant period spent in custody in connection with the offence. Under s 104(2)[b] consecutive 'term[s] of imprisonment' were to be treated as a single term. The applicant applied for judicial review of the Home Secretary's decision.

Held – The expression 'sentence of imprisonment' in s 67(1) of the 1967 Act was, like the expression 'term of imprisonment' in s 104(2), to be construed as referring to the aggregate of any consecutive sentences imposed at the same trial on an offender. It followed that where an offender was sentenced to consecutive sentences after being on remand in custody, the time spent on remand was deductible from the total sentence and not from each consecutive sentence when calculating the offender's release date, since a construction of s 67(1) which permitted time spent on remand to be deducted from each consecutive sentence produced results so absurd that it could not have been intended by Parliament.

---

a   Section 67, so far as material, is set out at p 429 b c, post
b   Section 104(2) is set out at p 429 e, post

Accordingly the application would be dismissed (see p 429 *j* to 430 *a*, p 434 *e h* to 435 *a e* and p 436 *j* to 437 *a*, post).

R v Governor of Blundeston Prison, ex p Gaffney [1982] 2 All ER 492 not followed.

Notes

For duration of sentence, see 11(2) *Halsbury's Laws* (4th edn reissue) para 1202, and for cases on the effect of time spent in custody on duration of sentence, see 15(2) *Digest* (2nd reissue) 275–276, *20770–20780*.

For the Criminal Justice Act 1967, ss 67, 104, see 34 *Halsbury's Statutes* (4th edn) 704, 709.

Cases referred to in judgments

Barnes v Jarvis [1953] 1 All ER 1061, [1953] 1 WLR 649, DC.

R v Governor of Blundeston Prison, ex p Gaffney [1982] 2 All ER 492, [1982] 1 WLR 696, DC.

R v Governor of HM Prison Styal, ex p Mooney [1996] 1 Cr App R (S) 74, DC.

R v Greater Manchester Coroner, ex p Tal [1984] 3 All ER 240, [1985] QB 67, [1984] 3 WLR 643, DC.

R v Secretary of State for the Home Dept, ex p Woodward and Wilson (24 June 1996, unreported), DC.

R v Secretary of State for the Home Office, ex p Read (1987) 9 Cr App R (S) 206, DC.

Application for judicial review

John Thomas Naughton applied, with the leave of the Divisional Court granted on 29 August 1996, for an order of certiorari to quash the decision of the Secretary of State for the Home Department on 23 August 1996 to cancel the current Home Office instructions to prison governors giving guidance, inter alia, on their duties to release prisoners, which the applicant contended applied to the calculation of his release date or, alternatively, an order of mandamus to require the respondent to recalculate the release date of the applicant. The facts are set out in the judgment of Simon Brown LJ.

Peter Weatherby (instructed by *John Howell & Co*, Sheffield) for the applicant.
David Pannick QC and *Pushpinder Saini* (instructed by the *Treasury Solicitor*) for the respondent.

Cur adv vult

4 September 1996. The following judgments were delivered.

SIMON BROWN LJ. No one could have failed to notice the recent political storm created by the various changes of approach adopted by the prison authorities to the calculation of certain prisoners' release dates. That storm, however, is merely the context in which this application came to be listed so urgently, with the substantive hearing following immediately upon the leave application itself. Political considerations have not the least part to play in the case. Rather, we are concerned here solely to determine which approach is the correct one. Is it the Home Office's original approach, now reinstated by order of the respondent Home Secretary? Or is it, as the applicant contends, the approach introduced in guidelines issued by the director general of the prison service on 15 August and then operated briefly until its cancellation on 23 August 1996?

The court is faced in short with a stark point of statutory construction. What is the true legal effect of the relevant legislative provisions? The specific point here at issue, let it be made plain at once, concerns prisoners serving consecutive sentences of imprisonment. Those serving concurrent sentences are not directly affected although, as will appear, their position is clearly of relevance.

First the facts, although it will readily be appreciated that the point for decision is one of general application and not, therefore, dependent upon the precise details of any particular applicant's case. The facts of this case, however, provide a convenient illustration of the problem arising.

The applicant is a prisoner at HM Prison Lindholme, Doncaster. He contends that he should have been released on 24 December 1995. On the Home Secretary's calculation, however, he still has time to serve.

He was first arrested on 26 September 1994 for possession of cannabis. He was remanded in custody and not admitted to bail until 9 January 1995, 106 days later. During this period he was sentenced to a short period of imprisonment for other offences pursuant to which he served 25 days in custody, namely between 18 November and 12 December 1994. Thus he was in custody *only* (the relevance of that emphasis will appear later) in connection with the proceedings for the cannabis offence for a total of 81 days of that initial period of 106 days.

On 23 March 1995, having by then been on bail for some two months, the applicant was arrested for burglary. He was again remanded in custody, henceforth, in connection with proceedings both for the cannabis offence and for the burglary.

Two hundred and thirty nine (239) days later, on 17 November 1995, the appellant was sentenced at the Crown Court at Sheffield to 18 months' imprisonment for each of those two offences, the sentences to run consecutively so as to produce a total of 36 months (1,094 days) imprisonment.

Since being sentenced, the appellant, by reason of indiscipline, was awarded four additional days in custody.

No one disputes that in the computation of his overall sentence and release date the applicant is entitled to credit in respect of 81 days plus 239 days less 4 days. It is the applicant's contention, however, that he is entitled to be credited with the second period of time spent on remand, the 239 days when he was on remand in respect of both offences, not just once, but twice. The respondent contests that submission, arguing that no period of remand can be credited against more than one element of a total term produced by consecutive sentences.

The issue of principle raised by the application has helpfully been crystallised by the parties in the following form:

'1 ... (1) A defendant is charged with offence X and offence Y. (2) He is remanded in custody on *each* charge, say for one year. (3) He is convicted on each charge. (4) He is sentenced to three years' imprisonment on each charge; those sentences to run *consecutively*. (5) On the true construction of [the legislation] should the remand time to be deducted from the sentence to be served by the prisoner be (a) one year or (b) two years. 2. In other words, should the time the prisoner serves be five years, deducting only the one year spent on remand from the total period of six years, or (b) four years, deducting one year from each of the three year sentences?' (Counsel's emphasis.)

It is time to set out the relevant statutory provisions. Section 67(1) and (1A) of the Criminal Justice Act 1967, as amended by s 49 of the Police and Criminal Evidence Act 1984, so far as relevant, provides:

'(1) The length of any sentence of imprisonment imposed on an offender by a court shall be treated as reduced by any relevant period ...

(1A) In subsection (1) above "relevant period" means—(a) any period during which the offender was in police detention in connection with the offence for which the sentence was passed; or (b) any period during which he was in custody—(i) by reason only of having been committed to custody by an order of a court made in connection with any proceedings relating to that sentence or the offence for which it was passed or any proceedings from which those proceedings arose; or (ii) by reason of his having been so committed and having been concurrently detained otherwise than by order of a court.'

The essential effect of the 1984 amendment was to introduce credit for police detention, in other words, to introduce the provision which is now s 67(1A)(a).

Those are the central statutory provisions in play. Section 104(2) of the 1967 Act, however, is also of importance:

'For the purposes of any reference in this Act, however expressed, to the term of imprisonment or other detention to which a person has been sentenced or which, or part of which, he has served, consecutive terms and terms which are wholly or partly concurrent shall be treated as a single term.'

These statutory provisions (together, on occasion, with ss 41 and 51(2) of the Criminal Justice Act 1991) have been considered by the Divisional Court in a series of four cases over the last 15 years (see *R v Governor of Blundeston Prison, ex p Gaffney* [1982] 2 All ER 492, [1982] 1 WLR 696, *R v Secretary of State for the Home Office, ex p Read* (1987) 9 Cr App R (S) 206, *R v Governor of HM Prison Styal, ex p Mooney* [1996] 1 Cr App R (S) 74 and *R v Secretary of State for the Home Dept, ex p Woodward and Wilson* (24 June 1996, unreported)). All four, however, were concerned with prisoners sentenced to *concurrent* terms of imprisonment, that is to say with the calculation of credit for periods of time spent on remand in custody (or in police detention) when a defendant is sentenced to two or more terms of imprisonment to be served concurrently. The present dispute, as stated, raises a distinct issue: how to deal with periods of remand in custody in respect of those sentenced to *consecutive* terms of imprisonment.

Put at its briefest, Mr Weatherby's argument for the applicant is essentially this. True, the *Gaffney* line of authority is concerned with concurrent sentences. Nevertheless it adopts and depends upon an approach to the construction of s 67 which necessarily carries with it the consequence for which he contends with regard to consecutive sentence cases. Surprising that result may be. It is, however, the only result consistent with the correctness of the *Gaffney* approach. If anomalous, then the law can be changed, the respondent being peculiarly well placed to change it. If the statute is ambiguous, then it is trite law that such ambiguity must be resolved in favour of the liberty of the subject.

Mr Pannick QC's opposing arguments are essentially twofold. First he submits that the applicant's contention, that time served on remand should be deducted from each consecutive sentence, produces results so absurd that the court should arrive at such a conclusion only if compelled to do so by the plainest of statutory language. Secondly, he submits that far from compelling such a perverse result, nothing in the legislation or in the *Gaffney* line of cases requires such a conclusion.

Mr Pannick's first submission is clearly a powerful one; indeed it scarcely requires elaboration. One has only to give an example of the consequences of the applicant's argument to recognise its absurdity. Two defendants are arrested and charged jointly with five burglaries. One is remanded in custody, the other granted bail. At trial a year later both are convicted and sentenced to consecutive terms of one year's imprisonment on each of the five counts, a total sentence of five years. Remission aside, on the applicant's case the remand prisoner walks free having spent but a single year in custody. His co-accused, however, has to serve the full five-year term. There can be no possible justification or logic for remand prisoners being thus advantaged. Really such a situation is almost too absurd to contemplate. Nor is it any answer to suggest that the courts could adjust their sentences to take account of this phenomenon. Not only would it throw over all established principles as to the imposition of consecutive sentences and the guideline decisions upon the appropriate level of sentencing for various offences, but on occasion it would also run up against problems of maximum sentences.

It is, however, when one comes to Mr Pannick's second submission that the difficulty in the case arises. This submission it is, which collides head on with the central point in Mr Weatherby's argument, the argument that fidelity to the *Gaffney* approach requires the applicant's construction to prevail.

It is necessary now, therefore, to turn to the *Gaffney* line of cases to see just what it is that they establish and the route by which they do so. The critical issue arising in these cases was, as stated, how periods of remand in custody should be treated in concurrent sentence cases. As I said in *R v Governor of HM Prison Styal, ex p Mooney* [1996] 1 Cr App R (S) 74 at 76:

> 'The issue can be put thus: whether, when a person is sentenced to more than one period of imprisonment to be served concurrently, the periods spent previously in custody should be deducted from each particular sentence to which they relate before calculating the release date by reference to the total sentence, or whether such periods in custody should be aggregated and the release date calculated simply by deducting that aggregate from the total sentence. The applicant advances the aggregate approach. The respondent deals with each sentence separately, calculating the release date by reference to the sentence with the latest expiry date, once that sentence has been identified after crediting the appropriate custody time attributable to it.'

Again, it is perhaps helpful to illustrate the basic problem by a factual example. Assume a defendant is arrested for burglary A and remanded in custody for six months. He is then released on bail and whilst on bail commits and is arrested for burglary B. He is then remanded in custody for a further six months after which he is tried for both. At trial he is convicted of both burglaries and sentenced to one year's imprisonment concurrently on each. Is he entitled to credit for the total period of one year spent on remand so that he immediately goes free, or only for six months so that he still (again, all questions of remission aside) has six months to serve? All four decisions in the *Gaffney* line of authority state that he still has six months to serve. They hold that the first six-month period on remand is served only in relation to burglary A, burglary B not even having been committed by then. True, the defendant is entitled to the full credit *a* of 12 months spent on remand in respect of burglary A, but that still leaves him with six months to serve in respect of burglary B.

It would certainly be burdensome and I think ultimately unhelpful to embark here upon a minute analysis of each of the four cases. For present purposes, I shall instead confine myself to the following comments. Although in the four cases the point arose in various different circumstances,—for example, in *Ex p*
b *Read* (1987) 9 Cr App R (S) 206 and *Ex p Woodward* (24 June 1996, unreported), although not *Ex p Wilson* (24 June 1996, unreported), the concurrent sentences were passed by different courts on different occasions—neither party before us suggests that these differences are of any materiality. The courts reached their conclusion on the point essentially by reference to the language of s 67 alone (described in *Ex p Gaffney* [1982] 2 All ER 492 at 494, [1982] 1 WLR 696 at 698 as
c 'a very difficult section'). Indeed, in *Ex p Gaffney* and *Ex p Read*, no other section was even referred to.

In *Ex p Mooney* the applicant for the first time sought to rely on provisions outside s 67 to illuminate its meaning, notably s 51(2) of the 1991 Act which is in substantially the same terms as s 104(2) of the 1967 Act. In giving the first
d judgment of the Divisional Court on that occasion I said ([1996] 1 Cr App R (S) 74 at 77):

'Mr Owen Davies [counsel for the applicant], in these proceedings, seeks to argue a point not apparently taken in either *ex parte Gaffney* or *ex parte Read*, although, as it seems to me, if a good point it was one which was
e available to the applicants in each. The point is this: that the phrase "sentence of imprisonment" in the opening line of section 67 should be interpreted to mean the same as the expression "term of imprisonment" as that expression is defined in section 51(2) of the 1991 Act, formerly section 104(2) of the 1967 Act. If that be right then every element of an eventual
f concurrent sentence is a sentence that carries with it the right to credit for pre-sentence periods spent in custody, irrespective of the offences in connection with which they were spent. In my judgment, however, it is plainly wrong. Section 51(2) simply does not address the question of deduction of time spent on remand. That is left to be dealt with in the specific provision in the 1967 Act, namely section 67 as amended. Section 67
g expressly adopts a particular approach, rather than the global or aggregate approach adopted for quite different purposes by section 51 [ie calculation of remission]. It is true, as Mr Davies points out, that Part II of the 1991 Act, to which section 51 applies, includes within it section 41, but section 41, by its opening words, begs rather than answers the question as to how section 67
h applies. Section 41 necessarily leaves its proper construction untouched. As to the proper construction of section 67, the language seems to me unambiguous: it clearly requires the same result here as in both the earlier cases. There is no material distinction on the facts, nor are the statutory provisions presently in play materially different.'

j It seems clear from that passage that we regarded the crucial words in s 67 to be the words 'sentence of imprisonment' in the first line, and that we understood those to refer to each individual sentence imposed rather than the total produced by the various different concurrent sentences. It might also appear that had we thought 'sentence of imprisonment' there referred to the total sentence imposed, a different result would have followed.

The decision in *Ex p Mooney* attracted adverse criticism from various academic commentators. One such was Dr David Thomas's commentary (see [1995] Crim LR 753–754):

'The position which emerges as a result of this decision and the earlier authorities cited in it seems obviously unfair to offenders who have spent time in custody on remand awaiting trial for one offence, and are eventually sentenced to concurrent sentences for other unrelated offences. If the offender spends (say) six months in custody awaiting trial for offence A, and is eventually sentenced to concurrent terms of two years for offence A and an unrelated offence, B, he will receive no credit for the time spent in custody on remand as it will not count against the sentence for offence B. If, however, he is sentenced to two consecutive terms of 12 months, he will get full credit for his time in custody, which will reduce the first sentence and thus shorten his total time in custody ... At its best, this decision produces one more anomaly and one more technicality which sentencers must be alert to recognise. This is particularly unfortunate, as the decision appears to be based on a misapprehension about the existing statutory framework. The decision appears to proceed on the assumption that Criminal Justice Act 1991, s. 51(2) has replaced Criminal Justice Act 1967, s. 104(2). It has not: Criminal Justice Act 1967, s. 104(2) appears to be still in force, and governs the interpretation of the 1967 Act ... If section 67 of the 1967 Act is interpreted in the light of this section (which was not mentioned in either *ex p. Gaffney* or *ex p. Read*) it seems impossible that the court could have come to the conclusion which it did in any of these cases.'

A similar point was made in *Current Sentencing Practice News* (1995) issue 5, p 6. (No one, be it noted, at that stage sought to suggest that the logical consequence of these decisions was what the applicant now contends for, with regard to consecutive sentence cases. Indeed, Dr Thomas's commentary plainly assumed the contrary.)

Those, then, were the circumstances in which the point concerning concurrent sentences came to be litigated for the fourth and final time just two months ago in *R v Secretary of State for the Home Dept, ex p Woodward and Wilson* (24 June 1996, unreported) (Russell LJ and Scott Baker J). This time, of course, the academic criticism was well in mind and s 104(2) (then recognised still to be in force) was at the very forefront of the argument. The main judgment was given by Scott Baker J, and a very full and careful judgment it is. The determinative passage reads thus:

'In my judgment, the key to the construction of s 67(1) lies in the expression "sentence of imprisonment" as opposed to the expression "term of imprisonment" in ss 104(2) and 51(2). It cannot, in my judgment, be doubted that by s 104(2), which clearly is applicable, these applicants each have a single term of imprisonment, but the question is what are the consequences of that single term, and that is a matter which is resolved not by s 104(2) but by s 67(1). Section 51(2) and s 104(2) are both general provisions, neither is concerned with how remand time and police detention time is to be deducted, that question is dealt with by s 67 of the 1967 Act in conjunction with s 41 of the 1991 Act. For my part, I have no doubt, bearing in mind the reasoning of Simon Brown LJ with which Curtis J agreed, that had that court been aware that s 104(2) of the 1967 Act was still in force, they

a   would have reached precisely the same conclusion ... In my judgment,
s 67(1) clearly envisages the particular approach. It has been so interpreted
by a number of authorities over the last 14 years. There is, so far as I am
aware, no decision to the contrary in the period of almost 20 years since the
1967 Act was envisaged. If Parliament had intended to change the law to the
aggregate approach it could easily have done so in one of the numerous
b   Criminal Justice Acts that have been passed in recent years. The reasoning
of Simon Brown LJ in *Ex p Mooney* prevails, and in my respectful view is
correct. Section 67 was intended to link periods in custody to particular
sentences for particular offences.'

The judge then explained why in his judgment no injustice or unfairness is
c   produced by such a construction: there would, he said—

'be no injustice provided the judge bears in mind the effect of any time
spent on remand or in police custody on the constituent elements of the
sentence he is minded to pass. Counsel should ensure that the judge is
informed of any periods that the defendant has spent in custody and the
d   offences to which they relate.'

We had said much the same in *Ex p Mooney*.
In the result, the judge saw 'no grounds for reopening a matter which seems to
me on the authorities now to be well settled' and, since Russell LJ agreed, the
court refused the applications for leave to move for judicial review.
e   In the light of those authorities and that reasoning Mr Weatherby's argument
is simple: if the words 'any sentence of imprisonment' in s 67(1) of the 1967 Act
are to be construed in the context of concurrent sentences as referring to the term
imposed for each individual offence—'the particular approach'—then so must
they be in consecutive sentence cases. And if they are, each consecutive sentence
f   then falls to be treated as reduced by any 'relevant period'. And that 'relevant
period' includes, by virtue of s 67(1A)(b)(i), the period spent on remand in
custody even though the remand related to more than one offence.
Mr Pannick seeks to meet this argument in one of two alternative ways. First
he submits (consistently with the *Gaffney* line of cases), that if it is necessary to
look at each individual sentence when computing the relevant period of
g   deduction, then nevertheless, the prisoner can only benefit once from any given
period spent on remand. If that period is deducted from the first consecutive
sentence, it cannot be claimed also in reduction of any other consecutive
sentence.
At one stage of the respondent's submissions (and certainly in his skeleton
h   argument) reliance was placed on the use of the word 'only' in s 67(1A)(b)(i) and
it was contended that 'where a person has been remanded in custody in relation
to two charges, he cannot say, in relation to each of them, that he had been
remanded in custody 'only' in relation to proceedings relating to that sentence or
that offence'. But that, in my judgment, cannot be right. No one disputes that
j   such a period can be brought into account at any rate once even though it relates
to more than one offence. It seems to me that Mr Weatherby is clearly correct in
submitting that the word 'only' is introduced simply so as to exclude periods
spent in custody whilst serving another sentence—precisely as this very applicant
did for 25 days of his initial 106-day period in custody. That is why no equivalent
words were necessary with regard to police detention provided for under
s 67(1A)(a).

Shorn of support from the word 'only', Mr Pannick's first argument appears *a*
then to owe rather more to common sense than to statutory construction. As a
matter of language, it is difficult to see how the section allows the 'relevant
period' to be computed differently for one consecutive sentence rather than
another.

His second argument is that regard should indeed be had to s 104(2) in this
context, so that one looks at the total sentence rather than its individual elements *b*
when computing the appropriate reduction for time spent in custody on remand.
Obviously this approach solves the problem of the present challenge entirely—at
the cost, however, of apparent inconsistency with the *Gaffney* approach: it
appears to involve using 'the global or aggregate' approach to s 67(1) rather than
'the particular approach' now established as appropriate in concurrent sentence
cases. *c*

Mr Pannick disputes any such inconsistency, contending rather that s 104(2)
can properly be invoked to assist in the construction and application of s 67 in
regard to the present issue, that being a quite different issue from the one arising
in the concurrent sentence cases. He points out that there is certainly no question
of double counting under the *Gaffney* principle—indeed, quite the reverse. Real *d*
inconsistency between the treatment of the two types of sentence, he submits,
would arise only if the applicant's present argument were to prevail.

It is time to state my conclusions upon these arguments, which I can do
relatively briefly.

The one result of s 67 which in my judgment Parliament could not possibly *e*
have intended, was that contended for by the applicant here. It would produce a
complete nonsense. Whatever may be said about the language of the section it
certainly does not lead clearly to that result. In truth, the only argument for the
section to be construed in that way derives from the *Gaffney* line of cases.
Powerful and logical though at first blush that argument may appear—and no *f*
doubt it was that power and logic which caused the prison service, so soon after
the decision in *Ex p Woodward and Wilson*, to introduce the new release
guidelines—in my judgment it cannot prevail. If, indeed, consistency with the
Gaffney approach would require consecutive sentences to be dealt with as the
applicant submits, then I should unhesitatingly conclude that the *Gaffney*
approach was wrong. The principle of stare decisis does not apply in the *g*
Divisional Court and we need not follow other decisions of this court when we
are 'convinced that [they are] wrong' (see *R v Greater Manchester Coroner, ex p Tal*
[1984] 3 All ER 240 at 248, [1985] QB 67 at 81). I would, if necessary, decline to
follow even such a well-established line of authority as this rather than produce
the absurd result contended for here. *h*

It is therefore unnecessary and, as it seems to me, inappropriate in the present
case to reach any final conclusion as to whether it is indeed possible to construe
s 67 sensibly, so far as consecutive sentences are concerned, consistently with the
correctness of the present approach in concurrent sentence cases. Suffice to say
that my preferred path of construction to Mr Pannick's undoubtedly sensible *j*
(indeed compelling) conclusion as to how consecutive sentence cases must be
treated is by way of s 104(2). If that route is indeed thought difficult to reconcile
with the *Gaffney* approach, so be it. Of one thing I am clear: whatever relevance
(if any) we might have attached to s 104(2) in *Ex p Mooney* [1996] 1 Cr App R (S) 74
had we known it remained in force, had we been alive to the present argument—
ie the consecutive sentence dimension to the case—I for my part would certainly

a not have described the language of s 67 as 'unambiguous' with regard to the correct treatment of concurrent sentence cases.

Whether in these circumstances the *Gaffney* approach could usefully be looked at yet again, despite its very decisive final examination and confirmation in *Ex p Woodward and Wilson*, is not for me to say. On any view it would plainly now be difficult to overthrow. I say no more than that over-precipitate action should

b clearly be avoided and that any further challenge should ideally go before a full Divisional Court presided over perhaps by the Lord Chief Justice. An alternative, of course, would be to legislate urgently for absolute clarity. As was said in *Ex p Read* (1987) 9 Cr App R (S) 206 at 209:

c 'The determination of a man's [latest date of release] is something which should be beyond dispute. Parliament must have intended the provision whereby the determination is made to be easy to apply.'

In *Ex p Woodward and Wilson* this too was said:

d 'If these applications have done nothing else, they have illustrated the urgent need for one consolidated Act of Parliament to deal with the law relating to sentencing.'

All that, however, is for the future, and not for this court. So far as the present challenge goes, although in all the circumstances we thought it right to give leave to move, we had no hesitation in dismissing it at the conclusion of the hearing.

e This judgment states my reasons for doing so.

POPPLEWELL J. I agree. It is unnecessary for me to repeat the facts or the statutory provisions to which Simon Brown LJ has just referred.

This application arises out of 'Instruction to Governors' IG50/1996 issued by a

f working party of the Home Office to governors of prisons under the signature of the director general of the prison service on 15 August 1996. Paragraph 8(5) of that instruction indicated that where consecutive sentences arise out of the same proceedings (ie where the cases are prosecuted together and one trial is held), then remand time which is applicable to *any* of the consecutive sentences will be added together to reduce the total sentence.

g That instruction was issued without the knowledge or agreement of the Secretary of State. It is no part of the court's function to express any view about that. On 23 August 1996 the Secretary of State countermanded that instruction, and it is against that decision of the Secretary of State that this application is made.

It is clear that that instruction substantially altered the method of calculation

h of the remand time which could be appropriately deducted from a prisoner's sentence when he received consecutive sentences.

The effect of the instruction can be best illustrated by an example raised during the course of argument. A prisoner commits ten burglaries, is arrested, and is remanded in custody for one year before he is tried. When he comes to be

j sentenced he receives a sentence of one year on each count consecutively (ie his total sentence is ten years). It is the applicant's argument that, as he has been remanded in custody for a year on each separate count, he is entitled to deduct that year from each year of his sentence so that his ten years sentence is thereby reduced by reason of a notional ten years of remand and he is entitled to be released immediately. For the purpose of these calculations all questions of parole are ignored.

Mr Weatherby accepts that that is an absurd situation. When the position of a co-defendant charged with the same offences, who is on bail, is considered the position becomes even more absurd. He will serve ten years, while his co-defendant would have served simply the one year on remand.

Mr Weatherby's reply to that situation is twofold. Firstly, that if it is absurd, it is for Parliament and not for the courts to correct it. Secondly, that by analogy with a number of decided cases of the Divisional Court relating to concurrent sentences, the instruction is in accordance with present law.

I turn therefore to these four cases. They are *R v Governor of Blundeston Prison, ex p Gaffney* [1982] 2 All ER 492, [1982] 1 WLR 696, *R v Secretary of State for the Home Office, ex p Read* (1987) 9 Cr App R (S) 206, *R v Governor of HM Prison Styal, ex p Mooney* [1996] 1 Cr App R (S) 74 and *R v Secretary of State for the Home Dept, ex p Woodward and Wilson* (24 June 1996, unreported).

It is not necessary to set out the individual facts of those cases, but the principle can be summarised in a simple example. A prisoner is arrested for offence A and remanded in custody for a period of six months. Thereafter he is on bail. He commits offence B, is arrested for that offence and is in custody for offence B for three months immediately preceding trial. When he comes to be sentenced he receives a concurrent sentence of one year on each offence. He will have served a total of nine months in prison on remand and received a term of imprisonment of 12 months. It might be thought therefore that the length of time that he had to serve was some three months.

However, that is not what the decisions say. The courts have decided that the first six months is to be ignored because while it may be set against the one year for offence A, there is only three months to be set against the one year for offence B. Therefore the prisoner is to serve a period of nine months. The first calculation, namely the deduction of nine months, is based on what is called the 'aggregate' argument; the second, namely the deduction of three months, is described as the 'particular' argument.

Based on those authorities, Mr Weatherby submits by analogy that a remand period of one year in respect of each of the ten offences in the example has to be deducted even though it has not actually been served. Therefore a prisoner is entitled to release because there is to be ascribed to him a period of one year remand in respect of each of the ten offences.

It seems to me that there are three answers to that argument. Firstly that those decisions are incorrect. At first sight, this may seem a somewhat bold criticism of decisions made by Lord Lane CJ, Woolf, Simon Brown and Russell LJJ, and Lloyd, Eastham, McCullough, Curtis, and Scott-Baker JJ, all of whom have experience in this field.

These decisions have not however, found favour with the academics. Dr David Thomas, the well-known criminologist in an article in *Current Sentencing Practice News* (1995) issue 5, p 6 disagrees with them and in [1995] Crim LR 753 suggests that they are wrong. The courts themselves have taken the view, in some cases, that the results may appear to be unjust and clearly they impose a very considerable burden on judges to ensure that there is not disparity between various prisoners.

I incline to agree that the effect of the Criminal Justice Act 1967, s 104(2) has not been fully appreciated by the courts. It is difficult to see what the purpose of s 104(2) is if it is not to treat the sentence passed as a single term and therefore, provided the periods on remand relate to those offences, to treat all the periods of remand also as a single term. If it is not related to s 67(1) of the 1967 Act it is *a* difficult to understand its purpose. None of the decisions have addressed this problem except to say boldly that they are unrelated.

Mr Pannick has submitted that the decisions in relation to concurrent sentences are correct and, more particularly, that the consistent approach which has remained for nearly 20 years, should be followed in order to give certainty. I entirely accept that this an area where certainty is desirable. Nothing is more *b* likely to cause distress and disquiet to prisoners than disputes in the court about the interpretation of s 67. But while certainty is a good thing, justice is even better.

Above all, it has to be remembered that the purpose of s 67 is to ensure that when the length of sentence which the prisoner actually has to serve is determined, the amount of time he has spent on remand is thereby to be *c* deducted so that for instance, compared with a co-defendant who is on bail, the total amount of time spent in prison is the same. Disparity is one of the commonest grounds of appeal in criminal cases. It equally follows that the period to be taken into account by way of deduction should be not less but certainly not more than the actual period served.

d It is not necessary for the purpose of this judgment, however, to do anything more than express some reservations as to the correctness of the decisions upon which Mr Weatherby relies as an analogy.

The second answer to Mr Weatherby's argument is that there is not an analogy. In the cases of concurrent sentences to which I have referred, the prisoner has actually served a period on remand. It is not notional. It is a fact. *e* The prisoner who serves a year and gets ten years consecutive has in fact only served one year. However unfair it may appear that the prisoner with a concurrent sentence is not entitled to credit for some period of the time he spent in custody on remand, it cannot give a prisoner who has *not* served time in custody on remand a corresponding advantage so as to receive credit for a period *f* which he has never served.

Mr Weatherby points out that s 67(1A)(a) which relates to the time spent by an offender in police detention is uncomplicated by any proviso, whereas sub-s (b)(i) has a wider connotation. It is Mr Pannick's contention, in relation to the phrase 'by reason only' in sub-s (b) that where a person has been remanded in custody in relation to two charges he cannot say, in relation to each of them, that he has *g* been remanded in custody *only* in relation to proceedings relating to that sentence or that offence. A prisoner cannot deduct from each sentence, remand time which has not been served specifically (ie only) in relation to that offence. Thus, there is only one period of remand in custody which constitutes a relevant period where there are concurrent remands, even in cases of consecutive sentences.

h There is nothing, in my judgment, in the cases relating to concurrent sentences which requires the court to treat a concurrent remand as if it is a consecutive remand or to treat a concurrent remand as if it were a series of separate remands attached to the individual offences subsequently treated as requiring a consecutive sentence. If any support for that view were needed apart from the *j* wording of s 67 I believe it is to be found in s 104(2).

The third reason for rejecting Mr Weatherby's argument is that it results in absurdity. The illustration in relation to a co-defendant who is on bail amply demonstrates this. Further, if the court were seeking to ensure that both accused in the example given serve the same period of time it would have to pass a sentence of 19 years on the prisoner who had spent one year in custody to equate with the ten years on the prisoner who had been on bail. That is because the prisoner who has spent one year in custody would get a deduction of ten years *a* from the 19 years by reason of the present argument but would already have spent one year in custody thus making a total of ten years in prison.

Mr Weatherby submitted that it is a canon of construction that any ambiguity in a statute affecting the liberty of the subject should be construed in favour of an accused. That is a valid submission, but another equally important canon of construction is to interpret legislation, so far as possible, to equate with common *b* sense. Happily, common sense is still, I believe, a part of the English common law. As Lord Goddard CJ said in *Barnes v Jarvis* [1953] 1 All ER 1061 at 1063, [1953] 1 WLR 649 at 652 '... a certain amount of common sense [must be applied] in construing statutes ...' Equally, there is always a presumption against construing an Act of Parliament so as to produce an absurd result.

It may be said that a court should not be deterred from enunciating the correct *c* principle of law because it may have startling or calamitous results. But I confess that I have approached the investigation of a legal proposition of this character with a strong prejudice in favour of the idea that there may be a considerable flaw in the argument somewhere. I am quite satisfied that there is. I regard this application as wholly unarguable. I agree that it must be dismissed. *d*

Application dismissed.

Dilys Tausz   Barrister.

R v Governor of Brockhill Prison, ex parte Evans
R v Governor of Onley Young Offender Institution, Rugby, ex parte Reid

QUEEN'S BENCH DIVISION

LORD BINGHAM OF CORNHILL CJ, ROSE LJ AND BLOFELD J

29 OCTOBER, 15 NOVEMBER 1996

Sentence – Reduction – Period spent in custody – Concurrent sentences – Defendant spending separate periods in custody pending sentence for separate offences – Defendant sentenced to concurrent periods of imprisonment – Period of custody by which sentence to be reduced – Criminal Justice Act 1967, s 67(1)(1A)(b)(i).

Where a defendant spent time in custody awaiting trial for more than one offence, and on conviction was sentenced to concurrent terms of imprisonment for those offences, the period by which the sentence is to be reduced under s 67(1)[a] and (1A)(b)(i)[b] of the Criminal Justice Act 1967 is the total period that the defendant spent in custody before sentence, and not merely the period spent in custody in respect of the offence for which the longest sentence was passed or, if the sentences were imposed on different occasions, for which the sentence was to expire last. However, any such period cannot be taken into account more than once, nor can any period be taken into account during which the defendant was in custody for some reason unrelated to the offences for which he was sentenced (see p 441 *d*, p 445 *c d*, 452 *j*, 453 *e* and p 454 *h*, post).

R v Secretary of State for the Home Dept, ex p Naughton [1997] 1 All ER 426 considered.

R v Governor of Blundeston Prison, ex p Gaffney [1982] 2 All ER 492, *R v Secretary of State for the Home Office, ex p Read* (1987) 9 Cr App R (S) 206 and *R v Governor of HM Prison Styal, ex p Mooney* [1996] 1 Cr App R (S) 74 disapproved.

Notes

For the duration of a sentence, see 11(2) *Halsbury's Laws* (4th edn reissue) para 1202, and for cases on the effect of time spent in custody on duration of sentence, see 15(2) *Digest* (2nd reissue) 275–276, 20770–20780.

For the Criminal Justice Act 1967, s 67, see 34 *Halsbury's Statutes* (4th edn) 704.

Cases referred to in judgment

R v Governor of Blundeston Prison, ex p Gaffney [1982] 2 All ER 492, [1982] 1 WLR 696, DC.

R v Governor of HM Prison Styal, ex p Mooney [1996] 1 Cr App R (S) 74, DC.

R v Greater Manchester Coroner, ex p Tal [1984] 3 All ER 240, [1985] QB 67, [1984] 3 WLR 643, DC.

R v Secretary of State for the Home Dept, ex p Naughton [1997] 1 All ER 426, DC.

R v Secretary of State for the Home Dept, ex p Woodward and Wilson (24 June 1996, unreported), DC.

R v Secretary of State for the Home Office, ex p Read (1987) 9 Cr App R (S) 206, DC.

Cases also cited or referred to in skeleton arguments

R v Gould [1968] 1 All ER 849, [1968] 2 QB 65, CA.

---

a   Section 67(1) is set out at p 444 *g h*, post

b   Section 67(1A) is set out at p 444 *j*, post

R v McKenna [1974] 1 All ER 637, [1974] 1 WLR 267, CA.

R v Parole Board, ex p Wilson [1992] 2 All ER 576, [1992] QB 740, CA.

R v Spencer [1985] 1 All ER 673, [1985] QB 771, CA; *rvsd* [1986] 2 All ER 928, [1987] AC 128, HL.

R v Taylor [1950] 2 All ER 170, [1950] 2 KB 368, CCA.

Williams v Fawcett [1985] 1 All ER 787, [1986] QB 604, CA.

Young v Bristol Aeroplane Co Ltd [1944] 2 All ER 293, [1944] KB 718, CA; *affd* [1946] 1 All ER 98, [1946] AC 163, HL.

Applications for habeas corpus and for leave to move for judicial review

R v Governor of Brockhill Prison, ex p Evans

The applicant, Michelle Carol Evans, was sentenced in the Crown Court at Cardiff on 12 January 1996, to four concurrent terms of imprisonment for offences of robbery, burglary, and assault occasioning actual bodily harm of which she had been convicted earlier. The longest term of imprisonment (and therefore the total sentence) was two years in respect of the robbery. The governor of Brockhill Prison, where the applicant was detained, maintained that the applicant was not due to be released until 18 November 1996 on the basis that under s 67(1) and (1A)(b)(i) of the Criminal Justice Act 1967 the two years was to be reduced only by the period of 73 days she had spent in custody in respect of the robbery before sentence. The applicant applied for a writ of habeas corpus ad subjiciendum and for leave to move for judicial review on the ground that the two years should be reduced by the total period of 135 days she had spent in custody in respect of the offences before sentence and that on that basis she was entitled to be released on 17 September 1996. The facts are set out in the judgment of the court.

R v Governor of Onley Young Offender Institution, Rugby, ex p Reid

The applicant Paul Reid was sentenced in the Crown Court at Snaresbrook on 7 May 1996 to five concurrent terms of imprisonment for offences of handling and burglary of which he had been convicted earlier. The longest term of imprisonment (and therefore the total sentence) was 27 months in respect of the burglaries. The governor of Onley Young Offender Institution, Rugby, where the applicant was detained, maintained that the applicant was not due to be released until 15 July 1997 on the basis that under s 67(1) and (1A)(b)(i) of the Criminal Justice Act 1967 the 27 months was to be reduced only by the period of 58 days he had spent in custody in respect of one of the burglaries before sentence. The applicant applied for a writ of habeas corpus ad subjiciendum and for leave to move for judicial review on the ground that the 27 months should be reduced by the total period of 310 days he had spent in custody in respect of the offences before sentence and that on that basis he was entitled to be released on 8 October or 5 November 1996. The facts are set out in the judgment of the court.

Edward Fitzgerald QC and *Peter Weatherby* (instructed by *John Howell & Co*, Sheffield) for the applicant Evans.

Michael Mansfield QC and *Martin Soorjoo* (instructed by *J R Jones*) for the applicant Reid.

Stephen Richards and *Michael Fordham* (instructed by the *Treasury Solicitor*) for the respondent governors.

Cur adv vult

a 15 November 1996. The following judgment of the court was delivered.

LORD BINGHAM OF CORNHILL CJ. If a defendant spends time in custody awaiting trial for a single offence, and if on conviction he is sentenced to a term of custody, the term he is required to serve will be reduced by the period he spent in custody before sentence (unless during that pre-sentence period he was in b custody for some reason unrelated to the offence for which he is sentenced).

If he spends time in custody awaiting trial for more than one offence, and if on conviction he is sentenced to consecutive terms of custody, the total term he is required to serve will be reduced by the total period he spent in custody before sentence, subject to the same exception as before, at any rate so long as the period spent on remand for any offence does not exceed the period to be served of the c consecutive sentence imposed for that offence.

These applications concern a third situation: where a defendant spends time in custody awaiting trial for more than one offence, and is on conviction sentenced to concurrent or overlapping terms of custody. To what extent is account to be taken, in assessing the term of custody to be served in pursuance of the sentence d in that situation, of time spent in custody (otherwise than for some unrelated reason) before the sentences were imposed? That is the problem the court is now called upon to resolve.

Michelle Carol Evans

e On 12 January 1996 the applicant, Michelle Carol Evans, was sentenced for four offences in the Crown Court at Cardiff. For robbery she was sentenced to two years' imprisonment; for each of two burglaries she was sentenced to nine months' imprisonment; for assault occasioning actual bodily harm she was sentenced to three months' imprisonment. All the sentences were concurrent. Her total sentence was therefore one of two years.

f The applicant had been arrested for burglary on 4 May 1995 and spent two days in police custody before being bailed. She had been re-arrested on 20 June 1995 and held in custody until 18 August 1995 before again being bailed. This period amounted in total to 62 days in custody. During the latter period of custody (20 June to 18 August, a period of 60 days) the applicant had also been held on the g assault charge. On the robbery charge, the applicant had been held in prison from 31 October 1995 until 11 January 1996, a total of 73 days. During this last period of custody she had not been remanded on the charges of burglary and assault but for the robbery alone.

The applicant now seeks an order of habeas corpus and leave to move for h judicial review. The respondent is the governor of Her Majesty's prison at Brockhill. The issue between the applicant and the respondent concerns her date of release.

The basis of the respondent's calculation is this. The sentence of two years is treated as one of 731 days. To calculate the date on which her sentence expires, j the respondent deducts the 73 days which the applicant spent in custody in relation to the robbery charge, this being the longest (and in the respondent's contention the dominant) sentence. On this basis the effective sentence is one of 658 days and expires on 30 October 1997. In order to calculate the applicant's conditional release date the respondent takes the length of the sentence (731 days) as reduced by the period spent on remand on the robbery charge (73 days), ie 658 days, and deducts 365 days, the period of the sentence which a short-term prisoner is not obliged to serve. This yields a total of 293 days to be served, to which must be added 19 additional days awarded on disciplinary grounds, yielding a release date of 18 November 1996.

The applicant accepts 731 days as the length of the sentence, but seeks to deduct from it 135 days (the sum of 62 days spent in custody for the burglary, including 60 days spent at the same time in custody on the assault charge, plus the 73 days in custody on the robbery charge) giving a total effective sentence of 596 days, which yields a sentence expiry date of 29 August 1997. To calculate her conditional release date the applicant takes this figure of 596 days and deducts 365 days (the period which need not be served by a short-term prisoner), obtaining a figure of 231 days. To this total of 231 days she adds the 19 additional days awarded on disciplinary grounds and achieves a release date of 17 September 1996. On this calculation the applicant should already have been released from prison.

The essential difference between the two modes of calculation is clear. The respondent allocates time spent in custody to the particular offence for which the applicant was at the relevant time held in custody. Thus, since the sentences were all imposed at the same time and the longest sentence imposed was that of 2 years for robbery, that period is reduced only by the 73 days which she spent in custody on that charge. The 62 days spent in custody on the burglary charge and the 60 days spent in custody on the assault charge do not, on this approach, reduce the period which the applicant is obliged to serve. The applicant does not seek to count twice the period of 60 days during which she was held in custody for both burglary and assault, but does claim that the 62 days spent in custody on the burglary charge and the 73 days spent in custody on the robbery charge should be added together and deducted from the length of the total sentence. The respondent's approach has been called the 'particular' approach, the applicant's 'the aggregate' approach.

Paul Reid

On 7 May 1996 in the Crown Court at Snaresbrook Blofeld J passed multiple concurrent sentences on this applicant, as follows:

(1) Handling	9 months	
(2) Burglary	27 months	
(3) Burglary	27 months	
(4) Burglary	27 months	
(5) Burglary	27 months.	

Although it proved impossible to achieve agreement of the facts until over a week after the hearing of the application before us had been concluded (and there is still a measure of disagreement), it appears that for offence (1) the applicant had before sentence spent three periods on remand: (a) from 21 November 1994 to 17 January 1995 (58 days); (b) from 20 January 1995 to 1 May 1995 (102 days); and (c) from 9 December 1995 to 7 May 1996 (150 days). For each of offences (2) and (3) he had been in custody for periods (b) and (c), but not (a); for offence (4) he had been in custody for period (c), but not periods (a) or (b); for offence (5) he had been in custody for part of period (c), from 11 March to 7 May 1996 (58 days), but not for periods (a) or (b), or (c) before 11 March 1996.

This applicant makes the same applications as the applicant Evans, but in this case the respondent is the governor of Onley Young Offender Institution, where he is held.

a   There is, again, a difference between the applicant and the respondent concerning the applicant's date of release. They agree that the sentence of 27 months is to be treated as 822 days. From this total the respondent deducts 58 days (the part of period (c) spent by the applicant on remand for offence (5)) to achieve an effective sentence of 764 days and a sentence expiry date of 9 June 1998. From the total so reached of 764 days he deducts 411 days (the half of the sentence which need not be served) to reach a total of 353 days to be served. To
b   that total must be added 82 additional days which the respondent says have been awarded under prison rules, giving a conditional release date of 15 July 1997.

The applicant deducts from the sentence of 822 days the total of 310 days spent on remand for all these offences, achieving an effective sentence of 512 days and a release date of 30 September 1997. From the total of 512 days he deducts 411
c   days (the half of the sentence which need not be served) to reach a total of 101 days to be served. With the addition of 54 disciplinary days (said by the applicant to be the total number of additional days awarded) he achieves a conditional release date of 8 October 1996. If the respondent is right and the applicant wrong about the number of additional days awarded, the conditional release date on this
d   approach would have been 5 November 1996.

It is plain from the record that when passing sentence the judge understood that the applicant would be released shortly, and intended that he should. The calculations now advanced by the respondent are not easy to reconcile with those supplied to the applicant's solicitor when his release date was first questioned; and the applicant's confidence cannot have been enhanced by a message from the
e   prison reading: 'Sorry about the diagram! I tried doing it twice but it looked so complicated even I couldn't understand it.'

The relevant statutory provisions
Section 33(1) of the Criminal Justice Act 1991 provides:

f
'As soon as a short-term prisoner has served one-half of his sentence, it shall be the duty of the Secretary of State ... (b) to release him on licence if that sentence is for a term of twelve months or more.'

In sub-s (5) a 'short-term prisoner' is defined to mean a person serving a sentence
g   of imprisonment for a term of less than four years. Section 51(2) of the 1991 Act reads:

'For the purposes of any reference in this Part, however expressed, to the term of imprisonment to which a person has been sentenced or which, or part of which, he has served, consecutive terms and terms which are wholly
h   or partly concurrent shall be treated as a single term.'

Since both these applicants received sentences for a term of more than 12 months but less than 4 years, treating the concurrent sentences as a single term, both are short-term prisoners within the meaning of the Act and entitled to release on licence after serving one half of their sentences.
j   Section 41 of the 1991 Act reads:

'*Remand time to count towards time served.*—(1) This section applies to any person whose sentence falls to be reduced under section 67 of the Criminal Justice Act 1967 ("the 1967 Act") by any relevant period within the meaning of that section ("the relevant period").

(2) For the purpose of determining for the purposes of this Part—(a)
whether a person to whom this section applies has served one-half or
two-thirds of his sentence; or (b) whether such a person would (but for his
release) have served three-quarters of that sentence, the relevant period
shall, subject to subsection (3) below, be treated as having been served by
him as part of that sentence ...'

Thus both applicants are obliged to serve one-half of their sentences, but in
determining whether they have done so the period to be served must be treated
as reduced by what s 67 of the 1967 Act defines as the 'relevant period'.

As originally enacted s 67 of the 1967 Act, so far as relevant, provided:

'(1) The length of any sentence of imprisonment imposed on an offender
by a court shall be treated as reduced by any period during which he was in
custody by reason only of having been committed to custody by an order of
a court made in connection with any proceedings relating to that sentence or
the offence for which it was passed or any proceedings from which those
proceedings arose, but where the offender was previously subject to a
probation order, an order for conditional discharge or a suspended sentence
in respect of that offence, any such period falling before the order was made
or suspended sentence passed shall be disregarded for the purposes of this
section ...

(4) Any reference in this Act or any other enactment (whether passed
before or after the commencement of this Act) to the length of any sentence
of imprisonment shall, unless the context otherwise requires, be construed
as a reference to the sentence pronounced by the court and not the sentence
as reduced by this section.'

The 1967 Act also provided, in s 104(2):

'For the purposes of any reference in this Act, however expressed, to the
term of imprisonment or other detention to which a person has been
sentenced or which, or part of which, he has served, consecutive terms and
terms which are wholly or partly concurrent shall be treated as a single
term'.

Section 67 has been amended and now provides:

'(1) The length of any sentence of imprisonment imposed on an offender
by a court shall be treated as reduced by any relevant period, but where he
was previously subject to a probation order, a community service order, an
order for conditional discharge or a suspended sentence in respect of that
offence, any such period falling before the order was made or suspended
sentence passed shall be disregarded for the purposes of this section.

(1A) In subsection (1) above "relevant period" means—(a) any period
during which the offender was in police detention in connection with the
offence for which the sentence was passed; or (b) any period during which
he was in custody—(i) by reason only of having been committed to custody
by an order of a court made in connection with any proceedings relating to
that sentence or the offence for which it was passed or any proceedings from
which those proceedings arose; or (ii) by reason of his having been so
committed and having been concurrently detained otherwise than by order
of a court ...'

Section 67(4) remains in force unamended. So does s 104(2).

The argument

The respondents contend that the particular approach is required by the language of s 67(1A)(b)(i) and its reference to a period during which an offender had been in custody 'in connection with any proceedings relating to that sentence or the offence for which it was passed'. Thus, it is said, time spent in custody in connection with proceedings relating to offence A cannot serve to reduce the sentence imposed for offence B. It is (the respondents argue) necessary to investigate what sentence was passed for what offence, and what period was spent in custody in connection with proceedings relating to that sentence or that offence. On this approach, s 104(2) of the 1967 Act and s 51(2) of the 1991 Act have little or no bearing: the earlier subsection was directed to the calculation, for example, of release dates; so too was the later subsection, which was also directed to determining whether a person was a long-term or short-term prisoner.

The applicants rely on s 51(2), alternatively s 104(2), and contend that since any reference to the term of imprisonment to which a person has been sentenced, however it may be expressed, is to be understood as treating consecutive terms and wholly or partly concurrent terms as a single term, and since (unless the contrary intention appears) words in the singular include the plural, the sentence or sentences passed by the court and the offence or offences for which it or they were passed, must be treated as giving rise, whether the sentences were concurrent or consecutive, to a single term, in reduction of which the whole period of pre-sentence custody (unless served for some unrelated reason) is to be set in calculating the release date.

The cases and the commentaries

In support of their contention the respondents are able to rely on four decisions of the Queen's Bench Divisional Court. The earliest of these was *R v Governor of Blundeston Prison, ex p Gaffney* [1982] 2 All ER 492, [1982] 1 WLR 696. In that case the applicant committed one group of offences (offence A) for which he was held in custody before trial for a short period. When he appeared in court sentence was deferred. He later committed another group of offences (offence B) for which he was held in custody for two months, being held in custody for offence B only. He appeared in court to be sentenced for both offence A and offence B. He was sentenced to 37 months' imprisonment for offence A and 36 months' imprisonment concurrently for offence B. The issue was whether, in calculating his release date, he could count against the 37-month sentence on offence A only the short period spent in custody on offence A or whether he could also set off the longer period spent in custody on offence B. He could set that longer period of custody against the slightly shorter sentence imposed on offence B, but that would not have the result of reducing the effective sentence he had to serve. Giving the first judgment Eastham J held that he could only set against the sentence for offence A the short period he spent in custody on offence A. He therefore upheld the particular approach. Lloyd J agreed. Lord Lane CJ also agreed, but added ([1982] 2 All ER 492 at 494, [1982] 1 WLR 696 at 698):

> 'It may be that the result appears to be unjust, but it is a result which we are forced to achieve by reason of the wording of s 67(1) of the Criminal Justice Act 1967.'

It does not appear that that authority was cited in the next case to come before a court, *R v Secretary of State for the Home Office, ex p Read* (1987) 9 Cr App R (S) 206. In that case the applicant had been convicted and sentenced for two robberies. For robbery A, he was arrested in November 1977 and held in custody until his conviction in May 1979 when he was sentenced to 15 years' imprisonment. For robbery B he was charged in July 1979 and bailed, although since he was already in custody he was not released. He was convicted in November 1979 and sentenced to 18 years' imprisonment, reduced on appeal to 16 years. A co-defendant, Sears, was also convicted of both robberies. He, however, was arrested for robbery A in November 1978, a year after the applicant. He also was convicted of robbery A in May 1979 and sentenced to 15 years. He also was charged with robbery B in July 1979, bailed (although not released since already in custody on robbery A), convicted in November 1979 and sentenced to 18 years (also reduced on appeal to 16 years). Since the criminal responsibility of the two robbers was at all times treated as the same, the applicant was aggrieved that he should spend a year longer in prison than his co-defendant, but receive no reduction to reflect that period of imprisonment. He sought a reduction in sentence on appeal to the Court of Appeal Criminal Division, but the court, although describing the position as anomalous, did not correct it. The applicant argued that since the prosecution for robbery B had been based on evidence which emerged from the trial for robbery A, the whole period of his confinement from November 1977 to his conviction of robbery B in November 1979 was in respect of robbery B. This argument was rejected. McCullough J, giving the leading judgment, said (at 209):

> 'The determination of a man's LDR [latest date of release] is something which should be beyond dispute. Parliament must have intended the provision whereby the determination is made to be easy to apply. This would not be so if the construction for which [counsel for the applicant] contends were correct.'

He upheld the particular approach for which the Secretary of State contended, and Woolf LJ agreed.

The next authority was *R v Governor of HM Prison Styal, ex p Mooney* [1996] 1 Cr App R (S) 74. In this case the applicant was on 29 November 1993 sentenced for a number of offences. For six offences of burglary (one of these being committed on 14 September 1993) she was sentenced to 30 months' imprisonment, all six sentences being concurrent. On eight counts of theft she was sentenced to six months' imprisonment concurrently with each other and concurrently with the 30 months' sentence. On four counts of going equipped and other offences she was sentenced to three months' imprisonment, those sentences being consecutive but concurrent with the sentence of 30 months. She was lastly sentenced to one day for burglary. Between February and September 1993, the applicant spent a total of 13 days in police custody in connection with various of these offences, but not in connection with the burglary committed on 14 September 1993. Between March and April 1993 the applicant spent a further 15 days in prison in respect of one or more of these offences, but not in respect of the 14 September 1993 burglary. At the date of sentence, she had thus spent 28 days in custody, but none of them related to the burglary of 14 September. The issue before the court was summarised by Simon Brown LJ in this way (at 76):

> 'The issue can be put thus: whether, when a person is sentenced to more than one period of imprisonment to be served concurrently, the periods spent previously in custody should be deducted from each particular sentence to which they relate before calculating the release date by reference to the total sentence, or whether such periods in custody should be

aggregated and the release date calculated simply by deducting that aggregate from the total sentence.'

That is essentially the issue which is before us. Having referred to the relevant legislation, under the mistaken belief that s 104(2) of the 1967 Act had been repealed and re-enacted as s 51(2) of the 1991 Act, and considered the previous authorities, Simon Brown LJ said (at 77):

'[Counsel for the applicant] in these proceedings, seeks to argue a point not apparently taken in either *ex parte Gaffney* or *ex parte Read*, although, as it seems to me, if a good point it was one which was available to the applicants in each. The point is this: that the phrase "sentence of imprisonment" in the opening line of section 67 should be interpreted to mean the same as the expression "term of imprisonment", as that expression is defined in section 51(2) of the 1991 Act, formerly section 104(2) of the 1967 Act. If that be right then every element of an eventual concurrent sentence is a sentence that carries with it the right to credit all pre-sentence periods spent in custody, irrespective of the offences in connection with which they were spent. In my judgment, however, it is plainly wrong. Section 51(2) simply does not address the question of deduction of time spent on remand. That is left to be dealt with in the specific provision in the 1967 Act, namely section 67 as amended. Section 67 expressly adopts a particular approach, rather than the global or aggregate approach adopted for quite different purposes by section 51. It is true, as [counsel for the applicant] points out, that Part II of the 1991 Act to which section 51 applies, includes within it section 41, but section 41, by its opening words, begs rather than answers the question as to how section 67 applies. Section 41 necessarily leaves its proper construction untouched. As to the proper construction of section 67, the language seems to me unambiguous: it clearly requires the same result here as in both the earlier cases. There is no material distinction on the facts, nor are the statutory provisions presently in play materially different.'

It was found to be unnecessary to address the competing policy arguments, but Simon Brown LJ added (at 78):

'I would, however, just touch on these because it is clearly important that the profession should know how matters stand and how properly to meet such difficulty as might otherwise be suggested to result from the construction of this provision presently adopted. Defending counsel must always be alive to the fact that not all periods spent in police or prison custody, prior to sentence, will necessarily count to a defendant's credit. That consideration should, in appropriate cases, be drawn to the sentencing judge's attention. My Lord, Curtis J., whose experience in this field is well nigh unrivalled, suggests that that already happens.'

Curtis J agreed. He said (at 78):

'It is for counsel then to make appropriate submissions to the sentencing judge who will take that matter into account in assessing the total appropriate period of punishment for the defendant's wrongdoing. This, in my experience, is already invariable practice since that Act came into force and especially since the decision in *ex parte Gaffney*.'

Ex p Mooney was the subject of comment in [1995] Crim LR 753. Dr D A Thomas
wrote (at 753–754):

> '... it seems obviously unfair to offenders who have spent time in custody
> on remand awaiting trial for one offence, and are eventually sentenced to
> concurrent sentences for other unrelated offences. If the offender spends
> (say) six months in custody awaiting trial for offence A, and is eventually
> sentenced to concurrent terms of two years for offence A and an unrelated
> offence, B, he will receive no credit for the time spent in custody on remand
> as it will not count against the sentence for offence B. If, however, he is
> sentenced to two consecutive terms of 12 months, he will get full credit for
> his time in custody, which will reduce the first sentence and thus shorten his
> total time in custody. A similar result will follow if offence B is taken into
> consideration, and he is sentenced to two years for offence A. The six
> months will reduce the effective duration of the two-year sentence.'

Dr Thomas pointed out that s 104(2) had not been repealed as the court had
thought, and suggested that if s 67 of the 1967 Act had been interpreted in the
light of this section (which had not been mentioned in either *Ex p Gaffney* or *Ex p
Read*) it seemed impossible that the court could have come to the conclusion
which it did in any of those cases.

Dr Thomas published a further and more detailed critique of this decision and
the preceding authority in *Current Sentencing Practice News* (1995) issue 4, pp 8–10.
He suggested (p 9):

> 'The basic principle is that time spent in custody will be deducted from the
> resulting sentence unless the offender was simultaneously in custody for
> some other reason.'

He repeated, tentatively, the suggestion that s 104(2) remained in force, and
attributed the court's decision in *Ex p Mooney* (in his view a mistaken decision) to
its failure to appreciate that fact. He also pointed to the serious injustice and
undesirable anomalies which the court's decision could produce—

> 'if the sentencing court can be persuaded (contrary to the usual and
> preferred practice) to pass a series of shorter consecutive terms with the
> same aggregate, he [the defendant] will retain all of the credit, as each of the
> periods of time on remand will be deducted from its related sentence. A
> defendant who has spent time in custody will be discouraged from pleading
> guilty to additional offences which have come to light more recently, for fear
> of losing the value of his remand time if concurrent sentences are passed. If
> he can have the other offences taken into consideration, he will preserve the
> value of his remand time, as the only sentence will be for the offences in
> relation to which the time was spent on remand, and the problem in *ex p.
> Mooney* will not arise.' (See p 10.)

Dr Thomas concluded:

> 'The real lesson of these cases is the desperate need to remedy the
> grotesque deficiencies of the statutory framework of sentencing, at least by
> a consolidation of the existing law into a single Act. The fact that the
> Divisional Court can go seriously wrong not once but three times, as a result
> of a failure to identify relevant statutory provisions, and in the course of
> doing so arrive at a result which is both unjust to individual defendants and

productive of yet more anomalies and technicalities is [the] clearest possible indication of the urgency of the problem.'

In *R v Secretary for the Home Dept, ex p Woodward and Wilson* (24 June 1996, unreported) the applicant Woodward had spent 143 days on remand before being sentenced to 33 months' imprisonment. He served part of that sentence, absconded, and committed further offences before he was again arrested. For those further offences, he again appeared in court and received concurrent sentences amounting in total to $3\frac{1}{2}$ years. The issue was whether he was entitled to set the 143 days on remand against the sentence of $3\frac{1}{2}$ years. The applicant Wilson had been sentenced to concurrent sentences of $3\frac{1}{2}$ years for a number of offences committed at different times. Before sentence, he had spent a total of 244 days on remand. Of that total, he had spent 84 days in custody before being released on bail. He had then committed further offences, for which he had again been arrested. He had then spent a further 160 days awaiting trial. The issue was whether the period of 84 days counted only against the sentences for the original offences (in which event they would not serve to reduce his effective sentence) or whether the whole period of 244 days should be set against the sentence of $3\frac{1}{2}$ years. On this occasion, the court had the benefit not only of the previously decided cases, but also Dr Thomas' criticism of them, and the court appreciated that s 104(2) of the 1967 Act remained in force. Giving the first judgment, Scott Baker J said:

'In my judgment the key to the construction of s 67(1) lies in the expression "sentence of imprisonment" as opposed to the expression "term of imprisonment" in ss 104(2) and 51(2). It cannot, in my judgment, be doubted that by s 104(2), which clearly is applicable, these applicants each have a single term of imprisonment, but the question is what are the consequences of that single term, and that is a matter which is resolved not by s 104(2) but by s 67(1). Section 51(2) and s 104(2) are both general provisions, neither is concerned with how remand time and police detention time is to be deducted, that question is dealt with by s 67 of the 1967 Act in conjunction with s 41 of the 1991 Act. For my part, I have no doubt, bearing in mind the reasoning of Simon Brown LJ with which Curtis J agreed, that had that court been aware that s 104(2) of the 1967 Act was still in force they would have reached precisely the same conclusion. There is clearly a distinction between s 51(2) and s 104(2) because s 51(2)applies only to the relevant Part of the 1991 Act whereas s 104(2) applies to the whole of the 1967 Act, but that distinction is, in my judgment, quite immaterial for the purposes of these applications and in particular for the purposes of the correct construction of s 67 of the 1967 Act. In my judgment, s 67(1) clearly envisages the particular approach. It has been so interpreted by a number of authorities over the last 14 years. There is, so far as I am aware, no decision to the contrary in the period of almost 20 years since the 1967 Act was envisaged. If Parliament had intended to change the law to the aggregate approach it could easily have done so in one of the numerous Criminal Justice Acts that have been passed in recent years. The reasoning of Simon Brown LJ in *Ex p Mooney* prevails, and in my respectful view is correct. Section 67 was intended to link periods of custody to particular sentences for particular offences. For my part, I cannot see any injustice or unfairness. One starts with the proposition that a defendant should be sentenced for each offence of which he has been convicted. The judge then has to consider the overall sentence that justice demands and for this reason, sentences are often ordered to be served concurrently, but I cannot see on the face of it why time spent in custody in respect of offence A should be credited against the sentence for offence B. There will, in my judgment, be no injustice provided the judge bears in mind the effect of any time spent on remand or in police custody on the constituent elements of the sentence he is minded to pass. Counsel should ensure that the judge is informed of any periods that the defendant has spent in custody and the offences to which they relate. If these applications have done nothing else, they have illustrated the urgent need for one consolidated Act of Parliament to deal with the law relating to sentencing.'

Russell LJ agreed. Leave to move for judicial review was refused.

On 4 September 1996 the Divisional Court (Simon Brown LJ and Popplewell J) gave judgment in *R v Secretary of State for the Home Dept, ex p Naughton* [1997] 1 All ER 426. The facts of the case, ignoring irrelevant details, were these. The applicant was arrested for unlawful possession of cannabis and spent 81 days in custody before being released on bail. He was later arrested for burglary and then spent a further period of 239 days in custody in connection with the proceedings both for the cannabis offence and the burglary offence. He was sentenced to 18 months' imprisonment for each of these offences, the sentences to run consecutively and so to produce a total of 36 months. It was common ground that in computing the applicant's release date he was entitled to credit for the two periods of 81 days and 239 days. He, however, adopting the particular approach upheld by the court in the decisions already referred to, contended that since for 239 days he had been held in custody on both of these two charges for which he received consecutive sentences, each of such sentences should be reduced by that period of 239 days. If periods spent on remand in relation to an offence were to reduce the sentence passed for that offence, then a prisoner was entitled to count the time twice. The Home Secretary challenged that contention.

In his judgment, Simon Brown LJ pointed out and illustrated the obvious absurdity to which that contention could give rise. But, in rejecting the particular approach to consecutive sentences, he was caused to doubt the correctness of that approach in relation to concurrent sentences, with which all the previous cases had been concerned. He concluded (at 434–435):

'The one result of s 67 which in my judgment Parliament could not possibly have intended, was that contended for by the applicant here. It would produce a complete nonsense. Whatever may be said about the language of the section it certainly does not lead clearly to that result. In truth, the only argument for the section to be construed in that way derives from the *Gaffney* line of cases. Powerful and logical though at first blush that argument may appear—and no doubt it was that power and logic which caused the prison service, so soon after the decision in *Ex p Woodward and Wilson*, to introduce the new release guidelines—in my judgment it cannot prevail. If, indeed, consistency with the *Gaffney* approach would require consecutive sentences to be dealt with as the applicant submits, then I should unhesitatingly conclude that the *Gaffney* approach was wrong. The principle of stare decisis does not apply in the Divisional Court and we need not follow other decisions of this court when we are "convinced that [they are] wrong" (see *R v Greater Manchester Coroner, ex p Tal* [1984] 3 All ER 240 at 248, [1985]

QB 67 at 81). I would, if necessary, decline to follow even such a well-established line of authority as this rather than produce the absurd result contended for here. It is therefore unnecessary and, as it seems to me, inappropriate in the present case to reach any final conclusion as to whether it is indeed possible to construe s 67 sensibly, so far as consecutive sentences are concerned, consistently with the correctness of the present approach in concurrent sentence cases. Suffice to say that my preferred path of construction to [counsel for the respondent's] undoubtedly sensible (indeed compelling) conclusion as to how consecutive sentence cases must be treated is by way of s 104(2). If that route is indeed thought difficult to reconcile with the *Gaffney* approach, so be it. Of one thing I am clear: whatever relevance (if any) we might have attached to s 104(2) in *Ex p Mooney* [1996] 1 Cr App R (S) 74 had we known it remained in force, had we been alive to the present argument—ie the consecutive sentence dimension to the case—I for my part would certainly not have described the language of s 67 as "unambiguous" with regard to the correct treatment of concurrent sentence cases.'

Popplewell J agreed, both as to the absurdity of the particular approach as contended for in relation to consecutive sentences and in expressing reservations as to the correctness of the decisions on concurrent sentences.

The conclusion reached in *Ex p Naughton* was, on the facts, plainly correct. But while the court clearly and rightly rejected the submission that the applicant could double count the 239 days spent in custody simultaneously for both the cannabis and burglary offences, the facts did not require the court to choose between the particular and aggregate approaches. Suppose that (as was the case) the applicant had spent 81 days on remand in relation to the cannabis charge alone and (as was not the case) 239 days on remand in relation to the burglary charge alone. Suppose that (as was the case) he was sentenced to 18 months and 18 months consecutive. He would have had to serve half the total of 36 months, namely 18 months. On these assumed facts he could, on the aggregate approach, have claimed to reduce the period he had to serve by the full period of 320 days spent on remand (as, on the actual facts, it was common ground he was entitled to do). But on those assumed facts, on the particular approach, that would not be accepted: he could set off the 239 days spent on remand against the term to be served on the burglary charge, leaving no period to serve (the 182 days to serve being outweighed by the 239 days served); but against the period to serve (182 days) for the cannabis offence the applicant would be able to set off only 81, leaving 101 days to serve. On this approach the applicant would gain credit for 263 days spent on remand, not 320. Although the facts in *Ex p Naughton* did not require the court to choose between these specific approaches, it seems that the court would have preferred the former.

We were shown a draft of an article by Dr Thomas reviewing these latest decisions (now published in *Current Sentencing Practice News* (1996) issue 4, p 10). In it, he points to objectionable anomalies in the existing law on concurrent sentence:

'A man spends six months in custody on remand in respect of one offence; he is subsequently sentenced to a total of two years' imprisonment for that offence and other offences for which he has been on bail. If the sentence is in the form of 12 months and 12 months consecutive, he will serve a further

six months; if the sentence is in the form of two years and two years
concurrent, he will serve 12 months. How can this anomaly be justified?
The Court of Appeal has for years, and on countless occasions, advised
sentencers that in a case involving multiple sentences, what matters most is
the totality of the composite sentence, not the make up of the individual
parts. This principle is totally inconsistent with the *ex parte Mooney* approach,
and a judge who follows it may produce a consequence which is the opposite
of what he intends. Take the case of a man who has spent nine months in
custody on remand for one set of offences, and has been on bail in respect of
another group of offences. If the sentencer's first thought is that he should
serve 18 months for the first set of offences and 18 months' consecutive for
the second set, making a total sentence of three years, the offender will have
to serve a further nine months in custody after sentence. His nine months in
custody on remand will count against the first of the consecutive sentences,
and he will have to serve half of the second sentence before release. He will
have been in custody for a total of 18 months overall. If the sentencer,
following the guidance of the Court of Appeal in many cases that he should
stand back and review the aggregate sentence, decides that taken as a whole
three years is too long, and that a fairer sentence would be 30 months on
each indictment concurrent, he will reduce the nominal length of the total
sentence by six months, but the rule in *ex parte Mooney* means that the
offender must now serve six months longer in custody than he would have
done under the original sentence of three years. His nine months on remand
will be deducted from only one of the two concurrent sentences of thirty
months, and he will have to serve another 15 months before being released
from the second concurrent sentence.'

Dr Thomas strongly argues that s 104(2) should lead the court to the conclusion
that the aggregate approach should be adopted in relation to concurrent as well
as consecutive sentences.

Conclusions

Section 33(1) of the 1991 Act requires the Secretary of State to release each of
these applicants after they have served one half of their sentences. In s 33(1) and
(5) 'sentence' must be interpreted in the light of s 51(2), which requires any
reference to a term of imprisonment, however expressed, to be treated as a single
term even though it is made up of consecutive or wholly or partly concurrent
terms. The length of the single term for this purpose is dependent on the
sentence as pronounced by the court: s 67(4) of the 1967 Act.

In the case of consecutive sentences, the single term is plainly the total of the
individual sentences ordered to be served consecutively. This is so whether the
sentences are imposed on the same occasion or different occasions.

If concurrent sentences are imposed on the same occasion, the single term will
in effect be the longest of the concurrent terms because that will be the last
sentence to expire. Where concurrent sentences are imposed on different
occasions they must still be treated as a single term, but the terminal date of the
sentence pronounced by the court will not necessarily be that of the longest of
the concurrent terms; it will, however, be the terminal date of the last sentence
to expire, which may or may not be the longest of all the sentences. In the case
of concurrent sentences it is not, obviously, a question of adding the relevant
sentences together but of seeing which expires last.

The references to 'sentence' in sub-ss (1) and (2) of s 41 of the 1991 Act must be read subject to s 51(2), as construed above. A short-term prisoner is accordingly to be treated as having served such part of the one half of his sentence he is required to serve as is to be regarded as a 'relevant part' of that sentence as defined in s 67(1A). For present purposes there appears to be no practical distinction between police detention in para (a) of that subsection and custody in para (b). It seems clear, as was held by the court in *Ex p Naughton*, that the expression 'only' in para (b)(i) is intended to preclude any account being taken of periods in custody unrelated to the offence or offences for which the relevant sentence or sentences were passed.

As we read them, s 51(2) and s 104(2) focus attention on the overall term ordered to be served as distinct from the terms, whether consecutive or concurrent, which contribute to or go to make up that overall term. Thus sentences of 9 months and 9 months consecutive is to be regarded as a single term of 18 months and the period to be served is 9 months, not 4 months and 4 months. On this construction it would, at first blush, seem illogical and inconsistent to revert to consideration of the individual sentences contributing to or making up the overall term in order to determine what period of custody on remand is to be set against each. The argument for doing so essentially rests on the singular language ('that sentence or the offence for which it was passed') in s 67(1A). But by s 6(c) of the Interpretation Act 1978 words in the singular include the plural unless the contrary intention appears. Since s 67(1A) applies to single as well as multiple sentences there was good reason to use the singular. Does a contrary intention appear? In our judgment it does not: as already indicated, we consider that logic and consistency support application of the statutory rule of interpretation. Considerations of justice point in the same direction. Time spent in custody in relation to any of the offences for which sentence is passed should serve to reduce the term to be served, subject always to the condition that time can never be counted more than once.

Had this rule been applied in *Ex p Gaffney*, the applicant would have gained the benefit of his second and longer period in custody, as he would if consecutive sentences of 19 and 18 months had been passed. In *Ex p Read* the applicant would not have had to serve a year longer than his equally guilty co-defendant. In *Ex p Mooney* the fact that the applicant had spent no time in custody for one of her many offences would not have deprived her of the benefit of the time she had spent in custody on all the others. In *Woodward* the applicant would have gained the benefit of the 143 days he spent on remand, although only once. In *Ex p Wilson* the applicant also would have gained the benefit of the full period spent on remand and not only part. On this approach the injustices highlighted by Dr Thomas, if not obviated, would be reduced.

In the course of an able and helpful argument Mr Stephen Richards for the respondents contended that the applicants' approach also would produce injustice. He put the following case:

> 'Consider the example of defendant A who is arrested for offence X, spends six months on remand in respect of offence X, is released on bail, commits offence Y and then spends a further three months on remand in respect of offence Y. He is then convicted and sentenced to nine months' imprisonment concurrent for each of offences X and Y. It is difficult to see why the sentence for offence Y should be reduced (allowing the defendant in this example to walk free) by reference to the time spent on remand in

respect of offence X before offence Y was even committed. Suppose further that there is a co-defendant B in respect of offence Y and that co-defendant B also spends three months on remand in respect of offence Y and receives nine months' imprisonment for that offence. Co-defendant B on any view still has six months until expiry of sentence. In all justice defendant A should have the same time until expiry of sentence in respect of offence Y. He should not *benefit* from the fact that he has spent time on remand for a different and earlier offence.'

The first of these cases involves no injustice: defendant A has spent twice as long in prison as the law requires. The second would indeed be an unjust result. But that is because it would be bad sentencing practice to impose the same sentence on A, who had committed two offences, one of them while on bail for the other, as on B who had only committed one offence. In the absence of good reason for doing otherwise, the sentencer would impose consecutive terms on A, or longer concurrent terms. In this way there would be no injustice.

It has been urged upon us, and we unreservedly accept, that we should not depart from previous decisions of this court unless we are satisfied that they are wrong. Our reluctance must be the greater when, as in this case, the authorities have quite rightly founded their practice on these decisions. We are, however, of the clear opinion that the construction previously put upon the legislative provisions we have reviewed was wrong. We are moreover of opinion that that construction is capable of producing, and has in some of the decided cases produced, injustice. Although differing with diffidence from the very clear view expressed by Curtis J, we feel bound to say that in the collective experience of this court it has not been the practice of sentencing judges to take account of the particular approach upheld in *Ex p Gaffney* when passing sentence. We have been referred to no reported case in which a judge has adopted that practice, nor has any of us adopted it. It is indeed evident that in one of the instant cases one of our number passed sentence in the belief that the defendant would, as he intended, be released very shortly. At the time of passing sentence the information necessary to decide, in applying the particular approach, what periods of pre-sentence custody would be taken into account and which would not would by no means always be available to the sentencing judge. It has in our experience been the practice to assume that all periods of custody before sentence, other than custody wholly unrelated to the offences for which sentence is passed, will count against the period of the sentence to be served.

We feel bound to conclude that the argument advanced on behalf of these applicants is correct and we are willing to grant appropriate relief.

The principle that a prisoner's release date should be beyond dispute, and that the provisions governing it should be easy to apply, is of great importance, for reasons both of fairness and good administration. It is not, on any showing, a test which the present provisions meet. They are not clear to the courts, or the legal profession, or prisoners or (it would seem) the prison authorities. They are certainly not simple. It appears that defendants are remaining in prison when the sentencing court did not intend that they should. The Law Commission has described it as an important feature of any criminal justice system that sentencing provisions should be accessible and comprehensible and has recommended the enactment of a comprehensive statutory consolidation of sentencing provisions. As already noted, Dr Thomas in August 1995 and this court in June 1996 drew *a* attention to the urgent need for such a statute. We hope that this may be seen as a task commanding a high degree of priority.

Applications granted. The court refused leave to appeal to the House of Lords but certified, under s 1(2) of the Administration of Justice Act 1960, that the following point of law of general public importance was involved in the decision namely: the correct method of *b* determining the 'relevant period' for the purposes of s 41 of the Criminal Justice Act 1991 and s 67 of the Criminal Justice Act 1967 in a case where an offender spent separate periods on remand in custody in respect of offences for which he is given concurrent sentences.

Dilys Tausz   Barrister.

Attorney General v MGN Ltd and others

QUEEN'S BENCH DIVISION

SCHIEMANN LJ AND BRIAN SMEDLEY J

17, 18, 19, 31 JULY 1996

Contempt of court – Publications concerning legal proceedings – Substantial risk of serious prejudice to fair trial – Extensive publicity being given to accused's violent behaviour and previous convictions prior to his arrest – Accused subsequently charged with wounding with intent and respondents publishing articles concerning pending trial – Criminal proceedings subsequently stayed – Whether publications creating substantial risk of serious prejudice to trial – Contempt of Court Act 1981, ss 1, 2.

Between May 1989 and March 1995 K and his girlfriend, T, who was a well-known television personality, were given saturation media coverage about their relationship. During that time disclosures were made about K's violent behaviour and his previous convictions. On 16 April 1995 K was arrested for assaulting T and another person and was charged the following day with wounding with intent contrary to s 18 of the Offences Against the Person Act 1861. On 18, 19 and 22 April newspapers owned by the first to fourth respondents published articles about the incident; further articles were published on 12 and 13 May by the third and fifth respondents respectively. K was subsequently committed to stand trial and a provisional trial date was fixed for 16 October 1995. However, he successfully applied for the proceedings to be stayed on the ground that the pre-trial press coverage of the case made it impossible for him to have a fair trial. Thereafter the Attorney General applied for orders against the respondents for contempt of court on the ground that the publication of the articles at that time had created a 'substantial risk that the course of justice [would] be seriously impeded or prejudiced' within s 2(2) of the Contempt of Court Act 1981 and that therefore they were guilty, under the strict liability rule set out in s 1 of that Act, of conduct tending to interfere with the course of justice in legal proceedings regardless of intent to do so.

Held – When deciding whether publications created a substantial risk that the course of justice in proceedings would be seriously impeded or prejudiced, within the meaning of s 2(2) of the 1981 Act, the court had to look at each publication separately as at the date of publication and consider the likelihood that it would be read by a potential juror, the likely impact of the article on an ordinary reader at the time of publication and its residual impact on a notional juror at the time of the trial. Furthermore, the mere fact that there was already some risk of prejudice by reason of earlier publications did not preclude a finding that the latest publication had created a further risk. In the instant case the saturation publicity which had been given over the previous years to the relationship between T and K and in particular to the disclosures which had been made as to K's violent behaviour on previous occasions and his previous convictions had continued until a month before the April incident and, in consequence, it could not be said that any one of the publications in April and May 1995 had created a greater risk of prejudice than that which had already been created. It followed that the publications were not in contempt of court and the Attorney General's applications would accordingly be dismissed (see p 460 *b* to *f*, p 463 *h j* and p 466 *f* j, post).

Notes

For publications intended or likely to prejudice fair trial or conduct of proceedings, see 9 *Halsbury's Laws* (4th edn) paras 8–14.

For the Contempt of Court Act 1981, ss 1, 2, see 11 *Halsbury's Statutes* (4th edn) (1991 reissue) 186.

Cases referred to in judgment

A-G v BBC (11 June 1996, unreported), DC.
A-G v English [1982] 2 All ER 903, [1983] 1 AC 116, [1982] 3 WLR 278, HL.
A-G v Guardian Newspapers Ltd [1992] 3 All ER 38, [1992] 1 WLR 874, DC.
A-G v Independent Television News Ltd [1995] 2 All ER 370, DC.
A-G v News Group Newspapers Ltd [1986] 2 All ER 833, [1987] QB 1, [1986] 3 WLR 365, CA.
A-G v Newspaper Publishing plc [1987] 3 All ER 276, [1988] Ch 333, [1987] 3 WLR 942, CA.
A-G v Times Newspapers Ltd (11 February 1983, unreported), DC.
Corbett v R (1988) 41 CCC (3d) 385, Can SC.
R v Cannan (1990) 92 Cr App R 16, CA.
R v Coughlan, R v Young (1976) 63 Cr App R 33, CA.
R v Lane [1970] 1 CCC 196, Ont HC.
R v West [1996] 2 Cr App R 374, CA.
Sunday Times v UK (1979) 2 EHRR 245, ECt HR.
Telegraph plc, Ex p [1993] 2 All ER 971, [1993] 1 WLR 980, CA.

Cases also cited or referred to in skeleton arguments

Central Independent Television plc, Re [1991] 1 All ER 347, [1991] 1 WLR 4, CA.
Dagenais v Canadian Broadcasting Corp (1994) 94 CCC (3d) 289, Can SC.
Duff v R (1979) 28 ALR 663, Aust Fed Ct.
Gisborne Herald Co Ltd v Solicitor General [1995] 3 NZLR 563, NZ CA.
Leary v BBC [1989] CA Transcript 905.
Phillips v Nova Scotia (1995) 98 CCC (3d) 20, Can SC.
R v Dixon (1989) 92 Cr App R 43, CA.
R v Evening Standard Co Ltd, ex p A-G [1954] 1 All ER 1026, [1954] 1 QB 578, DC.
R v Horsham Justices, ex p Farquharson [1982] 2 All ER 269, [1982] QB 762, DC and CA.
R v Kray (1969) 53 Cr App R 412, CCC.
R v McCann (1990) 92 Cr App R 239, CA.
R v Reade (1993) Independent, 19 October, CCC.
R v Savundranayagan and Walker (Note) [1968] 3 All ER 439, [1968] 1 WLR 1761, CA.
R v Taylor (1993) 98 Cr App R 361, CA.
R v Vermette (1988) 41 CCC (3d) 523, Can SC.
Stroble v California (1952) 343 US 181, US SC.
Victoria v Australian Building Construction Employees' and Builders Labourers' Federation (1982) 152 CLR 25, Aust HC.

Application

The Attorney General applied under RSC Ord 52 for committal orders against the respondents, MGN Ltd, Express Newspapers plc, News Group Newspapers Ltd, News (UK) Ltd and Associated Newspapers Ltd, for contempt of court committed by the publication of various articles pending the trial of Geoffrey Knights on the ground that they had thereby created a substantial risk that the course of justice would be seriously impeded or prejudiced. The facts are set out in the judgment of the court.

Sir Derek Spencer QC, S-G, Philip Havers QC and *Hugo Keith* (instructed by the Treasury Solicitor) for the Attorney General.
David Pannick QC and *Monica Carss-Frisk* (instructed by *Davenport Lyons*) for the first respondent.
David Eady QC (instructed by the *Simkins Partnership*) for the second respondent.
Andrew Caldecott QC (instructed by *Farrer & Co*) for the third and fourth respondents.
Jonathan Caplan QC (instructed by *D J Freeman*) for the fifth respondent.

Cur adv vult

31 July 1996. The following judgment of the court was delivered.

SCHIEMANN LJ.

INTRODUCTION

Before the court is an application by the Attorney General to punish various newspapers for alleged contempts of court committed by the publication of various articles pending the trial of Geoffrey Knights. The background is as follows.

On Sunday, 16 April 1995, Geoffrey Knights was arrested for assaulting Martin Davies and Gillian Taylforth following an incident outside Knights' and Taylforth's home address. On 17 April 1995 he was charged with wounding Martin Davies with intent contrary to s 18 of the Offences Against the Person Act 1861. He appeared before Hendon Magistrates' Court on Tuesday, 18 April and was granted bail. On 18, 19 and 22 April 1995 the first, second, third and fourth respondents published articles concerning him. On 12 and 13 May 1995 further articles were published by, respectively, the third and fifth respondents. On 13 June 1995 Mr Knights was committed to stand trial at the Crown Court at Harrow, and at a plea and directions hearing on 25 July 1995, a provisional trial date was fixed for 16 October 1995.

Before Judge Sanders on 29 September 1995, counsel for Mr Knights successfully applied for a stay of proceedings against Mr Knights on the basis that the pre-trial press coverage of the case made it impossible for Mr Knights to have a fair trial. In a judgment dated 3 October 1995, Judge Sanders stayed the proceedings. The Attorney General does not allege *intentional* contempt in relation to any of these publications but relies instead on the strict liability rule whereunder conduct may be treated as a contempt of court as tending to interfere with the course of justice in particular legal proceedings regardless of intent to do so.

The present application focuses, as these applications usually do, on the tension between two desiderata—(1) the desire that a person facing trial should face a tribunal which is not prejudiced against him by reason of matters which have not been proved in evidence, and (2) the desire that newspapers should be free to publish what they please.

This tension is particularly strong in cases which are of widespread public interest because of the notoriety of the persons or deeds involved[a]. The problems posed by this tension are real and recurring. The Solicitor General has drawn our attention to no less than three cases in the last six months where, to the Attorney

General's knowledge, a prosecution has been stayed indefinitely because of pre-trial publicity. Clearly that seriously prejudices the course of justice. There must be many others where a trial has had to be delayed or moved to a less convenient place and where it could be submitted that the course of justice has been seriously impeded[b].

The statutory provisions which govern liability for unintentional contempts are set out in the Contempt of Court Act 1981. That Act was enacted in the wake of the judgment of the European Court of Human Rights in *Sunday Times v UK* (1979) 2 EHRR 245, in which the court found by a majority that the newspaper's rights under art 10 of the European Convention of Human Rights (Convention for the Protection of Human Rights and Fundamental Freedoms (Rome, 4 November 1950; TS 71 (1953); Cmd 8969)) had been violated in that the restraint placed on its freedom of expression in reporting the Thalidomide proceedings was not necessary and had not been proportionate to the legitimate aim pursued. As Lloyd LJ observed in *A-G v Newspaper Publishing plc* [1987] 3 All ER 276 at 310, [1988] Ch 333 at 382:

'... the statutory purpose behind the 1981 Act was to effect a permanent shift in the balance of public interest away from the protection of the administration of justice and in favour of freedom of speech. Such a shift was forced on the United Kingdom by the decision of the European Court of Human Rights in *Sunday Times v UK* (1979) 2 EHRR 245, and was in any event foreshadowed by the recommendations of the Phillimore Committee [Report of the Committee on Contempt of Court ((1974) Cmnd 5794)].'

The crucial section in the present context is s 2, which states:

'(1) The strict liability rule applies only to publications, and for this purpose "publication" includes any speech, writing, programme included in a service or other communication in whatever form, which is addressed to the public at large or any section of the public.

(2) The strict liability rule applies only to a publication which creates a substantial risk that the course of justice in the proceedings in question will be seriously impeded or prejudiced.

---

a   In *R v West* [1996] 2 Cr App R 374 Lord Taylor CJ, delivering the judgment of the court, said that there was no doubt that the press coverage in advance of the trial was extensive and hostile to the Wests. He went on to say: '... however lurid the reporting, there can scarcely ever have been a case more calculated to shock the public who were entitled to know the facts. The question raised on behalf of the defence is whether a fair trial could be held after such intensive publicity adverse to the accused. In our view it could. To hold otherwise would mean that if allegations of murder are sufficiently horrendous so as inevitably to shock the nation, the accused cannot be tried. That would be absurd. Moreover, providing the judge effectively warns the jury to act only on the evidence given in court, there is no reason to suppose that they would do otherwise.' (See [1996] 2 Cr App R 374 at 385–386.)

b   Note in this context *A-G v Times Newspapers Ltd* (11 February 1983, unreported), where it was said: 'The course of justice is not just concerned with the outcome of proceedings. It is concerned with the whole process of the law including the freedom of a person accused of a crime to elect, so far as the law permits him to do so, the mode of trial which he prefers and to conduct his defence in the way which seems best to him and to his advisers. Any extraneous factor or external pressure which impedes or restricts that election or that conduct, or which impels a person accused to adopt a course in the conduct of his own defence which he does not wish to adopt, deprives him to an extent of the freedom of choice which the law confers upon him and is, in my judgment, not only a prejudice but a serious prejudice.'

(3) The strict liability rule applies to a publication only if the proceedings in question are active within the meaning of this section at the time of the publication ...'

THE PRINCIPLES GOVERNING THE APPLICATION OF THE STRICT LIABILITY RULE

These are as follows and are not the subject of serious dispute.

(1) Each case must be decided on its own facts[c].

(2) The court will look at each publication separately and test matters as at the time of publication (see A-G v English [1982] 2 All ER 903 at 918, [1983] 1 AC 116 at 141 per Lord Diplock and A-G v Guardian Newspapers Ltd [1992] 3 All ER 38 at 48–49, [1992] 1 WLR 874 at 885); nevertheless, the mere fact that, by reason of earlier publications, there is already some risk of prejudice does not prevent a finding that the latest publication has created a further risk[d]. [It was common ground that there was no room for reading the singular word 'publication' in s 2 of the 1981 Act as the plural in accord with s 6 of the Interpretation Act of 1978.]

(3) The publication in question must create some risk that the course of justice in the proceedings in question will be impeded or prejudiced by that publication.

(4) That risk must be substantial[e].

(5) The substantial risk must be that the course of justice in the proceedings in question will not only be impeded or prejudiced but *seriously* so.

(6) The court will not convict of contempt unless it is *sure* that the publication has created this substantial risk of that serious effect on the course of justice.

(7) In making an assessment of whether the publication does create this substantial risk of that serious effect on the course of justice the following amongst other matters arise for consideration: (a) the likelihood of the publication coming to the attention of a potential juror; (b) the likely impact of the publication on an ordinary reader at the time of publication; and (c) the residual impact of the publication on a notional juror at the time of trial. It is this last matter which is crucial.

One must remember that in this, as in any exercise of risk assessment, a small risk multiplied by a small risk results in an even smaller risk[f].

---

c   See A-G v News Group Newspapers Ltd [1986] 2 All ER 833 at 843, [1987] QB 1 at 18 per Parker LJ and A-G v BBC (11 June 1996, unreported), where Auld LJ said: 'The degree of risk of impact of a publication on a trial and the extent of that impact may both be affected, in differing degrees according to the circumstances, by the nature and form of the publication and how long it occurred before trial. Much depends on the combination of circumstances in the case in question and the court's own assessment of their likely effect at the time of publication. This is essentially a value judgment for the court, albeit that it must be sure of its judgment before it can find that there has been contempt. There is little value in making detailed comparisons with the facts of other cases.'

d   See A-G v Independent Television News Ltd [1995] 2 All ER 370 at 381: 'Mr Moses contended that it does not follow that because a risk had been created by the broadcast (on the night before) further publication in newspapers would not create fresh and added risk of prejudice. In other words, if several newspapers published prejudicial material, they cannot escape from liability by contending that the damage has already been done, because each affords its own additional risk of prejudice, or, as it might be said, each exacerbates and increases that risk. In my judgment, that submission is correct.'

e   In A-G v BBC Auld LJ said: '... the threshold of risk is not high, simply of more than a remote or minimal risk of serious prejudice.'

f   In A-G v Independent Television News Ltd [1995] 2 All ER 370 at 383 Leggatt LJ said: 'During the nine months that passed after anyone had read the offending articles, the likelihood is that he no longer would have remembered it sufficiently to prejudice the trial. When the long odds against the potential juror reading any of the publications is multiplied by the long odds against any reader remembering it, the risk of prejudice is, in my judgment, remote.'

(8) In making an assessment of the likelihood of the publication coming to the attention of a potential juror the court will consider amongst other matters: (a) whether the publication circulates in the area from which the jurors are likely to be drawn, and (b) how many copies circulated.

(9) In making an assessment of the likely impact of the publication on an ordinary reader at the time of publication the court will consider amongst other matters: (a) the prominence of the article in the publication, and (b) the novelty of the content of the article in the context of likely readers of that publication.

(10) In making an assessment of the residual impact of the publication on a notional juror at the time of trial the court will consider amongst other matters: (a) the length of time between publication and the likely date of trial[g], (b) the focusing effect of listening over a prolonged period to evidence in a case[h], and (c) the likely effect of the judge's directions to a jury.

This last matter in particular has been the subject of extensive judicial comment in two different contexts: in the context of a trial or an appeal from a trial verdict and in the context of contempt proceedings. There have been many cases where, notwithstanding such prejudicial publications, the convictions have not been quashed. However, undoubtedly there have also been occasions where convictions have been quashed notwithstanding judicial directions to the jury to ignore prejudicial comments in the media.

In the former category of cases what has been stressed is that the whole system of trial by jury is predicated upon the ability and willingness of juries to abide by the directions given to them by the judge and not to accept as true the content of a publication just because it has been published[i].

In libel cases where the issue is justification that is peculiarly the case. Confidence in a jury's capacity's to abide by judicial direction is reflected in the fact that they commonly have to consider evidence for one purpose, though not another, as in relation to joint offenders or multiple counts on one indictment. It has been pointed out that juries frequently acquit of some charges whilst convicting of others. Even in relation to sexual offences, where the risk of prejudice is self-evidently greater, Lord Taylor CJ commented on not under-estimating a jury's ability to do justice in such a context (see *R v Cannan* (1990) 92 Cr App R 16). As Lawton J put it in *R v Coughlan, R v Young* (1976) 63 Cr App R 33 at 37:

---

g   This was discussed both in *A-G v Independent Television News Ltd* [1995] 2 All ER 370 and in *A-G v News Group Newspapers Ltd* [1986] 2 All ER 833 at 843, [1987] QB 1 at 17–18, where Parker LJ explained: 'The imminence or remoteness of the proceedings will still vitally affect both the existence of a substantial risk of prejudice and the question whether, if there is such a risk, it is a risk that the course of justice will be seriously impeded or prejudiced. Both the risk and the degree of prejudice will, as it seems to me, increase with the proximity of the trial but it is not possible, and indeed would be contrary to the Act, to say that no publication earlier than a certain number of months before trial could be subject to the application of the strict liability rule. Each case must be decided on its own facts and a publication relatively close to trial may escape whereas another much further from trial will not do so by reason of the impact of its content on the reader, listener or viewer, as the case may be.' In the same case Donaldson MR had said ([1986] 2 All ER 833 at 841, [1987] QB 1 at 15): 'Proximity in time between the publication and the proceedings would probably have a greater bearing on the risk limb than on the seriousness limb, but could go to both.'

h   In *Ex p Telegraph plc* [1993] 2 All ER 971 at 978, [1993] 1 WLR 980 at 987 Lord Taylor CJ said: '... a court should credit the jury with the will and ability to abide by the judge's direction to decide the case only on the evidence before them. The court should also bear in mind that the staying power and detail of publicity, even in cases of notoriety, are limited and that the nature of a trial is to focus the jury's minds on the evidence before them rather than on matters outside the courtroom ...'

'Juries are capable of disregarding that which is not properly before them. They are expected to disregard what one accused says about another in his absence. If they can do that, which is far from easy, they can disregard what has been said in a newspaper.'

It can fairly be asked in this context, why, given the constraints on discovering the cogitations of a jury, should the courts be trusted to form a view as to what is going on or may go on in the jury's mind? A partial, but not wholly satisfactory, answer to that is that judges preside over very many trials; they see what seems to stick in witnesses minds; they watch jurors' reactions; they receive jurors questions and observe their verdicts; and so they do obtain some feel of what appears to stick in the mind and what appears to be influencing, at any event, a number of jurors. Another answer, different in kind, is to side-step the question and assert that, judging by the absence of legislation to the contrary, society is content to let judges make these judgments doing the best they can in what are undoubtedly difficult circumstances. Society requires a judgment to be made between conflicting desiderata and the judges are given the task of making it in individual cases. It is to be noted in this context that the admission into evidence at a trial of the accused's previous convictions has always been regarded as a potent ground of appeal and yet the courts have regularly maintained that, where previous convictions were properly admitted into evidence—for instance in order to do justice to a co-defendant—this will not form a potent ground of appeal. This is an example of the courts having to make a judgment between different desiderata.

THE PRESENT APPLICATIONS

The background to the present applications is that before the publications complained of, which start in April 1995, the lives of Mr Knights and his erstwhile girlfriend, Miss Taylforth, had long been of interest to the general public. This was in part the result of her having a major role in a popular television programme, with a consequential public interest in her love life, in part because of their activities together on the A1, where a police officer had made an arrest alleging activities of a sexual nature between them there, which arrest had been followed by a libel action concerned with the same activities, and in part because of Mr Knight's own colourful past.

---

i   In *Corbett v R* (1988) 41 CCC (3d) 385, a case which was concerned with the fairness of permitting the accused to be cross-examined as to his previous convictions, Dickson CJC said (at 401–403): 'It is of course, entirely possible to construct an argument disputing the theory of trial by jury. Juries are capable of egregious mistakes and they may at times seem to be ill-adapted to the exigencies of an increasingly complicated and refined criminal law. But until the paradigm is altered by Parliament, the court should not be heard to call into question the capacity of juries to do the job assigned to them. The ramifications of any such statement could be enormous ... There are many situations where the jury is permitted to hear and use evidence relevant to one issue, but not to another. In these situations, all that is required is a clear direction to the jury indicating what is permissible use and what is not. For example, in some cases, similar fact evidence is admissible to show some particular trait or design ... In the joint trial of co-accused, the confession of one accused is admissible against that accused only, and the jury must be instructed that such evidence cannot be taken into account in determining the guilt of the co-accused: see, *e.g.* ... *R v. Lane and Ross* ([1970] 1 CCC 196 at 201), where Addy J. stated as follows: "... I do not feel that, in deciding a question of this kind, one must proceed on the assumption that jurors are morons, completely devoid of intelligence and totally incapable of understanding a rule of evidence of this type or of acting in accordance with it. If such were the case there would be no justification at all for the existence of juries, and what has been regarded for centuries as a bulwark of our democratic system and a guarantee of our basic freedoms under the law would in fact be nothing less than a delusion."'

It is important to set out the dates of the previous publicity. In the exhibited documents there are many newspaper reports of incidents concerning these two. They start as long ago as 1989 when the News of the World published a report of Knights having been jailed for assault. In May 1989 there were further articles about the two and in December 1989 the People newspaper published an article referring to the fact that Knights had been charged with causing grievous bodily harm to an Australian businessman with whom he had been involved at the West End club, Stringfellows.

In January 1994 there was extensive reporting of the libel action brought by Miss Taylforth against the Sun newspaper in respect of the A1 incident. There was in the course of the reporting of that case a frequent reference to the fact that Knights had a prison record for violence. On Friday, 14 January 1994 the Sun published a banner headline with the words 'VIOLENT PAST' and a reference, chronologically, to the convictions of Mr Knights dating back to 1969. There was saturation coverage of that libel action for over two weeks including a report in The Times for Wednesday, January 26 detailing, with a photograph, the criminal record of Mr Knights dating back to 1969.

There was further reference in October 1994 in the People newspaper to the fact that Mr Knights was living in Spain, including a front page article on 9 October with banner headlines referring to Knights' violent past.

On 29 October in the Daily Mirror there was a further reference to Knights having been arrested for allegedly assaulting a police officer. In November there was a reference in the Sun newspaper to the fact that Miss Taylforth had had surgery after she had been beaten up by Knights.

In January 1995 Miss Taylforth was charged with driving under the influence of drink. That inevitably brought a further reference back to the libel action.

The publicity continued into March 1995 when Knights was convicted of assaulting a police constable and was fined £2,000. This was a month before the alleged assault which led to the publicity of which complaint is presently made.

It is not surprising in the light of that massive publicity over a period of some two years that Judge Sanders, when he was considering the question of abuse of process in October 1995, concluded: 'There could not be one member of the jury who had not read something about them.' He, of course, was considering the position in October, just before the trial was to begin and had to take into account more recent references in the press to the two principal participants—namely in August 1995—of which the Attorney General does not complain. We have to look mainly at the situation as it existed on 17 and 18 April 1995 and in the case of the Daily Mail the situation as it existed when Lynda Lee-Potter's article was published on 13 May. At that stage the trial was several months ahead. In deciding whether the publication of any particular article created a substantial risk of serious prejudice it has to be judged as at the date of the publication in the light of the saturation publicity given over previous months, indeed years, to the relationship between Miss Taylforth and Mr Knights and in particular to the disclosures which had been made previously of Mr Knights' violent behaviour on previous occasions and his previous convictions.

In some cases where there has been reference to previous convictions in the press the passage of time may result in those references being forgotten but nevertheless a subsequent reference to them may result in the recollection in the mind of a potential juror of those convictions and the incidents on which they were based. In this case it is to be remembered that the publicity given to Miss Taylforth and Mr Knights continued until a month before the incident in April 1995.

THE PUBLICATIONS OF WHICH COMPLAINT IS MADE

We have to look at each of these in the light of the principles outlined above and in the light of the foregoing history of publicity. We look at the respondents one by one.

The first respondent publishes the Daily Mirror. Complaint is made of the issues published on 18 April 1995 and that published on the following day.

The second respondent publishes the Daily Star. Complaint is made similarly of the contents of that newspaper in each of three editions published on 18 April 1995 and 19 April 1995.

The third respondent publishes the Sun and the fourth respondent published a newspaper called Today. Complaint is made of the edition of the Sun and that of Today published on 18 April. On 19 April Today published another article of which complaint is made and on 22 April and 12 May the Sun contained other material the subject of complaint.

The fifth respondent published the Daily Mail. That newspaper on 13 May contained a feature article written by Miss Lynda Lee-Potter after an interview with Gillian Taylforth, Knights' girlfriend.

We now turn to the individual articles of which complaint is made.

DAILY MIRROR

18 April 1995

The front page headline in letters one inch high reads 'KNIGHTS BEAT ME TO A PULP'. A statement attributed to the victim with a photograph of Knights and Miss Taylforth. On page 2 there was what purported to be a further quotation from Mr Davies, the victim, and a description of his injuries as described by a police officer and a suggestion by the writer that doctors feared that he might be blinded. Page 3 was entirely given over to the account of the incident with large photographs of Knights, Miss Taylforth and photographs of the scene. The article referred to the libel case brought by Miss Taylforth in 1994.

19 April 1995

On page 5 there was a photograph of Mr Knights in handcuffs arriving at court. Included in the article is a statement of his solicitor denying that he caused the injuries to Mr Davies.

As it seems to us, at any trial evidence would be bound to be given or agreed as to the extent of injuries. In those circumstances we do not believe that whatever remained in any juror's mind of this description of the injuries would be likely to affect his assessment of the evidence he would hear.

Applying the principles set out earlier in this judgment we do not consider that either of these publications created a substantial risk that the course of justice in the proceedings would be seriously impeded or prejudiced.

DAILY STAR

18 April 1995

On the front page of the second edition there is a reference in the main headline to Davies having been 'battered with iron bar', repeated in the text of the article. That was repeated on pages 2 and 3. Knights, it is said, 'went berserk with an iron bar'. The suggestion is made that the motive was Knights' jealousy over the relationship between Miss Taylforth and Mr Davies. There was a further reference to Knights 'wielding the bar above his head like a sword' and 'pounding his head with a hard-edged weapon, the iron bar'. This was wholly inaccurate: there was no weapon used. In the third edition the account has been toned down. Purporting to quote a neighbour the article contained the words 'A hard-edged weapon', the reference to the iron bar being deleted from the headline and the article itself. It refers to the possibility that Davies might lose an eye.

Having regard to the evidence of the number and location of the distribution of the first and second editions we regard the chance of these coming into the possession of someone who would turn out to be a juror at the Harrow Crown Court as very remote. So far as the third edition is concerned this is not so. However, applying the principles set out earlier in this judgment, we do not consider that this publication created a substantial risk that the course of justice in the proceedings would be seriously impeded or prejudiced.

19 April 1995

The Daily Star contained an article almost full page on page 7 referring to the fact that Knights had been granted bail with a condition that he should not contact Miss Taylforth or the 'alleged victim', Davies. His solicitor read out a statement to the press denying charges. That was also reported. On the same page a report of Davies' condition in hospital again referred to the possible loss of an eye. Applying the principles set out earlier in this judgment we do not consider that this publication created a substantial risk that the course of justice in the proceedings would be seriously impeded or prejudiced.

THE SUN

18 April 1995

The newspaper described the incident as 'a bust up' beneath a banner headline referring to the incident on the front page. On pages 4 and 5 there was a reference to Mr Davies being 'scarred for life' and looking like the Elephant Man. There were accounts allegedly given by neighbours who had been eye witnesses to the incident and who were therefore potential witnesses in any proceedings.

22 April 1995

There was a large photograph of Mr Davies, Mr Knights and Miss Taylforth, showing Davies' black eyes. This article reported both the charge and Knights' denial.

12 May 1995

There was an article on pages 26 and 27 reporting an interview with Miss Taylforth, which in fact is a somewhat sympathetic article, albeit making reference to Knights' and Miss Taylforth's stormy relationship.

Applying the principles set out earlier in this judgment we do not consider that any of these publications created a substantial risk that the course of justice in the proceedings would be seriously impeded or prejudiced.

TODAY

18 April 1995

The headline on page 1 gives a relatively short account of the incident but much material about the libel action which Miss Taylforth had brought against the Sun newspaper in January 1994.

19 April 1995

On the front page there is a reference to 'bust up' and on page 5 the solicitor's statement of denial was published. There was a graphic description of what were said to be Mr Davies' injuries.

Applying the principles set out earlier in this judgment we do not consider that any of these publications created a substantial risk that the course of justice in the proceedings would be seriously impeded or prejudiced.

THE DAILY MAIL

13 May 1995

The article by Lynda Lee-Potter purports to be based on an interview given by Miss Taylforth in which she described the stormy and violent relationship between herself and Mr Knights. There were, in that article, references to the fact that he had previously been convicted of an offence of violence and in particular a reference to the evidence which he had given in the libel action when he had been asked about his previous convictions. Despite the fact that the article occupied two pages with large photographs of Miss Taylforth and Knights, the reference to the incident on the night of the 17/18 April was really only one short paragraph with no detail as to how Mr Davies had received his injuries. The inference, however, from the context of the remainder of the article is that Knights had caused them and caused them unlawfully.

Applying the principles set out earlier in this judgment we do not consider that this publication created a substantial risk that the course of justice in the proceedings would be seriously impeded or prejudiced.

CONCLUSION

There is no doubt that the so called 'news items' or 'articles', excluding for the moment the article on 13 May in the Daily Mail, were all written in typical graphic tabloid style. They include large banner headlines, large photographs of all three of those involved in the incident. There is a measure of exaggeration in the description of the injuries sustained by Mr Davies and the language used is undoubtedly emotive. However, all in all it is difficult to see how any one of the publications in April and May 1995 created any greater risk of serious prejudice than that which had already been created.

We are not called upon to rule upon the correctness of Judge Sanders' decision to stay the proceedings in front of him and nothing in this judgment should be taken as doing so. A consequence of the need in contempt proceedings, in which respondents face imprisonment or a fine, to be sure and to look at each publication separately and the need in trial proceedings to look at risk of prejudice created by the totality of publications can be that it is proper to stay proceedings on the ground of prejudice albeit that no individual is guilty of contempt. One may regret that situation or one may take the view that this is the best answer to a difficult problem. We are not called upon to express our view on that matter.

What however clearly follows from our findings is that each of these applications by the Attorney General is dismissed.

Application dismissed.

Dilys Tausz   Barrister.

Mainwaring and another v Goldtech Investments Ltd

CHANCERY DIVISION

ROBERT WALKER J SITTING WITH TAXING MASTER ELLIS AND MR ANTHONY COWEN AS ASSESSORS

30, 31 JULY, 11 OCTOBER 1996

Costs – Taxation – Review of taxation – Jurisdiction – Litigant in person – Whether rule of court as to costs ultra vires – Whether pecuniary loss established – RSC Ord 62, r 18(3) – Supreme Court Act 1981, s 84(1)(2).

The plaintiffs, who were litigants in person, commenced proceedings against the defendant claiming unpaid salary and expenses. They obtained judgment in default and thereafter an order for costs was made by the Chief Taxing Master against the defendant's solicitors in the first plaintiff's favour in relation to the taxation of a bill of costs submitted by the defendant earlier in the proceedings. The first plaintiff submitted a bill of costs for £87,250, in which she sought to charge her time at a basic rate of £75 an hour, uplifted to £125 in respect of research and inquiries, and to £200 an hour in respect of preparation and advocacy and, on the Chief Taxing Master's direction, she lodged a detailed breakdown of the bill, together with an affidavit as to her pecuniary loss. On taxation, however, the master held that the first plaintiff had not established in her affidavit that she had suffered any pecuniary loss and, pursuant to RSC Ord 62, r 18(3), he allowed her to charge her time only at the rate of £8·25 per hour, which order he subsequently confirmed. The first plaintiff applied to the judge pursuant to Ord 62, r 35 for a review of the master's decision, contending, inter alia, (i) that Ord 62, r 18(3) was ultra vires and void in that it was beyond the scope of and unauthorised by s 84(1) and (2) of the Supreme Court Act 1981, which authorised the making of rules of court to regulate matters of practice and procedure, and (ii) that the burden of proof was on the solicitors, and that in the absence of any affidavit evidence in answer from them the master was not merely entitled but was bound to conclude that she had suffered pecuniary loss in relation to all, or at any rate the bulk, of the items of work claimed.

Held – (1) For the purposes of s 84(1) and (2) of the 1981 Act, costs were a matter of practice and procedure. Accordingly, the provisions of RSC Ord 62, r 18(3) were not ultra vires but were reasonable provisions defining and regulating the rights of a litigant in person to recover for work, expenses or loss under the Litigants in Person (Costs and Expenses) Act 1975. Moreover, those provisions were arguably generous in that the sum allowed an hour was above the rate of national average earnings (even on the basis of a 48-hour week) and was payable to a litigant who had suffered no pecuniary loss (see p 276 *j* and p 477 *b*, post).

(2) Whether a litigant in person had suffered significant loss of earnings was a matter peculiarly within his or her own knowledge. Accordingly, since it would be most unusual for the paying party to have to undertake the burden of proving a negative on a matter peculiarly within the receiving party's knowledge, and probably outside the paying party's own knowledge, the burden of proof was not on the defendant's solicitors but on the first plaintiff to establish her pecuniary loss. However, her affidavit had failed to do so and it would not be fair to the solicitors to give her a further opportunity to make good the deficiencies in it. The master's decision would therefore be affirmed (see p 477 *f* to *j*, p 478 *b* and p 479 *c* to 480 *b*, post).

Notes

For costs of litigant in person and review of taxation by order of the judge, see 37 *Halsbury's Laws* (4th edn) paras 750, 756.

For the Litigants in Person (Costs and Expenses) Act 1975, see 11 *Halsbury's Statutes* (1991 reissue) 896.

For the Supreme Court Act 1981, s 84, see ibid 1048.

Cases referred to in judgment

Buckland v Watts [1969] 2 All ER 985, [1970] 1 QB 27, [1969] 3 WLR 92, CA.
Calderbank v Calderbank [1975] 3 All ER 333, [1976] Fam 93, [1975] 3 WLR 586, CA.
Goldman v Hesper [1988] 3 All ER 97, [1988] 1 WLR 1238, CA.
Hart v Aga Khan Foundation UK [1984] 2 All ER 439, [1984] 1 WLR 994, CA.
Johnson v Reed Corrugated Cases Ltd [1992] 1 All ER 169.
Madurasinghe v Penguin Electronics (a firm) [1993] 3 All ER 20, [1993] 1 WLR 989, CA.
Pamplin v Express Newspapers Ltd [1985] 2 All ER 185, [1985] 1 WLR 689.

Review of taxation

The first plaintiff, Zipporah Mainwaring, applied for an order that two decisions on taxation of costs made by Chief Taxing Master Hurst, comprised in reasons dated respectively 6 September 1994 and 26 January 1995, and 21 June and 30 August 1995, made following disagreement between her and the defendant's solicitors, Lipkin Gorman, be reviewed. The first plaintiff was the paying party for the purposes of the first review and the receiving party for the purposes of the second review. The matter was heard in chambers but judgment was given by Robert Walker J in open court. The facts are set out in the judgment.

The first plaintiff appeared in person.
Andrew Post (instructed by *S J Berwin*) for Lipkin Gorman on the first review.
Peter Sheridan QC (instructed by *Lipkin Gorman*) for Lipkin Gorman on the second review.

Cur adv vult

11 October 1996. The following judgment was delivered.

ROBERT WALKER J. These are two reviews under RSC Ord 62, r 35 of two decisions on taxations of costs made by Chief Taxing Master Hurst (the master). Both arise out of litigation in which (after consolidation) Miss Zipporah Mainwaring and Mr Robert Lisle were the plaintiffs and a company called Goldtech Investments Ltd (Goldtech) was the defendant and counterclaimant.

The first decision, or group of decisions, is comprised in the master's reasons dated 6 September 1994, as supplemented by further reasons dated 26 January 1995. The second decision is comprised in reasons dated 30 August 1995, which in effect confirm a written decision dated 21 June 1995. I shall refer to the two reviews as 'the first review' and 'the second review' accordingly. Miss Mainwaring is the paying party for the purposes of the first review. She is the receiving party (under an order of the master made against Lipkin Gorman on 20 September 1991) for the purposes of the second review. I shall refer below to the position of Mr Lisle, the other plaintiff and defendant to counterclaim.

This introduction gives a hint of how complex and hard fought the litigation has been; and in order to explain the issues that arise on the reviews I must summarise the course of the litigation as briefly as I can.

The course of the litigation at first instance

The story begins in 1987 when Goldtech was incorporated with an issued share capital of two £1 shares. It was an English company but it was apparently intended by those who formed it to be non-resident for fiscal purposes. Those who were ultimately behind its formation seem to have been based in South Africa: it is in the nature of such companies to be opaque as regards their true ownership and management. They seem to have had plans for a substantial commercial operation, that is for gold coins to be minted at the Birmingham Mint and marketed in connection with the celebration of the millennium of the city of Dublin in 1988.

In November 1987 Mr Lisle was employed by Goldtech. Later Miss Mainwaring was employed by Goldtech. I know little about what they did but Whitford J was satisfied they were both experienced in the promotional field. Miss Mainwaring had previously been employed by Encyclopaedia Britannica International Ltd for eight years until 1986, when (in her own words) she took a sabbatical for personal reasons.

I need not try to go into the controversial events of late 1987 and early 1988. The true sequence of events may never be clearly established. But in March 1988 Miss Mainwaring and Mr Lisle commenced proceedings in the Chancery Division of the High Court against Goldtech claiming unpaid salaries and expenses of £40,000, and Miss Mainwaring (appearing as a litigant in person, as she has throughout all the substantive hearings and the taxations of costs) obtained a Mareva injunction on an ex parte application heard on 22 March 1988 by Hoffmann J. (I will refer to Miss Mainwaring and Mr Lisle together as 'the plaintiffs'; Miss Mainwaring has sometimes appeared as an advocate for both plaintiffs and sometimes only on her own behalf; the different capacities may not always be clearly and correctly recorded either in this judgment or in some earlier judgments.)

The Mareva had the practical effect of blocking a sum of $55,000 held by the Birmingham Mint, which itself became involved in other litigation in the Queen's Bench Division. On 12 April 1988 Goldtech started proceedings in the Chancery Division against the plaintiffs. Goldtech claimed a variety of relief against them, mostly connected with the general contention that they had no authority to act for Goldtech but were trying to take over its contractual and intellectual property rights. The two sets of proceedings were consolidated by an order made on 6 March 1989.

In the meantime, however, Goldtech had applied by notices of motion to discharge the Mareva injunction granted against it in the first action, and for injunctions against the plaintiffs to be granted to it in the second action. There was a three-day hearing before Whitford J and on 24 May 1988 he discharged the Mareva on the grounds of material non-disclosure, and granted injunctive relief to Goldtech. The plaintiffs were ordered to pay Goldtech's costs of the Mareva proceedings on the indemnity basis, to be taxed and paid forthwith.

These and subsequent events are recounted in more detail in a judgment of Hoffmann J delivered on 13 November 1989. After describing 'fierce hand-to-hand interlocutory fighting' over pleadings and discovery during the later part of 1988 and early in 1989, culminating in the order for consolidation, Hoffmann J described the next steps as follows:

'On 28 February 1989 Lipkin Gorman [Goldtech's solicitors] proceeded to tax their bill under the order of Whitford J. The amount claimed was £40,000, but Miss Mainwaring resisted item by item and to some effect, because the amount was considerably reduced. It was however a slow process and was adjourned to 25 April. By that time, Goldtech had decided to abandon the action. The Dublin Centenary year was over and for whatever reasons, the gold medal venture had been a total failure. The costs were mounting and Messrs Lipkin Gorman say that they had no confidence in the ability of Mr Lisle or Miss Mainwaring to meet a claim for damages or costs. The advice of counsel was taken. Finally on 25 April a meeting of Goldtech was held in Johannesburg at which it was decided to take no further steps in the litigation and to terminate Lipkin Gorman's retainer. As a result, Lipkin Gorman applied to come off the record. Miss Mainwaring applied to Browne-Wilkinson V-C for security for costs and on 18 May Browne-Wilkinson V-C ordered that unless Goldtech paid £25,000 into court the consolidated counterclaim should be dismissed with costs on an indemnity basis. There was no compliance and the counterclaim was dismissed On 28 June judgment by default was entered in favour of Miss Mainwaring and Mr Lisle on their claim for £39,722 and damages to be assessed, with costs on an indemnity basis. The taxing master gave no certificate in respect of the abandoned taxation under the order of Whitford J and ordered Goldtech to pay the costs. The result was therefore that Miss Mainwaring and Mr Lisle were wholly successful, but their victory has been empty because Goldtech has no assets in this country or probably in any other. Miss Mainwaring did not have the benefit of an order for security for costs which would ordinarily have been made against a non-resident company because the chief master had taken the view, which was not challenged on appeal, that the order for costs made in favour of Goldtech by Whitford J gave them a set-off which would be sufficient to cover the costs until the end of discovery. This was the point at which Goldtech abandoned the action.'

This judgment of Hoffmann J was given on an application by the plaintiffs for an order that Lipkin Gorman, as Goldtech's solicitors, should pay the costs of the consolidated actions. It was a wasted costs application under RSC Ord 62, r 11. The application was based on five separate grounds which Hoffmann J considered at some length in his judgment. But he concluded that none of the grounds was made out, and he dismissed the application (on which Lipkin Gorman appeared by counsel instructed by S J Berwin & Co). On 4 December 1989 Hoffmann J declined to award a gross sum in respect of costs under Ord 62, r 7(4), making no order as to costs of the application. Later in the same day he heard another application relating principally to documents (lodged on behalf of Goldtech) which had been handed to Miss Mainwaring by Master Gowers. Hoffmann J made an order restraining use of the documents and ordered the plaintiffs to pay half the costs.

Miss Mainwaring made a later application for leave to use the documents; this was dismissed with costs by Hoffmann J on 2 October 1991.

Appeals to the Court of Appeal

a   On 12 October 1990 the Court of Appeal (Dillon, Ralph Gibson and Leggatt LJJ) heard an appeal by the plaintiffs from the orders of Whitford J. The Court of Appeal allowed the appeal with costs, but only to the extent of discharging the indemnity costs orders made by Whitford J and the inquiry as to damages (suffered by Goldtech) directed by him (another inquiry, as to the damages

b   suffered by the plaintiffs proceeded and resulted in large but irrecoverable awards).

Goldtech was not represented before the Court of Appeal. Dillon LJ was critical of the individuals behind Goldtech and indeed of some of Goldtech's legal advisers (not including either counsel appearing before me on the reviews) but emphasised that in the absence of representation for Goldtech that was a prima

c   facie view. He concluded, however, that a party which sought to deceive the court, as Goldtech prima facie had, should not get costs on an indemnity basis.

On 24 January 1991 a differently constituted Court of Appeal (Russell, Butler-Sloss LJJ and Sir Christopher Slade) gave judgment on appeals by Miss Mainwaring from three judgments of Hoffmann J which I have already

d   mentioned: his refusal on 13 November 1989 to make a wasted costs order against Lipkin Gorman; his refusal on 4 December 1989 to give the plaintiffs their costs of the gross costs application; and his order (restraining use of documents obtained by Miss Mainwaring) made later on the same day. All three appeals were dismissed with costs, subject to an undertaking by Lipkin Gorman as to use of documents in the event of a complaint to the Law Society. The judgment of

e   the court, delivered by Sir Christopher Slade, runs in transcript to over 50 pages, the longest section being that concerned with the refusal of the wasted costs order.

The issues on the first review

f   The first review relates to four bills of costs in respect of which Miss Mainwaring was the paying party. Most of the orders for costs were made against Mr Lisle also, but apparently the bills were not served on him until long after their service on Miss Mainwaring. The master identified the four bills as follows: (A) costs under Hoffmann J's order dated 13 November 1989 (wasted costs); (B) costs under the order of the Court of Appeal dated 24 January 1991 (on appeal from

g   Hoffmann J); (C) costs (half) under the order of Hoffmann J dated 4 December 1989 (documents); (D) costs under the order of Hoffmann J dated 2 October 1991 (documents). These bills were taxed over several days, the last day being 18 September 1992.

On 9 October 1992 Miss Mainwaring put in written objections running to 11

h   paragraphs, some relating to several bills and some relating to particular bills. These objections were heard before the master on 15 December 1992 and 8 March 1993. Miss Mainwaring requested reasons in respect of five of the objections and the master gave these in writing on 6 September 1994, supplemented on 26 January 1995. Those five matters are the issues on the first

j   review.

(1) (Original objection 2 to bills A, B and C): Miss Mainwaring claimed the right to examine and take copies of the bills (if any) delivered by S J Berwin to Lipkin Gorman; the master, following Taylor LJ in *Goldman v Hesper* [1988] 3 All ER 97 at 101, [1988] 1 WLR 1238 at 1244, himself inspected the solicitor and own client bills but declined either to show them to Miss Mainwaring or to put the receiving party to its election.

(2) (Original objection 3 to bills A, B and C): Miss Mainwaring objected to the partner's hourly rate of £75 allowed on these bills; the master was satisfied that the rate was appropriate and he dismissed the objection.

(3) (Original objection 4 to bill A): Miss Mainwaring objected to the number of hours claimed for work by articled clerks. The master recorded in his reasons that he had been severely critical of the time claimed for articled clerks, and that no adequate response had ever been made to those criticisms. Nevertheless he allowed 189 hours as against 474 hours claimed.

(4) (Original objection 7 to bill A): Miss Mainwaring sought, but the master declined to award to her, the costs of the taxation.

(5) (Original objection 9 to bill B): Miss Mainwaring asked the master to disallow the costs of a report by Stoy Hayward. This related to value added tax (VAT) on bills to Goldtech. The costs of the report had been reduced but the master declined to disallow them in their entirety.

The first review: issue (1)

It is common ground that on a review under RSC Ord 62, r 35 the court can consider the matter afresh, and is not (at any rate apart from matters depending on the opinion of the taxing officer under Ord 62, r 18(2)) restricted to cases where the taxing master has exercised his discretion on a wrong principle, or in an wholly unreasonable way: see the decision of the Court of Appeal in *Madurasinghe v Penguin Electronics (a firm)* [1993] 3 All ER 20, [1993] 1 WLR 989, suggesting that the decision of the Court of Appeal in *Hart v Aga Khan Foundation UK* [1984] 2 All ER 439, [1984] 1 WLR 994 may at some time need to be reviewed. It is because I can look at the matter afresh that I have had the benefit of sitting with assessors with great experience of taxations. Nevertheless, the master has devoted several days of hearings to these taxations, and we have seen only a small part of the documentary material that was before him. Inevitably we have been most concerned with the general approach adopted by the master rather than with detailed assessment of particular items.

The first issue on the first review does raise a matter of principle, that is the problem of reconciling a party's right to legal professional privilege with the normal rule that an adjudicator should not look at and rely on documentary material proffered by one side without giving the other side the opportunity of seeing it and commenting on it: see what was said by Hobhouse J in *Pamplin v Express Newspapers Ltd* [1985] 2 All ER 185 at 186, [1985] 1 WLR 689 at 690–691. But taxation of costs, although a judicial process which is largely adversarial in character, does not have all the characteristics of substantive litigation. When a problem of privilege arises in the course of taxation, the taxing master has a discretion as to how to resolve it: see *Goldman v Hesper* [1988] 3 All ER 97 at 101, [1988] 1 WLR 1238 at 1244.

What the master did in this case was to look again himself at the solicitor and own client bills in order to satisfy himself that there was no infringement of the indemnity principle (under which the receiving party cannot recover any sum in excess of his liability to his own solicitor). It is open to me to review his exercise of discretion but I consider that his decision was (in all the circumstances as described above) the right one.

The first review: issues (2) and (3)

Miss Mainwaring's principal (though not her only) criticism of the partner's hourly rate of £75, for work done in 1989, is that a partner's hourly rate of only

a £70 was claimed for work done in 1991. She submits that this is self-evidently wrong. It is self-evidently inconsistent, since average hourly rates did rise significantly between 1989 and 1991. But it is possible that S J Berwin decided to charge Lipkin Gorman less than the full going rate in 1991 (indeed, Mr Andrew Post, who appeared for the solicitors on the first review, said as much on instructions). In other words it is possible, not that the 1989 rate was higher than
b it should have been, but that the 1991 rate was lower than it might have been. That is the conclusion that I have reached, after discussion with my assessors. I consider that the 1989 rate must be reviewed on its own merits, and that £75 is the proper rate for the master to have allowed.

I am however satisfied that I should depart from the master's decision as regards the number of hours claimed, on bill A, for work by articled clerks. That
c bill related to the wasted costs hearing before Hoffmann J, on which he gave judgment on 13 November 1989; and as I have already mentioned, on 4 December Hoffmann J heard (but made no order on) an application for a gross sum of costs. In support of that application Mr Nicholas Higham (a partner in S J Berwin who had the conduct of the defence of the wasted costs application)
d swore an affidavit to which he exhibited a printed-out timesheet which appears (it is not completely legible) to give the following particulars of hours worked by the two articled clerks (whom I will designate as A and B) during the period of weeks before the hearing. It appears to show A as having worked (in successive weeks) 11, 18, 18, 13, 21, 30, 36, 44, 44 and 54 hours. It shows B working for only just over six hours, making a total for articled clerks of about 307 hours. Mr
e Higham deposed in his affidavit that this timesheet was produced on his instructions and showed all the time recorded by him or his firm's fee-earners up to 10 November 1989. Yet the bill lodged for taxation claimed 474·76 hours (of which the master allowed 189·11 hours). As I have already noted, the master said in his reasons:

f   'I was severely critical of the time claimed in respect of the articled clerk[s], and no adequate response was ever made to those criticisms.'

But he went on:

         'However, for the reasons which I have already given it did not seem
g   appropriate to me to delete all the attendances which were not fully substantiated. Taxation is not an exact science (per Evans J in *Johnson v Reed Corrugated Cases Ltd* [1992] 1 All ER 169). I accordingly reached my view on the basis of what I felt was reasonable, having regard to the work which had to be done, and the amount of time which I felt should reasonably have been
h   spent in undertaking that work.'

Taxation of costs is certainly not an exact science, but (without necessarily saying that the master erred in principle) I think it right, on review, to attach more weight to the inadequate response made by S J Berwin to the master's severe criticisms. Mr Higham swore an affidavit, which I must assume to have been
j carefully prepared and checked, in support of an application for a gross costs order. The effect of that affidavit and exhibit, so far as now material, can be summarised in three propositions: (i) two articled clerks (A and B) were engaged on the case; (ii) A was engaged on the case almost full-time (142 hours in the last three weeks before the hearing); (iii) B's work was minimal (six hours). If any of those propositions was significantly wrong it should have been corrected, with an explanation, in a further affidavit by Mr Higham, the partner responsible. In

these circumstances a claim for over 470 hours for articled clerks, without *a*
explanation, is in my judgment totally unacceptable.

I could remit this matter to the master for him to consider this point again. But
that course would entail further time and expense and on the whole—even
though the effect is bound to be inexact—I think the right course is to resolve the
issue now, rather than remitting it to the master. I shall therefore reduce the
articled clerks' time on bill A by a further 50 hours and allow 139·11 hours. I am *b*
not overlooking that these costs are to be taxed on an indemnity basis; but in the
face of such an enormous unexplained discrepancy between the hours claimed
and the hours shown on the timesheet I am not satisfied that the work was done
at all, and so the question whether it was reasonable for the work to be done does
not arise[a].

c

The first review: issue (4)

The most general rule as to the costs of taxation, in RSC Ord 62, r 27(1), is that
the receiving party gets his costs of the taxation unless (see r 27(2)) 'it appears to
the taxing officer that in the circumstances of the case some other order should
be made as to the whole or any part of the costs'. The master disallowed the *d*
solicitors' costs of the taxation at an early stage, because of their delay, but did not
go further (despite being critical of the solicitors on other points) and did not
award Miss Mainwaring any costs.

For the court to direct that a successful plaintiff should not only be deprived of
his own costs, but should also pay all or part of the defendant's costs is an order
to be made only in the most exceptional circumstances, apart from a payment *e*
into court or a *Calderbank* offer (see *Calderbank v Calderbank* [1975] 3 All ER 333,
[1976] Fam 93). I accept Miss Mainwaring's submission that the question who is
the successful party on taxation (so far as it admits of a sensible answer) is a quite
different question from who has succeeded in the substantive litigation
determining liability and quantum. It more resembles a substantive hearing on *f*
quantum only after liability has been established or admitted. Nevertheless, it is
still an exceptional course to order the receiving party to pay the paying party's
costs of the taxation. Although Miss Mainwaring has had some success in the
taxation and the solicitors have attracted some criticism, she has been far from
wholly successful. I agree with the Chief Taxing Master's exercise of his
discretion on the matter of the costs of bill A and I will not vary his order. *g*

The first review: issue (5)

Where goods or services are supplied by a person registered for VAT to a
company which claims to be non-resident, the supplier may be entitled to invoice
the supply as zero-rated under the Value Added Tax Act 1983 and regulations *h*
made under that Act. The details may call for a little research but in the context
of this case the principles to be applied did not call for a lengthy report from
chartered accountants given only after discussion of the draft report with counsel.

Goldtech was a very shadowy entity, and the question of who controlled it at
different times may have been obscured by backdated documents (see Hoffmann *j*
J's judgment of 13 November 1989, though he rejected the charge that Lipkin
Gorman deliberately put forward false evidence). In the circumstances the

---

a   When judgment was delivered Miss Mainwaring pointed out that it omitted to rule on her
     objections in respect of assistant solicitors' hours. A reduction was ordered in respect of those
     hours, the details of which do not call for report.

a question whether Goldtech was at any particular time entitled to zero-rated invoices may be one of great obscurity. But the difficulty was basically a question of fact, and one that was not really addressed in the Stoy Hayward report exhibited to Mr Cukier's affidavit sworn on 29 November 1990. That affidavit does not in my view spell out the true facts about the VAT issue as fully or as clearly as was appropriate. The master said in his supplementary

b reasons that the whole subject of VAT had 'snowballed out of all proportion to the original difficulty'. But that was not to my mind something for which Miss Mainwaring was responsible. As the master said:

> 'The matter could have been resolved by the production of invoices to Goldtech showing that they had been charged to VAT. However, the
c > invoice that was produced to me appeared to be zero-rated.'

I cannot avoid the suspicion that the solicitors were in a position of some embarrassment over the question of VAT, and that they hoped to alleviate their embarrassment by playing up the complexity of the question. The real issue (whether the solicitors had breached the indemnity principle by claiming for VAT

d on zero-rated services) was one which could and should have been resolved more simply and unequivocally. In any event, it was not in my judgment reasonable, as between the parties, to obtain the Stoy Hayward report, even though leading counsel had advised it, and I shall disallow that item in its entirety.

The second review: ultra vires
e   Miss Mainwaring is by now a very experienced litigant in person, and so the terms of RSC Ord 62, r 18 (relating to litigants in person) are of particular interest to her. Before the master, and again on the second review, she has launched an attack on parts of r 18—that is the latter part of para (2) and the whole of para (3)—as being ultra vires and void.

f   Before considering her submissions on this point I must fill in the historical background. Before April 1976 a litigant in person, even if awarded costs, was entitled to no compensation for his or her time and trouble or loss of earnings but only to reimbursement of out-of-pocket expenses actually incurred. This was an old and well-established rule the reasons for which—whether good or bad—were examined and restated by the Court of Appeal in *Buckland v Watts* [1969] 2 All ER
g 985, [1970] 1 QB 27.

Parliament evidently took the view that the rule was not satisfactory and it was changed by the Litigants in Person (Costs and Expenses) Act 1975 with effect from 1 April 1976. The essential core of the 1975 Act is in the first part of s 1(1):

h   'Where, in any proceedings to which this subsection applies, any costs of a litigant in person are ordered to be paid by any other party to the proceedings or in any other way, there may, subject to rules of court, be allowed on the taxation or other determination of those costs sums in respect of any work done, and any expenses and losses incurred, by the litigant in or in
j   connection with the proceedings to which the order relates ...'

I will now set out RSC Ord 62, r 18 in its entirety:

'(1) Subject to the provisions of this rule, on any taxation of the costs of a litigant in person there may be allowed such costs as would have been allowed if the work and disbursements to which the costs relate had been done or made by a solicitor on the litigant's behalf together with any payments reasonably made by him for legal advice relating to the conduct of or the issues raised by the proceedings.

(2) The amount allowed in respect of any item shall be such sum as the taxing officer thinks fit but not exceeding, except in the case of a disbursement, two thirds of the sum which in the opinion of the taxing officer would have been allowed in respect of that item if the litigant had been represented by a solicitor.

(3) Where it appears to the taxing officer that the litigant has not suffered any pecuniary loss in doing any item of work to which the costs relate, he shall be allowed in respect of the time reasonably spent by him on that item not more than £9·25 per hour [that is the current rate, since 1 December 1995].

(4) A litigant who is allowed costs in respect of attending court to conduct his case shall not be entitled to a witness allowance in addition.

(5) Nothing in Order 6, rule 2(1)(b), or in rule 17(3) of, or Appendix 3 to, this Order shall apply to the costs of a litigant in person.

(6) For the purposes of this rule a litigant in person does not include a litigant who is a practising solicitor.'

Miss Mainwaring submits that the two-thirds limit in r 18(2) and the 'no pecuniary loss' provision in r 18(3) are beyond the scope of, and unauthorised by, the statutory power under which they were made, that is the Supreme Court of Judicature (Consolidation) Act 1925, s 99, now replaced by the Supreme Court Act 1981, ss 84ff. She contends that they are not matters relating to practice and procedure, but relate to the protection of solicitors' trade union differentials.

The master thought he had no power to decide this point but would have rejected these contentions. He referred to s 1(1) of the 1975 Act, emphasising the words 'subject to rules of court' and 'sums in respect of any work done' and said that if r 18 had been silent as to how those sums were to be ascertained, litigants in person would be no better off as a result of the 1975 Act. I cannot agree with that comment. If through some oversight the 1975 Act had come into force with no new rule in place to define the rights of litigants in person, then the taxing authorities of the courts and tribunals referred to later in s 1(1) would in my view have had a wide discretion (to be exercised judicially but unfettered by rules of court so long as no relevant rule existed) to allow reasonable sums for work done, and expenses and loss incurred, by a litigant in person.

However rules were made, and they regulate a litigant in person's rights unless they were beyond the scope of the statutory power. Section 99 of the 1925 Act allows rules of court to be made in order to regulate matters of practice or procedure (although that compendious phrase is not used in s 99, sub-s (1) of which breaks down the subject matter into ten separate paragraphs, including in para (e) 'for regulating any matters relating to the costs of proceedings in the Court of Appeal or the High Court'). Section 84(1) of the 1981 Act authorises rules of court to be made 'for the purpose of regulating the practice and procedure to be followed in the Supreme Court', and s 84(2) expressly provides for the rule-making power to include all matters of practice or procedure in the Supreme Court regulated by rules of court immediately before the commencement of the 1981 Act.

In my judgment it is clear that costs are a matter of practice and procedure, and that the provisions of r 18(2) and (3) to which Miss Mainwaring objects are reasonable provisions defining and regulating the rights of a litigant in person to recover for work, expenses or loss under the 1975 Act. Although Miss

Mainwaring did not in terms attack these provisions as unreasonable that thought was, I suspect, not far below the surface of her submissions. For my part I consider that the two-thirds rule is reasonable, so as not to provide any encouragement to persons who are not legally qualified to become, in effect, professional litigants in person. I also consider the 'no pecuniary loss' provisions in r 18(3) to be reasonable and indeed arguably generous, in view of the basic indemnity principle on which Miss Mainwaring relies in other contexts; £9·25 (replacing £8·25 and before that £8·00) an hour is a small sum for a high-achiever like Miss Mainwaring, but it is above the rate of national average earnings (even on the basis of a 48-hour week) and it is payable to a litigant who has suffered no pecuniary loss (for instance, because a sympathetic employer gives the litigant time off, with full pay, to conduct the litigation).

The second review: Miss Mainwaring's pecuniary loss

That brings me to the other point on the second review. On 27 July 1992 Miss Mainwaring commenced proceedings for taxation of her costs under the master's order of 20 September 1991 mentioned at the beginning of this judgment. Her bill amounted to £87,250 (plus VAT), reached by charging Miss Mainwaring's time at a basic rate of £75 an hour, uplifted to £125 in respect of research and inquiries, and to £200 an hour in respect of preparation and advocacy. The bill claimed not less than 30 hours for travelling and waiting, not less than 200 hours for research and inquiries, and not less than 300 hours for preparation and advocacy. Disbursements and overheads were included within this charge.

On 15 December 1992 the master directed Miss Mainwaring to lodge a chronology and a detailed breakdown of her bill, together with affidavit evidence of her pecuniary loss. She complied with this direction on 10 May 1993, but under protest at least so far as the affidavit was concerned. On 9 December 1994 Lipkin Gorman took out a summons for an order that Miss Mainwaring should provide further evidence of pecuniary loss. That summons was dismissed on the basis that her evidence was what she regarded as sufficient for her purposes. Miss Mainwaring has taken the view, both before the master and on this review, that the burden of proof is on Lipkin Gorman, and that in the absence of any affidavit evidence in answer from Lipkin Gorman the master was not merely entitled but was bound to conclude that she has suffered pecuniary loss in relation to all, or at any rate the bulk of the items of work set out in her detailed breakdown (which covers the period from September 1989 to June 1992, together with one further isolated item, her affidavit sworn at the master's direction in May 1993).

I do not think that Miss Mainwaring's contention as to the burden of proof can be right, either as a matter of common sense or as a matter of legal principle. In principle, the 1975 Act and the rules of court (Ord 62, r 18) made pursuant to it are intended to remedy the grievance (which was a real grievance) that a successful litigant in person could recover no more than out-of-pocket expenses even if he or she had suffered significant loss of earnings as a result of the litigation. But (subject to the minimum rate fixed by r 18(3)) there is no reason why the indemnity principle should not apply here too. Whether a litigant in person has suffered significant loss of earnings is a matter peculiarly within his or her own knowledge. Sometimes the position will be obvious and each side will accept it without the need for any affidavit evidence: at one extreme, for instance, a self-employed tradesman in a small but profitable way of business, who has more customers than he can cope with and can fill every working hour to advantage; at the other extreme, a retired civil servant with an index-linked pension who finds the conduct of litigation a more interesting pastime than bowls or crossword puzzles.

To my mind the formula 'where it appears' in r 18(3) (which appears elsewhere in Ord 62, for instance r 28(1) and is indeed a common expression in statutes and statutory instruments) says nothing, or almost nothing, about the burden of proof. It would be most unusual for the paying party to have to undertake the burden of proving a negative on a matter peculiarly within the receiving party's knowledge, and probably outside the paying party's own knowledge. In any case in informal—and not wholly adversarial—proceedings such as a taxation the burden of proof is something that can shift very readily. Miss Mainwaring had been appearing in person before the master intermittently over a period of many months. He must therefore have observed, because it is obvious, that she is intelligent, articulate, well-educated and under pensionable age; but he may not have known much more than that. He may have gleaned a little more about her background from the documents lodged with him, but that information would have been random and not directed to the issue in hand. Once it was known that Lipkin Gorman was challenging her bill, it was sensible, and well within the master's powers, for him to direct her to make an affidavit of pecuniary loss in support of a bill which, with VAT, amounted to well over £100,000. The fact that the bill charged VAT (but seems to have left blank Miss Mainwaring's VAT registration number) was by itself a matter of some interest.

I must therefore consider Miss Mainwaring's affidavit dated 7 May 1993, which she made under protest. A good deal of the affidavit is concerned with criticisms of the current treatment of litigants in person. Those criticisms may have force, and so far as they do it is to be hoped that changes following on the Woolf report will ameliorate the position; but the criticisms do not really help to establish that the deponent has suffered pecuniary loss. What Miss Mainwaring deposed to as regards her pecuniary loss amounted to this.

(a) The litigation started in March 1988 and she had devoted herself to it full-time 'ever since' [she made the affidavit in May 1993].

(b) She had to spend more time reading documents and authorities than if the issues had been identified in good time by the professionals on the other side.

(c) She worked for Encyclopaedia Britannica International Ltd for eight years until 1986, earning over £100,000 in the last year.

(d) She and Mr Lisle jointly obtained judgment (on the inquiry as to damages on Goldtech's undertaking) for over $2·8m for lost earnings for a period of little more than a year, ending in May 1989. This was presumably on an unopposed inquiry held when it was obvious that Goldtech could not pay damages.

(e) On 2 October 1991 Hoffmann J expressed regret that she should be devoting her whole life to litigation 'when you could, I am sure, have a much more rewarding existence in other ways'.

I accept Miss Mainwaring's evidence on points (b) to (e) above, but point (a) calls for some further examination. Miss Mainwaring's bill of costs covered a period of 34 months, from September 1989 to June 1992 (together with the isolated item of her most recent affidavit). During that period the only times of intense activity, so far as the taxation is concerned, were August 1990 (when she spent an unspecified number of hours on her ninth affidavit) and March to July 1991 (culminating in a three-day hearing before the master). Almost all the substantive first instance hearings were over by the end of 1989. The two hearings in the Court of Appeal were at the end of 1990 and at the beginning of 1991. I understood Miss Mainwaring to make some reference during the hearing to other litigation involving quite different parties (and it is mentioned in the master's reasons), but I have no clear picture of the history or significance of any other litigation.

I have to say that I find Miss Mainwaring's affidavit provides only the most tenuous evidence of what (if any) pecuniary loss she has suffered, either in lost salary or in lost profits of some self-employed activity, between September 1989 and June 1992. Among the matters which Miss Mainwaring does not cover in the affidavit are her training and qualifications; what work she did for Encyclopaedia Britannica; why she stopped working for that company; what paid employment she might have taken, but for the litigation, and at what remuneration, and what job offers she may have received and refused; alternatively what trade or profession she might have followed, with what likely customer or client base and with what prospects of profits; and finally, the significance of the blank VAT number on the first page of her detailed breakdown of costs.

The Chief Taxing Master discussed Miss Mainwaring's affidavit and concluded:

'Even if I accept, as I do, that Ms Mainwaring is a witness of truth, and that she is capable of earning a substantial salary, I am still without any evidence of her actual loss. The fact that she elected to devote herself full-time to this litigation is not sufficient. Ms Mainwaring states that it would have been a waste of everybody's time for her to apply for jobs which she had no intention of taking up, but I do not have any evidence of what employment was available to her during the relevant period. The employment market is constantly changing, and I cannot infer from the fact that Ms Mainwaring is employable that she would in fact have been employed had this litigation not taken place. Mr Sheridan complains that Ms Mainwaring does not explain what she does or how she supports herself. Mr Sheridan also points out that r 18 in its present form refers to pecuniary loss in doing any item of work. In other words, it would be necessary to look at each item of work and to see whether a pecuniary loss had been incurred in respect of it. In short, I have quite simply insufficient information to enable me to reach the conclusion that Ms Mainwaring has suffered pecuniary loss. She has gone part way to showing that she is in a situation where a pecuniary loss might arise, but has failed to produce evidence of what that pecuniary loss might be. In those circumstances I have no alternative but to allow the rate prescribed by the rule in respect of the work done by Mrs Mainwaring.'

I find myself in complete agreement with the master's conclusion on this point. I have carefully considered whether, since Miss Mainwaring is a litigant in person, she should be given an opportunity, even at this very late stage, to make good the manifold deficiencies in her affidavit. In the course of her submissions Miss Mainwaring has challenged the proposition that the court does show indulgence to litigants in person, and has suggested that the opposite is the case. I have to try to be fair to both sides in this long running and hotly contested matter.

After careful consideration I have come to the clear conclusion that I should not give Miss Mainwaring the opportunity of supplementing her affidavit sworn as long ago as 3 May 1993. Miss Mainwaring is not only intelligent and educated but is also, by now, a knowledgeable and experienced litigator. The tenuous content of her affidavit seems to have been a matter of deliberate choice on her part. It may have represented simply a stand on a matter of principle, or it may have resulted from principle mingled with other tactical considerations. Miss Mainwaring had the opportunity of changing her mind and supplementing her

affidavit when Lipkin Gorman issued their summons and again after that
summons was dismissed (see the master's reasons). I think it would be unfair to
Lipkin Gorman, and a waste of public resources, to give Miss Mainwaring
another opportunity to put in evidence (and, to be fair to her, she did not suggest
that course).

I shall not therefore make any alteration, on the second review, in the master's
decision.

Costs

Miss Mainwaring has had some limited degree of success on the first review
but none on the second (on which Mr Peter Sheridan QC appeared for the
solicitors). I shall if necessary hear submissions on costs but it may assist the
parties if I say that my present inclination is to make no order as to the costs of
the first review, and to order Miss Mainwaring to pay the costs of the second
review. It is desirable that any costs awarded on either review should if possible
be assessed at once. The parties should therefore exchange figures for the costs
of the reviews in advance of any further hearing.

Order accordingly.

Celia Fox   Barrister.

Shimizu (UK) Ltd v Westminster City Council

HOUSE OF LORDS

LORD BROWNE-WILKINSON, LORD GRIFFITHS, LORD LLOYD OF BERWICK, LORD COOKE
OF THORNDON AND LORD HOPE OF CRAIGHEAD

28, 29 OCTOBER 1996, 6 FEBRUARY 1997

*Town and country planning – Building of special architectural or historical interest –
Listed building – Alteration works – Works involving demolition of part of listed
building – Refusal of consent –Whether works amounting to alteration or demolition –
Whether building owner entitled to compensation for refusal of consent by Secretary of
State – Town and Country Planning Act 1990, s 336(1) – Planning (Listed Buildings
and Conservation Areas) Act 1990, s 27(1).*

The appellants purchased a listed building with consent to demolish the entire
building except for the façade, chimney breasts and chimney stacks, which were
considered to be of special architectural or historical interest. They wished to
redevelop the site and proceeded to demolish the building in accordance with the
listed building consent so that all that remained were the façade, the chimney
breasts and chimney stacks. The appellants then applied for listed building
consent to demolish the internal chimney breasts in order to provide an extra
floor to their proposed new development, which would add an estimated £1·8m
to the value of the development. The application was refused by the Secretary of
State. The appellants claimed compensation of £1·8m from the local planning
authority under s 27(1)[a] of the Planning (Listed Buildings and Conservation
Areas) Act 1990 (the Listed Buildings Act) on the grounds that removal of the
chimney breasts amounted to an 'alteration of ... a listed building' within the
meaning of s 27(1)(a) thereby entitling them to compensation because the works
did not constitute development and consent to the alteration had been refused by
the Secretary of State. The planning authority resisted the claim, but the Lands
Tribunal held that the proposed work constituted alterations to a listed building
under s 27(1)(a), with the result that compensation was payable by the planning
authority to the appellants. The Court of Appeal allowed an appeal by the
planning authority on the grounds that the concepts of 'demolition' and
'alteration' were mutually exclusive and that the removal of the chimney breasts
amounted to the demolition of a listed building or part of a listed building in
respect of which compensation was not payable under the section. The
appellants appealed to the House of Lords.

Held – (Lord Griffiths dissenting) The appeal would be allowed for the following
reasons—

(1) (Lord Cooke of Thorndon dubitante) Although the application of s 336(1)[b]
of the Town and Country Planning Act 1990 to the Listed Buildings Act by s 91(2)
of the Town and Country Planning Act meant that the term 'building' in the
Listed Buildings Act included 'any part of a building' unless the context otherwise
required, so that part of a building could be listed, it was possible to make sense

---

a   Section 27(1) is set out at p 491 *c d*, post
b   Section 336(1), so far as material, provides: '"Building" includes any structure or erection, and any
    part of a building ...'

of the term 'listed building' in the Listed Buildings Act without reading the term 'building' in that expression as including part of a listed building. Accordingly, the context of the Listed Buildings Act did not require the term 'listed building' to include part of that building. Whether work amounted to 'the alteration ... of a listed building' for the purposes of s 27(1)(a) of the Listed Buildings Act therefore had to be considered in the context of the whole, and not part only, of the structure that had been listed. Furthermore, 'demolition' referred to pulling down a building so that it was destroyed completely and broken up. It followed that works which involved the demolition of a part only of a listed building, falling short of the destruction of the whole listed building, fell within the expression 'alteration' and did not constitute demolition for the purposes of the Act unless the works to be carried out to the listed building as a whole were so substantial as to amount to a clearing of the whole site for redevelopment. Whether works were 'demolition' or merely 'alteration' was a question of fact in each case and the Lands Tribunal had been entitled to hold, on the facts, that the proposed works were works of alteration and not works of demolition (see p 483 *e*, p 485 *b*, p 491 *h* to p 492 *b h* to p 493 *a h j*, p 496 *b c j*, p 498 *e f j* and p 501 *d e*, post).

(2) (per Lord Cooke of Thorndon) There was nothing in s 27 to cut down the meaning of 'alteration or extension' of the Listed Buildings Act and prima facie the appellants were entitled to compensation, as each of the three conditions in s 27(1) was satisfied. The application could naturally be seen as being in essence for the alteration of a listed building and the fact that the Secretary of State's refusal was on the grounds that the works would involve the demolition or impairment of, or a threat to, features of special architectural or historic interest did not prevent the appellants from being entitled to compensation for the refusal of consent to the constructional work of alteration or extension (see p 485 *e* to *h*, post).

Notes

For compensation for refusal of listed building consent, see 46 *Halsbury's Laws* (4th edn reissue) para 930.

For the Town and Country Planning Act 1990, s 336, see 46 *Halsbury's Statutes* (4th edn) (1990 reissue) 877.

As from 25 July 1991, s 27 of the Planning (Listed Buildings and Conservation Areas) Act 1990 was repealed by the Planning and Compensation Act 1991, ss 31(3)(8), 84(6), Sch 19, Pt II, in relation to applications for listed building consent made on or after 16 November 1990.

Cases referred to in opinions

Customs and Excise Comrs v Viva Gas Appliances Ltd [1984] 1 All ER 112, [1983] 1 WLR 1445, HL.

Debenhams plc v Westminster City Council [1987] 1 All ER 51, [1987] AC 396, [1986] 3 WLR 1063, HL.

Furniss (Inspector of Taxes) v Dawson [1984] 1 All ER 530, [1984] AC 474, [1984] 2 WLR 226, HL.

London CC v Marks & Spencer Ltd [1953] 1 All ER 1095, [1953] AC 535, [1953] 2 WLR 932, HL.

R v North Hertfordshire DC, ex p Sullivan [1981] JPL 752.

Appeal

a Shimizu (UK) Ltd appealed from the decision of the Court of Appeal (Millett LJ and Sir Ralph Gibson; Russell LJ dissenting) ([1995] 1 EGLR 167) delivered on 20 December 1994 allowing an appeal by the respondent planning authority, the Westminster City Council (the compensating authority), from the decision of the Lands Tribunal (T Hoyes Esq, FRICS) ([1994] 1 EGLR 214) delivered on 21 May

b 1993 in which, on the trial of a preliminary issue, the tribunal held that the works at the listed building owned by the appellants on the western corner of Old Bond St and Piccadilly in London, which were the subject matter of an application for listed building consent which was refused by the Secretary of State for the Environment in a decision letter dated 4 June 1991, constituted alterations to or extensions of the listed building under s 27(1)(a) of the Planning (Listed

c Buildings and Conservation Areas) Act 1990, with the result that compensation was payable by the compensating authority to the appellants. The facts are set out in the opinion of Lord Hope of Craighead.

John Cherryman QC and *David Holgate* (instructed by *Freshfields*) for the appellants.

d *Michael Barnes QC* and *Viscount Dilhorne* (instructed by *C T Wilson*) for the compensating authority.

Their Lordships took time for consideration.

e 6 February 1997. The following opinions were delivered.

LORD BROWNE-WILKINSON. My Lords, I have had the benefit of reading in draft the speech to be given by my noble and learned friend Lord Hope of Craighead. I agree with it and for the reasons which he gives I would allow this

f appeal and restore the decision of the Lands Tribunal.

LORD GRIFFITHS. My Lords, I have the misfortune to differ from the majority of your Lordships and will therefore express my opinion shortly. I gratefully adopt the history and citation of the relevant sections of the Planning (Listed Buildings and Conservation Areas) Act 1990 set out in the speech of my noble and

g learned friend Lord Hope of Craighead.

The Prudential Assurance Co owned a block of buildings on the corner of Bond Street and Piccadilly. Part of the block, known as Qantas House, was a listed building. The obvious reason for the listing was the elegance of the façade of this building; a less obvious reason was apparently the importance of the

h chimney breasts and chimney stacks contiguous with the façade.

On 6 July 1988 the Prudential obtained listed building consent and planning permission to demolish the entire block with the exception of the façade and the chimney breasts and chimney stacks of Qantas House.

If the Prudential had applied to demolish the whole building including the

j chimney stacks and chimney breasts retaining only the façade and this had been refused they would not have been entitled to compensation. The Prudential might well have wished for permission to demolish the chimney stacks and chimney breasts because by doing so extra floor space would be available in the new building to be erected behind the façade. However although refusal would have resulted in loss of valuable floor space they would not have been entitled to compensation.

The building then changed hands and the appellants became the owners. The appellants proceeded to demolish the building in accordance with the listed building consent and by June 1990 all that remained were the façade and the chimney breasts and chimney stacks supported by temporary steel work. The appellants then applied for listed building consent to demolish the internal chimney breasts, which was refused on appeal by the Secretary of State. The reason why the appellants wished to demolish the chimney breasts was to provide more floor space, which they value at £1·8m.

In order to entitle themselves to claim this £1·8m of compensation, the appellants argue that the demolition of the chimney breasts and the infilling of the voids thereby created in the floors should be regarded not as a demolition of part of a listed building but as an alteration to a listed building the refusal of which entitles them to compensation of £1·8m.

Demolition and alteration in the context of the 1990 Act are overlapping concepts which must be applied with common sense to the facts of each particular case. In each case it will be a question of fact whether the work in question is to be regarded as demolition or alteration, and it will generally be inappropriate for an appellate court to interfere with the finding of fact of the Lands Tribunal. In this case, however, I am unable to accept the finding of the tribunal that the removal of the chimney breasts was an alteration rather than a demolition.

If the chimney breasts had been removed as part of the original site clearance they would unarguably have been 'demolished'. If the appellants had been refused leave to demolish them at that stage, as events prove they would have been, the appellants would have been entitled to no compensation, even though the only reason for wishing to demolish them would be to increase floor space to the value of £1·8m. Now for the same reason, extra floor space, the appellants wish to remove the chimney stacks at a later stage of the construction. In my view it is divorced from reality to regard what would have been demolition in the original site clearance as converted to an 'alteration' if carried out at a later stage.

I would stress that there is no alteration to the new building that was not necessarily involved in the demolition of the chimney breasts, namely extending the floor to the façade to cover the voids left by demolition of the chimney breasts.

Test the matter this way. The appellants acquired the building (on 2 November 1989) before any demolition had commenced. They could before starting demolition have applied for the planning consent to be varied to enable them to demolish the chimney breasts. This we know would have been refused. The appellants would have been thereby deprived of additional floor space, but would not have been entitled to compensation.

In fact they chose to demolish the building and then to apply to demolish the chimney breasts. And it is said that by making the application later rather than earlier they turn demolition into alteration and, hey presto, are entitled to £1·8m. My Lords, that does not seem right to me. Taking down and destroying the chimney breasts was part and parcel of the demolition of the old listed building whether it took place before or during the construction of the new building and I would dismiss the appeal.

The view I take does not depend on the construction of 'listed building'. But like Lord Cooke I am not persuaded that the statutory definition of 'building' should be excluded from the phrase 'listed building'. I certainly would not wish to decide the point without hearing argument from English Heritage and other

bodies likely to be affected by a fundamental change to the basis upon which the
legislation has hitherto been administered.

LORD LLOYD OF BERWICK. My Lords, I have had the benefit of reading in
draft the speech to be given by my noble and learned friend Lord Hope of
Craighead. I agree with it and for the reasons which he gives I too would allow
this appeal and restore the decision of the Lands Tribunal.

LORD COOKE OF THORNDON. My Lords, the appellants, having become
the owner of the listed building then known as Qantas House, on the western
corner of Piccadilly and Old Bond St, wished to enlarge the floor space by
removing old chimney breasts, extending the existing flooring and making it load
bearing for the support of the chimney stacks. Listed building consent under the
Planning (Listed Buildings and Conservation Areas) Act 1990 was sought, but
refused because the chimney breasts were considered of special architectural or
historical interest. The application had been made in June 1990 and subsequently
amended.

Section 27 of the 1990 Act made the provision for compensation on which this
appeal turns. The section was repealed in 1991 in relation to applications for
listed building consent made on or after 16 November 1990, but remains in force
for the purposes of the appellants' claim to compensation.

Prima facie the appellants are entitled to compensation, as each of the three
conditions in s 27(1) is satisfied. The application can naturally be seen as being in
essence for the alteration of a listed building. This is the only point in contention.
It is common ground that the works do not constitute development and that the
Secretary of State has refused consent.

The policy embodied in s 27 appears to have been in part that an applicant
could not obtain compensation for mere refusal of consent to demolition. That
is readily intelligible. It was for the refusal of consent to the constructional work
of alteration or extension that compensation was to be available. Subject to the
de minimis principle, it seems to me reasonably clear on the natural and ordinary
reading of the section that an applicant refused permission under the Act to carry
out such work of construction had a valid claim to compensation. A refusal
would normally be for the reason that the project would involve the demolition
or impairment of, or a threat to, features of special architectural or historic
interest; but such reasons, while explaining the refusal, did not eliminate the
former right of compensation. There was nothing in s 27 to cut down the
meaning of 'alteration or extension'.

On that short ground I would allow the appeal and restore the preliminary
decision of the Lands Tribunal.

My Lords, I must own to experiencing some difficulty in adopting in the route
to that result an interpretation which involves treating the expression 'listed
building' in ss 7 and 8 of the 1990 Act and elsewhere as not including part of a
listed building. I should have thought that, in combination, the relevant
definitions in s 91(1) and (2) of the Planning (Listed Building and Conservation
Areas) Act 1990 and s 336 of the Town and Country Planning Act 1990 have the
prima facie meaning that 'listed building' includes a part thereof; and it is at least
doubtful whether the various reasons which can be put forward to the contrary
are strong enough to enable one to say that the context *requires* the apparent
combined effect of the definitions to be rejected.

Merely arguable suggestions, or a limited degree of surplusage (possibly for clarity), seem grounds too slight to justify such a rejection, as does the fact that the discretionary powers in s 17(3) of the 1990 Act to impose a condition relating to works on 'the site' could not be exercised if there were no site. On the other hand, if a proposed alteration or extension will involve demolition of a part of a listed building it is understandable, albeit sometimes no doubt inconvenient, that notice of the proposal should be required to be given to the Royal Commission on Historical Monuments under s 8(2). Moreover, the government departments concerned in the administration of the Act, the member of the Lands Tribunal, the Court of Appeal and a High Court judge, and also perhaps counsel who appeared before your Lordships, had all understood the definitions to apply and so had regarded 'listed building' as including part thereof.

In these circumstances it does not seem to me easy to say that the context speaks with such clarity as to require a different meaning. In general those who draft legislation and those who are affected by it are entitled to assume that the courts will apply apparently relevant definitions unless they are clearly excluded. But, on the view which I have taken, a definite opinion on the point as to demolition of part of a listed building need not be expressed.

For the reason that the claim to compensation fell within s 27, I too would allow this appeal.

LORD HOPE OF CRAIGHEAD. My Lords, the question at issue in this case is whether the appellants' application for listed building consent for the removal of certain structures within a listed building was an application for the alteration or extension of that building within the meaning of s 27(1)(a) of the Planning (Listed Buildings and Conservation Areas) Act 1990. If it was, the appellants are entitled under s 27(2) to compensation from the respondent local planning authority (the compensating authority), as listed building consent for the removal of these structures was refused. Section 27 of the 1990 Act was repealed by ss 31(3) and 84(6) of and Pt II of Sch 19 to the Planning and Compensation Act 1991, so compensation under that section for the refusal of listed building consent is no longer available. But it will be necessary in order to decide this appeal to deal with some questions of more general interest about the structure of the legislation relating to the control of listed buildings.

The facts

The appellants are the owners of a site on the corner of Old Bond St and Piccadilly in London. The site extends from 56–60 Piccadilly to 45–50 Old Bond St. The building at 56–60 Piccadilly and 48–50 Old Bond St, which was known originally as 'The Corner' and more recently as 'Qantas House', is a listed building. The remainder of the site at 45, 46 and 47 Old Bond St is not listed. The building which is listed comprises a corner block of offices and shops. It is regarded as a fine example of the Edwardian baroque with Dutch influences. It was erected in 1905, to a design by Herbert Read and Robert Faulkner Macdonald, for Callard Stewart & Watt who operated tearooms popular with visitors to the Royal Academy. From the 1960s it was occupied by Qantas Airways, who carried out various works of modernisation and alteration to the interior and significant works of alteration to the ground floor frontages.

On 6 July 1988 Prudential Assurance, who then owned the site, were granted listed building consent and planning permission for the demolition of everything except the façades facing Piccadilly and Old Bond St and the chimney breasts and

a chimney stacks of the listed building, and for the redevelopment of the whole site
to provide shops, a wine bar and restaurant and offices. On 2 November 1989 the
appellants became the freehold owners of the site. Demolition began in March
1990. By June 1990 the building consisted only of the façades, chimney breasts
and chimney stacks supported by temporary steelwork.

On 22 June 1990 the appellants applied to the respondents for listed building
b consent for the removal of the chimney breasts at first, second, third and fourth
floor levels behind the Old Bond St façade. On 2 July 1990 the application was
amended to include the chimney breasts at fifth floor level. On 3 August 1990 a
further amendment was made to the application to include temporary and
permanent support to the chimney stacks. The respondents failed to determine
the application within the statutory eight-week period. The appellants then
c appealed against the deemed refusal to the Secretary of State of the Environment.
On 4 June 1991, after considering representations made by the appellants, by the
compensating authority and by English Heritage, the Secretary of State's
inspector dismissed the appeal. By that date the approved scheme of
redevelopment was at an advanced stage. Although the new fabric was
d incomplete internally, the roof and all the floors were in place and the temporary
steelwork within the building had all been removed.

A dispute then arose between the appellants and the compensating authority
as to whether the appellants were entitled to compensation for the refusal of
listed building consent for the removal of the internal chimney breasts. The
appellants referred their claim to the Lands Tribunal. On 8 July 1992 it was
e ordered that the following preliminary issues be determined at a preliminary
hearing on a date to be fixed:

'a) whether the works which were the subject matter of the application for
listed building consent which was refused by the Secretary of State for the
Environment in his decision letter dated 4 June 1991 constitute alterations to
f or extensions of a listed building under section 27(1)(a) of the Planning
(Listed Buildings and Conservation Areas) Act 1990, with the result that
compensation is accordingly payable by the Compensating Authority to the
Claimant; b) if compensation is payable, the date at which the amount of
compensation is to be assessed ...'

g On 21 May 1993 the Lands Tribunal ([1994] 1 EGLR 214) determined the first
preliminary issue in the appellants' favour. In respect of the second preliminary
issue it was agreed that the relevant date for the assessment of the amount of
compensation was 4 June 1991.

The issue which the member (T Hoyes Esq, FRICS) was asked to decide was
h one of fact, namely whether the removal of the chimney breasts constituted the
demolition or the alteration of a listed building within the meaning of the 1990
Act. It was accepted that if their removal was an alteration of the listed building,
compensation under s 27 would be payable. This was because sub-s (1)(a) of that
section provided that the section was to have effect where 'an application is made
j for listed building consent for the alteration or extension of a listed building'. It
was also accepted that if their removal amounted to the demolition of a listed
building or part of a listed building, compensation under that section would not
be payable. After reviewing the facts which had been established by the evidence,
the member reached the conclusion that the works constituted an alteration to a
listed building rather than the demolition of a part of a listed building. The
respondents then appealed by way of case stated to the Court of Appeal.

On 20 December 1994 the Court of Appeal (Millett LJ and Sir Ralph Gibson; Russell LJ dissenting) ([1995] 1 EGLR 167) allowed the appeal and set aside the decision of the Lands Tribunal. In his dissenting judgment Russell LJ (at 168) said that the question whether a particular activity was 'demolition' or 'alteration' of a building was essentially a question of fact to be determined in the light of all the relevant circumstances, that the court should not interfere in the finding of the Lands Tribunal if the member was entitled on the material before him to reach the conclusion that he did and that, as he was entitled to reach that conclusion, his decision should not be disturbed. The majority reached the opposite conclusion after a careful review of the relevant provisions of the 1990 Act. They held that, when s 27(1)(a) referred to 'an application for ... [consent] for the alteration ... of a listed building', the words in their context did not include an application for consent for works which consisted of or included demolition of part of a building. In their view the concepts of 'demolition' and 'alteration' were mutually exclusive, to the extent of precluding the demolition of a part of the building from amounting to an alteration of the whole. Millett LJ (at 170) made it clear that he reached this decision with reluctance and regret, but he said that he was persuaded that the opposite view could not be maintained in view of the provisions of s 8 of the Act, as they dealt separately with the authorisation of works of alteration or extension on the one hand and works of demolition on the other.

It should be noted that the discussion in the Court of Appeal was conducted throughout on the assumption that the statutory definition of the word 'building' in s 336(1) of the Town and Country Planning Act 1990 (the principal Act), which is extended to the 1990 Act by s 91(2) of that Act—namely that the expression 'building', except in so far as the context otherwise requires, includes 'any part of a building'—applies to the word 'building' where it appears in the phrase 'listed building' as used in the relevant sections of the 1990 Act. It was assumed not only that the expression 'listed building' includes any part of a listed building whenever that expression is used in the 1990 Act, but also that the system of control which the 1990 Act provides can be applied to any part of the listed building in the same way as it applies to the whole.

The history of the legislation

Special building controls in respect of buildings of special architectural or historic interest have formed part of the legislation relating to town and country planning since the 1930s. They were first introduced by s 17 of the Town and Country Planning Act 1932 and were extended by ss 42 and 43 of the Town and Country Planning Act 1944. The provisions of the 1932 and 1944 Acts were replaced by ss 29 and 30 of the Town and Country Planning Act 1947.

In its original form the mechanism which was available for the preservation of these buildings was an order known as a building preservation order. The effect of an order when made was to prohibit the demolition, alteration or extension of the building without the consent of the local authority. The expression 'listed building' was not used, but s 30 of the 1947 Act made provision for the compiling by the minister of lists of buildings of special architectural or historic interest. Subsection (6) of that section provided that, so long as any building was included in any such list, no person was to execute, or cause or permit to be executed, any works for the demolition of the building or for its alteration or extension in any manner which would seriously affect its character unless at least two months' notice had been given in writing of the proposed works to the local authority.

a   Failure to give such notice was an offence.   On receipt of the notice the local planning authority could either allow the works to proceed or make a building preservation order.   No distinction was made in regard to procedure between works of demolition on the one hand and works of alteration or extension on the other.

b   The provisions of the 1947 Act were repealed by s 223 of and Sch 15 to the Town and Country Planning Act 1962 and substantially re-enacted by ss 30, 32 and 33.   In Pts VI and VII of the 1962 Act there were re-enacted also various provisions for the payment of compensation following certain planning decisions restricting new development.   Part VIII re-enacted provisions which enabled an owner whose interests had been affected by various planning decisions or orders to require his interest in the land to be acquired by the local authority.   Section
c   125 enabled a building preservation order to make provision for payment of compensation by a local authority, and s 137 enabled a purchase notice to be served in the case of a building preservation order.

    Part V of the Town and Country Planning Act 1968 introduced a new basis of control by local authorities over buildings of special architectural or historic
d   interest.   This is the basis which, subject to some minor alterations, is now to be found in Pt I of the 1990 Act.   The provisions relating to building preservation orders were discontinued.   The control was now to be by means of the list approved by the minister.   The demolition of a listed building, or its alteration or extension in any manner which would affect its character as a building of special architectural or historic interest, was to be a criminal offence unless authorised
e   under that Part of the Act.   The expression 'listed building' was defined for the first time.   It was to mean a building which was for the time being included in a list compiled or approved by the minister under s 32 of the 1962 Act, which was to continue in force.

    The 1968 Act also dealt with various matters of procedure.   Authorisation for
f   the demolition, alteration or extension of a listed building was to be by means of written listed building consent granted by the local planning authority or by the minister.   Provision was made for the form and manner in which applications for listed building consent were to be made, for the notification to the minister of such applications made to it by the local planning authority and for the giving of directions by the minister to local planning authorities requiring them to notify
g   other bodies of such applications and of the decisions taken thereon.   Much of the system in regard to the form and manner of dealing with applications for listed building consent was to be dealt with by means of regulations made under the Act.   In the case of demolition, notice of the proposal to execute the works had also to be given to the Royal Commission on Historical Monuments, and time
h   had to be allowed before they were commenced for the commission to have reasonable access to the building for the purpose of recording it unless the commission stated in writing that they had completed their recording of the building or did not wish to record it (s 40(4) and (5)).   The procedures for compensation and for the service of a purchase notice on the local authority were
j   to be available in the event of a refusal or conditional grant of listed building consent.   Compensation could be claimed under s 43 only where listed building consent was refused for works of alteration or extension, and only if the works proposed did not constitute development or the development was such that planning permission therefor was granted by a development order.   A listed building purchase notice could be served on the local authority, irrespective of the nature of the proposed works, if the refusal rendered the land incapable of

reasonably beneficial use in its existing state (s 42). In *London CC v Marks & Spencer Ltd* [1953] 1 All ER 1095, [1953] AC 535 it was held that, while demolition works as such did not require planning permission, works which comprised demolition, site clearance and the erection of a new building on the site were operations for which planning permission would have been required but for the exception which was available in that case under s 78(1) of the 1947 Act. It appears that s 43 of the 1968 Act was framed on the basis that it was inappropriate to make provision for compensation in a case where the works proposed were demolition works, as any subsequent beneficial use of the site would require planning permission and compensation for refusal of planning permission was not generally available.

The provisions which I have just summarised duly found their way without material alteration into the Town and Country Planning Act 1971: see ss 54 to 56 of and Sch 11 to that Act. In 1990 the legislation relating to town and country planning was consolidated into four Acts, the principal Act and three separate Acts dealing with listed buildings and conservation areas, hazardous substances and consequential provisions respectively. The only provision in the principal Act which requires to be noticed is the definition of the expression 'building' in s 336(1) of that Act. As I have already mentioned, that definition by which the expression includes 'any part of a building' is extended to the 1990 Act by s 91(2) of that Act.

In the course of the hearing before your Lordships it became clear that in order to dispose of this appeal it was necessary to examine more closely the definition of the expression 'listed building' in the light of the definition of the expression 'building' which is given in the principal Act. The issue which arises in this case is a different one from that which was considered in *Debenhams plc v Westminster City Council* [1987] 1 All ER 51, [1987] AC 396. In that case it was necessary to consider the effect of the extended definition of 'listed building' which is now set out in s 1(5) of the 1990 Act by which any object or structure fixed to a building, or forming part of the land comprised within the curtilage of the building, is to be treated as part of the building. Lord Keith of Kinkel said that the word 'structure' was intended to convey a limitation to such structures as were ancillary to the listed building itself, for example the stable block of a mansion-house or the steading of a farmhouse, either fixed to the main building or within its curtilage, the concept which was envisaged being that of principal and accessory (see [1987] 1 All ER 51 at 55, [1987] AC 396 at 403). Thus the word 'structure' was not intended to embrace some other complete building in its own right. The question which we have to address is whether, given that the controls of the Act extend to every part of a listed building including such objects and structures as are to be treated as part of it, they must be applied in the same way to each part of the listed building as they apply to the whole. This is a problem of interpretation. Does the way in which the expression 'listed building' is used in the Act show that, having regard to the way the expression 'building' is used in this context, the controls are intended to be applied to the listed building seen as a whole? Or can they be applied, in a way which makes sense of the Act, to parts of the building only so that these parts are treated separately from the whole building? In order to answer these questions it is necessary to review the various provisions of the Act which are relevant to this issue.

The relevant provisions of the 1990 Act

a   Part I of the 1990 Act makes provision for the listing of buildings of special architectural or historic interest, the consequences of such listing, authorisation of works affecting listed buildings and the rights of owners to compensation and to serve listed building purchase notices. Part II of the Act, which deals with conservation areas, provides for the designation of conservation areas and the

b   control of demolition of certain buildings in conservation areas.

In Pt I the sections to which I shall need to refer are ss 1, 7 to 9, 17 and s 27. In Pt II the relevant section is s 74. The claim for compensation is made under s 27, which is the principal section which we have to construe. But in order to understand the meaning of the words used in it, it is necessary also to examine the other sections. Section 27(1) provides:

c   'This section shall have effect where—(a) an application is made for listed building consent for the alteration or extension of a listed building; (b) the works do not constitute development or they do so but the development is such that planning permission for it is granted by a development order; and

d   (c) the Secretary of State, either on appeal or on the reference of the application to him, refuses such consent or grants it subject to conditions.'

The words which we have to construe in order to understand the scope and effect of this subsection are the words 'alteration' and 'listed building'. Works of alteration to a building may take various forms, and the description which is to be applied to them will vary according to whether these works are to be seen in

e   the context of their effect on the whole building or on the parts only of the building where the work is to be done. An architect who is asked to design a scheme to alter a building in order to modernise it or improve its accommodation may propose that parts of the existing structure should be removed. He may say that he needs to do this in order to replace that part with a different part or that

f   he needs to do so in order to accommodate a new design which will not involve any replacement. He may describe what he proposes as the taking away or removal of that part, or he may say that that part needs to be demolished. But the various proposals which he makes and the words which he uses to describe them will all fall within the general description of works of alteration to the whole building. He would resist the idea that he was proposing demolition of the

g   building just because his scheme of alteration required the removal or demolition of parts of it in order to accommodate his scheme.

It seems then that it is not enough just to ask whether what is proposed amounts to works of alteration on the one hand to which the subsection will apply—or works of demolition on the other. Different answers may be given to

h   this question depending on what the structure is to which the expression is applied. The question has to be asked in the context of the whole phrase, including the words 'of a listed building'. Again, different answers may be given to the question depending on whether regard is to be had to the whole of the building or part of a building which has been listed or whether regard is to be had

j   only to the part of the building which is to be affected by the works. It is not satisfactory that the answer to the question should vary in this way, as different people may arrive at different answers according to the view which they take of what is meant by the words 'listed building'. This is likely to give rise to confusion or at least uncertainty in the application of the statute to the works which have been proposed. But if the expression 'listed building' in this context were to be read as meaning simply any building or part of a building which is for

the time being included in the list as a listed building—taking due account of the
extended definition in s 1(5) of the 1990 Act—so that the question whether what   *a*
is proposed amounts to an alteration is considered in the context of the whole,
and not part only, of what has been listed, the opportunity for different views
about the nature of the proposal would be minimised and the scheme of the Act
would be that much easier to understand.

Reduced to a question of statutory construction, therefore, the question is   *b*
whether the context in which the word 'building' is used here, where it appears
in the phrase 'listed building,' requires that the reference to 'any part of a
building' in s 336(1) of the principal Act be left out of account. In order to answer
that question it will be convenient now to examine more fully the way in which
the expression 'listed building' is used in the 1990 Act.

        c

The meaning of 'listed building'

Mr Barnes QC accepted that the difficulty which has arisen in this case is due
entirely to the extended meaning which is given to the word 'building' in the
principal Act as including 'any part of a building'. He said that in his approach to
the 1990 Act he had read the words 'any part of a building' into the phrase 'listed   *d*
building' on every occasion where this phrase appears in the Act. On this
approach it is easy to see how, if the chimney breasts are treated as part of a listed
building, their demolition cannot be treated as amounting merely to an alteration
of that part of the building. The purpose of the demolition was to remove the
chimney breasts entirely, not to alter them. If s 27(1)(a) is to be read as directing
that that section is to have effect where 'an application is made for listed building   *e*
consent for the alteration or extension of a listed building *or part of a listed
building*', one could without much difficulty say that the appellants' application
did not meet this requirement because it was an application to demolish a part of
the listed building—namely the chimney breasts—not to alter or extend that part
of the listed building.   *f*

But, for the reasons which I have already given, I do not think that it is
self-evident that the expression 'listed building' must be read in this way. Section
91(1) of the 1990 Act provides that, except in so far as the context otherwise
requires, 'listed building' has the meaning given in s 1(5). Section 1(5) is in these
terms:

        g

> 'In this Act "listed building" means a building which is for the time being
> included in a list compiled or approved by the Secretary of State under this
> section; and for the purposes of this Act—(a) any object or structure fixed to
> the building; (b) any object or structure within the curtilage of the building
> which, although not fixed to the building, forms part of the land and has   *h*
> done so since before 1st July 1948, shall be treated as part of the building.'

It is not said either in s 91(1) or in s 1(5) that the expression 'listed building'
includes any part of a listed building. The word 'building' where it appears on its
own must, of course—unless the context otherwise requires—be given the
extended meaning which it has in terms of s 336(1) of the principal Act. So the   *j*
word 'building' in the first line of s 1(5) of the 1990 Act must be read as including
any part of a building. Thus the entry which is included in the list may refer to a
whole building or to a part of a building according to what is necessary in the
opinion of the Secretary of State to achieve the purposes of the Act. Whatever is
included in the list will then fall within the expression 'listed building,' and it is
clear that the controls of the Act extend to the whole of what has been listed

a   including all its parts. But there is no direction in s 1(5) to the effect that wherever the expression 'listed building' is used the words 'any part of a listed building' may be substituted for that expression so that the controls of the 1990 Act may be applied separately to each part as well as to the whole building. The question whether these words may be substituted depends on the way in which the expression 'listed building' is used to provide these controls.

b   One can well understand why the word 'building' was given an extended meaning by the principal Act. There were likely to be many cases where it would be difficult to say precisely whether the structure which required to be dealt with under a particular provision of that Act was a building or was a part of a building, take a block of terraced houses or offices, for example, or where it would be necessary to extend the controls of that Act to what was undoubtedly only a part c   of a building. In the case of a listed building, however, all one needs to know, in order to identify the structure to which the controls in the 1990 Act apply, is what is the building or part of a building which is for the time being included in the list. Furthermore the direction in s 336(1) of the principal Act that the expression 'building' includes any part of the building does not purport to be an absolute d   rule. It applies 'except in so far as the context otherwise requires'. So it is necessary to examine the context in which the word 'building' appears, when it is used as part of the expression 'listed building,' in order to see whether the extended meaning should be given to it when it is used as part of this phrase.

Section 1(1) of the 1990 Act provides that, for the purposes of the Act and with a view to the guidance of local planning authorities in the performance of their e   functions in relation to 'buildings' of special architectural or historic interest, the Secretary of State shall compile lists of 'such buildings' or approve of such lists compiled by the Historic Buildings and Monuments Commission for England or by other persons or bodies of persons, and may amend any such list so compiled or approved. Section 1(3) provides that, in considering whether to include a f   'building' in a list compiled or approved under that section, the Secretary of State may take into account not only 'the building' itself but also any respect in which its exterior contributes to the architectural or historic interest of any group of buildings of which it forms a part, and the desirability of preserving any feature of 'the building' consisting of a man-made object or structure fixed to it or forming part of the land and comprised within its curtilage. I see no difficulty in g   reading the word 'building' wherever it appears in these two subsections as including 'any part of a building'. Circumstances may be envisaged where only a part of a building is of special architectural or historic interest, and where no good purpose would be served by extending the special control to the whole building. So content can be given here to the provision in s 91(2) that the word h   'building' in the 1990 Act is, except in so far as the context otherwise requires, to have the same meaning as in the principal Act.

Accordingly, when one comes to the definition of the expression 'listed building' in s 1(5) of the Act, namely that it means 'a building which is for the time being included in a list compiled or approved by the Secretary of State', the j   extended meaning can be given to the word 'building' in the passage which I have just quoted without difficulty. The expression 'listed building' can be taken to mean a building or part of a building which is for the time being included in the list. The definition then states that objects or structures fixed to the building, or within its curtilage, are to be treated as part of the building. The expression 'the building' in this part of the definition plainly means the listed building as already defined—that is to say the building, or any part of a building, which is for the time

being included in the list. I do not think that it is necessary to give the word
'building' when used in the expression 'listed building' the extended meaning in
order to make sense of this part of the definition. All this part of the definition is
telling us is that these objects or structures are to be treated, by accession, as part
of the structure whether it be a building or a part of a building which is for the
time being included in the list as a listed building.

Sections 7 to 9 of the 1990 Act provide for the control of works in respect of
listed buildings. The leading provision is s 7, which is in these terms:

> 'Subject to the following provisions of this Act, no person shall execute or
> cause to be executed any works for the demolition of a listed building or for
> its alteration or extension in any manner which would affect its character as
> a building of special architectural or historic interest, unless the works are
> authorised.'

There then follow s 8, which sets out the procedure for obtaining authorisation
for the proposed works, and s 9, which provides that a person who contravenes
s 7 or fails to comply with any condition attached to a listed building consent shall
be guilty of an offence.

I do not think that it is necessary to give the word 'building' in the expression
'listed building' its extended meaning in order to make sense of s 7. On the
contrary, the wording of s 7 suggests that the extended meaning of the word
'building' has no function here. All one needs to identify, in order to apply its
provisions, is the building or part of a building which is for the time being in the
list as a listed building: in other words, is the structure in question a listed
building? If it is, its demolition, assuming for the moment that this word means
the removal of the entire building, would be bound to affect its character as a
building of special architectural or historic interest, because if it were not of that
character it would not be in the list. Works of alteration or extension on the other
hand may or may not have that effect hence the qualification which applies to
these words for the purposes of s 7.

Section 8(2), which provides that works for the demolition of listed buildings
are authorised if inter alia notice of the proposal to execute the works has been
given to the Royal Commission, requires also (by para (c)) that after such notice
has been given either—

> '(i) for a period of at least one month following the grant of such consent,
> and before the commencement of the works, reasonable access to the
> building has been made available to members or officers of the Royal
> Commission for the purpose of recording it; or (ii) the Secretary of the Royal
> Commission, or another officer of theirs with authority to act on their behalf
> for the purposes of this section, has stated in writing that they have
> completed their recording of the building or that they do not wish to record
> it ...'

The requirement is for notice to be given to the Royal Commission before the
works are commenced. It assumes that consent for their execution has already
been granted. Under a separate requirement, which is the subject of directions
made by the Secretary of State under s 15(5) of the Act by means of a
departmental circular (Department of the Environment circular 8/87 (Historic
Buildings and Conservation Areas—Policy and Procedures) paras 81 and 82) all
applications for consent to demolish a listed building will already have been
notified to the Royal Commission, and all applications to alter, extend or

demolish any grade I or starred grade II building outside Greater London and any grade of listed building in Greater London will already have been notified to the Historic Buildings and Monuments Commission for England by the local planning authority before the applications are disposed of by granting or refusing consent.

The word 'building' in the passage which I have quoted from s 8(2) can be read as including any part of a building, because only a part of a building may have been included in the list as a listed building. But it does not seem sensible to qualify the word still further, if the word 'building' here is to mean the building which has been listed the 'listed building' which is referred to in the opening words of sub-s (2) by taking it as including any part of a listed building. When para (i) of sub-s (2)(c) refers to the giving of reasonable access to 'the building' and para (ii) refers to the completion of the recording of 'the building,' the context suggests that it is the listed building as a whole which is being contemplated. I think that the wording of this subsection supports the view that when the Act uses the expression 'listed building' it means simply the building, or part of a building, which is for the time being included in the list.

In the course of his opinion Millett LJ said that the expression 'part of a building' does not appear at all in the 1990 Act and that the definition of 'building' makes this unnecessary (see [1995] 1 EGLR 167 at 170). This observation is not however, with great respect, entirely accurate. Section 17(1) is in these terms:

'Without prejudice to the generality of section 16(1), the conditions subject to which listed building consent may be granted may include conditions with respect to—(a) the preservation of particular features of the building, either as part of it or after severance from it; (b) the making good, after the works are completed, of any damage caused to the building by the works; (c) the reconstruction of the building or any part of it following the execution of any works, with the use of original materials so far as practicable and with such alterations of the interior of the building as may be specified in the conditions.'

Strictly speaking, the words 'or any part of it' in para (c) of this subsection would not have been necessary if the definition of 'building' in the principal Act was to apply. In its context the word 'building' in s 17(1) clearly means the building, that is to say, the listed building with respect to which listed building consent is to be granted. The use of the words 'or any part of it' in para (c) is consistent with the view that the word 'building' does not have the extended meaning when it is used in the expression 'listed building'.

Further assistance can, I think, be found in the provisions of s 17(3):

'Listed building consent for the demolition of a listed building may be granted subject to a condition that the building shall not be demolished before—(a) a contract for the carrying out of works of redevelopment of the site has been made; and (b) planning permission has been granted for the redevelopment for which the contract provides.'

If the expression 'listed building' is to be read as including 'any part of a listed building', it would seem to follow that the removal of any part of it which did not amount merely to the alteration or extension of that part would amount to the demolition of the building for the purposes of sub-s (3). But the removal might be of a small part, such as the whole or part of a partition wall, the effect of which could not reasonably be said to produce 'a site' for redevelopment. Yet the

provisions of this subsection seem to have been framed on the assumption that
when a listed building is demolished there will then be a site for redevelopment.
In other words, its wording suggests that it is the whole of the listed building, not
a part of it, which must be affected by the works of demolition if its provisions are
to apply.

My Lords, I have not found any provision in Pt I of the 1990 Act where it is not
possible to make perfect sense of the expression 'listed building' in its context
without reading the word 'building' as including any part of a listed building. The
various places in which the word 'building' is used in this expression, when taken
together with the definition which is given to it by s 1(5), suggest that this word
should not be given its extended meaning where it appears in the phrase 'listed
building'. It is sufficient to give the word 'building' its extended meaning for the
purposes of this Act that the Secretary of State may include the whole or any part
of a building in the list. Once the whole or any part of a building has been
included in the list, however, it becomes a 'listed building' for the purposes of the
Act. The fact that only a part of a building has been included in the list then ceases
to have any significance. It is the entry in the list which identifies the structure
which is thereafter to be referred to as the 'listed building'.

It was suggested that the provisions of s 74, which appears in Pt II of the 1990
Act relating to conservation areas, were inconsistent with this interpretation.
Subsection (1) of s 74 provides that a building in a conservation area shall not be
demolished without the consent of the appropriate authority, and sub-s (3)
provides that various sections in Pt I of the 1990 Act have effect in relation to
buildings in conservation areas as they have effect in relation to listed buildings.
I do not think that there is any inconsistency, so long as it is appreciated that a
listed building can consist of a part of a building. Buildings in conservation areas
are put on the same footing as buildings of special architectural or historic
interest, or any part of a building which has that character, which is for the time
being included in the list. In the context of s 74(1), subject to any exceptions or
modifications in this regard which may have been prescribed under sub-s (3) of
that section, the reference to the demolition of a building in a conservation area
must be taken to mean the removal of the whole building, in the same way as
s 17(3) appears to contemplate works to a listed building which will produce a site
for redevelopment.

The meaning of 'demolition'

The meaning which I would give to the expression 'listed building' leaves little
room for discussion about the meaning of the word 'demolition' in this context.
But as it received close attention in the Court of Appeal I think that it is necessary
to examine the word more closely in order to see whether it is still possible to
support the view, contrary to that taken by the member in the Lands Tribunal,
that the works which were proposed in this case were works of demolition rather
than works of alteration or extension for the purposes of s 27(1) of the 1990 Act.

According to its ordinary meaning, the word 'demolish' when used in
reference to a building means to pull the building down—in other words, to
destroy it completely and break it up. I agree therefore with Millett LJ when he
said that demolition, with or without replacement, on the one hand and
alteration on the other are mutually exclusive concepts (see [1995] 1 EGLR 167 at
170). In relation to a building, its destruction and breaking up cannot constitute
a mere alteration. Once the works are over, the old building has gone. The
problem which led the majority in the Court of Appeal to hold that the works

which were proposed to the chimney breasts amounted to works of demolition and not alteration arose when they applied these words to a part only of the listed building—that is, to the chimney breasts, not to the whole building.

I can see the force of the observation, which appears in the same passage in Millett LJ's judgment and is then the subject of careful examination in the judgment of Sir Ralph Gibson, that the demolition and replacement of a part of a building cannot constitute an alteration of that part. The replacement of that part, as they pointed out, was to be a substitute for the old, not an alteration of it. Millett LJ then recognised, correctly in my opinion, that, while the demolition and replacement of part of a building cannot constitute the alteration *of that part* (his emphasis), it can constitute an alteration of the whole. He said that this approach would provide a test which was at once workable and provided some explanation of the legislative purpose in awarding compensation for the refusal of consent for alteration and withholding it for demolition. As he put it ([1995] 1 EGLR 167 at 170):

> 'The test would be whether the application, however worded, could fairly be described as an application to alter a listed building by demolishing or demolishing and replacing part. It would not matter how extensive the alterations were; major alterations qualify for compensation: indeed, the alterations must be significant enough to affect the character of the building or consent would not be required in the first place. What mattered would be what was left. The question would be whether those parts which were not to be demolished or demolished and replaced were sufficient to enable the application to be fairly described as an application to alter the building by demolishing part rather than as an application to demolish the whole or substantially the whole of the building.'

The provision in the Act which persuaded Millett LJ and Sir Ralph Gibson to reject this approach is s 8. This section deals separately with works of alteration or extension on the one hand and works of demolition on the other. It deals with the procedure for authorisation, where listed building consent is being sought. There is a difference in procedure between works of alteration or extension and works of demolition, although the procedure may perhaps more accurately be regarded as a single procedure with additional requirements in the case of demolition works. Where works of alteration or extension are involved, all that is needed is written consent for their execution given by the local authority or by the Secretary of State and that the works are then executed in terms of the consent and of any conditions attached to it. Where works of demolition are involved, notice of the proposal must also be given to the Royal Commission and one or other of the periods referred to in s 8(2)(c), which I have already quoted, must then be allowed to elapse.

The question whether the word 'building' in the phrase 'listed building' has the extended meaning given to it in the principal Act lies at the heart of the discussion about s 8 of the 1990 Act. As the majority in the Court of Appeal pointed out, if the demolition of part can also constitute an alteration of the whole, then such works will be authorised works if sub-s (1) of s 8 is satisfied even though notice has not been given to the Royal Commission in accordance with sub-s (2) before the works are commenced. I agree that it cannot have been the intention of Parliament that works for the demolition of a listed building should be authorised where the provisions of sub-s (1) only were satisfied. But I do not agree with the assumption on which this proposition has been based. In my opinion the whole difficulty is removed if the phrase 'listed building' is given the meaning which I have suggested should be given to it in the earlier part of this opinion. There can then be no question of the word 'demolition' within the meaning of the Act being applied to works of alteration which affect only part of a listed building.

It is important to notice also that the requirement to notify the Royal Commission under s 8(2) assumes that listed building consent for the execution of the works has already been granted by the local planning authority or by the Secretary of State. The purpose of this requirement is confined therefore to enabling the Royal Commission to obtain access to the building and record it before the commencement of the works. While the maintenance of an inventory of buildings of special architectural or historic interest is an important part of the commission's functions, this is not the stage at which it can express views as to whether it is appropriate for the proposal to receive listed building consent. An opportunity will already have been given to the commission and to the Historic Buildings and Monuments Commission to express any views at the earlier stage before the application is disposed of under the procedures laid down by the Secretary of State under s 15(5) by means of DOE circular 8/87. The structure of the legislation as it operates in practice cannot be understood without a full appreciation of the wide powers of regulation and direction which have been given in these matters to the Secretary of State and the way in which these powers have been exercised. For present purposes however it is sufficient to say that the requirement for notification in s 8(2) is concerned essentially with record keeping and not with the question whether or not listed building consent should be granted for the proposed works.

As I have said, s 8(2) can be read with perfect sense if the word 'building' is taken, in the context of these provisions, to mean simply the building or part of a building which is for the time being included in the list as a listed building. If that building or part of a building, the 'listed building', is to be pulled down, so that it will be destroyed completely and broken up, the works will amount to its destruction to which the additional procedure in s 8(2) will always apply. Works which involve the pulling down and breaking up of part of the building, falling short of its destruction, will fall within the expression 'alteration' which, if they would affect its character as a building of special architectural or historic interest, will require consent to be sought under s 8(1).

I should like to make it clear that I do not see the word 'demolition' as applying only where the proposal is that every single part of the listed building should be pulled down. It is now commonplace, especially in towns and cities, where the exterior of a building contributes to the architectural or historic interest of a group of buildings such as buildings in a terrace, for the façade to be left standing while clearing the remainder of the site for redevelopment. That indeed is what was done in this case. As s 17(3) has envisaged in the case of demolition works, planning permission for the redevelopment of the site was granted at the same time as the original proposals received listed building consent and conservation area consent. It seems to me to be plain that the original proposal was for the demolition of the listed building for all practical purposes, so that a scheme of redevelopment could be carried out. It went far beyond what could reasonably be described as its alteration, as the works were so extensive and so much was to be pulled down and taken away, although the façade and the chimney breasts and chimney stacks were to be retained. The question is ultimately one of fact for the decision of the Lands Tribunal, and I do not think that any more precise definition of this expression is required.

a   We were referred to Lord Diplock's observations in *Customs and Excise Comrs v Viva Gas Appliances Ltd* [1984] 1 All ER 112 at 116, [1983] 1 WLR 1445 at 1451, where he said that the word 'demolition' meant destroying the building as a whole. That case was concerned with a phrase in the description of an item in Group 8 of Sch 4 to the Finance Act 1972 relating to value added tax, where there was no reference to 'any part of a building'. What had to be construed was the

b   meaning of 'demolition' when it appeared in the phrase 'in the course of the construction, alteration or demolition of any building'. Mr Barnes said that that case was of no assistance here, because the words 'any part of a building' formed part of the definition in the 1990 Act and were thus relevant to this case. On the view which I have taken of the meaning of the expression 'listed building' that argument no longer applies. But I would prefer not to take Lord Diplock's

c   observation out of its context. In any event I do not think that what he said in that case can be taken to mean that, in the context of listed building consent, works which will involve the removal of so much of the old building as to clear a site for redevelopment cannot be held to amount to demolition works for the purposes of Pt I of the 1990 Act, and in particular for the purposes of s 8(2).

d   *Other matters*

(a) It should be noted that the view which I take of the meaning of the expression 'listed building' and of the distinction between works of 'demolition' and works of 'alteration' in this context is not the same as that which has been expressed in DOE circular 8/87 and in a prior decision in the Queen's Bench

e   Division of the High Court. In *R v North Hertfordshire DC, ex p Sullivan* [1981] JPL 752 Comyn J was referred to para 66 of DOE circular 23/77, which was in these terms:

f   'It is often asked whether works which do not involve total demolition of the building should, nevertheless, be regarded as "works for the demolition of a building". The Secretary of State cannot give an authoritative interpretation of the rules but draws attention to section 290(1) [of the 1971 Act] in which building is defined as including any part of a building but demolition of a part of the building should thus be regarded as the

g   demolition of the building for the purposes of section 55 and 77(a).'

That case was concerned with the question whether an extension of a listed building which involved the demolition of parts of the listed building constituted demolition within the meaning of the 1990 Act which required the proposal to be notified to various interested bodies by the local planning authority. The judge

h   (at 754) held that the dominant word in the provisions about demolition, alteration and extension was the word 'demolition', especially where, under the interpretation section, demolition was deemed to refer not only to a building but also to part of a building. As was observed in the comment on that decision, the problem raised by that case was how to find a wording which would distinguish

j   between fundamental demolitions and works which, although they involved a partial demolition of a building, were relatively minor. The commentator added that one easy solution would be to amend the law so that demolition of a building, in the context of listed buildings, did not include the demolition of part of a building but only the complete demolition of a building. It was recognised however that it might be considered that this would be too drastic, since it would mean that works which might fundamentally change a listed building would

come under less stringent procedures if they fell short of complete demolition
(see [1981] JPL 752 at 755).

On the approach which I favour to the meaning of these words no alteration
of the 1990 Act would be required. It will be sufficient to read the expression
'listed building' in the context of Pt I of the Act as meaning a building or any part
of a building which for the time being is included in the list. So demolition of a
part only of what is in the list as a listed building will not constitute demolition
for the purposes of this Part of the Act unless the works which are to be carried
out to the listed building as a whole are so substantial as to amount to a clearing
of the whole site for redevelopment.

(b) The advice which was given in DOE circular 23/77 has been carried one
stage further in regard to conservation areas, to which the provisions of the
Planning (Listed Buildings and Conservation Areas) Regulations 1990, SI 1990/
1519, apply, by a planning policy guidance note (PPG 15) issued by the
Department of the Environment and the Department of Natural Heritage in
September 1994, para 4.28 of which is in these terms:

> 'Section 336 of the principal Act states that a building includes "any part of
> a building." The demolition of part of a building should therefore be
> regarded as falling within the scope of conservation area control. What
> constitutes a demolition or demolition of part of a building must be a matter
> of fact and degree, to be decided in the particular case and ultimately by the
> courts. Routine works of repair, maintenance or replacement, including
> work involving such items as doors or windows, would not in the Secretary
> of State's view normally constitute demolition. Likewise, the removal of
> internal features, whether replaced or not, would not usually constitute a
> demolition and for the purposes of conservation area consent would not, in
> any event, have a material impact on the building's appearance or affect the
> character or appearance of the area.'

It follows from what I have said that the advice in that paragraph will require
to be reconsidered. Subject to such exceptions or modifications as may have been
prescribed by regulations under s 74(3) of the 1990 Act, it will no longer be correct
to say that, because of the definition of 'building' in the principal Act, the
demolition of part of a building in a conservation area should be regarded as
falling within the scope of conservation area control. In the context of s 74 of the
1990 Act, which requires to be read together with the legislation relating to listed
buildings in Pt I of that Act, the reference to demolition of a building means the
demolition of the whole building. But advice can still be given to the effect that
the question what constitutes the demolition of the whole building is a question
of fact and degree which will need to be decided on the facts of each case.

(c) It was submitted for the compensating authority that the application for
consent to remove the chimney breasts was part of a series of steps designed to
secure the overall aim of gaining consent to demolish the greater part of a listed
building. This argument was presented under reference to *Furniss (Inspector of
Taxes) v Dawson* [1984] 1 All ER 530, [1984] AC 474, on the view that there was a
premeditated scheme to achieve that end. But I agree with Sir Ralph Gibson that
the respondents cannot derive any assistance from the principles established in
Furniss v Dawson. As he put it, a claimant is entitled to make applications for
planning permission or for listed building consent at such time and in such
sequence as he chooses. Furthermore, there is no evidence here of a preordained
series of transactions. Ownership of the building changed between the date of

a the original applications and the application for consent for the removal of the chimney breasts before the Lands Tribunal, as the member has recorded, and it was common ground between counsel for the parties that there was no deliberate scheme by the appellants involving the fragmenting of the applications so as to secure and maximise compensation.

b (d) Various criticisms were made of the reasoning by which the member reached his decision that the removal of the chimney breasts constituted an alteration rather than demolition of part of a building. Millett LJ said that his reasoning could not be supported, as many of the considerations which influenced his decision were irrelevant to the question which he had to decide. In my opinion the force of these criticisms is removed by the approach which I have taken to the meaning of the expression 'listed building,' so I do not think that it is *c* necessary to go over this ground again.

Conclusion

For the reasons which I have given I consider that the question which had to be answered in this case is whether the proposed works for the removal of the chimney breasts constituted demolition of the listed building or its alteration or *d* extension. The member did not approach the question in this way, because he had regard to the extended meaning of the word 'building' in dealing with the issue, which he said was whether the proposed works amounted to the alteration or the demolition of part of the listed building. But in my opinion he was entitled to hold on the facts that the proposed works were works of alteration and not *e* works of demolition. That is sufficient to support the decision which he reached, as the question was essentially one of fact for him to decide.

I would therefore allow this appeal and restore the decision of the Lands Tribunal.

f *Appeal allowed with costs.*

Celia Fox   Barrister.

Semco Salvage and Marine Pte Ltd v Lancer Navigation Co Ltd
The Nagasaki Spirit

HOUSE OF LORDS

LORD MACKAY OF CLASHFERN LC, LORD GOFF OF CHIEVELEY, LORD MUSTILL, LORD LLOYD OF BERWICK AND LORD HOPE OF CRAIGHEAD

7, 8, 9 OCTOBER 1996, 6 FEBRUARY 1997

Shipping – Salvage – Salvage award – Special compensation for preventing or minimising damage to environment – Salvor entitled to special compensation of proportion of out-of-pocket expenses reasonably incurred in salvage operation and fair rate for equipment and personnel actually and reasonably used in salvage operation – Expenses – Fair rate – Whether fair rate should include profit element – International Convention on Salvage 1989, arts 13, 14.

The shipowners' vessel collided with another vessel off the coast of Malaysia and spilled part of its cargo of crude oil into the sea, causing both vessels to catch fire. The salvors agreed to salve both vessels and their cargo on the terms of Lloyd's Open Form 1990 for salvage, which provided that salvage was to be rendered in accordance with the traditional principle of 'no cure–no pay' and that the salvor's remuneration was to be fixed by arbitration in London. Having carried out the salvage of the shipowners' vessel, including putting out the fire on board and transhipping the balance of the cargo to another vessel, the salvors delivered the vessel to the owners in Singapore and claimed their salvage reward. The salvage arbitrator, in addition to the standard salvage award under art 13[a] of the International Convention on Salvage 1989, which had the force of law in the United Kingdom by s 224 of the Merchant Shipping Act 1995 and was incorporated into the Lloyd's Open Form, awarded special compensation under art 14[b] on the grounds that the salvage resulted in benefit to the environment by preventing a massive spillage from the shipowners' vessel. Article 14 provided that if the salvage operations prevented or minimised damage to the environment which the vessel or its cargo threatened to cause and the salvage reward under art 13 was less than the salvors' expenses, they were entitled to special compensation of up to 30%, or in special circumstances up to 100%, of their expenses. The salvors' 'expenses' were defined by art 14.3 as their 'out-of-pocket expenses reasonably incurred ... in the salvage operation and a fair rate for equipment and personnel actually and reasonably used in the salvage operation'. In calculating the special compensation, the arbitrator applied what he considered to be a fair daily rate for the salvor's tugs which included an element of profit for the salvors. On appeal, the appeal arbitrator disagreed with the salvage arbitrator on the grounds that 'expenses' could not include a profit element and reduced the special compensation to an amount which was less than the salvage award so that in fact no special compensation was payable. On appeal by the salvors, both the High Court judge and the Court of Appeal held that 'a fair rate for equipment and personnel actually and reasonably used in the salvage

---

a   Article 13, so far as material, is set out at p 508 *g* to *j*, post
b   Article 14 is set out at p 509 *a* to *d*, post

a operation' meant a rate of expense which took into account all indirect and
overhead expenses and the cost of having salvage facilities on standby and
instantly available and did not include remuneration or a profit element as they
should be included in the salvage award under art 13. The salvors appealed to the
House of Lords, contending that a 'fair rate' for special compensation was a fair
rate of remuneration having regard to the circumstances of the case, including
b the type of craft actually used and the type of work required, and which acted as
an incentive to the salvor by normally including a profit element but without
amounting to a salvage reward.

Held – For the purposes of art 14.3 of the 1989 convention, as incorporated into
Lloyd's Open Form 1990 for salvage, 'expenses ... incurred' by a salvor denoted
c amounts either disbursed or borne, not earned as profits. Accordingly, an award
of special compensation under art 14.2 was intended to recompense or reimburse
a salvor for his expenses in the event that his direct and standby costs exceeded
his salvage reward under art 13 and was not intended to yield or be a source of
profit. It followed that salvors entitled to special compensation for protecting the
environment were entitled to a fair rate of expense which was comprehensive of
d indirect or overhead expenses, including the additional cost of having resources
on standby and instantly available but not including a profit element. Since that
had been the basis of the appeal arbitrator's award of special compensation which
had been upheld by the judge and the Court of Appeal, the appeal would be
dismissed (see p 504 *a* to *d f*, p 512 *b d* to *g*, p 513 *e* to *g*, p 515 *f*, p 516 *c* to *g* and
e p 517 *b*, post).

Notes
For salvage reward and salvors' expenses, see 43 *Halsbury's Laws* (4th edn) paras
1053, 1067.

f **Case referred to in opinions**
Fothergill v Monarch Airlines Ltd [1980] 2 All ER 696, [1981] AC 251, [1980] 3 WLR
209, HL.

Appeal and cross-appeal
Semco Salvage and Marine Pte Ltd (the salvors) appealed from the decision of the
g Court of Appeal (Staughton and Swinton Thomas LJ; Evans LJ dissenting) ([1996]
1 Lloyd's Rep 449) delivered on 21 December 1995 dismissing their appeal from
the decision of Clarke J ([1995] 2 Lloyd's Rep 44) delivered on 30 March 1995
dismissing in turn their appeal from the decision of the appeal arbitrator, J F
Willmer QC, allowing an appeal by the shipowners, Lancer Navigation Co Ltd,
h from the award made by the salvage arbitrator, R F Stone QC, in which he
awarded the salvors special compensation of 3,135,893 Singapore dollars under
art 14 of the International Convention on Salvage 1989 in respect of their salvage
of the owners' vessel Nagasaki Spirit. The owners cross-appealed on the question
of the period for which a salvor was entitled to special compensation under art 14
j of the convention. The facts are set out in the opinion of Lord Mustill.

Geoffrey Brice QC and *Vasanti Selvaratnam* (instructed by *Hill Taylor Dickinson*) for
Semco.
Michael Thomas QC and *Simon Gault* (instructed by *Holman Fenwick Willan*) for the
owners.

Their Lordships took time for consideration.

6 February 1997. The following opinions were delivered.

a

LORD MACKAY OF CLASHFERN LC. My Lords, I have had the advantage of reading in draft the speech to be given by my noble and learned friend Lord Mustill. I agree with him for the reasons that he has given that the appeal and the cross-appeal should be dismissed, in each case with costs.

In relation to the appeal, I would in particular emphasise the importance of the *b* interpretation of the relevant words in their context. Although no doubt an interpretation clause defining expenses could specifically include an item or items that were not expenses it would more naturally be concerned with identifying particular heads or types of expenses. When the expenses as defined are repeatedly spoken of as incurred this appears to me to preclude the view that expenses as defined includes remuneration or profit. The use of the term 'rate' is *c* explained by the need to do more than identify a particular figure. The circumstances require a judgment of how much of the total expense incurred for equipment and personnel is fairly to be taken as applying to the equipment actually and reasonably used in the salvage operation in question taking into consideration the criteria referred to. *d*

For my own part, I would not have found it necessary to examine the travaux préparatoires in order to reach a decision on the central issue in this appeal. However, out of respect for the very full and detailed arguments to which your Lordships were treated, I am glad and grateful to my noble and learned friend that he has done so in such an admirable way, in an area of the law in which he is such an eminent authority, and has reached the conclusion that this analysis *e* strongly reinforces the view formed on the words themselves read in their context.

LORD GOFF OF CHIEVELEY. My Lords, I have had the benefit of reading in draft the speech to be given by my noble and learned friend Lord Mustill. I agree *f* with it, and for the reasons which he gives I would dismiss both the appeal and the cross-appeal.

LORD MUSTILL. My Lords, the law of maritime salvage is old, and for much of its long history it was simple. The reward for successful salvage was always large; for failure it was nil. At first, the typical salvor was one who happened on *g* a ship in distress, and used personal efforts and property to effect a rescue. As time progressed, improvements in speed, propulsive power and communications bred a new community of professional salvors who found it worthwhile to keep tugs and equipment continually in readiness, and for much of the time idle, waiting for an opportunity to provide assistance and earn a large reward. This *h* arrangement served the maritime community and its insurers well, and the salvors made a satisfactory living. It was however an expensive business and in recent years the capital and running costs have been difficult for the traditional salvage concerns to sustain. A number of these were absorbed into larger enterprises, less committed perhaps to the former spirit, and unwilling to stake *j* heavy outlays on the triple chance of finding a vessel in need of assistance, of accomplishing a salvage liable to be more arduous and prolonged than in the days of smaller merchant ships, and of finding that there was sufficient value left in the salved property at the end of the service to justify a substantial award. At about the same time a new factor entered the equation. Crude oil and its products have been moved around the world by sea in large quantities for many years, and the

a risk that cargo or fuel escaping from a distressed vessel would damage the flora and fauna of the sea and shore, and would impregnate the shoreline itself, was always present; but so long as the amount carried by a single vessel was comparatively small, such incidents as did happen were not large enough to attract widespread attention. This changed with the prodigious increase in the capacity of crude oil carriers which began some three decades ago, carrying with

b it the possibility of a disaster whose consequences might extend far beyond the loss of the imperilled goods and cargo. Such a disaster duly happened, at a time when public opinion was already becoming sensitive to assaults on the integrity of the natural environment. Cargo escaping from the wreck of the Torrey Canyon off the Scillies caused widespread contamination of sea, foreshore and wild life. The resulting concern and indignation were sharpened when the

c Amoco Cadiz laden with 220,000 tons of crude oil stranded on the coast of France, causing pollution on an even larger scale, in circumstances which rightly or wrongly were believed to have involved a possibly fatal delay during negotiations with the intended salvors.

To this problem the traditional law of salvage provided no answer, for the only

d success which mattered was success in preserving the ship, cargo and associated interests; and this was logical, since the owners of those interests, who had to bear any salvage award that was made, had no financial stake in the protection of anything else. This meant that a salvor who might perform a valuable service to the community in the course of an attempted salvage, by for example moving the vessel to a place where the escape of oil would be less harmful, would recover

e nothing or only very little, if in the end the ship was lost or greatly damaged. Something more was required to induce professional salvors, upon whom the community must rely for protection, to keep in existence and on call the fleets necessary for the protection of natural resources in peril. Some new form of remuneration must be devised. It is with an important aspect of the scheme

f worked out during long and hard-fought negotiations between the shipowning and cargo interests and their insurers on the one hand and representatives of salvors on the other, with participation by governmental and other agencies, that the present appeal is concerned.

It is important to make clear at the start that the solution devised in the 1980s was not to create a new institution: a kind of free-standing 'environmental

g salvage'. The services performed remain, as they have always been, services to ship and cargo, and the award is borne by those standing behind ship and cargo. The difference is that the sum payable to the salvor may now contain an additional element to reflect the risk to the environment posed by the vessel for which the services are performed. This element of 'special compensation' is

h based on the salvor's 'expenses' (as defined) and may be enhanced in cases where the salvage operations have actually prevented or minimised environmental damage. The reward for the salvage itself is assessed and apportioned between the vessel and other property interests as before, and the difference if any between the amount so awarded (or nil, if there is no award) and the amount of

j the special compensation is due to the salvor from the shipowner alone. Two issues are now before the House about the principles on which the special compensation should be assessed. Of these, one is much the more difficult. I will concentrate on this, leaving over the second point for a brief reference at the end.

The events which have led successively to hearings before Mr R F Stone QC as salvage arbitrator, Mr J F Willmer QC as appeal arbitrator, Clarke J ([1995] 2 Lloyd's Rep 44) sitting in the Commercial Court on appeal from the award of Mr

Willmer QC, the Court of Appeal ([1996] 1 Lloyd's Rep 449), and finally your Lordships, were summarised by Clarke J in terms which I am glad to adopt (see [1995] 2 Lloyd's Rep 44). At about 23.20 hours on 19 September 1992 the Nagasaki Spirit collided with the container ship, the Ocean Blessing. The collision occurred in the northern part of the Malacca Straits. At the time of the collision the Nagasaki Spirit was part laden with a cargo of 40,154 tonnes of Khafji crude oil. As a result of the collision, about 12,000 tonnes of the Nagasaki Spirit's cargo were released into the sea and caught fire. Both ships were engulfed by the fire. Only two members of the crew of the Nagasaki Spirit survived the fire. All the crew of the Ocean Blessing lost their lives. At about 09.00 hours on 20 September the appellants, Semco Salvage and Marine Pte Ltd (Semco), agreed to salve the Nagasaki Spirit and her cargo on the terms of Lloyd's Open Form 1990 (hereafter 'LOF 1990'). Later that day they agreed to salve the Ocean Blessing on the terms of the same form.

On the same day Semco mobilised a number of tugs, which proceeded to the position of the casualty. Semco fought the fire on the Nagasaki Spirit. They succeeded in extinguishing it at about 12.20 on 26 September. At about 17.00 hours on 26 September the Malaysian police expressed concern that the casualty might cause pollution. They ordered Semco to tow the Nagasaki Spirit away from the Malaysian coast. At about 14.03 hours on 3 October the Nagasaki Spirit was anchored in a position off Belawan in Indonesia. She remained at this anchorage until 24 October.

On 22 October the Indonesian authorities granted Semco permission for a ship to ship transfer of the cargo remaining on board the Nagasaki Spirit. On 24 October Semco moved the Nagasaki Spirit to a new position in order to transfer her cargo. Transhipment of the cargo from the Nagasaki Spirit to the Pacific Diamond was commenced at 00.25 hours on 29 October. The Nagasaki Spirit remained at the anchorage position until about 14.00 hours on 25 November when a tow to Singapore commenced. At 15.40 hours on 12 December the Nagasaki Spirit was redelivered to her owners afloat alongside the shipyard quay in Singapore.

Before turning to the relevant provisions of LOF 1990 a little of its history must be given. The move towards the evolution of what has been called a 'safety net', designed to provide an additional incentive for salvors to keep fleets on station, began during the late 1970s with two parallel initiatives. These first bore fruit in the 1980 revision of the Lloyd's Open Form, so as to make cl 1(a) read as follows:

'The Contractor agrees to use his best endeavours to salve the ... and/or her cargo bunkers and stores and take them to ... or other place to be hereafter agreed or if no place is named or agreed to a place of safety. The Contractor further agrees to use his best endeavours to prevent the escape of oil from the vessel while performing the services of salving the subject vessel and/or her cargo bunkers and stores. The services shall be rendered and accepted as salvage services upon the principle of "no cure–no pay" except that where the property being salved is a tanker laden or partly laden with a cargo of oil and without negligence on the part of the Contractor and/or his Servants and/or Agents (1) the services are not successful or (2) are only partially successful or (3) the Contractor is prevented from completing the services the Contractor shall nevertheless be awarded solely against the Owners of such tanker his reasonably incurred expenses and an increment not exceeding 15 per cent of such expenses but only if and to the extent that *a* such expenses together with the increment are greater than any amount otherwise recoverable under this Agreement. Within the meaning of the said exception to the principle of "no cure–no pay" expenses shall in addition to actual out of pocket expenses include a fair rate for all tugs craft personnel and other equipment used by the Contractor in the services and oil shall mean crude oil fuel oil heavy diesel oil and lubricating oil.'

b The history of this revision to the common form of salvage contract does not appear from the materials before the House, but it is possible to give an account of the contemporaneous efforts to reach an international solution, in the shape of a replacement for the Salvage Convention of 1910. Within a few months of the Amoco Cadiz disaster the International Maritime Organisation (the IMO) had *c* taken the matter in hand and prepared an initial report (which is not before the House). The problem was also addressed by the Comité Maritime International (the CMI), which agreed to co-operate in a study of the private law principles of salvage. The outcome was the establishment of sub-committee under the chairmanship of Professor E Selvig, which prepared a draft convention accompanied by a report. These documents were placed before a conference of *d* the CMI in Montreal during May 1981, by which time LOF 1980 with its safety net provision had come into force. The debates at Montreal led to a final draft, together with a report by Mr Bent Nielsen. For a time there was little further progress, but eventually a diplomatic conference led to the agreement of the International Convention on Salvage 1989. This did not come into force internationally until July 1996, when the necessary ratifications were achieved. *e* So far as English domestic law is concerned, the 1989 convention was given the force of law in the United Kingdom by the Merchant Shipping Act 1995, s 224. But the Act did not affect rights and liabilities arising out of operations started before 1 January 1996. Accordingly, the claim now under consideration is a private law claim, based on LOF 1990. The convention is relevant only because, *f* having partly been inspired by LOF 1980, it is now incorporated by reference into LOF 1990.

It is appropriate next to quote the relevant terms of LOF 1990 and the convention. The former provides:

g '1.(a) The Contractor shall use his best endeavours:—(i) to salve the [name of vessel] and/or her cargo freight bunkers stores and any other property thereon and take them to [specified port] or to such other place as may hereafter be agreed either place to be deemed a place of safety or if no such place is named or agreed to a place of safety and (ii) while performing the salvage services to prevent or minimize damage to the environment. *h* (b) Subject to clause 2 incorporating Convention Article 14 the services shall be rendered and accepted as salvage services upon the principle of "no cure– no pay." (c) The Contractor's remuneration shall be fixed by Arbitration in London in the manner hereinafter prescribed and any other difference arising out of this Agreement or the operations thereunder shall be referred to Arbitration in the same way …
j 2. Articles 1(a) to (e), 8, 13.1, 13.2 first sentence, 13.3 and 14 of the International Convention on Salvage 1989 ("the Convention Articles") set out hereafter are hereby incorporated into this Agreement. The terms "Contractor" and "services"/"salvage services" in this Agreement shall have the same meanings as the terms "salvor(s)" and "salvage operation(s)" in the Convention Articles.'

As regards the 1989 convention the following are material. Article 1 provides:

> '*Definitions*. For the purpose of this Convention ... (d) *Damage to the environment* means substantial physical damage to human health or to marine life or resources in coastal or inland waters or areas adjacent thereto, caused by pollution, contamination, fire, explosion or similar major incidents. (e) *Payment* means any reward, remuneration or compensation due under this Convention ...'

Article 8 provides:

> '*Duties of the salvor and of the owner and master* (1) The salvor shall owe a duty to the owner of the vessel or other property in danger: (a) to carry out the salvage operations with due care; (b) in performing the duty specified in subparagraph (a), to exercise due care to prevent or minimize damage to the environment ...
>
> (2) The owner and master of the vessel or the owner of other property in danger shall owe a duty to the salvor: (a) to co-operate fully with him during the course of the salvage operations; (b) in so doing, to exercise due care to prevent or minimize damage to the environment ...'

Article 12 provides:

> '*Conditions for reward* (1) Salvage operations which have had a useful result give right to a reward ...'

Article 13 provides:

> '*Criteria for fixing the reward* (1) The reward shall be fixed with a view to encouraging salvage operations, taking into account the following criteria without regard to the order in which they are presented below: (a) the salved value of the vessel and other property; (b) the skill and efforts of the salvors in preventing or minimizing damage to the environment; (c) the measure of success obtained by the salvor; (d) the nature and degree of the danger; (e) the skill and efforts of the salvors in salving the vessel, other property and life; (f) the time used and expenses and losses incurred by the salvors; (g) the risk of liability and other risks run by the salvors or their equipment; (h) the promptness of the services rendered; (i) the availability and use of vessels or other equipment intended for salvage operations; (j) the state of readiness and efficiency of the salvor's equipment and the value thereof ...
>
> (3) The rewards, exclusive of any interest and recoverable legal costs that may be payable thereon, shall not exceed the salved value of the vessel and other property.'

Article 14 provides:

> '*Special compensation* (1) If the salvor has carried out salvage operations in respect of a vessel which by itself or its cargo threatened damage to the environment and has failed to earn a reward under article 13 at least equivalent to the special compensation assessable in accordance with this article, he shall be entitled to special compensation from the owner of that vessel equivalent to his expenses as herein defined.
>
> (2) If, in the circumstances set out in paragraph 1, the salvor by his salvage operations has prevented or minimized damage to the environment, the special compensation payable by the owner to the salvor under paragraph 1

a   may be increased up to a maximum of 30% of the expenses incurred by the salvor. However, the tribunal, if it deems it fair and just to do so and bearing in mind the relevant criteria set out in article 13, paragraph 1, may increase such special compensation further, but in no event shall the total increase be more than 100% of the expenses incurred by the salvor.

b   (3) Salvor's expenses for the purpose of paragraphs 1 and 2 means the out-of-pocket expenses reasonably incurred by the salvor in the salvage operation and a fair rate for equipment and personnel actually and reasonably used in the salvage operation, taking into consideration the criteria set out in article 13, paragraph 1(h), (i) and (j).

    (4) The total special compensation under this article shall be paid only if and to the extent that such compensation is greater than any reward
c   recoverable by the salvor under article 13 …'

It is also necessary to set out the preamble to the 1989 convention, which although not directly incorporated in LOF 1990 is plainly relevant to a proper understanding of the provisions just quoted:

d   '*The States Parties to the present Convention,*

    Recognizing the desirability of determining by agreement uniform international rules regarding salvage operations,

    Noting that substantial developments, in particular the increased concern for the protection of the environment, have demonstrated the need to review the international rules presently contained in the Convention for the
e   Unification of Certain Rules of Law relating to Assistance and Salvage at Sea, done at Brussels, 23 September 1910,

    Conscious of the major contribution which efficient and timely salvage operations can make to the safety of vessels and other property in danger and to the protection of the environment,

f   *Convinced* of the need to ensure that adequate incentives are available to persons who undertake salvage operations in respect of vessels and other property in danger …'

The principal issue in the present appeal concerns the definition of 'expenses' in art 14(3), and in particular that part of it which includes in the expenses 'a fair
g   rate for equipment and personnel actually and reasonably used in the salvage operation …' Four elements have been identified as possible components of the 'fair rate': the direct costs to the salvor of performing the service; the additional costs of keeping the vessels and equipment on standby; a further element to bring the recoverable 'expenses' up to a rate capable of including an element of profit;
h   and a final element bringing the recovery up to the level of a salvage award. The respondent owners of the ship and bunkers (whom I will call 'the owners') accept that the first two elements are properly included. For their part, the appellants, Semco, concede that the fourth element cannot be included. In my opinion this understanding is plainly right, for reasons too plain to call for elaboration. The
j   dispute revolves around the third element. Semco assert, and the owners deny, that this too should feature in the calculation under art 14.3.

In a compressed form, which does less than justice to the reasoning, the opinions on this issue expressed by successive tribunals have been as follows. Much of the long and careful award of Mr Stone QC was concerned with a traditional salvage reward under art 13. This need not be described here. When he came to the 'special compensation', the arbitrator stressed the need for

encouragement. A professional salvor who had done his best but had in the event
failed to avert damage to the environment would not be encouraged to stay in
the business or try again if he merely received his expenditure, even if that took
account of idle time. To arrive at a 'rate' which is 'fair' it is necessary to have in
mind as a broad classification the type of work done, the scale of the job, whether
the towage was to a large or small vessel, whether or not there were crew and
machinery to assist, but not to the risks experienced and the benefit conferred. It
must be a rate which makes some contribution to future investment; but this
must be tempered by the fact that there will be further encouragement in the
event of success. It is of great assistance in assessing a fair rate to know the actual
cost and basic market rates, but a fair rate is none of these rates or a straight
mathematical computation of those rates.

The arbitrator's opinion is exemplified by the figures set out in the award. As
an example one may take the figures for the tug Salvenus. The basic daily cost
averaged over a full year including overheads was $US1,990. On a basis of 50%
utilisation the figure was $3,980 per day. A further uplift of 50% reflecting a
minimum actual service performed increased the figure to $5,970. Finally, a
figure was shown of $7,000 per day for a tug of that size engaged in a
straightforward commercial ocean towage of a vessel of a similar size without
taking into account specialist or extraordinary services. From these figures the
arbitrator built upwards to a fair rate of $16,000 per day. Applying a similar
approach to the other vessels and to personnel and equipment, the arbitrator
arrived at a figure for 'expenses' under art 14.3 of $3,623,180, equivalent in
Singapore dollars to $S5,967,671. After adding out-of-pocket expenses the total
allowed under art 14.3 was $S7,658,117.

Since in the present case the salvage resulted in benefit to the environment, the
arbitrator was required to apply the strange formula for enhancement of the
'expenses' contained in art 14.2. The difficulties caused by this formula, the
outcome of an unresolved conflict between the states and interests taking part in
the drafting of the convention, will no doubt have to be resolved before long, but
they do not arise on this appeal and need not be addressed now. It is enough to
record that the arbitrator applied an increment of 65%. The resulting figure was
$S12,635,893, which exceeded the salvage awarded under art 13 by $S3,135,893.
This was the special compensation, which now remains in dispute.

The appeal arbitrator disagreed with Mr Stone in several respects. First, and of
great significance in financial terms, he concluded that the award of traditional
salvage under art 13 was too low, by $S1,250,000. Secondly, on the award of
special compensation under art 14 he took a different line from Mr Stone, as
follows.

(1) Although the definition of expenses may be broad, it is still a definition of
expenses. It does not support the finding of a fair rate at such a level as by itself
to lead to an encouraging profit for the salvors, still less anything which would be
regarded as akin to salvage remuneration. The addition of an increment under
art 14.2 could all too easily lead to a figure which went well beyond compensation
and became salvage remuneration by the back door.

(2) The travaux préparatoires were inconsistent with a construction of art 14.3
as providing a rate which was encouraging, even before the addition of any
increment under art 14.2.

(3) A rate which reflected idle time and the availability of vessels but which did
not take into account the criteria of paras (h), (i) and (j) of art 13.1 would be too
low.

(4) The type and scope of the job would be a relevant factor in assessing the fair rate, if only because it would be reflected in the cost to the salvors of undertaking the services.

(5) The ability in certain cases to obtain an award of special compensation is an additional incentive, but it is a fall-back or safety net. It is only awarded when it is greater than any award recoverable for salvage. It follows that in any case where the services are substantial the salvage award ought to be more, and where possible significantly more, than what would be awarded by way of special compensation, unless the amount which can be awarded for salvage is constrained by the value of the salved fund.

Applying these and other considerations, the appeal arbitrator concluded that the total amount awarded by Mr Stone was much too high. He then performed three assessments, on each of which he differed from Mr Stone. The first was to reconsider the salvage award, which he regarded to be insufficiently encouraging; and he increased it to $S10,750,000. Your Lordships are not troubled with this question. Secondly, he arrived at his own figures for the expenses under art 14.3. For example, in respect of the Salvenus he awarded a rate of $7,500 per day, as against the arbitrator's figure of $US16,000. Finally, as to the increment under art 14.2 he agreed with the arbitrator's basic approach. On the figures for expenses under art 14.3, the appeal arbitrator would have regarded the arbitrator's uplift of 65% as too much. But, on the appeal arbitrator's own approach to expenses, this increment seemed fair and reasonable. The result was to increase the grand total under art 14.3 of $S5,216,404 to $S8,607,067. This was less than the salvage award, so that no special compensation was payable.

On appeal to Clarke J ([1995] 2 Lloyd's Rep 44) four principal questions were discussed, two relating to salvage and two to special compensation under art 14. As to the latter, the judge broadly accepted the arguments which the owners were later to repeat before this House, and accordingly upheld the general principles which the appeal arbitrator had sought to apply. But the judge did not agree with the way in which the appeal arbitrator had arrived at the figures which he had substituted for those of the arbitrator. As to salvage under art 13, the judge concluded that the appeal arbitrator was entitled in principle to differ from the award of the arbitrator, and that he was also entitled to cross-check between the amounts which he proposed to grant as salvage and as special compensation; but that since the figures for the latter were wrongly assessed the appeal arbitrator's salvage award might thereby have been distorted. He therefore remitted the matter to the appeal arbitrator to reconsider the quantification of salvage.

In the Court of Appeal a majority (Staughton and Swinton Thomas LJJ) agreed with Clarke J. As Staughton LJ put it ([1996] 1 Lloyd's Rep 449 at 455):

'... a fair rate ... means a rate of expense, which is to be comprehensive of indirect or overhead expenses and take into account the additional cost of having resources instantly available. Remuneration or uplift or profit is to be provided, if at all, under art. 14.2. Beyond that, what is a fair rate is a matter of judgment for the tribunal(s) of fact.'

Evans LJ took a different view, which I describe at a later stage. In the result the appeal on this aspect of the dispute was dismissed, since it was accepted that on the view of the majority no award of special compensation would ensue. Semco now appeal.

My Lords, leaving aside for the moment the interpretation preferred by Evans LJ, the rival contentions on the meaning of 'fair rate', as summarised in the parties' agreed statement of facts and issues, were as follows:

'... (i) is it a fair rate of remuneration having regard to the circumstances of the case, including the type of craft actually used and the type of work required (but in general terms) and a rate which acts as an incentive to a salvor (i.e. normally including a profit element but without amounting to a salvage reward or anything like it), as SEMCO contend; or (ii) does it mean a fair rate of expense which is to be comprehensive of indirect or overhead expenses and to include the additional cost of having resources instantly available, as the shipowners contend.'

My Lords, whichever alternative your Lordships prefer will not leave the parties and arbitrators in salvage disputes with any precise guidance on how to arrive at the special compensation. The fact is, however, that the assessment of salvage has never been an exact science, and the embellishment added by art 14.3 is well known to have been an uneasy compromise. At all events, although the possibilities are not exhausted by the two alternatives quoted, they are, in my view, more plausible than any others. On the choice between them, although weight has rightly been given to the history of the convention I prefer to begin with its words, read in the general context of the new regime. As to the words themselves, I feel little doubt that they support the narrower interpretation. The concept of 'expenses' permeates the first three paragraphs of art 14. In its ordinary meaning this word denotes amounts either disbursed or borne, not earned as profits. Again, the computation prescribed by art 14.3 requires the fair rate to be added to the 'out-of-pocket' expenses, as clear an instance as one could find of a quantification which contains no element of profit; and it surely cannot have been intended that the 'salvors' expenses' should contain two disparate elements. It is moreover highly significant that art 14.2 twice makes use of the expression 'expenses incurred' by the salvor, for in ordinary speech the salvor would not 'incur' something which yields him a profit. The idea of an award of expenses as a recompense, not a source of profit, is further reinforced by the general description of the recovery as 'compensation', which normally has a flavour of reimbursement. I acknowledge that this word has long been used to denote the amount recoverable as conventional salvage: see e g *Abbott on Merchant Ships* (5th edn, 1827) p 610. Nevertheless it is significant that a clear distinction is drawn in paras 1 and 4 of art 14 between compensation and reward, and the same contrast appears in art 1(e) quoted above.

This purely textual account of the text must now be measured against the aims of the convention. For Semco, Mr Brice QC emphasises that the explicit purpose of the new salvage regime is, in the words of the preamble, to provide 'adequate incentives' to keep themselves in readiness to protect the environment, and contends that a level of compensation which will furnish in cases where the efforts fail without the salvor's fault no more than direct and standby costs is not adequate for this purpose. My Lords, as to the purpose of the convention this is plainly right, but the careful submissions of counsel have not persuaded me that this 'teleological' method (as he described it) enables profitability to be written into expenses. I say this for two reasons.

In the first place I do not accept that salvors need a profit element as a further incentive. Under the former regime the undertaking of salvage services was a stark gamble. No cure no pay. This is no longer so, since even if traditional

salvage yields little or nothing under art 13 the salvor will, in the event of success
in protecting the environment, be awarded a multiple not only of his direct costs
but also the indirect standby costs, yielding a profit. Moreover, even if there is no
environmental benefit, he is assured of an indemnity against his outlays and
receives at least some contribution to his standing costs. Lack of success no
longer means 'No pay', and the provision of this safety net does suffice, in my
opinion, to fulfil the purposes of the new scheme.

Secondly, although Mr Brice disclaimed any intention to revive the method
adopted by the arbitrator, which was to treat art 14 as creating a salvage regime
parallel to that of art 13, the argument for Semco was in essence the same. The
omission from art 14.3 of paras (a) to (g) of art 13.1 shows that expenses are not
to be calculated on the same generous scale as an award for a successful salvage.
If such considerations enter the assessment of special compensation at all, this is
through the uplift under art 14.2. As Clarke J said ([1995] 2 Lloyd's Rep 44 at 51):

> '... the effect of the reference to matters such as promptness, availability,
> state of readiness and efficiency ... is not to transfer the concept of expense
> into something which goes beyond what could fairly be regarded as a type of
> expense. If that had been intended it could readily have been done by plain
> language.'

Furthermore, and in my view decisively, the promoters of the convention did
not choose, as they might have done, to create an entirely new and distinct
category of environmental salvage, which would finance the owners of vessels
and gear to keep them in readiness simply for the purpose of preventing damage
to the environment. Paragraphs 1, 2 and 3 of art 14 all make it clear that the right
to special compensation depends on the performance of 'salvage operations'
which, as already seen, are defined by art 1(a) as operations to assist a vessel in
distress.   Thus, although art 14 is undoubtedly concerned to encourage
professional salvors to keep vessels readily available, this is still for the purposes
of a salvage, for which the primary incentive remains a traditional salvage award.
The only structural change in the scheme is that the incentive is now made more
attractive by the possibility of obtaining new financial recognition for conferring
a new type of incidental benefit. Important as it is, the remedy under art 14 is
subordinate to the reward under art 13, and its functions should not be confused
by giving it a character too closely akin to salvage.

My Lords, the materials on which these opinions are founded are confined to
the instruments themselves, without recourse to the travaux préparatoires,
permissible where the meaning of an international agreement is found to be
unclear: see *Fothergill v Monarch Airlines Ltd* [1980] 2 All ER 696, [1981] AC 251.
Nevertheless, reference was made to them in argument without objection, and
they are a useful means of testing the tentative opinions already formed. Some
caution is however required. The documentary antecedents of the convention
are incomplete, and there is nothing before the House to indicate the origins of
the new safety-net provisions in LOF 1980. This is understandable, since that
form is neither the document sued upon, nor incorporated into it. Nevertheless,
it is plain from Professor Selvig's report that the first draft of the convention was
influenced by LOF 1980, and a full account of LOF 1990 cannot be given without
knowing the history of its predecessor.

Subject to these reservations, I find in the travaux préparatoires strong
reinforcement for the owners' interpretation of art 14. In particular: (1) it is made
quite clear throughout that the new remedy is linked to salvage and does not

stand on its own. (2) The report of Professor Selvig records that the
International Salvage Union proposed an amendment which would extend the
salvor's expenses to—

> 'a) the use and availability of vessels and other equipment intended for
> salvage operations and their standing costs; b) the time expended by the
> salvor and the out of pocket expenses reasonably incurred by the salvor in
> the services; c) the state of readiness of the salvors vessels and equipment
> intended for salvage operations; d) the level of investment and
> proffessionalism [sic] of the salvor.'

The sub-committee rejected this proposal, and it is significant that whilst items
a), b), and c), are broadly reflected in the ultimate text there is no counterpart to
item d).

(3) In Mr Bent Nielsen's commentary on the draft convention as it stood at the
end of the Montreal conference, which so far as concerned arts 14.1 and 14.3 was
almost identical to the form ultimately approved, there is nothing to suggest that
the members of CMI intended that the words of the draft might entitle the salvor
to a profits guarantee. On the contrary, the author noted in relation to the
predecessor of art 14.3: 'The reference to the criteria set out in [art 13.1 (h), (i) and
(j)] is important, in particular because it is thereby made clear that due account
shall be taken of the salvor's standing costs, overheads, etc., when determining
what is a fair rate in the particular case.'

(4) LOF 1980, which was undoubtedly one of the inspirations of the
convention, made use of the simpler formula 'the Contractor shall nevertheless
be awarded ... his reasonably incurred expenses'. It is even clearer here that the
salvor was not intended to make a profit; and there is nothing in the documentary
materials to suggest that the later expansion of the wording was meant to
produce a wholly different result.

Such preliminary documents as are available thus support the narrower
construction which I propose. Two other matters call for mention. First, your
Lordships were pressed with a submission that the meaning given to art 14.3 by
the judge and the Court of Appeal would be unworkable in practice. I cannot
accept this, for it seems to me that the ascertainment of the fair rate must
necessarily be performed with a fairly broad brush, albeit not so broad as the
fixing of the reward under art 13, and the uplift under art 14.2. Quite sufficient
information for such purposes could be derived from the salvor's books, as
indeed became clear when reference to materials from that source was made in
the course of argument.

Secondly, Miss Selvaratnam addressed the House on certain authorities
concerning the assessment of a fair rate of hire or other remuneration for services
performed in the absence, or outside the terms, of a binding contract. These
decisions would indeed have been germane if the purpose of art 14.3 had been to
give the salvor a reward, not directly defined by the contract, but generally
referable to a fair rate of remuneration. In the present case, however, I have
concluded for the reasons given that art 14.3 is not concerned with remuneration,
but with a more restricted basis of recovery, and the authorities cited therefore
do not assist.

These authorities do however point the way to an alternative argument for
Semco, which did not form part of their submissions in the Court of Appeal and
which was first proposed in the dissenting judgment of Evans LJ. It is best seen

a in the following passages from the judgment ([1996] 1 Lloyd's Rep 449 at
457, 459):

'In summary, I would hold that the Judge was wrong to exclude altogether
a possible "profit" element and that Mr. Stone erred in assessing the "fair
rate" as if it was a form of remuneration or reward. Broadly speaking, in my
judgment Mr. Willmer was correct to have regard to commercial or, where
b relevant, market factors as well as to the salvor's costs ...
I would hold that "fair" means "fair to both parties" and that "a fair rate"
for services provided in fact should be established by reference to what I
would call the commercial value of those services, disregarding the special
considerations which lead to the equivalent of enhanced rates for salvage
c services when the reward for a successful salvage is assessed ... If the
intended meaning was "a commercial rate for the particular service, taking
account of market rates when those may apply", then the chosen formula "a
fair rate" comes close to expressing it, in a context where a straightforward
reference to market rates was not possible, as both parties agree.'

d   My Lords, the difficulty which I find with this interpretation is two-fold. First,
the proposition gives no weight to the context which, for the reasons already
given, point directly away from anything resembling the kind of remuneration
which the salvor could expect, if not exactly in the open market, at least in some
approximation to it. There are elements in such remuneration which the safety
net was not in my opinion meant to embrace. Secondly, I believe that Evans LJ
e attached undue importance to the word 'rate', which was understood as
reflecting a notional periodical payment, to be multiplied-up to a figure forming
part of the expenses. It would, I can see, be only a short step from this to look for
a periodical basis of payment which could only be ascertained by reference to the
market for vessels or equipment of this kind. For my part, however, I believe the
f word 'rate' has sent the inquiry in the wrong direction. Whatever its ordinary
meaning, I believe that in the context of art 14 it simply denotes an amount
attributable to the equipment and personnel used, just as the expenses include an
amount attributable to out-of-pockets. This view is wholly consistent with the
French language version of the convention, where we find in art 14.4 the words
'les debours raisonnablement engagés par l'assistant dans les opérations
g d'assistance ainsi qu'une somme équitable pour le matériel et le personnel ...'
We were informed that the Spanish version of the text is to similar effect. I
believe that if there had been an opportunity to deploy before Evans LJ the
arguments which your Lordships have heard he might well have come to a
different conclusion. At all events, I must respectfully dissent from it.

h   Finally, whilst the French text is still in mind, I would draw attention to the
word 'indemnité' which appears in art 14 in the same places as 'compensation' in
the English version. Mr Brice correctly warned that this may be a 'false friend'
with indemnity in the English language, since one of its meanings does
correspond to a salary or other payment for work done. Nevertheless, I think
j that there is still a flavour of reimbursement for outlays, which accords with the
meaning I have already proposed.
My Lords, I have explored the matter at length in deference to the practical
importance of the question, the differences between the opinions expressed, and
the thoughtful argument of Mr Brice. Otherwise I would have been content
simply to express my agreement in every respect with the economical and
convincing judgment of Clarke J.

There remains a contingent cross-appeal by the owners, contingent because *a* the figures are such that it will arise only if Semco prevail on the principal issue under art 14.3, which in my opinion they do not. The question is whether the expenses comprise those incurred during the whole of the salvage operation, or only during the times when a threat to the environment is still in existence. Clarke J and all members of the Court of Appeal preferred the former opinion. In a spirited argument Mr Thomas supported the latter view, but your Lordships *b* did not think it necessary to invite a response from Mr Brice. I think the matter plain, and am content to adopt the reasons given by Clarke J for deciding that it is to the entirety of the operation that the expenses should be referred.

I therefore propose that the appeal and the cross-appeal should be dismissed, in each case with costs.

c

LORD LLOYD OF BERWICK. My Lords, I agree that the appeal and cross-appeal should each be dismissed for the reasons given by my noble and learned friend Lord Mustill. Since Mr Brice QC for Semco described the appeal as a test case of international importance on a point which has not so far been considered elsewhere, I underline what seem to me to be the salient points. *d*

(1) '... fair rate for equipment and personnel actually and reasonably used in the salvage operation' in art 14.3 means a fair rate of *expenditure*, and does not include any element of profit. This is clear from the context, and in particular from the reference to 'expenses' in art 14.1 and 2, and the definition of 'salvor's expenses' in art 14.3. No doubt expenses could have been defined so as to include *e* an element of profit, if very clear language to that effect had been used. But it was not. The profit element is confined to the mark-up under art 14.2, if damage to the environment is minimised or prevented.

(2) The first half of art 14.3 covers out-of-pocket expenses. One would expect to find that the second half of the paragraph covered overhead expenses. This is *f* what it does. If confirmation is needed, it is to be found in the reference to sub-paragraphs (h) to (j) of art 13.1 (which are apt to cover overhead expenses) and the omission of sub-paras (a) to (g).

(3) Mr Brice argued that the word 'rate' indicated more naturally a rate of remuneration rather than a rate of expenditure. But, as Lord Mustill points out, rate is the appropriate word when attributing or apportioning general overheads *g* to the equipment and personnel actually and reasonably used on the particular salvage operation.

(4) Mr Brice argued that if fair rate means rate of expenditure it would require 'a team of accountants' in every salvage arbitration, where the environment has been at risk. Mr Thomas QC's answer was that the basic rates in the present case *h* (not a straightforward one) were agreed without difficulty by the two firms of solicitors. In any event accountants are nowadays, as he says, a part of ordinary life.

(5) Although the meaning of art 14 is clear enough, and resort to the travaux préparatoires is therefore not strictly justified, I have never known a case where *j* the travaux point so strongly in favour of one party rather than another. The commentaries on the draft documents show conclusively what the salvors' representatives' were seeking to achieve during the international negotiations leading up to the 1989 convention, and how it was that sub-paras (h) to (j) found their way into that convention.

_a_ (6) Mr Brice made out a strong case that professional salvors of today need encouragement by way of remuneration over and above their expenses if they are going to stay in business. But that is not what they were seeking to achieve during the negotiations. Nor is it what was in fact agreed. I would dismiss the appeal.

_b_ **LORD HOPE OF CRAIGHEAD.** My Lords, I have had the benefit of reading in draft the speech to be given by my noble and learned friend Lord Mustill. I agree with it, and for the reasons which he gives I, too, would dismiss both the appeal and the cross-appeal.

Appeal and cross-appeal dismissed.

_c_

Celia Fox   Barrister.

Murphy and another v Young & Co's Brewery plc and another

COURT OF APPEAL, CIVIL DIVISION

BUTLER-SLOSS, PHILLIPS LJJ AND SIR JOHN BALCOMBE

21 OCTOBER, 20 NOVEMBER 1996

Costs – Order for costs – Payment of costs by non-party – Circumstances in which legal expenses insurer may be ordered to pay costs of proceedings – Plaintiffs bringing action against defendants for wrongful dismissal – Plaintiffs insured against legal expenses under agreement providing cover up to limit of £25,000 – Defendants obtaining judgment and applying for order that plaintiffs' insurer pay their costs – Insurer claiming that cover exhausted by plaintiffs' own costs – Whether insurer liable to pay defendants' costs – Supreme Court Act 1981, s 51(1).

The plaintiffs, who had been employed by the defendants to manage a public house, brought an action for wrongful dismissal against the defendants, who in turn counterclaimed for moneys payable by the plaintiffs under the agreement. The plaintiffs' legal expenses were funded by an insurance company under an agreement which provided them with cover up to a limit of £25,000 in respect of any claim arising out of the same cause of action. In the event, the plaintiffs' claim was dismissed and the defendants were awarded £16,000 on their counterclaim together with costs in the sum of £42,806. The plaintiffs were unable to pay the sums due under the judgment other than by instalments, and in those circumstances the defendants joined the plaintiffs' insurer in order to seek an order for costs against it. The insurance company contended that the plaintiffs had exhausted their right to indemnity in respect of the action, since their own costs exceeded the limit of £25,000, and that accordingly it could not be under any liability to meet the defendants' costs. The defendants, however, contended that since the insurance company had funded the plaintiffs' conduct of the litigation pursuant to a commercial agreement, and had exercised a degree of control over the conduct of the litigation, it could not seek to rely on that limit of liability. The judge held that there were no grounds for making an order for costs against the insurance company and dismissed the defendants' application. The defendants appealed.

Held – Although the court had power under s 51(1)[a] of the Supreme Court Act 1981 to order costs against a non-party, such as the insurers of an unsuccessful plaintiff's legal expenses, it would only make such an order where exceptional circumstance made it reasonable and just to do so, and the mere fact that the insurers had funded the litigation under a commercial agreement did not make it reasonable or just to order them to pay the costs of the adverse successful party. Since the insurance company in the instant case had not had any interest in the result of the litigation, or initiated it, or exercised control over its conduct, or wantonly or officiously intermeddled in it, the mere existence of legal expenses insurance with a limit of cover that had been exhausted was not enough to justify an order for costs against them. Accordingly, the appeal would be dismissed (see p 520 g h, p 529 f to j, p 530 g to j and p 531 d to f, post).

---

a   Section 51(1) is set out at p 520 g h, post

Notes
a For jurisdiction to award costs, see 37 *Halsbury's Laws* (4th edn) para 713, and for cases on the subject, see 37(3) *Digest* (Reissue) 230–233, 4273–4289.

For the Supreme Court Act 1981, s 51, see 11 *Halsbury's Statutes* (4th edn) (1991 reissue) 1019.

b Cases referred to in judgments
Aiden Shipping Co Ltd v Interbulk Ltd, The Vimeira [1986] 2 All ER 409, [1986] AC 965, [1986] 2 WLR 1051, HL.
Bahai v Rashidian [1985] 3 All ER 385, [1985] 1 WLR 1337, CA.
Bourne v Colodense Ltd [1985] ICR 291, CA.
Brendon v Spiro [1937] 2 All ER 469, [1938] 1 KB 176, CA.
c *Broxton v McClelland* (6 November 1992, unreported), QBD; *rvsd* [1995] EMLR 485, CA.
Calderbank v Calderbank [1975] 3 All ER 333, [1976] Fam 93, [1975] 3 WLR 586, CA.
Chapman Ltd v Christopher (23 May 1996, unreported), QBD.
Company, Re a (No 004055 of 1991) [1991] 1 WLR 1003.
d *Condliffe v Hislop* [1996] 1 All ER 431, [1996] 1 WLR 753, CA.
Cooper v Maxwell [1992] CA Transcript 273.
Davies (Joseph Owen) v Eli Lilly & Co [1987] 3 All ER 94, [1987] 1 WLR 1136, CA.
Framework Exhibitions Ltd v Matchroom Boxing Ltd [1992] CA Transcript 873.
Giles v Thompson [1993] 3 All ER 321, [1994] 1 AC 142, [1993] 2 WLR 908, HL.
e *Gleeson v J Wippell & Co Ltd* [1977] 3 All ER 54, [1977] 1 WLR 510.
Grovewood Holdings plc v James Capel & Co Ltd [1994] 4 All ER 417, [1995] Ch 80, [1995] 2 WLR 70.
Gupta v Comer [1991] 1 All ER 289, [1991] 1 QB 629, [1991] 2 WLR 494, CA.
Hayward v Giffard (1838) 4 M & W 194, 150 ER 1399.
f *Hill v Archbold* [1967] 3 All ER 110, [1968] 1 QB 686, [1967] 3 WLR 1218, CA.
Hollington v F Hewthorn & Co Ltd [1943] 2 All ER 35, [1943] KB 587, CA.
Land and Property Trust Co plc, Re [1991] 3 All ER 409, [1991] 1 WLR 601, CA.
Land and Property Trust Co plc, Re (No 2) (1993) Times, 16 February, [1993] CA Transcript 160.
Land and Property Trust Co plc, Re (No 3) [1991] BCLC 856.
g *McFarlane v E E Caledonia Ltd (No 2)* [1995] 1 WLR 366.
Oram v Hutt [1914] 1 Ch 98, [1911–13] All ER Rep 376, CA.
Orme v Associated Newspapers Group Ltd (1980) Times, 3 February, [1980] CA Transcript 809.
h *Palmer v Durnford Ford (a firm)* [1992] 2 All ER 122, [1992] QB 483, [1992] 2 WLR 407.
Pritchard v J H Cobden Ltd [1987] 1 All ER 300, [1988] Fam 22, [1987] 2 WLR 627, CA.
Roache v News Group Newspapers Ltd (1992) Times, 23 November, [1992] CA Transcript 1120.
j *Shah v Karanjia* [1993] 4 All ER 792.
Singh v Observer Ltd [1989] 3 All ER 777, CA; *rvsg* [1989] 2 All ER 751.
Symphony Group plc v Hodgson [1993] 4 All ER 143, [1994] QB 179, [1993] 3 WLR 830, CA.
Taylor v Pace Developments Ltd [1991] BCC 406.
Thistleton v Hendricks (1992) 32 Con LR 123.
Wild v Simpson [1919] 2 KB 544, [1918–19] All ER Rep 682, CA.

Cases also cited or referred to in skeleton arguments

Ainsbury v Millington [1987] 1 All ER 929, [1987] 1 WLR 379, HL.

Avandero (UK) Ltd v National Transit Insurance Co Ltd [1984] 2 Lloyd's Rep 613.

British Cash and Parcel Conveyors Ltd v Lamson Store Service Co Ltd [1908] 1 KB 1006, [1908–10] All ER Rep 146, CA.

Freshwater v Western Australia Assurance Co Ltd [1933] 1 KB 515, CA.

Hood's Trustees v Southern Union General Insurance Co of Australasia Ltd [1928] Ch 793, CA.

Harrington Motor Co Ltd, Re, ex p Chaplin [1928] Ch 105, CA.

Smith v Pearl Assurance Co Ltd [1939] 1 All ER 95, CA.

Tharros Shipping Co Ltd v Bias Shipping Ltd (No 3) [1995] 1 Lloyd's Rep 541.

Appeal

By notice dated 22 May 1995 the first defendant, Young & Co's Brewery plc (Youngs), appealed from the decision of Mr Griffith Williams QC sitting as a deputy judge of the High Court on 9 May 1995 whereby he dismissed their application that the second defendant, Sun Alliance and London Insurance plc (Sun Alliance), pay their costs of an action for damages for wrongful dismissal brought against them by the plaintiffs, Daniel Joseph Murphy and Christine Anne Murphy, whom the second defendant had insured under a legal expenses policy. The facts are set out in the judgment of Phillips LJ.

Andrew Hillier (instructed by *Druces & Attlee*) for Youngs.
Stuart Isaacs QC and *Neil Calver* (instructed by *Osborne Clarke*) for Sun Alliance.
The plaintiffs did not appear.

Cur adv vult

20 November 1996. The following judgments were delivered.

PHILLIPS LJ (giving the first judgment at the invitation of Butler-Sloss LJ). This is the first of two appeals which we heard together. They raise a common point. When an unsuccessful party has had its legal costs funded under legal expenses insurance, should the insurer be held liable to pay the successful party's costs?

Section 51(1) of the Supreme Court Act 1981 provides:

> 'Subject to the provisions of this or any other Act and to rules of court, the costs of and incidental to all proceedings in the civil division of the Court of Appeal and in the High Court, including the administration of estates and trusts, shall be in the discretion of the court, and the court shall have full power to determine by whom and to what extent the costs are to be paid.'

In *Aiden Shipping Co Ltd v Interbulk Ltd, The Vimeira* [1986] 2 All ER 409, [1986] AC 965 the House of Lords held that the jurisdiction provided by this section was not subject, as had been believed, to an implied limitation that costs could only be awarded against those who were parties to the litigation. Non-parties could be ordered to pay costs where justice so required. In the present case the successful defendants, Young & Co's Brewery plc (Youngs), joined the second defendants, Sun Alliance and London Insurance plc (Sun Alliance), in order to seek an order for costs against them. The trial judge, Mr Griffiths-Williams QC, sitting as a deputy judge of the High Court, rejected their application for this order. From his decision they now appeal.

The facts

a   The plaintiffs, Mr and Mrs Murphy, were employed by Youngs to manage a public house in Kew, called the Orange Tree. Youngs dismissed them, claiming that they had been in breach of their duties. Mr and Mrs Murphy brought this action, claiming wrongful dismissal. Youngs counterclaimed for 'food rent' payable under the agreement. The Murphys' claim was dismissed and Youngs

b   were awarded some £16,000 on their counterclaim, together with almost all the costs of the action. Those costs were taxed, on 11 March 1994, in the sum of £42,806. The Murphys said that they were unable to pay the sums due under the judgment other than by instalments. It was in these circumstances that Youngs sought an order for costs against Sun Alliance. Ironically, on the eve of the hearing of this appeal, the Murphys paid the last instalment necessary to

c   discharge their liability in respect of the costs of the action, but it was agreed by the parties, with the approval of the court, that the appeal should proceed, both because an important issue of principle is involved and because liability for the costs of the proceedings remains to be resolved.

d   *The insurance cover*

The Murphys were insured by Sun Alliance under the American Express Family Legal Expenses Plan. The relevant cover was expressed as follows:

'*Legal Benefits* a) Fees, expenses and other disbursements reasonably and properly incurred by the Appointed Representative [a solicitor, firm of solicitors or appropriately qualified person appointed to act for you] in

e   connection with any claim or legal proceedings including any costs incurred by Us. b) Costs and expenses of expert witnesses. c) Any costs payable by You following an Award of Costs by a Court or Tribunal in connection with a claim or proceedings ...'

f   The limit of cover in respect of any claim arising out of the same original cause was £25,000. Cover was subject to the following conditions:

'Our consent to pay Legal Benefits must firstly be obtained in writing. This consent will be given if You can satisfy Us that: (i) you have reasonable grounds for pursuing or defending the legal proceedings or (ii) it is

g   reasonable for Legal Benefits to be provided in a particular case. The decision to grant consent will take into account the opinion of Your Appointed Representative as well as that of Our own advisers. We may require You to obtain an opinion of Counsel on the merits of the claim or legal proceedings. If We refuse consent, You will be informed of the reasons

h   for Us doing so.   If You disagree You may invoke the Arbitration procedure ...'

The Murphys exhausted their right to indemnity in respect of this action, for their own legal costs exceeded the limit of £25,000. In these circumstances, Sun Alliance denied that they could be under any liability to meet Youngs' costs.

j   Youngs contended that it was just and reasonable that Sun Alliance should pay their costs and that the authorities demonstrated that it was appropriate for the court so to order on the facts of this case. I shall turn to those authorities shortly, but it is first convenient to identify the particular features of the case upon which Youngs relied. These were: (1) Sun Alliance funded the Murphys' conduct of the litigation; (2) Sun Alliance did so pursuant to a commercial agreement; and (3) Sun Alliance exercised a degree of control over the conduct of the litigation.

Youngs argued that in these circumstances to seek to rely on the limit of liability in answer to Youngs' claim was objectionable and contrary to public policy.

Sun Alliance for their part denied that they had exercised control over the litigation. They argued that legal expense insurance was in the public interest and that limits of cover were a usual and necessary feature of such insurance. Costs should only be ordered against a non-party in exceptional circumstances. There were no such circumstances in the present case and it would be contrary to public policy to hold Sun Alliance liable to pay costs beyond the limit of their cover.

The conclusions of the judge are set out in a short passage at the end of his judgment:

> 'Although I have been assisted by reference to authority, I am satisfied that I need only have regard to the general guidance offered by Lord Goff in *Aiden Shipping Co Ltd v Interbulk Ltd, The Vimeira* [1986] 2 All ER 409, [1986] AC 965 and to the particular facts of the case. Although I have referred to parts only of the evidence placed before me in the various affidavits of witnesses, I have reminded myself of all the evidence, and on that evidence I am not persuaded that there are grounds for making what is accepted is an exceptional order for costs against a non-party. There is no evidence of maintenance, of management or control, there are no public policy grounds for overriding a contractual limit of indemnity, the insurers have done nothing to undermine the position of the first defendants and there is no suggestion of mala fides on the part of the insurers.'

Aiden Shipping Co Ltd v Interbulk Ltd

The starting point for this court must be to consider what guidance, if any, is afforded by *Aiden Shipping* itself. Lord Goff said ([1986] 2 All ER 409 at 413, [1986] AC 965 at 975):

> '... it is not surprising to find the jurisdiction conferred under s 51(1), like its predecessors, to be expressed in wide terms. The subsection simply provides that "the court shall have full power to determine *by whom* ... the costs are to be paid". Such a provision is consistent with a policy under which jurisdiction to exercise the relevant discretionary power is expressed in wide terms, thus ensuring that the court has, so far as possible, freedom of action, leaving it to the rule-making authority to control the exercise of discretion (if it thinks it right to do so) by the making of rules of court, and to the appellate courts to establish principles on which the discretionary power may, within the framework of the statute and the applicable rules of court, be exercised.' (Lord Goff's emphasis.)

He continued ([1986] 2 All ER 409 at 416–417, [1986] AC 965 at 980–981):

> 'In the vast majority of cases, it would no doubt be unjust to make an award of costs against a person who is not a party to the relevant proceedings ... I do not, for my part, foresee any injustice flowing from the abandonment of that implied limitation. Courts of first instance are, I believe, well capable of exercising their discretion under the statute in accordance with reason and justice. I cannot imagine any case arising in which some order for costs is made, in the exercise of the court's discretion, against some person who has no connection with the proceedings in question. If any problem arises, the

Court of Appeal can lay down principles for the guidance of judges of first instance; or the Supreme Court Rule Committee can propose amendments to the Rules of the Supreme Court for the purpose of controlling the exercise of the statutory power vested in judges subject to rules of court.'

No guidance has yet been afforded by the Supreme Court Rule Committee. In these circumstances I think it important that, when dealing with individual cases, this court should try to formulate appropriate principles governing the exercise of the very wide jurisdiction that is accorded by s 51. At the same time it must be remembered that the ultimate question is what is reasonable and just on the facts of the individual case, so that principles are guidelines rather than fetters.

In *Symphony Group plc v Hodgson* [1993] 4 All ER 143 at 151–152, [1994] QB 179 at 191–192 Balcombe LJ made an analysis of the various circumstances in which the courts have been prepared to order a non- party to pay costs:

'(1) Where a person had some *management* of the action, e g a director of an insolvent company who causes the company improperly to prosecute or defend proceedings: see *Re Land and Property Trust Co plc* [1991] 3 All ER 409, [1991] 1 WLR 601, *Re Land and Property Trust Co plc (No 2)* (1993) Times, 16 February, *Re Land and Property Trust Co plc (No 3)* [1991] BCLC 856, *Taylor v Pace Developments Ltd* [1991] BCC 406, *Re a Company (No 004055 of 1991)* ([1991] 1 WLR 1003) ... and *Framework Exhibitions Ltd v Matchroom Boxing Ltd* [1992] CA Transcript 873. It is of interest to note that, while it was not suggested in any of these cases that it would never be a proper exercise of the jurisdiction to order the director to pay the costs, in none of them was it the ultimate result that the director was so ordered. (2) Where a person has maintained or financed the action. This was undoubtedly considered to be a proper case for the exercise of the discretion by Macpherson J in *Singh v Observer Ltd* [1989] 2 All ER 751, where it was alleged that a non-party was maintaining the plaintiff's libel action. However, on appeal the evidence showed that the non-party had not been maintaining the action and the appeal was allowed without going into the legal issues raised by the judge's decision: see *Singh v Observer Ltd* [1989] 3 All ER 777. (3) In *Gupta v Comer* [1991] 1 All ER 289, [1991] 1 QB 629 this court approached the power of the court to order a solicitor to pay costs under Ord 62, r 11 as an example of the exercise of the jurisdiction under s 51 of the Act 1981. (4) Where the person has *caused* the action. In *Pritchard v J H Cobden Ltd* [1987] 1 All ER 300, [1988] Fam 22 the plaintiff had suffered brain damage through the defendant's negligence. That resulted in a personality change which precipitated a divorce. This court held that the defendant's agreement to pay the costs of the divorce proceedings could be justified as an application of the *Aiden Shipping* principle (see [1988] Fam 22 at 51). (5) Where the person is a party to a closely related action which has been heard at the same time but not consolidated—as was the case in *Aiden Shipping* itself. (6) Group litigation where one or two actions are selected as test actions (see *Davies (Joseph Owen) v Eli Lilly & Co* [1987] 3 All ER 94, [1987] 1 WLR 1136).'

As Sir John Balcombe made clear in the course of argument in the present case, it was not his intention in *Symphony* to indorse these decisions as identifying circumstances in which it would necessarily be appropriate to order a non-party to pay costs. Those cases do, however, identify a number of factors which are of relevance when considering whether to make such an order. Balcombe LJ went on to identify a number of applicable principles ([1993] 4 All ER 143 at 152–154, [1994] QB 179 at 192–194):

'(1) An order for the payment of costs by a non-party will always be exceptional: see the *Aiden Shipping* case [1986] 2 All ER 409 at 416, [1986] AC 965 at 980 per Lord Goff. The judge should treat any application for such an order with considerable caution. (2) It will be even more exceptional for an order for the payment of costs to be made against a non-party, where the applicant has a cause of action against the non-party and could have joined him as a party to the original proceedings. Joinder as a party to the proceedings gives the person concerned all the protection conferred by the rules, e g the framing of the issues by pleadings, discovery of documents, the opportunity to pay into court or to make a *Calderbank* offer (see *Calderbank v Calderbank* [1975] 3 All ER 333, [1976] Fam 93), and the knowledge of what the issues are before giving evidence. (3) Even if the applicant can provide a good reason for not joining the non-party against whom he has a valid cause of action, he should warn the non-party at the earliest opportunity of the possibility that he may seek to apply for costs against him. At the very least this will give the non-party an opportunity to [apply] to be joined as a party to the action under Ord 15, r 6(2)(b)(i) or (ii). Principles (2) and (3) require no further justification on my part; they are an obvious application of the basic principles of natural justice. (4) An application for payment of costs by a non-party should normally be determined by the trial judge: see *Bahai v Rashidian* [1985] 3 All ER 385, [1985] 1 WLR 1337. (5) The fact that the trial judge may in the course of his judgment in the action have expressed views on the conduct of the non-party neither constitutes bias nor the appearance of bias. Bias is the antithesis of the proper exercise of a judicial function: see *Bahai v Rashidian* [1985] 3 All ER 385 at 388, 391, [1985] 1 WLR 1337 at 1342, 1346. (6) The procedure for the determination of costs is a summary procedure, not necessarily subject to all the rules that would apply in an action. Thus, subject to any relevant statutory exceptions, judicial findings are inadmissible as evidence of the facts upon which they were based in proceedings between one of the parties to the original proceedings and a stranger: see *Hollington v F Hewthorn & Co Ltd* [1943] 2 All ER 35, [1943] KB 587 and *Cross on Evidence* (7th edn (1990)) pp 100–101. Yet in the summary procedure for the determination of the liability of a solicitor to pay the costs of an action to which he was not a party, the judge's findings of fact may be admissible: see *Brendon v Spiro* [1937] 2 All ER 496 at 503, [1938] 1 KB 176 at 192 per Scott LJ, cited with approval by this court in *Bahai v Rashidian* [1985] 3 All ER 385 at 389, 391, [1985] 1 WLR 1337 at 1343, 1345. This departure from basic principles can only be justified if the connection of the non-party with the original proceedings was so close that he will not suffer any injustice by allowing this exception to the general rule. (7) Again the normal rule is that witnesses in either civil or criminal proceedings enjoy immunity from any form of civil action in respect of evidence given during those proceedings. One reason for this immunity is so that witnesses may give their evidence fearlessly: see *Palmer v Durnford Ford (a firm)* [1992] 2 All ER 122 at 125, [1992] QB 483 at 487. In so far as the evidence of a witness in proceedings may lead to an application for the costs of those proceedings against him or his company, it introduces yet another exception to a valuable general principle. (8) The fact that an employee, or even a director or the a   managing director, of a company gives evidence in an action does not normally mean that the company is taking part in that action, in so far as that is an allegation relied upon by the party who applies for an order for costs against a non-party company: see *Gleeson v J Wippell & Co Ltd* [1977] 3 All ER 54 at 58, [1977] 1 WLR 510 at 513. (9) The judge should be alert to the possibility that an application against a non-party is motivated by resentment

b   of an inability to obtain an effective order for costs against a legally aided litigant.'

These principles relate largely to questions of procedure which may impact upon the question of whether it is fair to order a non-party to pay costs.

c   *Procedure*
    In the present case Youngs joined Sun Alliance as second defendants in order to make an application for costs against them.   Sun Alliance objected, unsuccessfully to this joinder.   They have applied for leave to appeal against the order permitting the joinder.   At the time when it was considered that costs could only be ordered against a party to the action it was objectionable to join a party

d   simply to attempt to establish jurisdiction to make a costs order against him (see *The Supreme Court Practice 1997*, vol 1, para 15/4/6).   Now that it is clear that a non-party can be ordered to pay costs, it is plainly necessary for appropriate procedural steps to be taken to bring the non-party before the court so that he can make representations and, where appropriate, adduce evidence.   It seems to me

e   that the joinder of Sun Alliance effected in this case was a convenient way of achieving that end, although it may be that an originating summons would have been a more appropriate alternative.   In the event Sun Alliance did not press their application, without conceding that their joinder had been appropriate, and I propose to say no more about procedure.   I now turn to consider the cases in order to see whether they support Youngs' submission that Sun Alliance's

f   involvement in the funding and control of this litigation renders it reasonable and just that Sun Alliance should pay Youngs' costs.

The authorities
    On behalf of Youngs, Mr Hillier, whose submissions were clear, cogent and

g   concise, founded on a line of authority beginning with *Hill v Archbold* [1967] 3 All ER 110, [1968] 1 QB 686 to support the submission that 'where a person funds or contributes to the funding of litigation pursuant to an agreement for reward it will in general be fair and reasonable to require him to meet the costs of the successful adverse party'.

    In *Hill v Archbold* the issue was whether it was lawful for a trade union to fund

h   the legal costs of two officials of the union, who had been unsuccessful plaintiffs in a libel action.   It was contended that such support constituted the tort of maintenance.   *Oram v Hutt* [1914] 1 Ch 98, [1911–13] All ER Rep 376 was relied upon in support of this submission.   In the leading judgment, Lord Denning MR rejected this submission ([1967] 3 All ER 110 at 112, [1968] 1 QB 686 at 694–695):

j   'I do not think it right to take such a narrow point of distinction.   It is now over fifty years since *Oram v. Hutt* was decided.   I prefer to say plainly that *Oram* v. *Hutt* is no longer good law.   Much maintenance is considered justifiable today which would in 1914 have been considered obnoxious. Most of the actions in our courts are supported by some association or other, or by the State itself.   Very few litigants bring suits, or defend them, at their own expense. Most claims by workmen against their employers are paid for *a* by a trade union. Most defences of motorists are paid for by insurance companies. This is perfectly justifiable and is accepted by everyone as lawful, provided always that the one who supports the litigation, if it fails, pays the costs of the other side. It is the universal experience in this court that if a trade union or an insurance company supports a case and fails, it pays the costs of the other side. In the light of this experience, I am satisfied that if *b* *Oram* v. *Hutt* were to come before us today, we should hold that the union had a legitimate interest in the suit and were quite justified in maintaining it: remembering that if the suit had failed, the union would have paid the costs.'

In *Orme v Associated Newspapers Group Ltd* (1980) Times, 3 February Lord Denning MR again suggested that the question of whether or not the person *c* funding an action accepted liability for the costs of the other party could be critical in deciding whether such support constituted the tort of maintenance.

In *Singh v Observer Ltd* [1989] 2 All ER 751 an application was made for the disclosure of the identity of the person who was believed to be funding a plaintiff's claim for damages. In acceding to the application, Macpherson J observed (at 757): *d*

'During argument reference was made to common circumstances in which others pay for the litigation of a party, for example legally aided cases, insurance cases and union-assisted cases which make up much of today's non-jury list. But legal aid is statutory and so are the restrictions on recovery *e* of costs from the fund. The legal aid authorities can control the hardship which may be caused to successful litigants, who may not recover their costs, by requiring counsel to give fearless opinions as to the merits of a case as a condition of continuing legal aid. Insurance companies are subrogated to their insured's rights, and both they and unions invariably pay the costs of unsuccessful litigation. Otherwise, injustice could certainly result and I do *f* not believe that if, for example, unions decided simply to refuse to pay costs in these cases, the court would not step in.'

These three decisions were influential in leading Longmore J to order a non-party to pay the successful defendant's costs in *McFarlane v E E Caledonia Ltd (No 2)* [1995] 1 WLR 366. In that case a commercial company (Quantum) had funded a *g* plaintiff's unsuccessful claim for damages for personal injury on a contingency fee basis under which Quantum accepted no responsibility for the defendant's costs. In these circumstances Longmore J gave the following reasons for making an order under s 51 that Quantum pay the defendant's costs (at 373):

'It seems to me, therefore, that a judge sitting at first instance should follow *h* the dicta of Lord Denning M.R. in *Hill v. Archbold* ([1967] 3 All ER 110, [1968] 1 QB 686), approved as they have been in subsequent authorities. It may well be that it is not necessary to every case of lawful maintenance that the maintainer should accept a liability for a successful adverse party's costs; for example, a member of a family or a religious fraternity may well have a *j* sufficient interest in maintaining an action to save such maintenance from contractual illegality, even without any acceptance of liability for such costs. But in what one may call a business context (e.g. insurance, trade union activity, or commercial litigation support for remuneration) the acceptance of such liability will always, in my view, be a highly relevant consideration. The fact that Quantum has not accepted and does not accept any such liability seems to me to affect its contract with Mr. McFarlane with illegality as a matter of English law, quite apart from the additional illegality which arises from the champertous nature of the agreement. There is thus a double illegality in the present case. It is, moreover, the absence of any agreement to pay the adverse party's costs which is, to my mind, the more important illegality in the context of the defendants' summons. I have already said that an agreement with Mr. McFarlane to pay the costs for which he might become liable to the defendants would furnish a cogent reason for making an order that Quantum should pay such costs directly to the defendants. If the absence of any such agreement is one factor which renders illegal the maintenance contract between Quantum and Mr. McFarlane, it seems to me that the illegality also furnishes a cogent reason why, in the exercise of my discretion, an order should be made against Quantum to pay the defendants' costs. The fact that the maintenance contract is also champertous is in any event a further illegality in the present context.'

This reasoning falls to be contrasted with that of Vinelott J in the earlier case of *Shah v Karanjia* [1993] 4 All ER 792 at 810, where he said:

'I am not persuaded that the old law of maintenance offers any guide to the exercise of the court's discretion under s 51. It may be that in a case where it is plain or admitted that the action is brought by a nominal plaintiff at the expense and on behalf of another with an interest in the action (as in *Hayward v Giffard* ((1838) 4 M & W 194, 150 ER 1399)) or where it is funded by a trade union on behalf of a member or by a person liable to indemnify the plaintiff, the court could properly exercise its discretion by ordering the funder to pay the costs of the successful defendant, although the court would have to bear in mind the danger in exercising a summary jurisdiction of relying on a finding which would not be admissible in proceedings against the funder. However, all these cases fell outside the scope of the old law of maintenance and, if the court is to make an order, it much be, in the words of Lord Abinger CB, on the ground of justice and reason and in exercise of the jurisdiction under s 51.'

In the present case Mr Hillier did not suggest that the Sun Alliance funding of the Murphys constituted unlawful maintenance. He accepted the observation of Lloyd LJ in *Taylor v Pace Developments Ltd* [1991] BCC 406 at 410 that the statement of Lord Denning MR in *Hill v Archbold* was 'more a statement of universal practice than a binding legal principle, applicable to the exercise of the discretion in every case'. He submitted, however, that the court should not permit a non-party, who has funded an unsuccessful party, to avoid liability for the successful party's costs by purporting to contract out of such liability, either absolutely or, as here, by reason of a cap on the cover provided.

He further supported this submission by citing the following passage in the judgment of Kennedy LJ in *Condliffe v Hislop* [1996] 1 All ER 431 at 440, [1996] 1 WLR 753 at 762:

'... the court is entitled to protect its own procedures, and as Sir Thomas Bingham MR said in *Roache v News Group Newspapers Ltd* (1992) Times, 23 November the principle that in the ordinary way costs follow the event "is of fundamental importance in deterring plaintiffs from bringing and defendants from defending actions which they are likely to lose". If that principle is threatened, as for example if an insurer or a trade union were known to be giving financial support to a party without accepting liability for the costs of the other side if the supported party were to lose, then, as it seems to me, the court might, at least in some cases, be prepared to order that the action be stayed (cf *Wild v Simpson* [1919] 2 KB 544, [1918–19] All ER Rep 682, *Broxton v McClelland* (6 November 1992, unreported) and *Grovewood Holdings plc v James Capel & Co Ltd* [1994] 4 All ER 417, [1995] Ch 80, a case concerned with champerty, not maintenance). Normally the better course will be to let the action proceed to trial and then, if need be, consider the powers of the court under s 51 of the Supreme Court Act 1981 (as in *McFarlane's* case) ...'

The time has come to attempt to formulate some principles in the light of these decisions. My conclusions are as follows.

(1) In *Giles v Thompson* [1993] 3 All ER 321 at 360, [1994] 1 AC 142 at 164 Lord Mustill suggested that the current test of maintenance should ask the question whether—

'there is wanton and officious intermeddling with the disputes of others in [which] the meddler has no interest whatever, and where the assistance he renders to one or the other party is without justification or excuse.'

Where such a test is satisfied, I would expect the court to be receptive to an application under s 51 that the meddler pay any costs attributable to his intermeddling.

(2) Where a non-party has supported an unsuccessful party on terms that place the non-party under a clear contractual obligation to indemnify the unsuccessful party against his liability to pay the costs of the successful party, it may well be appropriate to make an order under s 51 that the non-party pay those costs directly to the successful party. Such an order may, for instance, save time and costs in short-circuiting the Third Parties (Rights against Insurers) Act 1930. *Bourne v Colodense* [1985] ICR 291 is a case where the court might well have thought fit to make such an order had it appreciated that it had jurisdiction to do so.

(3) Where a trade union funds unsuccessful litigation on behalf of a member the following factors, in addition to the funding itself, are likely to be present and, where they are, to make it appropriate to order the union to pay the successful party's costs should such an order be necessary: (a) an implied obligation owed by the union to its member to do so—see (2) above; (b) an interest on the part of the union in supporting and being seen to support the member's claim; (c) responsibility both for the decision whether the litigation is to be pursued and for the conduct of the litigation; and (d) expectation based on convention that the union will bear the costs of the successful party should the member lose.

(4) Where an unsuccessful defendant's costs are funded by insurers who have provided cover against liability, which is not subject to any relevant limit, the same considerations that I have set out under (3) are likely to apply.

(5) The position is more complex where a defendant's costs have been funded by insurers at risk under a policy under which their liability is limited to a sum which is insufficient to cover both liability and costs. This was the position in *Chapman Ltd v Christopher* (23 May 1996, unreported). In that case the plaintiffs were awarded damages in excess of £1m from an impecunious defendant who had the benefit of cover against liability for damages and costs up to a limit of £1m under his mother's household policy with Sun Alliance. Judge Zucker QC, sitting

as a judge of the High Court, made an order under s 51 that Sun Alliance pay the plaintiffs' costs for the following reasons.

'(1) The plaintiffs' claim from the outset exceeded and was known by Sun Alliance to exceed the limit of the indemnity, ie £1m. (2) Sun Alliance had the sole conduct and direction of the defence which it pursued in order to protect its own interest, ie its liability to pay out £1m under the insurance policy. I reject any suggestion that Sun Alliance was acting in the interests of Mr Christopher. (3) Sun Alliance knew from the outset that Mr Christopher had no means to meet any judgment or order for costs. (4) Each and every one of the defences put forward by Sun Alliance were either abandoned or failed. (5) By putting forward those defences, Sun Alliance and no one else caused the plaintiffs to incur costs of £250,000. (6) Sun Alliance further prejudiced the plaintiffs by keeping them out of their money for three years and seven months and, in the meantime, had the use of £1m.'

Having regard to these reasons it may be hard to fault the manner in which Judge Zucker exercised his discretion, but it is not clear to me why Sun Alliance will not be entitled to take account of the costs that they pay in consequence of his order when calculating their residual liability under the policy, in which case the plaintiffs will be no better off at the end of the day.

More generally, I am not persuaded that it will always be appropriate to order liability insurers to pay the plaintiffs' costs where they have unsuccessfully defended a claim made against their insured if the result of such an order will be to render them liable beyond their contractual limit of cover. It seems to me that the appropriate order may well turn on the facts of the particular case.

None of the considerations of principle set out above are directly relevant to the facts of the present case. Sun Alliance have funded the Murphys' litigation under a commercial agreement, but that is, it seems to me, the only ground that can validly be advanced in support of Youngs' contention that Sun Alliance should be ordered to pay their costs. In particular: (1) Sun Alliance have had no interest in the result of this litigation, save in so far as this has affected their liability to pay costs. (2) Sun Alliance did not initiate the litigation. They were contractually bound to fund it up to their limit of liability of £25,000 and would, in consequence, have been better off if the litigation had never been commenced. It has not been suggested, nor could it have been, that Sun Alliance could properly have refused their consent to this litigation. Counsel had advised the Murphys that they had 'a strong case'. (3) Sun Alliance exercised no control over the conduct of the litigation. (4) Sun Alliance cannot be accused of 'wanton and officious intermeddling' in the dispute. Legal expenses insurance is a respectable and well-recognised form of insurance and is subject to express regulation under statutory instruments pursuant to the Insurance Companies Act 1982.

For these reasons I do not consider that any of the authorities to which I have referred, or the principles that they reflect, answer the question of whether it is appropriate on the facts of this case to order Sun Alliance to pay Young's costs. The critical question is whether the mere fact that Sun Alliance have funded the Murphys' legal expenses under a policy of insurance, up to the limit of the cover under that policy, makes it reasonable and just that Sun Alliance should be ordered to pay Youngs' costs.

Mr Hillier referred us to *Thistleton v Hendricks* (1992) 32 Con LR 123. That case involved a claim by a builder against a house-owner and a counterclaim by the house-owner. The latter was successful and recovered damages of some £19,000 on the counterclaim. The builder's costs had been funded by his mother under loans motivated by maternal affection and made in the belief that her son's claim was bona fide. Judge Hicks QC, sitting as an Official Referee, ordered the mother to contribute £7,000 towards the house-owner's costs. In so doing he had particular regard to the following facts: (i) the mother knew that her son would be unlikely to be able to pay any costs ordered in favour of the house-owner; (ii) the builder was the plaintiff in the litigation; and (iii) the house-owner was a private individual. Judge Hicks considered that these circumstances justified his reaching a different conclusion from that of the Court of Appeal in *Cooper v Maxwell* [1992] CA Transcript 273. In that case the provisional liquidators of Bishopsgate Investment Management Ltd (BIM) had succeeded at first instance and on appeal in resisting an application by Mr Kevin Maxwell, a former director of BIM, that privilege against self-incrimination excused him from the obligation to answer questions put to him by the liquidators. Mr Maxwell's legal costs had been funded by his mother. The Court of Appeal held that the application made by Mr Maxwell had been made bona fide and on reasonable grounds. This led the court to the following conclusion, as stated at the end of the leading judgment of Dillon LJ:

'In these circumstances I am unable to see that it is required by justice that Mrs Maxwell, having elected to provide money for her son's costs and legal expenses, should be required also to pay the costs of the other side which has been successful against her son in the litigation for which the funds were used. The development of the authorities has not been that there will automatically be an order for costs against a person who is not a party to the proceedings if that person has funded the litigation. More is required. It is not suggested that a bank which funded litigation by providing an overdraft for a party to litigation on commercial terms would automatically be ordered to pay the other side's costs if the litigation was unsuccessful. The position could be different with a trade union which has an interest in funding the litigation of a member in the industrial field and habitually does pay the costs if the litigation fails. I do not see that there is anything in the circumstances of Mrs Maxwell in the present case which makes it right that the court should make an order against her to pay the costs of Mr Kevin Maxwell's unsuccessful appeal.'

This decision demonstrates a proposition that Mr Hillier has not sought to challenge. Funding alone will not justify an order against the funder under s 51. I do not consider that an order under s 51 will normally be appropriate where a disinterested relative has, out of natural affection, funded costs of a claim or a defence that is reasonably advanced.

Mr Hillier has urged that the special feature that makes it reasonable and just to make an order under s 51 in the present case is that the Sun Alliance has funded the Murphy's costs under a commercial agreement. This, it seems to me, reduces the central issue in this case to the following:

Should a legal expense insurer be permitted to cap its liability, or should the provision of such cover render the insurer liable to pay the costs of a successful adverse party, regardless of any contractual limit of liability?

For Sun Alliance, Mr Stuart Isaacs QC has argued that legal expense insurance is in the public interest. He has referred us to the approval of such insurance in the Final Report of Lord Woolf MR on Access to Justice, Overview section 1 para 12, in support of that submission. He has submitted that, if insurers are not *a* permitted effectively to limit their liability, they will be less ready to provide such cover.

As did the judge below, I accept the submission that legal expense insurance is in the public interest, particularly if it is on the terms of the cover in the present case. Such insurance not only provides desirable protection to the assured, it is of benefit to the adverse party in that (i) it is likely to ensure that careful *b* consideration is given to the merits of the litigation at an early stage, and (ii) it provides a potential source of funding of the adverse party's costs, should the assured be unsuccessful. The latter has proved illusory in the present case because of the limit of cover, but evidence before the court suggests that it is unusual for the limit of cover to be exceeded. That very evidence leaves me uncertain what the effect on the availability of such cover would be if legal *c* expense insurers were exposed to costs orders under s 51, but I do not believe that that question is critical to the answer in this case.

An order under s 51 that a non-party pay costs will only be justified when exceptional circumstances make such an order reasonable and just. In this judgment I have explored some of the categories of exceptional circumstances *d* that may justify such an order. This case does not fall into any of them. I have reached the conclusion that the existence of legal expenses insurance with a limit of cover that has been exhausted does not make it reasonable or just to order the insurer to pay the costs of the adverse successful party. For these reasons I would dismiss this appeal.

e **SIR JOHN BALCOMBE.** I have had the advantage of reading the draft judgment of Phillips LJ and I agree with him, and for the reasons which he gives, that this appeal should be dismissed. As will usually be the case, the legal expenses insurance with which we are here concerned did not relate to a specific piece of litigation, and this distinguishes this case from one where a third party funds a *f* particular claim and has a direct commercial interest in the outcome of that claim.

BUTLER-SLOSS LJ. I also agree that this appeal should be dismissed.

Appeal dismissed.

Paul Magrath Esq   Barrister.

Avon County Council v Hooper and another   *a*

COURT OF APPEAL, CIVIL DIVISION
BUTLER-SLOSS, ROCH AND HOBHOUSE LJJ
2, 22 FEBRUARY 1996

b

Social security – Services for sick and disabled persons – Recovery of charge for services – Minor severely mentally and physically handicapped at birth as a result of negligence of hospital – Local authority paying for maintenance of minor at special home – Health authority indemnifying minor and his estate against any liability to local authority in respect of claim to recover its costs in providing services – Local authority several years later seeking to charge for those services – Whether charge had to be made at time services provided – Whether right to indemnity amounted to sufficient means to pay charge – Health and Social Services and Social Security Adjudications Act 1983, s 17.

c

In June 1978 the first defendant's son, D, was born at a hospital run by the second defendant health authority. As a result of the hospital's negligence, D at birth *d* suffered serious brain damage due to foetal anoxia and was rendered severely mentally and physically handicapped. In November 1981 he was transferred from the hospital to a Leonard Cheshire Home, where he remained until his death in July 1991. The costs of maintaining D there were borne wholly by the plaintiff local authority in the discharge of its duties under s 29 of the National Assistance Act 1948 and Sch 8 to the National Health Service Act 1977 to provide *e* for the welfare of disabled persons and the care of persons suffering from illness. In 1989 an action brought by the first defendant, as D's next friend, against the health authority for negligence was settled on the terms that the health authority would pay D damages of £285,000. The settlement included provision to cover the cost of keeping D at the home from 15 November; and it was also a term of *f* the settlement that the health authority would indemnify D (and his estate) against any liability to the plaintiff for the cost of his care at the home prior to that date. On 21 June 1991 the plaintiff commenced an action against D pursuant to s 17ᵃ of the Health and Social Services and Social Security Adjudications Act 1983 to recover the cost of the provision of the services to him. The health authority contended that a charge was only recoverable under s 17 if it was made at the *g* time when the service was provided and the fact that D had a claim against the health authority did not amount to 'means' to pay for the purposes of s 17(3) of the Act. The judge rejected those contentions and gave judgment for the plaintiff. The defendants appealed.

h

Held – A local authority's power under s 17(1) of the 1983 Act to charge for services it provided had to be exercised reasonably, which meant that it had to have relevant and reasonable grounds for choosing to exercise that power. Further, for the purposes of s 17(3) of the 1983 Act 'means' meant the financial resources of a person, namely assets, sources of income, liabilities and expenses *j* and it also included a realisable asset. It followed that, since D had a right to be indemnified by the health authority against any liability for the cost of the services provided to him, he had the means to pay for them. Accordingly, as the local authority had acted reasonably in seeking to charge him for those services,

---

ᵃ   Section 17 is set out at p 535 *e* to *j*, post

it was entitled to recover the cost of providing them, notwithstanding that they
had been provided in the past. The appeal would therefore be dismissed (see
p 537 *a* to *f j*, p 538 *a b h j* and p 539 *f g*, post).

Notes

For a local authority's duty to provide welfare arrangements for handicapped
persons and their power to charge for such services, see 33 *Halsbury's Laws* (4th
edn) paras 925–927.

For the National Assistance Act 1948, s 29, see 40 *Halsbury's Statutes* (4th
edn) 33.

For the National Health Service Act 1977, Sch 8, see 30 *Halsbury's Statutes* (4th
edn) (1991 reissue) 914.

For the Health and Social Services and Social Security Adjudications Act 1983,
s 17, see 40 *Halsbury's Statutes* (4th edn) 311.

Case referred to in judgments

Pepper (Inspector of Taxes) v Hart [1993] 1 All ER 42, [1993] AC 593, [1992] 3 WLR
1032, HL.

Cases also cited or referred to in skeleton arguments

Perkins, Re, Poyser v Beyfus [1898] 2 Ch 182, [1895–9] All ER Rep 230, CA.
Plewa v Chief Adjudication Officer [1994] 3 All ER 323, [1995] 1 AC 249, HL.
Secretary of State for Social Security v Tunnicliffe [1991] 2 All ER 712, CA.

Appeal

By notice dated 18 July 1995 the defendants, Mrs Christine Elizabeth Hooper and
the Bristol and District Health Authority, appealed from the decision of Judge
Robert Taylor (25 BMLR 26) sitting as a deputy judge of the High Court in the
Bristol District Registry on 12 May 1995 whereby he entered judgment for the
plaintiff, the Avon County Council, for £232,002·90 (including interest) in respect
of its claim to recover pursuant to s 17 of the Health and Social Services and Social
Security Adjudications Act 1983 the costs of services provided for the first
defendant's son, Daniel Hooper, as a disabled person between 22 June 1985 and
15 November 1989. The facts are set out in the judgment of Hobhouse LJ.

John Grace QC and *John Beggs* (instructed by *Osborne Clarke*, Bristol) for the health
    authority.
Piers Ashworth QC and *Michael Roach* (instructed by *Peter Jennings*, Bristol) for the
    county council.
Mrs Hooper did not appear.

Cur adv vult

22 February 1996. The following judgments were delivered.

HOBHOUSE LJ (giving the first judgment at the invitation of Butler-Sloss LJ).
On 15 June 1978 Daniel Hooper was born at a hospital run by the Bristol and
District Health Authority. At birth, he suffered serious brain damage due to
foetal anoxia. Those responsible for caring for him and his mother, at the time of
his birth, had been negligent. As a result of their negligence, he was severely
handicapped both physically and mentally. He needed constant care. He did not
have a normal expectation of life. He died on 16 July 1991. Up until November

1981 Daniel was looked after in hospital, but he was then transferred to a Leonard
Cheshire Home in Dorchester, Dorset. From that date until his death he was
cared for full-time by those working at the home. The costs of maintaining
Daniel at the home until 15 November 1989 were wholly borne by the Avon
County Council in the discharge of its duties under s 29 of the National Assistance
Act 1948 and Sch 8 to the National Health Service Act 1977 to provide for the
welfare of disabled persons and the care of persons suffering from illness.

In this action, the county council is suing Mrs Hooper, as the administratrix of
the estate of Daniel and his former next friend to recover, under s 17 of the Health
and Social Services and Social Security Adjudications Act 1983, the cost of the
provision of the services to Daniel. The health authority was added as a second
defendant. The health authority was responsible for those whose negligence
caused Daniel's injuries. They have undertaken to indemnify Daniel and his
estate in respect of any liability that there might be under s 17 for the provision
of the services to Daniel. The present action, therefore, formally involves a claim
by the county council against Daniel (and his estate) but in substance is a dispute
between the county council and the health authority as to which of them should
bear the cost of Daniel's care at the Leonard Cheshire Home.

In 1981, at the time that the county council first became involved in the care of
Daniel, it was not aware of the full circumstances under which Daniel had
received his injuries, nor was it told of the belief that they had been caused by the
negligence of the health authority. The first that the county council learnt of this
was in 1986 when the county council received a letter from solicitors acting for
the health authority inquiring about who was bearing the cost of caring for
Daniel and who would bear the cost of future care. This came about because by
this time Daniel had, through his mother as next friend, commenced an action
against the health authority claiming damages for negligence. This fact having
been drawn to the attention of the county council, the county council thereafter
made it clear in correspondence, both to the solicitors acting for the health
authority and to those acting for Daniel, that the county council would expect
provision to be made in the damages awarded to Daniel for both the past and the
future cost of his care. The county council made it clear that it was not prepared
to waive whatever rights it had to recover the costs which they had incurred and
were continuing to incur. The health authority resisted this, but recognised that
the settlement of Daniel's claim would have to protect him against any liability
for those charges.

The settlement of Daniel's claim was negotiated in 1988, but not finally
incorporated into an agreed order and approved by the court until 15 November
1989. The agreed order provided for the health authority to pay Daniel damages
of £285,000. The settlement included provision to cover the cost of keeping
Daniel at the Leonard Cheshire Home from that date for the remainder of his life.
It was also a term of the approved settlement that, should Daniel be under any
liability to the county council for the cost of his care at the Leonard Cheshire
Home prior to that date, the health authority would indemnify Daniel (and his
estate) in respect of any such liability. Daniel was thereby enabled to meet
whatever might be his liabilities both in the past and in the future arising from his
care at the Leonard Cheshire Home.

The present action brought by the county council was not actually
commenced until 21 June 1991. It is now accepted that the claim in the action is
governed by s 9 of the Limitation Act 1980 and that any cause of action which
accrued more than six years before that date is statute-barred; it is common

a ground that any cause of action which the county council has under s 17 against Daniel accrued at the time of the provision of the services. Therefore, the subject matter of the present appeal is the cost of the provision of the services to Daniel between 22 June 1985 and 15 November 1989. The sum in issue is £232,002·90 (£111,686·39 plus £120,316·51 agreed interest).

b Since the issue in the action is now confined to the period since June 1985, we are not concerned, except as a matter of legislative history, with the charging provisions which preceded s 17 of the 1983 Act. Section 17 came into force on 1 January 1984 (by the Health and Social Services and Social Security Adjudications Act 1983 (Commencement No 1) Order 1983, SI 1983/974). It replaced the corresponding provisions of the National Assistance Act 1948 and the National Health Services Act 1977. The claim of the county council depends solely upon

c s 17 of the 1983 Act.

The point raised by this action is of some general importance. It can potentially arise whenever an individual has been injured by the negligence or actionable fault of another. The present case arose from medical negligence. It might have been a road accident or an industrial injury—or any situation where

d a person (whether a minor or not) has been seriously injured through another's fault. The liability of the tortfeasor to compensate the injured person gives the local authority which has provided services to the injured party an opportunity to argue that it can seek to recoup the cost of those services under s 17 of the 1983 Act. Thus, the question arises whether the cost is ultimately to be borne by the tortfeasor or the local authority.

e Section 17 comes in Pt VII of the 1983 Act, which deals with charges for local authority services. It reads:

'Charges for local authority services in England and Wales.—(1) Subject to subsection (3) below, an authority providing a service to which this section applies may recover such charge (if any) for it as they consider reasonable.

f (2) This section applies to services provided under the following enactments—(a) section 29 of the National Assistance Act 1948 (welfare arrangements for blind, deaf, dumb and crippled persons etc.); (b) section 45(1) of the Health Services and Public Health Act 1968 (welfare of old people); (c) Schedule 8 to the National Health Service Act 1977 (care of

g mothers and young children, prevention of illness and care and after-care and home help and laundry facilities); (d) section 8 of the Residential Homes Act 1980 (meals and recreation for old people); and (e) paragraph 1 of Part II of Schedule 9 to this Act.

(3) If a person—(a) avails himself of a service to which this section applies, and (b) satisfies the authority providing the service that his means are

h insufficient for it to be reasonably practicable for him to pay for the service the amount which he would otherwise be obliged to pay for it, the authority shall not require him to pay more for it than it appears to them that it is reasonably practicable for him to pay.

(4) Any charge under this section may, without prejudice to any other

j method of recovery, be recovered summarily as a civil debt.'

It is accepted that the relevant services were provided under s 29 of the 1948 Act and Sch 8 to the 1977 Act. It is also accepted that Daniel was a person who had availed himself of those services. The argument of the health authority was two-fold. First, as a matter of the construction of sub-s (1) the charge, if it is to be recoverable, must be made at the time the service is provided. Secondly, the fact that Daniel had a claim against the health authority, subsequently recognised by the consent order of November 1989, did not amount to 'means' for the purposes of sub-s (3).

Judge Robert Taylor, sitting as a deputy judge of the High Court, rejected these arguments and gave judgment for the county council for the sum which covered the cost of the services between 22 June 1985 and 15 November 1989. The judge said ((1995) 25 BMLR 26 at 32–33):

'There is nothing in any of the relevant statutory provisions which *expressly* prohibits a local authority from recovering a charge for a service which it has provided in the past. Furthermore, I have not been persuaded by any of the arguments advanced on behalf of the defendants that such a prohibition arises by necessary implication ... If any restriction upon a local authority's actions is to be implied into these provisions, the only one which seems to me to be necessary is a requirement that the local authority should act reasonably ... So far as the facts of the present case are concerned, it seems to me that, once the plaintiff knew that Daniel had a good claim against the second defendant, it was entitled to recover a charge for the full cost of services provided to Daniel in the past; and that it acted reasonably in seeking to recover such a charge when it did. Until the strength of Daniel's claim against the second defendant was established, it would have been very difficult if not impossible for any valid assessment of Daniel's means to have been made. Once it became clear that Daniel had a good claim against the second defendant, it followed that he had (in effect) always had the means to pay for the services with which he had been provided from the date of his admission to the Cheshire Home.' (Judge Robert Taylor's emphasis.)

The defendants appealed.

Before us, Mr John Grace QC developed his argument, on behalf of the appellants, in a number of ways. First, he relied upon the use of the present tense in sub-s (1): the authority 'providing' the service 'may recover' a charge if 'they consider' it reasonable. Similarly, sub-s (3) is expressed in the present tense— 'avails himself of a service ... and satisfies the authority providing the service that his means are insufficient'.

Secondly, he submitted that the scheme of the legislation under which welfare provision is made is that the provision should in principle be free of charge unless a charge for it is made at the time. Thus, unless the recipient of the service is told at the time it is provided that the service is to be charged for, it must be treated as a service which has been provided free. It was submitted that the statements of the minister when the 1983 Act was going through the House of Commons made it clear that the provision of services should be free unless the recipient was actually in a position to pay for them at the time. He argued that any different construction of the section would mean that after-acquired means, for example winning the lottery, could be used as a basis for subsequently charging for services which had at the relevant time been provided free.

Finally, he argued that the word 'means' was confined to available cash and that rights of indemnity for compensation from third parties could not properly be taken into account. He recognised that a local authority could, where a continuing service was being provided, say that from a certain date it would start to charge for that services; and he accepted that after the date of the consent order (15 November 1989), the charge could be made and that Daniel had the means *a* with which to pay it. But until Daniel had actually received the cash with which to pay, he had no means to do so.

The starting point for the evaluation of these arguments is s 17 itself. It is an empowering section. It gives a local authority the power, but not the obligation, to charge for the provision of the relevant services. It is implicit both in the language of the section and in the general law governing the activities of local

b authorities that the power must be exercised reasonably, that is to say, that the local authority must have relevant and reasonable grounds for choosing to exercise the power. Nothing turns upon how one construes the final words of the subsection 'such charge (if any) for it as they consider reasonable'. As a matter of language, these words carry the implication that the charge may be waived and that the local authority need only make any charge if it considers it reasonable to

c do so. Thus, there is an overriding criterion of reasonableness which governs the local authority's exercise of the power which is given by sub-s (1).

This criterion of reasonableness provides the primary answer to the arguments of Mr Grace. If the right to charge has been waived, clearly no charge can be recovered. If the service was provided in circumstances under which it would be

d unreasonable for the authority subsequently to charge for it, then the authority is not entitled later to seek to recover a charge. Similarly, if, having provided a service, the local authority seeks to recover a charge, it must be prepared to justify the reasonableness of doing so. The reasonableness of any conduct falls to be assessed at the time of the relevant conduct and having regard to all the

e relevant circumstances then existing. If the claim is first made some time after the provision of the services, the local authority must be prepared to justify the reasonableness of making the claim notwithstanding the delay. If the local authority is acting unreasonably, its claim will fail. If the local authority is acting reasonably, there is no basis in sub-s (1) for the person availing himself of the service to say that the local authority should not recover.

f If the local authority decides to charge and is acting reasonably in doing so, the person availing himself of the service has, in those circumstances, to satisfy the authority under sub-s (3) that his means are insufficient for it to be reasonably practicable for him to pay the amount which he would otherwise be obliged to pay. It is for the recipient of the service to discharge this burden of persuasion.

g He must show that he has insufficient means. The time at which he has to do this is the time when the local authority is seeking to charge him for the services. If his means have been reduced, as might be the case with a business man whose business had run into difficulties after his being injured, the reduction in his means is something upon which he would be entitled to rely as making it

h impracticable for him to pay, even though at an earlier date he might have been better off. The consideration under sub-s (3)(b) is the practical one: are his means such that it is not reasonably practicable for him to pay?

This also bears on the alternative argument of Mr Grace that only cash should be taken into account. This is too narrow a reading of sub-s (3). As a matter of

j the ordinary use of English, the word 'means' refers to the financial resources of a person: his assets, his sources of income, his liabilities and expenses. If he has a realisable asset, that is part of his means; he has the means to pay. The subject matter of paragraph (b) is the practicability of his paying. If he has an asset which he can reasonably be expected to realise and which will (after taking into account any other relevant factor) enable him to pay, his means make it practicable for him to pay.

Where the person has a right to be indemnified by another against the cost of the service, he has the means to pay. He can enforce his right and make the payment. There is nothing in any part of s 17 which suggests that it is intended that sub-s (3) should have the effect of relieving those liable to indemnify the recipient of the service for the cost of the service from their liability. On the contrary, it is clear that the intention of the section is to enable the local authority to recover the cost, save when it is unreasonable that it should do so or impracticable for the recipient to pay. The argument of the health authority would, if accepted, frustrate the clear intention of the section.

The other arguments of Mr Grace do not displace this conclusion. He cited *Pepper (Inspector of Taxes) v Hart* [1993] 1 All ER 42 at 64, [1993] AC 593 at 634, where Lord Browne-Wilkinson said:

'In my judgment, subject to the questions of the privileges of the House of Commons, reference to parliamentary material should be permitted as an aid to the construction of legislation which is ambiguous or obscure or the literal meaning of which leads to an absurdity. Even in such cases references in court to parliamentary material should only be permitted where such material clearly discloses the mischief aimed at or the legislative intention lying behind the ambiguous or obscure words.'

He submitted that s 17 was 'obscure' and that the ministerial statements resolved this obscurity in his favour. However, the section is not obscure or ambiguous; nor does it on its literal interpretation lead to any absurd result. Further, statements by the minister to the effect that 'we all want to avoid people with low incomes being charged', 'the new section provides adequate safeguards to ensure that charges are not imposed on people who lack the means to make proper payments for the services they require', 'the new clause is so flexible that it allows local authorities to impose charges only if they want to', do not add to (or detract from) what is already clear from the language of the section nor do they advance his argument.

He argued that there was a general principle that welfare benefits should be free. He referred to other provisions of the 1948 and 1977 Acts. These references did not however support his submissions. For example s 22(1) of the 1948 Act starts with the words 'Persons for whom accommodation is provided under this Part of this Act shall pay for the accommodation ...' Section 29 of the 1948 Act and Sch 8 to the 1977 Act each contained charging provisions before they were replaced by s 17 of the 1983 Act. Section 45 of the 1948 Act contains an express provision enabling the local authority to recover expenditure from any person who has misrepresented or failed to disclose any material fact.

He argued that, again as a matter of principle and as a result of the use of the present tense in s 17, the charges must be levied at the time of the provision of the services, like a shopkeeper asks a purchaser for the price at the time of sale or a hotel-keeper tells the visitor the room charge on arrival. He submitted that the recipient must be able, before he avails himself of the service to know whether the charge is acceptable to him and whether he wishes to go ahead. This is not a reasonable interpretation of the section. The primary duty of the local authority is to provide the services to those in need of them. The power to charge is consequential upon the provision of the service. Whether it is reasonable to charge has to be considered at an appropriate time which will not necessarily be before the time the services are rendered and will most probably be later when the local authority has put itself in possession of the relevant information.

Similarly, the question of means and the practicability of paying will very often have to be the subject of later inquiry and consideration. Once it is recognised that the local authority must act reasonably, the section can be seen to have a sensible and practical scheme which is not subject to the artificial restraint for which Mr Grace argues.

As regards the reasonableness of taking into account after acquired means under sub-s (3), no problem arises in the present case. Daniel's cause of action against the health authority was something of which he was possessed from before the time that the county council first provided him with any services. The reasonableness of the county council's conduct in demanding that the charges be paid once it learnt of his right of recovery was considered at the trial. The county council manifestly acted reasonably and no argument to the contrary has been advanced before us. Where a person only has a partial right of recovery or the right is doubtful, those factors may have to be taken into account in considering what is reasonable and what it is practicable for the person to pay. This case raises no problem of after acquired means.

It was suggested that, where the injured party's affairs are under the administration of the Court of Protection pursuant to the Mental Health Act 1983, this might provide some obstacle to the application of s 17 as I have interpreted it. This is not so. Sections 95 and 96 of that Act expressly recognise that the administration of the patient's affairs shall, subject always to the requirements of the patient, have regard to the interests of creditors and the desirability of making provision for obligations of the patient (even if they may not be legally enforceable. There is no conflict. Subsection (3) imposes a restriction having regard to what it is practicable for the person to pay; s 95 has regard to the requirements of the patient. The obligation of the local authority to act reasonably likewise will avoid conflict.

Accordingly, in my judgment the arguments of the health authority on the construction and correct approach to s 17 are not to be accepted. Daniel had at all material times sufficient means to make it practicable for him to pay. The county council has acted reasonably. The judgment of the judge was right and the appeal should be dismissed.

ROCH LJ. I agree.

BUTLER-SLOSS LJ. I also agree.

Appeal dismissed.

Paul Magrath Esq   Barrister.

Frost and others v Chief Constable of the South Yorkshire Police and others
Duncan v British Coal Corp

COURT OF APPEAL, CIVIL DIVISION

ROSE, HENRY AND JUDGE LJJ

15, 16, 17 JULY, 31 OCTOBER 1996

Negligence – Duty to take care – Nervous shock – Employer – Rescuer – Employee suffering psychiatric injury in the course of rescue – Police officers suffering psychiatric injury in aftermath of football stadium disaster caused by police negligence – Pit deputy suffering psychiatric injury after attending miner killed in colliery accident – Whether plaintiffs rescuers – Whether plaintiffs entitled to recover for psychiatric injury – Whether plaintiffs owed duty of care by employer as employees or rescuers.

In two separate appeals the issue arose as to the circumstances in which an employee could recover damages for psychiatric injury sustained as a result of tending a victim of his employer's negligence.

In the first appeal a number of police officers sued their employer, their chief constable, for damages in negligence for post-traumatic stress disorder suffered in the aftermath of a disaster at a football stadium. Three of the officers had been on duty at the stadium when 96 spectators died and 730 were injured as the result of crushing caused by a senior police officer's decision to open an outer gate to the ground without cutting off access to two spectator pens from which there was no exit. One of the officers had attempted to help free spectators from the pens and two of them had attended a makeshift morgue set up at the ground. Two other officers had been drafted in to help in the aftermath at the ground shortly after the disaster. All five officers had witnessed chaotic and gruesome scenes. The sixth officer had not been on duty at the ground and had acted as liaison officer between the hospital staff and the casualty bureau; she had also dealt with relatives and later went to the temporary morgue at the ground with personal effects. The officers' claim against the chief constable was based on a breach of his duty of care owed to them as their employer or as rescuers. The chief constable admitted that the disaster had been caused by negligence for which he was vicariously responsible and had accepted liability towards other officers more directly concerned in the events of the disaster, but denied that he owed any duty of care to the officers bringing the claim. He contended: that those officers were not within the category of secondary victims who could claim since they themselves had not been exposed to the physical danger which affected the victims and there were no ties of love and affection; that the employer/ employee relationship did not establish the necessary proximity; that the officers were professional rescuers in respect of whom it was not reasonably foreseeable that they would be affected by nervous shock; and that the officer's injuries were not shock induced. The judge dismissed the action on the grounds (i) that although a relationship analogous to master and servant existed between the chief constable and the plaintiffs, giving rise to a duty of care which embraced psychiatric illness, that duty did not arise where the police officer was a secondary victim, unless he could succeed as a rescuer, and such a duty could not place a a police officer in a better position than a bystander; and (ii) that only one plaintiff was a rescuer in law and he could not recover since, being a professional rescuer not intimately participating in the incident itself or in the immediate aftermath, it would not be just and reasonable that he could recover whereas a bystander could not. The plaintiffs appealed.

b In the second appeal the plaintiff was a pit deputy at a colliery when one of the men for whom he was responsible was crushed to death at the coal face. The plaintiff was about 275 metres away at the time, and arrived at the scene of the accident within four minutes. By then the victim was apparently already dead and the plaintiff's attempts to revive him were unsuccessful. The plaintiff subsequently developed a psychiatric illness and brought a claim against his employer who operated the colliery. The employer admitted that the accident to c the victim had been caused by negligence but denied owing a duty of care to the plaintiff. The judge dismissed the claim, holding that although the plaintiff had suffered a harrowing experience, what he had seen was an inanimate body which was no more than might be encountered at a road accident or the like which would not have affected a man of reasonable fortitude to the extent that the d plaintiff had been affected. The plaintiff appealed.

Held – (1) (Judge LJ dissenting) An employer who negligently caused physical injury to one employee was equally liable to a fellow employee of normal fortitude working on the same task who sustained psychiatric injury, either because of fear for himself or through witnessing what happened to his fellow e workman, since there was no justification for regarding physical and psychiatric injuries caused to an employee in such a situation as different kinds of injury with different requirements as to foreseeability of injury. Although in cases outside the master and servant relationship the courts had found it necessary, in identifying those to whom a duty of care was owed, to draw a distinction f between primary and secondary victims and to impose limiting criteria to determine those within the second category who could recover, in the master and servant context the duty of care existed by reason of that relationship. Accordingly, although a police officer could not complain against his employer, the chief constable, if he was injured in the course of his duties when deployed to prevent a riot or summoned to the scene of an accident, he did have a right of g action if his injury was caused by the antecedent negligence of the chief constable. Furthermore, a rescuer was in a special category and if and in so far as the distinction between primary and secondary victims was relevant to rescuers, a rescuer was in a primary relationship with the tortfeasor and therefore not subject to the limitations imposed on claims by secondary victims and it made no h difference that the rescuer was a professional rescuer (see p 545 f, p 546 d, p 548 j to p 549 a c h j, p 550 d to h, p 567 e to g and p 568 a b, post); *Chadwick v British Transport Commission* [1967] 2 All ER 945, *McLoughlin v O'Brian* [1982] 2 All ER 298, *Alcock v Chief Constable of the South Yorkshire Police* [1991] 4 All ER 907, *McFarlane v EE Caledonia Ltd* [1994] 2 All ER 1 and *Page v Smith* [1995] 2 All ER 736 j considered.

(2) Applying those principles, in the first appeal the defendant chief constable owed a duty of care to those police officers who were at the stadium and their appeals would accordingly be allowed. However, the chief constable owed no duty to the police officer on duty at the local hospital since she was not a rescuer and was not at the ground when the negligent loss of control occurred, and she was not therefore within the category of those officers to whom, being within the

area of risk when the incident occurred, a duty of care was owed by virtue of the master and servant relationship. It followed (Judge LJ concurring) that her appeal would be dismissed. In the second appeal, the plaintiff was not a rescuer since he was not geographically proximate when the incident occurred and by the time he arrived at the scene there was no danger to him or to the deceased. He was outside the area of risk of physical or psychiatric injury when the deceased was injured and he was not exposed to any unnecessary risk of injury when he attended the scene. Furthermore, his actions in rendering first aid were within the normal scope of his employment and were not attended by any unusually distressing features. It followed that the circumstances did not give rise to any breach of duty owed to the plaintiff by the defendants as employers and (Judge LJ concurring) his appeal would therefore be dismissed (see p 551 *c* to p 552 *j*, p 554 *c* to *e*, p 567 *g* and p 576 *d h*, post).

Notes
For liability for nervous shock, see 34 *Halsbury's Laws* (4th edn) para 8, and for cases on the subject, see 17 *Digest* (Reissue) 145–148, *378–393*.

Cases referred to in judgments
Alcock v Chief Constable of the South Yorkshire Police [1991] 4 All ER 907, [1992] 1 AC 310, [1991] 3 WLR 1057, HL; *affg* sub nom *Jones v Wright* [1991] 3 All ER 88, [1992] AC 310, [1991] 2 WLR 814, CA.
Associated Provincial Picture Houses Ltd v Wednesbury Corp [1947] 2 All ER 680, [1948] 1 KB 223, CA.
Bourhill v Young [1942] 2 All ER 396, [1943] AC 92, HL.
Burgess v Superior Court (1992) 831 P 2d 1197, Cal SC.
Caparo Industries plc v Dickman [1990] 1 All ER 568, [1990] 2 AC 605, [1990] 2 WLR 358, HL.
Chadwick v British Transport Commission [1967] 2 All ER 945, sub nom *Chadwick v British Railways Board* [1967] 1 WLR 912.
Chester v Waverley Corp (1939) 62 CLR 1, Aust HC.
Donoghue v Stevenson [1932] AC 562, [1932] All ER Rep 1, HL.
Dooley v Cammell Laird & Co Ltd [1951] 1 Lloyd's Rep 271, Assizes.
Dulieu v White & Sons [1901] 2 KB 669, [1900–3] All ER Rep 353, DC.
Galt v British Railways Board (1983) 133 NLJ 870.
Haynes v Harwood [1935] 1 KB 146, [1934] All ER Rep 103, CA.
Hill v Chief Constable of West Yorkshire [1988] 2 All ER 238, [1989] AC 53, [1988] 2 WLR 1049, HL.
Hughes v National Union of Mineworkers [1991] 4 All ER 278, [1991] ICR 669.
Jaensch v Coffey (1984) 155 CLR 549, Aust HC.
King v Phillips [1953] 1 All ER 617, [1953] 1 QB 429, [1953] 2 WLR 526, CA.
Knightley v Johns [1982] 1 All ER 851, [1982] 1 WLR 349, CA.
McFarlane v EE Caledonia Ltd [1994] 2 All ER 1, CA.
McLoughlin v O'Brian [1982] 2 All ER 298, [1983] 1 AC 410, [1982] 2 WLR 982, HL.
Mount Isa Mines Ltd v Pusey (1970) 125 CLR 383, Aust HC.
Ogwo v Taylor [1987] 3 All ER 961, [1988] AC 431, [1987] 3 WLR 1145, HL.
Page v Smith [1995] 2 All ER 736, [1996] AC 155, [1995] 2 WLR 644, HL; *rvsg* [1994] 4 All ER 522, CA.
Rigby v Chief Constable of Northamptonshire [1985] 2 All ER 985, [1985] 1 WLR 1242.
Robertson v Forth Road Bridge Joint Board, Rough v Forth Road Bridge Joint Board 1995 SLT 263, Ct of Sess.

a Salmon v Seafarer Restaurants Ltd* [1983] 3 All ER 729, [1983] 1 WLR 1264.
Wagner v International Rly Co (1921) 232 NY 176, NY Ct of Apps.
Ward v T E Hopkins & Son Ltd, Baker v T E Hopkins & Son Ltd [1959] 3 All ER 225,
   [1959] 1 WLR 966, CA.
Wigg v British Railways Board (1986) Times, 4 February.

b **Cases also cited or referred to in skeleton arguments**
Robertson v Bell 1969 SLT 119, Ct of Sess.
Yates v South Kirkby &c Collieries Ltd [1910] 2 KB 538, CA.

Appeals

c   *Frost v Chief Constable of the South Yorkshire Police and ors*
By notice dated 4 May 1995 the plaintiffs, Henry White, Mark Edward Bairstow,
Anthony Bevis, Geoffrey Arthur Glave and Janet Smith, who were police officers,
appealed from the order of Waller J made on 10 April 1995 whereby he dismissed
the plaintiffs' claims for damages for personal injury on the basis that there was
no duty owed to the plaintiffs on the part of the first defendant not to expose the
d plaintiffs to a foreseeable risk of psychiatric injury, that none of the plaintiffs had
been rescuers in the events at Hillsborough Stadium, Sheffield, on 15 April 1989,
that the psychiatric injuries which the plaintiffs sustained had not been
foreseeable, and that the negligence of the defendant had not caused those
injuries.   By respondent's notice dated 18 May 1995 the defendants, Chief
e Constable of South Yorkshire, Sheffield Wednesday Football Club and Eastwood
Partners (a firm), sought to affirm the decision.   The facts are set out in the
judgment of Rose LJ.

                        Duncan v British Coal Corp
f By amended notice dated 21 August 1995 the plaintiff, Walter Mein Duncan,
appealed from the order of Mr L B Stephen, sitting as a deputy circuit judge in the
Sheffield County Court made on 4 January 1995 whereby he dismissed the
plaintiff's claim for damages for personal injury against the defendants, British
Coal Corp, on the basis that although the plaintiff was owed a duty of care by the
defendants, the incident had not been of sufficient gravity to warrant the award
g of damages.   By amended respondent's notice dated 21 February 1996 the
defendants sought to affirm the decision.   The facts are set out in the judgment of
Rose LJ.

Benet Hytner QC and *Graham Platts* (instructed by *Russell Jones & Walker*, Leeds) for
h   the appellant police officers.
Andrew Collender QC and *Patrick Limb* (instructed by *Hammond Suddards*, Bradford)
      for the chief constable and second and third defendants.
W Bernard Phillips (instructed by *Keeble Hawson*, Sheffield) for Mr Duncan.
Richard Maxwell QC (instructed by *Nabarro Nathanson*) for British Coal Corp.

j   *Cur adv vult*

31 October 1996. The following judgments were delivered.

ROSE LJ. These two appeals raise questions as to the circumstances in which an
employee can recover damages for psychiatric injury sustained as a result of
tending a victim of his employer's negligence.

In the first appeal, five police officers challenge the decision of Waller J, who on 10 April 1995 dismissed their claims arising out of the disaster at Hillsborough Stadium in Sheffield on 15 April 1989. In the second appeal, a pit deputy challenges the decision of Mr L B Stephen, who on 4 January 1995 at Sheffield County Court, dismissed his claim arising from treating a man crushed to death by the admitted negligence of his employers.

It is convenient to deal first with the police officers' action.

The events at Hillsborough Stadium were horrific. Shortly after 3 pm, 96 football match spectators died and very many more were injured by crushing, sustained in pens 3 and 4 at the Leppings Lane end of the ground. The immediate cause of the disaster was a senior police officer's decision to open an outer gate without cutting off access to the pens. Liability for the deaths and injuries of those spectators has been admitted by the three defendants, the first of whom is the plaintiffs' chief constable. The defendants admit negligence in the present proceedings but dispute the existence of any duty to these plaintiffs.

By agreement, causation was not dealt with below. If, by reason of this court's decision on duty, it arises, causation will be remitted to a trial judge. However, as I understand the position, it is not in issue that the plaintiffs all sustained post-traumatic stress disorder. The Law Commission in *Liability for Psychiatric Illnesses* (Consultation Paper No 137, para 3.6) says that post-traumatic stress disorder is unique in psychiatric classification in that it contains an explicit assumption that the cause of the disorder is known. If this is correct (and we have heard no submissions on the point, though we heard rival contentions as to whether the plaintiffs' injuries were shock induced) it appears, at least prima facie, that causation seems likely to be established. Waller J made no specific finding as to whether psychiatric injury was foreseeable. However, the first defendant admits that, prior to April 1989, 'some police officers of ordinary fortitude suffered psychiatric illness without physical injury as a result of attending incidents involving death or serious injury or risk thereof'. It is also common ground that, from July 1988, the first defendant had a standing order in relation to the management of post-traumatic stress disorder, which identified the difficulty of predicting how any particular officer would react to an extreme incident. A force welfare officer and psychologist were at the stadium. Accordingly, in itself, foreseeability of psychiatric injury, at least by the first defendant, would appear to present no problem to the plaintiffs and, before us, it was not contended otherwise on behalf of the defendants. Accordingly, it is to the existence and breach of duty that I direct my consideration.

In his interim report on the disaster, Taylor LJ described the scene of carnage:

'It was truly gruesome. The victims were blue, cyanotic, incontinent: their mouths open, vomiting: their eyes staring. A pile of bodies lay and grew outside gate 3. Extending further and further onto the pitch, the injured were laid down and attempts made to revive them ... The scene was emotive and chaotic as well as gruesome'. (See Cm 765, p 15, para 8.3)

A temporary mortuary was opened in the stadium's gymnasium. Police officers played differing roles in different places. Thirty-seven brought claims. Liability has been admitted and damages assessed in relation to the 14 who either entered the pens or were active at the pens' fence. The roles played by the present plaintiffs represent the different types of activity carried out by the remaining 23 claimants. It was contended on behalf of each plaintiff, apart from Sgt Janet Smith, who was in the hospital mortuary, that he was a rescuer, but this was disputed by the defendants. Waller J found that only one of the plaintiffs, Insp White, was a rescuer and this is now challenged by the defendants.

Two grounds for founding liability were argued on appeal: first, breach of a duty of care by the chief constable, arising from the plaintiffs' service as police officers when acting under his direction and control; secondly, breach of a duty owed to them as rescuers. The plaintiffs did not pursue before us a third possibility canvassed unsuccessfully before the judge, namely that the plaintiffs were 'conduit pipes' led to believe that their own conduct had helped to bring about the disaster. The judge found, as to the first ground, that a relationship analogous to master and servant existed between the chief constable and the appellants, giving rise to a duty of care, embracing psychiatric illness, but that duty did not arise where the police officer was a 'secondary victim', unless he could succeed as a rescuer and such a duty could not place a police officer in a better position than a bystander. As to the second ground, only Inspector White was a rescuer in law and he could not recover since, being a professional rescuer not intimately participating in the incident itself or in the *immediate* aftermath, it would be 'unattractive' and not 'just and reasonable' that he could recover whereas a bystander could not: something akin to the 'fireman's rule' should apply in relation to psychiatric damage.

As to the first ground, Mr Hytner QC submitted that the scope of the duty owed by an employer and a chief constable in the position of an employer is the same whatever the nature of the employment, namely, to take reasonable care to avoid exposing the employee to unnecessary risk of physical or psychiatric injury. The normal work of steel erectors and stevedores, like that of police officers, exposes them to the risk of death and serious injury. This is part of the hazard of the particular job: but it does not exonerate the employer from the need to take reasonable care towards his employees. Mr Hytner accepts that a police officer injured when deployed to prevent a riot or summoned to the scene of an accident cannot complain against his chief constable. But he can complain if his injury whether physical or psychiatric, is due to antecedent negligence by the chief constable. It is for this reason that the plaintiff succeeded in *Knightley v Johns* [1982] 1 All ER 851, [1982] 1 WLR 349 to which, he submits, Waller J had inadequate regard. Where the duty exists, its scope cannot artificially be restricted by excluding from it psychiatric injury (see *Dooley v Cammell Laird & Co Ltd* [1951] 1 Lloyd's Rep 271, *Mount Isa Mines Ltd v Pusey* (1970) 125 CLR 383 and *Page v Smith* [1995] 2 All ER 736 at 752–753, 760–761, [1996] AC 155 at 181, 190 per Lord Browne-Wilkinson and Lord Lloyd of Berwick). *Robertson v Forth Road Bridge Joint Board, Rough v Forth Road Bridge Joint Board* 1995 SLT 263, a decision of the Inner House of the Court of Session on 2 March 1995, where it was held that an employer did not owe a duty of care to an employee who suffered nervous shock when he saw a fellow employee with whom he had been working on a joint task blown off the bridge to his death, was wrongly decided.

As to the second ground, Mr Hytner submitted that a rescuer is in a primary relationship with the tortfeasor (see Judge Cardozo in *Wagner v International Rly Co* (1921) 232 NY 176 at 180: 'The wrong that imperils life is a wrong to the imperilled victim; it is a wrong also to the rescuer ... The risk of rescue, if only it be not wanton, is born of the occasion. The emergency begets the man. The wrongdoer may not have foreseen the coming of a deliverer. He is accountable as if he had'). In *Ogwo v Taylor* [1987] 3 All ER 961, [1988] AC 431 the House of Lords rejected, as having no place in English Law, the American 'fireman's rule' (see [1987] 3 All ER 961 at 966, [1988] AC 431 at 448–449 per Lord Bridge of

Harwich), approving the decision of Woolf J in *Salmon v Seafarer Restaurants Ltd*
[1983] 3 All ER 729 esp at 736, [1983] 1 WLR 1264 esp at 1272, where he said: '...
there seems no reason why a fireman should be at any disadvantage when the
question of compensation for his injuries arises'. Waller J was wrong to rely on
Caparo Industries plc v Dickman [1990] 1 All ER 568, [1990] 2 AC 605 to conclude
that it would not be just, fair and reasonable for a professional rescuer to have a
remedy. Such a question only arises when consideration is being given to the
creation of a new category of plaintiff to whom a duty is owed, whereas, in the
present case, rescuers are an existing category. The only difference between
professional and non-professional rescuers is that the former are more hardened
and therefore it may be more difficult to foresee psychiatric injury to them, but
this does not change the scope of the duty owed. A tortfeasor owes a duty to a
rescuer (see *Haynes v Harwood* [1935] 1 KB 146, [1934] All ER Rep 103, *Ward v T E
Hopkins & Son Ltd, Baker v T E Hopkins & Son Ltd* [1959] 3 All ER 225, [1959] 1
WLR 966 and *Chadwick v British Transport Commission* [1967] 2 All ER 945, [1967]
1 WLR 912). Although a rescuer injured indirectly can be called a secondary
victim, he is in a primary relationship with the tortfeasor if and in so far as the
categorisation of primary and secondary victims is relevant to rescuers (see *Alcock
v Chief Constable of the South Yorkshire Police* [1991] 4 All ER 907 at 913–914, 923,
[1992] 1 AC 310 at 396, 407 per Lord Keith of Kinkel and Lord Oliver of
Aylmerton and *Page v Smith* [1995] 2 All ER 736 at 758, 759–760, and 760–761,
[1996] AC 155 at 187, 189 and 190 per Lord Lloyd).

With regard to who is a rescuer, *Chadwick v British Transport Commission* (which
was approved by the House of Lords in *McLoughlin v O'Brian* [1982] 2 All ER 298
at 302, 316, [1983] 1 AC 410 at 419, 438 per Lord Wilberforce and Lord Bridge,
and in *Alcock's* case per Lord Oliver) shows that, when a horrific catastrophe
occurs, the length of time over which and the precise manner in which the rescue
occurs is immaterial. Someone is a rescuer who in Judge Cardozo's language
answers the call of danger and goes to give relief. As Lord Oliver said in *Alcock's*
case:

'It is well established that the defendant owes a duty of care not only to
those who are directly threatened or injured by his careless acts but also to
those who as a result are induced to go to their rescue and suffer injuries in
so doing. The fact that the injury suffered is psychiatric and is caused by the
impact on the mind becoming involved in personal danger or in scenes of
horror and destruction makes no difference.' (See [1991] 4 All ER 907 at 923,
[1992] 1 AC 310 at 408.)

The fact that the peril has passed does not prevent recovery by a rescuer (see
Ward v T E Hopkins & Son Ltd and the dissenting judgment of Evatt J in *Chester v
Waverley Corp* (1939) 62 CLR 1 approved by Lord Bridge in *McLoughlin's* case
[1982] 2 All ER 298 at 316–317, [1983] 1 AC 410 at 439). If, as Lord Bridge said in
Ogwo v Taylor, the professional rescuer is not to be at a disadvantage, there is no
reason why he should be unable to recover for psychiatric injury.

For the defendants, Mr Collender QC stressed the distinction between primary
and secondary victims drawn in *Page v Smith* particularly by Lord Lloyd: a
primary victim suffers injury by reason of being directly involved in an accident
caused by the defendant's negligence; a secondary victim suffers injury by reason
of observing or apprehending harm done to another person involved in an
accident caused by the defendant's negligence, but he is not personally
threatened. The judge was correct to classify the appellants as secondary victims.

For a primary victim, the test is whether the defendant can reasonably foresee that his conduct will expose the plaintiff to the risk of personal injury, whereas, for a secondary victim, before damages for nervous shock can be recovered, the secondary victim must show that: (i) he falls within the category of person whose claim should be recognised, (ii) proximity, (iii) that the injury complained of was shock induced, and (iv) that injury by nervous shock to a person of normal fortitude was foreseeable (see *McLoughlin v O'Brian* [1982] 2 All ER 298 esp at 301–302 and 304–305, [1983] 1 AC 410 esp at 418–419 and 422 per Lord Wilberforce, *Alcock v Chief Constable of the South Yorkshire Police* [1991] 4 All ER 907 at 919, 933, [1992] 1 AC 310 at 402, 419–420 per Lord Ackner and Lord Jauncey and *Page v Smith* [1995] 2 All ER 736 at 758, [1996] AC 155 at 187 per Lord Lloyd).

In the present case, none of the officers was personally threatened by the negligently caused events. Mr Collender conceded that a rescuer might be a primary or a secondary victim depending on the circumstances and that the plaintiff in *Ward v T E Hopkins & Son Ltd* was a primary victim because he was overcome, like the other victims, by fumes. When the rescuer is not exposed to danger, he cannot be a primary victim but is in the category of secondary victim, together with those who have a tie of love and affection to the primary victim and involuntary participants. These plaintiffs had no tie of love and affection. The judge was correct to conclude that none of them considered themselves to be the involuntary cause of the disaster and they could not be rescuers because they did not extricate anyone from a situation of danger: once the peril has passed there can be comfort and treatment but no rescue, because, per Judge Cardozo in *Wagner v International Rly Co* (1921) 232 NY 176 at 181, 'there must be unbroken continuity between the commission of the wrong and the effort to avert its consequences'.

He sought to distinguish *Chadwick v British Transport Commission* on the basis that there was there a wealth of peril to the primary victim. (But, for my part, that does not appear to be the basis on which that case was decided. The judge said ([1967] 2 All ER 945 at 949, [1967] 1 WLR 912 at 918): '… I think that I must deal with this case on the basis that it was the horror of the whole experience which caused his reaction'.) Mr Collender concedes that in *Wigg v British Railways Board* (1986) Times, 4 February there was no peril to the plaintiff. He submits that a restrictive interpretation of 'rescuer' should be adopted and that it is insufficient for a rescuer who is a secondary victim to show that he has suffered psychiatric damage unless he is proximate to the accident in time and space: 'immediate aftermath' has been narrowly construed (see *McLoughlin v O'Brian* [1982] 2 All ER 298 at 305, [1983] 1 AC 410 at 422 per Lord Wilberforce). Professional rescuers have a higher resistance to nervous shock than the ordinary person, so injury to them is not so readily foreseeable. The judge was right to conclude that none of the plaintiffs' injuries could be said to be 'shock induced'. The existence of a master and servant relationship should not change the plaintiff's status from that of secondary victim to primary victim, as this would be inconsistent with the essential purpose of this type of employment contract and would place police officers at an unfair and unjustifiable advantage over lay persons.

As to the submission on behalf of the plaintiffs that the master and servant relationship enables the plaintiffs to establish a neighbourhood duty, this, Mr Collender said, is fallacious, as that relationship is not determinative of, but is incidental to, the question of whether the master is liable to the servant for nervous shock. *Knightley v Johns* [1982] 1 All ER 851, [1982] 1 WLR 349 was a straightforward case of breach of duty of the master and servant relationship and injury to a primary victim. He relied on Lord Hope's analysis of the authorities in *Robertson v Forth Road Bridge Joint Board, Rough v Forth Road Bridge Joint Board* 1995 SLT 263. The public would find it repugnant if claims by spectators failed if they could not establish a necessary relationship with a primary victim or they were insufficiently proximate to events, yet police officers, by virtue of the fact of their employment, would be placed in a different position in which they could recover. In any event, the existence of a master and servant relationship does not conclude the question of liability for nervous shock (see *Caparo Industries plc v Dickman* [1990] 1 All ER 568 at 574 and 581–582, 585, [1990] 2 AC 605 at 618 and 628, 633 per Lord Bridge (novel categories of negligence should be developed incrementally and a duty of care to avoid causing injury does not necessarily give rise to a duty to avoid purely economic loss) and per Lord Roskill and Lord Oliver (to like effect)). *Dooley v Cammell Laird & Co Ltd* [1951] 1 Lloyd's Rep 271, *Galt v British Railways Board* (1983) 133 NLJ 870 and *Wigg v British Railways Board* were based not on the master and servant relationship but on the plaintiffs' involuntary participation (see *Alcock*'s case [1991] 4 All ER 907 at 923–924, 933, [1992] 1 AC 310 at 408, 420 per Lord Oliver and Lord Jauncey). *Mount Isa Mines Ltd v Pusey* (1970) 125 CLR 383 was a rescue case. In *Page v Smith* [1995] 2 All ER 736, [1996] AC 155 and *McFarlane v EE Caledonia Ltd* [1994] 2 All ER 1 the master and servant relationship was not mentioned as being of any significance. Mr Collender relied on *McFarlane*'s case, where Stuart-Smith LJ said (at 14):

'As a matter of principle and policy, the court should not extend the duty to those who are mere bystanders or witnesses of horrific events unless there is a sufficient degree of proximity which requires both nearness in time and place and a close relationship of love and affection between plaintiff and victim'.

The need for proximity in relation to rescue is emphasised by the judgment of Judge Cardozo in *Wagner*. The judge was therefore right to say that Inspector White's claim failed on proximity even though he was a rescuer. He was also right to conclude implicitly, albeit not expressly, that the post-traumatic stress disorder each plaintiff suffered was not caused by shock.

In his reply, Mr Hytner submitted that a rescuer is in a category where a duty situation is recognised without reference to the criteria adumbrated in the *Caparo Industries* case. In the case of a rescuer there is no need to prove a tie of affection, and proximity merely defines who is a rescuer. In law and common sense a person will not be a rescuer once the dust has settled or he is merely giving aid and comfort in a place remote from the tort. The requirement of participation in the event is no more than a requirement that the rescuer be there in the immediate aftermath. These officers were present for the purposes of crowd control which continued to be their duty and so they were participating in the event. Without conceding that a rescuer's psychiatric illness must be shock induced, in the present case the illness of all these plaintiffs was shock induced. Spectators who carried bodies to the gym and saw the horrors there were rescuers and as entitled to recover compensation as police officers. Lord Hope's concern in *Robertson v Forth Road Bridge Joint Board* 1995 SLT 263 about the flood gates is not in point in a rescue case: in any event it is only very rarely that disasters of such horror occur. He accepted that foreseeability of psychiatric injury must be proved. It is a factor, in that regard, that a plaintiff is a professional rescuer of more than ordinary phlegm but this is a factor which affects foreseeability, not the scope of the duty owed to a professional rescuer. Although the plaintiff Hallam is not pursuing an appeal, Mr Hytner invited us to deal with the position of those like Hallam who went to the gym mortuary, and to rule whether such persons were within the ambit of rescue.

For my part, I am greatly indebted to counsel for their submissions in an area of law which is by no means free from difficulty. In the light of those submissions and the authorities to which we have been referred, I reach the following conclusions as to the principles to be applied.

(i) Since *Bourhill v Young* [1942] 2 All ER 396, [1943] AC 92, it has been recognised that the ambit of persons affected by negligence may extend beyond those actually subject to physical impact, particularly to rescuers. There, indeed, may be no one injured in a particular case by actual impact; but still a wrong may be committed to anyone who suffers nervous shock or is injured in an act of rescue' (see [1942] 2 All ER 396 at 405, [1943] AC 92 at 108–109 per Lord Wright).

(ii) Rescuers are in a special category (see *McLoughlin v O'Brian* [1982] 2 All ER 298 at 302, [1983] 1 AC 410 at 419 per Lord Wilberforce and *Alcock v Chief Constable of the South Yorkshire Police* [1991] 4 All ER 907 at 923–924, 934, [1992] 1 AC 310 at 408, 420–421 per Lord Oliver and Lord Jauncey).

(iii) The correctness of *Chadwick v British Transport Commission* [1967] 2 All ER 945, [1967] 1 WLR 912 has never been doubted (see *McLoughlin v O'Brian* [1982] 2 All ER 298 at 316, [1983] 1 AC 410 at 438 per Lord Bridge).

(iv) The ratio of *Chadwick's* case was that the catastrophe was such as would not normally be seen and it was the horror of the whole experience which caused the plaintiff's injury by shock (see [1967] 2 All ER 945 at 948, 949, [1967] 1 WLR 912 at 916, 918).

(v) *McLoughlin, Page v Smith* and *McFarlane* were not rescue cases and *Alcock* was not argued on that basis in the House of Lords. The relevance of the rescue cases in *McLoughlin* was that they were relied on, by way of analogy, to extend the category of persons to whom a duty of care is owed in relation to psychiatric injury.

(vi) Lord Lloyd's categorisation of primary and secondary victims in *Page v Smith* did not expressly or by implication have the rescue cases in mind: indeed none of them was cited either in the speeches or in argument. In any event, the present plaintiffs, (apart from Janet Smith who was not at the ground until long after the event) being directly involved, in the course of their employment, in the consequences flowing from their employer's negligence, were primary victims.

(vii) In *Alcock's* case Lord Oliver placed the rescue cases in the first group of nervous shock cases where the plaintiff was involved as a participant, rather than in the second group where the plaintiff was no more than a passive and unwilling witness of injury caused to others (see [1991] 4 All ER 907 at 922–923, [1992] 1 AC 310 at 407–408).

(viii) In the light of (vi) and (vii), Lord Lloyd's requirement in *Page v Smith* for foreseeability of psychiatric injury as a crucial ingredient where the plaintiff is a secondary victim and his statement that foreseeability of injury by shock is not enough in the case of a secondary victim are not presently in point. But his observation that 'There is no justification for regarding physical and psychiatric injury as different "kinds" of injury' is a generally applicable statement of the current law (see [1995] 2 All ER 736 at 758, 759–760 and 761, [1996] AC 155 at 187, 189 and 190 and also *Alcock* [1991] 4 All ER 907 at 922–923, [1992] 1 AC 310 at 408 per Lord Oliver). The same comments apply in relation to the speech of Lord Browne-Wilkinson in *Page v Smith*.

(ix) If firemen should not be at any disadvantage in relation to compensation for injury (see *Ogwo v Taylor* [1987] 3 All ER 961 at 966, [1988] AC 431 at 448 per Lord Bridge) there is to my mind no reason why policemen should be at a disadvantage.

(x) Whether a particular plaintiff is a rescuer is, in each case, a question of fact to be decided in the light of all the circumstances of the case. Among the factors to be considered, although none is in itself decisive, are the following: the character and extent of the initial incident caused by the tortfeasor; whether that incident has finished or is continuing; whether there is any danger, continuing or otherwise, to the victim or to the plaintiff; the character of the plaintiff's conduct, in itself and in relation to the victim; and how proximate, in time and place, the plaintiff's conduct is to the incident.

(xi) The analysis by the House of Lords in *Page v Smith* was not before Waller J in the instant case, although the Court of Appeal's decision in that case, which the House of Lords overturned, was before him. Furthermore, the Inner House of the Court of Session in *Robertson v Forth Road Bridge Joint Board* did not have *Page v Smith* before them: the court recognised, however, that active participation in the event might well have lead to recovery (see 1995 SLT 263 at 269 per Lord Hope). For my part, I doubt whether the English courts would today reach the same decision as that reached by the Scottish court in *Robertson's* case. Once it is accepted that there is no justification for regarding physical and psychiatric injuries as different kinds of injury, when an employer negligently causes physical injury to one employee, it seems to me to be impossible to contend that he is not equally liable to a fellow employee of normal fortitude working on the same task who sustains psychiatric injury, whether through fear for himself or through witnessing what happens to his fellow workman. Lord Hope said (at 269):

'It is difficult to see why the bystander in the case of a road accident should be denied his claim when a bystander who happens to be an employee but has nothing whatsoever to do with causing the incident is allowed to recover damages for this type of injury.'

In my respectful view the answer is that, whereas in cases outwith the master and servant relationship the courts have found it necessary, in identifying those to whom a duty of care is owed, to draw a distinction between primary and secondary victims and to impose limiting criteria to determine those within the second category who can recover, in the master and servant context a duty of care exists by reason of that relationship. The standard of care required in the discharge of that duty and the degree of proximity will of course vary from case to case according, among other matters, to the nature of the job and the degree of fortitude to be expected of the employee. So, for example, a rescuer, whether a policeman or layman, may recover against a tortfeasor for physical or psychiatric injury sustained during a rescue. An employee may, depending on the circumstances, recover against his employer for physical or psychiatric injury caused in the course of his employment by the employer's negligence. A mere bystander, whether a policeman or layman, who is not a rescuer and to whom no duty such as that arising from the master and servant relationship is owed by the tortfeasor, will not generally recover (*McFarlane v EE Caledonia Ltd* [1994] 2 All ER 1) and will only be able to do so if he is linked by ties of love and affection to a primary victim and otherwise fulfils the criteria for secondary victims enunciated in *McLoughlin*, *Alcock* and *Page v Smith*.

(xii) In none of the cases before the House of Lords since *Ogwo v Taylor* was the plaintiff either a servant of the defendant or a rescuer and although in *McFarlane*'s case the plaintiff was a servant, he was off duty at the time and no claim was made on the basis that his employers owed him a duty of care. This is a crucial matter which explains why some of the present plaintiffs may succeed, whereas the plaintiffs in *Alcock*'s case failed. The distinction is not due to any preference being given by the courts to policemen over laymen. It exists because the court has long recognised a duty of care to guard employees and rescuers against all kinds of injury, whereas, in deciding whether any duty of care exists towards plaintiffs who are not employees, rescuers, or primary victims, the courts have, in recent years, imposed specific criteria in relation to claims for psychiatric injury.

In the light of these principles I turn now to the individual plaintiffs each of whom, it seems to me, can, at least prima facie, claim to have sustained shock-induced trauma. Janet Smith was not on duty at the ground. At 4.15 pm she reported to Northern General Hospital in Sheffield where she was asked to strip bodies and complete casualty forms in the mortuary at the hospital. She acted as liaison officer between the hospital staff and the casualty bureau. During the evening she labelled two or three bodies for the purposes of identification. Later she went to the gymnasium at Hillsborough with personal effects. Her greatest anxiety was dealing with relatives and seeing the photographs in the gymnasium which enabled relatives to identify bodies. It is conceded by Mr Hytner that she was not a rescuer. She was not at the ground when the negligent loss of control occurred and she was not therefore within the category of those officers to whom, being within the area of risk when the incident occurred, a duty of care was owed by virtue of the master and servant relationship. What she subsequently did was no more than could properly be asked of any police officer in the ordinary carrying out of her duties following a serious incident. In my judgment, she is not entitled to recover.

Those in the position of Det Con Hallam were in the gymnasium at the ground when the disaster occurred. He sought to revive an apparently dead boy and, as more casualties arrived there was mayhem, with fans, relatives and police in the gymnasium. The bodies of the dead were very unpleasant to look at. Relatives had to be informed. The difference between Hillsborough and other incidents was the large number of dead and the fact that the vast majority were young people. In my judgment such officers were not rescuers because they were not sufficiently closely involved in the crushing incident or its immediate aftermath. They were, however, at the ground in the course of duty, within the area of risk of physical or psychiatric injury and were thus exposed, by the first defendant's negligence, to excessively horrific events such as were likely to cause psychiatric illness even in a police officer. There was therefore a breach of duty to such persons.

Pc Glave was ordered at 3 pm from the gymnasium to the far end of the ground from pens 3 and 4. Bodies were brought to that end. He helped to move bodies and obtained first aid. He carried three bodies into the gymnasium. He was on duty until 1.30 am the next morning. He was affected by the enormity of the tragedy with so many young and the sight of so many grieving relatives. In my judgment he was not a rescuer because he was not involved in the incident at the pens' end of the ground or its immediate aftermath. But he was, being at the ground in the course of duty, within the area of risk of physical or psychiatric injury and was thus, by the first defendant's negligence, exposed to these exceptionally horrific events. There was a breach of duty to him by the first defendant.

Anthony Bevis was on patrol elsewhere and was summoned to the gymnasium from where he went on the pitch at the opposite end from pens 3 and 4. He approached to within 20 yards of the pens' fencing and came across people lying dead. Bodies were being carried away. He applied mouth to mouth and heart massage to a boy who was already dead. He tried to resuscitate another man but he was also dead. The crowd were shouting and screaming and he was frightened. He went to a quiet room in the tunnel and stayed there for some time. Later he returned and helped form a line of officers controlling the crowd. Ultimately, he helped to clear the pitch of fans. He did not go into the gymnasium. On his way back to the police station he had to deal with a fight in Hillsborough Park. The sheer number of dead and injured affected him and he suffered from guilt for the fact that he could not help the brother of the young man who had asked him to help. In my view, he was a rescuer taking part in the immediate aftermath of the incident. He is entitled to recover.

Mark Bairstow arrived at the ground sometime after the incident and saw bodies lying near gate C. He went into pens 3 and 4 from where he could see bodies lying on the pitch. As he came out, he checked that the bodies which he had passed earlier were dead. He tried to assist other officers to give a boy heart massage and helped to carry out bodies to protect them from interference. His main feeling was of anger towards his superiors and it was this coupled with his feeling of inadequacy which distinguished Hillsborough from other incidents. In my judgment, although he was not within the area of risk of physical or psychiatric injury when the incident occurred, so that no duty was owed to him as a servant, he was, like Bevis, a rescuer who attended in the immediate aftermath of this incident. He is entitled to recover.

Insp White was at the ground from 10 am as part of the team in charge of crowd control. He saw congestion by gate C and he and other officers pulled out people fearing for their safety. Thereafter he entered the ground and could see blue faces at the perimeter fencing. Two were obviously dead. He joined a line of police officers passing injured and dead from the pens. One was a fifteen year old boy whose airways he tried to keep open. He saw others being carried away on boards and cardiac massage being applied by firemen whom he helped. At 4.20 pm he mustered his men, many of whom were distressed, and he tried to comfort them. He went to the gymnasium and helped to try and identify victims. He remained on duty until 11 pm. The real difference between Hillsborough and other incidents was the failure of the police to control the fans so that huge numbers of deaths resulted. In my judgment, he was plainly a rescuer participating in the immediate aftermath of the incident and a duty was owed to him both in that capacity and as an employee within the area of risk, which would not be owed to a mere bystander. There was a breach of duty to him.

Accordingly, for the reasons given, a duty of care was owed by the first defendant to these plaintiffs apart from Sergeant Smith, whose appeal I would dismiss. I would allow the appeals of Glave, Bevis, Bairstow and White and, if this is necessary, remit the question of causation in each of these cases for determination by a trial judge.

I turn to the second appeal and pay tribute to the admirable succinctness with which Mr Phillips for the plaintiff and Mr Richard Maxwell QC for the defendant dealt with the matter, they having been present throughout the argument in the first appeal.

a   The plaintiff was a pit deputy at Rossington colliery. On 6 February 1990 one of the men for whom he was responsible was crushed to death between the blade of a Webster bucket and the drive guard on a conveyor. At the time, the plaintiff was at the other end of the face about 275 metres away. He was contacted by telephone and was told there had been an accident. He ran down the face and arrived within four minutes. The deceased had been freed from the place where

b   he was crushed. He was clad in vest and pants in which he had been working. There was no sign of any injury or blood. He had no pulse and made no noise. He was not a friend or a relation of the plaintiff. There were six other men present. The plaintiff had been trained in first aid and gave mouth to mouth resuscitation for a period of about two hours, others helping him when he grew tired. Subsequently the plaintiff developed a psychiatric illness which it was

c   agreed was a proper head of claim if suffered as a result of witnessing or being near to an accident. It was also admitted that the deceased's injury was caused by the defendants' negligence.

     It was contended that the plaintiff was a rescuer. But the judge held that it was not necessary to go so far because the plaintiff had a duty imposed on him by the

d   Coal Board to attend accidents of this nature. The judge concluded that the accident gave rise to a foreseeable risk of injury to the plaintiff but that he had to decide whether or not the plaintiff was unduly susceptible. He concluded that, although the plaintiff had had a fairly harrowing time, what he had seen was an inanimate body which was no more than might be encountered at a road accident or the like. He concluded that he could not say that a man of reasonable fortitude

e   would be affected by the circumstances in which the plaintiff found himself.

     Mr Phillips submitted that the plaintiff, as a rescuer, was a primary victim of the accident and he relied in particular on Lord Oliver's speech in *Alcock v Chief Constable of the South Yorkshire Police* [1991] 4 All ER 907 at 922–923, [1992] 1 AC 310 at 407–408. Accordingly, the question of 'ordinary phlegm', which has to be

f   considered in relation to psychiatric injuries sustained by a secondary victim, does not arise. Post-traumatic stress disorder can result from events which are not catastrophic, as for example in *Page v Smith* [1995] 2 All ER 736 at 758, [1996] AC 155 at 187. It was inappropriate for the judge to take it upon himself to consider whether the plaintiff was unduly susceptible. It had never been suggested by the defendants that he was, and the question would only arise if the

g   plaintiff was a secondary victim.

     Mr Maxwell submitted that, before the trial judge, the main issue was whether or not psychiatric injury was reasonably foreseeable, because the position at that time was governed by the Court of Appeal decision in *Page v Smith* [1994] 4 All ER 522. In the light of the House of Lords decision, it is necessary to decide whether

h   the plaintiff was a primary or secondary victim and labelling him a rescuer does not determine the issue because, according to circumstances, even a secondary victim may be entitled to recover. The real question is whether the plaintiff can establish a breach of duty towards himself. The case was not pleaded or put on the basis that there was any failure to provide the plaintiff with a safe system of work in relation to first aid training or otherwise and, as a rescuer, it would only

j   be open to him to recover if he were either in an area of physical risk, (which he was not because he did not participate in the accident as a potential primary victim and was in no personal danger) or if he were subjected to a scene of horror and destruction in the immediate aftermath. On the facts, this last route was not open to the plaintiff in the light of the judge's correct finding that psychiatric injury was not reasonably foreseeable to a person of ordinary fortitude.

In my judgment, the deputy judge was correct to conclude that the circumstances of this incident were very different from those in *Chadwick v British Transport Commission* [1967] 2 All ER 945, [1967] 1 WLR 912 and the King's Cross fire disaster, in that the plaintiff was not observing horrifying circumstances. He was also correct to conclude that this did not necessarily mean that the plaintiff was unable to recover. However he did not, in my judgment pose the right question, in asking whether a man of reasonable fortitude would have been affected by the circumstances in which the plaintiff found himself. The prior, fundamental question was whether there was any breach of duty to the plaintiff either as a rescuer or as an employee.

Mr Duncan was not, in my view, a rescuer. What he did was proximate in time to the trapping of the deceased, but he was not geographically proximate when that incident occurred. When he arrived at the scene, there was no danger to him or to the deceased. Furthermore, the first aid which he rendered was plainly within the normal scope of his employment and was not attended by any unusually distressing features. From these matters, it also follows that the circumstances cannot be said to have given rise to any breach of duty owed to the plaintiff by the defendants as employers: he was outside the area of risk of physical or psychiatric injury when the deceased was injured and he was not exposed to any unnecessary risk of injury when he attended the scene.

Accordingly, the question of whether or not he was of ordinary or undue susceptibility did not arise. In my judgment, the judge was right to conclude that the claim failed, but it did so because there was no breach of any duty owed to the plaintiff. Had he been working with the deceased and seen the accident, the result may have been different.

I would dismiss this second appeal.

HENRY LJ. These are claims by police officers for damages for personal injury (psychiatric damage) brought against, inter alia, their chief constable for negligence (including the negligence of senior police officers in crowd control) which caused 96 spectators to be crushed to death (and about 730 injured) in horrific circumstances at Hillsborough Stadium on the occasion of the semi-final of the FA Cup, 1989.

The medical evidence

All those officers were on duty at the ground at the time, and, in the words of Professor Sims' medical report for the plaintiffs (which is accepted for purposes of deciding the legal questions we must consider)—

'were all amongst those who were intimately involved with one or more aspects of the disaster itself, and were therefore exposed to the psychological trauma of that occasion to a varying but significant extent.'

Professor Sims saw 70 police officers in all. The psychiatric damage caused was post-traumatic stress disorder and depressive illness. Post-traumatic stress disorder affected 60 of those seen. Those seen had previously been psychiatrically well, had no previous history of psychiatric illness, and no psychiatric treatment. In short, they were police officers who had coped with the exposure to death and injury that is an inevitable part of the normal police officer's working life.

That so many were affected reflects the nature of events sufficiently potent in their horror to cause post-traumatic stress disorder. Mullany and Handford *Tort Liability for Psychiatric Damage* (1st edn, 1993) p 35 informs me:

'The American literature currently defines [post-traumatic stress disorder] as requiring exposure to a psychologically distressing external event that is outside the range of usual human experience (so common experiences such as simple bereavement, serious illness, business or financial losses and marital conflict will not suffice) ... Stressors capable of producing the condition include military combat, natural disasters, intentionally caused disasters (such as confinement in concentration camps, subjection to torture or presence at bombing sites), and the situation with which we are concerned, accidental disasters.'

A footnote adds:

'After a devastating disaster it is not uncommon for as many as 50–80% of the survivors to develop [post-traumatic stress disorder]'.

(I am also indebted to the authors of that work for their comprehensive review and analysis of the authorities in several jurisdictions.)

I go to the detail of Professor Sims' report to identify the nature of the trauma, and the psychological pressure which contributed to the injuries cause by it. Professor Sims makes clear (p 5) that the trauma here is not instantaneous horror but rather prolonged exposure to horrifying and uncontrollable circumstances. He says (pp 37–38):

'It is important to consider the nature of psychological stress in this group of individuals. In fiction, and perhaps in a layman's view of shock as a psychological event, the individual experiences a grossly untoward event or situation with one or more sensory modalities but almost always vision, and is instantaneously "shocked" or traumatised. In practice this almost never occurs and it is in the nature of psychological trauma that exposure for several hours results in much more severe long-term symptoms than the instantaneous exposure to shock and then the removal of the aversive stimulus. This is different from the nature of psychological trauma caused by being put in an unsatisfactory situation or environment over months or years. Most of the subjects of this study were either exposed to severe psychological stress for about 2–4 hours (those near the fence) or for more than 6 hours (those in the emergency mortuary). In general, the longer the exposure to the traumatic situation, the greater was the degree of psychological distress subsequently.'

He went on to identify the recurring themes in the police officers accounts of what happened that day and its psychological impact on them.

I. Few officers could take useful urgent action, they had to be inactive and ineffective. Even those active were conscious of futility and helplessness, eg attempted mouth-to-mouth resuscitation of those already dead where it was difficult to tell the dead from the living. Taylor LJ in his Interim Report summarised the position thus (Cm 765, p 41, para 253):

'Despite the initial lack of leadership, many officers did all they humanly could to rescue and revive the victims. Many supporters who gave evidence paid tribute to these efforts. It is also fair to say that the number of officers who could at first be usefully involved at the two open gates was necessarily limited.' (and see, too, para 279).

II. The sheer number of deaths, the youth of the victims, the distress of relatives and friends, and the recognition of the senselessness of it all.

III. The hostility and abuse from the crowd they were controlling, with incidents of looting, spitting at police, throwing coins at them, all resulting in feelings of fear, isolation and failure. Indeed Taylor LJ concluded that the abuse and assaults by fans on ambulance and firemen in the course of their rescue work was probably because they were mistaken for police.

IV. The trauma of dealing with the dead bodies (and sitting with 'your' body pending identification) in the gymnasium and later the police mortuary—the number of victims resulting in cramped conditions and loss of dignity for the dead: 'You could not get to the other without sliding the top ones over' and dealing with the bodies: 'I tried to get the feet end, you don't remember feet'.

The theme was that this tragedy was something quite unique, outside normal police experience—the chaos, the helplessness, the guilt at not individually being able to achieve more, the shame that police crowd control decisions had caused or contributed to the disaster, and above all the time scale.

The effects of this psychological stress on the individuals concerned affected their whole lives: their jobs, their marriages, their family relationships, their social life.

The first conclusion that I draw from Professor Sims' report is that this tragedy was plainly a post-traumatic stress disorder stressor, namely a psychologically distressing external event quite outside the range of normal human or police experience, capable of causing 'marked or pervasive distress to almost anyone' (see the Law Commission's *Liability for Psychiatric Illnesses* (Consultation Paper no 137, para 3.5).

Second, that the length of the exposure and the circumstances of the exposure was the trauma that caused the psychiatric illnesses, rather than any sudden and immediate 'shock'. In so far as this conclusion may seem in conflict—and myself, I do not think that it is—with Lord Ackner's dicta (quoted by the trial judge) in *Alcock's* case that '"shock", in the context of this cause of action involves the sudden appreciation ... of a horrifying event', this is simply an example of what Lord Ackner referred to as an expansion of 'the liability for shock-induced psychiatric illness ... due to a better understanding of mental illness and its relationship to shock' (see [1991] 4 All ER 907 at 918, 916, [1992] 1 AC 310 at 401, 399). To make the meaning clear, I would have preferred to use the word 'trauma' for 'shock' as Professor Sims suggests. But what matters is not the label on the trigger for psychiatric damage, but the fact and foreseeability of psychiatric damage, by whatever process. Windeyer J in the High Court of Australia commented that in psychiatric damage cases, the law marches with medicine, but 'in the rear and limping a little' (see *Mount Isa Mines Ltd v Pusey* (1970) 125 CLR 383 at 395). Clearly the law should accept post-traumatic stress disorder rather than exclude it whether it is caused by sudden shock (properly defined) or not.

In those circumstances, it seems to me that the risk of psychiatric damage to police officers on duty at the ground as a result of negligent crowd control was plainly foreseeable. Those responsible for crowd control at sporting events (and particularly football) must be only too conscious (from examples here and overseas) of the scale of the disaster that negligence in crowd control and over-crowding can bring. And chief constables equally will be aware of the risks of post-traumatic stress disorder and psychiatric damage generally where police officers are exposed to such potent stressors. It is significant that the South Yorkshire Police standing order related to post-traumatic stress disorder, in saying 'that it is difficult to predict just how any particular officer will react to an extreme incident', made it clear that it did not affect just the already vulnerable or those who lack the 'customary phlegm' (the law significantly falling back on the language of ancient physiology). The numbers affected strongly suggest that ordinary police robustness is not protection against an experience such as this (a conclusion that would not surprise the doctors).

But foreseeability alone is not enough—to establish liability the plaintiffs must satisfy the proximity or neighbourhood principle expressed by Lord Atkin in *Donoghue v Stevenson* [1932] AC 562 at 580, [1932] All ER Rep 1 at 11.

I consider that question next.

Proximity and primary and secondary victims

The law on this issue has been jointly developed here and in Australia in a sequence of cases involving mothers claiming damages for psychiatric injury foreseeably caused to them by the emotional trauma of hearing and seeing the aftermath of the death or injury of loved ones (despite the fact that they were not present at the accident). In those cases it was unsuccessfully argued that once foreseeability of damage was established, the tort was complete. That submission reflected the reality of the position in the ordinary case of physical injury suffered in a road traffic accident or at work. Once it was held that the defendant/employer ought reasonably to have foreseen physical injury to the plaintiff, 'reasonable foreseeability of the risk is ... the only test that need be applied to determine liability' (see *Alcock v Chief Constable of the South Yorkshire Police* [1991] 4 All ER 907 at 913, 933, [1992] 1 AC 310 at 396, 419 per Lord Keith and also Lord Jauncey).

However, when the plaintiff was outside the area of risk of physical damage and suffered psychiatric damage, foreseeability of that damage was not enough. In *McLoughlin v O'Brian* [1982] 2 All ER 298, [1983] 1 AC 410, a plaintiff wife was told of a road accident to her husband and children and went to the hospital. There she learned that her youngest daughter had been killed, saw her husband and other children, and witnessed the nature and extent of their injuries. As a result of this she suffered psychiatric illness. The Court of Appeal refused her claim. The submission that reasonable foreseeability of that risk was the only test for negligence was rejected in the House of Lords, but despite that, the appeal was allowed. Lord Wilberforce quoted Lord Atkin's 'neighbour' principle in *Donoghue v Stevenson* [1932] AC 562 at 580, [1932] All ER Rep 1 at 11 and added:

> '... foreseeability must be accompanied and limited by the law's judgment as to persons who ought, according to its standards of value or justice, to have been in contemplation. Foreseeability, which involves a hypothetical person, looking with hindsight at an event which has occurred, is a formula adopted by English law not merely for defining, but also for limiting the persons to whom duty may be owed and the consequences for which an actor may be held responsible ... When it is said to result in a duty of care being owed to a person or class, the statement that there is a "duty of care" denotes a conclusion into the forming of which considerations of policy have entered. That foreseeability does not of itself, and automatically, lead to a

duty of care is I think clear.' (See [1982] 2 All ER 298 at 303, [1983] 1 AC 410 at 420.)

Then, having considered the policy argument (which I will consider later), their Lordships found for the plaintiff. They accepted that rescuers could recover (see [1982] 2 All ER 298 at 302, 316, [1983] 1 AC 410 at 419, 438 per Lord Wilberforce and Lord Bridge).

McLoughlin was applied two years later by the High Court of Australia in *Jaensch v Coffey* (1984) 155 CLR 549. The passage already quoted from Lord Wilberforce's speech was applied, but both Gibbs CJ (at 555) and Deane J (at 581) having made the point that foreseeability did not of itself and automatically lead to a duty of care, set out a limited exception to that rule:

'It is inevitable that, in cases falling within some closely settled areas of the law of negligence such as cases involving ordinary physical injury to an employee in an accident at his place of work or to one user of a public road involved in a collision with another, it will have been established in previous cases that the relationship between the parties necessarily possesses the requisite degree of proximity.'

These two categories of plaintiffs in relation to whom proximity was for all practical purposes presumed are to be added to the category of rescuers, which had already been recognised in *McLoughlin v O'Brian*. We are here concerned with the employer/employee category (which the Americans call the 'direct victim'). I recognise that police officers are not formally employees of the chief constable, but in relation to the duty owed by him to them, nothing here turns on that. The authority given for that by Deane J was *Mount Isa Mines Ltd v Pusey* (1970) 125 CLR 383. There the plaintiff went to the aid of two fellow employees, who had been severely burnt as a result the employers' negligence. In that case Windeyer J said (at 404):

'But in the present case the duty of care is not based simply on duty to a neighbour. It includes that, but arises independently from the legal relationship between the plaintiff and the defendant. It is the duty of care which a master has for the safety of his servant. Foreseeable harm caused by a master to the mind of his servant is just as much a breach of duty of care for him as harm to his body would be.'

Of this case, Deane J said ((1984) 155 CLR 549 at 597):

'While the case may, on proper analysis, lend support for a general proposition that an employer is liable for damages in respect of nervous shock sustained by an employee at his place of employment in circumstances where the employer has failed to take reasonable steps to avoid a reasonably foreseeable risk of injury in that form, *Pusey* is not authority for any such unqualified proposition in a case where the proximity involved in the relationship of employer and employee is not to be found.'

He went on (at 610) to make the point that where proximity was not provided by the master and servant relationship, then 'mere uninvolved observation' of injury to a person who was not a close relative would not found a duty unless the plaintiff was 'actively and foreseeably involved in an accident or its aftermath in a role such as that as a rescuer'.

That was the state of the authorities at the time of *Alcock v Chief Constable of the South Yorkshire Police* [1991] 4 All ER 907, [1992] 1 AC 310. This was a claim arising out the Hillsborough Stadium disaster, brought by friends and relations of spectators involved in the disaster, for the psychiatric damage they had suffered.

Their claims failed. Some failed because their relationship to the victim was not one of the established relationships which (because of their closeness) gave rise to a presumed duty, but was a remoter relationship *and* had not been proved to be sufficiently close in fact. Others failed because they had not established the requisite proximity—they were not directly involved as actors in the events, and they were not sufficiently close to the events. What they saw at the ground or on television did not depict recognisable individuals and so did not amount to sight or hearing of the event, and their mortuary visits were too late to be part of the immediate aftermath. As secondary victims, they failed the neighbour test.

That case, therefore, confirmed that foreseeability of psychiatric harm to the plaintiff was not enough where proximity was a requisite, and it set out to answer when that was. The case did so by distinguishing between a participant in the events who was a primary victim, and someone not directly involved as an actor, someone who was a witness, a spectator or bystander, unconnected with the event who was a secondary victim, and so subject to the strict policy criteria that resulted in the claims in *Alcock* failing. The matter is most fully dealt with in Lord Oliver's speech, but is echoed in the other speeches. He said ([1991] 4 All ER 907 at 922–923, [1992] 1 AC 310 at 406–407):

> 'There is, to begin with, nothing unusual or peculiar in the recognition by the law that compensatable injury may be caused just as much by a direct assault upon the mind or the nervous system as by direct physical contact with the body ... Cases in which damages are claimed for directly inflicted injuries of this nature may present greater difficulties of proof but they are not, in their essential elements, any different from cases where the damages claimed arise from direct physical injury and they present no very difficult problems of analysis where the plaintiff has himself been directly involved in the accident from which the injury is said to arise. In such a case he can properly be said to be the primary victim of the defendant's negligence and the fact that the injury which he sustains is inflicted through the medium of an assault on the nerves or senses does not serve to differentiate the case, except possibly in the degree of evidentiary difficulty, from a case of direct physical injury. It is customary to classify cases in which damages are claimed for injury occasioned this way under a single generic label as cases of "liability for nervous shock". This may be convenient, but in fact the label is misleading if and to the extent that it is assumed to lead to a conclusion that they have more in common than the factual similarity of the medium through which the injury is sustained—that of an assault upon the nervous system of the plaintiff through witnessing or taking part in an event—and that they will, on account of this factor, provide a single common test for the circumstances which give rise to a duty of care. Broadly they divide into two classes, that is to say, those cases in which the injured plaintiff was involved either mediately or immediately as a participant, and those in which the plaintiff was no more than a passive and unwilling witness of injury caused to others. In the context of the instant appeals, the cases of the former type are not particularly helpful, except to the extent that they yield a number of

illuminating dicta, for they illustrate a directness of relationship (and thus a
duty) which is almost self-evident from a mere recital of the facts.'

He then proceeded to define categories where the plaintiff who had suffered
psychiatric harm was the primary victim: (a) where the plaintiff was naturally and
obviously put in fear for her own safety (see *Dulieu v White & Sons* [1901] 2 KB
669, [1900–3] All ER Rep 353); (b) where the plaintiff was a rescuer and the act of
rescue was the child of the danger caused by the defendant's negligence (see
Chadwick v British Transport Commission [1967] 2 All ER 945, [1967] 1 WLR 912);
and (c) master and servant cases, where the employer's negligence for imperilling
a fellow workmate makes him an unwilling participant in the event, causing him
nervous shock, thus in *Dooley v Cammell Laird & Co Ltd* [1951] 1 Lloyd's Rep 271,
where a crane's load dropped because of a defective sling close to a hold where
the driver's fellow workmate was working. He sustained nervous shock, and
successfully sued his employer. Foreseeability was treated to be the issue:

> 'If the driver of the crane concerned fears that the load may have fallen
> upon some of his fellow workmen, and that fear is not baseless or
> extravagant, then it is, I think, a consequence reasonably to have been
> foreseen that he may himself suffer a nervous shock.'

The same principle is exemplified by two other cases mentioned by Lord Oliver,
Galt v British Railways Board (1983) 133 NLJ 870 and *Wigg v British Railways Board*
(1986) Times, 4 February. In the former case, a train driver suffered a heart attack
as a result of coming round a bend at speed and finding, through the defendant's
negligence, two railway workers on the track. The headnote reads: 'The
defendants owed him a duty to take reasonable care not to expose him to injury
from nervous shock.' In the latter case, a passenger was killed as a result of the
guard's negligence in not seeing that all doors were shut. The driver descended
from his cab, found the victim, and suffered nervous shock as a consequence.

It initially seemed to me clear that, on Lord Oliver's test, the police officers on
crowd control duty at Hillsborough were participants, and so primary victims.
This conclusion required reassessment in the light of *Page v Smith* [1995] 2 All ER
736 at 758, [1996] AC 155. But that authority (which I will consider later) does not
in the last analysis alter my initial view.

I regarded them as participants for the following reasons. They were on duty
under their service contracts. They were directly involved in the consequences
flowing from their employer's negligent actions in crowd control. They were on
duty at the ground close to the centre of the horror, dealing with the dead and the
injured and the fans, whether distressed or abusive. They had no choice but to
be there and be involved. It was that involvement which led to the frustrations
at being ineffective and helpless, to the guilt and the shame at the fact that
negligent police decisions had caused or contributed to the accident, to the
hostility and abuse they suffered, to the long hours of exposure, to horrors from
which any mere spectator could simply have averted his eyes. An off-duty
policeman at the match could, if his conscience permitted, have taken no part in
the events whatever, and gone home with the crowd (the match was abandoned
at 4.10 pm). No such course was open to those on duty. And on the medical
evidence, the longer the exposure, the greater the risk of psychiatric damage. To
put the other side of the coin, their employer's duty of care was owed to them
because they were not 'passive and unwilling witnesses of injury caused to
others', nor persons 'not directly involved as an actor' nor 'persons unconnected

with the event precipitated by [the] defendant's negligence' (see [1991] 4 All ER
907 at 923, 924 and 925, [1992] 1 AC 310 at 407, 408 and 410).

So at first reading, I would have been disposed to find that the police on duty
were primary victims because they were participants in the 'accident'—by which
I mean the incidents caused by their employer's negligence, *and* because they
were direct victims as their employer owed them a duty of care to protect them
from personal injury (psychiatric damage) cause by his negligence.

But a close reading of *Page v Smith* [1995] 2 All ER 736, [1996] AC 155 suggests
a narrower definition of primary victim. That was a road accident, caused by the
defendant's negligence. It was a collision of 'moderate severity' between two
cars. The plaintiff was physically uninjured, but the accident triggered a
recurrence of a post-viral fatigue syndrome, 'ME'. The court there held that
where there was a duty of care to avoid causing personal injury, then it mattered
not whether the injury sustained was physical or psychiatric or both. The plaintiff
was 'in' the accident, therefore a duty of care to avoid personal injury (physical
damage) was owed to him. So it mattered not whether the defendant should
have foreseen injury by psychiatric damage. But it is clear from Lord Lloyd's
judgment that where the plaintiff who has suffered psychiatric damage is not
within the area of likely physical impact (or zone of danger), then he must prove
that psychiatric damage was foreseeable:

> 'Foreseeability of psychiatric damage remains a crucial ingredient when
> the plaintiff is the secondary victim, for the very reason that the secondary
> victim is almost always outside the area of physical impact, and therefore
> outside the range of foreseeable physical injury.' (See [1995] 2 All ER 736 at
> 758, [1996] AC 155 at 187.)

That passage also makes it clear that, when dealing with road accidents at any
rate, the 'primary victim', in the sense there used, must be within the area of
physical impact. Waller J found that none of the police officers he was concerned
with were 'direct victims' of the crushing or had 'a reasonable fear of immediate
physical injury for themselves'. We know that the defendants had admitted
liability in relation to the 14 plaintiffs who entered the pens to remove fans who
were being crushed, though we do not know the basis for it: whether they were
regarded as rescuers, or whether as being within the area of physical impact. So
the remaining plaintiffs are secondary victims unless their employer's duty of care
not to cause them injury (whether physical or psychiatric) renders them primary
victims.

I am not sure that the labelling of each plaintiff as a primary or secondary
victim really matters, for two reasons. First, *McLoughlin v O'Brian* [1982] 2 All ER
298, [1983] 1 AC 410 makes clear that the relevance of that distinction lies only in
whether the proximity or neighbourhood test is (for practical purposes)
presumed to be satisfied or must be critically examined. Second, the employer/
employee cases show that even in such cases proximity may be a necessary test
and so should be so examined.

To demonstrate the second point, I have been dealing so far with police officers
who were on duty at the ground throughout, and involved with the dead and
dying, with the injured, and with the public. If they had not been there, or were
not on duty or so involved, then they would be unable to satisfy the neighbour
test. An obvious example is *McFarlane v EE Caledonia Ltd* [1994] 2 All ER 1. This
case involved the Piper Alpha disaster. That oil rig was owned and operated by
the defendants. They employed the plaintiff as a painter. At the time of the first

of a series of massive explosions on the rig, the plaintiff was off duty lying on his
bunk on a support vessel 550 metres away. That vessel had a second function as
a fire-fighting rescue vessel. In that role it steamed closer to the rig, and because
of the emergency it did not have time to evacuate non-essential personnel such
as the plaintiff. The closest the vessel got to the rig was some 50 metres. The
plaintiff was on deck watching. His only role as a potential 'rescuer' was to put
some blankets in a space cleared for potential use as a hospital. He suffered
psychiatric harm, and claimed damages first on the basis that he was in the actual
area of danger, second on the basis that he thought he was, and third on the basis
that he was a rescuer. No claim was made on the basis that his employers owed
him a duty of care, perhaps because the weakness of that claim. It was held by
the Court of Appeal that it was not foreseeable that non-essential personnel
would suffer injury. For instance, there was nothing to have stopped him seeking
refuge in the hangar, from where he could have seen nothing. Nor could it have
been reasonably foreseen that his very limited activities as a rescuer could have
exposed him to the risk of psychiatric damage. In the judgment of the court
Stuart-Smith LJ said (at 14):

> 'In my judgment both as a matter of principle and policy the court should
> not extend the duty to those are mere bystanders or witnesses of horrific
> events unless there is a sufficient degree of proximity, which requires both
> nearness in time and place and close relationship of love and affection
> between the plaintiff and the victim.'

I entirely agree with that conclusion. The fact that the plaintiff was employed by
the defendant, though remotely incidental to his presence as a bystander, was
irrelevant to any claim to being a participant. He was rightly treated as a
bystander.

A case closer to the line is *Robertson v Forth Road Bridge Joint Board, Rough v Forth
Road Bridge Joint Board* 1995 SLT 263, a decision of the Inner House of the Court
of Session. Three workmates had been working on the Forth Bridge. A gale was
blowing. They found a large thin piece of metal on the carriageway, which was
picked up and put on the open platform of a pick-up truck. Mr Smith sat on the
metal sheet, Mr Robertson drove the truck, and Mr Rough was driving a
following vehicle 'a few feet behind'. A sudden and violent gust of wind blew
both the sheet and Mr Smith off the back of the van and over the side of the
bridge. He was killed by the force of the impact, although he only fell a few feet
onto a girder. It was accepted that the defendants owed a duty to all three men
to take reasonable care for their safety, and were in breach of that duty to the
deceased. But they failed the proximity test, the Inner House finding: (i) they did
not have sufficiently close emotional ties to the deceased; (ii) they were not
rescuers; (iii) they were not in fear of their own lives; (iv) the employer/employee
cases (such as *Dooley, Galt, Wigg*), when properly understood, were limited to
cases where the plaintiff may have either caused the death or injury, or believed
that he was about to or had done so; and (v) on the facts they were not active
'participants' and so were legally indistinguishable from the category of
bystanders, not directly involved. Clearly the accident was over in a second, with
no chance for participation.

Lord Hope said (at 269):

> 'I conclude that where the employees are merely bystanders or witnesses,
> as the pursuers were in this case, the ordinary rule must apply. They must

a be assumed to be possessed of sufficient fortitude to enable them to endure the shock caused by witnessing accidents to their fellow employees. Unless they can bring themselves within one of the other recognised categories, their claim for damages for this kind of illness must be refused.'

I can understand the factual finding that those men were not 'active participants'—this accident was caused by a sudden gust of wind. Findings (i), (ii)
b and (iii) are obviously right. As a matter of analysis, (iv) is right, but Lord Hope correctly left the door open for 'active participants' (at 269):

'It is difficult to see why the bystander in the case of a road accident should be denied his claim, when a bystander who happens to be an employee but has had nothing whatever to do with the causing of the incident is allowed
c to recover damages for this type of injury. There appears to be no logical stopping point once the bystander type of case is admitted in the case of employees. On the other hand cases of active participation in the event form a distinct category, for the reasons already mentioned by Lord Oliver.'

d It seems to me likely that Lord Hope would have accepted that an employee 'active participant' was a primary victim just as a rescuer is. Both a rescuer and employee plaintiffs in Lord Hope's category (iv) may be outside the area of physical danger, certainly in the aftermath of an accident, yet still be vulnerable to post-traumatic stress disorder.

Whatever the language used in simple accident cases, it seems to be me that in
e circumstances such as this, all active participants in the events causing the psychiatric damage should be regarded as primary victims when the defendant is in breach of a pre-existing duty of care to them. Mullany and Handford *Tort Liability for Psychiatric Damage* (1st edn, 1993) p 13 inform me that the Californian Supreme Court has held that the limitations on bystander recovery (described by an American commentator as 'nearness, hearness and dearness') '... apply only to
f "bystander" cases, and not to "direct victim" situations, that is, cases where the plaintiff who suffers psychiatric injury is owed some pre-existing duty of care' (see *Burgess v Superior Court* (1992) 831 P 2d 1197, where a mother succeeded in an action for negligence for her 'emotional distress' for injuries caused to her child in childbirth).

g But however that may be, in my judgment those police officers who come within Lord Oliver's participants test satisfy the requirements of proximity (making them primary victims in his eyes), and, if it is wrong so to regard them, also satisfy Lord Lloyd's propositions restricting recovery by secondary victims in cases such as this:

h '(1) In cases involving nervous shock, it is essential to distinguish between the primary victim and secondary victims. (2) In claims by secondary victims the law insists on certain control mechanisms, in order as a matter of policy to limit the number of potential claimants. Thus, the defendant will not be liable unless psychiatric injury is foreseeable in a person of normal fortitude. These control mechanisms have no place where the victim is the
j primary victim. (3) In claims by secondary victims, it may be legitimate to use hindsight in order to be able to apply the test of reasonable foreseeability at all. Hindsight, however, has no part to play where the plaintiff is the primary victim. (4) Subject to the above qualifications, the approach in all cases should be the same, namely, whether the defendant can reasonably foresee that his conduct will expose the plaintiff to the risk of personal injury,

whether physical or psychiatric. If the answer is yes, then the duty of care is established, even though physical injury does not in fact occur. There is no justification for regarding physical and psychiatric injury as different "kinds of damage". (5) A defendant who is under a duty of care to the plaintiff, whether as primary or secondary victim, is not liable for damages for nervous shock unless the shock results in some recognised psychiatric illness. It is no answer that the plaintiff was predisposed to psychiatric illness. Nor is it relevant that the illness takes a rare form or is of unusual severity. The defendant must take his victim as he finds him.' (See *Page v Smith* [1995] 2 All ER 736 at 767–768, [1996] AC 155 at 197.)

To make this good, I deal with Lord Atkin's neighbourhood test first. He said:

> 'The liability for negligence … is no doubt based upon a general public sentiment of moral wrongdoing for which the offender must pay. But acts or omissions which any moral code would censure cannot in a practical world be treated so as to give a right to every person injured by them to demand relief. In this way rules of law arise which limit the range of complainants and the extent of their remedy. The rule that you are to love your neighbour becomes in law, you must not injure your neighbour; and the lawyer's question, "Who is my neighbour?" receives a restricted reply. You must take reasonable care to avoid acts or omissions which you can reasonably foresee would be likely to injure your neighbour. Who, then, in law is my neighbour? The answer seems to be—persons who are so closely and directly affected by my act that I ought reasonably to have them in contemplation as being so affected when I am directing my mind to the acts or omissions which are called in question.' (See *Donoghue v Stevenson* [1932] AC 562 at 580, [1932] All ER Rep 1 at 11.)

I have already set out Lord Wilberforce's commentary on this passage in *McLoughlin v O'Brian* [1982] 2 All ER 298 at 303, [1983] 1 AC 410 at 420.

In applying those passages the first point to make is that the policy question of proximity is very different when viewed from the standpoint of a 'direct victim' than from the standpoint of the traumatised relative where the focus is on the closeness of the relationship. In the latter case it is only after being satisfied as to the closeness of the plaintiff's relationship with the deceased, that one looks to see whether the tortfeasor should have had the plaintiff in contemplation (see Professor Goodhart's remarks about the 'unimaginative taxi-cab driver' in his commentary on *King v Phillips* [1953] 1 All ER 617, [1953] 1 QB 429 quoted by Lord Lloyd in *Page v Smith* [1995] 2 All ER 736 at 767–768, [1996] AC 155 at 192). Here, it seems to me obvious that the chief constable must have had police officers on crowd control duty in mind, and must have contemplated them as being directly affected. It is well known that negligent crowd control at football matches can produce catastrophic results, and self-evident that the police on duty would be bound to be there before, during and for some hours after the horror, and that both the American and international classifications for post-traumatic stress disorder make the point that events properly classified as such stressors can cause 'marked or pervasive distress to almost anyone' (see the Law Commission's *Liability for Psychiatric Illnesses* (Consultation Paper No 137, para 3.5)).

a So in my judgment, the literal part of the test is plainly satisfied. I come then to the policy parts, as identified by Lord Wilberforce in *McLoughlin v O'Brian* [1982] 2 All ER 298 at 303–304, [1983] 1 AC 410 at 421.

Lord Wilberforce identified four heads of policy argument. First, that any extension of the law might lead to a proliferation of claims, including possibly fraudulent claims. Second, any extension might be unfair to defendants, facing *b* them with numerically disproportionate claims. Third, to extend liability beyond direct and plain cases would increase evidentiary difficulties and lengthen cases. Fourth, any extension might be thought to be a matter for the legislature.

The first three of these are all 'floodgate' arguments. First, as to numbers, each plaintiff must establish the duty owed to him, that psychiatric injury to him was foreseeable, and that he was a participant doing his duty, and should not be *c* equated with a mere bystander. For instance, I do not imagine that police officers in the calm of the control room, watching TV monitors, would recover.

Second, that disasters capable of being post-traumatic stress disorder stressors against which 'customary phlegm' is not necessarily protective are rare, but when they happen do not spare the robust.

d Third, to the objection as to fraudulent claims, claims involving the identification of and compensation for psychiatric damage are today relatively commonplace in road traffic and workplace accidents. The risk of fraudulent claims succeeding is greatly reduced by objective psychological tests (see Law Commission, Consultation Paper No 137, para 4.8). Overall, I would put such risks as being no greater than in, say, cases involving back injuries where there is *e* often a wide gap between observable symptoms and complaints—yet the courts manage satisfactorily, or so I believe. It would in any event be curious to deny the majority of genuine claims for fear that a fraudulent claim might slip through the net. Fourth, if legislation is not contemplated, the common law can and should proceed in its traditional, cautious way: here the 'traditional *f* characterisation of the ... [employer/employee] situation' satisfies Lord Bridge's broad proximity label in *Caparo Industries plc v Dickman* [1990] 1 All ER 568 at 573–574, [1990] 2 AC 605 at 617–618, and thus satisfies Lord Lloyd's second and fourth proposition in *Page v Smith* [1995] 2 All ER 736 at 767–768, [1996] AC 155 at 197: where the defendant can reasonably foresee that his conduct will expose the plaintiff to psychiatric injury and the proximity control mechanisms are satisfied, *g* then the plaintiff should recover.

Waller J raised, but based no finding on, a different public policy objection. First, in an apparent misconception of the appellants' case he said:

> 'It is part of the police officer's duty to deal with situations which might *h* cause psychiatric injury to ordinary people and which it is known in fact do, on occasions, cause psychiatric injury to police officers. It is thus clear that it cannot be said simply in the case of a police officer that there is a duty not to expose that officer to the risk of psychiatric injury.'

That is so, but it is not the fact that the police officers were exposed to events *j* which foreseeably caused them psychiatric injury that founds their claim. Exposure to injury is a fact of police life. The essential ingredient of their cause of action is that they were so exposed because of the negligence of their employer, who was (subject to questions of neighbourhood and proximity) in breach of his duty to take reasonable care not to expose them to injuries from nervous shock. It is the *negligent* exposure to nervous shock that founds the liability, so it is nothing to the point to observe (correctly) that the chief constable owes no insurer's duty 'not to expose a police officer to injury by nervous shock', nor that there is here no allegation 'that there was any breach of duty in deploying the police officers at the scene'.

Nor is liability for negligence in crowd control precluded by *Hughes v National Union of Mineworkers* [1991] 4 All ER 278, nor by *Hill v Chief Constable of West Yorkshire* [1988] 2 All ER 238 at 240, [1989] AC 53 at 59 (as Waller J seemed to suggest).

Hughes' case concerned a picket line riot during the miners' strike. The negligence alleged was the deployment of an inadequate force of officers to control the disorder. In *Hill's* case the complaint was negligence in not apprehending the Yorkshire Ripper earlier. In each of those cases, the plaintiffs failed to recover essentially on public policy grounds. I quote from the headnote in *Hughes'* case:

'As a matter of public policy senior police officers charged with the task of deploying what might or might not be an adequate force of officers to control serious public order were not generally liable to individual officers under their command if those officers were injured by attacks from rioters, since to hold that a duty of care was owed in such circumstances would be significantly detrimental to the control of public order in that critical decisions which often had to be made by senior officers with little or no time for considered thought would be prejudiced if they were affected by the fear of a potential negligence claim by a subordinate if rioters injured that subordinate.'

It has been suggested that those decisions prevent (on public policy grounds) police officers from recovering when operational decisions expose them to risk, whereas they might recover in respect of policy decisions. However, that seems to me to be too broad a proposition. In *Hughes'* case May J considered *Knightley v Johns* [1982] 1 All ER 851, [1982] 1 WLR 349 (where the officer in charge of dealing with a road traffic accident did not follow laid down procedures and so gave orders which caused an officer to be injured) and *Rigby v Chief Constable of Northamptonshire* [1985] 2 All ER 985, [1985] 1 WLR 1242 (a decision of Taylor J dealing with negligence in firing a CS gas canister into a building to flush out an occupant when no fire-fighting equipment was available and there was a very real and substantial fire risk). Both of those were operational decisions where it was held that a duty was owed.

I find no difficulty in the result reached by any one of those four decisions. In *Hill* and *Hughes* it was for the police to decide on the priorities which dictated the scale of the response, and absent grounds for a *Wednesbury*-type challenge (see *Associated Provincial Picture Houses Ltd v Wednesbury Corp* [1947] 2 All ER 680, [1948] 1 KB 223), the decision was one for the exercise of their discretion. But in *Rigby* and *Knightley* and in this case, the police (by their negligence) were creating the very danger they were engaged to prevent. Public policy does not render the force immune in such circumstances.

In practice, much turns on the circumstances in which the negligent act or decision occurs; in calm or in the agony of the moment in a fast changing situation? And identification of the negligent act primarily responsible is not always straightforward. Here the fatal surge of spectators was when gate 3 was opened. Fears for the safety of the crowds outside struggling to get in might explain that decision in isolation. But working back from that, the negligence was not previously to cut off access to the central pens which were already overfull, a nor before that to make any attempt to limit the numbers in the central pens, nor to provide effective visual monitoring of crowd density in those pens. Labelling such acts and omissions 'operational' does not in my judgment mean either that spectators who were killed or injured by that negligence or the police officers who had to live through (and suffer psychiatric damage because of) the consequences of that negligence cannot, as a matter of public policy, recover

b damages for it. When planning for and dealing with crowd control on what should be a peaceful recreational occasion, I see no public policy justification for exempting chief constables (or other solvent or insured defendants whose negligence caused a major disaster) from the consequences of antecedent operational negligence which inevitably created one of the very dangers that the police presence was designed to prevent—namely fatal overcrowding.

c It follows that I regard the plaintiffs as having satisfied the proximity test, and that I see no public policy reasons why they should not succeed in their claims. So I differ from the trial judge in: (1) that in my judgment the plaintiffs have (as employees) a good cause of action against the first defendant, and so are, in the American parlance, 'direct victims'; (2) that (1) assists them in establishing that

d they were primary victims (or if not, participants in the events in Lord Oliver's sense); and (3) that it is wrong in fact and in law to regard them as 'bystanders'.

It also follows from what I have said and from those conclusions that even if the police officers were secondary victims, the successful plaintiffs can satisfy each of the controls restricting recovery by secondary victims found in Lord Lloyd's propositions quoted above.

e In conclusion, in addition to my views expressed above, I agree with Rose LJ's 12 propositions, with the following additions or reservations.

(vi) Nor did Lord Lloyd have employer/employee cases in mind, nor yet the long drawn-out exposure of those on duty to stressors caused by their employer's negligence which foreseeably might cause them psychiatric damage and would

f make them 'direct victims' in the American use of the phrase, or primary victims here.

(xi) I am less critical than him of the decision in *Robertson*, in that it seems to me to be a finding of fact—that they were bystanders—within the scope of the court's discretion on the facts as reported. That is to say, I understand how this could be treated as a *McFarlane* case, but I agree with what is said as to the law.

g I agree with Rose LJ's conclusions on the individual cases, and also with his dismissal of the appeal in Duncan v British Coal Corp.

My emphasis has been on the police officers as direct victims because of the employer/employee relationship. While that duty of care to them is a factor in a case such as this where their employer was negligent, I would expect a duty to

h be owed to them by any defendant who caused such a disaster as this. Deterrence is part of the public policy behind tort law. Prevention is better than cure, and potential defendants should face up to their safety responsibilities before rather than after an accident. I see no case for any relaxation of the rejection of the fireman's rule in *Ogwo v Taylor* [1987] 3 All ER 961 at 966, [1988] AC 431 at 449, as

j the judge seemed to favour.

I believe that where a plaintiff is a direct victim because of the duty that either his employer or the tortfeasor owes to him, that that should be the first head of recovery to be considered, because it might be wider and will not (so far as I can foresee) be narrower than any entitlement as a rescuer.

Dealing with the entitlement of a rescuer, it seems to me that public policy favours a wide rather than a narrow definition, to ensure that those brave and

unselfish enough to go to the help of their fellow men will be properly
compensated if they suffer damage as a result. I agree with what Rose LJ has said
as to rescuers.

Finally, I am aware that many people regard it as fundamentally unjust that the
police should recover damages for post-traumatic stress disorder sustained on
that terrible day while the relatives claiming in *Alcock*'s case failed. While
respecting their feelings of disappointment that the relatives failed, in this court
we can only consider whether these plaintiffs should recover on the different
principles of law applicable to them. In my judgment they should, and that
conclusion cannot properly be affected by my sympathy for the relatives.

JUDGE LJ. In his judgment Rose LJ has set out the material facts, including the
involvement of each individual plaintiff and the arguments advanced on his
behalf.

In summary, the plaintiffs, police officers on duty at Hillsborough Stadium,
witnessed horrific scenes and some gave direct assistance to those who had
already been injured or exposed to the risk of major or fatal injury. None of the
plaintiffs was exposed or believed he (or she) was exposed to physical injury and
the injuries actually sustained were psychiatric in nature. In such cases *Page v
Smith* [1995] 2 All ER 736, [1996] AC 155 underlined the critical importance of the
distinction between primary and secondary victims of negligence and identified
significant 'control mechanisms' to which claims by secondary victims are
subject.

The plaintiffs claim damages both as 'rescuers' and as quasi employees for the
failure of the chief constable (through other officers) to take reasonable care for
their safety, based on the proposition that whether as rescuers or quasi employees
they should as a matter of principle be regarded as primary rather than secondary
victims of the chief constable's negligence.

Rescuers

Police officers acting in the course of their duties are expected to respond to
unpleasant situations. They witness sights and accept risks to which ordinary
members of the public are not normally exposed: so do fire officers, and indeed
all who are employed in the emergency services. They are all nevertheless
entitled to recover damages for injury consequent on their efforts as rescuers
without any distinction in principle between them and civilians responding to the
same emergency: see *Haynes v Harwood* [1935] 1 KB 146, [1934] All ER Rep 103
(police officer), *Ward v T E Hopkins & Son Ltd, Baker v T E Hopkins & Son Ltd* [1959]
3 All ER 225, [1959] 1 WLR 966 (doctor) and *Ogwo v Taylor* [1987] 3 All ER 961,
[1988] AC 431 (fire officer) applying *Salmon v Seafarer Restaurants Ltd* [1983] 3 All
ER 729, [1983] 1 WLR 1264.

Accordingly, the fact that they are being paid for the services they offer on the
particular occasion does not permit the wrongdoer to escape liability or disqualify
police officers from claiming damages for injuries sustained while trying to avoid
or reduce the danger created by his negligence. As liability does not depend on
whether the rescuer is an individual with connections with the rescue services, or
retired from them, or on or off duty, or a civilian responding to the emergency,
those described as 'professional rescuers' cannot be regarded as under 'any
disadvantage'. That principle acknowledged, however, there is no warrant for
the conclusion that they should be more favourably treated than civilian rescuers
or professional rescuers who are off duty. Moreover, this principle does not

a

answer the question whether rescuers, professional or civilian, should be
regarded as primary or secondary victims of the original tortfeasor.

The first consideration is that for present purposes 'rescue' and 'rescuer' are
concerned with much wider activities than the words themselves may suggest.
Those who respond to an emergency not by rushing to the immediate scene of
an actual or impending disaster to alleviate it, but by taking part in a drawn out
operation to look and search for those who are apparently lost ('searchers') also
fall within the ambit of the principle. This indeed was the role of the rescuer
plaintiff in *Wagner v International Rly Co* (1921) 232 NY 176 from which the
formulation of principle by Judge Cardozo in the New York Court of Appeals has
been repeatedly adopted and followed in the UK as applying to rescue cases. In
Bourhill v Young [1942] 2 All ER 396, [1943] AC 92 Lord Wright regarded 'rescuers'
and 'searchers' as falling within the same principle and he recommended close
scrutiny of the dissenting judgment of Evatt J in *Chester v Waverley Corp* (1939) 62
CLR 1.

In that case the High Court of Australia considered the claim by a mother
whose seven-year-old child had failed to return home when expected and who,
having joined in the search for him, was present when his dead body was found
in a flood trench. Evatt J dissented from the view of the majority that the claim
for 'nervous shock' should be rejected. His judgment was subsequently
described by Lord Wilberforce in *McLoughlin v O'Brian* [1982] 2 All ER 298, [1983]
1 AC 410 as 'powerful' and by Lord Bridge as 'wholly convincing'. Evatt J said
((1939) 62 CLR 1 at 38):

> '... the rescuer who is injured in endeavouring to save ... or to prevent or
> mitigate the injurious consequences of the defendant's primary breach of
> duty is also owed a duty by the defendant ... The primary duty to take
> reasonable care to avoid inflicting injury coexists with a secondary duty to
> take care to avoid injuring rescuers ... Where a breach of the primary duty
> has occurred, there will also be a breach of the secondary duty, although the
> tort of negligence will be established only upon proof of injury to a particular
> plaintiff to whom either or both duties were owed. The same act or
> omission will constitute a breach of each duty ...'

He then summarised (at 44) the 'suggested' principles:

> 'I. In cases where the common law imposes on A a primary duty to take
> reasonable care to avoid action which is likely to cause injury to the person
> of another, it also imposed on A a secondary duty towards other persons
> because of their close association with the actual or apprehended casualties
> caused by a breach of his primary duty.
>
> II. The secondary duty is cast upon A because a reasonable person in his
> position would have foreseen the probability of injury being sustained ... (b)
> by those who will also be brought to the scene for the purpose of either
> preventing the casualty altogether, or of minimising injurious consequences,
> or in the course of a search to discover and rescue or aid any person who is
> feared on reasonable grounds to have been injured in the casualty.
>
> III. The common law imposes upon A a secondary duty towards the
> classes of persons referred to in II. to take reasonable care to avoid inflicting
> injury to the person of another.'

In this statement of principle, subsequently followed by Lord Wright, no
distinction is drawn between the 'rescue' cases and the 'search and rescue' cases,

into which *Chester's* case itself was grouped, and the question whether a searcher may recover damages in any particular circumstances falls to be decided within the same principle as those applied to rescuers. The principle therefore applies in many different circumstances. Thus, for example, unselfish members of the public will respond to the call from the police to turn out and assist in the search for a lost, possibly dead, child: police and other rescue agencies attend on these occasions as a matter of course: and as in *Chester's* case itself the searchers may include the parents or grandparents of a missing child, each with his or her particular emotional ties. Any one of them could find or come quickly onto the dreadful scene where the body of the dead or disfigured child was lying. Throughout the search none of them is at the slightest risk of physical injury and is in no fear for his own safety. To pursue the example further, if the child were found alive but injured at the bottom of an inadequately covered or supported shaft and one of the searchers, maybe a parent, perhaps a police officer, or possibly a volunteer from the local potholing club, were to enter the shaft and attempt to bring out the child he might well suddenly find himself exposed to serious risk of personal injury or even death. That is what happened in *Haynes v Harwood* [1935] 1 KB 146, [1934] All ER Rep 103, where the police officer was injured by a runaway horse, in *Chadwick v British Transport Commission* [1967] 2 All ER 945, [1967] 1 WLR 912, where the case was approached on the basis of the 'horror of the whole experience' but where the plaintiff in fact exposed himself to personal danger by crawling into the train wreckage, and *Ward v T E Hopkins & Son Ltd*, where Dr Baker's death might have been avoided if the rope around his waist had not become snagged, but was caused by the noxious fumes which had killed the men he was trying to save, and overwhelmed him. It would be surprising if these individuals, from civilians involved in a public spirited search to Dr Baker who died, all falling within the ambit of the rescue principle, should be categorised identically as primary victims.

The variety of circumstances can be underlined by considering those involved in the Hillsborough disaster itself, in addition to those who were killed or physically injured. As I understand it, claims by police officers and civilians who worked as rescuers within the fateful pens at Leppings Lane as the disaster unfolded were settled on the basis that they were at personal risk of physical injury and consequently liability for their claims has been accepted. Others present at the ground could without any derogatory implication be described as 'mere bystanders', witnessing unfolding events. Claims by them have not been pursued.

In *Alcock v Chief Constable of the South Yorkshire Police* [1991] 4 All ER 907, [1992] 1 AC 310 the Court of Appeal and the House of Lords were concerned with a series of claims not only by civilians who discovered what had happened through the media of television, but also by civilians who were present at the scene. Three cases detailed in the judgments merit particular attention.

Brian Harrison was inside the ground at Hillsborough and saw the incident as it developed. He realised that spectators in the two pens at the Leppings Lane terraces had either been killed or injured, and he also knew that both his brothers would be in these pens. As soon as the match was abandoned he tried unsuccessfully to find them. His precise movements are not described but there is nothing in them to suggest that he did not see something of the horrifying spectacle from close to it. He could reasonably be described as a searcher, but not a rescuer of others. Much later he was informed by telephone that his brothers had died. In the Court of Appeal and the House of Lords his claim failed.

a Robert Alcock's claim also failed. He was inside the stadium, witnessing and sickened by the unfolding incident. Because of a misunderstanding about the whereabouts of his brother-in-law he did not start to search for him until after leaving the ground. Much later, at about midnight, at the mortuary, he identified the body of his brother-in-law. The details of what he saw need no elaboration. The sights appalled him.

b John O'Dell was inside the ground and saw what was happening. He knew that his nephew was in the Leppings Lane terraces. He went to search for him. He looked among the bodies and assisted some of those staggering from the terraces, and continued with his search for his nephew. Later he discovered that his nephew was uninjured. He was therefore closely involved in the incident, and could be regarded as a searcher for his nephew, and a rescuer of unknown c spectators to whom he gave assistance. His appeal to the Court of Appeal against the dismissal of his claim was unsuccessful. His case was not considered in the House of Lords.

In summary, therefore, O'Dell was both a 'rescuer' and a 'searcher', Harrison was at least a 'searcher', and Alcock was to identify his deceased nephew's body d after having witnessed the incident at its worst and most painful. Each was assumed to have suffered psychiatric injury as a result of his involvement and activity during or in connection with the incident. Not one member of the Court of Appeal or the House of Lords considered that the claims by Harrison and Alcock could succeed and no member of the Court of Appeal considered that O'Dell's claim should succeed.

e Interestingly, the claim by William Pemberton, who had been successful at first instance, was not appealed. He was at the match but not inside the ground. He was asleep in the coach in which he had travelled with his son. After watching the incident unfold on the coach television he set out to search for his son. The details of his search are unclear, but it culminated in his identification of his son's f body much later at the temporary mortuary. He suffered consequent psychiatric illness. There was no appeal against his successful claim at first instance. It is difficult not to surmise that the decision not to appeal in his case was based on an appreciation of the force of the dissenting judgment of Evatt J in *Chester v Waverley Corp* (1939) 62 CLR 1, but neither the Court of Appeal nor the House of Lords expressed any views on this case.

g The main argument on behalf of O'Dell, Harrison and Alcock advanced in the Court of Appeal was based on liability to a searcher linked by an emotional or family relationship with the victim. Each member of the Court of Appeal had in mind the principles applied in rescue cases. In the House of Lords the well known rescue cases were cited in argument. In each of them the plaintiff was personally h at risk of physical injury or was or thought that he was the involuntary cause of injury or death to a third party.

Taking the matter as shortly as possible the reasons why the claims by Harrison and Alcock failed were expressed in language applicable to secondary victims:

j 'In neither of these cases was there any evidence of particularly close ties of love or affection with the brothers or brother-in-law.' (Per Lord Keith of Kinkel.)

'... there was not sufficient proximity in time and space to the accident ... there was no evidence to establish the necessary proximity which would make [Harrison's] claim reasonably foreseeable ... [Alcock] was not, in my

judgment, reasonably foreseeable as a potential sufferer from shock-induced
psychiatric illness ...' (Per Lord Ackner.)   *a*

'... the necessary proximity was lacking in their cases too, but I also agree
... that there is also lacking the necessary element of reasonable
foreseeability.' (Per Lord Oliver.)

'... none of the appellants having satisfied both the tests of reasonable
foreseeability and proximity I would dismiss all the appeals.' (Per Lord   *b*
Jauncey.) (See [1991] 4 All ER 907 at 915, 921–922, 931–932 and 937, [1992] 1
AC 310 at 398, 405–406, 417–418 and 424.)

In *Alcock*'s case Lord Oliver appeared to treat as a secondary victim someone
who had actually witnessed injury as a 'passive and unwilling witness'. In a
categorisation described in his own word as 'broad' he regarded a primary victim   *c*
as someone involved 'either mediately or immediately' as a participant, and it is
suggested, treated a rescuer coming to the 'aid of others, injured or threatened'
as a primary victim. Harrison and O'Dell were involved 'mediately' and Alcock
was arguably so involved. None of them could fairly be regarded as a mere
bystander or spectator. Nevertheless Lord Oliver agreed with the conclusion that
the claims by Harrison and Alcock should fail on the basis of the absence of   *d*
proximity and foreseeability.   Accordingly I do not regard his 'broad'
categorisation as supporting the conclusion that everyone falling within the
rescue principle must be regarded as a primary victim of the tortfeasor. If it did,
it would require reassessment in the light of *Page v Smith*.

In *Page v Smith* the plaintiff suffered recognisable psychiatric illness as a result   *e*
of involvement in a direct physical impact. Notwithstanding that his injuries
were psychiatric rather than physical he was entitled to recover damages. In a
speech with which Lord Ackner and Lord Browne-Wilkinson agreed, Lord Lloyd
analysed how on the three previous occasions when claims for damages for
nervous shock had been considered by the House of Lords, namely *Bourhill v
Young* [1942] 2 All ER 396, [1943] AC 92, *McLoughlin v O'Brian* [1982] 2 All ER 298,   *f*
[1983] 1 AC 410 and *Alcock* itself, the plaintiffs were 'outside the range of
foreseeable physical injury'. He categorised them as secondary rather than
primary victims. He accepted as the most 'appropriate terminology' the
distinction drawn by Lord Oliver between primary and secondary victims, that is
those directly involved in an accident and those who suffer from what they 'see   *g*
and hear'. In contrast with the three previous occasions when damages for
nervous shock had been considered by the House of Lords, he regarded Page as
'a participant. He was himself directly involved in the accident, and well within
the range of foreseeable physical injury. He was the primary victim.' Later he
encapsulated the distinction between the primary and secondary victim by   *h*
underlining that the 'secondary victim is almost always outside the area of
physical impact, and therefore outside the range of foreseeable physical injury'
(see [1995] 2 All ER 736 at 755, 758, [1996] AC 155 at 184, 187).

Lord Lloyd pointed out that in *Alcock*'s case Lord Keith of Kinkel's
consideration of the problem had focused on the nature of the injury which was
of the 'secondary sort' brought about by the infliction of physical injury or the risk   *j*
of physical injury upon another person. Lord Keith of Kinkel himself, considering
the observations of Lord Oliver, referred to the cases dividing broadly 'into two
categories':

'... those in which the plaintiff was involved as a participant in the incident
which gave rise to the action, and those in which the plaintiff was a witness

to injury caused to others, or to the immediate aftermath of an accident to others.' (See [1995] 2 All ER 736 at 739, [1996] AC 155 at 167.)

Lord Jauncey explained:

'Lord Oliver was considering proximity as determinative of the existence of a duty of care and drawing a distinction between a victim directly involved in an accident and one who merely witnessed '. (See [1995] 2 All ER 736 at 748, [1996] AC 155 at 176.)

Nothing in any of the speeches in *Page v Smith* suggests that whatever the extent of their participation, rescuers should automatically be regarded as primary victims. As Lord Lloyd made plain, claims by Harrison and Alcock were unsuccessful because they were secondary victims who had failed to establish the necessary degree of proximity in time and place and/or relationship. The failure of his claim did not mean that Harrison had failed to establish that he was a searcher within the rescue principle or that O'Dell was not at least a rescuer and searcher. Nevertheless, notwithstanding their positive roles (certainly in Harrison's case, and I would add a fortiori in O'Dell's case) which went well beyond those of a mere bystander or spectator, their claims were subject to the limitations applicable to secondary victims. Yet if the involvement of Harrison, Alcock and O'Dell had exposed them to the risk or apprehension of physical injury, I have no doubt that they would then have been regarded as primary victims whose claims for consequential psychiatric illness would have succeeded notwithstanding that they did not suffer any bodily injuries.

This conclusion is consistent with the reasoning in *Page* itself, and what was described by Lord Lloyd as the 'illuminating judgment' of Stuart Smith LJ in *McFarlane v EE Caledonia Ltd* [1994] 2 All ER 1. In the context of identifying a 'participant' Stuart Smith LJ identified three situations: first, the person within the 'actual area of danger created by the event'; second, the person who reasonably thinks that he is in such an area; and third, the rescuer who enters the actual area of danger because 'a tortfeasor who has put A in peril by his negligence must reasonably foresee that B may come to rescue him, even if it involves risking his own safety'. For present purposes the apparent inconsistency between this decision and some of the observations in *Alcock* about whether a bystander could ever recover for psychiatric illness does not require analysis. It is implicit in *McFarlane*'s case that presence in an area where psychiatric but not physical injury could reasonably be anticipated as a result of things seen and heard would not entitle a rescuer to be regarded as a primary victim.

I have therefore concluded that Mr Hytner QC's argument places too much weight on the categorisation of the plaintiffs in the present appeal as rescuers and thus avoids the necessary analysis of the precise activity and involvement of each individual at the scene. In my judgment those who fall within the 'rescue' principles should not automatically be regarded as primary victims of the tortfeasor's negligence. Some will, but some will not.

This conclusion does not minimise the protection rightly afforded to rescuers who respond to the cry for assistance. It simply underlines that those who respond do so in different ways and that by its very nature each emergency is different, sometimes altering dramatically as it unfolds, imposing changing demands on different rescuers. When damages are sought for psychiatric illness consequent on the response to an emergency, in my judgment the claim should be approached in the same analytical way as claims by other victims of negligence

whose cases will depend on whether they have been found to be primary or
secondary victims.

Service as police officers

As police officers the plaintiffs were not employees of the chief constable.
Nevertheless, by analogy with the obligations owed by an employer to his
employees, and subject to the demands imposed on police officers which expose
them in the course of their duties to the risk of personal injury and death, the chief
constable is required to protect them from and not expose them to unnecessary
risks. The claim under this head depends on the admitted negligence of police
officers for whom the chief constable was responsible, which created the danger
of injury and death to which those in the pens at Leppings Lane were exposed.
Page v Smith underlined that non-medical distinctions between physical and
recognisable psychiatric injury should be ignored and in my view also established
that notwithstanding the absence of physical injury an employer may be liable to
compensate his employee for psychiatric injury consequent on his (the
employer's) negligence. Therefore as the present plaintiffs suffered psychiatric
injury in the course of their endeavours to alleviate the risks or to cope with the
consequences of the original negligence, it is argued that they are entitled to
recover damages as primary victims of the negligence of those for whom the chief
constable was vicariously responsible.

I have already underlined that, in principle, a professional rescuer should not
be under any disadvantage compared with other rescuers but if the present
plaintiffs were to recover damages on the basis now under consideration as
primary victims, they would do so notwithstanding that civilian rescuers playing
similar roles at the disaster would not. Indeed, they would be regarded in exactly
the same way as brother officers and civilian rescuers who were exposed to the
risk (actual or apprehended) of physical injury and indeed the other primary
victims, the unfortunate spectators who as a result of being physically crushed in
the Leppings Lane pens sustained psychiatric injury. Mr Hytner argued that
these surprising results stem from the chief constable's responsibility for the
negligence which gave rise to the need for the police officers to carry out the
unpleasant tasks performed by the plaintiffs and the distinct duty owed to them
not as rescuers but as quasi employees.

Mr Hytner relied on the successful claim by the police officer in *Knightley v
Johns* [1982] 1 All ER 851, [1982] 1 WLR 349. The negligence of the fourth
defendant, a police inspector, arose from his failure to obey standing orders and
close the tunnel negligently blocked by the first defendant's vehicle, and his
express orders to a police constable to ride his motor cycle against the flow of
traffic round a blind bend to 'remedy his own negligence by a dangerous
manoeuvre'. The plaintiff was injured by a collision with a car driven in the
opposite direction on its correct side of the road. Hardly surprisingly his claim
against the police inspector succeeded: the defendant whose negligence had
originally caused the blockage of the tunnel escaped liability on the basis that the
effect of his negligence had been interrupted.

Knightley was a primary victim. If as a result of the impact he had sustained
psychiatric illness without physical injury he would have recovered damages in
accordance with *Page v Smith*. However, the liability of the police inspector to
him does not advance the present claims for compensation for psychiatric illness.
Without analysing the possible difficulties which might have arisen if the
negligence of the inspector had been limited to one or other rather than the

combined effect of both areas of his negligent behaviour, this decision demonstrates that the chief constable may be liable to police officers for injuries sustained by them when acting under orders to alleviate the consequences of earlier police negligence. In my judgment, however, it does not suggest that when such injuries are limited to psychiatric injuries by employees outside the area of physical danger, they should (whether police officers or civilians acting in the course of their employments) automatically be treated as primary victims.

Some attention was paid in *Alcock*'s case to successful claims by employees for psychiatric injury. Lord Oliver summarised the effect of *Dooley v Cammell Laird & Co Ltd* [1951] 1 Lloyd's Rep 271, *Galt v British Railways Board* (1983) 133 NLJ 870 and *Wigg v British Railways Board* (1986) Times, 4 February, as illustrations of the principle that an employee may recover for such damages as a primary victim when the negligence of his employer leads him to believe that he personally has or may have caused physical injury or death. What Lord Oliver did not suggest was that an employee suffering psychiatric injury as a result of negligence for which his employer was responsible should be regarded as a primary victim. Instead he proceeded to identify a particular basis on which the employees in the cases cited should be regarded as participants or primary victims, thus implying that an employee should not automatically be so regarded. No doubt a further basis on which an employee might be entitled to recover damages for psychiatric injury would be when his actions fell within the rescue principle (see *Mount Isa Mines Ltd v Pusey* (1970) 125 CLR 383). However, just because some employee rescuers should be treated as primary victims it does not follow that they all will. As this question was not directly addressed in *McFarlane*'s case it is enough to notice that the result in that case is consistent with this conclusion.

In *Robertson v Forth Road Bridge Joint Board, Rough v Forth Road Bridge Joint Board* 1995 SLT 263, in the Court of Session, the pursuers failed to establish liability for psychiatric injury caused to them when they witnessed a fatal accident to a fellow employee who, as a result of their employer's neglect, was blown off the back of a truck by a gust of wind. The argument for the pursuers was based on the relationship of employer and employee. Nevertheless after consideration of all the relevant authorities it failed. Lord Hope said (at 269):

> 'It is difficult to see why the bystander in the case of a road accident should be denied his claim, when a bystander who happens to be an employee but has had nothing whatever to do with causing the incident is allowed to recover damages for this type of injury ... Where the employees are merely bystanders or witnesses ... the ordinary rule must apply'.

As the victim was not a relative of either plaintiff, and the employer could not have foreseen that they would not possess the customary phlegm the claims failed. The decision reflected the developing legal principles in claims for damages for psychiatric injury underlined in *Alcock*'s case and the control mechanisms subsequently identified in *Page v Smith*. I respectfully agree with the decision in *Robertson*'s case, reinforced by *Page v Smith* and conclude that, in principle, an employee who establishes that his employer's breach of duty has caused him psychiatric illness is not automatically to be categorised as a primary victim of his employer's negligence. As with rescuers, depending on their involvement in the incident, some will be primary victims and others will be secondary victims, subject to the relevant control mechanisms. The same principle applies to claims by police officers against their chief constables.

I am fortified in this conclusion by the summary by Lord Lloyd in *Page v Smith* of the distinction drawn in the authorities that 'in cases involving nervous shock, it is essential to distinguish between the primary victim and secondary victims'. The application of this principle to each claim for damages for psychiatric illness requires that the identical question should be decided in relation to each victim of the same tortfeasor's negligence, irrespective of the formulation of the duty of which the tortfeasor is in breach, and accordingly without regard to whether the plaintiff was a civilian volunteer responding to the emergency and assisting at the disaster at Hillsborough, or a police officer present and acting in the course of his duties.

Conclusion

Without repeating Rose LJ's analysis of the parts played by each individual plaintiff I have considered each claim in the light of the principles set out in this judgment and on the assumption that each plaintiff suffered psychiatric illness consequent on his (or her) respective involvement in the disaster. The involvement of each plaintiff was brought about by the necessary efforts to mitigate the consequences of the earlier negligence by police officers for whom the chief constable was responsible and, save for Janet Smith, each came within the rescue principle in its broad unrestricted sense. Save in the limited sense that some of the plaintiffs were concerned about possible violent reactions from individuals in the crowd none was at any time present in an area where he (or she) was exposed to the risk (actual or apprehended) of physical injury arising from the chief constable's negligence. Like the plaintiffs in *Bourhill v Young* [1942] 2 All ER 396, [1943] AC 92, *McLoughlin v O'Brian* [1982] 2 All ER 298, [1983] 1 AC 410 and all the plaintiffs in *Alcock*'s case, but unlike the plaintiff in *Page v Smith*, these plaintiffs were all secondary and not primary victims. Accordingly, the control mechanisms applied. In each case the necessary proximity of relationship between the plaintiff and any person suffering injury or death was not established. Moreover, with the arguable exception of Inspector White the necessary proximity in time and place was also absent. Finally, despite Mr Hytner's contentions to the contrary there is no better basis for concluding that psychiatric injury was foreseeable in the case of any of the plaintiffs in the present appeal than it was for the plaintiffs all of whose claims failed in *Alcock* in the Court of Appeal or the House of Lords or both (see [1991] 4 All ER 907, [1992] 1 AC 310; *affg* sub nom *Jones v Wright* [1991] 3 All ER 88, [1992] AC 310).

For these reasons I would dismiss all the appeals.

Duncan v British Coal Corp

The appeal by Duncan also fails. Whether as a 'rescuer' or an individual who suffered psychiatric injury while in the course of his employment by the defendants, Duncan was not a primary victim of the defendant's negligence. Even if he could properly be described as a secondary victim his claim for damages for psychiatric injury did not escape the control mechanisms. There was no proximity in relationship, insufficient proximity in time and place to the accident in which the deceased was killed, and the psychiatric injury was not a foreseeable consequence of the defendant's negligence.

First appeal allowed in respect of four of the five police officers. Second appeal dismissed. Leave to appeal to the House of Lords refused.

L I Zysman Esq   Barrister.

Vernon v Bosley (No 1)

COURT OF APPEAL, CIVIL DIVISION

STUART-SMITH, EVANS AND THORPE LJJ

31 JANUARY, 1, 2, 5–8, 12, 13 FEBRUARY, 29 MARCH 1996

Negligence – Duty to take care – Nervous shock – Plaintiff suffering from post-traumatic stress disorder and pathological grief disorder – Plaintiff witnessing aftermath of car crash in which children killed – Plaintiff vulnerable to stress – Whether plaintiff entitled to recover damages for mental injury.

In August 1982 the plaintiff's two young children were passengers in a car driven by the defendant, their nanny, when it went off the road and crashed into a river. The plaintiff did not see the accident but was called to the scene shortly after, where he witnessed attempts to salvage the car when it was thought that the children might be still alive. The rescue attempt was unsuccessful and the children drowned. The plaintiff was at the time chairman and managing director of his own company, but in January 1986 his business failed and in 1992 his marriage broke up. He brought an action against the defendant claiming damages of more than £4m for her negligence, which he claimed had caused him mental or psychiatric injury by reason of the fact that he was an eye-witness of the unsuccessful rescue attempt. The defendant admitted that her negligence had caused the accident, but defended the claim on the ground that the plaintiff had suffered no more than normal grief reaction to the accident, that the failure of his business was due to his own fault and shortcomings as a businessman, as evidenced by his previous business career, and that if he was mentally ill the prime causes were the failure of his business and his marriage. The judge held that the plaintiff was entitled to recover damages in respect of his mental illness, but that such damages should not cover the loss of his business. The defendant appealed principally on the issue of liability.

Held (Stuart-Smith LJ dissenting) – (1) Although damages for normal grief and bereavement suffered as the result of another's negligence were not recoverable, a plaintiff in the position of secondary victim could recover damages for both post-traumatic stress disorder (ie the nervous shock of witnessing an accident or its immediate aftermath) or pathological grief disorder (ie grief which became so severe as to be regarded as abnormal and giving rise to psychiatric illness) provided the two preconditions for recovery of damages for psychiatric illness (ie nervous shock) were satisfied, namely that the plaintiff was in a close and loving relationship with the primary victim and was connected with the accident in time and place, ie as a bystander and direct viewer. The legal (as opposed to the medical) test determining recoverability was whether the plaintiff had suffered mental injury caused by the negligence of the defendant and not whether he had suffered post-traumatic stress disorder rather than pathological grief disorder. Accordingly, the secondary victim could recover damages for mental illness caused or at least contributed to by the actionable negligence of the defendant, notwithstanding that the illness could also be regarded as a pathological consequence of the bereavement which the plaintiff had inevitably suffered. It followed that damages payable to a plaintiff who was a secondary victim of a breach of a duty of care owed by the defendant and who suffered mental illness, which was properly regarded as a consequence both of his experience as a bystander and of an intense and abnormal grief reaction to the bereavement which he suffered, should not be discounted for his grief and the consequences of bereavement, even though his illness was partly so caused (see p 604 *e* to 605 *a d* to *h*, p 607 *e f*, p 611 *c d* and p 613 *d* to *f*, post).

(2) In the instant case, the judge had been entitled to conclude that the plaintiff suffered mental injury by reason of witnessing the aftermath of the accident in 1982 and that the accident was the initiating cause of his mental illness. It was impossible as a matter of common sense to distinguish between the effect upon the plaintiff's mind of seeing the accident, which was especially traumatic for him because he knew that his children were victims of it and were almost certainly dead, and the effects of grief and bereavement which became inevitable when he knew that they had in fact been killed. The appeal against liability would therefore be dismissed (see p 606 *e f* and p 607 *c d*, post).

Per curiam. The role of the expert medical witnesses is to inform the judge so as to guide him to the correct conclusions. It must be for the judge to gauge the weight and usefulness of such assistance as he is given and to reach his own conclusions accordingly. Expert witnesses are armed with the court's readiness to receive the expert evidence which it needs in order to reach a fully informed decision, whatever the nature of the topic may be, but their evidence ceases to be useful, and it may become counter-productive, when it is not marshalled by reference to the issues in the particular case and kept within the limits so fixed (see p 603 *a* to *c*, post).

Notes

For liability for nervous shock, see 34 *Halsbury's Laws* (4th edn) para 8, and for cases on the subject, see 17 *Digest* (Reissue) 145–148, 377–392.

Cases referred to in judgments

AB (child abuse: expert witness), Re [1995] 1 FLR 181.

Alcock v Chief Constable of the South Yorkshire Police [1991] 4 All ER 907, [1992] 1 AC 310, [1991] 3 WLR 1057, HL.

Allied Maples Group Ltd v Simmons & Simmons (a firm) [1995] 4 All ER 907, [1995] 1 WLR 1602, CA.

Birkett v Hayes [1982] 2 All ER 710, [1982] 1 WLR 816, CA.

Bonnington Castings Ltd v Wardlaw [1956] 1 All ER 615, [1956] AC 613, [1956] 2 WLR 707, HL.

Bourhill v Young [1942] 2 All ER 396, [1943] AC 92, HL.

Brice v Brown [1984] 1 All ER 997.

C (expert evidence: disclosure: practice), Re [1995] 1 FLR 204.

Calascione v Dixon (1993) 19 BMLR 97, CA.

Derby & Co Ltd v Weldon (1990) Times, 9 November, CA.

Elgindata Ltd, Re (No 2) [1993] 1 All ER 232, [1992] 1 WLR 1207, CA.

G (minors), Re (1994) 20 BMLR 10.

Hayes v Bowman [1989] 2 All ER 293, [1989] 1 WLR 456, CA.

Hinz v Berry [1970] 1 All ER 1074, [1970] 2 QB 40, [1970] 2 WLR 684, CA.

J (child abuse: expert evidence), Re [1991] FCR 193.

Jaensch v Coffey (1984) 155 CLR 549, Aust HC.

Jefford v Gee [1970] 1 All ER 1202, [1970] 2 QB 130, [1970] 2 WLR 702, CA.

McLoughlin v O'Brian [1982] 2 All ER 298, [1983] 1 AC 410, [1982] 2 WLR 982, HL.
Martin v Turner [1970] 1 All ER 256, [1970] 1 WLR 82, CA.
National Justice Cia Naviera SA v Prudential Assurance Co Ltd, The Ikarian Reefer
    [1995] 1 Lloyd's Rep 455, CA; *affg* [1993] 2 Lloyd's Rep 68.
Page v Smith [1995] 2 All ER 736, [1996] AC 155, [1995] 2 WLR 644, HL; *rvsg* [1994]
    4 All ER 522, CA.
Polivitte Ltd v Commercial Union Assurance Co plc [1987] 1 Lloyd's Rep 379.
R (a minor) (experts' evidence), Re [1991] 1 FLR 291.
Whitehouse v Jordan [1981] 1 All ER 267, [1981] 1 WLR 246, HL.

Cases also cited or referred to in skeleton arguments
Corbett v Barking Havering and Brentwood Health Authority [1991] 1 All ER 498,
    [1991] 2 QB 408, CA.
Fairhurst v St Helens and Knowsley Health Authority [1995] PIQR Q1.
Lipkin Gorman (a firm) v Karpnale Ltd [1992] 4 All ER 409, [1989] 1 WLR 1340, CA;
    rvsd in part [1992] 4 All ER 512, [1991] 2 AC 548, HL.
Nash v Southmead Health Authority [1993] PIQR Q156.
Smith v Huntley [1995] PIQR P475.
Spittle v Bunney [1988] 3 All ER 1031, [1988] 1 WLR 847, CA.
Thomas v Brighton Health Authority (7 November 1995, unreported), QBD.
Wilsher v Essex Area Health Authority [1988] 1 All ER 871, [1988] AC 1074, HL.

Appeal
The defendant, Katherine Bosley, appealed from the judgment of Sedley J ((1995)
28 BMLR 1) given on 30 January 1995 whereby he awarded the plaintiff, Peter
Vernon, the sum of £1,133,962·59 together with interest of £198,269 and costs on
the plaintiff's claim for damages for negligence. The facts are set out in the
judgment of Stuart-Smith LJ.

Dermod O'Brien QC and *Daniel Pearce-Higgins* (instructed by *Howard Palser
    Grossman Hermer & Partners*, Cardiff) for the defendant.
David Blunt QC and *Jonathan Marks QC* (instructed by *Osborne Clark*, Bristol) for the
    plaintiff.

Cur adv vult

29 March 1996. The following judgments were delivered.

STUART-SMITH LJ.

Introduction
    On 13 August 1982 the plaintiff's daughters, Philipa, aged 7, and Theresa, aged
3, together with a third child who was the daughter of friends, were being driven
in a Volvo motor car by the Vernons' nanny, the defendant. At Ynys Isaf
Ystradgynlais in Powys the defendant lost control of the car and it crashed down
a 30-foot bank into the fast flowing river which ran alongside the road. The
defendant managed to escape from the car. But the children were trapped. The
plaintiff and his wife, who both worked at a factory nearby, were called to the
scene by the police. When they arrived they watched the attempts of the rescue
services to retrieve the car and save the children. At one stage there was a
glimmer of hope that one of the girls might still be alive, but it was not to be. It

has never been disputed that the accident was caused by the defendant's negligence.

The plaintiff was born on 30 April 1942, he was therefore aged 40 at the time of the accident. His case was presented to the judge on the basis that he 'suffered a very severe degree of nervous shock and psychological trauma and subsequently developed a severe post-traumatic stress disorder (PTSD) complicated by a severe grief reaction'. It was said that by 1982 he was a successful businessman who, after a public school education and a career in the Army, had moved into executive employment with three major corporations in succession and then, using his accumulated skill and experience, had bought a viable and potentially prosperous business which he was in the process of building up when this tragedy struck. From then on, in spite of stoical efforts to sustain normality, he went to pieces; his business failed and he became unemployed and unemployable, socially inept and domestically insufferable. His wife and their three children born after the accident have now left him, and he lives an aimless and reclusive life. At 51, instead of success and fulfilment, he has, thanks to this accident, neither a present nor a future. His counsel, Mr Blunt QC, when opening the case, described him as a man shown by his career to have been—

> 'quite outstanding: intelligent and capable, confident, highly motivated, hardworking and ambitious, determined, courageous and reliant, a motivator of others, resourceful and imaginative, always anxious to acquire new skills, decisive, good at solving problems, someone who understood the value of careful planning and forethought, an enthusiast, full of initiative (if he perceived that a job needed to be done he rolled up his sleeves and got on with it and led from the front) and always ready to volunteer, someone who cared for his colleagues and subordinates, motivated them and commanded their respect.'

Mr Blunt accepted that his client had disagreements with colleagues and became 'ensnared by big company politics and reorganisations' but submitted that this is not untypical of the career of a high achiever; nor, he submitted, was the stress which from time to time the plaintiff suffered requiring minor medication. With his business success went 'a fulfilling social life, numerous interests and hobbies, and a loving and happy family life'.

At the time of the accident the plaintiff was chairman, managing director and majority shareholder of Paraero Ltd. This company, largely with the financial backing of the British Rail Pension Fund, had bought the assets of a company called Precision Circuits Ltd, in receivership. It was his case that as a result of witnessing the accident he was a changed man, his own level of performance was dramatically reduced and key personnel were no longer able to work with him and left. In the result Paraero went into receivership in January 1986 with the result that the plaintiff sustained capital and income losses of the order of £3m.

In addition to this it was the plaintiff's case that but for the effects of the accident he would have obtained employment in 1986 in the upper echelons of management of a multinational company, but effectively he was now unemployable. There was also a very substantial claim for past and future care on the basis that the plaintiff needed secretarial services, which had previously been provided by his wife until the marriage broke down and she left him in 1992.

He also required domestic help and a gardener because he was not capable of doing these things for himself.

The defendant has throughout accepted that the plaintiff fell into that category of person who may be awarded damages resulting from the nervous shock of witnessing an accident or its immediate aftermath. Her case was, and is, that the plaintiff did not suffer from post-traumatic stress disorder (PTSD), which is the term now used by psychiatrists in relation to this type of mental disorder, as opposed to a grief reaction, normal or abnormal (pathological grief disorder (or PGD)), which he would have suffered in any event if he had not witnessed the tragedy, but been told of it at a distance. The defendant further contended that the accident and its effect on the plaintiff was not causative of the collapse of Paraero; this was due to other factors and it would have collapsed when it did for the reasons it did irrespective of the accident.

Her case at the trial was that the plaintiff was a Walter Mitty character from the start, failing far more often than he succeeded at each stage of his life, making enemies through his own deficiencies of character and forever blaming others; a man who continuously refashioned his extremely modest achievements into a grandiose myth; who, having failed in a succession of employments, had bought at an overvalue an ailing company which was destined to founder for economic reasons and the plaintiff's defects of character; who has consistently with his life-long character blamed the failure of Paraero on everything and everybody but himself.

The defendant now accepts that the plaintiff is, or was at the date of trial, genuinely suffering from mental illness, though not to the extent alleged or requiring the care and support claimed. It is her case on appeal that the plaintiff failed to prove that this was due to the shock of witnessing the aftermath of the accident as opposed to a grief reaction at the death of his children and the effects of the collapse of the business, his inability to get employment thereafter, and perhaps also the effects of a head injury in December 1985, on a fragile personality which throughout his life had been prone to react badly to stress.

The trial began on 21 January 1994. The judge listened to 68 days of evidence, including that of four psychiatrists, three psychologists and three accountants spread over four periods. In addition he had extensive written submissions and two days of oral submissions. There was a vast amount of documentation and oral evidence relating to every phase of the plaintiff's life. His main judgment runs to 262 pages and was delivered on 30 January 1995. Further argument on reserved matters, such as interest and costs, took place, and the judge gave judgment on these matters on 10 May 1995.

The judge held that the plaintiff's present mental illness was one in respect of which he was entitled to recover damages. The precise basis upon which he so concluded will have to be examined later in this judgment, since it is the subject of the defendant's first and main challenge on this appeal.

He rejected the plaintiff's claim that the loss of his business, Paraero, was attributable to his illness, holding that it would have occurred when it did in any event. He rejected the plaintiff's case that he was destined to be high flyer and high earner in the top echelons of international companies, and in many respects he accepted the defendant's submissions in relation to his pre-accident personality. He awarded the plaintiff a total of £1,332,231·59 by way of damages

and interest. It is convenient to set out here the sums awarded by the judge, the
sums claimed by the plaintiff under various heads, and the interest on those sums.

Nature of claim	Amount claimed	Amount awarded	Interest
1. General damages		£37,500	£6,000
2. Past loss of earnings Less benefits	£747,455	£428,492·75 £16,842·36 £411,650·39	£173,636
3. Future loss of earnings	£1,045,725	£561,488	

4. Doctors' and psychologists' fees
  past
  future
	£4,545
	£1,820
		£4,545
		£1,400
			£2,286

5. Travelling expenses	£3,280	£2,884	£1,957

6. Sundries
  past
  future
		£3,487·72
		£3,159
			£2,442

7. Past care by Mrs Vernon
  secretarial
  domestic and other
	£69,975
	£9,304
		£20,000*	£11,950

8. Future care
  occupational therapy to 1999
  occupational therapy after 1999
  domestic help
  gardener/handyman
  nanny
  future secretarial assistance
	£51,452
	£18,300
	£41,743
	£13,430
	£32,543
	£6,443·97
		£51,452
		£14,640
		£41,574
		£3,952	

9. Loss of capital and profits in Paraero	£2,897,000		
Total Less future benefit	£4,943,015·97	£1,157,732·11 £23,770 £1,133,962·11	£198,271

* For reasons which will later appear, it is not clear what the basis of this award was.

In this appeal the defendant challenges the total award on the basis that the
judge wrongly held that the plaintiff suffered nervous shock from witnessing the
aftermath of the accident and mental illness in consequence. Alternatively, the
defendant challenges the special heads of damages contained under heads (2) and
(3) past and future loss of earnings, (7) past care by Mrs Vernon, (8) future care,
and the amount awarded by way of interest and costs in relation to the Paraero
issue, on which the defendant was successful.

Even though the judge awarded less than a quarter of the plaintiff's claim, it is
nevertheless surprising at first blush that the difference between witnessing the
tragedy, in the sense that the plaintiff came upon the scene during the rescue
attempts, and hearing of it at a distance, should result in an award of £1⅓ m.

The judge examined the plaintiff's career from his schooldays to the present in very great detail. He was able to do so because there was a mass of documentation which shed light upon his previous personality. A great deal of this had been kept by the plaintiff himself; other material was produced upon third party discovery and by subpoena, for example from the Ministry of Defence in relation to his army career and from the receivers in Paraero in relation to the reasons for the collapse of that company. This documentation led the judge to reject very substantially the plaintiff's view of himself as having been a success, at times throughout his career outstandingly so, who, but for the accident, would have made a great deal of money out of Paraero and then gone on to earn a high salary as chief executive or sales director of a multinational company. The judge felt himself unable to accept the plaintiff's evidence, save in so far as it was corroborated. He said that his present claims about his former qualities and achievements were frequently grandiose and absurd. He held that he confabulated, though this was due to his present illness.

Since the defendant in this appeal relies upon many of the judge's findings in relation to the plaintiff's previous career, it is necessary to set out, as briefly as possible, this history and the judge's findings.

[His Lordship then set out the plaintiff's career history, described the accident in which the children were killed and the plaintiff's reaction to it, and set out in detail the medical treatment the plaintiff had received since the accident. He continued:]

The law

In cases of physical injury to the plaintiff, it has to be established that the tortfeasor ought reasonably to have foreseen that his act or omission was liable to cause injury of some kind to the plaintiff. He must then prove that injury of that kind, though perhaps greater in extent than was foreseeable, was in fact caused by the act or omission of the defendant. Questions of causation do not as a rule present much difficulty to the court except in cases where there is a pre-existing condition which does, or is likely in the future, to cause disability, where there is a subsequent supervening event, or where there are two co-existing causes of injury. The judge will be guided by the opinions of doctors in reaching his conclusion. The courts are also familiar with cases of mental illness following physical trauma; this is the well-known post-traumatic neurosis, the trauma being the physical injury.

Although the courts have long recognised that psychiatric illness suffered independently of physical injury can amount to compensatable injury, considerable limitations have as a matter policy been placed on the scope of such actions. Thus in the case of a primary victim, that is to say one who suffers nervous shock and psychiatric illness in consequence of fear for his safety, the defendant is only liable if it is reasonably foreseeable that a person of ordinary phlegm would so suffer. If that is established, then it is immaterial that the plaintiff was himself a fragile person who suffers more severely as a consequence.

In the case of a secondary victim, that is to say one who suffers nervous shock as a result of witnessing a horrifying event and is put in fear for the safety of others, the law also imposes limitations. There must be proximity both in the relationship between the primary victim who is in danger and the secondary victim and in the way in which the secondary victim learns of the event. There must be a close relationship of affection and the secondary victim must see the event or its immediate aftermath, and the event must be one which is sufficiently horrific as to be likely to cause shock to a person of ordinary phlegm. It is common ground that in this case those conditions are satisfied. But there are two further requirements. The shock must be a 'sudden appreciation by sight or sound of a horrifying event, which violently agitates the mind' (see per Lord Ackner in *Alcock v Chief Constable of the South Yorkshire Police* [1991] 4 All ER 907 at 918, [1992] 1 AC 310 at 401) and the plaintiff must suffer from a recognised psychiatric illness. Over the last 15 years psychiatrists have come to call this illness post-traumatic stress disorder (PTSD). The trauma being the horrifying event in question; the symptoms of the illness include depression and anxiety, both of which the plaintiff suffers from.

A definition of PTSD which is widely recognised by psychiatrists is to be found in the *Diagnostic and Statistical Manual of Mental Disorders* (3rd edn) revised in 1987 (referred to as 'DSM-III-R'). The diagnostic criteria are:

'A. The person has experienced an event that is outside the range of usual human experience and that would be markedly distressing to almost anyone, e g., serious threat to one's life or physical integrity; serious threat or harm to one's children, spouse, or other close relatives and friends; sudden destruction of one's home or community; or seeing another person who has recently been, or is being, seriously injured or killed as the result of an accident or physical violence.

B. The traumatic event is persistently re-experienced in at least one of the following ways: (1) recurrent and intrusive distressing recollections of the event (in young children, repetitive play in which themes or aspects of the trauma are expressed), (2) recurrent distressing dreams of the event, (3) sudden acting or feeling as if the traumatic event were recurring (includes a sense of reliving the experience, illusions, hallucinations, and dissociative (flashback) episodes, even those that occur upon awakening or when intoxicated), (4) intense psychological distress at exposure to events that symbolize or resemble an aspect of the traumatic event, including anniversaries of the trauma.

C. Persistent avoidance of stimuli associated with the trauma or numbing of general responsiveness (not present before the trauma), as indicated by at least three of the following: (1) efforts to avoid thoughts or feelings associated with the trauma, (2) efforts to avoid activities or situations that arouse recollections of the trauma, (3) inability to recall an important aspect of the trauma (psychogenic amnesia), (4) markedly diminished interest in significant activities (in young children, loss of recently acquired developmental skills such as toilet training or language skills), (5) feeling of detachment or estrangement from others, (6) restricted range of affect, e g., unable to have loving feelings, (7) sense of a foreshortened future, e g., does not expect to have a career, marriage, or children, or a long life.

D. Persistent symptoms of increased arousal (not present before the trauma), as indicated by at least two of the following: (1) difficulty falling or staying asleep, (2) irritability or outbursts of anger, (3) difficulty concentrating, (4) hypervigilance, (5) exaggerated startle response, (6) physiologic reactivity upon exposure to events that symbolise or resemble an aspect of the traumatic event (e g., a woman who was raped in an elevator breaks out in a sweat when entering any elevator).

E. Duration of the disturbance (symptoms in B, C and D) of at least one month.

Specify delayed onset if the onset of symptoms was at least six months after the trauma.'

If a plaintiff is suffering from PTSD, and he is sufficiently close in relationship for it to be actionable, it is no defence to the defendant that the plaintiff was a fragile person who is likely to suffer more severely. This is simply an extension of the principle that the tortfeasor must take his victim as he finds him: see *Brice v Brown* [1984] 1 All ER 997.

But although it is foreseeable that a person who has witnessed an accident in which a loved one is killed is likely, indeed almost bound, to suffer the pangs of grief and bereavement, that is not something that sounds in damages: *Hinz v Berry* [1970] 1 All ER 1074, [1970] 2 QB 40. Nor in my judgment does it become actionable even if the grief becomes so severe as to be regarded as abnormal and gives rise to psychiatric illness, the symptoms of which may include depression and anxiety. Such an illness is referred to as pathological grief disorder (PGD); normal grief is usually spent in six to nine months from the bereavement. In *Alcock v Chief Constable of the South Yorkshire Police* [1991] 4 All ER 907 at 924–925, [1992] 1 AC 310 at 409–410 Lord Oliver said:

'... the law will not compensate such a person for the mental anguish and even illness which may flow from having lost a wife, parent or child or from being compelled to look after an invalid, although there is a statutory exception to this where the victim dies as a result of the accident and the victim is his widow or minor unmarried child ... Beyond this, however, the law in general provides no remedy, however severe the consequences of the distress or grief may be to the health or well-being of the third party and however close his relationship to the victim.'

There are in fact two separate illnesses, PTSD and PGD; their symptoms may in some respects be similar, ie include depression and anxiety, but their aetiology is different. The plaintiff in this case can recover if he can show that his present condition is PTSD, that is to say was caused or substantially contributed to by the shock of witnessing the event. He cannot do so if his condition is due to a grief reaction or other causes such as reaction to business stress. This is illustrated by the decision of this court in *Calascione v Dixon* (1993) 19 BMLR 97. The plaintiff suffered both PTSD, having seen the aftermath of an accident in which her son was killed, and PGD. The PGD was obviously based upon the death and bereavement, but normal grief had become abnormal in response to subsequent events which emerged at the inquest and subsequent criminal trial of the defendant. She recovered damages for the PTSD, but not the PGD.

In *Hinz v Berry* the plaintiff was a robust person and it was not altogether clear whether she suffered abnormal grief, though she did suffer what would now be described as PTSD. Lord Denning MR said ([1970] 1 All ER 1074 at 1075, [1970] 2 QB 40 at 42–43):

'In English law no damages are awarded for grief or sorrow caused by a person's death. No damages are to be given for the worry about the children, or for the financial strain or stress, or the difficulties of adjusting to a new life. Damages are however recoverable for nervous shock, or, to put it in medical terms, for any recognisable psychiatric illness caused by the breach of duty by the defendant ... Somehow or other the court has to draw a line between sorrow and grief for which damages are not recoverable; and nervous shock and psychiatric illness for which damages are recoverable.

The way to do this is to estimate how much the plaintiff would have suffered if, for instance, her husband had been killed in an accident when she was 50 miles away; and compare it with what she is now, having suffered all the shock due to being present at the accident. The evidence shows that she suffered much more by being present.'

Lord Pearson said ([1970] 1 All ER 1074 at 1077, [1970] 2 QB 40 at 45):

'It should not be for the whole of the mental anguish and suffering which she has endured during the last five or six years. It should be only for that additional element which has been contributed by the shock of witnessing the accident, and which would not have occurred if she had not suffered that shock. It is a difficult distinction to draw, but I think that the learned judge has laid a proper foundation and has found a right ground of decision, namely that where there is an extra element which has been added by the shock of witnessing the accident, that is a proper subject of compensation.'

This passage undoubtedly suggests that the plaintiff's grief and anguish was abnormal since it lasted for five or six years.

Mr Blunt submitted that it is only normal grief that has to be disregarded and not the grief reaction that is in fact sustained by the plaintiff. The judge accepted this submission, though he then went on to consider the alternative. I cannot accept this submission. It does not seem to me to have any logical basis. I do not see how a defendant can be required to take a plaintiff as he finds him, in this case a fragile personality, who was liable to and does react badly to stress, which is an individual and subjective approach, but disregards the plaintiff's actual reaction to bereavement which may well be more severe because of his personality, and have regard only to some objective standard of a reasonably robust man.

The judge thought his conclusion was supported by my decision in *Brice v Brown*. But with all respect to him, that case had no bearing on this problem. It was a straightforward case of what would now be regarded as PTSD; there was no question of grief or bereavement, since the plaintiff's daughter, who was apparently horribly injured in the accident, in fact made a good and fairly speedy recovery. But the plaintiff herself suffered much more severely because she had a fragile personality.

What the plaintiff is required to do, in my judgment, is to show on balance of probability that the illness from which he is suffering is caused, or substantially contributed to, by the shock, as defined by Lord Ackner, of witnessing the accident. Questions of causation and aetiology in psychiatric medicine are often very difficult because psychiatry is not a precise science. One could find no better example of this than the present case. After 68 days of evidence, about 22 of which seem to have been devoted mainly to medical evidence, the judge found himself unable to accept the opinions of the psychiatrists. Instead he took various parts of their evidence and fitted them to what he perceived to be the pre-accident personality of the plaintiff. The fact that the task is difficult, and I suspect in this case impossible, does not relieve the plaintiff of establishing his case; and if he cannot do so with reasonable clarity, it seems to me that he should fail.

Here there were at least five possibilities. (1) That the plaintiff was suffering from PTSD. (2) That he was suffering from a grief reaction which became pathological. (3) That he was suffering from a combination of PTSD and PGD. (4) That he suffered either PTSD or PGD, but this was superseded by worry and anxiety caused by business stresses. (5) That the PTSD and/or PGD rendered him more vulnerable to the stresses which he had to face when his business collapsed and he was unable to find employment.

This is not a case where damages for grief, even if it causes mental illness, is too remote in law. On ordinary grounds of foreseeability it is not too remote. But as a matter of policy the law stops short of giving damages in such a case; it is uncompensetable loss. In my opinion it does not help to say that the defendant was in breach of duty to the plaintiff because he was in sufficient proximity to the primary victims, and that he suffered mental illness as a result. And I do not think *Page v Smith* [1995] 2 All ER 736, [1996] AC 155, which was not relied upon by the plaintiff, assists. That was a case of a primary and not a secondary victim, and the limitations which apply in the latter case, including the limitation on recovery of damages for grief and bereavement, do not apply.

In my judgment, the decision of the House of Lords in *Bonnington Castings Ltd v Wardlaw* [1956] 1 All ER 615, [1956] AC 613 is of some assistance in illustrating the proper approach. The plaintiff was suffering from pneumoconiosis; there were two sources of dangerous dust in the defendant's factory which had contributed to the plaintiff's condition, one in respect of which they were in breach of statutory duty, which can be referred to as the actionable dust; in respect of the other they were not (the non-actionable dust). The House of Lords held that the onus was upon the plaintiff to prove that the actionable dust caused his illness in the sense that it made a material contribution to the disease. In the present case there is only one actionable cause of the symptoms experienced by the plaintiff, PTSD.

The judge's conclusions

The judge found himself unable to accept the opinions of any of the medical witnesses called before him. He said:

'I do not consider that I am limited to answering yes or no to a particular diagnosis posited by one or other party. The question I have to answer is the one posed above. Among the competing diagnoses and aetiologies are the signposts to a conclusion which must in the end be my own ... I believe that there is force in the contention made on the defendant's behalf that the expert witnesses who have treated the plaintiff, Dr Cuthill and Dr Lloyd, both psychiatrists, and the clinical psychologist, Mr Mackay, have all of them assumed the very thing which the plaintiff in this action is required to prove, namely that he is suffering from PTSD. All three were, of course, treating him, and Dr Lloyd inherited him as a patient at quite a late date. So it is principally upon Mr Mackay and Dr Cuthill that the criticism rests, and particularly upon the latter since it was he who switched from medico-legal diagnosis to treatment in reaction to Mr Vernon's distressed presentation at the first interview. I am not prepared to accept this as a valid critique of the professionalism of any of these witnesses, but it does present me with the problem that each has been working from an established hypothesis rather than setting out first to test the hypothesis against others. However, the two psychiatrists called for the defendant, Dr Swan and Dr Gaind, can be seen for reasons which I have already given to have become comparably "parti pris", again not through lack of professionalism but through the osmotic process which is an almost inevitable incident of litigation of this intensity. This is why I have found assistance in the evidence of all the expert witnesses but do not believe that any one of them has offered a satisfactorily comprehensive account of Mr Vernon.'

And there was the earlier criticism of Dr Cuthill, to which I have referred.

The plaintiff's primary case had been that he was suffering from PTSD complicated by a grief reaction. The judge did not find that the plaintiff was suffering from PTSD, at least as defined in DSM-III-R. In order to do so, he said that he would have to determine the conflict between the impulse that grief often brings to revisit the scene of death and the process of avoidance associated with PTSD. He would have to consider the significance of the plaintiff's river crossings during the holiday in Kenya, which the defendant's experts said was a contra-indication of PTSD. And he might have to resolve the dispute as to the significance of dreams. The plaintiff never claimed to dream about the actual event and there is no contemporaneous record from Dr Cuthill's notes that he experienced any nightmares relating to the accident; although later he said he had nightmares which Dr Mackay thought symbolically related to the accident.

He took the view, I think correctly, that it is possible to diagnose PTSD without rigid adherence to the criteria in DSM-III-R. And this is obviously so if there is no competing diagnosis. The difficulty with this approach is that the less the plaintiff's case fits these diagnostic criteria, the more difficult it is for him to satisfy the burden of proof.

The judge was much influenced by an article by Dr Murray Parkes, entitled 'Bereavement' (1985) 146 Br J Psychiatry 11. The article is not concerned with PTSD, but normal and abnormal (complicated) grief reactions or PGD. The author identifies some of the risk factors which predispose a person to such a reaction. There is no doubt that the plaintiff qualified both as to the circumstances of the death, being sudden, unexpected and untimely, and in horrifying circumstances, though actually witnessing the death is not one of the factors. The relationship with the victims and the previous personality of the plaintiff all predisposed him to a severe and complicated grief reaction. But I agree with Mr O'Brien QC that this article does not assist in the differential diagnosis of PTSD and PDG. And Dr Cuthill's evidence that someone who is predisposed to PDG because of their fragile personality is also predisposed for that reason to PTSD, does not assist.

As I have already indicated, I do not agree with the judge's construction of *Hinz v Berry*, namely all that he had to discount was the normal grief that a reasonably robust person suffers at the bereavement. But he continued:

'If the right test is personal to the plaintiff, then with more hesitation I nevertheless hold that more probably than not Mr Vernon would have grieved but eventually recovered as his wife did, had he learnt of the loss of his daughters but not actually witnessed it. Such a judgment can be no more than educated guesswork (which is another reason for thinking that the law does not call for it); much would depend, for example, on how the news was broken; but I find it possible to visualise a less immediate awareness permitting Mr Vernon to cope, as in the event he did not, with the loss.'

With all respect to the judge, I do not think guesswork, educated or otherwise, is sufficient to discharge the burden of proof, especially when he does not indicate what evidence he relies upon as educating his guess. Mr Blunt sought to support this finding by a reference to a later passage in the judgment where, I think, the judge expressed his final conclusion:

'It is because of the prominent role played by Mr Vernon's personality in the eventual loss of function that I think it safe to conclude that it was witnessing the accident that brought about [his present position]. The peculiarity of Mr Vernon's case lies in the complexity and fragility of the man: throughout his life personality and mental state have reacted upon one another, so that one cannot look in him for textbook conditions in isolation but must try, with the help of expert evidence, to understand as best one can the whole individual. Thus although his condition from the start included features both of post-traumatic stress disorder and of pathological grief, it was not a textbook example of either condition. The principal defect of the trauma, mediated by these features, was on a personality which, unable to cope with them, has given way to what is now an inextricable mixture of psychiatric disorder, personality disorder and, I strongly suspect iatrogenic bias in the manifestation of both. It is those paranoid and neurotic traits demonstrated by the defendant's evidence but not amounting before 1982 to true disorders which have been inflated by the trauma of the index event into major psychiatric and personality dysfunctions.'

But I cannot find any support in this passage for the conclusion that if he had not witnessed the event he would have grieved normally. It seems to me rather to point to the impossibility of determining that it was PTSD, even in its broadest sense, as the cause of the plaintiff's problems. This in effect was the burden of Dr Cuthill's evidence; he said it was impossible to distinguish between a grief reaction and PTSD in the plaintiff's case. And he conceded in cross-examination that in his first three consultations with the plaintiff that there was no symptom recorded in his notes that was necessarily referable to PTSD as opposed to grief reaction.

Having not accepted the opinions of any of the doctors, the judge proceeded to make his own diagnosis. Mr Blunt says he was entitled to do so; what he was doing was making findings as to the plaintiff's pre-accident personality and applying to that personality principles which he culled from the medical evidence. One of the problems about this is that the psychiatrists were able to find an answer to almost any proposition depending upon what precise view was taken of the history of the plaintiff's personality. Thus the judge explained the fact that the plaintiff did not avoid the scene of the accident, avoidance being one of the classic and necessary symptoms of PTSD, on the basis that it was 'very much a piece with Mr Vernon's personality and acquired sense of himself that he would have sought to outface the event by passing the spot, endeavouring—as he was doing socially and at work—to create an artificial sense of normality'. That hardly seems to explain how the plaintiff could return to the scene of the accident a few days after it occurred to take photographs with a view to making a possible claim against the local authority for having a dangerous road, or even going into the river to retrieve the accident warning sign from the car.

There is an important passage in the judgment. The judge quotes from a part of the plaintiff's evidence where he speaks of a fear while standing on the river bank that he would be unable to cope with his despair and control his business, and a premonition of its subsequent collapse. The judge's comment is as follows:

'For the most part the professional witnesses have treated this account, explicitly or implicitly, as another piece of post hoc confabulation. I am not so sure. The self-justificatory exegesis in the second part of the passage ("My subsequent behaviour and feelings should be considered in the light of this premonition" etc) is one of many examples of Mr Vernon's tendency to assert intellectual control over everything he is describing. But the "premonition" itself in my judgment rings true. This was a crisis of utter impotence without precedent in Mr Vernon's life.'

A number of points arise on this passage. But it is an example of the judge rejecting what appears to be the unanimous or virtually unanimous views of the professional witnesses. Secondly, he appears to be accepting that the plaintiff did have these thoughts. If so, as Mr O'Brien pointed out in his reply, it seems to indicate a process of rationalisation which is inconsistent with his mind being violently agitated by the sight, in Lord Ackner's phrase.

The judge returned to this point where he said:

'Mr Dougal Mackay, a clinical psychologist who has been treating Mr Vernon, suggested—and I find this useful—that the stress-prone, competitive and controlling type of personality which is Mr Vernon's may retreat from unmanageable stress into "learned helplessness" (see *Human Helplessness* (1980, ed Garber and Seligman) and that such a personality, faced with feelings of helplessness, may react dysfunctionally to grief (see Worden *Grief Counselling and Grief Therapy* (1982)).'

The article *Human Helplessness* is concerned with coronary heart disease; the particular point is that type A people, who the judge thought included the plaintiff, react badly to stress which they feel powerless to control. But I do not think there is any evidence that a sense of powerlessness to control a situation is a symptom of PTSD.

Although the judge accepted Mrs Vernon's account of the plaintiff's sleep disturbances which I have quoted, and the plaintiff's own account of nightmares in which he found himself grappling with intractable problems and physical dangers, he was not prepared to allocate them to the index event. This must surely be right, since the plaintiff made no mention of nightmares to Dr Cuthill till November 1983, when he attributed them to business worries. This is perhaps all the more striking when he had referred in the first consultation to the defendant's nightmares of the accident.

There is ample evidence in Dr Cuthill's and Dr Barker's notes that it was the plaintiff's worries about his business that was the major cause of stress in 1983 and onwards. That is what the plaintiff was telling both doctors and I see no reason to doubt it. There is an almost total absence of reference to the children in Dr Barker's notes. The comparatively few references in Dr Cuthill's notes seem to relate to grief. They do not indicate obsessional or intrusive thoughts about the accident and its circumstances, which is another hallmark of PTSD.

Basing himself on the lay evidence, the judge found that there was a change in the plaintiff in the months and years following the accident and before the collapse of the business. But that does not provide a reason to the cause of the change. The judge concluded:

'Precisely because these have been reactive and not endogenous changes, they have waxed and waned in relation to other life events. Thus during the lifetime of Paraero, and in spite of the succession of major problems bedevilling it, the stimulus of the job enabled him to function adequately in it, although not with the same grip as before; and correspondingly when the business failed, the anchorage it had provided went with it, with the result that from then on—apart from the again characteristic rally which nearly got him the McDonnell Douglas job—he sank into the kind of demanding helplessness which has seen the collapse of his marriage and the fading of all serious employment prospects. Of all these things the witnessing of the accident was not the sole cause, but it was the initiating cause of an uneven but perceptible sequence of mental deterioration and personality collapse in an already vulnerable individual.'

In the absence of acceptable medical evidence, I do not think the judge was justified in reaching this conclusion, any more than his educated guess that, but for seeing it, he would have grieved normally. It seems to me the judge was presented with an almost impossible task. He sought to tease out of a welter of evidence a case that was very far removed from the classic case of PTSD.

Although I disagree with his conclusions on the main and subsidiary issues, I would wish to pay this tribute to his judgment which in many ways is a tour de force. It reads like a biography as he traces in great detail through the plaintiff's career, interspersing the factual material with observations on the plaintiff's personality at every point in the history. He was not assisted by a clear definition of the issues, which seem to have shifted somewhat in the course of the trial. Nor was he assisted, as he should have been, by disinterested evidence from the medical professional witnesses who were allowed to range unchecked into almost every aspect of the case. In my opinion in this type of case in particular there is much to be said for the practice sometimes adopted in the Family Division of there being a psychiatrist appointed by the court. In the field of psychiatry it may be more difficult for those who have treated the plaintiff to approach the case with true objectivity. That was certainly the case here. Likewise, so far as the defendant's doctors were concerned, the judge thought they were parti pris. This may in fact at least have been due to the very extensive reading of the background of the case, at least so far as Dr Swan is concerned. Certain it is that the case would have been much shorter and would have been kept in more manageable bounds. But at present the rules of court do not permit this course. Unless the parties agree on a psychiatrist—these parties never would have—the court has no power to make such an order.

Mr O'Brien submitted that the judge ought to have accepted Dr Barker's diagnosis, since he commended his perception and, unlike all the witnesses who were called, he was not affected by bias. It is not altogether clear what Dr Barker's diagnosis was, though I think it is clear that he lent no support to the plaintiff's case that he was suffering from PTSD; rather it seems that he regarded the plaintiff as a stress prone individual who was reacting to his business worries. I do not think the judge was bound to accept his diagnosis in the absence of Dr Barker as a witness. What weight he gave to his opinion was a matter for him. But I consider that Dr Barker's notes and letters are very important because they make it clear what was affecting the plaintiff's mind from April 1986 onwards till the plaintiff fell out with him; this was his business worries.

The plaintiff had remained functional in the judge's definition of being able to attend to his business from the time of the accident till its collapse; it was only following that and his failure to get the McDonnell Douglas job that he went seriously downhill and became dysfunctional in the sense that the doctors advised him to give up looking for work, because he was becoming so depressed by his failure.

I have come to the clear conclusion that the plaintiff did not discharge the onus that was upon him of proving that the shock of witnessing the accident caused or substantially contributed to the illness from which he was suffering. That it did so, or was the initiating cause, without which presumably the other events in his life would not have had the same effect on him, seems to me to be speculation and guesswork. And for these reasons I would allow the appeal and dismiss the plaintiff's claim.

In view of the fact that Evans and Thorpe LJJ have reached an opposite conclusion on this aspect of the case and would dismiss the appeal, I must consider the separate heads of damage, interest and costs in respect of which the defendant appeals.

[His Lordship considered the matter of damages, interest and costs and continued:] The appeal will be allowed in part; judgment for the plaintiff for £1,133,962·11 together with interest of £198,271 and costs will be varied and judgment will be entered for the plaintiff for £643,425·56 together with interest to be calculated in accordance with this judgment and costs as set out above.

EVANS LJ. The only issue on liability is whether the plaintiff suffered personal injury by reason of the accident in which his own car, driven by his children's nanny, crashed into the River Tawe where it overturned and his two young children, together with a young friend of theirs, were drowned. He was not physically involved and there is no suggestion of physical injury to him. He claims that he was caused mental or psychiatric injury by reason of the fact that he was an eye-witness, not of the crash itself, but of the attempts which were made to salvage the car and to rescue the children. He saw these in company with his wife from the river bank.

That was in August 1982. He was at that time the managing director of a small private company (Paraero Ltd) which he had bought with the assistance of the British Rail Pension Fund in the previous year. He continued in that post until January 1986 when the company's business was placed in the hands of a receiver and much of its capital was lost. He did not succeed in finding fresh employment by the autumn of 1987 when he was advised by doctors that he should give up the search on account of his deteriorated mental condition. Since then he has devoted himself to preparing for this litigation which finally came to trial in January 1994. Meanwhile, his wife left him in September 1992 and his mental condition deteriorated still further. His performance in the witness box, spread over 27 days of the hearing, left the judge in no doubt that he was suffering from severe mental illness at that time.

Subsequently, the judge heard the evidence of six medical witnesses in the course of 24 hearing days. The total of the hearing was 68 days. In January 1995 the judge gave a 262-page judgment, which, if I may respectfully say so, is a tour de force, describing the whole of the plaintiff's life history in the light of the evidence which he had heard.

It is a matter of great concern that the hearing lasted so long and that the costs were so prodigiously high. The judge said: 'The reason is that practically every element, and every detail of every element, of the plaintiff's claim is contested on behalf of the defendant.' There is an undertone of criticism of the defendant or her representatives in that remark. This makes it necessary to consider the procedural history in a little more detail. There were, in my judgment, two principal reasons why the hearing was always likely to be prolonged. First, the plaintiff claimed more than £4m as damages, based on his allegation supported by highly reputable accountants and business consultants that the mental injury which he sustained by reason of witnessing the accident led to the failure of the

company's business in 1986. The size of the claim made it inevitable that the
defendant's representatives would spare little or no effort and expense in their
resistance to it. So far as the accountancy and business evidence was concerned,
this was kept within manageable bounds, but the second reason for the length
and cost of the hearing was the medical evidence which, in my judgment, got
completely out of hand, with the result that, in the judge's words, 'every aspect
of the plaintiff's life since leaving school' was examined in the course of the
evidence of expert and factual witnesses, mostly by reference to the unusually
large number of documents which the plaintiff himself was able to produce, or
which the parties were able to obtain from his former employers, the Ministry of
Defence (because he spent nine years from 1960 until 1969 in the army), and
other sources.

THE ISSUES
    Given the potential scope of this inquiry, it is lamentable in my view that
nothing whatsoever was done by either party to define the issues which were
raised by the medical evidence or to seek to limit the area of inquiry in some other
way. The pleadings conspicuously failed to perform this function. The plaintiff
gave particulars of injury as follows: '[The plaintiff] suffered a very severe degree
of nervous shock or psychological trauma and subsequently developed a severe
post-traumatic type of neurosis complicated by a severe grief reaction.'
    The defence, served in February 1988, admitted that the accident was caused
by the negligence of the defendant, who was the nanny who was driving the
plaintiff's car, and in its second paragraph said merely: 'No admissions are made
in respect of the pain, inconvenience, loss and damage which the plaintiff claims
to have suffered.'
    At that date the defendant's representatives had not consulted either of the two
doctors whom they called as expert witnesses at the trial, so presumably they
could not have reflected in that pleading any of the issues which subsequently
were raised. They instructed their first expert, Dr Gaind, shortly afterwards, and
there followed numerous requests for disclosure of further documents which
eventually the plaintiff was able to comply with to the extent indicated above. Dr
Gaind saw the plaintiff in April 1988. His report dated 7 December 1990 was
received by the plaintiff's solicitors on 21 May 1991. The contents of this report
gave some notice that the area of inquiry would be extensive and that issues
would be raised at the trial which did not begin to be identified in the defence.
    The case was set down for hearing in June 1993 on the defendant's application,
and at about that time leave was obtained to serve a further report from a second
medical expert witness, Dr Marion Swan. She saw the plaintiff for one day on 7
September 1993 and after thorough consideration of a large number of
documents supplied to her by the defendant's solicitors she produced a 38-page
report on 5 October 1993. Her conclusions were that the plaintiff and his wife had
suffered no more than the normal grief reaction of any parent following their
bereavement and the admittedly traumatic experience of seeing their daughters'
deaths, and that:

> 'I believe that Mr Vernon's business failed for reasons which were not
> associated with the accident but arose from factors in his medical,
> educational, family and work background and that such failure was more
> than probable given the background history of the matter and Mr Vernon's
> track record at the time when he became a company director.'

If any thought had been given at this time, which apparently it was not, to identifying the medical issues which this evidence raised, it would have amounted to a denial that the plaintiff suffered from mental illness after the accident, or that any such illness was caused by the accident, and that the failure of his business was caused, not by such injury as he alleged, but by the complex of other factors to which reference was made, including the plaintiff's 'track record' meaning the history of his business career before 1981. This allegation of an independent cause of the whole or a major part of the plaintiff's alleged loss should certainly have been pleaded, but it was not. This is more than a technical pleading point, if only because, had the pleadings been amended at that time, it would have become clearer than it was at the trial that the defendant's case, and Dr Swan's evidence in particular, went far beyond what she said in this report. Moreover, the question might well have been raised, but it was not, whether Dr Swan had the necessary expertise to give any opinion evidence as to the reasons why the business failed or the plaintiff's competence as a business man. She does not claim to have any experience of psychiatry or psychology in a business or industrial setting.

At or before the beginning of the trial, the defendant admitted that the relationship between the plaintiff and his daughters was close enough, and that he was sufficiently proximate in time and place to the accident in which they died, to give rise to a duty of care owed by the defendant to him in accordance with the principles established by the House of Lords decision in *Alcock v Chief Constable of the South Yorkshire Police* [1991] 4 All ER 907, [1992] 1 AC 310. She also accepted that the experience of witnessing the deaths of his own two young children was an event which might cause psychiatric damage to a person of normal fortitude. So the remaining issue on liability was whether the plaintiff sustained a mental injury which was caused by that experience. Because there was no admission that the plaintiff has suffered from mental illness (until the defendant conceded at the end of the trial that he was suffering from depression, a form of recognisable psychiatric illness, at the time of the trial, though not earlier), this issue sub-divided into two: had the plaintiff suffered from mental illness after witnessing the accident and losing his daughters in 1982, and if so, was that illness caused or contributed to by that experience?

The case for the defendant, as it appeared from her medical experts' reports, was: (1) the plaintiff was not and never had been mentally ill; (2) if he was, the illness occurred only after and as a result of the failure of his business in 1986 and his separation from his wife and their children, born since 1982, in 1992; (3) the failure of the business was caused by its initial lack of viability and/or the plaintiff's own shortcomings, both personal and as a businessman; (4) between 1982 and 1986 the plaintiff suffered from no more than the usual reactions of grief and bereavement which were to be expected from any person in his position; and (5) if the plaintiff was mentally ill at any time, it was no more than the manifestation as the result of stress of a personality disorder which he has suffered from since early childhood and which had appeared occasionally before 1982.

There were in addition issues as to the amount of damages, if the defendant was liable. In particular, the claims for loss sustained by reason of the failure of the business and for the plaintiff's failure to obtain fresh employment after 1986, which depended upon his employability and therefore upon his personality and his freedom from mental illness at that time, clearly overlapped the liability issues to such an extent that it was not easy to distinguish between them.

The evidence of the plaintiff and 38 witnesses, together with thousands of documents, including many which were relied upon under the Civil Evidence Act as evidence of the truth of facts, and even of opinions, stated in them, was directed to these complex issues. But the process was wholly undisciplined by pleadings or any other attempt to define in writing the issues which were raised. The plaintiff's representatives did suggest that the accountancy evidence, dealing primarily with the reasons why the business failed, could be reserved for a separate trial, but this was opposed by the defendant on the grounds that those issues were closely linked with the central issue on liability and that a second trial would become necessary in any event if the first was limited in that way. This objection succeeded and it cannot be said that it was wrong. But the sad fact remains that no other attempt was made to identify the issues which the proceedings were intended to resolve. The most powerful and the most obvious weapon in the forensic armoury against unnecessary time and expense is to define the issues in advance of the trial. It was not used.

The misfortunes do not end there. The extent to which the issues changed in the course of the hearing, and the defendant's case in particular, is strikingly demonstrated by a passage from the evidence of their leading expert witness, Dr Swan, when she was being examined in chief by Mr O'Brien QC on day 56. Her evidence was that by the end of 1986 the plaintiff 'must have become increasingly more distressed by his failure [to obtain fresh employment]'. She was asked about a condition described as 'learned helplessness' which had been observed in experiments on rats. The theory, she said—

> 'has been extrapolated to people who suffered so many blows in life that they would give up ... what I see as having happened to Mr Vernon is that he repeatedly failed on the career front. I think probably we have got to go back right to childhood and count all the blows that were whirled on him, his failure to get as many O levels as he had hoped',

and so through his army and business careers until—

> 'when the receivership happens he picks himself up again and does not really lower his sights. At the point when it comes to an end he falls apart.'

What is remarkable, as Mr Blunt QC observed in his submission to us, is that the catalogue of disasters as listed by her does not contain any mention of the 1982 accident or of the loss of his children. And on any view the witness had moved a considerable way from denying that the plaintiff suffered from any mental disorder, even after 1986.

Equally striking is the emergence of what became the defendant's principal submission before us, attacking the judge's conclusion that the plaintiff did sustain a mental injury by reason of witnessing the accident in 1982. The submission is that a crucial distinction exists between post-traumatic stress disorder (PTSD) and the feelings of grief and bereavement which follow naturally from the death of a loved one and which can themselves develop into a form of mental illness (pathological grief disorder, or PGD). This distinction has emerged in the medical literature since the early 1980s, and a classification is found in the *Diagnostic and Statistical Manual of Mental Disorders* published by the American Psychiatric Association in Washington DC. The revised third edition, known as DSM-III-R, is dated 1987. Mr O'Brien's submission is that the judge did not find that the plaintiff suffered from PTSD as so defined and that the evidence does not justify such a finding. Therefore, he submits, the plaintiff fails to establish the only kind of mental injury for which damages are recoverable at law, and any   *a* illness which may have manifested itself before 1986 was a consequence of the plaintiff's natural feelings of grief and bereavement. (The suggestion of a pre-existing personality disorder to which Dr Swan committed herself in her evidence was rejected by the judge, and the defendant does not appeal against this finding.)

This was a remarkable development of the defendant's case. There was no   *b* reference to PTSD or to PGD in Dr Swan's pre-trial report, but this may be explained by the fact that in her view as expressed in that report the plaintiff suffered no more than 'the pain and suffering as a consequence of [witnessing the accident] and the tragedy of bereavement such as it would affect any parents in such circumstances'. Dr Gaind saw the plaintiff in April 1988 and reported in   *c* December 1990. In his opinion, 'the death of his children did set him back a little but did not produce severe depression. Mr Vernon had grieved properly and recovered from bereavement within a short time'. His only reference to 'post-traumatic neurosis' was in relation to a minor road accident in which the plaintiff was or may have been concussed in December 1985 but which it is not now suggested has any bearing on the issues with which this appeal is concerned.   *d*

Dr Gaind's second report dated 16 August 1993 followed a further examination of the plaintiff on 21 July 1993. He diagnosed two distinct depressive disorders, the second being a depressive neurosis which had 'remained with him for many years'. He considered that the plaintiff had 'grieved properly and recovered from his bereavement within a short time', referring to 'Uncomplicated Bereavement',   *e* part of DSM-III-R. He concluded that the plaintiff suffered from paranoid psychosis 'which in spite of regular use of neuroleptics has been poorly controlled' and he added in the final sentence, 'Finally, I do not believe he does, or ever did, suffer from PTSD (post-traumatic stress disorder)' and he referred to the diagnostic criteria for PTSD as described in DSM-III-R. This seems to have   *f* been the first introduction of the DSM classification into the present case. The consequent need for differential diagnosis ie distinguishing between the illness described as PTSD, meaning, in legal terms, the consequences of involvement as a primary or a secondary victim of the shocking or traumatic event, and on the other hand feelings of grief and bereavement (uncomplicated bereavement) which may lead to the mental illness described as PGD, is now central to   *g* Mr O'Brien's submissions, for the reasons indicated above.

It is not clear, even now, how the defendant's case on the medical issues should be formulated in the light of the evidence given at the trial. It seems to come to this. She accepts that the plaintiff was suffering from mental illness at the time of the trial. She says that this was precipitated, first, by the failure of the company's   *h* business in January 1986 and his failure to obtain fresh employment thereafter, and by the fact that his wife with their children born since 1982 left him in September 1992. The underlying cause can be found, she says, in his medical and career history back to his schooldays. He has suffered throughout from a personality disorder which at times of stress, both before and after 1982, had   *j* resulted in degrees of mental illness and sometimes in physiological ie physical symptoms also. But she denies that the plaintiff suffered from 'nervous shock' by reason of his experience in August 1982, and she says that, if he did suffer from mental illness during the period between then and the failure of the business in January 1986, then that was no more than the extreme reaction to grief and bereavement which can be classified as 'pathological grief disorder' and is

a
described in the article by Dr Murray Parkes extensively quoted by the judge ('Bereavement' (1985) 146 Br J Psychiatry 11).

She denies that the plaintiff suffers or ever has suffered from the psychiatric illness classified as 'post-traumatic stress disorder'; in other words, that he sustained any mental injury from the experience of witnessing the accident in which his daughters were killed.

b
In these circumstances, it is hardly surprising that the judgment, masterly though it is, reads more as a biography of the plaintiff, mostly in chronological order, as seen by the judge after hearing the conflicting views of the medical expert witnesses.

This lengthy introduction to the issues raised by the appeal has been necessary because in my judgment the correct, if more mundane, approach is to identify the
c
issues and then ask in relation to each issue what the judge's findings were and whether or not they were supported by the evidence that he heard. Moreover, I consider that in the circumstances and for reasons which I shall give below regard should be had in the first instance to the factual evidence of lay witnesses rather than to the differing interpretations advanced by the expert witnesses of the facts
d
so established.

The principal issues, in my judgment, are simply these: (1) Did the plaintiff suffer from mental illness (a) after August 1982 and before January 1986; (b) after January 1986? (2) If so, was the mental illness caused or contributed to by his witnessing of the accident in August 1982? (3) If so, what is the correct measure of damages for the injury so caused?
e

(1)(a) *Did the plaintiff suffer from mental illness after 1982 and before January 1986?*

First, it is necessary to say something about terminology. The phrase traditionally used in the legal authorities is 'nervous shock' or 'mental shock'.
f
This was defined in *Hinz v Berry* [1970] 1 All ER 1074 at 1075, 1077, [1970] 2 QB 40 at 42, 44 as a 'recognisable psychiatric illness' per Lord Denning MR and Lord Pearson. It was suggested recently that the appropriate term might be 'mental trauma' (per Hoffmann LJ in *Page v Smith* [1994] 4 All ER 522 at 549) but 'trauma' is used to refer both to the injury and to its cause (the traumatic event). The medical literature which we have seen suggests that 'disorder' or 'mental
g
disorder' has become something of a term of art (PGSD and PGD are examples of its use). I do not see what advantage is gained by departing from the basic concept of 'mental illness' or 'mental injury'. The law is prepared to award damages for personal injury which extends beyond physical or organic injury to include psychiatric injury, meaning (literally) injury to the mind. Disorder of the
h
mind is no more than a metaphor, although a dramatic and useful one, as was Lord Ackner's graphic definition of 'shock' in *Alcock's* case [1991] 4 All ER 907 at 918, [1992] 1 AC 310 at 401:

> '"Shock", in the context of this cause of action, involves the sudden appreciation by sight or sound of a horrifying event, which violently agitates
j
> the mind.'   .

I shall therefore use the phrases 'mental illness' and 'mental injury' in the hope that they are sufficiently precise to convey the same meaning as 'recognisable psychiatric disorder' and the lawyers' favourite, 'nervous shock'.

A second preliminary observation is this. By definition, the mental illness in question is not necessarily accompanied by physical or organic injury, or even by any deterioration in physical health. To that extent its symptoms, therefore, are behavioural: conduct or speech which is regarded as 'inappropriate', meaning, as I understand it, not to be expected from a 'normal' person. This factor has some implications for the admissible scope of expert psychiatric evidence, because it may mean that ultimately the psychiatrist is expressing his or her own view as to the extent to which the observed behaviour departs from what is normal. (This does not mean and I do not suggest that there is no scope for such evidence, for there are many other respects in which it may be necessary to enable the judge to reach a fully informed conclusion; for example, to state from the witness' own experience how long the 'uncomplicated' reaction to grief and bereavement may last in a 'normal' person). It is for this reason in my judgment that the starting point for this particular inquiry is not the opinions of expert witnesses but the factual evidence of what the plaintiff said and did—how he behaved—during the periods in question.

[His Lordship then described the judge's assessment of the witnesses who deposed to the plaintiff's mental state. He continued:] The judge's overall finding on this issue, after considering the medical evidence, is:

'Of all these things the witnessing of the accident was not the sole cause, but it was the initiating cause of an uneven but perceptible sequence of mental deterioration and personality collapse in an already vulnerable individual.'

In so far as the finding rests upon the factual evidence, I do not consider that the defendant can even begin to suggest that it was not fully supported by evidence which the judge accepted and upon which he relied. There clearly was a change for the worse in the plaintiff's behaviour, conduct and speech, during the period after the accident and before 1986. The question is whether these were the symptoms of mental illness and, which is relevant rather to the question of causation, what the illness was.

The only medical witness who treated the plaintiff during this period was the consultant psychiatrist, Dr J M Cuthill, who practises in South Wales. The plaintiff was referred to him not by his general practitioner but by the solicitors who were handling his and his wife's claims arising out of the accident, in January 1983. Dr Cuthill saw him in March and immediately formed the view that he was in need of treatment which he himself undertook. Dr Cuthill's status as an expert witness was criticised by the judge, as were most if not all of the other experts who gave evidence at the trial, but the facts were as follows. Dr Cuthill continued to see and treat the plaintiff until 1987, and it was his diagnosis which formed the basis for the 'Particulars of injury' already quoted from the statement of claim, served in July of that year ('a very severe degree of nervous shock or psychological trauma and subsequently developed a severe post-traumatic type of neurosis complicated by a severe grief reaction'). He wrote to the plaintiff's GP on 11 March 1983:

'At the time of [the first] examination I felt it was imperative that he have some more active treatment, although he himself has been very reluctant to ask for it ... he continues to be exceptionally tense and has great difficulty in sleeping.'

After further examinations, Dr Cuthill wrote on 2 December 1983:

a   'I felt that he was more generally depressed ... and it would seem that he has for some years had spells of depression and has even had anti-depressant therapy.'

Pausing at this stage, before considering the opinion evidence of other expert witnesses, it seems to me that there is a clear basis in this historic evidence of what Dr Cuthill's diagnosis was for the judge's finding that not only was the plaintiff a b   changed man after 1982 but that his behaviour was symptomatic of mental illness during and after 1983.

So the question becomes, was the opinion evidence of the defendant's expert witnesses, Dr Gaind and Dr Swan, such that the judge's conclusion is demonstrably wrong? Effectively, they challenged the correctness of Dr Cuthill's c   diagnosis ten years after the event. Their primary evidence was that the plaintiff suffered no more pain and suffering then was inevitable, given the circumstances in which he suffered the loss of his children as they did. In so far as they were saying that the plaintiff did not suffer from any form of mental illness before 1986, their evidence clearly was rejected by the judge, and it is not necessary in my view to say more on this issue than that in my judgement he clearly was entitled, d   indeed he was correct, to do so. The main thrust of Mr O'Brien's submissions to us has been that the symptoms, whether of illness or not, were those of grief and bereavement rather than of post-traumatic stress. That issue lies more in the realm of causation, to which I shall come below.

e   (b) *Did the plaintiff suffer from mental illness after 1986 and before the date of trial?*

Although this is not formally admitted by the defendant, I do not believe that the contrary is seriously arguable. Dr Swan's evidence as to what were, in her view, the consequences first of the failure of the business in January 1986 and secondly of the plaintiff's wife and children leaving him in 1992, an extract from f   which I have quoted above, effectively admits that his mental condition deteriorated to the point of illness during this period. In her first report she said:

'It was at this point [1986] that he experienced a major mental breakdown and it would appear that he has never fully recovered from this ...'

g   There must have been some reason why this was not formally admitted, but I do not understand what it was.

(2) *Causation*

(a) Introduction

h   This is the issue which lies at the heart of the case. I would define it thus: does the evidence establish that the mental illness from which the plaintiff suffered between 1982 and 1986, and after 1986, was caused or contributed to by shock which he sustained by reason of seeing the accident and its aftermath in which his two daughters were drowned?

j   The starting point of this inquiry, in my judgment, is the defendant's formal concession that that experience was one which might cause psychiatric injury to a person of reasonable, which I take as meaning normal, fortitude. It is also, effectively, common ground that the plaintiff in 1982 when he underwent the experience was, in the judge's words, a vulnerable personality; not to the extent alleged by the defendant of suffering from a paranoid personality disorder, but because there were traits in his personality which made him particularly vulnerable to the effects of stress, both in his personal and his business life, as he had demonstrated often before.

It is also common ground that he suffered as distressing an experience as can be imagined. In Dr Swan's words:

> 'No one can consider that the accident involving Mr Vernon's children and their friend was anything other than tragic, eliminating as it did at one blow both of his offspring in the most gruesome circumstances imaginable ... The most distressing cases I have dealt with have probably been those where parents have witnessed the deaths of their children.'

These admitted facts, together with the finding which I would uphold that the plaintiff did suffer from mental illness after, but not before, August 1982, are sufficient in my judgment to establish at least a prima facie case that the illness was caused, or at least contributed to, by the traumatic experience. Put another way, it would seem remarkable that a vulnerable personality should have emerged unscathed from such an horrendous experience of that sort. This corollary of Dr Swan's evidence was not, it seems, pointed out directly to her, but it appears to me that it was a clear inference from the evidence which she gave.

But the burden of proving that there was such a connection between the experience and the illness remains with the plaintiff, and the defendant challenges it by ascribing the plaintiff's symptoms, not to illness resulting from the experience, but to his feelings of grief and bereavement, whether or not they led to illness (pathological grief disorder) in his case.

It is clear law that the plaintiff is only entitled to recover damages if he proves that his illness was caused or contributed to by the traumatic experience, as distinct from grief and bereavement: *Hinz v Berry* [1970] 1 All ER 1074, [1970] 2 QB 40. It is also established that the distinction between PTSD and PGD can be drawn when the medical evidence makes it appropriate to do so (*Calascione v Dixon* (1993) 19 BMLR 97) though it should be noted that in that case the judge's finding, which this court upheld, was that the PGD was 'an arresting or an intensification in the grief-healing process ... due to later events', including the activity or inactivity of the police and the subsequent inquest and trial of the defendant, a feature which is not present in this case, at least before 1986.

So the inquiry becomes whether the plaintiff's symptoms of illness were exclusively referable to grief and bereavement. If the evidence fails to establish that they were not, and that they were at least partly referable to his traumatic experience, then despite the apparent unlikelihood of the plaintiff being unaffected by the experience his claim for compensation must fail.

This is pre-eminently the issue to which the medical expert evidence was or should have been directed, and it becomes necessary at this stage to say something about these witnesses and the judge's findings about them.

(b) The (medical) expert witnesses

In his leading speech in *McLoughlin v O'Brian* [1982] 2 All ER 298 at 312, [1983] 1 AC 410 at 432–433 Lord Bridge of Harwich held that—

> 'the consensus of informed judicial opinion is probably the best yardstick available to determine whether, in any given circumstances, the emotional trauma resulting from the death or injury of third parties ... was ... the actual cause in fact, of the plaintiff's psychiatric or psychosomatic illness. But the word I would emphasise in the foregoing sentence is "informed". For too

a long earlier generations of judges have regarded psychiatry and psychiatrists with suspicion, if not hostility. Now, I venture to hope, that attitude has quite disappeared.'

So the role of the psychiatrist, like all other expert witnesses, is to inform the judge of matters which are relevant and within his area of expertise (and, I would add for completeness, which it cannot be assumed are already within the judge's
b own knowledge from experience of everyday life). But it cannot be suggested that the psychiatrist as a witness is not subject to the same disciplines as other expert witnesses. Their duties and responsibilities were set out by Cresswell J in *National Justice Cia Naviera SA v Prudential Assurance Co Ltd, The Ikarian Reefer* [1993] 2 Lloyd's Rep 68 and approved by this court, presided over by
c Stuart-Smith LJ ([1995] 1 Lloyd's Rep 455). Cresswell J said ([1993] 2 Lloyd's Rep 68 at 81–82):

'B. *THE DUTIES AND RESPONSIBILITIES OF EXPERT WITNESSES*   The duties and responsibilities of expert witnesses in civil cases include the following: 1. Expert evidence presented to the Court should be, and should be seen to
d be, the independent product of the expert uninfluenced as to form or content by the exigencies of litigation (*Whitehouse v. Jordan* ([1981] 1 All ER 267 at 276, [1981] 1 WLR 246 at 256–257) per Lord Wilberforce). 2. An expert witness should provide independent assistance to the Court by way of objective unbiased opinion in relation to matters within his expertise (see *Polivitte Ltd. v. Commercial Union Assurance Co. Plc.* ([1987] 1 Lloyd's Rep 379 at 386) per
e Mr. Justice Garland and *Re J* ([1991] FCR 193) per Mr. Justice Cazalet). An expert witness in the High Court should never assume the role of an advocate. 3. An expert witness should state the facts or assumption upon which his opinion is based. He should not omit to consider material facts which could detract from his concluded opinion (*Re J*). 4. An expert witness
f should make it clear when a particular question or issue falls outside his expertise. 5. If an expert's opinion is not properly researched because he considers that insufficient data is available, then this must be stated with an indication that the opinion is no more than a provisional one (*Re J*). In cases where an expert witness who has prepared a report could not assert that the report contained the truth, the whole truth and nothing but the truth
g without some qualification, that qualification should be stated in the report (*Derby & Co. Ltd. and Others v. Weldon and Others* ((1990) Times, 9 November) per Lord Justice Staughton). 6. If, after exchange of reports, an expert witness changes his view on a material matter having read the other side's expert's report or for any other reason, such change of view should be
h communicated (through legal representatives) to the other side without delay and when appropriate to the Court.'

Stuart-Smith LJ said ([1995] 1 Lloyd's Rep 455 at 496):

j '... the judge gave an admirable resumé of the duties and responsibilities of expert witnesses. We have no hesitation in endorsing it. We would, however, add one word of caution in relation to par. 4: That an expert should make it clear when a particular question or issue falls outside his expertise.'

Sadly, in the present case the judge did not receive the assistance from the expert witnesses which he was entitled to expect. Before I quote from the relevant parts of his judgment, I should identify the expert witnesses who were called. They were, for the plaintiff, first, Dr Cuthill to whom reference has already been made; he saw the plaintiff for what is called a 'medico-legal opinion' ie for the purposes of giving evidence in subsequent proceedings, and proceeded in fact to treat him from March 1983 until December 1987. Second, Mr Dougal Mackay, a chartered clinical psychologist who practises in Weston-super-Mare and who first saw the plaintiff in September 1986 and continued doing so until October 1993, the total period covered by his two reports. Third, Dr Gilbert Lloyd, a consultant psychiatrist practising in Gloucester who first saw the plaintiff in October 1991.

For the defendant, the two medical expert witnesses were Dr Gaind, a consultant neuropsychiatrist, and Dr Swan, a forensic psychiatry consultant in independent practice. Dr Gaind saw the plaintiff twice, in 1988 and 1993, and Dr Swan once, in 1993, for the purpose of preparing their reports. Each therefore was called as an independent expert whose first-hand knowledge of the plaintiff was limited to those examinations.

The reason why Dr Cuthill ceased treating the plaintiff was apparently one of geography. After the business ceased to occupy him in South Wales in early 1986 the plaintiff was mostly at home in Gloucestershire. His GP referred him to a consultant psychiatrist in Bristol, Dr Barker, in April 1986, who took over his treatment from Dr Cuthill in South Wales. Dr Barker was not called as a witness, though apparently he was not shown not to be available if either party had wished to do so. His manuscript notes and some correspondence were produced in evidence and the judge ruled that the documents were admissible as evidence of their contents, not limited to factual matters. But he declined to treat Dr Barker as an absent expert witness, and in my judgment he was entirely correct to do so.

With regard to the expert witnesses who were called, the judge said:

> 'I believe that there is force in the contention made on the defendant's behalf that the expert witnesses who have treated the plaintiff, Dr Cuthill and Dr Lloyd, both psychiatrists, and the clinical psychologist, Mr Mackay, have all of them assumed the very thing which the plaintiff in this action is required to prove, namely that he is suffering from PTSD ... I am not prepared to accept this as a valid critique of the professionalism of any of these witnesses, but it does present me with the problem that each has been working from an established hypothesis rather than setting out first to test the hypothesis against others. However, the two psychiatrists called for the defendant, Dr Swan and Dr Gaind, can be seen for reasons which I have already given to have become comparably "parti pris", again not through lack of professionalism but through the osmotic process which is an almost inevitable incident of litigation of this intensity.'

(He could have added, in my view, that the witnesses were invited or allowed to roam over large areas which were outside their medical expertise eg the plaintiff's performance as a businessman and the reasons for the failure of his business.)

In these circumstances, he proceeded to make his findings on the basis that it was necessary to form his own view, drawing upon the evidence of the various witnesses and the medical literature to such extent as he thought it appropriate to do so. Mr O'Brien submits that that was the wrong approach, and that if he found the expert witnesses' evidence unacceptable he should nevertheless have adopted the views expressed by Dr Barker, so far as they could be discerned from his notes and the letters which he wrote. I do not think that this submission can

a be right. Lord Bridge defined the role of the expert witnesses in this situation as that of 'informing' the judge so as to guide him to the correct conclusions. It must be for the judge to gauge the weight and usefulness of such assistance as he is given and to reach his own conclusions accordingly. And he was entitled, in my judgment, an already stated, to decline to go so far as to treat Dr Barker as an

b expert witness who happened not to have been called.

It is unfortunate that the trial was hijacked by the expert witnesses as it was. To pursue the metaphor, expert witnesses are armed with the court's readiness to receive the expert evidence which it needs in order to reach a fully informed decision, whatever the nature of the topic may be. But their evidence ceases to be useful, and it may become counter-productive, when it is not marshalled by

c reference to the issues in the particular case and kept within the limits so fixed. Identifying those limits is the primary responsibility of counsel and, if necessary, of the judge. When they are exceeded, or not made sufficiently clear, then the hearing is likely to be lengthened and the judge's task becomes more onerous than it already is. Properly informed, he must decide the issues to the best of his

d judgment, depending ultimately on the exercise of common sense in the light of the evidence he has heard. Lord Bridge in *McLoughlin v O'Brian* [1982] 2 All ER 298 at 315, [1983] 1 AC 410 at 437 also quoted from Lord Wright's speech in *Bourhill v Young* [1942] 2 All ER 396 at 406, [1943] AC 92 at 110 with regard to the proper ambit of the duty of care:

e   'The lawyer likes to draw fixed and definite lines and is apt to ask where the thing is to stop. I should reply it should stop where in the particular case the good sense of the jury, or of the judge, decides.'

(c) The law

f   For reasons which I hope will become apparent, it next becomes necessary, in my judgment, to consider the authorities which indicate the correct approach. These have been referred to by Stuart-Smith LJ and I would summarise their effect as follows. Although grief and suffering by others, even mental injury, is the foreseeable result of causing injury or death to a primary victim, the tortfeasor is not liable to those others for such consequences of his negligence

g unless two conditions are satisfied. For reasons of policy, the recovery of damages is limited to those in a close and loving relationship with the victim and who were themselves connected with the accident in time and place eg as a bystander and direct viewer: *McLoughlin v O'Brian* [1982] 2 All ER 298, [1983] 1 AC 410 and *Alcock v Chief Constable of the South Yorkshire Police* [1991] 4 All ER 907,

h [1992] 1 AC 310. Both conditions must be satisfied, and the person who seeks to recover damages must prove that he or she has suffered mental illness ('nervous shock') as the result of the traumatic experience: *Hinz v Berry* [1970] 1 All ER 1074, [1970] 2 QB 40.

This policy result has been achieved by limiting the scope of the defendant's

j duty of care to those who foreseeably were directly (the primary victim) or indirectly (the secondary victim) affected by the defendant's negligent act: see *Jaensch v Coffey* (1984) 155 CLR 549.

It is trite law that if the plaintiff is a person to whom a duty of care was owed, then damages are recoverable for the breach of the duty, subject to the damages claimed not being regarded as 'too remote' a consequence of the breach. That this is the correct approach in principle is confirmed, in my judgment, by the recent (majority) decision of the House of Lords in *Page v Smith* [1995] 2 All ER 736, [1996] AC 155. The defendant could reasonably foresee that the plaintiff might suffer physical injury, but not mental injury ('nervous shock'). Nevertheless, he was liable for the latter as well as the former, because he owed the plaintiff a duty of care and had caused a kind of injury for which damages are recoverable in law.

The present case is one where, admittedly, the defendant owed the plaintiff a duty of care and the duty was broken. In order to recover damages, the plaintiff has to prove that his involvement in the accident, though as a bystander, caused him mental injury. If so, then in principle he is entitled to recover damages for the illness he has suffered. But if he fails to prove that there was a causal link between his illness and his involvement in the accident, then his action fails.

Damages for mental injury do not include compensation for feelings of grief and bereavement which are not themselves symptomatic of illness; indeed, they are identified as the 'normal' consequences of such a bereavement, when it occurs. That the damages are limited in this way was established, in my view, by *Hinz v Berry*. This is not the policy-induced rule, recognised in *McLoughlin v O'Brian* and later decisions, which limits the scope of the duty of care, but rather a restriction on the heads of damage which may be recovered by a successful plaintiff. In technical legal terms, damages for 'normal' grief and suffering may be said to be too remote to be recoverable in law.

What if the plaintiff, who was a secondary victim and was owed a duty of care by the defendant, has suffered mental illness which properly should be regarded as a consequence both of his experience as a bystander and of an intense ie more than normal grief reaction to the bereavement which he suffered? This presupposes that the mental illness can be ascribed to both causes by medical science, rather than to one, and that the causes can be regarded as independent, or several, rather than joint ie combined causes of the resulting mental state. In such a case, are the damages limited to compensation for that part of the mental illness which can be ascribed to the experience rather than to the grief? As it has tended to be expressed in the present case, must the damage be discounted for grief and the consequences of bereavement, even if the plaintiff's illness was partly so caused?

In my judgment, this particular issue is not covered by the authorities, and I would hold that the damages for mental injury should not be discounted in this way. *Hinz v Berry* held that damages are not recoverable for feelings of grief and bereavement, but it was not suggested there that those feelings had worsened into illness or were partly the cause of the plaintiff's illness. In *Calascione v Dixon* (1993) 19 BMLR 97 the illness caused by grief (PGD) was found to have a subsequent post-accident cause. The question, in my view, is one of remoteness of damage and of the kinds of injury for which damages may be recovered. Mental injury suffered in consequence of witnessing at first hand an accident involving a loved one as its primary victim is actionable in law. In principle, damages are recoverable for injury caused partly by the negligence of the defendant, even if there was another cause and the negligence was only a contributory cause: *Bonnington Castings Ltd v Wardlaw* [1956] 1 All ER 615, [1956] AC 613 (this leads to the proposition that the plaintiff is entitled to recover damages for an injury caused *or contributed to* by the negligence of the defendant, provided that it was a 'substantial' or 'significant' contributory cause). Mental illness, as distinct from grief and other emotional sufferings resulting from bereavement, is a kind of injury which is recognised by the law. Therefore, I would hold that damages are recoverable for mental illness caused or at least contributed to by actionable negligence of the defendant ie in breach of a duty of care, notwithstanding that the illness may also be regarded as a pathological consequence of the bereavement which the plaintiff, where the primary victim was killed, must inevitably have suffered.

If this is a correct view of the law, then it has the following advantages for the trial of cases such as this. First, it is unnecessary to research into the niceties of psychiatric medicine in order to discover whether part, and if so what part, of the plaintiff's illness should be ascribed to bereavement rather than to the traumatic experience of witnessing the accident. Perhaps these are questions which even the experts find it difficult to answer—Dr Cuthill said more than once that he finds it impossible to do so, even now more than ten years since he first treated the plaintiff and after much research has been published. And it must be remembered that the only reason for making the inquiries, if they are necessary, is to set a limit to the damages which are recoverable by a plaintiff who has established the right to sue. The number of such persons is restricted, for policy reasons, in order to limit the exposure of defendants to claims by those who were only indirectly affected by their acts. I do not see any policy reason for limiting the damages in the way that is suggested, particularly when the line between recovery and non-recovery would or might depend upon a detailed psychiatric inquiry in every case. If the plaintiff was owed a duty of care, then he should recover, in my view, damages for the injury which he has sustained ie the illness from which he suffers. After all, even if his illness is partly attributable to the pathological consequences of grief and bereavement, it was nevertheless caused by the defendant's negligent act, and the policy reasons which limit the scope and number of those to whom a duty is owed do not provide equal justification for limiting the damages recoverable by those who can sue (see also *Clerk and Lindsell on Torts* (17th edn, 1995) para 7-51 'Policy and flexibility').

Secondly, the practical consequence of the submission for the defendant seems to be this. Only a plaintiff who had a close and loving relationship with the primary victim can recover damages, but the damages would have to be assessed so as to exclude the consequences of the bereavement which the plaintiff must have suffered, if the loved one was killed. This in my view would be an unrealistic and artificial exercise, just as the judge found that he could not do better than make an 'educated guess' as to what the extent of the plaintiff's grief reaction would have been if he had been a person of normal fortitude and not particularly vulnerable in circumstances of stress. If the law is, simply, that a plaintiff who is entitled to sue (who was owed a duty of care) can recover damages for mental illness caused or contributed to by his involvement as a secondary victim of the accident, notwithstanding that his illness may also be described as, in part, a pathological grief reaction to the bereavement which he has suffered, then it is unnecessary to embark on the process which the judge, not surprisingly, found both abstract and difficult in the present case.

(d) The evidence

It is essentially on this issue that I find myself constrained, reluctantly, to differ from the conclusion reached by Stuart-Smith LJ on this part of the case. I approach it, for the reasons given above, on the basis that the evidence of the lay ie the factual witness shows that the plaintiff's mental health declined after the accident to such an extent that he was showing symptoms of mental illness early in 1983, and in the light of the defendant's admission that he had an experience which, grief and bereavement apart, might cause mental injury to a person of reasonable fortitude—which he was not. The plaintiff's expert witness, Dr Cuthill, ascribed the illness in part to the post-traumatic consequences of that experience, and he was unable to distinguish between those consequences and symptoms of grief and bereavement which undoubtedly contributed to his mental deterioration also. The defendant's expert witnesses sought to distinguish between PTS and PGD as though they are universally recognised and mutually exclusive categories, or rather, labels for two such categories of mental illness, which I do not believe that they are. The publication DSM-III-R itself contains a number of cautions, including the following which was quoted by the judge:

> 'Although this manual provides a classification of mental disorders, no definition adequately specifies precise boundaries for the concept "mental disorder" ... There is no assumption that each mental disorder is a discrete entity with sharp boundaries (discontinuity) between it and other mental disorders, or between it and no mental disorder ...'

First, the defendant's experts' evidence does not persuade me that it is wrong to ask, if the plaintiff did suffer from mental illness after 1982 and before 1986, simply whether that illness was at least contributed to by the experience of witnessing the accident. If that question is asked, I find it impossible as a matter of common sense to distinguish between the effect upon his mind of seeing the accident, which was especially traumatic for him because he knew that his children were victims of it and were almost certainly dead, and the effects of grief and bereavement which became inevitable when he knew that they had in fact been killed. I do not see how he could avoid recalling what he had seen without the anguish of knowing that they were involved, nor remember them without recalling the awful circumstances in which they died. Indeed, part of Dr Swan's written evidence seems to suggest that the experience and the grief are necessarily interrelated in this way. She went so far in her second report as to say that, in her view—

> 'had Mr Vernon not witnessed the aftermath of the accident in the way that he did ... the grief that he subsequently experienced might have been worse, because he would have been likely to have had fantasies about the accident, even more distressing than the circumstances were.'

She also said:

> 'While it might appear to be common sense that the sight of the accident would cause nervous shock to Mr Vernon, I do not think that there is any evidence that this occurred.'

I would be strongly inclined to allow common sense a greater part: but it is sufficient for present purposes to note the linkage between grief and the experience which she allows may exist.

Secondly, the defendant's case was that the plaintiff suffered from a form of mental illness—paranoid personality disorder—long before the accident, and although this allegation failed, the judge nevertheless found, and both parties accept, that he was particularly vulnerable to stress and had been so throughout his adult life. Thus, he reacted adversely and sometimes with physical symptoms to various crises in his army (ages 18 to 27) and business (ages 28 to 40) careers. Yet the defendant's experts assert that he was unaffected, so far as his mental condition was concerned, by what they acknowledge was one of the most traumatic experiences that any person could have the misfortune to undergo. That would be surprising in any event, and it becomes unacceptable, in my view, when the evidence shows that he did become mentally ill after the accident; the illness cannot have been entirely caused by feelings of grief in which mental turmoil caused by his witnessing the accident played no part. The more vulnerable that he was, and the more frequently he had reacted aversely to stress before 1982, the less likely it seems to me that he was unscathed by witnessing the accident then.

I therefore would hold that the evidence proves that the plaintiff suffered mental injury by reason of the accident in 1982 and that this was contributed to, if not entirely caused, by the fact that he witnessed its aftermath as he did. But, strictly, my view on this issue is irrelevant. The judge held that witnessing the accident was the initiating cause of the plaintiff's mental decline which began after the accident and continued thereafter, with further impetus from the subsequent failure of the business in 1986 and the breakdown of his marriage in 1992. He also found that the failure of the business would not, of itself, have caused mental illness, because of the plaintiff's well-developed 'defence mechanisms' to that kind of event. There was evidence both factual and expert which supported these conclusions, and I do not feel that we should interfere with them.

I would also express my entire agreement with the judgment of Thorpe LJ, particularly with regard to the appellant's submission that damages can only be recovered for the kind of mental illness currently, but not universally, classified as PTSD, as distinct from PGD. As medical science advances, these or different categories may come and go. The duty of the courts, as I see it, is to take account of contemporary knowledge and to decide whether the plaintiff has suffered mental injury caused by the negligence of the defendant, and then to apply the policy limits on recovery which have been identified in *Alcock v Chief Constable of the South Yorkshire Police* [1991] 4 All ER 907, [1992] 1 AC 310 and elsewhere, and which may themselves change with the law.

(e) Causation post-1986

I have been troubled by the thought that the correct analysis of the plaintiff's symptoms since 1982 might be along the following lines. Already a vulnerable personality, he suffered mental illness in consequence of seeing the accident in August 1982, combined with effects of grief and bereavement upon his by-now-disordered mind. During the next three years, however, as he concentrated on the waning fortunes of his business, he effectively recovered from this illness, or at least it was overtaken by the effects of two further blows: the minor car accident in which he was concussed in December 1985, and then the collapse of his business in January 1986.

Because the defendant has denied throughout that the plaintiff was ill before 1986, or indeed until after his wife left in 1992, she has never stated her case in this way, even in the alternative, as regards the period before 1986. There is no evidence, therefore, directed to the question whether the plaintiff could have recovered by 1986 from mental illness caused by seeing the accident in August 1982. Her contention that any illness which he has suffered was solely caused by events in 1986 and subsequently was rejected by the judge. I have wondered whether it should be accepted to the limited extent referred to above ie that they caused a separate illness in and after 1986.

If that was the correct approach, then the plaintiff would be entitled to recover a presumably smaller amount by way of general damages, but only a negligible sum as special damages—the great majority is claimed to have been suffered after 1986.

I have come to the conclusion that it would be wrong to recast the case for the defendant in this way. No evidence was directed towards this possible explanation, and the explanation itself is no more than a partly-informed guess from the evidence that was given as to the plaintiff's mental state. We were not invited to consider it, and in my judgment we should not take it upon ourselves to do so.

I would add, in deference to Stuart-Smith LJ's view that some inference may be drawn as to what Dr Barker's evidence would have been, if his report had been available or he had been called as an expert witness, that Dr Barker saw the plaintiff for the first time in April 1986, and so he could only speak with first-hand knowledge of the plaintiff's mental health after the business had collapsed and what was on any view an aggravating factor had occurred (two, if the motor accident was significant also). Even if it is correct to infer that his evidence would have supported the defendant's case as to the cause of the plaintiff's condition at that time, this would not contradict Dr Cuthill's evidence that the plaintiff was ill before 1986 and that the cause or causes of the illness at that time were what Dr Cuthill believed them to be.

CONCLUSIONS

For these reasons, I would uphold the judge's finding that the plaintiff is entitled to recover damages for mental illness which he suffered after 1982, and with increased severity after 1986, and I agree with it on the basis of the evidence which he heard.

DAMAGES

It is sufficient for me to say that I agree with the judgment of Stuart-Smith LJ in all aspects of damages, interest and costs, for the reasons which he gives.

I would dismiss the appeal against liability but reduce the amount of the judgment accordingly.

THORPE LJ.

The issue of liability

In the latest House of Lords case, *Alcock v Chief Constable of the South Yorkshire Police* [1991] 4 All ER 907 at 926, [1992] 1 AC 310 at 411, Lord Oliver of Aylmerton classified what the plaintiff had to establish in order to succeed as follows:

'The common features of all the reported cases of this type decided in this country ... and in which the plaintiff succeeded in establishing liability are, first, that in each case there was a marital or parental relationship between the plaintiff and the primary victim, secondly, that the injury for which damages were claimed arose from the sudden and unexpected shock to the plaintiff's nervous system, thirdly, that the plaintiff in each case was either personally present at the scene of the accident or was in the more or less immediate vicinity and witnessed the aftermath shortly afterwards and, fourthly, that the injury suffered arose from witnessing the death of, extreme danger to, or injury and discomfort suffered by the primary victim. Lastly, in each case there was not only an element of physical proximity to the event but a close temporal connection between the event and the plaintiff's perception of it combined with a close relationship of affection between the plaintiff and the primary victim.'

Of these five features there was in the present case no issue as to numbers one, three and five. Liability turned upon the second and fourth features. The second feature requires the successful plaintiff to establish that he has suffered injury from nervous shock. In *Hinz v Berry* [1970] 1 All ER 1074 at 1075, [1970] 2 QB 40 at 42 Lord Denning MR said:

'Damages are however recoverable for nervous shock, or, to put it in medical terms, for any recognisable psychiatric illness caused by the breach of duty by the defendant.'

Subsequently in *McLoughlin v O'Brian* [1982] 2 All ER 298 at 301, [1983] 1 AC 410 at 418 Lord Wilberforce said:

'Although we continue to use the hallowed expression "nervous shock", English law, and common understanding, have moved some distance since recognition was given to this symptom as a basis of liability. Whatever is unknown about the mind-body relationship (and the area of ignorance seems to expand with that of knowledge), it is now accepted by medical science that recognisable and severe physical damage to the human body and system may be caused by the impact, through the senses, of external events on the mind. There may thus be produced what is as identifiable an illness as any that may be caused by direct physical impact.'

Lord Bridge of Harwich said ([1982] 2 All ER 298 at 311, [1983] 1 AC 410 at 431):

'The basic difficulty of the subject arises from the fact that the crucial answers to the questions which it raises lie in the difficult field of psychiatric medicine. The common law gives no damages for the emotional distress which any normal person experiences when someone he loves is killed or injured. Anxiety and depression are normal human emotions. Yet an anxiety neurosis or a reactive depression may be recognisable psychiatric illnesses, with or without psychosomatic symptoms. So, the first hurdle which a plaintiff claiming damages of the kind in question must surmount is to establish that he is suffering, not merely grief, distress or any other normal emotion, but a positive psychiatric illness.'

In the court below Mr O'Brien QC argued, amongst other things, that there were two essentially relevant medical diagnoses. The first was post-traumatic stress disorder (PTSD) and the second was pathological grief disorder (PGD). On his presentation, in order to succeed the plaintiff had to prove PTSD. If all he established was PGD then, in Mr O'Brien's submission, he failed on the application of the principle which he said was contained in the judgments in *Hinz v Berry* [1970] 1 All ER 1074 at 1075, [1970] 2 QB 40 at 43 and expressed in the following sentence in the judgment of the Lord Denning MR:

'Somehow or the other the court has to draw a line between sorrow and grief for which damages are not recoverable; and nervous shock and psychiatric illness for which damages are recoverable.'

It may be that Mr O'Brien was encouraged along this path by *Calascione v Dixon* (1993) 19 BMLR 97. From the judgment of Neill LJ it is clear that the case below proceeded on that footing. He quoted (at 101) the following passage from the judgment of French J:

'There are, as I hope will be apparent already, two psychiatric illnesses to consider: PTSD, the first; and PGD, the second. As to the first—PTSD—that is almost, by definition, a condition due to the accident, the collision or its aftermath. That is the trauma which forms part of the title of the condition. The second—pathological grief disorder—almost, though not quite, by definition is not.'

That Neill LJ approached the case on a wider basis seems to me plain by his definition of the issue in the appeal in the following paragraph (at 105):

'The crucial question to be answered in this case is whether the sights and sounds which Mrs Calascione experienced on 21 December 1985, caused or contributed to her PGD and, if so, for how long.'

I myself would be against confining in any way the type of 'recognisable psychiatric illness' which Lord Denning stated to be the medical definition of 'nervous shock'. *Hinz v Berry* was an appeal on quantum and not liability but the psychiatric illness for which damages were assessed was, according to the report of the consultant psychiatrist, 'morbid depression'. In *Brice v Brown* [1984] 1 All ER 997 at 1006 Stuart-Smith J, having cited the passages from the speeches in *McLoughlin v O'Brian*, said:

'Nevertheless all their Lordships in that case continued to use the phrase "nervous shock", albeit in inverted commas. I think it is a convenient phrase to describe mental injury or psychiatric illness to distinguish it from, on the one hand, grief and sorrow and, on the other, physical or organic injury. The psychiatric illness does not have to have any particular label or term of art applied to it.'

In fact the psychiatric condition proved by the plaintiff in that case was a hysterical personality disorder.

The evidence in the present case established that the diagnosis of PTSD seems to have entered medical literature in 1980 with the publication of DSM-III by the American Psychiatric Association. That classification was revised in 1987 and labelled DSM-III-R. It was the diagnostic classification in DSM-III-R that Mr O'Brien relied upon at the trial. DSM-III-R may provide the medical profession with a useful diagnostic tool but PTSD and its DSM-III-R classification should not, in my judgment, be adopted in personal injury litigation as the yardstick by which the plaintiffs' success or failure is to be measured. First, PTSD is not a bespoke measure for the purpose of nervous shock litigation. It was produced for other purposes and is itself of a much wider range; for instance a victim of sexual abuse may subsequently develop PTSD. Furthermore it is but one of many relevant psychiatric diagnoses. The fact that it is a diagnosis that necessarily involves a shock is not a reason for elevating it to the exclusion of other psychiatric illnesses that may be shock induced. Although in personal injury litigation it is sometimes said that the plaintiff must show shock to the nervous system or shock to the mind what ultimately is in issue is psychiatric illness whether it be the product of shock to the mind, to the nervous system or to the psyche. Second, medical science in this field is continuously expanding and evolving. The concept of PTSD is still relatively recent and its evolution is certainly not complete. Indeed in time it may be superseded by some different concept. Third, developmental disorders of personality as opposed to mental illness seem to me to be unusually difficult to classify and define in the concrete terms within which physical illness can usually be defined. Fourth, within the range of available expertise there is a wide divergence of stance and terminology between the psychiatrist who treats psychiatric illness largely chemically and the psychiatrist who favours a psychodynamic approach that emphasises the importance of the patient's unconscious. I suspect that the medical utility of the DSM-III-R classification would be differently assessed across this front line of medical expertise. Finally, DSM-III-R is not the only diagnostic manual. The World Health Organisation has produced the ICD-10 classification which defines PTSD in similar but nonetheless different terms.

Of course there is attraction in PTSD as a yardstick in these difficult cases for the reason expressed by French J. But if a plaintiff proves PGD as well as all the other necessary features of success as defined by Lord Oliver of Aylmerton in the passage cited, in my judgment he is entitled to succeed. PGD may be a recognisable psychiatric illness as is plainly demonstrated by the article by Dr Murray Parkes 'Bereavement' (1985) 146 Br J Psychiatry 11 relied upon by Sedley J. Perhaps because the article was submitted for publication in January 1984 it does not list PTSD as a specific psychiatric disorder in relation to bereavement.

Of course in the present case it was plainly strategically attractive to Mr O'Brien to present PTSD as defined by DSM-III-R as the essential yardstick since the plaintiff was clearly in difficulty in picking up sufficient ticks within boxes B, C and D of the diagnostic criteria. But psychiatric illness is too complex and insufficiently concrete to be subjected to such a rigid analysis. It is in my judgment regrettable that so much of the expert evidence at the trial was concentrated upon what seems to me to be clearly the wrong test. Sedley J was absolutely right to reject, as he did, the submission that the issue was PTSD as defined in DSM-III-R or nothing.

One of the most unfortunate aspects of this trial is that the expert evidence called by the parties failed to give the judge the help that he deserved. Of the three psychiatrists who had held clinical responsibility for the plaintiff's illness over more than a decade preceding trial only two were called and only the first had been approached for medico-legal opinion initially. The judge found that they, together with the behavioural psychotherapist to whom one of the three had referred the plaintiff were all flawed in that they had assumed the very thing that the plaintiff was required to prove. The two psychiatrists called by the defendant, neither of whom had any clinical experience of the plaintiff, he judged to be parti pris.

Of course there are both advantages and disadvantages for the expert in having carried a clinical responsibility for the plaintiff. From the doctor-patient relationship there might develop a sympathy for or identification with the plaintiff that jeopardises objectivity. Against that the clinician has the opportunity to develop an understanding of the plaintiff and his condition developed over an extensive relationship for which the assessment consultation of the medico-legal specialist can be no substitute.

Not only did Sedley J complain of these shortcomings in the expert witnesses but also of the fact that claims to legal professional privilege had denied him a sight of the letters by which they were instructed.

The use of psychiatric evidence in the Family Division expanded dramatically in the 1970s. Real difficulties were encountered with experts whose contributions were marred by lack of necessary experience, inadequate preparation, partiality or the failure to seek agreement, or at least reduction of issues, with other experts in the case in advance of trial. A number of judgments have been given at first instance in order to state clearly the requirements and the expectations of the court. A clear statement was made by Cazalet J in *Re R (a minor) (experts' evidence)* [1991] 1 FLR 291. Practical extensions were made by Wall J in *Re AB (child abuse: expert witness)* [1995] 1 FLR 181, *Re C (expert evidence: disclosure: practice)* [1995] 1 FLR 204 and *Re G (minors)* (1994) 20 BMLR 10. Of course proceedings in the Family Division are not purely adversarial. Proceedings under the Children Act 1989 or in wardship are quasi-inquisitoral. Even in ancillary relief proceedings authority clearly establishes the existence of a duty of full and frank disclosure owed by the litigant to the court arising out of the statutory function imposed on the judge by the Matrimonial Causes Act 1973. Thus, where experts come to testify and in so far as there is a conflict between the expert's duty to the court and his duty to the party instructing him, the duty to the court manifestly prevails. Once an expert is instructed, privilege does not attach to the resulting communication. The letter of instruction must be disclosed if called for as must be any report that results, even if it is fatal to the case of the party instructing the expert.

Some similar principles seem to govern the contributions of experts in the commercial court. In *National Justice Cia Naviera SA v Prudential Assurance Co Ltd, The Ikarian Reefer* [1993] 2 Lloyd's Rep 68 at 81 Cresswell J defined the duties and responsibilities of expert witnesses in civil cases, citing the decision of Cazalet J in *Re J (child abuse: expert evidence)* [1991] FCR 193. His statement was indorsed with one small caution in the subsequent judgment of this court.

[His Lordship then described the expert evidence and continued:] Now it may be that neither Dr Gaind nor Dr Swan were aware of their duties and responsibilities as defined in *The Ikarian Reefer*. As the judge found, they did not fulfil those duties and responsibilities, specifically because they lost objectivity and became parti pris. The area of expertise in any case may be likened to a broad street with the plaintiff walking on one pavement and the defendant walking on the opposite one. Somehow the expert must be ever mindful of the need to walk straight down the middle of the road and to resist the temptation to join the party from whom his instructions come on the pavement. It seems to me that the expert's difficulty in resisting the temptation and the blandishments is much increased if he attends the trial for days on end as a member of the litigation team. Some sort of seduction into shared attitudes, assumptions and goals seems to me almost inevitable. I would more tentatively hazard that it is likely to be easier for the expert holding a current NHS consultancy or a chair in medicine to maintain detachment than one whose principal responsibility is to undertake medico-legal work. The responsibilities and anxieties of the clinician presumably help to maintain a balanced perspective of the court room contribution.

Not only does the daily attendance of the expert jeopardise detachment but it inflates the cost of litigation. The practice direction that requires the parties to file a detailed schedule of costs expenditure which applies to financial claims in the Family Division is not known in personal injuries litigation. But in a written submission on the interest point from Mr Blunt QC he stated that the plaintiff's legal aid costs below were estimated to be £1,028,000. He put the defendant's costs below at £1m. Mr O'Brien subsequently commented that the figure was speculation but he did not take the opportunity to proffer any other figure. In the absence of information I would infer that the defendant's costs exceeded the plaintiff's since amongst their disbursements were the cost of daily attendance by Dr Gaind and Dr Swan for a substantial proportion of the hearing. That the legal costs of determining the plaintiff's entitlement should exceed £2m simply demonstrates that in the intensity of the fight all sense of proportion was lost.

Of course it is over two years since the opening of the trial. In that interim there has been the Lord Chief Justice's practice direction of 24 January 1995 on case management (see [1995] 1 All ER 385, [1995] 1 WLR 508). What it requires of the judge was anticipated by Sedley J, who on the sixty-fourth day imposed time limits on the evidence of the remaining witnesses and required counsel's submissions in writing. Then in June 1995 Lord Woolf's interim report, *Access to Justice*, was published. Chapter 23 in Section V demonstrates how widespread are the problems encountered by Sedley J with the medical experts. Although specific cases illustrating the general problem are no doubt legion this trial is hopefully amongst the most extreme. A number of the recommendations proposed in Ch 23 should ensure that it survives only as a memorial to bad past practice.

The views which I have expressed above on the medical issues and evidence lead me to the clear conclusion that the appeal on liability fails. Sedley J conducted a most profound and impressive analysis of the plaintiff's medical history, work history, and personality. In particular he analysed the plaintiff immediately prior to the accident, the accident and its aftermath, what had happened to the plaintiff, and the plaintiff at trial. The manner in which Sedley J expressed his findings and conclusions demonstrates the profundity and sophistication of his analytical survey. Of course in a judgment extending to no less than 262 pages the appellate advocate will always find material to justify a submission of inconsistency, oversight and misdirection in law. The judge was faced with an extremely complex task necessitating the review of a mass of evidence both documentary and oral. Within that mass there is ample that might have led to a verdict for the defendant. But the judge's appraisal led him to the conclusion that the plaintiff was entitled to succeed on liability and the appellant has not in my judgment demonstrated any misdirection on the route to that conclusion.

I am in agreement with the reduced quantification proposed by Stuart-Smith LJ. I am also in agreement with the need to increase the discount to reflect periods of unemployment to the figure which he has stated. I am also in agreement with his conclusions on the other areas of quantification, upon the claim to interest, and upon the issue of costs.

Appeal on liability dismissed. Appeal on quantum allowed.

Paul Magrath Esq   Barrister.

Vernon v Bosley (No 2)

COURT OF APPEAL, CIVIL DIVISION

STUART-SMITH, EVANS AND THORPE LJJ

22, 23 OCTOBER, 5–8 NOVEMBER, 13 DECEMBER 1996

Discovery – Discovery against parties to proceedings – Documents coming into party's possession after discovery but before judgment – Plaintiff claiming damages in respect of post-traumatic stress disorder after witnessing death of his two children in accident – Evidence in family proceedings revealing that plaintiff had substantially recovered – Judgment in family proceedings delivered before judgment in personal injury litigation – Changed prognosis not communicated to defendant, judge or Court of Appeal in personal injury litigation – Whether plaintiff under duty to disclose changes in his health and prognosis – Whether evidence as to changes in plaintiff's health and prognosis should be admitted on rehearing of appeal – RSC Ord 24.

Practice – Counsel – Litigant – Duty to court – Duty not to mislead court – Scope of duty.

In 1982 the plaintiff witnessed unsuccessful attempts to rescue his two daughters from a motor car which had plunged into a river while being driven by the defendant, their nanny. After the accident the plaintiff's mental condition deteriorated, his business failed, he was unable to obtain any other employment and his marriage broke down. The plaintiff brought an action against the defendant claiming damages in respect of nervous shock or psychiatric injury (ie post-traumatic stress disorder) sustained when he witnessed the aftermath of the accident. The judge upheld the plaintiff's claim that the witnessing of the aftermath of the accident was a substantial cause of his persistent and ongoing mental illness, but rejected his claim for failure of his business on the ground that it would have failed in any event. The defendant appealed to the Court of Appeal, which affirmed the judge's decision, although it reduced some of the heads of damage which he had awarded. However, before any final order was drawn up, the defendant's counsel received anonymously through the post copies of a county court judgment in earlier family proceedings between the plaintiff and his wife relating to their three children and the judgment of the Court of Appeal affirming it. The judgments revealed that the evidence in the family proceedings, in particular that of the plaintiff's two medical specialists, was that the plaintiff's psychiatric health had dramatically improved and that he was substantially, if not fully, recovered. The plaintiff's advisers knew of the changed prognosis before the judge gave judgment in the personal injury proceedings, although on their advice that prognosis was not communicated to the judge or to the Court of Appeal and it was unknown to the defendant's advisers. The defendant applied to the Court of Appeal for the appeal to be listed for rehearing, and for leave to adduce further evidence in the form of the reports of the plaintiff's two medical specialists and their evidence in the family proceedings, together with the evidence of other witnesses.

Held (Evans LJ dissenting) – (1) A party to civil litigation was under a continuing obligation under RSC Ord 24, r 1[a] until the conclusion of the proceedings to disclose all relevant documents whenever they came into his possession, unless

---

a   Rule 1, so far as material, is set out at p 624 *c*, post

they were clearly privileged from disclosure, notwithstanding that discovery by list or affidavit had already been made. Where, therefore, a document was disclosed to a party after he had closed his case, or the evidence as a whole was concluded, he should apply to the court to reopen the case in the light of the disclosure if the document was of real significance and there was otherwise a risk of injustice. It followed that the existence of the reports of the two medical experts, notes of evidence and the judgment in the family proceedings should have been disclosed to the defendant's advisers before the judge gave judgment. Moreover, since that evidence was relevant to the plaintiff's mental condition at the time of the judge's judgment and to the prognosis for the future and might have affected the assessment of general damages, future loss of earnings and the loss of future care and assistance, and since the events in question occurred so close to the trial, the court would admit it, as not to do so would be inequitable and would affront common sense or any sense of justice (see p 620 *j*, p 622 *f g*, p 623 *g*, p 626 *b* to p 627 *a g* to *j*, p 628 *b*, p 647 *b* and p 651 *e f*, post); *Mulholland v Mitchell (by his next friend Hazel Doreen Mitchell)* [1971] 1 All ER 307 applied; dictum of Hawkins J in *Mitchell v Darley Main Colliery Co* (1884) 1 Cab & El 215 at 216–217 approved; *James v Plummer* (1888) 23 LJNC 107 overruled.

(2) Having regard to that evidence, the further appeal would be allowed and the quantum of damages reduced accordingly (see p 631 *g* to p 632 *a*, p 647 *b* and p 653 *d* to *f*, post).

Per Stuart-Smith and Thorpe LJJ. Every litigant is under a duty not to mislead the court or his opponent until the judge has given judgment, and he does not discharge his duty simply by accepting the advice of his legal advisers: if the advice is incorrect, he is responsible for it vis-à-vis the other party to the civil litigation where the legal advisers are acting within the scope of their actual or ostensible authority. However, where the case has been conducted on the basis of certain material facts which are an essential part of the party's case, which are discovered before judgment to be significantly different, and there is a danger that the court will be misled, it is counsel's duty to advise his client that disclosure should be made, and if the client refuses to accept his advice (per Stuart-Smith LJ) he should not make the disclosure himself but should withdraw from the case; (per Thorpe LJ) in those circumstances, he has a duty to disclose the relevant material to his opponent and, unless there is agreement between the parties to the contrary, to the judge (see p 629 *e* to *h*, p 630 *f* to *h*, p 631 *a*, p 647 *b* and p 654 *a b*, post).

Notes

For disclosure of documents generally, see 13 *Halsbury's Laws* (4th edn) paras 37–55, and for cases on the subject, see 18 *Digest* (2nd reissue) 67–101, 571–876.

Cases referred to in judgments

Birds Eye Walls Ltd v Harrison [1985] ICR 278, EAT.
Blamire v South Cumbria Health Authority [1993] PIQR Q1, CA.
Derby & Co Ltd v Weldon (No 9) [1991] 2 All ER 901, [1991] 1 WLR 652.
Hughes v Singh (1989) Times, 21 April, [1989] CA Transcript 356.
James v Plummer (1888) 23 LJNC 107, DC.
L (a minor) (police investigation: privilege), Re [1996] 2 All ER 78, [1997] AC 16, [1996] 2 WLR 395, HL.
Ladd v Marshall [1954] 3 All ER 745, [1954] 1 WLR 1489, CA.
Lid Brokerage and Realty Co (1977) Ltd v Budd [1992] 2 WWR 453, Sask QB.

Livesey (formerly Jenkins) v Jenkins [1985] 1 All ER 106, [1985] AC 424, [1985] 2 WLR 47, HL.

Meek v Fleming [1961] 3 All ER 148, [1961] 2 QB 366, [1961] 3 WLR 532, CA.

Mitchell v Darley Main Colliery Co (1884) Cab & El 215; *rvsd on other grounds* (1884) 14 QBD 125, CA; *on appeal* (1886) 11 App Cas 127, [1886–90] All ER Rep 449, HL.

Mulholland v Mitchell (by his next friend Hazel Doreen Mitchell) [1971] 1 All ER 307, [1971] AC 666, [1971] 2 WLR 93, HL.

Murphy Stone Wallwork (Charlton) Ltd [1969] 2 All ER 949, [1969] 1 WLR 1023, HL.

National Justice Cia Naviera SA v Prudential Assurance Co Ltd, The Ikarian Reefer [1993] 2 Lloyd's Rep 68; *rvsd* [1995] 1 Lloyd's Rep 455, CA.

Ontario Bean Producers' Marketing Board v W G Thompson & Sons Ltd (Farm Products Marketing Board, third party) (1982) 134 DLR (3d) 108, Ont HC.

Saif Ali v Sydney Mitchell & Co (a firm) (P, third party) [1978] 3 All ER 1033, [1980] AC 198, [1978] 3 WLR 849, HL.

TNT Management Pty Ltd v Trade Practices Commission, Brambles Holdings Ltd v Trade Practices Commission (1983) 47 ALR 693, Aust Full Fed Ct.

Tombling v Universal Bulb Co Ltd [1951] 2 TLR 289, CA.

Ventouris v Mountain, The Italia Express [1991] 3 All ER 472, [1991] 1 WLR 607, CA.

With v O'Flanagan [1936] 1 All ER 727, [1936] Ch 575, CA.

Cases also cited or referred to in skeleton arguments

Abbey National Mortgages plc v Key Surveyors Nationwide Ltd (1995) 44 Con LR 22.

Aegis Blaze, The [1986] 1 Lloyd's Rep 203, CA.

Barrell Enterprises, Re [1972] 3 All ER 631, [1973] 1 WLR 19.

Bastow v Bagley & Co Ltd [1961] 3 All ER 1101, [1961] 1 WLR 1494, CA.

Black & Decker Inc v Flymo Ltd [1991] 3 All ER 158, [1991] 1 WLR 753.

Board v Thomas Hedley & Co Ltd [1951] 2 All ER 431, CA.

British Coal Corp v Dennis Rye Ltd (No 2) [1988] 3 All ER 816, [1988] 1 WLR 1113, CA.

Brown v Matthews [1990] 2 All ER 155, [1990] Ch 662, CA.

Bula Ltd v Tara Mines [1994] 1 IR 493, Ir SC.

Calcroft v Guest [1898] 1 QB 759, [1895–9] All ER Rep 346, CA.

Campbell v Tameside Metropolitan BC [1982] 2 All ER 791, [1982] QB 1065, CA.

Curwen v James [1963] 2 All ER 619, [1963] 1 WLR 748, CA.

Dinham v British Steel Corp [1986] CLY 1505.

Dolling-Baker v Merrett [1991] 2 All ER 890, [1990] 1 WLR 1205, CA.

Drennan v Brooke Marine Ltd (1983) Times, 21 June.

Essex CC v R (Note) [1994] Fam 167.

Goldman v Hesper [1988] 3 All ER 97, [1988] 1 WLR 1238, CA.

Goldstone v Williams Deacon & Co [1899] 1 Ch 47.

Great Atlantic Insurance Co v Home Insurance Co [1981] 2 All ER 485, [1981] 1 WLR 529, CA.

Guinness Peat Properties Ltd v Fitzroy Robinson Partnership [1987] 2 All ER 716, [1987] 1 WLR 1027, CA.

Harrison's Share under a Settlement, Re, Harrison v Harrison, Re Ropner's Settlement Trusts, Ropner v Ropner [1955] 1 All ER 185, [1955] Ch 260, CA.

Initial Services Ltd v Putterill [1967] 3 All ER 145, [1968] 1 QB 396, CA.

K and ors (minors) (disclosure of privileged material), Re [1994] 3 All ER 230, sub nom *Kent CC v K* [1994] 1 WLR 912.

Kenning v Eve Construction Ltd [1989] 1 WLR 1189.

Medway v Doublelock Ltd [1978] 1 All ER 1261, [1978] 1 WLR 710.
Millensted v Grosvenor House (Park Lane) Ltd [1937] 1 All ER 736, [1937] 1 KB 717, CA.
Minnesota Mining and Manufacturing Co v Rennicks (UK) Ltd [1991] FSR 97.
Myers v Elman [1939] 4 All ER 484, [1940] AC 282, HL.
Oxfordshire CC v M [1994] 2 All ER 269, [1994] Fam 151, CA.
Pittalis v Sherefetting [1986] 2 All ER 227, [1986] QB 868, CA.
Polivitte Ltd v Commercial Union Assurance Co plc [1987] 1 Lloyd's Rep 379.
Pritchard v J H Cobden Ltd [1987] 1 All ER 300, [1988] Fam 22, CA.
R (M J) (a minor) (publication of transcript), Re [1995] Fam 89.
Rondel v Worsley [1967] 3 All ER 993, [1969] 1 AC 191, HL.
Roux v Australian Broadcasting Commission [1992] 2 VR 577, Vic SC.
Shearson Lehman Hutton Inc v Maclaine Watson & Co Ltd [1989] 1 All ER 1056, [1988] 1 WLR 946.
Shocked v Goldschmidt (1994) Times, 4 November.
Sybron Corp v Barclays Bank plc [1985] Ch 299.
Warden v Peddington (1863) 32 Beav 639, 55 ER 251.

Application and appeal

Following the decision in *Vernon v Bosley (No 1)* [1997] 1 All ER 577 whereby the Court of Appeal (Evans and Thorpe LJJ; Stuart-Smith LJ dissenting) dismissed an appeal by the defendant, Katherine Sarah Bosley, from the decision of Sedley J on 30 January 1995 (28 BMLR 1) that she was liable to the plaintiff, Peter Frazer Vernon, for damages for nervous shock or psychiatric injury, but reducing the overall quantum of damages awarded by the judge, the defendant applied on 30 April 1996 for the appeal to be listed for rehearing and for discovery of and leave to adduce in further evidence certain documents whose existence had come to the defendant's attention since the Court of Appeal judgment. By amended notice of appeal dated 7 November 1996 the defendant appealed from the decision of Sedley J on quantum on the further grounds, inter alia, that the existing award had been based on a false basis and that a known improvement in the plaintiff's condition and prognosis should have been disclosed to the judge. On 23 October 1996 the Court of Appeal ruled that the defendant be allowed to admit further evidence. The facts are set out in the judgment of Stuart-Smith LJ.

Dermod O'Brien QC and *Daniel Pearce-Higgins* (instructed by *Howard Palser Grossman Hermer & Partners*, Cardiff) for the defendant.
David Blunt QC and *Jonathan Marks QC* (instructed by *Osborne Clarke*, Bristol) for the plaintiff.
Diana Cotton QC (instructed by the *Treasury Solicitor*) as amicus curiae.

Cur adv vult

13 December 1996. The following judgments were delivered.

STUART-SMITH LJ.

Background

On 29 March 1996 draft judgments were handed down by this court ([1997] 1 All ER 577) on the defendant's appeal from a judgment of Sedley J (28 BMLR 1) given on 30 January 1995 whereby he awarded the plaintiff £1,332,231·11 by way of damages and interest in respect of nervous shock or psychiatric injury sustained by him when he witnessed on 13 August 1982 unsuccessful attempts to rescue his two daughters from a motor car which had been driven into a river in South Wales by the defendant, who was employed by the plaintiff and his wife as a nanny.

The defendant never disputed that she had been negligent or that the plaintiff was a person, who, if he suffered nervous shock or psychiatric illness, usually referred to as post-traumatic stress disorder, as a result of witnessing the accident or, in this case its immediate aftermath, was entitled to recover damages. But she disputed that the plaintiff had suffered post-traumatic stress disorder, as opposed to a grief reaction albeit an extreme one. It was her case that any subsequent problems of depression and consequent disability were reactions to life's events, unconnected to the accident. The judge in essence upheld the plaintiff's claim that the witnessing of the aftermath of the accident was a substantial cause of the plaintiff's persistent and ongoing mental illness, though he rejected a claim for nearly £3m for the loss of capital and profits in a company called Parearo Ltd, the failure of which company the plaintiff contended was due to his reduced ability to conduct the affairs of the company properly. Sedley J held that it would have failed in any event.

On appeal to this court the defendant submitted, first, that the judge was in error in holding that the plaintiff had proved that he had suffered post-traumatic stress disorder, as opposed to a grief reaction, for which damages were not recoverable, or that his mental condition was attributable to his having witnessed the accident. On this issue the court was divided. I agreed with the defendant's submission and would have allowed the appeal in whole. Evans and Thorpe LJJ disagreed. The defendant also contested some of the heads of damage awarded by the judge, his award of interest and his decision on costs. By our draft judgment we reduced certain of his heads of damage, so that the total award of damages was reduced to £643,425·56 (though this was subject to an arithmetical error to which I shall refer hereafter), together with interest, calculated on a basis less favourable to the plaintiff than that awarded by the judge; we also altered the order for costs.

For reasons which will in due course appear, it is necessary to set out the various heads of damage claimed and the amount claimed by the plaintiff before Sedley J, the amount of the judge's award, whether or not it was subject to appeal and the amount awarded on appeal. It is not necessary to refer to the interest figures.

Nature of the claim	Amount claimed	Amount awarded by judge	Whether appealed	Award by the Court of Appeal
1. General damages**		£37,500	No	
2. Past loss of earnings	£747,455	£411,650·39	Yes	£276,937·64*
3. Future loss of earnings**	£1,045,725	£561,488	Yes	£266,533*
4. Doctors' and psychologists' fees past future	£4,545 £1,820	£4,545 £1,400	No No	

a 5. Past care by Mrs. Vernon				
secretarial	£69,975	£20,000	Yes	£9,304
domestic	£9,304			
b 6. Future care occupational therapy until 1999**	£51,452	£51,452	Yes	Nil
occupational therapy after 1999**	£18,300	£14,640	Yes	Nil
domestic help **	£41,743	£41,574	Yes	£10,233·60
gardener/handyman**	£13,430	£3,952	Yes	£3,952
nanny**	£32,543			
c future secretarial assistance**	£6,443·97			

*   These figures are subject to correction.

**   In respect of these claims the plaintiff's mental condition at the time of judgment by Sedley J and the future prognosis were or might well be relevant.

d   The claim for nearly £3m in respect of Parearo Ltd is no longer relevant, nor are relatively small claims for travelling and sundries, which the judge awarded.

When the draft judgments of this court were handed down issues arose as to the correct calculation of the past and future loss of earnings, which affected the calculation of interest. These matters were therefore adjourned in the hope that **e** the parties could agree; failing which the matter would have to be re-argued on these points. No such agreement had been reached and no final order of this court had been drawn up, when on or about 17 April 1996 Mr O'Brien QC received through the post from an anonymous sender copies of a judgment of Judge McNaught given on 6 January 1995 in the Gloucester County Court in certain proceedings under s 8 of the Children Act 1989 between Mr and Mrs **f** Vernon relating to their three children, together with a copy of the judgment of the Court of Appeal (Russell LJ and Wall J) delivered on 4 July 1995 (see [1995] CA Transcript 932), dismissing the plaintiff's appeal from the judgment of Judge McNaught.

These judgments reveal that the evidence before the Family Court was that Mr **g** Vernon's psychiatric health had dramatically improved since September 1993 and that he was substantially, if not fully recovered. This appeared to be the effect of the evidence of his medical specialists, Dr Lloyd, a consultant psychiatrist, and Mr Mackay, a clinical psychologist, both of whom had given evidence before Sedley J. It appeared to the defendant's legal advisors that this evidence was **h** materially different from the picture presented to Sedley J and this court, and in particular it might affect the judge's findings as to the plaintiff's state of health at the time of the judgment and the prognosis for the future. This would affect the level of general damages and also elements of future loss.

The present application

j   Accordingly, on 30 April 1996 the defendant applied to this court that the appeal be listed for rehearing, for discovery and inspection of the relevant reports and evidence and, by amendment, leave either of this court or Judge McNaught pursuant to r 4.23 of the Family Proceedings Rules 1991, SI 1991/1247, to inspect and take copies of the relevant documents and evidence. Initially the plaintiff resisted disclosure of the evidence. However, by letter dated 19 September 1996

his solicitors indicated that they waived any objection to discovery or privilege
and applied to Judge McNaught for leave under r 4.23 which was readily granted.

   In the result the court has had placed before it evidence adduced in the family
proceedings consisting of reports of Dr Lloyd and Mr Mackay and notes of their
oral evidence, affidavits, notes of evidence and transcript of evidence of Mr
Vernon and notes of evidence given by Mrs Vernon and transcripts of evidence
of two other witnesses given on a review hearing on 12 December 1995.

   It is desirable at this stage to set out the relevant history of the family
proceedings and the personal injury action. The writ in the latter was issued on
8 August 1985. In September 1992 Mrs Vernon left the matrimonial home. She
immediately applied for a residence order, which was granted on an interim basis.
In February 1993 she sought judicial separation, subsequently amended to a
petition for divorce. In March 1993 Mrs Vernon was granted a residence order in
relation to the children, reasonable contact to the plaintiff; she also applied to
oust the plaintiff from the matrimonial home. In April and May Mr Mackay and
Dr Lloyd furnished reports in the family proceedings to the effect that if the
plaintiff was ousted from the matrimonial home, he might commit suicide; these
reports were disclosed by the plaintiff in the personal injury litigation and used in
support of his case. In July Mrs Vernon withdrew her ouster application. In
October she was granted a divorce. In the personal injury action Dr Lloyd
provided a report dated 14 May 1993, and Mr Mackay one dated 18 November
1993. The trial started before Sedley J on 12 January 1994. Mr Vernon gave
evidence over many days during the early part of the trial. Mr Mackay and Dr
Lloyd gave evidence after the Easter break between 18 and 22 April. The
evidence as a whole was concluded on 14 July.

   On 8 August Mr Vernon applied for a residence order in respect of his children.
In support of his application reports were obtained from Mr Mackay and Dr
Lloyd. In their letters of instructions to these two experts dated 28 September
1994, Messrs Thring & Long (the plaintiff's matrimonial solicitors), said:

   'We need to show that his mental health has improved dramatically since
   the date of your report in May 1993 and moreover that it has improved again
   since the conclusion of his big personal injury case.'

There are two reports from Mr Mackay: the first is dated variously 14 or 17
October, the second dated 31 October or 1 November. Both purport to be
progress reports on the plaintiff from May 1993 to October 1994. They are in
broadly the same form, but there are substantial differences. I am not satisfied
that these differences are entirely due to the spontaneous second thoughts of Mr
Mackay as appeared to be his recollection when he gave evidence before us.

   On 24 and 25 October closing oral submissions were made to Sedley J.
Whether or not the plaintiff had seen Mr Mackay's report of 14 or 17 October by
then is not clear. He did know that he had made a dramatic and sustained
recovery, albeit he was still on medication. He was present throughout the oral
submissions to Sedley J. What is clear is that the plaintiff's legal advisers in the
personal injury litigation did not know at that stage of the contents of Mr
Mackay's report; nor did they know of the extent of the plaintiff's recovery. The
hearing before Judge McNaught began on 9 November and concluded on 28
December (it was not continuous) when the judge dismissed the plaintiff's claim
for residence. The plaintiff, Mr Mackay and Dr Lloyd gave evidence. Judge
McNaught gave judgment on 6 January 1995. He accepted that the plaintiff had
made a substantial recovery; there was no reason from the point of view of his

mental health why he could not look after the children. Sedley J gave his judgment on 30 January, though he dealt with further matters on 10 May.

There is one further matter in the proceedings before Judge McNaught which emerges from documentation put before this court in the last day or so. It is clear that Mrs Vernon was greatly concerned that if the latest information as revealed in the evidence of Mr Mackay, Dr Lloyd and the plaintiff was not communicated to Sedley J, he would be misled and his judgment given on a false basis, although this was against her own financial interest since she stood to gain from a large award. She feared that if the truth was not revealed she might be regarded as being party to a fraud on the insurers. She appears to have recognised that she could not reveal what was being said in the Children Act proceedings. But nevertheless the plaintiff was so concerned that she might do so, that he applied, on the advice of Mr Blunt and Mr Marks, for an ex parte injunction to restrain her from doing so. This was granted on 18 November 1994, but discharged when the judge gave judgment.

Furthermore, it is clear that Judge McNaught himself was very concerned that the picture presented to him was so significantly different from that which had been presented to Sedley J. This must have been apparent to the plaintiff, because on 17 November 1994, Osborne Clarke (the plaintiff's personal injury solicitors) wrote to Judge McNaught. They told the judge that leading counsel had advised that the plaintiff was not obliged to disclose the altered position. They indicated that it had not yet been decided whether the plaintiff would make voluntary disclosure. The judge was told that it was not appropriate for him to communicate with Sedley J, and if he did, the tort proceedings might be aborted. He was asked to confirm in writing that he would not do so. In the result no communication was made to Sedley J or the defendant's advisers.

The Court of Appeal dismissed the appeal from Judge McNaught on 4 July. There was a review hearing on dates between 27 November and 28 December 1995 at which a further report from Dr Lloyd was adduced in evidence. In January 1996 Judge McNaught made no variation in the residence order. Subsequently, however, Mrs Vernon agreed that the youngest child, who is ten years old, should reside with Mr Vernon, which he has done since then.

Mr Vernon was represented by different solicitors and counsel in the two sets of proceedings. But it is clear that counsel in these proceedings were aware of the change in opinion of Dr Lloyd and Mr Mackay well before Sedley J gave judgment. They advised that neither he, nor this court should be told of that change.

On 22 and 23 October we considered Mr O'Brien's application to be permitted to adduce further evidence in the form of the reports of Dr Lloyd and Mr Mackay and their evidence in the family proceedings, together with the evidence of other witnesses. Mr O'Brien submitted that the evidence could be admitted pursuant s 1 and/or s 4 of the Civil Evidence Act 1968 and that it was unnecessary for the witnesses to be called. Mr Blunt QC submitted that we should not reopen the case at all on the basis that the further evidence did not reveal a sufficiently significant difference between the evidence at trial and that revealed before Judge McNaught. But, he submitted that if we did, we should hear oral evidence, including that of the plaintiff and other witnesses, as well as the two experts.

This court's ruling of 23 October 1996

At the conclusion of the submissions of counsel, the court ruled that the further evidence should be admitted, since it was relevant to the plaintiff's mental condition at the time of Sedley J's judgment and to the prognosis for the future, which would or might affect the judge's assessment of general damages and the assessment made by both courts of future loss of earnings and the loss of future care and assistance. We directed that the only oral evidence should be that of Dr Lloyd and Mr Mackay. The plaintiff was anxious to call the former and we directed that he should attend, primarily for further cross-examination by Mr O'Brien, but also if need be to give evidence of the plaintiff's current state. So far as Mr Mackay's evidence was concerned, Mr O'Brien was content that we admitted the evidence he gave in the family proceedings as his evidence. Mr Blunt QC was undecided whether he wished him to be recalled. But in the event, following a further examination of the plaintiff, he was called. I must now give my reasons for the ruling made on 23 October.

Because the plaintiff had given disclosure and production of the relevant evidence and waived any privilege that might exist, it was unnecessary at that stage to consider these questions, or the linked question of counsel's duty to the court. But because of the importance of these questions and because they raised issues of public interest, we directed that we should hear arguments on the adjourned hearing. Mr Blunt QC conceded that this court was not functus officio.

RSC Ord 59, r 10(2) provides:

'The Court of Appeal shall have power to receive further evidence on questions of fact, either by oral examination in court, by affidavit, or by deposition taken before an examiner, but, in the case of an appeal from a judgment after trial or hearing of any cause or matter on the merits, no such further evidence (other than evidence as to matters which have occurred after the date of the trial or hearing) shall be admitted except on special grounds.'

In my judgment it is unnecessary to decide for the purpose of this case whether the evidence sought to be adduced related to matters which occurred before or after the date of the trial or hearing. They all occurred after the conclusion of the evidence before Sedley J; the substantial improvement in his health was known to Mr Vernon before submissions were made to Sedley J. The important change was known to the plaintiff's advisers before he gave judgment. But unless the matter was reopened before the judge at the instigation of the plaintiff or his advisers or they notified the defendant's advisers, there was no way in which the latter could have known of these matters earlier than they did. Evidence relating to the review by Judge McNaught in November/December 1995 occurred between judgment and hearing the appeal in the personal injury action.

It was accepted by Mr Blunt that the defendant could not by the exercise of reasonable diligence have obtained the fresh evidence either before Sedley J gave judgment or before the hearing of the appeal to this court. It was never suggested by Mr Blunt that if the defendant's advisers knew that proceedings had been heard in the Family Court (as to which we have no indication beyond the fact that the plaintiff was claiming in such proceedings that he could care for his children when they stayed with him), they should have appreciated the dramatic improvement in the plaintiff's health, or that his doctors' opinions had changed so dramatically in such a short time, so as to apply themselves to Judge McNaught to release the relevant documents.

In *Mulholland v Mitchell (by his next friend Hazel Doreen Mitchell)* [1971] 1 All ER 307, [1971] AC 666 the House of Lords held that the exercise by the Court of

Appeal of its discretion to admit fresh evidence as to matters arising after the date of the trial was largely a matter of discretion and degree. The principle that there should be finality in litigation should be borne in mind and evidence could not be admitted of every change which might have occurred since trial.

Lord Hodson said ([1971] 1 All ER 307 at 310, [1971] AC 666 at 676):

'In this case, I think that it can be fairly argued that the basis on which the case was decided at the trial was suddenly and materially falsified by a dramatic change of circumstances. An appeal on the whole question of damages is pending and it would be unsatisfactory for the court to deal with that appeal without taking into account the falsification, if such there be, of the basis of the trial judge's award. In the absence of the fresh evidence, the Court of Appeal would be restrained from dealing with the reality of the case before it.'

Lord Wilberforce said ([1971] 1 All ER 307 at 313, [1971] AC 666 at 679–680):

'I do not think that, in the end, much more can usefully be said than, in the words of my noble and learned friend, Lord Pearson, that the matter is one of discretion and degree (*Murphy's* case [ie *Murphy v Stone Wallwork (Charlton) Ltd*] [1969] 2 All ER 949 at 960, [1969] 1 WLR 1023 at 1036). Negatively, fresh evidence ought not to be admitted when it bears upon matters falling within the field or area of uncertainty, in which the trial judge's estimate has previously been made. Positively, it may be admitted if some basic assumptions, common to both sides, have clearly been falsified by subsequent events, particularly if this has happened by the act of the defendant. Positively, too, it may be expected that courts will allow fresh evidence when to refuse it would affront common sense, or a sense of justice. All these are only non-exhaustive indications; the application of them, and their like, must be left to the Court of Appeal. The exceptional character of cases in which fresh evidence is allowed is fully recognised by that court.'

One of the matters which I regard as significant in this case is that the events occurred so close to the trial. If Mr O'Brien's submission is correct that this evidence falsifies the assumptions and findings made by the trial judge and this court, then in my judgment it would be inequitable not to admit it. It would in Lord Wilberforce's words affront common sense or any sense of justice.

[His Lordship then considered the judge's findings as to the plaintiff's present and future condition, and reduced the general damages to £17,500, disallowed the claims for future domestic help and gardener/handyman, and, having referred to *Blamire v South Cumbria Health Authority* [1993] PIQR Q1 at Q5 per Steyn LJ in which the court held that the onus of proving what the plaintiff would have earned had he not been injured and what he was now likely to earn rested on the plaintiff throughout, concluded that the judge's conclusion that the plaintiff was unemployable could no longer be sustained and accordingly adjusted the earnings figures accordingly. His Lordship continued:]

Should the changes in the plaintiff's health and prognosis have been disclosed to the defendant, Sedley J and the Court of Appeal?

This raises important questions in relation to the litigant's obligation to give discovery of documents, disclosure of medical reports by doctors who have given evidence on matters relating to that evidence and the duty of the litigant and his

counsel not to mislead the court. On this we sought and obtained the assistance
of an amicus curiae, Miss Diana Cotton QC. Mr O'Brien submits that by one or
other or all three of these routes, namely discovery, disclosure of medical reports
or the requirement not to mislead the court, disclosure should have been made.
Mr Blunt asserts that a true understanding of the relevant obligations leads to the
opposite conclusion.

Discovery

The provisions as to discovery are contained in RSC Ord 24. Order 24, r 1(1)
provides:

> 'After the close of pleadings in an action begun by writ there shall, subject
> to and in accordance with the provisions of this Order, be discovery by the
> parties to the action of the documents which are or have been in their
> possession, custody or power relating to matters in question in the action.'

Provisions as to automatic discovery are contained in r 2 which applies to
actions where pleadings are closed (except for defendants in running down
actions). The obligation relates to documents 'which are or have been in his
possession'. Rule 3 applies to cases where there is not automatic discovery, but
the court makes an order. Again the same expression is used. The form of the
list or affidavit is prescribed by r 5. The form (No 26) provides for documents
which the litigant has in his possession custody or power to be listed in Sch 1 and
those which have been, but no longer are, in his possession custody or power to
be listed in Sch 2.

The use of the present and past tense is not apt in my judgment to cover
documents which have not yet come into existence at the time the list or affidavit
is made, though it will be apt to cover documents which were then in existence
but by error or oversight were omitted from the original. I do not accept Mr
O'Brien's submission that Ord 24, rr 2 and 3 are sufficient to cover all cases and
therefore r 1 must add something and that something is a continuing obligation
to give discovery. This was the view of the Federal Court of Australia on broadly
similar language in *TNT Management Pty Ltd v Trade Practices Commission, Brambles
Holdings Ltd v Trade Practices Commission* (1983) 47 ALR 693. In support of this
conclusion Sheppard J (at 708) cited *James v Plummer* (1888) 23 LJNC 107, which
his own research had unearthed. In that case there was a claim for forfeiture for
breach of covenant in a lease. An affidavit of documents was sworn by the
plaintiff in 1886, but on inspection it appeared that certain documents had been
omitted and an order was obtained in 1888 for a further and better affidavit. This
remedied the defect up to 1886, but it was contended by the defendant that
discovery should be given of documents which came into the plaintiff's
possession prior to the 1888 affidavit. The Divisional Court rejected this
contention. In the judgment of Manisty J (with whom Stephen J agreed) there is
no discussion of the construction of the relevant rule. The reasoning is that 'To
hold [otherwise] would ... be to cast a burden of intolerable weight upon litigants
and add enormously to the cost of litigation' (see 23 LJNC 107 at 108). I would
point out that it seems very unlikely that any relevant documents came into
existence after 1886 having regard to the nature of the action and none seem to
have been specified. *James v Plummer* has not been cited in any textbook since
Bray *Digest of Law of Discovery with Practice Notes* (2nd edn, 1910). It has effectively
been consigned to limbo.

In support of his submission that there is a continuing obligation to give
discovery Mr O'Brien relies upon *The Supreme Court Practice 1987* vol 1, para 24/
1/2, which is in these terms:

> '*Continuing obligation to give discovery*—Although one reading of O. 24, r. 1
> may suggest that discovery need be given only of documents which have
> come into a party's possession before the date of his list of documents, this is
> not the limit of a party's obligation to give discovery imposed by the rule.
> The obligation is general, and requires the disclosure of all relevant
> documents whenever they may come into a party's possession.   This
> requirement is supported by the linked principle that a party must not seek
> to take his opponent by surprise (*cf.* O. 18, rr. 8 and 9), and that he must not,
> by withholding relevant documents, mislead his opponent or the Court into
> believing that the statement in his list that he has given full discovery
> continues to be true (*Mitchell v. Darley Main Colliery Co* ((1884) Cab & El 215)).
> An obvious example is where a plaintiff, who is claiming damages for
> prospective loss of earnings, obtains new lucrative employment during the
> course of the action; this fact must be communicated to the defendant and
> further discovery must be made (or, at all events, offered).   In default, the
> plaintiff may be ordered to pay any costs occasioned by the failure to give
> discovery promptly.'

This has undoubtedly been the accepted practice in the legal profession at least
since this note first appeared in the 1988 edition of *The Supreme Court Practice*.   It
is right to say however that the authority cited in support of the note, namely
Mitchell v Darley Main Colliery Co (1884) 1 Cab & El 215, relates to a document, a
diary kept by and affording contemporaneous support for the evidence of one of
the principal witnesses, which had been in the possession, custody or power of
the defendants at the time the affidavit of documents was sworn, but had been
overlooked.   It was not disclosed until trial, whereupon the plaintiff's case
effectively collapsed.   It is not therefore authority for the proposition that
after-acquired documents (ie those that come into the possession of the party
after discovery by list or affidavit is made) must be disclosed.   But in my judgment
the reasoning of Hawkins J supports the proposition in the note.

The judge said (at 216–217):

> 'Now, in my opinion, a party, who, after filing an affidavit of documents,
> discovers a document of which his opponent has a right to have inspection,
> but which is not disclosed in the schedule because it has been forgotten, or
> overlooked, or supposed not to exist, is bound to inform his opponent of the
> discovery either by a supplementary affidavit, which I think is the proper
> course, or at least by notice; and he has no right to keep back all knowledge
> of the newly-discovered document simply because he was not aware of it at
> the time he swore his affidavit in obedience to the order for discovery.   To
> keep back under such circumstances a document known to be material,
> would, in my opinion, amount to a reprehensible want of frankness, and if,
> by reason of such conduct, unnecessary expense is entailed upon the party
> entitled to discovery, such unnecessary expense ought to be visited upon the
> party who ought to give it.   In the present case I am satisfied the defendants
> and their advisers were aware of the importance and materiality of the
> document; that the document was one which ought to have been disclosed;
> that there was no justification for not disclosing it as soon as it was found;

and that if it had been so disclosed, the whole of the expenses incurred by the plaintiff in his endeavour to prove that no subsidence had occurred to damage his property before the year 1882, would have been spared.'

In my judgment the rule stated in *The Supreme Court Practice* is not only the practice but the law, and in so far as *James v Plummer* is to a different effect it should be overruled. It is no longer relevant to modern litigation. I have reached this conclusion for a number of reasons.

First, the after-acquired document may alter the party's case, either for the better or worse as compared with that which is apparent from the documents hitherto disclosed. If the document is favourable to the party, late production may prejudice the other party and result in an adjournment, a belated attempt to settle the case or in the extreme example of *Mitchell's* case effectively a submission to judgment. In any event, it is likely to result in unnecessary expense and waste of court time. The parties and the court should do all in their power to avoid this.

Secondly, where the document is against the party, if it is not disclosed there is a risk that the other party and the court will be misled. The other party may be misled into settling the case on terms he would not otherwise do if he had known the true facts. The court may be misled into giving judgment on a basis that is no longer correct. The point is well made by Waite J in *Birds Eye Walls Ltd v Harrison* [1985] ICR 278. In the industrial tribunal there is no automatic discovery, but in that case the parties had voluntarily given discovery of documents they intended to rely upon, but the employers did not disclose a document which appeared to be contrary to their case.

Waite J said (at 287–288):

'Mr Tabachnik [for the employers] acknowledges, however, that this greater freedom in regard to discovery in the tribunals could not be permitted to provide a front for deception or unfair surprise. So he qualified his general submission by conceding that the complete freedom of a party to decide what documents he shall or shall not disclose to his opponent is curtailed by this principle. Any disclosure that he does make must not be so selective as to surprise unfairly, or mislead, the other side. No document, that is to say, should be withheld if the effect of non-disclosure would be to alter or conceal the true meaning of any document which has been voluntarily disclosed ... any party who chooses to make voluntary discovery of any documents in his possession or power must not be unfairly selective in his disclosure. Once, that is to say, a party has disclosed certain documents (whether they appear to him to support his case or for any other reason) it becomes his duty not to withhold from disclosure any further documents in his possession or power (regardless of whether they support his case or not) if there is any risk that the effect of withholding them might be to convey to his opponent or to the tribunal a false or misleading impression as to the true nature purport or effect of any disclosed document.'

Thirdly, Mr Blunt accepted that the court had inherent jurisdiction to make a further order for discovery in relation to after-acquired documents. This appears to me to be inconsistent with his principal submission that there is no obligation to give discovery save in accordance with the rules. After-acquired documents may well not fall within the provision of Ord 24, r 7 relating to further discovery, where the applicant for the order has to support his application by affidavit stating the belief of the deponent as to the existence of other documents in the possession a or power of his opponent. It seems to me the court would only have such a power if there was an obligation on the party concerned.

Fourthly, this seems to me to be explanation of the Canadian case, *Lid Brokerage and Realty Co (1977) Ltd v Budd* [1992] 2 WWR 453, a decision of the Saskatchewan Queen's Bench. Baynton J said (at 466 (para 31)):

b   'On the other hand, there is no Rule which precludes the court from making such an order pursuant to its inherent jurisdiction over the conduct of a legal action. As well, the concept of the ongoing disclosure and production of relevant documents is inherent in the Rules (e.g., r 218, 235, and 236). Although the penalty or consequences arising from the non-disclosure of after-acquired documents may be somewhat different than
c   those for non-disclosure of documents in possession or control at the time of disclosure under r 212, the principle of ongoing disclosure exists nonetheless. The framework of the Rules are focused primarily on the past or present possession and control of documents, and not on future possession or control. However, in this age of full disclosure and complex legal actions,
d   the Rules requiring disclosure of documents must be interpreted in the light of the realities of current litigation practice. I agree with counsel for the plaintiffs that from a practical consideration it is more expedient, in the circumstances of this case, to order an ongoing disclosure and production of documents than to deal with applications on a successive basis.'

e And the judge quoted the note in *The Supreme Court Practice 1988* with approval (see 2 WWR 453 at 468).

Fifthly, if the law is as Mr Blunt submits, it will mean in almost every case an application for discovery will have to be made immediately before trial or indeed during the trial, since a party who wished to stand on his rights would not make
f voluntary disclosure. The inconvenience and unnecessary additional expense and waste of time is wholly unacceptable. In very many personal injury actions the plaintiff's employment position, prospects and salary levels need to be brought up to the date of the trial. In my judgment there is no need for such an application. I understand that since the *TNT* case the rules in Australia have been changed to provide for continuing duty of discovery.

g Finally, Mr Blunt contrasted the existing Ord 24 with Lord Woolf's proposed draft Civil Proceedings Rules, r 7.12 of which provides that the duty of standard disclosure continues until the proceedings are concluded. For my part I do not regard this as a change to the existing law but a restatement.

If there is a continuing obligation to disclose after-acquired documents, up
h until what point of time does the obligation extend? Clearly in my view it must extend up to the close of the evidence; in most cases where judgment follows shortly afterwards, this in practice will no doubt suffice. But I can see no logical reason to take that as a cut-off point rather than the conclusion of the proceedings, as expressly provided in Lord Woolf's draft rules. If the party to
j whom discovery of the after-acquired document is disclosed has closed his case, or the evidence as a whole is concluded, he will have to obtain the leave of the judge to recall relevant witnesses or to reopen the case. Recalling witnesses does not usually present a serious problem. An application to reopen the case in the light of the disclosure is unlikely to be entertained unless the document is of real significance and there is otherwise a risk of injustice. An unwarranted application is likely to be visited with an order for costs.

It seems to me to be immaterial how the further discovery is made, whether by a further formal list or simply by letter. This will probably depend on the amount of documents involved. Moreover, I do not think the existence of documents that are clearly privileged need be disclosed. But this is subject to questions of disclosure of experts' reports to which I refer later.

In my judgment the existence of Mr Mackay's and Dr Lloyd's reports of October/November 1994, the notes of evidence and the judgment of Judge McNaught should have been disclosed to the defendant's advisers before Sedley J gave judgment.

Privilege

Mr Blunt submits that the reports of Mr Mackay and Dr Lloyd are subject to litigation privilege. I do not agree. These were reports obtained from experts in Children Act proceedings and such reports are not privileged (see *Re L (a minor) (police investigation: privilege)* [1996] 2 All ER 78, [1997] AC 16). The ratio decidendi of that case is not confined to wardship and care proceedings.

A document which does not attract legal professional privilege, does not do so simply because, if it had been brought into existence in other circumstances, it would have done so. Nor does a document not entitled to privilege become privileged merely because it is handed to a solicitor for the purposes of litigation (see *Ventouris v Mountain, The Italia Express* [1991] 3 All ER 472, [1991] 1 WLR 607).

Family Proceedings Rules 1991, r 4.23

Rule 4.23 provides:

'(1) Notwithstanding any rule of court to the contrary, no document, other than a record of an order, held by the court and relating to proceedings to which this Part applies shall be disclosed, other than to [persons which do not include the defendant] without the leave of the judge or district judge ...'

This rule could not in my view prevent the disclosure of the existence of the relevant documents in this case; but it would prevent disclosure of their contents without leave. This would have applied to all the documents with which we are concerned including the judgment of Judge McNaught, but not that of the Court of Appeal in the family proceedings, since judgment was given in open court. But had the defendant's advisers been alerted to the existence of the documents they could have applied for leave to Judge McNaught, who it appears to me would readily have granted it, or to the Court of Appeal after the appeal hearing.

Disclosure and exchange of expert's reports

Order 25, r 8 provides for automatic directions in personal injury actions. Where a party intends to place reliance at trial on expert evidence, he shall, within the appropriate time disclose the substance of that evidence to other parties in the form of a written report, which must be agreed if possible (see r 8(1)(b)(i)). If the reports are not agreed, the party can call the witness whose evidence has been so disclosed, but there is a limit of two medical experts (see r 8(1)(c)).

Order 38, rr 36 and 37 also applied in this case. The former provides that except by leave of the court or by agreement no expert evidence may be adduced in evidence unless the party seeking to adduce it has applied for directions under Ord 38, r 37 and complied with the direction or has complied with Ord 25,

r 8(1)(b). Where an application is made under Ord 38, r 36(1) then, unless the
court for special reasons otherwise orders, it shall direct that the substance of the
evidence be disclosed in the form of reports (see r 37(1)).

Mr Mackay's and Dr Lloyd's 1993 reports in the personal injury litigation were
exchanged pursuant to these provisions. Their reports in the family proceedings
relating to Mrs Vernon's ouster application were also disclosed. I have no doubt
that if reports to the same effect as those furnished in October/November 1994
had been in the possession of the plaintiff before they gave evidence they would
have to have been disclosed or else the witnesses could not have been called. This
is because it affected and related to the evidence that they were proposing to give.
I do not understand *Derby & Co Ltd v Weldon (No 9)* [1991] 2 All ER 901, [1991] 1
WLR 652 to be contrary to this proposition. In that case it was held that a party
was not required to give disclosure of an expert's evidence upon matters which it
is not proposed to call him to give evidence.

If a doctor whom it is proposed to call to give evidence relating to the plaintiff's
expectation of life writes in any accompanying letter or subsequently that he has
discovered that the plaintiff is suffering from a life-threatening disease unrelated
to the accident, that letter must clearly be disclosed, if the doctor is to be called to
give evidence on the question of expectation of life.

But I do not think these rules can be prayed in aid after the witness has given
evidence. Rather it is to the principle that the court or opponent must not be
misled that we must look.

Duty not to mislead the court

It is the duty of every litigant not to mislead the court or his opponent. He will
obviously mislead the court if he gives evidence which he knows to be untrue.
But he will also do so if, having led the court to believe a fact to be true, he fails
to correct it when he discovers it to be false. This duty continues in my opinion
until the judge has given judgment. An analogy can be drawn with the law
relating to misrepresentation. A representation which induces a contract which
is true at the time it is made, but is subsequently known by the representor to be
false before the contract is entered into is a misrepresentation (see *With v
O'Flanagan* [1936] 1 All ER 727, [1936] Ch 575).

Moreover, in my view the litigant does not discharge this duty simply by
accepting the advice of his legal advisers. He can no doubt rely upon such advice
as negativing any mens rea, so that he would not be guilty of the criminal offence
of attempting to pervert the course of justice. But if the advice is incorrect, he is
responsible for it vis-à-vis the other party to the civil litigation. This is the general
rule where legal advisers are acting within the scope of their actual or ostensible
authority.

In this case it is plain from the written submissions on general damages made
to Sedley J by the plaintiff's counsel that they placed reliance on the evidence of
both Mr Mackay and Dr Lloyd as to his current condition and prognosis and also
on the description of the plaintiff given by Mr Moxham (a social worker
employed by the Gloucestershire County Council), which was to the effect that
the plaintiff was incapable of looking after himself, evidence which the judge
substantially accepted. Yet at the time these submissions were made Mr Vernon
knew this description did not represent the true position. And shortly afterwards
his legal advisers knew the same. Unless the altered position was communicated
to the judge there was clearly a risk that he would give judgment on a basis that
was no longer true. And in my view that is exactly what happened.

Mr Blunt sought to rely on the distinction between actively misleading and passively standing by and watching the court be misled. This distinction was made in *Saif Ali v Sydney Mitchell & Co (a firm) (P, third party)* [1978] 3 All ER 1033, [1980] AC 198. The case concerned a barrister's duty, but the same principles apply to the litigant. Lord Diplock said ([1978] 3 All ER 1033 at 1042–1043, [1980] AC 198 at 220):

'A barrister must not wilfully mislead the court as to the law nor may he actively mislead the court as to the facts; although, consistently with the rule that the prosecution must prove its case, he may passively stand by and watch the court being misled by reason of its failure to ascertain facts that are within the barrister's knowledge.'

In *Tombling v Universal Bulb Co Ltd* [1951] 2 TLR 289 at 297 Denning LJ said:

'The duty of counsel to his client in a civil case—or in defending an accused person—is to make every honest endeavour to succeed. He must not, of course, knowingly mislead the Court, either on the facts or on the law, but, short of that, he may put such matters in evidence or omit such others as in his discretion he thinks will be most to the advantage of his client. So also, when it comes to his speech, he must put every fair argument which appears to him to help his client towards winning his case. The reason is because he is not the judge of the credibility of the witnesses or of the validity of the arguments. He is only the advocate employed by the client to speak for him and present his case, and he must do it to the best of his ability, without making himself the judge of its correctness, but only of its honesty.'

The classic examples of the distinction is the case where the barrister knows that his client has previous convictions, but the court and prosecution do not. He is not under an obligation to disclose the convictions, but he must not suggest that his client is a man of good character. Similarly, there may be several witnesses who can speak as to a certain matter of fact. Some may support one side, the others the opposite case. Neither the litigant nor his lawyers are bound to call in a civil case those witnesses who do not support their case.

But where the case has been conducted on the basis of certain material facts which are an essential part of the party's case, in this case the plaintiff's condition at trial and the prognosis, which were discovered before judgment to be significantly different, the court is not being misled by the failure of the defendant to put before it material of which she could or should have been aware, but by the failure of the plaintiff and his advisers to correct an incorrect appreciation which the court will otherwise have as a result of their conduct of this case hitherto. This can be illustrated by *Meek v Fleming* [1961] 3 All ER 148, [1961] 2 QB 366. Throughout the trial the defendant, a police officer, appeared in plain clothes and was addressed by his counsel as 'Mr'. In the ordinary way no possible objection could be taken to this; but what was known to the defence, but not known to the plaintiff or the court was that between the cause of action arising and trial, the defendant had been demoted to sergeant from chief inspector for being a party to an arrangement to practice a deception in a court of law in the course of his duty as a senior police officer. Although the matter only went to credit, the Court of Appeal ordered a retrial. The court had been misled because it was likely to have the impression, and indeed obviously did have the impression, that the defendant was still a chief inspector.

The duty of counsel

a   Where there is a danger that the court will be misled, it is the duty of counsel to advise his client that disclosure should be made. There is no reason to suppose that if Mr Vernon had been so advised in this case, he would not have accepted that advice. If the client refuses to accept the advice, then it is not as a rule for counsel to make the disclosure himself; but he can no longer continue to act. In

b the unlikely event that Mr Vernon did not accept the advice, then the non-appearance of counsel and solicitors before Sedley J on 30 January and 10 May 1995 would immediately have alerted the defendant's advisers, if not also the judge, that something was afoot. I have no doubt Mr O'Brien would have smelt a rat.

    In this case the position is complicated, at any rate so far as the proceedings

c before Judge McNaught are concerned, by r 4.23 of the Family Proceedings Rules 1991. But counsel's advice should in my view have included advice to Mr Vernon to seek the judge's leave to disclose the relevant evidence.

The position in the Court of Appeal

d   Here again Mr Blunt sought to draw the distinction between not disclosing that which he asserted (wrongly in my view) he had no duty to disclose and actively misleading the court. But in attempting so to do, counsel were walking a tight-rope and in my judgment did not succeed in staying on it. As I have already pointed out, counsel sought to uphold the judge's award of £67,000 for future occupational therapy on the basis of the assessment of Mrs Waterman (an

e occupational therapist) of the plaintiff's condition, which was similar to that of Mr Moxham, and his needs coupled with the Mackay/Lloyd prognosis. The latter was critical to the justification of a multiplier of 13.

    Similarly, so far as future domestic care and cost of gardening is concerned, counsel sought to justify the judges award of £41,000 and £3,900 on the basis of

f the judge's finding as to the plaintiff's present condition, as exemplified by Mr Moxham's description which was accepted by the judge, coupled with the Mackay/Lloyd prognosis. Here again the prognosis was essential in justifying a multiplier of 13 which the judge took.

    In relation to future loss of earnings, I consider we were misled into thinking on the basis of the judge's findings that the plaintiff was unemployable in the

g future. Although there might have been argument, as there had been in the recent hearing, as to the effect the new evidence should have on his loss of earnings claim, it seems to me unarguable that it might well have some effect. And for the reasons I have given, it has.

    I readily accept that the plaintiff's counsel did not deliberately intend to

h deceive the court and believed that the advice they gave Mr Vernon was sound. But in my judgment they made a serious error of judgment in failing to advise him on the need for disclosure. By an overtechnical construction of the rules and a failure to appreciate that their previous conduct of the case would result in the court reaching an unjust result unless disclosure was made, they found

j themselves in an impossible position. By the time the case came to this court they should have appreciated that they could no longer seek to uphold the judge's judgment on the four heads of future loss to which I have referred. I think it is unfortunate that counsel did not appreciate what appears to have been apparent to Mrs Vernon, Judge McNaught and apparently the plaintiff's own solicitor, Mr Bretton, until he was advised otherwise by counsel (see his affidavit of 18 November 1994, para 14). It is also unfortunate that when, towards the close of

the argument before us in February 1996, Mr O'Brien, who by then had some
suspicion but no tangible evidence of what had happened, applied for further
discovery, we were told by the plaintiff's counsel that the defendant was on a
fishing expedition and had not properly laid the foundation for further discovery,
with the result that this court summarily dismissed Mr O'Brien's application.

I would allow the further appeal and reduce the quantum of damages.

EVANS LJ. Because this will be a dissenting judgment, I begin with a summary
of the conclusions I have reached.

(1) I share the indignation which Stuart-Smith and Thorpe LJJ express at the
conduct of the plaintiff and his expert witnesses in the Family Court proceedings,
but I do not believe that it should have for these proceedings the consequences
which they propose.

(2) This is not a case where the plaintiff or the expert witnesses called on his
behalf gave evidence which was incorrect or expressed opinions which were
unjustified at the time when their evidence was given. To suggest that he or they
have 'changed their evidence' is not accurate.

(3) The further evidence which the expert witnesses gave before us in
November 1996 was not such as to destroy the basic assumptions upon which
their evidence was based when it was given in April 1994. That is an appropriate
test for the admission of fresh evidence for the purposes of an appeal: see
Mulholland v Mitchell (by her next friend Hazel Doreen Mitchell) [1971] 1 All ER 307,
[1971] AC 666. Their prognosis at the trial was accepted then by the defendants
and their expert witnesses. As the judge put it, the demands of consistency
prevented the defendants from challenging it. The same restraints would have
continued to operate if further evidence had been permitted before judgment
was given, and in my view they continue to operate now.

(4) The case and the appeal should be decided on the evidence given at the
trial, save in exceptional circumstances which do not arise here (see *Mulholland's*
case). Therefore, I do not agree that any duty of disclosure continued after the
close of evidence at the trial. The judge gave his judgment on the basis of the
evidence given at the trial, and this court was equally concerned to decide
whether his judgment was correct by reference to the evidence that was given.

(5) Neither the judge nor this court was under any illusion that the
unchallenged prognosis given by the plaintiff's expert witnesses in April 1994
might already have proved to have been unduly pessimistic by the time when
judgment was given, or when the appeal was heard, just as it might have been
over-optimistic, in which case the defendant's representatives would certainly
have objected to further evidence being introduced by the plaintiff.

(6) The fact of the plaintiff's recovery has to be distinguished from the
irresponsibility shown by two of his expert witnesses, in subsequently expressing
views in the family proceedings which are not easy to reconcile with their
evidence in this case, whether given in April 1994 or November 1996. If the fact
of improvement stood alone, I doubt whether the judge, if he had been asked, or
this court, would have contemplated allowing either party to open up this issue
after the original hearing. Unfortunately, the judge was already aware that the
expert evidence did not achieve that standard of independence which should
have characterised it. He found that the expert witnesses were parti pris, the
plaintiff's and the defendant's alike.

(7) Counsel for the plaintiff were correct to advise that there was no obligation
to disclose the documents in question in these proceedings, at the time when they

were received by the plaintiff and by them. Moreover, the documents did not lose their privileged status in these proceedings by reason of the confidentiality given to them by statute for the purposes of the family proceedings, in which the defendant and her representatives had and have no interest.

(8) Counsel for the plaintiff did not, in my judgment, either mislead the court or act improperly in any way. The consequences of holding that they did seem to me to go far beyond the confines of the present case, particularly with regard to views expressed by expert witnesses after their evidence has been given.

(9) Certain documents were sent anonymously to leading counsel for the defendant, in breach of statutory confidence and apparently in contempt of court. I am concerned that, so far as I am aware, no steps have been taken to discover who the sender was.

(10) This case already deserved a place in the history books or in some legal museum as an example of how costs and the length of proceedings can get entirely out of hand. Now we have a pendant to the appeal hearing, which was thought to be concluded by our judgments handed down on 29 March, and a useful reminder that interest rei publicae ut sit finis litium (it is in the public interest that proceedings should be brought to a timely end).

The trial

Sedley J assessed general damages, including future loss of earnings and future costs of professional (occupational therapy) and domestic help, by reference to the evidence which he heard between January and July 1994. After speeches in October 1994 he handed down his judgment in January 1995 (see 28 BMLR 1).

The amounts of damages awarded under the heads referred to above all depended on his assessment of the plaintiff's mental condition during the trial. The plaintiff gave evidence over a period of 30 days. He did so in a manner which left the judge in no doubt, but that he was suffering from mental illness at that time. It 'could not possibly have been feigned'. Eventually, and belatedly in view of their own experts' views, the defendants admitted this, whilst maintaining their contention both at trial and before this court that witnessing the accident in 1982, alone of all the stressful incidents which the plaintiff had experienced throughout his life, had not caused or contributed to his illness in any way.

The evidence also included the opinions of two of the plaintiff's expert witnesses. They were Dr Lloyd, a consultant psychiatrist who had been treating him since 1991 and was continuing to do so, and Mr Mackay, a consultant psychologist who saw him regularly until the beginning of the trial and had arranged to see him again when it was over. Both gave evidence shortly after the Easter vacation in April 1994, and both had had telephone conversations with the plaintiff during that vacation which caused them some alarm as to his mental state. They said that it had improved significantly since the previous September, 1993, and it was too soon to say whether the apparent relapse over Easter marked the ending of this improvement or was no more than a temporary setback.

Their evidence on this aspect of the case was not challenged by the defendants. Their expert witnesses, both of them highly qualified consultant psychiatrists, were in court for much of the plaintiff's evidence. Both produced supplementary reports which laid stress on the impression which the plaintiff had created on them whilst giving his evidence and when they had seen him at other times at the court. Dr Gaind on 21 March and Dr Swan as late as 26 June said that this had confirmed their views that he was not suffering from any mental illness or, if he was, that it was due to a personality disorder which had affected him since his

schooldays. Neither suggested that he would recover from that condition, and
no evidence was directed to the question whether he might or could do so, or
not. Nor did they say that if he was suffering from depression, that condition
would or might improve either in the short or the long term. So it is not
surprising that the Dr Lloyd and Mr Mackay were not challenged in
cross-examination in this respect: counsel for the defendant had no basis for doing
so. It would not have been easy for the defendant to suggest that the prognosis
was better than the witnesses said. As the judge put it, as regards prognosis 'the
defendant's answer is dictated by the demands of consistency'.

It followed that when the judge came to assess general damages and damages
for future loss, he did so on the basis that the plaintiff's current mental state,
meaning that which he observed for himself between January and October 1994
and which was examined in enormous detail during the evidence of all the expert
witnesses, would continue as a mental illness in the way described by Dr Lloyd
and Mr Mackay. He recognised that it might improve and he made some
allowance for this factor in his award.

It was obvious to all concerned, including the judge himself, that the figures
which he assessed in January 1995 were based in part on the prognosis given by
expert witnesses more than nine months before the date of his judgment.

It is now known that a dramatic improvement in the plaintiff's condition did
take place soon after he and his witnesses had given evidence. This was apparent
to his wife, from whom he was separated, because she made an application in
matrimonial proceedings on that basis in June 1994. It was not noticed however,
or was not considered significant, by the defendant's expert witnesses, who must
have continued to observe him closely until they completed their evidence in
July.

Then in October the solicitors acting for the plaintiff in the matrimonial
proceedings asked Dr Lloyd and Mr Mackay to prepare further reports on his
mental condition which they hoped would support his application for custody of
his three children, which was opposed by his wife. Dr Lloyd's report was
produced in those proceedings before Judge McNaught and he gave evidence in
November. Mr Mackay's report was sent to the wife's solicitors and to the court
without the plaintiff's express authority. It was highly favourable to the
plaintiff's application. Mr Mackay returned from an overseas visit and said that
it had been intended as a draft only. The plaintiff attempted to recover it but
Judge McNaught ruled that it should form part of the evidence and that Mr
Mackay should give evidence. This ruling was entirely consistent with the court's
duty to put the interests of the children above all other considerations. Mr
Mackay meanwhile produced a revised report and in due course he too gave
evidence.

What I will call the October 1994 reports by Dr Lloyd and Mr Mackay were
given by the plaintiff to the solicitors acting for him in these civil proceedings.
Strenuous efforts were made to ensure that the defendant in this action, or rather
the solicitors acting on her behalf on the instructions of her insurers, remained
unaware that they had been made and did not receive copies of them. The
plaintiff's solicitors were concerned lest the insurers would learn of the reports,
and the fact that subsequently a copy of Judge McNaught's judgment was sent
surreptitiously and in breach of confidence to Mr O'Brien QC, leading counsel for
the defendant, is some confirmation that their concern was justified.

Meanwhile, Mr David Blunt QC leading counsel for the plaintiff considered
whether the plaintiff or his representatives were bound to disclose the October

a reports to the defendant in those proceedings. He and Mr Marks QC (then junior counsel) advised that they were not, and no one suggests that their advice was not anxiously considered and conscientiously given. Mr O'Brien QC however submits that they were wrong.

The appeal

b The appeal hearing took place over 12 days in January/February 1996. At that time we were aware that proceedings had taken place, or were taking place, in the Family Court and that the plaintiff was putting himself forward as being in sufficiently good health to have custody of his children; in other words, that in his own eyes at least he had made a good enough recovery from his 1994 condition to justify such a claim.

c On 29 March 1996 we handed down our judgments, which by a majority upheld the judge's finding on liability but unanimously reduced the damages to about half the judge's figure (see [1997] 1 All ER 577).

There was no appeal against the general damages award of £37,500. The defendants therefore took no issue with regard to the judge's findings that the *d* plaintiff was suffering from mental illness at the time of the trial and that the prognosis was as the judge held it to be, in accordance with the unchallenged evidence as to what the April 1994 prognosis was. Opening the appeal, Mr O'Brien told us that it was conceded before Sedley J that the plaintiff was suffering from depression as a form of mental illness at the time of the trial. This concession is not mentioned in the judgment of Sedley J although it was in line *e* with the findings he made. The case which Mr O'Brien put to Dr Lloyd and Mr Mackay in cross-examination before us was inconsistent with that concession, and by a late amendment to the notice of appeal he sought leave to withdraw it for the purposes of the present application.

f *The defendant's application*

It is unnecessary to relate in detail the tortuous history of the defendant's application which eventually came before us on 22 October 1996. The defendant and his representatives, at first reluctant, agreed that leave should be sought from Judge McNaught to produce to the defendant's representatives copies of the papers in the matrimonial proceedings, including his judgment, which they *g* already illicitly had. The defendant's representative then applied in these proceedings for leave to introduce the October reports, the evidence given by Dr Lloyd and Mr Mackay and Judge McNaught's judgment as further evidence in the appeal, under the Civil Evidence Act 1968. The application was made in this form, surprisingly, so that the court should not be made aware of the current (1996) situation, apparently because Mr O'Brien anticipated that that might be *h* less favourable to the defendant than the situation disclosed by the reports in October/November 1994.

For my part, I had no hesitation in rejecting the application to adduce the 1994/1995 documents as further evidence in the appeal. If further evidence was *j* justified, it was to enable the court to know the up-to-date situation and to hear the witnesses' explanations of any differences in their evidence that had appeared.

What became the defendant's alternative application was that the witnesses should be recalled for further cross-examination so that they could be asked about their later evidence and reports. This was granted on November 1. There was no application to amend or add to the notice of appeal and we did not know then what the defendant's submissions would be, except that they would invite us to reject the witnesses' evidence given at the trial, as regards prognosis at least. There was and is no suggestion that the defendant's own expert witnesses are now able to support an attack on the evidence which the plaintiff's witnesses gave at the trial.

In these circumstances, I for my part would have rejected the alternative application also, if it was not for two factors. First, the public interest which exists when expert witnesses are involved. Briefly, I consider that expert witnesses, just as they have responsibilities to the court, should also have an opportunity to explain, and be required to explain, their evidence if subsequently the kind of criticism which is made by the defendant's representatives is levelled against them in the course of an appeal. Secondly, I agree with Thorpe LJ that the conduct of the parties is relevant to such an application (see *Hughes v Singh* (1989) Times, 21 April, [1989] CA Transcript 356 per Russell LJ) and that the plaintiff's conduct required investigation here.

The further hearing

Dr Lloyd and Mr Mackay were recalled for further cross-examination, and this took place over two full days on 5 and 6 November. The hearing was followed by submissions as to the correctness or otherwise of Mr Blunt's advice that the October 1994 reports should not then be disclosed. We received very great assistance in this issue from Miss Diana Cotton QC as amicus curiae, instructed on behalf of the Attorney General.

The purpose of the further hearing, therefore, was to enable Dr Mackay and Dr Lloyd to be cross-examined with regard to their April 1994 prognosis, on which the judge acted, and as to the current prognosis in November 1996. Their reports and evidence in October/November 1994 were relevant to this, but only in two ways. First, the plaintiff's condition at that time formed part of the history of the development of his illness during the period since April 1994. Secondly, if and to the extent that the witnesses were able to express opinions to Judge McNaught which were more favourable to the plaintiff than the evidence which they gave to Sedley J and now to us for the purposes of the damages claim, and were inconsistent with that evidence, then questions must arise as to their objectivity and reliability as expert witnesses.

Apart from this indirect relevance, there is no separate issue in these proceedings as to the state of the plaintiff's health in October/November 1994. For the purposes of the question whether the October 1994 reports should have been disclosed to the defendant's representatives when they came into the hands of the plaintiff and his solicitors, sometime early in November 1994, it is the contents of the reports which are relevant, rather than his actual state of health, because the allegation is that the reports should have been disclosed. There is no suggestion that his legal representatives knew what evidence the witnesses gave, or what the terms of Judge McNaught's judgment were, until after Sedley J gave judgment and possibly (we have not been told this) until after the hearing of the appeal.

The defendant's representatives also allege that the plaintiff himself was personally at fault in failing to disclose the reports to them in October/November 1994, and presumably later the evidence and the judgment also. This must mean that they contend that he should have applied to Judge McNaught for leave to make the disclosure, for without such leave the confidence of the matrimonial proceedings was protected by statute. In the event, Mr O'Brien attacked on a broad front, and he contended that the plaintiff and his legal representatives were all at fault in failing to disclose not only the October 1994 reports but also the fact of his improved condition and the evidence which was given to Judge McNaught and the resulting judgment.

I would say at the outset that, since the plaintiff did seek and obtain advice at least with regard to the reports from leading and junior counsel, and acted on that advice, the attack against him personally is groundless and should fail. Moreover, since he has not had an opportunity to answer the charges, the defendant's representatives having opposed his application to be recalled as a witness, I would hold that the charges against him should be rejected on that ground also.

The central allegation made against counsel, therefore, is that the October 1994 reports should have been disclosed to the defendant before Sedley J gave judgment in January 1995. If they were under any duty to do so, then the duty was broken in November 1994 and the breach continued until after the appeal hearing in January/February 1996. If there was no breach of duty, then a separate question arises as to the plaintiff's counsel's conduct of the appeal hearing itself, for the further allegation is made that counsel presented the plaintiff's case as respondent in a way which misled the court and was in breach of the Rules of Conduct of the Bar.

These are serious charges, and for my part I think it is regrettable that they have not been formulated except in general terms in various skeleton arguments by counsel for the defendant and in Mr O'Brien's oral submissions. It is right to add, however, that Mr Blunt was content to answer the charges in the same general terms as they were made, and like Mr O'Brien's his submissions concentrated on the question whether the October 1994 reports should have been disclosed during the following month.

The grounds on which it is said that they should have been disclosed are three. First, because the plaintiff was under a specific duty to do so, under RSC Ord 24, r 1. Secondly, because the reports constituted further evidence by expert witnesses, which were not privileged from disclosure or production in the present case, since they were made for the purpose of the family proceedings; even if they were privileged, their existence should have been disclosed so that the defendants could apply to that court for them to be produced. Thirdly, because the plaintiff's representatives thereafter conducted the case in such a way as to mislead the court, by continuing to rely on the evidence which was given at the trial without reference to the subsequent improvement in the plaintiff's mental health, as reflected in the October 1994 reports.

(1) Discovery

Order 24, r 1 reads:

> '(1) After the close of pleadings in an action begun by writ there shall, subject to and in accordance with the provisions of this Order, be discovery by the parties to the action of the documents which are or have been in their possession, custody or power relating to matters in question in the action ...'

The following provisions of Ord 24 include r 2(1), which requires the parties to an action to exchange lists of documents within 14 days after the close of pleadings; r 2(2), which exempts the defendant to any accident on land arising out of a vehicular collision from giving 'automatic' discovery under r 2(1); r 3, which gives the court power to order 'any party to a cause or matter (whether begun by writ, originating summons or otherwise)' to make a list or affidavit of documents 'which are or have been in his possession, custody or power'; r 5, which specifies the form the list must take; and r 7, which entitles the court to 'make an affidavit stating whether any document ... is, or has at any time been, in his possession ...'

Rule 1(1) is in general terms but, as it is expressly made subject to the following provisions of the order, the duty to give discovery imposed by it is performed in a number of specific ways, so that for example lists must be served within 14 days after close of pleadings by the parties to an action. The different rules all speak of documents which 'are or have been' in the possession etc of the party who is under a duty to disclose them.

Essentially, Mr O'Brien makes two submissions. First, that r 1(1) gives rise to a continuing duty which is independent of the particular examples of it in the following rules; and, secondly, that r 1(1) itself obliges the party to disclose after-acquired documents, meaning any which come into existence or which come into its possession etc for the first time after initial discovery takes place.

The second submission in my judgment turns the wording of r 1(1) upon its head. I do not understand how 'are' can mean 'will be' even if, as I think is submitted, 'have been' means 'are'. Nor do I see how a party can list or disclose documents which are not but will be in its possession at some future date. This submission was rejected by the Federal Court of Australia in *TNT Management Pty Ltd v Trade Practices Commission, Brambles Holdings Ltd v Trade Practices Commission* (1983) 47 ALR 693 and I respectfully agree.

The first submission, that r 1(1) imposes a continuing duty, is more substantial. It is supported by a note in *The Supreme Court Practice 1997* vol 1, para 24/1/2 and which first appeared there, we were told, in 1988. The note cites *Mitchell v Darley Main Colliery Co* (1884) Cab & El 215 as authority that 'The obligation is general, and requires the disclosure of all relevant documents whenever they may come into a party's possession'.

Another early authority, however, is to the contrary effect and it probably was not known to the learned editors of the White Book. This is *James v Plummer* (1888) 23 LJNC 107 which was discovered after diligent research by the judges in the *TNT* case (1983) 47 ALR 693 and upon which they relied when rejecting the submission now made before us.

In my judgment, *Mitchell v Darley Main Colliery Co* is authority only for the proposition that when a list (or affidavit) of documents is discovered subsequently to have been wrong or incomplete, because it failed to include a document which either was or had been in the party's possession etc when the list was made, then the party comes under a duty to correct the list as soon as the (pre-existing) document comes to light.

James v Plummer, on the other hand, is clear authority that there is no duty to give discovery of documents first acquired after the date of the affidavit or list. The rule then in force was Ord XXXI, which did not include the general obligation now found in Ord 24, r 1. The Federal Court of Australia approved of this judgment in the *TNT* case and I would hold that it is correct.

The question remains, however, whether a continuing obligation is imposed by r 1(1), which was introduced in 1962. If there is such a duty, the rules do not provide when or how the duty is to be performed. Does a fresh list have to be served on the other party whenever an after-acquired document comes into its hands, even a privileged document, the existence of which has to be disclosed? Or is the party required to up-date the list or lists which it has served, pursuant to the other rules of Ord 24, at a specific time or times thereafter—perhaps at the beginning of the trial? It is not easy to give practical answers to these questions and they lead to another significant query: for how long does the duty continue.

Until the close of evidence? Until judgment? Until final judgement after one or
a more appeals? Mr O'Brien was constrained to submit that the duty terminates on
judgment but revives if notice of appeal is given and then continues until
judgment by the Court of Appeal, and similarly in the event of an appeal to the
House of Lords.

I would reject this extreme and in my view unrealistic submission. I doubt
b whether it has been suggested before that the duty of disclosure continues after
judgment is given at the conclusion of the trial. More difficult is the question
whether there is a duty which continues until that time.

The note in *The Supreme Court Practice* is some indication that it is the current
practice to recognise such an obligation, although Mr Blunt QC and Miss Cotton
QC queried whether this is so. They were both inclined to accept, as I
c understood them, that it may well be the practice to produce after-acquired
documents to the other party, except where privilege is claimed, eg for reports or
further reports obtained from expert witnesses, but this is largely for reasons of
self-interest. Either the document assists the party's case, and he will be eager to
produce and rely on it, or it will make it difficult for him to give truthful evidence
d without revealing its existence. Moreover, there are particular circumstances,
such as when the plaintiff's schedule of special damage is served on the
defendant, or when pleadings are amended, in which the need for a further list
would be recognised. And the court has power at all times to order a party to
make a further list, either generally under r 3 or of specified documents under r 7.

The current situation, in my judgment, is that the parties to all forms of civil
e proceedings should recognise a duty to disclose after-acquired documents (in the
sense indicated above: documents which come into existence or are first acquired
after a list or affidavit has been served) which are relevant to an issue in the
proceedings and which are not privileged for the purposes of the discovery rules.
This duty is correlative to the court's power to order a further list or lists under
f r 3 and only in this sense is it a continuing duty under r 1. It does not require the
service of a further list or any particular formality, because the essence of the duty
is that relevant documents shall not be withheld, whether or not the party intends
to introduce them at the trial (cf the duty not to take the opposing party by
surprise at the trial (Ord 18, rr 8 and 9), as the note points out). This is consistent,
in my view, with current views as to the need to reduce costs and delay and to
g increase efficiency in civil proceedings, and with the decisions of the Canadian
courts in *Ontario Bean Producers' Marketing Board v W G Thompson & Sons Ltd
(Farm Products Marketing Board, third party)* (1982) 134 DLR (3d) 108 and *Lid
Brokerage and Realty Co (1977) Ltd v Budd* [1977] 2 WWR 453.

I therefore would broadly indorse the conclusions drawn by Paul Matthews in
h his article 'Ongoing discovery in English law' (1994) 144 NLJ 327 following the
Canadian and Australian judgments and the rediscovery of *James v Plummer*.
Order 24 does not in terms impose a continuing duty of disclosure, but the court
has power to make successive orders for discovery and in the exercise of its
inherent jurisdiction can order the future disclosure of after-acquired documents.
j I also agree with him that the precise nature of the continuing obligation can best
be formulated by amendment to the rules. I would go further than him,
however, in one respect. When the issue is whether a particular document
should have been produced to the other party before trial, the court can and
should hold that the failure was in breach of duty, assuming that the document is
relevant to an issue and is not privileged, for the reasons which I have given
above.

The next question is for how long the party remains under this duty. Putting to one side the defendants' submission that it revives even after judgment in the event of an appeal, there seem to be three possibilities: (1) the close of evidence at, or perhaps the beginning of, the trial, (2) the completion of closing addresses, which marks the end of the proceedings before the judge, and (3) when judgment is delivered.

I would reject (2), because the function of closing speeches is to assist the judge in reaching his conclusions of fact and law on the evidence which has been given. In principle, it seems to me, the duty ought to continue at least until the close of evidence. The question, therefore, is whether it continues thereafter until judgment is given.

I would hold, subject to one qualification which affects the party's representatives rather than himself, that no such duty continues after the evidence has closed. The reason essentially is one of principle. The trial process which is adversarial under our rules and traditions of procedure centres upon the evidence given at the trial itself. Only in special circumstances can evidence be given before the trial. Only in limited circumstances can a party add to, qualify or even contradict the evidence which has been given, after it has closed its case, and never without leave from the judge. When it is sought to introduce further evidence for the purposes of an appeal, the underlying principle is interest rei publicae ut sit finis litium. This is subject only to limited exceptions: the well-known three conditions in *Ladd v Marshall* [1954] 3 All ER 745, [1954] 1 WLR 1489 when the evidence existed at the time of the trial, and only in 'exceptional' circumstances when it has come into existence since the trial (see *Mulholland v Mitchell* [1971] 1 All ER 307, [1971] AC 666).

These are various practical applications, in my view, of a general principle that the judge decides the case on the evidence given at the trial. Both parties have the opportunity then to place their evidence before him, and only in special circumstances are they permitted to add to it after the stage commonly referred as the close of evidence has been reached. A general duty of disclosure continuing after that stage would be inconsistent with that general rule. One example will suffice. If the duty existed, it would extend to all relevant documents, even those which were of such trivial importance or marginal relevance that they could never be introduced in evidence, because the judge's leave would never be obtained.

The qualification I have referred to above is the duty not to mislead the court. This is the further ground which I shall consider separately below.

As regards discovery, therefore, I would hold that there is a duty to disclose relevant after-acquired documents, which continues until the close of evidence at the trial. It is not a duty to produce further lists or to disclose the existence of privileged documents, unless so ordered by the court under the specific provisions of Ord 24.

It may also be relevant (to the question whether there was a breach of the plaintiff's discovery obligations) that the defendant was under no obligation to give automatic discovery in the present case: Ord 24, r 2(2) so provides. If the plaintiff's duty was as extensive and continued for as long as the defendant now submits, even as regards experts' reports, it would produce a singularly one-sided and inequitable result.

(2) Further reports by expert witnesses

a   Independently of the rules regarding discovery of documents, Ord 25, r 8(1)(b) and Ord 38, rr 36 and 37 regulate the calling of expert witnesses at the trial. The former requires advance disclosure of the substance of expert evidence upon which the party 'intends to place reliance at the trial'. This applies only to personal injury actions, where it is one of the automatic directions which take

b   effect at the close of pleadings. Order 38, r 37 contains a similar provision for advance disclosure of the substance of expert evidence, which may be ordered in all cases, and r 36 prevents the parties from adducing expert evidence 'at the trial or hearing' where advance disclosure has not been made.

In his valuable summary of the duties of expert witnesses in *National Justice Cia Naviera SA v Prudential Assurance Co Ltd, The Ikarian Reefer* [1993] 2 Lloyd's Rep 68

c   at 81–82, subsequently approved by this court (see [1995] 1 Lloyd's Rep 455 at 496), Cresswell J included:

> '6. If, after exchange of reports, an expert witness changes his view on a material matter having read the other side's expert report or for any other reason, such change of view should be communicated (through legal
> d   representatives) to the other side without delay and when appropriate to the Court.'

These rules of practice, including the rules referred to above, are concerned solely, in my view, with the run-up to the expert witness's evidence at the trial. The reasons for them are practical and obvious. They are unrelated to any duty

e   to disclose documents and in my judgment they do not give rise to any duty which continues after the witness' evidence has been given.

It must often happen that after giving evidence a plaintiff's expert witness at least modifies some of the views he has expressed to the judge, for any number of possible reasons. The result in practice is that if he informs the party's

f   representatives, which he may not always do, then any document in which he does so is prima facie privileged from disclosure. In consequence, however, the defendant's expert witness is not cross-examined on the matters in question. This absence of cross-examination is likely to be noticed and commented on, and acted upon by the judge. I have never heard it suggested that counsel or the witness himself is under a duty to inform the judge expressly of what his changed views

g   are, and in my judgment no such duty exists. This again, however, is subject to the overriding duty not to mislead the court, to which I shall come below.

I therefore would reject the submission that because Mr Mackay and Dr Lloyd were expert witnesses there was some additional duty to disclose their October 1994 reports.

h

Privilege

It is convenient to deal at this stage with the question whether the October 1994 reports were privileged from production in these proceedings when they came into the hands of the plaintiff and of the solicitors and counsel instructed by

j   him in these proceedings.

Because they were prepared for the purposes of the Children Act proceedings they were subject to the statutory requirement of confidentiality under r 4.23 of the Family Proceedings Rules 1991, SI 1991/1247. This confidence could not be broken without leave from the judge of the Family Court. The House of Lords held in *Re L (a minor) (police investigation: privilege)* [1996] 2 All ER 78, [1997] AC 16 that such reports being prepared for non-adversarial family proceedings are not subject to litigation privilege. So, it is submitted, they were not privileged documents for the purposes of discovery in the present civil proceedings.

I find this a strange argument. The reports would have been privileged documents if they had been made for the purposes of these proceedings. The purpose of r 4.23 is to ensure the confidentiality of the family proceedings in the interests of the children whose welfare was at stake. It seems anomalous that the rule should have the indirect effect of obliging the plaintiff to produce in these proceedings, nominally to the defendant but in practice to her insurers and her legal representatives instructed by them, what he would otherwise be entitled to withhold from them. They have no conceivable interest in the welfare of the children, and the result would be not merely anomalous but also unjust.

In my judgment, the correct analysis is as follows. When the reports came into existence and were received by the plaintiff, he was obliged by r 4.23 not to disclose them except for the purposes of the family proceedings, without leave from the family judge. Strictly, he should not have given copies to the solicitors and counsel acting for him in these proceedings, as distinct from his legal representatives in the family proceedings (see r 4.23(b)). But he clearly was entitled to obtain advice as to whether or not they were privileged in these proceedings, and the good sense of asking for advice from his legal representatives in these proceedings means that any breach of the rules in this respect was technical only.

What advice should they have given? The reports could not be disclosed without obtaining leave from the family judge, and so the question became, was the plaintiff obliged to seek such leave in the circumstances of this case?

It should not be assumed, in my judgment, that leave would have been granted if the application had been made. Rather, the judge had to be satisfied that it was proper for leave to be given, and not inimical to the interests of the child. The question is, whether he could properly take account of the fact that by giving leave he would be destroying the privilege which the plaintiff was otherwise entitled to claim in the civil proceedings, and thereby giving the defendant an advantage over the plaintiff which he would not otherwise, that is apart from r 4.23, enjoy.

In my judgment, the family judge was bound to take this factor into account, for otherwise r 4.23 produces the anomalous and unjust result referred to above. It follows that the plaintiff's legal representatives were entitled to advise him that no such application need be made and that he was bound *not* to disclose the reports, or to waive privilege, if privilege existed, to the defendant in this action.

I therefore would hold that Mr O'Brien's submissions as to privilege lead to the opposite conclusion from that for which he contends. But this again is subject to the question whether the plaintiff or his representatives, by withholding the reports and the fact that they had been made, was in breach of his or their duties not to mislead the court, having regard to the evidence which the experts had already given. If any such breach was in prospect then that would justify the family judge in giving leave for the disclosure to be made.

Duty not to mislead the court

This usually is identified as a professional duty owed by the party's legal representatives, and I am doubtful whether the defendant's submission that it is also owed by the party himself is necessarily correct. I do not see how the party can be expected to do more than seek and act upon the advice of his legal representatives, and if that is done in good faith, as it was here, then I would have

thought that his duty was discharged, even if the advice proved to be incorrect.
If it was correct, then no breach of duty has occurred.

The defendant's submission (skeleton argument para D.3) is that—

'it was misleading for Sedley J. to be left with the evidence of Mr Mackay and Dr Lloyd to the effect that the plaintiff was currently suffering from chronic albeit variable depression and that the prognosis was poor when it was known before judgment that that evidence no longer represented the opinions of those two medical experts.'

This elides easily into the submission which was made orally that these two witnesses by reason of their October 1994 reports were known to have 'changed their minds' as regards the evidence they had given. That statement is not correct, except in the limited sense that by reason of the improvement in the plaintiff's condition after they gave evidence their current (October 1994) view as to (a) his condition, and (b) the prognosis for it, were different from the views which they held and expressed six months before. The evidence they gave bona fide in April 1994 was correct when it was given. It was not challenged by the defendant's experts and in large measure it was accepted by the judge. There was no reason for supposing in November 1994 that the evidence had been incorrect when it was given, and there is no basis for suggesting that now.

Their evidence in April allowed for the possibility that the improvement in the plaintiff's condition which they had observed from September 1993 would continue notwithstanding the relapse over Easter 1994, and the judge recognised and carefully analysed the likely therapeutic effect of a judgment which was in the plaintiff's favour, although not to the extent that he would have liked.

So the question becomes, was the judge misled by not being told that the plaintiff's recovery had been dramatically quicker and more complete than the expert witnesses had supposed that it would be, when they gave evidence at the trial?

It should be noticed at this stage that what the judge called 'the demands of consistency' would have become more pressing on the defendant and her representatives if the October 1994 reports had been made available to them. Clearly, the evidence weakened the plaintiff's case on damages. That was the reason no doubt why persistent efforts were made to prevent the reports from reaching them. But equally, it weakened the defendant's case on liability, because prompt recovery from depression was inconsistent with the ineradicable personality defects, which the defendant's expert witnesses asserted were the only form of mental illness from which the plaintiff was suffering during the period of the trial. It would be interesting to know whether the defendant's experts would have accepted in November 1994 that the plaintiff had recovered from the illness which they had acknowledged in July, or whether they would accept it now.

The fact that the evidence was double-edged would not excuse a failure in breach of duty to bring it to the attention of the court, but it does emphasise that if this had been done, both parties, not only the plaintiff, would reopen almost all of the many issues to which the expert evidence was directed at the trial. And the duty was owed to the court, not to the defendant, so that if the judge had been misled the defendant could not relieve the plaintiff's representatives of their duty so to inform the court.

The extent of counsel's duty not to mislead the court is defined by the contrasting decisions in *Tombling v Universal Bulb Co Ltd* [1951] 2 TLR 289 and

Meek v Fleming [1961] 3 All ER 148, [1961] 2 QB 366. Denning LJ said in the former case (at 297):

'The duty of counsel to his client in a civil case—or in defending an accused person—is to make every honest endeavour to succeed. He must not, of course, knowingly mislead the Court ... but, short of that, he may put such matters ... as in his discretion he thinks will be most to the advantage of his client.'

In *Tombling's* case the court was not misled, in *Meek v Fleming*, notoriously, it was. Both cases were concerned with the failure to put before the court evidence which was known to counsel at the trial. Neither, therefore, is directly relevant on its facts to the present case.

If material came into counsel's hands which suggested that the evidence which the witnesses gave in April 1994 was false to their knowledge when they gave it, then I would have no hesitation in holding that it was his duty so to inform the court. But that is not the present case.

Moreover, if subsequent events demonstrated that the evidence they had given could not have been correct, either factually as to the plaintiff's condition or as regards the prognosis at that time, then again, if there had been a significant inaccuracy, I would hold that the court should be told. Again, that is not this case.

The fact is that the October 1994 reports showed two things. First, that the plaintiff's recovery had been more marked than his expert witnesses had supposed that it would be, assisted in part by the fact that the long drawn-out trial was over. Secondly, it cast doubt on the reliability of Mr Mackay and Dr Lloyd as independent expert witnesses. Was the judge misled by not being informed of either of these?

I do not consider that he was. He knew that his judgment was based on the evidence given in April 1994. He knew that subsequent events might or might not have proved that the then prognosis, which was not challenged, was incorrect. Similarly, he knew that the expert witnesses whom he had heard in April/July 1994 might or might not have held the same views in January 1995 when he gave judgment as they did then. In short, his January 1995 judgment, including his assessments of future loss, was based on the prognosis as it was in, at latest, July 1994.

If he wondered whether or not the prognosis remained correct, then he would have to acknowledge that whereas one party might wish to put further evidence before him, the other would certainly object, unless it could be said that the evidence he had heard was incorrect when it was given.

In short, it seems to me that the plaintiff's counsel were entitled to take the view which they did, namely that they were under no duty to place the October 1994 reports before the judge.

What then was the extent of their duty to the Court of Appeal? In my judgment, there was no discovery obligation, for the reasons already given, and the October 1994 reports remained privileged, in the manner described above, in any event. That did not apply to the transcripts of evidence given before Judge McNaught, if the plaintiff had them, or to his judgment, but those documents were protected by the statutory requirement of confidentiality under r 4.23. Moreover, their existence was known to the defendant's representative before and during the appeal. They could have applied to the Family Court, but so far as I am aware they did not do so.

There was no mystery about the fact that family proceedings had taken place in which the plaintiff presumably was contending that he had recovered sufficiently to look after his children His claim might be and probably was supported by expert witnesses called on his behalf. The plaintiff was in court throughout the appeal hearing and if appearances are any guide he was no longer suffering from chronic or even serious mental illness as described by the judge. He had made some degree of recovery, and it was accepted on all sides that the question for this court was whether the judge's findings were correct on the basis of the evidence he had heard in 1994. It was obvious that his condition and prognosis in January 1996 were different from, and probably better than, they had been then. There was no suggestion that fresh evidence should be called in order to assess the plaintiff's condition and prospects at the time of the appeal. There was no issue before us as to general damages or as to the plaintiff's chances of obtaining future employment if his condition should improve. In these circumstances, I do not find convincing the suggestion that we were misled by not being informed that the plaintiff's recovery had been even better than we might have supposed. I would acquit his counsel of this further charge also.

Damages

The defendant, by amendment to the notice of appeal, now challenges the amounts awarded as general damages and in respect of future loss of earnings and future costs of professional and domestic help. Having received further evidence of the plaintiff's current (November 1996) condition and the prognosis for it, we clearly must take this further evidence into account when deciding what the proper amounts are.

I agree with Stuart-Smith LJ that for the reasons he gives the awards for future professional and domestic help cannot stand.

Two issues, in my judgment, arise with regard to general damages. The first is whether the plaintiff can be said to have recovered from his mental illness when he continues to need medication, although the daily amounts are much less than they were. The second is, what have been and will continue to be the consequences for him of the mental injury caused or contributed to by his witnessing the accident in 1982?

The need for medication exists because without it the plaintiff would continue to suffer from distressing and disabling symptoms of depression. Although the symptoms are kept at bay, the fact remains that he is mentally unwell, and I do not consider that he can properly be regarded as having recovered from the injury to his health. To have to take drugs on a daily basis, even in small quantities, is a disadvantage which should properly be compensated in damages, and in addition there are possible long-term consequences of the drug-taking itself and possible side-effects which might cause additional distress. The plaintiff himself has blamed some of his symptoms in the past on the drugs which were prescribed for him then. I therefore would not assess general damages on the basis that his recovery is complete.

The consequences of witnessing the accident in 1982, on the judge's findings and taking account of the evidence we have heard, have been that from 1986, when his business failed (as it would have done, in any event), until today he has been out of work and pre-occupied with this litigation, including a trial which lasted one year to judgment, and which the defendant's representatives, as the judge observed, did nothing to shorten or make less arduous by means of admissions or otherwise. His illness led directly to the break-up of his marriage in 1992. He and his wife are now divorced and the subsequent family proceedings have been far from amicable, due partly I would suppose to his mental ill-health. For many years he was in a state of chronic depression and in 1994 the judge found that he was socially and economically inept. Now that his health is improving he is at an age (54) when he would be fortunate to obtain regular paid employment, in current social and economic conditions, even without his history of prolonged mental illness.

The defendant's representatives did not suggest that the judge's award of £37,500 was excessive, given his findings as to the plaintiff's current (1994) condition and the unchallenged evidence that his prospects for recovery were small. The current situation according to the evidence we have heard is one where his social prospects are brighter, and continued medication will largely eliminate the symptoms of depression which might otherwise be manifest. There is also the possibility, small though it may be, of a worsening of his condition, particularly if these proceedings or his family problems turn out adversely for him.

The figure should clearly be reduced, leaving whatever element represented the past but with a smaller element for future disadvantage and loss. I would not reduce the award by as much as is proposed.

Future loss of earnings

There is no evidence directed to the plaintiff's chances of obtaining some form of paid employment apart from the impression which he gave the judge and the evidence of Mr Mackay and Dr Lloyd both at the trial and before us.

Neither witness accepted suggestions made to them in cross-examination that the plaintiff is now capable of obtaining and likely to obtain regular paid employment. It was also put to them that due to his various personality defects, the plaintiff would be unable to hold down any job for any length of time. This is the main reason for the 40% discount (from his assumed earnings if he had not suffered mental illness caused or contributed to by witnessing the accident) which we allowed in our earlier judgments.

Although the chances of the plaintiff obtaining some form of employment is now an issue in the appeal, the defendant has not sought leave to adduce any evidence directed towards this issue and has opposed the plaintiff's application to call further evidence, which it was unnecessary for him to call before.

I agree with Stuart-Smith LJ that that application could not be granted at this late stage of proceedings which are already in extra time. The consequence, in my judgment, is that it would be unfair to the plaintiff to accede to Mr O'Brien's submission that we should act upon published figures for average earnings, when these have not been explained in evidence and when the plaintiff, through no fault of his own, has had no opportunity of challenging their relevance to his case.

In my judgment, his chances of obtaining regular paid employment of any kind are speculative, and on the evidence of Dr Lloyd (Mr Blunt disclaimed reliance on Mr Mackay) there is no real chance of his doing so. I do not consider, on the evidence before us, that this court's assessments, based on the evidence given at the trial, should now be altered. Because of his improved condition the plaintiff no longer receives social security payments which were deducted from the damages figure. The discounted capital value is about £16,000. This represents rather more than 5% of the total award under this heading, and no injustice would be done if this potential reason for increasing the amount was disregarded also.

a On the issue regarding the calculation of future (lost) earnings, I agree with Stuart-Smith LJ that the plaintiff's submissions should be preferred.

THORPE LJ. I have had the advantage of reading in draft the judgment of Stuart-Smith LJ and I am in complete agreement with his reasoning and with the result that he proposes. I only differ from him on a comparatively small point as *b* to the extent of counsel's duty.

In my judgment on the appeal I commented upon the unsatisfactory contribution of the mental health professionals at the trial. I recorded the judge's finding that the plaintiff's experts, including of course Dr Lloyd and Mr Mackay, were flawed in that they had assumed the very thing that the plaintiff was *c* required to prove. I also recorded the judge's conclusion that the defendant's experts were parti pris. The reopening of this appeal has now revealed the degree to which at least Dr Lloyd and Mr Mackay amongst the plaintiff's witnesses were also partisan. Without any inkling of what the reopening of the appeal has subsequently revealed I commented upon the danger that an expert witness who has a well-established patient relationship with the plaintiff might develop *d* therefrom a sympathy for or identification with the plaintiff that jeopardised objectivity. I emphasised that mental health experts in the family justice system owe a duty to the court which in the event of conflict manifestly prevails over any duty to the party giving instructions. I criticised the defendant's experts for their partisan performance, suggesting that their loss of objectivity might be ascribed *e* to their daily attendance at the trial which had tempted them into sharing attitudes, assumptions, and goals with the defendant's litigation team. Had I then known what is now revealed I would have been equally if not more critical of Dr Lloyd and Mr Mackay. Whilst Stuart-Smith LJ rightly observes that the erroneous judgment of the plaintiff's counsel bears responsibility for the considerable extension of this appeal, and conceivably the appeal itself, the *f* dilemma from which the error stems was plainly created by the readiness of both Mr Mackay and Dr Lloyd to do their best to present the plaintiff's condition on different dates and in different proceedings in the light that seemed most helpful to the immediate cause, ignoring their equal or greater duty to the court and disregarding the very considerable inconsistencies that inevitably developed.

g In fairness to Mr Mackay and Dr Lloyd I will amplify the basis of those conclusions.

In evidence to this court Mr Mackay justified his pessimistic interpretation of the plaintiff's September 1993 recovery on the following three grounds: (1) the consultations which he had had with the plaintiff between September 1993 and *h* early 1994; (2) his observations of the plaintiff in and out of the witness box at the trial; and (3) his telephone conversation with the plaintiff on Maundy Thursday 1994. This evidence cumulatively had justified his opinion to Sedley J that the September 1993 recovery was a transient phenomenon. Dr Lloyd accepted that the only happening since September 1993 that influenced his pessimistic assessment was the telephone conversation he had had with the plaintiff over the *j* Easter vacation.

Manifestly the duty that these two experts owed to the judge in the Children Act proceedings, the welfare of children being at stake, was at the least to draw attention to these regressions if presenting a fundamental revision of the plaintiff's medical history between September 1993 and October/November 1994.

The plaintiff's solicitors in the family proceedings approached Dr Lloyd and Mr Mackay for reports on 8 August 1994. In the letter to Dr Lloyd the solicitor wrote:

'My understanding is that Peter's condition has improved significantly since [early 1993] and [his wife] has now made a fresh application to the court for Peter's eviction from his home.'

Presumably that understanding of significant improvement came from his client. A further letter was written to both experts on 2 September. The letter to Mr Mackay included this sentence:

'He argues that his health has improved dramatically but the Court is naturally going to be somewhat wary given Mr Vernon's psychiatric history.'

Further letters were written to the experts in identical terms on 28 September. Both letters enclosed a copy of a judgment given on 25 August on the plaintiff's application for an interim residence order. The revealing passage comes on the second page of the letter. It is worth quoting in full:

'We need to show that [Mr Vernon's] mental health has improved dramatically since the date of your report in May 1993 and moreover that it has improved again since the conclusion of his big personal injury case. On the positive side, we need to establish that he can do all that is required of a parent and that he is mentally perfectly fit to fulfill that capacity. I should also be grateful if you could address the issue of Mrs Vernon's Ouster Application. In your professional opinion, would it be right to take this man from his home and what might happen if he were ordered to leave. It is difficult to balance the two strands of the forthcoming hearing but we will need to convince the Judge not to impose an Injunction on Mr Vernon ordering him to leave but at the same time awarding him residence of the children instead of Mrs Vernon.'

The recipient does not have to read between the lines to discern that his instructions are to walk the tightrope leading to the grant of his application, dependant upon a clean bill of health, and the refusal of her application, on the ground that his psychiatric state would be too frail to withstand the reaction to an ouster order. This sort of attempt to influence the expression of expert opinion is to be deplored for the simple reason that it colludes in a partisan approach and ignores the expert's duty in Children Act proceedings to write every report as though his instructions came from the guardian ad litem.

The influence that this instruction had upon Mr Mackay's report is obvious. Having described his patient's improvement in September 1993 he continued:

'This improvement persisted during the ensuing months and, indeed, he coped extremely well with the stresses and strains of court attendances between January and July when his claims case was being heard.'

The triple strands of the evidence of regression which apparently influenced Mr Mackay's evidence to Sedley J in April 1994 are simply not referred to at all. Then, having reported on a consultation with the plaintiff on 11 October 1994, Mr Mackay pronounced full recovery from chronic depression. He added this paragraph:

'I have no doubt, whatsoever, that Mr. Vernon would prove to be not merely an adequate parent but in fact a "rock" upon which the children could confidently depend during the remainder of their childhood, and indeed throughout adulthood, for support, guidance and encouragement.'

He then turned to the reverse of the coin. He wrote:

'[An ouster injunction] would be particularly difficult for him to accept at this juncture for reasons radically different to those raised in my report of May 1993 when Mr. Vernon's personal welfare was a major consideration. Given that he has recovered from his chronic depression and is no longer distracted by his claims case, he feels better able than at any time in the past to provide his children with the support, guidance and encouragement they clearly require if they are to overcome their current difficulties and grow into mature, responsible and self-confident adults.'

The later report, upon which reliance was placed, was moderated by amendment and extension. But like Stuart-Smith LJ, I cannot accept that those changes were the product of Mr Mackay's spontaneous pen. I too found his evidence on this question unconvincing.

Dr Lloyd's response to his letter of instruction was more circumspect. In his introductory paragraph he made it plain that he was dealing with the plaintiff's residence order application alone. He then listed the papers in the case which he had read to aid him in the preparation of his report. They included the plaintiff's statement of 30 September 1994. In para 28 thereof the plaintiff had stated: 'My psychiatric situation has improved dramatically since the separation two years ago.' Dr Lloyd then dealt with the history from 7 May 1993 to date. What he said of spring 1994 was:

'I was required to attend court for fifteen days during the compensation trial and found Mr. Vernon to be smart, alert and attentive and able to conduct himself with dignity. There were occasions when he was emotionally distressed as a result of the evidence given in relation to the death of his two children, but this response was understandable and reasonable given the tragic loss.'

It is to be noted that there is no mention of the evidence, namely the telephone conversation he had with the plaintiff over the Easter vacation, which had led him to give such a pessimistic prognosis to Sedley J.

In the paragraph headed 'prognosis' appears this sentence:

'Following the death of his children he suffered from severe prolonged post-traumatic stress disorder the consequences of which were to cause a state of chronic depression which has improved quite dramatically in the last year.'

The same phrase appears in his comment on the court welfare officer's report:

'It is clearly the case that Mr. Vernon's depression has improved dramatically since this report was written—indeed he is no longer clinically depressed.'

The report ended with this conclusion:

'In my opinion Mr. Vernon is currently in good mental health and is not showing symptoms of depressive illness, although I feel he needs continuing pharmacological treatment and outpatient supervision to minimise the risk of relapse especially during this particularly stressful time. From the evidence available to me he appears to be both a capable and loving parent. I do not think there are compelling psychiatric grounds to prevent him from caring for his children on a full-time basis.'

These extensive quotations from the reports written by Mr Mackay and Dr Lloyd in October 1994 justify the conclusion that they were thoroughly partisan reports. Judge McNaught was entitled to an objective and complete statement of the recent medical history together with an unbiased prognosis as to the future in order to enable him to make a balanced assessment both of risk and of the welfare considerations. These reports simply do not meet the standards that are expected of experts in Children Act proceedings. However there are two mitigating circumstances. First, both experts had had extensive patient relationship with the plaintiff and both had been sucked into the personal injury litigation to the extent of each spending approximately three working weeks in court, only a small proportion of which was necessary for their testimony. In my judgment on the appeal I emphasised the danger of distortion from such factors in isolation. They are even more dangerous in combination. Second, neither expert had any worthwhile experience of Children Act proceedings. Mr Mackay said he had never previously been involved in a Children Act case and Dr Lloyd had had only very limited experience.

It seems to me that the demonstration of partisan commitment on this scale is corrosive of confidence in the value of the opinion not only then expressed but also previously and subsequently expressed. As Stuart-Smith LJ has said, the material in the Children Act proceedings might have affected the issue of liability as well as the issue of quantum. In finding for the plaintiff on liability Sedley J placed some reliance upon the opinion of both Mr Mackay and Dr Lloyd. Had he seen revealed their capacity to come to the plaintiff's aid in his residence order application he might have evaluated differently the support which they lent to his personal injury claim. Equally I find it difficult to avoid a degree of scepticism in evaluating the evidence which they have given to this court on the plaintiff's state throughout 1996.

The damaging significance of the further evidence to the plaintiff's case is, of course, highly relevant to the exercise of the discretion as to whether it should be admitted. In approaching that question I found particularly helpful the judgment of Russell LJ in *Hughes v Singh* (1989) Times, 21 April, [1989] CA Transcript 356. Having reviewed the authorities culminating in *Mulholland v Mitchell* [1971] 1 All ER 307, [1971] AC 666, Russell LJ said:

'It is, in my judgment, plain from these authorities to which I have referred that the Court of Appeal has indeed a wide discretion to exercise the power to receive fresh evidence, but that it should always be exercised sparingly with due regard to the need for finality in litigation. It is impossible to produce any sort of exhaustive list of the relevant considerations. But for my part I would emphasise that the following must always be material. (1) The extent to which the fresh evidence may affect the award of damages; the greater the extent the more likely and ready the Court of Appeal should be to admit the evidence. (2) The time element. It is not in my judgment necessary that fresh evidence should emerge before the case would ordinarily reach the Court of Appeal, but the closer to the date of trial the more likely it is that the evidence will be admitted. In this case I remind a myself that the fresh evidence emerged within a matter of four months of the trial. It emerged before, in the ordinary course of events, the matter would have reached this court, and of course it emerged at a time when already the plaintiff's advisors had lodged a notice of appeal directed to the issue of damages so far as the plaintiff's future was concerned. (3) The conduct of the parties. Any inequitable conduct on the part of a litigant is plainly

b relevant as other conduct may be in the course of the proceedings which have led to the mistaken assessment. At the end of the day, as Lord Wilberforce said in *Mulholland's* case, the evidence should be admitted in all cases where it would be an affront to one's sense of fairness not to admit it, and of course in applying that test the court takes into account all the circumstances—in my judgment before, during and after the trial.'

c

Applying that trio of considerations to this case, plainly the fresh evidence affects the amount of the plaintiff's award to a significant extent. Second, the time element goes strongly for admitting the evidence. The fresh evidence emerged before judgment, if not before submissions, even if it was not available to the defendants until a later stage. Third, there is plainly inequitable conduct

d on the part of the plaintiff who has deliberately advanced contradictory cases in contemporaneous proceedings in different courts to gain advantage in each. Certainly at the end of the day my sense of fairness would be affronted were technicalities successfully raised to exclude this material.

e *Discovery*

On this issue I am in complete agreement with the judgment of Stuart-Smith LJ. In his attempt to discredit the note in *The Supreme Court Practice 1987*, vol 1, para 24/1/2 Mr Blunt was obliged to rely upon *James v Plummer* (1888) 23 LJNC 107. The decision in that case is almost unreasoned and, as Stuart-Smith LJ has pointed out, it has been lost from legal sight for three quarters of a century. It

f would be patently absurd to resurrect it. To do so would be to destroy the sensible practice contained in the White Book note, to put this jurisdiction out of step with both Australia and Canada, and to introduce a practice so obviously out of step with the modern movement towards effective and cost saving procedures.

g *Privilege*

That the reports of Mr Mackay and Dr Lloyd were not the subject of litigation privilege is plainly established by the decision of the House of Lords in *Re L (a minor) (police investigation: privilege)* [1996] 2 All ER 78, [1997] AC 16. Mr Blunt's endeavours to distinguish that authority were quite unpersuasive.

h His first submission was that the authority should be restricted in its application to public law proceedings. The essential foundation of the decision of the House was that Children Act proceedings are not purely adversarial but quasi-inquisitorial. That is as true of private law proceedings as of public law proceedings. Equally in each the ultimate question is which of the available outcomes will best promote, or sadly in many cases least damage, the future

j welfare of the child. The approach to outcome frequently involves an assessment of risk and adult dangerousness. The court's inquiry cannot be deflected, inhibited, or disadvantaged by litigation privilege.

Mr Blunt's second submission was that the conclusion in *Re L* depended upon the circumstance that the reports in question were prepared from material which had been specifically directed to be made available to the expert for the purposes

of preparing the report. Here the order of 24 October 1994 made by consent was
only in these terms:

> '1. There be liberty to the Respondent to serve and file reports from:—i)
> Dr G Lloyd (Consultant Psychiatrist) by Wednesday, 2 November 1994 ii)
> Mr D Mackay (Clinical Psychologist) on or before Friday, 28 October
> 1994 ...'

Of course, as I have already demonstrated, Dr Lloyd had in his possession a
substantial proportion of the court papers before writing his report. Some were
sent to him by a letter of 26 October from the plaintiff's solicitors responding to
a request from Dr Lloyd's secretary. Strictly prior leave should have been
obtained from the judge. The failure to write that leave into the consent order of
24 October was plainly an error on the part of the plaintiff's solicitors. The
argument that in consequence of that failure a litigation privilege arises that
would not otherwise have arisen is little short of absurd.

Rule 4.23 of the Family Proceedings Rules 1991

In my judgment this rule has no bearing on the rival submissions as to whether
or not the material extracted from the Children Act proceedings relevant to this
appeal should have been disclosed to Sedley J. The purpose and effect of r 4.23 is
to ensure that the confidentiality of proceedings protects not just the days in
court but also the preliminary stages from first issue of proceedings and equally
the continuing future post judgment. The safeguard is provided by the rule and
applied by the court. However, if there is a legitimate need for the use of the
material in other proceedings the court exercises a discretion either to sanction or
refuse release on the application of principles established in a long line of
authority. Any party to the proceedings can apply to the court to exercise this
discretion. Had Mr Blunt shared Mr Bretton's (the plaintiff's solicitor) view that
evidence as to the plaintiff's state of recovery in October 1994 should be disclosed
to Sedley J, then an application to Judge McNaught would surely have resulted in
an order sanctioning release. Had the defendant's advisers had knowledge of this
evidence at that date it would have been open to them to apply to intervene in
the Children Act proceedings for the sole purpose of applying for the release of
the material. Certainly the plaintiff cannot rely upon r 4.23 to avoid any
obligation otherwise arising.

Duty not to mislead the court

The classic statement by Denning LJ in *Tombling v Universal Bulb Co Ltd* [1951]
2 TLR 289 at 297, cited by Stuart-Smith LJ, is clearly of enduring application. Its
application to the facts of individual cases can plainly give rise to finally balanced
outcomes. In that case Singleton LJ delivered what was in effect a dissenting
judgment. Counsel, Mr MacDermott, had established his client's address at 96
Church Road by putting to him the leading question, 'Do you live at 96 Church
Road, Stoneygate?' Like Singleton LJ I regard that as active and not passive
presentation. Denning LJ was apparently reassured by the evidence of Mr
MacDermott. He said:

> 'But after hearing Mr MacDermott I am quite satisfied that it was not done
> to mislead. This question was only asked so as to give the man's permanent

address, without disclosing the discreditable but irrelevant fact that he was at present in prison for a motoring offence.'

On the material in the report that strikes me as a charitable conclusion in the light of counsel's use of a leading question in preference to the proper form, 'Where do you live?'

Mr Blunt also relies upon the decision of the House of Lords in *Livesey (formerly Jenkins) v Jenkins* [1985] 1 All ER 106, [1985] AC 424. He argues that since the House rested the wife's obligation to disclose her intention to remarry only upon considerations special to ancillary relief proceedings under the Matrimonial Causes Act 1973, it follows that there is no wider duty applicable to other proceedings. I do not find the decision in *Livesey v Jenkins* of much relevance in determining the issue raised by this appeal. Of course in purely adversarial litigation where there is no particular duty of full and frank disclosure, a plaintiff is free to parade his strengths and hope that the defendant does not uncover his weaknesses. But quite different considerations must apply where the plaintiff elects to conceal from the court a material change of circumstance arising between the close of his case and the delivery of judgment.

On the facts of this case I am in complete agreement with Stuart-Smith LJ that the plaintiff was under a duty to report this material development to Sedley J. As I have already pointed out, his statement of 30 September, instructions for which must have been taken from him at an earlier date, contained the claim to dramatic improvement and the letter from his solicitor in the matrimonial proceedings written on 8 August referred to significant improvement. In my judgment it is simply unconscionable for a litigant to run contradictory cases in simultaneous proceedings in the hope of gaining advantage in each. In evaluating the plaintiff's responsibility it is significant to my judgment that he was ready enough to disclose the reports prepared by Mr Mackay and Dr Lloyd in 1993 for the divorce proceedings. At that stage he had an equal aim to establish a gloomy picture in both cases.

I am equally clear that Mr Blunt's decision to withhold the material was the result of a conscientious but erroneous exercise of judgment. I have every sympathy with Mr Blunt. After some 70 days of evidence in what was unquestionably as highly charged and arduous a personal injury case as it would be possible to conceive, the prospect of reopening evidential issues must have seemed unpalatable to say the least. There is only one point that I wish to make in relation to Mr Blunt's submissions in this field. He submitted that in the dilemma of decision counsel had only to look to the authorities and apply them to the circumstances. Counsel was not to be guided by his feelings on the issue in question. I cannot accept that counsel's approach should be so strictly cerebral. There is a value in instinctive and intuitive judgment. The more difficult the decision the greater that value. The course that feels wrong is unlikely to be the safe course to follow. In general terms the balance between the advocate's duty to the client and the advocate's duty to the court must reflect evolutionary change within the civil justice system. If evolutionary shifts are necessary to match civil justice reforms they should in my judgment be towards strengthening the duty to the court. Differing practices and procedures in the family justice system, the criminal justice system, and the civil justice system must be reflected in different requirements in, for instance, a criminal trial and a Children Act hearing.

The only difference of opinion that I hold from Stuart-Smith LJ is as to counsel's obligation if his client demurs in the communication of necessary material to the judge. If counsel's duty goes no further than requiring his withdrawal from the case there seems to me to be a remaining risk of injustice. Of course such an event leads to speculation. But more than one inference is there to be drawn. I would hold that in those circumstances counsel has a duty to disclose the relevant material to his opponent and, unless there be agreement between the parties otherwise, to the judge.

Appeal allowed.

Mary Rose Plummer   Barrister.

Tsikata v Newspaper Publishing plc

COURT OF APPEAL, CIVIL DIVISION
NEILL, WARD AND THORPE LJJ
22, 23, 24 JULY, 30 SEPTEMBER 1996

Libel and slander – Qualified privilege – Report of proceedings of public inquiry – Newspaper article referring to proceedings of special inquiry set up in Ghana to inquire into murder of three High Court judges – Special inquiry naming plaintiff as conspirator – Whether paragraph in article a 'report' and 'fair and accurate' – Whether report of special inquiry 'proceedings in public' – Whether publication 'not of public concern and ... not for the public benefit' – Defamation Act 1952, s 7(1)(3), Sch, para 5.

In June 1992 a national newspaper published an article about the forthcoming election in Ghana, which contained a paragraph stating: 'In June 1982, three High Court judges were kidnapped and executed at an army shooting range. A special inquiry [chaired by a High Court judge] into the killings recommended the prosecution of ten people, including [the head of state] Flt Lt Rawlings' close aide, Captain (Retired) Kojo Tsikata [the plaintiff], who was named as "the master mind" of the plot. Five people were prosecuted and executed, but not Captain Tsikata.' The plaintiff commenced a libel action against the publishers of the newspaper, and they in their defence claimed that the paragraph complained of was privileged, as a 'fair and accurate report of ... proceedings in public of a ... person appointed to hold a public inquiry by the government or legislature' of Ghana, by virtue of s 7(1) of and para 5 of the Schedule to the Defamation Act 1952. The plaintiff claimed that the paragraph complained of was not privileged on the grounds (i) that it was not a 'report' as it was published ten years after the events; (ii) that it was not 'fair and accurate' as it had failed to refer to events after the special inquiry, namely that the Attorney General had decided on receipt of the report of the inquiry that there was insufficient evidence to prosecute the plaintiff because, inter alia, the sole witness, K, who was one of the suspects, had made conflicting statements, and that shortly before he was executed he had confessed that he had invented his allegations against the plaintiff; (iii) that the report of the inquiry was not a 'proceeding in public' because, although the inquiry heard evidence in public, its report was submitted to the Attorney General and it was he who made it public; and (iv) that under s 7(3) of the 1952 Act any privilege had been lost because the passage of time meant that publication was 'not of public concern and ... not for the public benefit'. On the trial of a preliminary issue as to whether the paragraph complained of was published on an occasion of qualified privilege under para 5 of the Schedule to the 1952 Act or at common law, the judge held that it was so privileged. The plaintiff appealed.

Held – (1) For the purposes of para 5 of the Schedule to the 1952 Act, which had to be given a purposive and not a narrow or literal construction, a 'report' of proceedings did not have to be a contemporary report or an item of recent news and, as such, later events did not have any impact on its fairness and accuracy, which was to be measured by reference to that which it purported to relate. Further, the expression 'proceedings in public' was wide enough to encompass the final report of the special inquiry because even though that report was submitted to the Attorney General and not made public by the inquiry, the status

and procedure of the inquiry was such that its final report, being in effect its
judgment, formed part of the proceeding in public. It followed that the first two
sentences of the paragraph of the article complained of fell within the ambit of the
protection of qualified privilege afforded by para 5 of the Schedule to the 1952
Act, notwithstanding that the article had been published ten years after the events
referred to. However, the final sentence of the words complained of did not form
part of any report but was a statement as to subsequent events and therefore was
not protected by statutory privilege (see p 666 *g* to p 667 *c*, p 668 *c*, p 669 *b* to *j*,
p 670 *c d* and p 671 *c d f g*, post).

(2) Whether a publication lost the protection of qualified privilege under s 7(3)
of the 1952 Act because it was 'not of public concern … and not for the public
benefit' was a question of fact in each case. In the present case, the public were
legitimately concerned about the extent to which fundamental human rights and
freedoms were being upheld in Commonwealth countries, and there was a public
benefit in receiving information about the proceedings of a judicial inquiry and
the view it had taken of the plaintiff's actions since he had remained in high office
in the government whose part in the forthcoming elections was under critical
review. It followed that a prima facie defence had been made out and that the
circumstances in s 7(3) did not obtain. Accordingly, the appeal would be
dismissed (see p 667 *g*, p 668 *c*, p 670 *f j* to p 671 *d j* and p 672 *b*, post).

Notes

For qualified privilege of newspapers, see 28 *Halsbury's Laws* (4th edn) paras 128–
130, and for cases on the subject, see 32(1) *Digest* (2nd reissue) 350, 3282–3292.

For the Defamation Act 1952, s 7, Sch, para 5, see 24 *Halsbury's Statutes* (4th
edn) 113, 117.

As from a day to be appointed, s 7 and Sch, para 5 of the 1952 Act are to be
replaced by s 15 and Sch 1, para 3 of the Defamation Act 1996.

Cases referred to in judgments

A-G v Guardian Newspapers Ltd (No 2) [1988] 3 All ER 545, [1990] 1 AC 109, [1988]
  3 WLR 776, HL.
Blackshaw v Lord [1983] 2 All ER 311, [1984] QB 1, [1983] 3 WLR 283, CA.
Cook v Alexander [1973] 3 All ER 1037, [1974] QB 279, [1973] 3 WLR 617, CA.
New York Times Co v Sullivan (1964) 376 US 254, 11 L Ed 2d 686, US SC.
Perera v Peiris [1949] AC 1, PC.
Thorgeirson v Iceland (1992) 14 EHRR 843, ECt HR.

Cases also cited or referred to in skeleton arguments

Adam v Ward [1917] AC 309, [1916–17] All ER Rep 157, HL.
Andrews v Chapman (1853) 3 Car & Kir 286, 175 ER 558.
Australian Broadcasting Corp v Comalco Ltd (1986) 68 ALR 259, Aust Fed Ct.
Boston v W S Bagshaw & Sons [1967] 2 All ER 906, [1966] 1 WLR 1126, CA.
Brent Walker Group plc v Time Out Ltd [1991] 2 All ER 753, [1991] 2 QB 33, CA.
C v DPP [1995] 2 All ER 43, [1996] AC 1, HL.
Campbell v Spottiswoode (1863) 3 B & S 769, 122 ER 288.
Chapman v Lord Ellesmere [1932] 2 KB 431, [1932] All ER Rep 221, CA.
Derbyshire CC v Times Newspapers Ltd [1993] 1 All ER 1011, [1993] AC 534, HL.
*Dunford Publicity Studios Ltd v News Media Ownership Ltd, Dunford v News Media
  Ownership Ltd* [1971] NZLR 961, NZ SC.
Globe and Mail Ltd v Boland (1960) 22 DLR (2d) 277, Can SC.

Hill v Church of Scientology of Toronto (1994) 114 DLR (4th) 1, Ont CA.

Horrocks v Lowe [1974] 1 All ER 662, [1975] AC 135, HL.

Kingshott v Associated Kent Newspapers Ltd [1991] 2 All ER 99, [1991] 1 QB 88, CA.

Lingens v Austria (1986) 8 EHRR 407, ECt HR.

London Artists Ltd v Littler [1968] 1 All ER 1075, [1968] 1 WLR 607; *affd* [1969] 2 All ER 193, [1969] 2 QB 375, CA.

Macdougall v Knight (1890) 25 QBD 1, CA.

Macdougall v Knight & Son (1886) 17 QBD 636, CA; *affd* (1889) 14 App Cas 194, HL.

Mitchell v Hirst Kidd & Rennie Ltd [1936] 3 All ER 872, Assizes.

Montereale v Longmans Green & Co (1965) Times, 23 February.

Stern v Associated Newspapers plc [1996] CA Transcript 538.

Templeton v Jones [1984] 1 NZLR 448, NZ CA.

Toogood v Spyring (1834) 1 Cr M & R 181, [1824–34] All ER Rep 735, 149 ER 1044.

Watts v Times Newspapers Ltd (Schilling & Lom (a firm), third party) [1996] 1 All ER 152, [1996] 2 WLR 427, CA.

Webb v Times Publishing Co Ltd [1960] 2 All ER 789, [1960] 2 QB 535.

Appeal

By notice dated 28 November 1994 the plaintiff, Kojo Tsikata, appealed from the decision of Jonathan Sumption QC, sitting as a deputy judge of the High Court on 28 October 1994, declaring on the trial of a preliminary issue that the words complained of in the plaintiff's libel action against Newspaper Publishing plc had been published on an occasion of qualified privilege. The facts are set out in the judgment of Neill LJ.

Michael Tugendhat QC and *Richard Parkes* (instructed by *Bindman & Partners*) for the plaintiff.

Sydney Kentridge QC and *Andrew Caldecott QC* (instructed by *Oswald Hickson Collier*) for the defendant.

Cur adv vult

30 September 1996. The following judgments were delivered.

NEILL LJ.

Introduction

For about 11 years between 1981 and 1992 the government in Ghana was a military regime under the control of Flt Lt Rawlings and the Provisional National Defence Council (the PNDC). In 1992, however, it was announced in Ghana that there was to be a referendum and that the referendum would be followed by an election and a return to civilian rule. The election was due to take place in November 1992.

In the months leading up to the election there was speculation as to whether Mr Rawlings would be a candidate for the office of President in the new civilian government.

On 18 June 1992 the Independent newspaper published, among a number of articles on foreign affairs, an article about the forthcoming election under the heading 'Can populist Rawlings win the people's votes?' The article had the further heading 'Supporters of the Ghanaian military leader are preparing the ground for a return to democracy, writes Karl Maier in Accra'. In the latter part of the article reference was made to the fact that many people wanted a change from the military rule which Mr Rawlings personified. The article continued:

'Ghanaians, whose nation symbolised the hopes and dreams of African nationalism and independence from Britain 35 years ago, are embarrassed at being ruled by the military, especially one which, in Ghanaian terms, has been a fairly bloody affair. While ordinary Ghanaians giggle at Flt. Lt. Rawlings' renowned populist touch, such as working alongside farmers to bring in the harvest, his many opponents are sure to evoke the memories of the scores of people, including three heads of state, executed by his regime. After taking power for the second time Flt. Lt. Rawlings and his PNDC set up Committees for defence of the revolution and a system of public tribunals which the New York-based human rights group, Africa Watch, has described as "a mockery of justice".'

It is the next paragraph in the article which forms the subject matter of the present proceedings:

'In June 1982, three High Court judges were kidnapped and executed at an army shooting range. A special inquiry into the killings recommended the prosecution of ten people, including Flt. Lt. Rawlings' close aide, Captain (Retired) Kojo Tsikata, who was named as "the master mind" of the plot. Five people were prosecuted and executed, but not Captain Tsikata.'

At the time of the publication of the article Mr Tsikata had responsibility within the PNDC for foreign affairs and national security.

The article, and in particular the paragraph to which I have drawn attention, came to the notice of Mr Tsikata. He instructed solicitors and on 26 March 1993 a writ was issued against Newspaper Publishing plc, the publishers of the Independent. In para 4 of the statement of claim, which was served on 8 April 1993, it was alleged that the words in the paragraph in which Mr Tsikata was named meant and were understood to mean in their natural and ordinary meaning 'that [Mr Tsikata] had in June 1982 masterminded the kidnap and murder of three High Court judges and that he had escaped being prosecuted and executed for his crime'.

On 11 June 1993 the publishers served their defence. In para 4 of the defence it was pleaded by way of admission that the words meant and were understood to mean that a special inquiry to be set up by the government of Ghana had named Mr Tsikata as the mastermind behind a conspiracy to murder three High Court judges and that the inquiry had accordingly recommended that Mr Tsikata be prosecuted. In para 5, however, it was pleaded that the words were published on an occasion of qualified privilege.

On 20 December 1993 it was ordered by Master Hodgson that, pursuant to RSC Ord 33, r 3, the following question or issue should be tried by a judge alone as a preliminary issue:

'Whether the words complained of herein were published on an occasion of qualified privilege whether by virtue of the provisions of paragraph 5 of Part I of the Schedule to the Defamation Act 1952 or at common law.'

The events of 1982 and 1983

Before coming to the decision of the judge on the trial of the preliminary issue it will be convenient to say something about the events of 1982 and 1983.

On 30 June 1982 three Ghanaian High Court judges and a retired army officer
a were abducted and murdered. At that time Mr Tsikata was the head of national
security of the PNDC.

Following these murders a law was passed (PNDC Law 15 of 1982) establishing
a board to be known as the Special Investigation Board (Kidnapping and Killing
of Specified Persons) (the SIB) in order to investigate the kidnapping and killing
b of the three High Court judges and of Major Acquah, the retired army officer.
Section 3 of Law 15 set out the functions of the SIB. Section 3(1) provided:

> 'It shall be the duty of the Board—(a) to investigate the kidnapping and
> killing of [the three judges and the army officer who were named]; (b) to
> investigate any other matter which appears to the Board to be reasonably
c > related to the foregoing; and (c) to submit its findings to the Attorney
> General for necessary action to be taken thereon.'

By s 5(1) of Law 15 it was provided that the proceedings of the board should be
in public but where the board deemed it necessary in the national interest it might
sit in camera. The Law was signed by Mr Rawlings as chairman of the PNDC.
d In due course five members were appointed to the SIB under the chairmanship
of Crabbe J. During the next few months the SIB heard 60 witnesses, including
Mr Tsikata and Mr Amartey Kwei, a former member of the PNDC. On 5
November 1982 the board presented an interim report to the Attorney General,
and on 30 March 1983 the final report was submitted.
e The final report included a summary of the board's findings and
recommendations. I should refer to some of the paragraphs in the summary
which contained cross-references to the paragraphs in the report itself.

> '21 Having regard to the whole evidence, it is clear that the plan to kidnap
> and to kill the four specified persons was masterminded by Captain Tsikata
f > (para 292).
> 22 Accordingly, it is recommended that Captain Tsikata should be
> arrested immediately and placed in custody to await trial (para 293) ...
> 29 On the evidence as a whole, it is clear that Captain Tsikata ... Sgt.
> Alolga Akata-Pore and Joachim Amartey Kwei ... were all implicated in the
> conspiracy to kidnap the three judges and the retired army major. Indeed
g > Amartey Kwei described Captain Tsikata ... as "the architect of the plot"
> (para 340).'

In May 1983, after studying the report, Mr G E K Aikins, the Attorney General
and the PNDC Secretary for Justice prepared a document setting out his
h comments on the SIB report. In para 3 of these comments the Attorney General
referred to the final report of the SIB:

> 'In that report the Board confirmed its adverse findings against [four
> named individuals] and recommended that they should be prosecuted for
> conspiracy to commit murder and the murder of the three High Court
j > judges and the retired army officer. The Board also recommended that J.
> Amartey Kwei should be prosecuted for conspiring with the four suspects
> mentioned above to commit murder. In addition the Board recommended
> that five other persons should also be prosecuted for their part in joining the
> conspiracy with the criminal purpose of killing the four victims. The five
> suspects are [four named individuals] and Captain Kojo Tsikata (Rtd.).'

In the following paragraphs of the comments the Attorney General stated his view that there was evidence to support the charge of conspiracy to commit murder against some of the individuals named in the board's report and the charge of murder against others. In para 7 he rejected the opinion that had been expressed by the Bar Association that the Attorney General was obliged to prosecute the whole of the findings of the board and leave it to the court to judge on the sufficiency or otherwise of the evidence against the accused. He stated in para 11 that the SIB was primarily an investigation board and that, even if Law 15 had stated (which it did not) that the findings of the SIB should be prima facie evidence of the facts found, the Attorney General still had a discretion as to whether or not a person named should be put before the court.

In para 19 of his comments the Attorney General dealt specifically with the case of Mr Tsikata. He said:

'In connection with Captain Kojo Tsikata, to whom the Board devotes a substantial part of its report, the finding of the Board that he was the "mastermind" of the whole affair is extremely difficult to reconcile with the detailed evidence before the Board, which the Board accepted, of preparations undertaken by Amartey Kwei independently of Captain Tsikata, and long before Amartey Kwei claims that he was briefed by Captain Tsikata on 30 June 1982. Even leaving aside Captain Tsikata's vehement denials and the evidence of two witnesses ... which tended to indicate that Captain Tsikata was at the Castle at the critical time when he was supposed to have been with Amartey Kwei, it is clear that Amartey Kwei, whom the Board described as "the hub of the conspiracy", gave a number of inconsistent statements and that his story was not confirmed by L/Cpl. Amedeka or indeed any other persons involved in the events of 30 June 1982. If Captain Tsikata were to be prosecuted, the State would have to rely wholly on the evidence of Amartey Kwei, who is himself regarded as a key participant in the offence charged. A part of Amartey Kwei's evidence, which the Board considered critical, namely the part concerning a note allegedly sent by Captain Tsikata through Amartey Kwei to Amedeka where Amartey Kwei claims that he was told by Amedeka that the contents of the note contained a coded message instructing the killings, would even be inadmissible third-hand hearsay.'

The Attorney General then examined what he described as the inconsistencies in Mr Amartey Kwei's statements. He concluded:

'71 With all these inconsistencies in his statements it will be difficult to use Amartey Kwei as a credible witness against Captain Tsikata. Moreover the only material witness L/Cpl. Amedeka who could connect Captain Tsikata to the crime of conspiracy to commit murder has denied ever obtaining any note from Amartey Kwei and most of the allegations made by Amartey Kwei against Captain Tsikata have been denied by L/Cpl. Amedeka.

72 What is more the evidence of Amartey Kwei taken in its entirety cannot even implicate Captain Tsikata in the crime of conspiracy to kidnap much more to commit murder.

73 I am unable to find on record any other strong corroborative evidence which will enable the prosecution to sustain a case to answer against Captain Tsikata at the close of the case for the prosecution when they are charged together. Even if Captain Tsikata is charged separately the evidence of Lance

Corporal Amedeka will neutralise the little effect Amartey Kwei's evidence may have on the case against Captain Kojo Tsikata.'

On or about 31 May 1983 the Attorney General held a press conference at which he released to the public the SIB's final report as well as his own written comments on the report. Both the SIB's report and the Attorney General's comments were reported in the Ghanaian press during the course of the next few days.

Mr Amartey Kwei, L/Cpl Amadeka and three other persons were subsequently prosecuted for conspiracy to murder the three High Court judges and the retired army officer. The accused, other than Mr Kwei, were also charged with murder. The trial took place before a public tribunal. At the conclusion of the trial all five accused were found guilty of the charges alleged against them and were sentenced to death. L/Cpl Amadeka was not present at the trial as he had evaded arrest.

The trial was held in public. Mr Tsikata gave evidence for the prosecution. In the course of his evidence Mr Tsikata denied having ordered Mr Kwei to commit the murders. Mr Kwei was invited by the tribunal to cross-examine Mr Tsikata to challenge this evidence, but he declined to do so. Later, however, he made an unsworn statement from the dock, in the course of which he repeated what he had said about Mr Tsikata's role in the crime. The tribunal concluded that Mr Kwei's failure to cross-examine was to be treated as an admission of Mr Tsikata's evidence.

On 18 August 1983 Mr Kwei was executed by firing squad. Immediately before his execution he made statements confessing that he had invented his allegations against Mr Tsikata. It seems that this confession was made first to a clergyman who attended Mr Kwei just before his death and later to Flt Lt Rawlings himself, who attended at the execution ground. The conversation with Mr Rawlings was tape recorded and the tape was subsequently played back at a press conference. Mr Kwei's confession was reported in the issue of the People's Daily Graphic dated 22 August 1983.

It is to be noted that Mr Tsikata himself was not prosecuted, though the allegations against him were considered by the tribunal.

The trial of the preliminary issue

The preliminary issue was tried by Mr Jonathan Sumption QC sitting as a deputy judge of the High Court. In his judgment dated 28 October 1994 the judge referred to the events of 1982 and 1983. In the judgment he said:

'I make no findings, because I do not need to, about whether the diverse conclusions of the Special Investigation Board, the Attorney General and the Public Tribunal about Captain Tsikata's role were right or wrong. For present purposes all that matters is that those were the views which they expressed.'

The judge then turned to consider the law. For this purpose he had to examine both the common law of qualified privilege and the impact of the relevant provisions of the Defamation Act 1952. He referred to the background to the statutory privilege as follows:

'Historically, qualified privilege meant a state of affairs which negatived legal malice and meant that the plaintiff had to prove malice in fact. The classic form of qualified privilege, which depends on a social or moral duty to communicate information and a reciprocal duty or interest in receiving it, was never easy for a newspaper to invoke, because a newspaper necessarily publishes its contents indiscriminately. The courts, however, have always recognised that the reporting of certain matters to the public at large is in the public interest because those matters relate to some aspect of the community's public affairs which it is right should be in the public domain, even if they are defamatory and may be untrue.'

He drew attention to the fact that at an early stage qualified privilege at common law became attached to judicial and parliamentary proceedings, but that it was uncertain how much further it extended. He referred to the opinion of Lord Uthwatt in *Perera v Peiris* [1949] AC 1 at 21, where he said:

'Reports of judicial and parliamentary proceedings and, it may be, of some bodies which are neither judicial nor parliamentary in character, stand in a class apart by reason that the nature of their activities is treated as conclusively establishing that the public interest is forwarded by publication of reports of their proceedings. As regards reports of proceedings of other bodies, the status of those bodies taken alone is not conclusive and it is necessary to consider the subject-matter dealt with in the particular report with which the court is concerned. If it appears that it is to the public interest that the particular report should be published privilege will attach.'

The judge had already set out the relevant provisions of the 1952 Act. Section 7, so far as is material, is in these terms:

'(1) Subject to the provisions of this section, the publication in a newspaper of any such report or other matter as is mentioned in the Schedule to this Act shall be privileged unless the publication is proved to be made with malice ...
(3) Nothing in this section shall be construed as protecting the publication ... of any matter which is not of public concern and the publication of which is not for the public benefit.'

In this case we are concerned with a report of the class identified in para 5 of Pt I of the Schedule to the 1952 Act. Paragraph 5 provides:

'A fair and accurate report of any proceedings in public of a body or person appointed to hold a public inquiry by the government or legislature of any part of Her Majesty's dominions outside the United Kingdom.'

It is common ground that the definition of Her Majesty's dominions in para 14 of the Schedule includes Ghana.

It is clear from the judgment that the arguments which were addressed to the judge were similar to those which were advanced before this court. It is therefore sufficient if I state the judge's conclusions quite shortly, though by taking this course I mean no disrespect to his helpful and illuminating judgment. I hope I can fairly summarise his conclusions as follows.

(1) There is no general defence in the law of defamation of fair information on a matter of public interest. One has to look at the facts of the individual case.

(2) Nor does English law recognise a general qualified privilege in respect of the criticism of public men, as now exists in the United States since the decision of the Supreme Court in *New York Times Co v Sullivan* (1964) 376 US 254, 11 L Ed 2d 686.

a (3) A balance has to be struck between the free flow of information on public affairs and the protection of private reputations. The matters which come within the scope of public interest for this purpose may vary from one generation to another.

(4) The court must bear in mind art 10 of the Convention for the Protection of Human Rights and Fundamental Freedoms (the European Convention on *b* Human Rights) (Rome, 4 November 1950; TS 71 (1953); Cmd 8969). It was to be noted that in *A-G v Guardian Newspapers Ltd (No 2)* [1988] 3 All ER 545 at 660, [1990] 1 AC 109 at 283 Lord Goff observed that there is no difference of principle between English law and art 10 of the European Human Rights Convention as to where the point of balance is to be found. The judge also reminded himself of the dictum of the European Court of Human Rights in *Thorgeirson v Iceland* (1992) 14 *c* EHRR 843 at 865 that 'freedom of expression constitutes one of the essential foundations of a democratic society'.

(5) On the issues raised by s 7 of the 1952 Act and by para 5 of the Schedule he concluded: (a) that once the final report of the SIB had been published it became a 'proceeding in public' of the board; (b) that the first two sentences in the *d* paragraph complained of by Mr Tsikata constituted a 'fair and accurate report' of the proceedings of the SIB, and (c) that the matters set out in the first two sentences were of public concern and the publication of those two sentences was for the public benefit.

The judge said that he considered that the impact of s 7(3) of the 1952 Act was the real question at issue in the case. He rejected the argument on behalf of Mr *e* Tsikata that the mere passage of time had made it impossible any longer to satisfy the conditions set out in s 7(3). He also rejected the submission that the recommendation of the SIB had been so discredited since its original publication in May 1983 that the privilege could no longer be invoked. In the course of dealing with this argument the judge said:

f
'I would for my part be prepared to accept that in extreme cases an allegation which might have been contemporaneously reported with the benefit of qualified privilege may be so conclusively and publicly discredited thereafter that its further publication is no longer in the public interest. But the common feature of all these examples is that the defamatory statement *g* has been authoritatively or conclusively refuted. The mere accumulation of evidence for the contrary proposition is irrelevant. If the matter remains open to legitimate debate, the privilege attaching to the report of a public body's conclusions about it is unaffected.'

h He rejected the contention that the views of the Attorney General or the decision of the public tribunal put the question of Mr Tsikata's involvement in the events of 30 June 1982 beyond controversy.

(6) In the result the statutory privilege extended to the first two sentences only, but the third sentence in the paragraph was privileged at common law. In *j* the penultimate paragraph of his judgment he said:

'If (as I have already held) there is a sufficient public interest in the publication of the findings of a statutory inquiry that a member of the government should be prosecuted for a political murder, then it seems to me that the same public interest justifies the reporting of the response of that same government.'

Accordingly the judge granted a declaration that the words complained of by Mr
Tsikata were published on an occasion of qualified privilege.

Mr Tsikata has now appealed.

The appeal

Before turning to the arguments advanced in support of the appeal it will be
convenient to set out again the paragraph complained of:

> 'In June 1982, three High Court judges were kidnapped and executed at an
> army shooting range. A special inquiry into the killings recommended the
> prosecution of ten people, including Flt. Lt. Rawlings' close aide, Captain
> (Retired) Kojo Tsikata, who was named as "the master mind" of the plot.
> Five people were prosecuted and executed, but not Captain Tsikata.'

It was argued on behalf of Mr Tsikata that no part of this paragraph was
capable of being protected by the defence of qualified privilege. The publishers
purported to rely on qualified privilege at common law and on the statutory
privilege provided for in para 5 of Pt I of the Schedule to the 1952 Act but, it was
submitted, neither the first nor the third sentences of the paragraph constituted a
report 'of any proceedings' and the second sentence did not meet the conditions
required for a defence of statutory privilege. Nor was any part of the paragraph
protected by common law privilege.

In addressing the issue of statutory privilege counsel for Mr Tsikata accepted
that the judge had correctly identified the four questions to be answered.

(a) Was the final report of the SIB a 'proceeding in public' of the SIB?

(b) Were the words complained of a 'report' of it in the sense in which that
word appears in para 5 of the Schedule?

(c) If it was a 'report' of proceedings of the SIB, was it a fair and accurate one?

(d) Were the matters contained in the relevant part of the article matters of
'public concern' the publication of which was 'for the public benefit' within the
meaning of s 7(3) of the 1952 Act?

On the first question counsel drew attention to the fact that, though the oral
evidence (save in respect of a few witnesses) was heard in public, the report was
submitted to the Attorney General. It was the Attorney General who made the
report public. The task of the SIB was comparable to that of a prosecuting
authority charged with the duty of investigating an alleged crime. The SIB had
no power to make its findings public. Moreover, the proceedings on 31 May 1983
when the report was 'published' were proceedings conducted by the Attorney
General and not by the SIB. In his skeleton argument counsel expanded this
suggested distinction between the proceedings of the Attorney General and the
proceedings of the SIB as follows:

> 'Had these events taken place in the United Kingdom the publication of the
> findings on 31 May 1983 might have fallen within paragraph 12 of the
> Schedule (a fair and accurate report or summary of a notice issued for the
> information of the public by or on behalf of an officer of state) but not within
> paragraph 10(c) which is the domestic equivalent of paragraph 5.'

On the second question counsel for Mr Tsikata submitted that the second
sentence of the paragraph was not in any event a 'report' within the meaning of
the Act. The kind of report contemplated by para 5 of the Schedule was a report
published to the public as an item of news. The whole paragraph was merely a

a commentary on past events which might have been published in a book and was not a report which the public was interested to receive as a piece of news.

On the third question counsel submitted that if (which he did not accept) the report of the SIB was a report of proceedings in public it became public at the moment it was published by the Attorney General on 31 May 1983. In these circumstances a report of the SIB's findings could not be a fair and accurate report

b if published to the exclusion of the Attorney General's comments. The report and the comments were released to the public simultaneously. Furthermore, a fair and accurate report required some reference to the later developments in the case including Mr Kwei's retraction of his allegations.

As was pointed out in *Cook v Alexander* [1973] 3 All ER 1037, [1974] QB 279, a report to be fair and accurate must constitute a fair presentation of that which

c took place on the relevant occasion. The purpose of the statutory defence is to enable the public to be informed, usually by a brief summary, of proceedings of importance and interest which in the nature of things few people could have attended themselves.

The fact that the reference to the findings of the SIB was published without

d regard to the comments of the Attorney General or the subsequent events including Mr Kwei's retraction was also of crucial importance in considering the impact of s 7(3) of the 1952 Act. The publication of this stale allegation was not of public concern nor was the publication for the public benefit, particularly as the allegation had been publicly withdrawn by the person who had made it. Furthermore, though the public might be concerned with the suitability of Flt Lt

e Rawlings as a candidate for election as President, the reference to Mr Tsikata was quite unnecessary.

Counsel drew our attention to a passage in the judgment of Stephenson LJ in *Blackshaw v Lord* [1983] 2 All ER 311 at 327, [1984] QB 1 at 26, where he said:

f   'Where damaging facts have been ascertained to be true, or been made the subject of a report, there may be a duty to report them ... provided the public interest is wide enough ... But where damaging allegations or charges have been made and are still under investigation ... or have been authoritatively refuted ... there can be no duty to report them to the public.'

g In the present case, it was said, the Attorney General gave detailed reasons for rejecting the SIB's recommendation to prosecute Mr Tsikata and analysed the inconsistencies in Mr Kwei's statements. In addition it was important to bear in mind that Mr Kwei had not cross-examined Mr Tsikata at the trial and, indeed, before his execution had retracted his accusation altogether. In the circumstances there had been an 'authoritative refutation' of the allegations against Mr Tsikata.

h In addition counsel referred to s 15(3) of the Defamation Act 1996, which re-enacted the condition that statutory privilege would not attach to the publication of matter which was not of public concern or where the publication was not for the public benefit.

Counsel also dealt with the suggested defence of qualified privilege at common

j law, which was the only defence relied on in respect of the third sentence in the words complained of. Counsel submitted that there was no room for the application of a common law privilege where Parliament had laid down the scope of the protection to be conferred by statute and indeed had recently considered the matter again at the time when the Defamation Bill was being scrutinised earlier this year. The decision of the Privy Council in *Perera v Peiris* had to be treated with care because it preceded the enactment of the 1952 Act.

These are formidable arguments.

Counsel for the publishers sought to counter them by pointing to the evolution of the defence of qualified privilege, both at common law and later by statute which had been developed to protect the publication of reports of parliamentary and judicial proceedings. As time went by the protection was extended to proceedings of tribunals and other public bodies. In deciding whether a privilege attached to any particular publication, the court was concerned, it was submitted, to examine both the status of the body whose deliberations had been reported and the subject matter with which it was concerned. One might add that it is also relevant to take account of the extent to which the conclusions of the body concerned can be said to have been reached after detailed examination.

Counsel for the publishers also submitted that except (possibly) in the case of a complete refutation the question of qualified privilege has to be looked at in the first instance by reference to the report itself. In this case the findings of the SIB stood on their own.

If one applied a purposive construction to para 5 of the Schedule, it was said, the first two sentences (which had to be read together) constituted a fair and accurate report of the proceedings in public of the SIB. It was not to the point that the final report of the SIB was in fact submitted to the Attorney General and then published by him at the news conference on 31 May 1983.

Conclusions

I propose to deal first with the issue of statutory privilege. It is convenient to consider this issue in two stages. (a) Whether the words complained of, or any of them, are covered by para 5 of the Schedule to the 1952 Act. (b) Whether, though prima facie covered by s 7(1) of the Act and para 5, protection is lost because of the provisions of s 7(3).

Paragraph 5 applies to a 'fair and accurate report of any proceedings in public of a body or person' appointed to hold a public inquiry by the government of Ghana.

I agree with the judge that the final sentence of the words complained of did not form part of any report. This sentence is a statement as to subsequent events. Accordingly the sentence is not protected by statutory privilege. It was not argued that para 4 of the Schedule had any relevance.

I turn to the first two sentences of the words complained of, which, in my view, have to be read together. The first sentence identifies the subject matter of the report.

It will be remembered that it was argued on behalf of Mr Tsikata that the recommendation in the final report was not a report at all because it was published as a piece of information long after the event, that the final report was not a proceeding in public because it was sent to the Attorney General and only made public by him on 30 May 1983 and that, because it failed to include the contemporary comments of the Attorney General, it was not fair and accurate.

I am satisfied that s 7(1) and para 5 of the Schedule should be construed so as to give effect to the clear intention of Parliament and not by the adoption of a narrow linguistic approach.

One starts with the status and procedure of the SIB. The SIB was charged with investigating a matter of great public concern in Ghana. The chairman was a High Court judge. The proceedings took place in public and save for a few witnesses whose evidence was held in camera the oral evidence was heard in public. It is true that the final report was submitted to the Attorney General, but this circumstance did not in my view prevent the final report, as being in effect the judgment of the SIB, forming part of the proceeding in public.

Nor do I think that for the purposes of para 5 the protection which would have covered a report in a newspaper published at the beginning of June 1983 ceased to exist, because the report of the proceedings was published nearly ten years later. To be covered by para 5 a report of proceedings does not have to be a contemporary report or an item of recent news. Furthermore, for the purposes of para 5, the fairness and accuracy of a report has to be measured by reference to that to which it purports to relate. Later events, whether a successful appeal or arising in some other way, may raise doubts as to the propriety of publishing a report and may be very relevant to the considerations which arise under s 7(3), but in my view they do not have an impact on the fairness and accuracy of the report itself.

I now come to s 7(3) because, like the judge, I consider that the questions which arise under s 7(3) constitute the real matters at issue.

It will be remembered that it was argued on behalf of Mr Tsikata that there was no need in 1992 to mention his name at all. This argument, however, can be disposed of quite easily. Mr Tsikata continued to be a member of the government in 1992 and he provided the suggested link with the events of 1982.

The much more difficult question to my mind is whether the publishers can claim that it was for the public benefit to publish a reference to the recommendations of the SIB without at the same time (a) giving the public any information about the Attorney General's comments and the reasons which he gave for declining to accept the SIB's recommendations and (b) referring to Mr Kwei's subsequent retraction of his allegations that Mr Tsikata was involved in the killings.

I confess that I have found this to be a more difficult point than did the judge. In the end I think the solution is to be found by considering the basis on which this privilege exists and the surrounding facts. The law provides that in certain circumstances and in relation to certain types of subject matter a newspaper is entitled to qualified protection if it publishes a fair and accurate report of proceedings in public before a tribunal in a Commonwealth country. A newspaper may not know what happened subsequently nor may the newspaper be in a position to assess the quality or effect of any later denials or refutations.

Each case must depend on its own facts. But in this case it seems to me that a prima facie defence is made out and that the conditions in s 7(3) are satisfied.

I turn now to the third sentence in the words complained of and the question of qualified privilege at common law.

The decision of the Privy Council in *Perera v Peiris* provides guidance as to the scope of the qualified privilege which exists at common law for reports of the proceedings of this nature. Parliament, however, has conferred a statutory privilege in certain circumstances by the provisions enacted in the 1952 Act. In these circumstances the fact that the first two sentences of the words complained of might have been protected by common law privilege is no longer of importance except in so far as it throws light on the possible protection of the third sentence.

I have come to the conclusion, as did the judge, that if the facts stated in the third sentence had any defamatory meaning the publication of them was prima facie protected by qualified privilege as being part of the matters relating to the proceedings which the public were entitled to know. I would therefore hold that the third sentence was protected by qualified privilege at common law.

I should make it quite clear, however, that what I have said is wholly without prejudice to the question whether the defence of qualified privilege can be defeated by proof of malice. The care which was exercised in relation to this publication and the reasons why, as it could be said, only one side of the story was told will no doubt require careful examination.

For the reasons which I have endeavoured to outline I would dismiss the appeal.

WARD LJ. I agree with Neill LJ's judgment. With diffidence, but with deference to the compelling submissions addressed to us on the delicate and important balance between the integrity of personal reputation and the freedom of the press, aspects of which I did not conceal were troubling me, I state shortly how I came to my conclusions.

The following questions seem to me to need answers.

(1) *What were the 'proceedings in public of a body ... appointed to hold a public inquiry by the government' of Ghana?*

Were they: (a) only those sittings of the Special Investigation Board (Kidnapping and Killing of Specified Persons) (the SIB) which were open to members of the public, or (b) did the proceedings comprise not only the evidence, submissions, rulings, etc occurring in the public hearings but also the report of the body's conclusions even though the board itself did not make its findings public but only submitted the report to the Attorney General, as it was required to do, 'for the necessary action to be taken thereon, or (c) bearing in mind that it was the Attorney General who made the report public, did the 'proceedings in public' incorporate his public refutation of the report and his reasons for exonerating the plaintiff and for not prosecuting him?

There is no issue about (a) because the public sittings were at least part of, if not the whole of, the proceedings but this does not advance the case because the defendant's publication did not relate to that part. To my mind there is no difficulty about (c) and about excluding the Attorney's comments on the board's report. 'Proceedings' are defined to be the proceedings of 'a body appointed to hold an inquiry'. The Attorney held no such appointment. He could not be part of the appointed body nor could he become part by doing what he had to do, namely take action on the report.

Question (b) is not so easy to answer. There is force in the submission that the proceedings in public ended with the last open sitting of the board. Whilst 'proceedings in public of an international court' provided for in para 3 of the Schedule to the Defamation Act 1952 might ordinarily include the most important part of the proceedings—the judgment—that would invariably be delivered in open court. A public inquiry by contrast usually submits its conclusions to the government which decides whether to publish or not. Mr Tugendhat QC submits that had these events taken place in the United Kingdom, the publication of the findings may have fallen within para 12, which covers 'any notice or other matter issued for the information of the public by or on behalf of any government department, officer of state ... or chief officer of police' but does not fall under para 10(c), which deals with the reports of 'proceedings at any meeting or sitting' of any 'commission, tribunal, committee or person appointed for the purposes of any inquiry by ... a Minster of the Crown'. He submits that para 10(c) is the domestic equivalent of para 5. I cannot accept that submission. Paragraph 10(c) must be narrower because it refers to the report of proceedings *at any meeting or sitting.* Paragraph 5 has no such limitation. If the reports to be protected under para 5 were intended to be confined to reports of the meetings and sittings of the board, para 5 could have expressly so provided as was done in para 10(c). Something more than the meetings and sittings must be envisaged.

In my judgment a literal construction of the Schedule is not appropriate. If it were, para 12 is wide enough to apply but neither party submits that can be right. That literal approach would produce the absurdity that a judgment of the Supreme Court of the United States of America might not be covered but a notice issued by the Chief Officer of Police in Ruritania might be. A purposive construction must be given to the Schedule. The purpose was to avoid the common law investigation into the origin and status of the inquiring body and to categorise those whose reports would automatically enjoy privilege. Common sense informs us that the proceedings of a public inquiry begin with the evidence but end with the findings. Save exceptionally the findings are published in the public interest. Those conclusions are what the public want to know and what the newspapers want to report. The purpose of the Act must be to give such reporting protection. 'Proceedings' should be widely enough construed to cover the culminating act of the board if those findings are made public in the ordinary course of events. That may vary from case to case but the facts here are so close to the facts of *Perera v Peiris* [1949] AC 1 that a statutory privilege must be inferred in place of the common law privilege which would previously have been enjoyed.

(2) What constitutes a 'report' of those proceedings?

On the face of it, to write the first two sentences: (1) '... three High Court Judges were ... executed ...' and (2) 'A special inquiry ... recommended the prosecution of ... (the Plaintiff) ... as the mastermind of the plot' is to give some narration of and so give a 'report' of the proceedings. The first sentence, whilst not itself alluding to the report, is necessary to introduce the commentary and only the punctuation separates it from the second sentence. They must be read together. On the other hand, the third sentence deals with events that followed and cannot, therefore, be a report of the proceedings which can thereby gain statutory privilege.

In my judgment, it is a report if it is an account of or a résumé of the proceedings. There is no limitation of time or editorial purpose as Mr Tugendhat contends. There is no requirement of the kind found in s 3 of the Law of Libel Amendment Act 1888 relating to judicial proceedings that the report must be published contemporaneously with the proceedings. Current reporting was not required by s 4 of that Act (the forerunner of the provisions before us). Nor do I see any justification for a distinction between a report as a news item and a report as a political commentary. The role of the press is to inform the public of fact as well as by comment based on fact.

(3) Was the report a 'fair and accurate report of [the] proceedings'?

The report correctly summarises the board's findings and there can be no challenge to its accuracy.

Fairness is essentially a matter of balance. A certain degree of selectivity is given to the reporter who, subject of course to malice, can report a résumé only provided that the impression he recounts would approximate with the opinion of the reader of the whole of the document thus summarised. The theory is that the reporter represents the public—he is their eyes and ears and he has to do his best, using his professional skill, to give them a fair and accurate picture of what he saw or heard. In *Cook v Alexander* [1973] 3 All ER 1037 at 1042, [1974] QB 279 at 288, a case involving a parliamentary sketch, Lord Denning MR gave this test:

'... he need not report it verbatim, word for word or letter by letter. It is sufficient if it is a fair presentation of what took place so as to convey to the reader the impression which the debate itself would have made on a hearer of it. Test it this way. If a member of the House were asked: "What happened in the debate? Tell me about it." His answer would be a sketch giving in words the impression it left on him, with more emphasis on one thing and less emphasis on another, just as it stuck in his memory.'

The report must be a fair report 'of any proceedings'. The proceedings are the board's proceedings and do not include the Attorney's reasons for rejecting their findings. For the purpose under consideration, the required balance has to be struck internally and the Attorney's view does not come into that equation. Fairness is established.

(4) *Is this a publication of matter 'which is not of public concern and the publication of which is not for the public benefit'?*

This is the most troublesome question for me. If the answer is Yes, then by virtue of s 7(3) of the 1952 Act protection is lost. At common law the essence of the privilege, as it is expressed in *Perera v Peiris* [1949] AC 1 at 21 is: 'If it appears that it is to the public interest that the particular report should be published privilege will attach.'

I venture to think that the public interest may be measured by the degree of public concern and public benefit. I agree that the public is legitimately to be concerned about the extent to which fundamental human rights and freedoms are being upheld in Commonwealth countries. The assassination of the three judges was a gross attack on the freedom of the law. It was an act so reprehensible that the public of the United Kingdom had a concern to know about it and to know that a judicial inquiry had laid the blame squarely on the plaintiff. But that was not the only view taken of his responsibility. The Attorney analysed the board's findings and pointed to inconsistencies he found in it. The plaintiff gave evidence for the prosecution of the others named in the inquiry, and his denial of his involvement was not challenged and so was accepted by the military tribunal. His accuser apparently recanted in the face of the firing squad. There was, therefore, another side to the story. I am not sure how much of that was known to the journalist. What has caused me great anxiety is whether the public truly gain benefit from this article if they are only told half the truth about the matter in issue. Should reputation suffer such a sacrifice to give freedom to the press? At the end Mr Kentridge QC persuaded me that there is a public benefit in receiving this information. Its source was a judicial inquiry whose status derived from a law passed to empower it. The inquiry was conducted along judicial lines. The plaintiff had the opportunity to put his case. The subject matter was of the gravest relevance to the conduct of affairs in Ghana and the due administration of its government. The plaintiff was then a special adviser to the ruling council and was responsible for the security services. He was a close aide of Flt Lt Rawlings. Moreover, and crucially, he remained in high office in the government whose part in the forthcoming elections was under critical review.

He is not part of history though his actions may be. There is a benefit in knowing what view the inquiry had taken of him. Their status commands some respect. To require a newspaper so thoroughly to investigate subsequent events and report them in order to place the whole picture before the public in order to exclude damage to individual reputation is to make unacceptable inroads into the press' role as the public watchdog. It transforms investigative journalism from a virtue to a necessity. A degree of flexibility must be allowed and that will vary from case to case. Here I have been persuaded that the publication of the report is entitled to its qualified privilege.

(5) Is the third sentence privileged?

This can only enjoy a common law privilege if publication is in the public interest. The information conveyed by this sentence is so closely related to the first two that the same considerations will apply to protect it.

I agree the appeal should be dismissed.

THORPE LJ. I have had the advantage of reading in draft the judgment of Neill LJ and I am in complete agreement with it. The unusual facts of this case give rise to a point that I as a newcomer to this field have not found easy. If the first publication of the report of a public inquiry is by a government minister at a press conference and if simultaneously the minister publishes his own report, reasoning his rejection of the recommendation contained in the public inquiry report, I considered as a matter of strong first impression that subsequent newspaper reports should not be entitled to invoke any special defence to a plea of defamation if they had chosen to report only the criticism contained in the public inquiry report and to omit any reference to the minister's simultaneous dissenting report. However, I was persuaded by Mr Kentridge QC's submission that s 7 of the 1952 Act allows that outcome.

There can be no doubt, in my judgment, that the report of the Special Investigation Board (Kidnapping and Killing of Specified Persons) (the SIB) falls within the terms of para 5 of the Schedule to the 1952 Act. The board conducted its inquiry in public and its report was subsequently made public by the Attorney General. It would be quite unrealistic to construe para 5 narrowly to distinguish between the public hearings of the board and the publication of the report not by the board but by the Attorney General. The report is an essential part of the proceedings of the board and its proceedings were throughout essentially public.

Strictly analysed only the second of the three sentences complained of reports the outcome of the SIB. Although it is no more than the briefest of summaries it could not be said to be unfair or inaccurate in itself. Thus it is entitled to statutory protection under s 7 unless that protection is forfeit under s 7(3). The issue raised under s 7(3) is agreed by both parties to be the nub of this appeal.

Events in Ghana at the date of publication seem to me to show beyond doubt that the article complained of addressed matters of public concern and was of benefit to the public in that it enabled the substantial body of the readership interested in current foreign affairs to form a more balanced judgment on the issues in and outcome of the pending Ghanaian election. Of course it is said that benefit to the public was sacrificed by such a selective presentation of the history of events in 1983. To be of true benefit the public should have been informed not only of the condemnation of the SIB but also of the Attorney General's report with its reasoned rejection of the recommendation of the SIB. Mr Kentridge's response is that the Independent was entitled to report the accusatory findings of

the SIB as a distinct outcome and without reference to subsequent or even
contemporaneous qualification. He founds that submission principally on *Perera
v Peiris* [1949] AC 1 and *Blackshaw v Lord* [1983] 2 All ER 311, [1984] QB 1. Only
authoritative refutation has the effect of removing the qualified privilege which
otherwise attaches to the report. I conclude that that submission is justified by
the authorities. Whether or not a report is on a matter of public concern and for
the public benefit within the terms of s 7(3) is a question of fact and in this case by
agreement that question of fact was to be determined by the judge. There seems
little guidance as to what constitutes authoritative refutation. It seems that the
phrase was coined by Stephenson LJ in *Blackshaw v Lord* and I accept Mr
Kentridge's submission that it is most easily illustrated by the case of a criminal
charge subsequently conceded to have been mistakenly brought alternatively
subsequently dismissed. Mr Tugendhat's submission that here was an a fortiori
situation I did not find convincing. The facts found by the SIB led them to the
conclusion that the plaintiff was the mastermind of the conspiracy to murder.
They reached that conclusion having heard sworn evidence from those seeking
to exonerate themselves. The Attorney General rejected their recommendation
on the ground that in his judgment he would not secure a conviction against the
plaintiff. The subsequent events during the trial before the public tribunal and
the circumstances surrounding the execution of Joachim Kwei seemed to me to
be of doubtful weight. But the judge gave careful consideration to these and
other circumstances before reaching the conclusions which he did. Despite Mr
Tugendhat's able submissions no error in those conclusions has been
demonstrated to me.

Appeal dismissed.

Paul Magrath Esq   Barrister.

Wells v Wells
Thomas v Brighton Health Authority
Page v Sheerness Steel Co plc

COURT OF APPEAL, CIVIL DIVISION
HIRST, AULD AND THORPE LJJ
17–20, 24 JUNE, 23 OCTOBER 1996

Damages – Personal injury – Amount of damages – Assessment – Anticipated future losses and expenses – Appropriate test.

When assessing damages for anticipated future losses and expenses in personal injury cases, the court should fix the award on the assumption that the plaintiff will adopt a prudent investment strategy once he receives the award and include in his portfolio a substantial proportion of equities, rather than taking the minimum risk. Accordingly, the court should continue to adopt the conventional approach when fixing the quantum of damages awarded by applying a multiplier consistent with a return of 4·5% on the capital sum, rather than fixing the multiplier by reference to the return on index-linked government securities (see p 675 *g*, p 693 *e* to *g*, p 694 *h* to p 695 *c*, p 696 *b* to *e* and p 697 *h j*, post).

Notes
For the measure of damages in personal injury cases, see 34 *Halsbury's Laws* (4th edn) paras 78–87, and for cases on the subject, see 36(1) *Digest* (2nd reissue) 479–504, 4159–4266.

Cases referred to in judgment
Auty v National Coal Board [1985] 1 All ER 930, [1985] 1 WLR 784, CA.
Casey v East Anglian Regional Health Authority (1 November 1993, unreported), QBD.
Cookson v Knowles [1978] 2 All ER 604, [1979] AC 556, [1978] 2 WLR 978, HL.
Croke (a minor) v Wiseman [1981] 3 All ER 852, [1982] 1 WLR 71, CA.
Duxbury v Duxbury (1985) [1990] 2 All ER 77, [1992] Fam 62, [1991] 3 WLR 639, CA.
F v F (Duxbury calculation: rate of return) [1996] 1 FLR 833.
Hodgson v Trapp [1988] 3 All ER 870, [1989] AC 807, [1988] 3 WLR 1281, HL.
Hunt v Severs [1994] 2 All ER 385, [1994] 2 AC 350, [1994] 2 WLR 602, HL; *rvsg* [1993] 4 All ER 180, [1993] QB 815, [1993] 3 WLR 558, CA.
Lim Poh Choo v Camden and Islington Area Health Authority [1979] 2 All ER 910, [1980] AC 174, [1979] 3 WLR 44, HL.
Livingstone v Rawyards Coal Co (1880) 5 App Cas 25, HL.
Lodge v Simpson (18 December 1995, unreported), QBD.
Mallett v McMonagle [1969] 2 All ER 178, [1970] AC 166, [1969] 2 WLR 767, HL.
Malone v Harrison [1979] 1 WLR 1353.
Mitchell v Mulholland (No 2) [1971] 2 All ER 1205, [1972] 1 QB 65, [1971] 2 WLR 1271, CA.
Nott v Ward (13 December 1994, unreported), Ch D.

Pickett v British Rail Engineering Ltd [1979] 1 All ER 774, [1980] AC 136, [1978] 3 WLR 955, HL.

Preston v Preston [1982] 1 All ER 41, [1982] Fam 17, [1981] 3 WLR 619, CA.

Robertson v Lestrange [1985] 1 All ER 950.

Smith v Waltham Forest Health Authority (19 March 1996, unreported), QBD.

Taylor v O'Connor [1970] 1 All ER 365, [1971] AC 115, [1970] 2 WLR 472, HL.

Walsh v Glessio (16 February 1996, unreported), QBD.

Wright v British Railways Board [1983] 2 All ER 698, [1983] 2 AC 773, [1983] 3 WLR 211, HL.

Young v Percival [1974] 3 All ER 677, [1975] 1 WLR 17, CA.

Cases also cited or referred to in skeleton arguments

Anderson v Davis [1993] PIQR Q87.

Birkett v Hayes [1982] 2 All ER 710, [1982] 1 WLR 816, CA.

Bradburn v Great Western Rly Co (1874) LR 10 Ex 1, [1874–80] All ER Rep 195.

British Transport Commission v Gourley [1955] 3 All ER 796, [1956] AC 185, HL.

Cassel v Riverside Health Authority (formerly Hammersmith and Fulham Health Authority) [1992] PIQR Q168, CA.

Cunningham v Camberwell Health Authority [1990] 2 Med LR 49, CA.

Duller v South East Lincs Engineers [1981] CLY 585.

Futej v Lewandowski (1980) 124 SJ 777.

Goldfinch v Scannell [1993] PIQR Q143, CA.

Harries v Church Comrs for England [1993] 2 All ER 300, [1992] 1 WLR 1241.

Housecroft v Burnett [1986] 1 All ER 332, CA.

Hussain v New Taplow Paper Mills Ltd [1988] 1 All ER 541, [1988] AC 514, HL.

Janardan v East Berkshire Health Authority [1990] 2 Med LR 1.

McIlgrew v Devon CC [1995] PIQR Q66, CA.

Nestle v National Westminster Bank plc [1994] 1 All ER 118, [1993] 1 WLR 1260, CA.

O'Brien's Curator Bonis v British Steel plc 1991 SLT 477, Ct of Sess.

Parry v Cleaver [1969] 1 All ER 555, [1970] AC 1, HL.

Roberts v Johnstone [1989] QB 878, CA.

Shearman v Folland [1950] 1 All ER 976, [1950] 2 KB 43, CA.

Smoker v London Fire and Civil Defence Authority [1991] 2 All ER 449, [1991] 2 AC 502, HL.

Whiteley, Re, Whiteley v Learoyd (1886) 33 Ch D 347, CA.

Appeals

Wells v Wells

By notice dated 26 July 1995 the defendant, Derek Sydney Wells, appealed from the decision of Judge Wilcox, sitting as a judge of the High Court on 13 June 1995 ([1996] PIQR Q62), whereby he awarded the plaintiff, his wife Margaret Thelma Wells, suing by her daughter and next friend Susan Smith, the sum of £1,619,332 in damages and interest in respect of his admitted liability for injuries suffered by her in a road accident. The facts are set out in the judgment of the court.

Thomas v Brighton Health Authority

By notice dated 18 January 1996 the defendant, Brighton Health Authority, appealed from the decision of Collins J on 7 November 1995 ([1996] PIQR Q44) whereby he awarded the plaintiff, James Oliver Thomas, suing by his mother and next friend Susan Thomas, the sum of £1,307,963 in damages in respect of its

admitted liability for injuries sustained by the plaintiff as a result of
maladministration of a drug to the plaintiff's mother during labour. The facts are
set out in the judgment of the court.

Page v Sheerness Steel Co plc

By notice dated 30 January 1996 the defendant, Sheerness Steel Co plc, appealed
from the decision of Dyson J on 4 December 1995 ([1996] PIQR Q26) whereby he
awarded the plaintiff, Kelvin Page, the sum of £906,000 in damages in respect of
the defendant's admitted liability, as the plaintiff's employer, for injuries
sustained in the course of his employment. The facts are set out in the judgment
of the court.

John Leighton Williams QC and Richard Methuen (instructed by Linda Y Oliver,
Worthing) for Mr Wells.

Christopher Purchas QC and George Gadney (instructed by Waterson Hicks) for Mrs
Wells.

Kieran Coonan QC and Christina Lambert (instructed by Hempsons) for Brighton
Health Authority.

Robert Owen QC and Philip Havers QC (instructed by Compton Carr) for James
Thomas.

John Leighton Williams QC and Richard Methuen (instructed by Lawrence Graham)
for Sheerness Steel.

Christopher Purchas QC and Matthias Kelly (instructed by Russell Jones & Walker) for
Mr Page.

Cur adv vult

23 October 1996. The following judgment of the court was delivered.

HIRST LJ.

INTRODUCTION

These three appeals raise matters of considerable importance concerning the
assessment of damages for anticipated future losses and expenses in personal
injuries litigation. This is the judgment of the court, to which we have each
contributed.

All three cases are tragic ones, and nothing we say in this judgment in any way
diminishes their inherent gravity.

Mrs Thelma Wells, then aged nearly 58, sustained very grievous head injuries
in a road accident in which her husband, the appellant, was the driver, and for
which he admitted liability. She was awarded approximately £1·619m by Judge
Wilcox sitting as a judge of the High Court on 13 June 1995.

James Thomas was born suffering from cerebral palsy in the Royal Sussex
County Hospital, which is under the aegis of the Brighton Health Authority, who
admitted liability for maladministration of a drug to his mother, during labour.
He is now aged seven and was awarded approximately £1·307m by Collins J on
7 November 1995.

Mr Kelvin Page, then aged 28, suffered brain damage as a result of an accident
at work when in the employment of Sheerness Steel Co plc, who admitted
liability. He was awarded approximately £906,000 damages by Dyson J on 4
December 1995.

The respective appellants appeal against the quantum of damages awarded. The three cases are reported successively (see [1996] PIQR Q26, Q44, Q62).

[Their Lordships noted that each appeal raised detailed questions in relation to individual items of assessment and continued:]

However, overarching all three cases is a general point of principle as to the appropriate multiplier to be applied to the annual amount assessed for future losses and expenses (the multiplicand). In each case the judge, having heard expert evidence from both sides, departed from the well-established conventional approach of applying a multiplier consistent with a return of 4%–5% pa on the capital sum, and fixed the multiplier by reference to the return on Index Linked Government Securities (ILGS) at 3% pa, with the result that the multiplier was very significantly higher, and the damages greatly increased.

During the same period, the same point arose in a number of similar cases, but the judges declined to apply the ILGS multiplier and adhered to the conventional guidelines. As a result the law on this point has been thrown into the melting pot, with the very severe consequence that there is presently a stalemate in major personal injuries claims due to uncertainty as to the appropriate multiplier.

The adoption of the ILGS yardstick followed the recommendations of the Ogden Working Party (see *Actuarial Tables with explanatory notes for use in Personal Injury and Fatal Accident cases* (2nd edn, 1994)) and of the Law Commission Report *Structured Settlements and Interim and Provisional Damages* (Law Com No 224) (September 1994), to both of which we refer in detail below.

The Damages Act 1996 received the Royal Assent on 24 July 1996. In the debates during the passage of the Bill through the House of Lords, the Lord Chancellor stated that he awaits the outcome of this appeal, both in relation to the exercise of his powers under s 1 of the Act, and also in connection with the implementation of s 10 of the Civil Evidence Act 1995, which is not yet in force.

Section 1 of the 1996 Act provides:

'(1) In determining the return to be expected from the investment of a sum awarded as damages for future pecuniary loss in an action for personal injury the court shall, subject to and in accordance with rules of court made for the purposes of this section, take into account such rate of return (if any) as may from time to time be prescribed by an order made by the Lord Chancellor.

(2) Subsection (1) above shall not however prevent the court taking a different rate of return into account if any party to the proceedings shows that it is more appropriate in the case in question.

(3) An order under subsection (1) above may prescribe different rates of return for different classes of case.

(4) Before making an order under subsection (1) above the Lord Chancellor shall consult the Government Actuary and the Treasury; and any order under that subsection shall be made by statutory instrument subject to annulment in pursuance of a resolution of either House of Parliament.

(5) In the application of this section to Scotland for references to the Lord Chancellor there shall be substituted references to the Secretary of State.'

Section 10 of the 1995 Act provides:

'*Admissibility and proof of Ogden Tables.*—(1) The actuarial tables (together with explanatory notes) for use in personal injury and fatal accident cases issued from time to time by the Government Actuary's Department are

a   admissible in evidence for the purpose of assessing, in an action for personal
     injury, the sum to be awarded as general damages for future pecuniary loss.
     (2) They may be proved by the production of a copy published by Her
     Majesty's Stationery Office.
     (3) For the purposes of this section—(a) "personal injury" includes any
     disease and any impairment of a person's physical or mental condition; and
b   (b) "action for personal injury" includes an action brought by virtue of the
     Law Reform (Miscellaneous Provisions) Act 1934 or the Fatal Accidents Act
     1976.'

     PART I–THE GENERAL POINT OF PRINCIPLE

c   *The present guidelines—the conventional approach*
     The basic rule, which has stood for over a century, and which is accepted on
     all sides in the present appeals, is that the damages are to be assessed on the basis
     that the fundamental purpose of an award is to achieve as nearly as possible full
     compensation to the plaintiff for the injuries sustained (see *Livingstone v Rawyards
     Coal Co* (1880) 5 App Cas 25 at 39 per Lord Blackburn, quoted with approval by
d   Lord Scarman in *Lim Poh Choo v Camden and Islington Area Health Authority* [1979]
     2 All ER 910 at 917, [1980] AC 174 at 187, and also in *Pickett v British Rail
     Engineering Ltd* [1979] 1 All ER 774 at 796, [1980] AC 136 at 168).
     Later in his judgment in *Lim's* case [1979] 2 All ER 910 at 921, [1980] AC 174 at
     190–191, Lord Scarman also stated that the court must be vigilant to avoid 'not
e   only duplication of damages but the award of a surplus exceeding a true
     compensation for the plaintiff's deprivation or loss' (see also per Lord Bridge in
     Hodgson v Trapp [1988] 3 All ER 870 at 873–874, [1989] AC 807 at 819).
     In *Hodgson v Trapp* [1988] 3 All ER 870 at 878–879, [1989] AC 807 at 826 Lord
     Oliver of Aylmerton, with whom the other members of the Appellate
f   Committee agreed, stated:

     'The underlying principle is, of course, that damages are compensatory.
     They are not designed to put the plaintiff, or his estate in the event of his
     death, in a better financial position than that in which he would otherwise
     have been if the accident had not occurred. At the same time, the principle
     of making a once for all award necessarily involves an assessment both of the
g   probable duration and extent of the financial disadvantages resulting from
     the accident which the plaintiff will suffer in the future and of the present
     advantage which will accrue to him from payment in the present of a capital
     sum which he would not otherwise have had and which represents his future
     income loss. In the making of that assessment, account has also to be taken
h   of a number of unpredictable contingencies and in particular that the life
     expectancy from which the calculation starts may be falsified in the event by
     supervening illness or accident entirely unconnected with the event for
     which compensation is being awarded. Such an assessment cannot,
     therefore, by its nature be a precise science. The presence of so many
j   imponderable factors necessarily renders the process a complex and
     imprecise one and one which is incapable of producing anything better than
     an approximate result. Essentially what the court has to do is to calculate as
     best it can the sum of money which will on the one hand be adequate, by its
     capital and income, to provide annually for the injured person a sum equal
     to his estimated annual loss over the whole of the period during which that
     loss is likely to continue, but which, on the other hand, will not, at the end

of that period, leave him in a better financial position than he would have been apart from the accident. Hence the conventional approach is to assess the amount notionally required to be laid out in the purchase of an annuity which will provide the annual amount needed for the whole period of loss.'

Later in the same speech he said ([1988] 3 All ER 870 at 884–886, [1989] AC 807 at 833–834):

'There are, I think, four considerations which have to be borne in mind at the outset. First and foremost is the fact that the exercise on which the court has to embark is one which is inherently unscientific and in which expert evidence can be of only the most limited assistance. Average life expectations can be actuarially ascertained, but to assess the probabilities of future political, economic and fiscal policies requires not the services of an actuary or an accountant but those of a prophet. Second, the question is not whether the impact of taxation is a factor legitimately to be taken into account at all but to what extent, if at all, it is right to treat it as a separate, individual and independent consideration which justifies the making of additional provision conditioned not by the loss sustained but by the way in which the provision made for that loss is assumed to be dealt with by the recipient. Third, what the court is concerned with is the adequacy of a fund of damages specifically designed to meet the loss of future earnings and the cost of future care. It cannot, I think, be right in assessing the adequacy of that fund to take into account what the plaintiff may choose to do with other resources at his command, including any sums which he may receive by way of compensation for other loss or injury. If he chooses, for instance, to retain other sums awarded to him for, for example, loss of amenity or pain and suffering, and to supplement his income by investing them so as, incidentally, to put himself into a higher tax bracket, that cannot, in my judgment, constitute a legitimate ground for increasing the compensatory fund for loss of future earnings and future care. That fund must, in my judgment, be treated as a fund on its own for the purposes of assessing its adequacy. Fourth, it must not be assumed that there is only one way in which the plaintiff can deal with the award and there has, I think, to be borne in mind Lord Diplock's analysis of the underlying basis of the method by which the multiplier is selected. In practice, of course, the probability is that the plaintiff who receives a high award will treat the fund as a capital fund to be retained and invested in the most advantageous way. But the award has been calculated by reference to the cost of purchasing an appropriate annuity; and since the fund is at his complete disposal it is open to the plaintiff actually so to apply it either in whole or in part. If that were done, the capital proportion of each annual payment, calculated by dividing the cost of the annuity by the life expectation of the annuitant at the date of purchase, would be free from tax and the balance alone would be taxable. It is, I suppose, conceivable that that proportion could attract tax at the higher rate but it would require a very large annuity before a significant additional fiscal burden was attracted ... In my opinion, the incidence of taxation in the future should ordinarily be assumed to be satisfactorily taken care of in the conventional assumption of an interest rate applicable to a stable currency and the selection of a multiplier appropriate to that rate. Both in *Cookson v Knowles* [1978] 2 All ER 604, [1979] AC 556 and in *Lim's case* [1979] 2 All ER

910, [1980] AC 174 this House was prepared to envisage that there might be
very exceptional cases where it could be positively shown by evidence that
justice required it, in which special allowance might have to be made for
inflation and, inferentially, for tax. Such cases are not, I suppose, impossible,
although for my part I do not find it easy to envisage circumstances in which
evidence could satisfactorily establish that which is inherently uncertain.'

In order to meet these criteria the court had over the years developed the
conventional approach described by Lord Diplock in *Cookson v Knowles* [1978] 2
All ER 604 at 608, 611, [1979] AC 556 at 567–568, 571–572 (in the comparable fatal
accidents field) as follows:

'When the first Fatal Accidents Act was passed in 1846, its purpose was to
put the dependants of the deceased, who had been the bread-winner of the
family, in the same position financially as if he had lived his natural span of
life. In times of steady money values, wage levels and interest rates this
could be achieved in the case of the ordinary working man by awarding to
his dependants the capital sum required to purchase an annuity of an amount
equal to the annual value of the benefits with which he had provided them
while he lived, and for such period as it could reasonably be estimated they
would have continued to enjoy them but for his premature death. Although
this does not represent the way in which it is calculated such a capital sum
may be expressed as the product of multiplying an annual sum which
represents the "dependency" by a number of years' purchase. This latter
figure is less than the number of years which represents the period for which
it is estimated that the dependants would have continued to enjoy the benefit
of the dependency, since the capital sum will not be exhausted until the end
of that period and in the meantime so much of it as is not yet exhausted in
each year will earn interest from which the dependency for that year could
in part be met. The number of years' purchase to be used in order to
calculate the capital value of an annuity for a given period of years thus
depends upon the rate of interest which it is assumed that money would
earn, during that period. The higher the rate of interest, the lower the
number of years' purchase. Thus to give an illustration that is relevant to the
instant case, the capital value of an annuity for the full 16 years which would
have elapsed if the deceased had lived to work until he was 65 would require
the 11 years' purchase adopted as multiplier by the judge at an assumed
interest rate (whether he worked it out or not) of $4\frac{3}{4}$ per cent; whereas it
would need only seven years as multiplier if the assumed interest rate were
12 per cent ... Quite apart from the prospects of future inflation, the
assessment of damages in fatal accident cases can at best be only rough and
ready because of the conjectural nature of so many of the other assumptions
on which it has to be based. The conventional method of calculating it has
been to apply to what is found on the evidence to be a sum representing "the
dependency", a multiplier representing what the judge considers in the
circumstances particular to the deceased to be the appropriate number of
years' purchase. In times of stable currency the multipliers that were used
by judges were appropriate to interest rates of four per cent to five per cent
whether the judges using them were conscious of this or not. For the
reasons I have given I adhere to the opinion Lord Pearson (in *Taylor v
O'Connor* [1970] 1 All ER 365 at 379, [1971] AC 115 at 143) and I (in *Mallett v*

McMonagle [1969] 2 All ER 178 at 190, [1970] AC 166 at 175) had previously expressed which was applied by the Court of Appeal in *Young v Percival* ([1974] 3 All ER 677 at 686–688, [1975] 1 WLR 17 at 27–29), that the likelihood of continuing inflation after the date of trial should not affect either the figure for the dependency or the multiplier used. Inflation is taken care of in a rough and ready way by the higher rates of interest obtainable as one of the consequences of it and no other practical basis of calculation has been suggested that is capable of dealing with so conjectural factor with greater precision.'

In the same case Lord Fraser of Tullybelton described the correct method as follows ([1978] 2 All ER at 615–616, [1979] AC 556 at 576–577):

'I pass to the second question, which is whether the award should be increased to make allowance for inflation after the date of trial. What is relevant here is not inflation in general, but simply increases in the rate of earnings for the job in which the deceased person would probably have been employed. The reason for the increase is irrelevant. There would be no justification for attempting to protect dependants against the effects of general inflation, except to the extent that they might reasonably expect to have been protected by increases in the deceased person's earnings. At first sight it might seem reasonable that the award for the period after the date of trial should be increased in some way "to allow for inflation in the future". But I am satisfied that an increase on that ground would not merely be impossible to calculate on any rational basis, but would also be wrong in principle. The measure of the proper award to a widow (who is generally the main dependant and to whom alone I refer, brevitatis causa) is a sum which, prudently invested, would provide her with an annuity equal in amount to the support that she has probably lost through the death of her husband, during the period that she would probably have been supported by him. The assumed annuity will be made up partly of income on the principal sum awarded, and partly of capital obtained by gradual encroachment on the principal. The income element will be at its largest at the beginning of the period and will tend to decline, while the capital element will tend to increase until the principal is exhausted. The multipliers which are generally adopted in practice are based on the assumption (rarely mentioned and perhaps rarely appreciated) that the principal sum of damages will earn interest at about four or five per cent, which are rates that would be appropriate in time of stable currency, as my noble and learned friend Lord Diplock pointed out in *Mallett v McMonagle* [1969] 2 All ER 178 at 190, [1970] AC 166 at 176. But in times of rapid inflation the rate of interest that can be earned by prudent investment in fixed interest securities tends to be high, as investors seek to protect their capital and also to obtain a positive rate of interest. At the date of the trial in this case (May 1976) it was possible to obtain interest at a rate of approximately 14 per cent in gilt-edged securities, and so long as inflation continues at its present rate of approximately 10 per cent, experience suggests that the interest element in the widow's assumed annuity will be appreciably higher than the four or five per cent on which the multiplier is based. What she loses by inflation will thus be roughly equivalent to what she gains by the high rate of interest, provided she is not liable for a high rate of income tax. In that sense it is possible to obtain a large measure of protection against inflation by prudent investment, although the theory that protection was to be had by investment in equities is now largely exploded. I have referred to the "assumed" annuity because of course the widow may not choose to apply her award in the way I have mentioned; it is for her to decide and she may invest it so as to make a profit or she may squander it. But the defendant's liability should be calculated on the basis of an assumed annuity.'

Viscount Dilhorne and Lord Scarman agreed with Lord Diplock and Lord Fraser.

Thus the discount rate of 4%–5% has become generally established, and it has also been settled that the court should ignore both inflation, and also the incidence of tax, save perhaps in the case of very high levels of damages (see per Lord Oliver in *Hodgson v Trapp*).

The assumption in cases where very large awards are involved has been that the plaintiff will seek advice as to the ways in which the money can be managed to the best advantage, and that there will be a normal spread of investments (see *Taylor v O'Connor* [1970] 1 All ER 365 at 372, 379, [1971] AC 115 at 134, 143 per Lord Morris of Borth-y-Gest and Lord Pearson).

Lim's case is the culmination of the above series of House of Lords authorities in the period 1970–1980, and, in addition to the passages already quoted, contains a further passage in the speech of Lord Scarman (with whom Lord Diplock, Viscount Dilhorne and Lord Simon of Glaisdale agreed) which seems to us of particular relevance in the present case ([1979] 2 All ER 910 at 923, [1980] AC 174 at 193):

> 'The law appears to me to be now settled that only in exceptional cases, where justice can be shown to require it, will the risk of future inflation be brought into account in the assessment of damages for future loss. Of the several cases to this effect I would cite as of particular importance *Taylor v O'Connor* [1970] 1 All ER 365, [1971] AC 115 and *Young v Percival* [1974] 3 All ER 677, [1975] 1 WLR 17. It is perhaps incorrect to call this rule a rule of law. It is better described as a sensible rule of practice, a matter of common sense. Lump sum compensation cannot be a perfect compensation for the future. An attempt to build into it a protection against future inflation is seeking after a perfection which is beyond the inherent limitations of the system. While there is wisdom in Lord Reid's comment in *Taylor v O'Connor* [1970] 1 All ER 365 at 368, [1971] AC 115 at 130 that it would be unrealistic to refuse to take inflation into account at all, the better course in the great majority of cases is to disregard it. And this for several reasons. First, it is pure speculation whether inflation will continue at present, or higher, rates, or even disappear. The only sure comment one may make on any inflation prediction is that it is as likely to be falsified as to be borne out by the event. Secondly, as Lord Pearson said in *Taylor v O'Connor* [1970] 1 All ER 365 at 378, [1971] AC 115 at 143, inflation is best left to be dealt with by investment policy. It is not unrealistic in modern social conditions, nor is it unjust, to assume that the recipient of a large capital sum by way of damages will take advice as to its investment and use. Thirdly, it is inherent in a system of compensation by way of a lump sum immediately payable, and, I would think, just, that the sum be calculated at current money values, leaving the recipient in the same position as others, who have to rely on capital for their support to face the future. The correct approach should be, therefore, in the

first place to assess damages without regard to the risk of future inflation. If it can be demonstrated that, on the particular facts of a case, such an assessment would not result in a fair compensation (bearing in mind the investment opportunity that a lump sum award offers), some increase is permissible. But the victims of tort who receive a lump sum award are entitled to no better protection against inflation than others who have to rely on capital for their future support. To attempt such protection would be to put them into a privileged position at the expense of the tortfeasor, and so to impose on him an excessive burden, which might go far beyond compensation for loss.'

Time and again the courts have emphasised that this exercise is not a precise science. Thus, in the very recent case of *Hunt v Severs* [1994] 2 All ER 385 at 396–397, [1994] 2 AC 350 at 365–366 Lord Bridge of Harwich, with whom the other members of the Appellate Committee agreed, stated as follows with reference to the Ogden Tables (1st edn) which were referred to in argument:

'The assessment of damages is not and never can be an exact science. There are too many imponderables. For this reason, the courts have been traditionally mistrustful of reliance on actuarial tables as the primary basis of calculation, approving their use only as a check on assessments arrived at by the familiar conventional methods; see, for example, *Taylor v O'Connor* [1970] 1 All ER 365 at 377, [1971] AC 115 at 140 per Lord Pearson. We are told by counsel that the practice has changed in recent years and that actuarial tables tend to figure more prominently in the evidence on which courts rely. This may well be so. But before a judge's assessment of the appropriate multiplier for future loss, which he has arrived at by the conventional method of assessment and which is not attacked as being wrong in principle, can properly be adjusted by an appellate court by reference to actuarial calculations, it is essential, in my judgment, that the particular calculation relied on should be precisely in point and should be seen as demonstrably giving a more accurate assessment than the figure used by the judge. The passage I have cited from the judgment of the Court of Appeal ([1993] 4 All ER 180 at 210, [1993] QB 815 at 841) appears to show the court as treating the circumstance that both doctors in evidence estimated the plaintiff's expectation of life at 25 years as establishing the "fact" or "assumption" that she would live for 25 years and thus converting the process of assessing future loss into "a simple arithmetical calculation". I cannot think that this was a correct approach to the evidence. A man or woman in normal health, at a given age, no doubt has an ascertainable statistical life expectancy. But in using such a figure as the basis for assessment of damages with respect to future losses, some discount in respect of life's manifold contingencies is invariably made. Moreover, when the Court of Appeal referred to the *Kemp and Kemp* table as showing "that the allowance for mortality must be very small", they were not making an appropriate comparison of like with like. The figure of 14·8 taken from the *Kemp and Kemp* table refers, as already indicated, to a woman of 35 with an average expectation of life. From the life table, also set out in *Kemp and Kemp*, we see that this expectation is 44·6 years. Thus the fact that only a small allowance for mortality is appropriate in relation to the average woman's expectation of survival from the age of 35 to the age of 60 cannot be a reliable guide to the allowance for mortality appropriate to a severely injured woman aged 29 with a total expectation of life estimated by doctors as no more than 25 years.'

The Ogden Working Party Report

The Ogden Working Party Report was prepared by a working party comprising representatives of the actuarial and legal professions, chaired by Sir Michael Ogden QC, and published under the auspices of the Government Actuaries Department by HMSO in its second edition in 1994. It is headed 'Actuarial Tables with explanatory notes for use in Personal Injury and Fatal Accident Cases'.

The tables themselves set out multipliers which enable the user to assess the present capital value of the plaintiff's future annual loss or future annual expense calculated to take account of the chances that he will die young, or live to be very old, based on population mortality. The expectation of life of course differs for men and women. Calculations are also given for the adjustment of the multiplier for other risks or contingencies, e g unemployment or illness, reflecting individual circumstances in relation to occupation and to region.

The explanatory notes instruct the reader in detail how to use the tables and the adjustments. They also very strongly advocate the adoption of the ILGS discount rate as the appropriate multiplier in place of the conventional 4%–5%, with arguments which were taken up by the Law Commission.

The Law Commission Report

The Law Commission Report (Law Com No 224) is entitled 'Structured settlements and interim and provisional damages'.

The research on which its recommendations were based is described in the report as follows:

'1.7 At the same time as our consultation exercise was taking place, the Commission was carrying out empirical research on damages. Social and Community Planning Research, an independent non-profitmaking institute specialising in social surveys, carried out a linked programme of quantitative and qualitative research for us, while Professor Hazel Genn, of Queen Mary and Westfield College, London, coordinated the project on our behalf. She is now preparing a report which we hope to publish later this year. We commissioned an in-depth survey of a nation-wide representative sample of 761 people who had received awards of damages for personal injury. The study had three specific aims, which were to explore what levels and what sorts of damages people receive for personal injuries, how people use their compensation payments and why they used the funds in the way reported, and to explore recipients' feelings about the adequacy of the settlement in meeting their needs, both at the time the award was made and at the time of interview. Interviews were conducted with people who had received damages at any time from two years ago up to ten years ago (the accidents occurred between 1967 and 1991), and we stratified the claims into four size bands according to the amount of damages received: Band 1 being settlements between £5,000 and £19,999, Band 2 being settlements between £20,000 and £49,999, Band 3 being settlements between £50,000 and £99,999, and Band 4 being settlements of £100,000 or more. Most of the interviews were held in the spring of 1993.'

Having recommended that the Ogden Tables should be admissible in evidence in actions for personal injuries where it is desired to establish the capital value of any future pecuniary loss, the report discusses the discount rate as follows:

'Use of ILGS rates to discount lump sums

2.24 We also described in the consultation paper how, despite elaborate calculations concerning mortality, the assessment of future pecuniary loss could be falsified by application of an inappropriate discount rate to the multiplier. The present interest rates and projections of future movements are both subject to continuous adjustment. At present, however, the general presumption is that the court will always abide by its figure of a 4–5% return on investment as appropriate in determining the discount. Insurance companies do not take decisions based on such simplistic assumptions. Annuities involve such companies in making a promise to make payments over a long period of time on the basis of much more sophisticated methods of predicting future interest rates and of hedging the risk of interest rate movements. We therefore suggested in the consultation paper that the need for actuarial methods to be given greater prominence goes hand in hand with the need for more thought to be given to the choice of the appropriate discount rate when selecting multipliers in individual cases.

2.25 The multiplier approach is very flexible in that it can incorporate virtually any assumption about "contingencies and chances", and about interest rates. Its use, however, seemed to us to be inappropriate unless use is also made of the most up-to-date information. We suggested in the consultation paper that to make enlightened assumptions about mortality rates would not lead to much greater accuracy in the assessment of damages so long as very crude assumptions about interest rates were being made. Our provisional view was that courts should make more use of information from the financial markets in discounting lump sums to take account of the fact that they are paid today. One way of doing this would be to enable courts to refer to the rate of return on ILGS as a means of establishing an appropriate rate of discount. The purpose of this would be to obtain the best reflection of market opinion as to what real interest rates will be in future. The question upon which we sought the views of consultees was whether it would be reasonable to use the return on ILGS as a guide to the appropriate discount.

2.26 Almost two-thirds of those who responded to this question supported the use of the ILGS rates to determine more accurate discounts. These consultees agreed that the assumption of a 4–5% rate of return over time is crude and inflexible and can lead to over- or under-compensation and hence to injustice. The General Council of the Bar told us that National Savings index-linked savings certificates produced 3·25% compound between 1980 and 1990, and that the Family Division generally used a 5% discount rate, but because this was before the deduction of tax, such a discount amounted to 3–3·75% net of tax. A number of consultees argued that it was inconsistent to apply a 2% rate to plaintiffs for loss of interest on capital used for housing. One QC noted that the real rate of return for top tax payers on building society savings has been consistently less than 2% since 1978 and for much of that period there has been a negative return.

2.27 Comments were made to the effect that the current discount rate is "excessively favourable to defendants", that plaintiffs are "consistently short-changed", and that 4–5% is "wholly unrealistic", "unfair" and "no more than a judicial exercise in defendant-weighted approximation". While a third of those who responded opposed our suggestion about ILGS rates, a quarter of these in fact favoured the use of other methods (such as a new and regularly reviewed fixed rate), thereby also recognising the arbitrary nature of the 4–5% rate assumption. Another concern of those who opposed the suggestion was that any new system would be more complex than the existing one, which had the attraction of simplicity and consistency. These responses suggested that if a new system is practical and does not significantly add to costs, it would be acceptable.

2.28 We share the views of the majority of those who responded to us, that a practice of discounting by reference to returns on ILGS would be preferable to the present arbitrary presumption. The 4–5% discount which emerged from the case law was established at a time when ILGS did not exist. ILGS now constitute the best evidence of the real return on any investment where the risk element is minimal, because they take account of inflation, rather than attempt to predict it as conventional investments do. Capital is redeemed under ILGS at par and index-linked to the change in the Retail Price Index (RPI) since issue. Income remains constant in real terms, rising with increases in the RPI. There is no premium available for risk because there is no risk.

2.29 While it cannot, of course, be said with certainty that plaintiffs would always invest lump sum damages in ILGS, it is reasonable to assume they are naturally risk-averse, and the evidence from the Edinburgh study confirms the reasonableness of this assumption. Our own study was particularly revealing on this point. Spending of the award was related not only to the amount of damages received but also to the period between settlement and interview by SCPR. The proportion of recipients with about half or more of their damages still to spend by the time of interview increased from 24% in Band 1 to 35% in Band 2, 53% in Band 3, with a very slight drop to 51% in Band 4. Only one in ten in Band 4 had spent all their damages. For settlements within 3 years prior to interview, 71% of those with the smallest awards had spent over half of their damages, and only a third of those with the largest awards had done so. The longer the time since settlement, the smaller the difference between Bands: for settlement over 4 years ago, 56% of Band 2 recipients had spent over half their award, but the figure for those in Band 4 was still less at 45%. We believe that these figures show that those with serious injuries, who receive larger awards, are most concerned to preserve their funds for the future, and this would naturally make them risk-averse.

2.30 Our study revealed more direct evidence of this tendency. The most common method of saving a compensation award was to use a building society account, followed by a bank account. In all Bands, recipients were more likely to save their money in bank or building society accounts or in savings certificates than to invest in stocks or securities. As the amount of the award increased, however, so did the likelihood of investing in stocks or securities. Only one in ten recipients in Band 1 invested some of their compensation money in stocks or securities compared with six in ten of those in Band 4. The likelihood of getting advice about investment also increased significantly by size of award, from 26% in Band 1 to 84% in Band 4. We consider this to be clear evidence that those who receive large awards, where the choice of multiplier, and hence the level at which it is discounted, is crucial, are most concerned to preserve the value of their damages and to make good investments. This lends considerable weight to our assumptions about ILGS.

2.31 We are also convinced that ILGS rates can be used in a practical way to achieve a discount rate which is more realistic. We believe that ILGS should always be looked at, but that the parties should have the opportunity to adduce evidence as to alternatives they consider more appropriate if they so wish. For example, it may in the future be arguable that returns on ILGS are unduly depressed compared to those on other investments, and it is therefore important to keep flexibility in the system. We therefore *recommend that there should be legislative provision: (2) Requiring courts, when determining the return to be expected from investment of the sum awarded in any proceedings for damages for personal injury (including proceedings under the Fatal Accidents Act 1976 and the Law Reform (Miscellaneous Provisions) Act 1934), to take account of the net return to the plaintiff on an index-linked government security (Draft Bill, Clause 6(3)).'*

The Law Commission then recommend that the legislation should only permit departure from the ILGS rate where it can be shown that an alternative rate would be more suitable in the individual case.

A draft Bill containing clauses implementing these recommendations was appended to the report.

The expert evidence

Expert evidence was called by both sides in all three cases and was strongly relied upon by both the appellants and the respondents from their respective viewpoints.

In Wells v Wells, the respondent called Mr J H Prevett OBE, who is a partner in Bacon & Woodrow, actuaries and consultants, and a Fellow of the Institute of Actuaries. He was a member of the Ogden Working Party, and in his short report he simply indorsed their recommendations (and of course inferentially those of the Law Commission), and put forward ILGS as the appropriate guideline by reference to their real return as published daily in the Financial Times. The respondent did not call an accountant.

The appellant called Mr Michael Topping, a partner in Messrs Frenkel Topping & Co, chartered accountants, who stated that he considered the appropriate discount rate applicable to the case was the conventional 4%–5% range.

Citing the policy of the Court of Protection (see below) he stated that, as the award would almost certainly be invested in a mixed basket of securities split approximately 70% equities and 30% gilts, the yields on equities should be taken into account when adopting the appropriate discount rate upon which to base the multiplier. These have over the medium to long term exceeded 4%–5%, as demonstrated by the BZW Equity and Gilt Study, showing the average annual real rates of return on equities after deduction of basic rate taxes, as summarised by Mr Topping for each of the periods to 31 December 1992 on an investment made on 1 January in each of the years from 1973 to 1992 as follows:

	%		%
1973	3·7	1983	11·2
1974	6·6	1984	10·2
1975	12·4	1985	8·7
1976	8·8	1986	8·0
1977	10·6	1987	6·1
1978	9·0	1988	6·7
1979	9·5	1989	7·2
1980	11·1	1990	2·6
1981	10·8	1991	13·1
1982	12·0	1992	15·7

Mr Topping also provided a table setting out in greater detail the performance of equities by reference to their average annual real rate of return from 1961 onwards which showed that, although in most years there was a positive yield, in some years, particularly in 1968 and 1972, there was a negative yield for a subsequent period of up to ten years, before a positive yield emerged.

In Page v Sheerness Steel Co plc Mr Prevett again gave evidence for the respondent, who did not call an accountant. His report was on the same lines as in Wells v Wells, but he also gave much more extensive oral evidence, stating that while he had no experience of advising plaintiffs in setting up investment funds, he had for all his life advised trustees of pension funds, where it was important that the assets should match the liabilities; once the fund was closed, with benefits in payment and liabilities fixed, he would recommend the investment of the entire fund in ILGS, so as to minimise the risk of the fund not being able to meet its liabilities due to inflation. He thought that the position of a plaintiff was comparable, and that ILGS was the natural investment for his award, whereas investment in a mixed basket of equities and other stocks would carry a high degree of risk.

The appellant called Mr Hugh Gregory, a partner in Messrs Robson Rhodes, chartered accountants. Having cited the policy of the Court of Protection, the terms of the Trustee Investment Act 1961 and the BZW table, he said he considered that it was reasonable to follow the Court of Protection investment strategy of about 70% in equities and 30% in gilts, on which the return was significantly higher than that on ILGS, as demonstrated by the following BZW table:

Returns in period 1983–1994

	Geometric mean %	Arithmetic mean %
Nominal returns		
Equities	17·14	17·85
Conventional gilts	10·97	11·38
Index-linked gilts	7·08	7·36
Cash	10·45	10·49
Real returns		
Equities	11·70	12·45
Conventional gilts	5·82	6·29
Index-linked gilts	2·11	2·41
Cash	5·32	5·33

In addition, the appellant called on subpoena Mr Bruce Denman, who is in charge of the investment branch at the Public Trust Office dealing with Court of Protection cases where there is an outside receiver. He stated that where a person comes under their jurisdiction, they will normally formulate an investment policy for that individual in the light of his or her circumstances at the time, which would probably dictate a different approach from an entire investment in ILGS. Where a long-term scheme is involved, a segregated portfolio would normally be set up, including as the main part (70% or thereabouts) UK equities together with unit and investment trusts, as well as keeping money in cash and investments in gilts. In cross-examination he stated that even if the court adopted a new approach and assessed the award of damages on the basis of what would be a reasonable return on ILGS as recommended by the Law Commission, the hands of the Court of Protection would not be tied, and they would probably stick to their normal investment strategy of setting up a segregated portfolio as described above.

In Thomas v Brighton Health Authority the respondent called Mr Philip Haberman, a partner in Messrs KPMG, chartered accountants. He compared the multiplier/multiplicand approach as akin to an annuity calculation, and recommended ILGS as suitable securities for providing an annuity on the footing that they provide a regular unfluctuating income with no need to resort to frequent or premature sales of capital. Other advantages were that a portfolio of ILGS could be set up to allow for anticipated withdrawals of capital to be made at or close to the maturities of individual stocks (thus almost eliminating the risk of unplanned capital depletion), and that ILGS are liquid and readily realisable in an emergency. This policy was comparable to that adopted by life insurers and by the managers of closed pension schemes.

Mr Haberman defined 'prudent management of the portfolio' as avoiding unnecessary risks, matching the riskiness of the investments selected to the needs of the plaintiff, and avoiding excessive dealing and hence the need to recover high levels of dealing costs. These criteria were met by investment in ILGS, in contrast to investment in equities which is inherently risky since both capital and income can vary widely, and can even disappear altogether if the company goes into liquidation; although these risks can be reduced by selecting a portfolio of equities, this can only eliminate the risks of individual investments relative to the market as a whole, and cannot reduce the risks inherent in the market itself. Volatility in real capital value led to the risk that planned sales of capital would have to be made at unfavourable points in the investment cycle, and volatility in income led to the risk of having to make unplanned excessive sales of capital in the early years, in both instances depleting the fund. This was well illustrated by the performance of equities in unfavourable years as shown in the Topping table.

Mr Haberman recognised that the long-term average rate of return on equities currently lies in the range of 4%–5%, but said it is important to note that the higher return which this represents, in excess of the (almost) risk free returns generated from ILGS, is compensation for the risks involved in equities.

In cross-examination Mr Haberman acknowledged that when giving evidence in Casey v East Anglian Regional Health Authority (1 November 1993, unreported) he had recommended a portfolio comprising 80% ILGS and 20% equities, but said that he had subsequently changed his mind, and throughout his cross-examination he adhered to the views described above that 100% ILGS is appropriate.

The appellant called Mr Peter Dickerson, a partner in Messrs Baker Tilly, chartered accountants. He stated that in his opinion Mr Haberman drew a closer comparison between personal injuries awards and a conventional purchased annuity than is justified by the facts. The touchstone for investment of a plaintiff's award was to avoid rigidity in future cash flow, and to maximise the opportunities for flexibility to meet possible changing needs, always bearing in mind the wide range of uncertainties for which the court is required to allow.

ILGS were not the appropriate form of investment for a number of reasons. The assumption that they are virtually risk-free applies only if, once an investment is made, it is held to maturity, and also only if a pattern of holdings can be purchased at the date of the award to meet the predicted requirements; neither of these criteria was made easy by the pattern of ILGS currently available, as set out in a table furnished to us during the hearing:

ILGS AVAILABILITY

Short	*Medium*	*Long*
to 5 years	5 to 15 years	15+ years
1996	2001 2003	2016
1998	2004 2005	2020
	2006 2009	2024
	2011 2013	2030

In recent years, further tranches of existing ILGS have been issued, but no gaps have been filled, and no issue has been made with a redemption date beyond the year 2030.

Secondly, changes in market rates of return on ILGS are affected by changes in the capital values at which they are bought and sold in the market. These are illustrated by the following table which was furnished to us during the hearing covering the years 1990 to 1994:

GROSS RETURN ON INDEX-LINKED GOVERNMENT SECURITIES

DATE		GROSS RETURN (%)	AFTER DEDUCTION OF TAX AT 25%	AFTER DEDUCTION OF TAX AT 40%
1994	Jan.	2·93	2·20	1·76
	Feb.	3·26	2·45	1·96
	Mar.	3·41	2·56	2·05
	Apr.	3·50	2·63	2·10
	May	3·90	2·93	2·34
	June	3·95	2·96	2·37
	July	3·98	2·99	2·39
	Aug.	3·76	2·82	2·26
	Sept.	3·86	2·90	2·32
	Oct.	3·89	2·92	2·33
	Nov.	3·86	2·90	2·32
	Dec.	3·88	2·91	2·33

DATE	GROSS RETURN (%)	AFTER DEDUCTION OF TAX AT 25%	AFTER DEDUCTION OF TAX AT 40%
1993 Jan.	3·71	2·78	2·23
Feb.	3·47	2.60	2.08
Mar.	3·41	2·56	2·05
Apr.	3·57	2·68	2·14
May	3·56	2·67	2·14
June	3·52	2·64	2·11
July	3·38	2·54	2·03
Aug.	3·24	2·43	1·94
Sept.	3·18	2·39	1·91
Oct.	3·14	2·36	1·88
Nov.	3·08	2·31	1·85
Dec.	2·86	2·15	1·72
1992 Jan.	4·29	3·22	2·57
Feb.	4·29	3·22	2·57
Mar.	4·57	3·43	2·74
Apr.	4·49	3·37	2·69
May	4·31	3·23	2·59
June	4·35	3·26	2·61
July	4·58	3·44	2·75
Aug.	4·72	3·54	2·83
Sept.	4·11	3·08	2·47
Oct.	3·67	2·75	2·20
Nov.	3·88	2·91	2·33
Dec.	3·83	2·87	2·30
1991 Jan.	4·14	3·11	2·48
Feb.	4·16	3·12	2·50
Mar.	4·14	3·11	2·48
Apr.	4·14	3·11	2·48
May	4·22	3·17	2·53
June	4·36	3·27	2·62
July	4·39	3·29	2·63
Aug.	4·31	3·23	2·59
Sept.	4·22	3·17	2·53
Oct.	4·23	3·17	2·54
Nov.	4·30	3·23	2·58
Dec.	4·45	3·34	2·67
1990 June	4·21	3·16	2·53
July	4·30	3·23	2·58
Aug.	4·32	3·24	2·59
Sept.	4·35	3·26	2·61
Oct.	4·34	3·26	2·60
Nov.	4·17	3·13	2·50
Dec.	4·18	3·14	2·51

The actual interest paid remains fixed in real terms, in the case of most ILGS at 2% of the nominal value adjusted for inflation. If the market rate is above 2%, that market rate of return is obtained by purchasing ILGS at a discount, so that part of the return is obtained in the form of a premium in excess of the purchase price (in real terms) payable only on maturity. This produces the further disadvantage that the cash flow on interest payments is normally less than the real rate of return, thus increasing the need to realise capital regularly.

a   Thirdly, if investments need to be sold to meet unanticipated changes in the timing of the plaintiff's needs, the wide fluctuations in market rates of interest, and hence in the value of ILGS, can expose him to a considerable level of risk.

Fourthly, since the prices and returns on all ILGS are influenced by the same factors, they will tend to move in unison, so that there can be no policy of investing in a spread of such securities to ensure that the risk is spread.

b   Mr Dickerson questioned the validity of Mr Haberman's comparison with life insurers and closed pension funds, since in both these instances the insurance company or pension provider has entered into a fixed commitment where future expenditure was pre-determined, whereas those responsible for investing a plaintiff's fund have no fixed liabilities, but are required in his best interests to cater for a range of estimated future needs which might well change over time.

c   Consequently the latter should invest in a fund which produces the highest reasonable real return after tax without incurring undue risk.

The BZW analysis indicated that a portfolio with a substantial equity content, but with a component of non-equity investment available to meet short-term needs, stands a reasonable chance of balancing risk against return in a way which

d   should be acceptable to plaintiffs and their advisers. While it was true that equity values do suffer some volatility, such volatility has historically only been in the short term; in the long term, real equity values have shown a continual upward progression so that whatever past investment date is chosen, an attractive long-term return has invariably been achieved.

e   In conclusion, in common with the other two appellants' experts, Mr Dickerson recommended that a prudently managed balanced investment portfolio would comprise not less than 70% equities.

The three judgments

In *Wells v Wells* [1996] PIQR Q62 Judge Wilcox cited the Law Commission's

f   recommendations and their draft Bill, which he said had changed the climate of opinion, and which he appeared to assume would be fully implemented. As a result he rejected Mr Topping's approach, accepted Mr Prevett's, and adopted a multiplier based on ILGS.

In *Thomas v Brighton Health Authority* [1996] PIQR Q44 at Q52–Q53 Collins J stated:

g
'I am conscious of the value of guidelines and the desirability of endeavouring to achieve some degree of certainty and consistency, if only because cases can the more easily be settled if the relevant principles are known. It has understandably taken a very long time for the courts to

h   consider change, but the evidence before me persuades me that, consistently with the requirement that damages should compensate and provide, so far as possible, that the plaintiff is put into the position he would have been in but for the defendant's negligence, it is right to take account of the ILGS. It seems to me that, unless authority precludes me from so doing, I ought to recognise the existence of a means, which, to follow Lord Diplock's words,

j   is capable of dealing with so conjectural a factor with greater precision. I am not impressed with the argument espoused by Mr Dickerson that the prudent plaintiff will invest in equities and obtain 4 to 5 per cent. So long as the courts assume such an investment in fixing the multiplier, plaintiffs will be forced to invest in that way to prevent the money running out. The argument is thus circular. The court will not consider what an individual plaintiff may choose to do with his money. He may decide to seek a larger return, but at least the sum available should be sufficient to cover the risk involved in so doing. There have been some attempts to persuade judges to have regard to ILGS. All but one have hitherto failed. The first was *Robertson v. Lestrange* ([1985] 1 All ER 950), a decision of Webster J. He was pressed with *Wright v. British Railways Board* ([1983] 2 All ER 698, [1983] 2 AC 773), which was said to justify the new approach. I respectfully agree with Webster J. that that case did not directly assist. The evidence at that time did not support the contention that damages would be invested in ILGS as opposed to the conventional type of investments. It seems to me that I have the evidence which Webster J. lacked. I think, too, that Webster J. may have over-emphasised the need for there to be evidence that all competent advice would recommend investing the award in ILGS, since, so long as the award was based on 4 to 5 per cent, such advice would hardly be likely to be given. Further, he was clearly unimpressed with the evidence of the expert called by the plaintiff. The next attempt was in *Casey v. East Anglian R.H.A.* before Gage J. in November 1993. Gage J. summaries the contentions of the parties … The evidence before him focused on the recommendation as to how the award should be invested. For the reasons I have given, I think of greater importance is how an annuity can sensibly be provided, although it must be demonstrated that such a method of investment would be appropriate for a plaintiff to use. After referring to the relevant authorities, Gage J. said this: "In my judgment, what Mr Justice Webster said in *Robertson v. Lestrange* holds good today, although, for myself, I would not go quite as far as Mr Justice Webster did. My view is that the court should not depart from the convention unless satisfied on the evidence in a particular case that there is a reason peculiar to that case to do so or that investment in equities giving a return of 4–5 per cent no longer satisfied the requirement of prudent investment management given the object and life of the fund". It will be apparent that I respectfully disagree with his approach. The test is not whether it would be prudent to invest in equities but whether to invest in ILGS would achieve the necessary object with greater precision.'

In *Page v Sheerness Steel Co plc* [1996] PIQR Q26 at Q35 Dyson J stated:

'In my view Mr Purchas is right in submitting that the court is not concerned with how a particular plaintiff will choose to invest his damages. A wealthy plaintiff might choose to use the money to buy a yacht. That is irrelevant. The court is concerned to calculate a sum which is sufficient, if invested, to yield a return which will as closely as possible match the income lost by the plaintiff and/or the expenditure that he will incur from time to time as a result of the injuries sustained. Until the advent of ILGS, a plaintiff who wished to invest his damages so as to obtain a return which would as closely as possible compensate him for his lost income, no more and no less, had no choice but to invest in a balanced portfolio of blue chip equities, gilts and so on. There was no other way of seeking to get as close as possible to the position in which he would have been if he had not suffered a loss of earnings. Now there is a far more precise investment tool for achieving this purpose. I agree with what Collins J. said in *Thomas v. Brighton Health Authority* ([1996] PIQR Q44). The question is not whether it would be prudent for a plaintiff to invest in equities but whether to invest in ILGS a would achieve the necessary object of compensation with greater precision. I have no doubt that it does.'

In both *Thomas* and *Page* the judges also accepted the respondent's expert evidence in preference to the appellant's.

b *The other recent decisions*

These are: *Casey v East Anglian Regional Health Authority* (1 November 1993, Gage J), *Lodge v Simpson* (18 December 1995, Garland J), *Walsh v Glessio* (16 February 1996, Gage J) and *Smith v Waltham Forest Health Authority* (19 March 1996, French J).

As already noted, in each of these four cases the self-same arguments were c addressed, the ILGS multipliers were rejected, and the conventional guidelines adopted, for reasons similar to those advanced by the appellants in the present appeals.

The appellants' submissions

d Mr John Leighton Williams QC on behalf of Mr Wells and of Sheerness Steel Co plc, and Mr Kieran Coonan QC on behalf of the Brighton Health Authority, submitted that there is no reason for change from the conventional approach, which is still sound in law.

They unequivocally accepted the basic rule that damages are to be assessed on the basis that the fundamental purpose of an award is to achieve as nearly as e possible full compensation for the injuries sustained. But they submitted that the judges fell into error by concluding that from this it followed: (i) that the award of damages must be fixed on the assumption that the plaintiff is entitled to invest it taking the minimum risk, and (ii) that the test is not whether it would be prudent to invest in equities but whether to invest in ILGS would achieve the f necessary object with greater precision.

On the contrary, as the authorities showed, the plaintiff is in no different position from the ordinary investor, and the court can and should assume that he and his advisers will invest prudently. Prudent investment required the choice of a basket of securities including a preponderance of equities. Furthermore ILGS, because of the gaps, their non-availability beyond the year 2030, and the g substantial fluctuations in their market value, are by no means risk-free.

They submitted that the Law Commission's reasoning was unsound, and based on inadequate research. The correct approach was that adopted by the appellants' experts.

h *The respondents' submissions*

Mr Christopher Purchas QC on behalf of Mrs Wells and Mr Page, and Mr Robert Owen QC on behalf of James Thomas, submitted that the only way of satisfying the fundamental purpose of an award of damages, namely to achieve as nearly as possible full compensation to the plaintiff for the injuries sustained, was j to fix it on the assumption that he was entitled to invest it taking the minimum risk, ie to invest in ILGS; and that the correct test was that adopted in the courts below, namely that the court should not ask whether it was prudent to invest in equities, but whether to invest in ILGS would achieve the necessary object with greater precision. The ultimate object was to produce a present value for the future recurring loss with the greatest conceivable degree of accuracy. As a result the plaintiff was not to be treated as equivalent to an ordinary investor, since he had suffered loss, and received in compensation damages on a once-for-all basis as his sole protection for the foreseeable future.

Prior to the inception of ILGS in 1982, there was no practical way of dealing with the problem, and in particular guarding against future inflation, other than by the conventional approach, but that has all changed, as the Ogden Working Party and the Law Commission Report showed, with the result that the court can now see what return is available once inflation is taken out by reference to ILGS. It followed that, had ILGS been available in the 1970s, Lord Diplock and his colleagues would surely have adopted ILGS as a better alternative and a more appropriate benchmark; this they suggested was strikingly illustrated by the frequent references in the speeches of Lord Diplock and others to an annuity or an assumed annuity.

The great advantage of ILGS is that the return is certain, both interest and capital are protected against inflation, the yields are visible on a daily basis, and consequently the future is protected as securely as possible. By contrast, equities are risky, as illustrated by the evidence showing that in some years, particularly 1968 and 1972, an investment in equities would have shown a negative return over several subsequent years.

They further submitted that, when fixing the multiplicand at the first stage, all relevant factors were taken into account, and appropriate discounts applied in accordance with the relevant degrees of probability, with the result that at the end of the first part of the exercise the court had converted those probabilities into a notional certainty; by contrast, at the second stage, when selecting the multiplier, probabilities did not enter into the picture, and the sole function of the court was to select that figure which would most precisely ensure that the plaintiff was fully compensated. As Mr Purchas put it vividly at the conclusion of his argument, ILGS is the only way you can guarantee the plaintiff gets his money back.

They accepted that there was a degree of risk in ILGS, but one that paled into insignificance compared with equities. Consequently, if the multiplier was based on the conventional approach, the element of risk would not be reduced to the greatest possible degree, so that in the result the plaintiff would be under-compensated.

Furthermore, even if contrary to their argument prudence was a relevant consideration, their expert evidence demonstrated that ILGS was the most prudent investment.

Analysis and conclusions

There is, as already stressed, no dispute as to the basic rule, namely that the damages are to be assessed on the basis that the fundamental purpose of an award is to achieve, as nearly as possible, full compensation for the injuries sustained by the plaintiff.

The two critical and closely linked questions which lie at the heart of the present problem are whether the respondents are right in their two propositions that, in order to achieve this object: (i) the award must be fixed on the assumption that the plaintiff is entitled to invest it taking the minimum risk; and (ii) the test is not whether it would be prudent to invest in equities but whether to invest in ILGS would achieve the necessary object with the greatest precision.

In support of the first proposition the respondents sought to draw a contrast between an ordinary investor on the one hand and a plaintiff on the other, portraying the latter in some special category, since he has suffered damage, and

receives a once-for-all award which is his sole protection for the future. But in
our judgment this contrast is fallacious, and the plaintiff is in no different case
from the ordinary investor, as Lord Scarman stressed in the final passage quoted
above from *Lim's* case [1979] 2 All ER 910 at 923, [1980] AC 174 at 193–194; to
treat him in some different category from the ordinary investor would place him
unwarrantably in a privileged position. This statement of principle, made
unanimously by the House of Lords (including Lord Diplock), is in our judgment
of paramount importance in the present context, and confronts the respondents
with grave difficulty.

In addition the respondents laid great stress on the references in several of the
judgments to an annuity or an assumed annuity. We very much doubt whether
the use of these words signified anything more than that the calculation is to be
made on the footing that both capital and income will be exhausted at the end of
the prescribed span. Moreover, there is nothing elsewhere in these judgments
suggesting any intention to sanction the 'risk-free' test (contrast *Lim's* case).

The respondents also sought to portray the multiplicand, once firmly
established during the first stage of the exercise, as converting an assessment of
probabilities into a notional certainty; and they submitted that at the second
stage, the fixing of the multiplier is in effect a mere mathematical function,
regardless of probabilities, to return the plaintiff to his pre-accident position with
maximum precision.

We cannot accept either of these submissions. The multiplicand is the product
of an assessment of a combination of a wide range of future probabilities, and
cannot be regarded as anything more that the best and most conscientious
estimate of the plaintiff's future losses and needs, which will always remain
uncertain; thus the concept of a notional certainty is unsound. To adopt Lord
Scarman's comments in *Lim's* case, unfortunately the only certainty is that,
particularly in long-term cases, the projection will prove wrong to some extent
one way or the other.

So far as the second stage is concerned, in our judgment the suggestion that, in
fixing the multiplier, the court is making a judgment which is little more that a
mathematical exercise is erroneous, as Lord Bridge stressed in *Hunt v Severs* [1994]
2 All ER 385 at 396–397, [1994] 2 AC 350 at 365–366 in the passage quoted above.
Furthermore, at this second stage, no less than at the first, the probabilities come
into play in order to arrive at the appropriate discount when fixing what Lord
Scarman described in *Lim's* case as a 'fair multiplier'. In the process of assessing
this discount the court must take into account not only financial considerations
such as the accelerated payment and the availability of capital as well as income
to meet future expenses, but also, bearing in mind life's manifold contingencies,
the degree of likelihood that the particular plaintiff may not live out his full
expectation of life; and, in the case of future loss of earnings, that he might not
have continued to work throughout his full working span, or (in the case of a
child) that he might never have become an earner (see *Cookson v Knowles* [1978] 2
All ER 604 at 608, [1979] AC 556 at 568 per Lord Diplock, *Lim's* case [1979] 2 All
ER 910 at 925, [1980] AC 174 at 196 per Lord Scarman, *Hunt v Severs* [1994] 2 All
ER 385 at 396–397, [1994] 2 AC 350 at 365–366 per Lord Bridge and *Croke (a minor)
v Wiseman* [1981] 3 All ER 852 at 862, [1982] 1 WLR 71 at 83 per Griffiths LJ).
These factors are of course helpfully addressed with a considerable degree of
sophistication in the Ogden Tables (2nd edn) which will no doubt be of
considerable assistance in the future; but they cannot of course cater for every
relevant circumstance, affecting the individual plaintiff, which will enter into the

final assessment, as for example in *Hunt v Severs* in the case of a severely injured plaintiff aged 29 as quoted above.

Thus we reject the respondents' first basic proposition.

We now turn to the respondents' second basic proposition as to the appropriate test. The appellants, we think rightly, strongly rely on the repeated emphasis in the authorities upon prudent investment. The respondents suggest that this only related to the guidelines then in force, and has been outmoded by the advent of ILGS. We disagree. It is for the court to hold the balance evenly between both sides, and just as the plaintiff is entitled to an award which achieves as nearly as possible full compensation for the injuries sustained, so also we think the defendant is entitled to take advantage of the presumption that the former will adopt a prudent investment strategy once he receives his award. Furthermore, the court, which, as already noted, is dealing with probabilities when fixing the multiplier, can and should pay regard to the high probability that the plaintiff will invest prudently; any other approach would be artificial.

We therefore also reject the respondents' second basic proposition.

What then is prudent investment strategy?

We concentrate for the present on the long-term awards of which the present three are typical instances at the top end.

Of the expert accountant witnesses called, only Mr Haberman (supported by Mr Prevett's actuarial evidence) dissented from the view that a basket of investments including a substantial proportion of equities is appropriate. We do not find his reasoning convincing, since it seems to be based on the assumption that the respondents' two basic propositions, which we have rejected, were sound. We much prefer the evidence of the appellants' experts, and are satisfied that their recommendations as to prudent investments are sound.

Undoubtedly, equities are more risky than ILGS. Undoubtedly in some individual years investing in equities would have yielded a negative return in the ensuing period (the same applies albeit less severely to ILGS). However, the figures produced by the appellants' experts, and in particular the BZW tables, seem to us to demonstrate that, over longer periods of years, equity investment has been sound.

We are also strongly influenced by two other aspects. (i) With the sole exception of short-term cases, the policy of the Court of Protection, as described in Mr Denman's evidence, and as illustrated by their published Investment Policy (latest edition, February 1996), which was made available in the course of the hearing before us, is to include 70–80% equities in a wide spread of high yielding investments chosen from Common Investment Funds, unit trusts, investment trusts, individual United Kingdom ordinary shares, and convertibles. Common Investment Funds are a collection of three unit trusts professionally managed and only available for funds held in court, which provide a convenient method of obtaining a good spread of investment, both in equities and fixed interest securities. This is on the footing, specifically stated in the policy document, that 'some risk is acceptable'. Only in the short-term cases of five years or less is a portfolio based on short-dated gilts adopted, on the footing that in this limited class of case 'very little risk is acceptable'. As French J observed in *Smith v Waltham Forest Health Authority* (19 March 1996, unreported) the Court of Protection is an organisation which is 'hardly noted for its gambling instinct'. (ii) Under the terms of the Trustee Investment Act 1961 trustees are obliged to split their investment equally between narrow and wider range investments unless otherwise directed by the terms of the trust itself; and recently, under the

a Charities (Trustee Investment Act 1961) Order 1995, SI 1995/1092, the
permissible ratio between wider and narrow range investment has been extended
to 75:25 in the case of charities.

The respondents contend that trusts are not comparable, because the trustees
must balance the interest of present and future beneficiaries, whereas those in
charge of the investment of a personal injuries award are solely concerned with
b the individual plaintiff. However, we do not think this undermines the validity
of the comparison in the present context, since it is implicit in the policy of the
legislature that investment of a substantial proportion of the capital of a trust in
wider range funds is inherently sound; and in any event a prudent plaintiff in a
long-term case will also seek to balance present and future needs to safeguard his
c capital position during the later stages of his life.

We are not impressed by Mr Haberman's comparison with life insurance and
closed pension schemes, which we do not regard as comparable to personal
injuries awards, not least because of the inevitable uncertainty of the estimates
underlying the multiplicand, to which we have already referred; this uncertainty
d we think, tells strongly in favour of the flexibility afforded by equities, which may
be a particular advantage to a plaintiff if in due course the multiplicand proves to
have been fixed on an unduly optimistic assessment. ILGS, by contrast, are
inherently rigid.

While of course we fully accept that ILGS are less risk-prone than equities, they
e do none the less carry some element of risk, which includes the drawbacks
identified by Mr Dickerson. We note particularly the gaps and the present cut-off
in 2030, which would (for example in the *Thomas* case), make an ILGS-based
investment strategy difficult, since his expectation of life extends well beyond that
year. No doubt, as the experts accepted, further ILGS stocks will be issued, but
in the light of the recent policy of issuing further tranches of existing stocks rather
f than new ones, it does not seem to us necessarily to follow that the present gaps
will be filled, or future gaps avoided.

It follows that we do not accept that, had ILGS been available in the 1970s,
Lord Diplock and his colleagues would have been likely to select them in
preference to the conventional guidelines. In support of this submission the
g appellants also relied on Lord Diplock's conclusion in *Wright v British Railways
Board* [1983] 2 All ER 698, [1983] 2 AC 773 that, to assess the appropriate discount
for past loss of interest, ILGS is the best yardstick; but, as is clearly demonstrated
by the judgment of Oliver LJ in *Auty v National Coal Board* [1985] 1 All ER 930,
[1985] 1 WLR 784, the exercise there being undertaken was quite different from
h the assessment of future loss.

For all these reasons we consider that the present guidelines are still valid and
we are not persuaded that the case has been made out for the courts of their own
motion to adopt ILGS in their place. Consequently the present conventional
discount rate of 4.5% should continue to apply.
j
Counsel for all parties urged us to recommend a single guideline to apply
across the board. We were concerned that this might unfairly disadvantage
plaintiffs in short-term cases (say within the Law Commission Bands 1 to 3)
where, as the Law Commission's evidence shows and the Court of Protection
recommends, they would be likely to invest in gilts or building societies rather
than in equities. However, as the following table from Kemp and Kemp *The*

Quantum of Damages vol 1, para 8–055 shows, in these cases the rate of the percentage discount makes practically no difference:

| Years | Multiplier calculated with allowance for rate of interest of: | | | | | | | | Years |
	1·5%	2%	2·5%	3%	3·5%	4%	4·5%	5%	
1	1·0	1·0	1·0	1·0	1·0	1·0	1·0	1·0	1
2	2·0	2·0	2·0	1·9	1·9	1·9	1·9	1·9	2
3	2·9	2·9	2·9	2·9	2·9	2·8	2·8	2·8	3
4	3·9	3·8	3·8	3·8	3·7	3·7	3·7	3·6	4
5	4·8	4·8	4·7	4·6	4·6	4·5	4·5	4·4	5
6	5·7	5·7	5·6	5·5	5·4	5·3	5·3	5·2	6
7	6·6	6·5	6·4	6·3	6·2	6·1	6·0	5·9	7
8	7·5	7·4	7·3	7·1	7·0	6·9	6·7	6·6	8
9	8·4	8·2	8·1	7·9	7·7	7·4	7·6	7·3	9
10	9·3	9·1	8·9	8·7	8·5	8·3	8·1	7·9	10
11	10·1	9·9	9·6	9·4	9·2	8·9	8·7	8·5	11
12	11·0	10·7	10·4	10·1	9·8	9·6	9·3	9·1	12
13	11·8	11·5	11·1	10·8	10·5	10·2	9·9	9·6	13
14	12·6	12·2	11·8	11·5	11·1	10·8	10·5	10·1	14
15	13·4	13·0	12·5	12·1	11·7	11·3	11·0	10·6	15
16	14·2	13·7	13·2	12·7	12·3	11·9	11·5	11·1	16
17	15·0	14·4	13·9	13·4	12·9	12·4	12·0	11·6	17
18	15·8	15·1	14·5	14·0	13·4	12·9	12·4	12·0	18
19	16·5	15·8	15·2	14·5	13·9	13·4	12·9	12·4	19
20	17·3	16·5	15·8	15·1	14·5	13·9	13·3	12·8	20
21	18·0	17·2	16·4	15·6	15·0	14·3	13·7	13·1	21
22	18·8	17·8	17·0	16·2	15·4	14·7	14·1	13·5	22
23	19·5	18·5	17·5	16·7	15·9	15·2	14·5	13·8	23
24	20·2	19·1	18·1	17·2	16·3	15·5	14·8	14·1	24
25	20·9	19·7	18·7	17·7	16·8	15·9	15·2	14·4	25
26	21·6	20·3	19·2	18·1	17·2	16·3	15·5	14·7	26
27	22·2	20·9	19·7	18·6	17·6	16·7	15·8	15·0	27
28	22·9	21·5	20·2	19·0	18·0	17·0	16·1	15·3	28
29	23·6	22·1	20·7	19·5	18·3	17·3	16·4	15·5	29
30	24·2	22·6	21·2	19·9	18·7	17·6	16·7	15·8	30
31	24·8	23·2	21·7	20·3	19·1	17·9	16·9	16·0	31
32	25·5	23·7	22·1	20·7	19·4	18·2	17·2	16·2	32
33	26·1	24·2	22·6	21·1	19·7	18·5	17·4	16·4	33
34	26·7	24·7	23·0	21·4	20·0	18·8	17·6	16·6	34
35	27·3	25·2	23·4	21·8	20·3	19·0	17·9	16·8	35

Clearly the Ogden Tables are very useful as a check, and we therefore favour the sanction of their admissibility as proposed in s 10 of the 1995 Act, together with those parts of the explanatory notes which are truly explanatory. This recommendation does not however apply to those parts of the explanatory notes which espouse ILGS as the appropriate guideline.

Our departure from the Law Commission's and the Ogden Working Party's recommendations, which of course deserve considerable respect, causes us some concern.

a Counsel for the appellants directed strong criticism against the Law Commission's reliance on a sample of no more than 761 people, but we do not feel we are qualified to form a view either way on that aspect.

However, it is noteworthy that this sample was broken down into only four bands, of which Band 4 started at the comparatively low level of £100,000. In that band no less than 84% took investment advice, and no less than 60% invested in *b* stocks and securities, no doubt pursuant to the advice they received. With all respect, this does not seem to us to support the Law Commission's assumption in favour in ILGS for Band 4, particularly at the top end of the range. In the lower bands, for reasons already given, the selection of the discount rate has minimal significance.

It is also noteworthy that, according to para 10.3 of the Law Commission *c* Consultation Paper *Personal Injury Compensation: How much is enough? A study of the compensation experiences of victims of personal injury* (Law Com No 225) (17 October 1994), no less than of 77%–78% of the sample were satisfied with the way in which they had saved or invested their money.

We would add that many of the considerations which have influenced our *d* conclusion are not debated in either report, in both of which there seems to be an implicit assumption, which we have rejected, that the two basic propositions advanced by the respondents are sound.

Finally in this part of our judgment, we wish to mention the Duxbury Tables and the publication issued by the Family Bar Association entitled 'At a glance', to which our attention was drawn, and which, based on computer technology, have *e* developed a very sophisticated mechanism for assessing future financial dependencies after divorce. This technique may, with suitable adaptation, provide a useful step forward in personal injuries cases in the future while adhering to the present guidelines, particularly, for example, in the treatment of tax, where the present multiplier/multiplicand method seems somewhat crude. *f* This would be worthy of investigation as a much more modest measure of reform. We would, however, wish to make it clear that in our opinion such a review should be undertaken by a body on which not only lawyers and actuaries but also accountants and investment advisers are represented. For all its good work, it seems to us that it would have been a great advantage to the Ogden Working Party, which was composed of eminent lawyers and actuaries, to have *g* included within its membership both accountants and investment advisers; so far as we can judge the former were not involved at all, and the latter were only involved to the extent that assistance from a well-known firm of stockbrokers was acknowledged. We attach an appendix on this topic written by Thorpe LJ.

The appellants' appeals on the general point of principle are therefore allowed.

h [Their Lordships proceeded to consider the individual cases, reduced the awards in each of them and continued:]

FINAL CONCLUSION

In the result all three appeals succeed to the extent we have stated in this *j* judgment. Mrs Wells' cross-appeal succeeds only in relation to the Court of Protection fees. James Thomas's and Kelvin Page's cross-appeals fail.

Appendix

THORPE LJ. From 1 January 1971 the court on dissolving a marriage acquired jurisdiction to make provision for the former wife's financial dependency by way of equitable redistribution of assets. Subsequent decisions emphasised the desirability of a single capital award to achieve a clean break between the spouses. The broad basis upon which such a capital sum was to be calculated was first established by the decision of this court in *Preston v Preston* [1982] 1 All ER 41, [1982] Fam 17. The case decided that the recipient of the capital award had to have resort both to the principal sum as well as to the interest that it earned in meeting her needs. Hollings J specifically referred to civil claims when he said ([1982] 1 All ER 41 at 59, [1982] Fam 17 at 40):

'If it seemed that [the judge] was assessing the amount of the lump sum by reference to the income to be derived from it, without regard to the freedom of the wife to expend capital, then there could indeed have been an error of principle in the judge's approach, for it is, in my judgment, wrong to assess a lump sum by reference to the amount of gross or net income it could produce, since, in cases such as this, where the lump sum is provided for no one specific purpose, the recipient must be expected to expend in one way or another both capital and income: cf awards of damages (and, for example, *Malone v Harrison* [1979] 1 WLR 1353 under the Inheritance (Family Provision) Act 1975).'

At that point there was no established method by which judges should calculate the sum needed by the recipient during her whole life dependency on the assumption that the award would be exhausted at the end of her actuarial span. The judges might have looked to the multiplier/multiplicand method used in the Queen's Bench Division and, incidentally, used by Hollings J in the Inheritance Act case of *Malone v Harrison*. But since the field was untrammelled by precedent, Mr Lawrence, a partner in Messrs Coopers & Lybrand who was particularly experienced in Family Division litigation, considered what would be the most precise means of calculation. His solution, as ultimately developed, was to harness the computer by devising a program into which could be fed in each case the individual characteristics that would determine the outcome. First it was necessary to calculate what sum the recipient required to meet her needs in the first year of the dependency. Second it was necessary to calculate the duration of the dependency, either by instructing an actuary in the individual case or by reference to the English Life Tables. Finally it was necessary to feed the computer with required assumptions as to the rate of yield, the rate of capital appreciation, the rate of inflation and the current tax structure. Obviously the program was flexible to meet variations in anticipated future need and receipts. For instance if an expensive car needed to be replaced every four years that could be built into the program. Equally if a vested reversionary interest was expected to come into possession at an estimated future date that circumstance could be reflected in the calculations that the computer was programmed to carry out. So programmed, the computer calculated for each year of the dependency the receipts, the disbursements including tax precisely calculated, and the consequent value of the fund at the year end. At the end of the final year of dependency the value of the fund was close to zero. At the beginning of the first year the fund stood at that figure which enabled it to perform its obligation to meet the calculated outgoings on a year by year basis. If the value of the fund were expressed as a graph it would show the initial value climbing in the early years as the combination of yield and capital appreciation exceeded outgoings to a point approximately three quarters of the way through the dependency in the average case, after which the recipients' needs are met largely by capital realisation and the graph line plunges steeply to zero. Mr Lawrence introduced this method for

the first time in *Duxbury v Duxbury* determined by Reeve J in 1985. The judge
a accepted Mr Lawrence's methodology. The husband appealed to this court on
another issue. In the leading judgment Ackner LJ said ([1990] 2 All ER 77 at 78–
79, [1992] Fam 62 at 63):

> '... the resultant figure is £540,000 and, according to expert evidence which
> has not been challenged before us, this sum is required to produce over the
b > assumed future expectation of life of Mrs Duxbury of 35 years, she being at
> the date of the hearing 45 years old, an income which is spendable (that
> means after tax) of £28,000 per annum approximately. When I say that this
> sum is required, resort is to be made both to the income which it can produce
> and to the capital, so that over the 35 years she can thus maintain herself, the
c > assumption being, and it is all theoretical, that at the end of the 35 years the
> whole of that fund will have been spent.'

Thereafter Mr Lawrence's methodology acquired the name of the case in
which he had introduced it. It has become the universal method of calculating
the extent of the applicant's award in substantial clean-break cases. The efficacy
d of the method has never, to my knowledge, been successfully challenged and that
is no doubt a tribute to its worth. Whilst in the aftermath of *Duxbury* it was
customary for accountants to be instructed in each case to prove the
computations, since 1991 the Family Law Bar Association has published annually
essential court tables for ancillary relief (entitled 'At A Glance'). These tables
include Duxbury calculations which enable a judge to see in any case what is the
e life expectancy of any applicant between the ages of 42 and 76 and what capital
sum would be required to provide for round figure expenditure from £10,000 pa
to £100,000 pa throughout that dependency. So since the arrival of 'At A Glance'
it has only been necessary to involve the forensic accountants in unusual or
difficult cases.

f   The use of the multiplier/multiplicand method in Inheritance Act claims was
short-lived. Once the utility of the computer program method became apparent
it was adopted for the resolution of large scale claims in the Chancery Division
once the dependency was admitted or proved. A recent example is *Nott v Ward*
(13 December 1994, unreported).

There can be no doubt that the introduction of computer technology to the
g calculation of a future dependency produces results that, although inevitably
speculative, are more specifically calculated and more likely to match reality than
those achieved by the cruder method of multiplier and multiplicand. This was
recognised by the Bar Council in its submission to the Law Commission (see
Structured Settlements and Interim and Provisional Damages (Consultation Paper No
h 125)). The submission included an appendix, 'A simple damages problem, a
typical common law multiplier/multiplicand calculation and a Duxbury
calculation' (para 2.3). Later in para 2.10 the authors concluded:

> 'We would not exclude the multiplier/multiplicand approach as
> appropriate in the vast majority of simple cases ... On the other hand,
j > Duxbury calculations will provide a fairer answer and should therefore have
> a place in more complex cases, as we have demonstrated.'

The authors of the report included the Family Division junior, Mr Nicholas
Mostyn, the principal author of 'At A Glance'. It seems to me surprising that the
Law Commission Report *Structured Settlements and Interim and Provisional
Damages* (Law Com No 224) (September 1994) referred to the submission of the

Bar Council without even recording their conclusion that Duxbury calculations should have a place in more complex cases. This may be because professional debate had centred upon not whether the multiplier/multiplicand method should be replaced but upon whether in using the multiplier/multiplicand method the court should make the conventional assumption of net yield at the rate of 4·5% or at the rate of 3% generally available from ILGS. Professional debate was probably so centred since it was upon that issue that the Ogden Committee concentrated in its reports.

The multiplier/multiplicand method by contrast is less sophisticated, having its origins in an age prior to the introduction of computer technology. What is it in essence? It is described in Kemp and Kemp *The Quantum of Damages* vol 1, para 6-006 as 'a crude way of taking into account the relevant contingencies such as mortality and the receipt of a lump sum as compensation for a stream of future losses'. More specifically it is said (para 6-008):

> '[The courts] take account both of contingencies and the discount for a lump sum by applying an arbitrary multiplier to the multiplicand ... One can say "arbitrary" because the multiplier is not calculated in a precise or logical manner.'

On the other hand, in another sense the selection of the appropriate multiplier is by no means arbitrary as the courts tend to select a multiplier which accords with that selected in comparable cases by other courts over the years. Thus a pattern has emerged. Practitioners likewise tend to study the pattern and assume that, in the particular case with which they are concerned, the court will choose a multiplier that accords with the pattern.

An endeavour to substitute a more mathematical approach was made in *Mitchell v Mulholland (No 2)* [1971] 2 All ER 1205, [1972] 1 QB 65. The court evaluated an income loss to the respondent over the period of 29 years from trial to assumed retirement at age 65. The judge adopted a multiplier of 14. The discount from 29 to 14 was, of course, intended to reflect both the benefit of accelerated receipt of future earnings by way of single immediate capital payment and the avoidance of future risks such as redundancy and early death. The respondent unsuccessfully contended for what was described by the court as an actuarial approach. What the respondent proposed was that the court should take his assumed net salary for each of the 29 future years and discount 3·625% for each year of accelerated receipt. Thus in the twenty-ninth year the discount factor was applied 29 times. The summation of the calculations for each of the future years was then further discounted to reflect the possibility of periods of unemployment resulting from contingencies. The approach was rejected by this court. The emphasis in the judgments on the limitations of actuarial assumptions does not seem to me to meet the point that the respondent proffered a more precise calculation of his loss by arithmetical method. In my judgment the deficiency of the method advanced in *Mitchell v Mulholland* was that it attempted greater precision, and therefore a more scientific mode, only in relation to the flow of future income and not in relation to other factors capable of more precise formulation.

The Ogden tables represent the modern challenge to the hallowed multiplier/multiplicand method. It seems to me that they have much in common with the method advocated in *Mitchell v Mulholland*. Both might be described as discounted income-flow calculations. The Ogden method calculates the duration of loss, simply in the case of a working life by counting the number of *a* years from the respondent's age at trial to the age of retirement, and in the case of a whole life by taking the figure from English Life Table 14. So for a 50-year-old respondent the whole life figure is 24. At a 4% investment (or discount) rate an initial investment of £14·80 would produce £1 p a spendable for 24 years. So the tables show a multiplier of 14·8 for such a case.

b Again in my judgment the deficiency of the Ogden method is that it makes no attempt at similar precision in calculating other relevant considerations, and particularly the incidence of tax. The problem of tax is described in para 10 of section A of the Tables as follows:

c 'Thus, if it is decided that the rate of interest to be used to value the loss, without allowing for tax, is (say) 3½ per cent and the plaintiff will pay no tax, the figure of present value is to be found by using the multiplier in the column headed 3½ per cent. If, however, he will pay 25% tax on the income from his compensation, so that the net income he receives will be at the rate of only 75% of 3½ per cent, that is at 2·625%, then the best figure is to be found in the column headed 2½ per cent. However, it should be borne in mind that as the capital is gradually exhausted the total income obtainable

d from the interest upon it will fall; and the rate of tax payable may therefore also fall. This may mean that the deduction to be made for tax should be a smaller percentage than the rate of tax apparently applicable at the outset.'

However, although the problem is identified there is only the barest suggestion of a solution. The assumption of a 25% flat rate of tax currently made

e in the Queen's Bench Division (despite the reduction of basic rate to 24%) is in my judgment crude, unrealistic, and favourable to plaintiffs. The reality is that the individual taxpayer is entitled to allowances and the income above is then taxed by the application of varying and increasing rates to specific bands of income. In an average case a taxpayer currently only pays tax amounting to 25%

f of taxable income if his taxable income approaches £40,000 p a. Even in the case of a very substantial award the overall incidence of tax expressed as a percentage of overall receipts will not approach 25%. By way of instance I again take the case annexed to the Bar Council's submission to the Law Commission. The plaintiff's needs would by a Duxbury calculation be met by an award of £823,245 assuming the current Family Division yield of 4·25% and 1996/97 tax rates. Over the 38

g years of dependency total receipts by way of capital and income amount to nearly £3·4m upon which tax of £380K is levied. So tax expressed as a percent of receipts plus tax emerges as almost precisely 10%. This seemingly low percentage is explained by the fact that much of the receipt, particularly in later years, comes from capital realisations. Since the introduction of indexation relief within capital

h gains tax and since the Duxbury computation is currently programmed on the basis that capital growth equates to the rate of inflation, no allowance need be made for capital gains tax on realisations. Obviously if too great an incidence of tax is assumed the resultant award will overcompensate a plaintiff since provision is made for more tax than will be levied.

j From this review of the three modes I reach the following conclusions.
(1) Duxbury is to be preferred to both the multiplier/multiplicand and Ogden modes in substantial cases because, although it shares with Ogden a more precise attempt to calculate the future discounted income flow, it has these important additional advantages.
(a) The program attempts a realistic arithmetical calculation of the incidence of tax year by year throughout the period for which compensation is provided.

Of course it can be said that the resulting figure is speculative and imprecise in that it necessarily makes assumptions as to future rates of tax which future budgets will inevitably confound. However, it is surely preferable to attempt greater accuracy, and with it greater fairness to litigants, than to apply in all cases a crude assumption that is demonstrably unsound. Certainly the Duxbury method offers a specific solution to the problem posed in para 10 of section A, namely that in the early years when expenditure is largely met from income the incidence of tax will be comparatively great, whereas in the later years when expenditure is largely funded from capital realisations the incidence of tax will be comparatively low.

(b) The Duxbury method enables specific assumptions as to changes in needs and receipts in future years to be programmed. This flexibility is particularly convenient in cases in which there may be a finding of variable levels of expenditure resulting from changing needs and circumstances, alternatively in cases in which future capital receipts can be anticipated. Particular examples drawn from Family Division experience might be an applicant who at the conclusion of the children's education will move to a jurisdiction where higher rates of tax are levied; alternatively an applicant who will be free to realise a substantial part of the capital provided for a home selected to meet the needs of the family during the children's education. It is important to emphasise that Duxbury is only a program. Whilst it makes general assumptions, such as future rates of inflation and capital appreciation, it makes none specific to the individual plaintiff. It is for the judge to determine what assumptions should fairly be made in relation to the individual plaintiff and to instruct the computer to make its calculations accordingly.

(2) The 6% gross yield conventionally assumed in the multiplier/multiplicand method is probably currently too high. The rate of yield from ILGS is perhaps too low, although if expressed as 3% net it is only marginally below the current Duxbury assumption of 4·25% gross or 3·18% net were 25% to be deducted for tax. The Damages Act 1996 allows for periodic review of the assumed rate of yield. That flexibility must have advantages over the comparative rigidity of the multiplier/multiplicand assumption.

(3) No single assumption adopted in the calculation of awards of damages should be reviewed in isolation. The current multiplier/multiplicand assumption of 6% gross yield, disadvantageous to a plaintiff, is offset by the advantageous assumption of an overall 25% tax on total receipts. Were the appellants to succeed in establishing the ILGS rate of yield and then to discount it by 25% they would have turned a minus and a plus into two pluses. (That may perhaps explain why the expert evidence on which the respondents relied stated that the ILGS 3·76% gross rate of return was equivalent to 3% net. Mathematically a 25% tax deduction would produce a net rate of 2·82%.)

(4) Any review of these highly technical considerations bearing on methodology should be attempted in the first instance not by way of landmark appeals but by an interdisciplinary committee of experts. The Ogden Committee obviously provides the model but surely it should be expanded to include judges, forensic accountants, and investment fund managers. Whatever value there is in this appendix is in considerable measure the result of interdisciplinary work. I have discussed it in draft with both Mr Lawrence and Mr Mostyn and I acknowledge the great contributions that each has made to its development.

(5) The principal objective of such a reviewing committee should be to advise on the method that most effectively achieves three objectives. (a) It must be fair

a to the victim of the tortfeasor. (b) It must be not unfair to the insurance industry which from its premium income indemnifies the tortfeasor. (c) It must be relatively simply expressed and relatively straightforward in application, thereby aiding the determination of individual cases by compromise and avoiding any unnecessary introduction of expert reports and evidence in those cases that have to be determined by trial.

b (6) It seems difficult to conceive that one method would be universally applicable. It is obvious that a computer program would only be considered for the computation of large awards. To take the Law Commission's classification, the computer program would seem to have nothing to offer in cases within Bands 1, 2 and 3. But that should present no practical obstacle. In ancillary relief litigation there has never been any difficulty in perceiving the boundary between

c the case that requires a Duxbury computation and the case that does not.

(7) There does not seem to be a distinction of fundamental principle between providing for the future needs of plaintiffs in personal injury litigation and applicants in proceedings under the Matrimonial Causes Act 1973 or the Inheritance (Provision for Family and Dependants) Act 1975. As part I of our

d judgment emphasises the victim of tort is not entitled to privileged status as an investor. In so far as Holman J drew distinctions in *F v F (Duxbury calculation: rate of return)* [1996] 1 FLR 833 he did so in reliance on passages in the judgment of Collins J in *Thomas v Brighton Health Authority* ([1996] PIQR Q44), which we have disapproved.

e *Appeals allowed.*

Mary Rose Plummer   Barrister.

R v Acott

HOUSE OF LORDS

LORD MUSTILL, LORD NOLAN, LORD NICHOLLS OF BIRKENHEAD, LORD STEYN AND LORD HOFFMANN

28 NOVEMBER 1996, 20 FEBRUARY 1997

Criminal law – Murder – Provocation – Direction to jury – Defendant charged with mother's murder – Prosecution suggesting defendant provoked into losing self-control – No evidence of active provocation – Whether evidence of specific act or words of provocation resulting in a loss of self-control required before judge obliged to leave issue of provocation to jury – Homicide Act 1957, s 3.

The appellant, who lived with his mother, was charged with her murder after she had been found dead from multiple injuries. The appellant denied that he was responsible for his mother's death and claimed that his mother had sustained her injuries as the result of a fall, his unskilled efforts to resuscitate her and a further fall when he tried to pick her up. At the appellant's trial two pathologists testified for the Crown that the mother had died as a result of a sustained attack but a third pathologist testified for the defence that the mother's injuries could be explained on the basis of the appellant's account. During cross-examination counsel for the prosecution repeatedly put to the appellant the possibility that he had lost his self-control and attacked his mother because she had berated him, treated him like a child and taken advantage of the fact that he was financially dependent on her, but the appellant denied such a suggestion. The trial judge left the case to the jury on the basis that the appellant was either guilty or not guilty of murder without leaving any issue of provocation to the jury. The appellant was convicted. He appealed to the Court of Appeal on the ground that the prosecution having introduced a possible reason for the killing which gave rise to the defence of provocation, the trial judge should have left the issue of provocation to the jury and directed them on it. The appeal was dismissed on the ground that there had to be some evidence, either direct or inferential, of what was said or done to provoke the accused before the trial judge required by s 3[a] of the Homicide Act 1957 to leave the issue of provocation to the jury, and there was no such evidence. The appellant appealed to the House of Lords.

Held – In the absence of any evidence, emerging from whatever source, which suggested the reasonable possibility that the defendant might have lost his self-control due to the provoking conduct of the deceased, the question of provocation did not arise and should not be put to the jury, since without some evidence of the nature of the provocation the jury could not determine either the subjective or the objective condition under s 3 of the 1957 Act, namely whether the provoking conduct of the deceased caused the defendant to lose his self-control and whether the provocation was enough to make a reasonable man do as the defendant did. If there was no evidence of a specific act or words of provocation resulting in a loss of self-control, but merely the speculative possibility that there had been an act of provocation, it would be wrong for the judge to direct the jury to consider provocation. In such a case there was simply

---

a   Section 3 is set out at p 710 *fg*, post

a no triable issue of provocation. In deciding what issues must be left to the jury the judge had to be guided by the state of the evidence. Suggestions in cross-examination could not by themselves raise an issue of provocation where the evidence, on the most favourable view for the defendant, revealed no issue. Since there was no evidence of specific provoking conduct on the part of the mother the inference that the appellant had lost his self-control and attacked his
b mother was mere speculation and was not sufficient by itself to give rise to an issue of provocation. The appeal would therefore be dismissed (see p 707 j, p 708 a, p 710 g to p 711 a f g, p 712 b to e h and p 713 b to d j, post).

Dicta of Lord Devlin in *Lee Chun-Chuen v R* [1963] 1 All ER 73 at 77 applied.

Decision of the Court of Appeal [1996] 4 All ER 443 affirmed.

c **Notes**

For provocation as a defence to a charge of murder, see 11(1) *Halsbury's Laws* (4th edn reissue) paras 438–439, and for cases on the subject, see 14(2) *Digest* (2nd reissue) 33–48, 5260–5409.

For the Homicide Act 1957, s 3, see 12 *Halsbury's Statutes* (4th edn) (1994
d reissue) 280.

Cases referred to in opinions

Lee Chun-Chuen v R [1963] 1 All ER 73, [1963] AC 220, [1962] 3 WLR 1461, PC.

Logan v R [1996] 4 All ER 190, [1996] AC 871, [1996] 2 WLR 711, PC.

e *Mancini v DPP* [1941] 3 All ER 272, [1942] AC 1, HL.

DPP v Camplin [1978] 2 All ER 168, [1978] AC 705, [1978] 2 WLR 679, HL.

R v Duffy [1949] 1 All ER 932, CCA.

R v Stewart [1995] 4 All ER 999, CA.

f **Appeal**

Brian Gordon Alfred Acott appealed with leave of the Court of Appeal (Criminal Division) against the decision of that court (Hirst LJ, Rougier and Mitchell JJ) ([1996] 4 All ER 443) delivered on 8 March 1996 dismissing his appeal against his conviction of murder at the Central Criminal Court before the Recorder of London and a jury on 19 June 1995 for which he was sentenced to life
g imprisonment. In dismissing the appeal the Court of Appeal (Criminal Division) certified that a point of law of general public importance (see p 708, post) was involved in the decision. The facts are set out in the opinion of Lord Steyn.

h *Michael Gale QC* and *Louis French* (instructed by *Sharpe Pritchard*) for the defendant.

Heather Hallett QC and *Russell Flint* (instructed by the *Crown Prosecution Service*) for the Crown.

j Their Lordships took time for consideration.

20 February 1997. The following opinions were delivered.

LORD MUSTILL. My Lords, I have had the advantage of reading in draft the speech prepared by my noble and learned friend Lord Steyn, and for the reasons which he gives, I, also, would dismiss this appeal.

LORD NOLAN. My Lords, for the reasons given in the speech to be delivered by my noble and learned friend Lord Steyn, which I have read in draft and with which I agree, I, too, would dismiss the appeal.

LORD NICHOLLS OF BIRKENHEAD. My Lords, for the reasons given by my noble and learned friend Lord Steyn, with which I agree, I, also, would dismiss this appeal.

LORD STEYN. My Lords, on 19 June 1995 at the Central Criminal Court the appellant was convicted of the murder of his mother. He appealed to the Court of Appeal (Criminal Division) on a number of grounds. In a reserved judgment the Court of Appeal dismissed his appeal ([1996] 4 All ER 443). The appeal to your Lordships' House is directed to one issue only, namely the ruling of the Court of Appeal on provocation.

In his summing up to the jury the Recorder of London had not left the issue of provocation to the jury. On appeal to the Court of Appeal (Criminal Division) counsel for the appellant submitted that the recorder should have left the issue of provocation to the jury and should have directed the jury upon it. In giving the judgment of the court Rougier J stated that the vital question was 'what sort of evidence must exist before the judge's duty to leave the issue of provocation to the jury is triggered?' Rougier J considered this question in some detail. In a careful judgment he concluded that 'there was no evidence to enable the jury to come to any determination as to what provocation, if any, was offered to the appellant'. He held that the recorder came to the correct conclusion in not leaving the issue of provocation to the jury. In these circumstances the court dismissed the appeal. The Court of Appeal (Criminal Division) certified that there was a point of law of general public importance involved in the decision to dismiss the appeal, namely:

> 'In a prosecution for murder, before the judge is obliged to leave the issue of provocation to the jury, must there be some evidence, either direct or inferential, as to what was either done or said to provoke the alleged loss of self-control?'

The Court of Appeal granted leave to appeal.

Given the narrow focus of the appeal it is possible to summarise the background to the case briefly.

The trial

The trial took place in June 1995 before the Recorder of London. The prosecution case was as follows. In 1993 the appellant lived with his mother. He was 48 years old and his mother was 78 years of age. At 9.15 pm on 17 February 1993 the appellant, in a state of agitation, telephoned for an ambulance. He said that his mother had been injured as the result of a fall. The ambulance men met the appellant in his mother's bungalow and found the deceased dead on the floor of the hallway. An examination showed that the deceased had sustained multiple injuries, particularly in the area of the head, face and neck.

The appellant was of good character. He was a mild man. He worked until 1991 when he gave up his job and moved to Rainham to live with his mother. The appellant tried to obtain another job but he was unsuccessful. After exhausting his savings he became financially dependent on his mother. He found his dependence on his mother somewhat irksome. But in his interviews and at the trial he repeatedly said he was very fond of his mother. There was other evidence to the same effect. In accordance with a recent will of his mother he was her sole beneficiary.

When questioned by the police, and at the trial, the appellant consistently denied that he was responsible for his mother's death. He said his mother had come to his bedroom to say 'goodnight' and almost immediately afterwards he heard her fall. He said he tried to help her but she fell again. He tried to pick her up and she again fell heavily. He tried to resuscitate her, he thumped her chest and slapped her face in an effort to bring her round. He said her injuries had been caused by her falls and his unskilled efforts to resuscitate her.

Three pathologists testified: two pathologists, with varying degrees of emphasis, said that the deceased died as a result of a sustained attack; and a third pathologist testifying on behalf of the defence said the injuries were explicable on the basis of the defendant's account.

The appellant's case at the trial was therefore that he had not attacked his mother and that he was entitled to a complete acquittal. Counsel in their speeches and the recorder in his summing up treated it as a case involving a single issue. The recorder directed the jury that 'This is murder or nothing'. The jury rejected the appellant's explanation and, having been given the directions required by law in regard to burden and standard of proof, the jury convicted the appellant of murder by a majority verdict.

The evidence said to justify a direction on provocation

It is now possible to summarise the materials relied on by the appellant in support of the argument before the Court of Appeal, which was repeated before your Lordships' House, that the judge ought to have left provocation as an issue to the jury. First, counsel for the appellant pointed out correctly that leading counsel for the Crown had repeatedly put to the appellant in cross-examination that he had lost his self-control and attacked his mother. Counsel for the Crown cross-examined on the basis that the appellant had been angered by his mother treating him like a little boy and berating him. Counsel for the appellant submitted that the Crown had made provocation an issue and that accordingly the judge should have summed up on provocation. Instead, counsel for the appellant said, the judge reminded the jury of these passages in the evidence but failed to leave the issue of provocation to the jury.

Counsel for the appellant further argued that the extent of the injuries to the deceased was testimony to a frenzied attack which was prima facie indicative of a loss of self-control. Moreover, counsel argued that this inference was reinforced by the cumulative effect of the following factors: the appellant was unemployed; he was in the humiliating position of having to ask his mother for money; the evidence was that she sometimes treated him like a little boy; she was given to black moods; and apparently sometimes she drank excessively.

The decision of the Court of Appeal

Rougier J said that the issue of provocation caused the court some anxiety. He was willing to accept that there was evidence tending to suggest that the appellant lost his self-control. After analysing the statute and the authorities, he concluded ([1996] 4 All ER 443 at 453):

'In our judgment, having considered the authorities, before a judge is required by the statute to leave the issue of provocation to the jury, there must be some evidence of provocation in its active sense, in other words some evidence of *what* was done or *what* was said to provoke the homicidal reaction. Such evidence will, in the vast majority of cases, be direct. It is possible that it could arise by inference—for instance if, shortly before his death, the deceased was heard to say that he proposed to go and taunt the defendant upon a matter whereon the latter was known to be particularly sensitive. But it is not enough that the evidence should merely indicate that the defendant had lost his temper, *possibly* as a result of some unidentified words or actions, for people occasionally work themselves into a fury and erupt with no external provocation at all. If it were otherwise, the jury would have no material upon which they could make the objective judgment demanded by the statute. To direct them to determine whether the provocation in question was enough to make a reasonable man do as the defendant did, without the slightest inkling of what the provocation was, would be to ask the impossible ... From the foregoing it follows that since there was no evidence to enable the jury to come to any determination of fact as to what provocation, if any, was offered to the appellant, we do not consider that it was incumbent on the recorder to put the issue before them, and he was right not to do so.' (Rougier J's emphasis.)

These are the conclusions of the Court of Appeal which were challenged on appeal to your Lordships' House.

The general principles

Before I turn directly to an analysis of the issues on this appeal it is necessary to summarise the principles of law so far as they may affect this appeal. Section 3 of the Homicide Act 1957 reads as follows:

'Where on a charge of murder there is evidence on which the jury can find that the person charged was provoked (whether by things done or by things said or by both together) to lose his self-control, the question whether the provocation was enough to make a reasonable man do as he did shall be left to be determined by the jury; and in determining that question the jury shall take into account everything both done and said according to the effect which, in their opinion, it would have on a reasonable man.'

Section 3 moderated the strict requirements of the common law defence of provocation. Section 3 can be divided into three parts: (1) the provoking conduct; (2) causatively relevant loss of self-control; and (3) the objective criterion whether the provocation was enough to make a reasonable man do as the defendant did. For the purposes of examining the constituent elements of provocation it is only necessary to consider the classic case of provocation of an accused person *by the deceased*. First, in respect of the provoking conduct s 3 abolished the common law rule that words alone could not amount to provocation. It did so by using the general words 'whether by things done or by things said or by both together'. The meaning of these words is plain and by using the shorthand expression 'provoking conduct' I do not intend to put a gloss on the words of the statute. Secondly, the question is whether the provoking conduct of the deceased caused the defendant to lose his self-control. This is usually called the subjective condition. In the absence of any evidence, emerging from whatever source, suggestive of the reasonable possibility that the defendant might have lost his self-control due to the provoking conduct of the deceased, the question of *a* provocation does not arise. Thirdly, the section provides that the question whether the provocation was enough to make a reasonable man do as he did shall be left to be determined by the jury. This part of the section provides for an external or objective standard. This provision is explained by the concluding provision that in determining the objective question the jury shall take into account everything done and said according to the effect which, in their opinion,

b it would have on a reasonable man. The purpose of this part of the section is well settled. After the adoption of the reasonable man test in the second half of the last century, judges withdrew cases where the defendant wished to rely on provocation on the basis of rules or supposed rules which were judicially developed. By converting commonsense criteria into fixed rules of law judges empowered themselves to invoke those rules to withdraw cases from the jury.

c Thus the rule was laid down that disproportionate retaliation may bar the defence, or, as it was later put, that the retaliation must bear a reasonable relationship to the provocation received: see *Mancini v DPP* [1941] 3 All ER 272, [1942] AC 1 and *R v Duffy* [1949] 1 All ER 932; see also generally *Logan v R* [1996] 4 All ER 190 at 202–203, [1996] AC 871 at 887. Plainly proportionality was a highly relevant matter to a defence of provocation. But the perceived mischief

d was that judges withdrew cases from the jury on the ground of fixed rules of law. In *DPP v Camplin* [1978] 2 All ER 168, [1978] AC 705 the House of Lords held that s 3 abolished all previous rules linked with the objective requirement as to what can or cannot amount to provocation (see [1978] 2 All ER 168 at 173, [1978] AC 705 at 716 per Lord Diplock). At the same time s 3 abolished the power of the

e judge to withdraw provocation as an issue on the ground that there was no evidence on which the jury could find that a reasonable man would have been provoked as the defendant was: *DPP v Camplin*. Henceforth the objective requirement was to be regarded as an issue of fact, or, more realistically as a matter of opinion, within the sole province of the jury. But importantly, in the context of the present appeal, it remained the duty of the judge to decide whether

f there was evidence of provoking conduct, which resulted in the defendant losing his self-control. If in the opinion of the judge, even on a view most favourable to the accused, there is insufficient material for a jury to find that it is a reasonable possibility that there was specific provoking conduct resulting in a loss of self-control, there is simply no issue of provocation to be considered by the jury

g (see *Lee Chun-Chuen v R* [1963] 1 All ER 73 at 77, [1963] AC 220 at 229 per Lord Devlin).

Standing back from the minutiae of s 3, A J Ashworth (now Professor Ashworth) in *The Doctrine of Provocation* [1976] CLJ 292 at 317–318 described the core features of the modern law of provocation in terms which are helpful in the

h context of the present appeal. He said:

'Provocation mitigates moral culpability to the extent that a person acted in a less-than-fully-controlled manner in circumstances in which there was reasonable justification for him to feel aggrieved at the conduct of another.

j The law's subjective condition operates to ensure that it was not a revenge killing, but rather a sudden and uncontrolled reaction to perceived injustice. The objective condition looks to the element of partial justification and, inevitably, to the conduct of the provoking party. It requires of the jury an assessment of the seriousness of the provocation, and a judgment as to whether the provocation was grave enough to warrant a reduction of the crime from murder to manslaughter. This question of sufficiency is one of degree, and the legal rules, although they can take the court so far, cannot determine this ultimate question. Of course there will be clear cases—as, for example, where a teenage son loses control and attacks his bullying father— and there will be doubtful cases—as, for example, where a husband kills his wife during a quarrel over infidelity, which the parties had more or less accepted for a considerable time. Each case is for the decision of the jury, properly directed as to the law.'

This passage emphasises that it is an integral part of the idea of provocation that the deceased aroused the anger of the defendant and made him lose his self-control. It explains how the jury cannot determine either the subjective or the objective condition without some evidence of the nature of the provocation.

The proposition that the Crown made provocation an issue

Counsel for the appellant argued that the Crown made provocation an issue by putting to him in cross-examination that he attacked his mother as a result of a loss of self-control caused by momentary anger at the way in which his mother treated him. The appellant throughout denied these suggestions, and he insisted that his relationship with his mother was good and that she had done nothing to anger him. The cross-examination produced no evidence of provoking conduct or of a loss of self-control. In deciding what issues must be left to the jury a judge must be guided by the state of the evidence. Suggestions in cross-examination cannot by themselves raise an issue of provocation where the evidence, on the most favourable view for the defendant, reveals no issue. It follows that I would reject this way of putting the appellant's case.

The relevant evidence

The disposal of the appeal therefore depends on the state of the evidence. Like Rougier J I am willing to infer from the injuries of the deceased that there was a reasonable possibility that the appellant lost his self-control and attacked his mother in anger. But by itself that is not enough. The question is whether there is any evidence of specific provoking conduct. As the issues became refined during the helpful oral submissions of both counsel, it became clear that counsel for the appellant was submitting in this part of his argument that from the fact of loss of self-control and the evidence that the appellant was sometimes treated by his mother as a little boy it is a rational inference that the appellant's loss of self-control might have followed upon a specific provoking element albeit perhaps of a trivial and 'last straw' variety. Subject to his earlier argument already discussed, counsel for the appellant accepted that if such an inference is not justified, the appeal must fail. In my judgment that concession was rightly made. It is a short point not of law but of logic and common sense. The recorder plainly took the view that the evidence did not justify an inference of a specific provoking event. In my view the evidence was insufficient to support the suggested inference. It was not a reasonable possibility arising on the evidence: it was mere speculation. In these circumstances the appeal must fail on the facts.

The certified question

Strictly, the certified question need not be answered in order to dispose of the appeal. But it seems possible to summarise the legal position in terms which might be helpful. Section 3 is only applicable 'if there is evidence ... that the person charged was provoked (whether by things done or things said or by both together) to lose his self-control'. A loss of self-control caused by fear, panic,

a sheer bad temper or circumstances (e g a slow down of traffic due to snow) would
   not be enough.   There must be some evidence tending to show that the killing
   might have been an uncontrolled reaction to provoking conduct rather than an
   act of revenge.   Moreover, although there is no longer a rule of proportionality
   as between provocation and retaliation, the concept of proportionality is
   nevertheless still an important factual element in the objective inquiry.   It
b necessarily requires of the jury an assessment of the seriousness of the
   provocation.   It follows that there can only be an issue of provocation to be
   considered by the jury if the judge considers that there is some evidence of a
   specific act or words of provocation resulting in a loss of self-control.   It does not
   matter from what source that evidence emerges or whether it is relied on at trial
   by the defendant or not.   If there is such evidence, the judge must leave the issue
c to the jury.   If there is no such evidence, but merely the speculative possibility
   that there had been an act of provocation, it is wrong for the judge to direct the
   jury to consider provocation.   In such a case there is simply no triable issue of
   provocation.   I would hold that *in such circumstances* our law of provocation
   knows no principle that 'the jury must not be deprived of their opportunity to
d return a perverse verdict': see the commentary by Sir John Smith on *R v Stewart*
   [1995] 4 All ER 999 in [1995] Crim LR 67 but compare his later commentary on *R
   v Acott* [1996] 4 All ER 443 in [1996] Crim LR 665.
        Counsel for the appellant invited your Lordships to go further and state what
   would be sufficient evidence of provocation to justify a trial judge in leaving the
   issue of provocation for the jury to consider.   The invitation was attractively put.
e But it must be rejected.   What is sufficient evidence in this particular context is
   not a question of law.   Where the line is to be drawn depends on a judgment
   involving logic and common sense, the assessment of matters of degree and an
   intense focus on the circumstances of a particular case.   It is unwise to generalise
   on such matters: it is a subject best left to the good sense of trial judges.   For the
f same reason it is not useful to compare the facts of decided cases on provocation
   with one another.
        For my part the certified question can be answered in the general way in which
   I have indicated.   But the reasoning in this judgment is subject to the overriding
   principle that the legal burden rests on the Crown to disprove provocation on a
   charge of murder to the required standard of proof.   In *Lee Chun-Chuen v R* [1963]
g 1 All ER 73 at 77, [1963] AC 220 at 229 Lord Devlin summed up the legal position
   as follows:

        'It is not of course for the defence to make out a prima facie case of
        provocation.   It is for the prosecution to prove that the killing was un-
        provoked.   All that the defence need do is to point to material which could
h   induce a reasonable doubt.'

   That remains the position.
   I would dismiss the appeal.

j **LORD HOFFMANN.** My Lords, for the reasons given in the speech delivered by
   my noble and learned friend Lord Steyn, which I have read in draft and with
   which I agree, I, too, would dismiss the appeal.

Appeal dismissed.

                                                    Celia Fox   Barrister.

Kawarindrasingh v White

COURT OF APPEAL, CIVIL DIVISION

LORD WOOLF MR, ALDOUS AND BROOKE LJJ

5 NOVEMBER 1996

Costs – Taxation – Review of taxation – Judge's discretion – District judge reconsidering taxation of litigant in person's bill of costs – Application to judge for review of district judge's decision – Whether judge bound by district judge's decision – Whether judge having discretion to reconsider application afresh – CCR Ord 38, r 24(4)(6).

The plaintiff, who at all material times resided in India, entrusted the conduct of his county court claim for damages for breach of contract to his brother in England. In the course of the proceedings, in which the brother appeared as a litigant in person, two costs orders were made in the plaintiff's favour and a bill of costs for £425 was submitted on his behalf. On taxation, the district judge allowed only £67·66 of the bill; and he subsequently reconsidered and confirmed his order on two separate occasions. The plaintiff applied to the judge pursuant to CCR Ord 38, r 24(4) for a review of the district judge's taxation. The judge held that since his jurisdiction was limited to an inquiry as to whether the district judge had had regard to any irrelevant considerations, failed to take into account any relevant considerations or was clearly wrong, there were no grounds on which he could interfere with the district judge's decision. The plaintiff applied to the Court of Appeal for leave to appeal against the judge's decision.

Held – On an application under CCR Ord 38, r 24(4) for a review of a district judge's decision on a reconsideration of the taxation of a litigant in person's bill of costs, or an application under RSC Ord 62, r 35 for a review of taxation, the judge had, by virtue of CCR Ord 38, r 24(6)[a], or RSC Ord 62, r 35(4), the same powers in relation to the subject matter of the application as the district judge or taxing master. Accordingly, the judge's discretion was not fettered by the manner in which the district judge or taxing master had exercised his discretion. It followed in the instant case that the judge's view as to the limits of his jurisdiction was wrong, and since in conducting his review he had not purported to exercise his own original discretion in relation to the matters in dispute, it would be wrong to deprive the plaintiff of the opportunity of the taxation being reviewed by the judge on the correct basis. The application for leave to appeal would therefore be treated as a full hearing, an order nisi allowing the appeal would be granted and the application would be remitted to the judge for a decision on the correct basis (see p 718 *b* to *d g* to *j* and p 719 *e* to *j*, post).

Madurasinghe v Penguin Electronics (a firm) [1993] 3 All ER 20 followed.

Dictum of Cumming-Bruce LJ in *Hart v Aga Khan Foundation (UK)* [1984] 2 All ER 439 at 445–446 not followed.

Notes

For review of taxation of costs in the county court, see 10 *Halsbury's Laws* (4th edn) paras 647, 648.

a   Rule 24(6), so far as material, is set out at p 716 *j*, post

Cases referred to in judgments

Associated Provincial Picture Houses Ltd v Wednesbury Corp [1947] 2 All ER 680, [1948] 1 KB 223, CA.

Cooper v Cooper, Parish (intervener), Williams (party cited) [1936] 2 All ER 542, CA.

Evans v Bartlam [1937] 2 All ER 646, [1937] AC 473, HL.

Hart v Aga Khan Foundation (UK) [1984] 2 All ER 439, [1984] 1 WLR 994, CA.

Madurasinghe v Penguin Electronics (a firm) [1993] 3 All ER 20, [1993] 1 WLR 989, CA.

Application for leave to appeal

The plaintiff, Lieut Col Kawarindrasingh, applied to the Court of Appeal for leave to appeal from the order of Judge Morrell made in the Peterborough County Court on 25 October 1995 dismissing his application under CCR Ord 38, r 24(4) for a review of the district judge's taxation of his bill of costs in respect of two costs orders granted in his favour. The facts are set out in the judgment of Brooke LJ.

The plaintiff appeared in person.

The defendant did not appear.

BROOKE LJ (delivering the first judgment at the invitation of Lord Woolf MR). This is an application by a plaintiff, Lieut Col Kawarindrasingh, for leave to appeal from an order of Judge Morrell made in the Peterborough County Court on 25 October 1994 on a review of a taxation of costs. The judge held that there were no grounds for interfering with the district judge's decision that the costs should remain taxed in the sum of £67·66 in contrast to the sum of £425 claimed by the plaintiff. The judge refused leave to appeal and the plaintiff now renews his application for leave to appeal before this court.

The relevant orders for costs were made as long ago as 1986 and 1987. They were made in the context of a claim, which was originally started in August 1984 in the Ashby-de-la-Zouch County Court, in which the plaintiff claimed damages for breach of contract limited to £5,000 against a defendant, Mr White, who was engaged in the business of buying and selling dogs on a farm near Leicester. The dispute was concerned with a payment of air freight charges in connection with a plan to ship two puppies bred by the defendant by air to the plaintiff in India. At all material times the plaintiff has lived in India and he entrusted the conduct of this action not to an English solicitor but to his brother, who lives in England.

In due course the proceedings were transferred to the Peterborough County Court where, on 9 January 1986, Mr Registrar Martin made an order that the defendant should swear and serve on the plaintiff within 14 days an affidavit verifying his list of documents and that the costs of the application should be the plaintiff's in any event.

On 13 February 1987 in the same county court, Mr Registrar Whitehirst ordered that the application before him, presumably by the defendant, should be dismissed and that the defendant should pay the plaintiff's costs and expenses in any event. The action proceeded but the details of what occurred later are not before this court and are not relevant to the present application.

On 14 June 1992 a bill of costs was submitted on the plaintiff's behalf relating to those two orders. This bill amounted to £425. It was headed 'Taken as Costs of Plaintiff's Representative as Plaintiff in Person at Current Rates ...' The bill was taxed on 2 July 1993. The costs which were allowed were stated as follows:

'Costs allowed for one attendance in 1986	£15
Costs allowed for one attendance in 1987	£20
Preparation 1986 (half hour)	£8·66
Preparation 1987 (half hour)	£12
Plus travel	£12
Total	£67·66'

In addition a taxing fee of £3·40 was allowed but the costs of taxation were otherwise disallowed.

There followed a long period during which the same district judge reconsidered and confirmed his earlier taxation on two separate occasions. The plaintiff then sought a review by the judge. On 25 October 1994 Judge Morrell conducted his review without assessors. In a written judgment dated 31 October 1994 he said that he could find no grounds upon which he should interfere with the decision of the district judge. He considered that he was bound by the judgment of this court in *Hart v Aga Khan Foundation (UK)* [1984] 2 All ER 439, [1984] 1 WLR 994 to decide the review in accordance with the principles set out in *Associated Provincial Picture Houses Ltd v Wednesbury Corp* [1947] 2 All ER 680, [1948] 1 KB 223. He reviewed the district judge's order on this basis and decided that he had not had regard to any irrelevant considerations, or failed to take into account relevant considerations, and it could not be said that his opinion was clearly wrong.

Judge Morrell was aware of the fact that in *Madurasinghe v Penguin Electronics (a firm)* [1993] 3 All ER 20 at 24, [1993] 1 WLR 989 at 994 McCowan LJ had suggested that the decision in *Hart*'s case might require reconsideration on some future occasion, but he said that since this was a taxation of the costs of a litigant in person he was bound by the decision in *Hart*'s case.

The plaintiff now seeks leave to appeal against this judgment. Rules relating to costs in the county court are contained in CCR Ord 38. Order 38, r 17, whose predecessor was introduced as a consequence of the enactment of the Litigants in Person (Costs and Expenses) Act 1975, makes provision for the costs of a litigant in person. Order 38, r 17(4) states:

'Where the costs of a litigant in person are taxed or assessed without taxation—(a) he shall not be allowed more than such sum as would be allowed in the High Court in respect of the time reasonably spent by him in doing any work to which the costs relate if in the opinion of the court he has not suffered any pecuniary loss in doing the work, and (b) the amount allowed in respect of any work done by the litigant in person shall not in any case exceed two-thirds of the sum which in the opinion of the court would have been allowed in respect of that work if the litigant had been represented by a solicitor.'

At the heart of this application is an issue of considerable public importance relating to the nature of a judge's jurisdiction when he or she hears an application for a review of taxation, made pursuant to Ord 38, r 24(4), by a party who is dissatisfied with the district judge's decision on a reconsideration of a taxation. Order 38, r 24(6) provides, so far as is material:

'... on the hearing of the application the judge may exercise all such powers and discretion as are vested in the [district judge] in relation to the subject matter of the application.'

Order 38, r 24(7) gives the judge the power to appoint two assessors, if he sees fit, one of whom must be a district judge. In the present case Judge Morrell decided not to avail himself of this power.

In my judgment, Ord 38, r 24(6) reproduces in a codified form the familiar principles which govern the jurisdiction of a judge on an interlocutory appeal from a master or district judge. These are clearly set out in the speech of Lord Atkin in *Evans v Bartlam* [1937] 2 All ER 646 at 648–649, [1937] AC 473 at 478:

'I stay only to mention a contention of the respondent that, the master having exercised his discretion, the judge in chambers should not reverse him unless it was made evident that the master had exercised his discretion on wrong principles. I wish to state my conviction that, where there is a discretionary jurisdiction given to the court or a judge, the judge in chambers is in no way fettered by the previous exercise of the master's discretion. His own discretion is intended by the rules to determine the parties' rights, and he is entitled to exercise it as though the matter came before him for the first time. He will, of course, give the weight it deserves to the previous decision of the master, but he is in no way bound by it. This, in my experience, has always been the practice in chambers, and I am glad to find it confirmed by the recent decision of the Court of Appeal in *Cooper v. Cooper* ([1936] 2 All ER 542), with which I entirely agree.'

As Judge Morrell was well aware, a difficulty had arisen in relation to the interpretation of his powers because of something said by Cumming-Bruce LJ in a two-judge division of this court in *Hart v Aga Khan Foundation (UK)* [1984] 2 All ER 439, [1984] 1 WLR 994. This was an appeal from a judgment of Lloyd J, sitting with assessors, on a review of a taxation by Master Berkeley of the plaintiff's costs. As in the present case, the plaintiff was a litigant in person. One of the issues in that case related to the number of hours a solicitor would have taken to undertake a certain item of work. Earlier in his judgment Cumming-Bruce LJ had recited the terms of RSC Ord 62, r 28A , and in particular para (2). He said ([1984] 2 All ER 439 at 445–446, [1984] 1 WLR 994 at 1006):

'In my view there is no material before this court which could entitle this court to interfere with the decision of the judge sitting with assessors on the quantum of the notional time that a solicitor would have taken in respect of the item for preparation for trial. As a matter of construction r 28A(2) proceeds on the basis that it is for the taxing master to form an opinion on what would have been allowed. On a review, where a judge is sitting with assessors, it is in my view clearly open to the court sitting with such assessors, on review of the opinion of the taxing master, to vary the opinion of the taxing master either as to the number of hours that a notional solicitor would have taken or as to the fee that a notional solicitor would have obtained on taxation. But it is clear from the terms of the judgment that there was in the opinion of the court, sitting with assessors, no sufficient ground shown for substituting a different opinion for the opinion of the taxing master. The approach, in my view, is the approach which is relevant whenever legislation confides to a court the determination of fact or opinion to a specified person or body. It is open to a court on review to reject the opinion of the taxing master only if it is shown on the *Wednesbury* principles (see *Associated Provincial Picture Houses Ltd v Wednesbury Corp* [1947] 2 All ER 680, [1948] 1 KB 223) that the taxing master had regard to irrelevant considerations, or failed to take into account relevant considerations, or if the court is satisfied that the opinion of the taxing master on the facts was clearly wrong.'

As Judge Morrell also knew, this passage was considered by a three-judge division of this court in *Madurasinghe v Penguin Electronics (a firm)* [1993] 3 All ER 20, [1993] 1 WLR 989. That appeal, like the present, was connected with the taxation of costs in the county court. McCowan LJ adopted the same interpretation of Ord 38, r 24(6) as I would adopt in the present case. He said ([1993] 3 All ER 20 at 23, [1993] 1 WLR 989 at 993):

'The vital words are "all such powers and discretion as are vested in the district judge in relation to the subject matter of the application". In my judgment, since the district judge and the judge have the same powers and discretion in relation to the subject matter of the application the judge's discretion cannot be fettered by the manner in which the district judge exercised his discretion. It follows that I consider the judge was plainly wrong in believing himself to be bound by *Hart v Aga Khan Foundation* only to interfere if he thought that the registrar or district judge had not taken into account something he ought to have taken into account or had taken into account an irrelevant matter or that his opinion was clearly wrong.'

McCowan LJ went on to say ([1993] 3 All ER 20 at 24, [1993] 1 WLR 989 at 994):

'I would only add this in relation to the decision of this court in *Hart v Aga Khan Foundation*. As I have indicated, it is clearly distinguishable from the present case. But, in my judgment, that case may require reconsideration on some future occasion if it becomes directly in point, since it is open to question whether the court on that occasion took account of RSC Ord 62, r 35(4), which stipulates that a judge, on a review of taxation, "may exercise all such powers and discretion as are vested in the taxing officer".'

The present application provides an appropriate occasion for this court to resolve any doubts which may still linger as to the nature of a judge's jurisdiction on an application to review a taxation of costs, whether made by a taxing officer or by a district judge, and whether made by a firm of solicitors or a litigant in person under RSC Ord 62, r 35(4), or under CCR Ord 38, r 24(6), whose words are identical, mutatis mutandis, so far as the provisions relating to the judge's powers and discretion are concerned. The words, as McCowan LJ said in *Madurasinghe's* case, mean exactly what they say.

In my judgment, Judge Morrell was wrong, as a matter of law, to hold that his jurisdiction was limited to an inquiry as to whether the district judge's order could be faulted on *Wednesbury* grounds, although in the light of the apparently conflicting decisions of the Court of Appeal, it is hardly surprising that he decided to follow what was said in *Hart*, which was another case concerned with a litigant in person, particularly as the current edition of *The County Court Practice* (1996) drew attention to this distinction.

So far as the merits of the application are concerned, the plaintiff claimed to be entitled to recover the costs of his brother as his representative as plaintiff in person at what he described as 'current rates':

'Time spent on the trips—10 hours home to home @ £32 per hour £320
Preliminaries—1·5 hours (Including 1 application with letter of confirmation
when solicitor misled the court—and preparation time) £48
Expenses (train fare and refreshments) £25
Preparing the Bill £32
£425.'

The district judge said of these items:

'(1) The amounts I allowed for attendances were those I considered
appropriate for a lay representative attending a relatively simple
interlocutory application in 1986 and 1987. (2) I assessed the appropriate
preparation time in respect of each application as half an hour. I allowed
two-thirds of the then charging rate for that preparation. No specific and
separate claim was made in respect of a letter. (3) These applications could
have been made by agents. In any event "refreshments" would not be
allowed in respect of a short interlocutory application. (4) There was no
attendance and the bill was half a page and improperly drawn. The
statement on costs did not assist me save to establish that the actual expenses
were £12 which is what I allowed.'

It is quite clear, in my judgment, that in conducting his review Judge Morrell did
not purport to exercise his own original discretion in relation to the matters in
dispute. He said that with one exception the plaintiff's submissions were directed
to matters which were exclusively within the discretion of the district judge. He
commented that the rates allowed by the district judge were by no means
derisory. He went on to consider one matter which it was said that the district
judge failed to take into account, and held on the facts that the plaintiff's claim in
this regard was misconceived.

In my judgment, it would be wrong for this court to deprive the plaintiff of his
opportunity to have the judge review this taxation on the correct basis, since we
do not have the expertise, in the absence of expert assistance, to determine that
this application for a review was doomed to fail.

This is, however, only an application for leave to appeal. The defendant took
no part in the original taxation or the review before the judge. In my judgment,
the appropriate course for this court to take today would be to grant leave to
appeal, treat this hearing as the full hearing of the appeal, and make an order nisi
allowing the appeal and remitting the plaintiff's application for a review by the
judge at the Peterborough County Court on the correct basis. This order should
be drawn up but not perfected for six weeks. The court should send a copy of the
order forthwith to the defendant and, if he sees fit, he may make an application
to this court within that six week period for a direction that the order should not
be perfected and for an opportunity to be heard on the appeal.

ALDOUS LJ. I agree.

LORD WOOLF MR. I also agree. With the order there will be a copy of the
transcript of Brooke LJ's judgment so that the defendant can have an opportunity
of seeing it as well. As the applicant is hard of hearing, I direct that he should
receive a copy of our judgment. Because this was an application for leave, there
are no reporters present in court. As Brooke LJ indicated, the matter is a point of
some general importance and in those circumstances the judgment shall be

drawn to the attention of the law reporters. In the event of there being no application, the matter should be restored before the court pursuant to the direction which Brooke LJ made in his judgment.

In addition, it seems to me that this is a situation where it should be said in fairness to the judge of the county court that I do not think any criticism justified for his taking the course which he did. Brooke LJ has already indicated that his decision was not surprising. I can say for my part that I understand why he regarded himself as bound by the decision in *Hart's* case. The matter has now been considered by a three-judge court and, therefore, the situation is different.

Appeal allowed.

L I Zysman Esq   Barrister.

Ali and others v Christian Salvesen Food Services Ltd

COURT OF APPEAL, CIVIL DIVISION

WAITE, SAVILLE AND OTTON LJJ

9, 18 OCTOBER 1996

Contract – Implied term – Circumstances in which term should be implied – Reasonable that term should be implied – Intention of parties as collected from words of agreement and surrounding circumstances – Collective agreement made between employers and trade unions for annualisation of pay – Employment contract providing for annualised hours – Employee dismissed before year end – Whether term to be implied for payment for hours worked in excess of basic week – Wages Act 1986, s 1(1).

The appellant employers adopted a collective agreement, negotiated with recognised trade unions, which introduced a system of annualised pay whereby employees were paid a standard wage (varying according to the grade of the employee concerned) on the basis of a roster providing for a total of 1,824 hours to be worked during the 12 months from 1 June 1992. Those hours, and the applicable standard wage, were calculated on the basis of an assumed 40-hour working week averaged out over a 12-month period and adjusted to take account of holiday entitlement. No specific provision was made in either the collective agreement or the individual employment contracts of employees for the eventuality that an employee might cease work for any reason before the 12-month period was completed. One of the respondents was an employee who was made redundant at a time when he had worked only 22 of the 52 weeks shown on his roster for the year. He claimed that he had worked in excess of 40 hours per week during his employment and applied to an industrial tribunal for a declaration that he was entitled to be paid pro rata for the alleged excess and that his employers' failure to pay him constituted an unauthorised deduction from his wages under s 1(1)[a] of the Wages Act 1986. The industrial tribunal dismissed the application on the ground that, in the absence of specific provision to cover the eventuality of premature termination of employment during the currency of the roster, the respondent had to be content with the standard wage which the collective agreement had ensured him, regardless of the hours actually worked. The Employment Appeal Tribunal allowed his subsequent appeal, holding that there ought to be implied into the individual and collective agreements, as a matter of law, a term that would entitle an employee whose employment was terminated by the employer before the end of the pay year to be paid the standard hourly rate for the hours actually worked by him in excess of 40 hours per week. The case was remitted to the industrial tribunal for recalculation of an award on that basis. The employers appealed.

Held – Where a collective agreement had been freely and carefully negotiated with trade unions representing a substantial labour force, it was in the nature of the agreement that it should be concise and clear. Accordingly, if any topic had

---

a   Section 1(1), so far as material, provides: 'An employer shall not make any deduction from any wages of any worker employed by him unless the deduction ... is required or authorised to be made by virtue of ... any relevant provision of the worker's contract ...'

been left uncovered by such an agreement, the natural inference was not that there had been an omission so obvious as to require judicial correction, but rather that the topic had been omitted advisedly from the terms of the agreement on the ground that it was seen as too controversial or too complicated to justify any variation of the main terms of the agreement to take account of it. It followed that the respondent employee was not entitled to be paid for the alleged excess, since the agreement itself did not specify what was to happen in such an eventuality and there was no justification for an implied term covering the contingency of a premature termination of contracts of employment. The appeal would therefore be allowed and the industrial tribunal's decision restored (see p 725 *e*, p 726 *c* to *g* and p 727 *d e*, post).

Notes
For implied terms generally, see 9 *Halsbury's Laws* (4th edn) paras 351–362, and for cases on the subject, see 12(1) *Digest* (2nd reissue) 403–424, *3282–3382*.

As from 22 August 1996, s 1(1) of the Wages Act 1986 was replaced by s 13(1) of the Employment Rights Act 1996.

For the Employment Rights Act 1996, s 13, see 16 *Halsbury's Statutes* (4th edn) (1997 reissue) 576.

Case referred to in judgments
Liverpool City Council v Irwin [1976] 2 All ER 39, [1977] AC 239, [1976] 2 WLR 562, HL.

Cases also cited or referred to in skeleton arguments
Lake v Essex CC [1977] ICR 577, CA.
Mears v Safecar Security Ltd [1982] 2 All ER 865, [1982] ICR 626, CA.

Appeal
By notice dated 18 July 1995 Christian Salvesen Food Services Ltd (the employers) appealed with leave from the decision of the Employment Appeal Tribunal ([1996] ICR 1) on 9 June 1995, allowing appeals by the respondent employees, Osmond Ali, J E High, S L Green, T R Matthews and S Bessey, from the decision of an industrial tribunal sitting at Norwich on 7 December 1993, which had dismissed their claims under the Wages Act 1986. The facts are set out in the judgment of Waite LJ.

Peter Wallington (instructed by *Edward Lewis*, agent for *Sarah Booth*, Edinburgh) for the employers.
Andrew Glennie (instructed by *Nicholsons*, Lowestoft) for Mr Ali and Mr Green.
The other employees did not appear.

Cur adv vult

18 October 1996. The following judgments were delivered.

WAITE LJ. This appeal arises from the adoption by employers of a collective agreement, negotiated with the unions concerned, for what is termed the 'annualisation' of wages. We are told that such agreements have achieved some popularity, in cases where trade is seasonal, as an alternative to the ordinary incidence of basic rate pay and overtime, which is liable in such trading conditions a   to produce capricious or unfair results for either side. Annualisation agreements provide the workforce with an assured overall wage calculated (like a salary) on an annual basis: at the same time they preserve flexibility for management in appointing hours of work to fit fluctuations in seasonal demand. We are also told that this is the first occasion on which such an agreement has arisen for consideration in this court.

b   The appellants, Christian Salvesen Food Services Ltd, are engaged in the processing and storage of vegetables. They have a workforce of about 150 at their cold store and factory in Lowestoft, Suffolk. On 6 September 1991 and 16 April 1992 they negotiated with two unions (the Amalgamated Engineering Union and the Transport and General Workers' Union respectively) collective agreements
c   which were both to run from 1 June 1992. There is no material distinction between the terms of the two agreements, and I will refer to them together as 'the collective agreement'. They provided, in summary, that the workforce, which had previously been paid on a traditional arrangement as hourly paid workers entitled to overtime if and when worked in any particular week, should
d   be paid a standard wage (varying according to the grade of the employee concerned) on the basis of a roster providing for a total of 1,824 hours to be worked during the 12 months from 1 June 1992 to 31 May 1993. Those hours, and the applicable standard wage, were both calculated broadly on the basis of an assumed working week (when averaged out over the whole 12-month period) of 40 hours, adjusted to take account of holiday entitlement. Each employee
e   entered at the same time into an individual contract of employment running from the same date, which incorporated the collective agreement. Specific provision was made in the individual contracts of employment for termination by either side on seven days' notice.

f   No specific provision was made, in either the collective agreement or the individual employment contracts, for the eventuality that an employee might cease work for any reason before the 12-month period was completed and the 1,824 hours had been worked. That has provided the occasion for the present proceedings, which arise in the following circumstances. Mr Ali, respondent to this appeal, was an employee who was made redundant at a time when he had
g   worked only 22 of the 52 weeks shown on his roster for the year. He claimed that the hours he had worked over that period exceeded the 'norm' of working hours by reference to which his standard wage had been calculated, and he applied to an industrial tribunal for a declaration as to his entitlement to be paid pro rata for that alleged excess. The industrial tribunal dismissed his claim, holding that in
h   the absence of specific provision to cover the eventuality of premature termination of employment during the currency of the roster Mr Ali must be content with the standard wage which the collective agreement had ensured him, regardless of the hours actually worked. On appeal the Employment Appeal Tribunal ([1996] ICR 1) took a different view, holding that there ought to be
j   implied into the individual and collective agreements, as a matter of law, a term that would entitle an employee whose employment is terminated by the employer before the end of the pay year to be paid the standard hourly rate for the hours actually worked by him in excess of 40 hours per week. The case was remitted to the industrial tribunal for an award to be calculated on that basis. From that decision the employers now appeal to this court.

The facts

The governing terms of engagement are set out in the judgment of the
Employment Appeal Tribunal and need not be repeated. It is undisputed that
their effect is as follows. Each employee was presented at the outset of his
engagement on 1 June 1992 with a roster showing hourly night and day shifts
which he would be required to work throughout the ensuing twelve months.
The total of such shifts amounted to less than 1,824 hours, the average rostered
hours being about 1,700. The difference between the rostered figure and the
1,824 hours was known as 'banked hours'—ie additional hours which the
employee could be called upon to work up to the limit of 1,824. Once that limit
was passed the employee would become entitled to time and a half for each hour
worked in excess of 1,824.

Mr Ali was an employee in grade 2 (multi-skilled) qualifying for a standard
wage of £240 per week. By the time that he was made redundant on 28 October
1992, he had worked 22 of his rostered 52 weeks and had achieved a total of 858
hours. He claimed that this total exceeded by 104 hours the 'norm' by which his
standard wage of £240 per week had been calculated. This case has been brought
to test an issue of principle affecting not only Mr Ali but other redundant
employees in similar circumstances (some of whom are or were parties to the
proceedings). Because it is accepted by the employers for the purposes of this
appeal that the total of the hours worked by Mr Ali by the date of his dismissal
does represent at least *some* increase on the norm which provided the basis for his
standard wage, it is unnecessary to go into the detailed basis for that calculation
(which may or may not be accurate—depending, among other factors, upon the
effect of including holiday provision in the 1,824 hour calculation). It is also
accepted by the employers that if the implied term for which Mr Ali contends is
allowed by the court, he is entitled to have a pro rata reward for the excess hours
calculated at the (standard) rate of £240 per week recoverable as an unauthorised
deduction from his wages under the enactment in force at the date of his
dismissal—namely the Wages Act 1986 (now re-enacted by the Employment
Rights Act 1996).

It was found by the industrial tribunal (adopting in this respect a statement
made by Mr Wallington in his skeleton argument to that tribunal on behalf of the
employers) that in the course of the discussions which preceded the making of the
agreements:

> 'The collective parties did discuss the question of what would happen at
> the end of the year and the [employers] made it clear that there would be no
> additional payments unless the employee worked more than 1,824 hours, ie
> all rostered hours and banked hours, and additional rostered hours; and no
> recovery [by the employers] if the employee worked fewer hours because
> shifts were cancelled for lack of work'.

It will be convenient to refer to this for short as 'the discussion finding'.

The argument

The implied term for which Mr Glennie, counsel for Mr Ali, contends is
expressed by him as follows:

> 'In the event of termination of the contract by the employer before the
> employee has worked 1,824 hours in any roster year (excluding extra hours
> for which he has been paid), the employee will be paid for the hours actually

a worked by him in excess of the notional weekly hours up to the date of termination (excluding extra hours for which he has been paid), payment to be at the standard hourly rate specified in the contract.'

It was accepted, for the purposes of argument only (since matters of detailed computation are not agreed), that the 'notional weekly hours' in that formula b refer to the 35·7 hours which are achieved by dividing 1,824 by the 52 weeks of the roster year.

Mr Glennie's submission (which prevailed before the Employment Appeal Tribunal) is that this term should be implied on the basis: (a) that it was an obvious inference from the collective and individual agreements, because the parties cannot have intended the obvious injustices which would follow if it were c not implied; and/or (b) that, without it, the agreement is incomplete. This was a contract for hourly paid employment. It is a legal incident of such a contract that an employee is to be paid for the hours which he has actually worked, regardless of when his employment is terminated.

The first submission rests on the well-known 'officious bystander' test, and the d second on the principle approved by the House of Lords in *Liverpool City Council v Irwin* [1976] 2 All ER 39, [1977] AC 239. No reliance is placed on the other established heads for term implication—business efficacy, and custom and practice.

The submission of Mr Wallington (which prevailed before the industrial e tribunal) is as follows.

(1) There is no justification for the claimed (or any other) term being implied into an agreement which was freely negotiated on a collective basis and contains 'swings and roundabouts' for each side. The redundant employee is by no means the only case for which the agreements make no express provision. Sometimes f premature determination of the employment contract would work to the advantage of the employer; at other times it would benefit the employee. Take the converse of this case—the employee who is found, when his employment is terminated before the end of the roster period, to have worked fewer hours than the assumed norm. Consistency would suggest that if the applicant is right, there ought to be an implied term providing for 'claw-back' by the employer of the g wages which on that footing would be overpaid. The applicant does not however contend for the implication of any such term.

(2) The contracts were clear in their general operation. The fact that there were eventualities for which no provision was made did not render them incomplete. Such omissions are to be expected when an agreement is being h negotiated collectively to cover many different grades and occupations and to ensure, in a market where there is wide fluctuation in seasonal demand, the mutual advantage of certainty of reward on the one side and flexibility of working power on the other.

Mr Glennie's riposte to the reference in submission (1) to the absence of any j contention for an implied term for 'claw-back' for the employers was to rely on the discussion finding. That showed, in his submission, that 'claw-back' was an aspect fully covered by oral discussion, and the absence of any reference to it in the agreements themselves could not therefore be prayed in aid in support of any contention that this was an agreement which left uncovered the converse case (for which no implied term is claimed or conceded) of the prematurely dismissed employee who has worked less than his norm of hours.

Conclusion

The importation of an implied term depends, in the final analysis, upon 'the intention of the parties as collected from the words of the agreement and the surrounding circumstances' (see *Chitty on Contracts* (27th edn, 1994) vol 1, para 13-003. The collective agreement itself and the individual contracts are wholly silent as to consequences of a premature termination of the employment contract in individual cases before the end of the rostered term. This is not therefore a case where the contractual documents create by their wording an internal context in favour—or for that matter against—the implication of the proposed term. What of the surrounding circumstances?

The circumstances which are in my view crucial to the present case are that this was a collective agreement negotiated across a broad front for a substantial labour force. It represented a carefully negotiated compromise between two potentially conflicting objectives—the desire on the one hand of the employees to have an assured rate of weekly pay spread over a long period to which they would be entitled regardless of hours actually worked; and the desire on the other hand of the employers to avoid the high cost of paying overtime rates for work done at periods of peak demand. It is in the nature of such an agreement that it should be concise and clear—so as to be readily understood by all who are concerned to operate it. One would expect the parties to such an agreement to set their face against any attempt to legislate for every possible contingency. Should there be any topic left uncovered by an agreement of that kind, the natural inference, in my judgment, is not that there has been an omission so obvious as to require judicial correction, but rather that the topic was omitted advisedly from the terms of the agreement on the ground that it was seen as too controversial or too complicated to justify any variation of the main terms of the agreement to take account of it.

When the collective and individual agreements are approached in that light, I find, for my part, that Mr Wallington's submissions are wholly persuasive. This was an agreement which, by its very nature, would require it to be applied to many eventualities that it did not, and could not realistically, cover specifically. The omission of any reference at all to the contingency of a premature termination (for any reason) of the contracts of employment before the end of the roster period may at first sight be surprising, but it becomes less so when regard is had to the immensity of the task of legislating for every eventuality resulting from such termination. There are numerous possibilities, differing according to the circumstances in which the employment contract is terminated. They include (to mention only a few) the employee who falls sick and has to be dismissed on grounds of incapacity before his roster has been worked; the employee who is dismissed during the currency of the roster for misconduct; and the zealous latecomer—that is to say the employee who comes late into the roster (after it has been running for (say) nine months) and then works hours substantially in excess of the norm but still falling well short of the 1,824 total. To devise terms to cover all those contingencies would involve an unacceptable level of elaboration, and even then it could not be confidently asserted that the agreement was apt to cover every possible development occurring during the unworked currency of the roster. Once it is apparent that the situation for which it is sought to imply a term is only one of the numerous eventualities on which the agreement is silent, it becomes difficult, if not impossible, to devise for any particular eventuality, a term of which it can be predicated with certainty that the *a* negotiating parties would inevitably have been of one mind about it if a decision had been taken to make specific provision for it in the agreement. The point is also well made, in my view, that the absence of any reciprocal arrangement for 'claw-back' against the prematurely dismissed employee who has worked less than the norm of hours makes it even more difficult to imply the particular term that is claimed here. The discussion finding provides no answer *b* to that objection. Even assuming (which I personally doubt) that it is permissible, when construing a document for the purpose of determining whether an implied term is to be inferred in it or not, to have regard to an oral representation by one party that he would interpret the agreement in a particular way, the representation in that particular instance was restricted to the situation obtaining at the end of the 1,824 hours working, and had no connection with cases of *c* premature termination.

I bear very much in mind that the Employment Appeal Tribunal is equipped, through its lay members, with an industrial expertise which this court cannot match. When that is acknowledged, however, and when tribute is paid to the clear and helpful way in which the reasoning of the appeal tribunal is set out in *d* the judgment delivered on their behalf, this does nevertheless appear to me to be a very plain case against the implication of the proposed (or any) term.

I would allow the appeal and restore the decision of the industrial tribunal.

SAVILLE LJ. I agree.

e **OTTON LJ.** I also agree.

Appeal allowed. Leave to appeal to the House of Lords refused.

Paul Magrath Esq   Barrister.

Camdex International Ltd v Bank of Zambia (No 2)

COURT OF APPEAL, CIVIL DIVISION

SIR THOMAS BINGHAM MR, ALDOUS AND PHILLIPS LJJ

22 MAY 1996

Practice – Pre-trial or post-judgment relief – Mareva injunction – Injunction restraining removal of assets out of jurisdiction – Variation of injunction – Defendant wishing to exclude Zambian bank notes ordered by it for issue in Zambia from scope of injunction – Defendant willing to pay considerable price to recover bank notes – Whether removal of bank notes from jurisdiction constituting dissipation of an asset available to satisfy judgment debt – Whether bank notes having value in open market to plaintiff – Whether maintaining injunction amounting to holding defendant to ransom – Whether application to vary empty application – Whether injunction should be varied in exercise of court's general equitable discretion.

The central bank of Zambia was a judgment debtor and subject to a Mareva injunction granted to the plaintiff judgment creditor. As inflation was very high in Zambia, the defendant bank had arranged for the printing in the United Kingdom of a large quantity of high value bank notes for issue in Zambia in replacement of lower denomination notes, and those notes were bound by the injunction. Accordingly, although it had not satisfied any part of the judgment debt through lack of funds, since it had other debts and substantial obligations to the International Monetary Fund and the World Bank, the bank applied to the court for the bank notes to be exempted from the injunction, on the ground that the issue of the notes in Zambia was of great importance to the Zambian economy. The judge refused the application, holding that the notes had a real value because the bank would be likely to wish to repurchase them from the plaintiff for a considerable price, that the injunction was not being used to exert any kind of improper pressure on the bank or hold it to ransom; that, in the absence of an application for a stay of execution of the judgment, the application was an empty one since, even if the injunction was varied, the notes still remained liable to the process of execution; and that he would not exercise the court's general equitable discretion in the bank's favour unless and until it showed an intention of honouring its obligations pursuant to the judgment. The bank appealed to the Court of Appeal.

Held – (1) The purpose of a Mareva injunction was to prevent the removal or dissipation of assets by a prospective or actual judgment debtor, with the object or effect of denying a claimant or judgment creditor satisfaction of his claim or judgment debt. In the instant case, however, the bank, in wishing to transfer the bank notes to Zambia, would not be dissipating any asset available to satisfy the judgment debt because the notes had no value in the open market to the plaintiff or other creditors of the bank; and to maintain the injunction merely because the bank was willing to pay a considerable price to recover the notes would amount to holding it to ransom. Moreover, notwithstanding that no application had been made for a stay of execution of the judgment, the bank's application was not an empty one, since the relaxation of the injunction to permit removal of the bank a notes would improve the bank's position and the court was not in any case concerned with any question of execution (see p 732 *j* to p 733 *d*, p 734 *a* to *d* and p 735 *e j* to p 736 *c*, post).

(2) Furthermore, although a judgment debt should, in the ordinary way and in any ordinary situation, be paid, the fact that the bank was a body to whom the ordinary procedures of bankruptcy and winding up were not available, that on

b the evidence severe national hardship to the people of Zambia would follow if the state defaulted in its international obligations and that the concern of the bank to try to ensure that repayments due to the World Bank and the International Monetary Fund were not the subject of default was legitimate, constituted extraordinary circumstances affecting the exercise of the court's general equitable discretion to which the judge had given inadequate weight. Accordingly, and

c since on the evidence the people of Zambia would suffer very substantial damage if the injunction was not modified, the appeal would be allowed and the injunction varied so as to exclude the bank notes from its scope (see p 733 *d e g* to *j*, p 734 *e*, p 735 *a b* and p 736 *c*, post).

d **Notes**
For Mareva injunctions, see 37 *Halsbury's Laws* (4th edn) para 362, and for cases on the subject, see 28(4) *Digest* (2nd reissue) 197–214, *5326–5392*.

Case referred to in judgments
Deutsche Schachtbau- und Tiefbohrgesellschaft mbH v Ras Al Khaimah National Oil Co
e   [1987] 2 All ER 769, [1990] 1 AC 295, [1987] 3 WLR 1023, CA; *rvsd* [1988] 2 All ER 833, [1990] 1 AC 295, [1988] 3 WLR 230, HL.

Cases also cited or referred to in skeleton arguments
Iraqi Ministry of Defence v Arcepey Shipping Co SA (Gillespie Bros & Co intervening), The Angel Bell [1980] 1 All ER 480, [1981] QB 65.
f *PCW (Underwritng Agencies) Ltd v Dixon* [1983] 2 All ER 158; *varied* [1983] 2 All ER 697n, CA.

Appeal
The defendant, the Bank of Zambia, appealed from the decision of Morison J
g given in the Commercial Court on 17 May 1996 whereby he dismissed the defendant's application to discharge or vary a Mareva injunction granted by Sir John Wood sitting in chambers on 4 April 1996 in favour of the plaintiff, Camdex International Ltd, so as to exempt from the injunction, bank notes in Zambian currency ordered by the defendant which were held within the jurisdiction. The facts are set out in the judgment of Sir Thomas Bingham MR.
h
Michael Brindle QC and Richard Handyside (instructed by Lovell White Durrant) for the defendant.
Timothy Charlton QC and Alan Roxburgh (instructed by Baker & McKenzie) for the plaintiff.

j
SIR THOMAS BINGHAM MR. This is an application by the defendant for leave to appeal and, should leave be granted, an appeal against a decision of Morison J given in the Commercial Court on 17 May 1996.
The plaintiff in these proceedings is a judgment creditor and the defendant is the central bank of Zambia. The detailed background to the proceedings is not relevant for present purposes. It is apparent from the documents before us that

there were financing agreements made between the central bank of Kuwait and the defendant under which considerable sums of money were payable by the defendant to the central bank of Kuwait.

In due course there was an assignment of the benefit of a number of claims by the central bank of Kuwait to the plaintiff, a Bahamian company, which issued proceedings against the defendant. In those proceedings the plaintiff obtained summary judgment in its favour on 18 September 1995 for the sum of £80m, which has now increased, with the addition of interest, to some £120m.

The defendant appealed against that judgment to the Court of Appeal but its appeal was dismissed on 3 April 1996 (see [1996] 3 All ER 431, [1996] 3 WLR 759). Although the defendant is seeking leave to appeal to the House of Lords, there is currently no stay in existence. However, there is an undertaking by the plaintiff to preserve the fruits of any execution it may succeed in levying within the jurisdiction until the proceedings in the House of Lords have come to an end, whether by refusal of leave or by determination of an appeal. It is accepted that the plaintiff is to be treated as a judgment creditor with an unsatisfied judgment debt.

Immediately following the dismissal of the appeal on 4 April 1996, Sir John Wood, sitting in chambers, granted the plaintiff a worldwide Mareva injunction against the defendant. The defendant applied to Newman J to set aside that injunction, and achieved partial success in as much as the territorial scope of the injunction was narrowed down to this jurisdiction. Newman J, however, rejected a submission made by the defendant that it should be free to dispose of its assets in the ordinary course of business. The judge distinguished the position of a judgment creditor from that of an ordinary claimant who has yet to establish his claim, and the decision of Newman J is not subject to appeal. Indeed, it is accepted on behalf of the defendant that it was correct and that a judgment debtor is not free, as a defendant may be, to dispose of its assets in the ordinary course of business.

The defendant has not satisfied the judgment debt or any part of it. The reason for that is quite clear from the evidence before us, which is that it lacks the funds to do so. The defendant has debts which we are told amount externally to some $US7bn, and it has assets of some $US115m of which less than half are unencumbered. It has substantial obligations to international institutions such as the International Monetary Fund and the World Bank. It is quite plain that the economic predicament of the country would be even more severe were it to default on its repayment obligations. As is apparent from the figures I have given, it has other creditors besides the plaintiff and it is quite plain that the Zambian economy is in a far from healthy condition.

The defendant, the central bank, is responsible for managing and issuing currency in Zambia. The local medium of exchange is the Kwacha. The evidence shows that as a result of inflation very much greater denominations of Kwacha are needed in order to conduct business and the country finds itself with too many notes in low denominations of which, accordingly, citizens need very large numbers in order to do business. It has not quite reached the position such as existed in pre-war Germany, as one gathers from the evidence, but, none the less, the picture that is painted is that the volume of bank notes which it is necessary to handle in order to do business has become so great as to act as a shackle on the efficient conduct of economic life.

a   Against that background, the defendant wished to obtain, and issue, a very large quantity of high value Kwacha notes for issue in Zambia in replacement, or partial replacement, of lower denomination notes. To that end it placed an order with De La Rue plc, the well-known security printers, for the production of bank notes. Those notes have been printed and are available in this country, but they have not yet been delivered to the defendant and are not yet, as we understand, b   the defendant's property, although they have been paid for.

The defendant accepts that these bank notes are bound by the Mareva or, in any event, will be the moment they become the property of the defendant. It was this situation which led to the application before the judge. The defendant applied to Morison J that the bank notes should be exempted from the Mareva injunction. The bedrock of the defendant's case was that the issue of these notes c   by the defendant in Zambia was of great importance to the Zambian economy and that accordingly the notes should be freed for that purpose.

The point was made that only the defendant as the central bank could issue the notes and also that they were of negligible value save to the defendant. Therefore, it was argued that they should be released since the function of a d   Mareva injunction is to safeguard the value of assets and not to act as a means of enhancing the value of those assets. The plaintiff on the other hand, in argument before the judge, stressed, as Mr Charlton QC has cogently done today, that the issue should be seen as an essentially simple one. The plaintiff is a judgment creditor. It is entitled to payment. It faces a debtor who has no intention to pay and, furthermore, the plaintiff says, it faces a debtor who will do what it can to e   evade payment. The plaintiff submitted to the judge that the relaxation of the Mareva which the defendant was seeking would be of no benefit to the defendant since the bank notes would still be liable to execution and the defendant, for whatever reason, had made no application to stay execution.

The plaintiff further took issue with the suggestion that the bank notes were of no value, save to the defendant, pointing out that their value to the defendant f   gave them a value since the defendant would be willing to pay what was judged to be a considerable sum to obtain possession of them, even if they were not saleable to a third party. The plaintiff, however, did not accept that they were not necessarily saleable to any third party and drew attention to a letter which was before the judge from Zambia Consolidated Copper Mines Ltd (ZCCM), through g   its solicitors, in which the receipt of Kwacha was discussed.

The plaintiff submitted to the judge that the defendant had no right to pick and choose among its creditors to decide which it would pay or which assets it should expose to execution. These bank notes were, it was submitted, an asset and were therefore subject to execution like any other asset. The defendant's response to h   this submission was to suggest that, in effect, it was being held to ransom. The plaintiff, it was said, was saying: 'We have control of your asset, it may be of no value to us but it is of great value to you, therefore we shall hold it until you pay us off.'

For the defendant there was also an appeal to the general equitable discretion of the court to grant or withhold injunctions. It was urged upon the judge that j   in all the present circumstances it would be inappropriate to refuse relaxation of the injunction to the extent sought.

It is plain from his judgment, of which we have a transcript, that the judge attached importance to the fact that there was before him no application for a stay. He accepted a submission made by Mr Charlton, on behalf of the plaintiff, that this application was an empty one since, even if the injunction was varied,

the bank notes still remained liable to the process of execution. He also rejected
the defendant's argument that it was being held to ransom. He said:

> 'It seems to me that the Mareva injunction is not being used to exert any
> kind of improper pressure on the bank or to hold it to ransom, which is the
> description used by Mr Brindle QC. It simply preserves within this juris-
> diction assets, including the bank notes, upon which Camdex may execute.
> Those notes, in my judgment, have a real value because the Bank will be
> likely to wish to repurchase them from Camdex for a considerable price if the
> contents of their affidavit evidence is true.'

The judge further rejected Mr Brindle's appeal to the general equitable discretion
of the court. He said:

> 'The Mareva injunction is being used properly in aid of execution and, in
> any event, in the light of the bank's attitude towards the court's judgment, I
> am not inclined to exercise my discretion in their favour unless and until they
> show an intention of honouring their obligations pursuant to the judgment.
> That being so, I shall give the bank liberty to reapply, if it has demonstrated
> an intention of honouring the court's orders which have been made and
> making an application under RSC Ord 47 as Newman J indicated that they
> might wish to do.'

Before this court, both parties have essentially repeated their submissions made
to the judge. Mr Brindle has repeated both his arguments, although he has
somewhat modified his first argument in order to meet the contention that this
is an empty application. As the defendant understands the position, it is not free
to renegotiate the De La Rue contract so long as the Mareva injunction is in force,
but contends that if the Mareva injunction were varied and the relaxation were
granted to the extent sought, then it would be able, and would certainly seek, to
renegotiate the contract with De La Rue so as to ensure that the property in the
bank notes did not pass to the defendant while the bank notes were still within
the jurisdiction. In that manner there would be no risk of execution. In this way
he submits that the defendant could achieve its essential objective.

Mr Charlton again submits that the defendant is in effect seeking to obtain the
benefit of a stay without applying, as it should, under Ord 47 and suggests that
the defendant has to some extent changed its grounds. His submission is that if
the defendant wanted a stay it should apply for it, and that the reason why it did
not apply for it was because it knew that such an application, if made, would be
unsuccessful.

This application arises in what is certainly, in my experience, a novel situation,
where the enforcement of a claim is said to threaten, or certainly jeopardise, the
economic survival of a state. In such a situation, one would expect to find a claim
made for sovereign immunity. It is, however, plain that in the agreement
between the central bank of Kuwait and the defendant there was an express and
irrevocable waiver of any right to plead sovereign immunity and so that issue
does not arise.

It seems to me that in a situation such as this, it is important to go back to first
principles. A Mareva injunction is granted to prevent the dissipation of assets by
a prospective judgment debtor, or a judgment debtor, with the object or effect of
denying a claimant or judgment creditor satisfaction of his claim or judgment
debt. Here, it is plain that the defendant wants to transfer these bank notes to

a   Zambia. In doing so it would not, as it seems to me, dissipate any asset available to satisfy the judgment debt because the asset has, in the open market, no value. It is not an asset of value to the plaintiff or other creditors of the defendant if it were put up on the market and sold. It is true that the denial of this asset to the defendant would put the defendant in a position of such extreme difficulty that the defendant would seek to pay a price beyond the market value of the asset in order to recover it, but that is, as it would seem to me, what would in ordinary b parlance be described as holding someone to ransom. I do not for my part consider that this is an empty application. The relaxation of the injunction to permit removal of the bank notes would, in my judgment, improve the position of the defendant. This court is not at this stage immediately concerned with any question of execution. It is enough to note that the defendant could, if so advised, c make an application for a stay of execution if this relaxation of the injunction were granted. It might be that the need for such an application would be obviated by a variation of the agreement with De La Rue plc.

This court is not concerned with that issue which is not immediately before it, but is concerned as to whether the injunction should stand without variation. In d response to Mr Brindle's first argument, I would hold that it should not. I would add that I would also accede to Mr Brindle's argument based on more general equitable grounds. I remind myself that this is the judge's discretion and not an original discretion in this court, and the judge's exercise of his discretion is not to be lightly displaced. On the other hand, I feel driven to conclude that the judge did give inadequate weight to the quite extraordinary circumstances affecting the e exercise of the equitable jurisdiction in this case. He said that he did have misgivings about a private institution acquiring a central bank's rights and advancing those interests in preference to those of other international governmental or quasi-governmental organisations. However, he went on to say that he was faced with a judgment debtor who had decided to make enforcement f as difficult as possible, and who was seeking to remove from the jurisdiction an asset which was of considerable value to itself and which it might be willing to purchase from the judgment creditor once execution had been levied upon it.

Of course one agrees with the judge, without qualification, that a judgment debt should, in the ordinary way and in any ordinary situation, be paid. It is, however, relevant that the defendant is a body to whom the ordinary procedures g of bankruptcy and winding up are not available. The situation is one in which, on the evidence, severe national hardship to the people of Zambia would follow if the state defaulted in its international obligations.

It would seem to me that the defendant, grievously short of funds as it plainly is, cannot be at fault if it seeks to pay its creditors on a pro-rata basis, even if that h means that each of them recover very little. It must be a legitimate concern of the defendant to try and ensure that the repayments due to the World Bank and the International Monetary Fund are not the subject of default. This seems to me a setting so unlike that in which the ordinary Mareva jurisdiction falls to be exercised, that the learned judge did fall into error in failing to recognise this new j dimension of the problem with which he was confronted.

With regard to ZCCM I agree with Phillips LJ and would wish to associate myself with what he is to say about that.

I would, for my part, grant leave to appeal and would allow the appeal directing that there be a variation of the existing Mareva injunction so as to exclude from its scope the bank notes currently held by De La Rue plc.

ALDOUS LJ. I agree with the judgment that has just been given by Sir Thomas Bingham MR and would only add a few words which I believe are in support. The purpose of Mareva relief is, and always has been, to prevent a defendant from removing from the jurisdiction his assets or dissipating them. It is not, and never has been, an aid to obtaining preference for repayment from an insolvent party.

In this case the plaintiffs seek to resist the defendant's application to remove the bank notes from the ambit of the Mareva injunction. They have no market value, but the plaintiff believes that the defendant would, or ought, to pay for them if they were seized upon a writ of fi fa. They say that maintenance of the injunction in the form that it is, does not amount to a ransom. That is a view which does not reflect reality. The notes have no value, but the defendants want them so that they can be issued in Zambia. What the plaintiffs are saying is: 'If you do not pay your debt which you owe to us, we will not release the bank notes from the injunction. How much will you pay to avoid the damage and inconvenience caused?' That is no doubt a commercial attitude, but it is not one for which a Mareva injunction should be properly granted. The bank notes have at the moment no value and to remove them from the jurisdiction cannot amount to dissipation of assets. The view taken by the judge that they were assets was wrong. They only had a market value when issued in Zambia.

I, like Sir Thomas Bingham MR, also believe that the injunction should be modified as a matter of discretion. The evidence to which we were directed in the affidavit of Mr Holland, sworn on 16 May 1996, is, I believe, relevant. In that affidavit, he sets out in detail the consequences that would happen if the injunction was not modified. He refers to the fact that the Zambian currency has devalued to such an extent that the notes presently in circulation are of denominations that are too low for practical day-to-day use. As a result, a very large number of notes must be carried by persons in Zambia. He goes on to say that he has been informed by the deputy governor of the bank, Dr Situmbeko Musokotwane, that the bank has engaged in an extensive advertising and publicity campaign in Zambia with a view to bringing out the fact that new high denomination notes are to be introduced into the country. Those efforts have made the population aware of the design of the notes so as to reassure them of their value. He says that he has been informed by the deputy governor that some of the new notes have already been sent to Zambia. They have not as yet been issued, but the process of delivering them to commercial banks in Zambia has started; to continue that process is critical to maintaining monetary and economic stability. Further, the notes were to be issued at the end of May and that has been widely publicised. He goes on to draw attention to the fact that the Mareva had the effect of freezing the notes in the hands of De La Rue with the result that the bank is very concerned that it cannot even issue the notes that have already been sent to Zambia and if the Mareva is maintained, it will not be able to issue the ones that are the subject of this dispute. Mr Holland draws attention to the difficulties that that will have on the money supply in Zambia. He says that, in theory, notices could be given in Zambia to the effect that new notes are not, and will not, be treated as being legal tender, but says that this potentially has difficult and could have catastrophic consequences on the Zambian economy. Mr Holland also gave evidence that many of the notes in circulation in Zambia were damaged and unusable. If those notes were not replaced, there was likely to be an inadequate money supply with consequential loss.

a   In my view, that evidence establishes the very substantial damage which residents of Zambia will suffer if the injunction is not modified. In this case the evidence is, I believe, overwhelming in establishing that the court should not extend the injunction to cover the bank notes.

I, therefore, have come to the same conclusion as that reached by Sir Thomas Bingham MR.

b   **PHILLIPS LJ.** A Mareva injunction granted after judgment is a comparatively rare form of such relief. In *Deutsche Schachtbau- und Tiefbohrgesellschaft mbH v Ras Al Khaimah National Oil Co* [1987] 2 All ER 769 at 780, [1990] 1 AC 295 at 317 Donaldson MR said:

c   '"The Mareva innovation, which time has shown to be one of the most imaginative, important and, on the whole, most beneficient of modern times, lay in giving a plaintiff some degree of protection *before* he became a judgment creditor and in anticipation that he would become one. Judgment creditors had little need of new protection since they were usually adequately protected by their right to levy execution by a writ of fieri facias, *d*   attachment of debts or the appointment of a receiver.' (Donaldson MR's emphasis.)

A Mareva can properly be granted after judgment in circumstances, which must be rare, where this is necessary to prevent the removal or dissipation of an asset before the process of execution can realise the value of that asset for the benefit *e*   of the judgment creditor. That is not this case. The reality here is that the unissued bank notes, which are the subject matter of the application, are not assets which would be of any interest or benefit to a sheriff executing a writ of fi fa.

Mr Charlton QC urged us to find that there was a third party who was a *f*   potential purchaser of these notes for value. That third party is a governmental organisation, Zambia Consolidated Copper Mines Ltd (ZCCM), the state owned copper mining organisation against whom garnishee proceedings are currently taking place. Mr Charlton made the same submission before the learned judge, and this is what he said in relation to it:

g   'I was shown a letter from a firm of solicitors called Eversheds who act on behalf of ZCCM and reference is made to the potentiality of ZCCM making payments to Camdex against the equivalent amount of Kwacha in exchange. I do not intend to go into the dispute which is involved in applications between Camdex and ZCCM by way of garnishee proceedings, but it seems *h*   to me, on a reading of this letter, that it is obvious that Eversheds are referring to Kwacha which has been issued in the way described in the affidavit filed on behalf of the bank in this case, and not to notes which Camdex have seized under a writ of fi fa in this jurisdiction and then handed over to ZCCM.'

j   Mr Charlton has shown us that letter and I have reached precisely the same conclusion as the learned judge. The letter does not suggest to me that ZCCM would constitute a purchaser to whom the sheriff could properly sell these unissued bank notes for value.

The reality is that these bank notes have no market value whatsoever. They are a worthless and potentially embarrassing quantity of scrap paper of some

19 tons in weight. They are, however, of great practical significance to the defendant as they are needed by the defendant to fulfil its role as central banker in Zambia. Because of this, if they are detained, the consequences will be such as to result in the defendant being prepared to pay a significant sum to buy their release. In these circumstances, it seems to me, that the Mareva is being used in relation to these bank notes not for the purpose of preserving an asset that will be of value in the process of execution, but in an attempt to pressurise the defendant into discharging part of its liability under the judgment. That is not a legitimate use of the Mareva injunction.

For this reason, and for the wider reasons of policy given by Sir Thomas Bingham MR and Aldous LJ, I agree that leave to appeal should be granted, that this appeal should be allowed and the Mareva injunction varied as Sir Thomas Bingham MR has indicated.

Appeal allowed. Leave to appeal to House of Lords refused.

L I Zysman Esq   Barrister.

Director of Public Prosecutions v McKeown
Director of Public Prosecutions v Jones

HOUSE OF LORDS

LORD GOFF OF CHIEVELEY, LORD MUSTILL, LORD STEYN, LORD HOFFMANN AND LORD CLYDE

11, 12 NOVEMBER 1996, 20 FEBRUARY 1997

Road traffic – Breath test – Device – Print-out produced by device – Inaccuracy of device – Malfunctioning of computer in way which was not relevant to accuracy of contents of print-out – Clock attached to computer producing print-out from device inaccurate – Whether print-out inadmissible in evidence of drink-driving charge – Police and Criminal Evidence Act 1984, s 69(1) – Road Traffic Offenders Act 1988, s 16.

In two separate appeals the issue arose whether a document produced by a breathalyser device using a computer display and print-out was admissible as evidence of driving with an excessive proportion of alcohol in the breath and failing without reasonable excuse to provide a specimen of breath if the device did not accurately record the time of the breath test but in all other respects operated satisfactorily. In the first appeal the respondent was charged with driving with an excessive proportion of alcohol after a breath test showed her to be over the prescribed limit. However, the time shown on the print-out of the breathalyser device was 1 hr 13 mins slow, as was noted at the time. One hour of the discrepancy was accounted for by the fact that the device was set to Greenwich Mean Time, not to British Summer Time, which was an hour ahead. The remaining discrepancy was not accounted for. In the second appeal the respondent was tested on the same device a week later and failed to provide a proper test. He was charged with failing without reasonable excuse to provide a specimen of breath. The print-out showing the failure was noted to be 1 hr 15 mins slow. Both respondents were convicted by justices on the basis of print-outs produced by the device which were tendered in evidence by the prosecution under s 16[a] of the Road Traffic Offenders Act 1988, which provided that evidence of the proportion of alcohol in a specimen of breath could be given by the production of a statement automatically produced by the device by which the proportion of alcohol in a specimen of breath was measured together with a certificate signed by a constable that the statement related to a specimen provided by the defendant at the date and time shown in the statement. The respondents appealed to the Divisional Court, which allowed their appeals on the ground that the inaccuracy of the timing mechanism in the device rendered documents produced by it inadmissible under s 69(1)[b] of the Police and Criminal Evidence Act 1984, which provided that a statement in a document produced by a computer was not admissible as evidence unless at all material times the computer was operating properly, or if not, that any respect in which it was not operating properly or was out of operation was 'not such as to affect the production of the document or the accuracy of its contents'. The Director of Public Prosecutions appealed to the House of Lords.

---

a   Section 16, so far as material, is set out at p 740 *e* to *h*, post
b   Section 69(1) is set out at p 741 *c d*, post

Held – The appeals in both cases would be allowed for the following reasons—
(1) Section 69 of the 1984 Act was concerned with the way in which a
computer dealt with information to generate the statement which was being
tendered as evidence of a fact which it stated. The words 'not such as to affect
the production of the document or the accuracy of its contents' in s 69(1)(b) of the
1984 Act were to be read subject to the overall qualification that para (b) referred
to those aspects of the document or its contents which were material to the
accuracy of the statement tendered in evidence. All that s 69 required as a
condition of the admissibility of a computer-generated statement was positive
evidence that the computer had properly processed, stored and reproduced
whatever information it received. Accordingly, the malfunctioning of a
computer in a way which was not relevant did not affect the admissibility in
evidence of a statement generated by it. A malfunction was relevant if it affected
the way in which the computer processed, stored or retrieved the information
used to generate the statement tendered in evidence. Other malfunctions did not
matter (see p 739 *f g*, p 744 *c* to *f* and p 746 *f*, post).
(2) In the first appeal there was evidence before the justices that the clock
display did not affect the proper functioning of the computer in processing the
information from the breath analyser and therefore the print-out from the
breathalyser device was admissible evidence on which they were entitled to
convict the respondent. In the second appeal the respondent was required to
provide two specimens of breath for analysis by means of an 'approved' device.
The fact that the clock on the device was inaccurate did not mean that it was no
longer an 'approved' device, nor did that inaccuracy provide a 'reasonable excuse'
for the respondent's failure to provide a specimen, since there had to be some
causal connection between the excuse and the failure to provide the specimen.
The respondent's failure to provide a specimen, as evidenced by the device,
provided a proper basis for his conviction (see p 739 *f g*, p 744 *j* to p 745 *b e h j* and
p 746 *a* to *d f*, post).

Notes

For breath tests in relation to driving with excess alcohol, see 40 *Halsbury's Laws*
(4th edn) para 489ff.

For the Police and Criminal Evidence Act 1984, s 69, see 17 *Halsbury's Statutes*
(4th edn) (1993 reissue) 222.

For the Road Traffic Offenders Act 1988, s 16, see 38 *Halsbury's Statutes* (4th
edn) (1995 reissue) 1062.

Cases referred to in opinions

Castle v Cross [1985] 1 All ER 87, [1984] 1 WLR 1372, DC.
R v Skegness Magistrates' Court, ex p Cardy [1985] RTR 49, DC.
Statue of Liberty, The, Sapporo Maru (owners) v Statute of Liberty (owners) [1968] 2 All
ER 195, [1968] 1 WLR 739.

Appeals

DPP v McKeown

The Director of Public Prosecutions appealed with leave of the Appeal
Committee granted on 2 November 1995 from the decision of the Divisional
Court of the Queen's Bench Division (Kennedy LJ and Alliott J) delivered on 27
May 1994 allowing the appeal of Sharon Marie McKeown against her conviction

a by justices sitting for the petty sessional division of Halton, Cheshire, on 20 April
1993 on a charge of driving after consuming so much alcohol that the proportion
in her breath exceeded the prescribed limit of 35 microgrammes of alcohol in 100
millilitres of breath, contrary to s 5(1) of the Road Traffic Act 1988. The facts are
set out in the opinion of Lord Hoffmann.

b   *DPP v Jones*
The Director of Public Prosecutions appealed with leave of the Appeal
Committee granted on 2 November 1995 from the decision of the Divisional
Court of the Queen's Bench Division (Kennedy LJ and Alliott J) delivered on 27
May 1994 allowing the appeal of Christopher Gerrard Jones against his conviction
by justices sitting for the petty sessional division of Halton, Cheshire, on 4 May
c 1993 on a charge of failing without reasonable excuse to provide a specimen of
breath when required to do so, contrary to s 7(1) of the Road Traffic Act 1988.
The facts are set out in the opinion of Lord Hoffmann.

d *Anthony Scrivener QC, Steven Everett* and *Andrew S R Clarke* (instructed by the *Crown
Prosecution Service*) for the Crown.
Michael Beloff QC and *Renée Calder* (instructed by *Byrne Frodsham & Co*, Widnes)
for the respondent McKeown.
Nigel J Ley (instructed by *Nyland & Beattie*, Widnes) for the respondent Jones.

e Their Lordships took time for consideration.

20 February 1997. The following opinions were delivered.

LORD GOFF OF CHIEVELEY. My Lords, I have read in draft the speech
f prepared by my noble and learned friend Lord Hoffmann. For the reasons he
gives I would allow the Director's appeals in both cases.

LORD MUSTILL. My Lords, I have had the advantage of reading in draft the
speech prepared by my noble and learned friend Lord Hoffmann. For the reasons
which he gives I would allow the Director's appeals in both cases.

g
LORD STEYN. My Lords, I have read in draft the speech prepared by my noble
and learned friend Lord Hoffmann. For the reasons he gives I would allow the
Director's appeals in both cases.

h **LORD HOFFMANN.** My Lords, these two appeals concerning convictions
under the Road Traffic Act 1988, one for driving with an excessive proportion of
alcohol in the breath and the other for failing without reasonable excuse to
provide a specimen of breath, both arise out of the fact that in late July 1992 the
computer clock in the Lion Intoximeter 3000 in use at Widnes Police Station was
displaying a time about an hour and a quarter slow. In neither case was there any
j dispute about the correct time at which the Intoximeter was used; in fact, the
precise time was not a matter of any importance. In the one case the Intoximeter
recorded that the motorist had twice the prescribed limit of alcohol in both
specimens of her breath; in the other, the first specimen was more than four times
the prescribed limit, after which the motorist deliberately refused to provide a
second. Nevertheless the Divisional Court accepted that the inaccuracy of the

clock reading vitiated both convictions and against that decision the Director of
Public Prosecutions appeals to your Lordships' House.

By s 5(1) of the 1988 Act it is an offence to drive a motor vehicle on a road after
consuming so much alcohol that the proportion in his breath exceeds the
prescribed limit of 35 microgrammes of alcohol in 100 millilitres of breath. By
s 7(1) a constable investigating whether a person has committed an offence under
s 5 may require him to provide two specimens of breath for analysis by means of
a device of a type approved by the Secretary of State and by s 7(6) a person who
without reasonable excuse fails to provide a specimen when required to do so
pursuant to sub-s (1) is guilty of an offence.

The Lion Intoximeter 3000 is a device approved by the Secretary of State for
the purposes of s 7(1). It consists of an analyser which measures the alcohol
content of the breath by means of an electrical signal; a computer which converts
the signal into digital form with a visual display on which the result of the test is
shown and a printer on which it can be printed out; and a breath simulator which
provides air containing a measured quantity of alcohol so that the constable
operating the machine may check whether it is calibrating correctly. The
standard procedure is for the machine to be tested before and after the analysis of
the two specimens provided by the motorist.

The usual way in which evidence of the proportion of alcohol in the breath is
proved in court is by certificate under s 16 of the Road Traffic Offenders Act 1988.
This provides as follows:

'(1) Evidence of the proportion of alcohol ... in a specimen of breath ...
may, subject to subsections (3) and (4) below ... be given by the production
of a document or documents purporting to be ... (a) a statement
automatically produced by the device by which the proportion of alcohol in
a specimen of breath was measured and a certificate signed by a constable
(which may but need not be contained in the same document as the
statement) that the statement relates to a specimen provided by the accused
at the date and time shown in the statement ...

(3) Subject to subsection (4) below—(a) a document purporting to be such
a statement or such a certificate (or both such a statement and such a
certificate) as is mentioned in subsection (1)(a) above is admissible in
evidence on behalf of the prosecution in pursuance of this section only if a
copy of it either has been handed to the accused when the document was
produced or has been served on him not later than seven days before the
hearing ...

(4) A document purporting to be a certificate (or so much of a document
as purports to be a certificate) is not so admissible if the accused, not later
than three days before the hearing or within such further time as the court
may in special circumstances allow, has served notice on the prosecutor
requiring the attendance at the hearing of the person by whom the
document purports to be signed ...'

The section is a specialised exception to the hearsay rule which, on compliance
with its conditions, enables evidence which the constable could have given orally
to be given instead by a certificate admissible on mere production. But the
requirement that the certificate and statement be served on the accused and that
they should not be admissible if the accused gives notice that he requires the
constable who signed the certificate to attend the hearing means that the
procedure is for practical purposes consensual. If such notice is given, or the

a prosecution is unable to comply with the conditions, the prosecution must prove its case by other admissible evidence. This will in practice mean calling the officer who operated that Intoximeter to testify to the results of the test by reference to what he saw on the visual display and what the machine printed out. Such first-hand evidence of what was displayed or recorded on a mechanical measuring device is real evidence *b* admissible at common law: see *Castle v Cross* [1985] 1 All ER 87, [1984] 1 WLR 1372, applying *The Statue of Liberty, Sapporo Maru (owners) v Statute of Liberty (owners)* [1968] 2 All ER 195, [1968] 1 WLR 739. But when the measuring device, as in this case, includes a computer, the evidence is not admissible unless it satisfies the requirements of s 69 of the Police and Criminal Evidence Act 1984:

c '(1) In any proceedings, a statement in a document produced by a computer shall not be admissible as evidence of any fact stated therein unless it is shown—(a) that there are no reasonable grounds for believing that the statement is inaccurate because of improper use of the computer; (b) that at all material times the computer was operating properly, or if not, that any respect in which it was not operating properly or was out of operation was *d* not such as to affect the production of the document or the accuracy of its contents ...'

These provisions are supplemented by para 8 of Sch 3:

e 'In any proceedings where it is desired to give a statement in evidence in accordance with section 69 above, a certificate—(a) identifying the document containing the statement and describing the manner in which it was produced; (b) giving such particulars of any device involved in the production of that document as may be appropriate for the purpose of showing that the document was produced by a computer; (c) dealing with any of the matters mentioned in subsection (1) of section 69 above; and (d) *f* purporting to be signed by a person occupying a responsible position in relation to the operation of the computer, shall be evidence of anything stated in it; and for the purposes of this paragraph it shall be sufficient for a matter to be stated to the best of the knowledge and belief of the person stating it.'

g That is the statutory background to the two cases under appeal. Although both are concerned with the effect of the inaccuracy of the time display upon the validity of the conviction, the offences charged were different and the legal issues are not the same. I shall therefore consider first the case of Ms McKeown, who was convicted under s 5(1) and then that of Mr Jones, who was convicted under *h* s 7(6).

Late on 21 July 1992 Ms McKeown was observed to be driving erratically in Liverpool Road, Widnes, arrested on suspicion of being over the limit and taken to Widnes Police Station. There she was required to provide specimens of breath for analysis. The Lion Intoximeter 3000 was operated by Sgt O'Dell. He tested *j* the machine and it calibrated correctly. By this time it was about a quarter after midnight; the sergeant's watch said 00.13 am. But the time display on the machine read 23:00. Part of the discrepancy was explained by the fact that, as the print-out made plain, the machine was set to GMT. But there was no explanation of the balance. Ms McKeown provided the required two specimens, both of which registered 78; well in excess of the prescribed limit of 35. Afterwards Sgt O'Dell tested the machine again and once more it calibrated correctly. He filled

in the standard form of witness statement for use in such cases, attaching the
print-out from the Intoximeter but noting on his statement 'Time shown on
print-out is 1 hr 13 mins slow'.

Ms McKeown was charged under s 5(1). She was served with the statement of
Sgt O'Dell and also a statement of Dr Paul Williams, a director of Lion
Laboratories Ltd, which supplies the Intoximeter to the police. It said that the
alcohol analytical system and breath sampling system were separate from the
circuitry which controlled the accuracy of the clock. Inaccuracy in the time
display could have absolutely no effect on the accuracy of the readings obtained
on breath samples.

On 27 November 1992, shortly before the case was due to be heard, Ms
McKeown's solicitors wrote to the Crown Prosecution Service (the CPS) saying
that the statement of Dr Williams 'cannot be accepted'. They also asked to be
supplied with 'all relevant design documents and the circuit diagram'. On 7
December 1992 the CPS wrote back saying that Dr Williams would give evidence
but refusing to produce diagrams or documents. In the event the case did not
come on till 20 April 1993, but there was no application until the hearing, when
the defence applied for an order that Dr Williams should produce the documents
and diagrams. The justices refused the application.

As the time inaccuracy meant that Sgt O'Dell was unable to certify, in
accordance with s 16 of the Road Traffic Offenders Act 1988, that the statement
automatically produced by the Intoximeter related to 'a specimen provided by
the accused at the date and time shown in the statement', he was called to give
evidence and testified to the conduct of the test and the readings on the visual
display and print-out which I have described. Dr Williams also gave evidence.
He said that he was not an electronics expert and did not understand the circuitry
of the Intoximeter clock but that the clock had no bearing on the accuracy of the
breath readings. The justices accepted this evidence and found, as later recorded
in the case stated, that the Intoximeter was not affected by the clock and that the
statements as to the breath readings it produced were accurate.

It is convenient at this stage to deal with two procedural questions which were
raised by the justices in the case stated. The first was whether they were right to
refuse the application for production of documents. The application was made
under s 97(1) of the Magistrates' Courts Act 1980:

> 'Where a justice of the peace ... is satisfied that any person ... is likely to be
> able to ... produce any document ... likely to be material evidence ... at the
> summary trial of an information ... and that that person ... will not
> voluntarily produce the document ... the justice shall issue a summons
> directed to that person requiring him to attend before the court ... to
> produce the document ...'

It has repeatedly been said that there is no provision for discovery of documents
for a summary trial in a magistrates' court and that s 97(1) should not be used as
a disguised attempt to obtain discovery: see *R v Skegness Magistrates' Court, ex p
Cardy* [1985] RTR 49. The circuit diagrams would have been meaningless
without explanation and Dr Williams, who disavowed any expertise in
electronics, would not have been able to explain them. The proceedings would
have had to be adjourned for the documents to be examined by an expert on
behalf of the accused. Whether they would then have had any relevance is
entirely speculative: the defence made no attempt to lay a foundation for their
application by evidence of how a circuit diagram might demonstrate that,

a contrary to Dr Williams' empirical observations, the inaccuracy of the time reading did in fact have some effect on the breath analysis. I think that the justices were right to reject the application.

The second question is whether, given Dr Williams' lack of expertise in electronics, his expert evidence was admissible on the question of the reliability of the device. In my view Dr Williams was entitled to give this evidence by *b* reason of his familiarity with the working of the Lion Intoximeter 3000. It is notorious that one needs no expertise in electronics to be able to know whether a computer is working properly. Dr Williams was qualified to say that he was familiar with Intoximeters which displayed the time incorrectly but nevertheless produced correct breath analyses. Sgt O'Dell, who tested his Intoximeter to see whether it was calibrating correctly, was able to give evidence to the same effect. *c* This was evidence on which the justices were entitled to make their finding that the statements produced by the device were accurate.

This brings me to the chief question in Ms McKeown's case, which is whether the evidence of the Intoximeter's breath analysis satisfied the requirements of s 69(1) of the 1984 Act. If it did not, there was no other evidence of the alcohol *d* content in her breath and her conviction cannot stand. It will be recalled that s 69(1) deals with the admissibility of 'a statement in a document produced by a computer' as evidence of 'any fact stated therein'. In order for the statement to be admissible, it must be shown, in accordance with sub-s (1)(b)—

e 'that at all material times the computer was operating properly, or if not, that any respect in which it was not operating properly or was out of operation was not such as to affect the production of the document or the accuracy of its contents ...'

A 'statement' has the same meaning as in s 10(1)(c) of Pt I of the Civil Evidence Act 1968, where it includes 'any ... device in which ... data ... are embodied so as *f* to be capable ... of being reproduced therefrom'. This would include the memory of a computer.

I shall for the moment assume that the inaccuracy in the time display meant that 'the computer ... was not operating properly'. The question is therefore whether that was 'such as to affect the production of the document or the accuracy of its contents'. If the words are read literally, it did. The document said *g* that the first test had occurred at 23.00 GMT when it was in fact 00.13 BST. As to one hour, the discrepancy is merely as to the way in which the time was expressed—23.00 GMT is the same time as 00.00 BST. But the remaining 13 minutes cannot, I think, be dismissed as de minimis. The inaccuracy of the time reading therefore affected the accuracy of a part of the contents of the document.

h In my view, however, the paragraph was not intended to be read in such a literal fashion. '[T]he production of the document or the accuracy of its contents' are very wide words. What if there was a software fault which caused the document to be printed in lower case when it was meant to be in upper case? The fault has certainly affected the production of the document. But a rule which *j* excluded an otherwise accurate document on this ground would be quite irrational. To discover the legislative intent, it is necessary to consider the purpose of the rule.

The first thing to notice is that s 69 is concerned solely with the proper operation and functioning of a computer. A computer is a device for storing, processing and retrieving information. It receives information from, for example, signals down a telephone line, strokes on a keyboard or (in this case) a device for

chemical analysis of gas, and it stores and processes that information. If the
information received by the computer was inaccurate (for example, if the
operator keyed in the wrong name) then the information retrieved from the
computer in the form of a statement will likewise be inaccurate. Computer
experts have colourful phrases in which to express this axiom. But s 69 is not in
the least concerned with the accuracy of the information supplied to the
computer. If the gas analyser of the Intoximeter is not functioning properly and
gives an inaccurate signal which the computer faithfully reproduces, s 69 does not
affect the admissibility of the statement. The same is true if the operator keys in
the wrong name. Neither of these errors is concerned with the proper operation
or functioning of the computer.

The purpose of s 69, therefore, is a relatively modest one. It does not require
the prosecution to show that the statement is likely to be true. Whether it is
likely to be true or not is a question of weight for the justices or jury. All that s 69
requires as a condition of the admissibility of a computer-generated statement is
positive evidence that the computer has properly processed, stored and
reproduced whatever information it received. It is concerned with the way in
which the computer has dealt with the information to generate the statement
which is being tendered as evidence of a fact which it states.

The language of s 69(1) recognises that a computer may be malfunctioning in
a way which is not relevant to the purpose of the exclusionary rule. It cannot
therefore be argued that any malfunction is sufficient to cast doubt upon the
capacity of the computer to process information correctly. The legislature clearly
refused to accept so extreme a proposition. What, then, was contemplated as the
distinction between a relevant and an irrelevant malfunction? It seems to me that
there is only one possible answer to that question. A malfunction is relevant if it
affects the way in which the computer processes, stores or retrieves the
information used to generate the statement tendered in evidence. Other
malfunctions do not matter. It follows that the words 'not such as to affect the
production of the document or the accuracy of its contents' must be read subject
to the overall qualification that the paragraph is referring to those aspects of the
document or its contents which are material to the accuracy of the statement
tendered in evidence.

Paragraph (a) of s 69(1), which deals with improper use of the computer,
clearly has this meaning. The statement is inadmissible only if there are
reasonable grounds for believing that the improper use has caused the statement
tendered in evidence to be inaccurate. It was argued that because para (b) uses
different language and speaks of the 'production of the document or the accuracy
of its contents' rather than being concerned, as in para (a), with the accuracy of
'the statement', it must have a different meaning. I shall not speculate on the
reasons why the draftsman thought it necessary to deal with improper use of the
computer separately from the question of whether it was in proper working
order. But there cannot have been any difference in the purpose of the two
paragraphs: in both cases the legislature was concerned with the reliability of the
statement tendered in evidence as a properly processed and reproduced piece of
information. On the point now in issue I think it would be quite irrational if the
effect of the two paragraphs was not the same.

The justices had before them a certificate signed by Sgt O'Dell under para 8 of
Sch 3 stating that to the best of his knowledge and belief the requirements of
s 69(1) had been complied with. In the absence of contrary evidence, they were
entitled to accept this certificate as sufficient to satisfy s 69(1). The question is

a   then whether they were obliged to regard the inaccuracy of the clock display as contrary evidence. The justices also had evidence from Dr Williams and Sgt O'Dell, which they were entitled to accept, that the clock display was not affecting the proper functioning of the computer in processing the information from the breath analyser. Having accepted this evidence, there was in my view nothing to displace the effect of Sgt O'Dell's certificate.

b   I have considered the matter on the assumption that the error in the clock display showed that the computer was not operating properly. I should say, however, that I am not satisfied that this conclusion should have been drawn. Computer clocks, like any others, have to be set to the correct time and the most obvious explanation for the 15-minute discrepancy was that someone had made a mistake when he last set the clock. This would not have anything to do with c the computer not operating properly. Furthermore, if the error lay in the clock mechanism itself, I doubt whether it would constitute part of 'the computer' for the purposes of s 69(1). The section, as I have said, is concerned with the processing and storage of information and not with the accuracy of the information supplied. The clock, although no doubt physically in the same box d as the computer, is something which supplies information to the computer rather than being part of the processing mechanism. But I do not explore this question any further because there was no evidence about why the time was inaccurate and I prefer to base my decision on the construction of s 69(1). In my view, there was admissible evidence upon which the justices were entitled to convict Ms McKeown and the Director's appeal in her case should be allowed.

e   Mr Christopher Jones was brought into Widnes Police Station about a week after Ms McKeown. He had driven his car onto a roundabout and appeared to be very drunk indeed. He provided one specimen of breath, which registered 148; more than four times the prescribed limit. He then did not blow hard enough to provide a second specimen. The visual display and print-out indicated that the f test had aborted. The officer who operated the machine and gave evidence at the trial was Sgt Draycott. Like Sgt O'Dell, he noted that the time display was inaccurate by his watch; in his case, by an hour and 15 minutes, but the discrepancy of two minutes from the evidence in the earlier case is as likely to have been in the policemen's watches as an indication that the computer clock had fallen further behind.

g   Mr Jones was charged under s 7(6) of the 1988 Act with failing without reasonable excuse to provide a specimen of breath when required to do so in pursuance of s 7(1). At the trial he gave evidence that he had tried his best but was overcome by a fit of coughing. The justices rejected his explanation, found that he had deliberately refused to blow into the machine as instructed and h convicted.

It was submitted on behalf of Mr Jones that he could not lawfully be required to provide breath for an Intoximeter with an inaccurate clock. But s 7(1) says only that a constable may require a person under investigation to 'provide two specimens of breath for analysis by means of a device of a type approved by the j Secretary of State'. There is nothing about the approved device having to have an accurate clock. The Lion Intoximeter was an approved type of device and it seems to me impossible to argue that, by reason of the inaccuracy in its clock, the device at Widnes Police Station could no longer be described as a Lion Intoximeter. The point is reinforced by sub-s (3)(b), which says that a constable may not require a specimen of blood or urine to be provided at a police station except in specified circumstances, one of which is that 'a device or a reliable

device of the type mentioned in subsection (1)(a) … is not available at the police
station …' This clearly contemplates, as one would expect, that a device may be
'unreliable' and yet of the type approved by the Secretary of State.

Secondly, it was argued that the inaccuracy in the clock was a 'reasonable
excuse' for Mr Jones's failure to provide a specimen. The difficulty about this
argument is that Mr Jones never claimed to have the slightest notion that there
was anything wrong with the time on the clock. His defence before the justices,
on which he was disbelieved, was that the inadequacy of the specimen had not
been his fault. It is therefore hard to see how the clock could have been an
'excuse' for his failure to provide a specimen. I do not say that an excuse must be
something which the accused had in mind when he failed or refused to provide
the specimen. It would, for example, have been an excuse that he was
unconscious when the request was made. But the concept of an excuse requires
that it must have been a reason why the specimen was not provided. There must
have been some causal connection between the excuse and the failure to provide
the specimen. In this case, there was none.

In any case, even if Mr Jones had noticed that the clock was slow, I do not think
that this would have been an excuse. If it was obvious that the device was in no
state to analyse his breath correctly, he might reasonably have objected to going
through a pointless exercise. But this would have been far from obvious and the
evidence before the justices showed that it would have been wrong.

Finally, it was submitted for Mr Jones that the only admissible evidence that his
second breath specimen was inadequate was the computer reading showing that
the test had aborted. If this was inadmissible for failure to comply with s 69(1),
he could not be convicted. The arguments against the admissibility of the
computer evidence were the same as those which I have already rejected in the
case of Ms McKeown. It follows that in my view this point also fails and the
Director's appeal in Mr Jones's case should also be allowed.

LORD CLYDE. My Lords, I have had the advantage of reading in draft the
speech prepared by my noble and learned friend Lord Hoffmann. For the reasons
which he gives I would allow the Director's appeals in both cases.

Appeals allowed.

Celia Fox   Barrister.

Thomas v Commissioner of Police of the Metropolis

COURT OF APPEAL, CIVIL DIVISION

SIR RICHARD SCOTT V-C, EVANS AND SAVILLE LJJ

28, 29 OCTOBER, 28 NOVEMBER 1996

Rehabilitation – Rehabilitation of offenders – Spent conviction – Reference to spent conviction in civil proceedings – Action against police for assault, damage to property, false imprisonment and malicious prosecution – Judge granting application to cross-examine plaintiff as to two previous spent convictions – Whether judge right to do so – Whether justice could be done without doing so – Whether substantial wrong or miscarriage had been occasioned – Rehabilitation of Offenders Act 1974, ss 4(1), 7(3).

Following a charity performance at the London Arena, the plaintiff, who was a limbo dancer, was arrested by two police officers outside the stage door entrance and charged with threatening behaviour. In due course the plaintiff was tried in the magistrates' court and acquitted of the charge and thereafter he brought an action against the commissioner for damages for assault, damage to property, false imprisonment and malicious prosecution. The plaintiff claimed that he had been subjected to abusive and racist remarks and brutally manhandled by the arresting officers and arrested without lawful cause, which they denied. During the trial, the judge was asked, in the absence of the jury, to determine whether two previous convictions of the plaintiff could be put to him in cross-examination. Both convictions were spent for the purposes of the Rehabilitation of Offenders Act 1974 and were therefore prima facie inadmissible by virtue of s 4ᵃ of that Act, unless they fell within the exception provided for by s 7ᵇ of the Act. The convictions were for unlawful wounding in October 1980, for which he had been given a suspended prison sentence, and for criminal damage in October 1993, for which he had been fined. The judge, pursuant to s 7(3) of the 1974 Act, ruled that the plaintiff could be cross-examined as to the two convictions on the grounds that justice could not be done except by admitting the convictions, because if they were not admitted, the jury would be left with an impression of the plaintiff and his credibility which might not be totally accurate and fair. When the jury returned, the two convictions were put to the plaintiff in cross-examination and he admitted them. At the conclusion of the trial, the jury found for the plaintiff on his claims for assault and damage to property and for the defendant on the claims for false imprisonment and malicious prosecution, and awarded damages accordingly. The plaintiff appealed, contending that under s 7(3) of the 1974 Act a judge could only admit evidence of spent convictions where they were relevant to an issue in the case, and not where they were relevant merely as to credit.

Held (per Evans and Saville LJJ) – Under s 7(3) of the 1974 Act a trial judge could, in the exercise of his discretion, admit evidence as to the previous spent convictions of a party or witness, if satisfied that justice could not otherwise be

---

a   Section 4, so far as material, is set out at p 750 *j* to p 751 *b*, post

b   Section 7, so far as material, is set out at p 751 *d* to *h*, post

done, not only if those convictions were relevant to an issue in the case, but also if they were relevant merely as to credit. However, some degree of relevance was a precondition for admitting the evidence, and therefore if the previous convictions were such that a reasonable jury could not properly take them into account when deciding whether to believe the witness or not, the evidence should not be admitted. Moreover, since such evidence had some potential for prejudice, the judge should weigh the degree of relevance against the amount of prejudice and should only admit the evidence if satisfied that otherwise the parties would not have a fair trial or the witness's credit could not be fairly assessed. In the instant case, the judge had not misdirected himself as to the test he should apply, and since the more serious of the convictions was of some marginal relevance and was also of limited prejudice, it could not be said that his decision was an invalid exercise of discretion under s 7(3) of the Act. Even if it had been (Sir Richard Scott V-C concurring), the court would not have ordered a new trial because the jury's knowledge of the spent convictions had made no difference to the result and no substantial wrong or miscarriage of justice had been occasioned by the admission of the evidence. Accordingly, the appeal would be dismissed (see p 759 a b, p 761 h, p 762 b to d, p 763 g, p 764 b to p 765 e j and p 766 b e to j, post).

Notes
For admissibility of spent convictions, see 11(2) *Halsbury's Laws* (4th edn reissue) paras 1078–1084, and for cases on the subject, see 15(2) *Digest* (2nd reissue) 604, 24396–24398.

For the Rehabilitation of Offenders Act 1974, ss 4, 7, see 12 *Halsbury's Statutes* (4th edn) (1994 reissue) 634, 643.

Cases referred to in judgments
Clifford v Clifford [1961] 3 All ER 231, [1961] 1 WLR 1274.
Dickinson v Yates, Lettice v Chief Constable of the Lancashire Constabulary [1986] CA Transcript 554.
R v Nye (1982) 75 Cr App R 247, CA.
R v P [1991] 3 All ER 337, [1991] 2 AC 447, [1991] 3 WLR 161, HL.
Reynolds v Phoenix Assurance Co Ltd [1978] 2 Lloyd's Rep 22, CA.

Cases also cited or referred to in skeleton arguments
Kirk v Laine Theatre Arts [1995] CLY 1712, Cty Ct.
Morris v Johnson Matthey & Co Ltd (1967) 112 SJ 32, CA.
O'Brien v Martin (2 April 1996, unreported), QBD.
Selvey v DPP [1968] 2 All ER 497, [1970] AC 304, HL.

Appeal
By notice dated 4 April 1995 the plaintiff, Gabriel Thomas, appealed from the verdict and award of the jury in respect of his claim for damages for assault, damage to property, false imprisonment and malicious prosecution against the defendant, the Commissioner of Police of the Metropolis, on the grounds, inter alia, that the trial judge, Sir Michael Davies, sitting as a judge of the High Court, had erred in law in ruling on 27 February 1995, in the absence of the jury, that the plaintiff could be cross-examined as to two previous convictions, both of which were spent for the purposes of the Rehabilitation of Offenders Act 1974. The facts are set out in the judgment of Sir Richard Scott V-C.

a Lord Gifford QC and *Paul Kishore* (instructed by *Harris & Co*) for the plaintiff.
Jonathan Loades (instructed by the *Solicitor, Metropolitan Police*) for the defendant.

Cur adv vult

28 November 1996. The following judgments were delivered.

b **SIR RICHARD SCOTT V-C.** This appeal raises two issues. One is a point of general interest concerning the Rehabilitation of Offenders Act 1974. The other is a point regarding quantum of damages.

The appellant, Mr Thomas, was plaintiff in the court below. The respondent, defendant below, is the Commissioner of Police of the Metropolis.

c The litigation arises out of an incident that took place at about 2 am on 28 May 1990. The plaintiff, a limbo dancer of considerable reputation, had been giving a charity performance at a telethon arranged by London Weekend Television at the London Arena in the Docklands. After the performance, Mr Thomas left the London Arena via the stage door entrance.

d A security guard was on duty at the door. It appears to be common ground that immediately before Mr Thomas left the premises, an altercation of sorts had taken place between him and the security guard. Nothing turns on the content of the altercation, but in the street outside the stage door when Mr Thomas emerged were two police officers. They arrested Mr Thomas. They say that he was swearing, making a lot of noise and, in short, making a nuisance of himself.

e They say that he pushed one of the officers in the chest and told him to 'fuck off'. They therefore arrested him for threatening behaviour. Mr Thomas has throughout denied this version of the incident. He says that, on leaving the London Arena, he was forcefully confronted by the two officers and made the object of abusive and racist remarks. He was, he says, brutally manhandled by the officers in the course of the arrest, an arrest for which, he says, there was no reasonable or lawful cause.

f The police deny that they used excessive force in effecting the arrest. They say that Mr Thomas was struggling violently while they were endeavouring to arrest him and that they had to use some degree of force to achieve their purpose.

It is common ground that Mr Thomas was taken by the police to Limehouse Police Station where he was detained in police custody until being released on police bail at 9.20 am the same morning.

g At the police station Mr Thomas was charged with the offence of threatening behaviour. He was tried on this charge on 27 November 1990 at Thames Magistrates' Court. He was acquitted.

h On 23 March 1993 Mr Thomas commenced proceedings in the High Court against the commissioner. He claimed damages for assault, for damage to his property occasioned by the assault, for false imprisonment and for malicious prosecution. Exemplary damages were claimed.

The false imprisonment claim was based on the allegation that the police had
j had no lawful occasion to arrest him and that his detention subsequent to the arrest was consequently unlawful. The malicious prosecution case was based on allegations that the officers deliberately made false statements in support of the threatening behaviour charge. As for the assault and damage to property case, it was not in dispute that in the course of the arrest Mr Thomas had sustained physical injuries and damage to his clothing. He had been medically examined in the police station following his arrest and the medical reports made that clear.

The first issue on the assault and damage to property case was whether the police had had any lawful occasion to arrest him. If they had not, the assault case would be bound to succeed as, also, would the false imprisonment case. But if the police had had lawful occasion to arrest Mr Thomas, in which event the false imprisonment case would fail, Mr Thomas would still be entitled to succeed on his assault claim if the police, in arresting him, had employed a degree of force that was in all the circumstances excessive.

Mr Thomas's action against the commissioner came for trial before Sir Michael Davies and a jury in February 1995. It was a case in which the credibility of Mr Thomas on the one hand and the two police officers on the other hand would be crucial. Mr Thomas's wife had been a witness to most of the scene outside the London Arena stage door. She gave evidence corroborating Mr Thomas's version of the incident. It might have been expected that one side or the other would have called the security guard, but neither did so. So the issue as to what had actually happened in the early morning of 28 May 1990 outside the stage door was bound to involve a conflict of evidence between Mr Thomas, supported by his wife, and the two police officers.

Mr Thomas gave evidence-in-chief. His wife had not yet given evidence. At the conclusion of his evidence-in-chief and before cross-examination began, the question was raised with the judge, in the absence of the jury, whether two previous convictions which Mr Thomas had had could be put to him in cross-examination. On 13 October 1980 Mr Thomas had been convicted in the Crown Court at Canterbury for the offence of unlawful wounding and sentenced to 18 months' imprisonment suspended for two years. And on 18 October 1983 at Margate Magistrates' Court he had been convicted of criminal damage, fined £50 and ordered to pay £24·71 compensation.

The question whether these convictions could be put to Mr Thomas in cross-examination required consideration to be given to the relevant provisions of the Rehabilitation of Offenders Act 1974. The main purpose of the Act was 'to rehabilitate offenders who have not been reconvicted of any serious offence for periods of years' (see the Preamble). Section 1 of the 1974 Act introduced the concept of a 'spent' conviction. On the expiration of a specified period of years after conviction, the 'rehabilitation period', the conviction would, provided it had not led to an 'excluded' sentence and provided the offender had not during the rehabilitation period received an 'excluded' sentence on any subsequent conviction, be treated as 'spent'. Neither of Mr Thomas's sentences had been an 'excluded' sentence (see s 5(1) of the 1974 Act). The rehabilitation period applicable to the unlawful wounding conviction was ten years. So the conviction had become spent on 13 October 1990. The rehabilitation period applicable to the criminal damage conviction was five years. So that conviction had become spent on 18 October 1988.

Section 4(1) of the 1974 Act sets out the effect of a conviction becoming 'spent'. It provides as follows:

'Subject to sections 7 and 8 below, a person who has become a rehabilitated person for the purposes of this Act in respect of a conviction shall be treated for all purposes in law as a person who has not committed or been charged with or prosecuted for or convicted of or sentenced for the offence or offences which were the subject of that conviction; and, notwithstanding the provisions of any other enactment or rule of law to the contrary, but subject as aforesaid (a) no evidence shall be admissible in any

a proceedings before a judicial authority exercising its jurisdiction or functions in Great Britain to prove that any such person has committed or been charged with or prosecuted for or convicted of or sentenced for any offence which was the subject of a spent conviction; and (b) a person shall not, in any such proceedings, be asked, and, if asked, shall not be required to answer, any question relating to his past which cannot be answered without
b acknowledging or referring to a spent conviction or spent convictions or any circumstances ancillary thereto.'

I draw attention to the breadth of the words 'for all purposes in law' and 'notwithstanding the provisions of any other enactment or rule of law to the contrary'.

c It is clear from s 4(1) that, unless the case could be brought within either s 7 or s 8 of the 1974 Act, Mr Thomas's spent convictions could not be put to him in cross-examination. Section 8 relates to defamation actions and has nothing to do with this case. Section 7 sets out a number of limitations to s 4(1). Nothing turns on sub-s (1) of s 7. Subsection (2) provides:

d 'Nothing in section 4(1) above shall affect the determination of any issue, or prevent the admission or requirement of any evidence, relating to a person's previous convictions or to circumstances ancillary thereto—(a) in any criminal proceedings before a court in Great Britain (including any appeal or reference in a criminal matter) ... (f) in any proceedings in which
e he is a party or a witness, provided that ... he consents to the determination of the issue or, as the case may be, the admission or requirement of the evidence notwithstanding the provisions of section 4(1).'

Subsection (3), however, is the critical provision for present purposes. It provides as follows:

f 'If at any stage in any proceedings before a judicial authority in Great Britain (not being proceedings to which, by virtue of any of paragraphs (a) to (e) of subsection (2) above or of any order for the time being in force under subsection (4) below, section 4(1) above has no application, or proceedings to which section 8 below applies) the authority is satisfied, in the light of any
g considerations which appear to it to be relevant (including any evidence which has been or may thereafter be put before it), that justice cannot be done in the case except by admitting or requiring evidence relating to a person's spent convictions or to circumstances ancillary thereto, that authority may admit or, as the case may be, require the evidence in question notwithstanding the provisions of subsection (1) of section 4 above, and may
h determine any issue to which the evidence relates in disregard, so far as necessary, of those provisions.'

The statutory criterion prescribed by sub-s (3) for the admission into evidence of spent convictions is that the judicial authority must be 'satisfied ... that justice
j *cannot* be done in the case *except*' by admitting the spent convictions into evidence. This language expresses a very stringent criterion. If the criterion is satisfied, the judicial authority has power to admit, 'may admit', the spent convictions. It is difficult, however, to construct a case in which the criterion has been satisfied but in which the judge could properly decide not to exercise his power to admit the spent convictions. Accordingly, although expressed in terms of a discretionary power, I find it difficult to regard the judicial authority's power

to admit or to refuse to admit spent convictions into evidence as constituting a discretionary power in the normal sense. If the judicial authority is not satisfied that 'justice cannot be done' except by admitting the convictions, there is no power to admit them. If the judicial authority is so satisfied it seems to me that, in reality, there would be no option but to admit them.

I return to the narrative of the present case. Sir Michael Davies heard submissions as to whether or not the spent convictions should be admitted into evidence. In the course of these submissions he was told that Mr Thomas had pleaded guilty to the unlawful wounding charge and that the unlawful wounding had arisen out of a domestic dispute between Mr Thomas and his wife. What, if any, detail was given to the judge regarding the criminal damage charge is not disclosed by the papers before us.

On 27 February 1995 the judge gave an interlocutory judgment with his ruling on the issue. He ruled that the plaintiff could be cross-examined on the two convictions. He gave the reasons for his ruling in the following passage from his judgment:

'Now, as I have indicated, in this particular case the plaintiff claims damages against the police, as in D's case for assault and wrongful arrest, false imprisonment and malicious prosecution, and it is quite plain that his credibility is crucial to his case. There is other evidence which the court will hear from his wife, who saw something if not everything of what the plaintiff alleges to have happened, and there is medical evidence. But the plaintiff's evidence is—and I repeat the word—crucial. In the witness box, as Lord Gifford has pointed out, he has certainly not been asked any question to elicit the answer, "I am a man of perfectly good character, I am a man of no previous convictions". Of course, he would not be asked such a question because that would have been inviting an answer which would either let in his convictions or would have been totally misleading if he had given the answer I have suggested. One must not overlook—and I have listened carefully to his evidence and watched him give his evidence—that he does give the impression (and this is something I can say in giving this ruling because of the effect it makes on me at this stage and so it may have an effect on a jury, although I would not, of course, say this to the jury) or did until this matter was mentioned, of being a man quiet spoken, apparently sincere, well-educated and generally in every way an upright citizen. Now, that is a matter of his credit, and it does seem to me that, if these convictions are not admitted, the jury will be left in the situation in which they may have what in the result is an impression of him and his reliability and credibility which may not be totally accurate and fair. I remind myself once again that the very existence of the Rehabilitation of Offenders Act 1974 means that on occasions, unless the court finds circumstances to say otherwise, an inaccurate picture may be presented. But the loophole—if that is not an unfair word—has been deliberately left by specific provision by the legislature, and I repeat those words, "Justice cannot be done in a case except by admitting the evidence". I have, in what is not an easy point to decide, the clear feeling that justice would not be done by refusing to admit these convictions. Of course, the jury will have to be told, and I certainly shall tell them later, that it would be totally wrong because of those previous convictions if they involved, as on the face of it they did, some form of violence that it follows that he used violence on this occasion, which of course is what the defendant is in effect asserting. Also, of course, the jury will have in mind that those convictions are spent—they will be told that— and they were in any event a good many years ago. But, in the end, the court, as *D*'s case made clear, is left with a discretion. The usual principles apply. The court must look at the provisions of the law—I have done—and it must look carefully at the facts and any possibility of injustice in either event. But this is somewhat different from a criminal case because, of course, the plaintiff is a plaintiff, he is not a defendant, and he is bringing this case. I do not think any great assistance, if any at all, is to be obtained from the much older Act, the Criminal Evidence Act 1898, or of criminal proceedings and the rules and practices there in general. I have done my best to apply my mind to the relevant factors and in the circumstances the court's ruling is that the defendant may cross-examine the plaintiff on these two convictions.'

The judge's two references to *D*'s case were reference to *Dickinson v Yates, Lettice v Chief Constable of the Lancashire Constabulary* [1986] CA Transcript 554. The judge had been referred to a footnote in Clayton and Tomlinson *Civil Actions against the Police* (2nd edn, 1992) in which reference had been made to the case. Following the judge's ruling on 27 February 1995 Lord Gifford QC, counsel for Mr Thomas both here and below, procured transcripts of the Court of Appeal judgments in *Dickinson*'s case and invited the judge to reconsider his ruling in the light of those judgments. The judge, having done so, gave a short supplemental judgment on 28 February in which he confirmed his ruling of the previous day. He repeated the reasons for his ruling and said:

'... in a sentence there is the overall impression, made upon me at any rate, of the plaintiff appearing to be a man of complete probity and high standing. Secondly, his case does involve matters in which his credit is of paramount importance.'

The consequence of the judge's ruling was that the two convictions were put to Mr Thomas in cross-examination. He admitted them. Nothing more than that was made of them in cross-examination. No mention at all was made of them in the final submissions made to the jury by counsel for the commissioner. Lord Gifford, in his final submissions to the jury, invited the jury to disregard them.

The judge, in his summing up to the jury on 6 and 7 March 1995, said this about the convictions:

'Fourthly, there is the question of the plaintiff's two previous convictions. This is rather important, members of the jury, if you will allow me to say so. In October 1980, for unlawful wounding, he was sentenced to 18 months' imprisonment which was suspended for two years, and he was ordered to pay some costs. Now, on the face of it, that is quite an important offence and the fact that he was sentenced to imprisonment is a matter which demonstrates that, although there were obviously, if I may say so in fairness to him, mitigating circumstances because the sentence was suspended. In October 1983 at Margate Magistrates' Court for criminal damage he was fined £50. Members of the jury, because those convictions happened a good many years ago and were not of the gravest kind, the [defendant's counsel] was not entitled to ask him about them without the leave of the court. It was so that I could decide that matter, and I promised I would tell you why you left court, that you were asked earlier in the case to leave court. I ruled, applying the guidelines which are given for judges in these matters, that, in the interests of justice, it was right that you should know about those two convictions, because otherwise—if I may say so, on all the rest of the evidence we have had, Mr Thomas appears to have led a perfectly respectable and law-abiding life—you would not have heard the full picture. But now you have heard, which I did not know at that time, the plaintiff's explanation of those offences. The unlawful wounding, he says, was in effect part of a domestic dispute with his wife, although he admitted he had wounded her and pleaded guilty. The other offence of damage was in connection with a broken glass. Now, you are entitled to bear those convictions in mind according to how seriously you consider they weigh, when considering what lawyers call the plaintiff's credit. That is whether he is believable or not. Ask yourselves does that make any difference, now we have seen and heard him in the witness box over quite a long period of time, as to whether we believe him that those years ago, in the circumstances he has described, he had these convictions? If you do not think it makes any difference, ignore them. If you think it makes some difference, give them some weight. But what is absolutely vital is that not only should you not overestimate their importance, but that you must not fall into the trap of saying he was violent on certainly the first of those two occasions and the other offence involves causing damage, and therefore he is likely to have been violent this time. That would be totally unjust and totally unfair and I know you will not do it because the fact that he misbehaved those years ago does not mean he misbehaved on this occasion. It goes to credit only.'

The judge mentioned the convictions again when instructing the jury on quantum of damages. He said:

'I should have said earlier, when dealing with conduct, that of course the character of the plaintiff is something that you are also entitled to take into account, and here you may think that there is nothing you should take into account in regard to the plaintiff's character. He did not misbehave except in the way that is alleged in the facts of the incident itself. He is not somebody who goes around continually making false complaints against the police, or taunting the police or anything of that sort, inviting conduct on the part of the police on which he can subsequently sue, and, if you may think that those convictions really—they are not relied on by the defence for this purpose—may be ignored when you are considering the question of compensation, you should do so.'

There are several other passages in the judge's summing up which I will mention later in connection with the quantum of damages issue.

Following discussion between the judge and counsel the questions to be put to the jury were agreed upon.

There were four questions on liability. On these, the jury found for Mr Thomas on his claim for assault and on his claim for damage to property. They must, therefore, have accepted his evidence in preference to that of the police officers as to the extent of force and violence used in arresting him. On the claims for false imprisonment and malicious prosecution, the jury found for the commissioner. They must, therefore, have accepted the evidence of the police officers that Mr Thomas appeared to them to be behaving in a threatening manner outside the stage door of the London Arena and that in making the statements that led to Mr Thomas's prosecution they believed in the truth of what they were saying.

The questions for the jury on quantum of damages in respect of the assault and damage to property claims were the following:

'1. On the claim for damages for assault, how much do you award (a) for loss of earnings? (b) for pain and suffering? (c) Do you award exemplary damages? If so how much? ...

3. On the claim for damage to property, how much do you award?'

On the assault claim, the jury awarded Mr Thomas £15,815 general damages and £16,185 special damages. On the damage to property claim, the jury awarded Mr Thomas £310. The total, with interest of £4,091, amounted to £36,401. So, on 8 March 1995 the judge ordered that judgment in that sum be entered for Mr Thomas. The awarded sum was, however, less than the amount of a sum that had been paid into court. The consequence was that Mr Thomas obtained an order for costs up to 3 February 1995 but had to pay, or allow to be set-off, the commissioner's costs from 3 February 1995.

Mr Thomas's notice of appeal seeks an order for a new trial both on liability and on damages. The grounds of appeal are: (i) that the judge erred in law in allowing Mr Thomas to be cross-examined on his spent convictions; and (ii) that the general damages award of £15,815 was manifestly inadequate and/or impossible to reconcile with the special damages award of £16,185.

The most important question to be decided is, obviously, whether or not a new trial should be ordered. There are two hurdles the appellant must surmount. First, this court must be persuaded that the judge erred in law in ruling that the spent convictions could be put to Mr Thomas. Second, the court must be of the opinion that 'some substantial wrong or miscarriage has been thereby occasioned' (RSC Ord 59, r 11(2)).

As to the spent convictions issue, the starting point, in my judgment, should be the purpose of the 1974 Act and the language of s 7(3). The 1974 Act was intended to allow persons convicted of the less serious offences to become, after a suitable period of time, rehabilitated. It was intended to allow the stain of the conviction to be wiped from the record. The language of s 7(3) is entirely consistent with that purpose. A spent convention is not to be allowed into evidence unless the judge is 'satisfied ... that justice cannot be done' otherwise. A spent conviction and the circumstances surrounding it might show some propensity of the relevant individual to do or omit to do some act, the commission or omission of which by the individual was an issue in the case. The spent conviction and the circumstances surrounding it might cast light on an aspect of the individual's character, eg dishonesty, that was of relevance to an issue in the case. In the present case, however, the convictions that were allowed in showed neither any relevant propensity on Mr Thomas's part (the judge expressly directed the jury in his summing up to that effect), nor any relevant aspect of character such as dishonesty or a record of having lied on oath. The reason why the offences were allowed in by the judge was, as appears from both his rulings, that Mr Thomas appeared to be well-spoken and respectable and the judge seems to have thought that that appearance was, in view of the convictions, a possible misrepresentation. I am of the clear opinion that that cannot be enough to satisfy the statutory criterion. Mr Thomas's convictions and their circumstances were not suggested to be probative of any issue in the case. They were not suggested to be relevant to his credibility in the sense that they showed him to be a man who had previously lied in giving sworn testimony or to be a man who has dishonest tendencies. In what sense then could it be said that the convictions were relevant to credit? I do not see what answer could be given unless it be said that the status of an individual is relevant to his credit and that a person who has suffered a spent conviction in the past is not entitled to present himself as a respectable upright citizen. This is an answer which I would have no hesitation in rejecting. If Mr Thomas's case had been tried before a judge alone I cannot believe that any judge would have placed weight on these spent convictions when deciding whether to believe Mr Thomas or to believe the police officers. If a judge would not have done so, how could it be said that 'justice cannot be done' unless the spent convictions' were admitted? Moreover, if it were right to admit these spent convictions in order to correct Mr Thomas's presentation of himself as a respectable upright citizen, would it have been any different if Mr Thomas had had spent convictions for, say, sexual offences, or offences of cruelty to animals? I have chosen an example of spent convictions with no conceivable probative value in respect of any issue in the present case. How would spent convictions for sexual offences or offences of cruelty to animals assist on the issue of credibility? Would the offenders be less likely to be telling the truth in cases concerning allegations of assault by the police than persons who had not been so convicted? If, as I think, the answer must be No, there would, as it seems to me, be no basis on which the s 7(3) test could be satisfied. So too with Mr Thomas's spent convictions.

The answer can, in my judgment, be no different in a case being heard by a jury than in a case being heard by a judge. If a judge would not himself attribute weight to spent convictions, he is not, in my judgment, entitled to allow the jury to be told about them. The s 7(3) test could not, in my judgment, have been satisfied.

In his 27 February ruling the judge expressly disavowed any reliance on the practice in criminal cases. He was right to do so. None the less I have an uneasy suspicion that the approach adopted by the judge in the present case may have had its origin in the approach that would have been adopted in a criminal case. Section 7(1) excludes criminal cases from the effect of s 4(1). Section 1(f) of the Criminal Evidence Act 1898 prevents an accused being asked, or if asked being required to answer, any questions about his previous conviction unless—

'(i) the proof that he has committed or been convicted of such other offence is admissible evidence to show that he is guilty of the offence wherewith he is then charged; or (ii) he has personally or by his advocate asked questions of the witness for the prosecution with a view to establishing his good character ... or the nature or conduct of the defence is such as to involve imputations on the character of the prosecutor or the witnesses for the prosecution ...'

Paragraph (i) of s 1(f) of the 1898 Act allows previous convictions to be put to an accused if they have probative value in the case. For the purposes of s 7(3) of the 1974 Act, the probative value of spent convictions might well satisfy a judge that justice could not be done unless they were allowed in. Paragraph (ii) of s 1(f) allows previous convictions to be put to an accused if he has endeavoured to establish his good character either by calling witnesses himself or by giving evidence himself to that effect or by cross-examining the prosecution witnesses. If a party in a civil action did these things, it might well be that the s 7(3) test would be satisfied. Sir Michael Davies seems to have had this in mind when, in a his 27 February ruling, he commented that Mr Thomas had not in his examination-in-chief been asked any question to elicit an answer establishing his good character or the absence of previous convictions. Immediately after those comments the judge went on to refer to the 'impression' given by Mr Thomas 'of being a man quiet spoken, apparently sincere, well-educated and in every way an upright citizen' and to express the fear that this impression might have an effect

b on the jury and, bearing in mind the spent convictions, might be 'an impression of him and his reliability and credibility which may not be totally accurate and fair'. These passages in the judge's ruling may have owed something to remarks made in the Court of Appeal judgment in R v Nye (1982) 75 Cr App R 247, a case with which this very experienced judge would certainly have been familiar. The court was giving guidance as to the manner in which criminal courts should deal

c with spent convictions. Talbot J said (at 250–251):

d '... it is entirely a question for the discretion of the judge. It may well be that the past spent conviction ... happened when the defendant being tried was a juvenile, for instance for stealing apples, a conviction of many years before. In those circumstances quite plainly a trial judge would rule that such a person ought to be permitted to present himself as a man of good character. At the other end of the scale, if a defendant is a man who has been convicted ... of some offence of violence, and his conviction has only just been spent, and the offence for which he is then standing trial involves some

e violence, then it would be plain ... that a trial judge would rule that it would not be right for such a person to present himself as a man of good character. The essence of this matter is that the jury must not be misled and no lie must be told to them about this matter. The exercise of the discretion of the trial judge in the cases which fall between the two extremes referred to must be carried out having regard to the 1974 Act and to the practice direction (see [1975] 2 All ER 1072, [1975] 1 WLR 1065). It should be exercised, so far as it

f can be, favourably towards the accused person.'

Paragraph (ii) of s 1(f) also allows an accused's previous convictions to be put to him if the accused is attacking the character of prosecution witnesses. But the judge has a discretion to exclude such evidence even though admissible under s 1(f).

g There is no doubt but that the present case involves, necessarily, a serious attack on the characters of the police officers involved in the incident. The police officers are alleged to have assaulted Mr Thomas, to have subjected him to racial abuse, to have lied in their police statements, to have given false evidence in the magistrates' court. If the present case had been a criminal case with Mr Thomas

h the accused, s 1(f)(ii) would, subject to the trial judge's discretion to exclude, have permitted Mr Thomas's spent convictions to be put to him on credit. And it may be that the judge, for much the same reasons as those given by Sir Michael Davies, would not have exercised his discretion to exclude the evidence.

But the approach established in criminal cases is not, in my judgment, an

j appropriate approach in civil cases. In civil cases, unlike criminal cases, s 4(1) applies. Section 4(1), subject to the s 7(1) exceptions, is intended to allow an individual whose convictions are spent 'to present himself as a person of good character' (see Talbot J in R v Nye). It cannot, in my judgment, be a sufficient reason for holding the s 7(3) test to be satisfied that the individual is so presenting himself. In a civil case in which spent convictions have no probative value on any issue in the case and do not provide any rational support for a suggestion that the individual might not be telling, or might not have told, the truth on one or other issue in the case, the fact that the individual's evidence or the nature of the case sued on involve imputations on the character of the other party or other witnesses in the case does not, in my judgment, justify admitting the spent convictions into evidence. That fact does not meet the test that 'justice cannot be done except' by admitting the evidence.

In my judgment, for the reasons I have given the judge's ruling whereby the spent convictions were allowed to be put to Mr Thomas was based on an error in law. There were, in my judgment, no circumstances in the case which could have enabled the judge to be satisfied that justice could not be done unless the spent convictions were admitted. On this point, in my judgment, the appeal is entitled to succeed.

The next question is whether there should be a new trial. In my judgment, there should not. I have not formed the opinion, necessary if a new trial is to be ordered, that the jury's knowledge of these two spent convictions has occasioned any substantial wrong or miscarriage of justice. There are a number of factors to be taken into account.

(i) Apart from simply putting the two spent convictions to Mr Thomas, counsel for the commissioner made nothing of them. He did not suggest to the jury that they reduced Mr Thomas's credibility.

(ii) The judge, in his summing up, told the jury that they were 'entitled to bear those convictions in mind according to how seriously you consider they weigh, when considering what lawyers call the plaintiff's credit. That is whether he is believable or not'. The judge went on: 'Ask yourselves does that make any difference ... If you do not think it makes any difference, ignore them. If you think it makes some difference, give them some weight.' But he then emphasised that it was 'absolutely vital' that the jury should not overestimate the importance of the convictions. He warned the jury that the convictions did not make it more likely that Mr Thomas had been violent on this occasion. To think otherwise would, he said, 'be totally unjust and totally unfair'. The convictions, he said, went 'to credit only'.

(iii) The jury, in the event, preferred Mr Thomas's evidence to the evidence of the police officers on the assault issue. This was the issue on which, more than on any other, there was a direct conflict of evidence. Mr Thomas's credit did not suffer from the jury's knowledge of the spent convictions.

(iv) On the false imprisonment case the jury must have accepted that, from the police officers' point of view, they had reasonable grounds for making the arrest. And on the malicious prosecution case, they must have believed the police officers' evidence that they had made their police statements bona fide believing the contents to be true and without any unlawful intentions towards Mr Thomas. In neither of these respects was Mr Thomas's evidence or his credibility necessarily of critical importance.

(v) Finally, I have, I hope, already made clear in this judgment my own view of the irrelevance of the two spent convictions on any issue arising in the case or on the credibility of the evidence Mr Thomas had given or might give in the case. This view seems to me to be a matter of common sense. I do not see why I should attribute to the jury a view of the importance of the convictions that differs in any substantial way from my own.

Saville LJ, in the course of argument, pointed out the Morton's fork on which Lord Gifford's arguments were impaled. If the convictions were of no more than trivial relevance to the issue of credibility, there is no reason to suppose that the a jury gave them any real weight. If, on the other hand, the convictions were of real relevance, then the judge was right to let them in.

For the reasons I have given, I do not believe that the admission into evidence of these spent convictions made any difference to the result of the case. I think the judge was wrong to let them in but am not persuaded that any substantial wrong or miscarriage of justice was thereby occasioned.

b I would refuse the request for a new trial.

I turn now to the narrow issue of damages. Lord Gifford's submissions on this issue were as follows.

(i) Mr Thomas's evidence at the trial was that the injuries he had sustained in the assault had prevented him from continuing to perform as a limbo dancer.

c Limbo dancing was not simply a pastime that gave him great satisfaction and enjoyment, but was one from which he was able to earn substantial sums of money. In a schedule of special damages that was submitted to the jury, Mr Thomas estimated that over 1988 and 1989 his average yearly earnings from limbo dancing were £4,560. £4,560 p a would be £3,420 net of tax. Calculated at a rate of £3,420 p a, special damages to compensate Mr Thomas for the loss of

d limbo dancing earnings over the period from, say, 1 June 1990 (i e a few days after the assault) to the end of February 1995 (i e a few days before the award) would be £16,245. In the event, the jury awarded £16,185 special damages. There were no special damage items other than loss of limbo dancing earnings that could have justified this sum. Accordingly, the inference is justified that the jury

e accepted Mr Thomas's evidence that his injuries had prevented him over the period in question from continuing to earn fees for limbo dancing.

(ii) Mr Thomas's evidence was that his incapacity, caused by his injuries, to earn fees for limbo dancing would continue beyond the date of the trial. It would have been perverse for the jury to have accepted his evidence of his incapacity to continue limbo dancing in the period up to the date of trial, but to have judged

f him capable of limbo dancing thereafter.

(iii) The evidence of the medical expert, Mr Britton, called on behalf of Mr Thomas, was that the particular injury inflicted in the course of the assault that had produced the limbo dancing incapacity was incurable. The final sentence of his report dated 25 October 1993 said: 'At best his recovery will take many

g months, and he may be left with permanent loss of flexibility within these tissues [ie Mr Thomas's back] which will reduce the possibility of return to full-time dancing.' Mr Thomas was born on 25 August 1957, was 37 years old at the time of the assault and gave evidence that but for the assault he could have continued professional limbo dancing until he was 50 years of age.

h (iv) Accordingly, based on the jury's award of special damages, the jury ought to have included in their general damages award an element reflecting Mr Thomas's future loss of limbo dancing earnings. This item of loss should have been calculated at the same rate, £3,420 p a, multiplied by a suitable factor. In his summing up the judge suggested that if the jury were of opinion that Mr Thomas had a sound claim for loss of future earnings, a multiplier of 10 might be

j appropriate. Thus calculated, the general damages should have included a sum of £27,350 for loss of future earnings.

(v) In addition, general damages should have included a sum for pain and suffering and for the sense of deprivation Mr Thomas would feel in being unable to continue the limbo dancing which had up to the time of the assault given him such pleasure. £20,000 was suggested as a suitable figure.

(vi) Accordingly, the general damages award of £15,815 was, it was submitted, grossly inadequate.

Lord Gifford had two supplemental points. He submitted that the judge's direction had not adequately dealt with the loss suffered by Mr Thomas in being deprived of the pleasure of limbo dancing. He submitted also that the judge had erred in law in not requiring the jury to make separate awards for (i) future loss of earnings and (ii) pain and suffering and loss of amenity. There is nothing, in my judgment, in this last point. The questions that the jury were to be invited to answer were agreed between counsel and the judge. The agreed questions did not require the separate awards now contended for. The judge directed the jury on the basis of the agreed questions. It is not open to Lord Gifford now to complain that one of the agreed questions ought to have been subdivided.

As to the loss of amenity point, there is, in any judgment, nothing in that either. The judge directed the jury that they were entitled to include in the award of damages an item to reflect Mr Thomas's loss of the enjoyment of limbo dancing if they found that he had been so deprived.

The main point at issue, however, is whether Mr Thomas can impugn the general damages award on the ground that the amount was grossly inadequate to reflect his loss of future earnings and pain and suffering.

It is important on this point to repeat that the jury were not invited to give separate awards. The £15,815 was a comprehensive award. One of the consequences of a jury trial is that the jury, unlike a judge, do not give reasons for their decisions. Mr Thomas, having chosen a jury trial at which to prosecute his causes of action, must put up with that consequence.

In his summing up the judge put clearly before the jury that Mr Thomas was making a claim for loss of future earnings. He put to the jury the suggestion that 10 might be a suitable multiplier. He told the jury to 'face the fact that the plaintiff's case is that he has suffered these very substantial past, and will suffer these more substantial future, loss of earnings and should be compensated'. But he went on to remind the jury that the 'defendant says this is a very exaggerated claim; he is entitled, if we are liable at all, to something for loss of earnings for a limited period of time; but he is certainly not entitled to anything in the future either in respect of his limbo dancing or his employment as a teacher'. So the issue of loss of future earnings was put fairly and squarely to the jury.

Moreover, the plaintiff's schedule of special damages contained a claim for 'future loss of earnings' in which a 10-year multiplier was applied to an annual earnings figure of £12,147. It may have been confusing to the jury to find 'future loss of earnings' dealt with in a special damages schedule, but it is clear that they were fully apprised of the extent of Mr Thomas's loss of earnings claim.

It is to be borne in mind also that the defendant's counter-schedule of special damage averred that 'after 28th November 1991 at the latest the Plaintiff would have been able to resume fully his work as a dancer'. So there was an issue between the parties, which the jury had to resolve, as to the length of the period in respect of which Mr Thomas was entitled to recover lost limbo dancing earnings. The judge put the issue to the jury unambiguously. He said: 'The issue is for how long would he have been unable to work ...'

In my judgment, there being no fault in the judge's summing up on damages, this is not a case in which this court would be justified in interfering with the jury's damages award.

First, although the inference that the special damages of £16,185 must have reflected loss of limbo dancing earnings up to the date of trial is a possible one, it *a* is not necessarily right. Mr Thomas was claiming also damages to reflect his alleged loss of earnings as a teacher. This was a relatively weak claim but was left by the judge to the jury. It is simply not possible to know whether some, and if so what, part of the £16,185 was attributable to the teaching claim. And it is equally impossible to know what, if any, part of the £15,815 general damages was attributable to loss of future earnings, as a limbo dancer or as a teacher, or to pain *b* and suffering, or loss of amenity.

I do not accept that the only, or even that the most likely, inference to be drawn from the general damages and special damages figures is that the jury made an error of law or were in some way perverse.

It follows that in my judgment this appeal should be dismissed.

c **EVANS LJ.** Until 1974 there was little restriction, if any, on the right to cross-examine a witness in civil proceedings as to his or her previous convictions. It was commonly accepted that such convictions could affect the creditworthiness of the witness, even when, as was often the case, the convictions themselves and the circumstances which gave rise to them had no direct *d* relevance to any issue before the court. Sometimes the convictions were so insignificant or so obviously irrelevant, even to credit, that the questioner was discouraged, perhaps by a formal ruling but usually by some other expression of disapproval by the judge. And in a jury trial the judge would be reluctant to exclude evidence which a reasonable jury could take into account when deciding where the truth lay. So the scope for judicial intervention was limited.

e The common law position was stated by Cairns J in *Clifford v Clifford* [1961] 3 All ER 231 at 232, [1961] 1 WLR 1274 at 1276 as follows:

'The range of permissible cross-examination as to credit is, however, a very wide one. It has never, I think, been doubted that a conviction for any offence could be put to a witness by way of cross-examination as to credit, *f* even though the offence was not one of dishonesty.'

The 1974 Act introduced the concept of spent convictions. Depending on the gravity of the offence and the length of sentence imposed for it, after a certain period of up to ten years a defendant who is not further convicted becomes a rehabilitated person, and by s 4(1) the offence is expunged for all purposes from *g* his record. No reference may be made to it, whether in or out of court, subject to the provisions of the 1974 Act. As Lord Denning MR said in *Reynolds v Phoenix Assurance Co Ltd* [1978] 2 Lloyd's Rep 22 at 24:

'The man has to be treated as if he had never been convicted at all ... If he *h* is asked whether he has been convicted, he need not answer. He can say "No".'

Section 4(1), however, is expressly made subject to s 7(3). The judicial authority, meaning (here) the trial judge, has a discretionary power to allow the previous convictions of a party to be adduced in evidence when the interests of *j* justice so require. In *Reynolds'* case the spent conviction was relevant or potentially relevant (depending on the trial judge's findings as to 'materiality' for insurance purposes) to a liability issue in the case. In *Dickinson v Yates, Lettice v Chief Constable of the Lancashire Constabulary* [1986] CA Transcript 554 the Court of Appeal upheld the judge's ruling which excluded the evidence in a case where, if the evidence had been given, it could not have been regarded as relevant to any issue in the case and would have been admitted solely in relation to credit. I respectfully agree with Nourse LJ that s 7(3) has imposed a further (statutory) requirement in addition to the common law test, which he defined as 'materiality'.

In the present case, the judge ruled that evidence of previous convictions could be admitted. The question is whether that was a proper exercise of the discretion given to him by s 7(3).

One begins with the 1974 Act. Section 7(3) is expressed as a qualification to the general rule of exclusion in s 4(1), and its terms demonstrate that the evidence must be excluded unless the judicial authority, ie the trial judge, is 'satisfied ... that justice cannot be done ... except by admitting [it]'. So there is a strong presumption against permitting cross-examination or admitting the evidence, but the section also emphasises that the discretion is a broad one. The judge may take into account 'any considerations which appear to [him] to be relevant' and the overriding requirement is that 'justice shall be done'. In the context of civil proceedings, this means taking account of the interests of both parties, and justice requires that there shall be a fair trial between them.

This marks a clear distinction from criminal cases, where the interests of the defendant tend to be pre-eminent. But it is in criminal cases that the concepts of relevance and admissibility of such evidence have been most often considered. Those authorities are now the subject of the Law Commission's meticulous and scholarly consultation paper, *Evidence in Criminal Proceedings: Previous Misconduct by a Defendant* (No 141) (1996). Certain features of them should be noticed for the purposes of this appeal.

The criminal authorities

First, evidence of previous convictions may sometimes, although rarely, be admissible as relevant, ie logically probative of an issue in the particular case.

This test of relevance is satisfied in the 'similar facts' cases, most recently *R v P* [1991] 3 All ER 337, [1991] 2 AC 447. Relevance in this sense is a question of law, but the House of Lords also affirmed that the evidence may nevertheless be excluded by the trial judge, if its probative force is outweighed by its potential for prejudice to the defendant. The reason why the limits of admissibility were narrowly drawn was explained by Lord Devlin in his *Trial by Jury* (1956 Hamlyn Lectures p 114) as follows:

'Similarly, a knowledge of the accused's previous convictions might often help in determining whether or not he had committed the crime, but because with a jury the prejudice created might outweigh its value, the evidence, again except for limited purposes, is not allowed.'

This is one example of the judicial function in a jury trial. Lord Devlin continued (p 115):

'... so the judge determines relevancy by admitting categories of evidence according to the principles settled by precedent and admitting particular pieces of evidence according to his own judgment. In both cases the law is at work in the task of limitation and definition by the drawing of general and particular lines.'

Secondly, cross-examination of the defendant, if he gives evidence, is restricted by the well-known provisions of s 1(f) of the Criminal Evidence Act 1898, but it is clear that when cross-examination is allowed previous convictions may be referred to which are not relevant to any issue in the case, ie not logically

probative in the sense referred to above. The underlying principle is that they
may be taken into account by the jury when considering the creditworthiness of
the defendant, or as it is sometimes put, they are regarded as 'relevant to credit',
meaning that the jury can properly take them into account in deciding whether
to believe the defendant when he gives evidence.

The assessment of credit is not exclusively a logical process. Juries invariably
are directed to use their 'knowledge of human nature' when deciding whether a
witness is telling the truth, and the law not only permits but requires them to
form their subjective though collective view, taking such account of demeanour,
motive, consistency and other characteristics of the person they have seen giving
evidence as they think fit. In this broad sense, certain matters can be described as
'relevant to credit', but this is something different from relevance meaning
logically probative of an issue.

Thirdly, the distinction is made between the defendant's *credibility*, which is
said to be supported by evidence of previous good character and damaged by
evidence of past convictions, and his *propensity* towards the kind of conduct
which is charged against him. This may be negatived by evidence of good
character but clearly it is enhanced if the previous convictions include any which
the jury could regard as establishing such propensity, even where they are not
admissible under the narrower confines of the 'similar facts' rule. When
dishonesty is alleged, proof of previous dishonesty on an unrelated occasion
could be regarded as such. This provides another degree of meaning for
'relevant', because a previous conviction which tends to establish 'propensity'
could well be taken into account by a jury whether assessing credibility or guilt,
although the jury is directed not to do so as regards guilt unless the evidence is
'logically probative' within the similar fact rule. It is when such evidence is
admissible under that rule or when the previous convictions might properly be
put to the defendant in cross-examination, which could be given disproportionate
weight by the jury as regards relevance or propensity, that the judge is most likely
to exercise his power to exclude it or them on grounds of undue prejudice to the
defendant.

Civil cases

Though it is necessary to allow for the fact that in criminal cases the
circumstances are different, nevertheless in my judgment these authorities are
relevant to the exercise of the judge's discretion in civil cases to permit the
introduction of past 'spent' convictions under s 7(3).

Lord Gifford QC's first submission is that there is no scope for exercising the
power except when the previous conviction or the circumstances relating to it are
relevant to an issue in the case, meaning as I understand it 'relevant' within the
terms of the similar fact rule. This would exclude past convictions which are
relevant, if at all, only to credit, and also those which might show 'propensity'
without themselves being logically probative of any issue in the case. I would
reject this submission. Given that previous convictions can sometimes be
'relevant to credit' then it follows, in my judgment, that in such cases the interests
of justice must require that such evidence should be admitted before the jury,
rather than withheld from it, when credit is in issue. Moreover, a past conviction
for dishonesty could be said to be directly relevant to credit, a fortiori if the
conviction was for giving perjured evidence in court.

His second submission is, in effect, that the evidence must be excluded unless
it is 'relevant', not merely to credit, but in the broader of the two senses referred

to above. This is equivalent to saying that the past conviction must show some
degree of propensity towards the kind of conduct which is in issue in the instant a
case. Here, he submits, a conviction for domestic violence has no relevance, in
that sense of the word, to the question whether the plaintiff was abusive or
offered violence to the police. Moreover, since the plaintiff pleaded guilty to the
previous charge, it has no relevance to his creditworthiness either.

In my judgment, it would be wrong to restrict the scope of the judge's b
discretion under s 7(3) except by reference to the words of the statute—the
interests of justice—and equally wrong to limit the facts which he may properly
take into account—any considerations which appear to him to be relevant. The
criminal authorities are useful because they have formulated a number of
concepts which it may be helpful for him to identify and give such weight to as
he considers appropriate in the circumstances of the particular case. But he c
should equally bear in mind, in my judgment, that the concepts are not
independent of each other and they may often overlap. For example, the more
'relevant' the previous conviction is, the more likely it is to be prejudicial to the
party giving evidence, because some degree of propensity will be shown in
addition to any damage caused to his credibility as a witness. The fact is that any d
previous conviction is likely to be prejudicial to the party or witness to whom it
is put, unless it is so obviously trivial and irrelevant that it must be disregarded by
a reasonable jury (e g a minor motoring offence). These fail the test of relevance
however it is formulated, and the need to exclude them probably will not arise,
because only an over-enthusiastic cross-examiner would seek to rely upon them
in any event. e

Furthermore, when the question is whether the party is telling the truth on a
central issue in the case, then his creditworthiness is bound up with the decision
on that issue itself. In the present case, the jury had to decide whether the
plaintiff's or the police officers' version of alleged assault was correct, and this
required them to decide whose evidence to accept. f

Section 7(3) therefore calls, in my view, for a single exercise of judgment by the
trial judge, and it follows that this court cannot interfere unless, in accordance
with general principles, the judge misdirected himself as to the test he should
apply or where his decision was obviously wrong. Here, there was no
misdirection and Sir Michael Davies reconsidered his ruling after being referred g
to the unreported judgments in *Dickinson v Yates, Lettice v Chief Constable of the
Lancashire Constabulary.* Can it be said that his ruling was obviously wrong?

The question raised by s 7(3) has to be answered by the judge, although it is not
a matter of law, nor can it be answered by logic or by any process of reasoning
alone. A negative answer would be required, in my judgment, where the h
previous conviction was so obviously irrelevant both to the issues in the case and
to the moral standing of the witness that a reasonable jury could not properly
take it into account when deciding whether to believe him or not. But the
interests of justice are synonymous with a search for the truth, and the judge has
to recognise that a reasonable jury may take a wide range of factors into account
when deciding which witnesses to believe and therefore where the truth lies. It j
is also his responsibility, in my judgment, to consider whether the likely
significance of the fact of a previous conviction in the jury's eyes is such that they
may be unfairly prejudiced against the witness in question, when deciding
whether to accept his evidence, or not. The adverb 'unfairly' is a necessary
qualification, because some prejudice is inevitable except in cases of total and

obvious irrelevance where, as stated above, the evidence should be excluded in any event. When relevance and prejudice co-exist, then the judge can carry out a similar though not identical balancing exercise to that which is required in 'similar facts' (criminal) cases by virtue of *R v P*; he can decide whether the potential prejudice to one party outweighs the prima facie right of the other party to introduce evidence of previous convictions, even if they are 'relevant' only to credit, meaning that they could influence the decision of a reasonable jury whether to accept a witness's evidence, or not.

In summary: some degree of relevance, including relevance to credit, is a sine qua non requirement for admitting the evidence. If it has any relevance, then it has some potential for prejudice. The degree of relevance can be weighed against the amount of prejudice, and other factors may be taken into account. The judge must be satisfied that the parties will not have a fair trial, or that a witness's credit cannot be fairly assessed, unless the evidence is admitted. The statutory exclusion does not apply if, in his view, the interests of justice otherwise dictate.

In the present case, the more serious of the convictions was of marginal relevance, even to credit, but of limited prejudice also; hence the dilemma to which Saville LJ refers. Sir Michael Davies decided that it was necessary in the interests of justice that the jury should have a full picture of the plaintiff and his past history, not limited by his deemed good character under s 4(1) of the 1974 Act. It cannot be said, in my judgment, that that was not a valid exercise of his discretion under s 7(3).

Two footnotes. First, s 7(3) implies that the judicial authority is separate from the tribunal of fact, which is factually correct when as here the s 7(3) decision is taken by a judge and the evidence then admitted, if it is admitted, before a jury. If the judge is himself the tribunal of fact then, if he rules that the evidence should not be admitted, he has to put it out of his mind and decide the case without reference to it. This is never an easy exercise, and in my judgment a considerable responsibility rests upon counsel, not to seek leave to refer to previous convictions except in a case where it is clearly arguable that they should be admitted under s 7(3). It would be wrong even to make an application which had no realistic prospect of success.

Secondly, the Law Commission's Paper contains details of research which was carried out using mock juries in order to assess the effects of admitting this kind of evidence in criminal cases. One factor which emerged was that knowledge of a previous conviction for a sexual offence was disproportionately likely to prejudice the jury against the defendant, regardless of the nature of the offence for which he was standing trial. This could mean that in a civil case where s 7(3) applies and there is no issue of a sexual nature the judge would more readily recognise that the potential for prejudice outweighed any 'relevance to credit' which such a conviction might otherwise have. But by the same token if the previous sexual misconduct was potentially relevant, then although the prejudice would be greater the judge might decide that justice could not be done between the parties unless the evidence was admitted.

For these reasons I would dismiss the appeal on liability. I also agree entirely with Sir Richard Scott V-C's reasons for refusing a new trial, even if the cross examination on previous convictions was wrongly permitted, and for not interfering with the award of damages.

I too would dismiss the appeal.

SAVILLE LJ. It seems to me that Lord Gifford QC's argument finds itself impaled upon the horns of a dilemma, from which there is only one escape route.

Lord Gifford's basic submission is that the judge was wrong to admit the evidence of the spent convictions on the issue of credibility, since he was wrong to conclude that justice could not otherwise be done within the meaning of s 7 of the 1974 Act.

To my mind that submission can only be correct if the evidence of the spent convictions had so little relevance to the issue of credibility that its exclusion from the trial could not properly have made any material difference to the outcome. If the evidence could properly have made a material difference, then it seems to me self-evident that justice indicates that it should not be excluded.

Lord Gifford's second main submission was that this court should order a new trial, since there was a real prospect that the jury was influenced by the evidence of the spent convictions in their assessment of the credibility of his client.

On the face of it, therefore, Lord Gifford's argument seems to contain two inconsistent assertions, one that the evidence could have made no material difference and so should have been excluded; and the other, that it might well have made a material difference so that there should be a new trial.

In my view, the only escape route from this would be if it could be shown not only that the evidence could not properly have made a material difference, but also that the jury might well have unreasonably or perversely thought it did. In his reply it seemed to me that Lord Gifford did in the end seek to make this submission.

There is, however, nothing to suggest that the jury acted in this way. The judge's direction to the jury on this evidence was, in my judgment, impeccable; in particular he warned them in no uncertain terms not to treat the evidence as going to propensity but merely, if they thought it of assistance, as something to take into account when assessing the weight to give to the plaintiffs evidence. Furthermore, the fact that the jury decided in favour of the plaintiff on the issue of assault, where his credibility as opposed to that of the police officers was all important, seems to me to indicate that the jury accepted his evidence. The fact that the jury did not find in favour of the plaintiff on the issues of false imprisonment and malicious prosecution does not, in my judgment, take the matter any further, since there are many aspects of these claims which did not depend on the veracity of the plaintiff.

It is possible that I might myself have excluded the evidence on the grounds that it had little or no relevance to the credibility of the plaintiff, but since I accept that others could reasonably hold the opposite view, it seems to me that it would be wrong to substitute this possible view for that held by the judge who had the advantage, which I do not, of actually conducting the trial and thus of being able better to judge what justice required to be done.

In these circumstances, I am not persuaded that there has been any miscarriage of justice and I would accordingly dismiss the appeal on this point.

As to damages I also agree that the appeal should be dismissed. Lord Gifford's argument depends on one vital premise: namely that the jury must have awarded loss of earnings up to the date of trial. To seek to demonstrate this, Lord Gifford submitted that if one takes the plaintiff's final figures for loss of earnings as a limbo dancer, but excludes his claimed uplift of 50% on past figures; if one also excludes any recovery for the claim for loss of earnings as a teacher, and if one *a* then takes the period of loss up to the date of trial, the arithmetical result comes quite close to the amount awarded by the jury as special damages.

I am quite unpersuaded that this is more than speculation. It seems to me that there are a variety of ways in which the jury could properly have reached the amount they awarded, e g by taking a shorter period and by awarding something for loss of teaching income or by way of uplift on past earnings. Thus to my mind

b Lord Gifford fails to demonstrate that the jury must have erred as he suggested they did.

Appeal dismissed.

Celia Fox   Barrister.

Jones v Vans Colina

COURT OF APPEAL, CIVIL DIVISION

NOURSE, ROCH AND SCHIEMANN LJJ

15, 16 MAY, 30 JULY 1996

Vexatious proceedings – Leave to institute or continue proceedings – Setting aside leave – Defendant to proposed proceedings applying to set aside leave – Court setting aside leave – Whether court having power to do so – Whether proposed defendant having locus standi to apply to set aside leave – Whether proposed defendant party to proceedings – Supreme Court Act 1981, s 42(3) – RSC Ord 32, r 6.

In 1989 a civil proceedings order was made against the plaintiff under s 42(1)[a] of the Supreme Court Act 1981, which prevented him thereafter from instituting proceedings in any court without the leave of the High Court. In 1993 the plaintiff applied ex parte for and was granted leave in the High Court under s 42(3) of the 1981 Act to institute proceedings in the county court for possession against the defendant, who was the tenant of one of his flats. Following the issue and service of the proceedings on him, the defendant issued a summons under RSC Ord 32, r 6[b] seeking to have the leave set aside. The judge found that the proceedings had been instituted as a device to achieve an ulterior purpose and that there had been material non-disclosure to the original judge and set aside the leave. At a subsequent hearing of a summons issued by the defendant to amend the judge's order, it was held that the judge had had no power to set aside the grant of leave and therefore the order purporting to do so was a nullity and so incapable of amendment. The defendant appealed to the Court of Appeal, contending that it was a fundamental rule of justice that an order made ex parte could be set aside by the party against whom it had been made.

Held – The power of the court under Ord 32, r 6, to set aside an order made ex parte only applied to an order made in proceedings in which the person seeking to have it set aside was either a party or entitled to be made one. However, on an application under s 42(3) of the 1981 Act for leave to institute proceedings, the proposed defendant was not a party to the application, nor was he entitled to be made one. It followed that the defendant had had no locus standi to apply to set aside the grant of leave and the court had had no power to accede to it. Accordingly, the appeal would be dismissed (see p 772 e and p 773 e to p 774 a e to g, post).

R v Highbury Corner Magistrates' Court, ex p Ewing [1991] 3 All ER 192 and *Ex p Ewing (No 2)* [1994] 1 WLR 1553 considered.

Becker v Noel [1971] 2 All ER 1248n not followed.

Notes

For vexatious litigants, see 37 *Halsbury's Laws* (4th edn) para 143, and for cases on the subject, see 37(2) *Digest* (Reissue) 255–257, 1665–1670.

For the Supreme Court Act 1981, s 42, see 11 *Halsbury's Statutes* (4th edn) (1991 reissue) 1008.

---

a   Section 42, so far as material, is set out at p 771 *d* to *f*, post

b   Rule 6 is set out at p 771 *g* post

Cases referred to in judgments

a *A-G v Jones* [1990] 2 All ER 636, [1990] 1 WLR 859, CA.
Becker v Noel [1971] 2 All ER 1248n, [1971] 1 WLR 803n, CA.
Becker v Teale [1971] 3 All ER 715, [1971] 1 WLR 1475, CA.
C, Re (1989) Times, 14 November.
Ewing, Ex p (No 2) [1994] 1 WLR 1553, CA.
b *Pearlberg v Varty (Inspector of Taxes)* [1972] 2 All ER 6, [1972] 1 WLR 534, HL.
R v Highbury Corner Magistrates' Court, ex p Ewing [1991] 3 All ER 192, [1991] 1 WLR 388, CA.
WEA Records Ltd v Visions Channel 4 Ltd [1983] 2 All ER 589, [1983] 1 WLR 721, CA.
Young v Bristol Aeroplane Co Ltd [1944] 2 All ER 293, [1944] KB 718, CA; *affd* [1946]
c 1 All ER 98, [1946] AC 163, HL.

Cases also cited or referred to in skeleton arguments

Minister of Foreign Affairs Trade and Industry v Vehicles and Supplies Ltd [1991] 4 All ER 65, [1991] 1 WLR 550, PC.
d *Onslow v IRC* (1890) 25 QBD 465, CA.
R v Secretary of State for the Home Dept, ex p Herbage (No 2) [1987] 1 All ER 324, [1987] QB 1077, CA.

Appeal

e By notice dated 19 May 1995 the defendant, Gordon Charles Vans Colina, appealed with leave from the decision of Sir John Wood sitting as a judge of the High Court in the Queen's Bench Division on 25 April 1995 whereby he refused to amend Ognall J's order setting aside the orders of Tuckey and Bell JJ granting the plaintiff, Marcus David Jones, leave to institute proceedings and thereafter to amend such proceedings pursuant to his ex parte application made under *f* s 42(3) of the Supreme Court Act 1981. The facts are set out in the judgment of Nourse LJ.

William Crowther QC and Paul Storey (instructed by Hooper & Wollen, Torquay) for Mr Vans Colina.

g Mr Jones appeared in person.

Cur adv vult

30 July 1996. The following judgments were delivered.

h **NOURSE LJ.** Although the procedural history of this case is complex, the question to which it has given rise can be shortly stated. Where a vexatious litigant has been given leave, ex parte, under s 42(3) of the Supreme Court Act 1981 to institute legal proceedings, can the defendant to those proceedings apply to the court to set the leave aside? That question has been answered in the *j* negative by Sir John Wood, sitting as a judge of the High Court in the Queen's Bench Division. Now we have to say whether we agree with him or not.

Marcus David Jones was formerly a member of the Bar. On 20 March 1989 a civil proceedings order was made against him by a Queen's Bench Divisional Court under s 42(1) of the 1981 Act. His appeal to this court was dismissed (see *A-G v Jones* [1990] 2 All ER 636, [1990] 1 WLR 859). Mr Jones owns the freehold of a block of flats in Torquay which are let on long leases. In June 1993, for

reasons bad or good, he wished to institute proceedings in the Torquay County
Court against the tenant of one of the flats, Gordon Charles Vans Colina.

On 25 June 1993, as required by RSC Ord 32, r 11(1)(g), Mr Jones applied in
person to the Queen's Bench judge in chambers, Tuckey J, for leave to institute
the proceedings under s 42(3). In accordance with the practice governing such
applications, no originating process, fee or affidavit was required, although it
would no doubt have been open to the judge to ask for an affidavit had he
thought it appropriate. The only document put before him was a draft of the
proposed particulars of claim. The judge's order, which bears the stamp of the
court dated 25 June 1993 but no reference to any record, reads thus:

'*Ex parte Marcus David Jones.*

Upon hearing the applicant in person it is ordered that: The applicant do
have leave to issue proceedings in the county court for the relief set out in
the draft particulars of claim initialled by the judge and annexed hereto.'

We have not seen a copy of the particulars of claim in draft, but only in the
form in which they were issued and later amended. It appears from our copy that
Mr Jones initially claimed possession and damages for breach of covenant, the
stated ground for possession being that the entirety of the rent payable by virtue
of a supplemental lease dated 15 December 1977 was in arrear as from that date.
Lower down it was stated that the annual rent payable under the supplemental
lease was a peppercorn. It must have escaped the judge's eye that possession was,
therefore, claimed for non-payment of some 15 peppercorns, which presumably
had never been demanded in the first place.

The proceedings were issued on 7 July 1993. Five days later, on 12 July, Mr
Jones obtained a further order from Bell J, giving him leave to serve the
proceedings in the amended form initialled by the judge and annexed thereto.
That order is, with the necessary variations, in the same form as Tuckey J's order,
except that it bears the case number of the county court proceedings. The
amendment pleaded an alternative ground for possession, namely failure to
comply with a notice served under s 146 of the Law of Property Act 1925.

The proceedings having been served on him, on 3 August 1993 Mr Vans Colina
issued a summons in the Queen's Bench Division seeking an order that the orders
of Tuckey and Bell JJ be set aside. After two ineffective hearings, the summons
came before Ognall J on 4 November 1993, when he made the order sought,
refused Mr Jones leave to institute proceedings and gave Mr Vans Colina most of
his costs. Mr Jones did not submit that there was no power to make the order
sought. On the submissions which were made to him, the judge was clearly right
to make it. He formed a clear view that the proceedings were a device or
stratagem by Mr Jones to achieve an ulterior purpose and that there had been
material non-disclosure to Tuckey J. There being no proceedings in the High
Court in which it could be made, the judge's order was headed:

'IN THE TORQUAY COUNTY COURT
BEFORE MR JUSTICE OGNALL
SITTING IN THE QUEEN'S BENCH DIVISION OF THE HIGH COURT OF JUSTICE ...'

It bore two county court case numbers.

Mr Vans Colina then went to the Torquay County Court in order to tax the
costs he had been awarded by Ognall J. The district judge, hardly surprisingly,
took the view that he had no power to tax costs awarded in the High Court. He
dismissed the application and ordered Mr Vans Colina to pay Mr Jones' costs. Mr

a Vans Colina then issued a summons in the Queen's Bench Division of the High Court seeking to amend Ognall J's order by deleting the words 'In the Torquay County Court', together with the relevant case number. That summons came before Sir John Wood on 13 December 1994, when Mr Jones submitted that Ognall J had had no power to make the order he did, so that it was a nullity which could not be amended. Sir John Wood, being of the opinion that there was an arguable point on jurisdiction, adjourned the summons so that an amicus curiae could be instructed.

The matter came back before Sir John Wood in April 1995, when the amicus made submissions in support of Mr Vans Colina. The judge's view was that Ognall J had had no power to set aside the leave given by Tuckey and Bell JJ, so that his order was a nullity, which he, Sir John Wood, had no power to amend. On 25 April he dismissed the summons but gave Mr Vans Colina leave to appeal to this court. Notice of appeal was duly entered. The appeal has been argued on Mr Vans Colina's behalf by Mr Crowther QC. The amicus has not appeared in this court. Mr Jones, as he has at every stage of the case, has appeared in person.

The power for the court to make, inter alia, a civil proceedings order is contained in s 42(1) of the 1981 Act. So far as material, sub-s (1A) provides:

'In this section—"civil proceedings order" means an order that—(a) no civil proceedings shall without the leave of the High Court be instituted in any court by the person against whom the order is made ...'

Subsections (3) and (4) provide:

'(3) Leave for the institution or continuance of, or for the making of an application in, any civil proceedings by a person who is the subject of an order for the time being in force under subsection (1) shall not be given unless the High Court is satisfied that the proceedings or application are not an abuse of the process of the court in question and that there are reasonable grounds for the proceedings or application ...
(4) No appeal shall lie from a decision of the High Court refusing leave required by virtue of this section.'

Order 32, r 6 provides: 'The Court may set aside an order made *ex parte*.'

The primary submission advanced on behalf of Mr Vans Colina, both here and below, was that it is a fundamental rule of justice that an order made ex parte may be set aside on the application of the party against whom it has been made. In this court, Mr Crowther has relied on an observation of Donaldson MR in *WEA Records Ltd v Visions Channel 4 Ltd* [1983] 2 All ER 589 at 593, [1983] 1 WLR 721 at 727:

'... there is no doubt that the High Court has power to review and to discharge or vary any order which has been made ex parte. This jurisdiction is inherent in the provisional nature of any order made ex parte and is reflected in RSC Ord 32, r 6.'

Mr Crowther also relied on *Becker v Noel* [1971] 2 All ER 1248n, [1971] 1 WLR 803n. There, Cusack J had given Mrs Dorothy Becker, a vexatious litigant, leave, ex parte, to issue a writ against Mr and Mrs Noel, who applied to set the writ aside and also the leave to issue it. Cusack J acceded to the application, holding that the leave given to Mrs Becker was an order and was covered by Ord 32, r 6. On her ex parte application in person to this court, Lord Denning MR said:

'I am quite clear that not only may the court set aside an order made ex
parte, but where leave is given ex parte it is always within the inherent
jurisdiction of the court to revoke that leave if it feels that it gave its original
leave under a misapprehension on new matters being drawn to its attention.'
(See [1971] 2 All ER 1248 at 1248, [1971] 1 WLR 803 at 803.)

The application was dismissed.

The first reason given by Sir John Wood for concluding that there was no
power to set aside the leave was that, since s 42(4) describes the refusal of leave
as a 'decision', the grant of leave under s 42(3) is not an 'order' within Ord 32, r 6.
He found support for that view in the difference in wording between s 42(4) and
its predecessor, s 31(1)(l) of the Supreme Court of Judicature (Consolidation) Act
1925 as amended, which provided that no appeal should lie from an 'order'
refusing leave for the institution or continuance of legal proceedings by a
vexatious litigant. He thought that, since the 1981 Act was not a consolidating
Act, the change in wording must have been deliberate. It seems that, on this
ground, the judge would have distinguished *Becker v Noel*, which was decided
when the 1925 Act was still in force. He also regarded himself as bound by
observations in this court in *R v Highbury Corner Magistrates' Court, ex p Ewing*
[1991] 3 All ER 192, [1991] 1 WLR 388 and in *Ex p Ewing (No 2)* [1994] 1 WLR 1553
respectively.

While I am unable to support the whole of the judge's reasoning, I am in no
doubt that his decision was correct. I approach the question in this way. The
power expressed in Ord 32, r 6 can only apply to an order made in proceedings in
which the person seeking to have it set aside is either a party or entitled to be
made one. The court could not accede to an application made by a person who
had no locus standi to make it. On an application under s 42(3) for leave to
institute proceedings, the proposed defendant is neither a party to the application
nor is he entitled to be made one.

In *Becker v Teale* [1971] 3 All ER 715 at 716, [1971] 1 WLR 1475 at 1476, another
case in which Mrs Dorothy Becker had been given leave to institute proceedings,
Davies LJ said:

'... it is to be remembered that the application, in the first instance at any
rate, is ex parte, though the judge may cause notice of the application to be
given to the Attorney-General so that he may be represented.'

It appears from those observations that Davies LJ assumed that there could be no
question of joining the proposed defendant. He was not entitled to be made a
party to the application. The Attorney General was in a different position
because it was he who had brought the proceedings in which the applicant had
been declared a vexatious litigant. It was he, and only he, who had the locus
standi to appear on the application (see also the observations of Brooke J in *Re C*
(1989) Times, 14 November).

In *R v Highbury Corner Magistrates' Court, ex p Ewing* [1991] 3 All ER 192, [1991]
1 WLR 388 it was held by this court that a person against whom a civil
proceedings order has been made must be given leave under s 42(3) before he can
apply for leave to apply for judicial review under Ord 53, r 3. In delivering
judgment, Lord Donaldson MR gave guidance as to how such cases should be
handled in the future. He thought that the applications under s 42(3) and Ord 53,
r 3 should both be made to a judge dealing with the Crown Office list. Having
pointed out that if the judge refused leave under s 42(3), that would be an end of

the matter because s 42(4) denied the applicant a right of appeal, he said ([1991] 3
All ER 192 at 197, [1991] 1 WLR 388 at 393):

> 'If he gives leave, the respondent will be unable to attack the leave under s 42
> because that is final, but he may be able to attack the leave under Ord 53. At
> that stage the vexatious litigant, having obtained his leave under s 42, will be
> treated in all respects as if he were not subject to the order.' (My emphasis.)

In *Ex p Ewing (No 2)* [1994] 1 WLR 1553 Mr Ewing, having been refused leave
to institute proceedings by the High Court, sought to get round the effect of
s 42(4) by making a renewed application for leave to this court under Ord 59,
r 14(3). In that endeavour he was unsuccessful. In delivering the judgment of the
court, Bingham MR said (at 1558):

> 'If, in every such case, the litigant could simply escape section 42(4) of the
> Act by making a renewed application to the Court of Appeal that section
> would be emasculated and the obvious intention of Parliament frustrated.
> Ord. 59, r. 14(3) must in our judgment be read subject to section 42(3) and
> (4) of the Act, the plain intention of which is that jurisdiction to give or refuse
> leave shall be entrusted to the High Court and its decision shall be final. *If
> the High Court grants leave the prospective respondent cannot attack the decision,* if
> leave is refused that is the end of the matter: see *Ex parte Ewing* ([1991] 3 All
> ER 192 at 197, [1991] 1 WLR 388 at 393) *per* Lord Donaldson of Lymington
> MR.' (My emphasis.)

While I cannot agree with Sir John Wood that the observations made in the
two *Ewing* cases are of more than persuasive authority in the decision of the
question that now confronts us, they are certainly valuable as demonstrating an
assumption that a defendant to proceedings for the institution of which leave has
been given under s 42(3) cannot apply to set the leave aside. Coupled with the
limitations which must be put on Ord 32, r 6 and the observations of Davies LJ in
Becker v Teale, I think that they provide a solid basis for affirming Sir John Wood's
decision in this case. Moreover, I believe that his conclusion is confirmed by a
proper appreciation of s 42(4). That subsection provides that no appeal by a
vexatious litigant shall lie from a decision refusing leave under sub-s (3). Mr
Crowther submitted that that provision impliedly permitted an appeal by a
defendant to the proceedings, on which footing he must equally be entitled to
apply to set the leave aside. I do not agree. I think that s 42(4), by referring to an
appeal only by the vexatious litigant, confirms that the proposed defendant is not
entitled to be made a party to the application under s 42(3).

There remains the decision of this court in *Becker v Noel*, which appears not to
have been cited in either of the *Ewing* cases and which Mr Crowther submitted
was binding on us here. Certainly, I am unable to distinguish it on the ground
suggested by Sir John Wood. I think that, notwithstanding the language of
s 42(4), the grant of leave under s 42(3) is properly to be described as an 'order'
and, other considerations apart, that it would fall naturally within Ord 32, r 6.
Nor can it be distinguished on the ground that there the application was made
after the issue of the proceedings. Lord Denning MR's remarks apply directly to
the setting aside of the leave. Nor, since there is no conflicting decision but only
dicta, is it possible to apply the first exception to the rule in *Young v Bristol
Aeroplane Co Ltd* [1944] 2 All ER 293, [1944] KB 718. I think that we must either
hold that it is not in reality a binding decision, since as it was given on an
interlocutory point without the benefit of argument or mature consideration, or

apply the third exception and say that it was given per incuriam. Either way, I do not think that we should follow it.

I desire to add three further points. First, Mr Jones referred us to a number of other cases where leave given for the institution of proceedings cannot be reviewed by the proposed defendant or respondent. Of the authorities cited, the most helpful is *Pearlberg v Varty (Inspector of Taxes)* [1972] 2 All ER 6, [1972] 1 WLR 534, where it was held by the House of Lords that a taxpayer was not entitled to be heard on an application to a general or special commissioner for leave to make an assessment to income tax under s 6 of the Income Tax Management Act 1964, the function of the commissioner in deciding whether or not to grant leave being an administrative one.

Secondly, the circumstances of this case suggest that a repetition of some further observations of Davies LJ in *Becker v Teale* [1971] 3 All ER 715 at 716, [1971] 1 WLR 1475 at 1476 may be timely:

'In my view the jurisdiction which is given by that section to a judge in chambers to give leave for the institution or continuance of proceedings by a vexatious litigant is a jurisdiction that should be very carefully exercised. Ex hypothesi the person has already "habitually and persistently and without any reasonable ground instituted vexatious proceedings"; and there is a high onus cast on such a person when he or she applies to the judge for the leave mentioned in the section.'

Thirdly, it is clear that the ground on which Ognall J set aside the orders of Tuckey and Bell JJ would, if established afresh, be a ground for striking out the county court proceedings under CCR Ord 13, r 5. Indeed, it is important to emphasise that a defendant to proceedings for which leave has been given under s 42(3) will always have the opportunity of effectively impugning the leave by making an application under that rule or RSC Ord 18, r 19.

I would dismiss this appeal.

ROCH LJ. I agree.

SCHIEMANN LJ. I also agree.

Appeal dismissed. Leave to appeal to the House of Lords refused.

L I Zysman Esq   Barrister.

Fellowes (or Herd) and another v Clyde Helicopters Ltd

HOUSE OF LORDS

LORD MACKAY OF CLASHFERN LC, LORD NICHOLLS OF BIRKENHEAD, LORD HOFFMANN, LORD HOPE OF CRAIGHEAD AND LORD CLYDE

14, 15, 16 JANUARY, 27 FEBRUARY 1997

Carriage by air – Carriage of passengers – Domestic carriage – Limitation of carrier's liability – Negligence – Exclusion of liability – Police officer on surveillance duties on board helicopter operated by respondents under time charter to police – Police officer killed when helicopter crashed – Whether police officer being carried for reward – Whether officer's dependants having common law remedy against respondents for pilot's negligence – Carriage by Air Acts (Application of Provisions) Order 1967, arts 3, 4, Sch 1, Pt III, arts 17, 22.

The appellants were the dependants and relatives of a Scottish police officer who was killed while on board a helicopter which crashed during a snow storm. The officer was a member of his police force's helicopter unit and his duties were to carry out aerial surveillance and detection within the region covered by his force. The helicopter was supplied and operated by the respondent company under a contract between the respondents and the police authority which provided that the helicopter would be used principally within the force's region with the proviso that flights might be required beyond the region in exceptional circumstances. The contract, which was for a specified period, further provided that the helicopter was to be used exclusively for police use under police instructions, that it was to carry police markings and equipment, that it was to be piloted by and under the control of a civilian pilot employed by the respondents but under the directions and instructions of the police surveillance officers on board acting as observers. The appellants brought an action against the respondents claiming damages at common law on the ground that the accident had been caused by the negligence of the pilot of the helicopter employed by the respondents. The respondents contended that the appellants' claim was barred by arts 3[a] and 4[b] of the Carriage by Air Acts (Application of Provisions) Order 1967 because the police officer's presence on board the helicopter was 'non-international' carriage to which the modified Hague Rules set out in Sch 1 to the 1967 order applied and therefore the respondents' liability, although strict, was limited under arts 17[c] and 22[d] of Sch 1 to approximately £93,850. Under art 3, the 1967 order applied to all carriage by air in the United Kingdom, not being carriage to which the Hague Rules applied, and art 4 had the effect of extending the modified Hague Rules to air carriage which was not international. The appellants contended that the 1967 order did not operate to limit the respondents' liability and, in particular, did not exclude the respondents' liability to the

---

a	Article 3, so far as material, provides: 'This Order shall apply to all carriage by air, not being carriage to which the amended Convention [ie the Hague Rules] applies.'

b	Article 4 is set out at p 779 *b*, post

c	Article 17 is set out at p 781 *g*, post

d	Article 22, so far as material, provides: 'In the carriage of persons the liability of the carrier for each passenger is limited to the sum of eight hundred and seventy-five thousand francs ...'

appellants at common law, on the grounds that the contract between the respondents and the police authority was not a contract of carriage, that the police officer neither accepted nor consented to the terms of the contract, that he was not on board the helicopter as a passenger and he was not a party to any contract of carriage. The Lord Ordinary dismissed the action and on appeal his decision was upheld by the Court of Session. The appellants appealed to the House of Lords.

Held – Although the police officer was on board the helicopter for the purpose of carrying out his police duties, he had no responsibility in respect of the operation of the aircraft, which was solely under the control of the pilot, and consequently the activities which he carried out while on board could not to be regarded as contributing to the carriage of himself or the other persons on board. He was therefore properly to be regarded as a passenger so far as the performance of the contract of carriage for reward was concerned. Moreover, while the normal case falling within the ambit of Sch 1 to the 1967 order was a contract of carriage entered into for the transportation of a passenger on a pre-determined route from one place to another, the articles of Sch 1 were so widely expressed that they encompassed carriage under what was, in effect, a time charter of the helicopter from the respondents to the police authority. It followed that the police officer's presence on board the helicopter at the time of the crash constituted 'carriage of persons ... by aircraft for reward' within art 1 of Sch 1 and the respondents were the 'carrier' in respect of that carriage, with the result that the limitations of liability set out in arts 17 and 22 applied to the carriage of the police officer. Accordingly the appeal would be dismissed (see p 781 *efh* to p 782 *a c* to *e*, p 785 *j* to p 786 *d f* to *h*, p 787 *a* to *c*, p 790 *j* to p 791 *a*, p 792 *a*, p 793 *g*, p 794 *b* and p 795 *d*, post).

Grein v Imperial Airways Ltd [1936] 2 All ER 1258 and *Holmes v Bangladesh Biman Corp* [1989] 1 All ER 852 distinguished.

Notes

For non-international carriage of passengers by air, see 2 *Halsbury's Laws* (4th edn reissue) para 1629–1639.

For the Carriage by Air Acts (Application of Provisions) Order 1967, arts 3, 4, see 3 *Halsbury's Statutory Instruments* (1995 reissue) 28.

Cases referred to in opinions

Aéro-Club de l'Aisne v Klopotowska (1970) 24 RFDA 195, Cour de Cassation.
Barnes v Service Aérien Français (1993) 47 RFDA 343, Paris Cour d'Appel.
Block v Cie Nationale Air France (1967) 386 F 2d 323, US Ct of Apps (5th Cir).
Fothergill v Monarch Airlines Ltd [1980] 2 All ER 696, [1981] AC 251, [1980] 3 WLR 209, HL.
Grein v Imperial Airways Ltd [1936] 2 All ER 1258, [1937] 1 KB 50, CA.
Holmes v Bangladesh Biman Corp [1989] 1 All ER 852, [1989] AC 1112, [1989] 2 WLR 481, HL.
Johnson Estate v Pischke (1989) 1 S & B Av R 337, Sask QB.
M'Kay v Scottish Airways Ltd 1948 SC 254, Ct of Sess.
Megarity v Law Society, Gayway Linings Ltd v Law Society [1981] 1 All ER 641, [1982] AC 81, [1981] 2 WLR 335, HL.
Mertens v Flying Tiger Line Inc (1965) 341 F 2d 851, US Ct of Apps (2nd Cir).
Mexico City Aircrash, Re (1983) 17 Avi 18,387, US Ct of Apps (9th Cir).

a *Moss v Penman (No 2)* 1994 SLT 602, Ct of Sess.
Ortet v Georges (1976) 30 RFDA 490, Paris Cour d'Appel.
Shiloh Spinners Ltd v Harding (No 2) [1973] 1 All ER 966, [1973] 1 WLR 518, HL.
Sidhu v British Airways plc, Abnett (known as Sykes) v British Airways plc [1997] 1 All
ER 193, [1997] 2 WLR 26, HL.
Sté Mutuelle d'Assurance Aériennes v Gauvain (1967) 21 RFDA 436, Cour de
b   Cassation.
Sulewski v Federal Express Corp (1991) 23 Avi 17,685, US Ct of Apps (2nd Cir).
UTA v Fichou (1983) 38 RFDA 444, Cour de Cassation.
Warren v Flying Tiger Line Inc (1965) 352 F 2d 494, US Ct of Apps (9th Cir).

Appeal
c The pursuers, Pauline Mary Fellowes (or Herd), suing as widow of her husband
and on behalf of her four children, and Jessie McDonald or Herd or Rivera,
appealed from the decision of the Second Division of the Inner House of the
Court of Session (the Lord Justice Clerk (Ross) and Lord Morison; Lord Murray
dissenting) (1996 SLT 976) delivered on 5 May 1995 refusing their reclaiming
d motion from the decision of the Lord Ordinary (Milligan) delivered on 24 March
1994 sustaining the plea of the defenders and respondents, Clyde Helicopters Ltd,
and dismissing the appellants' claim against the respondents for damages for
negligence at common law in respect of the death of the first appellant's husband,
Sgt Malcolm Herd. The facts are set out in the opinion of Lord Mackay of
Clashfern LC.
e

Michael S Jones QC (of the Scottish and English Bars), *G J B Moynihan* and *Shona
Haldane* (both of the Scottish Bar) (instructed by *Leigh Day & Co*, agents for
Balfour & Manson, Edinburgh, acting for *Levy & McRae*, Glasgow, and by
Reynolds Porter Chamberlain, agents for *John G Gray & Co SSC*, Edinburgh,
f acting for *John Wilson & Co*, Glasgow) for the appellants.
R S Keen QC and *R B M Howie* (both of the Scottish Bar) (instructed by *Beaumont
& Son*, agents for *Maclay Murray & Spens*, Glasgow) for the respondents.

Their Lordships took time for consideration.

g 27 February 1997. The following opinions were delivered.

LORD MACKAY OF CLASHFERN LC. My Lords, Sgt Malcolm Herd was
killed in a helicopter crash on 24 January 1990. The first appellant is his widow,
suing as guardian of their four children. The second appellant is Sgt Herd's
h mother.
At the time of his death Sgt Herd was a member of the Police Helicopter Unit
of the Strathclyde Police Force. His duties were to carry out aerial surveillance
and detection within Strathclyde. The helicopters used by the Helicopter Unit
were supplied by the respondents, Clyde Helicopters Ltd, in terms of a contract
j between them and Strathclyde Regional Council as police authority for
Strathclyde. On the date of his death Sgt Herd and two colleagues were carrying
out their duties on board one of these helicopters. During the flight a snow storm
was encountered as a result of which the pilot, an employee of the respondents,
became lost, an engine failure occurred and the helicopter collided with a block
of flats on the south side of Glasgow, as a result of which Sgt Herd sustained fatal
injuries.

The appellants are suing the respondents for reparation in respect of the death of Sgt Herd, basing their claim on allegations of common law negligence on the part of the respondents' pilot. The respondents maintain that the claim in respect of common law negligence is excluded by the Carriage by Air Acts (Application of Provisions) Order 1967, SI 1967/480, and particularly the provisions of arts 3 and 4 of and Sch 1 to, that order, and that their liability is confined to liability under that order, which I shall refer to as 'the 1967 order.'

The Lord Ordinary (Lord Milligan) gave judgment in favour of the respondents on this issue and on a reclaiming motion the Second Division of the Court of Session (the Lord Justice Clerk (Ross) and Lord Morison; Lord Murray dissenting) (1996 SLT 976) adhered to the interlocutor of the Lord Ordinary. From that judgment the appellants appeal to this House.

The history of the legislation of which the 1967 order forms part is clearly described in *Holmes v Bangladesh Biman Corp* [1989] 1 All ER 852 at 854–856, 857–859 and 865–869, [1989] AC 1112 at 1124–1126, 1129–1131, 1139–1144 in the speeches of Lord Bridge of Harwich and Lord Jauncey of Tullichettle. I need not repeat it here except to say that I shall have occasion later to comment on a passage quoted in both of these speeches from Greene LJ in *Grein v Imperial Airways Ltd* [1936] 2 All ER 1258 at 1277, [1937] 1 KB 50 at 74, which is also referred to by Lord Hope of Craighead in *Sidhu v British Airways plc, Abnett (known as Sykes) v British Airways plc* [1997] 1 All ER 193 at 202, [1997] 2 WLR 26 at 36. Like Lord Bridge of Harwich I shall refer to 'the Warsaw rules' (set out in Sch 2 to the 1967 order), 'the Hague Rules' (set out in Sch 1 to the Carriage by Air Act 1961) and 'the United Kingdom rules' (set out in Sch 1 to the 1967 order).

As history shows, the 1967 order was made under powers conferred upon Her Majesty by Order in Council by s 10 of the 1961 Act to—

'apply the First Schedule to this Act [ie the Hague Rules (made at the Warsaw Convention and amended at The Hague in 1955)], together with any other provisions of this Act, to carriage by air, not being carriage by air to which the Convention [ie the Hague Rules] applies, of such descriptions as may be specified in the Order, subject to such exceptions, adaptations and modifications, if any, as may be so specified.'

No submissions have been made in this appeal based upon the terms of the power to make the Order in Council and I turn immediately to the terms of the 1967 order as they are said to apply in the present case.

By art 3 the 1967 order applies to all carriage by air, not being carriage to which the Hague Rules apply. In terms of art 1(1) of Pt I of Sch 1 to the 1961 Act the Hague Rules apply to—

'all international carriage of persons, baggage or cargo performed by aircraft for reward. It applies equally to gratuitous carriage by aircraft performed by an air transport undertaking.'

In terms of art 1(2) 'for the purposes of' the Hague Rules—

'the expression *international carriage* means any carriage in which, according to the agreement between the parties, the place of departure and the place of destination, whether or not there be a break in the carriage or a transhipment, are situated either within the territories of two High Contracting Parties or within the territory of a single High Contracting Party if there is an agreed stopping place within the territory of another state, even if that state is not a High Contracting Party. Carriage between two points within the territory of a single High Contracting Party without an agreed stopping place within the territory of another state is not international carriage for the purposes of [the Hague Rules].'

Article 4 of the 1967 order provides:

'Schedule 1 to this Order shall have effect in respect of carriage to which this Order applies, being either—(a) carriage which is not international carriage as defined in Schedule 2 to this Order, or (b) carriage of mail or postal packages.'

International carriage is defined in Sch 2 by para 3(2) as follows:

' "International carriage" means any carriage in which, according to the contract made by the parties, the place of departure and the place of destination, whether or not there be a break in the carriage or a transhipment, are situated either within the territories of two States Parties to the [Warsaw Convention], or within the territory of a single such State, if there is an agreed stopping place within the territory subject to the sovereignty, suzerainty, mandate or authority of another State, even though that State is not a party to the [Warsaw Convention].'

In the present case the specification of the contract between the respondents and Strathclyde Regional Council contains the provision:

'The aircraft will be used principally within Strathclyde region. Flights beyond the geographical boundaries of Strathclyde region may, however, be required under exceptional circumstances.'

Accordingly, it is clear that in general the aircraft would not be used beyond the boundaries of Strathclyde region and therefore outside the boundaries of the United Kingdom, and there is certainly no question of any arrangement in respect of the fatal flight that it should go outside the bounds of the Strathclyde region. No question therefore arises in the present case that the Hague Rules could apply in the circumstances of the fatal flight, nor that it could involve international carriage as defined in Sch 2 to the 1967 order (the Warsaw rules). It follows that Sch 1 to the 1967 order has effect in law in respect of any carriage by air involved in the fatal flight.

Before proceeding to consider the application of Sch 1 to the circumstances of this case it is necessary to set out some further facts. In terms of their contract the respondents were obliged to be prepared to carry such numbers of people and equipment as required by the chief constable or his authorised representatives as might reasonably be required for the operation of the contract. The contract required the respondents to provide a complete air support service to Strathclyde police over a five month period, the aircraft operating on a private operator basis, with the Chief Constable of Strathclyde Police or his authorised representatives as the responsible person, from whom the respondents would take all reasonable instruction. The aircraft were to operate from an operating base within a radius of ten miles of Strathclyde Police Headquarters and the respondents were required to supply the aircraft for the exclusive use of Strathclyde police, during the period of the contract providing pilotage, all maintenance services, full ground facilities, including an operating base and hangarage, all fuel, insurance cover and such other facilities necessary for the performance of the contract. The

contract contained a description of the aircraft required and provided that the
following equipment considered essential for police operations was to be
supplied by the respondents: (1) 'Nitesun' or equivalent powered searchlight
facility, capable of being operated by remote control within the cabin. (2) A night
sight device. (3) A public address system, stabilised binoculars or night glasses.

Since the aircraft was to operate predominantly at low level, the respondents
were also required to specify what method would be used to ensure that Civil
Aviation Authority minimum height conditions would be maintained. The
aircraft were in addition required to be provided with facilities for the
transportation of stretcher cases, with under-slung cargo lifting facilities, with
navigation and instrumentation to appropriate standard to enable operation
within the hours of darkness, with provision for police radio link and with
flotation equipment, since Strathclyde region encompasses a number of islands.
It was required that the aircraft livery was to be in police colours incorporating
the lettering 'Police' on the aircraft nose, sides and in large letters on the
underside. The respondents were also required to provide a helicopter landing
pad situated within ten miles of Strathclyde Police Headquarters with office
accommodation adjacent to the landing pad including refreshment facilities for
crew members and support staff during standby periods, for a minimum of five
persons at any one time. This suggests that the word 'crew' in this context
included police officers. The contract period was 150 consecutive days from the
commencement of the contract, Strathclyde police guaranteed to undertake a
minimum of 350 flying hours during that period, and the basic contract price was
£198,000.

The duties of Sgt Herd and his police colleagues while they were on board the
helicopters, provided in pursuance of the contract, were to direct the surveillance
operations on which the helicopters were engaged; to give the necessary
instructions to the pilots; to inform the pilots of the manoeuvres which they
wished them to carry out and generally to act as observers and to provide
information to the pilots during the course of each flight. On the occasion of the
fatal flight the respondents' pilot was Captain Graham Pryke, who was solely
responsible for the flying of the helicopter and all decisions related thereto.

Although, as I have said, the contract itself provided that the respondents'
aircraft would operate on a private basis, the respondents aver that the Civil
Aviation Authority subsequently ruled that the contract amounted to a public
transport commission and that all flights performed under and in terms of the
contract should accordingly be deemed to be flights for the purposes of public
transport. This allegation is not dealt with in the appellants' pleadings and in my
opinion nothing turns upon it in the circumstances of this case.

Against this background of fact the case for the appellants is that the 1967 order
did not operate to limit the respondents' liability and, in particular, that it did not
exclude the respondents' liability to the appellants at common law. In support of
this submission they argue that the regional council contract was not a contract
of carriage, that Sgt Herd neither accepted nor consented to the terms of the
regional council contract, that he was not on board the helicopter as a passenger
and neither was he a party to any contract of carriage.

The respondents, on the other hand, maintain that the 1967 order did apply to
limit the liability of the respondents in respect of the death of Sgt Herd and, in
particular, that it excluded liability to the relatives of Sgt Herd for negligence at
common law. They argue that Sgt Herd was being carried on the helicopter for
reward with the agreement of the respondents, that he was a passenger, that the

respondents had agreed to the carriage of Sgt Herd on the helicopter, that he was
there in pursuance of a contract between the police authority and the
respondents which provided for the carriage of such a police officer and that he
was a person whom the chief constable in the circumstances had required the
respondents to carry in terms of the contract between the police authority and
the respondents, and, in the discharge of his duties as a police officer under the
direction of the chief constable, Sgt Herd, they say, implicitly consented to such
carriage.

Although a number of decisions of both the United Kingdom courts and of the
courts of the United States of America, of Canada and of France were referred to
in argument, none of them deals directly with the application of the 1967 order
to circumstances such as obtain in the present case and therefore I propose to
consider the matter firstly, by seeking to apply the relevant words of the 1967
order to the circumstances of the present case, and then to consider whether any
of the decisions cited cast doubt on the validity of the conclusion thus reached.

Article 1 provides:

'This Schedule applies to all carriage of persons, baggage or cargo
performed by aircraft for reward. It applies equally to gratuitous carriage by
aircraft performed by an air transport undertaking.'

It appears to me clear that Sgt Herd was being carried by the respondents'
helicopter at the time of his death. Indeed in their written case on this appeal the
appellants state: 'Transportation was "accessory—albeit necessary" to the
purposes of the contract.'

That carriage was performed by the respondents in terms of the requirement
to carry such numbers of people and equipment as required by the chief constable
or his authorised representatives and that was a stipulation to be carried out,
among others, in return for the sum contracted to be paid by the regional council
to the respondents under the contract. I therefore conclude that the result of
reading the words of this article in their ordinary meaning is that Sch 1 applies to
the carriage of Sgt Herd on the fatal flight.

Article 17 provides:

'The carrier is liable for damage sustained in the event of the death or
wounding of a passenger or any other bodily injury suffered by a passenger,
if the accident which caused the damage so sustained took place on board the
aircraft or in the course of any of the operations of embarking or
disembarking.'

In my view it is clear that the respondents were the carrier in respect of the
carriage of Sgt Herd. It is true that Sgt Herd was on the aircraft for the purpose
of carrying out his duties as a member of the Police Helicopter Unit, but from the
facts as alleged, which I have quoted above, it is clear that he had no responsibility
whatever in respect of the operation of the aircraft, which was solely under the
control of the pilot, and therefore in my opinion the activities which Sgt Herd was
carrying on while on the aircraft are not to be regarded as contributing in any way
to the carriage of himself or the other persons on board. He therefore is properly
regarded as a passenger.

Article 22 states (and it has been affected by subsequent modifications to the
way in which the limitation of liability is calculated which are not relevant for our
present consideration so that it is sufficient to say that it provides) that 'In the

carriage of persons the liability of the carrier for each passenger is limited ...' This
appears to me to apply directly to liability for Sgt Herd and for his death.

Article 24(2) provides:

> 'In the cases covered by article 17 the provisions of the preceding
> paragraph also apply, [that is to say "any action for damages, however
> founded, can only be brought subject to the conditions and limits set out in
> this Convention"] without prejudice to the questions as to who are the
> persons who have the right to bring suit and what are their respective rights.'

This provision appears to me plainly to exclude any action for damages except
in accordance with the conditions and limits set out in Sch 1, and accordingly
effectively to limit the claims of the appellants to liability as provided for in art 17,
leaving the distribution of the total amount available between the persons having
right thereto in the proportions to be determined by the general law, in this case
the law of Scotland.

Article 25 is not founded on in this case.

It appears to me that what I have said so far is sufficient to demonstrate that the
result contended for by the respondents is correct, subject to consideration of any
argument that would throw doubt on the validity of the construction which I
have put upon the articles of Sch 1 so far referred to. In particular, it does not
appear to me that the application of Sch 1 requires that Sgt Herd should have
been carried under a contract to which he was a party or under a contract of any
particular type if he was being carried for reward.

Article 30(1) provides:

> 'In the case of carriage to be performed by various successive carriers each
> carrier who accepts passengers, baggage or cargo is subjected to the rules set
> out in this Schedule, and is deemed to be one of the contracting parties to the
> contract of carriage in so far as the contract deals with that part of the
> carriage which is performed under his supervision.'

This article has no application to the circumstances of the present case but it is
founded on as indicating that Sch 1 proceeds on the assumption that there will be
a contract of carriage if Sch 1 applies. In my opinion this article can be given effect
appropriately by saying that where a person is carried by an aircraft for reward or
gratuitously by an aircraft being operated by an air transport undertaking there
must be a contract, which is, for the purposes of art 30, the contract of carriage.
I should also note in passing that art 31 clearly contemplates that stipulations with
regard to carriage by air could be contained within a contract which deals with
other matters, for example, for carriage partly by any other mode of carriage than
by air. Equally, art 32 can in my view be explained in the same way as I have
suggested as available in respect of art 30. The reference to contract of carriage
in art 33 I think is of no particular significance. I should also point out that art 25A
of Sch 1 applies to servants or agents of the carrier who would not themselves
generally, be parties to any contract of carriage. This is relevant to the question
of whether the 1967 order is to be considered as effective in law, providing
general rules with regard to the liability of the carrier in respect of the contract of
carriage, or as imposing on the contract statutory rules which the contracting
parties are not entitled to agree to vary or contravene. Undoubtedly art 30 denies
effect to clauses or special agreements entered into before the damage occurred
by which the parties purpose to infringe the rules laid down by Sch 1, whether by
deciding the law to be applied or by altering the rules as to jurisdiction, but in my

a opinion the general words of art 24 are naturally construed as having effect as general rules of law rather than merely as statutory contractual terms. This view is supported in my opinion by the terms of s 1(1) of the 1961 Act itself, which provides that reading short the Hague Rules shall—

b 'so far as they relate to the rights and liabilities of carriers, carriers' servants and agents, passengers, consignors, consignees and other persons, and subject to the provisions of this Act have the force of law in the United Kingdom in relation to any carriage by air to which the Convention applies ...',

and in my opinion the opening words of s 10(1), which as I have said is the empowering section for the 1967 order, empower the application of Sch 1 to this *c* Act together with any other provisions of this Act to carriage by air dealt with by the 1967 order. It is I think therefore natural to take it that when this power is exercised it is so exercised in a way that relates to the rights and liabilities not only of parties to the contract but also to those of other persons affected by the ordinary meaning of the terms of the 1967 order unless there is some express or *d* implied limitation in the 1967 order itself in respect of those to whom it applies.

Although Greene LJ in *Grein v Imperial Airways Ltd* [1936] 2 All ER 1258 at 1278–1279, [1937] 1 KB 50 at 74–77 in the passage cited by Lord Bridge of Harwich and Lord Jauncey of Tullichettle in *Holmes v Bangladesh Biman Corp* [1989] 1 All ER 852 at 858 and 867, [1989] AC 1112 at 1129 and 1141 refers to the convention provisions operating by imposing statutory terms upon contract of carriage, this *e* aspect of the matter was not an issue in your Lordships' House in *Holmes v Bangladesh Biman Corp* and, in the decision in *Grein v Imperial Airways Ltd* itself, Greene LJ did in fact deal with the position of the relatives on the footing that it was covered by the terms of the convention in the result.

As I have said, in the very well prepared and careful argument to which your *f* Lordships were treated, a number of decisions were referred to. None of them dealt with the terms of the 1967 order with which your Lordships are concerned in the present case. In so far as they dealt with the Warsaw Convention either as originally agreed upon, or as modified at the Hague, they dealt with provisions very substantially different in important respects from those with which we are concerned in the 1967 order. In particular, the ticketing provisions are *g* fundamental in those conventions to the limitation of liability, since the delivery of a ticket with the appropriate notice of limitation is generally essential to the application of the limitation provisions which involves a relationship between, for example, the passenger and the carrier which is not necessary in the 1967 order.

h The cases in the United States and Canada and all but two of the French decisions could be explained on the basis that if there is a relationship between the carrier and the person carried in addition to, or distinct from, the relationship of the person carried and the carrier, such as, for example, where the person being carried is an employee of the carrier with duties connected with the conduct of *j* the flight, the liability under such relationship is not affected by limitations on the liabilities incurred as carrier.

I now turn to look at the decisions which have been relied upon from foreign courts in some more detail. The first is *Block v Cie Nationale Air France* (1967) 386 F 2d 323 which was a case in which the Atlanta Art Association arranged for a flight from the United States to France and return, Air France being the operator of the plane in respect of which each passenger was issued with a ticket which

referred to the Warsaw Convention liability limitation when it was held that the
Warsaw Convention applied to it. In the majority judgment the United States
Court of Appeals for the Fifth Circuit gave an account of the history of the
Warsaw Conference and resulting convention which is of interest and
supplements to some extent the history to which I have already referred of the
statutory provisions in this country given in *Holmes v Bangladesh Biman Corp*. In
particular, the court quoted an explanation given by Secretary of State Cordell
Hull in transmitting the Warsaw Convention to the United States Senate in 1984
in these terms (386 F 2d 323 at 327):

> 'It is believed that the principle of limitation of liability will not only be
> beneficial to passengers and shippers as affording a more definite basis of
> recovery and as tending to lessen litigation, but that it will prove to be an aid
> in the development of international air transportation, as such limitation will
> afford the carrier a more definite and equitable basis on which to obtain
> insurance rates, with the probable result that there would eventually be a
> reduction of operating expenses for the carrier and advantages to travellers
> and shippers in the way of reduced transportation charges ... The principle
> of placing the burden on the carrier to show lack of negligence in
> international air transportation in order to escape liability, seems to be
> reasonable in view of the difficulty which a passenger has in establishing the
> cause of an accident in air transportation.'

A good deal of the judgment was taken up with examining whether the Warsaw
Convention could apply to charter flights and concluded that it could apply to
some while it might not apply to others. The court said (at 333–334):

> '... all that is needed to establish the requisite contract is a promise, an
> undertaking, on the part of the carrier to transport the passenger, and the
> consent of the passenger. [This is on the basis that the company in that case
> was an air transportation enterprise.] The contract plays a role fundamental
> to the objectives of the Warsaw Conference. The obligations arising from
> the contract between the carrier and the passenger carry out the Conference
> goal that the rules of limited liability be known to both parties. This
> knowledge enables the passenger to determine in advance the amount of
> insurance he needs; permits the carrier's insurer to gauge the carrier's
> long-term risk, and act accordingly; and, finally, advises the carrier as to what
> law it need conform its transportation documents. This rationale—that the
> flight arrangements must be based upon an agreement because only in that
> way can the necessary knowledge or foreseeability be achieved—implies
> that as long as there exists an agreement between the carrier and the
> passenger as to transportation and as to places of *departure* and *arrival*, any
> agreement between the owner-carrier and a third person, the charterer, is
> irrelevant to Warsaw purposes.'

That observation applies to the Warsaw Convention in the light of the ticketing
provisions, but as I have already noted the ticketing provisions are absent from
the 1967 order which applies in the present case. The court said (at 334):

> 'The existence of the airline-passenger relationship is not destroyed by the
> fact that a third party negotiated the agreement and signed the charter.'

a   Accordingly, when one allows for the fact that the ticketing provisions of the Warsaw Convention are not included in the 1967 order, there is nothing in this decision to cast doubt on the view which I have taken.

In *Sulewski v Federal Express Corp* (1991) 23 Avi 17, 685, a decision of the United States Court of Appeals for the Second Circuit, the deceased was a mechanic held to be travelling not as a passenger but as an employee of the air carrier and b   accordingly the court held that the limitations did not apply to him.

In *Mertens v Flying Tiger Line Inc* (1965) 341 F 2d 851 the Warsaw Convention was held not to apply since the ticket contained only an unreadable notice of limitation and it was not delivered to the passenger until after he had boarded the aircraft. In *Warren v Flying Tiger Line Inc* (1965) 352 F 2d 494 it was again held that the Warsaw Convention did not apply as the ticket had not been timously c   delivered. The decision in *Re Mexico City Aircrash* (1983) 17 Avi 18,387 turned on whether or not the persons being carried were being carried merely as passengers of the airline or in their capacity as employees of the airline. Without examining the decision in detail I think it is sufficient to say that the question whether or not the Warsaw Convention applied was decided to depend on whether or not the d   person carried was an employee of the carrier and travelling in that capacity, in which case the Warsaw Convention would not apply, whereas, if though an employee, the person being carried was being carried truly as a passenger with no responsibility in connection with the operation of the flight and without being obliged to travel as an employee on that particular flight, the convention would apply.

e   I turn now to *Sté Mutuelle d'Assurance Aériennes v Gauvain* (1967) 21 RFDA 436, a French decision on the domestic law of France which is quite different from the 1967 order with which this case is concerned. In *Gauvain* there was a contract of instruction between the parties as a result of which the trainee pilot was on board the aircraft at the time of the accident. This I think is sufficient to preclude f   application of the Warsaw Convention in so far as the operator of the aircraft had obligations to the trainee pilot over and above those of a carrier in any event. This case was followed in Canada in *Johnson Estate v Pischke* (1989) 1 S & B Av R 337. *Aéro-Club de l'Aisne v Klopotowska* (1970) 24 RFDA 195 was in respect of a test flight which certainly involved obligations distinct from that of mere carriage between a person on the aircraft and the club operating the aircraft. *Ortet v* g   *Georges* (1976) 30 RFDA 490 was concerned with an aerial survey for which the instructions were contained in a verbal arrangement not at all detailed and which certainly did not specifically provide for carriage and in which the arrangements for remuneration were not detailed. *Barnes v Service Aérien Français* (1993) 47 RFDA 343 was a case of rescue in which it appears clear that the private h   helicopters of the public limited company Service Aérien Français, whose work involved the provision of aid to persons in difficulty, were placed at the disposal of the state-financed civilian rescue organisation as rescue means to be used in the event of an accident occurring on the ski slopes, and that no remuneration was provided for in favour of the company, Service Aérien Français, for any of its j   operations, not even for those of its pilots and assistants. Finally, in *UTA v Fichou* (1983) 38 RFDA 444 there was clearly a contract of employment between the carrier and the person injured.

This brief examination of the authorities that were referred to in my opinion gives no occasion to alter the view which I have formed on the basis of applying the words of the 1967 order to the circumstances of the present case where there was no arrangement of any kind between Sgt Herd and the respondents except that of a person carried to the carrier. I also agree with my noble and learned friend, Lord Hope of Craighead that the other considerations with which he has dealt fully do not require an alteration of the view which I had formed.

I also agree with him that it is appropriate to deal with the legal aid situation in the manner he has proposed.

I am therefore of the opinion that this appeal should be refused, that the appellants should be found liable as assisted persons to the respondents in the costs of this appeal, that their liability should be modified to nil and that the Scottish Legal Aid Board should be found liable to the respondents, subject to this being intimated to them and their having an opportunity to respond, in the costs of the respondents in this appeal.

LORD NICHOLLS OF BIRKENHEAD. My Lords, I have had the advantage of reading in draft the speech of my noble and learned friend Lord Mackay of Clashfern LC. For the reasons he gives, with which I agree, I would dismiss this appeal.

LORD HOFFMANN. My Lords, I have had the advantage of reading in draft the speech of my noble and learned friend Lord Mackay of Clashfern LC. For the reasons he has given, I, too, would dismiss this appeal.

LORD HOPE OF CRAIGHEAD. My Lords, the question in this appeal is whether the Carriage by Air Acts (Application of Provisions) Order 1967, SI 1967/480, applies so as to regulate the liability of the carrier, where a police officer who was on board an air support unit helicopter sustained fatal injuries when it was being operated by the respondents under a contract with Strathclyde Regional Council as the police authority. It is not disputed that, if the 1967 order applies, the provisions of Sch 1 to the 1967 order provide the exclusive cause of action and sole remedy for the appellants, who claim damages from the respondents for the loss which they have sustained as a result of the death of the police officer.

I do not think that this question gives rise to any real difficulty on the facts of this case if their ordinary meaning is to be given to the words used in the 1967 order and in the relevant articles of Sch 1. Article 3 of the 1967 order states that the order is to apply to all carriage by air, not being carriage to which the amended convention (that is, the convention concerning international carriage by air known as 'the Warsaw Convention as amended at the Hague 1955') applies. Article 1 of Sch 1 states that the schedule applies to all carriage of persons, baggage or cargo performed by aircraft for reward. Article 17 states that the carrier is liable for damage sustained in the event of the death or wounding of a passenger or any other bodily injury suffered by a passenger, if the accident which caused the damage so sustained took place on board the aircraft or in the course of any of the operations of embarking or disembarking.

Sgt Herd was being carried by air in the helicopter when it crashed, and the carriage was being performed for reward by the respondents under their contract with the police authority. It is not suggested that the surveillance and detection duties on which Sgt Herd was engaged at the time involved him at any stage in the handling of the helicopter. It is a matter of admission that the flying of the helicopter was a matter for which the pilot, Captain Pryke, was solely responsible. Although Sgt Herd was on board the helicopter in the course of his duties as a police officer, he was there merely as a passenger so far as the performance of the contract of carriage for reward was concerned. There is no suggestion that he was travelling on a route from one place to another which had been pre-determined by the contract with the carrier before the helicopter became airborne. The contract between the respondents and the police authority was one by which the helicopter was made available to the police authority under what was in effect a time charter. It appears that its primary function was to enable police officers to carry out police operations while the helicopter was in the air. But the terms of the order and the relevant articles of Sch 1 are so widely expressed that these features of the present case, which distinguish it from the ordinary case where a contract of carriage is entered into for the transportation of a passenger on a route which has been pre-determined, are not sufficient to prevent the application of the rules as set out in Sch 1 to the liability of the respondents to Sgt Herd's relatives for the consequences of his death.

The point which has caused me difficulty is whether the 1967 order and the relevant articles can properly be given such wide meaning, in view of the context in which the 1967 order was made and the extent of the power which was being exercised. The 1967 order was made under s 10 of the Carriage by Air Act 1961 and s 5(2) of the Carriage by Air (Supplementary Provisions) Act 1962. The 1962 Act gave force of law in the United Kingdom to the convention which was adopted at Guadalajara, Mexico on 18 September 1961 which was supplementary to the Warsaw Convention of 12 October 1929 as amended at the Hague on 28 September 1955. We are not concerned here with the 1962 Act. In the present case it is the Warsaw Convention concerning international carriage by air as amended at the Hague, to which force of law was given by the 1961 Act, which provides the relevant background. The long title to the 1961 Act states that it is an Act to give effect to that convention and to enable the rules contained in it to be applied, with or without modification, in other cases and, in particular, to non-international carriage by air. Section 10(1) of the 1961 Act provides:

'Her Majesty may by Order in Council apply the First Schedule to this Act, together with any other provisions of this Act, to carriage by air, not being carriage by air to which the Convention applies, of such descriptions as may be specified in the Order, subject to such exceptions, adaptations and modifications, if any, as may be so specified.'

In *Holmes v Bangladesh Biman Corp* [1989] 1 All ER 852, [1989] AC 1112 it was held that the 1967 order could have no wider scope and effect than was clearly authorised by the enabling power conferred by s 10(1) of the 1961 Act. The question which arose for decision in that case was whether the 1961 Act and the 1967 order were intended by Parliament to apply to an air accident in Bangladesh on an internal domestic flight which was not governed by any international convention. The language and structure of the 1967 order was wide enough to have that effect, but it was held that the power in s 10(1) had to be construed subject to the presumption that Parliament was not to be taken, by the use of general words, to legislate in the affairs of foreign nationals who did nothing to bring themselves within its jurisdiction. Lord Bridge of Harwich said ([1989] 1 All ER 852 at 855–856, [1989] AC 1112 at 1126):

'... the 1967 order can have no wider scope and effect than is duly authorised by the power conferred by s 10 of the 1961 Act to legislate by Order in Council. If that power is unlimited, the scope of its exercise by the order will be a matter to be determined on the true construction of the order.

But if on the true construction of s 10 the enabling power is itself limited, then it is axiomatic that the order cannot exceed that limit. Accordingly, it seems to me that the essential prior question to be answered, before attempting to construe the order, is whether the words in s 10, "carriage by air ... of such descriptions as may be specified", ought to be read as subject to any limitation.'

In the present case the presumption against extra-territorial legislation is not in issue, as the accident occurred in the United Kingdom when the police officer was engaged on duties within the area of his police authority. But it is plain both from the long title to the 1961 Act and from the wording of s 10 that the enabling power was given so that a modified version of the convention might be enacted to provide a set of rules governing all carriage by air not falling within the definition of 'international carriage' to which the convention applies. As Lord Bridge pointed out, there are thus now three sets of rules in the law of the United Kingdom and other British territory which govern different categories of carriage by air (see [1989] 1 All ER 852 at 855, [1989] AC 1112 at 1126). These are the Hague Rules in Sch 1 to the 1961 Act, the Warsaw rules in Sch 2 to the 1967 order and the United Kingdom rules in Sch 1 to the 1967 order.

In regard to the general character and purpose of the Warsaw and the Hague Rules, which are authorised to be applied by Order in Council to non-convention carriage by air with or without exceptions, adaptions and modifications, he said that the rules have these features in common ([1989] 1 All ER 852 at 858, [1989] AC 1112 at 1129):

'They impose liability on the carrier without proof of fault in respect of the death of or injury to passengers and damage to or loss of baggage or cargo which the carrier, however, may rebut by proving certain matters in relation to the relevant causative event. They impose limits on the amount recoverable in respect of the relevant death, injury, loss or damage. They nullify contractual provisions tending to relieve the carrier of liability or to lower the applicable limits of liability. They allow, however, recovery against the carrier of an amount in excess of the relevant limit if the claimant can prove certain matters in relation to the relevant causative event. Actions for damages pursuant to the rights given by the rules can only be brought subject to the rules and are to the exclusion of other remedies. Such actions must be brought within a time limit. Perhaps most important of all, each set of rules contains a provision to prevent avoidance of the rules by any contractual term "deciding the law to be applied". Thus, if a carrier undertakes carriage by air to which the rules apply, he cannot contract out of the rules by a choice of law clause.'

Lord Bridge then quoted from Greene LJ's judgment in *Grein v Imperial Airways Ltd* [1936] 2 All ER 1258 at 1278–1279, [1937] 1 KB 50 at 74–77, where the philosophy underlying the Warsaw Convention is described. In the course of this part of his judgment, Greene LJ said that, when by the appropriate machinery, the rules are given the force of law in the territory of a High Contracting Party they govern the contractual relations of the parties to the contract of which, to use language appropriate to the legal systems of the United Kingdom, they become statutory terms (see [1936] 2 All ER 1258 at 1277, [1937] 1 KB 50 at 74). Lord Bridge then said ([1989] 1 All ER 852 at 859–860, [1989] AC 1112 at 1131):

a   'The United Kingdom rules have the same common features as those to which I have drawn attention in the Warsaw and Hague Rules. In authorising the application of such rules, based on or adapted from the Hague Rules, to non-convention carriage by air, what categories of such carriage may Parliament have reasonably had in contemplation as the proper subject matter of United Kingdom legislation? Just as the character of

b   "international carriage" in the convention definition is determined by reference to the places of departure and destination and agreed stopping places "according to the agreement between the parties", so may the potential categories of non-convention carriage to which the United Kingdom rules might apply be similarly distinguished. It seems to me that four distinct categories fall for consideration. (1) Carriage in which the

c   places of departure and destination and any agreed stopping places are all within the United Kingdom or other British territory. (2) Non-convention carriage involving a place of departure or destination or an agreed stopping place in a foreign state and a place of departure or destination or an agreed stopping place in the United Kingdom or other British territory.

d   (3) Non-convention carriage between places of departure and destination in two foreign states with no agreed stopping place in the United Kingdom or other British territory. (4) Carriage in which the places of departure and destination and any agreed stopping places are all within the territory of a single foreign state, being either a convention or a non-convention country.'

e   I think that it is reasonably clear from these passages that what both Lord Bridge and Greene LJ had in mind when they were describing carriage by air in this context was carriage in pursuance of a contract in which, according to the agreement with the parties, there was a place of departure and a place of destination and, where appropriate, an agreed stopping place. That indeed is the

f   way in which the expression 'international carriage' is defined for the purposes of the Hague Rules in art 1(2) of Sch 1 to the 1961 Act. The references to passenger tickets and other documents of carriage in Ch II of these rules support this approach. The definition in art 1(2) of Sch 1 to the 1961 Act has been omitted from the United Kingdom rules in Sch 1 to the 1967 order, as also have the provisions of Ch II in regard to documents of carriage. But other provisions in

g   the rules which refer to a contract of carriage have been retained: see arts 30(1), 31(2) and 32. And the potential categories of non-convention carriage which Lord Bridge identified were all described by him with reference to the places of departure and destination and any agreed stopping place.

Two of these categories were appropriate subjects of United Kingdom

h   legislation, as the places were all within the United Kingdom or other British territory or involved a place of departure or destination or an agreed stopping place there as well as a place in the territory of a foreign state. Two of them were not, as the places were all in foreign states or within the territory of a single foreign state. Lord Bridge mentioned with approval the submission for the

j   respondents that, like the conventions themselves, the United Kingdom rules had as one of their primary objectives the elimination of conflict of laws problems and that such problems would be as likely to arise, if not excluded by uniform rules, from non-convention as from convention carriage (see [1989] 1 All ER 852 at 860, [1989] AC 1112 at 1132). He emphasised again the obvious desirability, in relation to carriage in category (2), as in relation to 'international carriage' within the convention definition, of uniform rules applicable by British courts for the avoidance of the kind of conflict of laws problems discussed by Greene LJ in the passage from his judgment in *Grein v Imperial Airways Ltd* [1936] 2 All ER 1258 at 1278–1279, [1937] 1 KB 50 at 74–77, which he had quoted. The concept of a contract of carriage in which the places of departure and destination and any agreed stopping place were agreed between the parties before the passenger embarked on the aircraft runs right through the whole of his discussion of the purpose and effect of these rules.

The aspects of this case which I have found most troublesome are (1) that there was here no contract between Sgt Herd and the respondents in regard to which the rules in Sch 1 of the 1967 order could be said to have become statutory terms, and (2) that the contract between the respondents and the police authority in pursuance of which he was a passenger on the helicopter did not provide for a place of departure or destination or any agreed stopping places. The hours of operation of the helicopter and the places to which it was to fly were left open, to be determined by police operational requirements. The helicopter was available to be used for whatever purposes these requirements made necessary. These might involve a journey from one place to another, or a journey in which a round trip was undertaken to provide support to police operations from the air before returning to the place of origin. A description of the categories of carriage by air by reference to the way in which passengers are normally carried by airline operators is wholly inappropriate for the kind of carriage by air which was involved in this case, where the helicopter was made available to the police authority as a means of conducting police operations from the air.

As I mentioned in *Sidhu v British Airways plc, Abnett (known as Sykes) v British Airways plc* [1997] 1 All ER 193 at 202, [1997] 2 WLR 26 at 36 under reference to the discussion of this point in *Fothergill v Monarch Airlines Ltd* [1980] 2 All ER 696, [1981] AC 251, it is now well established that a purposive approach should be taken to the interpretation of international conventions which have the force of law in this country. If the United Kingdom rules had been designed to deal exclusively with carriage performed within the United Kingdom, there might have been no need to follow this approach in the interpretation of the United Kingdom rules which were derived from the conventions. But the same rules apply also to non-convention carriage involving a place of departure or destination or an agreed stopping place in a foreign state and a place of departure or destination or an agreed stopping place in the United Kingdom or other British territory, in order to eliminate the same kind of conflict of laws problems as between these two states as those which gave rise to the conventions. Schedule 1 to the 1967 order was not made in order to give effect to any treaty obligations of the United Kingdom, but uniformity of interpretation is nevertheless important. All those who are involved in carriage by air, whether as carriers or as passengers, and their insurers should be able to assume that the same law applies no matter where the event occurs or where the forum is for the dispute: *Grein v Imperial Airways Ltd* [1936] 2 All ER 1258 at 1277–1278, [1937] 1 KB 50 at 74–75 per Greene LJ. In this situation I think that it is appropriate to have regard to the purpose and subject matter of the conventions and to decisions of foreign courts in regard to the conventions in order to resolve the issue whether the phrase 'carriage by air' in art 1 of Sch 1 to the 1967 order is wide enough to involve the circumstances in which Sgt Herd was being carried by the helicopter when it crashed and he was killed.

So far as the purpose and subject matter of the conventions is concerned, the question is whether there is anything in them which is in conflict with the

a respondent's argument that a wide construction should be given to these words in the United Kingdom rules. Having had the benefit of studying the minutes of the International Conference on Private Aeronautical Law at Warsaw from 4 to 12 October 1929 in the course of the argument in *Sidhu's* case [1997] 1 All ER 193 at 202, [1997] 2 WLR 26 at 36, I do not believe that there is any such conflict. The discussion at the Warsaw Convention was of course concerned only with

b international carriage by air. There was no need for any agreement as to carriage performed within the territory of one state, as in that situation there was not likely to be any difficulty about the law which was applicable. The whole discussion took place also in the context of what was known at that time about the uses to which aircraft could be put. It was understandable, and probably inevitable, that that discussion should have been carried on with reference to the

c practice of the airline industry at that time, by which aircraft were increasingly coming to be used as a means of transporting people and goods from one place to another under contracts of carriage with a variety of provisions about liability, limitation of liability, time limits and jurisdiction. The Warsaw Convention did not purport to deal with all matters relating to contracts of international carriage

d by air. But it is clear that what was sought to be achieved was a uniform international code which could be applied to all such contracts. One of the objects of the convention was to encourage the development of the airline industry, which it was felt might be unduly inhibited by the increasing legal complexity of conducting a business of that kind across international frontiers. The aim was to reduce the opportunity for litigation and to provide a more

e definite and equitable basis on which airline operators could negotiate rates with their insurers.

The terms of the convention seem to me to support this approach. Article 1(1) of the Warsaw Convention, which was repeated without amendment in the Hague Convention, states that it applies to 'all' international carriage of persons,

f baggage or cargo performed by aircraft for reward, and 'equally' to gratuitous carriage by aircraft performed by an air transport undertaking. There are some express exclusions, such as in respect of domestic carriage in view of the definition of international carriage in art 1(2) and in respect of mail and postal packages in art 2(2)—neither of which apply to the rules in Sch 1 to the 1967 order. But the starting point is the generality of effect indicated by the use of the

g word 'all'. The nationality or place of business of the carrier is irrelevant, as all carriers who undertake international carriage, as defined in art 1(2), of passengers, baggage or cargo by aircraft are bound by the convention. There is nothing in the convention to indicate that the purpose for which the passenger, baggage or cargo was on the aircraft has any bearing on the question whether the

h convention applies.

In my opinion the convention agreed at Warsaw, as amended at The Hague, was intended to be, and is, capable of accommodating changes in the practice of airlines and aircraft operators with regard to the purposes of which aircraft are used to carry people and goods, and in the contractual arrangements in

j pursuance of which people and goods are carried by air for reward. For this reason I think that it is proper to read Lord Bridge's discussion in *Holmes v Bangladesh Biman Corp* [1989] 1 All ER 852, [1989] AC 1112 and Greene LJ's judgment in *Grein v Imperial Airways Ltd* [1936] 2 All ER 1258, [1937] 1 KB 50 from which he quoted as having been framed with reference to the particular subject matter with which they were dealing at the time. In each of these cases the subject matter was carriage by air of the ordinary kind in pursuance of a contract between the airline and the passenger by which places of departure and destination had been agreed. It seems to me, that when regard is had to the desire to lay down a uniform international code which would achieve equity between the carrier and the user of his services, there is no necessary conflict between what they said in these cases and the wider interpretation of the phrase 'carriage by air' for which the respondents contend in this case.

As for decisions in the foreign courts, we were referred to several French cases which appeared to indicate that the view has been taken consistently in the French courts that it is necessary to consider the purpose for which the passenger is being carried on the aircraft, and that where this is to go to work either on or from the aircraft while it is airborne this is not for the purpose of transport within the meaning of the convention. In *Sté Mutuelle d'Assurance Aériennes v Gauvain* (1967) 21 RFDA 436, it was held by the Cour de Cassation that the law of 2 March 1957 by which the rules of the Warsaw Convention were applied to domestic air transport within France did not apply to regulate the liability of the air carrier for the death of a student pilot while undergoing a flying lesson. In *Aéro-Club de l'Aisne v Klopotowska* (1970) 24 RFDA 195 the accident occurred during a test flight, which did not have the purpose of carrying people or goods from one point to another according to the definition of air transport in art 113 of the Civil Aviation Code, so it was held by the Cour de Cassation that the law of 2 March 1957 did not apply. In *Ortet v Georges* (1976) 30 RFDA 490 the aircraft had been leased for the taking of aerial photographs and it was held by the Cour d'Appel de Paris that the flight did not have the character of air transport. The same approach was taken in *Barnes v Service Aérien Français* (1993) 47 RFDA 343, where a helicopter was being used to airlift a man who had suffered a skiing accident to hospital and the Cour d'Appel de Paris held that the provisions of the Warsaw Convention as applied by Law 321.3 of the Civil Aviation Code did not apply.

These decisions all support the argument which Mr Jones presented with great skill on behalf of the appellants that Sgt Herd was on board the helicopter not in pursuance of a contract of carriage but in pursuance of his duties as a police officer. But we were shown a commentary on the decision in *Aéro-Club de l'Aisne v Klopotowska* which suggests that opinion in France was divided on this point, and that some decisions in the French courts had taken the view that the law of 2 March 1957 was of general application to all cases where there is air transport. In any event the fact that the jurisprudence in one country has adopted an interpretation of the convention which supports Mr Jones's argument is not in itself a compelling reason for holding that we should follow the same approach in our interpretation of art 1 of Sch 1 to the 1967 order. As in *Sidhu's* case [1997] 1 All ER 193 at 211, [1997] 2 WLR 26 at 45, where it was observed that the United States from which a number of decisions were cited in that case was only one jurisdiction amongst many, the same point can be made about cases cited from the French courts. It cannot be assumed that the view which appears to have been formed in France is the same as that which would be taken in other countries which are party to the conventions.

The only other jurisdictions from which decisions were cited to us were Canada and the United States. In the Canadian case of *Johnson Estate v Pischke* (1989) 1 S & B Av R 337 it was held that a trainee pilot who had been at the controls of an aircraft engaged on an international flight was not a passenger for the purposes of the Warsaw Convention. That case however was concerned with the meaning to be given to the word 'passenger,' not with the question what was meant by 'carriage by air' for the purposes of the convention. Halvorson J

a said (at 342) that he had drawn support for his conclusion from the decision in *Sté Mutuelle d'Assurance Aériennes v Gauvain* (1967) 21 RFDA 436, but he made it clear that he preferred to base his decision on the meaning of 'passenger' and not on the question whether the flight was the type of flight which was governed by the convention. None of the United States cases, all of which were decisions in the Federal Courts on appeal except *Block v Cie Nationale Air France* (1967) 386 F 2d
b 323, was concerned with that issue. In *Re Mexico City Aircrash* (1983) 17 Avi 18,387, in which the person killed was a flight attendant who although employed by the airline was not working on the flight as she was travelling from her home to Mexico City where she was to work as a flight attendant on another flight, and *Sulewski v Federal Express* (1991) 23 Avi 17,685, in which the person killed was an aircraft mechanic who had been assigned to the flight by the airline, the question
c was whether these persons were on the aircraft at the time of the accident as passengers. *Mertens v Flying Tiger Line Inc* (1965) 341 F 2d 851 and *Warren v Flying Tiger Line* (1965) 352 F 2d 494 were both concerned with the requirement for a ticket to be provided to the passenger before boarding the aircraft for an international flight subject to the convention.

d *Block v Cie Nationale Air France* (1967) 386 F 2d 323 was concerned with the question whether the Warsaw Convention applied to a voyage charter by which an aircraft had been chartered to carry passengers on an international flight. The charter had been negotiated by a third party on behalf of the passengers. The case is of interest because of the opinion which was expressed by Judge Wisdom (at 330) that the charter flight could not come within art 1(2) of the convention if the
e places of departure, stopping places and destination of the flight were not stated in the charter and that the application of the convention is premised upon a contract of carriage that arises from the relationship between a carrier and the passengers. He said (at 334) that for a flight to come within the scope of the Warsaw Convention the carrier must have agreed to carry the passenger and that
f both the carrier and the passenger must have consented to the particular route. Here again these observations at first sight would seem to support Mr Jones's argument. But I have not found anything in the discussion of that case to indicate that Judge Wisdom had in mind the question whether a flight of the kind which was being undertaken in this case was included within 'carriage by air' within the meaning of that phrase as used in the convention.
g On balance therefore, while I have not found the decision in this case to be an easy one, I have come to the conclusion that we are not compelled by the conventions which form the background to the 1967 order or by the decisions in the foreign courts to which we were referred to depart from the plain meaning of the words used in Sch 1 to the 1967 order. Although this decision may seem harsh
h in the present case, it should not be forgotten that one of the advantages of excluding the rules of the common law is that the United Kingdom rules are designed to impose liability on the carrier without proof of fault in respect of the death of or injury to passengers and to nullify contractual provisions the effect of which would be to relieve the carrier of liability or to restrict his liability in
j amount. These are significant advantages, as it may be very difficult to prove where fault lies when an aircraft has been destroyed in an air crash and all those who were on board the aircraft have lost their lives, and in view of the opportunities which would otherwise be available to those who provide carriage by air to exclude or restrict their liability. In *M'Kay v Scottish Airways Ltd* 1948 SC 254 at 263 the Lord President (Cooper) remarked on the amazing width of the conditions and the effort which had evidently been made to create a leonine

bargain under which the passenger took all the risks and the carrier accepted no
obligations. In that case a mother's claim for damages for her son's death was
held to have been excluded by the conditions printed on the ticket which had
been issued to the son as a fare-paying passenger. A bargain of that kind would
now be vulnerable to the provisions of the Unfair Contract Terms Act 1977, but
the rules in Sch 1 to the 1967 order provide greater certainty so that both parties
to the arrangement may now know where they stand and can make their own
arrangements with their insurers accordingly.

For these reasons and for the reasons given by my noble and learned friend
Lord Mackay of Clashfern LC, I, also, agree that this appeal must be dismissed.

I should like to add some observations with regard to the motions which were
made to us on the matter of expenses. This appeal has been brought by Mrs Herd
in her capacity not as an individual, although she is a pursuer in that capacity in
the Court of Session, but only as guardian of her four children and by Mrs Rivera,
who is the mother of Sgt Herd. The appellants had the benefit of civil legal aid
for the purpose of the proceedings in your Lordships' House under s 14 of the
Legal Aid (Scotland) Act 1986 and reg 4 of the Civil Legal Aid (Scotland)
Regulations 1987, SI 1987/381. As each of them was given the benefit of legal aid
on a nil contribution, it is appropriate that their liability under the award of
expenses which must follow from the respondents' success in this appeal should
be modified to nil under s 18(2) of the 1986 Act.

Mr Keen then asked us to make an order under s 19 of the 1986 Act for the
payment out of the Scottish legal aid fund of the expenses which had been
incurred by the respondents in this appeal. Mr Jones pointed out in his reply that
s 19(1) of the 1986 Act, as amended by para 8 of Sch 4 to the Legal Aid Act 1988,
provides that such an award may only be made in any proceedings which are
'finally decided' in favour of an unassisted party. He submitted that a decision in
this appeal would not finally determine the proceedings in this case, as it must
now be returned to the Court of Session for a proof to be heard on other matters
which are still in dispute.

In *Moss v Penman (No 2)* 1994 SLT 602 the pursuer in a sheriff court appeal
successfully resisted an appeal to the Inner House by the defender on a question
of relevancy. It was held that on a proper construction of the provisions of s 19
of the 1986 Act it was for the court in which the proceedings were 'finally
determined' to deal with this matter, and that the motion which was made at the
stage of the disposal of that appeal was premature. At first sight that decision may
be thought to support Mr Jones' submission that Mr Keen's motion for an order
under s 19 to be made at this stage was premature. But in *Megarity v Law Society,
Gayway Linings Ltd v Law Society* [1981] 1 All ER 641, [1982] AC 81 it was held that
on the true construction of the Legal Aid Act 1974 all proceedings on appeal to an
appellate court in any action, cause or matter were to be treated as separate
proceedings from the proceedings in the same action in the court of first instance
from which the appeal was brought, and that an interlocutory appeal to the Court
of Appeal constituted separate proceedings for the purposes of s 13 of that Act.
Lord Diplock pointed out that, where there was an appeal to an appellate court,
the only court that could make an order under s 13(1) was the appellate court, as
s 13(3) plainly contemplated that, in the event of an appeal, an order relating to
the unassisted party's costs at first instance might be made by the appellate court
by which the proceedings were finally decided: see [1981] 1 All ER 641 at 648,
[1982] AC 81 at 107; see also *Shiloh Spinners Ltd v Harding (No 2)* [1973] 1 All ER
966, [1973] 1 WLR 518. Section 13(1) of the 1974 Act was in similar terms to

a   s 19(1) of the Scottish 1986 Act as amended by the Legal Aid Act 1988, Sch 4, para 8, and the corresponding subsection in the 1986 Act to s 13(3) of the 1974 Act is s 19(3).

    Without wishing to cast doubt on the soundness of the decision in *Moss v Penman (No 2)*, except to point out that the Inner House was not referred to *Megarity v D J Ryan & Sons Ltd (No 2)* or *Shiloh Spinners Ltd v Harding (No 2)* in the *b*   course of the discussion in that case, I consider that the matter is resolved, so far as your Lordships' House is concerned, by what was decided in *Megarity's* case. The appellants were given legal aid for the purpose of this appeal, which has now been finally determined, and there is no appeal from a decision in your Lordships' House. For these reasons this is the appropriate stage for an order under s 19 to be made. I consider that, subject to an opportunity being given to the Scottish *c*   legal aid board to make representations to the contrary, it would be just and equitable that such an order be made in this case.

    LORD CLYDE. My Lords, I have had the advantage of reading in draft the speech of my noble and learned friend Lord Mackay of Clashfern LC. For the *d*   reasons he has given, I, too, would dismiss this appeal.

Appeal dismissed.

Celia Fox   Barrister.

R v Secretary of State for the Home Department, ex parte Rahman

a

COURT OF APPEAL, CIVIL DIVISION

STAUGHTON, HOBHOUSE AND HUTCHISON LJJ

b

5 NOVEMBER, 11 DECEMBER 1996

Immigration – Illegal entrant – Detention pending deportation – Habeas corpus – Evidence – Hearsay – Whether court entitled to take into account hearsay evidence relied on by Secretary of State on application for habeas corpus.

c

In 1989 the appellant came to the United Kingdom from Bangladesh, having obtained a certificate of entitlement to the right of abode in order to join his father, S, who was a British citizen by registration. Thereafter, two denunciatory letters asserting that he was not S's son led entry clearance officers in Bangladesh to make inquiries through interpreters of the inhabitants of two local villages as to the appellant's true name and paternity. The villagers' responses were translated and, together with an interview of the appellant, they satisfied the Secretary of State that the appellant was not S's son and that he had obtained the certificate of entitlement by deception. The appellant was served with notice that he was an illegal entrant and detained under para 16 of Sch 2 to the Immigration Act 1971 pending his deportation. The appellant applied for a writ of habeas corpus, contending that as the villagers' evidence was hearsay and so inadmissible, the court could not take it into account in determining whether the Secretary of State had proved that he was an illegal entrant. The judge held that he could take into account all the material on which the Secretary of State had relied, even if it was hearsay, and that that material was sufficient to establish that the appellant was an illegal entrant. The appellant appealed to the Court of Appeal.

d

e

f

Held – In determining whether a person was an illegal entrant on an application for habeas corpus, the court could take into account all the material on which the Secretary of State had legitimately relied in reaching his decision and was not confined to considering only such evidence as was presented in strictly admissible form. The court could therefore take into account hearsay evidence, as the Secretary of State was entitled to do, while making the appropriate allowance for that fact in the weight which it attached to that evidence. It followed that the judge had been right to take into account the villagers' evidence. Moreover (Hutchison LJ dissenting), having regard to all the available material, including the villagers' evidence, the fact that the appellant was not S's son and so had obtained the certificate of entitlement by deception had been proved to the requisite standard. Accordingly, the appeal would be dismissed (see p 799 *g*, p 802 *j*, p 803 *d* to *g*, p 807 *e* to *g*, p 814 *f*, p 815 *a* to *d*, p 817 *b g h*, p 819 *j*, p 821 *f g* and p 822 *a b*, post).

g

h

j

Khawaja v Secretary of State for the Home Dept [1983] 1 All ER 765 applied.

R v Brixton Prison Governor, ex p Ahson [1969] 2 All ER 347 not followed.

Decision of Collins J [1996] 4 All ER 945 affirmed.

Notes

a For entitlement to apply for writ of habeas corpus ad subjiciendum, see 1(1) *Halsbury's Laws* (4th edn reissue) para 245.

For meaning of hearsay, circumstances in which admissible and weight to be attached to it, see 17 *Halsbury's Laws* (4th edn) paras 11, 53, 55.

For illegal entry, see 4(2) *Halsbury's Laws* (4th edn reissue) para 118.

b For the Immigration Act 1971, Sch 2, para 16, see 31 *Halsbury's Statutes* (4th edn) (1994 reissue) 109.

Cases referred to in judgments

Associated Provincial Picture Houses Ltd v Wednesbury Corp [1947] 2 All ER 680,
c   [1948] 1 KB 223, CA.

Bater v Bater [1950] 2 All ER 458, [1951] P 35, CA.

Ejaz v Secretary of State for Home Affairs [1978] CA Transcript 777.

Eshugbayi Eleko v Officer administering the Government of Nigeria [1931] AC 662,
    [1931] All ER Rep 44, PC.

d *Guerin, Re* (1888) 60 LT 538, DC.

Khawaja v Secretary of State for the Home Dept [1983] 1 All ER 765, [1984] AC 74,
    [1983] 2 WLR 321, HL.

R v Brixton Prison Governor, ex p Ahson [1969] 2 All ER 347, [1969] 2 QB 222, [1969]
    2 WLR 618, DC.

e *R v Secretary of State for the Home Dept, ex p Ahmad* [1983] CA Transcript 234.

R v Secretary of State for the Home Dept, ex p Miah [1990] 2 All ER 523, [1990] 1 WLR
    806, CA.

R v Secretary of State for the Home Dept, ex p Patel [1986] Imm AR 515, CA.

R v Secretary of State for the Home Dept, ex p Yasmeen (11 February 1982,
f   unreported), DC.

R v Secretary of State for the Home Office, ex p Muse [1992] Imm AR 282.

Zamir v Secretary of State for the Home Dept [1980] 2 All ER 768, [1980] AC 930,
    [1980] 3 WLR 249, HL.

Cases also cited or referred to in skeleton arguments

g *Carltona Ltd v Comrs of Works* [1943] 2 All ER 560, CA.

R v Oldham Justices, ex p Cawley [1996] 1 All ER 464, [1997] QB 1, DC.

R v Secretary of State for the Home Dept, ex p Yasin [1996] Imm AR 62.

h Appeal

By notice dated 22 July 1996 the appellant, Saidur Rahman, appealed from the decision of Collins J ([1996] 4 All ER 945) made on 26 June 1996, whereby he dismissed the appellant's application for a writ of habeas corpus ad subjiciendum seeking his release from Bedford Prison where he had been detained as an illegal entrant under para 16 of Sch 2 to the Immigration Act 1971. The facts are set out
j in the judgment of Hutchison LJ.

Michael Shrimpton (instructed by *Saf Awan*, Luton) for the appellant.
Mark Shaw (instructed by the *Treasury Solicitor*) for the Secretary of State.

Cur adv vult

11 December 1996. The following judgments were delivered.

HUTCHISON LJ (giving the first judgment at the invitation of Staughton LJ). This is an appeal from the judgment of Collins J ([1996] 4 All ER 945) given on 26 June 1996 refusing leave for the issue of a writ of habeas corpus. The appellant had sought to challenge the legality of his detention, as an illegal entrant, pursuant to para 16 of Sch 2 to the Immigration Act 1971. The two issues before the judge were: (1) whether certain evidence relied on by the Secretary of State was admissible; and (2) whether, even if that evidence was admissible, the totality of the evidence before the court was sufficient to satisfy the onus of proof of deception to the required standard in accordance with the test laid down by the House of Lords in *Khawaja v Secretary of State for the Home Dept* [1983] 1 All ER 765, [1984] AC 74.

The judge held in favour of the Secretary of State on both issues and Mr Shrimpton for the appellant contends that he was wrong to do so.

I shall try to summarise the facts as briefly as possible.

The appellant claims to be the son of Abdus Somed and his wife, Momjan Bibi, and to have been born into their family in Bangladesh on 29 July 1967. Abdus Somad, by virtue of his registration in 1960 as a citizen of the United Kingdom and Colonies, enjoyed British citizenship and, in 1989, was living in the United Kingdom. On 29 May 1989 the appellant, who had expressed the wish to join his alleged parents, was interviewed by an entry clearance officer at the British High Commission in Dhaka and was granted a certificate of entitlement to the right of abode in the United Kingdom, where he accordingly arrived in 1989. He applied for and on 20 November 1990 obtained a British passport.

In January 1991 the appellant returned to Bangladesh. On 7 April 1991 his wife, Rina Akhter (whom he had married on 18 February 1988), and a boy named Rone Ahmed whom she represented to be the child of herself and the appellant, applied for a certificate of entitlement to join the appellant in the United Kingdom. On 4 November Rina Akhter gave birth to a boy, Jone Ahmed, and he was added to the application.

The appellant returned to the United Kingdom on 22 July 1991, no doubt anticipating that he would soon be followed by Rina and the two boys. However, while her application was still pending the Secretary of State, in October 1991, received a denunciatory letter claiming that the boy Rone was not the appellant's and Rina's son but the son of Rina's sister and that the appellant was not whom he claimed to be but a man named Mohammed Surab Ali Talukder. A second denunciatory letter was received in April 1992. It, too, asserted that the appellant was not the son of Abdus Somed.

Not surprisingly, on receipt of the first letter inquiries were instituted and, though it will be necessary to return to the details, the outcome of those inquiries can be said to be as follows.

(a) The appellant and Rina, having initially maintained their position that Rone was their son, eventually (anticipating the results of DNA tests that had been undertaken) conceded that he was not and that he was indeed their nephew.

(b) The Secretary of State, through entry clearance officers in Bangladesh, instituted inquiries about the appellant in two villages. The first, Holdarpur, was Abdus Somad's village where the appellant claimed to have been born and brought up. The second (where the inquiry took place after the commencement of these proceedings), was Nittarchok, the village of a man called Suraj Ali Talukder, said in the letters to be the appellant's true father. The approach a adopted was to show villagers photographs of the appellant and see whether and what they knew about him. The questioning was effected through interpreters, on whom the entry clearance officers (who did not speak the dialect of the villagers) were dependent. The result of the inquiries (I am not at present dealing with the question of admissibility) very strongly supported the allegations in the letters, in that virtually everyone interviewed in Holdapur asserted that the man

b in the photograph was not the son of Abdus Somed, whom they knew; and virtually everyone interviewed in Nittarchok recognised the photograph as that of Surab Ali son of Suraj Ali. Moreover, and of particular importance, there was evidence that Abdus Somed and Rina, both of whom were seen in Holdapur, admitted that the appellant was not Abdus Somed's son. It is common ground that this evidence, if presented in an admissible form and uncontradicted, is such

c as could justify the conclusion that deception had been established to the requisite high standard. It is also common ground that, unless at least some of the village visits evidence is taken into account, there is not sufficient evidence to support that conclusion.

Before considering the two issues in detail I should complete my account of the

d history by relating further events leading up to this appeal.

On learning of the results of the Holdarpur visit, the Immigration Department arranged for the appellant to be interviewed by an immigration officer on 3 August 1993 and, on concluding that he was an illegal entrant, that officer served the relevant notice on him authorising his detention pending his removal from the United Kingdom. On 11 August the appellant applied for leave for judicial

e review of that decision and for a writ of habeas corpus. On 16 August Clarke J, refusing bail, gave certain directions and it appears to have been accepted that the matter should proceed as an application for habeas corpus. Subsequently the appellant was released on bail pending the outcome of his application. For whatever reason, the hearing before Collins J did not take place until June 1996.

f By then of course the second village visit had taken place and those advising the appellant had obtained evidence on which he relied to refute that put forward by the Secretary of State.

The first issue

g The question to which the first issue gives rise can be formulated in this way. When a court is obliged to inquire into the truth of a question of fact on which an administrative decision has been based, is it entitled to look at all the material on which the decision-maker legitimately relied (as well of course as looking at any additional material placed before it) or is it confined to considering such evidence as is presented in strictly admissible form?

h Collins J admitted evidence of the village visits and, in particular, of the interviews, which was tendered in a manner familiar in judicial review proceedings—namely by means of affidavits from immigration officers including affidavits from entry clearance officers who were present at the visits. This evidence may be summarised as follows.

j (1) Mr Leighton, an officer in the Immigration and Nationality Department with responsibility for cases involving illegal entrants, deposed to the facts and exhibited documents in reliance on Home Office files and information provided by other officials. In the present context it is necessary to focus on his evidence about the first village visit—the second had not taken place when he swore his affidavits. What Mr Leighton did was to exhibit the report of the entry clearance officer about the visit and, in the body of his affidavit, summarise its effect. The report records that the visit occurred on 15 February 1993 and that two entry clearance officers were present—Mr Casserly with an interpreter named Navir and Miss Davies with an interpreter named Fozli. It records that Mr Casserly conducted the 'compound inquiry' (which included the interviews with Abdus Somed and Rina Akhter) and Miss Davies the 'walkabout inquiry', in which she interviewed four villagers. Between them, and apart from Abdus Somed and Rina Akhter, they recorded interviews, in question and answer form, with eleven villagers. The precise terms of those questions and answers are not material in the present context—their general effect has already been stated.

(2) There was also an affidavit from Mr Casserly, who said that he was an entry clearance officer at Dhaka between November 1988 and July 1993; that he and Miss Davies made the visit to Holdarpur; and that the report was the report that he and Miss Davies had compiled. It is clear that he had very considerable experience in conducting such visits, which he explained are often the only means of testing a claimed identity or relationship. He described how such visits are made unannounced, with interpreters, and conducted as this one was. He referred to taped records of the interviews, from which he wrote up his report the same evening, after a day in which a number of such visits had been carried out. In this connection we were told by Mr Shaw—and it is not I think disputed—that the entry clearance officer on such occasions uses his tape recorder not to record what the villager or the interpreter say, but by dictating into it, as an aide-mémoire, what he heard—in other words using it in lieu of a notebook.

(3) As to Nittarchok, there was an affidavit from another immigration officer, Mr Clements, who had by then taken over from Mr Leighton, in which Mr Clements dealt with this visit in a manner similar to that in which Mr Leighton had dealt with the other. He produced the report of the visiting entry clearance officer, Mr Simpson. He said that, in this case, he had listened to the tape dictated by Mr Simpson during the visit and that it was, in all essentials, accurate.

(4) Mr Simpson himself swore an affidavit in June 1996, describing how he went to Nittarchok with an interpreter (Fozli) on 1 December 1993. He said that he remembered the visit because he was asked to make a special trip as a matter of importance. He verified his reports—consisting as they did of the verbatim (present tense) transcript of the tape and a written up version.

Mr Shrimpton's argument, before the judge and in this court, was that all of this evidence was inadmissible, because it was hearsay—or, as the judge said, double hearsay because of the interposition of the interpreters (see [1996] 4 All ER 945 at 947). It would therefore, Mr Shrimpton argued, be inadmissible in legal proceedings in this country and was similarly inadmissible on the factual issue which, in accordance with the principles derived from *Khawaja's* case, the judge had to determine. Mr Shrimpton's argument is not—as at one time I understood it to be—that there are different rules as to admissibility depending on whether the challenge is by way of judicial review or habeas corpus. On the contrary, his contention is that the distinction lies in the difference between a challenge on conventional *Wednesbury* grounds (see *Associated Provincial Picture Houses Ltd v Wednesbury Corp* [1947] 2 All ER 680, [1948] 1 KB 223)—where he concedes hearsay evidence is readily admitted—and a challenge, as in illegal entry cases, which involves the court's satisfying itself as to a precedent fact. Thus, he argues, since in any illegal entry case it is for the Secretary of State to prove to the satisfaction of the court to the relevant high degree of probability that the facts relied on as justifying the immigration officer's conclusion are true, that can only be done by admissible evidence, and it matters not whether the claim is for a judicial review or habeas corpus. I emphasise this submission because there are passages in the judgment of Collins J which strongly suggest that he understood that the argument advanced before him depended largely on a suggested distinction between a challenge mounted by way of judicial review and one seeking a writ of habeas corpus.

Counsel began by referring to a passage in the judgment of Lord Atkin in b *Eshugbayi Eleko v Officer administering the Government of Nigeria* [1931] AC 662 at 670, [1931] All ER Rep 44 at 49:

c 'In accordance with British jurisprudence no member of the executive can interfere with the liberty or property of a British subject except on the condition that he can support the legality of his action before a court of justice. And it is the tradition of British justice that judges should not shrink from deciding such issues in the face of the executive. The analogy of the powers of the English Home Secretary to deport aliens was invoked in this case. The analogy seems very close. Their Lordships entertain no doubt that under the legislation in question, if the Home Secretary deported a British d subject in the belief that he was an alien, the subject would have the right to question the validity of any detention under such order by proceedings in habeas corpus, and that it would be the duty of the Courts to investigate the issue of alien or not.'

e This is a passage on which reliance was placed by the House of Lords in *Khawaja's* case, and it does not seem to me that it assists the appellant, since it does not touch upon the issue in the present case. It is, in my judgment, primarily to *Khawaja's* case that we must look for guidance as to that issue. Before turning to that case, however, I shall mention some of the other authorities on which Mr Shrimpton relies.

The first is the decision of the Divisional Court in *R v Brixton Prison Governor,* f *ex p Ahson* [1969] 2 All ER 347, [1969] 2 QB 222. There, the critical issue was whether the applicants had landed clandestinely less than 24 hours before—as the law then stood they could only be refused admission or removed if that were so. Reliance was placed on the inference which it was suggested could be drawn from the circumstances in which they were apprehended—wandering on a sunny g morning with wet shoes and trousers, some with sand on them. However, the Home Office also sought to rely on admissions made by one of the men, who was not before the court, that they had indeed all entered within the previous 24 hours. Objection was taken to the admissibility of his statements and Mr Shrimpton adopted the argument advanced by Mr Quintin Hogg QC that they h were hearsay and should not be admitted, since the individual in question had not sworn an affidavit. He adopted as his own Mr Hogg's argument that: 'Once the court has embarked on an inquiry it is under an obligation to discover the truth in applying the ordinary presumptions and rules of evidence.' (See [1969] 2 QB 222 at 225.)

Moreover, counsel submitted, the court, by a majority, held that the statement j was inadmissible. Collins J did not accept this, since in his view, while it was clear that Ashworth J regarded the statements in question to be inadmissible and Blain J regarded the objection as going only to weight, Lord Parker CJ did not make it clear whether his refusal to have regard to it was based on inadmissibility or weight. What Lord Parker CJ said was ([1969] 2 All ER 347 at 350–351, [1969] 2 QB 222 at 230):

'Further, according to the police, the Indian to whom I referred admitted that he had been with the other 11 Pakistanis, and that they had all landed that morning ... However, it is only right to say that the evidence in regard to that is pure hearsay, because the Indian concerned has not sworn an affidavit and has not given evidence before this court, and accordingly I disregard anything which it is said that he, the Indian, said.'

Bearing in mind that the evidence had been admitted de bene esse, and that there had been advanced a clear challenge to admissibility based on its being hearsay, I understand Lord Parker CJ to have based his decision on its inadmissibility, and I therefore accept that this is an example of a case where, on an application for habeas corpus where the issue was illegal entry, hearsay evidence was excluded. I do not regard the unreported decision of this court in *Ejaz v Secretary of State for Home Affairs* [1978] CA Transcript 777 as an authority the other way. That was a habeas corpus case decided, of course, before *Khawaja's* case had established the principle already referred to. The court was therefore considering whether, on such material as he was entitled to have regard to, the Secretary of State's decision that Mr Ejaz was an illegal entrant was one which could be shown to be erroneous on conventional *Wednesbury* grounds. The point taken for the appellant was that the Secretary of State himself was entitled to have regard only to evidence which would be admissible in a court of law, and this court decisively rejected that contention. Nothing was said which to my mind bears on the question whether, now that it is appreciated that the court's obligation is to decide whether the Secretary of State's decision was right, we are entitled to have regard to material properly before him which would not be admissible in evidence.

However, while in my view *Ex p Ahson* provides some support for Mr Shrimpton's argument (and *Ejaz's* case is not inconsistent with that argument) I cannot regard the former decision, which is not binding on this court, as a significant authority on the issue I am considering, particularly in the light of passages to which I have yet to refer in the speeches in *Khawaja's* case.

Mr Shrimpton also relied on *Re Guerin* (1888) 60 LT 538. This case, he argues, shows that there is and remains a right to trial by jury of an issue of fact arising in habeas corpus proceedings and submits that it was not to be imagined that on such a trial the court would countenance the admission of hearsay evidence. Disregarding for a moment Collins J's pertinent observation that an application for jury trial in such a case in England would, in 1996, fall upon singularly stony ground, it seems to me that if, for whatever reason, it is proper as a matter of principle to have regard to hearsay evidence, there is no reason why it should not be received in a jury trial and evaluated, as to weight, by the jury.

While reference was made, both by Mr Shrimpton and Mr Shaw for the respondent, to various other authorities, I do not consider that (*Khawaja's* case apart) they are of assistance. There is, it seems to me, no doubt that:

(1) The Secretary of State and the immigration officers through whom he acts are entitled to have regard to reports and other sources of information available to them in order to form conclusions on which they base their decisions—Mr Shrimpton does not suggest the contrary, and any number of authorities could be cited to establish as much.

(2) In cases where a decision to detain a person as an illegal entrant is challenged, whether in proceedings for judicial review or habeas corpus or both, it is for the Secretary of State to prove to an appropriately high degree of probability, that the person concerned is an illegal entrant.

(3) If it be correct that in such cases the court is precluded from taking into account material that the Secretary of State legitimately had regard to in reaching his decision, a number of consequences would follow. The court would often be deciding the question on the basis of material wholly different from and much less persuasive than that on which the Secretary of State had relied; the applicant also would be prevented from adducing hearsay evidence; the excluded evidence might, nevertheless, be very cogent; and the practical result would be either that there was a strong incentive to persons who were illegal entrants to mount a challenge to prima facie perfectly proper decisions or that the Secretary of State would be forced to require, before making his decision, that the material on which he relied satisfied all the strict requirements of admissibility in a court of law. Mr Shrimpton would say that such consequences are far from being undesirable, would impose a salutary discipline on the Secretary of State's approach to such important issues, and reflect the law as, at least in respect of habeas corpus applications, it is and always has been.

It is my view, as it was the view of Collins J and as Mr Shaw for the Secretary of State submits, that the answer to the question posed by this first issue is to be found in the speeches of their Lordships in *Khawaja*'s case. I shall make reference to various passages in those speeches, but before doing so I can anticipate my conclusions as to their effect by saying that I am in entire agreement with the way in which Collins J put the matter. Having acknowledged that habeas corpus had been and remained an important weapon in the hands of the court against attempts to restrict the liberty of the individual in an unauthorised fashion, he continued ([1996] 4 All ER 945 at 952):

'However in reality, in my judgment, as Lord Scarman indicated, one has to look at the context in which the remedy has been sought. Here the context is a decision of the Secretary of State that the individual in question was an illegal entrant. That is an administrative decision which he has to form by virtue of the responsibilities placed upon him by the Immigration Act 1971. If that decision is challenged, the court has to decide for itself on looking at the material which was available to the Secretary of State or which is available to the court if there is further material before the court ... Of course, it is a matter for the Secretary of State to decide how he chooses to present that material. If he chooses to present it in such a way as is hearsay or hearsay upon hearsay then he runs the risk that the court will attach that much less weight to it.'

As Collins J pointed out, the facts of the other case that was decided at the same time as *Khawaja* (that of *Khera v Secretary of State for the Home Dept*) included material in an affidavit by an immigration officer, that Khera had made to a medical officer who examined him an untrue statement to the effect that he was unmarried—a crucial matter affecting his entitlement to enter. There was no evidence before the court from the medical officer or from anyone who had been present at the examination. Yet none of their Lordships questioned the admissibility of this evidence. While it has to be recognised that apparently no submission was made that the evidence was inadmissible, that does not deprive the passages I am about to cite of authority or, at the very least, of the strongest persuasive effect.

I begin by citing a lengthy passage from the speech of Lord Wilberforce. He had pointed out that such cases involved, first, a determination by the authorities that the person in question *was* an illegal entrant and, secondly, a discretionary decision by the Secretary of State to remove him and meanwhile to detain him,

and that the nature of review by the courts of the first stage required different
formulation from that of the second. He continued ([1983] 1 All ER 765 at 774–   *a*
775, [1984] AC 74 at 100–101):

> 'It is, I think, helpful to test the above analysis by considering what actually
> happens in "illegal entrant" cases. A person is found in this country in
> circumstances which give rise to doubt whether he is entitled to be here or   *b*
> not; often suspicions are provoked by an application made by him to bring
> in his family. So investigations are made by the Home Office, under powers
> which it undoubtedly has under the 1971 Act (s 4 and Sch 2, paras 2 and 3).
> Inquiry is made, of him and other witnesses, when and how he came to the
> United Kingdom, what documents he had, what leave, if any, to enter was
> given. Further inquiry may have to be made in his country of origin: often   *c*
> this is done through the High Commission there and through the entry
> clearance officer from whom he may have obtained an initial clearance.
> Sometimes very extensive inquiries have to be made. In *R v Secretary of State
> for the Home Dept, ex p Yasmeen* (11 February 1982, unreported), the officer
> made a visit to the village where it was said that the applicant had married,
> taking photographs of her and her alleged husband, or fiancé. These he   *d*
> showed to a group of four or five women, he spoke to other women and then
> to a group of eight to ten people. He interviewed the fiancé. He sent a report
> to the Home office. On this an immigration officer interviewed the applicant
> and put to her the report of the entry clearance officer. That officer
> concluded that in spite of her denials, the applicant was married. The whole   *e*
> case was then reviewed by an officer of the Home Office who took the view
> that she was an illegal entrant, for reasons which he stated. The point is, and
> I tried to make this in *Zamir v Secretary of State for the Home Dept* ([1980] 2 All
> ER 768, [1980] AC 930), that the conclusion that a person is an illegal entrant
> is a conclusion of fact reached by immigration authorities upon the basis of
> investigations and interviews which they have power to conduct, including   *f*
> interviews of the person concerned, of an extensive character, often abroad,
> and of documents whose authenticity has to be verified by inquiries. Now
> there is no doubt that the courts have jurisdiction to review the facts on
> which the Home Office's conclusion was reached; there is no doubt that
> procedural means exist, whether under the head of habeas corpus or of   *g*
> judicial review, for findings of fact to be made, by the use of affidavit
> evidence or cross-examination upon them or oral evidence. There is no
> doubt that, questions of liberty and allegations of deception being involved,
> the court both can and should review the facts with care. The sole question
> is as to the nature of this review. How far can, or should, the court find the   *h*
> facts for itself, how far should it accept, or consider itself bound to accept, or
> entitled to accept, the findings of the administrative authorities? On
> principle one would expect that, on the one hand, the court, exercising
> powers of review, would not act as a court of appeal or attempt to try or retry
> the issue. On the other hand, since the critical conclusion of fact is one
> reached by an administrative authority (as opposed to a judicial body) the   *j*
> court would think it proper to review it in order to see whether it was
> properly reached, not only as a matter of procedure, but also in substance
> and in law.'

To my mind that passage is entirely consistent with the contentions of the
respondent and the decision of Collins J, and if there were any doubt about that

a it is dispelled by what Lord Wilberforce said ([1983] 1 All ER 765 at 777–778, [1984] AC 74 at 105):

'I would therefore restate the respective functions of the immigration authorities and of the courts as follows. (1) The immigration authorities have the power and the duty to determine and to act on the facts material for *b* the detention as illegal entrants of persons prior to removal from the United Kingdom. (2) Any person whom the Secretary of State proposes to remove as an illegal entrant, and who is detained, may apply for a writ of habeas corpus or for judicial review. On such an application the Secretary of State or the immigration authorities if they seek to support the detention or removal (the burden being upon them) should depose to the grounds on *c* which the decision to detain or remove was made, setting out essential factual evidence taken into account and exhibiting documents sufficiently fully to enable the courts to carry out their function or review. (3) The court's investigation of the facts is of a supervisory character and not by way of appeal (it should not be forgotten that a right of appeal as to the facts exists under s 16 of the 1971 Act even though Parliament has thought fit to impose *d* conditions upon its exercise). It should appraise the quality of the evidence and decide whether that justifies the conclusion reached, eg whether it justifies a conclusion that the applicant obtained permission to enter by fraud or deceit. An allegation that he has done so being of a serious character and involving issues of personal liberty, requires a corresponding degree of *e* satisfaction as to the evidence. If the court is not satisfied with any part of the evidence it may remit the matter for reconsideration or itself receive further evidence. It should quash the detention order where the evidence was not such as the authorities should have relied on or where the evidence received does not justify the decision reached or, of course, for any serious procedural irregularity.'

f Lord Bridge of Harwich, having stated his views as to the standard of proof in such cases, said ([1983] 1 All ER 765 at 792, [1984] AC 74 at 124–125):

'I would add that the inherent difficulties of discovering and proving the true facts in many immigration cases can afford no valid ground for lowering *g* or relaxing the standard of proof required. If unlimited leave to enter was granted perhaps years before and the essential facts relied on to establish the fraud alleged can only be proved by documentary and affidavit evidence of past events which occurred in some remote part of the Indian subcontinent, the court should be less, rather than more, ready to accept anything short of convincing proof. On the other hand, it must be accepted that proof to the *h* appropriate standard can, and in the vast majority of cases will, be provided, in accordance with the established practice of the Divisional Court, by affidavit evidence alone. I understand all your Lordships to be agreed that nothing said in the present case should be construed as a charter to alleged *j* illegal entrants who challenge their detention and proposed removal to demand the attendance of deponents to affidavits for cross-examination. Whether to permit cross-examination will remain a matter for the court in its discretion to decide. It may be that the express discretion conferred on the court to permit cross-examination by the new procedure for judicial review under RSC Ord 53 has been too sparingly exercised when deponents could readily attend court. But however that may be, the discretion to allow cross-examination should only be exercised when justice so demands. The cases will be rare when it will be essential, in the interests of justice, to require the attendance for cross-examination of a deponent from overseas. If the alleged illegal entrant applying for habeas corpus, certiorari or both, files an affidavit putting in issue the primary facts alleged against him he will himself be readily available for cross-examination, which should enable the court in the great majority of cases to decide whether or not he is a witness of truth. If he is believed, he will succeed in his application. If he is disbelieved, there will be nothing to stop the court relying on affidavit evidence, provided it is inherently credible and convincing, to prove the fraud alleged against him, even though it has not been tested by cross-examination.'

This passage, I accept, does not in terms touch on the question raised in the present case, but it is entirely consistent with the view that it is with questions of weight rather than admissibility that the court is concerned when considering whether the decision that the appellant was an illegal entrant was a correct decision. That this is so appears clearly from Lord Scarman's speech, from which I need cite only one brief extract ([1983] 1 All ER 765 at 784, [1984] AC 74 at 114):

'... the facts relied on as justification [for detention] must be proved to the satisfaction of the court. A preponderance of probability suffices: but the degree of probability must be such that the court is satisfied. The strictness of the criminal formula is unnecessary to enable justice to be done: and its lack of flexibility in a jurisdiction where the technicalities of the law of evidence must not be allowed to become the master of the court could be a positive disadvantage inhibiting the efficacy of the developing safeguard of judicial review in the field of public law.'

Lord Templeman said ([1983] 1 All ER 765 at 794, [1984] AC 74 at 100 at 127):

'In many cases material facts relevant to an appeal can only be ascertained from the country of origin of the applicant to which he is removed. The adjudicator and the tribunal are not bound by strict rules of evidence but may receive on behalf of the applicant, and on behalf of the immigration authorities, written representations and reports of investigations which may take some time and involve inquiries as to identity, births, marriages, deaths and other circumstances in remote countrysides.'

A little later Lord Templeman said ([1983] 1 All ER 765 at 795, [1984] AC 74 at 100 at 128–129):

'In habeas corpus and judicial review proceedings evidence will be by affidavit, subject to cross-examination at the discretion of the court. It may be necessary for the court to reach a conclusion on the available information and without the benefit of oral evidence or of a prolonged investigation in the country of origin of the entrant. If fraud has been concealed for a number of years, witnesses or recorded statements may not be available to provide affidavits as to the circumstances in which those statement were prepared, composed and signed. Those statements may appear before the court as exhibits to affidavits from persons in whose custody the statements have been preserved. It will be for the court to determine what weight to attach to any of the information proved. It will be for the court to consider any explanations furnished by the entrant and his witnesses and to judge the a   reliability of the entrant under cross-examination. In Khera's case, for example, it is said that there was available a record of Khera's medical examination bearing the thumb-print or signature of Khera himself and the signature of the medical officer. The record is said to have contained the statement that Khera was unmarried. The medical officer might or might not have been available, and might or might not have recollected the

b   interview. Faced with any such record Khera himself could have given evidence and been cross-examined as to the recorded statement that he was unmarried. It would have been open to the court on consideration of the record   and   other   circumstances,   and   on   consideration   of   the cross-examination of Khera, to have decided that fraud was not made out.

c   But it would also have been open to the court to conclude that Khera had lied to the medical officer, and to disbelieve any proffered explanation that the record had been prepared previously to Khera's marriage, or that Khera from Amritsar had failed to make himself understood to anyone present at the interview in Delhi. It would also have been open to the court to infer that Khera had told a lie to the medical officer and subsequently kept silent to the

d   immigration officer about his marriage because he must have appreciated that his marriage had defeated or prejudiced his chances of obtaining admission to the United Kingdom. But in the event the immigration authorities failed to produce any record of the medical examination which in correspondence they claimed to exist.'

e   I agree with Collins J, who cited most of the above passage and said ([1996] 4 All ER 945 at 951):

'It is perfectly plain, in my judgment ... that Lord Templeman was not suggesting that the material was not admissible. What he was indicating was that it was for the court to decide its weight.'

f   I need not cite a passage from the speech of Lord Scarman ([1983] 1 All ER 765 at 782, [1984] AC 74 at 111) in which he explained why, in this context, the approach of the courts should be the same whether the challenge to the finding that the appellant was an illegal entrant was mounted by way of habeas corpus or judicial review because, as I have said, Mr Shrimpton does not dispute that this is so. His

g   submission is that the strict rules of evidence would apply to both forms of challenge. The passages I have cited from Khawaja's case and the reasoning of Collins J lead me to conclude that this submission must be rejected, and that accordingly the disputed evidence was rightly admitted.

h   *The second issue*
The question for the court is whether we are satisfied that the appellant was an illegal entrant, which depends on whether we are satisfied that he is not, as he claims to be, the son of Abdus Somed. Collins J directed himself that, whereas it was technically correct to apply the civil standard of proof (in accordance with

j   *Khawaja's* case in reality the criminal standard must be invoked because, where one is dealing with a case such as this, nothing less than that sort of approach seemed to him to be appropriate.
In so far as the judge was recognising that, in a case where a finding of illegal entrance involved imputing to the immigrant serious fraudulent conduct, the degree of probability must be so great as closely to approximate to the criminal standard I would not quarrel with his approach. But if he intended to go further

I cannot agree, since as Lord Scarman explained in a passage I have already cited from his speech in *Khawaja's* case, the distinction is of importance.

What makes the present case to an extent unusual is that, as I have already mentioned, the crucial evidence on which the respondent relies is that of the village visits which is, in strict evidential terms, double hearsay. No affidavits from the villagers or the interpreters were adduced by the respondent. Moreover, the description of this evidence as crucial is amply justified, for without it the respondent, as Mr Shaw on his behalf concedes, would not have a sustainable case. Plainly, therefore, the first step is to subject that evidence to critical evaluation.

Mr Shrimpton, who does not challenge the credit or competence of the entry clearance officers, submits that there were nevertheless grounds for treating the evidence they give as of little weight. He argues that the officers depended entirely on the veracity and accuracy of the interpreters, as to whom we know nothing beyond their names (a single name in each case); there is not even any indication as to what dialect they were speaking, no verification of their competence in that dialect; and no indication of their experience as interpreters. All of these matters could have been covered by affidavit evidence from the interpreters and the entry clearance officers, and to have obtained such evidence would have been a simple and by no means onerous matter. Moreover, says Mr Shrimpton, the absence of affidavits from the villagers themselves—he contends they should have been obtained—is compounded by the fact that tape recordings of what they said were not available: had they been it would have been possible to verify exactly what they did say. As it is, the court is left with highly unsatisfactory evidence to which little weight should be attached (even before regard is had to the contradictory affidavits adduced by the appellant). There are, Mr Shrimpton submits, very real grounds for doubting the reliability of this double hearsay evidence. In what I believe was a recognition of the difficulty of maintaining the suggestion that the interpreters might simply be mistaken as to the import of what the villagers were saying, Mr Shrimpton suggested that it was quite possible that they were interpreting the villagers' answers in such a way as to make it seem that the villagers were saying what they, the interpreters, knew or believed their employers wished to hear.

I accept that, particularly because it forms so important a part of the respondent's case, there are various steps that could, and should, have been taken to present this evidence in a more convincing manner. It would have been a simple matter to place before the court affidavit evidence as to the following matters. (1) The competence and experience of the interpreters. (2) The dialect or dialects in which the conversations with the villagers were conducted. (3) The fact that the interpreters had to the best of their ability, skill and knowledge faithfully interpreted the questions and answers. (4) The accuracy, at least in general terms, of the entry clearance officers' records of what was said by the villagers.

None of these matters would have involved the respondents in unreasonably onerous procedural steps; such as, it might legitimately be suggested, would have been involved in obtaining affidavit evidence from each of the villagers.

Nevertheless, I have to say that I regard the evidence as to the results of the village visits as highly persuasive evidence to which very considerable weight must be attached, for the following reasons.

(1) The absence of any challenge to the veracity or accuracy of the entry clearance officers greatly diminishes the force of the points on which Mr

a Shrimpton relies. The procedure adopted on the visits and the nature of the questions asked were such that it would in my view be virtually inconceivable that the interpreters could have been mistaken or that they could have been purporting to interpret the villagers' answers in such a manner as deliberately to convey the opposite of what they were saying. It seems to me that even a person lacking the experience of the entry clearance officers in such procedures would

b readily have been able to appreciate if that was happening: the process of showing a photograph and inquiring if the person depicted is known to the interviewee is so simple that even a person ignorant of the language in use would readily get the drift of the exchanges. As Collins J said ([1996] 4 All ER 945 at 956):

c '... it is usually fairly easy to tell whether they are saying yes or no when asked ... [if they] recognise someone, even without an interpreter being present, and also experienced entry clearance officers would, one expects, be able to recognise when names were stated, even if they could not understand the language otherwise.'

d (2) There is not a scrap of material to support the suggestion that the interpreters were incompetent, partial or dishonest.

(3) Of particular significance is the record of the exchanges with Abdus Somad and Rina Akhter on the visit to Holdarpur. Given their importance I ought to cite from the record of these interviews exhibited to Mr Leighton's affidavit and verified by the entry clearance officer concerned, Mr Casserly:

e 'On arrival at the applicant's compound we were met by [Abdus] Somed. He took us into the house and the principal applicant was there holding the child. She told me the child was called Jone.

Q. That's your only child, isn't it? A. No, I've got one called Rone.

Q. No, but the blood test has shown that Rone's not your child. A. Yes,

f that's right, I've only got one son.

Q. Why did you try to take your sister's child to UK? A. Well, it's a poor country. Everybody wants to help one another.

Q. Now can you tell me what your husband's real name is because I know it's not Saidur Rahman. A. It's Saidur Rhaman.

I then turned to Abdul Somed.

g Q. You've not been truthful with us, Mr Somed. You have taken a boy to UK who's not your son. Your niece's husband is not your son, is he? A. I brought him up.

Q. The whole village has told us that he's not your son, he's not even from this village. Now please tell me the truth. A. He's a poor child. I brought

h him up, so I took him to UK.

Q. Who is he really? A. Well, I'm a sick man, I can't really remember everything.

Q. I'm sure you can remember who that boy really is.

He didn't reply. I then put the same question to the principal applicant.

j A. His name is Surab, and his real name is Saidur.

Q. Which village is Surab from? A. He's from Nittarchok. It is near Hobiganj:

Q. And who is his real father? A. [Suraj] Ali.

Q. And why did your uncle take that boy to the UK? A. He brought him up and took him to UK. We are only three sisters, we've got no brothers so later on my uncle arranged the marriage ...

I then asked [Abdus] Somed one final question.

Q. Did you receive money for taking this boy to UK? A. No, I just took him to help him.

I terminated my enquiry there.'

(4) The force and inferentially the accuracy of the evidence as to the Holdarpur visit is confirmed by the complementary findings on the later Nittarchok visit. Moreover, I identify three pieces of evidence in relation to that visit as having particular significance. First, there is the fact that whereas many of the villagers identified the photograph of the appellant as that of Surab Ali, son of Suraj Ali, some did not recognise the photograph: evidence hardly consistent with the suggestion of partiality or deception on the part of the interpreter. Secondly, there is Mr Simpson's evidence that two men were observed apparently endeavouring to persuade villagers not to talk to Mr Simpson's party. Thirdly, there is the evidence that, as they made their way across the fields after the interviews had finished, they were accosted by a man who had pursued them from the village who said, according to what Mr Simpson recorded through the interpreter, that the photograph was of Surab Ali and that the two men already mentioned were Surab Ali's brothers.

In all the circumstances, and despite the absence of what I believe it is fair to say would have been more or less formal affidavits from the interpreters, I am persuaded that it is really impossible to accept that there is any sensible reason for doubting the veracity and accuracy of the respondent's evidence as to the results of the village visits. The importance of this conclusion is obvious: once the notion of inaccuracy, partiality or dishonesty on the part of the interpreters is dismissed, and it is accepted that the villagers said essentially what is attributed to them the only possible explanation for their answers is, as the appellant suggested in interview after the Holdapur visit, that the villagers were lying. While it might be possible to suggest motives of jealousy—which is what he did in interview— for the villagers' alleged lies, the same surely cannot be said in relation to Abdus Somed and Rina Akhter, nor do I read the appellant's interview as asserting that *they* were lying; rather I would interpret his answers as an assertion that it was those who attributed damaging answers to the latter two witnesses who were lying. It is plain from Rina Akhter's affidavit that she, too, asserts that the account of her answers in interview was simply untrue. (The appellant in his affidavit says that on the same evening as the visit had taken place she telephoned him and told him that she was subjected to pressure, to which she did not succumb, to admit that he was not Saidur Rahman). As I have said, I simply cannot accept this, particularly when it is remembered that the credit of the appellant and Rina Akhter is gravely compromised by their admitted attempt at deliberate deception in relation to the boy Rone. Thus this particular part of the village visits evidence, all of which is in the highest degree persuasive, carries particular weight.

The appellant, however, argues that even so, the other evidence to which he can point is such as to raise such doubts on the deception issue as ought to prevent this court from concluding that it has been established to the requisite high degree of probability that he is not Abdus Somad's son. I summarise the evidence relied on.

(1) I have already mentioned, and given my reason for attaching scant significance to, the affidavit evidence of the appellant and Rina Akhter.

(2) A number of affidavits have been sworn by inhabitants of the two villages—some of them by witnesses who were interviewed and some by

others—all giving an account generally to the opposite effect to that attributed to the interviewees. There is also an affidavit sworn by Abdus Somed asserting that he is the appellant's father. The Holdarpur affidavits, in particular, suffer from the disadvantage that those with interviewees are all in virtually identical terms, including the sentence:

'In February 1993 in Holdarpur village, I was approached by some people who showed me some photographs of Saidur Rahman and Rina Akhter. They asked me my name. I was asked if I knew him and I said yes. I do not remember saying anything else.'

The other affidavits from Holdarpur are also essentially in common form, though plainly not too much ought to be made of that.

(3) Some reliance is placed on records of such things as savings accounts and transactions in relation to land, in which the father/son relationship is stated. Since, however, these post-date Rina Akhter's application they seem to me to carry no significant weight.

(4) More to the point, the appellant relies on the birth certificate, of which two copies are to be found in the papers. This certificate purports to record the birth on 29 July 1967 in Holdarpur of Saidur Rahman and his father's name as Abdus Somed. A curious feature of this certificate is that it states that the birth was registered on 30 January 1972 (in one copy) and 30 September 1972 (in another copy). The two certificates are dated, respectively 18 October 1990 and 27 October 1986. To the evidence of Mr Simpson, based on long experience, that it is a simple matter to obtain a false birth certificate in Bangladesh (evidence inferentially confirmed by the false certificate produced for the child Rone) Mr Shrimpton responds by pointing out that it would have been a simple matter for the Secretary of State to have the register checked, and that there is no evidence of his having done so.

(5) Finally, the appellant points to a letter on a blue airletter form bearing a post mark dated 19 June 1972 purporting to be written the previous day by Abdus Somed to his mother in Bangladesh. This letter and a translation were before the judge, though it seems that little weight was attached to it and the judge does not mention it. Before us, Mr Shrimpton placed great reliance on it, for this reason. The letter seems to have been written with the object of advancing Abdus Somed's intention to procure the admission of members of his family to the United Kingdom, where he was lawfully living. In the body of the text on the first page is the sentence: 'I had written requesting the children's birth certificates for which I am still waiting to learn whether you will be able to send them or not. If you can then you should write and let me know'. Then one finds, on the second page, the following:

'MOMJAN BIBI WIFE
1. LUTHFA BEGUM (daughter) 13–11–61
2. HAFIZA BEGUM (daughter) 5–5–64
3. SAIDUR RAHMAN (son) 29–7–67
4. SAIFUR RAHMAN (son) 28–1–69
I give you the children's dates of birth.

While the comment can be made that, at least to a European, it is surprising to find a father, whose wife is at the time in Bangladesh, telling his mother, also in that country, what are the dates of birth of his children, the fact is that, though afforded the opportunity to examine this letter, the respondent's advisers have not felt able to advance any evidence casting doubts on its genuineness and, in particular, on its date. It therefore provides some telling evidence that, as long *a* ago as 1972, the vital relationship was being asserted by Abdus Somed.

I have anxiously considered all of this evidence in order to determine whether, when weighed against what I have earlier accepted is the very cogent evidence of the village visits, it is of significant effect. I have found the question a difficult one to determine but in the end I have concluded, differing in this respect from *b* Collins J, that a loyal application of the principles embodied in *Khawaja's* case makes it impossible to say that the evidence as a whole is sufficiently convincing to satisfy the stringent burden of proof which the respondent must satisfy. I shall endeavour to explain my reasons as briefly as I can:

(1) I do not feel able, as Collins J did, in effect to dismiss all the village affidavits adduced on the appellant's behalf. True it is that, particularly given their standard *c* form, the affidavits sworn by those who had been interviewed by the entry clearance officers appear unconvincing. However, there are also the affidavits of a number of witnesses whose testimony cannot be impugned by pointing to previous inconsistent statements, and I do not consider that their sworn statements ought to be dismissed out of hand as fabrication. On the contrary, *d* they provide some material to contradict the respondent's evidence. I should, however, make it clear that, were this the only material on which the appellant could rely, I should not have been persuaded in his favour.

(2) The birth certificates, apparently regular and genuine, are also in my view prima facie entitled to some credence. A United Kingdom birth certificate would be received in our courts and accorded appropriate weight unless and until *e* shown to be a forgery; and I do not consider that merely to adduce evidence that false certificates can easily be obtained in Bangladesh suffices to deprive such a document of some prima facie weight, which it is, in my view, entitled to be given. As I have pointed out, if the certificates are false this could have been simply and easily demonstrated by producing evidence of the content of the *f* register.

(3) It is, however, the letter of 18 June 1972 that has been the decisive factor in compelling me to the decision I have reached. If this letter is genuine—and the contrary has not been alleged—then it establishes that as early as June 1972 the relationship was being asserted. This, it will be remembered, is about the same time as, according to the birth certificates, the birth was registered. If it is *g* suggested that this is consistent with Abdus Somed's having determined to 'adopt', as his own son, the son of Suraj Ali and thereafter bring him up (see the passages from his interview which I have already cited and that accordingly the letter is of no significance, there are in my view grave difficulties about such a suggestion, because of its inconsistency with the evidence on which the *h* respondent primarily relies—that of the village visits. On the suggested hypothesis, the appellant would have been aged about five at the time of the supposed 'adoption'. It would follow, as it seems to me, that the inhabitants of Holdarpur *would* have known him as Abdus Somed's son, albeit one who was 'adopted' at an early age; and those of Nittarchok would, if they had not forgotten *j* that he was Suraz Ali's son, at least have said something about his disappearing at the age of 5. Moreover—a not unimportant consideration in my view—this hypothesis has never been part of the respondent's case; the delay between the stated date of birth and registration has never been the subject of any investigation (for example, to determine whether in Bangladesh it is unusual); and, as I have indicated, absolutely nothing in the village visit evidence appears

a to support it. In these circumstances, I consider that this letter is a telling piece of evidence in favour of the claimed relationship.

(4) While I have now completed the summary of the reasons for my inability to feel satisfied that the appellant is not Abdus Somed's son, I wish to add a word about one matter which, unexplained, might seem puzzling to anyone considering this case, who might wonder why the existence or otherwise of the b crucial relationship had not been resolved by DNA testing. Abdus Somed and his wife are now dead, but the alleged brother, Saifur Rahman and two daughters survive, and as I understand it, a test which would in practice be decisive would, were the parties willing, be practicable. The appellant deals with the matter in his affidavit from which it appears that the respondent requested the production of DNA evidence and the appellant was willing to provide it, but according to c him was prevented during his father's life time by logistical problems and his father's illness from arranging a test with him as the comparator; and thereafter by his brother and sisters' refusal to co-operate in one. He explains their refusal by what he says is open hostility between himself and Saifur, whom he believes to be anxious for financial reasons to have him deported. It seems that he believes d that Saifur was the author of the denunciatory letters. While I should make it clear that, were this explanation for the appellant's failure to undergo a DNA test shown to be untrue, I would regard his refusal (as it would then appear to be) as a potent piece of evidence against him, no evidence has been placed before us which seeks to refute his account.

In the light of the conclusions stated, I would allow this appeal on the second e issue and quash the order for detention.

HOBHOUSE LJ. On this appeal from the judgment of Collins J ([1996] 4 All ER 945), the appellant Mr Saidur Rahman, represented by Mr Shrimpton, makes two basic submissions. The first, which is a submission of law, is that the court, in f deciding whether a person is an illegal entrant, may only have regard to evidence admissible at common law. The second, which is a submission of fact, is that Collins J should, even taking into account all the available evidence, have concluded that it was not proved that the appellant was an illegal entrant.

The legal submission
g   I need not repeat the history of this matter which has already been set out in the judgment of Hutchison LJ. The challenged decision was that of the immigration officer dated 3 August 1993 which declared that the appellant was an illegal entrant. It informed him that he was therefore 'a person who is liable to be detained pending completion of arrangements dealing with you under the h [Immigration Act 1971]' and that it was proposed 'to give directions for your removal from the United Kingdom in due course'. His detention meanwhile was authorised and he was thereafter detained. On 11 August he commenced these proceedings. He applied for a writ of habeas corpus requiring the Secretary of State to release him and for the judicial review of the decision that he was an j illegal entrant. On 16 August Clarke J refused to grant summarily the application for the writ of habeas corpus or to order release on bail: he directed a further hearing. He also directed that the matter should proceed as an application for habeas corpus and that the judicial review application should stand withdrawn. This assumed that the appellant would continue to be detained in custody. However, on 28 August the appellant was granted temporary admission and was released. Under these circumstances it would have been more satisfactory and

more accurate if the proceedings by way of judicial review had then been reinstated and the habeas corpus application had been treated as spent. However that did not occur and both before Collins J and this court the proceedings were treated formally as applications for a writ of habeas corpus. I consider that this was unfortunate procedurally but it has not affected the substance of the points which have to be considered.

Mr Shrimpton at one point in his argument sought to found upon a difference between applications for a writ of habeas corpus and applications for judicial review. He referred to the differences of subject matter and historical origin. The writ of habeas corpus is of ancient origin and is enshrined in the Habeas Corpus Act 1816. In the historical past it has given rise to trials before juries. The Rules of the Supreme Court include, in Ord 54, provisions for regulating applications for writs of habeas corpus. In contrast, there is the right to apply for judicial review and the various remedies which the court is able to order on such applications. The relevant order is Ord 53. Mr Shrimpton argued that where the application was for a writ of habeas corpus or for any remedy which related to personal liberty, the court should apply strict rules of the admissibility of evidence. He submitted that, if, contrary to his primary submission, there was a difference between habeas corpus and judicial review proceedings, the present proceedings were habeas corpus proceedings and the narrower rule should be applied. But his primary submission was that in the present context no such distinction should be made and that however the proceedings were formalised the same rules of evidence should apply.

It is common ground that the governing authority is *Khawaja v Secretary of State for the Home Dept* [1983] 1 All ER 765, [1984] AC 74 and that where the Secretary of State seeks to declare a person an illegal entrant, the Secretary of State must prove that he is in fact an illegal entrant. It is accepted, albeit reluctantly by Mr Shrimpton, that the standard of proof is the 'flexible' civil standard, that is to say, the balance of probabilities having regard to the seriousness of the matters that have to be proved and the general assumption that a person has acted legally not illegally. It is further accepted that the immigration officer or an adjudicator is entitled to take into account all the material placed before him either from the person concerned or those representing him or from those who have conducted inquiries on behalf of the Secretary of State (see *Ejaz v Secretary of State for Home Affairs* [1978] CA Transcript 777). This is an important point to which I will have to revert. It is a point which must be borne in mind when reading the speeches in the House of Lords in *Khawaja*'s case.

Prior to the decision of the House of Lords in *Khawaja*'s case it had been the law, based upon earlier authorities, that it was for the Secretary of State to determine whether or not a person was an illegal entrant and that that determination could only be challenged on conventional judicial review grounds: provided that the Secretary of State had reasonable grounds for concluding that the person was an illegal entrant his decision could not be interfered with in the absence of some procedural irregularity. Whilst this was still the law, the question of admissibility of evidence had been considered by the Court of Appeal in *Ejaz*'s case. The Court of Appeal had to consider an application for a writ of habeas corpus by a person who had been declared by the Secretary of State to be an illegal entrant and was detained in custody at HM Remand Centre Brockhill. The argument was that the Secretary of State was only entitled to take into account evidence which would be admissible in a court of law. He had taken into

a account other material including the statement of an informer. The Court of
Appeal rejected this argument. Roskill LJ said:

> 'In my judgment there is no reason why the Secretary of State should not,
> if he thinks fit, act upon evidence—hearsay evidence from an informer—
> giving it such weight, if any, as he thinks it proper to give.'

b Megaw LJ agreed. He referred to counsel's argument—

> '... that the Secretary of State, in considering the evidence in this matter,
> was obliged to take into account only evidence which would be properly
> admissible in a court of law. That wide proposition, I think, is wholly
> unsustainable; and if it were to be accepted it would give rise to very great
c > difficulties to applicants, among others.'

That is a decision of the Court of Appeal regarding the admissibility of evidence
when the relevant matter has to be considered by the Secretary of State. Its
application to the Secretary of State is accepted by Mr Shrimpton before us, but
he submits that the decision in *Khawaja* requires that different rules of
d admissibility must be applied once the decision of the Secretary of State is
challenged, whether by way of habeas corpus or judicial review, in the courts. I
do not accept this submission.

The speeches in *Khawaja's* case were unanimous in dismissing the appeal and,
in substance, in the reasons which led to this conclusion. However it is clear that
on some aspects Lord Wilberforce adopted a view which was less favourable to
e applicants than that of the other members of the House. Although Mr Shrimpton
sought to found arguments on the passage in the speech of Lord Wilberforce, it
is clear that it does not assist him. Lord Wilberforce said ([1983] 1 All ER 765 at
777–778, [1984] AC 74 at 105):

> 'The court's investigation of the facts is of a supervisory character and not
f > by way of appeal (it should not be forgotten that a right of appeal as to the
> facts exists under s 16 of the 1971 Act even though Parliament has thought fit
> to impose conditions upon its exercise). It should appraise the quality of the
> evidence and decide whether that justifies the conclusion reached, eg
> whether it justifies a conclusion that the applicant obtained permission to
g > enter by fraud or deceit. An allegation that he has done so being of a serious
> character and involving issues of personal liberty, requires a corresponding
> degree of satisfaction as to the evidence. If the court is not satisfied with any
> part of the evidence it may remit the matter for reconsideration or itself
> receive further evidence. It should quash the detention order where the
h > evidence was not such as the authorities should have relied on or where the
> evidence received does not justify the decision reached or, of course, for any
> serious procedural irregularity.'

The other speeches are no more helpful to the applicant. Lord Scarman whose
speech was mainly concerned with the 'precedent fact' point, stressed that the
j law was not to be governed by procedural or historical differences between
habeas corpus and judicial review. He said ([1983] 1 All ER 765 at 782, [1984] AC
74 at 111):

> 'There are, of course, procedural differences between habeas corpus and
> the modern statutory judicial review. *Zamir v Secretary of State for the Home
> Dept* ([1980] 2 All ER 768, [1980] AC 930) was a case of habeas corpus; in the

instant cases the effective relief sought is certiorari to quash the immigration officer's decision. But the nature of the remedy sought cannot affect the *a* principle of the law. In both cases liberty is in issue ... Whatever the process, the party seeking relief carries the initial burden of showing he has a case fit to be considered by the court. Accordingly, faced with the jealous care our law traditionally devotes to the protection of the liberty of those who are subject to its jurisdiction, I find it impossible to imply into the statute words *b* the effect of which would be to take the [relevant statutory power] out of the "precedent fact" category.'

Having discussed the questions of burden and standard of proof, Lord Scarman concluded ([1983] 1 All ER 765 at 784, [1984] AC 74 at 114):

'Accordingly, it is enough to say that, where the burden lies on the *c* executive to justify the exercise of a power of detention, the facts relied on as justification must be proved to the satisfaction of the court. A preponderance of probability suffices; but the degree of probability must be such that the court is satisfied. The strictness of the criminal formula is unnecessary to enable justice to be done: and its lack of flexibility in a *d* jurisdiction where the technicalities of the law of evidence must not be allowed to become the master of the court could be a positive disadvantage inhibiting the efficacy of the developing safeguard of judicial review in the field of public law.'

Lord Templeman also referred to the evidence which may be taken into account *e* ([1983] 1 All ER 765 at 794–795, [1984] AC 74 at 127–128):

'In many cases material facts relevant to an appeal can only be ascertained from the country of origin of the applicant to which he is removed. The adjudicator and the tribunal are not bound by strict rules of evidence but may receive on behalf of the applicant, and on behalf of the immigration *f* authorities, written representations and reports of investigations which may take some time and involve inquiries as to identity, births, marriages, deaths and other circumstances in remote countrysides ... If the court is not satisfied that the entrant obtained leave to enter by fraud, the court will protect the entrant against detention and removal. I agree with my noble *g* and learned friend Lord Scarman that the burden of proving that leave to enter was obtained by fraud and that consequently the entrant is an illegal entrant liable to arrest and expulsion can only be discharged by the immigration authorities manifesting to the satisfaction of the court a high degree of probability. It does not follow that the court must disregard written statements by witnesses who are not available for cross-examination *h* or documents which are not supported by direct written or oral evidence as to the circumstances in which they came into existence. In habeas corpus and judicial review proceedings evidence will be by affidavit, subject to cross-examination at the discretion of the court. It may be necessary for the court to reach a conclusion on the available information and without the *j* benefit of oral evidence or of a prolonged investigation in the country of origin of the entrant. If fraud has been concealed for a number of years, witnesses of recorded statements may not be available to provide affidavits as to the circumstances in which those statements were prepared, composed and signed. Those statements may appear before the court as exhibits to affidavits from persons in whose custody the statements have been

a
preserved. It will be for the court to determine what weight to attach to any of the information provided. It will be for the court to consider any explanations furnished by the entrant and his witnesses and to judge the reliability of the entrant under cross-examination.'

b
The tenor of all these quotations which I have made from the speeches is an acceptance of evidence which does not necessarily meet the criteria of admissibility for a court conducting a trial. It is implicit that the court can take into account all relevant material making appropriate allowance for the weight which is to be attached to it which, of course, does not exclude the view that certain evidence should be disregarded if it is not worthy of any weight. *Khawaja*'s case, far from being supportive of the legal submission of Mr

c
Shrimpton, is in my judgment directly contrary to it. The same conclusion is implicit in the judgments in *R v Secretary of State for the Home Dept, ex p Miah* [1990] 2 All ER 523, [1990] 1 WLR 806 and *R v Secretary of State for the Home Office, ex p Muse* [1992] Imm AR 282.

There is a further and more fundamental objection to Mr Shrimpton's argument. The Secretary of State and those acting on his behalf are under an

d
obligation to determine whether or not a person is an illegal entrant and, if they conclude that he is, to make the appropriate declaration and authorise his removal and, if necessary meanwhile, his detention. In so determining they must take into account all material evidence whether it would be admissible in court or not. If their determination is in accordance with the evidence, it is valid and

e
lawful as are the steps taken in consequence. However, on Mr Shrimpton's argument, if the entrant challenges the determination in the courts, what was valid may, because of the exclusion of some of the material evidence, have to be held invalid. This cannot be correct. The original determination was at the time it was made either valid or invalid: the entrant either was or was not an illegal entrant. Further, if the court quashes the decision of the Secretary of State so that

f
he has to reconsider it (see also Lord Wilberforce above), the fresh decision will again have to be made on evidence which the court would be debarred from taking into account.

I consider that the relevant law is correctly encapsulated in the unreported words of May LJ in *R v Secretary of State for the Home Dept, ex p Ahmad* [1983] CA

g
Transcript 234 adopted by Glidewell LJ in *R v Secretary of State for the Home Dept, ex p Patel* [1986] Imm AR at 515 at 523:

'The role of the Court in these cases is to consider all the available material and to decide for itself whether it has been satisfied by the Secretary of State that the applicant for habeas corpus or certiorari is an illegal entrant ...'

h
The first ground of appeal therefore fails.

The factual submission
Turning now to the factual submission and taking into account 'all the

j
available material' and bearing in mind the burden of proof which is upon the Secretary of State and its standard, I must consider for myself whether, like the immigration officer, on behalf of the Secretary of State, and Collins J, I am satisfied that the appellant was an illegal entrant. No issue arises in this case as to what representations were made: the question is simply whether it has been proved that they were false. This in turn depends upon whether the appellant was, as he claims to have been, the son of Abdus Somed. It is not in dispute that

applicants for leave to enter the United Kingdom may have a strong motivation to lie and that documents emanating from Bangladesh may either be forgeries or contain false statements. Apparently genuine documents are of course evidence to be taken into account but should not be regarded as conclusive and may be false or misleading. Such is the common knowledge and experience of immigration officers and accepted by Mr Shrimpton in this case. But before considering the evidence relied upon by the appellant it is necessary to consider and evaluate the evidence relied upon by the Secretary of State. I repeat, it is for the Secretary of State to point to evidence which properly leads to the conclusion that the appellant is an illegal entrant. If the Secretary of State cannot do so, this appeal must succeed.

The evidence by which the immigration officer's conclusion has to be justified is the evidence obtained on the visits to the villages of Holdarpur and Nittarchok. The former took place in February 1993 after the application of the appellant's wife and alleged son for certificates of entitlement and the receipt by the Secretary of State of the anonymous denunciatory letters. It was the evidence obtained on the visit to Holdarpur which led to the immigration officer calling the appellant in for interview in August 1993 and, having heard his explanations, declaring him an illegal entrant. The visit to Nittarchok took place in December 1993 by which time the appellant was aware of the evidence which was being relied upon by the Secretary of State and the names of those who had previously been interviewed.

The evidence relating to the respective visits was given on affidavit by officers responsible for carrying out those visits. They produced their records and specifically deposed to their accuracy. The officers' integrity and expertise was not challenged or questioned by any contrary evidence. Although they had to act through interpreters, there was no evidence which would support any criticism of the competence or integrity of those interpreters. I mention this because of certain submissions made forensically by Mr Shrimpton which sought to cast doubt upon the integrity and competence of those involved. There was no evidential basis for any such submissions. The most that could be said was that the tape recordings used at the time of the first visit had, in accordance with the ordinary and understandable practice of the relevant officers, been re-used and the tapes recording the notes of the officers conducting the second visit were not of a sufficiently good quality to be usable at the time of the proceedings before Collins J. The comments made by the appellant himself upon the evidence of the visits were to the effect that the villagers were activated by malice or jealousy to tell untruths about the appellant. In the evidence relied on by the appellant, even in the affidavit of his wife Rina Akhter dated 8 December 1995, there is no allegation of any improper conduct on the part of the officers in conducting the interviews. Therefore (subject to the submission based upon the more recent affidavits put in by the appellant, which I will come back to) the attack on what the villagers have been recorded as saying depends upon drawing the inference that they were not telling the truth but telling deliberate lies.

The village of Holdarpur was the village of the Rina Akhter and her uncle Abdus Somed. They were both living there in February 1993. If the appellant was indeed the son of Abdus Somed it would be expected that he would be known in the village and that the villagers would be aware that the Rina Akhter's husband was a blood relation of her and of her uncle. Further, they would identify the appellant as being from her own village. The officers took with them a photograph of the appellant. Most villagers did not recognise him at all. The a few that did recognised him as being from another village and not related to his wife or her uncle. Most of the villagers knew that her husband was from another village. One of the officers visited the compound of Abdus Somed where the appellant's wife was also living. She admitted that she had fraudulently attempted to pass off her sister's child as her own in an attempt to obtain leave to enter the United Kingdom. Abdus Somed was then asked whether he was the

b father of the appellant and gave answers which implicitly admitted that he was not. The appellant was 'a poor child—I brought him up, I took him to UK'. In the presence of Abdus Somed the same question was put to the appellant's wife. She answered that the appellant was 'from Nittarchok' and his real father was one '[Suraj] Ali'.

c   'Q. Why did your uncle take that boy to the UK? A. He brought him up and took him to UK. We are only three sisters, we've got no brothers so later on my uncle arranged the marriage.'

Finally, Abdus Somed was asked whether he received money for taking 'this boy' to the United Kingdom and he answered: 'No, I just took him to help him'.

d   This evidence is cogent. It has been proved by the best means that could be expected in the circumstances—an affidavit from the interviewing officer and copies of his notes and reports. It is strongly probative of the fact that although brought up by Abdus Somed, the appellant was not his son. All the persons involved were acting without any personal interest in the matter. The wife and

e her uncle gave answers contrary to their interest and there is a very strong inference that what they said on that occasion was true.

In interview on 3 August 1993 the appellant was asked about this evidence. He told the interviewing officer that he knew about the visit because 'I heard it later on the telephone'. His response was that the villagers including Abdus Somed and the appellant's wife had been telling lies. Abdus Somed 'always says one

f thing at one time then the next moment he says something else'. He has a 'mental condition'. He gave no other explanation of the evidence notwithstanding that he already knew of the visit.

The visit to Nittarchok was also significant. There, the villagers recognised the photograph of the appellant and volunteered that he was the son of Suraj Ali.

g Suraj Ali could not be interviewed as he had died some two years before. Two men appeared to be attempting to prevent the villagers from talking to the immigration officer. They were identified as brothers of the appellant (and sons of Suraj Ali). One villager who had refrained from speaking in the village caught up with the officer about a mile and a half from the village to inform him that he

h was right that the appellant was the son of Suraj Ali and that the appellant's brothers were attempting to stop villagers telling the officer that.

Again this is cogent evidence. The officer was experienced and disinterested. The evidence he collected was all one way and confirmed what the appellant's wife had said about his paternity. This evidence was, in my judgment, more than

j sufficient to prove that the appellant was not the son of Abdus Somed, that he had obtained entry to the United Kingdom by fraud, and that he was an illegal entrant.

What, then, was the evidence by which the appellant sought to answer this evidence? He is not himself creditworthy and he had the clearest interest in telling lies. The same applies to his wife. The only evidence from her is in an affidavit of December 1995. She says she told the officers that it was not true that her husband was from Nittarchok and the son of Suraj Ali. She said: 'He is my first cousin, I have known him all my life and I am married to him.'

Other affidavits were obtained from persons living in Holdarpur or Nittarchok, including from some of those who had been interviewed in 1993. The affidavits are dated between June 1995 and February 1996. Most of them are in a common form. Those of villagers from Holdarpur say that the deponent identified both the photograph of the wife and of the appellant and that the appellant and his wife are cousins. Those from Nittarchok say that the deponent does not know who the appellant is. They say that this is what they told the officer who interviewed them. I do not consider that these affidavits carry weight in comparison with the evidence obtained by the officers in 1993. Nor do I consider that they discredit the evidence of the officers themselves or throw doubt upon the accuracy of their records or the reliability of the evidence they collected. Some further affidavits from villagers at Holdarpur, not previously interviewed, again generally in a common form, state that they know the appellant as a co-villager and son of the late Abdus Somed. I make the same comment.

Other documentary material has been produced by the appellant referring to him as the son of Abdus Somed. I consider that this material has to be evaluated in the light of the evidence that Abdus Somed brought up the appellant. It is consistent with this that Abdus Somed may have treated him as his son even though he was not. The description of the appellant as 'the son of Abdus Somed' clearly goes back some way. If there is a conflict between such evidence of reputation and the evidence obtained on the first village visit, I prefer the evidence of the first village visit. It is a fair comment that it is hard to reconcile the appellant having been brought up, in the conventional sense, by Abdus Somed and having the reputation of being his son with the evidence that he was not well known in Holdarpur.

There are three other pieces of evidence to which I should specifically refer. The first is the birth certificate. Two documents have been produced, one purporting to be a duplicate of the other. They both purport to be certified extracts from the birth register of a town in Bangladesh. The entry in the register is said to have been of the birth of a child bearing the appellant's name in the village of Holdarpur on 29 July 1967. But the date of registration is said to have been either 30 January 1972 or 30 September 1972. The certificates themselves are dated October 1986 and October 1990. These documents appear to be genuine. There is nothing on their face which justifies any different conclusion, although it must be recognised that there is always a risk that they are not genuine. Mr Shrimpton has made the powerful comment that if it is the case of the Secretary of State that these certificates are not genuine then the fact could easily be proved by checking the register. There is no evidence that any such check was made. No comment has been made, although the fact has been noticed, that the registration did not take place until the child was four or five years old. In the absence of other evidence I infer that these documents are consistent with Abdus Somed not being the true father of the appellant but a person who, as he himself said, had brought the appellant up treating him as his son.

I consider that a similar view is to be taken of a letter which can be reliably dated to 1972. There is no evidence to show that this document is not what it appears to be, a letter from Abdus Somed to his mother in India asking her to assist in getting birth certificates for 'the children' with a view to arranging their entry into the United Kingdom. Abdus Somed apparently thought it necessary to a tell his mother in this letter the name of his wife and who his children were and what were their sexes and dates of birth. I consider that this letter is as consistent with the appellant being brought up by Abdus Somed from an early age as his son as with the appellant being his natural son.

Finally, there are the letters of denunciation which were sent to the immigration authorities denouncing the appellant. These letters were clearly
b provoked by the application made in respect of the appellant's nephew passing him off as his son. But they also related to the claim of the appellant to be the son of Abdus Somed. Anonymous letters are an unimpressive form of evidence; I give them little weight. It is remarkable, however, that the statements in them have since been confirmed by independent evidence. So far as the parenthood of the nephew is concerned, this has since been proved by DNA profiling and has
c been admitted. The letters are therefore entitled to some weight. At the time that the immigration officer had to take the relevant decision the letters still had to be treated as anonymous. However, the appellant himself has since asserted that he knows the authorship of the letters. One, he says, was written by his 'brother', the son of Abdus Somed, and the other was written by a friend of that
d man on his instructions. The appellant says that his 'brother' was motivated by jealousy and spite and was fabricating lies to cause him trouble. If, as the appellant asserts, these letters were written or dictated by the son of Abdus Somed, I consider that they are entitled to significantly more weight. No doubt that man was serving his own interests but he was a person well placed to know the true facts and the truth of what he said has since been independently
e corroborated.

I have had the advantage of reading in draft the judgment prepared by Hutchison LJ. He has not been persuaded by this evidence that the appellant was not the natural son of Abdus Somed. I respect his view but my own assessment is that the evidence of the village visits is so strong that one must conclude that
f the appellant was not the natural son of Abdus Somed and that the contrary evidence does not suffice to displace this conclusion.

It follows that in my judgment the appeal must be dismissed.

STAUGHTON LJ. For the reasons given by Hobhouse and Hutchison LJJ, I agree that we are entitled to take into account all the evidence that was before the
g Secretary of State, in addition to any other evidence that is available to us. When the issue is whether one man is the son of another man, as in this case, the only first hand evidence which could be obtained would be that of the mother, or possibly of the taking of blood samples and their interpretation by a scientist. In those circumstances it is in the nature of things likely that the Secretary of State
h will sometimes have to rely on other evidence from a number of sources, which may be near at hand or far away, and where the evidence may have to be gathered by intermediaries.

The second issue is whether Saidur Rahman is proved not to be the son of Abdus Somed. It is accepted that the standard of proof is not that prevailing in a criminal
j case. Rather it is that which applies when an allegation of crime is part of an issue to be decided in what is not a criminal case. There is then, as it were, ordinarily a presumption to be placed in the scale which favours innocence, because ordinary people do not ordinarily commit crimes. The weight of that presumption varies; as Denning LJ said in *Bater v Bater* [1950] 2 All ER 458, [1951] P 35 quoting Best CJ, 'in proportion as the crime is enormous, so ought the proof to be clear' (see [1951] P 35 at 37). Here, any presumption which once existed that

Saidur Rahman would not be guilty of deceit in an immigration context is rebutted; it is now admitted that he was guilty of such deceit in connection with *a* a child who was said to be his son in 1991.

For the reasons given by Hobhouse LJ, I agree with his and the judge's view that Saidur Rahman is proved not to have been the son of Abdus Somed. It is true that the notion of an informal adoption by the latter faces difficulties, as mentioned by both Hobhouse and Hutchison LJJ. And unless there was some *b* such informal adoption it is difficult to explain the letter of 18 June 1972. But that letter was clearly written for the record. I regard its evidential value as distinctly suspect, whereas the evidence in favour of the Secretary of State's conclusion is coherent and convincing. I, too, would dismiss this appeal.

Appeal dismissed. Leave to appeal to the House of Lords refused.   *c*

L I Zysman Esq   Barrister.

R v Surrey Coroner, ex parte Wright

QUEEN'S BENCH DIVISION (CROWN OFFICE LIST)
TUCKER J
5, 6, 14 JUNE 1996

Coroner – Inquest – Assessor – Extent of assessor's role at inquest – Patient dying under general anaesthetic – Coroner sitting with consultant anaesthetist as assessor – Assessor questioning witnesses and providing expert evidence – Whether coroner having authority to invite assessor to sit at inquest – Whether assessor able to give expert evidence himself – Coroners Rules 1984, r 20.

Coroner – Inquest – Verdict – Lack of care – Patient dying under general anaesthetic – Coroner making finding of fact that there had been lack of care – Whether coroner able to return verdict of lack of care.

In 1992 W, a fit 27-year-old man, was admitted to hospital for surgery to remove his wisdom teeth. He was given a general anaesthetic but he never regained consciousness and died a week later owing to cerebral anoxia, as a result of his airway being obstructed. At the inquest the coroner sat with an assessor, a consultant anaesthetist, as an adviser on anaesthetic and resuscitation procedures, and invited him to question witnesses and to give evidence. The coroner found as a fact that there had been a lack of care but held that that was not a verdict he could return under the Coroners Rules 1984 and the Coroners Act 1988, and so returned a verdict of accidental death. The applicant, who was W's mother, applied for judicial review of the coroner's decision, on the grounds, inter alia, that the coroner had no power under the 1988 Act or at common law to invite an assessor to sit with him, that in any event the role of the assessor in both examining witnesses and providing expert evidence offended the rules of natural justice, and that the coroner had erred in law in holding that he could not return a verdict of lack of care.

Held – The application would be refused for the following reasons—

(1) A coroner was entitled to invite an assessor to sit with him if he considered it necessary having regard to the technical nature of the evidence which might have to be considered. Moreover, under r 20 of the 1984 rules the assessor could examine witnesses who gave technical evidence provided it was done under the control of the coroner and was restricted to matters within the assessor's special experience. However, the role of an assessor could not extend to his giving expert evidence himself, since there was a danger that the evidence of such a witness might attract the special confidence of the coroner and might carry greater weight than would otherwise be the case. It followed that the coroner had erred in allowing the assessor to do so. Nevertheless, since a thorough investigation had been carried out and it had not been shown that the fact that the assessor had given evidence would have made any material difference to the outcome, it was not necessary or desirable in the interests of justice to order a fresh inquiry to be held, or to substitute the court's verdict for that of the coroner (see p 830 *d g* to *j*, p 831 *d* and p 832 *e f*, post).

(2) It was not open to a coroner to return a verdict of lack of care. However, it was open to him, in appropriate circumstances, to return a verdict of death as

result of neglect, provided the 'neglect' had been continuous or at least non-transient neglect. Since, in the instant case, that was not an appropriate description of the negligent lack of care that was alleged to have led to W's death, it followed that the coroner was entitled to record the decision which he did (see p 831 *h* to p 832 *d*, post); dictum of Bingham MR in *R v North Humberside and Scunthorpe Coroner, ex p Jamieson* [1994] 3 All ER 972 at 990 applied.

Notes

For the examination of witnesses at inquests, see 9 *Halsbury's Laws* (4th edn) para 1095.

For the Coroners Act 1988, see 11 *Halsbury's Statutes* (4th edn) (1991 reissue) 552.

For the Coroners Rules 1984, see 5 *Halsbury's Statutory Instruments* (1994 reissue) 359.

Cases referred to in judgment

Associated Provincial Picture Houses Ltd v Wednesbury Corp [1947] 2 All ER 680, [1948] 1 KB 223, CA.
R v A-G, ex p Ferrante [1995] CA Transcript 135.
R v Birmingham and Solihull Coroner, ex p Cotton (1995) 160 JP 123, DC.
R v Carter (1876) 45 LJQB 711.
R v Divine, ex p Walton [1930] 2 KB 29, [1930] All ER Rep 302, DC.
R v East Berkshire Coroner, ex p Buckley (1992) 157 JP 425, DC.
R v Hammersmith Coroner, ex p Peach [1980] 2 All ER 7, [1980] QB 211, [1980] 2 WLR 496, CA.
R v Inner London North District Coroner, ex p Linnane [1989] 2 All ER 254, [1989] 1 WLR 395, DC.
R v North Humberside and Scunthorpe Coroner, ex p Jamieson [1994] 3 All ER 972, [1995] QB 1, [1994] 3 WLR 82, CA.
Richardson v Redpath Brown & Co Ltd [1944] 1 All ER 110, [1944] AC 62, HL.
Woods v Wilson Sons & Co Ltd (1915) 8 BWCC 288, HL.

Cases also cited or referred to in skeleton arguments

Lane v D D Leitch & Son (1921) 55 ILT 161, Ir CA.
R v Adomako [1994] 3 All ER 79, [1995] 1 AC 171, HL.
R v HM Coroner for Inner London North District, ex p Linnane (No 2) (1990) 155 JP 773, DC.
R v HM Coroner for North Northumberland, ex p Armstrong (1987) 151 JP 773, DC.
R v Poplar Coroner, ex p Chaudhry (1992) Times, 20 October, [1992] CA Transcript 911.
R v Poplar Coroner, ex p Thomas [1993] 2 All ER 381, CA.
R v Shrewsbury Coroner's Court, ex p British Parachute Association (1987) 152 JP 123, DC.
R v South London Coroner, ex p Thompson (1982) 126 SJ 625, DC.
R v Southwark Coroner, ex p Hicks [1987] 2 All ER 140, [1987] 1 WLR 1624, DC.

Application for judicial review

Irene Wright applied with the leave of Dyson J granted on 5 October 1995 for an order of certiorari to quash the decision of the Her Majesty's Coroner for Surrey on 13 October 1994 that her son, Vassell Wright, had died accidentally and an order of mandamus to require a further inquest to be held by another coroner with a jury. The facts are set out in the judgment.

Raymond Croxon QC and *Delphine Breese-Laughran* (instructed by *J R Jones*) for the applicant.

Ian Burnett (instructed by *J H Jessup*, Kingston upon Thames) for the coroner.

Cur adv vult

14 June 1996. The following judgment was delivered.

TUCKER J. This is an application for judicial review pursuant to leave granted by Dyson J. The decision under challenge is that of HM Coroner for Surrey, who on 13 October 1994 concluded that Mr Vassell Wright died by accident.

The originating application is dated 24 February 1995, so it is about six weeks out of time. However, I am satisfied that the delay is attributable to problems in obtaining legal aid for which no blame should be attributed to the applicant. In view of this, and also of the facts that leave was granted without any reservation, and that counsel for the respondent takes no point on the matter, I consider that there is good reason for extending the period within which the application can be made, and I do so.

The applicant is the mother of the deceased. He was a fit 27-year-old young man, who on 27 November 1992 was admitted as a day surgery patient to Ashford General Hospital for relatively minor dental surgery to remove his wisdom teeth. He received a general anaesthetic for the purposes of the surgery. But unfortunately he never regained consciousness, and died on 5 December 1992. It is accepted that the cause of death was cerebral necrosis due to cerebral anoxia. It is clear that the deceased must have suffered an obstruction to his airway.

An inquest was held at the Ashford Hospital on 4 and 29 March 1993. The inquest was then adjourned for the police and the Crown Prosecution Service to consider whether the death should give rise to criminal charges, but no charges were laid. This is what accounts for the 18-month delay before the coroner was able to announce his verdict.

The relief sought in this application is for an order of certiorari to quash the decision of the coroner and an order of mandamus requiring a further inquest to be held by another coroner, sitting with a jury.

The grounds on which the relief is sought are as follows. (1) The coroner failed to have proper regard to the requirements of s 8(3)(d) of the Coroners Act 1988 and failed to direct himself to empanel a jury. The subsection provides:

'If it appears to a coroner, either before he proceeds to hold an inquest or in the course of an inquest begun without a jury, that there is reason to suspect ... (d) that the death occurred in circumstances the continuance or possible recurrence of which is prejudicial to the health or safety of the public or any section of the public, he shall proceed to summon a jury in the manner required by subsection (2) above.'

(2) The coroner sat with an assessor, Dr Ziderman, a consultant anaesthetist, as an adviser on anaesthetic and resuscitation procedures. The applicant submits that there is no provision in the 1988 Act or at common law for a coroner to sit with an assessor. (3) Having arranged that Dr Ziderman should sit with him as an assessor, the coroner invited him to ask questions of witnesses and later to give evidence and then to assist him in making his decision, contrary to the rules of natural justice. (4) The coroner sent the Dinamap equipment manufactured by Critikon USA, which did not at the material time operate to warn the nurse of the

blockage of the patient's airway and consequential deprivation of oxygen, back to the manufacturers in the United States for inspection, thus depriving the deceased's relative of having it inspected by an independent expert before or at the hearing contrary to the rules of natural justice. (5) The coroner did not properly investigate or consider certain matters of fact set out in the affidavit of Imran Khan which were relevant to the issue of the causation of death and raised matters of public concern. The only matter not otherwise referred to is the allegation that the coroner failed to make any finding as to the face mask used on the deceased and therefore may have missed a possible contributing factor to the death of the deceased, who was Afro-Caribbean. Though not referred to in the affidavit, the applicant's counsel, Mr Croxon QC, has also sought to raise the question of confusion as to who was in charge of the patient's treatment once the 'crash team' had arrived. (6) Although making a finding of fact that there had been a lack of care which led to the death of Vassell Wright, the coroner erred in law in holding that this was not a verdict he could give within s 11(5) of the 1988 Act and r 36 of the Coroners Rules 1984, SI 1984/522, having regard to *R v North Humberside and Scunthorpe Coroner, ex p Jamieson* [1994] 3 All ER 972, [1995] QB 1.

I can dispose of two of these matters right away.

Ground (4): the Dinamap equipment

This complaint is misconceived. It now appears from the coroner's office that the hospital returned this equipment to its suppliers before the death occurred, and that the suppliers returned it to the manufacturers in the United States. The coroner's jurisdiction arose only on the death. He played no part in the dealings with the equipment. It is unfortunate that it was not available for inspection. However, the applicant does not appear to have raised the issue with the coroner at the inquest. And it is difficult to see what the coroner could have done about it in any event.

It was not suggested in the grounds set out in Form 86A that the coroner should have asked why the equipment had been returned.

I agree with Mr Burnett, counsel appearing on behalf of the coroner, that this point could not and cannot engage public law remedies.

Ground (5): the face mask

In my opinion the coroner made a clear finding as to the colour of the mask. There was conflicting evidence as to whether it was green or transparent. There was evidence from a witness, Sister Chana, that it was 'a clear mask'—not tinged green. The coroner found in two passages that it was a transparent mask. This was a finding which he was entitled to make.

There was no obstacle to observing cyanosis even in an Afro-Caribbean patient.

The jury issue

Mr Croxon, who also represented the applicant at the inquest, applied three times to the coroner for him to empanel a jury, but his applications were refused. The coroner sat with an assessor but without a jury. Having regard to the wording of s 8(3)(d) the issue for me to determine is whether any reasonable coroner, on the basis of the material before him at this inquest, could have failed to have reason to suspect that the death occurred in circumstances the continuance or possible recurrence of which was prejudicial to the health and safety of the public. The circumstances upon which Mr Croxon relied were, first, the suggestion that a green mask was used on a black patient; second, that the *a* Dinamap monitor was in regular use; and third, the dispute over control of the crash team.

In considering whether or not the coroner acted unreasonably in the *Wednesbury* sense (see *Associated Provincial Picture Houses Ltd v Wednesbury Corp* [1947] 2 All ER 680, [1948] 1 KB 223) in deciding to proceed without a jury, it is material to bear in mind the purposes for which an inquest is held. These are

b defined by r 36 of the 1984 rules as follows:

> '(1) The proceedings and evidence at an inquest shall be directed solely to ascertaining the following matters, namely—(a) who the deceased was; (b) how, when and where the deceased came by his death; (c) the particulars for the time being required by the Registration Acts to be registered concerning

c the death.

> (2) Neither the coroner nor the jury shall express any opinion on any other matters.'

Rule 42 provides that no verdict shall be framed in such a way as to appear to determine any question of (a) criminal liability on the part of a named person, or

d (b) civil liability.

In his affidavit, Mr Burgess, the coroner, sets out his reasons for not empanelling a jury. At para 8 he says that it did not appear to him either before the inquest began or in the course of it, that there was reason to suspect that the death occurred in circumstances the continuance or possible recurrence of which

e was prejudicial to the health or safety of the public or any section of it. Mr Croxon criticised the use of the word 'suspect' in this context, but the criticism is in my opinion without foundation, since it is the word used in the section to which the coroner had to have regard.

At para 9 the coroner described the difficulty of drawing a line between a case

f involving a one off incident, which would not call for a jury, and one in which a system was at fault in a way which, if unchecked, might result in further injury or death. He deposes to the fact that he formed the view that this was an isolated death in which s 8(3)(d) was not engaged.

Mr Croxon referred me to the decision of the Divisional Court in *R v Inner London North District Coroner, ex p Linnane* [1989] 2 All ER 254, [1989] 1 WLR 395.

g It was in that case common ground that the phrase 'if it appears to a coroner' governs the whole of s 8(3), so as to leave the decision of whether to summon a jury under that subsection solely to the coroner. His decision can only be overturned if he has misdirected himself in some material respect. I agree with Mr Croxon's submission that should it appear to the coroner that there is reason

h to suspect, then he is obliged to proceed to summon a jury. The question is as I have already formulated it, or (put another way) whether the coroner misdirected himself in some material respect in reaching his decision that this was a one off incident not requiring a jury.

In *Ex p Linnane* Taylor LJ referred to observations made by members of the Court of Appeal in *R v Hammersmith Coroner, ex p Peach* [1980] 2 All ER 7, [1980]

j QB 211 which he said were helpful in considering what is the purpose of para (d) in s 8(3). Lord Denning MR said ([1980] 2 All ER 7 at 10, [1980] QB 211 at 226):

> 'Having regard to these illustrations, it seems to me that the suggestions made by Bridge LJ in the course of the argument gives a good indication of the "circumstances" in which a jury must be summoned. It is when the circumstances are such that similar fatalities may possibly recur in the future,

and it is reasonable to expect that some action should be taken to prevent their recurrence.'

Bridge LJ said ([1980] 2 All ER 7 at 10, [1980] QB 211 at 226–227):

'The key to the nature of that limitation is to be found, I think, in the paragraph's concern with the continuance or possible recurrence of the circumstances in question. This indicates to my mind that the paragraph applies to circumstances of such a kind that their continuance or recurrence may reasonably and ought properly to be avoided by the taking of appropriate steps which it is in the power of some responsible body to take.'

Sir David Cairns said ([1980] 2 All ER 7 at 11, [1980] QB 211 at 228):

'The reference to "continuance or possible recurrence" indicates to my mind that the provision was intended to apply only to circumstances the continuance or recurrence of which was preventable or to some extent controllable. Moreover, since it is prejudice to the health or safety of the public or a section of the public that is referred to, what is envisaged must, I think, be something which might be prevented or safeguarded by a public authority or some other person or body whose activities can be said to affect a substantial section of the public.'

Mr Croxon submits that the fact, as found by the coroner, that the hospital has since the death of Mr Wright revised the policy as to the tuition of those who might be called upon to take part in resuscitation of itself shows why the coroner was in breach of his obligation. And it is submitted that although the coroner ultimately found that a transparent mask was used on this occasion, green masks were available for use, there was a dispute as to which type *had* been used, and the matter was one which called for investigation, as also was the apparent failure of the alarm on the Dinamap equipment. As to this latter point, the fact was, that the particular piece of equipment had been sent away and was no longer in use. There was no evidence that it contained an inherent fault.

Mr Burnett, on the coroner's behalf, has referred me to an unreported decision of the Court of Appeal in *R v A-G, ex p Ferrante* [1995] CA Transcript 135 in which Bingham MR referred to the case as being—

'plainly a case which in the coroner's judgment did not appear to be a case of systemic default, in other words, a case in which the system was so much at fault that, if nothing was done, there would be other deaths.'

The question of confusion as to who was in charge once the crash team arrived is not a matter which was expressly or clearly referred to in Mr Khan's affidavit and therefore it is not one with which the coroner has dealt in his own affidavit. It was something which was raised in the evidence at the inquest and which was dealt with by the coroner in his review of the evidence. He states that 'whilst, in this instance, it is possible that the outcome would have been no different, nevertheless, the event has shown the shortcomings in both training and co-operation'.

This matter has caused me some concern. It might be regarded as the strongest of the circumstances upon which Mr Croxon relied in submitting that a jury should have been empanelled. Nevertheless, having given the matter careful consideration, I am not persuaded that the coroner misdirected himself in any material respect, or acted unreasonably in the *Wednesbury* sense. The question of who was in charge on this occasion was entitled to be regarded as an individual rather than a systemic failing.

In my opinion the coroner's decision not to summon a jury cannot be stigmatised as wrong in a public law sense.

The assessor

So far as counsel are aware, this is the first occasion on which a court has had to consider the legality of a coroner sitting with an assessor.

Mr Croxon was correct when he submitted that there is no express provision in the 1988 Act for the coroner to sit with an assessor. There is provision in another statute, the Regulation of Railways Act 1871, for the appointment of an inspector or other person having legal or special knowledge to assist in holding an inquest on the death of a person occasioned by a railway accident.

It is well recognised that judges of the High Court from time to time sit with an assessor. The statutory basis for this is s 70 of the Supreme Court Act 1981, sub-s (1) of which provides:

'In any cause or matter before the High Court the court may, if it thinks it expedient to do so, call in the aid of one or more assessors specially qualified, and hear and dispose of the cause or matter wholly or partially with their assistance.'

This is reflected in RSC Ord 33, r 2, which provides that a cause or matter or any question or issue arising therein may be tried before '(c) a judge with the assistance of assessors, or (d) an Official Referee with or without the assistance of assessors' and in r 6, which provides that 'trial of a cause or matter with the assistance of assessors under section 70 of the Act shall take place in such a manner and on such terms as the Court may direct'.

In Admiralty proceedings, Ord 75, r 25(2) provides for trial with or without assessors, whether Elder Brethren of Trinity House, nautical assessors or other assessors. And on a review by a judge of a decision of a taxing officer, Ord 62, r 35(5) refers to the power of the court to appoint not less than two assessors, of whom one shall be a taxing officer and one a practising solicitor. And see s 70(3) of the 1981 Act: 'Rules of court shall make provision for the appointment of scientific advisers to assist the Patents Court ...' So too in the county court, s 63 of the County Courts Act 1984 enables a judge to summon to his assistance one or more persons (a) of skill and experience in the matter to which the proceedings relate; and (b) who may be willing to sit with him and act as assessors.

Nevertheless, in the absence of any express provision in the 1988 Act and where there is reference in another statute dealing with specific situations, does a coroner have a general power to sit with an assessor? Mr Croxon submits that he does not, and that it offends the rules of natural justice for a coroner to have an assessor sitting alongside him as an expert witness, appearing to have the same power as the coroner himself. In the present case the matter was further complicated by the fact that the coroner allowed the assessor to examine a number of the witnesses, and then called him to give evidence himself as an expert witness.

In his affidavit the coroner deposes to the fact that the practice of a coroner sitting with an assessor in difficult technical cases is relatively common. He says he has done so himself on perhaps a dozen occasions. He makes the point that an inquest is (as the name suggests) an inquisitional proceeding without parties, and that the coroner cannot rely on the attendance of lawyers fully instructed to ask searching questions of the witnesses.

Mr Burnett's researches show that as long ago as 1876, coroners were sitting with assessors. He cites *R v Carter* (1876) 45 LJQB 711 concerning the inquest on Mr Charles Bravo, in which an assessor clearly took part. Mr Burnett's submission is that, that being the established practice, it was retained in force by s 45(5) of the Coroners Act 1887, and by s 36(5) of the 1988 Act. There is certainly nothing in either statute to suggest that the practice has been forbidden.

In both the textbooks on this subject, the authors recognise that the practice exists. Thus in *Thurston's Coronership* (3rd edn, 1985) para 16.16 it is stated: 'The coroner may sit alone ... or with any assessor whom he may choose.' At para 16.17 there is a reference to an informal assessor, contrasting this with an official assessor appointed under the 1871 Act. And interestingly it is said: '... other persons may sit with the coroner at his invitation as in a difficult anaesthetic medical case when, for example an anaesthetist may be so invited.'

And in *Jervis on Coroners* (11th edn, 1993) para 12.17 it is accepted that a coroner may invite an expert of some kind to sit with him as an assessor where particular expertise will be required even to understand the significance of the evidence, but the coroner must be careful to avoid any suggestion that his decisions or conclusions are being made for him by such assessor. In my judgment, what was the established practice for at least 120 years, remains so today, and it is entirely permissible for a coroner to call for the assistance of an assessor to sit with him if he considers it necessary having regard to the technical nature of the evidence which may have to be considered. The present case falls into that category. In my opinion the coroner was justified in sitting with an assessor, and cannot properly be criticised for having done so.

But what role should the assessor play in the proceedings? In particular, in the present case was it manifestly wrong so as to amount to unlawfulness to allow the assessor to examine witnesses and then to give evidence himself?

Rule 17 of the 1984 rules provides that an inquest should be held in public. One of the grounds of complaint is that the coroner allowed the assessor to assist him in making his decision, contrary to the rules of natural justice. In so far as this suggests that the coroner consulted privately with the assessor before reading his decision, I reject the complaint. I accept the coroner's evidence contained in para 4 of his affidavit that after the conclusion of the evidence he did not discuss the circumstances of the death with Dr Ziderman.

Rule 20 deals with the entitlement to examine witnesses. Among the persons having this right is 'any other person who, in the opinion of the coroner, is a properly interested person' (para (2)(h)). This gives the coroner a wide discretion to allow anyone to question witnesses. I doubt whether the rule was framed with assessors in mind. Nevertheless, it is wide enough to include them, and in my opinion it would unnecessarily curtail the functions of an assessor, and hence the value of his assistance to the coroner, if he were to be prevented from asking any relevant question of a witness giving technical evidence provided this is done under the coroner's control, and is restricted to matters within the assessor's special experience. In my judgment there can be no objection to the assessor asking the questions which he did ask in the present case.

Rule 40 provides: 'No person shall be allowed to address the coroner or the jury as to the facts.' Despite concern expressed by Mr Croxon at the time, the coroner called Dr Ziderman to give evidence, and he was in due course cross-examined by counsel. Mr Croxon submitted that this offended the rules of natural justice, in that it did not appear to be right to have the assessor sitting

a beside the coroner at one stage, and then at a later stage giving evidence before
   him as an expert witness.

   In *Richardson v Redpath Brown & Co Ltd* [1944] 1 All ER 110, [1944] AC 62 the
   House of Lords considered the position of a medical assessor in an application
   under the Workmen's Compensation Acts. Viscount Simon LC referred to Lord
   Parmoor in *Woods v Wilson Sons & Co Ltd* (1915) 8 BWCC 288 at 311 as having
b aptly defined the medical assessor's function as being 'not to supply evidence but
   to help the judge ... to understand the medical evidence', a view in which Lord
   Parker concurred (see [1944] 1 All ER 110 at 113, [1944] AC 62 at 71). The real
   ground of objection in that case was that the medical assessor was unsworn and
   could not be cross-examined.

   It was submitted by Mr Burnett that the calling of the assessor to give evidence
c and exposing him to cross-examination had the effect of overcoming this
   mischief, and that it was important that the assessor's involvement should take
   place in public.

   However, in my opinion, the role of an assessor should not extend to his giving
   expert evidence. There is a danger that it might appear (whether justifiably or
d not) that the evidence of such a witness might attract the special confidence of the
   coroner, and might carry greater weight than would otherwise be the case. It is
   better that the roles of assessor and expert witness should be kept separate.
   However well-intentioned, as I accept it was, I feel the coroner fell into error in
   allowing Dr Ziderman to fulfil both these functions.

e *The verdict*
   The conclusion of the coroner in his inquisition as to the death was 'That the
   deceased died by Accident'. However, the coroner had earlier referred to it
   seeming to be a clear case of lack of care. He said: 'Without being specific, those
   who had care of him failed to maintain his airway and death resulted from such
f failure.' However, the coroner felt that he was prevented from returning a
   verdict to that effect by reason of the judgment of the Court of Appeal in *R v North
   Humberside and Scunthorpe Coroner, ex p Jamieson* [1994] 3 All ER 972, [1995] QB 1.
   The coroner set out at length the passage in the judgment of Bingham MR which
   he felt was binding upon him. Having considered that judgment, the coroner felt
   obliged to say that a verdict of lack of care or neglect would not be an appropriate
g conclusion.

   Mr Croxon criticises this decision of the coroner's. He submits that in the
   present case the patient handed himself over to the care of professional people,
   who rendered him unconscious, and who thereafter let him down. Mr Croxon
   asks rhetorically: 'If this is not a case of lack of care, what is?' He submits that *Ex
h p Jamieson* has not altered the law but has merely clarified it. Basing himself on
   the decision of the Divisional Court in *R v East Berkshire Coroner, ex p Buckley*
   (1992) 157 JP 425 which he says was cited without disapproval in *Ex p Jamieson*,
   Mr Croxon submits that it is still open to a coroner to record a 'lack of care'
   verdict.

   I do not agree with this submission. It cannot stand with the words of Bingham
j MR in his judgment in *Ex p Jamieson* [1994] 3 All ER 972 at 990, [1995] QB 1 at 25
   (para (8)). In the light of that judgment I do not see how the coroner could have
   returned a verdict of 'lack of care'.

   However, Bingham MR went on to deal further with the matter (see [1994] 3
   All ER 972 at 990, [1995] QB 1 at 25 (para (9))). It is open to the coroner to record
   a verdict of death as a result of neglect, in a case where he considers such a verdict
   to be appropriate. Mr Croxon urges me alternatively to substitute such a verdict

in the present case—the form of words he proposes are that 'Vassell Wright died on 5 December 1992 of cerebral necrosis due to cerebral anoxia sustained whilst unconscious and recovering from anaesthetic at Ashford Hospital, as a result of neglect'.

Mr Croxon submits that, at the relevant time, the patient was in a dependent position due to anaesthesia, and that there was a failure to provide medical attention for him when he obviously needed it.

However, in my opinion, the 'neglect' referred to by Bingham MR in *Ex p Jamieson* means continuous or at least non-transient neglect. It is not an appropriate description of the negligent lack of care which is alleged to have led to the death in the present case.

I have been referred to the decision of the Divisional Court in *R v Birmingham and Solihull Coroner, ex p Cotton* (1995) 160 JP 123. I adopt the words of McCowan LJ (at 129). In my judgment, matters of negligence are better decided in a civil action by a judge alone trying a pleaded case. I am told that such an action has been commenced in the present case, and that the health authority have admitted liability. It is difficult to see what further advantage is to be obtained from any different verdict. In my opinion the coroner was perfectly entitled to record the decision which he did. It was certainly not an irrational conclusion.

Discretion

That leads me to the question whether, in view of the part played by the assessor, I ought to grant relief. These matters occurred long ago. Memories of witnesses will have faded. A thorough investigation was carried out. I am not persuaded that the fact of the assessor having given evidence will have made any material difference to the outcome.

Having regard to the decision of the court in *R v Divine, ex p Walton* [1930] 2 KB 29, [1930] All ER Rep 302, I do not consider it necessary or desirable in the interests of justice to order a fresh inquest to be held, or to substitute any verdict of my own.

The application is accordingly refused.

Application refused.

Dilys Tausz   Barrister.

a # MD Foods plc (formerly Associated Dairies Ltd) v Baines and others

HOUSE OF LORDS

b LORD GOFF OF CHIEVELEY, LORD MUSTILL, LORD NICHOLLS OF BIRKENHEAD, LORD HOFFMANN AND LORD CLYDE

22, 23 JANUARY, 27 FEBRUARY 1997

c *Restrictive trade practices – Registration of agreement – Excepted agreements – Agreement for the supply of goods – Exclusive supply agreement containing non-competition clause – Party undertaking not to sell goods by way of retail to supplier's customers – Party breaching agreement by obtaining supplies elsewhere but claiming agreement void because it had not been registered – Whether non-competition clause relating exclusively to goods supplied in pursuance of agreement – Whether agreement containing restrictions in respect of sale, or acquisition for sale, of other d goods of same description – Whether agreement exempted from registration – Restrictive Trade Practices Act 1976, ss 6(1), 9(3)(7), Sch 3, para 2.*

The respondent milkman entered into a five-year milk supply agreement with the appellant dairy company under which (by cl 4(1)) he agreed to buy from the company and the company agreed to supply to him all the milk he needed for sale e in his milk round business. The agreement contained mutual non-competition clauses, which in the case of the respondent was expressed in the form (in cl 4(3)) that the respondent undertook 'not to sell milk by way of retail to any customers of the Company', and the company agreed not to sell milk to the customers of the respondent's business. The respondent found that he could obtain milk, f including the company's milk, more cheaply from sources other than directly from the company. When he began obtaining his milk from outside sources, the company commenced proceedings to obtain an interlocutory injunction, alleging a breach of cl 4(1). The respondent contended that his obligation to buy all his milk from the company was void because the agreement had not been registered under the Restrictive Trade Practices Act 1976. He contended that the restriction g in cl 4(3) made the agreement registrable under s 6(1)[a] of the Act because it was an agreement between two persons carrying on business in the supply of goods under which restrictions were accepted by the parties in respect of either 'the terms or conditions on … which goods are to be supplied' within para (c) or 'the persons … to … or from whom … goods are to be supplied or acquired' within h para (f). The company contended that the agreement fell within the exemptions from registration contained in s 9(3)[b] and para 2[c] of Sch 3 to the Act because (i) under s 9(3) the non-competition clause, cl 4(3), was to be disregarded in determining whether the agreement should be registered since cl 4(3) was a 'term which relate[d] exclusively to the goods supplied … in pursuance of the

j ─────────────────────────────

a Section 6(1), so far as material, provides: '(1) This Act applies to agreements … between two or more persons carrying on business within the United Kingdom in the … supply of goods … under which restrictions are accepted by two or more parties in respect of …(c) the terms or conditions on … which goods are to be supplied … (f) the persons … to … or from whom … goods are to be supplied or acquired …'

b Section 9(3), so far as material, is set out at p 838 *b*, post

c Paragraph 2, so far as material, is set out at p 837 *f*, post

agreement' and no account was to be taken of it, and (ii) under para 2 of Sch 3 the
Act did not apply if the only restrictions accepted by the parties were '(a) by the
party supplying the goods, in respect of the supply of goods of the same
description to other persons; or (b) by the party acquiring the goods, in respect of
the sale, or acquisition for sale, of other goods of the same description'. The
judge held that the agreement was not registrable and continued the injunction.
On appeal, the Court of Appeal held that the agreement was registrable and
discharged the injunction. The company appealed to the House of Lords.

Held – (1) In order to attract the exemption in para 2 of Sch 3 to the 1976 Act, an
agreement had to be one under which no relevant restrictions were accepted
beyond those falling within sub-paras (a) and (b) of para 2. However, the
respondent's obligation not to sell to the company's customers milk supplied to
him by the company was outside the exemption provided by sub-para (b), since
that obligation was a restriction accepted in respect of the sale of the very goods
acquired under the agreement, not a restriction in respect of the sale of other
goods of the same description. Accordingly, taken by itself, para 2 of Sch 3 did
not operate to exempt the agreement between the company and the respondent
from the requirement of registration under the 1976 Act   (see p 835 *d e*, p 837 *g j*
and p 841 *a b*, post).

  (2) However, the effect of s 9(3) of the Act was that the restriction imposed by
cl 4(3) had to be disregarded to the extent that it applied to milk supplied by the
company and para 2 of Sch 3 had to be applied on that footing, in accordance with
s 9(7)[d], which provided that in determining whether an agreement was exempt
from registration under Sch 3 no account was to be taken of restrictions which
were required to be ignored under s 9(3). On that basis, to the extent that it
applied to milk obtained elsewhere, cl 4(3) imposed a restriction which fell within
sub-para (b) and consequently the agreement was exempted from registration by
the joint effect of s 9 and para 2 of Sch 3. The appeal would therefore be allowed
(see p 835 *d e*, p 838 *g j*, p 839 *c* and p 841 *a b*, post); dictum of Stamp J in *Re
Schweppes Ltd's Agreement (No 2), Registrar of Restrictive Trading Agreements v
Schweppes Ltd* [1971] 2 All ER 1473 at 1489 disapproved.

Notes

For exempted agreements, see 47 *Halsbury's Laws* (4th edn reissue) paras 229–244.
   For the Restrictive Trade Practices Act 1976, ss 6, 9, Sch 3, para 2, see 47
Halsbury's Statutes (4th edn) 328, 333, 378.

Case referred to in opinions

*Schweppes Ltd's Agreement, Re (No 2), Registrar of Restrictive Trading Agreements v
   Schweppes Ltd* [1971] 2 All ER 1473, (1971) LR 7 RP 336, [1971] 1 WLR 1148.

Appeal

MD Foods plc (formerly Associated Dairies Ltd) appealed with leave granted by
the Court of Appeal from the decision of the Court of Appeal (Stuart-Smith, Hirst
and Schiemann LJJ) ([1996] ICR 183) delivered on 23 June 1995 allowing the
appeal of the respondent, Andrew Baines, from the judgment and order made by
Sir John Vinelott sitting as a judge of the High Court in the Chancery Division

---

d   Section 9(7), so far as material, is set out at p 838 *c d*, post

a ([1995] ICR 296) on 21 October 1994 whereby he held that the respondent's application for summary determination under RSC Ord 14A of a question arising in an action brought by the appellants against the respondent, Philip Anthony Denby and Eric Taylor, namely that the exclusive purchase obligation in cl 4(1) of the milk supply agreement entered into by the appellants and the respondent on 10 August 1989 was unenforceable, failed. The facts are set out in the opinion of Lord Nicholls of Birkenhead.

Kenneth Parker QC and *Mark Brealey* (instructed by *Pinsent Curtis*, Leeds) for the appellants.

Peter Roth (instructed by *Oglethorpe Sturton & Gillibrand*, Lancaster) for the respondent.

Their Lordships took time for consideration.

27 February 1997. The following opinions were delivered.

LORD GOFF OF CHIEVELEY. My Lords, I have had the advantage of reading a draft of the speech of my noble and learned friend Lord Nicholls of Birkenhead. For the reasons he has given, I would allow this appeal.

LORD MUSTILL. My Lords, I have had the advantage of reading a draft of the speech of my noble and learned friend Lord Nicholls of Birkenhead. For the reasons he has given, I, too, would allow this appeal.

LORD NICHOLLS OF BIRKENHEAD. My Lords, Mr Andrew Baines is a milk roundsman in Lancaster. He buys milk from a wholesale supplier, and delivers it from house to house onto the doorsteps of his customers. In August 1989 he entered into a five-year milk supply agreement with Associated Dairies Ltd, now known as MD Foods plc. The company agreed to supply to Mr Baines, and Mr Baines agreed to buy from the company, all the milk he needed for sale in his business. His 'business' meant his existing milk distribution business, together with any milk distribution business he might acquire in future not already tied to another milk supplier. If force majeure prevented the company from maintaining supplies, Mr Baines could obtain milk elsewhere as a temporary measure. The agreement contained mutual non-competition clauses. The company agreed not to sell milk to the customers of Mr Baines' business; Mr Baines agreed not to sell milk by way of retail to any customers of the company. The latter restriction lies at the heart of this case. I must set out the form in which it was expressed:

> '4 ... [Mr Baines] hereby undertakes and agrees with the Company ... (3) During the continuance of this Agreement (except with the prior written consent of the Company) not to sell milk by way of retail to any customers of the Company ...'

Milk roundsmen are under increasingly severe competition from milk sales by shops, especially supermarkets. If a milk roundsman's business is to survive, the difference between the price of milk on sale in shops and the price of the milk he delivers to the homes of his customers must not become too large. So it was a matter of grave concern to Mr Baines when the company, more than once, increased the price it charged him for his milk. He had to increase his own prices to his customers, or see his profit margin eroded.

In January 1992 he started taking his milk supplies from an outside source, where he could obtain milk more cheaply. Other sources could obtain milk, ironically from the company itself, at one or two pence per pint less than the price charged by the company to Mr Baines. They were not tied by an exclusive supply agreement and they were able to negotiate better terms. One of these sources was Mr Baines' own father, who also was a milk roundsman.

The company started High Court proceedings against Mr Baines and obtained interlocutory injunctive relief. One of his defences was that his obligation to buy all his milk from the company was void because the agreement had not been registered under the Restrictive Trade Practices Act 1976. An application to determine this issue under RSC Ord 14A came before Sir John Vinelott, sitting as a judge of the High Court in the Chancery Division ([1995] ICR 296). He held, in favour of the company, that the agreement was not registrable. He declined to discharge the injunction.

The Court of Appeal, comprising Stuart-Smith, Hirst and Schiemann LJJ ([1996] ICR 183), reached the contrary conclusion. By now the agreement had expired by effluxion of time, but the validity of the agreement remained a live issue: partly because of the company's liability on its cross-undertaking in damages, but more especially because the agreement was in the company's standard form. The Court of Appeal upheld Mr Baines' contentions and ordered an inquiry as to the damages he had sustained by reason of the injunction. With the leave of the Court of Appeal the company appealed to your Lordships' House.

Some points of common ground can be noted. Clause 4(3), plainly, applied to milk supplied to the milkman under the agreement. It is common ground that in two circumstances the agreement could apply to milk which had not been supplied under the agreement. The milkman's obligation not to sell milk to customers of the company would apply if he obtained milk supplies elsewhere while the company was temporarily unable to supply him. The obligation would also apply if he obtained milk from a third party to whom he was bound by an exclusive supply agreement.

It is also accepted that if cl 4(3) had been drafted in a different form, although having precisely the same ambit, the agreement would not have been registrable. This would be so if cl 4(3) had been drafted in two linguistically separable pieces, to the following effect:

'(3) … not to sell by way of retail to any of the customers of the company any milk supplied to him (a) by the company or (b) by any source other than the company.'

The question is whether this difference in form makes all the difference so far as registrability is concerned.

The basic scheme of the 1976 Act is familiar. Certain agreements are made subject to registration in a register maintained by the Director General of Fair Trading. The agreements may concern goods (Pt II of the Act) or services (Pt III). In respect of agreements of which particulars have been registered, the court is given power to declare whether restrictions, or provisions for the furnishing of information, by virtue of which the Act applies are contrary to the public interest. Any restrictions or information provisions found by the court to be contrary to *a* the public interest are void and unenforceable. The sanction for non-registration is that all restrictions accepted under the agreement, and all information provisions made under the agreement, are void and it is unlawful to enforce them.

This case concerns restrictive agreements relating to goods. Section 6(1), so far as material, provides that the Act applies to agreements between persons carrying
b on business within the United Kingdom in the production or supply of goods under which restrictions are accepted by two or more parties in respect of, among other matters, prices to be charged or recommended, the terms on which goods are to be supplied, the quantities to be produced or supplied or, in para (f), the persons from whom goods are to be acquired or to whom goods are to be supplied.

c Mr Baines' milk supply agreement was an agreement between persons carrying on business within the United Kingdom in the supply of goods. It is common ground that under this agreement Mr Baines and the company accepted several relevant restrictions, by which I mean restrictions falling within s 6(1). Mr Baines' obligation to buy all his milk from the company, the company's
d obligation not to sell milk to customers of Mr Baines' business, and Mr Baines' obligation under cl 4(3) not to sell milk to customers of the company are all restrictions which come within s 6(1)(f). Thus, unless exempted, particulars of the agreement were registrable.

There are two relevant exemptions. Under s 28 the Act does not apply to the agreements described in Sch 3. Paragraph 2 of Sch 3 concerns exclusive dealing
e agreements. Omitting immaterial words for ease of comprehension, para 2 provides:

> 'This Act does not apply to an agreement for the supply of goods between two persons ... under which no such restrictions as are described in section
f 6(1) above are accepted ... other than restrictions accepted ... (a) by the party supplying the goods, in respect of the supply of goods of the same description to other persons; or (b) by the party acquiring the goods, in respect of the sale, or acquisition for sale, of other goods of the same description.'

Taken by itself, para 2 does not operate to exempt Mr Baines' agreement from
g the Act. Some of the restrictions in the agreement fall within sub-paras (a) and (b). The company's obligation not to sell milk to Mr Baines' customers is within sub-para (a). Mr Baines' obligation to buy all his milk from the company is an obligation not to buy milk elsewhere. This falls within sub-para (b). So also does his obligation under cl 4(3) so far as it relates to milk *not* supplied by the company.
h Mr Baines' obligation not to sell milk to customers of the company is within sub-para (b) so far as it relates to milk not bought from the company because that is a restriction accepted by him, as the person acquiring goods under the agreement, in respect of the sale of other goods of the same description.

However, Mr Baines' obligation not to sell to the company's customers milk supplied to him *by the company* is outside sub-para (b). This obligation is a
j restriction accepted in respect of the sale of the very goods acquired under the agreement, not a restriction in respect of the sale of *other* goods of the same description. This being so, the agreement is not within the para 2 exemption, if the paragraph is taken by itself, because to be within the paragraph the agreement must be one under which no relevant restrictions are accepted beyond those falling within sub-paras (a) and (b).

I can now turn to the second relevant exemption. Paragraph 2 in Sch 3 does not stand alone. Section 9 sets out a number of provisions which are to be disregarded in determining whether the Act applies. Section 9(3) provides:

> 'In determining whether an agreement for the supply of goods ... is an agreement to which this Act applies ... no account shall be taken of any term which relates exclusively to the goods supplied ... in pursuance of the agreement.'

Section 9(7) then spells out how this is to work in a case where Sch 3 is sought to be applied:

> 'Any reference in Schedule 3 to this Act to—(a) such restrictions as are described in section 6(1) above ... shall be construed, in relation to any agreement, as not including references to restrictions ... of which, by virtue of any provision of this section, account cannot be taken in determining whether the agreement is one to which this Act applies by virtue of this Part, or of restrictions accepted ... by any term of which account cannot be so taken.'

The issue on this appeal concerns the meaning and application of s 9(3). Mr Baines' case is that s 9(3) has no application to the milk supply agreement. The starting point of his argument is that, as already noted, the restriction which excluded the milk supply agreement from the para 2 exemption was Mr Baines' obligation not to sell to customers of the company milk supplied to him by the company. This restriction is part of the restriction accepted by Mr Baines under cl 4(3). Clause 4(3) applied, however, not only to milk supplied to Mr Baines under the agreement. Clause 4(3) applied also to milk bought elsewhere in the two circumstances in which Mr Baines was entitled to obtain milk from other suppliers. Hence, the argument continues, cl 4(3) is not a 'term which relates exclusively to goods supplied ... in pursuance of the agreement'. This being so, the argument concludes, s 9(3) is inapplicable, with the consequence that para 2 of Sch 3 operates according to its own terms. If that is correct, it follows, as already seen, that the agreement is not exempted from registration.

Sir John Vinelott rejected this argument. He held ([1995] ICR 296 at 301–302) that the effect of s 9(3) was that the restriction imposed by cl 4(3) must be disregarded to the extent that it applied to milk supplied by the company. In accordance with s 9(7), para 2 of Sch 3 must then be applied on that footing. On that footing, to the extent that it applied to milk obtained elsewhere, cl 4(3) imposed a restriction within sub-para (b). Hence the agreement was not registrable. It was exempted by the joint effect of s 9 and para 2 of Sch 3.

The Court of Appeal disagreed with the judge. Schiemann LJ, giving the principal judgment, held ([1996] ICR 183 at 193–194) that the approach adopted by the judge was not open to him. The Act adopted a mechanistic approach so far as registrability is concerned. Section 9 drew a distinction throughout between terms and restrictions. Clause 4(3) was not a term which related exclusively to milk supplied by the company. The fact that different drafting may produce a situation in which the statute does not require the furnishing of particulars is not a potent argument, in the context of this statute, for applying the Act in an artificial way. A restrictive agreement should only be outside the Act altogether if it is clearly outside.

I prefer the judge's view. At the outset it should be noted that the Act applies to agreements and arrangements, however made ('any agreement or *a* arrangement'), and whether legally enforceable or not: see s 43(1). An agreement may be made in writing in a single document or in more than one document, or by correspondence, or by word of mouth, or partly in one way and partly in another. An agreement may be inferred from a course of conduct. A restriction may be accepted expressly or impliedly (see s 43(1)). An agreement which provides encouragement to comply with conditions regarding price and so forth

b is treated as an agreement under which restrictions are accepted in respect of those conditions (s 6(3)).

Section 9(3), which must be seen against this background, cuts down the width of s 6. As I read the Act, the purpose of s 9(3) is to provide that in the case of every agreement for the supply of goods, however the agreement was made, there shall be left out of account that part of its content which relates exclusively to the

c goods supplied. In determining whether the Act applies account shall be taken only of the remainder of the content of the agreement. Similarly, in respect of agreements for the application of any process of manufacture to goods, which are also within the scope of s 9(3). A corresponding approach is applicable to the equivalent provision in s 18(2), regarding agreements as to services.

d Thus s 9(3) calls for an examination of the provisions of an agreement, not in a formalistic way akin to a blue pencil test, but having regard to the substance of their content. A restriction which applies both to goods supplied and to other goods is to be disregarded so far as it relates only to the goods supplied. So far as it relates to other goods the restriction is outside the scope of the s 9(3) exemption, and the statutory provisions of the Act are to be applied accordingly.

e If Stamp J intended to suggest otherwise in his passing observation in *Re Schweppes Ltd's Agreement (No 2), Registrar of Restrictive Trading Agreements v Schweppes Ltd* [1971] 2 All ER 1473 at 1489, (1971) LR 7 RP 336 at 373, I am unable to agree with him.

Any other approach would lead to frankly absurd results. It would mean that

f in a statute concerned with competition policy and the public interest, registrability and scrutiny by the court would depend on the form in which a restriction was framed and not upon the substance of the restriction. Two agreements could contain exactly the same restrictions: one would be registrable, the other not. It would mean that an agreement, entered into in one form, would not be registrable, but it would become registrable if at a later date the drafting

g were tidied up and two restraints were telescoped into a single clause in an amended agreement. Parliament cannot have intended this. These distinctions without a difference would bring the Act into disrepute.

I do not believe that the interpretation of the Act which I prefer does any violence to the statutory language. 'Term', used in relation to an agreement, is a

h loose expression. Its meaning is not confined to a linguistically discrete provision. In ordinary usage one refers to the 'terms' of an agreement when referring generally to the provisions of the agreement. In ordinary usage one states that a particular obligation is a 'term' of an agreement, meaning thereby simply that it is a contractual obligation. This is so even if the obligation is expressed in the agreement as part of a larger, linguistically indivisible obligation.

j The context supports this usage of 'term'. This meaning produces a workable and sensible result, the suggested alternative does not. Section 9(3) is intended to be applicable to all agreements, and term must bear a meaning capable of being applied across the range of different forms in which an agreement, as widely defined in the Act, can come into being. Mr Baines' interpretation of s 9(3), which involves looking at the form in which the provision is expressed, could not be applied to implied agreements or implied terms where, ex hypothesi, a restriction was accepted without its being expressed in any form. In such cases the substance of the restriction is capable of being identified and s 9(3) applied accordingly, but there could be no criteria for deciding which of several possible forms in which the restriction might be expressed is the form to be adopted for the purposes of s 9(3). Further, an attempt to apply the 'form' interpretation to an oral agreement could involve a bizarre analysis of precisely what words were used and by whom in the course of a discussion at a meeting or over the telephone. There remain express terms of written agreements. In such cases Mr Baines' interpretation could be applied, but for the reason already given, with an arbitrariness of result which would bemuse a businessman.

In Mr Baines' submissions and in the Court of Appeal judgments reliance was placed on the contrast in language in s 9 between 'term' and 'restriction'. This was seen as supporting the view that 'term' is not synonymous with, or co-extensive with, 'restriction'. Linguistic arguments of this character should be handled warily. They are a legitimate and useful aid in statutory interpretation, but they are no more than this. Sometimes a difference in language is revealing and therefore important, other times not. In the process of statutory interpretation there always comes a stage, before reaching a final decision, when one should stand back and view a suggested interpretation in the wider context of the scheme and purpose of the Act. After all, the object of the exercise is to elucidate the intention fairly and reasonably attributable to Parliament when using the language under consideration. It is wrong to rely upon linguistic dissimilarities as indicative of an intended meaning with far reaching consequences when those consequences, seen in the wider context of the Act as a whole, lack all rhyme and reason.

That is the position in the present case. Mr Baines' interpretation of s 9(3) gives rise to the serious difficulties spelled out above. In seeking to minimise the significance of these difficulties, Mr Roth submitted that having to register an agreement imposes no hardship. The consequence is to enable restrictions in an agreement to be scrutinised, in the public interest. This is no answer. The scheme of the Act is that only registrable agreements call for scrutiny. An agreement is either registrable in accordance with the provisions of the Act, or it is not. There is no reason for supposing Parliament intended that the obligation to register should depend upon what is essentially an irrelevancy: the precise form in which a restriction is expressed, as distinct from its substance.

I should add a final observation. The test for registration under the Act should be as simple and clear as possible. The interpretation of s 9(3) which I prefer furthers this laudable aim. On any view it is necessary to analyse a restriction by identifying the circumstances in which it may operate. No reason has been suggested why, this having been done, it should be necessary to go on and attempt to apply the 'linguistically separable' test. The statutory registration test is mechanistic in the sense that if an agreement contains relevant restrictions it is registrable unless exempted, regardless of whether the restrictions have any significant economic consequences. But there is no warrant for interpreting the Act as elevating form over substance when identifying the existence or scope of restrictions or when applying the statutory exemptions.

I would allow this appeal, set aside the order of the Court of Appeal and restore the order of the judge.

a **LORD HOFFMANN.** My Lords, I have had the advantage of reading a draft of the speech of my noble and learned friend Lord Nicholls of Birkenhead. For the reasons he has given, I, too, would allow this appeal.

LORD CLYDE. My Lords, I have had the advantage of reading a draft of the speech of my noble and learned friend Lord Nicholls of Birkenhead. For the *b* reasons he gives I, too, would allow this appeal.

Appeal allowed.

Celia Fox   Barrister.

Bentley and another v Gaisford and another   *a*

COURT OF APPEAL, CIVIL DIVISION
SIR RICHARD SCOTT V-C, ROCH AND HENRY LJJ
25, 26 JUNE, 21 OCTOBER 1996

b

*Solicitor – Lien – Retaining lien – Lien over documents in respect of unpaid costs –
Solicitor discharged during course of action – Client instructing new solicitor – First
solicitor handing documents over to second solicitor – Second solicitor undertaking to
hold documents to first solicitor's order in respect of outstanding fees and disbursements
– Second solicitor photocopying documents and transmitting copies to client –*   *c*
*Undertaking containing no express embargo on photocopying – Whether second
solicitor in breach of undertaking.*

The plaintiff solicitors had been retained by a Chinese company to act for them
in an arbitration. The company later terminated that retainer and instructed the
plaintiffs to send all the relevant documents to the defendants, another firm of   *d*
solicitors which had been instructed in their place. The plaintiffs agreed to the
request on the defendants' undertaking to hold the documents to their order in
respect of outstanding fees and disbursements, but no express limit was placed on
the purposes for which the defendants would be using the documents. A partner
dealing with the matter in the defendant firm, acting in good faith and in   *e*
pursuance of what he regarded as his duty to his client, copied all the documents
and transmitted the copies to the client thereby effectively rendering the
plaintiffs' lien worthless. Thereafter, the plaintiffs sent a bill for £14,550 for their
costs to the client and informed the defendants of the bill sent, reminding them
that they still had a right of lien. They then called for the return of all the
documents held by the defendants that were subject to the retaining lien and all   *f*
copies or notes of the contents of the documents. The defendants made available
all the original documents, but refused to return any copies or notes of
documents that they had made, denying that the retaining lien extended to them.
The plaintiffs contended that, in copying the documents and sending the copies
to the client, the defendant partner was in breach of the undertaking given to the
plaintiffs to hold the documents to their order and they accordingly issued   *g*
proceedings against the partner and the defendant firm, seeking: (i) the delivery
up of all documents subject to the retaining lien; (ii) an injunction restraining the
defendants from making any use of the documents or any copies of them; and (iii)
compensation for breach of the undertaking. The judge dismissed the plaintiffs'
application, holding that in the absence of a copying embargo the defendants had   *h*
not breached the undertaking in taking the photocopies and sending them to the
client. The plaintiffs appealed.

Held (Sir Richard Scott V-C dissenting) – Where a solicitor claiming a retaining
lien over documents for a client's unpaid fees transferred them to another   *j*
solicitor to hold to his order or account, the lien was preserved and the solicitor
claiming the lien was entitled to every security not inconsistent with the progress
of the cause. Accordingly, the wholesale copying of the documents by the
defendants and dispatch to their client was in breach of their undertaking to hold
the documents to the plaintiffs' order, since it would effectively destroy rather
than maintain the security and would have to be justified on the basis that the

a arbitration required that disclosure then. The appeal would therefore be
   allowed. However, it would be inappropriate to grant the plaintiffs any of the
   relief they sought, since the client now had the documents relating to the
   arbitration and it was too late to restrain the defendants from deploying or using
   them in the arbitration; it would also be inappropriate to order compensation
   because the defendant partner's conduct was not inexcusable and such as likely
b to merit reproof (see p 854 *e*, p 856 *a* to *c f*, p 857 *b* to *h*, p 859 *b* to *d f*, p 860 *e* to *h*
   and p 861 *f* to *j*, post).

      Dictum of Lord Cottenham LC in *Heslop v Metcalfe* (1837) 3 My & Cr 183 at 190
   and of Balcombe LJ in *Udall v Capri Lighting Ltd* [1987] 3 All ER 262 at 269 applied.

   Notes
c For a solicitor's lien for unpaid costs, see 44(1) *Halsbury's Laws* (4th edn reissue)
   paras 244–253, and for cases on the subject, see 44 *Digest* (Reissue) 341–366, *3278–
   3998*.

   Cases referred to in judgments
d *A v B* [1984] 1 All ER 265.
   Caldwell v Sumpters (a firm) [1972] 1 All ER 567, [1972] Ch 478, [1972] 2 WLR 412,
      CA; *rvsg* [1971] 3 All ER 892, [1972] Ch 478, [1971] 3 WLR 748.
   Gamlen Chemical Co (UK) Ltd v Rochem Ltd [1980] 1 All ER 1049, [1980] 1 WLR 614,
      CA.
e *Grey, Re* [1892] 2 QB 440, CA.
   Hemsworth, Re, ex p Underwood (1845) De G 190.
   Heslop v Metcalfe (1837) 3 My & Cr 183, 40 ER 894.
   Home Office v Harman [1982] 1 All ER 532, [1983] 1 AC 280, [1982] 2 WLR 338, HL.
   Hughes v Hughes [1958] 3 All ER 179, [1958] P 224, [1958] 3 WLR 500, CA.
f *Lake v Lake* [1955] 2 All ER 538, [1955] P 336, [1955] 3 WLR 145, CA.
   Myers v Elman [1939] 4 All ER 484, [1940] AC 282, HL.
   Udall v Capri Lighting Ltd [1987] 3 All ER 262, [1988] QB 907, [1987] 3 WLR 465,
      CA.
   Watkins v A J Wright (Electrical) Ltd [1996] 3 All ER 31.
g *Watson v Lyon* (1855) 7 De G M & G 288, 44 ER 113, LJJ.

   Cases also cited or referred to in skeleton arguments
   Al-Kandari v J R Brown & Co (a firm) [1987] 2 All ER 302, [1987] QB 514; *rvsd* [1988]
      1 All ER 833, [1988] QB 665, CA.
h *Barclays Bank plc v Weeks Legg & Dean* (9 February 1996, unreported), QBD.
   Goldcorp Exchange Ltd (in receivership), Re [1994] 2 All ER 806, [1995] 1 AC 74, PC.
   Haddonstone Ltd v Sharp [1996] CA Transcript 79.
   Hastingwood Property Ltd v Saunders Bearman Anselm (a firm) [1990] 3 All ER 107,
      [1991] Ch 114.
j *Henderson v Merrett Syndicates Ltd, Hallam-Eames v Merrett Syndicates Ltd, Hughes v
      Merrett Syndicates Ltd, Arbuthnott v Feltrim Underwriting Agencies Ltd, Deeny v
      Gooda Walker Ltd (in liq)* [1994] 3 All ER 506, [1995] 2 AC 145, HL.
   Kelly v Cooper [1993] AC 205, PC.
   Morris, Re [1908] 1 KB 473, CA.
   Mutter v Eastern and Midlands Rly Co (1888) 38 Ch D 92.
   Robb v Green [1895] 2 QB 315, [1895–9] All ER Rep 1053, CA.

Appeal

The plaintiffs, Keith Anthony Charles Bentley and Hewett & Co (a firm of solicitors), appealed from the order of Judge William Crawford QC sitting as a judge of the High Court in the Queen's Bench Division on 12 March 1996, whereby he dismissed their action commenced by originating summons dated 5 December 1995 claiming (i) the delivery up by the defendants, Robert Edmund Gaisford and Sinclair Roche & Temperley (a firm of solicitors in which Mr Gaisford was a partner), of all documents subject to the plaintiffs' retaining lien, (ii) an injunction restraining the defendants from making use of the documents or any copies of them and (iii) compensation for breach of the undertaking to hold the documents to the plaintiffs' order in respect of outstanding fees and disbursements. The facts are set out in the judgment of Sir Richard Scott V-C.

John Cherryman QC and *David Bailey* (instructed by *Hewett & Co*) for the plaintiffs.
Peter Gross QC and *David Allen* (instructed by *Sinclair Roche & Temperley*) for the defendants.

Cur adv vult

21 October 1996. The following judgments were delivered.

SIR RICHARD SCOTT V-C. This case raises a point of principle regarding the scope of a solicitor's undertaking given by Messrs Sinclair Roche & Temperley (SRT), the respondent defendants, to Messrs Hewett & Co, the appellant plaintiffs.

Hewett & Co acted for China Everbright Trading Co (CET), a Chinese company whose principal offices were in Beijing, and who were engaged in a commercial dispute with Armada Bulk Carriers Ltd arising out of a charterparty dated 26 November 1994. The partner in Hewett & Co dealing with the matter was Mr Bentley.

The dispute had been referred to arbitration in London. By the end of August 1994, an interim award had been made and CET's defence and intended counterclaim were due.

By fax dated 30 August 1995, CET terminated Hewett & Co's retainer. The fax instructed Hewett & Co 'to send immediately upon receipt of this letter all documents and communications between or among you and all the parties involved in the arbitration case' to Mr Robert Gaisford of Sinclair Roche & Temperley. In a fax to Hewett & Co of the same date SRT confirmed that they had been instructed to act for CET in the arbitration and asked to be provided 'with your files and other documents in relation to this matter as soon as possible'. Hewett & Co had, in their work done pursuant to their retainer, earned fees and made disbursements. They were entitled, until they received payment of their fees and disbursements, to exercise a retaining lien over all the documents and papers which had come into their possession as CET's solicitors (see 44(1) *Halsbury's Laws* (4th edn reissue) para 245).

In response to the request in the two faxes of 30 August that they send their files and documents to SRT, Hewett & Co, in a fax to SRT of 31 August said:

> 'Upon receiving your undertaking to hold the documents/our file to our order in respect of outstanding fees/disbursements we shall put out papers for collection.'

a   It is to be noted that this fax did not in terms express any limit on the use to which SRT might put the documents. SRT's reply, by fax, also sent on 31 August, said:

> 'We thank you for your fax today regarding our request that you provide us with the files of documents and papers in relation to this matter. While we agree to hold them to your order that is without prejudice to the
b   following point. We understand from our clients that the question of fees has never been raised with them and it is their clear understanding that Tekso are responsible for your fees. Obviously this is a matter which will have to be sorted but sooner rather than later but the matter of greater urgency is, of course, that we shall have the files in order to take the necessary steps to protect our clients' interests. We are arranging to collect
c   them from your offices as agreed.'

There are two comments to be made on this fax. First, it indicated at least the possibility of a dispute about CET's liability for Hewett & Co's fees. Second, and more important, it, too, contained no express limitation on the purposes for which SRT would be using the documents.

d   The documents were collected on the same day.

The undertaking from SRT, sought and given by the two faxes of 31 August 1995 to which I have referred, is the undertaking in question in these proceedings. It is not in doubt that the effect of the undertaking by SRT 'to hold' the documents to Hewett & Co's 'order in respect of outstanding fees/disbursements' was effective to preserve Hewett & Co's retaining lien. The
e   nature of a solicitor's retaining lien is set out in 44(1) *Halsbury's Laws* (4th edn reissue) para 247:

> 'A solicitor having a retaining lien over property in his possession is entitled to retain the property as against the client and all persons claiming through
f   him ... until the full amount of the solicitor's taxed costs payable by the client is paid. The client has no right to inspect the documents or to take copies of them, but delivery of documents which the client requires will be ordered upon payment of the solicitor's costs being secured, as by payment into court ...'

g   The termination by the client of his solicitor's retainer and the engagement of a new solicitor does not deprive the former solicitor of his retaining lien. Provided he has not been discharged for misconduct (and Hewett & Co were not discharged for misconduct), the former solicitor cannot, until his fees are paid or properly secured, be compelled to hand over the papers to the new solicitor (see
h   *Hughes v Hughes* [1958] 3 All ER 179 at 180, [1958] P 224 at 227–228 per Hodson LJ).

If, therefore, a solicitor's retainer is terminated during the course of litigation, the retaining lien presents obvious difficulties for the client and the new solicitor. The new solicitor will need the documents in order to protect the client's interests in the continuing action. But the former solicitor's bill may be disputed;
j   taxation of the bill may take some time; and the other party or parties to the action are not likely to be content to allow the action to become quiescent while their opponent sorts out his obligations to his former solicitor.

The Law Society has provided guidance to its members as to what they should do in these circumstances. In *The Guide to the Professional Conduct of Solicitors* (6th edn, 1993) para 12.18(4) the following guidance is given:

'Where a solicitor is properly exercising a lien in respect of unpaid costs, following his or her discharge by the client during the course of proceedings, the Law Society recommends that the solicitor's papers should be released to the successor solicitor subject to a satisfactory undertaking as to the outstanding costs being given in lieu of the lien. There is, however, no duty on the original solicitor to accept an undertaking.' *a*

The undertaking recommended by the Law Society was not sought by Hewett & Co in the present case. Instead they simply sought, and received, an undertaking that the documents would be held to their order in respect of outstanding fees and disbursements.

The effect of such an undertaking has received some judicial attention. *c*

In *Caldwell v Sumpters (a firm)* [1972] 1 All ER 567, [1972] Ch 478 solicitors with a retaining lien over the former client's title deeds sent the deeds to the new solicitors under cover of a letter stating that 'these deeds and documents are being sent to you on the understanding that you will hold them to our order, pending the payment of our fees ...' The new solicitors declined to give the undertaking that was sought but none the less kept the deeds and used them for *d* the purposes of their work on behalf of the client. It was common ground that if the new solicitors had agreed to hold the deeds and documents to the order of the former solicitors, the retaining lien would have been preserved notwithstanding that actual possession of the deeds and documents had for the time being been relinquished to the new solicitors. *e*

The Court of Appeal, differing from Megarry J (see [1971] 3 All ER 892, [1972] Ch 478), held that since the deeds and documents had been sent on the express understanding that they would be held to the order of the former solicitors, they could be retained by the new solicitors only on that basis. Since the new solicitors had not returned the documents they were treated as having given the *f* undertaking that had been sought. The court held that a retaining lien was not lost by parting with physical possession if the circumstances showed that the lien was being expressly or impliedly reserved. *Watson v Lyon* (1855) 7 De G M & G 288, 44 ER 113 was cited as authority. In that case documents subject to a retaining lien were sent by the solicitors entitled to the lien to another firm of solicitors 'to hold them on our account'. It was held that the retaining lien was *g* thereby preserved. It is important to notice, however, that neither in *Watson v Lyon* nor in *Caldwell v Sumpters* was the court concerned to consider what use the new solicitors could make of the documents while they remained in their (the new solicitors') possession. The issue was whether the original solicitors could insist on the return of the documents, ie whether their retaining lien had been *h* lost when the documents came into the possession of the new solicitors.

In the present case, therefore, there is no doubt but that the undertaking requested by Hewett & Co and given by SRT was effective to preserve Hewett & Co's retaining lien while the documents were in the hands of SRT. What is at issue, however, is the use to which SRT, consistently with that undertaking, were *j* entitled to put the documents while they remained in their possession. It is common ground that SRT were under an obligation to return the documents to Hewett & Co on demand. It is common ground also that if Hewett & Co had given any express order forbidding some particular use of the documents, SRT would have been obliged to comply with that direction. But in the absence of any express direction, and in this case there was none, what were SRT, consistently *a* with their undertaking to Hewett & Co and with the preservation of the retaining lien, entitled to do with the documents?

Having posed the question, let me continue with the narrative.

During the evening of 31 August, or on the morning of 1 September 1995, Mr Gaisford, a partner in SRT, read the documents and had copies of them made. Later on 1 September Hewett & Co asked for the return of two correspondence

b files. The correspondence files were made available for collection by SRT and collected by Hewett & Co the same day. The copies that SRT had made of the documents in the correspondence files were not included. Hewett & Co did not know that the documents had been copied.

On 14 September 1995 Hewett & Co sent CET a bill for their costs. The bill sought payment of £13,750 in respect of fees and £800 in respect of

c disbursements. By letter of the same date Hewett & Co informed SRT of the bill sent to CET and reminded SRT that 'we still have a right of lien'.

By letter to SRT of 15 September 1995 Hewett & Co called for the return to them of the remaining documents held by SRT that were subject to the retaining lien and called expressly for all copies or notes of the contents of the documents

d to be delivered to them.

SRT at once made available for collection all the original documents delivered to them by Hewett & Co that they, SRT, still held but did not deliver up any of the copies or notes that had been made.

By letter to Hewett & Co dated 19 September 1995 SRT refused to return any copies or notes of the documents that they, SRT, had made. SRT denied that the

e retaining lien extended to those copies or notes.

In subsequent correspondence between Hewett & Co and SRT, Hewett & Co were informed that SRT had had photocopies made of all the documents subject to the retaining lien and that the copies, or perhaps copies of the copies, had been sent to CET in China for CET's perusal. In an affidavit sworn in these

f proceedings, Mr Gaisford explained that his own perusal of the documents had led him to be concerned about certain aspects of the manner in which Hewett & Co had dealt with the arbitration proceedings, and that he had believed it necessary in the discharge of his own firm's duty to CET to bring the matters of concern to CET's attention and to seek instructions from them. Hewett & Co firmly refute the inference that their conduct while acting for CET has given rise

g to any legitimate complaint by CET, but it is accepted that Mr Gaisford's concern on reading the documents was reasonable, and that in copying the documents and sending the copies to CET for instructions he acted reasonably and bona fide in discharge of what he believed to be his duty to CET. It is, however, contended on behalf of Hewett & Co that in copying the documents and sending the copies

h to CET Mr Gaisford was in breach of the undertaking given to Hewett & Co to hold the documents to Hewett & Co's order.

By originating summons of 5 December 1995 these proceedings were commenced, with Hewett & Co, and Mr Bentley as plaintiffs and SRT and Mr Gaisford as defendants. The relief claimed was: (i) the delivery up of all

j documents subject to the retaining lien; (ii) an injunction restraining the defendants from making any use of the documents or any copies of them and; (iii) compensation for breach of the undertaking.

There is no doubt but that Hewett & Co's retaining lien is still in existence. The bill for £14,550 remains unpaid. Hewett & Co have commenced proceedings against CET and also against Tekso Ltd, an associate company of CET said to have undertaken responsibility for Hewett & Co's fees. Leave to serve out of the jurisdiction on CET and Tekso has been granted. In the meantime Hewett & Co remain entitled to a retaining lien.

It is of some importance that the originating summons is entitled 'In the matter of the Solicitors Act 1974' and invokes the jurisdiction of the court over solicitors. The undertaking given by SRT no doubt had contractual effect but the obligations arising under a solicitor's undertaking go beyond contractual effect. They are obligations which a solicitor has a professional duty, as well as a contractual duty, to observe. Breach is, prima facie, professional misconduct. It has been held by the Court of Appeal that the jurisdiction to order compensation to be paid by solicitors found guilty of misconduct ought not to be exercised unless 'the conduct of the solicitor is inexcusable and such as to merit reproof' (see *Udall v Capri Lighting Ltd* [1987] 3 All ER 262 at 269, [1988] QB 907 at 917 per Balcombe LJ).

On 12 March 1996 Judge William Crawford QC, sitting as a judge of the High Court, dismissed the action. He held that it was not a breach of the undertaking for Mr Gaisford to have taken copies of the documents and sent them to SRT. Hewett & Co and Mr Bentley have appealed.

The undertaking given by SRT to Hewett & Co was short and simple. It was an undertaking by SRT to hold the documents to the order of Hewett & Co. Hewett & Co's fax of 31 August made clear that the purpose of the undertaking was to preserve Hewett & Co's retaining lien. SRT's fax in response made clear that SRT understood that that was the purpose of the undertaking.

It is well established that a solicitor with a retaining lien is entitled at will to allow or to refuse the erstwhile client and any new solicitor access to the documents and is entitled at will to allow or to refuse to allow any copies of the documents to be taken. It was so held in *Re Hemsworth, ex p Underwood* (1845) De G 190. In *Re Hemsworth*, however, the documents were still in the actual possession of the solicitor entitled to the lien. The dicta in the case are no guide as to the position that arises if the solicitor (solicitor A) passes the documents to a new solicitor (solicitor B) on solicitor B's undertaking to hold the documents to the order of solicitor A in order to preserve the retaining lien.

In every such case the documents will have been handed over to solicitor B for a purpose. It is possible, conceptually speaking, to envisage a case in which solicitor B is not entitled to read the documents, or to allow anyone to read the documents, or to take copies of the documents, or to make notes of the contents of the documents, without the express consent of solicitor A. All these are things that solicitor A, if he had retained actual possession of the documents, would have been entitled by virtue of his retaining lien to allow or to refuse to allow as he might choose: see *Re Hemsworth*. To allow any of these things to be done would, to some degree, reduce the value of the retaining lien. So, is it possible to conclude that the undertaking by solicitor B to preserve the lien should require solicitor B to obtain solicitor A's consent for any of these things to be done? I do not think so. The documents must have been handed over by solicitor A to solicitor B in order for solicitor B to make some use of them. It could not sensibly be contended that the use of them for the purpose for which they were handed over would be a breach of solicitor B's undertaking to hold the documents to solicitor A's order.

Solicitor A would, of course, be well advised, when parting with the documents subject to his retaining lien, to express the purposes for which the documents could, without further recourse to solicitor A, properly be used by solicitor B. In the absence of any express permission or express prohibition a communicated by solicitor A to solicitor B, it would nearly always be possible from the circumstances of the case to imply some particular permitted use; it might sometimes be possible to imply some particular prohibition. But in asking what use ought in a particular case to be regarded as authorised by implication, or prohibited by implication, two aspects of the matter, likely to be present in every case, must, in my judgment, be kept in mind.

b First, solicitors' undertakings cast a heavy burden of observance on the solicitors who give them. A solicitor's undertaking which is not clear in its terms and which leaves it uncertain what the solicitor may or may not do is unsatisfactory. The court should not, in my judgment, interpret a solicitor's undertaking in a manner more restrictive or onerous than a reasonable solicitor giving the undertaking would expect. Second, it must be borne in mind that

c solicitor B will owe a duty to his client, the erstwhile client of solicitor A. Unless a prohibition clearly imposed by solicitor A so requires it, the court should not, in my judgment, interpret solicitor B's undertaking in such a manner as to place solicitor B in risk of breach of his duty to his client.

d In the present case, as I have already observed, no express permission or prohibition as to use of the documents was given by Hewett & Co to SRT. But the documents were plainly handed over for use by SRT on behalf of CET in connection with the pending arbitration. Mr Cherryman QC, counsel for Hewett & Co, contended that all that Mr Gaisford was entitled to do with the documents was to read them. He was not entitled to allow anyone else to read them and was not entitled to copy them. To do so, Mr Cherryman submitted, was not

e consistent with preserving the retaining lien. I regard this submission as unreal. Mr Gaisford must, at the least, have been entitled to copy the documents to counsel so that counsel could peruse them, give advice on points arising out of them and settle any necessary documents or pleadings required for the purposes of the arbitration.

f Mr Cherryman's fall-back position was that, in any event, Mr Gaisford was not entitled to copy the documents wholesale to CET. This submission requires more careful attention to be paid to the basis on which the documents were handed over and the reason why Mr Gaisford copied them to CET.

The documents were handed over by Hewett & Co for use by SRT on CET's behalf in connection with the arbitration. It has been suggested that it should be

g inferred that the permitted use was limited to use for the purpose of preparing CET's overdue defence and counterclaim. I do not regard this limitation as justified. It is not mentioned in any of the communications between Hewett & Co and SRT at the time the undertaking was sought and given. To infer such a limit to the permitted use that could be made of the documents would, in my

h view, be thoroughly unfair to Mr Gaisford to whom no such limitation was suggested at the time. Moreover, even the limited purpose of using the documents to settle the defence and counterclaim might well have required some of the documents to be copied to CET with a request for instructions. In my judgment, the only safe and fair inference that can be drawn from the

j communications between Hewett & Co and SRT is that the documents were being made available to SRT for them to use in connection with the arbitration.

Mr Gaisford, on reading the documents, became concerned about the manner in which, in certain respects, Hewett & Co had been conducting the arbitration. That was why the documents were copied by Mr Gaisford to CET. It might well have been a breach of Mr Gaisford's duty to CET to have refrained from drawing the contents of the documents to CET's attention. If Hewett & Co had expressly stipulated that the documents should not be copied to CET, Mr Gaisford would have had to comply with that prohibition or to refrain from accepting the documents on those terms. Having accepted the documents on terms which did not expressly include any such prohibition, and in circumstances in which the necessary implication of such a prohibition was not obvious to Mr Gaisford (nor I may say to the judge below or to myself), it would, in my view, be thoroughly unfair to Mr Gaisford to treat him as having given a solicitor's undertaking to abide by such a prohibition. In making copies of the documents and sending the copies to CET he acted in good faith in pursuance of his duty to his client; in so doing, he was using the documents for a purpose connected with the arbitration. I agree with the judge that Mr Gaisford was not in breach of his undertaking.

Even if, contrary to the views I have expressed, the taking of copies of the documents was a breach of SRT's undertaking to hold the documents to Hewett & Co's order, I would not regard this as a case in which an order for compensation ought to be made.

It is accepted that Mr Gaisford acted in good faith and in pursuance of what he regarded as his duty to his client. If he was, unwittingly, in breach of the undertaking, his breach was brought about by the failure of Hewett & Co, in seeking the undertaking, to be explicit as to what Mr Gaisford could and could not do with the documents. In these circumstances, I do not regard Mr Gaisford's conduct as inexcusable or as meriting reproof.

If there is no case for compensation for breach of SRT's undertaking, there is no other peg on which to hang a case for compensation or damages. It has been suggested that SRT's actions in copying the documents and sending the copies to SRT should be regarded as being actions in breach of the retaining lien. This is not, in my judgment, a correct analysis. A retaining lien gives no more rights than its name suggests. It is a right to retain possession of documents against the claim to possession of their legal owner, the client. The right to retain the documents can be relaxed whenever and in whatever manner the solicitor entitled to the right from time to time chooses. A relaxation, whether by allowing perusal or copying or whatever, would leave the retaining lien extant, although it would to some extent reduce its value. It would not involve any breach of the retaining lien. The clandestine removal or some other unauthorised handling of the documents would, however, constitute a tortious interference with the solicitor's possession of the documents and, accordingly, would constitute a trespass to goods for which damages could be claimed. The trespass would be actionable at the suit of the solicitor whose right to possession of the documents had been interfered with. In the present case, the only issue is whether the use made by SRT of the documents was a breach of the undertaking they had given to Hewett & Co. If it was not, there is no basis on which that use could be described as an interference with Hewett & Co's possession of the documents. The case was, rightly, not put below or in this court on the footing that the use made of the documents gave rise to any other cause of action than that of the breach of the undertaking.

As to the claim by Hewett & Co for delivery up of the copies of the documents still retained by or under the control of SRT, that claim is, in my judgment, misconceived. The copies were made by and became the property of SRT on behalf of their client, CET. The copies were never in the possession of Hewett & Co. The retaining lien never extended to those copies. If, contrary to my view, the making of the copies constituted a breach of SRT's undertaking or should be regarded as an unauthorised interference with Hewett & Co's possession of the a copied documents, the remedy must be a financial one. The court would not, in my judgment, be justified in extending the retaining lien so as to include documents which came into existence after the termination of the retainer and which had never been in the possession of the solicitor claiming the lien. In my judgment, if a financial remedy is not available there is an end of the matter.

For these reasons, too, I would dismiss the appeal.

b I have had the advantage of reading in draft the judgments of Roch and Henry LJJ. They propose an order that the appeal of the appellant plaintiffs be allowed notwithstanding that no substantive order in their favour is to be made. As will have appeared from my judgment, I am in agreement with them that no substantive order in favour of the appellants should be made. I desire, however,

c to make clear my opinion that where, as here, an appeal has failed to achieve any of the substantive relief for which it was brought, an order that the appeal be allowed is a misrepresentation of the result. If the purpose of such an order is to serve as a vehicle for an order for costs in favour of the ostensibly successful, but in reality unsuccessful, party, it is an unnecessary device. The court has in any event a full discretion in respect of costs. The question whether an order of this

d court should express an appeal to be allowed or to be dismissed should, in my opinion, depend upon whether the appellant has or has not succeeded in obtaining on appeal some substantive relief not obtained below or in obtaining the discharge of some substantive relief granted below. The result of this appeal is that neither of these things has been obtained.

e In *Lake v Lake* [1955] 2 All ER 538, [1955] P 336 it was held by the Court of Appeal that appeals lay against orders made, not against the reasons given for the making of the orders. That principle has, so far as I am aware, never been doubted (see also *The Supreme Court Practice 1997* vol 1, para 59/1/6). Since an appeal cannot be brought against reasons but only against the order made, it seems to me to follow that an appeal which fails to achieve any alteration in the

f order is an appeal which has failed notwithstanding that the appellant may have succeeded in undermining the reasons given by the trial judge. In my opinion, for the reasons I have given, the concurring judgments of Roch and Henry LJJ on this appeal ought to lead to an order that the appeal be dismissed. The order to be made, however, must be the order they have prescribed.

g

ROCH LJ. The appellants and the respondents are solicitors. On 30 August 1995 the China Everbright Trading Co, to whom I shall refer as 'CET', terminated their retainer of the appellants to act for them in their arbitration with Armada Bulk Carriers Ltd, and instructed the appellants to send immediately to the

h respondents: 'All the documents and communications between you and all the parties involved in the arbitration case ...' The same day the appellants replied by fax that they would hold off doing anything until the following morning and they reminded CET that the time for filing the defence and counterclaim submissions would expire at the close of business the following day, 31 August

j 1995.

The respondents also faxed the appellants asking if the appellants: 'Would kindly provide us with your files and other documents in relation to this matter as soon as possible.' The fax was headed with the name of the ship, the chartering of which was the basis of the arbitration.

On 31 August 1995 the appellants sent the respondents a fax in these terms:

'1. Please find enclosed copy fax from Tekso setting out background to delay in preparing documents in support of defence/counterclaim submissions, as discussed yesterday. Time for service expires today.

2. Upon receiving your undertaking to hold the documents/our file to our order in respect of outstanding fees/disbursements we shall put out papers for collection.'

The respondents replied by fax the same day:

'We thank you for your fax today regarding our request that you provide us with the files of documents and papers in relation to this matter. While we agree to hold them to your order, this is without prejudice to the following point. We understand from our clients that the question of fees has never been raised with them and it is their clear understanding that Tekso are responsible for your fees. Obviously this is something which will have to be sorted out sooner rather than later but the matter of greater urgency is of course that we should have the files in order to take the necessary steps to protect our client's interest. We are arranging to collect them from your offices as agreed.'

The following day, 1 September, the appellants faxed the respondents, heading the fax with the name of the ship the subject of the arbitration. The fax read:

'We refer to our telephone conversation/your fax of the 31st August 1995 in this matter. Following our above telephone conversation you have agreed to provide your undertaking that the papers are to be held to our order. We have been in discussion with Mr Bentley who is handling the matter at our firm and the position is that until Mr Bentley's return we would like to have the correspondence files 1 and 2 returned to us. We are quite content for you to retain the rest of the documents for the time being to be held to our order. Please confirm by return that you will have these files ready for our collection by us from your offices.'

It is not certain whether the partner in the respondents dealing with the matter, Mr Gaisford, received that fax which was sent during the afternoon of 1 September 1995. Prior to that fax being sent, the evidence of Mr Gaisford is to the effect that, having read the appellants' files during the evening of 31 August, he became so concerned that he arranged for the files to be copied in their entirety and that that was done on the morning of 1 September. Whether that fax reached Mr Gaisford or not, it is clear that the respondents' request for the return of the two correspondence files did because on 1 September the respondents faxed the appellants in these terms, the fax again being headed with the name of the ship:

'We refer to our telephone conversation today and return herewith your correspondence files as requested. However, we would point out that the correspondence in relation to this matter is of course documentation to which our clients are entitled and we look forward to receiving their return as soon as Mr Bentley is back from holiday.'

Copies of the copies taken by the respondents of the appellants' files were faxed during the morning of 1 September to CET in Beijing. In his affidavit, Mr Gaisford deposed:

a   'I resolved to copy the documents because I thought it to be in the best
interests of my clients. I believed then and I believe now that it was both
right and proper for me to have the documents photocopied. Diminishing
the value, which of course I had never undertaken to protect, of Hewitt and
Co's lien was not and is not in my view a relevant consideration to my
photocopying the documents. In any event this did not even figure in my
b   mind at the time. Had it entered my mind it would not have deterred me for
a moment and with the benefit of hindsight I continue to believe that I acted
properly, lawfully, in accordance with our undertaking and in the best
interests of my client.'

Mr Gaisford goes on to depose:

c   'My understanding was and remains that my firm was obliged to return the
original documents to Hewitt and Co on their demand. Our obligation was
no more nor less than that.'

In so deposing, Mr Gaisford raises the essential issue in this case, namely the
d   conflict between a solicitor's duty to his client, and a solicitor's obligations to
another firm of solicitors who have handed over their files in reliance on their lien
to those files because their fees have not been discharged by the client.
In fact, in order to be in a position to return the original documents to the
appellants on demand, the respondents had an obligation to retain possession and
to preserve the documents. That is conceded by Mr Gross QC for the
e   respondents. It is his submission that that was the full extent of the respondents'
obligations to the appellants in respect of those documents.
The judge agreed and the judge held that the obligations arose out of the
respondents' undertaking and that those obligations were threefold. The judge
began his conclusions in this way:

f   'I conclude therefore: (i) that in undertaking to hold the documents to the
plaintiffs order, the defendants undertook (a) to keep the original documents
safely, ensuring so far as they could they were not defaced, destroyed or
stolen, (b) not to part with possession of the documents and (c) to return
them promptly on demand; (ii) that while the defendants were under a
g   fiduciary duty to the plaintiffs in relation to the documents, the limits of that
duty were exactly the same as those owed under the undertaking, and were
co-terminous with it; (iii) the defendants did not undertake that they would
not photocopy the documents nor that they would not retain any
photocopies that they made; (iv) the defendants were accordingly entitled to
photocopy the documents, and to retain the photocopies; (v) that the
h   plaintiffs in order successfully to prevent photocopying or copying of the
documents by the defendants should have insisted upon a different form of
undertaking or, if that was not forthcoming, should not have released the
documents.'

j   The solicitor's lien gives the solicitor the right to retain any deed, paper or
personal chattel which has come into his possession in the course of his
employment and in his capacity as solicitor with the client's sanction. The
solicitor can retain these items against his former client, where the client has
terminated the solicitor's instructions and against all persons claiming through
the former client until the full amount of the solicitor's taxed costs are paid. The
solicitor can prevent those persons inspecting the documents and prevent them

taking copies of the documents, unless a court orders otherwise, which the court will only do in certain limited cases.

The solicitor's lien is ended by the solicitors, whom I shall call the first solicitors, parting with the documents over which the lien is claimed, but not if possession is given to the solicitors replacing them, (whom I shall call the second solicitors) to hold to their order or to hold for their account. In these cases the legal possession of the documents remains in the first solicitors. None of these propositions is controversial.

What is controversial is the effect of the transfer of the documents by the first solicitor to the second solicitor. Is the second solicitor bound by the undertaking which he has given expressly or impliedly, or does the solicitor's lien survive and if so in what form?

The judge's judgment in this case rests essentially on two reasons. First, that the second solicitor's power to deal with the documents handed to him by the first solicitor depends upon the extent of the undertaking that he has given to the first solicitor, and that an undertaking to hold the documents to the first solicitor's order means no more than the three matters identified in his first conclusion. Secondly, that there is a valid distinction to be drawn between the solicitor's lien and the value of the solicitor's lien. In my view both those assumptions made by the judge require examination.

The case law establishes that where solicitor one transfers the documents to solicitor two to hold to solicitor one's order, the lien of solicitor one is preserved. Solicitor one retains the legal possession of the documents, albeit that the physical possession is now with solicitor two. This will be so although solicitor two in terms states that he is not prepared to give any undertaking to solicitor one concerning his use of the documents: see *Caldwell v Sumpters (a firm)* [1972] 1 All ER 567, [1972] Ch 478. In that case the Court of Appeal consisting of Salmon and Stamp LJJ decided that the preservation of the lien does not depend on any prior arrangement or agreement to preserve the lien. That had been the decision of Megarry J at first instance (see [1971] 3 All ER 892, [1972] Ch 478), but it was rejected by the Court of Appeal. The appellant's counsel opened his appeal by saying ([1972] Ch 478 at 490):

'Megarry J. was wrong in concluding that it was necessary for the defendants to establish that there was an agreement. Neither logic nor authority compels that conclusion. It is sufficient that there should be an intention not to abandon the lien.'

In his judgment, in dealing with the submission that the first solicitors had made a mistake in parting with physical possession of the documents without a prior agreement or arrangement by the second solicitors to observe the lien, Salmon LJ said ([1972] 1 All ER 567 at 570, [1972] Ch 478 at 495):

'In my judgment, however, Sumpters had made no mistake. The letter and all the surrounding circumstances show that they did not intend to abandon their lien nor to part with legal possession of the documents. They offered them to their brother solicitors to hold as their agents on their behalf so that they might be enabled to prepare a draft contract of sale. To my mind it is plain that Margolis & Co were under a legal obligation to return the documents to Sumpters or make them available to Sumpters on Sumpters's request.'

In his judgment Stamp LJ observed ([1972] 1 All ER 567 at 572, [1972] Ch 478 at 497):

> 'In my judgment it is also the law that where a solicitor having a possessory lien on his former client's papers puts them in the hands of a third party to hold them to the order of the solicitor or for the account of the solicitor, the lien is not destroyed because the possession of the transferee becomes the possession of the solicitor. In my judgment it makes no difference that the transferee is the solicitor of the owner of the papers. If this were not the law, powerful considerations of convenience and indeed, in some cases but not this, of honest dealing, would be frustrated ... The first proposition was that if a solicitor having a lien on a document places it in the hands of an agent (and it was necessarily conceded in this case that the solicitor to the other party can be an agent) instructing him to hold the document to the account or order of the former solicitor, the possessory lien is not defeated because the possession of the transferee is the possession of the transferor.'

The next question is the form in which the lien is preserved? What is the extent of the lien once the documents have been handed to the second solicitor; what are its incidents?

The judge found that the lien survived to the extent set out in his first conclusion. Mr Gross for the respondents supports that finding. He submits that the lien is a retaining lien and solicitor two has only to retain the documents in the state in which they were handed to him and return them or handle them as and when instructed by solicitor one. In the meantime he can make such use of the documents as he pleases, even if such use renders the lien of solicitor one totally meaningless. There will be cases where solicitor two will not be able to act so as to render the lien totally worthless, for example where the documents handed to him include documents such as title deeds where the client will have a continuing need for the original because the original has an intrinsic value. In the present case, solicitor two has acted so as to remove completely, on the evidence, the need of the client to seek to obtain the originals in solicitor one's files from solicitor one. The judge has decided that to obtain wider protection, solicitor one should not have relied upon the words 'hold to our account' but should have required undertakings not to copy the documents for any purpose other than the preparation of a defence and counterclaim and not to supply their clients with any copy. But this reasoning assumes that it is necessary to obtain from solicitor two an undertaking or undertakings before the lien survives at all. That is clearly contrary to way this court decided *Caldwell v Sumpters*.

The second assumption is that there is a valid distinction to be drawn between the value of the lien and the lien itself. There are dicta referring to the value of the lien in those cases where solicitor one has terminated his retainer. An example is *A v B* [1984] 1 All ER 265. In such cases it is stated that the court will order the handing over of documents by solicitor one to solicitor two to hold them subject to solicitor one's lien, even if that rendered the lien useless. In my view that is not drawing a distinction between the value of the lien and the lien itself, it is merely a way of stating the legal principle applicable in a case where solicitor one discharges himself during the course of proceedings. It can be observed that even in such cases, the court does not order the handing over of the documents in every instance but will weigh the principle that a litigant shall not be deprived of material relevant to the conduct of the case and so driven from the judgment seat, if that would be the result of permitting the lien to be sustained,

against the principle that litigation should be conducted with due regard to the
interest of the court's own officers, who should not be left without payment for a
what was justly due to them.

In such cases, the court will make an order consistent with the principle stated
by Lord Cottenham LC in *Heslop v Metcalfe* (1837) 3 My & Cr 183 at 190, 40 ER
894 at 897: 'I think the principle should be, that the solicitor claiming the lien,
should have every security not inconsistent with the progress of the cause.' Here b
Lord Cottenham LC was referring to the client's action. His speech in that case
was cited with approval by the members of this court in *Gamlen Chemical Co (UK)
Ltd v Rochem Ltd* [1980] 1 All ER 1049, [1980] 1 WLR 614.

In my judgment this principle can be applied to cases such as the present where
solicitor one transfers documents to solicitor two to hold to his order. Mr Gross
argues that such a rule would create practical difficulties for solicitor two and for c
the client, because neither could be sure what use they were permitted to make
of the documents. Consequently if solicitor one wishes to limit the uses to be
made of the documents by solicitor two he should spell it out and obtain detailed
undertakings limiting those uses precisely. In my view, this suggested path will
lead to as many problems as the application of the principle contained in Lord d
Cottenham LC's speech. It is a method which will involve delay and probably
create considerable correspondence between solicitors. If solicitor one obtains
detailed undertakings, for example that the documents are to be used solely for
the preparation of the defence and counterclaim, this would still require solicitor
two to decide what use he could properly make of the documents consistent with
such an undertaking. e

The decided cases would indicate that the practice of solicitors who have been
dismissed by their clients but whose fees have not be fully discharged, handing
their files to the new solicitors to hold to 'our account' or to hold 'to our order' is
well established. Because the present case is the first of its kind I would conclude
that it is a practice which has lead to little difficulty in the real world. f

I would allow this appeal and hold that in copying every document in every file
and sending copies of all those documents to the client, the respondents were in
breach of the appellants' lien. In making that finding I must make it clear that I
would not wish to cast any doubt upon the good faith or integrity of Mr Gaisford
who I am sure held the views contained in his affidavit and acted as he did in the
belief that he was properly discharging his duty to his client and acting in a way g
which was not a breach of the appellants' lien.

The conclusion that the respondents urge on us would have the effect, in my
opinion that the third course open to solicitor one, identified by the judge in
para 10 of his judgment, namely that 'he can preserve his lien by delivering the
papers and documents to the new solicitor subject to an undertaking that they be h
held to his order or on his account' would, in practice disappear. Solicitor one
could not preserve his lien in this way because it would always be open to
solicitor two to destroy the lien by doing what the respondents did in this case,
namely copying every document and providing the client with a copy of each
document. Although the Law Society supports the use of the first course of j
action identified by the judge in that paragraph of his judgment, it would be
regrettable if the third method were to be lost.

There remains the question as to the relief that should be given to the
appellants. The appellants sought in effect three remedies: first, the delivery up
of the papers and documents including any photocopies taken of those
documents that were handed to the respondents to hold to the appellants' order;

a second, that the respondents be restrained from deploying or using such papers or documents in connection with the arbitration; and, third, that the respondents compensate the appellants for breach of their undertaking.

In my judgment this is one of those rare cases where it is inappropriate to order any relief. CET now have the necessary papers and documents relating to the arbitration, albeit that they are copies of the documents which were originally

b held by the appellants, and in those circumstances it would be pointless to order the respondents to deliver up the copies that they have of those documents. For the same reason it is too late to order that the respondents be restrained from deploying or using such papers or documents in the arbitration.

Neither is this a case in which, in my view, it is appropriate to order

c compensation. The principles upon which the courts will order a solicitor to pay compensation for breach of an undertaking are set out in *Udall v Capri Lighting Ltd* [1987] 3 All ER 262, [1988] QB 907, a decision of this court. The principles upon which a court should act are set out in the judgment of Balcombe LJ (see [1987] 3 All ER 262 at 268–269, [1988] QB 907 at 916–918). Simple breach of the undertaking is not sufficient to lead to an award of compensation under the

d summary jurisdiction of the courts to deal with breaches of undertaking by solicitors. Compensation is only available where the conduct of the solicitor is inexcusable and such as to merit reproof (see [1987] 3 All ER 262 at 269, [1988] QB 907 at 917 (proposition 2)).

I have already expressed the views I have formed upon the conduct of Mr

e Gaisford in dealing with the documents in the way he did and it follows that, in my opinion, his conduct was neither inexcusable nor such as to merit reproof. He was acting, as he thought in the light of the information he gleaned from the documents, properly in the interest of his clients. That he had grounds for being of that view on matters which were contained in the documents was conceded by the first appellant in his affidavit.

f I have had the advantage of reading the judgment of Henry LJ, and of seeing the orders that he proposes. Consequently, I would allow the appeal, reverse the finding of the court below that the respondents were not in breach of the appellants' lien and discharge the orders dismissing the appellants' application and the further order that the appellants pay the respondents' costs of the

g proceedings in that court, but I would, exercising this court's discretion, decline to grant any of the relief sought by the appellants.

HENRY LJ. I have read and agree with the judgment of Roch LJ, and the order that he proposes. Here the appellant solicitors (Hewett & Co, acting through Mr

h Bentley) were discharged in mid-litigation by their clients (CET), but were not discharged for misconduct. Therefore they continued to enjoy the full protection of their retaining lien over all their clients' documents that had come into their possession in the course of their retainer. That lien (and the legal protections that go with it) was not discharged, waived in any way or altered by their delivery of

j those documents to the respondent solicitors (Sinclair Roche & Temperley (SRT), acting through Mr Gaisford), because they made it clear that that delivery was subject to their lien, by use of the standard phrase 'upon receiving your undertaking to hold the documents/our file to our order in respect of outstanding fees/disbursements'. On that basis, they delivered the documents to SRT. They thereupon ceased to enjoy physical possession of the documents, but retained legal possession of them.

Hewett's essential complaint is that immediately on receipt of those documents, Mr Gaisford on behalf of SRT promptly copied all those documents to the clients, thereby effectively rendering the lien worthless.

The respondent solicitors justified their action on two grounds, one general, which would apply whenever documents subject to the retaining lien are received by the solicitor taking over litigation after the client has discharged his former solicitor, and the second particular to these documents.

In relation to the general ground, the respondent solicitors asserted that, as the retaining lien had been applied only to the original documents, it was no breach of the lien to photocopy all the documents, and, as the photocopies are not the subject of the lien, they may then be sent to the clients (though, of course, the originals could not be). For the respondents, a Mr Murray had already explained to their clients that the lien meant little because of what he asserted to be the freedom to copy and keep or distribute the documents, and Mr Gaisford (who took the decision to copy and deliver to the clients) though deposing that he was ignorant that that advice had been given, says he agrees with it. They explain that it is necessary to distinguish between preserving the lien, and preserving the value of the lien. If the beneficiary of the lien wishes to preserve its value (and I interpose the rhetorical question 'Which solicitor would not?') then he must specifically add some 'no copying' embargo on his lien, or refuse to part with possession of the documents unless the second solicitors are prepared to pay his taxed costs. This general ground was put forward by the respondents and accepted by the judge as permitting unfettered copying and distribution.

Mr Gaisford's second justification is that, on reading the documents, he felt it was his duty to copy them to his clients because of their contents. As his firm's facsimile of 31 August makes clear, their original instructions were that a company called Tekso were responsible for the appellants' fees in the arbitration. According to Mr Gaisford, the clients, CET, were alleging fraud against Tekso, on the basis that Tekso had fraudulently induced them to lend their name as charterers of a vessel, while Tekso was the real charterer. They believed that Mr Bentley was in reality acting for Tekso, that he had shares in Tekso, and so was in a position where, at lowest, his financial interest conflicted with his duty to his clients. On the basis of the documents delivered pursuant to the lien, Mr Gaisford believed there was substance in those suggestions of impropriety in Mr Bentley's acting for CET in the arbitration, on the basis that in reality he was acting for and in Tekso's best interests (which were not those of CET). He felt it was his duty to pass on this information to his clients, and accordingly, he did so, and advised them of their legal rights.

While Mr Bentley vehemently denies that he was in breach of duty to his client, he accepts that in the light of his then state of knowledge the concerns referred to by Mr Gaisford were 'both genuine and reasonable'. But he submits that that did not justify the wholesale copying and dispatch of the entire file to CET.

So Hewetts felt they had justifiable cause for complaint and redress against Mr Gaisford and SRT. Their complaint was essentially for breach by Mr Gaisford and SRT of the subsisting lien subject to which the respondents had taken the documents.

Three possible remedies were open to Hewetts: (1) if there was a cause of action, by action at law; (2) by an application to the High Court to exercise its inherent jurisdiction to take summary action against solicitors (as officers of the a court) for their misconduct; (3) by an application to the Law Society alleging professional misconduct.

Here Hewetts chose to proceed by the second method, namely summary proceedings under the court's inherent disciplinary jurisdiction over its officers. That jurisdiction empowers the court to order (inter alia) the solicitor to perform undertakings, or to give compensation to make good the loss cause by his breach

b of duty. Here the first head of relief sought was the return of all copies of the documents, and the second an injunction against using the copies (or copies of them) in the arbitration. I agree with Roch LJ that it is too late to make either order. It would be to lock the stable door after the horse has bolted: once the China-based clients have the documents, to order the solicitors to return the 'original' copies is futile, and the court does not act in vain. Nor can they (or the

c court by order in this action) prevent CET from using them in the arbitration. Hewetts remedy, if any, is compensation.

Against that background, I come to the issues in this case.

The trial judge founded his judgment on what I have called the general point, namely that the continued presence of the retaining lien does not (absent a

d copying embargo) prevent wholesale copying and distribution of the documents subject to that lien to the lay clients in the case. His conclusion contains no restraint on the right to copy the documents and return the copies. He did not rely on the particular circumstances based on Mr Gaisford's suspicions, holding that those suspicions merely emphasised the importance of the decision, and were not otherwise relevant. I regard it as unfortunate that he took that view and

e that course. It seems to me that SRT and Mr Gaisford's case was stronger on their second justification for the copying, namely that in all the circumstances he felt it was his duty, and I would have been assisted by the judge's conclusions on that aspect of the matter. I will revert to this point.

I agree with Roch LJ that the judge was wrong on the general point. The

f submission made, in the fifth decade of the photocopier, that when you accept documents subject to a general lien in the ordinary form ('hold to our order') you can in all circumstances immediately copy all documents so covered to your client is one I have never met in practice, and which has no authority behind it. Were it not a novel suggestion, as I believe it to be, then one would expect authority dealing with the point, and/or that retaining liens would in practice be

g hedged about with 'no copying' qualifications, and/or would have become obsolete. None of these things has happened. To revert to my rhetorical question: any solicitor seeking to preserve his retaining lien for his unpaid fees (but public spiritedly not wishing to cause unnecessary difficulties for his client in the litigation (notwithstanding the discharge of his retainer)) would wish to

h prevent the documents being copied to the client, and would provide accordingly if the lien did not already give him that protection in law.

I agree with Roch LJ that, though many comparisons may be drawn between solicitors' undertakings and the acceptance of property subject to lien, the obligation attached to the retaining lien is (unless qualified by some individual

j undertaking) fundamentally a matter of law and not a matter of agreement. Thus in *Caldwell v Sumpters (a firm)* [1972] 1 All ER 567, [1972] Ch 478 the second solicitors were bound by terms they had never agreed to because they were imposed by law. So the cases resistant to the implication of terms in solicitors' undertakings have no significance here. The question is whether the law implies protection against unfettered copying and distribution. The better analogy is the kind of implied undertaking the law imposes as to documents disclosed on

discovery: not to use such documents for a collateral or ulterior purpose (for the
implied term and its enforceability, see *Home Office v Harman* [1982] 1 All ER 562
at 538, 543, [1983] 1 AC 280 at 304, 312). Where such a term is implied into a legal
obligation, ignorance of the implied term is not a defence to disciplinary
proceedings, but goes to mitigation of sentence (see *Watkins v A J Wright
(Electrical) Ltd* [1996] 3 All ER 31 at 42–43).

What use of the documents subject to the lien does the law permit in the
ordinary case where the documents are held to the first solicitors' order? The
public policy matters to be considered in answering this question are: (a) the
public interest in the orderly conduct of litigation; (b) the public interest in
solicitors who are discharged, but not for misconduct, being paid for their proper
services. As the court emphasised in *Hughes v Hughes* [1958] 3 All ER 179 at 181,
[1958] P 224 at 229:

> 'This lien should be preserved in the public interest in order that litigation
> may be properly conducted with due regard to the interest not only of
> litigants but also of the officers of the court who serve those interests.'

(c) The public interest that the solicitors in (b) who have it within their power
to disrupt litigation by their refusal to release documents the subject of their lien
should be encouraged not to do so. Implicit in this is that, at the very least, the
co-operative solicitor, not discharged for misconduct, should not be worse
treated under the law than the solicitor who discharges himself in mid-litigation.
Such a case was *Heslop v Metcalfe* (1837) 3 My & Cr 183, 40 ER 894, referred to by
Roch LJ. Roch LJ accepts that the limitation put on the use that may be made of
the documents is to give the solicitor claiming the lien 'every security not
inconsistent with the progress of the cause'. I agree with him that such a
limitation on the use to be made of documents delivered subject to the solicitor's
lien contains such an implicit undertaking. That test was laid down nearly 160
years ago, and there is nothing to indicate that it has been found to be
unworkable. In my judgment, that test is properly implied in the circumstances
we have here. The application of that would permit copying to the client only
where the progress of the cause required it. That was not the test the judge
applied, nor the question he addressed. That test would not permit the
immediate wholesale copying and transmission of the documents subject of the
lien to the client. Such wholesale disclosure would effectively destroy rather than
maintain the security, and would have to be justified on the basis that the
arbitration required that disclosure then. This question was not addressed by the
judge.

I therefore am of the opinion that the judge was wrong to hold that the
respondent solicitors were justified in their wholesale copying of the documents
to their clients under the general ground of justification the judge based his
judgment on.

It follows that in my judgment the appellants were right, and the respondents
wrong, in their basic contention.

There is then the question of remedy. I have already considered and rejected
the injunctive relief claimed. So the only remedy open to Hewetts under the
procedure they have chosen is an order for compensation against Mr Gaisford
and SRT. The circumstances in which the court may exercise its summary
disciplinary jurisdiction over its officers are summarised in *Udall v Capri Lighting
Ltd* [1987] 3 All ER 262, [1988] QB 907. I get from that authority four relevant
propositions (to be found [1987] 3 All ER 262 at 268–269, [1988] QB 907 at 916–

a 918 unless otherwise stated): (i) the court acts where there has been professional misconduct 'although the jurisdiction is compensatory and not punitive, it retains a disciplinary slant' acting 'to enforce honourable conduct on the part of the Court's own officers' (see *Re Grey* [1892] 2 QB 440 at 443); (ii) while the general rule is that the remedy is only available where the conduct of the solicitors is 'inexcusable and such as to merit reproof ... a mere mistake or error of judgment

b is not generally sufficient'; this is qualified by the rule that: (iii) failure to implement a solicitor's undertaking (to which I would equate failure to observe the legal obligations imposed by receiving documents subject to another's lien) is prima facie misconduct, even though there has been no dishonourable conduct or 'personal obliquity'. But this in its turn is subject to the proviso that the solicitor 'may be able to give an explanation for his failure to honour his

c undertaking which may enable the Court to say that there has been no misconduct in the particular case'; (iv) the remedy is discretionary (see Lord Wright in *Myers v Elman* [1939] 4 All ER 484 at 508, [1940] AC 282 at 318): 'The summary jurisdiction thus involved a discretion both as to procedure and as to substantive relief.'

d   Should the court grant compensatory relief in the exercise of its discretion?
    The difficulty the court here has is that the court below did not consider the validity of what I have call Mr Gaisford's second or particular justification for the copying of the documents, which copying would prima facie be a breach of the terms on which he received the documents.
    Had the judge considered this in detail, he might or might not have found that

e the documents copied were documents properly copied 'in the progress of the cause' having given proper weight to the lien. But he did not investigate that issue. We have not the material before us to know whether that test was satisfied. Normally, therefore, the case would be one for remission for investigation and findings on the real issue.

f   But, having regard to Mr Bentley's fair acknowledgement that Mr Gaisford's concerns (given his then state of knowledge) were 'both genuine and reasonable', I for my part would not find it necessary to remit this matter for further finding on the issues as to breach and relief, because, now that the explanation has been both given and accepted, it does not seem likely that any court would find his conduct to be 'inexcusable and such as to merit reproof', even following a finding

g of breach of lien.
    Against that background, I turn to the question of the order to be made on this appeal. In all the circumstances, I agree with the finding and order proposed by Roch LJ, despite the fact that these proceedings have concluded without the appellants obtaining the discretionary compensatory relief sought. First, this

h litigation has the 'disciplinary slant' already referred to. Second, the appellants were quite justified in bringing it. What might have been Mr Gaisford's defence only emerged in his affidavit. Third, the respondents put their case too high and were wrong in law in so doing. It was the way they put that that caused the judge's mistake and distracted him from addressing his mind to the real question.
    Though I do not consider it a necessary or appropriate use of the time of the court

j below now to investigate whether or not the wholesale copying was justified under the true test, it would not seem to me to be right to dismiss this appeal simply on the basis that no compensation was recovered.

Appeal allowed.

Mary Rose Plummer   Barrister.

Hillsdown Holdings plc v Pensions Ombudsman and others

QUEEN'S BENCH DIVISION (CROWN OFFICE LIST)
KNOX J
5–7, 14, 17 JUNE, 12 JULY 1996

Pension – Pension scheme – Maladministration of pension scheme – Jurisdiction of Pensions Ombudsman – Trust deed authorising transfer of assets and liabilities to another approved scheme but prohibiting transfer of assets to employer and amendment of scheme for that purpose – Trustees transferring assets and liabilities of scheme to another pension scheme –Trustees of other scheme amending scheme to enable payment of surplus funds to employer – Whether exercise of power to transfer used for collateral purpose – Jurisdiction of ombudsman with regard to remedies – Liability of employer to make repayment – Pension Schemes Act 1993, s 151(2).

H plc was the parent company of a group which participated in a pension scheme (the FMC scheme). In 1989, following negotiations with H plc and on legal advice, the trustees of the scheme transferred the entire assets and liabilities of the fund to another pension scheme (the HF scheme) pursuant to r 21[a] of the FMC rules, which authorised transfers of liabilities to other approved schemes provided such transfers did not seriously prejudice any member or pensioner. Prior to that transfer, the FMC scheme had a substantial actuarial surplus of funds in excess of permitted Revenue limits, but there was no provision under the scheme enabling the trustees to repay surplus funds to participating employers, save on a winding up, and the scheme could not be amended to confer such a power. Shortly after the transfer, an agreement previously negotiated between H plc and the FMC trustees to augment the benefits of FMC members and to pay the surplus funds to H plc was put into effect, and the rules of the HF scheme were changed to permit that payment to H plc, which was also made the administrator of the scheme. Thereafter H plc was paid sums in excess of £11m after tax. A pensioner, supported by 51 other complainants, complained to the Pensions Ombudsman that the transfer of the assets of the FMC scheme to the HF scheme and the amendment made to the HF scheme to enable the payment of surplus funds to be made to H plc were in breach of trust. The ombudsman found that while the FMC trustees had acted in the members' best interests in agreeing to the transfer of assets the sole purpose of that transfer was to secure a payment of surplus to H plc which was prohibited by the FMC trust deed and rules and that therefore the trustees were in breach of trust in using the transfer power under r 21 to secure such payment. Accordingly, he held that the transfer constituted maladministration and involved injustice to the pensioners in that they received a reduction in the security of their benefits and were deprived of the opportunity of further benefit increases and directed that H plc refund the surplus payments. H plc appealed. The issues arose: (i) whether the transfer was impeachable; (ii) whether the ombudsman had jurisdiction under s 151(2)[b] of the 1993 Act to direct steps to be taken to remedy any injustice caused by

---

a Rule 21 is set out at p 870 *j* to p 871 *d*, post
b Section 151, so far as material, is set out at p 867 *g* to *j*, post

a maladministration to anyone other than the complainant with whose complaint he was dealing; and (iii) if so, whether his power was limited to directing only those steps which a person could be compelled to take by the court.

Held – (1) The purpose of the FMC trustees in exercising the power in r 21 was a composite one of giving effect to the bargain struck with H plc, a major element of which was the payment of surplus to H plc. Since that element was
b outside the proper ambit of r 21, that exercise constituted an improper use of the power for a collateral purpose. Accordingly, the transfer was an improper and invalid exercise of the power and, notwithstanding that the FMC trustees had acted in what they considered to be the best interests of the members, it was an act of maladministration, albeit that it was done with the advice and concurrence of an appropriately experienced solicitor, since it was intrinsically in breach of
c trust and damaging to the interests of the members (see p 883 h j and p 884 g to p 885 d, post); Re Vauxhall Motors Pension Fund, Bullard v Randall [1989] 1 Pensions LR 49 distinguished.

(2) Under s 151(2) of the 1993 Act the ombudsman had jurisdiction to direct steps to be taken by the trustees or managers of a scheme with a view to
d remedying any injustice caused to anyone by maladministration. Accordingly, where the remedy discerned as appropriate by the ombudsman was one which was equally applicable in relation to a large number of other authorised complainants on the same facts and it was a remedy to which the particular claimant in question was entitled, he had jurisdiction to direct steps which granted that remedy, notwithstanding that there was no express provision in the
e Act or relevant regulations for representation orders. Moreover, although the FMC scheme had been wound up after the assets were transferred to the HF trust, the pension trust had continuing trusts and therefore the appropriate order was an order or determination that funds improperly taken out of the trust should be put back (see p 896 j to p 897 a f to h, post); Target Holdings Ltd v Redferns
f (a firm) [1995] 3 All ER 785 considered.

(3) The ombudsman did not have jurisdiction to direct an employer or trustee to replace funds improperly removed from a pension scheme unless the court itself could so order. In the circumstances H plc could have been held liable by a court as a constructive trustee because, although it honestly believed itself to be
g entitled to do and receive what it did, it had taken an active part in persuading the trustees to agree the breach of trust, had used a threatening technique of persuasion to induce the breach of trust and was unjustly enriched. It followed that the ombudsman had jurisdiction to order H plc to refund the surplus and the appeal would therefore be dismissed (see p 898 c d, p 899 c to h, p 902 j to p 903 f and p 905 a, post); Westminster City Council v Haywood [1996] 2 All ER 467
h distinguished; Miller v Stapleton [1996] 2 All ER 449 considered.

Notes

For occupational pension schemes generally, see 33 Halsbury's Laws (4th edn)
j para 973.

Cases referred to in judgment

Barnes v Addy (1874) LR 9 Ch App 244, LC and LJJ.

Carl-Zeiss-Stiftung v Herbert Smith & Co (a firm) (No 2) [1969] 2 All ER 367, [1969] 2 Ch 276, [1969] 2 WLR 427, CA.

Chase Manhattan Bank NA v Israel-British Bank (London) Ltd [1979] 3 All ER 1025, [1981] Ch 105.

Courage Group's Pension Schemes, Re, Ryan v Imperial Brewing and Leisure Ltd [1987] 1 All ER 528, [1987] 1 WLR 495.

Farrar v Farrars Ltd (1888) 40 Ch D 395, CA.

Hastings-Bass (decd), Re, Hastings v IRC [1974] 2 All ER 193, [1975] Ch 25, [1974] 2 WLR 904, CA.

Henderson v Henderson (1843) 3 Hare 100, [1843–60] All ER Rep 278, 67 ER 313, V-C.

Imperial Group Pension Trust Ltd v Imperial Tobacco Ltd [1991] 2 All ER 597, [1991] 1 WLR 589.

Kirkness (Inspector of Taxes) v John Hudson & Co Ltd [1955] 2 All ER 345, [1955] AC 696, [1955] 2 WLR 1135, HL.

Lipkin Gorman (a firm) v Karpnale Ltd [1992] 4 All ER 512, [1991] 2 AC 548, [1991] 3 WLR 10, HL.

Mettoy Pension Trustees Ltd v Evans [1991] 2 All ER 513, [1990] 1 WLR 1587.

Miller v Stapleton [1996] 2 All ER 449.

Montagu's Settlement Trusts, Re, Duke of Manchester v National Westminster Bank Ltd (1985) [1992] 4 All ER 308, [1987] Ch 264, [1987] 2 WLR 1192.

National Trustees Co of Australasia Ltd v General Finance Co of Australasia Ltd [1905] AC 373, PC.

Pauling's Settlement Trusts, Re, Younghusband v Coutts & Co [1961] 3 All ER 713, [1962] 1 WLR 86; *rvsd in part* [1963] 3 All ER 1, [1964] Ch 303, [1963] 3 WLR 742, CA.

Pepper (Inspector of Taxes) v Hart [1993] 1 All ER 42, [1993] AC 593, [1992] 3 WLR 1032, HL.

Perrins v Bellamy [1899] 1 Ch 797, CA.

Target Holdings Ltd v Redferns (a firm) [1995] 3 All ER 785, [1996] AC 421, [1995] 3 WLR 352, HL.

Thompson's Settlement, Re, Thompson v Thompson [1985] 2 All ER 720, [1986] Ch 99, [1985] 3 WLR 486.

Tito v Waddell (No 2) [1977] 3 All ER 129, [1977] Ch 106, [1977] 2 WLR 496.

Topham v Duke of Portland (1863) 1 De G J & S 517, 46 ER 205, LJJ; *affd* (1864) 11 HL Cas 32, [1861–73] All ER Rep 980, 11 ER 1242, HL.

Vatcher v Paull [1915] AC 372, [1914–15] All ER Rep 609, PC.

Vauxhall Motors Pension Fund, Re, Bullard v Randall [1989] 1 Pensions LR 49.

Westdeutsche Landesbank Girozentrale v Islington London BC [1996] 2 WLR 802, [1996] AC 669, [1996] 2 All ER 961, HL.

Westminster City Council v Haywood [1996] 2 All ER 467, [1996] 3 WLR 563.

Wild v Pensions Ombudsman (1996) Times, 17 April.

Wright v Morgan [1926] AC 788, [1926] All ER Rep 201, PC.

Cases also cited or referred to in skeleton arguments

Agip (Africa) Ltd v Jackson [1992] 4 All ER 451, [1990] Ch 265, CA.

Baden v Société Générale pour Favoriser le Développement du Commerce et de l'Industrie en France SA (1982) [1992] 4 All ER 161, [1993] 1 WLR 509.

Brook's Settlement Trusts, Re [1968] 3 All ER 416, [1968] 1 WLR 1661.

Charterbridge Corp Ltd v Lloyds Bank Ltd [1969] 2 All ER 1185, [1970] Ch 62.

Cowan de Groot Properties Ltd v Eagle Trust plc [1992] 4 All ER 700.

Cowan v Scargill [1984] 2 All ER 750, [1985] Ch 270.

Dolphin Packaging Materials Ltd v Pensions Ombudsman (1993) Times, 2 December.

a   *El Ajou v Dollar Land Holdings plc* [1994] 2 All ER 685, CA.
Hallett's Estate, Re, Knatchbull v Hallett, Cotterell v Hallett (1880) 13 Ch D 696,
     [1874–80] All ER Rep 793, CA.
Harries v Church Comrs for England [1993] 2 All ER 300, [1992] 1 WLR 1241.
LRT Pension Fund Trustee Co Ltd v Hatt [1993] Pensions LR 227.
McDonald v Horn [1995] 1 All ER 961, CA.
b   *Space Investments Ltd v Canadian Imperial Bank of Commerce Trust Co (Bahamas) Ltd*
     [1986] 3 All ER 75, [1986] 1 WLR 1072, PC.
Stannard v Fisons Pension Trust Ltd [1991] Pensions LR 225, CA.

Appeal

c   By originating motion dated 6 November 1995 Hillsdown Holdings plc
(Hillsdown) appealed from the determination of the first respondent, the
Pensions Ombudsman, made on 11 October 1995 whereby: (i) he held that FMC
Superannuation and Pension Scheme Trustees Ltd (the FMC trustees) had acted
in breach of trust under r 21 of the trust deed and rules of the scheme when it
transferred the assets and membership of the scheme to the fourth respondent,
d   HF Meat and Foods Processing Pension Scheme Trustees Ltd (the HF trustees),
on 17 November 1989 and when it exercised its power under cl 11 of the HF
scheme trust deed so as to amend the trust deed and rules of the HF scheme on
4 December 1989 to provide for the payment of a surplus from the HF scheme to
Hillsdown; and (ii) directed that Hillsdown return with interest the gross surplus
payments from the HF scheme which the HF trustees had made. The second and
e   third respondents, Robert Eric Burt and Alan James Bothwell, were pensioners of
the FMC scheme and complainants. The fourth respondent did not appeal
against the ombudsman's decision but was joined to the appeal on its own
application by order of Carnwath J dated 1 May 1996. The facts are set out in the
judgment.

f
David Oliver QC, Nicholas Warren QC and *Nigel Giffin* (instructed by Herbert Smith)
     for Hillsdown.
Christopher Nugee (instructed by *Paisner & Co*) for the Pensions Ombudsman.
Nigel Inglis-Jones QC and *Richard Hitchcock* (instructed by *Nabarro Nathanson*) for
g   the HF trustees.
Mr Burt and Mr Bothwell appeared in person.

Cur adv vult

h   12 July 1996. The following judgment was delivered.

KNOX J. Hillsdown Holdings plc (Hillsdown) appeals by way of originating
motion dated 6 November 1995 from a determination of the Pensions
Ombudsman dated 11 October 1995 (the determination) and asks for it to be set
aside. By the determination the Pensions Ombudsman directed the return with
j   interest by Hillsdown of gross payments of surplus from a pension fund, the HF
Meat and Foods Processing Pension Scheme (the HF scheme), which the trustees
thereof (the HF trustees) made to Hillsdown in December 1989 and June 1990.
The HF trustees were enabled to make those payments of surplus to Hillsdown
only because there had been on or shortly after 17 November 1989 a transfer to
them, to form part of the HF scheme, of all the assets and liabilities of another
pension scheme, the FMC Superannuation and Life Assurance Scheme (the FMC

scheme). The FMC scheme prior to that transfer had a substantial surplus but under the FMC scheme deed and the rules made thereunder not only was there *a* no available provision enabling repayment of surplus to the employers under the FMC scheme, of which Hillsdown was one, but there was also a provision prohibiting amendments resulting in the transfer of any assets held by the FMC trustees to any of the employers thereunder, subject to an irrelevant exception on the dissolution of the FMC scheme. The FMC scheme did contain a provision *b* allowing transfers of liabilities and, by implication, of assets to other defined schemes and that power of transfer, which was the one used to effect the transfers from the FMC scheme to the HF scheme, did not itself contain any express terms prohibiting, or indeed permitting, transfer of assets to employers by the trustees of the transferee scheme. What I have said so far is a very condensed summary of events and provisions of the relevant documents which I must return to in *c* greater detail, but it will serve as a very summary explanation of the context for the Pensions Ombudsman's essential conclusion which was that the transfer process from the FMC scheme to the HF scheme constituted what he called a fraud on the power but which might perhaps be more broadly and less technically described as the improper use of a power for a purpose other than the use for *d* which the power was granted.

I start with the relevant legislation which conferred the power on the Pensions Ombudsman to make the determination and which confers the power on this court to hear and determine the appeal before me.

Section 145 of the Pension Schemes Act 1993 includes in sub-s (1):

e

'For the purpose of conducting investigations in accordance with this Part ... there shall be a commissioner to be known as the Pensions Ombudsman.'

That Part was Pt X of the 1993 Act and it included the following provisions:

146.—(1) The Pensions Ombudsman may investigate and determine any complaint made to him in writing by or on behalf of an authorised *f* complainant who alleges that he has sustained injustice in consequence of maladministration in connection with any act or omission of the trustees or managers of an occupational pension scheme or personal pension scheme.

(2) The Pensions Ombudsman may also investigate and determine any dispute of fact or law which arises in relation to such a scheme between—(a) *g* the trustees or managers of the scheme, and (b) an authorised complainant, and which is referred to him in writing by or on behalf of the authorised complainant ...'

'Authorised complainant' is defined by sub-s (7) in terms which include '(a) a member of the scheme, (b) the widow or widower, or any surviving dependant, *h* of a deceased member of the scheme ...' 'Member' is defined by sub-s (8) in relation to a pension scheme in terms which include a person '(a) who is or has been in pensionable service under the scheme ...' The original authorised complainant was Lord Bradbury, a pensioner of the FMC scheme, but after his death the Pensions Ombudsman's predecessor in that office agreed to consider *j* the complaint of Mr R E Burt, whom the Pensions Ombudsman treated as the lead complainant although he was supported by 51 other complainants, including Lord Bradbury's widow and Mr A J Bothwell, also a pensioner under the FMC scheme. The complaint investigated by the Pensions Ombudsman was that of Mr Burt who wished it to be supported by the documents relating to the complaint earlier submitted by Lord Bradbury. Both Mr Burt and Mr Bothwell a are parties to the appeal as second and third respondents, but they have not been represented before me although Mr Bothwell has written two letters to the court and both gentlemen have been present during the hearing. There is no dispute but that Mr Burt and Mr Bothwell are within the definition of 'authorised complainant' as was Lord Bradbury.

Section 146(4) of the 1993 Act conferred a power on the Secretary of State to
b provide by regulations that Pt X of the 1993 Act should apply in relation to (inter alios) the employer in relation to any category of employment to which an occupational pension scheme relates as it applies in relation to the trustees of such a scheme. That power was exercised by the Personal and Occupational Pension Schemes (Pensions Ombudsman) Regulations 1991, SI 1991/588 (made under the enactment which the 1993 Act re-enacts), with the result pursuant to reg 2
c thereof that the Pensions Ombudsman may, in relation to an occupational pension scheme, investigate and determine any complaint or dispute involving an authorised complainant and the employer to which the scheme relates and where the Pensions Ombudsman commences any such investigation the provisions of what is now Pt X of the 1993 Act apply in relation to the employer
d as they would apply in relation to the trustees of such a scheme.

The Pensions Ombudsman has wide powers in relation to the conduct of investigations by him, including the power to hear oral evidence but this latter power was not exercised in the present case. What happened procedurally was that the three entities against whom allegations of maladministration causing injustice were made, that is to say the FMC trustees, the HF trustees and
e Hillsdown, were all invited to answer in writing the complaints made by the complainants and did so. Mr Burt made observations in reply and the Pensions Ombudsman gave all concerned a sight of a draft determination upon which they had an opportunity of commenting and did so, before the Pensions Ombudsman issued the determination in its final form. The procedure therefore was all in
f writing which is before the court.

The statutory provisions regarding the Pensions Ombudsman's determinations are contained in s 151 of the 1993 Act, which, so far as relevant, reads:

'(1) Where the Pensions Ombudsman has conducted an investigation
g under this Part he shall send a written statement of his determination of the complaint or dispute in question—(a) to the authorised complainant in question; and (b) to the trustees or managers of the scheme in question; and any such statement shall contain the reasons for his determination.

(2) Where the Pensions Ombudsman makes a determination under this Part ... he may direct the trustees or managers of the scheme concerned to
h take, or refrain from taking, such steps as he may specify in the statement referred to in subsection (1) or otherwise in writing.

(3) Subject to subsection (4), the determination by the Pensions Ombudsman of a complaint or dispute, and any direction given by him under subsection (2), shall he final and binding on—(a) the authorised
j complainant in question; (b) the trustees or managers of the scheme concerned; and (c) any person claiming under them respectively.

(4) An appeal on a point of law shall lie to the High Court ... from a determination or direction of the Pensions Ombudsman at the instance of any person falling within paragraphs (a) to (c) of subsection (3) ...'

Section 146(6) of the 1993 Act provides:

'The Pensions Ombudsman shall not investigate or determine a complaint or dispute—(a) if before the making of the complaint or the reference of the dispute proceedings have been begun in any court in respect of the matters which would be the subject of the investigation ...'

The terms in which Parliament has chosen to define the remedial powers of the Pensions Ombudsman in s 151(2) are remarkably widely stated. All that is said is that he may direct the taking or refraining from taking such steps as he may specify. That some limits must be placed upon the steps is self-evident but that subsection is silent on the subject and, unless one is to resort to what would to a lawyer be a counsel of despair and leave the limits to the unfettered discretion of the Pensions Ombudsman, so as to put him under the traditional palm tree, limits must be sought elsewhere. It was not suggested by any party before me that there are no limits upon the Pensions Ombudsman's powers to direct steps to be taken or not to be taken. The appeal to the court on a point of law suffices to show, if it needs to be shown, that the Pensions Ombudsman must operate within the law.

The limitations on the power given to the Pensions Ombudsman are to be found in the definition of his function, namely the investigation and determination of (i) complaints alleging injustice in consequence of mal-administration and (ii) disputes of facts or law. As Robert Walker J has said in *Westminster City Council v Haywood* [1996] 2 All ER 467 at 475, [1996] 3 WLR 563 at 571, after a valuable summary of the Pensions Ombudsman's functions in the context of other pre-existing ombudsmen:

'It is ... easy to see the general legislative purpose behind these wide provisions, including the Pensions Ombudsman's unusual powers (not shared by other ombudsmen) to decide questions of law and give directions that are enforceable. A very important part of the legislative purpose was to provide a quick, inexpensive and informal means of settling complaints and disputes about occupational pensions, especially where an individual or small group of individuals (whether employees or pensioners) find themselves in conflict with trustees who have large resources and may sometimes (rightly or wrongly) be thought to be more attentive to the views of the employer than to those of the employees or pensioners.'

I would only add to that, that the object of providing a quick inexpensive and informal means of settling complaints was equally aimed at large cases where a large group of individual members was involved in such a dispute. The great majority of a large group of members would individually be likely to have resources far too slender to contemplate litigation in such a technical, difficult and thereby expensive, field of law.

Two important questions on the Pensions Ombudsman's jurisdiction were argued before me. The first was the extent to which the Pensions Ombudsman in directing steps to be taken by trustees or employers was entitled to include steps which went beyond curing the injustice through maladministration sustained by the complainant whose complaint he was investigating so as to permit the Pensions Ombudsman to direct the taking of steps which would in his view rectify any injustices through the same maladministration suffered by other persons, notably persons who would have been authorised complainants but did not make complaints to the Pensions Ombudsman.

The second question argued was whether the Pensions Ombudsman was
limited in his choice of steps which he could lawfully direct to be taken, notably
by an employer, to those which that person could be compelled to take by legal
proceedings brought by the complainant and other persons (if any) for whose
benefit steps could, pursuant to the answer to the first question above, be directed
to be taken.

Both these important questions only arise if the central issue, whether the
transactions whereby assets were transferred from the FMC scheme to the HF
scheme and payments made out of the latter to Hillsdown, can now be
impeached, and to that I now turn.

The primary facts

The FMC scheme was originally constituted by a definitive trust deed dated 24
July 1955 and made between the Fatstock Marketing Corp Ltd, later called 'FMC
Ltd', and other parties but it is not necessary to go back to any earlier version of
that trust deed and rules thereunder than that which came into force with effect
from 17 September 1981 and is contained in schedule V to a deed dated 21 March
1983 by which the provisions of the original trust deed of 24 July 1955 were
amended. I shall refer to this version as 'the 1983 FMC trust deed and rules'.
Under its provisions 'the Corporation' was defined as 'FMC Ltd'. The 1983 FMC
trust deed also included the following relevant provisions.

By cl 3 the trustees (an expression defined as the trustees for the time being
thereof) undertook to administer the FMC scheme in accordance with the
provisions of the FMC trust deed and the rules. Clause 4 read:

'(a) ANY company being a subsidiary of or associated with the Corporation
may with the approval of the Corporation undertake by Deed with the
Trustees to be bound by the provisions of this Deed and of the Rules as an
Employer and may thereafter remain an Employer for the purposes of the
Scheme but not if by so doing it would cause the Scheme to cease to have the
approval of the Commissioners of Inland Revenue as an exempt approved
scheme under Chapter II of Part II of the Finance Act 1970 or any statutory
modification or re-enactment thereof for the time being in force.

(b) Notwithstanding the terms of paragraph (a) of this Clause a company
which is for the purposes of Section 154(1) of the Companies Act, 1948 a
subsidiary of the Corporation or of any other Employer will if the
Corporation so directs and subject to the prior approval of the
Commissioners of Inland Revenue become an Employer without executing
a Deed similar to that described in paragraph (a) of this Clause but such
company shall by a resolution of its board of directors undertake that it will
comply with its obligations as an Employer under this Deed and the Rules.
Any company which becomes an Employer pursuant to this subclause may
thereafter remain an Employer but not if by so doing it would cause the
Scheme to cease to have the approval of the Commissioners of Inland
Revenue as an exempt approved scheme under Chapter II of Part II of the
Finance Act 1970 or any statutory modification or re-enactment thereof for
the time being in force.'

Clause 5(a) read:

'EACH of the Employers undertakes to pay to the Trustees by way of
contribution such sums as on the advice of the Actuary shall from time to

time be required in addition to such from as are received by way of
contributions from members of the Scheme to secure the benefits payable
under the Scheme.'

Clause 14 provided:

'THE Trustees with the consent of the Employers which shall be witnessed
by the Corporation on behalf of itself and the other Employers being a party
to the Deed of Amendment shall be entitled by Deed to alter modify or add
to all and any of the provisions of this Deed and the Rules. Provided that no
such alteration modification or addition shall:—(a) operate so as in the
opinion of the Actuary (as defined in the Rules) substantially or unfairly to
prejudice the rights or interests of any Member of the Scheme or of any
person receiving any benefit under the Scheme by virtue of the membership
of any deceased Member in so far as such rights or interests have been
secured by virtue of service with any of the Employers prior to the date of
such alteration modification or addition except with the written consent of
the person whose rights or interests are so prejudiced, or (b) cause any
alteration in the main purpose of the Scheme, or (c) cause any of the assets
held by the Trustees under the trusts hereof to be used otherwise than for
the purposes of the Scheme, or (d) result in the transfer of any of the assets
held by the Trustees under the trusts hereof to any of the Employers but
subject to the provisions of Clause 17(a)(iii) hereof. The Trustees shall notify
in writing each Member affected by any alteration, modification or addition
so made by them.'

It was common ground that the prohibition on transfers of assets to the
employers (subject to the exception in cl 17(a)(iii) dealing with ultimate surplus
on winding up) was inserted because of the then current requirements of the
Inland Revenue for approval of such schemes.

Clause 17 dealt with how the fund was to be dealt with on the termination of
the FMC scheme and it will suffice for my purposes to say it required net assets
after discharge of liabilities to be applied by providing for the purchase of
annuities for pensioners and others such as widows and deferred pensioners and
by cl 17(a)(iii) it was provided that any balance remaining thereafter should be
applied to increase within the permitted limits approved by the Commissioners
of Inland Revenue the pensions and annuities for which provision had earlier
been directed to be made and subject thereto any ultimate balance should be
returned to the employers.

The 1983 FMC scheme rules included the following relevant provisions
besides normal provisions for benefits in defined circumstances. 'The
Corporation' was defined as 'FMC Ltd'. 'The Group' was defined as—

'FMC Ltd and those of its subsidiary and associated companies which
undertake in accordance with clause 4 of the Definitive Trust Deed to be
bound by the provisions thereof and of the Rules.'

'Employer' was defined as 'any company for the time being comprised in the
Group'. Rule 21(a) is at the centre of this appeal. It was not in the rules as
originally formulated but was inserted at an uncertain date before 21 March 1983
and read:

'TRANSFERS OF OBLIGATIONS (a) The Trustees may at any time or times
with the consent of the Corporation and the Employers concerned and after

a obtaining the advice of the Actuary but otherwise in their discretion make arrangements upon such terms as they shall think fit for the transfer to some other retirements benefits scheme (approved under Chapter II of Part II of the Finance Act 1970 or Section 208 or Section 222 of the Income and Corporation Taxes Act 1970 or any other fund scheme or arrangement approved by the said Commissioners for the purposes of this Clause) of *b* which the then Members concerned are or will thereupon become Members of the total or partial responsibility for securing and making payment of all or any particular benefits under the Scheme in respect of all or some of the Members (including, without prejudice to the generality of the foregoing, all the Members in or formerly in the service of a particular one of the Employers). *Provided always that*: (i) no such transfer shall without his *c* consent increase the liability of any Member to make contributions; and (ii) the Trustees shall not implement any transfer under this Rule which in their opinion after obtaining the advice of the Actuary will or may seriously prejudice any person who is a Member or pensioner at the proposed transfer date.'

d Rule 22 provided for a duly qualified actuary to be appointed and included as one of his duties from time to time at the request of the corporation (and in any event once every five years after 1 July 1971) to make an actuarial valuation of and report to the trustees and employers on the scheme, together with such recommendations as he might think fit.

e Rule 23 is also of considerable importance. It read:

'SURPLUS AND DEFICIENCY   (a) If any periodic valuation by the Actuary shall disclose any surplus which the Actuary shall certify not to be required to cover the immediate and prospective liabilities of the Scheme the same shall be applied in accordance with the directions of the Trustees (who shall *f* in relation to such application seek and have regard to but not be bound by the advice of the Actuary) in any either or both of the following ways, namely: (i) the holding of a reserve to meet any subsequent loss or deficiency; (ii) the reduction of future contributions of Members and/or Employers; (iii) an increase in the amount of any pensions then in course of *g* payment or deferred pensions allocated but no such increase may be made if it would result in any deferred pensions exceeding the maximum pension approvable by the Commissioners of Inland Revenue at retirement or in any pensions in the course of payment being increased by an amount proportionally greater than any increase in the Index since *h* commencement; (iv) subject to the permitted limit an increase or improvement in the terms of all or any of the pensions or other benefits prospectively payable under the Rules. (b) If any periodic valuation by the Actuary shall disclose any deficiency or anticipated deficiency in the funds held for the purposes of the Scheme the Trustees shall (having regard to the advice of the Actuary and to any additional contributions to the Fund which *j* the Employers may indicate their willingness to pay) make alterations to or modifications of the Rules to remedy the deficiency by one or other of the following means, namely: (i) an increase in the rate of Employers and/or Members' contributions; (ii) a reduction in the amount of all or any particular benefits not yet in course of payment (other than deferred pensions already allocated) for which the Rules provide ...'

There followed an irrelevant proviso limiting certain categories of reduction upon which nothing turns for present purposes.

The last of the important rules was r 35, which provided:

'REDUCTION SUSPENSION OR TERMINATION OF EMPLOYER'S LIABILITY   (a) The Employers or any of them may at any time reduce suspend or terminate their liability to pay contributions under the Scheme by giving notice to the Trustees and without the concurrence of the Members. Upon receipt of such notice the liability of the Employer by which it was given shall be reduced suspended or terminated to the extent therein defined except in respect of payments due on or before the date of expiry of such notice and the Trustees shall notify individually in writing each Member who is affected by the contents of such notice ...'

The interrelation of rr 23 and 35 is a subject to which I must return, but it will suffice at this stage to note that r 23 confers a duty and powers upon the FMC trustees to give directions as to the application of a surplus certified by the actuary not to be required to cover the immediate and prospective liabilities of the FMC scheme and that neither the corporation nor the employer are required or entitled to give advice, let alone directions on the subject, by the terms of r 23. It is also to be observed that none of the possible modes of application of surplus provided for by r 23 includes a payment to the employers. At most there can be a reduction of employers' contributions, but where there is a large surplus it may well be that the employer is already not contributing. This was the position in relation to Hillsdown after 1985 in the FMC scheme. Rule 35, on the other hand, confers a unilateral right on the employers or any of them to reduce, suspend or terminate their liability. No question arises of a right in the trustees, members or pensioners to be consulted about, let alone consent to, any exercise of that power.

Hillsdown acquired the issued share capital of FMC plc in 1983. It was not until 30 November 1987 that the power in r 21 was exercised so as to create machinery for Hillsdown to become the corporation in place of FMC. The actual change was achieved by two stages in deeds executed on 30 November 1987 and 1 December 1987. By the first of those deeds the trustees added to the 1983 FMC trust deed a cl 22, which read:

'(1) If with the consent of the Corporation (unless it has been wound up) the New Corporation enters into an agreement with the Trustees under which the New Corporation undertakes the liabilities of the Corporation under the Fund the Corporation shall thereupon be released from all obligations under the provisions of the Scheme which shall thereafter have effect as if the New Corporation had been the "Corporation" therein referred to.

(2) For the purpose of this Clause "New Corporation" means any of the Employers (other than the Corporation) or any other subsidiary or associated company which enters into the agreement which is referred to in sub clause (1) above.'

By the deed of the following day, 1 December 1987, Hillsdown with the consent of FMC covenanted with the FMC trustees to observe and perform such of the provisions in the 1983 FMC trust deed and rules as were to be observed and performed by the corporation and FMC was released by the FMC trustees with Hillsdown's approval as the corporation under the FMC scheme. By this slightly convoluted path Hillsdown became the corporation in place of FMC. The a validity of the substitution of Hillsdown for FMC Ltd as the corporation was sought to be challenged before me by Mr Nugee on behalf of the Pensions Ombudsman although it was not challenged in the complaints to the Pensions Ombudsman and that is a subject to which I must return later.

The transactions which were the subject of the complaints to the Pensions Ombudsman and the subject of the determination were set in train initially by a
b letter dated 3 May 1989 written by the actuaries to Mr Jackson at Hillsdown, the employer, and not to the trustees. It included the following:

> 'As you are aware, we are in the process of carrying out an actuarial valuation of the FMC Superannuation Scheme as at 6 April 1988.'

c I interpose that it is common ground that such a valuation was indeed being done by the actuary as part of his duty to carry out periodical valuations. The letter continued:

> 'At the last valuation a substantial surplus was disclosed and it is likely that given investment conditions over the intervaluation period, the surplus will
d have increased. It is therefore important that the company come to a view on its attitude to surplus, not just for the FMC Scheme, but also for the other schemes in the group. Of course the flexibility available to the company is now restricted and the Inland Revenue will not allow surpluses to be carried forward indefinitely. This means the company will have to come to a decision on how any surplus disclosed at this valuation will have to be
e distributed. There are a number of choices open to the company. They can improve members' pension rights and/or suspend their contributions; the company could suspend its contributions but only for a maximum period of five years; the company could admit other companies to the Scheme; the company could take a repayment of surplus but subject to a penal tax charge
f of 40 per cent and of course the company could carry out a combination of the above. Alternatively the company could do nothing and thereby lose part of the fund's tax exempt status. I suggest that you come to a firm decision on your attitude to surplus and the trustees are made fully aware of your intentions.'

g This was not of course advice from a legal adviser but it is an unfortunate feature of this series of events that it is this letter, which ignored the fact that r 23 of the 1983 FMC scheme rules placed the duty to decide what to do with a surplus disclosed by a periodic valuation upon the FMC trustees alone, and not upon Hillsdown as employer, set the tone for the ensuing negotiations. This is shown by the letter which Mr Jackson for Hillsdown sent to the trustees of the FMC
h scheme the next day, 4 May 1989, in which he said:

> 'As you are aware there are now considerable restraints imposed by the Inland Revenue on the ability of a scheme to continue to carry forward surpluses from one valuation to the next. As a result of this, the company
j has decided that should a surplus emerge as a result of the current or any future valuation this will be used solely to reduce the company's contribution rate. The company feels that the benefits of the scheme are at a competitive and generous level and the company will not be considering any improvement to benefits in the foreseeable future. If the surplus is such that a contribution holiday for the FMC Schemes will not comply with the Inland Revenue's requirements then the company will restructure its other

pension arrangements in such a way as to ensure that the surplus is brought within the prescribed limits. In practice this will mean adhering the various other group companies to the FMC Schemes and enjoining them in the company contribution holiday.'

Four days later, on 8 May 1959, Mr Jackson for Hillsdown first raised the suggestion of a transfer of the FMC scheme assets and liabilities to the HF trustees as part of the HF scheme by writing again to the secretary to the FMC trustees. After describing the HF scheme and saying that it would in time become the only vehicle for future pension provision he went on:

'The company now requests that the trustees give consideration to agreeing to transfer all of the assets and liabilities of the FMC Superannuation Scheme to the new HF Scheme by virtue of the powers enjoyed by them under Rule 21—TRANSFERS OF OBLIGATION of the Trust Deed and Rules dated 21st March 1983. If the trustees agree to transfer the assets and liabilities of the Scheme then the Company will agree to introduce the following substantial benefit improvements in the new scheme. 1) In respect of active members of the FMC Scheme:—An immediate uplift in the pension accrued to date by 5 percent of the value of the pension. For future leavers *all* of their pension accrued to the date of leaving will be indexed at 5 per cent p.a. (rather than just the post 1/1/85 accrued pension). 2) In respect of current pensioners: An enhancement exercise to increase their pensions in payment by 5 per cent. 3) In respect of deferred pensioners:—An enhancement of 5 per cent of the value of their deferred pension.'

The FMC trustees held a meeting on 15 May 1989 with the FMC scheme actuary and Mr Ellison, a solicitor from a firm specialising in pensions advice, and another person described as a pensions consultant. The Pensions Ombudsman was provided with an unsigned draft of a report to the FMC trustees which contained the advice given by Mr Ellison. This referred to and quoted from rr 21 and 23 of the 1983 FMC rules and in relation to r 21 referred to what was called the *Vauxhall* decision (see *Re Vauxhall Motors Pension Fund, Bullard v Randall* [1989] 1 Pensions LR 49), saying that following that decision—

'it is now clear that the trustees have the power, even where there is no power to return surplus to the employer, to transfer in bulk fashion to another scheme which does have such a power, in certain circumstances.'

What the circumstances were was not elaborated further. On the issue, described as one of the main questions for the trustees to decide, whether the FMC trustees had power to comply with Hillsdown's request to transfer all the assets to the HF trustees pursuant to r 21, it was said that the question divided into four parts. The first two were whether the specific conditions mentioned in r 21 itself were met, the third read:

'Whether directions as to the use of the surplus prohibit transfer to another scheme without such constraints to meet the requirements of clause 23.'

The fourth was whether it was in the interests of the members generally. On whether, if there was power, the FMC trustees should exercise it, the advice was that they should take into account what would happen if they did not agree and whether they had achieved the best for their beneficiaries in the circumstances, considering the overriding powers of the employer. Finally, it was said that a before coming to a final decision, the FMC trustees had the power if they thought it necessary, either to obtain the consent of the members or to apply to the court for ratification (perhaps on a construction summons) or to obtain counsel's opinion. It was added that the trustees might feel that none of the above steps was necessary as the issues were now simple and clear-cut and there was considerable experience in the repatriation of surpluses. Overall there is no doubt

b that the legal advice received by the FMC trustees was to the effect that they did have the power, if they thought they had struck the best bargain they could realistically hold out for, to agree to the proposals by Hillsdown.

The minutes of the FMC trustees' meeting of 15 May 1989 included the following:

c   'Consideration was given to the letters received from the company dated the 4th May 1989 and the 8th May 1989. Mr Ellison confirmed that the company were under no obligation to approve any pension augmentation unless they so choose. It was agreed that the trustees should consider the types of augmentation they might wish for members of the Scheme and see

d   if it was at all possible to persuade the company to make an increase over and above that set out in their letter of the 8th May. It was considered that some thought should be given as to whether any benefit improvement might be weighted towards those with longer periods of service. It was agreed that once the advisors had had an opportunity to evaluate these ideas the trustees would meet again to formulate what they might seek in the way of benefit

e   improvement from the employer.'

This resulted in a counter-offer being made by the FMC trustees on 28 June 1989 in a letter signed by Mr B C Legg, who was one of the FMC trustees and a director of Hillsdown and was acting as secretary to the FMC trustees. One of the other FMC trustees, Mr H Solomon, was also a director of Hillsdown. It was

f in his capacity as secretary to the FMC trustees that Mr Legg wrote the letter of 28 June 1989. This included the following:

        'If the trustees agreed to the bulk transfers requested, it would involve the incidental transfer of about £15m of actuarial surplus. As I am sure you

g   appreciate, we have to ensure that this would be in the best interests of our members. We understand that the surplus may be reduced by additional benefits being awarded by the company to a particular group of employees and we also appreciate that the company could continue to introduce new members into the Scheme, both of which actions could adversely affect the

h   amount of surplus and possibly the maintenance of the desired security target of 100%. In addition we fully understand the company's powers to close the Scheme. Nonetheless, after careful consideration, we feel the offer to enhance the benefits could be considerably improved and we attach with this letter our proposals which in value amounts to approximately three times your original offer.'

j The precise details of the offer are not material but they included a proposal that in addition to the benefits proposed by Hillsdown, costed at £1,050,000, there should be additional benefit improvements costed at £2,040,000. This found little favour with Hillsdown, which replied by a letter from Mr Jackson dated 10 July which included the following:

'I am afraid that if the trustees current attitude persists the company will have no alternative but to revise its plans and revert to its former practice of admitting new employees into the FMC Scheme. This would of course include the substantial and rapidly growing HF Scheme.'

And a little further on under the heading 'The quantum of surplus':

'Moreover you should realise that the company will suffer a substantial tax burden in its share of the surplus. Thus whilst the surplus is nominally £15m the impact of taxation reduces this to £9m. We feel that out of this figure we might be able to offer an improvement in the region of £1m.'

Mr Legg for the trustees came back on 14 July 1989 saying inter alia:

'We are also greatly concerned about the tone of your letter which does appear to be some sort of veiled threat. Even if all you say is true—and we do not for one moment accept that this is so—you really must appreciate that we have a clear duty to our members to ensure that we get the best deal possible for them.'

Hillsdown's reply by Mr Jackson dated 9 August 1989 included the following:

'It is apparent to us that you and the trustees are missing the point of the proposed re-organisation and that your attitude is coloured by this misconception. As far as the company is concerned we are simply seeking to accelerate a release of surplus that will accrue to the company in any event by way of a contribution holiday. We have estimated that the current surplus can be absorbed over 5 years by admitting the other allied Group Companies to the FMC Scheme, a course of action that we are now strongly minded to take. In these circumstances there would be no benefit improvement whatsoever for the members and the full benefit of the currant surplus would be enjoyed by the company. The financial advantage that the company might gain by withdrawing the surplus in one or perhaps two years is therefore not to be measured in terms of the absolute value of the surplus—since this will accrue in any event. Rather one should only consider the extra financial gain arising from the earlier use of these "contribution holiday years", a much lower figure indeed. We have calculated that the extra benefit to the company of obtaining the earlier use of these monies is in the region of £1m. In the light of this our offer of £1m for benefit improvements is extremely generous indeed. Given the above we do not feel there is much to be gained by continuing these discussions since the advantage to the company of having a refund rather than a contribution holiday is not that substantial, especially when you realise that a refund bears tax at 40% while a contribution holiday only effectively bears tax at our then marginal rate. The company is therefore minded to withdraw our offer of £1m surplus completely, if we do not have written agreement to our proposals within seven days.'

The FMC trustees with their actuarial and solicitor advisers met to consider this letter of 9 August on 4 September 1989. The minutes of that meeting included the following:

'After legal and actuarial advice, the trustees reached the conclusion that the company's argument for recovery of surplus was a strong one. In particular, there was a real and strong possibility that the company would a   make good its threat to water down the surplus by introducing new members, which it was fully permitted to do, to the detriment of the existing beneficiaries. After discussion the trustees agreed to approach the company to see whether they would improve their offer from £1m to £1.5m, which was considered by the advisers to be a reasonable compromise.'

b   Following meetings for further discussion Mr Jackson for Hillsdown wrote on 25 September 1989 to Mr Legg setting out the terms Hillsdown was prepared to offer. They were stated as follow:

c   'If the trustees agree to a reconstruction of the FMC pension arrangements and in particular use their power under Rule 21 ... to transfer all the assets and liabilities of the FMC ... Scheme to the HF ... Scheme, then the company will agree to the use of £1·3m of the surplus for the improvement of members' benefits.'

d   Curiously, there is no record of a formal letter of acceptance but there is no doubt that the FMC trustees did agree to this proposed compromise of the differences expressed earlier in the correspondence. It was not suggested that the FMC trustees acted otherwise than in accordance with the professional advice given to them nor, a fortiori, was it suggested that they acted otherwise than in good faith.

On 5 October 1989 the individuals who were the FMC trustees were replaced by the FMC Trustee Co, whose full name was FMC Superannuation and Pension Scheme Trustees Ltd, and which I refer to hereafter as 'the FMC trustee'. Those

e   individuals were Mr Legg, already mentioned above, Mr Solomon (now Sir Harry Solomon) chairman of Hillsdown, Mr A Hewitt and Mr C Jay. They were all four directors of the FMC trustee when it became the trustee of the FMC scheme.

By a deed dated 31 October 1989 the FMC trustee, with Hillsdown's consent,

f   amended the 1983 FMC trust deed so as to provide for the FMC scheme to be wound up and the FMC trustee released if the responsibility for paying all benefits in respect of past and present members of the scheme was transferred.

The HF trustee was a limited company a majority of whose directors were trustees of the FMC trustee or, when that trusteeship changed to the limited company, were directors of that company, the FMC trustee. The directors of the

g   HF trustee included the chairman of Hillsdown and the latter's company secretary. There were not shown to the Pensions Ombudsman on behalf of the HF trustee any minutes of board meetings of the HF trustee in relation to the transfer to it from the FMC trust and it is apparent from the determination that he did not accept as a fact that all the directors of the HF trustee knew about the

h   negotiations with the FMC trustee. The HF scheme was regulated by a definitive trust deed dated 28 December 1984 (the HF trust deed). It was until 1989 a relatively small scheme with only 80 participating employees until 6 April 1989 when it was expanded by the admission of some 800 additional members and Hillsdown became what was called in the HF trust deed 'the Founder' in place of

j   its subsidiary Hillsdown Ltd, which traded as Lockwoods Foods. The HF scheme in the autumn of 1989 had about £1m assets but no significant actuarial surplus. The HF trust deed contained a wide power to accept the assets of a retirements benefits scheme which had been operating for the benefit of the employees of a particular employer. It was not disputed but that the HF trustee had the power to accept the assets of the FMC trust. This was done through two deeds of 17 November 1989. By the first of those two deeds FMC and 14 other companies

which were employers under the FMC scheme were admitted to participate in
the HF scheme with the consent of Hillsdown as the founder thereof and of the
HF trustee and covenanted to observe and perform the provisions of the HF
scheme. In the second deed dated 17 November 1989 (which I shall refer to as
'the transfer agreement' and which was therein thus described) and made
between Hillsdown, the FMC trustee, the HF trustee and FMC and the other 14
companies that had just been admitted to the HF scheme (called 'the employers')
there were recitals that Hillsdown and the employers agreed to the transfer
thereby effected, that the actuary to the FMC scheme by a letter dated 18 October
1989 had advised that the transfer neither would nor might prejudice any person
who was a member or pensioner of the FMC scheme and that Inland Revenue
consent had been obtained. The operative part contained an agreement by the
FMC trustees to transfer the assets of the FMC scheme to the HF trustee. The
latter agreed to accept those assets and to accept into membership of the HF
scheme all persons to whom the assets transferred related and to undertake
responsibility for securing and paying all benefits under the FMC scheme, to
ensure that thereafter the liability of any member thus transferred to make
contributions to the HF scheme should not be increased without his consent and
to ensure that no such transferred member would or might be seriously
prejudiced as a result of the transfer.

There is no doubt that the assets of the FMC trust were indeed transferred on
or soon after 17 November 1989 to the HF trust although the precise date is not
established. The next step was taken 17 days later on 4 December 1989 when the
HF trustee with the consent of Hillsdown as the founder of the HF trust, a
position which it had acquired on 8 June 1989, exercised a power in cl 11 of the
HF trust deed to alter the terms thereof. This power was conferred on the HF
trustee in very wide terms and only required the consent of the founder and its
concurrence in the deed. There were no restrictive conditions attached to its
exercise. The amending deed of 4 December 1989 inserted into the HF rules a
provision for the founder (ie Hillsdown) to be the administrator of the scheme
and another provision in the following terms:

'*Reduction of Surpluses*   If the Founder shall decide to take action in
accordance with Schedule 22 of the Income and Corporation Taxes Act 1988
to reduce the amount of the Fund the Founder shall decide which of the
permitted methods is to be used to effect that reduction and appropriate
action shall be taken accordingly PROVIDED THAT if a payment is to made out
of the Fund the Administrator shall determine the apportionment out of the
total paid and in particular may direct that either: (i) the payment shall be
made to the Founder; or (ii) the payment shall be made to one or more of the
Employers (including the Founder) and if to more than one such Employer
in such proportions as the Administrator may at its sole discretion decide.'

The actuary to the HF scheme valued the HF scheme as at 17 November 1989,
ie immediately after the transfer of assets from the FMC trust, as having a past
service surplus of £20,394,000. That figure was arrived at by deducting from the
assessed value of the HF scheme's assets the liabilities in respect of current
pensioners, deferred pensioners and active members in respect of past service.
There was obviously no calculation involving liabilities in respect of future
service of active members or a fortiori future members.

The scene was now set for the payment to Hillsdown for which it had
negotiated. On 21 December 1989 £3,288,000, after the deduction of tax of

£2,192,000, was paid to Hillsdown by the HF trustee. On 25 June 1990 a further £7,774,200, after deduction of tax of £5,182,800, was paid to Hillsdown by the HF trustee. Both sums of tax were accounted for by the HF trustee to the Inland Revenue. The liability to tax arose under s 601 of the Income and Corporation Taxes Act 1988, which makes the tax recoverable from the employer, ie Hillsdown.

So far as benefit increases in accordance with the bargain struck between Hillsdown and the FMC trustee were concerned the response by the HF trustee to the complaint made to the Pensions Ombudsman against the HF trustee included a statement that augmentation of the benefits of the former FMC scheme members, pensioners and deferred pensioners as previously negotiated between the FMC trustees and Hillsdown was put into effect. The pensioners'

share of this augmentation was claimed by Mr Burt to be a 2% increase in pension on 1 May 1990. On the other hand, Hillsdown's response included a statement that the package of benefit augmentation within the HF scheme was subsequently costed at slightly in excess of £3·4m, in excess of the FMC trustees' estimate of £1·3m because salary levels proved to be higher than those used for

the original costing. Those uncertainties are not of major significance since there was no claim that the bargain struck between Hillsdown and the FMC trustees was not honoured by Hillsdown.

Active members of the FMC scheme were informed of the merger of the scheme with the HF scheme, but not of the payments to Hillsdown of surplus. Pensioners were not even informed of the merger let alone the payment of funds

to Hillsdown for a number of years. Mr Burt discovered that the merger had occurred in early 1992. No issue directly arises for decision by the court regarding this failure of communication but it provides the explanation for the delay that occurred before the validity of the actions taken in the autumn of 1989 was first challenged.

The Pensions Ombudsman's determination

The Pensions Ombudsman dealt with the complaints against the FMC trustee, the HF trustee and Hillsdown in that order. In relation to the FMC trustee he considered, first, whether the transfer from the FMC scheme to the HF scheme was contrary to the 1983 FMC trust deed and rules and, so far as the express

restrictions stated in r 21 itself were concerned, concluded that if the transfer was in the members' best interests the express terms of r 21 did not prevent payments being made to the HF scheme for the express purpose of effecting a payment of surplus to Hillsdown. No challenge was advanced by Hillsdown to that conclusion nor was it suggested to be wrong by Mr Nugee.

Secondly, the Pensions Ombudsman dealt with the question whether there were implied restrictions on the use of r 21. Under this head he criticised the reliance on the *Vauxhall* decision by the solicitor advising the FMC trustee, which I have quoted above, as misleading and he held that the *Vauxhall* decision was no more than a decision on the construction of a particular clause. That conclusion

was challenged by Mr Oliver QC for Hillsdown. I deal with this below. The Pensions Ombudsman went on to hold that the doctrine of frauds on the power applied. He said:

'The transfer power was exercised in order that the HF Scheme could make a payment of surplus to Hillsdown which was prohibited from receiving any such payment from the FMC Scheme ... I have to conclude

that the *sole* reason for the bulk transfer from the FMC Scheme to the HF
Scheme was to secure a payment of surplus to Hillsdown. Although the
transfer comes within the meaning of a fraud on a power, the underlying
basis of the doctrine is the idea of purpose. It cannot be stated that the
transfer went beyond the purpose of Rule 21 without considering the status
of the proviso against payments of surplus in Clause 14.' (The ombudsman's
emphasis.)

The Pensions Ombudsman, basing himself on cl 14 of the 1983 FMC trust
deed, held that the question of a payment of a surplus to Hillsdown was not
negotiable—the FMC trustee was not empowered to grant a payment of surplus.
This led to his conclusion that the use of the transfer power in order to secure a
payment of surplus to Hillsdown was contrary to the purposes of the FMC
scheme and that the FMC trustee was in breach of trust in using the power in this
way. This is the critical conclusion in the determination and it was challenged by
Mr Oliver on behalf of Hillsdown. An important feature of that challenge was the
Pensions Ombudsman's finding that the FMC trustee did act in the members'
best interests in agreeing to the transfer of assets to the HF scheme. He reached
that conclusion on the basis that the deal struck between Hillsdown and the FMC
trustee, whereby in exchange for an immediate reduction in the security of their
accrued benefits the FMC scheme members received increased benefits, was in
the latter's best interests because otherwise Hillsdown was going to absorb the
surplus over five years by the admission of new employing companies. The loss
of security was compensated he found by the benefit increases. Nevertheless, the
Pensions Ombudsman found there was a breach of trust in using the transfer
power to secure a payment of surplus to Hillsdown which was prohibited by the
trust deed and rules of the FMC scheme. This constituted maladministration and
involved injustice to Mr Burt and those supporting him in that they received a
reduction in the security of their benefits and were deprived of the opportunity
of further benefit increases.

The appeal by Hillsdown against this central finding was put on three basic
grounds. (i) There was no such implied limitation as the Pensions Ombudsman
found to exist on the power conferred by r 21, namely that it could not be used
to achieve a purpose which could not have been carried out through an
amendment to the FMC scheme. (ii) Even if that limitation existed the finding
that the FMC trustee transgressed it was unsustainable. (iii) Even if there were
a breach of trust the finding of maladministration occasioning injustice was
inconsistent with the express finding that the FMC trustee acted in the best
interests of the members of the FMC scheme and could not stand.

As to the first of these grounds the particular phrase in the determination used
in Mr Oliver's submission for Hillsdown was in fact posed as a question to be
answered rather than a finding and it somewhat obscures the difference between
two quite separate legal concepts. The first is that, as a matter of construction,
implications may be made restricting general provisions in a document such as
pension fund rules. This can only be done within defined limits such as where it
is shown that the implication is necessary to give business efficacy to the
document in question. I accept that no case for any such implication was shown
in the present case nor do I consider that the Pensions Ombudsman for all his
references to implications intended so to decide. Quite separate from this
concept, is that upon which the Pensions Ombudsman did in my view rely,
namely that powers may not be exercised for a purpose or with an intention

a   beyond the scope of or not justified by the instrument creating the power. This
principle is commonly referred to as that of frauds on the power and the Pensions
Ombudsman cited the classic statement by Lord Parker of Waddington in *Vatcher
v Paull* [1915] AC 372 at 378, [1914–15] All ER Rep 609 at 612 from which I have
taken a sentence. As Lord Parker went on to say in relation to powers of
appointment, the context in which the doctrine of frauds on the power
b   developed:

'The real vice of an appointment on condition that the appointee shall
benefit the appointor or a third party is that the power is not used with the
single purpose of benefiting its proper objects but in order to induce the
appointee to confer a benefit on a stranger ...' (See [1915] AC 372 at 379,
c   [1914–15] All ER Rep 609 at 613.)

The first issue to be decided in relation to the question whether there was an
improper and invalid exercise of power in r 21 is what was the purpose or
intention of the FMC trustee in making the transfer to the HF trust on 17
d   November 1989. Mr Oliver for Hillsdown argued that the reason and purpose
why the power was exercised as it was, was in fact to secure the augmentation of
benefits to members or, if one looks at the problem on a literal basis, the purpose
of the exercise of the power was to transfer the assets to another scheme and
thereby achieve the price that was to be paid for the benefit of the beneficiaries of
the FMC scheme. Strong criticism was made of the sentence I have quoted from
e   the determination in which the Pensions Ombudsman said that the sole reason
for the bulk transfer was to secure a payment of surplus to Hillsdown. In my view
the purpose of the FMC trustee in exercising the power in r 21 was to give effect
to the bargain which had been struck between Hillsdown and the FMC trustee.
That bargain had two essential features, first, the payment of surplus to
f   Hillsdown and, secondly, the augmentation of members' benefits. As Mr Oliver
put it in opening the appeal:

'I squarely confront the position in this case that the purpose of these
transactions was to ensure that there could be a return of surplus to
Hillsdown in circumstances where the trust deed of the FMC Scheme did not
g   on its terms permit it.'

If it was the purpose of the transactions, it was also in my view one at least of the
purposes of the exercise of the r 21 power. No one suggested that there was not
a bargain struck between the FMC trustee and Hillsdown and the argument in
h   support of the appeal very properly fully accepted the existence of that bargain.
I accept that if the Pensions Ombudsman intended to define the purpose of the
exercise of the power under r 21 in saying that the sole reason for it was to secure
the payment of surplus to Hillsdown, he was in error but I am not satisfied that
he was doing anything more than identifying why the power under r 21 was used.
j   It was a way, and probably the only way, in which Hillsdown could secure a very
large part of the surplus in the FMC scheme. However that may be, I am satisfied
that the purpose was as I have stated it. Nor is that conclusion escaped by
describing the payment to Hillsdown as the price for securing the desired benefit.
The person who pays a price for an article out of a fund under his control has
inevitably, as part of his purpose, both the acquisition of the article and the
payment of its price. No doubt his motive is to secure the article. But motive and

purpose are not the same and it is the latter that counts. As Turner LJ said in
Topham v Duke of Portland (1863) 1 De G J & S 517 at 571, 46 ER 205 at 227:

> '... it is one thing to examine into the purpose with which an act is done,
> and another thing to examine into the motives which led to that purpose ...'

So he declined to examine the propriety of the motive of the appointor in that
case, the Duke of Portland, which was that the duke disapproved of the proposed
marriage of one of his daughters to Colonel, later Sir William, Topham.

The Vauxhall decision
    The solicitor advising the FMC trustee relied heavily on the *Vauxhall* decision.
This was *Re Vauxhall Motors Pension Fund, Bullard v Randall* [1989] 1 Pensions LR
49, a decision on motion of Browne-Wilkinson V-C. The report only contains the
words of the judgment but it would appear that the motions were motions for
interlocutory injunctions against trustees of a pensions fund in circumstances
which bear a strong resemblance to the facts of the FMC scheme. 'The Vauxhall
fund', as I call it for short, had an actuarial surplus but under the trust deed
governing it there was as Browne-Wilkinson V-C said: 'To put it at its lowest no
power to return any surplus of the fund to the employer contributors'. What was
proposed was a scheme where the Vauxhall fund trustees with the consent of
some members would pay over assets to trustees of new pension funds under
which assenting members would get larger benefits but the surplus assets would
under the terms of the new scheme be returnable to the subscribing companies.
There was also a fixed intention for such a return to take place. The plaintiffs did
not assent and, although the report does not say so in terms, brought motions to
restrain the trustees from implementing the scheme. The power to transfer to
another approved pension scheme was couched in general terms but it contained
a proviso (among others) requiring the trustees to notify the transferee, ie the
other approved scheme to which assets were to be transferred, of any restrictions
applicable to a certain category of assets. It was contended on behalf of the
plaintiff non-assenting members that one such restriction which needed to be
notified was a proviso to the general power contained in cl 55 of the trust deed to
alter the terms thereof. That proviso was to the effect that no alteration should
be made which would have the effect of, inter alia, resulting in the payment to
the employer companies of any part of the trust fund. Browne-Wilkinson V-C
prefaced his judgment by saying that, contrary to the usual practice, he was asked
to decide on motion a short point of construction which was the only point raised
in the proceedings and that, since the matter was urgent, he had acceded to the
request and his judgment was therefore on the true construction of various
clauses in the trust deed. The actual point of construction decided, the ambit of
the words 'such restrictions' in the proviso to the power to transfer assets to
another approved fund is of no relevance and I do not take time to state it. What
is relied upon is the passage at the end of Browne-Wilkinson V-C's judgment,
where he is recorded as having said (at 53):

> 'Say that clause 55 [the clause giving power to alter the terms of the trust
> deed] is or is capable of being a restriction on the assets. The only restriction
> imposed by clause 55 itself is a restriction on the power to amend the 1982
> trust deed. I can not for myself see how such a restriction can be imported
> into the operation of the new trust deeds in any way that has any meaning.
> There can be no doubt that the restriction is a restriction on the amendment

a

of the 1982 deed, a restriction which could not affect the funds in the hand of the new trustees. Mr Turner-Samuels [counsel for the plaintiff dissentient members] went further to suggest ... that Proviso C to clause 55 in some way imposed a general restriction on the assets in the fund. I am bound to say I cannot see that that is so. Proviso C is simply a limitation on a power of amendment. It is not a restriction affecting an asset as such. Therefore in my judgment the claim based on the construction of the trust deed which the plaintiffs have put forward is not correct ...'

b

The argument advanced to me by Mr Oliver was that the proviso C to cl 55 in the *Vauxhall* case closely resembled the proviso to cl 14 of the 1983 FMC trust deed and the finding of Browne-Wilkinson V-C that the former could not affect the funds in the hands of new trustees should apply here. Secondly, that the restriction on the power of amendment of a trust deed was just that and not a restriction on assets. Thirdly, he submitted that if the argument which the Pensions Ombudsman has adopted in the determination was correct it would have prevented Browne-Wilkinson V-C deciding the case in the way he did decide it.

c

d

In my view Mr Oliver's submissions are correct in so far as they concern the construction of the FMC trust deed and the *Vauxhall* case is, I think, authority for the proposition, beyond the narrow and presently irrelevant point of construction actually decided in it, that one cannot as a matter of construction get an implication restricting the ambit of the power in r 21 of the 1983 FMC rules by reference to the proviso to cl 14 of the 1983 FMC trust deed. On the other hand, it is no authority on the question whether the power to transfer was proposed to be used for a collateral purpose in a way which would constitute a fraud on the power. There is absolutely no trace of that having been argued and it is clear that Browne-Wilkinson V-C did not regard himself as doing more than decide a question of construction. The highest the case can be put is to say that the argument on fraud on the power was open to the dissentient plaintiffs and was not taken. That might well have been enough to estop them thereafter from raising the point in relation to that particular transaction on the lines of the principle stated in *Henderson v Henderson* (1843) 3 Hare 100, [1843–60] All ER Rep 278, but it does not make Browne-Wilkinson V-C's decision a precedent on a subject not addressed by him because not argued before him, far less a binding precedent. For my part, therefore, I agree with the Pensions Ombudsman that the *Vauxhall* decision is not a relevant authority on the question of fraud on the power and that far too weight was placed upon it by the solicitor advising the FMC trustee.

e

f

g

h

There is therefore no impediment in the *Vauxhall* decision to a finding that the FMC trustee's exercise of the power in r 21 constituted a fraud on the power, or in more modern parlance an improper use of the power for a collateral purpose. The purpose for which it was exercised was the composite one of giving effect to the bargain struck with Hillsdown of which a major element was that of a payment of surplus to Hillsdown. That was well outside the proper ambit of r 21 which was to enable transfers of obligations and assets to other approved funds securing pension rights for members. In my view the Pensions Ombudsman was right in calling the transfer a fraud on the power.

j

It was also argued for Hillsdown that the inclusion of specific limitations on the r 21 power to transfer supported the proposition that it would be wrong to read other limitations in. This too seems to me a valid point so far as it goes which is

on any question of construction but it does not in my view touch the question
whether the power was used for a collateral purpose. A traditional power of
appointment may well be hedged about with restrictions: a common one inserted
for tax reasons is to exclude as an object any person to whom the settlor is
married. No doubt as a matter of construction the power of appointment should
not be impliedly restricted any further than the express exclusion warrants but
that is of no relevance to an issue which might arise on any given appointment
whether there had been a collateral purpose in the appointment such as to render
it ineffectual.

The finding that the FMC trustee acted in the best interests of the members

I accept that if the Pensions Ombudsman intended to find that what the FMC
trustee actually did was, when viewed objectively, something which operated in
the best interests of the FMC members, that would conflict with a finding that the
FMC trustee was guilty of maladministration which caused injustice to Mr Burt
and the other complainants. This is really no more than a recognition that that
which is beneficial causes no injustice. Maladministration and breach of trust are
neither synonymous nor coterminous. There can be maladministration without
a breach of trust; for example failure to give information when it should be given,
as indeed incurred in the present case. There can also be breaches of trust
without there being maladministration. Lord Lindley in *National Trustees Co of
Australasia Ltd v General Finance Co of Australasia Ltd* [1905] AC 373 at 375–376
corrected counsel's citation of his own quotation (in *Perrins v Bellamy* [1899] 1 Ch
797 at 798) of what Selwyn LJ used to say, probably extra-judicially, viz: 'The
main duty of a trustee is to commit *judicious* breaches of trust', to read 'the great
use' of a trustee is to commit such breaches. Unauthorised but successful
investments are a very common example of such breaches. Closer to this case is
what Robert Walker J said in *Westminster City Council v Haywood* [1996] 2 All ER
467 at 481–482, [1996] 3 WLR 563 at 578: 'It is not necessarily maladministration
for a decision maker to take a wrong view of the law.' A little later he continued:

> 'Taking and acting on a wrong view of the law may be maladministration
> if the decision-maker knows, or ought to know, that the state of the law is
> uncertain and that those who may be adversely affected by the uncertainty
> need to be warned about it.'

In my view, the Pensions Ombudsman had ample material before him upon
which to conclude that to transfer the entire assets of the fund to another set of
trustees by a transaction which was ineffectual because it amounted to an
exercise of a power at least in part for a collateral and unauthorised purpose was
an act of maladministration although it was done with the advice and
concurrence of an appropriately experienced solicitor. I do not consider that
there is a conflict between that conclusion of the Pensions Ombudsman and his
finding that the FMC trustee acted in the best interests of the members of the
FMC scheme because that latter finding was in my view directed at an
appreciation of what the FMC trustee was trying to do. The FMC trustee was
under the impression at all material times (a) that Hillsdown was in a position
over a period of some five years to obtain for itself by a policy of adhering further
employers to the FMC scheme coupled with a suspension of its contributions
under r 35, the whole of the surplus in the FMC scheme and (b) that it was open
to FMC trustee properly to conduct negotiations with Hillsdown regarding the
amount of surplus which Hillsdown should receive.

The FMC trustee held those views perfectly honestly. No one suggested the
a contrary to me. The Pensions Ombudsman agreed with the former of those
impressions and disagreed with the latter. In my view, in saying that the FMC
trustee acted in the best interests of the members, he was doing no more than
assess the quality of their intentions. What they did was intrinsically in breach of
trust and damaging to the interests of the members but, given the impressions
b that they had honestly formed, they were intending to act in the best interests of
the members. If and to the extent that the Pensions Ombudsman in his
determination concluded that objectively speaking what the FMC trustee did was
beneficial to the members, I agree with Mr Oliver's submission that such a finding
was repugnant to the rest of the determination but I would resolve the conflict,
not by saying, as Mr Oliver would have me do, that the finding of
c maladministration causing injustice cannot stand, but rather by saying that the
finding, if there was one, that what the FMC trustee did was beneficial to the
members is in the circumstances a perverse finding which should be rejected. As
I have attempted to explain I do not believe that the Pensions Ombudsman's
finding was intended by him to extend beyond an assessment of the quality of the
d FMC trustee's intentions and on that footing no finding of perversity is needed or
indeed called for.

Was the FMC trustee acting under a mistake in negotiating with Hillsdown?

I turn now to deal with an argument addressed to me by Mr Nugee that the
FMC trustee in striking the deal that was negotiated with Hillsdown was acting
e under a mistaken view of the respective powers of Hillsdown and the FMC
trustee.

The substitution of Hillsdown as 'the Corporation' in the FMC scheme

Before me the validity of the creation by the deed dated 30 November 1987 of
f the power to substitute another company for FMC as the new corporation was
sought to be challenged by Mr Nugee for the Pensions Ombudsman, although it
had not been challenged at any stage before the Pensions Ombudsman who
made no comment upon it, nor did he investigate or make any findings about the
circumstances obtaining on or around 30 November and 1 December 1987. Mr
g Nugee accepted that it would not be right for this court to deal with a point of
law not raised before the Pensions Ombudsman if factual findings were needed
for its elucidation and those findings had not been embarked upon, let alone
made. On that basis he accepted that it would not now be practicable or right for
me to deal with the exercise of the power to appoint Hillsdown as 'the
Corporation' in place of FMC. He relied on what Millett J said in *Re Courage*
h *Group's Pension Schemes, Ryan v Imperial Brewing and Leisure Ltd* [1987] 1 All ER 528
at 542, [1987] 1 WLR 495 at 511:

> 'In my judgment, the validity of a power of substitution depends on the
> circumstances in which it is capable of being exercised and the characteristics
j > which must be possessed by the company capable of being substituted; while
> the validity of any purported exercise of such a power depends on the
> purpose for which the substitution is made. The circumstances must be such
> that substitution is necessary or at least expedient in order to preserve the
> scheme for those far whose benefit it was established; and the substituted
> company must be recognisably the successor to the business and workforce
> of the company for which it is to be substituted. It is not enough that it is a

member of the same group as, or even that it is the holding company of, the company for which it is substituted. It must have succeeded to all or much of the business of the former company and have taken over the employment of all or most of the former company's employees. In my judgment, the proposed power to substitute IBL's ultimate holding company for IBL in undefined circumstances is far too wide, alters and is capable of defeating the main purpose of the schemes, and is ultra vires.'

Mr Nugee relied on the distinction drawn by Millett J between the validity of a power of substitution of the principal company in a pensions scheme on the one hand and the validity of the exercise of such power by an actual substitution on the other. While accepting that the latter demanded, as indeed Millett J himself said in terms, an examination of the circumstances surrounding the substitution, he submitted that to judge the validity of the creation of the power of substitution it was enough to look at the power itself and assess whether it was validly created by looking at the circumstances in which it was stated to be exercisable. I am not persuaded that such a hard and fast line can be drawn between the creation of a power of substitution and its exercise. It would not in my view be right to disregard the surrounding circumstances in assessing the validity of the deed of 30 November 1987 while taking them into account in relation to the validity of the deed of 1 December 1987.

It seems to me that the whole transaction would need to be investigated before a proper view could be formed regarding the validity of either of the deeds executed on successive dates.

An additional reason for not opening at this stage the question of the validity of the substitution of Hillsdown as the corporation in the FMC scheme is that there had been three employers added to the FMC scheme after Hillsdown's substitution on 1 December 1987 and August of 1989. There was no investigation of this aspect of the matter before the Pensions Ombudsman and it would not in my view be right to allow a new point of law to be raised at this late stage which might well have repercussions upon transactions in the past under which rights have probably accrued without those concerned being at least warned, if not represented.

The balance of power between Hillsdown and the FMC trustee

Upon the basis that it is too late to challenge the substitution of Hillsdown as the corporation in the FMC scheme, there remains the question where the balance of power lay as between Hillsdown, as the corporation, and the FMC trustee in the FMC scheme in relation to the surplus. This needs to be addressed in order to assess Mr Nugee's argument that the FMC trustee was acting under a mistake in making the bargain which it did make with Hillsdown. I propose to consider first the FMC trustee's rights and duties and then those of Hillsdown.

The FMC trustee's rights and duties in relation to surplus

Clause 19 of the 1983 FMC trust deed required the FMC trustees to cause a periodic valuation to be made by the actuary as provided by the rules and to deal with any surplus appearing on such valuation in accordance with r 23 which I have already set out. The provision in the rules (under r 22(b)(iii) regarding periodic valuations) was that one should be made in any event once in every five years after 1 July 1971. Regulation 8(3) of the Occupational Pensions Schemes (Disclosure of Information) Regulations 1986, SI 1986/1046 (the disclosure *a* regulations), which was in force from 1 November 1986, required actuarial valuations to be obtained as at the later of 1 November 1987 and the day falling three years and six months after the previous valuation obtained before 1 November 1986. There was evidence before the Pensions Ombudsman that the actuary had embarked upon a valuation as at 6 April 1988 and the presumption is that this was in compliance with the obligation under the combined effect of the disclosure regulations and r 22(b)(iii). The formal valuation had not been

b obtained but there was an obligation under reg 8(5) as it stood in the summer of 1989 for it to be obtained as soon as reasonably practicable after the date as at which it was to be made. The FMC trustee had in fact been warned that a surplus would be shown by the valuation. The situation therefore was that the FMC trustee was under a duty to see that the valuation was obtained as soon as

c reasonably practicable and it was known to be pending. Once the valuation was obtained the FMC trustee would come under an obligation to see that it was applied in accordance with their directions (after taking and having regard to the advice of the actuary) in one or more of the permitted ways specified in r 23(a). This resulted in my view in there being an existing obligation at all times after 6

d April 1988 and in particular by the summer of 1989 on the FMC trustee to deal with the surplus as directed by r 23(a) as and when the surplus was certified by the actuary. It would have been improper for the FMC trustee to regard itself as not being under any such obligation unless and until the surplus was certified even though the obligation could only be discharged once the surplus was certified or, alternatively but improbably, if a deficit rather than a surplus had

e been certified. The maxim 'equity looks on that as done which ought to be done' would in my view clearly apply here so as to create the obligation to deal with surplus under r 23 even though the size of the surplus could not be exactly known.

The next problem raised in argument before me was exactly what the surplus
f envisaged by r 23(a) was. The relevant words in r 23(a) are 'any surplus which the actuary shall certify not to be required to cover the immediate and prospective liabilities of the Scheme ...' In my view the liabilities in question are limited to those ascertainable as either immediate or prospective on the date as at which the valuation is made. Immediate liabilities would cover those liabilities that existed as liabilities. Typically that would include the pension of a pensioner and it would

g include the future payments as well as any existing arrears of such a pension. Prospective liabilities would in my view cover liabilities which could be seen to be in prospect and were susceptible of calculation by recognised actuarial techniques. Typically, that would include the pension of an active member not yet retired but who if he survived his retirement would become entitled to a

h pension. I do not take time to debate whether a deferred pensioner's right to his or her deferred pension would be an immediate or prospective liability. It certainly would be one or the other and for my purposes it matters not which. On the other hand, I would exclude as a prospective liability the liabilities that would come upon the FMC trustee if there was a prospect on the date as at which

j the surplus was to be certified of another employer being adhered to the FMC scheme in the future. The chance of such an event occurring is not included in the phrase 'immediate and prospective liabilities' however high the odds of it happening in the future. It is not a chance which is susceptible of actuarial evaluation and is radically different from such chances as mortality and fluctuations in interest rates. It is of course possible that the actuary, when consulted by the FMC trustee pursuant to r 23(a) before the FMC trustee decided how to apply a surplus, might properly in giving his advice have regard certainly to events which had occurred since the date as at which the surplus was certified, *a* such as the adherence of an additional employer and, depending upon his professional judgment as to its relevance, to events which were known to be very likely to occur in the near future.

Mr Oliver's argument for Hillsdown was that what is known as the aggregate method of valuation illustrated what r 23 was directed at. His description of the *b* aggregate method was accepted by Mr Nugee as accurate and it was stated as follows:

> 'The aggregate method values the liabilities of the scheme for total service (i.e past and future service of members); it also values the assets which are (a) the assets actually held by the trustees at the time of the valuation, and (b) *c* the discounted value of future contributions from members; the shortfall (if there is one) of assets as compared with liabilities is then eliminated by fixing a contribution rate from the employers to bring the scheme into balance.'

Since all the assets actually held by the trustees at the time of valuation are included, it follows that there is already taken into account any part of those *d* assets which might otherwise be regarded as surplus. Mr Oliver drew the conclusion, also in his argument, that it was only if no employers' contributions were necessary because the assets actually held and the discounted value of future contributions from members exceeded the liabilities for total service that there was a real surplus of assets over liabilities which could be applied under r 23. *e* That conclusion, in itself quite accurate as an analysis of using the aggregate method, seems to me of itself to demonstrate that the aggregate method is quite inappropriate in relation to the operation of r 23. The principal reason for this is that r 23 specifically provides for one of the methods whereby the trustees can apply the surplus once identified to be in reduction of the employers' contributions. No method which necessarily involves the employers' *f* contribution being at zero can possibly fit with the system envisaged by r 23(a) for ascertaining surplus. It was also pointed out that the aggregate method would also be inappropriate in relation to r 23(b), which deals with the situation where there is no surplus but a deficiency or anticipated deficiency and gives as one of the trustees' available remedies the increase of the rate of the employers' contributions. The application of the aggregate method as submitted by Mr *g* Oliver would involve there always being a deficiency for the purposes of r 23 in any situation where the sum of the assets held by the trustees and the discounted future members' contributions was less than the total service liabilities and is not only irreconcilable with the possibility of increasing the employers' rate of contributions which is ex hypothesi non-existent but also a result which cannot *h* have been contemplated.

I am not of course criticising the aggregate method as an appropriate technique for calculating a modified contribution rate, regard being had to the existence of a surplus. Not only am I very conscious that I am ill-equipped to do that but also I am only concerned with the true construction of r 23 and it is only in that *j* connection that I express the decided view that the aggregate method, which is doubtless highly appropriate as a technique for calculating a modified contribution rate, is quite inappropriate as a technique for calculating a surplus under r 23.

I should mention that I am not expressing any further views as to the appropriate actuarial techniques for arriving at a surplus or deficiency under r 23.

a That is a matter for the actuary's professional judgment and may even be a subject upon which different techniques would be preferred by different experts. So long as the technique adopted is not one which, like the aggregate method, is directed at finding the appropriate contribution rate given the existing surplus or deficiency of assets, I see no problem in leaving the matter to the actuary's expertise.

b Finally on this aspect I would say that there does not appear to have been any question raised at any stage in the actual negotiations which took place between the FMC trustee and their advisers on the one side and Hillsdown on the other concerning the appropriate actuarial techniques for calculating surplus under r 23. Nor is there any trace of a suggestion having been made at the time that the aggregate method should be adopted. The issue arose both in Mr Oliver's

c argument regarding the true construction of r 23 and in Mr Nugee's argument regarding the extent to which the trustees needed to obtain Hillsdown's agreement to the application of a surplus revealed by a periodical valuation by the actuary.

d *Hillsdown's powers*

Hillsdown had power under cl 4(b) of the 1983 FMC trust deed to adhere other employers in the group of which it was the holding company and it is not necessary for me to deal with the position under cl 4(a) on the footing that FMC and not Hillsdown was the corporation because I have earlier held that the

e question whether Hillsdown was effectively substituted as the corporation can not now properly be raised. So I conclude that Hillsdown had this power and did not have to obtain the trustees' consent to its exercise. On the other hand, I accept Mr Nugee's submission that this power was one which Hillsdown held subject to the implied obligation in contracts of employment that powers should not be exercised so as to destroy or seriously damage the relationship of

f confidence and trust between the employer and its employees and former employees. This implication was made by Browne-Wilkinson V-C in *Imperial Group Pension Trust Ltd v Imperial Tobacco Ltd* [1991] 2 All ER 597, [1991] 1 WLR 589, the year after he decided the *Vauxhall* case [1989] Pensions LR 49, in relation to a power to give or withhold consent to an increase in pension benefits.

g Browne-Wilkinson V-C used the expression 'the obligation of good faith' as a form of shorthand for the implication set out above and in adopting it I should like to emphasise that it is a convenient shorthand only and, in particular, does not carry the implication that a failure to observe the implied obligation involved would amount to bad faith in the pejorative sense in which that expression is often used.

h The practical implications which Browne-Wilkinson V-C drew from the obligation of good faith were, in the *Imperial Group* case [1991] 2 All ER 597 at 607, [1991] 1 WLR 589 at 598–599, described as follows:

j '... the obligation of good faith does require that the company should exercise its rights (a) with a view to the efficient running of the scheme established by the fund and (b) not for the collateral purpose of forcing the members to give up their accrued rights in the existing fund subject to this scheme.'

In the context which existed in the *Imperial Group* case, he went on to say in relation to (b) above that in the context of a closed class of employees the power to consent to benefit improvements could not be used consistently with the obligation of good faith—

'for the purpose of coercing that class to give up its rights under the existing trust. The duty of good faith requires the company to preserve its employees' rights and pension fund, not to destroy them. If there are financial and other considerations which require the fund to be determined, so be it. But if the sole purpose of refusing to consent to an amendment increasing benefits is the collateral purpose of putting pressure on members to abandon their existing rights (including the right to surplus on determination) in my judgment the company would not be acting in good faith.'

The other power which Hillsdown had was to suspend or determine its contributions under r 35. Clearly that power was given to it for its own benefit and there can be no question of fiduciary duty being owed in relation to its exercise. But where it does seem to me that the obligation of good faith would have applied to restrain Hillsdown's unilateral pursuit of its own interests without a proper regard to those of its employees and retired employees would have been in a combined operation of the power to adhere further employers while at the same time suspending its contributions which would otherwise have been payable in respect of them for the purpose of running down a surplus certified to have arisen ex hypothesi in relation to the service of the employees of other employers which were in the FMC scheme before the date as at which the surplus was certified. I say this for two reasons. The first is that the surplus thus certified was in the disposition of the trustees alone under the express terms of r 23(a) and Hillsdown had no right to interfere with its exercise and, secondly, because it would in my view constitute a breach of the implied obligation of good faith on the one hand to enlarge the class of employers and so bring in large categories of new members and at the same time to decline to make contributions in respect of such new members for the purpose of running off a surplus which had arisen in relation to other members who were members at the time as at which the surplus was certified. It is one thing for an employer to take a contributions holiday in respect of a category of existing members and quite another to introduce a large class of new members and take a contributions holiday in relation to them so as to accelerate the effect of the contributions holiday in relation to the existing members.

It was suggested to me that there is an apparent tension between the passages which I have quoted from Browne-Wilkinson V-C's judgment in the *Imperial Group* case and the passage in Millett J's judgment in the *Courage* case in which he contemplates as perfectly proper a process of bargaining between the trustees of a pension fund and the employer in the context of a desire by an employer to obtain payment of at least part of a surplus and a desire by the trustees to secure increased benefits for their members. The last sentence of the penultimate paragraph of Millett J's judgment in the *Courage* case [1987] 1 All ER 528 at 545, [1987] 1 WLR 495 at 515 reads:

'Where the employer seeks repayment, the trustees or committee can be expected to press for generous treatment of employees and pensioners, and the employer to be influenced by a desire to maintain good industrial relations with its workforce.'

a Clearly a process of negotiation is there envisaged and it may be asked how one reconciles a freedom to negotiate with a duty to observe the implied obligation of good faith. I see no irreconcilable conflict in the two nor indeed anything out of line with many facets of employment relations where it is common for employers whilst under that implied obligation nevertheless to be free to negotiate with employees or their representatives. There is however an

b important distinction, which was not observed in the present case, between negotiating over issues in which both parties have a locus standi, a legitimate interest to preserve, on the one hand, and negotiating over a matter where one party has no legitimate interest to preserve and therefore no locus standi, on the other. In this case the mode of application of the surplus, once ascertained pursuant to r 23(a), was a matter for the FMC trustee alone, subject to

c consultation with the actuary. Hillsdown was not in a position to ask for a share of the surplus as a term of giving its consent because its consent was not needed. That is not to say that the FMC trustee should have cut itself off altogether from and ignored the principal employer under its scheme; but there is a very wide gulf between active bargaining for substantial financial payments and consultation

d with a view to ensuring that pension fund trustees take a decision which fits in, so far as practicable and permissible, with an employer's industrial strategy. The situation envisaged in Millett J's judgment, where negotiation in the shape of bargaining was contemplated with approval, was one where each side had something to give or withhold by way of necessary consent and there was no absolute bar on what was sought to be achieved, e g a change in the relevant rules

e to get rid of a prohibition upon the payment of funds to the employer.

Overall therefore my conclusion on the above analysis of the respective rights and duties of the FMC trustee and Hillsdown is that the Pensions Ombudsman was correct in his analysis that 'the question of a payment of surplus to Hillsdown was not negotiable—FMC Trustee was not empowered to grant a payment of

f surplus' although I would base that conclusion not solely on the terms of and implications from cl 14 of the 1983 FMC trust deed, although it is a relevant background factor, but on a wider consideration of the rights and duties of the FMC trustee. The Pensions Ombudsman also said that the FMC trustee was not entitled to enter into negotiations of the type envisaged by Millett J in the *Courage* case. I would agree with that but I would add that Hillsdown was not entitled to

g enter into such negotiations, both because it was seeking to persuade the FMC trustee to do that which it ought not to have done and because it was itself in breach of its implied obligation of good faith in doing so.

The HF trustee

h I can deal much more briefly with the complaint against the HF trustee. The Pensions Ombudsman found that the power of amendment in cl 11 of the HF trust deed was wide enough to permit the introduction of amendments to permit payment of surplus to an employer. That was not challenged.

However, the Pensions Ombudsman went on to find in his determination that

j the HF trustee was in breach of its duty to act in the best interests of its members in effecting the amendment which permitted payment to Hillsdown without seeking to bargain with Hillsdown for some advantage to its members as the price for such an amendment. In reaching that conclusion the Pensions Ombudsman placed much stress upon the fact that the transfer agreement whereby the FMC scheme assets were agreed to be transferred to the HF scheme was dated 17 November 1989 whereas the amendment to the HF scheme was not

made until 4 December 1989. The Pensions Ombudsman did not accept that the
HF trustee was under a contractual obligation to give effect to the bargain struck   *a*
between the FMC trustee and Hillsdown because there was no sufficient
evidence of that, given the absence of any relevant HF trustee board minute and
the fact that, although two of the members of the board of the HF trustee were
also members of the FMC trustee, not all were. He also held that any moral
obligation there might be on the HF trustee to give effect to the bargain between   *b*
the FMC trustee and Hillsdown was insufficient to justify the HF trustee in failing
to carry out its duty to bargain with Hillsdown on behalf of its members.
Accordingly, he upheld the complaint against the HF trustee.

I do not think that decision can stand because it ignores the fact that the HF
trustee would have had no defence to a claim to restitution of the assets paid and
transferred over to it by the FMC trustee pursuant to the bargain between the   *c*
FMC trustee and Hillsdown if it, the HF trustee, had declined to implement what
it undoubtedly had clear notice of, namely the bargain regarding the application
of the assets. Not only would it have been morally wrong for the HF trustee to
accept assets known by it to be transferred to it solely for the purpose of
implementing a particular bargain and then claim to keep those assets without   *d*
giving effect to that bargain but it would also have been legally indefensible to
claim to retain the assets and ignore and refuse to implement the known basis
upon which the assets were transferred. Mr Nugee did not contend for the
contrary. It is unnecessary for me to deal with the question whether there was a
legally binding obligation on the HF trustee to implement the bargain between
the FMC trustee and Hillsdown. Nor do I find it necessary to resolve questions   *e*
how far it is proper for trustees to give effect to moral obligations which may
conflict with the economic benefit of the beneficiaries. In the event, the
complaint against the HF trustee is largely academic in that no relief was granted
as against them although they are involved in the implementation of the relief
which was granted. There was no appeal by the HF trustee against the   *f*
determination and they were represented before me largely on the ground that
questions arise in connection with the implementation of the relief granted upon
which the HF trustee clearly should be heard. I did have the benefit of
submissions by Mr Inglis-Jones QC on behalf of the HF trustee and they did
extend to deal with certain aspects other than the issue of relief.

g

Hillsdown

The complaint against Hillsdown was upheld by the Pensions Ombudsman on
the basis that it was a breach of Hillsdown's duty of good faith for it to induce the
FMC trustee to act in breach of trust by committing a fraud on the power.

On the other hand he also held that, in the light of the prospective loss of full   *h*
tax exemption if the surplus in the FMC scheme was not reduced to the level
permitted by the Inland Revenue, Hillsdown would not have been in breach of
its duty of good faith had it adopted, as a means of avoiding the prospective tax
liability, the option of opening the membership to other group employers whose
employees had pensions which were underfunded or unfunded. I have already   *j*
expressed the view that the combination of that option with the exercise of
Hillsdown's power to suspend or terminate its contributions as a means of
running off a surplus which had been certified to exist for the purposes of r 23 in
relation to a membership which did not include the new members thus
introduced would constitute a breach of the implied obligation of good faith. To
that extent I disagree with the Pensions Ombudsman's conclusion regarding

a Hillsdown's powers. In my view he overestimated Hillsdown's powers in relation to the surplus as at 6 April 1988 but this is of relatively small importance given that in my view he was right in holding that there was a breach of that implied obligation of good faith in inducing the FMC trustee to act in breach of trust by the misuse of the power in r 21, a conclusion with which I agree. My reasons for agreeing with the conclusion is not the same as the Pensions

b Ombudsman's in reaching it and the difference is significant because, as will be seen later, it impinges on the question of remedies. I consider it to be significant that the process of negotiation used by Hillsdown, the threat to absorb surplus over five years by adhering other categories of employees coupled with the threat to use the power in r 35 to suspend or terminate employers' contributions was intrinsically a breach of the implied obligation of good faith so that not only was

c Hillsdown seeking to persuade the FMC trustee to commit a fraud on the power but also the technique by which that process of persuasion was brought to bear was intrinsically one which Hillsdown was not in my view entitled to use in relation to the surplus in the FMC scheme as at 6 April 1988. Mr Oliver's argument against the conclusion that Hillsdown induced the FMC trustee to

d commit a fraud on the power was based on the fact which is clearly established that neither Hillsdown nor the FMC trustee thought that what they were negotiating about would, if carried into effect, constitute a use of a power for a collateral and improper purpose and both were perfectly honest in that belief which was largely induced by advice from a reputable professional source. That argument would have had much more force had it not been for the additional

e factor that Hillsdown was in my view using as a negotiating tactic a threat to do something which was intrinsically improper. The case is therefore not just one of a third party negotiating with a trustee in such a way as, unbeknown to either the third party or the trustee, would cause the trustee to commit a breach of trust, but of a third party by threatening to do something which he was not entitled to do, persuading the trustee to do that which neither of them appreciated would

f constitute a breach of trust.

For those reasons I consider that the finding that Hillsdown was guilty of maladministration causing injustice was correctly made although my reasons for reaching that conclusion are not the same as the Pensions Ombudsman.

Before I turn to the question of remedies and the powers in that behalf of the

g Pensions Ombudsman I must deal with two additional arguments advanced by Mr Nugee for attacking the validity of the transfer agreement of 17 November 1989. The first was that the FMC trustee so misunderstood where the balance of power lay as between the FMC trustee and Hillsdown in thinking that Hillsdown was entitled to obtain the benefit of the surplus in the FMC scheme as at 6 April 1988 by adhering additional employers and suspending or terminating the

h liability to make employer's contributions, that there was a failure on the FMC trustee's part to take into account considerations which ought to have been taken into account. The next step in the argument was that if the FMC trustee had correctly appreciated what Hillsdown's powers were the FMC trustee would not have exercised its discretion to enter into the transfer agreement and the

j conclusion is that the court would in these circumstances have power to set the transfer agreement aside. The principle upon which that would be done was stated by Warner J, applying in a pension fund context the decision of the Court of Appeal in *Re Hastings-Bass (decd), Hastings v IRC* [1974] 2 All ER 193, [1975] Ch 25, in *Mettoy Pension Trustees Ltd v Evans* [1991] 2 All ER 513 at 552–553, [1990] 1 WLR 1587 at 1621 as follows:

'... where a trustee acts under a discretion given to him by the terms of the
trust, the court will interfere with his action if it is clear that he would not   *a*
have acted as he did had he not failed to take into account considerations
which he ought to have taken into account.'

He went on to hold that the extent of the trustee's duty to take into account
relevant considerations was not affected by the quality of the advice received by
the trustee (see [1991] 2 All ER 513 at 556, [1990] 1 WLR 1587 at 1625–1626). This   *b*
argument was not addressed by the Pensions Ombudsman because he did not
accept an important premise upon which the argument was founded, namely
that the FMC trustee misunderstood Hillsdown's powers to absorb the FMC
scheme surplus as at 6 April 1988 over a five-year period. For reasons already
given, I do consider that the FMC trustee did misunderstand Hillsdown's powers   *c*
in that connection and it follows that I do consider that the court would have
been entitled to intervene under the *Hastings-Bass* principle. I have no doubt that
the attitude of the FMC trustee in the negotiations with Hillsdown was critically
affected by the conviction perfectly honestly, but in my view erroneously,
formed that Hillsdown could properly absorb the surplus in question over a
five-year period. However, since this does not add anything to the conclusion   *d*
which I have earlier reached that the FMC trustee's purported exercise of the
power conferred by r 21 was a fraud on the power, it is not in my view necessary
to explore this aspect further and, in particular, I need not decide how far it would
be proper on appeal to deal with a point of law not raised before the Pensions
Ombudsman or dealt with by the determination. My impression is that it would   *e*
be proper to deal with points of law not raised below or dealt with in the
determination under appeal if, but only if, the resolution of the point of law does
not involve an investigation of facts which have not been investigated. Since the
Pensions Ombudsman's jurisdiction is largely inquisitorial it would in my view
be proper to include among points of law, which can properly be investigated on
appeal from his determination, points of law which could have been dealt with   *f*
by him on the material before him but were not. There is a clear distinction
between appeals from the Pensions Ombudsman and appeals to the Employment
Appeal Tribunal from industrial tribunals, where a more restrictive approach to
the taking of new points of law on appeal prevails.

The second additional argument advanced by Mr Nugee for attacking the   *g*
validity of the transfer agreement of 17 November 1989 was that it was liable to
be set aside as having been made in breach of the self-dealing rule. That rule was
shortly stated by Megarry J in *Tito v Waddell (No 2)* [1977] 3 All ER 129 at 241,
[1977] Ch 106 at 241 as follows:

'The self-dealing rule is (to put it very shortly) that if a trustee sells the trust   *h*
property to himself, the sale is voidable by any beneficiary ex debito justitiae,
however fair the transaction.'

In the present case there were two persons, Mr Solomon and Mr Legg, who had
a foot in three camps in that they were directors of Hillsdown (Mr Solomon was
chairman), they were directors of the FMC trustee having previously been   *j*
individual FMC trustees, and they were directors of the HF trustee. It is primarily
in relation to the dual capacity regarding Hillsdown and the FMC trustee,
between which bodies the critical bargaining took place, that the point is made.
There is no doubt that Mr Legg in particular played an active part on behalf of the
FMC trustee because he conducted the correspondence for them. Mr Nugee's

a submission was to the effect that the self-dealing rule applied so as to render a transaction voidable, no matter how fair and proper it was, if in the negotiations leading up to the transaction there was at least one person who was either a trustee or a director on both sides with a conflict of duties. That was not his formulation, which was that there was here an agreement between trustees and a company of which two of the trustees were directors and as such it would seem

b prima facie to be liable to be set aside ex debito justitiae at the request of any beneficiary. Even on that formulation it is only a prima facie result and is therefore not a necessary one. But apart from that point, which may be no more than verbal, I am not satisfied that the self-dealing rule is as hard and fast as to require a negotiation between pension fund trustees and the employer to be set aside automatically and without investigation if one or more of the trustees are

c directors of the employer. I accept that, unless there is an express provision in the relevant trust deed permitting a trustee to act in negotiations with the employer under the scheme notwithstanding that the trustee is a director or employee of the company, the fact that negotiations have been conducted by persons one of whom had a conflict of duties puts upon those who say the transaction in

d question should be upheld the onus of proving that it was indeed reasonable and proper. That of course involves an investigation of the facts.

In the present case there is nothing in the determination about the possible impact of the self-dealing rule. The nearest that one approaches to it is in the recital of Mr Burt's complaint, which includes the following:

e 'He [that is Mr Burt] believes that the decision was taken because the individuals who were directors of FMC Trustee were also directors of Hillsdown and that they failed to distinguish their competing fiduciary duties. His complaint against Hillsdown in this regard was that it brought undue influence to bear on FMC Trustee.'

f It might be thought that this would have alerted the Pensions Ombudsman to the possible application if not of the self-dealing rule at least of a necessity for Hillsdown to show that there was in fact no operative conflict of duties in the negotiating process. But the fact is that no separate investigation on those lines was conducted although, as has already appeared, the bargain itself was investigated in some detail.

g My reasons for holding that negotiations of the type conducted between Hillsdown and the FMC trustee are not automatically liable to be set aside at the request of a beneficiary are that the self-dealing rule does not in my view extend in its full stringency that far. The high-water mark is the decision of Vinelott J in Re Thompson's Settlement, Thompson v Thompson [1985] 2 All ER 720, [1986] Ch 99

h in which a transaction amounting either to an assignment or a surrender and regrant of a lease between trustees on the one hand and a company on the other was held voidable under the self-dealing rule because one of the trustees was also a director and, with his wife, majority shareholder in the company. The transaction was therefore within the self-dealing rule. The significance of the

j decision for Mr Nugee's argument was that Vinelott J, in reply to an argument that the self-dealing, as opposed to the fair-dealing, rule only applied if there was a sale or purchase by trustees of trust property or something analogous to it, said ([1985] 2 All ER 720 at 730, [1986] Ch 99 at 115):

'I do not think the self-dealing rule can be so confined. It is clear that the self-dealing rule is an application of the wider principle that a man must not

put himself in a position where duty and interest conflict or where his duty
to one conflicts with his duty to another (see in particular the opinion of Lord
Dunedin in *Wright v Morgan* [1926] AC 788 at 797, [1926] All ER Rep 201 at
205) which I have cited. The principle is applied stringently in cases where a
trustee concurs in a transaction which cannot be carried into effect without
his concurrence and who also has an interest in or owes a fiduciary duty to
another in relation to the same transaction. The transaction cannot stand if
challenged by a beneficiary because in the absence of an express provision in
the trust instrument the beneficiaries are entitled to require that the trustees
act unanimously and that each brings to bear a mind unclouded by any
contrary interest or duty in deciding whether it is the interest of the
beneficiaries that the trustees concur in it.'

Where a limited company is involved on one side there is however in my view
on the authorities a less rigid line. That seems to me to be demonstrated by *Farrar
v Farrars Ltd* (1888) 40 Ch D 395, which fell on the fair-dealing side of the line
where the individual concerned was interested in that he had a small
shareholding and *Re Thompson's Settlement*, which, as already mentioned, fell on
the self-dealing side of the line where the individual was a substantial shareholder
and director. It suffices for my purpose to say that the position is not so clear-cut
that the self-dealing rule applies to render the transfer agreement voidable that it
would be right at this stage for me to hold that that was established as a point of
law where the point of law was not dealt with in the determination nor were the
relevant facts, such as the extent, if any, to which Mr Solomon and Mr Legg were
involved on behalf of Hillsdown, investigated and established as facts upon which
an appeal could be founded.

The Pensions Ombudsman's jurisdiction regarding remedies

Two important issues arise here. The first is whether the Pensions
Ombudsman has jurisdiction to direct steps to be taken under s 151(2) of the 1993
Act with a view to remedying any injustice caused by maladministration to
anyone other than the complainant with whose complaint he is dealing, in this
case Mr Burt. A half-way house on this issue would be to hold that steps could
be directed to be taken in relation to the complaints actually received by the
Pensions Ombudsman. They totalled 51 besides Mr Burt's. There were some
1,100 members of the FMC scheme. The 52 complaints were stated by the
Pensions Ombudsman to be in substance identical. Mr Oliver not surprisingly
recognised that his submission that only Mr Burt's injustice caused by
maladministration (if there was one) could be the subject of remedial steps was
not an attractive one because it would require separate treatment of all
complaints and effectively prevent an effective system of taking a test case.
Nowhere in the Act or the relevant regulations is there express provision for
representation orders. In my view the argument advanced for thus limiting the
Pensions Ombudsman's jurisdiction not only leads to inconvenient results but is
also unsound in principle.

The jurisdiction is defined in s 151(2) of the 1993 Act in very wide terms. I have
already set it out and there is no express limitation on the steps which the
Pensions Ombudsman can direct to be taken or refrained from. Where, as here,
the remedy discerned as appropriate by the Pensions Ombudsman is one which
is equally applicable in relation to a large number of other authorised
complainants on the same facts and it is a remedy to which the particular claimant

a in question is entitled then I have no doubt that there is jurisdiction to direct steps which grant that remedy. What has happened here upon the view which the Pensions Ombudsman in my view has correctly taken is that as a result of a breach of trust a large sum of money has been paid out of a pension trust to an employer. Where there is a continuing trust the remedy of a beneficiary under the trust which has payments made out of it in breach of trust is to have the trust

b fund restored. This rule has lately come under the scrutiny of the House of Lords in *Target Holdings Ltd v Redferns (a firm)* [1995] 3 All ER 785, [1996] AC 421. Lord Browne-Wilkinson said ([1995] 3 All ER 785 at 793, [1996] AC 421 at 434):

> 'The basic right of a beneficiary is to have the trust duly administered in accordance with the provisions of the trust instrument, if any, and the general law. Thus, in relation to a traditional trust where the fund is held on
c > trust for a number of beneficiaries having different, usually successive, equitable interests, eg A for life with remainder to B), the right of each beneficiary is to have the whole fund vested in the trustees so as to be available to satisfy his equitable interest when, and if, it falls into possession. Accordingly, in the case of a breach of such a trust involving the wrongful
d > paying away of trust assets, the liability of the trustee is to restore to the trust fund, often called "the trust estate", what ought to have been there.'

Lord Browne-Wilkinson went on to hold that this well-established principle did not apply to a bare trust and that was the essential issue in the decision. Mr Inglis-Jones submitted that because the FMC scheme had been wound up, as it
e was shortly after the assets were transferred to the HF trust, the appropriate rule to apply was that appropriate to a bare trust as set out in *Target Holdings Ltd v Redferns (a firm)* by the House of Lords so that each complainant would have to establish the individual quantum of injustice which he or she would have suffered—in effect a claim to damages. I am quite unable to accept that
f submission. Bringing the scheme to an end cannot be allowed to obscure the fact that what has happened and what calls for an appropriate remedy is that assets have improperly been taken out of a trust fund which had at the time continuing trusts to be performed. To suggest that those responsible for that improper act can mitigate or alter the quantum of their liability by determining the scheme is a startling proposition which I am quite unable to accept. I appreciate that with
g a pension fund events keep on happening, members retire and die, so there is no permanence at all in entitlement out of the fund. That no doubt complicates the issues regarding appropriate remedies, but it does nothing to persuade me that the appropriate remedy, even for a single complainant who shows that assets have been improperly taken out of a pension trust with continuing trusts, is not
h an order or determination that they should be put back.

Can the Pensions Ombudsman make orders that the court could not make?
This is both an important and difficult issue upon which there has been some measure, at least temporarily, of difference of opinion between my brethren Carnwath and Robert Walker JJ. The particular question upon which their
j opinions diverged was whether the Pensions Ombudsman had jurisdiction to direct the payment of compensation for distress and inconvenience caused by maladministration. In *Miller v Stapleton* [1996] 2 All ER 449 at 465 Carnwath J obiter and reluctantly was inclined to agree that the Pensions Ombudsman had no power to direct such payment in circumstances where the court would not do so. In *Westminster City Council v Haywood* [1996] 2 All ER 467 Robert Walker J held

that there was power to direct the payment of reasonable compensation for distress and inconvenience and upheld just such an award and, finally, in *Wild v Pensions Ombudsman* (1996) Times, 17 April Carnwath J said that it seemed to him right that he should follow Robert Walker J's decision in spite of the doubts which he expressed in *Miller's* case unless and until the matter was considered by a higher court. It would not I think be fair to assume that because Carnwath J's readiness to follow Robert Walker J's decision was limited to the period before the matter was considered by a higher court that he intended to convey that the higher court in question would decide the point differently from Robert Walker J. Nevertheless both judges recognised that the point was a difficult one upon which there were cogent arguments either way. Those arguments are set out in those judgments and I do not take time to repeat them. My own view, in the different context of a complaint against an employer in respect of maladministration causing injustice to members in participation in a transaction involving the improper payment out of sums which in large measure found their way, as they were from the outset intended to do, into the employer's hands, is that it would not be permissible for the Pensions Ombudsman to require the employer to refund the sums it received unless the court would be in a position to make such an order. In reaching that conclusion I have not taken into account, as Mr Inglis-Jones submitted that I should, what was said in the House of Commons Standing Committee by the Under-Secretary of State during the debate on what has become the Pensions Act 1995 (see HC Official Report, SC D (Pensions Bill), 20 June 1995). In relation to a concern expressed by the then Pensions Ombudsman that while he could recommend compensation for distress, delay and inconvenience suffered by a complainant, he could not direct such compensation to be paid, the Under-Secretary of State said (col 758):

'If he were able to direct that that [sic] compensation be paid, he would have powers greater than those of any other ombudsman or of the courts. It would not be appropriate for the ombudsman to have those powers. The ombudsman's powers are correctly delineated by existing law and by the extensions introduced in the Bill.'

While I accept that that is a clear expression of the Under-Secretary of State's understanding of the law as it then stood, I do not consider that it is admissible within the very narrow confines laid down by Lord Browne-Wilkinson in *Pepper (Inspector of Taxes) v Hart* [1993] 1 All ER 42 at 64, [1993] AC 593 at 634 in a speech with which the majority of the House agreed. He said:

'... subject to the questions of the privileges of the House of Commons, reference to parliamentary material should be permitted as an aid to the construction of legislation which is ambiguous or obscure or the literal meaning of which leads to an absurdity. Even in such cases references in court to parliamentary material should only be permitted where such material clearly discloses the mischief aimed at or the legislative intention lying behind the ambiguous or obscure words.'

In my view what the Under-Secretary of State said in 1995 cannot amount to material clearly disclosing the legislative intention in the Pension Schemes Act 1993, or a fortiori, the earlier Act, the Social Security Act 1990, which the 1993 Act re-enacted. I appreciate that it is permissible to have regard to a later Act in order to construe earlier legislation, if but only if, the earlier legislation is ambiguous:

see *Kirkness (Inspector of Taxes) v John Hudson & Co Ltd* [1955] 2 All ER 345, [1955] AC 696. I also appreciate that the Pensions Act 1995 amended (inter alia) s 151 of the 1993 Act and effectively re-enacted it as amended. Nevertheless, there is I believe a clear line to be drawn between parliamentary material evidencing the intention behind legislation then going through Parliament on the way to the statute book and parliamentary material evidencing the understanding of

b ministers of the current state of the law. It seems to me that what the Under-Secretary of State said on 20 June 1995 falls into the latter category and falls outside what *Pepper v Hart* allows into evidence. It would follow that I consider that Robert Walker J was in my view rightly not told that he could get assistance from *Hansard* under the principle in *Pepper v Hart* (see *Westminster City Council v Haywood* [1996] 2 All ER 467 at 480, [1996] 3 WLR 563 at 576).

c   My main reasons for holding the view that I have expressed regarding the Pensions Ombudsman's inability to direct an employer or trustee to replace funds improperly removed from a pension scheme unless the court itself could so order are twofold. First, it seems to me that there is a real distinction between ordering compensation for inconvenience and distress caused by

d maladministration as an adjunct to the power to remedy injustice caused by maladministration which, in line with Robert Walker J's decision, I take to be permissible, and requiring the repayment of what might well be, and in this case were, very substantial sums by way of payment out from a pension fund, on the other hand. It is trite law that pension funds must operate within the law and it does not seem to me right that there should be a different answer to the question

e 'are you legally liable to repay this sum' according to the tribunal to which resort is had so that the answer is: 'If I am sued in court, No, but if a complaint is made to the Pensions Ombudsman, Yes.' The injustice through maladministration must in this case consist of the detriment suffered by the payment out itself and is in no sense ancillary as are claims to compensation for inconvenience and

f distress. My second reason is tied up with the first and is that s 146(6)(a) of the 1993 Act prevents the Pensions Ombudsman from investigating a complaint if before the complaint is made proceedings have been begun in court in respect of the matters which would be the subject of the investigation. That suggests that the two are intended to be mutually exclusive alternatives and it would be strange if it was contemplated that the alternatives would or might produce

g different results as to the substance of the dispute. I can well imagine that the two tribunals would be contemplated as having radically different procedures and it may be types of relief but I would not expect differences on such fundamental matters as whether there was a liability to repay capital sums. Also there would be a possibility of abuse if it were possible to avoid an impending complaint to the

h Pensions Ombudsman by a well-timed application for the determination of a dispute of fact or law.

Is Hillsdown liable in law to make repayments?
The Pensions Ombudsman said in his determination:

j   'Since the transfer took place in breach of trust, the assets were received by HF Trustee as constructive trustee and the payment made to Hillsdown was received by Hillsdown as constructive trustee.'

I fear that cuts some well-known corners in the law of constructive trusts. Notably, as Mr Oliver submitted, receipt of trust property by a third party does not, without more, constitute the recipient a constructive trustee. The categories of constructive trust in this field are usually referred to as 'knowing assistance' and 'knowing receipt' cases of constructive trust. In either category some form of knowledge is required. The knowing assistance cases are not relevant here since Hillsdown did receive the sums paid out by the HF trustee which came from the FMC scheme and was not guilty of any such dishonest conduct as is requisite in knowing assistance constructive trusts.

The knowing receipt cases on the other hand are rather more complex. I was referred by Mr Oliver to *Carl-Zeiss-Stiftung v Herbert Smith & Co (a firm) (No 2)* [1969] 2 All ER 367, [1969] 2 Ch 276, where claims that the defendant solicitors were liable to account as constructive trustees for sums received on account of their fees from the West German Zeiss foundation, all of whose assets were claimed to belong to the plaintiff East German foundation. Both facts and law were in dispute but what was not in dispute was the integrity of the solicitors. All that was said against them was that they had notice of the East German foundation claim that moneys paid to them belonged beneficially to the latter. The claim against the solicitors failed but the reasons given by the members of the Court of Appeal were not identical. Danckwerts LJ held that knowledge of a claim was not sufficient to amount to notice of a trust or of misapplication of the moneys (see [1969] 2 All ER 367 at 372–373, [1969] 2 Ch 276 at 290). He approved of a passage taken from 38 *Halsbury's Laws* (3rd edn) para 1450, which included the following:

'A person does not, however, become a constructive trustee merely by acting as the solicitor or agent of trustees in transactions within their legal powers, although the transactions may be of a character of which a court of equity would disapprove, unless he receives and becomes chargeable with some part of the trust property, or unless he knowingly assists in a dishonest and fraudulent act on the part of the trustees.' (See [1969] 2 All ER 367 at 373, [1969] 2 Ch 276 at 291.)

The passage is largely based on the classic statement by Lord Selborne LC in *Barnes v Addy* (1874) LR 9 Ch App 244 at 251–252 which Danckwerts LJ quoted. Danckwerts LJ rejected the argument that all the allegations in the statement of claim had at that interlocutory stage to be assumed to be true saying ([1969] 2 All ER 367 at 375, [1969] 2 Ch 276 at 293):

'That will not do. What we have to deal with is the state of the defendants' knowledge (actual or imputed) at the date they received payments of their costs and disbursements. At that date they cannot have had more than knowledge of the claims ... It is not a case where the West German foundation were holding property on any express trust.'

Sachs LJ emphasised the difference between knowledge and notice and held that 'cognisance of what has been termed "a doubtful equity" is not enough' to fix a stranger with constructive trusteeship (see [1969] 2 All ER 367 at 378, [1969] 2 Ch 276 at 296). He also held that the solicitors were not under a duty to the plaintiffs to investigate the validity of the claims either as to the facts or the law. Sachs LJ said this, which Mr Oliver naturally relied upon ([1969] 2 All ER 367 at 379, [1969] 2 Ch 276 at 298):

'It does not, however, seem to me that a stranger is necessarily shown to be both a constructive trustee and liable for a breach of the relevant trusts even if it is established that he has such notice. As at present advised, I am inclined to the view that a further element has to be proved, at any rate in a case such as the present one. That element is one of dishonesty or of consciously acting improperly, as opposed to an innocent failure to make what a court may later decide to have been proper enquiry. That would entail both actual knowledge of the trust's existence and actual knowledge that what is being done is improperly in breach of that trust—though, of course, in both cases a person wilfully shutting his eyes to the obvious is in no different position than if he had kept them open.'

Edmund Davies LJ put the matter on a broad basis in the following passage ([1969] 2 All ER 367 at 381–382, [1969] 2 Ch 276 at 300–301):

'English law provides no clear and all-embracing definition of a constructive trust. Its boundaries have been left perhaps deliberately vague, so as not to restrict the court by technicalities in deciding what the justice of a particular case may demand. But it appears that in this country unjust enrichment or other personal advantage is not a sine qua non ... Nevertheless, the concept of unjust enrichment has its value as providing one example among many of what, for lack of a better phrase, I would call "want of probity", a feature which recurs through and seems to connect all those cases drawn to the court's attention where a constructive trust has been held to exist. SNELL'S EQUITY (26th edn, 1966) at p. 201, expresses the same idea by stating that: "A possible definition is that a constructive trust is a trust which is imposed by equity in order to satisfy the demands of justice and good conscience, without reference to any express or presumed intention of the parties." It may be objected that, even assuming the correctness of the foregoing, it provides no assistance, inasmuch as reference to "unjust enrichment", "want of probity" and "the demands of justice and good conscience" merely introduces vague concepts which are in turn incapable of definition and which, therefore, provide no yardstick. I do not agree. Concepts may defy definition and yet the presence in or absence from a situation of that which they denote may be beyond doubt. The concept of "want of probity" appears to provide a useful touchstone in considering circumstances said to give rise to constructive trusts, and I have not found it misleading when applying it to the many authorities cited to this court. It is because of such a concept that evidence as to "good faith," "knowledge" and "notice" plays so important a part in the reported decisions. It is true that not every situation where probity is lacking gives rise to a constructive trust. Nevertheless, the authorities appear to show that nothing short of it will do. Not even gross negligence will suffice.'

Edmund Davies LJ emphasised the reluctance of the law to make agents liable as constructive trustees.

The *Zeiss* case is obviously factually distinguishable primarily on the basis that it was concerned with a claim to make an agent acting within the scope of his authority liable as a constructive trustee. Moreover, the solicitors plainly had no connection whatever with the breach of trust relied upon in the action. On the other hand, Sachs and Edmund Davies LJJ did emphasise the general need for want of probity, but in doing so Edmund Davies LJ accepted the usefulness of the concept of unjust enrichment as providing one of many examples of want of probity as he saw it.

The other authority on constructive trusts of the knowing receipt category to
which Mr Oliver referred was *Re Montagu's Settlement Trusts, Duke of Manchester v
National Westminster Bank Ltd* (1985) [1992] 4 All ER 308, [1987] Ch 264. In that
case the settlor and tenant for life under an old-fashioned strict settlement which
included a settlement of chattels had handed over to him various settled chattels
in breach of an obligation imposed on the trustees of the settlement to select
chattels suitable to be settled as family heirlooms. The life tenant was only
entitled to receive what was left of the settled chattels after that selection was
made and it never was. Megarry V-C found that the life tenant had notice, both
actual and imputed through his solicitor, of the terms of the settlement but did
not personally know that he was not entitled to take absolutely the chattels that
were made over to him by the trustees and in those circumstances he declined to
hold the life tenant liable as a constructive trustee. That was a case where to a
lawyer, if he read the relevant clause (numbered 14B) attentively, it was clear that
there was a duty on the trustees to make a selection of heirlooms and not a mere
power to do so. To a layman however the situation was not obvious and there
was an affirmative finding that the life tenant, who was not a lawyer, did not
know that he was not absolutely entitled to the chattels handed over to him. *Re
Montagu's Settlement Trusts* is, in my view, authority for the proposition that a
person to whom trustees hand over property in breach of trust will not be treated
as a constructive trustee unless he had actual knowledge or deliberately shut his
eyes to the fact that the property was trust property or wilfully and recklessly
failed to make such inquiries as a reasonable and honest man would make. There
was a tracing claim in so far as tracing was possible but in the event that did not
prove possible. Here again the facts, although closer to the present case than
those in the *Zeiss* case, are in my view clearly distinguishable in that the life tenant
did not have a hand in the trustees' breach of trust otherwise than as the recipient
of what he thought he was entitled to receive. It was a case like the one before
me of an honest muddle in that no one involved acted dishonestly and the
trustees who committed the breach of trust had advice throughout but not good
advice. The critical distinguishing feature in my view is that, in the case before
me, Hillsdown were the instigators of the breach of trust, albeit that they did not
appreciate that what was involved was a breach of trust. Moreover, the
instigation took the form of a threat to do something which in my view
Hillsdown as a matter of construction of the 1983 FMC trust deed was not
entitled to do and the whole process of negotiation consisted of unwarranted
interference with the duty of the FMC trustee after consulting the actuary to
decide how to apply the surplus in the FMC scheme as at 6 April 1988.

Mr Oliver relied upon the fact that there was nothing in the 1983 FMC trust
deed either by way of express provision or by way of necessary implication in
terms prohibiting what was done. I have dealt with this argument in connection
with the finding that there was a fraud on the power and need not do more than
repeat that there may very easily be a fraud on the power if a power is used for a
collateral purpose without there being an infringement of the letter of the power,
e g an appointment to an object of the power which is only vitiated because there
is a collateral agreement with the appointor to benefit a stranger.

I would respectfully adopt what Megarry V-C said in *Re Montagu's Settlement
Trusts* [1992] 4 All ER 308 at 330, [1987] Ch 264 at 285:

'In considering whether a constructive trust has arisen in a case of the
knowing receipt of trust property, the basic question is whether the

conscience of the recipient is sufficiently affected to justify the imposition of such a trust.'

In my view, there has to be set in the scales over against the fact that Hillsdown honestly believed itself to be entitled to do and receive what it did and received the following factors. (a) Hillsdown took a very active part in persuading the FMC trustee to agree to what was a breach of trust. (b) Hillsdown's technique in that persuasion was to threaten to do something which Hillsdown was not entitled to do because: (i) it involved a combination of adhering additional employers and suspending employers' contributions in a manner which would have been a breach of implied good faith, as that expression is used by Browne-Wilkinson V-C in the *Imperial Group* case; (ii) it involved an interference with a discretion given exclusively to the FMC trustee under r 23(a) in relation to the surplus as at 6 April 1988. (c) Hillsdown was unjustly enriched by the receipt of £18·4m less 40% tax and the FMC trust was the poorer by the same sum gross of that tax. There can be no doubt about the enrichment save possibly as regards quantum. As to its being unjust, in my view one only has to compare the position of Hillsdown who successfully wielded a big but misguided stick with that of the members of the FMC scheme who were never told anything of what was being done as regards the payment of surplus to Hillsdown to see which way the scales of justice fall.

Although it can be said in a sense that Hillsdown was an innocent instigator of a breach of trust in that it did not appreciate that a breach of trust was involved, it was also in a sense guilty because it played an active part in what was in my view an improper threat to interfere with that with which it had no right to interfere. That seems to me to constitute a quite different and lesser degree of innocence from that of the solicitors in the *Zeiss* case and the tenant for life in *Re Montagu's Settlement Trusts*.

For those reasons, I conclude that, subject to possible defences, Hillsdown could have been held liable by a court as a constructive trustee of the sums which it received from the HF trustee.

Support can also be found for not permitting the instigator of a breach of trust to rely on his ignorance of the fact that the transaction which he instigated constituted a breach of trust in the authorities which deal with the allied questions (a) whether a beneficiary who has instigated or acquiesced in a breach of trust can nevertheless sue the trustee who is otherwise liable for the breach of trust and (b) whether a beneficiary who has thus initiated or acquiesced is liable to have his interest impounded to indemnify the trustee who has been made liable at the suit of other beneficiaries. The authorities were reviewed by Wilberforce J in *Re Pauling's Settlement Trusts, Younghusband v Coutts & Co* [1961] 3 All ER 713 at 729–730, [1962] 1 WLR 86 at 107–108, when he concluded that, subject to the court considering whether it is fair that a beneficiary who has been concerned in a transaction should be able to turn round and sue the trustees for breach of trust, it was not necessary that he should know that what he is concurring in is a breach of trust provided that he fully understands what it is he is concurring in. The Court of Appeal in *Re Pauling's Settlement Trusts* [1963] 3 All ER 1 at 20, [1964] Ch 303 at 353 put the question of acquiescence very broadly saying 'a party cannot be held to have acquiesced unless he knew or ought to have known what his rights were'. It is also to be noted that the principle set out by Wilberforce J in *Re Pauling's Settlement Trusts* above is described in Goff and Jones *The Law of Restitution* (4th edn, 1993) p 96 as a somewhat harsh rule.

If my conclusion on constructive trusteeship is wrong, there remain the alternative formulations of unjust enrichment, mistake and a tracing claim. As to unjust enrichment, I doubt whether at this stage of the development of English law it is appropriate for a judge at first instance to give effect to a claim in restitution where a claim in constructive trust fails. The authority upon which reliance would be placed for such an attitude would doubtless be *Lipkin Gorman (a firm) v Karpnale Ltd* [1992] 4 All ER 512, [1991] 2 AC 548, where such a form of proceeding in the context of a common law claim for money had and received succeeded. I have already stated my opinion that there was unjust enrichment here and in the circumstances I think it will suffice if I express my view on the defences which Mr Oliver relied upon by way of change of position. The first was the consent by Hillsdown to pension increases in the HF scheme and the second was the payment of tax. I do not accept that either of them would constitute an adequate defence of change of position. The consent to pension increases was not in my view something which was, so far as the FMC trust was concerned in respect of which the unjust enrichment really occurred, within Hillsdown's gift. Hillsdown had no right of veto there, certainly so far as the surplus in the FMC scheme was concerned. It is in my view right to regard the unjust enrichment claim as arising in the FMC scheme because the payments to the HF trustee and thence to Hillsdown were negotiated and carried through as a package deal. The HF trust was no more than a conduit pipe. On that basis Hillsdown did not do more than allow in part that which ought to have been done in the whole, ie apply the surplus as permitted by r 23(a). That does not seem to me to constitute a defence by way of change of position.

Equally the liability to tax should not in my view be allowed as a defence except to the extent that Hillsdown is unable to recover the tax. The Commissioners of Inland Revenue were not represented before me and there was no argument as to the recoverability of the tax paid. The fact that the tax was actually paid by the HF trustee on behalf of Hillsdown is neither here nor there. The liability to tax was Hillsdown's and there is no relevant change of position in having to pay the tax leviable on the footing that the transaction was lawful. On the other hand, I do accept that Hillsdown should not be made to account for irrecoverable tax. But that would merely be mitigation of liability and not enough to ground a defence on change of position.

So far as mistake is concerned, I do not consider that the situation is significantly different from that regarding constructive trusteeship which I have dealt with above. The validity of the decision in *Chase Manhattan Bank NA v Israel-British Bank (London) Ltd* [1979] 3 All ER 1025, [1981] Ch 105 is at best doubtful after the House of Lords decision in *Westdeutsche Landesbank Girozentrale v Islington London BC* [1996] 2 All ER 961 at 996–997, [1996] AC 669 at 714–715.

The tracing claim was not explored by the Pensions Ombudsman in the determination and without any findings of fact on the subject it does not seem to me right to express views beyond saying that, since Hillsdown was clearly not a purchaser for value without notice, a tracing claim would in principle lie against it in respect of traceable assets as at the date when it had notice of the claimants' rights. When that was and how far there were then traceable assets remains unresolved. Had it been necessary to do so the matter could have been remitted for the relevant findings to be made but in the light of the view I have formed on constructive trusteeship that is not necessary.

a I therefore conclude that so far as Hillsdown's liability to refund in principle is concerned the appeal should be dismissed but there are a number of points on the exact remedy to be granted which were not argued before the principal issues on liability were decided. I propose, therefore, subject to any arguments of counsel on the subject, to give an opportunity for submissions on remedies to be made. That the remedy should be proportionate to the injustice suffered is not, I *b* imagine, likely to be challenged. How that is to be achieved may be less simple.

Order accordingly.

Mary Rose Plummer   Barrister.

Re T (a minor) (wardship: medical treatment)

COURT OF APPEAL, CIVIL DIVISION

BUTLER-SLOSS, WAITE AND ROCH LJJ

27, 30 SEPTEMBER, 24 OCTOBER 1996

Medical treatment – Child – Invasive surgery – Mother refusing consent – Child born with life-threatening liver defect – Medical opinion that liver transplant which would prolong child's life had good chance of success – Mother refusing consent to operation because of pain and distress it would cause to child – Whether mother's views relevant – Whether in child's best interests to require him to undergo liver transplant.

A child who was born with a life-threatening liver defect underwent an operation at the age of three and a half weeks. The operation was unsuccessful and caused the child considerable pain and distress. The medical prognosis was that he would not live beyond two and a half years without a liver transplant. Three consultant paediatricians expressed the view that the child was suitable for a liver transplant, that although liver transplantation was one of the most major and complicated forms of surgery the operation had a good chance of success and that, if it did succeed, the child would be likely to have many years of normal life. The mother refused to give her consent to the operation because she was not willing to permit the child to undergo the pain and distress of invasive surgery. The mother later moved out of the jurisdiction to join the child's father. The local authority, at the consultants' instigation, applied to the court for permission to carry out the operation, notwithstanding the mother's opposition and for the child to be returned to the jurisdiction in order that the operation could be carried out. The judge held that the mother was being unreasonable in withholding consent in the face of the medical opinion in favour of the operation, that it was in the child's best interests to undergo a liver transplant and that permission should be granted. The mother appealed.

Held – In determining whether permission should be granted to carry out invasive surgery which might prolong the life of a child born with a life-threatening defect when a parent refused to consent to the operation, the paramount consideration was the welfare of the child and not the reasonableness of the parent's refusal of consent. However, since in the instant case the welfare of the child depended on the mother, who would be expected to care for him through surgery and for many years after, her views were relevant and the judge had erred in deciding that her decision was unreasonable in the light of the unchallenged clinical opinion in favour of the operation. The judge had failed to assess the relevance or the weight of the mother's concern as to the benefits to her child of the surgery and post-operative treatment, the dangers of failure both long term as well as short term, the possibility of the need for further transplants, the likely length of life and the effect on her child of all those concerns, together with the strong reservations expressed by one of the consultants about coercing the mother into playing a crucial part in the aftermath of the operation and thereafter. Having regard to those matters, the fact that the mother would be required to return to the jurisdiction, possibly without the father, in which case she would have to manage unaided, and that the court would be directing her to take on a total commitment when she did not agree with the proposed surgery,

a it would not be in the best interests of the child to give consent and require him
to be returned to the jurisdiction for the purpose of undergoing liver
transplantation. The appeal would therefore be allowed (see p 913 *g h*, p 914 *a* to
f, p 915 *a b h j*, p 916 *b d f g*, p 917 *d*, p 918 *b e*, p 919 *f* and p 920 *c*, post).
Dicta of Lord Donaldson MR in *Re J (a minor) (wardship: medical treatment)*
[1990] 3 All ER 930 at 934, 936 applied.

b *Re B (a minor) (wardship: sterilisation)* [1987] 2 All ER 206, *Re B (a minor)
(wardship: medical treatment)* (1981) [1990] 3 All ER 927 and *Re Z (a minor) (freedom
of publication)* [1995] 4 All ER 961 considered.

Notes

c For consent to medical treatment generally, see *30 Halsbury's Laws* (4th edn
reissue) para 39, and for cases on the subject, see *33 Digest* (2nd reissue) 483–485,
2712–2715.

Cases referred to in judgments

d *B (a minor) (wardship: medical treatment), Re* (1981) [1990] 3 All ER 927, [1981] 1
WLR 1421, CA.

B (a minor) (wardship: sterilisation), Re [1987] 2 All ER 206, [1988] AC 199, [1987] 2
WLR 1213, HL.

Bolam v Friern Hospital Management Committee [1957] 2 All ER 118, [1957] 1 WLR
582.

e *G v G* [1985] 2 All ER 225, [1985] 1 WLR 647, HL.

J (a minor) (wardship: medical treatment), Re [1990] 3 All ER 930, [1991] Fam 33,
[1991] 2 WLR 140, CA.

W (a minor) (medical treatment), Re [1992] 4 All ER 627, [1993] Fam 64, [1992] 3
WLR 758, CA.

f *Z (a minor) (freedom of publication), Re* [1995] 4 All ER 961, [1996] 2 WLR 88, CA.

Cases also cited or referred to in skeleton arguments

Airedale NHS Trust v Bland [1993] 1 All ER 821, [1993] AC 789, HL.

C (a minor) (wardship: medical treatment), Re [1989] 2 All ER 782, [1990] Fam 26, CA.

g *D (a minor) (wardship: sterilisation), Re* [1976] 1 All ER 326, [1976] Fam 185.

Frenchay Healthcare NHS Trust v S [1994] 2 All ER 403, [1994] 1 WLR 601, CA.

Gillick v West Norfolk and Wisbech Area Health Authority [1985] 3 All ER 402, [1986]
AC 112, HL.

Harben v Harben [1957] 1 All ER 379, [1957] 1 WLR 261.

h *Hope v Hope* (1854) 4 De G M & G 328, [1843–60] All ER Rep 441, 43 ER 534, LC.

J v C [1969] 1 All ER 788, [1970] AC 668, HL.

Liddell's Settlement Trusts, Re, Liddell v Liddell [1936] 1 All ER 239, [1936] Ch 365,
CA.

P (a minor), Re [1986] 1 FLR 272, CA.

j *P (G E) (an infant), Re* [1964] 3 All ER 977, [1965] Ch 568, CA.

R v Sandbach Justices, ex p Smith [1950] 2 All ER 781, [1951] 1 KB 62, DC.

Sidaway v Bethlem Royal Hospital Governors [1985] 1 All ER 643, [1985] AC 871, HL.

W (a minor) (contact), Re [1994] 2 FLR 441, CA.

W (an infant), Re [1971] 2 All ER 49, [1971] AC 682, HL.

Willoughby (an infant), Re (1885) 30 Ch D 324, CA.

Appeal

The mother of a baby boy, C, appealed from the decision of Connell J made on *a* 17 September 1996 whereby he held, on an originating summons issued by the local authority in whose area C and his mother had been residing, that it was in C's best interests to undergo surgery for a liver transplantation, that permission be granted to perform the surgery notwithstanding the refusal of the mother to consent to it, and for the child to be returned to the jurisdiction for the purpose *b* of such surgery. The facts are set out in the judgment of Butler-Sloss LJ.

Robert Francis QC and *Andrew Hockton* (instructed by *Pannone & Partners*) for the mother.

David Harris QC and *Yvonne Coppel* (instructed by *Susan Orrell*) for the local *c* authority.

Gordon Murdoch QC and *Huw Lloyd* (instructed by the *Official Solicitor*) for the guardian ad litem.

Cur adv vult

d

24 October 1996. The following judgments were delivered.

BUTLER-SLOSS LJ. C was born on 10 April 1995 suffering from biliary atresia, a life-threatening liver defect. The unanimous medical prognosis is that he will not live beyond the age of two to two and a half without a liver transplantation. It is equally the unanimous clinical opinion of the consultants that it is in his *e* interests to undergo the operation when a donor liver becomes available. The parents, who were trained as health care professionals and are both experienced in the care of young sick children do not wish the operation to take place. The main issue before the judge and on appeal before this court is whether the court should overrule the decision of the parents and consent to the operation. It arises *f* as a specific issue in respect of which the court is asked to exercise its inherent jurisdiction.

The background to this tragic and deeply worrying case is as follows. The parents are not married but have a stable relationship. They decided to apply for jobs in a distant Commonwealth country (country AB). The father went to country AB in September 1995 while C and his mother remained in England with *g* her family. In February 1996 the mother took C to visit his father but returned with him in April to England. They went back to country AB in June 1996 and remain there now. The mother gave evidence to Connell J in the proceedings, the subject of this appeal, by video link.

Once C's liver defect was diagnosed the medical advice at the local hospital was *h* for him to undergo an operation called 'Kasai' with the hope that this would improve his condition. The parents agreed and he underwent the operation at the age of three and a half weeks but the outcome was unsuccessful. The mother's view of the proposed liver transplantation operation has been much influenced by the circumstances of the 'Kasai' operation and the pain and distress *j* caused to the baby both by it and by the consequential treatment. She and the father came to the conclusion, having sought medical advice, that if the 'Kasai' operation proved unsuccessful, they would not wish their baby to undergo major transplant surgery.

The mother and child were then referred to one of the few hospitals which carry out liver transplantation operations, which I shall call 'hospital X'. She met a the consultant paediatrician, Dr A, and her team and between September and November 1995 C was assessed for his suitability and found to be suitable to have the transplantation operation.   The mother was supplied with printed information about the operation, called Liver Transplantation An Introduction Fact Sheet 10. It said that it was—

b   'one of the most major forms of surgery. It is more complicated than other transplant operations on other organs and is only considered when other forms of treatment no longer maintain a good quality of life … The team will discuss the results of the tests with the parents and tell them whether their child or baby is a suitable candidate for transplant. It is a very big decision to make on the part of the family and every assistance will be given

c   to help to make the decision. If the family choose not to proceed with the transplantation once they are acquainted with the facts, this decision is respected. The child and family will continue to receive the necessary medical and nursing care to give him / her the best quality of life.'

The mother did not consent to the carrying out of the operation. Dr A made d it clear to the mother that it was in the best interests of C that the operation be carried out and could not accept the mother's reasons for refusing to consent. Inevitably, the relationship between Dr A and the mother became strained. Dr A told the mother that the hospital would seek legal advice if the mother did not consent. The mother obtained a second opinion from a consultant paediatrician, Dr P at hospital Y, another centre of liver transplant operations. Dr P set out his e conclusions in a letter dated 6 December 1995 which was sent to the mother's GP. Despite referring to adverse factors, which are no longer of significance in the light of later evidence, Dr P wrote:

'I would consider an excellent result of transplantation to be many years of life with normal growth and development with no treatment necessary f other than immunosuppression, and there is certainly a good chance that such an outcome could be achieved.'

He and his team strongly urged the mother to consent to the offer of transplantation at hospital X, but said that if she and the father after further consideration did not consent, that decision should be respected.

g C was placed on the urgent transplant list at hospital X. The mother then took him to country AB against the advice of Dr A. Whilst there, C was under the care of a consultant paediatrician, but there are no facilities for a liver transplant operation in that country. A suitable liver became available at hospital X while the mother was abroad with the baby, but the hospital was unable to get in touch h with the mother and the opportunity was lost. Dr A's team formed the view that the mother was not acting in the best interests of C and they took legal advice. The matter was referred to the local authority of the mother's area who involved their child protection team. The police in country AB were informed and visited the mother. The child was found to be well and happy. They concluded, j supported by the local social services, that no action was needed.

On the return of the mother and C to England in April they were again referred to hospital Y and Dr P was asked to take over the care of C. The mother continued to oppose the carrying out of the operation. Dr P discussed the matter with her at length on several occasions. He and his team formed the view that she was a loving and devoted mother, and, from her professional background, an unusually well-informed parent. They concluded that her reluctance to submit her son to the operation was founded in love and care for him. She was to the best of her ability discharging her duty of trust to her child and her decision should be respected.

The mother then returned to country AB with C and on 17 July 1996 the local authority sought the leave of the court to commence proceedings under the provisions of s 100(3) of the Children Act 1989. Their application was granted by Hollis J on 27 August 1996. The Official Solicitor was appointed guardian ad litem of the child and he instructed a consultant surgeon, Mr R, from hospital Z.

At the substantive hearing of the application of the local authority, Connell J heard evidence from Dr P, Mr R and Dr A, all distinguished consultants in this specialist field. Dr P accepted the opinion of Mr R as to the likely success of the transplant operation. In their reports and in their oral evidence the three doctors were unanimous that the prospects of success were good and that this operation was in the best interests of the child. Dr A and her team were prepared to carry out the operation without the consent of the mother if the court gave consent. The judge felt that the breakdown in the relationship between the mother and the team of Dr A made hospital X unsuitable in the best interests of C. Dr P and his team, while strongly recommending the operation, would wish to respect the decision of the mother and would not be prepared to perform the operation without her consent. Mr R was prepared to carry out the operation but could not answer for his team in the event that the mother did not consent.

The local authority in their originating summons sought the answers to three specific questions: (1) whether it was in the best interests of C to undergo surgery for a liver transplantation; (2) for permission to be granted to perform the surgery notwithstanding the refusal of the mother to consent, and (3) for the child to be returned to the jurisdiction for the purpose of such surgery. They were neutral before the judge and the proposed surgery was strongly advocated by C's guardian ad litem.

Connell J, on 17 September 1996, in a careful, comprehensive and sensitive judgment reviewed the reasons for the mother's refusal to consent and said:

'In my judgment it has proved impossible for this mother to accept the main burden of the advice of the doctors, which is to the effect that if C does not undergo a transplant he will die within the next 12 to 18 months. Clinging to her own ability to provide expert care for this little boy, and observing his apparent improvement in health, I am satisfied that she has not as yet really been able to face up to the clear and unanimous conclusion of the doctors that transplantation would be in his best interests. Whilst I can understand her difficulties, I conclude that her refusal to accept the unanimous advice of the doctors is not the conduct of a reasonable parent.'

He answered the three questions posed by the local authority in the affirmative and directed the return of the mother with C to the jurisdiction within 21 days in order to undergo the surgery for liver transplantation. He directed that the child be presented to hospital Y or hospital Z for assessment for transplantation. He concluded:

'In reaching a decision in cases such as this case the court is required to balance a number of factors. I have considered that quality of life which is likely to be available to the little boy post transplantation, and I have considered the pain and suffering which is likely to be undergone either with or without transplantation. There is of course a strong presumption in a favour of preserving life, but this is not an absolute rule. It is clear that C will die without transplantation, that treatment is available to him, and that it is recommended as in his best interests by the three doctors who gave evidence to the court. In all the circumstances, and in the light of all the evidence, I reach the clear conclusion that it is appropriate to make orders as sought.'

b He expressed the hope that the mother might change her mind and consent to the operation. He gave leave to appeal.

On the appeal Mr Francis QC, for the mother, informed us that the mother has not changed her mind and that she continued to be supported in her views by the father. He challenged the judge's conclusion that the mother's refusal to consent was unreasonable. He relied heavily upon the opinion of Dr P that he and his
c team respected the mother's decision and would not seek to go behind it and their view of the enormous importance of the total co-operation of the mother to the operation and the consequential treatment. In most medical situations there was more than one answer. The doctor's view was based upon clinical grounds, but where the welfare of a child required a family decision that decision if
d reasonable ought to be respected and the inherent jurisdiction of the court ought not to be exercised to overrule it. The more borderline the decision, the more weight should be given to the parent's view.

He stressed the possibility of further operations and further treatment and the effect upon the mother and upon the child. The choice was to allow the child a short life where he was well and happy for most of the time and would be likely
e to die peacefully or to cause him to undergo major invasive surgery with a good success rate but all the risks, discomfort and distress for a young child and a lifetime of drugs and the possibility of further invasive surgery and other treatment. The consequence of the decision was to commit the mother to a lifetime of care of the child with the requirement of total commitment to the
f treatment. The importance of the element of morale was not to be underestimated. The mother would find it very difficult to support the treatment, despite her specialist training and her devotion to the child. Since transplant operations have only been performed for 14 years on children, the statistics were inadequate as a guide for the future. He drew a distinction between extending life and allowing a child to die prematurely. The mother's
g decision was within that band of reasonable decisions with which the court should not interfere and coerce the mother.

Mr Harris QC, for the local authority, and Mr Murdoch QC, for the Official Solicitor as guardian ad litem of C, strongly supported the decision of the judge that the transplant operation was in the interests of C. They argued that the
h judge was entitled to come to the conclusion that the mother's refusal of consent was unreasonable in the light of unanimous medical opinion, that this was the accepted treatment and the surgery gave the child a good chance of an extended and a reasonable quality of life. The test was welfare of the child and not the reasonableness of the parent. The view of the parents was only one factor in the
j welfare test. We were reminded of the enormous strides which continue to be made in medical knowledge and techniques which supported the good prospects of success for the child. There was no reason to suppose that, if the operation was carried out, this mother with her special abilities would not respond to the needs of the child and care for him with devotion and competence. Mr Murdoch stressed that the practical difficulties were not insuperable and should be met if or when they arose.

I turn to consider previous decisions which set out the principles to be followed in an application such as this which invokes the inherent jurisdiction of the High Court. In recent years the medical profession and local authorities have increasingly sought declarations or directions from the High Court in difficult medical issues which involve ethical as well as medical considerations, for instance, abortion or sterilisation. Applications have also been made to the court in a number of cases which might affect the continued life of the child or adult. In the past applications in respect of children were made within the ambit of wardship. It is however clear that wardship is a mechanism within which to seek the decision of the High Court and it is not necessary to make the child a ward in order to invoke the inherent jurisdiction of the court (see Bingham MR in *Re Z (a minor) (freedom of publication)* [1995] 4 All ER 961 at 986, [1996] 2 WLR 88 at 113).

A line of cases from 1981 has, in my judgment, clearly established the approach of the court to these most difficult and anxious questions. In *Re B (a minor) (wardship: medical treatment)* (1981) [1990] 3 All ER 927, [1981] 1 WLR 1421 the child was born suffering from Down's Syndrome and from an intestinal blockage which required to be relieved by an operation if she were not to die within a few days. The surgeon respected the wishes of the parents not to consent to the operation and decided not to operate. The judge took the same view. This court allowed the appeal and held that the question for the court was whether it was in the best interests of the child that she should have the operation and not whether the wishes of the parents should be respected. In that case, the evidence disclosed that if the operation was performed the child would live the normal span of life of a mongol.

The House of Lords in *Re B (a minor) (wardship: sterilisation)* [1987] 2 All ER 206, [1988] AC 199 held that a court exercising wardship jurisdiction, when reaching a decision on an application to authorise an operation for sterilisation of the ward, was concerned with only one primary and paramount consideration, the welfare of the child.

This court in *Re J (a minor) (wardship: medical treatment)* [1990] 3 All ER 930, [1991] Fam 33 considered the future medical management of a severely brain-damaged premature baby with a considerably shortened life expectancy. Lord Donaldson MR said ([1990] 3 All ER 930 at 934, [1991] Fam 33 at 41):

'... it is sensible to define the relationship between the court, the doctors, the child and its parents. *The doctors* owe the child a duty to care for it in accordance with good medical practice recognised as appropriate by a competent body of professional opinion (see *Bolam v Friern Hospital Management Committee* [1957] 2 All ER 118, [1957] 1 WLR 582). This duty is, however, subject to the qualification that, if time permits, they must obtain the consent of the parents before undertaking serious invasive treatment. *The parents* owe the child a duty to give or to withhold consent in the best interests of the child and without regard to their own interests. *The court* when exercising the parens patriae jurisdiction takes over the rights and duties of the parents, although this is not to say that the parents will be excluded from the decision-making process. Nevertheless in the end the responsibility for the decision whether to give or to withhold consent is that of the court alone.' (Lord Donaldson MR's emphasis.)

He concluded ([1990] 3 All ER 930 at 938, [1991] Fam 33 at 46–47):

a
'*Re B* seems to me to come very near to being a binding authority for the proposition that there is a balancing exercise to be performed in assessing the course to be adopted in the best interests of the child. Even if it is not, I have no doubt that this should be and is the law. This brings me face to face with the problem of formulating the critical equation. In truth it cannot be done with mathematical or any precision. There is without doubt a very strong

b
presumption in favour of a course of action which will prolong life, but, even excepting the "cabbage" case to which special considerations may well apply, it is not irrebuttable. As this court recognised in *Re B*, account has to be taken of the pain and suffering and quality of life which the child will experience if life is prolonged. Account has also to be taken of the pain and suffering involved in the proposed treatment itself ... But in the end there will be cases

c
in which the answer must be that it is not in the interests of the child to subject it to treatment which will cause increased suffering and produce no commensurate benefit, giving the fullest possible weight to the child's and mankind's, desire to survive.'

d
In *Re Z (a minor) (freedom of publication)* [1995] 4 All ER 961, [1996] 2 WLR 88 the main issue was whether the child was to be identified and allowed to participate in a television film about her upbringing. The question whether the courts should intervene in a situation where a mother exercised her parental responsibilities bona fide and reasonably was directly before this court. Bingham MR said ([1995] 4 All ER 961 at 986, [1996] 2 WLR 88 at 113):

e
'I would for my part accept without reservation that the decision of a devoted and responsible parent should be treated with respect. It should certainly not be disregarded or lightly set aside. But the role of the court is to exercise an independent and objective judgment. If that judgment is in accord with that of the devoted and responsible parent, well and good. If it

f
is not, then it is the duty of the court, after giving due weight to the view of the devoted and responsible parent, to give effect to its own judgment. That is what it is there for. Its judgment may of course be wrong. So may that of the parent. But once the jurisdiction of the court is invoked its clear duty is to reach and express the best judgment it can.'

g
From the decisions to which I have referred which bind this court, it is clear that when an application under the inherent jurisdiction is made to the court the welfare of the child is the paramount consideration. The consent or refusal of consent of the parents is an important consideration to weigh in the balancing

h
exercise to be carried out by the judge. In that context, the extent to which the court will have regard to the view of the parent will depend upon the court's assessment of that view. But as Bingham MR said in *Re Z*, the court decides and in doing so may overrule the decision of a reasonable parent.

Applying those principles to the present appeal, the first argument of

j
Mr Francis that the court should not interfere with the reasonable decision of a parent is not one that we are able to entertain even if we wished to do so. His suggestion that the decision of this mother came within that band of reasonable decisions within which a court would not interfere would import into this jurisdiction the test applied in adoption to the refusal of a parent to consent to adoption. It is wholly inapposite to the welfare test and is incompatible with the decision in *Re Z*.

In my view however, the judge erred in his approach to the issue before the court. He accepted the unchallenged clinical opinion of the three consultants and assessed the reasonableness of the mother's decision against that medical opinion. Having held that the mother was unreasonable, he accepted that the liver transplant would be likely to prolong the life of C and in the absence of any reasonable argument to the contrary, he came to the clear conclusion that he should consent to the operation. Since he had already decided the mother's approach was unreasonable, he did not weigh in the balance reasons against the treatment which might be held by a reasonable parent on much broader grounds than the clinical assessment of the likely success of the proposed treatment. Some of the objections of the mother, such as the difficulties of the operation itself, turned out, from the evidence of Mr R, to be less important than the mother believed. Underlying those less important objections by the mother, was a deep seated concern of the mother as to the benefits to her son of the major invasive surgery and post-operative treatment, the dangers of failure long term as well as short term, the possibility of the need for further transplants, the likely length of life, and the effect upon her son of all these concerns. The judge did not assess the relevance or the weight of such considerations in his final balancing exercise.

In particular, he did not consider at that stage the evidence of Dr P and his strong reservations to the effect of coercing, (as Dr P put it), this mother into playing the crucial and irreplaceable part in the aftermath of major invasive surgery not just during the post-operative treatment of an eighteen month old baby but also throughout the childhood of her son. She would inevitably be the primary carer, (no one suggested that this baby should be taken into care) and would be expected to care for him for many years through surgery and continuing treatment while she, on her present view, believed that this course was not right for her son. The total commitment of the caring parent, in Dr P's view, was essential to the success of the treatment. Mr Harris suggested to us that Dr P's evidence supporting the mother's approach lacked logic and was woolly. That suggestion is, in my view, to underestimate the experience of a distinguished consultant paediatrician in a specialist and still experimental area of medicine. Moreover, his evidence was supported by the advice given to parents by hospital X in its Fact Sheet 10.

I have well in mind the important principles set out by the House of Lords in *G v G* [1985] 2 All ER 225, [1985] 1 WLR 647 and that this most experienced judge saw the witnesses and, in particular, the mother. If the decision in this case was a matter of assessing the clinical opinions of the doctors, the judge was clearly right to prefer their views to the mother who could not be as well qualified to give an opinion.

But this matter has to be looked at more broadly. The mother certainly told the judge that she recognised her son had only a short time to live if no operation was performed. She was focusing, it seems to me, on the present peaceful life of the child who had the chance to spend the rest of his short life without the pain, stress and upset of intrusive surgery against the future with the operation and treatment taking place. That is an alternative point of view to that to which the judge came and with some hesitation, I doubt that he was right to deem the mother to be unreasonable in her assessment of the broader perspective of whether this operation should be carried out. But in any event, the reasonableness of the mother was not the primary issue. This mother and this child are one for the purpose of this unusual case and the decision of the court to consent to the operation jointly affects the mother and son and it also affects the a father. The welfare of this child depends upon his mother. The practical considerations of her ability to cope with supporting the child in the face of her belief that this course is not right for him, the requirement to return probably for a long period to this country, either to leave the father behind and lose his support or to require him to give up his present job and seek one in England were not put by the judge into the balance when he made his decision.

b Despite the conclusion of the judge, which I have set out above, I do not believe that he put into the balance these broader considerations. Consequently, in my view his exercise of discretion was flawed and I am satisfied that his decision cannot stand.

It falls therefore for this court to make the decision whether to consent to the operation and require the return of the child to the jurisdiction. I agree with Mr
c Murdoch that this court ought not to make a decision on so difficult and delicate an issue mainly on the problems of ordering the return of the child when he is out of the jurisdiction, or in ignorance of whether hospital Z would in fact carry out the operation if the mother continued in her refusal to consent. But they are none the less relevant considerations which, in my judgment, have to be taken
d into account in the balancing exercise, although they are not determinative. More important than those considerations is, to my mind, the evidence of Dr P and the emphasis he placed throughout his evidence upon the requirements both of the consent of the parents and of a total commitment by the caring parent to the proposed treatment. He foresaw grave difficulties in carrying out the operation and the treatment without that wholehearted support of the mother.

e In Re W (a minor) (medical treatment) [1992] 4 All ER 627, [1993] Fam 64, a case about the medical treatment of a girl of 16 suffering from anorexia nervosa, Lord Donaldson MR said that there were two purposes to seeking consent, clinical and legal:

f 'The clinical purpose stems from the fact that in many instances the co-operation of the patient and the patient's faith or at least confidence in the efficacy of the treatment is a major factor contributing to the treatment's success.' (See [1992] 4 All ER 627 at 633, [1993] Fam 64 at 76.)

That passage applies, in my judgment, with equal force to the need for the confidence in and the commitment to the proposed treatment by the principal
g carer on the unusual facts of this case. Unlike the intestinal obstruction of the Down's Syndrome baby which could be cured by a simple operation, C's problems require complicated surgery and many years of special care from the mother.

The reservations of Dr P, to which he held despite concessions he made in his
h evidence, remain of great significance and importance. His view that the decision of a loving, caring mother should be respected, ought to be given great weight, and are reinforced by the Fact Sheet 10 provided by hospital X. The alternative of the court giving the consent and passing back the responsibility for the parental care to the mother and expecting her to provide the commitment to the child after the operation is carried out in the face of her opposition is in itself fraught
j with danger for the child. She will have to comply with the court order, return to this country and present the child to one of the hospitals. She will have to arrange to remain in this country for the foreseeable future. Will the father stay in country AB and work or come with her to England, giving up his job and having to seek another job? If he does not come she will have to manage unaided. How will the mother cope? Can her professionalism overcome her view that her

son should not be subjected to this distressing procedure? Will she break down? How will the child be affected by the conflict with which the mother may have to cope? What happens if the treatment is partially successful and another transplant is needed? The mother may not wish to consent to the further surgery. Is the court to be asked again for consent to the next operation?

The welfare of the child is the paramount consideration and I recognise the 'very strong presumption in favour of a course of action which will prolong life' and the inevitable consequences for the child of not giving consent. But to prolong life, as Lord Donaldson MR recognised in somewhat different circumstances, is not the sole objective of the court and to require it at the expense of other considerations may not be in a child's best interests. I would stress that, on the most unusual facts of this case with the enormous significance of the close attachment between the mother and baby, the court is not concerned with the reasonableness of the mother's refusal to consent but with the consequences of that refusal and whether it is in the best interests of C for this court in effect to direct the mother to take on this total commitment where she does not agree with the course proposed. The effect of the evidence of Dr P respecting the mother's decision and the prospect of forcing the devoted mother of this young baby to the consequences of this major invasive surgery lead me to the conclusion, after much anxious deliberation, that it is not in the best interests of this child to give consent and require him to return to England for the purpose of undergoing liver transplantation. I believe that the best interests of this child require that his future treatment should be left in the hands of his devoted parents. Once the pressure of this litigation is over it may be the parents will reconsider whether they should remain in country AB or should return to this country and attend at hospital Y with a view to a further assessment for the purpose of carrying out the operation. That, however, will be a matter for them and not for this court.

I would allow this appeal and would answer the three questions posed in the originating summons in the negative and would set aside the orders of the judge.

WAITE LJ. I agree. The law's insistence that the welfare of a child shall be paramount is easily stated and universally applauded, but the present case illustrates, poignantly and dramatically, the difficulties that are encountered when trying to put it into practice. Throughout his clear and able judgment, the judge demonstrated his appreciation of the dilemma to which the case gives rise. Loving and devoted parents have taken, after anxious consideration, a decision to withhold consent to operative transplant treatment. Although it is relatively novel treatment, still unavailable in many countries, doctors of the highest expertise have unanimously recommended it for this child on clinical grounds, taking the view that it involves a relatively minor level of risk which they regard as well worth taking in the child's long-term interests (which in this instance include an extension of life itself). The parents' opposition is partly instinctive and (being based on their own awareness of the procedures involved) partly practical. It has sufficient cogency to have led one of the principal medical experts in the field of this operation to say that his team would decline to operate without the mother's committed support.

What is the court to do in such a situation? It is not an occasion—even in an age preoccupied with 'rights'—to talk of the rights of a child, or the rights of a parent, or the rights of the court. The cases cited by Butler-Sloss LJ are uncompromising in their assertion that the sole yardstick must be the need to *a* give effect to the demands of paramountcy for the welfare of the child. They establish that there are bound to be occasions when such paramountcy will compel the court, acting as a judicial parent, to substitute the judge's own views as to the claims of child welfare over those of natural parents—even in a case where the views of the latter are supported by qualities of devotion, commitment, love and reason. The judge, after anxious consideration, reached

b the conclusion that this case provides such an occasion. Was he right to do so?

Of course if his decision was founded on a correct application of legal principle, it is unassailable, however tempted individual members of an appellate court might be to substitute a judgment of our own. These decisions, not least because they are so difficult and finely balanced, are best left to the discretion of the experienced judges who have the task, often a lonely and worrying one, of

c weighing the numerous delicate elements (including the view taken of the parties and witnesses) which enable a cumulative picture to be formed of the demands of welfare in a particular case, and taking the momentous decision which the child patient cannot take for himself.

In this instance, however, in agreement with Butler-Sloss LJ, I consider that the

d judge was betrayed into an error of law by his concern with the need to form a judgment about the reasonableness of the mother's approach. An appraisal of parental reasonableness may be appropriate in other areas of family law (in adoption, for example, where it is enjoined by statute), but when it comes to an assessment of the demands of the child patient's welfare, the starting point—and the finishing point too—must always be the judge's own independent assessment

e of the balance of advantage or disadvantage of the particular medical step under consideration.

In striking that balance, the judge will of course take into account as a relevant, often highly relevant, factor the attitude taken by a natural parent, and that may require examination of his or her motives. But the result of such an inquiry must

f never be allowed to prove determinative. It is a mistake to view the issue as one in which the clinical advice of doctors is placed in one scale and the reasonableness of the parent's view in the other. Had the judge viewed the evidence more broadly from the standpoint of his own perception of the child's welfare when appraised in all its aspects, he would have been bound, in my view, to take significant account of other elements in the case. Those include the

g parents' ties in country AB, and—crucially—the evidence of Dr P.

No one disputes that in the aftermath of the operation the child would remain in the primary care of the mother. Dr P maintained a very clear view that—even assuming that the operation proved wholly successful in surgical terms—the child's subsequent development could be injuriously affected if his day-to-day

h care depended upon the commitment of a mother who had suffered the turmoil of having her child being compelled against her will to undergo, as a result of a coercive order from the court, a major operation against which her own medical and maternal judgment wholeheartedly rebelled.

All these cases depend on their own facts and render generalisations—

j tempting though they may be to the legal or social analyst—wholly out of place. It can only be said safely that there is a scale, at one end of which lies the clear case where parental opposition to medical intervention is prompted by scruple or dogma of a kind which is patently irreconcilable with principles of child health and welfare widely accepted by the generality of mankind; and that at the other end lie highly problematic cases where there is genuine scope for a difference of view between parent and judge. In both situations it is the duty of the judge to allow the court's own opinion to prevail in the perceived paramount interests of the child concerned, but in cases at the latter end of the scale, there must be a likelihood (though never of course a certainty) that the greater the scope for genuine debate between one view and another the stronger will be the inclination of the court to be influenced by a reflection that in the last analysis the best interests of every child include an expectation that difficult decisions affecting the length and quality of its life will be taken for it by the parent to whom its care has been entrusted by nature.

I too would allow this appeal and substitute the order proposed by Butler-Sloss LJ.

ROCH LJ. This is a desperately difficult case.

The medical evidence was, as the judge stressed, unanimous on the prognosis for this child if he did not receive a transplanted liver; he will die in a matter of months. The doctors went further and said that despite those matters which mean that the child is not the ideal recipient of a liver transplant, he was nevertheless a good candidate with good prospects for a favourable outcome.

On the other hand, no one suggests that the child's parents are not responsible parents who are devoted to this child or that they have not spent much time and thought in reaching their decision that their son should not undergo a liver transplant and the treatment that will inevitably follow such an operation. The evidence indicated that because of their training and experience they are 'uniquely well qualified' to make a decision. In my view, it cannot be said on the evidence that was before the judge that their decision was unreasoned.

What principles should apply to a case such as this? The paramount principle is that the court must make the decision which it considers to be in the best interests of the child. In reaching that decision how should the court treat the decisions of parents? I would gratefully adopt the words of Bingham MR in *Re Z (a minor) (freedom of publication)* [1995] 4 All ER 961 at 986, [1996] 2 WLR 88 at 113, where he said:

> 'I would for my part accept without reservation that the decision of a devoted and responsible parent should be treated with respect. It should certainly not be disregarded or lightly set aside. But the role of the court is to exercise an independent and objective judgment. If that judgment is in accord with that of the devoted and responsible parent, well and good. If it is not, then it is the duty of the court, after giving due weight to the view of the devoted and responsible parent, to give effect to its own judgment. That is what it is there for. Its judgment may of course be wrong. So may that of the parent. But once the jurisdiction of the court is invoked its clear duty is to reach and express the best judgment it can.'

The issue then is what is in the best interests of the child? One factor in determining that issue to be taken into account by the court is the decision of devoted and responsible parents. It is, I would suggest, misleading to ask, once it is accepted that the parents are devoted and responsible, whether their decision is reasonable or unreasonable because parents who are responsible and devoted will almost certainly reach a decision which falls within the range of decisions which can be classed as reasonable. If the decision falls outside the range of permissible decisions, it is unlikely that the parents are responsible and devoted parents who have sought only to decide in the best interests of their child.

a
In my judgment, the judge mislead himself by categorising the parent's decision as being unreasonable. I can see nothing to justify the judge's conclusion that the child's mother is deluding herself that with her care the child miraculously will survive beyond that period of time forecast by the doctors, or that the parents have failed to grasp the improvements in operating technique and subsequent treatment which have taken place in the field of liver

b
transplantation in recent years, particularly in view of Dr P's evidence of the protracted and thorough discussions he has had with the mother.

If the proper stance for parents is that whenever there is a treatment which may prolong the life of their child, then that treatment should be accepted, a decision not to accept that treatment would be unreasonable. But in my opinion that cannot be and will not be the answer in every case. Nor are such decisions

c
to be taken solely with medical factors in mind. The presumption in favour of the sustaining of life is not irrebuttable and perhaps has less weight where the issue is whether to prolong or not to prolong life by means of organ transplantation.

The view of the parents in a liver transplant case has two aspects. First, if, as

d
here, the parents are devoted and responsible and have the best interests of their child in mind, then their views are to be taken into account and accorded weight and respect by the court when reaching its decision. Second, the views of the parents have a clinical significance because in the absence of parental belief that a transplant is the right procedure for the child, the prospects of a successful

e
outcome are diminished. This factor explains the stance adopted at hospital Y. It may also explain the passage in Fact Sheet 10, published by the Children's Liver Disease Foundation and given to the mother in this case, in which this sentence appears: 'If the family choose not to proceed with the transplantation once they are acquainted with the facts, this decision is respected.'

f
I have formed the view that the judge was wrong to categorise the parent's decision as unreasonable and to disregard it in the balancing exercise he had to perform; the judge, therefore, misdirected himself, and we, in this court should exercise the court's inherent jurisdiction.

There are formidable practical difficulties in this case which stand in the way of implementing the order which the judge in fact made. The child's father works

g
abroad. The mother and the child and the father at present are living together. If the mother does not comply with the order, it is not certain whether the courts of the country in which they live will assist in any proceedings to oblige the mother to comply or how long such proceedings would take. The order involves the child and the mother returning to this country, although the financial ability

h
of the family to pay for that is uncertain, particularly if it is necessary for a doctor to accompany the child during the journey. The return of the child to this country must involve both mother and child in distress which will arise from leaving the father and their home, and that must in turn increase the risk that such a journey poses for this child. On arrival in this country it is clear that the

j
operation could not be performed at hospital Y, the hospital that the mother would choose were she disposed to seek a transplant for her child, because that hospital will not perform such an operation without the mother's willing consent. There is another possible centre at which such an operation might be performed, hospital Z. Whereas the surgeon at that centre has indicated that he would be prepared to perform such an operation although the mother was not consenting, it is not clear whether the remainder of the medical team at that

centre would be of his view or whether they would take the view set out in Fact Sheet No 10.

Then there is the question of treatment following the operation. Are the mother and child to stay in this country? If they are to stay, for how long? If further transplant operations become necessary will the mother give or withhold her consent? What will be the position if at such time the mother and child have returned to country AB?

At present the evidence indicates that this child has a happy and secure life with his parents in country AB. It is true that that life will be a very short life which will end when the child is still a baby, but at a time before the child can become aware of the significance of his condition and its consequences.

I do not consider that it is in the child's best interests to disrupt his present life by the court giving its consent to his undergoing a liver transplant operation and ordering the mother to return with him to this country with all the distress and uncertainties that that will inevitably entail for the child in the special circumstances that exist in this case.

I agree that this appeal should be allowed.

Appeal allowed. Leave to appeal to the House of Lords refused.

Paul Magrath Esq   Barrister.

Johnson and another v Davies and another

CHANCERY DIVISION

JACOB J

29 NOVEMBER, 5 DECEMBER 1996

Insolvency – Voluntary arrangement – Solvent co-debtors – Effect of arrangement on solvent co-debtors – Plaintiff shareholders sureties under lease taken by company – Plaintiffs selling shares and purchasers agreeing to indemnify them against claims under lease – Plaintiffs meeting claim under lease and seeking indemnity from purchasers – Individual purchaser entering into voluntary arrangement with creditors – Plaintiffs voting for arrangement at creditors' meeting – Whether arrangement extinguishing liability of solvent co-debtors to plaintiffs – Whether arrangement releasing co-debtors from debt by operation of law.

In 1989 the plaintiffs, who were sureties under a lease taken by a company in which they owned practically all of the shares, sold their shares in the company to the two defendants and a third person, H. The company subsequently failed and a claim was made against the plaintiffs under the lease, which they met. Thereafter H entered into an individual voluntary arrangement with his creditors under Pt VIII of the Insolvency Act 1986. The plaintiffs were given notice of the creditors' meeting and voted for the arrangement and were consequently deemed to be parties to the arrangement and bound by it pursuant to s 260(2)[a] of the 1986 Act. The plaintiffs brought proceedings against the defendants to recover the sum they had had to pay under the lease, alleging that the defendants and H had in the share sale agreement agreed to indemnify them against all claims arising therefrom, and applied for summary judgment under RSC Ord 14. The defendants contended that the effect of H's voluntary arrangement was to extinguish their liability to the plaintiffs on the grounds that a co-debtor was released by operation of law when a debt was taken into account in a debtor's voluntary arrangement, or at least where the creditor had voted for it. The deputy district judge dismissed the plaintiffs' application and the plaintiffs appealed.

Held – By virtue of s 260(2) of the 1986 Act a voluntary arrangement bound every person who had notice of, and was entitled to vote at, the creditors' meeting as if he were a party to the arrangement. However, such persons were bound solely by the statute and the voluntary arrangement, whether or not the creditor had voted for it, did not constitute a contract with the debtor, nor did it affect the creditors' rights against third parties unless it expressly said so. Since, in the instant case, the voluntary arrangement only released H from his liability to the plaintiffs and did not seek to deal with the position between the plaintiffs and third parties, it did not have the effect of releasing solvent third party co-debtors and so had not extinguished the defendants' liability to the plaintiffs. The defence therefore failed and the appeal would accordingly be allowed (see p 924 h, p 925 b c f and p 928 b h j, post).

RA Securities Ltd v Mercantile Credit Co Ltd [1995] 3 All ER 581 applied.

---

a   Section 260 (2), so far as material, is set out at p 924 h j, post

Notes

For the effect and implementation of individual voluntary arrangements, see 3(2) *Halsbury's Laws* (4th edn reissue) paras 100–109, and for a case on the subject, see 4(1) *Digest* (2nd reissue) 174, *1514*.

For the Insolvency Act 1986, s 260, see 4 *Halsbury's Statutes* (4th edn) (1987 reissue) 904.

Cases referred to in judgment

Bradley-Hole (a bankrupt), Re [1995] 4 All ER 865, [1995] 1 WLR 1097.
Burford Midland Properties Ltd v Marley Extrusions Ltd [1994] BCC 604.
Deanplan Ltd v Mahmoud [1992] 3 All ER 945, [1993] Ch 151, [1992] 3 WLR 467.
EWA (a debtor), Re [1901] 2 KB 642, CA.
Finch v Jukes [1877] WN 211.
March Estates plc v Gunmark Ltd [1996] 32 EG 75.
Mytre Investments Ltd v Reynolds [1995] 3 All ER 588.
Pybus v Gibb (1856) 6 E & B 902, 119 ER 1100.
RA Securities Ltd v Mercantile Credit Co Ltd [1995] 3 All ER 581.
Watts v Aldington, Tolstoy v Aldington (1993) Times, 16 December, [1993] CA Transcript 1578.

Cases also cited or referred to in skeleton arguments

AE Realisations (1985) Ltd, Re [1987] 3 All ER 83, [1988] 1 WLR 200.
Commercial Banking Co of Sydney Ltd v Gaty [1978] 2 NSWLR 271, NSW SC.
Doorbar v Alltime Securities Ltd [1996] 2 All ER 948, [1996] 1 WLR 456, CA.
Garner's Motors Ltd, Re [1937] 1 All ER 671, [1937] Ch 594.
Hill v Anderson Meat Industries Ltd [1972] 2 NSWLR 704, NSW CA.
Hindcastle Ltd v Barbara Attenborough Associates Ltd [1996] 1 All ER 737, [1997] AC 70, HL.
Jacobs, Ex p, re Jacobs (1875) LR 10 Ch App 211.
Megrath v Gray, Gray v Megrath (1874) LR 9 CP 216.
Naeem (a bankrupt), Re (No 18 of 1988) [1990] 1 WLR 48.
Wilson v Lloyd (1873) LR 16 Eq 60.

Appeal

By notice dated 23 May 1996 the plaintiffs, Robert Arthur Johnson and Anne Johnson, appealed from the decision of Deputy District Judge Radcliffe on 14 May 1996 in the Brighton District Registry refusing their application for summary judgment under RSC Ord 14 in respect of their claim against the defendants, Suzanne Davies and Nicholas Cole, for moneys due under an indemnity agreement made between the parties. The facts are set out in the judgment.

Christopher Wilson (instructed by *Aldrich Crowther & Wood*, Brighton) for the plaintiffs.
Clifford Darton (instructed by *Judge Sykes & Harrison*) for the first defendant and (instructed by *Edward Harte & Co*, Brighton) for the second defendant.

Cur adv vult

5 December 1996. The following judgment was delivered.

JACOB J. This is a plaintiffs' appeal from the decision dated 14 May 1996 of Deputy District Judge Radcliffe sitting in the Brighton District Registry. The application was for summary judgment under the provisions of RSC Ord 14 and a determination of a number of points of law pursuant to Ord 14A. Although the sum involved is comparatively small the appeal raises a question of general importance in relation to the effect of an individual voluntary arrangement (IVA) under the provisions of the Insolvency Act 1986. It was extremely well argued by counsel on both sides and I am grateful to them both.

b THE FACTS

The plaintiffs are two individuals, Robert Arthur Johnson and Anne Johnson. Originally they owned practically all the shares in a company. The company took a lease from a landlord, L. The plaintiffs were sureties under that lease. In 1989 the plaintiffs sold their shares in the company to three individuals, namely the two present defendants, Suzanne Davies and Nicholas Cole, and a Mr Hopkins.
c They also resigned their directorships and ceased to have any connection with the company. The plaintiffs say that by virtue of the share sale agreement the purchasers (namely the defendants and Mr Hopkins) agreed to indemnify the plaintiffs against all claims arising out of the lease. The next they heard was in 1993 when they were informed that the company had failed and that a claim was
d being made against them on the indemnity they had given in the lease. They had to meet that claim and accordingly seek to rely on the indemnity from the defendants contained in the share sale agreement. The lease has now come to an end, so there is no problem about any ongoing liability for rent. The plaintiffs claim from the defendants what they had to pay, after appropriate adjustments with which I am not concerned.
e
On 19 April 1994, following the relevant procedural steps pursuant to the 1986 Act, Mr Hopkins entered into an IVA with his creditors. The plaintiffs were given notice of the meeting and voted for the IVA. As it happens if they had voted against the proposal for an IVA it would not have got the necessary 75% in value majority called for by r 5.18 of the Insolvency Rules 1986, SI 1986/1925. One of
f the defendants, but not the other, was also given notice of the meeting. Under the IVA the creditors were to be paid 11p in the pound. Two provisions of the IVA read as follows:

g '4. When all monies to be made available under these proposals have been realised and distributed to creditors in accordance with the terms herein I [ie Mr Hopkins] will be released from any further liability to them relating to claims in respect of which they were entitled to participate in this Voluntary Arrangement.

h 15. When all assets to be made available under these proposals have been realised and distributed to the creditors in accordance with the terms herein, I will be released from any further liability to them relating to claims in respect of which they were entitled to participate in this Voluntary Arrangement.'

j In summarising these facts I have omitted what is now agreed to be an immaterial complication, namely that at one point L granted a concurrent lease to another company. This was the subject of a point taken by the defendants before the deputy district judge. He held against the defendants on this point. Mr Darton, for the defendants, sensibly concluded that the judge was right on this point and abandoned it. He likewise abandoned another point about whether or not the 1989 agreement was a guarantee or an indemnity.

THE ISSUES

That leaves two issues to be determined. First have the plaintiffs proved to the *a* standard of Ord 14 that the defendants gave the indemnity relied upon and second, does the IVA with Mr Hopkins release the defendants?

Was there an indemnity?

The problem is this: the plaintiffs are unable to produce the original of the 1989 share sale agreement. The best they can do is rely upon the following matters: *b* that a draft, signed by the first plaintiff for both plaintiffs was in the possession of the defendants, that the shares in the company were undoubtedly paid for and transferred to the defendants and Mr Hopkins, that the defendants and Mr Hopkins took over the company, and that the plaintiffs' solicitor recalls that the defendants did sign the agreement. Further there is contemporaneous *c* correspondence supporting the existence of a contract. The solicitor deposes that he has been unable to find the signed agreement. The defendants do not say there was no contract or that the draft contract produced in fact contains the terms to which they agreed. They just say they do not remember.

The deputy district judge took the view that the evidence of the plaintiffs' solicitor was not a firm enough foundation for Ord 14 and that his recollection *d* may be successfully challenged on cross-examination. However, the defendants are in this difficulty: there plainly was an agreement of some sort. They are unable to suggest any agreement other than that signed by the plaintiffs. It is wholly improbable that the plaintiffs would not have taken an indemnity. And Mr Darton fairly and sensibly accepted that the evidence (apart from a possible *e* challenge to the solicitor's recollection) would not change at trial. I think in the circumstances there is no realistic prospect of the plaintiffs being unable to prove that there was indeed an indemnity.

The effect of the IVA

This is a pure point of law. The defendants say that the effect of the IVA with *f* Mr Hopkins is to extinguish their liability to the plaintiffs. They say first that any co-debtor is released by operation of law when the debt is taken into account in a debtor's IVA. Recognising that this would include the case where the creditor had voted against the IVA (producing the monstrous result that a creditor would, against his will, lose a perfectly good claim against a solvent co-debtor) they say alternatively that at least this is the case where the creditor votes for the IVA. *g*

The solution to the problem depends, on one view, on the correct juridical analysis of an IVA. Is the arrangement to be regarded as 'quasi-contractual' (as Mr Darton put it) or is it an arrangement whose effect is simply provided for in the statute? Section 260(2) of the 1986 Act provides:

h

'The approved arrangement ... (b) binds every person who in accordance with the rules had notice of, and was entitled to vote at, the meeting (whether or not he was present or represented at it) as if he were a party to the arrangement.'

In *RA Securities Ltd v Mercantile Credit Co Ltd* [1995] 3 All ER 581 I had to consider *j* the effect of the corresponding parallel provision relating to company voluntary arrangements in the 1986 Act, namely s 5. I said (at 585):

'Turning back to s 5, does "binds every person" have any effect outside the voluntary arrangement? I think not. The effect of the binding is solely as between the parties bound, those entitled to vote, whether they did or not. An outsider, such as T1, can get no assistance from the terms of the

a voluntary arrangement as such. Of course if something is actually done as a result of the arrangement (e g property transferred, or as might have but did not happen here, surrender of a lease) then an outsider can rely upon that. But his right to rely upon it must result from an actual act done, not the arrangement.'

I remain of that view. It is unnecessary to spell out of the statute anything more than that. I see no reason to think that when a creditor votes for or against an IVA he is doing anything more than just voting for or against a statutory binding. He is not entering into a contract with the debtor or with his co-creditors and he is not purporting (unless the document expressly says so) to touch his rights against third parties. Either the IVA is approved, when it has the legal consequences set out in the Act, or it is not, in which case the debtor will probably go into bankruptcy. And I remain of the view that an IVA (or a company voluntary arrangement) does not have the effect of releasing perfectly solvent co-debtors. The Act does not say it does and I do not see why in principle it should have that effect. As I said in the *RA Securities* case (at 584):

'The purpose of voluntary arrangements is to enable a company (or individual, for which case provision is made in Pt VIII) to come to a composition with creditors so that the more drastic step of liquidation or bankruptcy can be avoided, if possible. It is better to keep the show on the road than close it down even if creditors have to accept less than their nominal (but not achievable) entitlement. The whole scheme is not for the benefit of solvent parties who happen to owe debts also owed by the debtor. It would in my judgment be unfair if a solvent debtor escaped liability as a sidewind of the voluntary arrangement system.'

Mr Darton accepted that an IVA did not constitute a contract. But, he said, that did not matter. It still operated to extinguish the debt. He relied on the principle that the release of one joint debtor (or covenantor) will release the other joint debtors (or covenantors) unless the creditor's (covenantee's) rights against the latter are reserved, referring to *Re EWA (a debtor)* [1901] 2 KB 642 and *Deanplan Ltd v Mahmoud* [1992] 3 All ER 945, [1993] Ch 151. In *Re EWA* Collins LJ said:

'If this legal consequence had been pointed out to the bank at the time, they might have said that that was not what they intended, but that is a factor common probably to all cases in which a release is given to one of two joint debtors. The person giving it may not realize the full legal consequences of it as regards the release of the co-debtor; but that is not, in my opinion, a sufficient ground for reading into the document something that is not expressed in it; and unless you find in it something qualifying the general words, it appears to me that the legal consequences of the general words of discharge must follow, notwithstanding that those consequences may go beyond what the person giving the document would have intended if they had been pointed out to him at the time, and he had had an opportunity of addressing his mind to them.' (See [1901] 2 KB 642 at 649–650.)

And in the *Deanplan* case three reasons for the rule were identified by Judge Paul Baker QC: (1) there is only one obligation; (2) the covenantee cannot have both the promised performance and some other performance which he agrees to accept; and (3) unless the co-covenantors are also released they could claim a right of contribution or indemnity from the covenantor who entered into the release (see [1992] 3 All ER 945 at 959–960, [1993] Ch 151 at 170). Mr Darton said that even if the arrangement was purely statutory, so reason (2) did not apply, reasons (1) and (3) still did. As to reason (1) I do not think that an IVA operates to destroy the obligation as such. It merely binds the creditor (by virtue of s 260(2)) to an alternative. In practice that alternative is merely payment of a sum less than that which is due. If he agreed to accept less directly with the debtor, it is worth noticing that his agreement would have no consideration and would not be binding—it could hardly then amount to accord and satisfaction releasing a co-debtor.

As to reason (3) there is some force in what Mr Darton says. If a co-debtor is not released then he may upset it by claiming contribution from the debtor. This may pose a problem where he is not bound by the IVA (eg because he was not given notice or had only a contingent claim). He could go against the debtor and possibly upset the IVA, though the possibility of a further IVA varying the first would exist. Mr Darton adds this would be particularly unfair on the co-debtor if, as Rimer J held in *Re Bradley-Hole (a debtor)* [1995] 4 All ER 865, [1995] 1 WLR 1097 the assets the subject of an IVA did not vest in a trustee in bankruptcy but remained in a trust of which the trustee was the nominee of the IVA. (I was told that this decision has been questioned on the basis that normally a debtor cannot put his assets beyond the reach of creditors by putting them into a trust. I do not think it is necessary for me to consider it further here.)

But although there is some force in what Mr Darton says, I do not think it is sufficient to hold that the accord and satisfaction rule applies to an IVA. Most significantly the Act does not say it does. Further if the rule did apply no creditor, sensibly advised, would ever vote for an IVA when he had a solvent co-debtor to go against. This in practice could frustrate many a proposed IVA. It is true that the co-debtor may attack the debtor if not himself bound, but in practice there may be little point. And the creditor will often get more recovery from the debtor via an IVA (thus indirectly benefiting the co-debtor) than via a bankruptcy. Here, for instance, Mr Hopkins paid 11p in the pound, which, on the figures in the IVA proposal, is more than a bankruptcy would have been likely to yield.

Mr Darton suggested that the creditor could protect his right against co-debtors by insisting upon an express reservation of his right at the meeting. If he did not get it, then he could be protected by an appeal to the court under s 262. Implicit in this suggestion is that the court would never allow a creditor to lose his right against a co-debtor, which is not an explicit limitation on the court's powers. In practice the consequence of such an insistence would be that many an IVA would fail at the outset.

Before turning to the second way the plaintiffs put their case I should touch upon certain further matters concerning my decision in the *RA Securities* case. First, I commented on a passage in Andrews and Millett *Law of Guarantees* (1st edn, 1992). I said ([1995] 3 All ER 581 at 586–587):

> 'This does not adopt the *Chitty* view, suggesting as a better analysis the notion that a voluntary arrangement is in effect a statutory variation of pre-existing contractual rights. It follows, the authors argue, that the common law effect of discharge of a surety by a consensual discharge of the debtor (without reservation of a right against the surety) will apply in a voluntary arrangement. This analysis to my mind turns a statutory binding into a consent and is in error.'

I remain of that view. The authors, in *Andrews and Millett* (2nd edn, 1995) p 244 say:

a   'In *RA* Jacob J disapproved this argument on the ground that a statutory binding cannot be equated with a consent. However it is difficult to see why the fact that the satisfaction of the debt under the voluntary arrangement is statutory rather than consensual on a creditor by creditor basis should make any difference to the result. Indeed in *Finch v Jukes* [1877] WN 211, it was held that a surety for performance of obligations under a building contract

b   was discharged when the obligations of the principal were altered by an Act of Parliament.'

The authors then, in a footnote, cite *Pybus v Gibb* (1856) 6 E & B 902, 119 ER 1100 and observe that neither this case nor *Finch's* case was cited to me in the *RA Securities* case. That is true, but I do not think either case relevant. In both what

c   happened was that the defendant had agreed to act as surety for obligation X, but, by Act of Parliament, that obligation had been varied to obligation Y. The court asked in each case whether the position of the surety was so altered that he must be treated as being discharged—the inquiry being the extent of the difference between X and Y.

d   Next it may be observed that the *RA Securities* case has not been questioned in three subsequent cases, namely *Burford Midland Properties Ltd v Marley Extrusions Ltd* [1994] BCC 604, *Mytre Investments Ltd v Reynolds* [1995] 3 All ER 588 and *March Estates plc v Gunmark Ltd* [1996] 32 EG 75. Now it is true that in the *Burford* case Judge Cooke QC, sitting as a deputy judge of the High Court, took the contractual route, holding that on the construction of the IVA concerned, third parties were not absolved. And in *March Estates plc v Gunmark* Lightman J allowed

e   for the possibility that an IVA may affect third party rights. He said (at 76–77):

f   'A voluntary arrangement may expressly or by necessary implication regulate the rights *inter se* of a creditor of the company and of third parties liable for the same debt: consider *Burford Midland Properties Ltd v Marley Extrusions Ltd* [1994] BCC 604. Exceptional circumstances may justify this course. But if this is to be the case, the intention to regulate such rights must be made plain on the face of the proposal. Of course notice of the meeting must also be given to those affected. In this way, those affected will know what is at stake, can make representations and vote at the meeting

g   accordingly, and if necessary can within the statutory 28-day period apply to the court under section 6 of the Act (as to which see below) to revoke or suspend the approval of the meeting if this provision in the proposal unfairly prejudices their interests. But in the absence of either of these statutory safeguards to the interests of those affected being complied with, any arrangement can only affect the company alone, leaving unaffected the

h   rights of the creditor against third parties. The voluntary arrangement may statutorily absolve the company from liability without absolving or releasing from liability any other party and will ordinarily be construed as reserving all rights of creditors against other parties: see *RA Securities* and *Mytre Investments Ltd v Reynolds* [1995] 3 All ER 588.'

j   I do not think this in any way conflicts with my view that an IVA is in itself a mere statutory binding. If it expressly or by necessary implication deals with the position as between a creditor and a co-debtor that binding may have an effect. If the co-debtor is a party to the IVA he may be bound directly by statute. If he is not a party then he cannot take advantage directly of the IVA. In some cases there may be machinery which could operate to prevent the creditor from going against the third party, for instance a plea of estoppel by convention (which I have not investigated) or, by the third party turning on the debtor who, by virtue of the IVA, would be able to prevent the creditor from proceeding against the third party.

The significance of the conclusion that an IVA operates to bind the parties to it merely by statute as compared by contract is that it is for the statute to spell out the consequences. It does not absolve solvent third party co-debtors: it merely binds the parties to the IVA. This IVA only releases Mr Hopkins from liability to the plaintiffs and does not seek to deal with the position between the plaintiffs and third parties. It is not a necessary implication that it goes any further.

Further, however, even if an IVA is to be regarded as something like a contract it is a question of construction as to whether it releases third parties. This IVA does not say it does. Mr Wilson, for the plaintiffs, drew my attention to the Court of Appeal case of *Watts v Aldington, Tolstoy v Aldington* (1993) Times, 16 December. A large sum by way of damages and costs had been awarded to Lord Aldington against Count Tolstoy and a Mr Watts. Lord Aldington entered into a settlement with Mr Watts whereby a much lesser sum was accepted (along with other matters providing a consideration). A term of the settlement provided:

'That Lord Aldington undertakes to accept the said sum in full and final settlement of the judgment and orders referred to above and any liability howsoever arising before today's date which could involve any payment directly or indirectly to Lord Aldington.'

Even though that clause was a good deal more explicit than the clause here, the Court of Appeal held that it did not absolve Mr Watt's co-debtor, Count Tolstoy. Morritt J's solution to the problem—that the agreement was merely an agreement not to sue (the well-settled escape route from the rule in *Re EWA*)—was rejected. But each of Neill, Steyn and Simon Brown LJJ held that the rule in *Re EWA* (which they accepted, reluctantly in the case of Steyn LJ, was binding) did not apply where the presumed intention of the parties was not to absolve the co-debtor, such intention to be learned from the language used and the surrounding circumstances. They were willing, in the circumstances of that case, to imply such a term. I would do likewise in this case. In particular, since this is not one of actual contract, one must focus on what was the intention of the creditors. Clearly if they voted against the IVA they could not be consenting to a release of the co-debtor. If they voted for the IVA I see no reason why, unless that was expressly what was involved in what they were voting for, they should be held to have voted for a release of a co-debtor. On the contrary, if the voter was asked 'are you voting for a release' the answer would clearly be a testy No.

In the result the IVA defence fails. I am not sorry. I think it would be absurd if the two sureties were better off because there was a third surety who failed (although contributing something to payment of the debt), than if they had stood alone. Similarly it would be very bizarre if the creditors were worse off because they had a further surety in addition to the two defendants. The actual result means that instead of shouldering a third of the liability, each of the defendants will have to take on something like 45%. That does not seem particularly unfair.

Accordingly the appeal succeeds. I will hear counsel.

Appeal allowed.

Celia Fox   Barrister.

Harrow London Borough Council v Johnstone

HOUSE OF LORDS

LORD BROWNE-WILKINSON, LORD JAUNCEY OF TULLICHETTLE, LORD MUSTILL, LORD HOFFMANN AND LORD CLYDE

4, 5 NOVEMBER 1996, 13 MARCH 1997

Landlord and tenant – Tenancy – Joint tenancy – Determination – Determination of secure tenancy held by two or more joint tenants – Determination of tenancy by one joint tenant by notice to quit without consent of the other – Tenant giving notice to quit to landlord while subject to non-molestation order – Landlord taking possession proceedings against other tenant – Whether notice to quit constituting breach of non-molestation order – Whether landlord in contempt by taking possession proceedings.

In 1989 the respondent and his wife became secure tenants of a council house owned by the appellant council. In 1994 the wife left taking the children with her. The husband remained in possession of the house and on 3 February obtained an injunction restraining the wife, whether by herself 'or by instructing or encouraging any other person', from using or threatening violence against the husband or in any way harassing or otherwise interfering with him or taking action 'to exclude or attempt to exclude' him from the house. The wife applied to the council for other accommodation. The council was sympathetic to the wife's request but, in accordance with its policy not to provide accommodation to persons who already had a council tenancy, suggested that the wife first serve notice on it quitting and delivering up possession of the house. The wife did so, whereupon the council served notice on the husband that his tenancy would terminate on 25 April. The husband informed the council of the existence of the injunction but the council nevertheless brought proceedings in the county court for possession of the house when the notice to quit expired. The county court judge dismissed the possession proceedings on the ground that the wife's notice to quit was not genuine because it formed part of the council's plan to rehouse her, that by giving the notice the wife was in breach of the injunction and that the council had aided and abetted that breach and were in contempt of court. The council appealed to the Court of Appeal which dismissed the appeal. The council appealed to the House of Lords.

Held – Where a husband and wife were joint tenants of a council house and an injunction was granted prohibiting the wife from excluding or attempting to exclude the husband from the property, the injunction was not intended to be a mandatory order requiring the wife to co-operate in preserving the rights created under the joint tenancy pending their future adjustment, but simply to ensure that she did not prevent him from exercising his rights of occupation under the joint tenancy. It followed that by giving notice to quit to the council the wife was not in breach of the terms of the injunction. Furthermore, since at the time the notices to quit were given no proceedings to obtain proprietary relief were in existence, no inference of an intention to frustrate the aim of proceedings could be drawn from the council's dealings with the wife because there were no proceedings to frustrate, and without such an intention an allegation of contempt was unsustainable. Accordingly, there was no ground on which it could be held that the dealings of the council with the wife and the husband were completely ineffectual; and consequently by the time of the possession proceedings the husband's interest under the tenancy had come to an end by effluxion of time, so that there was no longer any ground on which he could deny the council the right to resume possession of the house. The appeal would therefore be allowed (see p 931 *b c*, p 937 *b* to *d*, p 938 *h j*, p 939 *h j*, p 940 *b c* and p 941 *b*, post).

Hammersmith and Fulham London BC v Monk [1992] 1 All ER 1 applied.

A-G v Times Newspapers Ltd [1991] 2 All ER 398 distinguished.

Per Lord Hoffmann. If a non-molestation order contains an order restraining the joint tenant against whom the order is directed from serving a notice to quit terminating the tenancy without the consent of the joint tenant remaining in occupation that in itself will not vitiate a notice to quit served nevertheless. Furthermore, it is doubtful whether a notice to quit, or the termination of a tenancy pursuant to the notice, is a 'disposition' within the meaning of s 37(2)(b) of the Matrimonial Causes Act 1973 under which the court may set aside the notice as a 'reviewable disposition', since a notice to determine a periodic tenancy is not equivalent to the assignment or surrender of that tenancy (see p 940 *c* to *e g* to *j*, post).

Notes

For notices to quit, see 27(1) *Halsbury's Laws* (4th edn reissue) paras 191–196.

Cases referred to in opinions

A-G v Leveller Magazine Ltd [1979] 1 All ER 745, [1979] AC 440, [1979] 2 WLR 247, HL.

A-G v Newspaper Publishing plc [1987] 3 All ER 276, [1988] Ch 333, [1987] 3 WLR 942, Ch D and CA.

A-G v Times Newspapers Ltd [1991] 2 All ER 398, [1992] 1 AC 191, [1991] 2 WLR 994, HL.

Chapman v Honig [1963] 2 All ER 513, [1963] 2 QB 502, [1963] 3 WLR 19, CA.

Hammersmith and Fulham London BC v Monk [1992] 1 All ER 1, [1992] 1 AC 478, [1991] 3 WLR 1144, HL.

Newlon Housing Trust v Al-Sulaimen (1997) The Times, 24 January.

Roche v Roche (1981) Fam Law 243

Shipman v Shipman [1991] 1 FLR 250

Appeal

Harrow London Borough Council appealed with leave granted by the Appeal Committee on 21 July 1995 from the decision of the Court of Appeal (Russell LJ and Sir Roger Parker; Hobhouse LJ dissenting) ((1995) 93 LGR 435) delivered on 16 March 1995 dismissing the council's appeal from the order made by Judge Hunter sitting at the Willesden County Court on 9 August 1994 dismissing the council's application for possession of the dwelling house at No 5 Waghorn Road, Harrow, Middlesex, occupied by the respondent, Maurice Johnstone. The facts are set out in the opinion of Lord Mustill.

Andrew Arden QC and *Frank Feehan* (instructed by *R Vergine*, Harrow Legal Services) for the council.

Nicholas Underhill QC and *Adrian Jack* (instructed by *Rosenbergs*) for the respondent.

Their Lordships took time for consideration.

a 13 March 1997. The following opinions were delivered.

LORD BROWNE-WILKINSON. My Lords, I have had the opportunity of reading in draft the speech of my noble and learned friend Lord Mustill and, for the reasons he gives, I would allow this appeal.

b I have also had the advantage of reading in draft the speech of my noble and learned friend Lord Hoffmann. I prefer to express no view on the two points to which he refers, which do not arise for decision in the present case.

LORD JAUNCEY OF TULLICHETTLE. My Lords, I have had the opportunity of reading in draft the speech of my noble and learned friend Lord Mustill and, for the reasons he gives, I would allow this appeal.

c

LORD MUSTILL. My Lords, on 14 June 1989 the respondent husband, Maurice Johnstone, and his wife Laura entered into a joint tenancy agreement with the appellants, Harrow London Borough Council, relating to 5 Waghorn Road, Kenton, Middlesex. The agreement provided, by cl 19, that the tenants might

d terminate the tenancy by giving four weeks' written notice to the council, expiring on a Monday. This was a secure tenancy under the Housing Act 1985.

The couple moved into the house and lived there, latterly with their two young children, until February 1994. The marriage ran into difficulties, and it appears that during 1992 the wife commenced divorce proceedings. These were

e not immediately pursued, and did not reach the stage of a decree until 1995. Meanwhile, matters had come to a head at the beginning of February 1994. Precisely what happened is not in evidence, but it is clear that (a) the wife left the house, taking the children with her, and (b) the husband made applications to Willesden County Court, based on allegations that his wife had assaulted him and had attempted to eject him from the house. These applications were, first, for an

f injunction under the Domestic Violence and Matrimonial Proceedings Act 1976 and, secondly, for a prohibited steps order under s 10 of the Children Act 1989. On 3 February 1994 the matter came before Judge Krikler who made two orders, evidently ex parte. One was a 'prohibited steps order' requiring that the elder boy should not be removed from the jurisdiction. The second must be quoted in full:

g   'Laura Johnstone is forbidden (whether by himself [sic] or by instructing or encouraging any other person) (1) To use or threaten violence against the applicant or in any way to harass or otherwise interfere with her [sic] (2) To exclude or attempt to exclude the applicant from 5 Waghorn Road, Kenton, Harrow, Middlesex. This order shall remain in force until further order of

h   the court.'

No return date was given for a further hearing. It is not known whether the order was served on the wife, or when she first got to hear of it. No application has been made to discharge the order.

j Since the husband remained in possession of the house and the wife was unwilling to return she needed somewhere else to live and applied to the council, which was willing to rehouse her. It was, however, contrary to council policy to provide accommodation to someone who already had a council tenancy. Accordingly, the council set about regaining possession of 5 Waghorn Road, and for this purpose they suggested to the wife that she should serve on them a notice, in the event dated 22 March 1994, that she would—

'quit and deliver up possession of 5 Waghorn Road, Kenton jointly held by
me as your tenant on 25 April 1994 or at the end of the period of my tenancy
which will expire next after the expiry of four weeks after the service of this
notice on you.'

By a letter dated 30 March 1994, which did not arrive until 15 April, the
council's housing services forwarded to the husband a copy of the notice and told
him that his tenancy would come to an end on 25 April. As soon as the husband
received the letter he went to the housing services' office and told the relevant
official about the injunction.

The husband remained in the house, and on 17 June 1994 the council
commenced proceedings for possession in Willesden County Court. Not having
received legal aid until the day before the hearing, the husband did not file a
defence, but he did so when the matter came before Judge Hunter on 9 August
1994. Its substance was that by giving the notice the wife was acting in breach of
the injunction and was in contempt of court. By bringing the proceedings when
it was aware of the injunction the council had aided and abetted the wife in that
breach and was itself in contempt of court, and the proceedings were an abuse of
the process of the court. The judge accepted this submission and dismissed the
claim. His reasoning was: (1) The letter was not a genuine notice to quit
because it formed part of the council's plan to rehouse the wife. (2) The wife
should probably have tried to get the injunction varied. When the council
learned of the position on 15 April the position could have been rectified. Instead
the proceedings were instituted. (3) By giving the notice the wife was in breach
of the injunction. The council had aided and abetted the breach and 'in a sense'
were in contempt of court. (4) The judge had grave doubts about the validity of
the notice which was procured by the council for its own convenience. (5) In
any event even if the notice were valid the judge would not grant possession as
this would be perpetuating the breach.

In addition, it seems that the judge had doubts, notwithstanding *Hammersmith
and Fulham London BC v Monk* [1992] 1 All ER 1 at 3, [1992] 1 AC 478 at 483, as to
whether a notice by one tenant alone was sufficient to bring the tenancy to an end
under cl 19.

On an appeal by the council there was a marked difference of opinion among
the members of the court (see (1995) 93 LGR 435). Russell LJ reasoned as follows:
(i) The wife might well have been in contempt of court by serving the notice to
quit. (ii) More importantly, the local authority should be so regarded because
with knowledge of the injunction they sought possession although her husband
was protected from eviction at her suit. The fact that the council was not a party
to the injunction was not to the point. (iii) The institution of the proceedings was
an interference with the administration of justice because it sought to achieve a
result which, whilst the injunction was still in progress, was not open to the wife
whose act was an essential link in the obtaining of possession by the council: see
A-G v Newspaper Publishing plc [1987] 3 All ER 276, [1988] Ch 333.

Sir Roger Parker agreed with Russell LJ in the result, but reached it by a
different route as follows: (i) There was no doubt that the intention of the
county court when granting the injunction was that the husband should remain
in possession of the premises until further order and that the wife should not take
any action to exclude him from such occupation. (ii) *Hammersmith and Fulham
London BC v Monk* did not avail the wife. There was no difference between a
mandatory order to assent by silence and an order not to give a notice. The act

a enjoined was the giving of notice. (iii) Even if the court had not contemplated the possibility of an interference with property rights, it was concerned to prevent a result, namely, the exclusion of the husband from occupation, or an attempt to procure that result, by whatever means. (iv) Since the wife was clearly in breach, it followed that in instituting and pursuing the proceedings after it learned of the injunction, the council was in abuse of the process of the court. (v) Quite apart

b from this it was aware that the marriage was in difficulties and must be taken to have been aware that the fate of the joint tenancy might be a matter to be dealt with in divorce proceedings. It should not have proceeded in such circumstances without any inquiry. (vi) The question whether the notice was invalid had not been pursued, but in any future proceedings it might be for consideration whether clause 19 of the tenancy, read with the Housing Act 1985 and the

c Matrimonial Homes Act 1983 would take the case out of the decision in *Hammersmith and Fulham London BC v Monk*.

Hobhouse LJ disagreed with the conclusion and the reasoning of the other members: (i) In the light of *Hammersmith and Fulham London BC v Monk* he distinguished the wife's letter from an ordinary notice to quit. It merely signified

d her unwillingness to continue as a joint tenant for the succeeding period. (ii) The letter related solely to her unwillingness to extend further the period of the joint tenancy. It was not a positive act. (iii) To require her to give her consent would have required a different kind of order from the one actually made; and there was no suggestion that the application for the order was made on any such basis. (iv) The council's possession action derived from the fact that the husband no

e longer had any right to remain in the house. Neither she nor the council excluded him from the house in breach of the order; he no longer had any right to be there. (v) As to the alternative argument that the council's conduct was abusive because of the possibility of a further order in the divorce proceedings, there was no factual basis for saying that in such proceedings the husband would be

f assigned any rights in respect of the house.

These divergences of view foreshadowed the arguments now before the House. Central to them all is the decision of this House in *Hammersmith and Fulham London BC v Monk*. Without the added feature of the county court's order, the facts were very similar to the present. The question was whether a notice given by one joint tenant alone was sufficient to terminate the tenancy. In a

g speech with which the other members of the House agreed, Lord Bridge of Harwich analysed and rejected the argument that the determination of a periodic tenancy by notice is analogous to the determination of a lease for a fixed term in the exercise of a break clause. I must quote from the speech at length. First, his Lordship approached the question a priori ([1992] 1 All ER 1 at 2–3, [1992] 1 AC

h 478 at 482–483):

'For a large part of this century there have been many categories of tenancy of property occupied for agricultural, residential and commercial purposes where the legislature has intervened to confer upon tenants extra-

j contractual rights entitling them to continue in occupation without the consent of the landlord, either after the expiry of a contractual lease for a fixed term or after notice to quit given by the landlord to determine a contractual periodic tenancy. It is primarily in relation to joint tenancies in these categories that the question whether or not notice to quit given by one of the joint tenants can determine the tenancy is of practical importance, particularly where, as in the instant case, the effect of the determination will

be to deprive the other joint tenant of statutory protection. This may appear
an untoward result and may consequently provoke a certain reluctance to
hold that the law can permit one of two joint tenants unilaterally to deprive
his co-tenant of "rights" which both are equally entitled to enjoy. But the
statutory consequences are in truth of no relevance to the question which
your Lordships have to decide. That question is whether, at common law, a
contractual periodic tenancy granted to two or more joint tenants is
incapable of termination by a tenant's notice to quit unless it is served with
the concurrence of all the joint tenants. That is the proposition which the
appellant must establish in order to succeed. As a matter of principle I see no
reason why this question should receive any different answer in the context
of the contractual relationship of landlord and tenant than that which it
would receive in any other contractual context. If A and B contract with C
on terms which are to continue in operation for one year in the first place and
thereafter from year to year unless determined by notice at the end of the
first or any subsequent year, neither A nor B has bound himself contractually
for longer than one year. To hold that A could not determine the contract
at the end of any year without the concurrence of B and vice versa would
presuppose that each had assumed a potentially irrevocable contractual
obligation for the duration of their joint lives, which, whatever the nature of
the contractual obligations undertaken, would be such an improbable
intention to impute to the parties that nothing less than the clearest express
contractual language would suffice to manifest it. Hence, in any ordinary
agreement for an initial term which is to continue for successive terms unless
determined by notice, the obvious inference is that the agreement is
intended to continue beyond the initial term only if and so long as all parties
to the agreement are willing that it should do so. In a common law situation,
where parties are free to contract as they wish and are bound only so far as
they have agreed to be bound, this leads to the only sensible result. Thus the
application of ordinary contractual principles leads me to expect that a
periodic tenancy granted to two or more joint tenants must be terminable at
common law by an appropriate notice to quit given by any one of them
whether or not the others are prepared to concur ...'

His Lordship then examined the reported decisions to see whether they
displaced his reasoning, and continued ([1992] 1 All ER 1 at 4, [1992] 1 AC 478
at 484):

'Hence, from the earliest times a yearly tenancy has been an estate which
continued only so long as it was the will of both parties that it should
continue, albeit that either party could only signify his unwillingness that the
tenancy should continue beyond the end of any year by giving the
appropriate advance notice to that effect. Applying this principle to the case
of a yearly tenancy where either the lessor's or the lessee's interest is held
jointly by two or more parties, logic seems to me to dictate the conclusion
that the will of all the joint parties is necessary to the continuance of the
interest.'

Lord Bridge concluded his analysis ([1992] 1 All ER 1 at 9, [1992] 1 AC 478 at
490–491):

'Finally, it is said that all positive dealings with a joint tenancy require the
concurrence of all joint tenants if they are to be effective. Thus, a single joint

a   tenant cannot exercise a break clause in a lease, surrender the term, make a
disclaimer, exercise an option to renew the term or apply for relief from
forfeiture. All these positive acts which joint tenants must concur in
performing are said to afford analogies with the service of notice to
determine a periodic tenancy which is likewise a positive act. But this is to
confuse the form with the substance. The action of giving notice to
b   determine a periodic tenancy is in form positive; but both on authority and
on the principle so aptly summed up in the pithy Scottish phrase "tacit
relocation" the substance of the matter is that it is by his omission to give
notice of termination that each party signifies the necessary positive assent
to the extension of the term for a further period.'

c   My Lords, in the light of these principles it seems to me quite beyond doubt
that, absent the special procedural background, the wife's notice to the council of
22 March 1994 was effective to allow the joint tenancy to terminate on the expiry
of the notice. I am unable to see how cl 19 of the tenancy agreement could lead
to any other result, nor has anything in the 1985 Act been identified which could
d   alter the position. The husband's right to remain in occupation, and the security
of tenure which he had hitherto enjoyed, came to an end on the due date for
renewal. Other things being equal, the husband remained in the house without
legal warrant, and the council was entitled to take steps to remove him.
        The question is whether, in the particular circumstances, other things were
indeed equal. The husband maintains that they were not, for two quite distinct
e   reasons. The first depends on the injunction of 3 February 1994. It is said that,
by giving the notice of 22 March 1994, the wife was in breach of the injunction
and that all the subsequent acts of the wife and the council are either inherently
flawed or were abusive and hence unenforceable.
        An examination of this argument must begin with the terms of the injunction.
f   Did the requirement that the wife should not 'exclude or attempt to exclude' the
husband from the house prohibit her from notifying the council that the tenancy
would not be renewed? As background, it is useful to consider what powers
might have been available to the judge when he ordered the wife not to 'exclude'
the husband from the house. The following were mentioned in the course of
g   argument. (I set out the legislation as it existed at the relevant time, since this was
the context of the injunction.)
        (1) Under s 24(1) of the Matrimonial Causes Act 1973 the court could make a
property adjustment order requiring one spouse to transfer to the other any
property to which the former was entitled. This power arose only on the
h   granting of a decree of divorce.
        (2) Under s 7 of and paras 1 and 2 of Sch 1 to the 1983 Act where one spouse
was entitled jointly with the other spouse to occupy a dwelling house as a secure
tenant the court could direct that there should be transferred to and vested in the
latter the interest which the former had in the dwelling house by virtue of the
lease. This power arose only on the granting of a decree of divorce.
j
        (3) Under s 9 of the 1983 Act, read with s 1 thereof, in cases where two spouses
were each entitled by virtue of (inter alia) contractual or statutory rights to
occupy a dwelling house, the court had power to make an order prohibiting,
suspending or restricting the right of one spouse to exercise the right of
occupation, or requiring that spouse to permit its exercise by the other. The
court was required when making use of this power to have regard to the conduct

of the spouses, their respective needs and financial resources and the needs of the children.

(4) Under s 37 of the 1973 Act the court, if satisfied that one spouse was about to make a disposition or otherwise deal with property with the intention of frustrating or impeding the enforcement of an order for financial relief claimed by the other spouse under (inter alia) s 24 of that Act (see item 1 above), could make an order restraining the former from doing so or otherwise protecting the claim. Such an order could only be made in the proceedings in which the relief under s 24 was claimed.

(5) Under s 1 of the 1976 Act the court had the power to make an order (a) restraining one spouse from molesting the other, (b) restraining one spouse from molesting a child living with the other, (c) excluding one spouse from the matrimonial home, and (d) requiring one spouse to enter and remain in the matrimonial home. The power could be exercised whether or not any other relief was claimed in the proceedings. 'Molesting' has been interpreted as including such a degree of 'harassment' as to call for the intervention of the court. The order could be made ex parte but should be strictly limited in time; and it should refer specifically to the statute under which the jurisdiction was assumed. (See, generally, *The County Court Practice* 1996, p 1043, note headed 'Procedure'.)

(6) It has been held that the court has jurisdiction under its general statutory powers of granting injunctive relief to make orders protecting financial and proprietary remedies which may be awarded in the future even if s 37 of the 1973 Act is not available because the prescribed conditions are not satisfied: see *Shipman v Shipman* [1991] 1 FLR 250, and see also *Roche v Roche* (1981) Fam Law 243.

Looking though this list it is plain that most of the items on it have no bearing on Judge Krikler's order. Relief under s 24 of the 1973 Act and Sch 1 to the 1983 Act could be granted only on decree and at that time there was none. The order obviously was not made under s 9 of the 1983 Act, as the discretionary balancing exercise required of the court could not have been performed ex parte on the material put before the judge. And the order could not have been made under s 37 of the 1973 Act, since this was available only on an application made in matrimonial proceedings and the husband's application was not so made.

There remain the last two grounds on which Judge Krikler might have exercised jurisdiction. The choice between them seems quite clear. Let us look at how the case proceeded. The husband's application was led by an affidavit alleging that the wife had assaulted him and locked him out of the house. The application was typed on a printed form reciting the 1976 Act. It invited the court to make orders:

'That [the wife] be forbidden ... from: (1) To use or threaten to use violence upon the applicant. (2) To harass threaten pester or otherwise interfere with the applicant. (3) To leave and not return to the former matrimonial home situate and known as 5 Waghorn Road, Kenton, Harrow, Middlesex. (4) To remove or attempt to remove the children of the family from the day to day care of the applicant or attempt to remove from the jurisdiction',

and concluded with the words: 'And that the respondent not prevent the applicant from returning to 5 Waghorn Road ... '

Regrettably, even on this second appeal neither side is able to provide any information about what happened when this application came before the judge.

a It is not even known whether the ex parte application was followed, as it should have been, by inter partes proceedings; and if so, with what result. What we do know, however, is that an injunction was made in the terms already recited: an injunction which so far as is known the wife has never sought to discharge or vary.

b My Lords, reading this application together with the statute which it invoked and with the terms of the order as made it is in my view absolutely plain that the prohibition against excluding the husband was not intended to be a mandatory order requiring the wife to co-operate in maintaining in force the rights created by the joint tenancy pending the adjustment of those rights on a future date in proceedings not yet started. The application was made at a time of crisis when the husband had been locked out of the house and wanted to get back in. His

c concern was that his wife had excluded him from the exercise of the rights of occupation which he undoubtedly possessed under the joint tenancy. There is no sign in the documents of an apprehension on his part that the rights themselves were under threat and would require protection by an order requiring the wife to keep the tenancy in being. If the court was to grant something on the lines of

d a mandatory Mareva-like injunction the first step was to ask for one. This the husband did not do. Instead he invited the court to make an order designed to ensure that the molestation of which she was accused did not happen again. The 1976 Act was the right vehicle for such an order, and although the injunction actually issued did not follow precisely the wording of the Act I have no doubt that this was the foundation of the order which Judge Krikler intended to make

e and did make. As such it was concerned with the exercise of rights under the tenancy and not with the continued existence of the rights themselves.

On this view the husband's first line of argument fails at the outset.

There remains the husband's second line of argument, based not on the husband's rights but on the general interest of preserving the integrity of the

f judicial process. It was based primarily on *A-G v Times Newspapers Ltd* [1991] 2 All ER 398, [1992] 1 AC 191, reinforced by *A-G v Leveller Magazine Ltd* [1979] 1 All ER 745, [1979] AC 440. The former case arose from successive attempts by newspapers to publish materials drawn from a work named *Spycatcher*, said to infringe the confidentiality of information about the activities of the British security services. In one set of proceedings the Attorney General was seeking a

g final injunction against certain newspapers to restrain the publication of such materials and had obtained an interlocutory injunction pending trial. This injunction attracted widespread publicity. Later, the Sunday Times began to serialise extracts from *Spycatcher*, which by now was on the verge of sale in the United States. The Attorney General instituted further proceedings against the

h proprietors of that newspaper and its editor, alleging that although they were not parties to the injunction they had knowingly impeded the proper conduct of the confidentiality action in which it had been granted, since once material was made public the purpose of that action was gone. This submission prevailed in your Lordships' House.

j My Lords, the decision in *A-G v Times Newspapers Ltd* could not by any stretch be applied directly to the present appeal. It depended on four circumstances. There were proceedings in existence between the Attorney General and the first group of defendant newspapers which would be fruitless if anyone made public the information whose confidentiality the proceedings were brought to assert. There was in force an injunction, admittedly not directed to anyone except the first group of newspapers, but obviously intended to stop the publication by any medium of materials which would compromise the pending proceedings. The editor and publishers of the Sunday Times knew of the injunction and understood its purpose. Accordingly, they knew that if they published extracts from the book they would frustrate both the purpose of the injunction and the purpose of the action itself. Their choice to publish was treated by the courts below (and this was no longer challenged before the House) as justifying the inference of an intention to interfere with the course of justice.

None of these features is present here. It could not I think seriously be maintained that *A-G v Times Newspapers Ltd* binds the House to decide in favour of the husband. The argument on his behalf is more oblique. Before addressing it I must point out one feature which does not stand in its way. At first sight the most conspicuous difference between *A-G v Times Newspapers Ltd* and the present case lies in the existence of an injunction which although not directed to other newspapers had the obvious purpose of preventing just the kind of act which the Sunday Times deliberately carried out. References to this injunction recur throughout the arguments and judgments, and its presence overshadows the entire case. Nevertheless, it was not the mainspring of the decision, for every member of the House was at pains to emphasise that the submission for the Attorney General did not depend on giving the injunction any binding effect on the Sunday Times. It is not perhaps entirely clear what the reasoning of the House would have been if the injunction had not existed at all. A lead towards the answer is, I believe, given by Lord Oliver of Aylmerton ([1991] 2 All ER 398 at 420, [1992] 1 AC 191 at 224):

'If the court has taken into its hands the conduct of the matter to the extent of ordering the interim preservation of the interest of the plaintiff so that the issue between him and the defendant can be properly and fairly tried, it has to be accepted that that is what the court had determined that the interests of justice require. The gratuitous intervention of a third party intended to result in that purpose being frustrated and the outcome of the trial prejudiced must manifestly interfere with and obstruct what the court has determined to be the interests of justice. Those interests are not dependent upon the scope of the order.'

This reasoning shows, I believe, that even where there is no injunction to make explicit the importance of preserving the subject matter of an action until trial a wanton destruction of that subject matter, with the intention of impeding a fair and fruitful trial, is capable of being a contempt of court; and indeed I would myself have been willing to recognise this possibility even without the guidance of the House.

It does, however, appear to me that even on this footing the differences from *A-G v Times Newspapers Ltd* are fatal to this branch of the husband's case. No proceedings designed to yield proprietary relief were in existence at the relevant time. There was no reason for the council to be aware of any aspect of the matrimonial relationship except that the wife had moved out and was serious enough about wanting to live separately to apply for rehousing. No inference of an intention to frustrate the aim of the proceedings could be drawn from the council's dealings with the wife (whatever exactly they were) since there were no proceedings to frustrate. Without such an intention an allegation of contempt would be quite unsustainable, even if the activities of the wife and the council did stand in the way of whatever remedies in relation to the tenancy the husband might subsequently have tried to obtain.

a Counsel for the husband were thus compelled to advance an argument much more extreme than any relied upon in *A-G v Times Newspapers Ltd*, to this effect. Faced with a spouse who showed real signs of desiring a permanent end to the marriage the council should have foreseen that there already were, or in the future might be, proceedings in which the court would be called on to address the proprietary rights of the spouses, including the valuable (if vulnerable) security of

b tenure of the house; it should also have foreseen that the destruction of the tenure would cause irreparable damage to the husband, since the loss of his tenancy coupled with the rehousing of the wife might critically determine the question of where the young children lived; even if it was not at first in possession of enough information to form a judgment the council should have informed itself by making inquiries; and having done so should have abstained from joining with

c the wife in any course of action which might put out of the husband's reach the possibility of obtaining some kind of relief in any proceedings which he or the wife might, in the parlous state of the marriage, ultimately come to begin.

My Lords, I acknowledge the appeal of this argument in human terms. We know insufficient of the marital discord to say that the wife was in the wrong, but

d at least there was sufficient merit on the husband's side for him (rather unusually, given the reversal of gender) to obtain an anti-molestation order which the wife has never tried to displace. Nevertheless, I see no ground to treat the notice by the wife as ineffectual, and still less to convict the council of a wrongful intention to frustrate the ends of justice. Exactly what passed between the council and the wife has never been investigated, as it should have been if they were to be held in

e contempt. One may, however, test the matter by envisaging a situation where the wife came to the council and simply asked to be rehoused; where the official explained that this could not be done because she was already a tenant; where she told the official that she no longer wanted to keep the joint tenancy in being and asked what to do; where the official recommended that she should take legal

f advice; and where her lawyer, familiar with the principle of *Hammersmith and Fulham London BC v Monk*, prepared the notice which was in fact served. Would it be possible to say that anyone involved had acted in contempt of court? Surely not. All one needs, then, to reach the present case is to telescope the course of events. The contrast between this case and *A-G v Times Newspapers Ltd* is obvious. There, the newspaper defiantly acted in detriment to the obvious

g interests of justice. Here, the council simply carried through the logic of its housing policy, that one person could not have two council tenancies at the same time. I find it impossible to hold that by putting its statutory duty as housing authority before the interests of a matrimonial relationship of which it was not the guardian the council contemptuously subverted the authority of the court or

h intentionally nullified the aims of any legal proceedings. This being so I can see no ground upon which it could be held that the dealings of the council with the wife and the husband were completely ineffectual, leaving the parties in the same position as if the notice had never been given. The conclusion is to my mind inescapable that by the time the matter reached Judge Hutton the interest of the

j husband under the tenancy had come to an end by effluxion of time, so that there was no longer any ground on which he could deny the council the right to resume possession of the house.

These conclusions are sufficient to dispose of the appeal, and I therefore abstain from expressing a decided opinion on the matters discussed in the speech of my noble and learned friend Lord Hoffmann. As at present advised, however, I would respectfully agree with the first of the points which he makes, and as to the second it is important to note the concession made by counsel in *Newlon Housing Trust v Al-Sulaimen* (1997) The Times, 24 January. The correctness of this concession may, I believe, have to be examined if the point comes before the courts again.

However this may be, in my opinion the judgment of Hobhouse LJ was right, and I would allow this appeal. Much may have happened in the years since the question was before Judge Hunter, and the whole merits of the matrimonial situation may by now be seen in a different light. Nevertheless, I consider that the council was entitled to an order for possession in August 1994, I would propose to your Lordships that such an order should now be made.

LORD HOFFMANN. My Lords, I have had the opportunity of reading in draft the speech of my noble and learned friend Lord Mustill and I agree that, for the reasons which he gives, this appeal should be allowed. The order made by Judge Krikler did not restrain the wife from serving a notice to quit upon the council. But since there is likely sooner or later (probably sooner) to be a case in which, at the time when the notice was served, an order to this effect had been or could have been made under one or other of the jurisdictions enumerated by my noble and learned friend, I would offer some observations on what the consequences would be.

In my view, the existence of an injunction could not in itself vitiate the notice given by the wife. The principle laid down by this House in *Hammersmith and Fulham London BC v Monk* [1992] 1 All ER 1, [1992] 1 AC 478 is that the term created by the grant of a periodic joint tenancy is defined by reference to the absence of a notice by the landlord or one or other of the joint tenants signifying that he is not willing that it should continue. If this negative condition is not satisfied, the term comes to an end. For my part, I do not see how the existence of an injunction against the wife in proceedings to which the landlord was not a party and of which it had no knowledge could enable a court to deem the negative condition to be satisfied. The case against doing so would be much stronger than in *Chapman v Honig* [1963] 2 All ER 513, [1963] 2 QB 502 in which a notice to quit was held valid notwithstanding that the landlord seeking to uphold its validity had himself given it in contempt of court. In this case the landlord would not have given the notice or been party to any contempt.

If no injunction had been granted before service of the notice, there may be a question as to whether the joint tenant remaining in occupation can resist an order for possession by invoking the jurisdiction under s 37(2)(b) of the Matrimonial Causes Act 1973 to set aside the notice as a 'reviewable disposition'. In the recent case of *Newlon Housing Trust v Al-Sulaimen* (1997) The Times, 24 January it was conceded by counsel that the notice, or the termination of the tenancy pursuant to the notice, was a 'disposition' within the meaning of the section. But, as at present advised, I feel bound to express my doubt as to whether this concession was rightly made. A notice to determine a periodic tenancy is not in my view equivalent to the assignment or surrender of that tenancy. There is no interest which passes to the landlord, whether intact or so as to merge in his reversion. At the time when the notice takes effect, there is nothing to assign or surrender. What happens is simply that the interest comes to an end in accordance with the conditions by which it is defined, just as a life interest comes to an end upon the death of the tenant for life. In neither case is there in my view a disposition. The definition of 'disposition' in s 37(6) is non-exhaustive and therefore perhaps inconclusive, but it should be noted that the jurisdiction to *a* grant injunctions under 37(2)(a) is much wider than the jurisdiction to set aside dispositions under s 37(2)(b). The former exists not merely when the respondent is about to make a disposition but also when he is about to 'deal with' any property. I express no view upon whether giving notice would be a 'dealing' with the joint tenancy, but the expression is plainly wider than 'disposition' and this in my view makes it unlikely that Parliament intended 'disposition' to be given in *b* this context an unnaturally wide meaning.

LORD CLYDE. My Lords, I have had the advantage of reading a draft of the speech of my learned and noble friend Lord Mustill and for the reasons he gives I too would allow this appeal.

c *Appeal allowed.*

Celia Fox   Barrister.

R v Secretary of State for the Home Department, ex parte Fininvest SpA and others

QUEEN'S BENCH DIVISION

SIMON BROWN AND GAGE J

2, 3, 4, 23 OCTOBER 1996

Evidence – Foreign tribunal – Evidence for purpose of criminal proceedings – Request for assistance in obtaining documents – Serious fraud investigation by Italian prosecuting authorities – Secretary of State acceding to request – Whether request for assistance in obtaining 'evidence' – Criminal Justice (International Co-operation) Act 1990, s 4(2A) – European Convention on Mutual Assistance in Criminal Matters 1959, art 2(a).

Evidence – Foreign tribunal – Evidence for purpose of criminal proceedings – Request for assistance in obtaining documents – Serious fraud investigation by Italian prosecuting authorities – Fraud allegedly involving illicit donations to political party – Secretary of State acceding to request – Whether Secretary of State bound to consider whether or not request concerned political offence – European Convention on Mutual Assistance in Criminal Matters 1959, art 2(a).

The Italian prosecuting authorities sent a letter of request under the provisions of the European Convention on Mutual Assistance in Criminal Matters 1959 (implemented in the United Kingdom by the Criminal Justice (International Co-operation) Act 1990) to the Home Secretary requesting assistance in obtaining documents held by CMM, a company whose offices were in London. The documents were relevant to an investigation of a fraud in which the applicants, an Italian company and its present and previous presidents, were alleged to be involved. It was alleged that over 100bn lire had been removed from the company and used for criminal purposes, and a prosecution was already afoot against the third applicant for making illicit donations to a former Prime Minister and Leader of the Italian Socialist Party. The request was referred by the Home Secretary to the Serious Fraud Office under s 4(2A)[a] of the 1990 Act. The Serious Fraud Office implemented the request by obtaining and executing a search warrant authorising entry to CMM's premises under s 2 of the Criminal Justice Act 1987. The applicants applied for judicial review of, inter alia, the Home Secretary's decision to refer the request to the Serious Fraud Office, contending: (i) that the letter of request described the documents sought so widely that it could not properly be regarded as one for assistance in obtaining 'evidence' for the purposes of s 4 of the 1990 Act but was merely a fishing expedition; and (ii) that the Home Secretary should have considered whether or not the request concerned 'a political offence [or] an offence connected with a political offence' within the meaning of art 2(a)[b] of the convention and, had he done so, he would have concluded that it did and refused assistance to the Italian authorities.

---

a   Section 4(2A) is set out at p 946 *f* to *h*, post
b   Article 2(a) is set out at p 957 *c*, post

a **Held** – (1) The 1990 Act made provision for the obtaining of evidence in connection with a criminal investigation provided that the Home Secretary was satisfied that an investigation into a particular offence was being conducted and that there were reasonable grounds for suspecting that it had been committed. Accordingly, since the permissible area of search in the context of a criminal investigation had inevitably to be wider than where that investigation was b complete, and the prosecution's concern was rather to prove an already investigated and 'instituted' offence, the scheme created by the 1990 Act necessitated the examination of more material than would ultimately constitute evidence at a trial. It followed that since the investigation for which the material was requested involved a wide-ranging international fraud, and the request was as precise and focused as it could sensibly be in the circumstances, the request c could properly be said to be for the obtaining of evidence and not for the purposes of a fishing expedition (see p 951 *a* to *f h* to p 952 *a*, post); *Rio Tinto Zinc Corp v Westinghouse Electric Corp* [1978] 1 All ER 434 and *Re State of Norway's Application (No 1)* [1989] 1 All ER 661 distinguished.

(2) The question whether an offence was 'political' for the purposes of art 2(a) d of the convention had to be determined by the law of the requested state. However, although the Home Secretary was bound to consider art 2(a), he was not bound to reach a decision as to whether or not the offences were, or were connected with, political offences, since he could have decided that in any event he would not exercise his discretion under art 2(a) to refuse co-operation with the Italian authorities. Moreover, the making of illegal donations to a political party, e although an offence committed in a political context, could not be regarded as political per se (ie political irrespective of motive or circumstance), since the offence was merely one against the ordinary law enacted for the proper ordering of the democratic process in Italy. Nor was it made political because the offender hoped to change government policy by buying political influence, or because the f judiciary, by prosecuting him, hoped to clean up politics. The application would therefore be dismissed (see p 957 *f* to *h*, p 958 *b* to *d*, p 959 *b g h*, p 960 *d* to *f* and p 962 *c f* to *j*, post); *Schtraks v Government of Israel* [1962] 3 All ER 529, *Tzu-Tsai Cheng v Governor of Pentonville Prison* [1973] 2 All ER 204 and *T v Secretary of State for the Home Dept* [1996] 2 All ER 865 considered.

g **Notes**

For cases in which assistance may be given, see 17 *Halsbury's Laws* (4th edn) para 326.

For the Criminal Justice (International Co-operation) Act 1990, s 4, see 12 *Halsbury's Statutes* (4th edn) (1994 reissue) 1413.

h For the Criminal Justice Act 1987, s 2, see ibid 1103.

Cases referred to in judgments

Associated Provincial Picture Houses Ltd v Wednesbury Corp [1947] 2 All ER 680, [1948] 1 KB 223, CA.

j *Castioni, Re* [1891] 1 QB 149, [1886–90] All ER Rep 640, DC.

Fothergill v Monarch Airlines Ltd [1980] 2 All ER 696, [1981] AC 251, [1980] 3 WLR 209, HL.

Meunier, Re [1894] 2 QB 415, DC.

Norway's (State) Application, Re (No 1) [1989] 1 All ER 661, [1987] QB 433, [1986] 3 WLR 452, CA; *affd* [1989] 1 All ER 745, [1990] 1 AC 723, [1989] 2 WLR 458, HL.

R v Central Criminal Court, ex p Propend Finance Property Ltd, R v Secretary of State for the Home Dept, ex Propend Finance Property Ltd [1996] 2 Cr App R 26, DC.

R v Reading Justices, ex p Berkshire CC [1996] 1 Cr App R 239, DC.

R v Southampton Crown Court, ex p J [1993] Crim LR 962, DC.

Rio Tinto Zinc Corp v Westinghouse Electric Corp [1978] 1 All ER 434, [1978] AC 547, [1978] 2 WLR 81, HL.

Schtraks v Government of Israel [1962] 3 All ER 529, [1964] AC 556, [1962] 3 WLR 1013, HL.

T v Secretary of State for the Home Dept [1996] 2 All ER 865, [1996] AC 742, [1996] 2 WLR 766, HL.

Tzu-Tsai Cheng v Governor of Pentonville Prison [1973] 2 All ER 204, [1973] AC 931, [1973] 2 WLR 746, HL.

Williams v Summerfield [1972] 2 All ER 1334, [1972] 2 QB 512, [1972] 3 WLR 131, DC.

Cases also cited or referred to in skeleton arguments

Buchanan (James) & Co Ltd v Babco Forwarding and Shipping (UK) Ltd [1977] 3 All ER 1048, [1978] AC 141, HL.

Carltona Ltd v Comrs of Works [1943] 2 All ER 560, CA.

Della Savia v Ministere Public de la Confederation (1969) 72 ILR 618.

Golden Chemical Products Ltd, Re [1976] 2 All ER 543, [1976] Ch 300.

Oladehinde v Secretary of State for the Home Dept [1990] 3 All ER 393, [1991] 1 AC 254, HL; affg [1990] 2 All ER 367, [1991] 1 AC 254, CA and DC.

R v Central Criminal Court, ex p Adegbesan [1986] 3 All ER 113, [1986] 1 WLR 1292, DC.

R v Crown Court at Inner London Sessions, ex p Baines & Baines (a firm) [1987] 3 All ER 1025, [1988] QB 579, DC.

R v Governor of Winson Green Prison, Birmingham, ex p Littlejohn [1975] 3 All ER 208, [1975] 1 WLR 893, DC.

R v Lewes Crown Court, ex p Hill (1990) 93 Cr App R 60, DC.

R v Maidstone Crown Court, ex p Waitt [1988] Crim LR 384, DC.

R v Nottingham Justices, ex p Lynn (1984) 79 Cr App R 238, DC.

R v Southwark Crown Court, ex p Sorsky Defries (1995) Times, 21 July, DC.

Application for judicial review

Fininvest SpA, Fedele Confalonieri (Fininvest's president) and Silvio Berlusconi (a former president of the corporation, its principal shareholder and from March to December 1994, Prime Minister of Italy), applied with leave granted by Tucker J on 13 June 1996 for, inter alia, an order of certiorari to quash the decision of the Secretary of State for the Home Department to refer a request from the Italian prosecuting authorities for assistance in obtaining documents held by a company in London to the Director of the Serious Fraud Office under s 4 of the Criminal Justice (International Co-operation) Act 1990. The facts are set out in the judgment of Simon Brown LJ.

Clare Montgomery QC, Edward Fitzgerald QC and *Julian Knowles* (instructed by *Peters & Peters*) for the applicants.

James Turner (instructed by *Treasury Solicitor*) for the Home Secretary.

Andrew Radcliffe (instructed by the *Solicitor for the Serious Fraud Office*) for the Serious Fraud Office as an interested party.

Cur adv vult

a
23 October 1996. The following judgments were delivered.

SIMON BROWN LJ. This motion involves a wide-ranging series of challenges directed at the implementation by the United Kingdom authorities of an Italian letter of request. The applicants are respectively Fininvest SpA, a large Italian corporation with interests in advertising, publishing and broadcasting; Mr
b Confalonieri, Fininvest's president since 1991; and Mr Berlusconi, Fininvest's previous president and their principal shareholder, a member of the Italian Chamber of Deputies, leader of the Forza Italia political party and, from March to December 1994, Prime Minister of Italy.

The applicants and others are alleged by the Italian prosecuting authorities to be involved in a huge fraud, a fraud whereby at least 100bn lire (about £51m
c sterling) has been surreptitiously removed from Fininvest and used for criminal purposes. Prosecutions are already afoot against Mr Berlusconi respectively for bribing Revenue inspectors (Proceeding No 12731/94) and for making illicit donations of 10bn lire to Mr Craxi, the former Prime Minister and leader of the Italian Socialist Party (Proceeding No 9811/93). Such donations were illicit
d because they were made without proper authority of Fininvest's board of directors and without proper records; Italian law requires transparency of political payments both from donors and recipients.

The applicants and others are now being investigated too in relation to other offences involved in this overall fraud, notably offences of false accounting within the Fininvest group whereby the source of these large sums was concealed.
e It was in connection with these investigations that the Secretary of State for the Home Department received from the Public Prosecutor in Milan a letter of request dated 21 March 1996, supplemented by a further letter dated 9 April 1996, sent under the provisions of the European Convention on Mutual Assistance in Criminal Matters (Strasbourg, 20 April 1959; TS 24 (1992); Cm 1928),
f implemented in the United Kingdom by the Criminal Justice (International Co-operation) Act 1990.

By that letter, the Italians requested assistance in obtaining documents relevant to the allegations of false accounting, in particular documents held by CMM Corporate Services Ltd (CMM) at an address in Regent Street. CMM is a company founded by Mr David Mills, a solicitor and now a partner in Messrs
g Withers.

The request was referred by the Home Secretary to the Director of the Serious Fraud Office (the SFO) under s 4(2A) of the 1990 Act (introduced by amendment by the Criminal Justice and Public Order Act 1994, s 164).

The SFO implemented the request under their powers contained in the
h Criminal Justice Act 1987, similarly amended in 1994 to provide for a s 4(2A) reference by the Home Secretary. They did so in part under s 2(4) of the 1987 Act by seeking and obtaining a search warrant authorising entry to CMM's premises to search there for specified documents, and in part under s 2(3) of the 1987 Act by serving upon Mr Mills a notice requiring him to produce specified documents.
j Seven days was initially allowed under the s 2(3) notice, a period since from time to time extended whereby the notice still remains outstanding.

The search warrant was issued by the Bow Street metropolitan stipendiary magistrate on 15 April 1996 and executed that day with the full co-operation of CMM. The documents removed were (with the consent of the applicants' then solicitors) examined by representatives of the Italian authorities to ascertain which were relevant and which were required for transmission to Italy. Some of

the documents taken have since been returned to CMM; the rest were sent by the
SFO to the Home Secretary.   None, pending this challenge, have been *a*
transmitted to Italy. The Italian representatives, however, have communicated
certain information as to their contents to the Italian prosecuting authorities
whereby certain further arrests have since been made.

The present challenges are directed: (1) to the Home Secretary's decision to
refer the request to the SFO; (2) to the SFO's decision to seek a search warrant; *b*
(3) to the Bow Street stipendiary magistrate's decision to issue the warrant; (4) to
the terms of the s 2(3) notice; (5) to the transmission of information by the Italian
representatives to their prosecuting authority.

The grounds of these challenges are many and various. Some go to more than
one of the steps under attack.   Principally, however, they are three-fold,
concerned respectively with: (a) the width of the request (and, in turn, of the *c*
warrant and notice), (b) the justifiability of seeking (and issuing) a search warrant,
and (c) the question whether this case involves political offences.

It is time to set out the material parts of the main statutory provisions in play,
providing as these do the essential framework within which all these challenges
fall to be considered. *d*

First, s 4 of the 1990 Act as amended provides:

'(1) This section has effect where the Secretary of State receives—(a) from
a court or tribunal exercising criminal jurisdiction in a country or territory
outside the United Kingdom or a prosecuting authority in such a country or
territory; or (b) from any other authority in such a country or territory which *e*
appears to him to have the function of making requests of the kind to which
this section applies, a request for assistance in obtaining evidence in the
United Kingdom in connection with criminal proceedings that have been
instituted, or a criminal investigation that is being carried on, in that country
or territory ... *f*
(2A) Except where the evidence is to be obtained as is mentioned in
subsection (2B) below [ie in Scotland], if the Secretary of State is satisfied—
(a) that an offence under the law of the country or territory in question has
been committed or that there are reasonable grounds for suspecting that
such an offence has been committed; and (b) that proceedings in respect of
that offence have been instituted in that country or territory or that an *g*
investigation into that offence is being carried on there, and it appears to him
that the request relates to an offence involving serious or complex fraud, he
may, if he thinks fit, refer the request or any part of the request to the
Director of the Serious Fraud Office for him to obtain such of the evidence
to which the request or part referred relates as may appear to the Director to *h*
be appropriate for giving effect to the request or part referred ...
(5) In this section "evidence" includes documents and other articles.'

Next, s 2 of the 1987 Act as amended provides:

' ... (1B) The Director shall not exercise his powers on a request from the *j*
Secretary of State acting in response to a request received from an overseas
authority within subsection (1A)(b) above unless it appears to the Director
on reasonable grounds that the offence in respect of which he has been
requested to obtain evidence involves serious or complex fraud ...
(3) The Director may by notice in writing require the person under
investigation or any other person to produce at such place as may be

a specified in the notice and either forthwith or at such time as may be so specified any specified documents which appear to the Director to relate to any matter relevant to the investigation or any documents of a specified description which appear to him so to relate; and—(a) if any such documents are produced, the Director may—(i) take copies or extracts from them; (ii) require the person producing them to provide an explanation of any of them;
b (b) if any such documents are not produced, the Director may require the person who was required to produce them to state, to the best of his knowledge and belief, where they are.

(4) Where, on information on oath laid by a member of the Serious Fraud Office, a justice of the peace is satisfied, in relation to any documents, that there are reasonable grounds for believing—(a) that—(i) a person has failed
c to comply with an obligation under this section to produce them; (ii) it is not practicable to serve a notice under subsection (3) above in relation to them; or (iii) the service of such a notice in relation to them might seriously prejudice the investigation; and (b) that they are on premises specified in the information, he may issue such a warrant as is mentioned in subsection (5)
d below ...

(8A) Any evidence obtained by the Director for use by an overseas authority shall be furnished by him to the Secretary of State for transmission to the overseas authority which requested it ...'

The Home Secretary's decision to refer the request to the SFO is attacked on
e two main grounds. First, it is said that the request was not properly to be regarded as one 'for assistance in obtaining *evidence*'; rather, it is said, the request invites merely an extensive fishing expedition, something which the Home Secretary has no jurisdiction to entertain or to refer on to the SFO. Second, it is said that the Home Secretary was bound to consider whether or not the request concerned 'a political offence [or] an offence connected with a political offence'
f (within the meaning of art 2(a) of the 1959 convention), and that had he done so in the light of the information which the Italians were duty bound, but failed, to put before him, he must, or at least could, properly have concluded that it did, a conclusion which would have provided him with a specific discretion to refuse assistance to the Italian authorities. To this political issue I shall come at the end,
g once the facts are more fully described.

I start with the width of the request, a question which arises more obviously in relation to the search warrant and the s 2(3) notice; more obviously because, provided only and always that the request is essentially one for evidence, the possibility that it extends too far is not, the Home Secretary submits and I accept, something that need concern him; rather it is a matter for consideration by the
h SFO if the request is referred to them (as it would be a matter for the court in those cases, unlike the present, where the Home Secretary nominates a court under s 4(2)).

Examination of this part of the case necessarily involves further reference to the facts, in particular those set out in the letters of request and in the information
j sworn by Mr Dickson of the SFO to obtain the search warrant.

The criminal offence under investigation is described in the letter of request thus:

'False accounting ... in that acting together and with a single purpose they fraudulently falsified the annual balance sheets of Fininvest in order to conceal the creation, administration and use of very large sums of money,

by: (a) fraudulent money transfers; and (b) false commercial operations; and
(c) payments for consulting services which did not exist. Very large sums of
money were booked to overseas companies which were outside the
consolidated balance sheet of Fininvest. Under Italian law, the offences
aggravated both because of the damage which has been done to Fininvest
and because of its continuing nature. By surreptitious and unrecorded
means, monies from the overseas companies have been used for criminal
purposes such as illicit payments to politicians. The monies booked to the
overseas companies were financed both by Silvio Berlusconi Finanziariasa
SA (now SFII SA), a Luxembourg company which was the Fininvest foreign
treasury company, and by Istifi spa, the Fininvest Italian treasury company.
The administrative arrangements were made under the direction of
executives of Fininvest.'

The letter then explains in rather more detail how the fraud was committed and
why assistance is sought from the United Kingdom authorities in connection with
documents held by CMM and Mr Mills:

'Fininvest is a large Italian holding company which has interests in
broadcasting, television and advertising. Through a network of further
holding companies of which he held, in each case, a majority of the shares,
Silvio Berlusconi, until recently Prime Minister of Italy, controlled Fininvest.
The investigation into Fininvest has discovered a very large fraud whereby,
for different reasons and by different methods, the persons under
investigation all acting under the direction of Silvio Berlusconi, worked
together to remove large sums of money secretly from Fininvest. This
operation included the laundering of money. The manner in which the
Fininvest Group operated was that none of the companies within the Group
received or paid out their own funds. Within Italy, there was a single
treasury company, Istifi spa, which made all payments and received all funds.
Outside Italy, there was, again, a single treasury company, Silvio Berlusconi
Finanziaria SA (now SFII SA), which fulfilled the same function. As part of
the fraud, a substantial number of overseas companies were created, many
in such jurisdictions as Panama, the British Virgin Islands and the Channel
Islands. These overseas companies are listed in Schedule I attached hereto.
Initially, these overseas companies were administered by fiduciaries in
Switzerland. A number of different financial operations were employed.
These are some examples. 1. A company within the Fininvest group would,
either directly or through a third party, conclude an agreement with an
overseas company whereby, in return for a fee from the Fininvest company,
services of various kinds would apparently be provided. In fact such services
were never provided and the effect was simply to move money out of
Fininvest to the overseas company. 2. A similar method of removing
money was for the company in the Fininvest Group either directly or
through a third party to purchase share rights from the overseas company.
Again, this was illusory, and no rights were actually acquired. 3. A different
type of operation arose where, using funding from Fininvest through a third
party, overseas companies purchased quoted shares in companies in the
Fininvest Group, the apparent intention being to inflate the price of the
shares. That this operation was a sham was clear from the fact that the
shares, which were bearer shares, remained at all times in the possession of
the same fiduciary. The ultimate destination of the money going to the

a overseas companies is still the subject of investigations. It is possible to say, however, that some of it has been removed in cash from banks in Switzerland. In respect of one particular payment, however, there is documentary evidence that in 1991, Lire 10 billion (approximately 4m Sterling) was paid into an account in the name of an overseas company at SBS, a bank in Lugano. This sum was then transferred to the account of

b Northern Holding at the Trade Development Bank of Geneva, Switzerland. This account is operated by a fiduciary who represents Bettino Craxi, an Italian Deputy (ie a Member of Parliament) who has been Prime Minister of Italy and also President of the Socialist Party of Italy. The money was then transferred from that account to BIL, a Luxembourg bank, where it was credited to the account of Bellhart Holding. One of the people permitted to

c operate the Bellhart Holding account is a man called Al Kateeb, a representative of the PLO. As a result of a Commission Rogatoire which was sent to Switzerland, and the actions of the examining magistrate in Lugano, we have discovered that the persons under investigation considered it too dangerous to continue to have the overseas companies administered from Switzerland, and therefore moved their administration to London. We have

d discovered that this is being undertaken by a company called CMM Corporate Services Limited (now owned by a company called Edsaco Limited) which is located at Sceptre House, 169/173 Regent Street, London W1R 7FB. The name "CMM" originated with a law firm called Carnelutti Mackenzie Mills. This firm no longer exists, and nor does the firm

e of Mackenzie Mills & Co which succeeded it. Mr. David Mackenzie Mills of that former firm is presently a partner in the firm of Withers, which is located at 12 Gough Square, London EC4A 3DE. Mr. Mills has been very much involved in administering these overseas companies, and this does not appear to have ceased since he became a partner in Withers. In that the

f overseas companies are now administered by CMM Corporate Services Limited/Edsaco Limited with the assistance of Mr. Mills, I believe that documents material to our investigation are likely to be found both at Septre House and in the possession of Mr Mills at the firm of Withers. I have set out a description of these documents in Schedule II attached hereto. Apart from Mr Mills, it appears that the other current directors of CMM Corporate

g Services Limited/Edsaco Limited are J R Beardsley, D F Lavin, Ms Tanya Maynard, A Sarikhani and M J Wickers. Others who have been, and may still be, involved are Anthony R Indaimo and Jeremy W Le M Scott who are both presently partners in the firm of Withers.'

The letter then indicated the particular form of assistance requested and why.
h This, however, goes (as does also the supplementary letter of request) rather to the separate issue of whether or not a search warrant was justified here, and to that I shall return later. Suffice it for present purposes to note only that the Italian authorities were seeking in particular to obtain the documents specified in schedule 2 to the request, a schedule which commences thus:

j 'all documents of the description set out below, or files of documents containing documents of the description set out below, which are connected to, or relate in any way to, Fininvest or any companies in its Group, or any of the persons named in this letter of request including persons under investigation, or any companies or entities set out in Schedule I hereto [a list of overseas companies] for the period 1st January 1989 to the present day', and which then recites a long list of categories of business documentation.

Mr Dickson's information repeated much of the contents of the letter of *a* request, explained why he was applying for a search warrant (a matter to which I shall return) and scheduled the documents being sought (described almost identically as in the letter of request save that the schedules were somewhat reordered). A warrant was issued duly authorising entry to CMM's Regent Street premises to search for the scheduled documents. Six named Italians were *b* permitted to accompany any police constable executing the warrant. This had been specifically requested for obvious good reason: the documents related to highly complex matters and many were in Italian. The Italians were there to advise where necessary as to which documents fell within the terms of the warrant.

The s 2(3) notice served on Mr Mills described the documents to be produced *c* by him precisely as they were described in the search warrant. There have, we are told, been extensive subsequent discussions between Mr Mills and the SFO as to just what documents he has which should be produced.

The applicants' arguments for contending that the warrant and the s 2(3) notice, as well as the letter of request itself, were impermissibly wide, run *d* essentially as follows.

(1) 'Evidence' (the word used in s 4(1)(b) and (2A) of the 1990 Act) has an established meaning in this context, ie in the field of mutual assistance.

Amongst the various formulations encapsulating this meaning are that the evidence required is '... direct evidence for use at a trial as contrasted with *e* information which may lead to the discovery of evidence ...' (see *Rio Tinto Zinc Corp v Westinghouse Electric Corp* [1978] 1 All ER 434 at 450, [1978] AC 547 at 619 per Viscount Dilhorne). Or that it is the antithesis of fishing:

> '[Fishing] arises in cases where what is sought is not evidence as such, but information which may lead to a line of inquiry which would disclose *f* evidence. It is the search for material in the hope of being able to raise allegations of fact, as opposed to the elicitation of evidence to support allegations of fact, which have been raised bona fide with adequate particularisation.' (See *Re State of Norway's Application (No 1)* (1986) [1989] 1 All ER 661 at 684, [1987] QB 433 at 482 per Kerr LJ.) *g*

(2) The documents sought in the present case fall foul of that test. This is so in three particular respects. (a) The formula adopted in schedule 2 'all documents [of descriptions so wide as to encompass virtually all business documentation] ... which are connected to, or relate in any way to [anyone named in the request]' was held in the *Westinghouse* case, where the request was *h* for 'any memoranda, correspondence or other documents relevant thereto', to be too wide. It does not attempt to identify any particular transaction or activity. It has all the hallmarks of a fishing expedition. (b) The period of time encompassed by the request, '1st January 1989 to the present day' is too wide, in particular in that it extends some 15 months after the closing of the account on 31 *j* December 1994 in connection with the second, later, false accounting charge. (c) The documents are sought provided only that they relate to 'any of the persons named in this letter'. That includes, for instance, Mr Mills himself and the other named individuals concerned with CMM. In the result, the description read literally is apt to include, for example, Mr Mills' own personal correspondence and bank statements. That plainly goes too far.

a Plausible though at first blush these arguments appear, in my judgment (with but a single qualified exception in respect of the named persons) they prove unsustainable on closer examination. In the first place, I would accept the respondents' contention that what is meant by the word 'evidence' in the present context is not identical to its established meaning in the legislation under consideration in the *Westinghouse* case and in *Re State of Norway's Application*

b (*No 1*). True, as the applicants point out, the evidence obtainable under the Evidence (Proceedings in Other Jurisdictions) Act 1975 included that required for civil proceedings, whether already instituted or contemplated, and that required for criminal proceedings provided they are already instituted. But it was not until the 1990 Act that a provision was made for obtaining evidence in connection with 'a criminal investigation', providing only, as s 4 makes plain, that the Home

c Secretary is satisfied both that an investigation into a particular offence is being carried on and that there are reasonable grounds for suspecting that it has been committed.

Inevitably there is some flexibility in the whole concept of evidence—not even the applicants submit, for example, that what may be sought under the 1990 Act

d must be 'likely to be material evidence' within the meaning of s 97(1) of the Magistrates' Courts Act 1980, as explained in *R v Reading Justices, ex p Berkshire CC* [1996] 1 Cr App R 239. When, therefore, one is speaking of 'evidence' in the context of a criminal investigation, the permissible area of search must inevitably be wider than once that investigation is complete and the prosecution's concern is rather to prove an already investigated and 'instituted' offence.

e The 1990 Act in short created a wholly new scheme for mutual assistance with regard to criminal investigations, a scheme under which it would plainly be necessary to examine altogether more material than would ultimately constitute evidence at any trial. True, the word 'evidence' continues to be used, but Parliament cannot thereby have intended to confine assistance within the

f relatively narrow limits prescribed by the *Westinghouse* case and *Re State of Norway's Application (No 1)*. That in effect would be to defeat the very change being brought about by the 1990 Act. The terms of art 1 of the 1959 convention should in this regard be noted:

g '1. The Contracting Parties undertake to afford each other, in accordance with the provisions of this Convention, the widest measure of mutual assistance in proceedings in respect of offences the punishment of which, at the time of the request for assistance, falls within the jurisdiction of the judicial authorities of the requesting Party ...'

In my judgment, that consideration of itself is sufficient to defeat the applicants'

h central contentions here with regard to the width of disclosure sought in this case. What is under investigation here is, after all, as the respondents point out, a wide-ranging, multi-faceted, international fraud involving far-reaching allegations against a large number of individuals in connection with an even larger number of companies. Considering, moreover, that it is at the

j investigative stage, one could hardly look to greater particularisation of the offences than is contained in the letter of request. So far from this being a fishing expedition, specific allegations of fact are made concerning the setting up of an elaborate network of overseas companies and the various ways in which the false accounting has been committed. The documentation which it is believed will establish or support these allegations is (or rather was) with CMM and Mr Mills. In short, the request for assistance here is not, as the applicants contend, vague

and speculative; rather it is as precise and focused as such a request could sensibly
be in these circumstances. It is impossible to know just what documents are both a
in London and relevant. To discover that, it is necessary to find, examine and
appraise them. Given, however, that these are the type of documents invariably
germane to any major company fraud investigation, and that these overseas
companies are now administered by CMM, it is highly likely that many will be
relevant. And in so far as any of the documents seized prove not to be, they will b
not be transmitted to Italy. It is perhaps helpful in this regard to note also this
passage from the judgment of the Swiss Federal Court dealing with the
applicants' challenge to the Commission Rogatoire there:

> 'The question of knowing whether the information requested in the
> context of an application for assistance is necessary or of use in the c
> proceedings underway in the applicant State, in general, must be left up to
> the assessment of the latter's authorities. The State applied to does not, in
> fact, have the means to be able to pronounce on the advisability of adopting
> certain evidence and cannot, therefore, put its own power of assessment in
> place of that of the foreign authority carrying out the enquiries.' d

As for the period encompassed by the request, extending as it does beyond the
periods of false accounting under investigation, that seems to me plainly
justifiable in the present circumstances: self-evidently documents postdating the
closing of accounts are likely to refer back to the accounting period and in any
event they may reveal the subsequent movement of assets or shares allegedly e
employed in the fraud. The position here could hardly be more different from
that under consideration by Lord Widgery CJ in *Williams v Summerfield* [1972] 2
All ER 1334 at 1338, [1972] 2 QB 512 at 518, when, with reference to s 7 of the
Bankers' Books Evidence Act 1879, he suggested that the period of disclosure of
bank accounts be limited to the period strictly relevant to the charge before the f
justices.

The one criticism I do accept is, as stated, with regard to the named persons
and the consequences of a literal application of the terms of the search warrant
and the s 2(3) notice in that regard. In my judgment, however, it would be quite
wrong to strike down these instruments on that account. The search warrant has
now long since been executed and there is no suggestion that such obviously g
inappropriate documents as theoretically would fall within its scope were in fact
taken. On no view did the infelicitous formulation of the schedule constitute the
sort of serious breach of statutory safeguard that Auld J was referring to in *R v
Southampton Crown Court, ex p J* [1993] Crim LR 962 when this court declined to
allow the warrant there to stand, albeit, one should note, even then on the basis h
that the police investigation would not be prejudiced because a fresh warrant
could be sought and meantime the documents would be held safe.

As for the outstanding s 2(3) notice, the intended scope of which is already
under discussion between the SFO and Mr Mills, I see no reason why agreement
should not readily be reached to confine it to what may sensibly be called the j
Fininvest documents. Plainly the SFO have no possible interest in seeing Mr
Mills' own personal papers. Had it been necessary, I would have regarded this as
a clear case for 'excising inappropriate material [to] produce a request which is
acceptable and proper' (see *Re State of Norway's Application (No 1)* (1986) [1989] 1
All ER 661 at 691, [1987] QB 433 at 491 per Glidewell LJ). In my judgment,
however, this is not necessary here.

a Before concluding this part of the case, there is one further group of arguments I should notice. We were treated to elaborate submissions from both sides as to the significance of the word 'information' in s 2(2) of the 1987 Act, a provision which I need not read and which was not, of course, invoked in the present case.

The applicants, as I understand it, point to the contrast between 'information' and 'evidence', submit that 'information' is wider and more accurately represents *b* what was the subject of the request here, and argue that compliance with such a request goes beyond what is permissible under s 4(2A) of the 1990 Act (which confines assistance to obtaining evidence). The SFO's powers under s 2(2) could, they submit, only properly be used in a domestic context.

Not so, submit the respondents. They argue, first, that the word 'information' is used in s 2(2) (and in s 2(10)) merely in contradistinction to documents and that *c* it would be inappropriate to use the word 'evidence' there because what is disclosed is only ever admissible in evidence where the s 2(8) conditions are satisfied. Second, and in any event, they submit that s 4(2A) of the 1990 Act, introduced in 1994 by the same amending legislation as introduced also the implementing provisions in the 1987 Act, contemplates, as indeed does s 2(1A)(b) *d* of the 1987 Act itself, the full use of the SFO's powers. In other words, the 'director's investigation powers' conferred by s 2, draconian as they may be, are no narrower with regard to requests for mutual assistance in overseas investigation cases than they are in the domestic context. The SFO can, in short, use their s 2(2) power in a mutual assistance case although, as I repeat, they did not do so here.

e It is sufficient to say that I accept the respondents' arguments on these matters also; the applicants can accordingly derive no possible assistance from the use of the word 'information' in s 2(2).

I would accordingly reject all the applicants' claims for relief with regard to the suggested excessive width of the letters of request, the search warrant and the *f* s 2(3) notice.

I must turn next to a further discrete ground of challenge advanced against the Home Secretary's referral of this request to the SFO, the contention that before making such referral he was required, but failed, to consider whether there was dual criminality in respect of these offences. Whatever strictly is the position in *g* law, I have to say that this seems to me, on any view, a wholly barren point: the clear fact is that Mr Dickson of the SFO deposed in his information that 'the facts set out in the Request would, if they had taken place in England, constitute offences of, inter alia, conspiracy to defraud and false accounting'. It is, indeed, impossible to suppose that the Home Secretary himself, had he addressed the *h* point, could have concluded otherwise.

The applicants contend, however, that relevant questions of extra-territoriality could have arisen here under English law and that the Home Secretary was bound to consider them. I therefore briefly address the substantive point: should he have done so? The applicants' argument here fixes upon the language of the *j* precondition to referral in s 4(2A) of the 1990 Act: that 'it appears to [the Home Secretary] that the request relates to an offence involving serious or complex fraud'.

The SFO's powers under the 1987 Act, of course, only arise in cases involving 'serious or complex fraud': see s 1(3) of that Act. It follows, submit the applicants, that the offence in question must necessarily always constitute such an offence prosecutable under English law.

In my judgment this is a hopeless argument. The 1990 Act is at pains to indicate when dual criminality is required and when it is not. The relevant starting point is art 5 of the 1959 convention, which, so far as relevant, allows any contracting party to—

'1. ... reserve the right to make the execution of letters rogatory for search or seizure of property dependent on one or more of the following conditions: (a) that the offence motivating the letters rogatory is punishable under both the law of the requesting Party and the law of the requested Party ...'

The United Kingdom duly reserved that right and when thereafter, in s 7 of the 1990 Act, Parliament came to deal with the 'search or seizure of property', it provided in terms that the offence in question must 'constitute a serious arrestable offence if it had occurred in any part of the United Kingdom': see s 7(1) and (2)(b).

The one other requirement of dual criminality to be found in the 1990 Act is with regard to fiscal offences under s 4(3):

'Where it appears to the Secretary of State ... that the request relates to a fiscal offence in respect of which proceedings have not yet been instituted he shall not exercise his powers under [the earlier provisions] unless ... (b) he is satisfied that the conduct constituting the offence would constitute an offence of the same or a similar nature if it had occurred in the United Kingdom.'

That was permissible not because of art 5 of the 1959 convention but rather because of art 2(a), which permits assistance to be refused not only if the request concerns a political offence but also if it concerns a fiscal offence, and which therefore allows conditions to be imposed, as here, in s 4(3)(b).

These instances are in striking contrast to the language of s 4(2A)(a), which requires only that the offence be one 'under the law of the country or territory in question'.

In short, even were these false accounting offences, contrary to the fact, not offences under English law too, it would matter nothing. Assistance would still be required.

Subject then to what I have called the political issue, that disposes of the challenge to the Home Secretary's referral of this request to the SFO and I can move next to the SFO's decision to seek a search warrant against CMM and, in turn, the magistrate's decision to grant it. These decisions, it is said, were unjustified on the facts. More particularly it is argued that s 2(4)(a)(iii) of the 1987 Act was not satisfied here, ie that there were no reasonable grounds for believing that the service of a s 2(3) notice on CMM 'might seriously prejudice the investigation'. I should record here the applicants' acknowledgment that the challenges to these two decisions (the SFO's to seek, and the magistrate's to grant, a search warrant) are identical; on the facts of this case either both must succeed or neither.

Once again it is necessary to return to the facts to see the basis upon which this search warrant was sought. This is to be found in para 15 of Mr Dickson's information:

'I have considered carefully whether it would be appropriate to obtain the specified documents by service on CMM Corporate Services Limited/Edsaco Limited and Mr Mills of Notices under Section 2(3) of the Act. Other *a* things being equal, this is the normal way in which the Director would obtain such documents. I have noted (but no more) the request of the Assistant Public Prosecutor in Milan that the specified documents be obtained by means of a search warrant. In the case of Mr Mills, who is a professional man and a member of a highly respected professional firm, I believe that he would comply with a Notice to produce such documents as

b he has in his possession at his professional premises. I therefore intend to serve a Notice on him at the same time as any warrant which this court may grant is executed. In respect of CMM Corporate Services Limited/Edsaco Limited, however, I have come to the conclusion that service of such a Notice in relation to the specified documents might seriously prejudice the investigation, by allowing the opportunity for some or all of the specified

c documents to be concealed, destroyed or removed from the United Kingdom. I have come to this conclusion for three reasons: (a) Those persons running CMM Corporate Services Limited/Edsaco Limited must be aware that what they have done in managing the companies set out in Schedule III is fraudulent and might render them liable to prosecution in

d Italy. That in itself would give them a strong incentive to comply with a Notice, and to destroy or remove the documents. (b) It is extremely worrying that the persons under investigation considered it too dangerous to continue to have the overseas companies administered from Switzerland, and therefore moved their administration to London. Quite apart from believing that enforcement action would not be taken in London, this

e suggests that CMM Corporate Services Limited/Edsaco Limited were considered a "safe" repository of the specified documents. (c) The fact that the documents have already been moved once (from Switzerland) suggests that those involved would not hesitate to do the same again.'

f Most of what is set out there closely reflects the fears expressed by the Italians in their letters of request. The second letter, I should note, referred to evidence that had then come to light that Tanya Maynard, one of CMM's directors, had required those responsible for holding the documents in Switzerland to transfer them to CMM in London. This she did on 10 April 1995, very shortly after Italian letters of request were sent to Switzerland on 8 and 24 March. If there was an

g innocent explanation for this, none has ever been provided. Prosecuting authorities are, submit the respondents, entitled to a measure of scepticism in this sort of situation.

Not so, say the applicants. They argue that there was no sufficient evidential basis for a search warrant here and that it is fanciful to suggest that people

h running a company administration service such as CMM provides have a sufficient knowledge of the significance of their actions to allow an inference to be drawn that they themselves are involved. Unless, moreover, it could be said that those representing the directing mind of the company would destroy or remove the documents, there could be no sufficient reason for not seeking a s 2(3) order against CMM. This, after all, could have been served upon Mr Mills

j himself; it could have required production of the documents 'forthwith'; and it would have been attended by grave sanctions—up to six months imprisonment for non-compliance (s 2(13)), and up to seven years imprisonment were anyone to destroy or dispose of relevant documents (s 2(16) and (17)).

The applicants seek to attack these decisions in two ways. First, it is said that the SFO ought to have carried out further investigation than they did to determine for themselves whether so extreme a step as a search warrant was justified against an apparently respectable company like CMM (a company *a* owned since 1994 by Edsaco Ltd, itself a wholly owned subsidary of the Union Bank of Switzerland), most of whose clients are wholly unconnected to Fininvest. That an obligation lies upon the SFO to satisfy themselves of the justifiability of whatever course they take cannot be doubted: see *R v Central Criminal Court, ex p Propend Finance Property Ltd, R v Secretary of State for the Home Dept, ex p Propend Finance Property Ltd* [1996] 2 Cr App R 26 at 36. In my judgment, however, the *b* SFO did all that could reasonably be required of them in this regard. In the first place they were themselves already in direct discussions with the Italian prosecutors before ever this request was referred to them. Second, as Mr Dickson has deposed in these proceedings, he instigated certain inquiries of CMM through the metropolitan police. Third, it is plain that the SFO exercised their own independent judgment in the matter; that, indeed, is apparent from para 15 *c* of Mr Dickson's information.

The second ground of attack is that there was here simply no reasonable basis for seeking this search warrant. That, however, as the applicants recognise, can only be advanced as a *Wednesbury* challenge (see *Associated Provincial Picture Houses Ltd v Wednesbury Corp* [1947] 2 All ER 680, [1948] 1 KB 223) and in my *d* judgment it is quite impossible to say here that, on the material before them, it was irrational either for the SFO to seek or for the magistrate to grant this search warrant.

I turn next to the challenge to the transmission to Italy of information gleaned by the Italian representatives following upon the execution of the search warrant. This, it is contended, breached the requirement in s 2(8A) of the 1987 Act that any *e* evidence obtained by the SFO should be furnished to the Home Secretary for transmission abroad, a requirement reflected in Mr Dickson's assurance to the applicants' then solicitors by letter dated 17 April 1996 that 'the documents will be transmitted by us to the Home Office in the usual way for onward transmission to Italy'. *f*

By that same letter, however, Mr Dickson confirmed the arrangement already agreed with those solicitors that the Italian representatives would continue to examine the documents, as they had during the search itself, so as to limit what was to be sent to the Home Office to the documents or copies needed for the investigation. The Italian representatives made no notes of the documents, a fact confirmed by the terms of a report which they wrote on return to Italy on 19 *g* April:

'... the information given in this report could contain some inaccuracies as it is simply the fruit of an effort to memorise the information made by the writer.' *h*

In those circumstances I accept the respondents' submission that it cannot be said that there has yet been any transmission to Italy of 'evidence' (defined by s 4(5) of the 1990 Act to include documents) contrary to s 2(8A), or of the documents contrary to the assurance. Nor do I think it right to criticise the Italian representatives for reporting back to their superiors in Italy to the best of their *j* ability, or the SFO for not seeking assurances from the Italians that they would not do so. This frankly seems to me to have been neither realistic nor necessary.

This challenge too, therefore, I would reject.

I come finally to the political issue, the applicants' argument being that had the Home Secretary correctly directed himself on the law and been properly informed on the facts, he would have regarded each of these offences as 'a

political offence [or] an offence connected with a political offence' within the
meaning of art 2(a) of the 1959 convention, and thus been entitled to refuse
assistance to the Italian authorities. Without such a discretion, I should note, the
Secretary of State had no alternative under the convention but to comply with
the request. I have already set out the terms of art 1(1); for good measure art 19
provides that 'reasons shall be given for any refusal of mutual assistance'. No
other basis for refusal (save the width of the request with which I have already
dealt) has been suggested.

It is time to set out the relevant part of art 2:

> 'Assistance may be refused: (a) if the request concerns an offence which the
> requested Party considers a political offence, an offence connected with a
> political offence, or a fiscal offence ...'

The first question arising on this part of the case is whether the Home Secretary
had to have regard to art 2(a) at all. In fact he did have regard to it, but if, as he
argues, he was not in law required to do so, then even assuming he misdirected
himself on the point, it would not matter.

In contending that he was not bound to consider art 2(a) at all, the Home
Secretary relies in particular upon the lack of any such requirement in the
domestic legislation, a silence contrasting with the express provision made by
s 4(3) for fiscal offences. In my judgment, however, the argument is plainly
unsound. Section 4(3) deals merely with some and by no means all fiscal offence
requests and it does so, moreover, by removing the discretion which otherwise
would exist with regard to them. This leaves other fiscal offence requests to be
considered, just like any political offence requests, under the remaining
provisions of s 4, which expressly confer upon the Home Secretary a general
discretion in the matter. It seems to me quite impossible to contend that in
exercising this general discretionary power the Home Secretary is entitled to
ignore the express discretion arising under art 2. The Secretary of State would in
my judgment plainly be overlooking a material consideration if, for example, he
simply forgot the existence of art 2(a).

That is not to say, however, that the Home Secretary was bound to reach a
decision as to whether or not these offences were themselves, or were connected
with, political offences. He could instead, had he wished, have decided that
whether or not they were (whether or not in other words a discretion arose under
art 2(a)) he would not in any event exercise it to refuse co-operation with the
Italian authorities in the particular circumstances of this case. Had he followed
that course, or, indeed, had he deposed in the present proceedings that, even had
he reached a contrary view on the political offence question, he would still have
decided to comply with the request, his decision would in my judgment be proof
against this particular ground of challenge, irrespective of whether or not he
directed himself correctly on the substantive issue.

As it is, however, the Home Secretary has deposed, by Mr Sonnenberg who
dealt with this request, that:

> 'The request of 21st March 1996 referred to "illicit payments to politicians".
> I considered that the payments referred to were offences of bribery and
> corruption. I did not consider that the offences described in the request,
> namely of false accounting and use of monies for criminal purposes such as
> illicit payments to politicians, were political offences or offences connected
> with political offences. Accordingly, although I had article 2(a) of the

Convention well in mind, I did not need to consider possible refusal of
assistance thereunder.'

In the result, we do not know what decision the Home Secretary would have
taken in the case had he concluded that these were or were connected with
political offences. Likely though it might appear that he would in any event have
co-operated with this request, it accordingly becomes necessary to address the
substantive question.

The next issue to arise is: according to whose law is the question whether or
not an offence is political to be determined, that of the requesting state or that of
the requested state? Although the applicants contend that this is to be determined
by reference to the law of the requesting state, or perhaps both states, that seems
to me wholly inconsistent with the express words of art 2(a): '... an offence which
the requested Party considers a political offence ...' That formulation to my
mind distinguishes the position here from that ordinarily arising under
international conventions when the courts seek if possible to maintain
consistency between the decisions of different jurisdictions: see e g *Fothergill v
Monarch Airlines Ltd* [1980] 2 All ER 696, [1981] AC 251 and *T v Secretary of State for
the Home Dept* [1996] 2 All ER 865 at 891, [1996] AC 742 at 779 per Lord Lloyd. In
my judgment the issue here is to be determined according to English law.

I must touch now on a short point arising on the facts. As indicated in the
passage already cited from his affidavit, Mr Sonnenberg thought all the illicit
payments to politicians involved offences of bribery and corruption. That is now
conceded to be mistaken: some of these payments were unlawful simply because
they were political contributions made without the requisite transparency and
authority. The Italian authorities should, the applicants contend, have made this
clear to the Home Secretary so that he could exercise his art 2(a) discretion with
a proper understanding of the facts. I agree, and I further agree that in these
circumstances the appropriate question to ask is whether, had the true facts been
known to him, the Home Secretary would, or even could, have regarded these
offences as political.

It is necessary at this stage to clarify precisely what offences here are said to be
political. As I understand the applicants' argument, it is that one of the two sets
of existing proceedings in Italy (Proceeding No 12731/94 for making illicit
donations of 10bn lire to Mr Craxi) is political, and that the false accounting
charges in respect of which the request is made are offences connected with it.
From time to time in the argument Mr Fitzgerald QC appeared to submit that the
false accounting offences themselves must be regarded as political, on the
grounds that the Italian authorities are not in truth interested in prosecuting them
for their own sake but rather are concerned to bring the applicants to book for
making illegal political contributions. On analysis, however, that seems to me
essentially the same argument as saying that the respective offences are
connected. In other words, it cannot avail the applicants to establish that the
motive underlying investigation of the false accounting offences is a desire to
punish the applicants for making illicit political donations unless only the making
of such donations is itself a political offence. To make good their argument,
therefore, the applicants must in my judgment establish that the making of illicit
political donations is indeed a political offence. That I believe to be the critical
question on this part of the case.

In this regard I should first note that the respondents, rightly in my view,
accept: (a) that the fact that other funds produced by this fraud were used for
bribing Revenue inspectors—on no view a political offence—cannot avail them:

a the false accounting allegations make no distinction between the various uses to which the concealed funds were put; and (b) that the false accounting offences are indeed connected to those offences presently being prosecuted in Italy, in the sense that the very purpose of the false accounting was to disguise the source of the illicit payments so that in reality the respective offences are closely interrelated (and perhaps connected too by virtue of the prosecutor's motivation

b in pursuing both, although, as I have indicated, that to my mind adds nothing to the argument).

Is then the making of illegal political donations (hereafter called, for convenience, 'the present offence') a political offence? In submitting that it is, the applicants advance two main arguments: first, that the present offence is intrinsically a political offence, in the same category as, say, treason and sedition,

c all of them offences against the state. Alternatively, they say that it must be regarded as a political offence because of the motivation of the offender in committing it, or of the requesting state in prosecuting it.

The whole concept of political crime is well recognised to be one of considerable difficulty. There are many reported cases in the field, most of high

d authority, and within them innumerable dicta illuminating various aspects of the problem. Many of these authorities were cited to us. Rather, however, than attempting any wide-ranging review of the law, I shall concentrate instead upon what seem to me to be the few key passages of present relevance.

The applicants rely here upon three dicta in particular. First, in support of their argument that the present offence is per se a political offence, this from Lord

e Reid's speech in *Schtraks v Government of Israel* [1962] 3 All ER 529 at 533–534, [1964] AC 556 at 581:

'We must, I think, approach the interpretation of the subsection [s 3(1) of the Extradition Act 1870 which bars extradition of a fugitive criminal for an offence of a "political character"] with two things in mind. In the first place,

f offences obviously of a political character are not within the scope of extradition at all: for example, there is no mention in [the Act] of treason, sedition or any other offence of that kind ...'

I am ready to assume that there are indeed certain offences of an intrinsically political character (although, as the respondents point out, the murder of the

g Sovereign, if carried out for purely personal reasons, albeit by definition treason, might not be thought a political offence). Even making this assumption, however, I find it impossible to regard the present offence as political per se, ie political irrespective of motive or circumstance. The applicants argue that it is so simply because it relates to the funding of the political process. I disagree. Rather

h it seems to me merely an offence against the ordinary law enacted for the proper ordering of the democratic process in Italy—no different from, say, voting twice at an election. It is, of course, an offence committed in a political context. In my judgment, however, that does not make it a political offence.

The second dictum upon which the applicants principally rely is this from Lord

j Lloyd's recent speech in *T v Secretary of State for the Home Dept* [1996] 2 All ER 865 at 899, [1996] AC 742 at 786–787:

'A crime is a political crime for the purposes of art 1F(b) of the 1951 convention [Convention relating to the Status of Refugees (Geneva, 28 July 1951; TS 39 (1954); Cmd 9171; a provision excluding the protection of asylum for those guilty of "serious non-political crimes"] if, and only if (1) it is committed for a political purpose, that is to say, with the object of overthrowing or subverting or changing the government of a state or inducing it to change its policy; and (2) there is a sufficiently close and direct link between the crime and the alleged political purpose. In determining whether such a link exists, the court will bear in mind the means used to achieve the political end, and will have particular regard to whether the crime was aimed at a military or governmental target, on the one hand, or a civilian target on the other, and in either event whether it was likely to involve the indiscriminate killing or injuring of members of the public. Although I have referred to the above statement as a definition, I bear in mind Lord Radcliffe's warning in *Schtraks v Government of Israel* [1962] 3 All ER 529, [1964] AC 556 that a question which was first posed judicially more than 100 years ago in *Re Castioni* [1891] 1 QB 149, [1886–90] All ER Rep 640 is unlikely now to receive a definitive answer. The most that can be attempted is a description of an idea.'

Viscount Radcliffe in *Schtraks'* case [1962] 3 All ER 529 at 539, [1964] AC 556 at 589, one may note, had suggested that 'the court's reluctance to offer a definition has been due ... to the realisation that it is virtually impossible to find one that does not cover too wide a range'.

The words in Lord Lloyd's formulation upon which the applicants here focus are 'inducing [the government] to change its policy'. It is, they submit, an obvious inference to be drawn from the basic facts of this case that the present offence was committed to influence government policy in some way: one does not clandestinely pay vast sums of money to a political party without such a purpose. I for my part am disposed to accept this submission and draw the suggested inference, an inference, I would note, yet more readily drawn had the position been as Mr Sonnenberg misunderstood it to be, ie had all the payments involved bribery and corruption; it is for this reason that in my judgment the factual misunderstanding is immaterial, the actual position being a fortiori to what it was understood to be.

What, however, I cannot accept is that any offence committed with a view to inducing a change in government policy is ipso facto to be regarded as a political offence. The difficulty comes in defining just when it will be and when it will not. Lord Lloyd's formulation was, of course, in the context of violent crime. But that, I recognise, is not itself a necessary precondition of political offending; see eg this from Lord Reid's speech in *Schtraks'* case [1962] 3 All ER 529 at 535, [1964] AC 556 at 583:

'... I do not see why the section should be limited to attempts to overthrow a government. The use of force, or it may be other means, to compel a sovereign to change his advisers, or to compel a government to change its policy may be just as political in character as the use of force to achieve a revolution. And I do not see why it should be necessary that the refugee's party should have been trying to achieve power in the state. It would be enough if they were trying to make the government concede some measure of freedom, but not attempting to supplant it.'

A little later, moreover, Lord Reid contemplates asylum for—

'a refugee who had committed an offence, perhaps of a non-violent kind, as part of a campaign to induce or compel an autocratic government to grant a measure of civil or religious liberty [even had there been] no disturbance of public order ...' (See [1962] 3 All ER 529 at 535, [1964] AC 556 at 584.)

a Just when, then, can such an offence properly be characterised as political by virtue of the offender's purpose or motivation? In addressing this question in the present context I find considerable help in the following passage from Lord Radcliffe's speech in *Schtraks'* case [1962] 3 All ER 529 at 540, [1964] AC 556 at 591–592:

b 'In my opinion the idea that lies behind the phrase "offence of a political character" is that the fugitive is at odds with the state that applies for his extradition on some issue connected with the political control or government of the country. The analogy of "political" in this context is with "political" in such phrases as "political refugee", "political asylum" or "political prisoner." It does indicate, I think, that the requesting state is after c him for reasons other than the enforcement of the criminal law in its ordinary, what I may call its common or international, aspect. It is this idea that the judges were seeking to express in the two early cases of *Re Castioni* ([1891] 1 QB 149, [1886–90] All ER Rep 640) and *Re Meunier* ([1894] 2 QB 415) when they connected the political offence with an uprising, a disturbance, an d insurrection, a civil war or struggle for power: and in my opinion it is still necessary to maintain the idea of that connexion. It is not departed from by taking a liberal view as to what is meant by disturbance or these other words, provided that the idea of political opposition as between fugitive and requesting state is not lost sight of: but it would be lost sight of, I think, if one were to say that all offences were political offences, so long as they could be e shown to have been committed for a political object or with a political motive or for the furtherance of some political cause or campaign. There may, for instance, be all sorts of contending political organisations or forces in a country and members of them may commit all sorts of infractions of the criminal law in the belief that by so doing they will further their political f ends: but if the central government stands apart and is concerned only to enforce the criminal law that has been violated by these contestants, I see no reason why fugitives should be protected by this country from its jurisdiction on the ground that they are political offenders.'

g Before finally dealing with the offender's motivation, it is convenient to cite the third dictum relied upon by the applicants, that which brings the prosecutor's motivation too into play in determining whether or not an offence is political. This is from Lord Diplock's speech in *Tzu-Tsai Cheng v Governor of Pentonville Prison*, [1973] 2 All ER 204 at 209–210, [1973] AC 931 at 946:

h 'The purpose of the restriction [again, s 3(1) of the Extradition Act 1870], as it seems to me, was two-fold. First, to avoid involving the United Kingdom in the internal political conflicts of foreign states. Today's Garibaldi may well form tomorrow's government. And, secondly, the humanitarian purpose of preventing the offender being surrendered to a jurisdiction in j which there was a risk that his trial or punishment might be unfairly influenced by political considerations. As indicated by the inclusion of the second part of the restriction [barring extradition where it is sought "with a view to try or punish him for an offence of a political character"] it was suspicion of the motives of requisitioning states in seeking the surrender of fugitive criminals who were political opponents of the government of that state which underlay both the requirements of [s 3(1)] of the Act.'

In asserting here that the applicants risk 'trial or punishment ... unfairly influenced by political considerations', Mr Fitzgerald places before us extensive writings describing the Italian magistracy's 'Mani Pulite' ('clean hands') crusade, and submits that these writings clearly reveal a power struggle between the two arms of state, the judiciary and the executive. The prosecutor here, he contends, is concerned 'to make a political example of certain prominent politicians for "political" ends'.

It is time to state my conclusions on the political issue and this I can do really quite briefly.

I do not accept for one moment that the Italian magistracy's desire to expose and punish corruption in public and political life, and the conflict that that has created between the judges and the politicians there, operates to transform the present offences into political ones. It is a misuse of language to describe the magistrates' campaign as being for 'political ends', or their approach to Mr Berlusconi as one of political persecution. On the contrary, all that I have read in this case suggests rather that the magistracy are demonstrating both their proper independence from the executive and an even-handedness in dealing equally with the politicians of all political parties. If one applies Lord Radcliffe's dictum in *Schtraks'* case [1962] 3 All ER 529 at 540, [1964] AC 556 at 591–592 that there should be no protection for offenders 'if the central government stands apart and is concerned only to enforce the criminal law', one finds in the present context the magistracy standing apart as the relevant arm of central government and the politicians (or some of them) as the offenders against whom 'the criminal law in its ordinary ... aspect' is being enforced. It is, indeed, somewhat ironical that the applicants here are seeking to be regarded as political offenders in respect of offences committed in part whilst Mr Berlusconi himself was actually in office.

More fundamentally, however, I reject the applicants' basic proposition that making payments to politicians or political parties (whether by way of bribes or illicit donations to my mind matters not) constitutes political offending in any relevant sense. It is not intrinsically political, nor is it made so because the offender hopes to change policy by buying political influence, nor because the judiciary by prosecuting him hope to clean up politics. In short, none of the applicants' arguments, whether taken individually or cumulatively, begin to persuade me that the present offences are political. I just cannot see corrupt political contributors as 'today's Garibaldis' (per Lord Diplock), or seekers after 'freedom' (per Lord Reid), or 'political prisoners' (per Lord Radcliffe).

It follows that I would reject this final ground of challenge also and, in the result, dismiss the motion.

I add just this footnote. I am conscious of having referred throughout this judgment to offending of one sort or another. It is imperative to recognise, however, that none of the applicants has yet been convicted of anything and that nothing I have said should be thought to raise the least presumption of guilt against them.

GAGE J. I agree.

Application dismissed.

30 October 1996. The Appeal Committee of the House of Lords (Lord Lloyd of Berwick, Lord Steyn and Lord Hope of Craighead) refused leave to appeal.

Dilys Tausz   Barrister.

R v Blake

a

COURT OF APPEAL, CRIMINAL DIVISION
HIRST LJ, McCULLOUGH AND TOULSON JJ
29, 31 JULY 1996

b

Wireless – Broadcasting – Broadcasting without licence – Using wireless telegraphy station without licence – Defendant unaware he was transmitting – Whether offence of strict liability – Whether presumption that mens rea required displaced – Wireless Telegraphy Act 1949, s 1(1).

c
The defendant, a disc jockey, was charged with two counts of using a station for wireless telegraphy without a licence on two separate dates contrary to s 1(1)[a] of the Wireless Telegraphy Act 1949. On arraignment, the defendant submitted that although he had known that he was using the broadcasting apparatus, since he had believed he was making a demonstration tape and had not been aware that he was in fact transmitting, he had a defence to the charges as the prosecution needed to
d establish mens rea. The recorder rejected that submission and ruled that the offence created by s 1(1) was an absolute offence of strict liability. The defendant thereupon changed his plea to guilty and was sentenced to a fine of £150 on each count, £900 costs and forfeiture of all the equipment under s 14(3) of the 1949 Act. The defendant appealed against conviction.

e
Held – The purpose behind making unlicensed transmissions a serious criminal offence was one of social concern in the interests of public safety, since unauthorised pirate broadcasts interfered with public service communications used by the emergency services and air traffic controllers, and thereby posed a grave risk to wide sections of the public. Moreover, the imposition of an absolute
f offence would encourage greater vigilance on the part of those establishing or using a station, or installing or using the apparatus, to avoid committing the offence and would operate as a deterrent. Accordingly, although there was a presumption in favour of a requirement of mens rea, that presumption was in the circumstances displaced. It followed that under s 1(1) of the 1949 Act the prosecution had to establish merely that the defendant knew he was making use
g of the apparatus, and did not need to show that he was doing so with a guilty mind because the section created an absolute offence. The appeal would therefore be dismissed (see p 966 d e, p 968 e to h, and p 969 h j, post).
     Dictum of Lord Scarman in *Gammon (Hong Kong) Ltd v A-G of Hong Kong* [1984] 2 All ER 503 at 508 applied.

h
Notes
For the necessity for wireless telegraphy licence, see *45 Halsbury's Laws* (4th edn) para 505.
     For the Wireless Telegraphy Act 1949, ss 1, 14, see 45 *Halsbury's Statutes* (4th
j edn) (1994 reissue) 32, 54.

Cases referred to in judgment
Gammon (Hong Kong) Ltd v A-G of Hong Kong [1984] 2 All ER 503, [1985] AC 1, [1984] 3 WLR 437, PC.

---

a   Section 1(1), so far as material, is set out at p 965 j, post

R v Brown [1996] 1 All ER 545, [1996] AC 543, [1996] 2 WLR 203, HL.
R v Howells [1977] 3 All ER 417, [1977] QB 614, [1977] 2 WLR 716, CA.
R v Hussain (1980) 72 Cr App R 143, CA.
R v Steele [1993] Crim LR 298, CA.
R v Waller [1991] Crim LR 381, CA.
R v Wells Street Metropolitan Stipendiary Magistrate, ex p Westminster City Council
   [1986] 3 All ER 4, [1986] 1 WLR 1046, DC.
Rudd v Secretary of State for Trade and Industry [1987] 2 All ER 553, [1987] 1 WLR
   786, HL.
Sweet v Parsley [1969] 1 All ER 347, [1970] AC 132, [1969] 2 WLR 470, HL.
Warner v Metropolitan Police Comr [1968] 2 All ER 356, [1969] 2 AC 256, [1968] 2
   WLR 1303, HL.

Cases also cited or referred to in skeleton arguments
Alphacell Ltd v Woodward [1972] 2 All ER 475, [1972] AC 824, HL.
Chilvers v Rayner [1984] 1 All ER 843, [1984] 1 WLR 328, DC.
Customs and Excise Comrs v Air Canada [1991] 1 All ER 570, [1991] 2 QB 446, CA;
   rvsg [1989] 2 All ER 22, [1989] QB 234.
R v Bezzina, R v Codling, R v Elvin [1994] 3 All ER 964, [1994] 1 WLR 1057, CA.
R v Brockley (1993) 99 Cr App R 385, CA.
R v Miller [1975] 2 All ER 974, [1975] 1 WLR 1222, CA.
Whiley v DPP [1995] Crim LR 39, DC.

Appeal against conviction
Albert Philip Blake appealed with leave of Ebsworth J against his conviction in
the Crown Court at Wood Green on 19 March 1996 before Mr Recorder
Carey QC on a plea of guilty of two offences under s 1(1) of the Wireless
Telegraphy Act 1949 for which he was sentenced to a fine of £150 on each, £900
costs and forfeiture of all his equipment pursuant to s 14(3) of the Act, on the
ground that as he had not known he was actually transmitting that amounted to
a defence under s 1(1). The facts are set out in the judgment of the court.

Philip Levy (assigned by the Registrar of Criminal Appeals) for the appellant.
Jonathan N Davies (instructed by Hatten Asplin & Glenny, Barking) for the Crown.

                                                          Cur adv vult

31 July 1996. The following judgment of the court was delivered.

HIRST LJ. On 18 March 1996 in the Crown Court at Wood Green, before Mr
Recorder Carey QC, the appellant, Mr Albert Philip Blake, pleaded guilty on
re-arraignment, after legal argument and a ruling by the recorder, to two counts
of using a station for wireless telegraphy without a licence on two separate dates.
On 19 March he was sentenced to a fine of £150 on each count, £900 costs and
forfeiture of all the equipment under s 14(3) of the Wireless Telegraphy Act 1949,
as amended. He now appeals against conviction by leave of the single judge.
    The facts are that on various dates in February 1995 radio investigation officers
heard an unlicensed radio station called 'Ragga' transmitting on the VHF
broadcasting band. On the evening of 15 February the disc jockey identified
himself as 'Casanova'. The transmissions were traced to a tower block in Holly
Street, E8. A radio link to the distant studio was identified and the source of
emission was traced to Newton Road, N15. From there, a second microwave
radio link was traced to low-rise flats in Cunningham Road, N15. The premises

a were searched during a transmission and the appellant was discovered alone in the flat standing in front of record decks, playing music and wearing a set of headphones. A cable ran to the kitchen where a microwave transmitter and a suitable aerial were found. When the transmitter was switched off, the broadcast ceased.

b The appellant told the radio investigation officer that his disc jockey name was Casanova and gave the hours during which he transmitted and the frequency on which the transmissions took place: he also signed a contemporaneous note of the interview confirming its accuracy. Following caution, the question and answer session went as follows:

'Q. What time did you start your show tonight? A. Nine.
c Q. What DJ name do you use? A. Casanova.
Q. Have you any records in the studio room? A. Yes, some in a bag and some singles.
Q. Are the records on the turntable yours? A. Yes.
Q. What's the name of the station? A. Ragga.
d Q. When was the last time you transmitted on Ragga? A. Two weeks ago.
Q. Was that from here? A. Yes.
Q. What frequency do you transmit on? A. 99·6.
Q. Did you install the apparatus? A. No.
Q. What time did you come here tonight? A. Nine.
Q. How did you get in? A. The guy that was before me let me in.
e Q. What time did he leave? A. He left when I came in.
Q. So you have been on your own since 9 o'clock? A. Yes.'

The equipment seized included a number of cassettes, two record decks, a compact disc player, a stereo audio mixer, a microphone, a microwave
f transmitter and aerial, assorted cables and leads, various papers and posters, one transmitter and one microwave receiver.

Having regard to the appellant's activity at the time of the search, and also to the clear statements made by him in the interview, there was no dispute that he knew he was using the broadcasting apparatus in the studio. His defence was that he believed he was making demonstration tapes at the time and so did not know
g that he was, in fact, transmitting.

The question which the recorder had to decide on when he gave his ruling was whether, as the prosecution contended, the offence created by s 1(1) of the 1949 Act is an absolute offence of strict liability, or whether, as the defence contended, the prosecution needed to establish mens rea. The recorder upheld the
h prosecution's submission on this point, at which juncture the appellant changed his plea to one of guilty.

Section 1(1) provides, so far as relevant, as follows:

'*Licensing of wireless telegraphy.*—No person shall establish or use any station for wireless telegraphy or instal or use any apparatus for wireless
j telegraphy except under the authority of a licence in that behalf granted under this section—(a) by the Secretary of State (unless it is a television licence), or (b) if it is a television licence, by the BBC; and any person who establishes or uses any station for wireless telegraphy or instals or uses any apparatus for wireless telegraphy except under and in accordance with such a licence shall be guilty of an offence under this Act ...'

It is common ground between the two parties (1) that the word 'use' is to be
interpreted in its natural and ordinary meaning (cf *Rudd v Secretary of State for*
Trade and Industry [1987] 2 All ER 553, [1987] 1 WLR 786 and *R v Brown* [1996] 1
All ER 545, [1996] AC 543); and (2) that the relevant general law was accurately
summarised by Lord Scarman giving the judgment of the Board in the Privy
Council case of *Gammon (Hong Kong) Ltd v A-G of Hong Kong* [1984] 2 All ER 503 at
508, [1985] AC 1 at 14, applying the earlier and very well-known decision of the
House of Lords in *Sweet v Parsley* [1969] 1 All ER 347, [1970] AC 132, as follows:

> 'In their Lordships' opinion, the law relevant to this appeal may be stated
> in the following propositions (the formulation of which follows closely the
> written submission of the appellants' counsel, which their Lordships
> gratefully acknowledge): (1) there is a presumption of law that mens rea is
> required before a person can be held guilty of a criminal offence; (2) the
> presumption is particularly strong where the offence is "truly criminal" in
> character; (3) the presumption applies to statutory offences, and can be
> displaced only if this is clearly or by necessary implication the effect of the
> statute; (4) the only situation in which the presumption can be displaced is
> where the statute is concerned with an issue of social concern; public safety
> is such an issue; (5) even where a statute is concerned with such an issue, the
> presumption of mens rea stands unless it can also be shown that the creation
> of strict liability will be effective to promote the objects of the statute by
> encouraging greater vigilance to prevent the commission of the prohibited
> act.

The history of s 1(1) is of some relevance. In its original form in 1949 it was in
substantially the same terms as in its present wording, and the prescribed penalty
on summary conviction was imprisonment for a period not exceeding three
months or a fine not exceeding £100, or both. However, the 1949 Act was
amended by ss 168, 169 and 170 of the Broadcasting Act 1990, which made two
relevant changes.

(1) Three new sections were added as follows:

> '1A. *Offence of keeping wireless telegraphy station or apparatus available for*
> *unauthorised use.*—Any person who has any station for wireless telegraphy or
> apparatus for wireless telegraphy in his possession or under his control and
> either—(a) intends to use it in contravention of section 1 of this Act; or (b)
> knows, or has reasonable cause to believe, that another person intends to use
> it in contravention of that section, shall be guilty of an offence.
>
> 1B. *Offence of allowing premises to be used for purpose of unlawful*
> *broadcasting.*—(1) A person who is in charge of any premises which are used
> for making an unlawful broadcast, or for sending signals for the operation or
> control of any apparatus used for the purpose of making an unlawful
> broadcast from any other place, shall be guilty of an offence if—(a) he
> knowingly causes or permits the premises to be so used; or (b) having
> reasonable cause to believe that the premises are being so used, he fails to
> take such steps as are reasonable in the circumstances of the case to prevent
> the premises from so being used ...
>
> 1C. *Prohibition of acts facilitating unauthorised broadcasting.*—(1) If a
> person—(a) does any of the acts mentioned in subsection (2) in relation to a
> broadcasting station by which unauthorised broadcasts are made, and (b) if
> any knowledge or belief or any circumstances is or are specified in relation

a to the act, does it with that knowledge or belief or in those circumstances, he shall be guilty of an offence.

(2) The acts referred to in subsection (1) are—(a) participating in the management, financing, operation or day-to-day running of the station knowing, or having reasonable cause to believe, that unauthorised broadcasts are made by the station; (b) supplying, installing, repairing or

b maintaining any wireless telegraphy apparatus or any other item knowing, or having reasonable cause to believe, that the apparatus or other item is to be, or is, used for the purpose of facilitating the operation or day-to-day running of the station and that unauthorised broadcasts are made by the station; (c) rendering any other service to any person knowing, or having reasonable cause to believe, that the rendering of that service to that person

c will facilitate the operation or day-to-day running of the station and that unauthorised broadcasts are so made; (d) supplying a film or sound recording knowing, or having reasonable cause to believe, that an unauthorised broadcast of the film or recording is to be so made; (e) making a literary, dramatic or musical work knowing, or having reasonable cause to believe,

d that an unauthorised broadcast of that work is to be so made; (f) making an artistic work knowing, or having reasonable cause to believe, that an unauthorised broadcast including that work is to be so made; (g) doing any of the following acts, namely—(i) participating in an unauthorised broadcast made by the station, being actually present as an announcer, as a performer or one of the performers concerned in an entertainment given, or as the

e deliverer of a speech; (ii) advertising, or inviting another to advertise, by means of an unauthorised broadcast made by the station; or (iii) publishing the times or other details of any authorised broadcasts made by the station or (otherwise than by publishing such details) publishing an advertisement of matter calculated to promote the station (whether directly or indirectly),

f knowing, or having reasonable cause to believe, that unauthorised broadcasts are made by the station.'

(2) The penalty was increased by prescribing a term of imprisonment not exceeding six months or a fine not exceeding the statutory maximum, or both, on summary conviction and imprisonment for a term not exceeding two years, or a

g fine, or both, on conviction on indictment.

On behalf of the appellant, Mr Levy submitted that the word 'use' itself implied mens rea and was synonymous with 'make use of' or 'employ for a purpose'. This, he submitted, was underlined by the insertion of the three new sections in 1990 which he suggested create a whole range of new offences which would have

h been unnecessary if the prosecution's interpretation of the subsection were correct. He drew special attention to s 1C(2)(g), which makes it an offence, inter alia, knowingly to participate in an unauthorised broadcast made by the station or being actually present as an announcer. Clearly, he submitted, a disc jockey with the necessary mens rea would be caught under s 1C(2)(g) yet, if the prosecution were right, he would already have been caught under s 1(1) itself

j without the need to prove mens rea.

Finally, Mr Levy placed strong reliance on the principles laid down in the *Gammon* case and submitted that the present case did not fall within the exceptions laid down in paras (4) and (5).

On behalf of the prosecution, Mr Davies stressed that s 1(1) is silent on mens rea and that, in consequence, it was properly to be construed as creating an absolute offence, in contrast to the three new sections, 1A, 1B and 1C, with their

express use of the word 'knowingly'. Moreover, he submitted that any
presumption to the contrary was displaced by the aspects of social concern and
public safety addressed by s 1(1), seeing that unauthorised pirate broadcasts
frequently interfere with public service communications used by the police, the
fire service, and the ambulance service, and also by air traffic control. It was thus
important that there should be a strong deterrent and an encouragement to
greater vigilance to prevent the commission of the prohibited offence.

In support of the latter argument, he relied on *R v Wells Street Metropolitan
Stipendiary Magistrate, ex p Westminster City Council* [1986] 3 All ER 4, [1986] 1
WLR 1046, where the Divisional Court (Watkins LJ and Sir Roger Ormrod) held
that s 55(1) of the Town and Country Planning Act 1971, which prohibits the
execution of various works to a listed building, was an absolute offence. Having
expressly cited the principles laid down in the *Gammon* case, the court held that
s 55(1) clearly related to an issue of social concern and that the creation of strict
liability would be effective to promote the objects of the statute by encouraging
greater vigilance, and by furnishing a deterrent to those tempted to breach it (see
[1986] 3 All ER 4 at 8–9, [1986] 1 WLR 1046 at 1050–1051 per Watkins LJ).

The solution to this case, which we have not found easy, clearly lies in the
application of the five principles laid down by Lord Scarman in the *Gammon* case.
In our judgment, since throughout the history of s 1(1), an offender has been
potentially subject to a term of imprisonment, the offence is 'truly criminal' in
character, and it follows that Mr Levy is correct in submitting that the
presumption in favour of mens rea is particularly strong. However, it seems to
us manifest that the purpose behind making unlicensed transmissions a serious
criminal offence must have been one of social concern in the interests of public
safety for the reasons given by Mr Davies, since undoubtedly the emergency
services and air traffic controllers were using radio communications in 1949,
albeit in a much more rudimentary form than nowadays. No doubt the much
greater sophistication of these modes of communication, and the wider
prevalence of pirate radio stations 40 years on, led to the substantial increase in
the penalty in 1990.

Clearly, interference with transmissions by these vital public services poses a
grave risk to wide sections of the public. We, therefore, consider that the test laid
down in para (4) in the *Gammon* case is met.

Furthermore, we are satisfied that the test in para (5) is also met, since the
imposition of an absolute offence must surely encourage greater vigilance on the
part of those establishing or using a station, or installing or using the apparatus,
to avoid committing the offence, eg in the case of users by carefully checking
whether they are on air; it must also operate as a deterrent. The case is thus in
our judgment, mutatis mutandis, comparable with *Ex p Westminster City Council*,
perhaps a fortiori, since here public safety is the main consideration and, in our
view, a consideration of paramount importance.

We do not find the parliamentary history of great assistance either way. On
the one hand, we do not think Mr Davies is entitled to invoke, for the purpose of
the construction of s 1(1), newly inserted sections which were not in existence
when it was enacted. On the other hand, we are not persuaded by Mr Levy's
alternative analysis, since it seems to us that, looked at in the round, the new
sections were probably intended to sweep up a number of broadcasting activities,
nearly all of which would fall outside the scope of s 1(1), and which, because of
their more peripheral character, were made subject to the requirement of the
proof of mens rea. Inevitably, in such circumstances, there is likely to be some

a overlap, as in the case of an announcer or disc jockey under s 1C(2)(g), on which Mr Levy particularly relied.

The real significance of the amendments, we think, is to underline the deep concern of Parliament to deter pirate broadcasting, by bringing within the purview of the prohibition not only those directly responsible for establishing or using the station or installing or using the apparatus (under s 1(1) itself), but also b (by the amendment) persons less directly involved, who are engaged in connected activities, subject in the latter case to the more onerous burden of proof.

We think that the proper approach to s 1(1) is closely akin to the approach adopted to the absolute offence of possessing a firearm without a certificate contrary to s 1 of the Firearms Act 1968, which Mr Davies cited to us for the c purposes of comparison. This is described in *Archbold's Criminal Pleading Evidence and Practice* (1996 edn) paras 24-5. Section 1(1) provides:

> 'Subject to any exemption under this Act, it is an offence for a person—(a) to have in his possession, or to purchase or acquire, a firearm to which this section applies without holding a firearm certificate in force at the time, or d otherwise than as authorised by such a certificate ...'

The *Archbold* commentary is as follows:

> 'Section 1(1) creates absolute offences. In *R. v. Hussain*, 72 Cr. App. R. 143, C.A. (a case concerning s. 1(1)(a)), the court held (applying *Warner v.* e *Metropolitan Police Commr*, ([1968] 2 All ER 356, [1969] 2 AC 256) H.L., a drugs case) that if the prosecution prove that the defendant knowingly had in his possession an article which in fact is a firearm as defined in the 1968 Act (see s. 57(1), *post*, §24–72), then the offence is committed, and the fact that the defendant did not know that the article in his possession was a firearm within f the Act for which a certificate was required is immaterial ... Similarly, in *R. v. Waller* [1991] Crim. L.R. 381, C.A., following *Hussain*, the defendant was held to have been rightly convicted under section 1(1) where he took possession of a friend's bag which, unknown to him, contained a firearm and not, as he thought it might, a crowbar; and in *R. v. Steele* ([1993] Crim. L.R. 298, C.A., following *Waller*, a conviction was upheld where the defendant g had custody of the bag for only a matter of minutes and could not reasonably have been expected to know that it contained a firearm. Accordingly, an honest and reasonable belief that a modern reproduction is an antique firearm ... is no defence to a charge of possessing a firearm without a certificate contrary to section 1(1)(a): *R. v. Howells* ([1977] 3 All ER 417, [1977] h QB 614), C.A. ...'

So here, by analogy, it is incumbent upon the prosecution to establish that the defendant knew he was making use of the apparatus, but they need not show that he was doing it with a guilty mind. Thus, for example, if a remark made by a bystander near the studio was accidentally picked up by the microphone and j broadcast, the bystander would not be liable.

In these circumstances, we are satisfied that s 1(1) does create an absolute offence and it follows that this appeal will be dismissed.

Appeal dismissed. Leave to appeal to the House of Lords refused.

N P Metcalfe Esq   Barrister.

Nelson v Nelson   *a*

COURT OF APPEAL, CIVIL DIVISION

McCOWAN, PETER GIBSON AND WALLER LJJ   *b*

18 NOVEMBER, 6 DECEMBER 1996

Solicitor – Payment of costs by solicitor personally – Application for solicitor to pay costs personally – Solicitors instructed by undischarged bankrupt in property claim – Solicitors unaware of client's bankruptcy – Solicitors not acting improperly, *c* *unreasonably or negligently – Solicitors commencing action and obtaining Mareva injunction – Injunction discharged on client admitting he was a bankrupt – Judge ordering solicitors to pay costs of proceedings – Whether proper exercise of discretion.*

In March 1995 the plaintiff instructed a firm of solicitors to protect his interest in *d* a property which his son, the first defendant, was in the process of selling under a power of attorney. At the time the plaintiff was an undischarged bankrupt but he did not disclose that fact to the solicitors. On hearing that the property had been sold, the solicitors obtained over the telephone a Mareva injunction against the defendants, but the injunction was discharged on the return date when the *e* plaintiff admitted in the course of cross-examination that he was a bankrupt. On the question of costs, the judge held that there was no basis for making a 'wasted costs' order against the solicitors under s 51(6) and (7) of the Supreme Court Act 1981, since they had been misled by the plaintiff and had acted neither improperly, unreasonably nor negligently. However, he proceeded to make an *f* order for costs on an indemnity basis against the solicitors under the inherent jurisdiction of the court, on the grounds that although they had been wholly innocent in the matter, by virtue of s 306(1)[a] of the Insolvency Act 1986 they had had no authority to act for the plaintiff, had behaved in a manner analogous to that of a breach of warranty of authority and were thereby in breach of their duty to the court. The solicitors appealed.   *g*

Held – Where a solicitor commenced proceedings on behalf of a client, he did not thereby represent that the client had a good cause of action, but merely that he had a client who bore the name of the party to the proceedings and who had authorised them. In the instant case, the plaintiff did not have a good cause of *h* action, as any interest he had in the property had vested in his trustee in bankruptcy. Nevertheless, since a bankrupt was entitled to bring any action except one relating to his property he had had the capacity and the authority to retain a solicitor, and therefore the solicitors had had the plaintiff's authority in commencing the proceedings and had warranted no more than that. They were *j* not consequently in breach of their duty to the court and, in the light of his findings of fact as to their conduct, the judge should have exercised his discretion as to costs in their favour. Accordingly, the appeal would be allowed (see p 972 *h*, p 973 *a* to *e*, p 974 *h* to p 975 *c* and p 978 *e* to *j*).

a   Section 306(1) is set out at p 972 *d*, post

Notes

a For definition and form of a solicitor's retainer by his client, see 44(1) *Halsbury's Laws* (4th edn reissue) paras 99–103, and for the effect of a solicitor acting without a client's authority in contentious business, see ibid para 132.

For the Insolvency Act 1986, s 306, see 4 *Halsbury's Statutes* (4th edn) (1987 reissue) 947.

b
Cases referred to in judgments

Heath v Tang, Stevens v Peacock [1993] 4 All ER 694, [1993] 1 WLR 1421, CA.
Moss, Re (1866) LR 2 Eq 345.
Motion v Moojen (1872) LR 14 Eq 202.
Myers v Elman [1939] 4 All ER 484, [1940] AC 282, HL.
c *Ridehalgh v Horsefield* [1994] 3 All ER 848, [1994] Ch 205, [1994] 3 WLR 462, CA.
Tolstoy-Miloslavsky (Count) v Lord Aldington [1996] 2 All ER 556, [1996] 1 WLR 736, CA.
Yonge v Toynbee [1910] 1 KB 215, CA.

d
Cases also cited or referred to in skeleton arguments
Boaler v Powell [1910] 2 KB 229, CA.
Collen v Wright (1857) 8 E & B 647, [1843–60] All ER Rep 146, 120 ER 241.
Fricker v Van Gutten [1896] 2 Ch 649, CA.
Geilinger v Gibbs [1897] 1 Ch 479.
Payne v Dicker (1871) LR 6 Ch App 578.
e *Savage, Re* (1880) 15 Ch D 557.
Udall v Capri Lighting Ltd [1987] 3 All ER 262, [1988] QB 907, CA.

Appeal

By notice dated 3 January 1996 and amended on 8 October 1996 Messrs Aslam Heath, a firm of solicitors, appealed with leave of Saville LJ from the decision of
f Judge Marr-Johnson, sitting as a judge of the High Court on 16 May 1995 whereby, inter alia, he ordered the solicitors to pay the costs of an application on behalf of the plaintiff, Joseph Nelson, for a Mareva injunction against the defendants, Matthew Dixon Nelson, Joseph St Rose and Pardeep Pabila, including the costs of the hearing and the application for costs, to be taxed on an
g indemnity basis (in default of agreement) and paid forthwith. The facts are set out in the judgment of McCowan LJ.

Guy Mansfield QC (instructed by *Barlow Lyde & Gilbert*) for the solicitors.
Richard Evans (instructed by *H Omar & Co*) for the third defendant.
h The first and second defendants did not appear.

Cur adv vult

6 December 1996. The following judgments were delivered.

j **McCOWAN LJ.** This is an appeal brought with leave of Saville LJ from an order made on 16 May 1995 of Judge Marr-Johnson, sitting as a judge of the High Court, that the plaintiff's solicitors should pay the costs of the application for a Mareva injunction including the costs of the hearing of 31 March 1995 and the hearing of the application for costs of 16 May 1995, to be taxed on an indemnity basis (in default of agreement) and paid forthwith.

The judge found that Mr Mensah-Dankwah was at all material times a solicitor with the appellant solicitors and that he was instructed by the plaintiff, Joseph

Nelson, to act for him and, in particular, to take all appropriate steps to protect *a* what he claimed was his interest in 18 Arundel Gardens, Ilford, Essex. The plaintiff was at the time an undischarged bankrupt but he did not disclose that fact to the solicitors. The solicitors instructed counsel and they obtained a Mareva injunction for the plaintiff on the telephone from Owen J on 18 March 1995. On the return day for the injunction, namely 31 March 1995, as a result of an admission made by the plaintiff in cross-examination, the appellant solicitors *b* learned for the first time that the plaintiff was an undischarged bankrupt.

The judge in his judgment said that he had heard evidence from Mr Mensah-Dankwah and found that he acted with ordinary diligence throughout. He continued: 'Nor has his firm acted in a negligent manner. The true position is that the plaintiff had grossly misled the solicitors.' The judge therefore held that there was no basis for making a 'wasted costs' order under s 51(6) and (7) of *c* the Supreme Court Act 1981, the solicitors having acted neither improperly, unreasonably nor negligently. Instead, the judge purported to make the order for costs against the appellant solicitors under the inherent jurisdiction of the court over solicitors, based upon the following argument of the defendants.

Reliance was placed upon s 306(1) of the Insolvency Act 1986, which reads: *d*

> 'The bankrupt's estate shall vest in the trustee immediately on his appointment taking effect or, in the case of the official receiver, on his becoming trustee.'

Therefore, the defendants argued to the judge that the solicitors had no authority *e* to act for the plaintiff in this case, behaved in a manner analogous to that of a breach of warranty of authority and were thereby in breach of their duty to the court. The judge accepted this argument and said:

> 'There is a common misfortune here by both solicitors and defendants alike but, on balance, the authorities have decided that the loss should fall *f* upon the solicitors and not the parties. I accept therefore that this action was brought without authority and therefore, though satisfied that the plaintiff's solicitors are wholly innocent in this matter, they must pay the costs.'

In justification of ordering that the costs be on an indemnity basis, he said that *g* 'there was no reason why the defendants should be out of pocket at all'.

Before this court Mr Richard Evans for the third defendant relied on RSC Ord 80, r 2(1), which reads: 'A person under disability may not bring, or make a claim, in any proceedings except by his next friend ...' Mr Evans suggested that the situation in the case of an undischarged bankrupt is comparable. I cannot agree. *h* A bankrupt is entitled to bring any action except one relating to his property. Thus, he can bring an action for personal injury or defamation. This means that he has the capacity and the authority to retain solicitors. What is lost is the right to bring certain types of action.

Mr Evans placed heavy reliance on *Motion v Moojen* (1872) LR 14 Eq 202. For my part, however, I find this case of no assistance at all. It was decided before the *j* Supreme Court of Judicature Act 1875 and decided no more than that when a bankrupt pursues an action in the administration of his bankruptcy he has to bring it in the Bankruptcy and not the Chancery court.

We were also referred, as was the judge, to *Yonge v Toynbee* [1910] 1 KB 215, *Ridehalgh v Horsefield* [1994] 3 All ER 848, [1994] Ch 205, *Myers v Elman* [1939] 4 All ER 484, [1940] AC 282, *Heath v Tang, Stevens v Peacock* [1993] 4 All ER 694, [1993]

1 WLR 1421 and *Count Tolstoy-Miloslavsky v Lord Aldington* [1996] 2 All ER 556, [1996] 1 WLR 736.

I see nothing in these authorities to contradict the contention of Mr Mansfield QC, for the solicitors, that a solicitor who lends his name to the commencement of proceedings is saying: (1) that he has a client; (2) that the client bears the name of the party to the proceedings; and (3) that that client has authorised the proceedings. He does not represent that the client has a good cause of action. What the plaintiff in the present case was lacking was a good cause of action, since any action in respect of a claim to 18 Arundel Gardens was vested in his trustee in bankruptcy.

In my judgment, in commencing these proceedings the solicitors had authority from the plaintiff to do so and warranted no more than that. In particular, they are not to be taken to be warranting that the plaintiff had a good cause of action vested in him.

In those circumstances, I see no breach on the part of the solicitors of their duty to the court. Indeed, such a finding seems to me to be inconsistent with the judge's other findings, first, that the solicitors were wholly innocent in the matter and, second, that they were not properly subject to a wasted costs order. At the very least he should have recognised that he had a discretion whether to make the solicitors pay any costs of the case.

In the light of the judge's findings of fact as to the conduct of the solicitors, any such discretion should have been exercised in favour of the solicitors.

I would add that, in my judgment, in the light of those findings, it could not properly be considered a suitable case for indemnity costs.

For these reasons, I would allow the appeal.

PETER GIBSON LJ. The central question on this appeal is not, pace Mr Evans for the third defendants the effect of the bankruptcy order upon the rights of the bankrupt in relation to the property owned by him. That effect is plain, having regard to s 306 of the Insolvency Act 1986, which vested in the trustee in bankruptcy property such as the bankrupt's claimed interest in 18 Arundel Gardens, Ilford on the bankruptcy. Instead, the question to be answered is whether the bankrupt had the capacity to retain a solicitor to commence the proceedings which he did commence. Those proceedings are not a nullity such as would have been the case if the plaintiff did not exist. But they were liable to be stayed or struck out because the bankrupt did not have any interest in the property, such interest as he did have prior to the bankruptcy order having vested in the trustee in bankruptcy. They might be stayed pending the decision of the trustee in bankruptcy to take over the proceedings. Alternatively, if the trustee did not wish to do so, a defendant could apply to strike out the action. The substantive order made by Judge Marr-Johnson was, entirely correctly, that the action be struck out unless the trustee in bankruptcy of the plaintiff showed cause.

Mr Evans submitted that by virtue of s 306 of the 1986 Act a solicitor who acts on behalf of a bankrupt does so without authority. He described the position as analogous with that of a solicitor who acts on behalf of a mentally disabled person or a minor. But the analogy does not seem to me apt. Subject only to one limited exception, the rules governing procedure in the Supreme Court and in the county court respectively do not permit a person under disability to bring an action except by his next friend (RSC Ord 80, r 2(1) and CCR Ord 10, r 1(1)). The exception is that by s 47 of the County Courts Act 1988, a minor may prosecute an action in a county court for any sum of money not exceeding the county court limit which may be due to him for wages or piece-work or for work as a servant in the same manner and as if he were of full age. There is no such procedural bar for the bankrupt.

There are a number of actions which a bankrupt may bring notwithstanding s 306 of the 1986 Act. He may bring any action in which the claim is personal to himself and affects his person or his reputation. Thus, he may bring an action in defamation, for personal injury, in assault and in negligence where his person or reputation is injured. He may bring an action as assignee, and there are other actions which the bankrupt has been held to have been able to bring (see e g *Chitty on Contracts* (27th edn, 1994) vol 1, para 20-041).

Yet it is said by Mr Evans, supporting the decision of the judge, that the bankrupt is not able to retain a solicitor to bring proceedings to assert a property claim when the property is vested in the trustee in bankruptcy. That seems to me to confuse an effective cause of action with an effective retainer, as Mr Mansfield QC submitted. If a person who has completed an effective assignment in accordance with s 136 of the Law of Property Act 1925 of a chose in action retains solicitors to enforce that chose in action but omits to tell them of the assignment, the retainer is, in my judgment, effective notwithstanding that he has no effective cause of action. I cannot see why the position is not the same in a case where, in effect, there has been an assignment by virtue of s 306 of the 1986 Act.

Mr Evans drew our attention to the *Law Society's Guide to the Professional Conduct of Solicitors* (6th edn, 1993) p 265, para 12.17, in which it is stated: '3. The retainer may be determined by operation of law, e.g. the client's or solicitor's bankruptcy or mental incapacity.' Although no authority is cited in support, in *Re Moss* (1866) LR 2 Eq 345 at 348 Lord Romilly MR held that if the client becomes bankrupt, and the assignees do not employ the firm of solicitors, that is a discharge by the client of the solicitors. Lord Romilly MR gives no reasons for this view, but his proposition is said to be correct in 44(1) *Halsbury's Laws* (4th edn reissue) para 116, note 6 on three grounds:

> '... (1) the bankruptcy should terminate the authority of the solicitor which he may have warranted to third persons ... (2) the solicitor is probably acting on the faith of his client's credit and bankruptcy makes it impossible for the client to fulfil his obligations in respect of future services and disbursements; and (3) the relationship of solicitor and client is confidential and fiduciary, and the solicitor never agreed to act for the trustee in bankruptcy.'

For my part, I have considerable doubt whether the mere fact of a solicitor's client becoming bankrupt automatically operates to discharge the solicitor's retainer. Of the three reasons given in *Halsbury*, the first raises the question of what authority a solicitor does have when he accepts a retainer to bring proceedings for a client and what warranty he gives by bringing the proceedings in the client's name. Prima facie, his authority is to bring the proceedings in the name of the client and I do not see that he warrants more than that he has a retainer from the client who exists and has authorised the proceedings and against whom a costs order can be made. He does not warrant that the client has a good cause of action or that the client is solvent. Whether the client has made representations to the solicitor as to his ability to pay for future services and disbursements depends on the facts of the particular case. It is of course true that the relationship of solicitor and client is confidential and fiduciary and that the solicitor is hardly likely to have agreed to act for the trustee in bankruptcy, but that does not in itself entail the automatic discharge by the bankruptcy of the retainer.

a   Accordingly, I am not persuaded by the reasoning in *Halsbury*. In any event, the present case is not one relating to the termination of an existing retainer but one which raises the question whether a retainer ever came into being.

For the reasons given, in my judgment, the retainer did come into being. The bankrupt had the legal capacity to retain a solicitor and he gave authority to the appellants by instructing them to bring the proceedings in his name. In some
b   cases, a solicitor who brings proceedings which are doomed to failure will be at risk of being found guilty of improper or negligent conduct and it may be questioned whether he was knowingly a party to the bringing of an action which he knew to be improperly brought. The judge's findings in the present case exonerate the appellants of any charge of culpable conduct.

It follows that the basis on which the judge ordered the appellants to pay the
c   costs cannot be sustained. I, too, would allow the appeal.

WALLER LJ. The plaintiff at all material times was an undisclosed bankrupt. On 6 March 1995 the plaintiff instructed Mr Mensah-Dankwah, a solicitor with Messrs Aslam Heath, the appellant firm, to act for him, and in particular, to take
d   all appropriate steps to protect what the plaintiff claimed was his interest in 18 Arundel Gardens, Ilford, Essex. At this stage, the plaintiff did not disclose the fact that he was an undischarged bankrupt. The solicitors exchanged correspondence with solicitors for the first defendant, who was the son of the plaintiff and who, acting under a power of attorney which the plaintiff disputed, was in the process of selling 18 Arundel Gardens. The solicitors sought an undertaking that the
e   property would not be dealt with, but the response received, by letter of 13 March 1995, from solicitors for the first defendant was that the property had been sold 'last week' and that they had remitted the proceeds to the first defendant 'on Friday'.

The solicitors obtained emergency legal aid and an application was made for a
f   Mareva injunction supported by an affidavit sworn by the plaintiff. On 18 March 1995 an injunction was obtained (over the telephone) from Owen J against all three respondents. A written statement of claim was issued and served with the injunctions on the first and third defendants.

On 27 March 1995 the first defendant told his solicitors of the plaintiff's bankruptcy. A search confirmed the bankruptcy and revealed a creditor's notice
g   and bankruptcy inhibition registered against the plaintiff's home, 18 Belgrave Road, not the property the subject of the proceedings. It also appeared that the plaintiff had not told the Official Receiver of any interest in 18 Arundel Gardens, the subject of the proceedings. On 28 March 1995 the solicitors were notified of the bankruptcy but it was not until 31 March 1995 on the return date of the
h   Mareva injunction that the plaintiff admitted that he was a bankrupt.

On 31 March 1995 the Mareva injunction was discharged and the question of costs was adjourned until 15 May 1995. On 16 May 1995 Judge Marr-Johnson, sitting as a judge of the High Court, made an order that the solicitors pay all the costs of the plaintiff's application for a Mareva injunction on 18 March 1995
j   including those of the hearing of 31 March 1995.

The judge's findings and reasons

The defendants did not allege, in their application for the solicitors to pay the costs, that the firm had conducted the action in an unreasonable or improper manner, but alleged that they had been negligent. The judge, however, found that Mr Mensah-Dankwah 'acted with ordinary diligence throughout' and that his firm had not 'acted in a negligent manner'. He found that the plaintiff had *a* 'grossly misled his solicitors'. The judge, accordingly, declined to make any order against the solicitors on the grounds of negligence.

What, however, the judge did find was that so far as the authorities cited to him went they appeared to show: (1) that where a solicitor commences an action on behalf of a party, he impliedly warrants that he has the authority of that party; (2) that where a party does not have the capacity to instruct a solicitor to commence *b* an action, but an action is nevertheless commenced, there is a breach or something analogous to a breach of that warranty; and (3) that it matters not whether the solicitor is entirely without fault, the result will be that the solicitor is liable to the party against whom proceedings have been taken for all the costs incurred.

We, too, were taken to certain of the authorities, and Mr Mansfield QC sought *c* to persuade us, first, that even if a solicitor commenced proceedings without authority, the liability to pay costs was not absolute. He submitted that the court was only exercising its inherent jurisdiction when it made an order in such a situation and the exercise of that jurisdiction depended on establishing a breach of duty to the court. He relied on certain passages in the speeches of Viscount Maugham, Lord Wright and Lord Porter in *Myers v Elman* [1939] 4 All ER 484, *d* [1940] AC 282 supported, as he suggested, by passages in the judgments of the Court of Appeal in *Ridehalgh v Horsefield* [1994] 3 All ER 848, [1994] Ch 205 and *Count Tolstoy-Miloslavsky v Lord Aldington* [1996] 2 All ER 556, [1996] 1 WLR 736. My understanding of his submission was that he was suggesting that unless some fault in the conduct of the solicitor over and above an entirely innocent *e* commencement of proceedings without authority could be established, the jurisdiction did not exist. His alternative submission on this aspect was that there, in any event, remained a discretion, even if the court had the power under its inherent jurisdiction to award costs.

His second submission was that in any event a distinction must be drawn between the situation in which a plaintiff's cause of action will be defeated *f* because he or she is the wrong plaintiff, and the situation in which the plaintiff has no capacity to instruct a solicitor. His submission was that a bankrupt has the capacity to instruct a solicitor and to commence an action, but in relation to an action concerning property which has vested in his trustee in bankruptcy, the defendant simply has a right to stay the proceedings because the bankrupt is the *g* wrong plaintiff, ie has no locus standi. Mr Mansfield submitted that no solicitor warrants that his client has a cause of action; at most he warrants that he has the authority of the client to bring the action.

The submission of Mr Evans was, first, that a bankrupt simply has no capacity to instruct solicitors in relation to matters that have vested in the trustee in *h* bankruptcy citing *Motion v Moojen* (1872) LR 14 Eq 202 and *Heath v Tang* [1993] 4 All ER 694, [1993] 1 WLR 1421, second, accordingly the solicitors were acting without authority and, third, that the cases showed that however innocent, solicitors who act without authority will be liable for the costs on a basis analogous to damages for breach of warranty of authority citing *Yonge v Toynbee* [1910] 1 KB 215. *j*

In my view, Mr Mansfield is right when he says that in a case where the court orders a solicitor to pay the costs when he is acting without authority, the court is acting under its inherent jurisdiction. But I do not think that it follows that in all cases something other than the mere fact that the solicitor is acting without authority would have to be established. Lord Porter in *Myers v Elman* [1939] 4 All ER 484 at 521, [1940] AC 282 at 336, approving Swinfen Eady J in *Yonge v Toynbee*, a is only pointing out that the solicitor is not being made liable for a breach of warranty of authority because the solicitor is not being sued and is not a party to the action. As Swinfen Eady J put it, the court is exercising its authority over its officers upon the footing that a solicitor assuming to act in an action for one of the parties, warrants his authority (see [1910] 1 KB 215 at 234). Furthermore, (a) none of their Lordships questioned the correctness of Yonge's case, in which a

b solicitor had totally innocently continued to act for a person of unsound mind, and was found liable for the costs of the other party. (b) Rose LJ in Count Tolstoy's case [1996] 2 All ER 556 at 565, [1996] 1 WLR 736 at 746, far from supporting any theory that fault was a necessary ingredient of the liability for a solicitor acting without authority, contemplates liability for so acting 'even unwittingly'.

c   The only support for the view that it should always be necessary to establish some improper, unreasonable or negligent act over and above the mere fact that an action had been commenced or continued without authority comes from the tentative view expressed by Ward LJ in Count Tolstoy's case [1996] 2 All ER 556 at 570, [1996] 1 WLR 736 at 751. He there suggested that even in relation to

d commencing actions without authority, liability should now be judged under s 51(6) and (7) of the Supreme Court Act 1981. As I have said, that view was tentative and since it would, in my view, involve overruling many previous decisions including Yonge's case, I do not for my part agree with it.

     What, however, I do think is that it is important to appreciate that if the court

e is exercising its supervisory jurisdiction, there may be more than one route to the same conclusion. In other words, there may be cases in which in one sense the want of authority analogy will be used, but there will also be a degree of negligence on the part of the solicitor which would render him liable in any event. Thus, there is little doubt, if the solicitor commences an action without obtaining the authority of a corporation, the solicitor will be liable for the costs

f incurred by a party who relied on the solicitor having such authority, but the route could as well have been by the negligence route as the breach of warranty of authority route. Similarly, if the solicitor commences an action for a bankrupt in relation to a cause of action which is vested in the bankrupt's trustee, there will on most occasions be negligence bringing into play the jurisdiction which does

g not depend on an analogy with breach of warranty of authority.

     It is in a situation in which a solicitor is entirely innocent but may be acting without authority that it becomes really important to analyse the basis on which he may be held liable to pay the costs of the opposing party. There is no question that if the person for whom the solicitor purports to act does not exist, eg a

h defunct corporation, the solicitor is, on the analogy of breach of warranty of authority, held liable to pay the costs. Similarly, if the capacity of the would-be client is such that the client is simply not able to instruct a solicitor, the solicitor will be held liable to pay the costs on the same analogous basis, eg a minor or a person of unsound mind. Yonge's case is an example of the latter case. But, in such cases, it is, I think, of some importance (1) that the persons or entities simply

j have no power to retain solicitors at all; and thus (2), applying the analogy of want of authority, it need go no further than warranting that the solicitors have a principal who has authorised them, as opposed to a warranty that the solicitor has the principal who is himself authorised. There is a distinction between those warranties, and in exercising its supervisory jurisdiction it seems to me important to analyse precisely what warranty by analogy should be imposed on a solicitor if he is to be rendered liable in costs.

I would have thought that the court is not concerned to make a solicitor *strictly* liable simply because the person who instructs him turns out not to be the right plaintiff, as opposed to ensuring that there is a party against whom the opposing party can obtain an order for costs. Even in the latter context, a solicitor does not warrant that his client is solvent, albeit if he brings an action for an insolvent client there may be circumstances where the solicitor's conduct of such proceedings will render him liable as in *Count Tolstoy-Miloslavsky v Lord Aldington* [1996] 2 All ER 556, [1996] 1 WLR 736.

How then should an action brought on behalf of a bankrupt be viewed? A bankrupt may bring proceedings as regards property acquired after adjudication before intervention of the trustee, and may bring actions in respect of personal rights, and indeed may even bring actions in relation to property which has transferred to his trustee but which the trustee authorises him to keep. So on any view there are circumstances in which the bankrupt can retain a solicitor and instruct him to bring proceedings. However, that said, the language used by, for example, Hoffmann LJ in *Heath v Tang* [1993] 4 All ER 694 at 697, [1993] 1 WLR 1421 at 1423 is of the 'incapacity' of the bankrupt to bring proceedings where those proceedings relate to property including any causes of action which have vested in the trustee as a result of adjudication. Furthermore, *Williams and Muir Hunter on Bankruptcy* (19th edn, 1979) p 247 suggest a bankrupt in relation to such actions 'cannot bring any action or other legal proceedings to enforce rights relating to "his property"', reliance being placed on, inter alia, *Motion v Moojen* (1872) LR 14 Eq 202. Thus, if one poses the question did the bankrupt Mr Nelson have the power to commence these actual proceedings, I think the answer to that question is that he did not. But that does not necessarily provide the answer to the question. If the warranty which by analogy should be implied is that the solicitor had the authority of the person entitled to enforce the rights in relation to the property, then that warranty would be broken. If, however, all that was warranted was that the solicitor had a retainer from Mr Nelson and Mr Nelson was a person against whom a costs order could be made, that warranty was complied with.

In my view, the latter warranty is the maximum that should be applied by analogy. I should finally make clear two things. First, because even in the want of authority case the court is exercising its inherent jurisdiction, it must be right to say that the court ultimately has a discretion. But second, it is of such importance that solicitors do not commence proceedings without authority leaving the opposing party without even a person or entity against whom an order for costs can be obtained, that it is difficult to contemplate circumstances where, if the lack of authority leads to that result, the discretion would be exercised in favour of the solicitors. The warranty by analogy, however, is not a warranty of solvency or that the costs will be recovered, it is that the plaintiff exists and has authorised the proceedings and no more.

I would thus, on the judge's findings of fact that the solicitors in this case were totally innocent, allow the appeal.

Appeal allowed.

Paul Magrath Esq   Barrister.

a Bence Graphics International Ltd v Fasson UK Ltd

COURT OF APPEAL, CIVIL DIVISION
OTTON, AULD AND THORPE LJJ
1, 2, 3 JULY, 17 OCTOBER 1996

b

Contract – Damages for breach – Measure of damages – Defendants supplying defective goods to plaintiffs for manufacture of product and onward sale – Defect becoming apparent only after onward sale – Plaintiffs seeking to recover purchase price of goods from defendants – Whether correct measure of damages being difference in market value of goods or plaintiffs' actual losses under and arising from onward sale – Sale of Goods Act 1979, s 53(3).

c

The defendants supplied cast vinyl film to the value of £564,328·54 to the plaintiffs who used it to manufacture decals which were used in the shipping industry to identify bulk containers. It was a term of the contract that the film would survive in a good legible condition for at least five years, but the film degraded *d* prematurely and rendered many of the decals illegible. The plaintiffs received extensive complaints from their customers about the poor performance of the film and were forced to retain about £22,000 worth of unused and defective material. The plaintiffs thereafter commenced proceedings against the defendants for damages for breach of contract. The defendants admitted liability *e* for breach of warranty as to the quality of the goods and the judge, applying s 53(3)[a] of the Sale of Goods Act 1979, which provided that the prima facie measure of damages for such a breach was the difference between the value of the goods at the time of delivery to the buyer and the value they would have had if they had fulfilled the warranty, awarded the plaintiffs damages of £564,328·54 *f* with interest, on the grounds that this was the measure of damages which the parties would have contemplated as being recoverable in the event of a breach of warranty when the contract was made. The defendants appealed contending, inter alia, that the judge had misdirected himself as to the correct measure of damages, since the principal issue was the parties' contemplation of the nature of the financial loss which the defendants would be likely to suffer in the event of a *g* breach, and that therefore the plaintiffs were only entitled to recover damages for losses under or arising from a breach of contract for onward sales.

Held (Thorpe LJ dissenting) – Where a defendant supplied goods to a plaintiff containing a latent defect which became apparent only after the goods were *h* converted in a manner contemplated by both parties and then sold on, the measure of damages to which the plaintiff was entitled from the defendant for breach of contract was the actual loss suffered by the plaintiff under or arising from a breach of contract for onward sales. The prima facie measure of damages under s 53(3) of the 1979 Act was displaced in such circumstances since it was the *j* plaintiff's liability to the ultimate user that was contemplated by the parties as the measure of damages. In the instant case, the defendants knew that the film was used exclusively to manufacture decals which the plaintiff then sold on, and that therefore a breach of warranty would result in claims for damages being made by subsequent purchasers against the plaintiff. It followed that at the time of making

---

a   Section 53 is set out at p 983 *b* to *e*, post

their contract the parties were aware of facts which indicated to both that the loss, in the event of a breach, would not be the difference between the value of the goods delivered and the market value and accordingly that measure of damages ceased to be appropriate. It followed that the judge had erred in holding that the prima facie measure of damages had not been displaced. The appeal would therefore be allowed and the case would be remitted for assessment of damages (see p 987 *a*, p 989 *j* to p 990 *c f*, p 991 *b* to *e* and p 996 *d* to *f*, post).

Slater v Hoyle & Smith Ltd [1918–19] All ER Rep 654 not followed.

Notes

For measure of damages for breach of warranty in respect of goods which are then sold on, see 41 *Halsbury's Laws* (4th edn) paras 890–891.

For the Sale of Goods Act 1979, s 53, see 39 *Halsbury's Statutes* (4th edn) (1995 reissue) 115.

Cases referred to in judgments

Biggin & Co Ltd v Permanite Ltd (Berry Wiggins & Co Ltd, third parties) [1950] 2 All ER 859, [1951] 1 KB 422; *rvsd* [1951] 2 All ER 191, [1951] 2 KB 314, CA.

Bostock & Co Ltd v Nicholson & Sons Ltd [1904] 1 KB 725.

Dexters Ltd v Hill Crest Oil Co (Bradford) Ltd [1926] 1 KB 348, [1925] All ER Rep 273, CA.

Hadley v Baxendale (1854) 9 Exch 341, [1843–60] All ER Rep 461, 156 ER 145, Ex.

Hall (R & H) Ltd v W H Pim Junr & Co Ltd (1927) 30 Ll L Rep 159, HL.

Hammond & Co v Bussey (1887) 20 QBD 79, CA.

Heron II, The, Koufos v C Czarnikow Ltd [1967] 3 All ER 686, [1969] 1 AC 350, [1967] 3 WLR 1491, HL.

Holden (Richard) Ltd v Bostock & Co Ltd (1902) 18 TLR 317, CA.

Kasler and Cohen v Slavouski [1928] 1 KB 78.

Kendall (Henry) & Sons (a firm) v William Lillico & Sons Ltd, Holland Colombo Trading Society Ltd v Grimsdale & Sons Ltd, Grimsdale & Sons Ltd v Suffolk Agricultural and Poultry Producers Association Ltd [1968] 2 All ER 444, [1969] 2 AC 31, [1968] 3 WLR 110, HL.

Pagnan (R) & Flli v Corbisa Industrial Agropacuaria Ltda [1971] 1 All ER 165, [1970] 1 WLR 1306, CA.

Parsons (H) (Livestock) Ltd v Uttley Ingham & Co Ltd [1978] 1 All ER 525, [1978] QB 791, [1977] 3 WLR 990, CA.

Rodocanachi Sons & Co v Milburn Bros (1886) 18 QBD 67, CA.

Slater v Hoyle & Smith Ltd [1920] 2 KB 11, [1918–19] All ER Rep 654, CA.

Victoria Laundry (Windsor) Ltd v Newman Industries Ltd (Coulsdon & Co Ltd, third party) [1949] 1 All ER 997, [1949] 2 KB 528, CA.

Wertheim v Chicoutimi Pulp Co [1911] AC 301, [1908–10] All ER Rep 707, PC.

Williams Bros v Ed T Agius Ltd [1914] AC 510, [1914–15] All ER Rep 97, HL.

Cases also cited or referred to in skeleton arguments

Aryweh v Lawrence Kostoris & Son Ltd [1967] 1 Lloyd's Rep 63, CA.

British Westinghouse Electric and Manufacturing Co Ltd v Underground Electric Rly Co of London Ltd [1912] AC 673, [1911–13] All ER Rep 63, HL.

Chao (t/a Zung Fu Co) v British Traders and Shippers Ltd (NV Handelsmaatschappij J Smits Import-Export, third party) [1954] 1 All ER 779, [1954] 2 QB 459.

Cullinane v British 'Rema' Manufacturing Co Ltd [1953] 2 All ER 1257, [1954] 1 QB 292, CA.

a   *Finlay (James) & Co v Kwik Hoo Tong Handel Maatschappij* [1929] 1 KB 400, [1928]
        All ER Rep 110, CA.
    Minster Trust Ltd v Traps Tractors Ltd [1954] 3 All ER 136, [1954] 1 WLR 963.
    Monarch Steamship Co Ltd v Karlshamns Oljefabriker (A B) [1949] 1 All ER 1, [1949]
        AC 196, HL.
    Randall v Newson (1877) 2 QBD 102, CA.
b   *Randall v Raper* (1858) EB & E 84, 120 ER 438.
    Robophone Facilities Ltd v Blank [1966] 3 All ER 128, [1966] 1 WLR 1428, CA.
    Smith v Green (1875) 1 CPD 92.

Appeal

c   By notice dated 9 January 1995 and amended on 7 June 1995 the defendants,
Fasson UK Ltd, appealed from the decision of Morland J sitting at Liverpool on
14 December 1994 whereby he awarded the plaintiffs, Bence Graphics
International Ltd, damages of £564,328·54 plus interest in their action against the
defendants for breach of contract, on the ground that the judge had misdirected
himself as to the correct measure of damages. The facts are set out in the
d   judgment of Otton LJ.

Stephen Grime QC and *David Heaton* (instructed by *Lace Mawer*, Manchester) for
    the defendants.
Andrew Moran QC and *Anthony Edwards* (instructed by *Hill Dickinson Davis
e   Campbell*, Liverpool) for the plaintiffs.

Cur adv vult

17 October 1996. The following judgments were delivered.

f   **OTTON LJ.** The defendants, Fasson UK Ltd, appeal from a judgment of
Morland J whereby he ordered that there be judgment for the plaintiffs, Bence
Graphics International Ltd, for £564,328·54 together with interest. The
defendants seek to set aside the judgment and assert that in substitution there be
judgment for the plaintiffs for the sum of £22,000 (being the admitted value of
returned goods) together with interest or alternatively that there be a new trial
g   or that an assessment of damages according to the correct measure (being that
contended for by the defendants) be directed in any event.
     The sole issue raised on this appeal is whether the correct measure of damages
was (as the judge found) the difference in market value or the actual losses (if any)
suffered by the plaintiffs under or arising from a breach of contract for onward
h   sales.

Background
     The defendants were one of a small number of suppliers of cast vinyl film, one
of the uses for which is to manufacture decals which are used to identify bulk
j   containers, this being the only end use intended in the case of film sold by them
to the plaintiffs. The plaintiffs' manufacturing process involved screen printing
words, numbers or symbols on the film and cutting it to size. The decals were
then attached to the containers by reason of the self-adhesive character of the
vinyl. Between 1981 and 1985 the defendants supplied to the plaintiffs film to the
value of £564,328·54. This was to produce in excess of 100,000 decals. Of the
decals manufactured from the defendants' film, 93% went for use on Sea

Containers Ltd (SCL), who were an important customer of the plaintiffs and who
imposed their own specifications for containers and decals on manufacturers.   *a*
SCL owned the containers and leased them to shipping lines and others so that
the containers passed out of physical possession of the owners for the vast
majority of their life and were used all over the world.

It was common ground that the standard requirement in the container
industry for such decals was that they should have a 'guaranteed minimum five   *b*
year life'. The defendants know this to be so. Moreover, it was a term of the
contract between the parties that the film would be of such a nature as to survive
in use in good legible condition for a period of five years at least.

The plaintiffs alleged that the film did not fulfil the warranties with which it
was sold, was not reasonably fit for its intended purpose and was not of   *c*
merchantable quality. The reason for the defective condition was that the
polymer constituting the film had insufficient stabiliser against the effects of
ultraviolet light and became degraded upon such exposure. The defendants were
at pains in their promotional literature to assure customers that their film would
be of such a nature as to survive in use in good legible condition for a period of   *d*
five years at least. The Dutch manufacturing associate of the defendants
incorrectly formulated the film sold to the plaintiffs by putting insufficient UV
stabiliser in the film so that, in use, it tended to degrade over a period eventually
making some decals illegible. There were extensive complaints from customers
of SCL about the poor performance of the film. However, only one claim
relating to 349 Tsujii containers was met by the plaintiffs who applied new decals   *e*
at their expense and the defendants paid an agreed amount to the plaintiffs in
compensation. There was also an intimation of a claim from SCL which has so
far not been pursued. The plaintiffs retained about £22,000 worth of unused and
defective material.

By the statement of claim served in August 1988 the plaintiffs claimed for the   *f*
difference in value (ie the recovery of the whole purchase price). By an
amendment served three years later the claim was enlarged to include an
alternative claim for indemnity against 'all claims' by customers of the plaintiffs.
The defendants sought to rely on exclusion clauses contained in their standard
trading terms. However, on the penultimate and final days of the trial, the
defendants made several admissions including that their terms did not operate so   *g*
as to exclude or limit their liability for any breach and that they were in breach of
their warranty that their product was durable for five years. Thus, in the
concluding stages of the trial the only issue left to Morland J was the proper
measure of damage. The defendants conceded that, at least, the plaintiffs were
entitled to be reimbursed in the sum of £22,000 in respect of the stock returned   *h*
to them. Morland J accurately summarised the position thus :

> 'In the present case the plaintiffs have not suffered a loss in the shape of a
> claim for damages from their customers in respect of the decals processed by
> them from the defective Fasson 940 sold to them by the defendants to whom   *j*
> they have paid the contract price. Although they have suffered no such loss,
> they have been exposed and *remain exposed* to claims from their customers
> and they have been put to the expense of investigating and answering
> complaints. Also their commercial reputation may have suffered.' (My
> emphasis.)

a   Morland J found applying s 53(3) of the Sale of Goods Act 1979 that the plaintiffs were entitled to the difference between the value of the goods at the time of delivery and the value they would have had if they had fulfilled the warranties.

At the heart of this appeal is the defendants' assertion that the judge misdirected himself in defining the issue as to the proper measure of damages which fell for determination.

b   Section 53 of the 1979 Act provides:

'*Remedy for breach of warranty.*—(1) Where there is a breach of warranty by the seller, or where the buyer elects (or is compelled) to treat any breach of a condition on the part of the seller as a breach of warranty, the buyer is not by reason only of such breach of warranty entitled to reject the goods; but he

c   may—(a) set up against the seller the breach of warranty in diminution or extinction of the price, or (b) maintain an action against the seller for damages for the breach of warranty.

(2) The measure of damages for breach of warranty is the estimated loss directly and naturally resulting, in the ordinary course of events, from the

d   breach of warranty.

(3) In the case of breach of warranty of quality such loss is prima facie the difference between the value of the goods at the time of delivery to the buyer and the value they would have had if they had fulfilled the warranty.

(4) The fact that the buyer has set up the breach of warranty in diminution

e   or extinction of the price does not prevent him from maintaining an action for the same breach of warranty if he has suffered further damage.'

Section 54 provides:

'*Interest, etc.*—Nothing in this Act affects the right of the buyer or the seller

f   to recover interest or special damages in any case where by law interest or special damages may be recoverable, or to recover money paid where the consideration for the payment of it has failed.'

The 1979 Act lays down the basic principles for remoteness of damage in language derived from the leading case of *Hadley v Baxendale* (1854) 9 Exch 341,

g   [1843–60] All ER Rep 461, where the main proposition was:

'Where two parties have made a contract, which one of them has broken, the damages which the other party ought to receive in respect of such breach of contract should be such as may fairly and reasonably be considered either as arising naturally, ie, according to the usual course of things, from such

h   breach of contract itself, or such as may reasonably be supposed to have been in the contemplation of both parties, at the time they made the contract, as the probable result of the breach of it.' (See (1854) 9 Exch 341 at 354, [1843–60] All ER Rep 461 at 465 per Alderson B.)

j   The principles in *Hadley v Baxendale* have been interpreted and restated by the Court of Appeal (see *Victoria Laundry (Windsor) Ltd v Newman Industries Ltd (Coulsdon & Co Ltd, third party)* [1949] 1 All ER 997, [1949] 2 KB 528 and in the House of Lords in *The Heron II, Koufos v C Czarnikow Ltd* [1967] 3 All ER 686, [1969] 1 AC 350). In the latter case, the word 'directly' is eliminated and more emphasis is placed on the 'reasonable contemplation' of the parties. Such moderately differing formulations of the common law principles for remoteness of damage in contract are still based on *Hadley v Baxendale*. Lord Reid in *The Heron II, Koufos v C Czarnikow Ltd* [1967] 3 All ER 686 at 691, [1969] 1 AC 350 at 385 stated:

> 'The crucial question is whether, on the information available to the defendant when the contract was made, he should, or the reasonable man in his position would, have realised that such loss was sufficiently likely to result from the breach of contract to make it proper to hold that the loss flowed naturally from the breach or that loss of that kind should have been within his contemplation.'

Lord Upjohn stated—

> 'the broad rule as follows: what was in the assumed contemplation of both parties acting as reasonable men in the light of the general or special facts (as the case may be) known to both parties in regard to damages as the result of a breach of contract ...' (See [1967] 3 All ER 686 at 717, [1969] 1 AC 350 at 424.)

The so-called second rule in *Hadley v Baxendale* applies when the loss caused by the breach of contract is greater than, or different from, what it would have been in 'normal' circumstances. The rule is that—

> 'if the special circumstances under which the contract was actually made were communicated by the plaintiffs to the defendants, and thus known to both parties, the damages resulting from the breach of such a contract, which they would reasonably contemplate, would be the amount of injury which would ordinarily follow from a breach of contract under the special circumstances so known and communicated.' (See (1854) 9 Exch 341 at 354, [1843–60] All ER Rep 461 at 465.)

Section 53(2) lays down the basic rule in terms of *Hadley v Baxendale*. The second rule is not expressly incorporated in the 1979 Act but is considered to be impliedly accepted by the wording of s 54: 'Nothing in this Act affects the right of the buyer or the seller to recover ... special damages in any case where by law... special damages may be recoverable ...' (see *Benjamin's Sale of Goods* (4th edn, 1992) p 1768).

The judgment

The judge approached the problem thus:

> 'In my judgment ... the main issue which I have to determine in this action ... is whether the prima facie measure damages is displaced by some other measure. At the time the contracts were made what may the court reasonably suppose to have probably been in the contemplation of the parties as to the *remedy* to be available to the plaintiffs in the event of breach of the warranty of quality, assuming the parties to have applied their minds to the contingency of there being such a breach ... Unless the court is satisfied on the balance of probabilities that some other *measure of damages* was objectively in the contemplation of the parties when the contract was made, the prima facie measure set out in s 53(3) remains un-displaced if as the result of transactions by the buyer with other parties either the buyer may recover a windfall or the seller's liability may be limited to the prima facie measure albeit that the buyer's loss is much greater ... A plaintiff will only be restricted in his claim for damages (by reduction from the prima facie

a measure) as a result of special circumstances when those special circumstances have been brought home to him in such a way as to show that he has accepted or is taken to have accepted the risk *that he will not be able to claim damages in respect of defective goods supplied to him unless his customer of his processed goods brings a claim against him.* Not only at the time that the contract was made must the parties be viewed objectively to have

b contemplated that the plaintiff is taking the risk of having his normal measure of damages restricted in the event that his customer does not claim against him although he may still suffer loss because his customer may not re-order from him because of the defective quality of the goods supplied to him but also they must be taken to have contemplated that the defendant is taking the risk that the damages awarded against him will not be limited to

c the prima facie measure but that he will be exposed to a potential open-ended liability that he will have to indemnify the plaintiff in respect of any claim made by a customer against him. The defendants have failed to satisfy me on the balance of probabilities that having regard to all the circumstances in which the contract was made the parties must be taken to have contemplated that the s 53(3) measure of damages was displaced.' (My

d emphasis.)

Mr Stephen Grime QC, on behalf of the defendants, submits that Morland J misdirected himself in defining the issue as to the measure of damages which fell for determination. He submits that the principle issue which Morland J had to

e decide was as to whether, at the time of the making of the relevant contracts, the parties contemplated that the loss which would be suffered by the plaintiff in the event of a serious breach of warranty of quality resulting in premature deterioration in service of the decals made from the defendants' goods was (i) diminution in the value of goods supplied by the defendants or (ii) liability in damages to purchasers of the decals together with loss of business and goodwill

f and any incidental loss and expense. Morland J wrongly defined the issue as being as to the parties' contemplation of the legal remedy which was available to the plaintiff in the event of breach of contract rather than as to their contemplation of the nature of the financial loss which the plaintiff would be likely to suffer upon breach.

g Mr Grime advanced the following propositions:

'1. In case of sale of goods where a term as to quality is broken, the measure of damages depends upon the contemplation of the parties as to the consequence of a breach of the type committed, such contemplation being based on either their imputed or actual knowledge at the time of contracting.

h 2. There will be imputed to parties knowledge of facts which they had learnt as to the nature and background of their respective businesses (first limb of Hadley v Baxendale so called). 3. In [the 1979 Act] s 53(3) words "prima facie" are not an expression of special quality or merit being attached to difference in value measure but more a reflection of the trading/mercantile

j conditions of times. Where the sale contract is not made between merchants dealing in a market the displacement burden is a light one. 4. Actual knowledge of special circumstances may extend the ambit of potential damages (S. 54). 5. In some cases the finding as to contemplation of the parties as to the consequences of breach may be to show that breach will give rise to difference in value measure under s. 53(3) *and* special damages under s. 54. The claimant will not be limited if he wishes to choose one or both.

6. In other cases the finding as to contemplation of the parties as to the   *a*
consequences of breach will show that the possible measures are
alternatives. 7. Where the measures are alternatives it is for the court to
choose the correct measure, not the claimant. 8. Where the court chooses
one or other measure, the effect of the choice may reduce the amount of
damages which may be claimed or increase it.' (Mr Grime's emphasis.)

b

Mr Andrew Moran QC, on behalf of the plaintiffs, submits that Morland J did
not misdirect himself in defining the issue as to the measure of damages which
fell for determination. The issue was whether the loss claimed by the respondent
was too remote a consequence of a breach of contract. In approaching this issue
Morland J was correct to proceed to the measure prescribed by s 53(2) and (3) of   *c*
the 1979 Act as the starting point and then to consider whether on the facts of this
case, the defendants had satisfied him that the prima facie measure was displaced
by some other measure. This was to be resolved by asking the question: what
loss to the plaintiffs is it reasonable to suppose would have been in the
contemplation of the parties as a 'serious possibility' or 'a not unlikely result' had   *d*
they had in mind the breach when they made their contract? The time of
assessment is the time of making the contract. Morland J both correctly defined
the issue and expressed a proper approach to its resolution. Section 53(2) lays
down a rule defining the measure of damages as a particular 'loss' and s 53(3) is
the exposition of how 'such loss' is ordinarily calculated.

e

Mr Moran advanced the following propositions:

'1. In a case of sale of goods when a term as to quality is broken the court
should resolve any issue as to the measure of damage by first recourse to
section 53 [of the 1979 Act]. In doing so the court is objectively ascertaining   *f*
what loss would have been in the contemplation of the parties at the time of
making the contract had they been made aware that a breach of the type
which in fact occurred would occur. 2. The reference to "loss" in paragraph
1 does not involve the precise detail of the damage or the precise manner of
its happening it is enough for the innocent party to show that loss of that kind
is not unlikely or a serious possibility. 3. The parties are deemed to   *g*
contemplate loss which directly and naturally results in the ordinary course
of events. In the ordinary course of events when goods of defective quality
are delivered such loss is prima facie the difference in value. This principle is
of universal application and not confined to mercantile or trading conditions
of the time when the predecessor of the Act appeared. 4. Additional actual   *h*
or imputed knowledge proved by a party seeking to rely on it, may
demonstrate that particular loss would have been in the contemplation of
the parties either i) as a serious possibility of additional loss or, ii), (as in a
chain sale proper) as the exclusive kind of loss that might be suffered. In i)
the party suffering loss may confine his claim to the loss which the parties are   *j*
deemed to contemplate as in para 3 above, or he may add a claim for
additional loss in contemplation. In ii) he is confined to a claim for the
exclusive loss so contemplated. 5. It is for the Judge to resolve as a question
of fact whether such additional knowledge as is relied on, demonstrates that
some exclusive alternative loss was in contemplation.'

Conclusion

a

I take as my starting point that s 53(3) of the 1979 Act lays down only a prima facie rule, from which the court may depart in appropriate circumstances. The burden of proof lies upon the person who seeks such a departure. The plaintiffs do not suggest that it is only open to a buyer to rebut the presumption. In my view, there is no reason in logic or principle why a seller cannot, in appropriate

b circumstances, seek to discharge the burden and displace the presumption (and see *Biggin & Co Ltd v Permanite Ltd (Berry Wiggins & Co Ltd, third parties)* [1950] 2 All ER 859 at 868–869, [1951] 1 KB 422 at 435–436).

The situation often arises where the buyer seeks to displace the presumption and recover losses other than the diminution in value. Where a seller knows that the buyer intended to resell the goods and ought reasonably to have

c contemplated that a breach of his undertaking as to the description or condition of goods would be not unlikely to cause the buyer to lose the profit he hoped to make on the resale, or potential sub-sale, the buyer may recover damages in respect of such loss of profits caused by a breach of the seller's undertaking (see *Chitty on Contracts* (27th edn, 1994) para 41–315).

d Situations arise where the court is satisfied and finds as a fact that it was within the contemplation of the parties, at the time of making the contract that:

'(a) the buyer intended to resell, or probably would do so, and that his sub-buyer would probably resell, and so on, so that there would be a series of sub-sales or "string contracts" of the same goods; and (b) that each

e contract in the series would, or probably would, contain the same, or a similar, contractual undertaking as to the description or condition of the goods; and (c) that it was not unlikely that a breach of the seller's undertaking would cause the buyer and each sub-buyer in the series to be in breach of his undertaking to his own buyer; and (d) that it was not unlikely that, in the case of such a breach, the ultimate buyers would recover damages from their

f sellers, so that liability would in turn be passed up the chain of sellers and buyers. In these circumstances, the buyer who has paid to his sub-buyer damages and costs for breach of the undertaking in the first contract of sub-sale (which the sub-buyer claimed from the buyer, as the result of similar payments of compensation between successive sub-buyers down the chain)

g may recover the amount paid by him to the sub-buyer, together with his own reasonable costs in reasonably defending the sub-buyer's claim against him; the damages and costs paid or incurred by the buyer are taken as the measure of damages for the seller's breach of the original contract.' (See *Chitty* para 41–321.)

h (See *Hammond & Co v Bussey* (1887) 20 QBD 79 and *Kasler and Cohen v Slavouski* [1928] 1 KB 78.)

In the present case there was no series or 'string' contracts. The same goods were not sold on. Even so, the string contract cases illustrate graphically how the court is permitted to and will depart from the presumption in order to do justice

j between the parties based on a finding of fact of what the parties reasonably contemplated.

If the buyer uses the goods to make some product out of them the value of the goods is not taken. In *Richard Holden Ltd v Bostock & Co Ltd* (1902) 18 TLR 317 where sugar was sold to brewers to be used for brewing beer and because of arsenic in the sugar, the beer was rendered poisonous and was destroyed by the brewers, the value of the beer at its market price in their cellars was allowed, inter alia, as damages. Similarly, in *Bostock & Co Ltd v Nicholson & Sons Ltd* [1904] 1 KB 725 where commercial sulphuric acid warranted free from arsenic was used by the buyer for making brewers sugar, one of its ordinary uses, he recovered not only the price paid for the acid rendered worthless to him by the breach of warranty but the value of other ingredients spoilt by being mixed with the acid.

In *McGregor on Damages* (15th edn, 1988) para 808 it is stated:

> 'In all these cases, it is once again vital that the use to which the goods have been put by the buyer is one that the seller either contemplated or must be taken to have contemplated: otherwise the damage will be too remote. If the buyer adopts the ordinary use of the goods, as where food sold for human consumption is eaten by him, or adopts one of the ordinary and well recognised uses although not the only one, as in *Bostock* v. *Nicholson*, or adopts even a use which is not the predominant one provided it is a use which is sufficiently common, as in *Hardwick Game Farm* v. *Suffolk Agricultural Poultry Producers Association* ([1968] 2 All ER 444, [1969] 2 AC 31) where contaminated groundnut extractions were supplied for compounding into poultry food and the compound was fed to pheasants and partridges, he will recover under the first rule in *Hadley* v. *Baxendale*. If however he puts them to some special use, he will recover only if this intention is communicated to the seller, i.e. under the second rule in *Hadley* v. *Baxendale*. Here, as elsewhere, the dividing line between the first and second rules is not always clear in the cases.'

Mr Moran, in argument, invoked the principle that where the seller delivers defective goods but the buyer is nevertheless able to perform a sub-contract by delivering the goods to his sub-buyer, the buyer's damages against the seller cannot be reduced by taking this into account. He relied upon the decision of the Court of Appeal in *Slater v Hoyle & Smith Ltd* [1920] 2 KB 11, [1918–19] All ER Rep 654, where the buyer bought cotton cloth from the seller in order to fulfil another contract which the buyer had already made with a sub-buyer. The seller delivered cloth which was not up to the contractual quality, but the buyer was able to perform the sub-contract by delivering the same cloth. The sub-buyer paid the full price under the sub-contract. The buyer sued the seller for damages. The court awarded the buyer damages assessed at the normal measure, namely the difference between the market price, at the time and place of delivery of cloth up to the contractual quality, and the market price, at the time and place of delivery of the cloth actually delivered. Scrutton LJ said ([1920] 2 KB 11 at 23, [1918–19] All ER Rep 654 at 659):

> 'If the buyer is lucky enough, for reasons with which the seller has nothing to do, to get his goods through on the sub-contract without a claim against him, this on principle cannot affect his claim against the seller any more than the fact that he had to pay very large damages on his sub-contract would affect his original seller.'

In my judgment, the decision in *Slater* can be narrowly distinguished from the instant case. In *Slater's* case the sub-sale was of the same goods albeit after bleaching; the seller did not know of the contemplated sub-sale. In the instant case, the goods were substantially converted or processed by the buyer and the sellers were aware of the precise use to which the film was to be put at the time the contract was made. I recognise Auld LJ's reservations.

a   This last case must be considered in the light of the dicta of Devlin J in *Biggin & Co Ltd v Permanite Ltd* [1950] 2 All ER 859 at 868–869, [1951] 1 KB 422 at 435–436:

> *b*   'Damages which arise under the so-called "second rule" in *Hadley* v. *Baxendale* are sometimes referred to as if they were an increased sum which the plaintiff could obtain if he could show "special circumstances", or as if the rule embodied a measure of damage specially beneficial to the plaintiff which he could invoke if he fulfilled the necessary conditions. It is, no doubt, true that it generally operates in favour of a plaintiff rather than against him, but I think that it is capable of doing either … It has often been held … that the profit actually made on a sub-sale which is outside the contemplation of the parties cannot be used to reduce the damages measured by a notional loss in market value. If, however, a sub-sale is within the contemplation of the parties, I think that the damages must be assessed by reference to it, whether the plaintiff likes it or not. Suppose that the only fault in the compound was its incompatibility with bitumen felt, the chance that it might produce bad results would certainly reduce its market value before use. But if it is the plaintiff's liability to the ultimate user that is contemplated as the measure of damage and if in fact it is used without injurious results so that no such liability arises, the plaintiff could not claim the difference in market value, and say that the sub-sale must be disregarded. I say this so as to make it clear, that although I have come to the conclusion that, if the plaintiffs' basic claim fails, they can to some extent rely on the alternative of difference in market value, it is not because I think the plaintiffs have an option in the matter.'

Lord Pearce in *The Heron II, Koufos v C Czarnikow Ltd* [1967] 3 All ER 686 at 712, [1969] 1 AC 350 at 416 made a similar point when he said:

> *f*   '… of course the extension of the horizon need not always *increase* the damage; it might introduce a knowledge of particular circumstances, e g, a subcontract, which show that the plaintiff would in fact suffer *less* damage than a more limited view of the circumstances might lead one to expect.' (Lord Pearce's emphasis.)

g   In my judgment, once the goods had been converted in a manner which was contemplated by the parties, *Slater's* case has no application, the damages must be assessed by reference to the sub-sale 'whether the plaintiff likes it or not'. Thus, the plaintiff does not have the option to choose which outcome is most favourable to him. It is for the court to determine the correct measure of *h*   damage, not the aggrieved party. Where the court determines the proper measure, the effect of the choice may reduce the amount of damages claimed or increase it.

With this analysis I address the issue as to what was within the contemplation of the parties. The evidence showed that there was a close and protracted *j*   business relationship between the parties from which it can be readily inferred that the defendants had detailed knowledge of the plaintiffs' business. The end use of the film was exclusively for container decals. The defendants knew that the plaintiffs then supplied the decals to container manufacturers and the manufacturers subsequently supplied the containers (suitably marked by the decals) to subsequent purchasers. The sellers knew that the plaintiffs' customers demanded five-year durability of their product.

Moreover, the sellers would have known that any defect in the film would not have been detected on delivery or in the process of manufacture. The defect, i e the breach, would have caused deterioration of decals in service with the result that the ultimate users of the containers (lessees of the owners) would complain to and claim damages against the container owners who would in turn make claims against the container manufacturers. The manufacturers in turn would make claims for damages against the plaintiffs which the plaintiffs would be 'not unlikely' obliged to meet. Moreover, the defendants would expect to be liable for the value of unmerchantable film processed by the plaintiff and of unsaleable raw materials supplied by the defendants.

These factors, to my mind, point indubitably against a loss of value basis and towards a measure of damage based upon the plaintiff's liability to the subsequent or ultimate users of the plaintiffs product in which the defendants' goods were an integral part and, in the event of a breach of the warranty as to quality, the plaintiffs' liability to those others would be triggered.

It is not without significance that after the breach had been discovered, the remedy sought by the plaintiffs in correspondence was one of indemnity and not the difference of value of the goods. However, when the statement of claim was served in 1988 it was solely for the difference in value. The obvious inference to draw is that by that time the plaintiffs had realised that the claim for indemnity and the peripheral claims were of lesser value than a claim for the market value. It is true that the statement of claim was amended in 1991 to include, in the alternative, an indemnity against all claims by customers of the plaintiff. However, at trial they pressed for relief under the s 53(3) of the 1979 Act presumption.

Thus, in my view, at the time of making their contract the parties were aware of facts which indicated to both that the loss would not be the difference between the value of the goods delivered and the market value and accordingly, the prima facie measure ceased to be appropriate.

Finally, Morland J in rejecting the defendant's case at trial said:

> 'Mr Heaton's submission is that the measure of damages recoverable by the plaintiff is in effect an indemnity in respect of claims by their customers made against them. The weakness of the Heaton submission is demonstrated by the *nebulousness* of what Mr Heaton called an indemnity. Was it unlimited in amount? The purpose for which the vinyl was made was for processing into decals. A degraded decal, that is not having the five-year durability quality, could result in the loss of a container and the goods within it, the value of which could be large or small. It could also result in a container and its goods going to a wrong destination. Did the indemnity cover such losses which might well be of a magnitude out of all proportion to the price of the vinyl when sold to the plaintiffs or the price of the decal, the vinyl processed by the defendants when sold on to their customers? Did the indemnity only cover claims the defendants were legally obliged to satisfy or did it cover claims which could be defeated by reason of the Limitation Act but which would be commercially suicidal not to satisfy? Did the indemnity cover claims successfully defended in respect of costs of successfully defending claims arising out of the breach of warranty. Did it cover the costs of processing and investigating complaints?' (My emphasis.)

I do not see any 'nebulousness' of what Mr Heaton called an indemnity. The defendants will only be liable to indemnify the plaintiffs in respect of any liability *a* which they may be held to have incurred to third parties. The difficulties posed by the trial judge are, to my mind, more apparent than real and would be a matter for determination in any subsequent action by third parties and in third party proceedings against the defendants.

I accept Mr Grime's submission that Morland J attached weight to the supposed difficulties in assessment, that adoption of the measure of damages *b* contended for by the defendant would create when such difficulties as may exist were irrelevant to the issue which Morland J had to decide.

It follows that, with respect to Morland J, I consider his reasoning and conclusion cannot be sustained. If the plaintiff had sought to rebut the presumption they would have succeeded with ease. Any argument by the defendants that the correct measure of damage was the difference in value would *c* have been doomed to failure. I am satisfied, therefore, that Morland J erred in law in holding that the prima facie measure of damages for breach of warranty of quality provided for by s 53(3) of the 1979 Act was not displaced.

Accordingly, I would allow the appeal, substitute a judgment for £22,000 with any appropriate interest and direct that the case be remitted for assessment of *d* damages.

AULD LJ. I agree with the conclusion of Otton LJ and his general reasoning, but wish to add some words on the effect of s 53(3) of the Sale of Goods Act 1979 and on mercantile contracts where the parties obviously contemplate that the buyer will sell on the subject matter of the contract in its existing or in an altered form *e* or as part of some other thing.

As to s 53(3), there is, in my view, a danger of giving it a primacy in the code of s 53 that it does not deserve. The starting point in a claim for breach of a warranty of quality is not to determine whether one or other party has 'displaced' the prima facie test in that subsection. The starting point is the *Hadley v Baxendale* *f* principle ((1854) 9 Exch 341, [1843–60] All ER Rep 461) reproduced in s 53(2) applicable to a breach of any warranty, namely an estimation on the evidence, of 'the … loss directly and naturally resulting, in the ordinary course of events, from the breach of warranty'. The evidence may be such that the prima facie test in s 53(3) never comes into play at all.

The *Hadley v Baxendale* principle is recovery of true loss and no more (or less), *g* namely to put the complaining party, so far as money can do it, in the position he would have been if the contract been performed. Where there is evidence showing the nature of the loss that the parties must be taken to have contemplated in the event of breach, it is not to be set aside by applying the prima facie test in s 53(3) simply because calculation of such contemplated loss would *h* be difficult. Equally, it should not be set aside in that way so as to produce a result where the claimant will clearly recover more than his true loss.

Where, as here, the contract of sale is between two merchants both of whom contemplate that the subject matter of the sale is to be sold on in whatever form, it offends the *Hadley v Baxendale* principle to rule out mutual contemplation by *j* them of damage arising from the buyer's onward sale simply because the subject matter is to be altered or incorporated in another product, or because the terms of the sub-sale may not be identical to those in the sale. It is equally offensive to that principle to describe the subject matter, as Mr Moran QC did, as 'worthless' or of 'no value' to the buyer at the time of delivery if it appeared then to be of the contract quality and he was able to incorporate it in his product and sell it on without claim or provable prospective claim. Put shortly, and drawing on the analysis of Scarman LJ in *H Parsons (Livestock) Ltd v Uttley Ingham & Co Ltd* [1978] 1 All ER 525 at 537, [1978] QB 791 at 807, the sort of question the judge should have asked is: 'What would the parties have thought about the probable loss to the buyer in the event of a latent defect in film at the time of delivery later causing trouble?'

Those observations run contrary to the judgments of this court in *Slater v Hoyle & Smith Ltd* [1920] 2 KB 11, [1918–19] All ER Rep 654, though they are of a piece with the approach of Devlin J in *Biggin & Co Ltd v Permanite Ltd* (*Berry Wiggins & Co Ltd, third parties*) [1950] 2 All ER 859, [1951] 1 KB 422. In my view, the time has come for *Slater*'s case to be reconsidered at least in the context of claims by a buyer for damages for breach of warranty where he has successfully sold on the subject matter of the contract in its original or modified form without claims from his buyers. With respect to Otton LJ, I do not think that the case is materially distinguishable from the present on the two bases that he suggests.

As to the first, the seller's knowledge of the buyer's intended use of the goods, the report in *Slater*'s case states that the seller did not know of the buyer's onward sale contracts. However, that must simply mean that he did not know of the specific contracts; for there can be no doubt that, in contracting to sell 3,000 pieces of unbleached cloth of a certain quality, the seller knew that he was dealing with a commercial buyer who would sell them on either unprocessed or processed to some degree, and must be taken to have contemplated that loss could result from such onward sales if the cloth was not of the required quality. The fact that the seller in this case had more detailed knowledge of the use to which the buyer would put the film is not a material distinction in determining the measure of damages as distinct from their precise calculation.

Second, as to what happened to the goods, the buyer in *Slater*'s case did in fact process them before selling them on; he bleached the unbleached pieces of cloth. That does not seem to me to be materially different for this purpose from incorporating the goods in a manufactured product for onward sale.

The Court of Appeal in *Slater*'s case had to reason around two decisions to the effect that where there has been delivery of goods to the buyer his onward sale may be taken into account in the assessment of damages. The first was a decision of the Privy Council in *Wertheim v Chicoutimi Pulp Co* [1911] AC 301, [1908–10] All ER Rep 707, where their Lordships held that the damages for late delivery should take account of the price actually obtained by the buyer in his onward sale. Lord Atkinson, giving the judgment of the Board, said ([1911] AC 301 at 307–308, [1908–10] All ER Rep 707 at 711):

'... it is the general intention of the law that, in giving damages for breach of contract, the party complaining should, so far as it can be done by money, be placed in the same position as he would have been in if the contract had been performed ... That is a ruling principle. It is a just principle. The rule which prescribes as a measure of damages the difference in market prices at the respective times above mentioned is merely designed to apply this principle and ... it generally secures a complete indemnity to the purchaser. But it is intended to secure only an indemnity. The market value is taken because it is presumed to be the true value of the goods to the purchaser. In the case of non-delivery, where the purchaser does not get the goods he purchased, it is assumed that these would be worth to him, if he had them, what they would fetch in the open market; and that, if he wanted to get others in their stead, he could obtain them in that market at that price. In a   such a case, the price at which the purchaser might in anticipation of delivery have resold the goods is properly treated, where no question of loss of profit arises, as an irrelevant matter: Rodocanachi [Sons & Co] v. Milburn [Bros] ((1886) 18 QBD 67). The purchaser not having got his goods should receive by way of damages enough to enable him to buy similar goods in the open market. Similarly, when the delivery of goods purchased is delayed, the

b   goods are presumed to have been at the time they should have been delivered worth to the purchaser what he could then sell them for, or buy others like them for, in the open market, and when they are in fact delivered they are similarly presumed to be, for the same reason, worth to the purchaser what he could then sell for in that market, but if in fact the purchaser, when he obtains possession of the goods, sells them at a price

c   greatly in advance of the then market value, that presumption is rebutted and the real value of the goods to him is proved by the very fact of this sale to be more than market value, and the loss he sustains must be measured by that price, unless he is, against all justice, to be permitted to make a profit by the breach of contract, be compensated for a loss he never suffered, and be

d   put, as far as money can do it, not in the same position in which he would have been if the contract had been performed, but in a much better position.'

Lord Atkinson's reasoning in that case, in particular, the distinction between cases of non-delivery and late delivery and the relevance of the onward sale price in the latter case, was approved and restated by Lord Dunedin in the House of

e   Lords in Williams Bros v Ed T Agius Ltd [1914] AC 510 at 522–523, [1914–15] All ER Rep 97 at 101–102, a case of non-delivery. He said:

'It is certain that Lord Atkinson, who delivered the judgment in that case, did not think that he was going against Rodocanachi's Case for he says so in terms. Nor, in my mind, is there any discrepancy between the two

f   judgments. Wertheim's Case was a case, not of delivery withheld, but of delivery delayed. The buyer, therefore, got the goods, and the only damage he had suffered was in delay. Now, delay might have prejudiced him; but the amount of prejudice was no longer a matter of speculation, it had been put to the test by the goods being actually sold; and he was rightly, as I think, only held entitled to recover the difference between the market price at the

g   date of due delivery and the price he actually got. But when there is no delivery of the goods the position is quite a different one. The buyer never gets them, and he is entitled to be put in the position in which he would have stood if he had got them at the due date. That position is the position of a man who has goods at the market price of the day—and barring special

h   circumstances, the defaulting seller is neither mulct in damages for the extra profit which the buyer would have got owing to a forward resale at over the market price ... nor can he take benefit of the fact that the buyer has made a forward resale at under the market price.'

j   See also Lord Atkinson ([1914] AC 510 at 529, [1914–15] All ER Rep 97 at 102) and the unusual case of R Pagnan & Flli v Corbisa Industrial Agropacuaria Ltda [1971] 1 All ER 165, [1970] 1 WLR 1306, where a buyer, having initially rejected goods because of their defective quality, later accepted them after negotiating a reduced price which was less than the market price for similar goods at the date of the seller's breach. The Court of Appeal held that the prima facie market price rule in s 53(3) of the 1979 Act did not apply because the buyer had suffered no loss.

In *Slater's* case all the members of the court were disinclined to extend the
decision in *Wertheim's* case to a claim for breach of warranty of quality. Bankes
LJ confined it in any event to a sub-sale of the identical goods, relying on
reasoning of Lord Dunedin in the *Williams Bros* case [1914] AC 510 at 523, [1914–
15] All ER Rep 97 at 101–102 about the difficulty of establishing damages based
on the terms of a sub-sale in a non-delivery case (see [1920] 2 KB 11 at 15, [1918–
19] All ER Rep 654 at 655–656). Warrington LJ appears to have been of the
view—though he did not explain why—that s 53(3) of the Sale of Goods Act 1893
[corresponding to s 53(3) of the 1979 Act] was the right principle governing
delivery of inferior goods to those provided for by the contract and that what the
buyer did with the goods was irrelevant (see [1920] 2 KB 11 at 17–18, [1918–19]
All ER Rep 654 at 656–657). Scrutton LJ expressed the view that the *Rodocanachi*
principle as to non-delivery applied equally to delivery of inferior goods, because
if the buyer fulfils his sub-contract by buying in the market, he is left with the
inferior goods at their market value against the market value of sound goods (see
[1920] 2 KB 11 at 21–22, [1918–19] All ER Rep 654 at 658–659). Alternatively, if
he applies the inferior goods to a sub-sale the damages he may have to pay to his
buyer may be calculable differently from those in the contract with his seller. He
acknowledged that, on this approach, the buyer may recover more than his true
loss, but he cited examples of the same principle resulting in a recovery of less
than the true loss.

With respect to the Court of Appeal in that case, and to the authors of the
supporting comments in *McGregor* para 774 and *Chitty* note 91 to para 41–300, it
seems to me that they wrongly: (1) overlooked the basic rule in s 53(2) as to what
would have been in the ordinary and natural contemplation of the parties in a
commercial contract such as it was, namely, that the buyer could well be
prejudiced in his onward dealing with the goods if they were defective; (2)
disregarded the reasoning of the Privy Council in *Wertheim* as approved and
restated by Lord Dunedin and Lord Atkinson in *Williams Bros v Ed T Agius Ltd*,
that where there has been delivery in a mercantile contract and it can be seen
what the buyer has done with the goods, it is possible and proper to measure his
actual loss by reference to that outcome; (3) had too much regard to practicality
at the expense of principle in relying on possible difficulties of establishing
causation and of assessment where the goods sold have been subjected to some
process or where the terms of the contract and sub-contract may for that or some
other reason be different; and (4) were seemingly content to award a buyer more
than the evidence clearly showed he had lost.

As Devlin J made plain in his consideration in *Biggin & Co Ltd v Permanite Ltd*
[1950] 2 All ER 859 at 869, [1951] 1 KB 422 at 436, of the supposed two rules in
Hadley v Baxendale, the critical matter in determining the earlier question as to the
applicability or not of the prima facie rule in s 53(3) is the contemplation of the
parties:

'... there is only one area of indemnity to be explored, and that is what is
within the prevision of the defendant as a reasonable man in the light of the
knowledge, actual or imputed, which he has at the time of the contract. It
has often been held ... that the profit actually made on a sub-sale which is
outside the contemplation of the parties cannot be used to reduce the
damages measured by a notional loss in market value. If, however, a sub-sale
is within the contemplation of the parties, I think that the damages must be
assessed by reference to it, whether the plaintiff likes it or not ... if it is the

a plaintiff's liability to the ultimate user that is contemplated as the measure of
damage and if in fact it is used without injurious results so that no such
liability arises, the plaintiff could not claim the difference in market value and
say that the sub-sale must be disregarded.'

Morland J directed himself broadly to the question of the notional
contemplation of the parties in the event of a latent defect in the film putting the
b buyer in breach of his contract to the container manufacturers. However, apart
from a brief summary of the relevant circumstances and posing a series of
unanswered questions about uncertainties as to the extent of the damages if
calculated on that basis, he has not made a reasoned finding as to their notional
contemplation. His approach was a paraphrase of a passage in *McGregor* para 264,
c relating to contracting parties' knowledge of 'special circumstances'. He asked
whether there were 'special circumstances' known at the time to the buyer which
he should be taken as having accepted so as to restrict his claim '(by reduction
from the prima facie measure)' or by which the seller should have contemplated
exposing himself to an 'open-ended liability' of indemnity.

In my view, that was a wrong approach. This was not a 'special circumstances'
d case or one where the possible damages were so remote or open-ended as not to
have been within the parties' contemplation. It was eminently a case in which
they would have contemplated that, in the event of a breach by the seller
discovered only after the decals had been in use, the buyer might wish to pass on
to it claims for damages from dissatisfied customers.

e I add a few words about chain contracts. In *Dexters Ltd v Hill Crest Oil Co
(Bradford) Ltd* [1926] 1 KB 348, [1925] All ER Rep 273 Bankes, Warrington and
Scrutton LJJ expressed the view, obiter, that all the contracts in a chain must be
the same if recoverable damages are to be passed along the chain. However, as
the editors of *McGregor* para 815 observe, that approach is 'a little too strict'. The
matter was considered by Devlin J in *Biggin & Co Ltd v Permanite Ltd* [1950] 2 All
f ER 859 at 867, [1951] 1 KB 422 at 433. He said that he agreed with the reasoning
that lay behind the view, namely that material variations in contracts down the
line could lead to contractual claims for damages not contemplated by the
original seller. However, he clearly regarded the matter as one of fact for
determination in each case, not as a rigid principle of law that all contracts in the
g chain must be in the same terms. He said ([1950] 2 All ER 859 at 867, [1951] 1 KB
422 at 435):

'I respectfully adopt this principle, but I have still to determine how it
should be applied in this case, and also what degree of variation in
description breaks the chain ... To understand the application of the
h principle it is necessary to understand its basis. Like every principle in this
branch of the law, it stems from the broad rule that the damage is to be
measured by those consequences of the breach which the parties as
reasonable men would, if they had thought about it, have foreseen and
accepted as natural and probable. If the variation to a description is such that
j it is impossible to say whether the injury that ultimately results would have
flowed from the breach of the original warranty, the parties must as
reasonable men be presumed to have put the liability for the injury outside
their contemplation as a measure of compensation. If this is, as I believe, the
nature of the principle, it must be applied very differently according to
whether the injury for which the defendant is being asked to pay is a market
loss or physical damage. In the former case (which I think is what the lords

justices were considering in *Dexter*) any variation that is more than a matter of words is likely to be fatal, because there is no way of telling its effect on the market value. In the latter case the nature of the physical damage will show whether the variation was material or not.'

As Mr Stephen Grime QC submitted, on behalf of the seller, the point is essentially one of causation, namely whether there is sufficient similarity between the sale contract and the subsequent contract(s) to enable a finding that breach by the seller of the sale contract has in fact caused the breach of the subsequent contract(s). Clearly, as he also submitted, a substantial change to goods sold as a result of the buyer subjecting them to a manufacturing process may break the chain of causation between the breach of the contract sued upon and any claim arising under a subsequent contract. However, that is unlikely on the facts of this case—a five-year film life without deterioration was stipulated by the container owner, the container manufacturer and the decal manufacturer, the buyer, in the contracts into which they respectively entered along the chain.

I, therefore, conclude, as Otton LJ has done, that this is plainly a case in which the parties must be taken as having contemplated that any latent defect in the vinyl film at the time of delivery or at the time of conversion by the buyer into the decals, might when later discovered, render the buyer vulnerable to claims for damages which it would wish to pass back to the seller. On the material before Morland J, there appears to have been no material differences between the contracts in the chain which would have put damage claimed at any point in the chain outside the imputed contemplation of the buyer and seller, given their knowledge that the vinyl film and the decals into which it was converted were required to serve their purpose for a minimum of five years. I am accordingly of the view that the appeal should be allowed and that there should be an order in the terms stated by Otton LJ.

THORPE LJ. Where a contract is breached the natural objective of the legal system is to compensate the injured party fairly. Where a manufacturer supplies a defective product to his customers as a consequence of the use within the process of a raw material that did not possess the qualities warranted by the supplier, the manufacturer is fairly compensated by recovering from the supplier the cost of settling claims made by his customers together with the profit lost on those sales, and perhaps prospective sales. Compensation so calculated would in the vast majority of cases considerably exceed the price that the manufacturer paid for the raw materials. I make those generalisations to illustrate the conclusion that the facts underlying this appeal are exceptional.

The condition of sale governing the supply of the product to the plaintiffs dealt with liability under para 11 in these terms:

'(c) The Seller's aggregate liability to the Purchaser whether for negligence breach of contract misrepresentation or otherwise shall in no circumstances exceed the cost of the defective, damaged or undelivered Goods determined by net price invoiced to the Buyer in respect of any occurrence or series of occurrences. (d) The Seller's prices are determined on the basis of the limits of liability set out in this Condition. The Purchaser may by written notice to the Seller request the Seller to agree a higher limit of liability provided insurance cover can be obtained therefor.'

a Thus, the parties must be taken to have contemplated the consequence of possible future breach within the terms of those sub-paragraphs.

When problems of discolouration and disintegration of the decals arose in the summer of 1985, the plaintiffs did not know the cause but the defendants did. The defendants took steps to remedy the deficiency in future supplies, concealing its realisation and its reaction from the plaintiffs.   When the plaintiffs
b subsequently asserted the true cause of the defect, the defendants refuted the assertion by spurious reliance on test results that were not germane. Despite this unmeritorious history, the defendants vigorously contested the issue of liability. The plaintiffs' managing director gave lengthy evidence.   On the sixth day the defendants made substantial admissions.   On the seventh day they added the admission that all the material supplied to the plaintiffs between 1980–1985
c inclusive was defective in that by reason of its lack of ultraviolet stabiliser it had a tendency to discolour or degrade within the five-year period for which it was warranted durable. The defendants were therefore left with the issue of quantum of the resultant damage. The statement of claim sought the return of the contract price of £564,328·54.   By subsequent amendment, it sought an indemnity in
d respect of all claims made or to be made against the plaintiffs caused by or attributable to the supply by the defendants of defective film. But the defendants' endeavour to persuade Morland J to assess damages on the alternative basis pleaded by amendment had to be weighed not only in the light of the concessions but also upon the evidence of the plaintiffs alone, since the defendants elected to call no evidence. In the course of his evidence, Mr Bence, for the plaintiffs, had
e asserted that the defective film supplied was worthless, since it lacked the essential durability, and that, accordingly, the plaintiffs were entitled to the return of the price paid.

Of course, the reality was that he had had no conception that the material was defective until 1985 and had processed it to supply decals to manufacturers whose
f ultimate dissatisfaction had only given rise to modest claims. Despite that reality, Morland J was entitled to find that the product was worthless for want of durability and that finding has always been accepted by the defendants. But that is simply an unusual feature of the developments post the defendants' breach and it is the consequence of the latent character of the defect.

g The issue fought by the defendants following the concessions on the sixth and seventh days had to be resolved by the application of ss 53 and 54 of the Sale of Goods Act 1979 to the contract from formation to breach. By the terms of s 53(3) the plaintiffs had a prima facie entitlement to the return of the contract price. At trial, Mr Heaton mounted an argument under s 54, or the second limb in *Hadley v Baxendale* (1854) 9 Exch 341, [1843–60] All ER Rep 461.   Throughout this appeal
h Mr Stephen Grime QC has contended under the first limb of s 53 that the plaintiffs' prima facie entitlement is displaced by the parties' exclusive contemplation of an alternative measure of damages. Mr Grime criticises with justification the use of the word 'remedy' in the judgment.   But in the end, Morland J made a finding which in my judgment is decisive of this appeal.   His
j ultimate conclusion was in these terms:

'The defendants have failed to satisfy me on the balance of probabilities that having regard to all the circumstances in which the contract was made the parties must be taken to have contemplated that the s 53(3) measure of damages was displaced.'

That was a finding of fact made on the evidence of the plaintiffs. I accept Mr
Moran QC's submission that that finding is unassailable in this court. The
consequence of the finding was judgment for damages equivalent to the price
paid for the defective goods. The plaintiffs accepts that the judgment is
comprehensive of all claims arising from the breach and that should they face
future claims from those they supplied they cannot look to the defendants for
indemnity or any other contribution.

Before reaching his essential contribution, Morland J reviewed the relevant
authorities at some length. As the sophisticated argument in this appeal
demonstrates, this is not an easy field of case law to summarise or to reconcile.
But in my judgment, Mr Moran is right to emphasise the distinction between
authorities which determine cases involving a string of contracts and cases
involving the supply of a raw material to a manufacturer or processor who
converts the material to, or incorporates it within, some other product for supply
to his customers. As Mr Moran submits, in the former class of case the buyer
changes role and becomes himself the seller, the selfsame goods passing along a
conduit of contracting parties on identical terms save as to price. In such cases
(exemplified by *R & H Hall Ltd v W H Pim Junr & Co Ltd* (1927) 30 Ll L Rep 159),
the exclusive contemplation of the parties is very different in the event of breach
of a quality warranty. In the latter type of case, the contemplation of the supplier
and the manufacturer is less confined and will depend upon all the circumstances
of the case. Here Morland J decided the contemplation of the parties on the
evidence of the plaintiffs alone.

Although the arguments have ranged wide over authority which, as Auld LJ
demonstrates, is difficult if not impossible to reconcile, I would dismiss this
appeal on the simple ground that Morland J's conclusion was justified on the
evidence and no sufficiently substantial misdirection in law has been
demonstrated.

Appeal allowed. Leave to appeal to the House of Lords granted.

Paul Magrath Esq   Barrister.

a
Issa and another v Hackney London Borough Council

COURT OF APPEAL, CIVIL DIVISION

NOURSE, SAVILLE AND BROOKE LJJ

b

18, 19 NOVEMBER 1996

Nuisance – Statutory nuisance – Premises in such a state as to be prejudicial to health or a nuisance – Local authority premises – Plaintiffs living in premises with parents – Local authority convicted of criminal offence in relation to state of premises – Plaintiffs
c *bringing civil action for damages for ill-health resulting from state of premises – Whether commission of criminal offence rendering local authority liable in civil action for damages for loss or damage thereby suffered by plaintiffs – Public Health Act 1936, ss 92(1)(a), 94(2), 99.*

d The plaintiffs lived with their parents in accommodation owned by the defendant local authority. In 1988 an environmental health consultant concluded that the condition of the premises, which were severely affected with condensation and associated mould growth, was prejudicial to health and therefore constituted a statutory nuisance under Pt III of the Public Health Act 1936. Thereafter the defendants pleaded guilty to an offence under ss 92(1)(a)[a] and 99[b] of the 1936 Act
e and were fined £500 pursuant to s 94(2)[c] of the Act. The plaintiffs, by their father and next friend, subsequently commenced civil proceedings against the defendants for damages for ill-health resulting from the condition of the premises. The assistant recorder decided as a preliminary issue that the criminal offence for which the defendant had been convicted rendered them liable for any
f loss thereby suffered by the plaintiffs and, finding for the plaintiffs on the issue of causation, awarded the plaintiffs damages. The defendants appealed to the Court of Appeal.

Held – Part III of the 1936 Act was a self-contained code dealing with the abatement of statutory nuisances under which the power to impose a fine was
g only one of several methods of enforcement for which provision was made by the Act. It followed that, since criminal sanctions were not the only method of enforcement provided, there was no ground for construing that part of the Act so as to incorporate the creation of a civil cause of action. Accordingly, the appeal would be allowed, the assistant recorder's awards of damages discharged and the
h plaintiffs' actions dismissed (see p 1004 *e* to *h*, p 1005 *g* and p 1008 *f g*, post).

Notes
For construction of statute to ascertain whether an action lies for breach of duty, see 45 *Halsbury's Laws* (4th edn) paras 1282–1285.

j   For summary abatement of nuisances, see 38 *Halsbury's Laws* (4th edn) paras 410–423, and for a case on the subject, see 36(2) *Digest* (2nd reissue) 162, 1279.

---

a   Section 92, so far as material, is set out at p 1002 *g h*, post
b   Section 99 is set out at p 1003 *g h*, post
c   Section 94, so far as material. is set out a p 1003 *a* to *e*, post

As from 1 January 1991 Pt III of the Public Health Act 1936 was replaced by Pt III of the Environmental Protection Act 1990.

For the Environmental Protection Act 1990, Pt III, see 35 *Halsbury's Statutes* (4th edn reissue) 901.

Cases referred to in judgments

Coventry City Council v Doyle [1981] 2 All ER 184, [1981] 1 WLR 1325, DC.
Cutler v Wandsworth Stadium Ltd [1949] 1 All ER 544, [1949] AC 398, HL.
Doe d Bishop of Rochester v Bridges (1831) 1 B & Ad 847, [1824–34] All ER Rep 167, 109 ER 1001.
Habinteg Housing Association v James (1994) 27 HLR 299, CA.
Herbert v Lambeth London Borough (1991) 24 HLR 299, DC.
Lonrho Ltd v Shell Petroleum Co Ltd (No 2) [1981] 2 All ER 456, [1982] AC 173, [1981] 3 WLR 33, HL.
McCall v Abelesz [1976] 1 All ER 727, [1976] QB 585, [1976] 2 WLR 151, CA.
McNerny v Lambeth London Borough (1988) 21 HLR 188, CA.
Quick v Taff-Ely BC [1985] 3 All ER 321, [1986] QB 809, [1985] 3 WLR 981, CA.
R v Crown Court at Liverpool, ex p Cooke [1996] 4 All ER 589, DC.
R v Newham Justices, ex p Hunt, R v Oxted Justices, ex p Franklin [1976] 1 All ER 839, [1976] 1 WLR 420, DC.
Summers v Salford Corp [1943] 1 All ER 68, [1943] AC 283, HL.

Cases also cited or referred to in skeleton arguments

Birmingham DC v Kelly (1985) 17 HLR 572, DC.
Botross v Hammersmith and Fulham London Borough (1994) 27 HLR 179, DC.
Cavalier v Pope [1906] AC 428, HL.
Lambeth London BC v Stubbs (1980) 78 LGR 650, DC.
McGhee v National Coal Board [1972] 3 All ER 1008, [1973] 1 WLR 1, HL.
Rickless v United Artists Corp [1987] 1 All ER 679, [1988] QB 40, CA.
Sandwell Metropolitan BC v Bujok [1990] 3 All ER 385, [1990] 1 WLR 1350, HL.
Thornton v Kirklees Metropolitan BC [1979] 2 All ER 349, [1979] QB 626, CA.
Wilsher v Essex Area Health Authority [1988] 1 All ER 871, [1988] AC 1074, HL.

Appeal

By notice dated 17 November 1995 the defendants, Hackney London Borough Council, appealed with leave of Beldam LJ granted on 2 November 1995 from the order of Mr Assistant Recorder Crawford made on 17 August 1995 in the Central London County Court whereby he awarded the plaintiffs, Yasin Issa and Imran Issa, suing by their next friend and father, respectively damages and interest of £5,851·50 and £4,494·50 in respect of the defendants' breach of duty in committing an offence under Pt III of the Public Health Act 1936. The facts are set out in the judgment of Nourse LJ.

Richard Drabble QC and *Ian Lewis* (instructed by *Christopher Hinde,* Hackney) for the defendants.
Lorna Tagliavini (instructed by *Moss & Co*) for the plaintiffs.

NOURSE LJ. Shortly stated, the question on this appeal is whether s 94(2) of the Public Health Act 1936 (Power of court to make nuisance order if abatement notice disregarded), by making it a criminal offence to make default in complying *a* with the notice, also renders the person guilty of the offence liable in a civil action for damages at the suit of any person who thereby suffers loss or damage.

The plaintiffs, Yasin and Imran Issa, were born in 1975 and 1978 respectively. They are two of the four sons of Mr and Mrs Ali Ahmed Issa. Until 1983 the family lived in Lancashire. In November of that year they moved to London and lived at various addresses until 7 April 1985, when Mr and Mrs Issa were granted
b a joint tenancy of 21 Malmsmead House, Kingsmead Estate, London E9, a property owned by the defendants, the Hackney London Borough Council. At that time the plaintiffs were aged nine and seven respectively.

On 25 October 1988 Mr Bill Page, an environmental health consultant, made a report based on a visit to 21 Malmsmead House some two and a half weeks earlier, in which he recorded that the premises were severely affected with
c condensation and associated mould growth and concluded that their condition was such that he was satisfied that they were prejudicial to health and therefore a statutory nuisance as defined by s 92(1)(a) of the 1936 Act. On 12 June 1989 the defendants pleaded guilty at Wells Street Magistrates' Court to an offence under that provision and s 99 of the Act. They were fined £500, with £1,400
d compensation and £2,023·80 costs being awarded to Mr Issa. An order was made for the nuisance to be abated within 56 days, the necessary works being completed in December 1989.

In July 1992 the plaintiffs, suing by Mr Issa as next friend, brought separate actions against the defendants in the Shoreditch County Court which were later transferred to the Central London County Court, where they were tried together
e by Mr Assistant Recorder Crawford in August 1995. The plaintiffs claimed damages for ill-health allegedly suffered as a result of the condition of the premises, in particular through the aggravation of the asthma from which they both suffered. On 15 August the assistant recorder decided, as a preliminary issue, that the criminal offence for which they had been convicted rendered the
f defendants liable for any loss or damage thereby suffered by the plaintiffs. He then proceeded with the trial. On 17 August, having decided the issue of causation in favour of the plaintiffs, he awarded the first plaintiff, Yasin, damages and interest amounting to £5,851·50 and the second plaintiff, Imran, damages and interest amounting to £4,494·50.

The assistant recorder refused the defendants leave to appeal to this court.
g However, leave was granted on consideration of the documents by Beldam LJ as the single judge. Three issues were raised by the notice of appeal: first, the question of law identified at the beginning of this judgment; second, the question whether, if a civil liability arose, there was sufficient evidence of causation to establish liability; third, the question whether the period for which the defendants
h were liable (if at all) to the plaintiffs terminated with the abatement of the statutory nuisance in December 1989. In opening the appeal yesterday, and for reasons applicable to this case but not necessarily to any other, Mr Drabble QC, for the defendants, abandoned their case on the second and third issues. Argument then proceeded on the question of law.

j In dealing with that question it is important to emphasise at the outset that Pt III of the 1936 Act, now replaced by Pt III of the Environmental Protection Act 1990, is of wide and frequent application as between local authorities as regulatory bodies on the one hand and those who cause, suffer or permit statutory nuisances to occur on the other, whereas the circumstances of the present case, where it is a local authority as landlords who are responsible for the nuisance, must be comparatively rare. But if the Act gives the plaintiffs a civil

remedy against the defendants, it must equally give one to all those who suffer
loss or damage as a result of statutory nuisances caused, suffered or permitted in
the far more numerous cases referred to, most of whom, however, will already
have a cause of action at common law.

As an introduction to his consideration of Pt III of the 1936 Act, Mr Drabble
cited 45 *Halsbury's Laws* (4th edn) para 1285, headed 'Effect of provision of
statutory remedy for breach of duty':

> 'There is a general rule that where a new obligation is created by statute
> which at the same time provides a special means of enforcing it, that
> performance cannot be enforced in any other manner. However, this rule is
> subject to the ordinary rules as to the construction of statutes. Where the
> only manner of enforcing performance for which the statute provides is by
> means of criminal proceedings, there are two classes of exception to this
> general rule. The first is where the obligation was imposed for the benefit or
> protection of a particular class of individuals. The second is where the
> statute creates a public right and a particular member of the public suffers
> particular direct and substantial damage other and different from that which
> was common to the rest of the public.'

The authorities cited in support of the first sentence are *Doe d Bishop of Rochester
v Bridges* (1831) 1 B & Ad 847 at 859, [1824–1834] All ER Rep 167 at 169–170 per
Lord Tenterden CJ and *Cutler v Wandsworth Stadium Ltd* [1949] 1 All ER 544,
[1949] AC 398. The principal authority cited in support of the third, fourth and
fifth sentences is the speech of Lord Diplock in *Lonrho Ltd v Shell Petroleum Co Ltd
(No 2)* [1981] 2 All ER 456 at 461, [1982] AC 173 at 185–186.

Part III of the Act is headed 'Nuisances and offensive trades'. Under the
subheading 'General duty of local authority', s 91 provides:

> 'It shall be the duty of every local authority to cause their district to be
> inspected from time to time for the detection of matters requiring to be dealt
> with under the provisions of this Part of this Act as being statutory nuisances
> within the meaning of the next succeeding section.'

Sections 92 to 99 then follow under the subheading 'Nuisances which may be
dealt with summarily'. So far as material, s 92 provides:

> '(1) Without prejudice to the exercise by a local authority of any other
> powers vested in them by or under this Act, the following matters may,
> subject to the provisions of this Part of this Act, be dealt with summarily, and
> are in this Part of this Act referred to as "statutory nuisances", that is to say:—
> (a) any premises in such a state as to be prejudicial to health or a nuisance ...'

Section 93 provides:

> 'Where a local authority are satisfied of the existence of a statutory
> nuisance, they shall serve a notice (hereafter in this Act referred to as "an
> abatement notice") on the person by whose act, default or sufferance the
> nuisance arises or continues, or, if that person cannot be found, on the owner
> or occupier of the premises on which the nuisance arises, requiring him to
> abate the nuisance and to execute such works and take such steps as may be
> necessary for that purpose ...'

There are then two provisos, which I need not read.

a I now come to s 94, of which sub-ss (1) and (2) provide:

'(1) If the person on whom an abatement notice has been served makes default in complying with any of the requirements of the notice, or if the nuisance, although abated since the service of the notice, is, in the opinion of the local authority, likely to recur on the same premises, the authority shall cause a complaint to be made to a justice of the peace, and the justice shall

b thereupon issue a summons requiring the person on whom the notice was served to appear before a court of summary jurisdiction.

(2) If on the hearing of the complaint it is proved that the alleged nuisance exists, or that although abated it is likely to recur on the same premises, then, subject to the provisions of subsections (4) and (5) of this section the court

c shall make an order (hereafter in this Act referred to as "a nuisance order") for either, or both, of the following purposes—(a) requiring the defendant to comply with all or any of the requirements of the abatement notice, or otherwise to abate the nuisance, within a time specified in the order, and to execute any works necessary for that purpose; (b) prohibiting a recurrence of the nuisance, and requiring the defendant, within a time specified in the

d order, to execute any works necessary to prevent a recurrence; and may also impose on the defendant a fine not exceeding level 4 on the standard scale. Where a nuisance proved to exist is such as to render a building, in the opinion of the court, unfit for human habitation, the nuisance order may prohibit the use of the building for that purpose until a court of summary

e jurisdiction, being satisfied that it has been rendered fit for human habitation, withdraws the prohibition.'

I need not read any other subsections of s 94. Section 95 provides, by sub-s (1), for a further fine by way of penalty for contravention of a nuisance order and, by sub-s (2), for abatement of the nuisance by the local authority where a nuisance

f order has not been complied with.

Section 99, to which the sidenote is 'Power of individual to make complaint as to statutory nuisance', must be read in full:

'Complaint of the existence of a statutory nuisance under this Act may be made to a justice of the peace by any person aggrieved by the nuisance, and

g thereupon the like proceedings shall be had, with the like incidents and consequences as to the making of orders, penalties for disobedience of orders and otherwise, as in the case of a complaint by the local authority, but any order made in such proceedings may, if the court after giving the local authority an opportunity of being heard thinks fit, direct the authority to

h abate the nuisance.'

It was under that subsection that Mr and Mrs Issa brought the defendants before the magistrates' court in this case.

In *R v Newham Justices, ex p Hunt, R v Oxted Justices, ex p Franklin* [1976] 1 All ER

j 839, [1976] 1 WLR 420 it was held by the Divisional Court, first, that s 99 enabled an individual to bring proceedings by information in a magistrates' court and thereby invoke against a local authority the penal provisions of s 94 and, secondly, that it was not a necessary preliminary to those proceedings that an abatement notice should be served. In *Coventry City Council v Doyle* [1981] 2 All ER 184, [1981] 1 WLR 1325 it was held by the Divisional Court that, on the wording of s 94(2), the relevant date for determining whether the alleged nuisance exists is the date of the hearing before the magistrates. Accordingly, if it has by that time been abated, no offence is committed.

Mr Drabble submits, first, that the question depends on the true construction of Pt III of the 1936 Act as a whole; secondly, that it must be construed as at the date of its enactment. So much is accepted by Miss Tagliavini, for the plaintiffs. But that is the extent of the common ground. Mr Drabble submits that this is a plain case where the general rule stated in 45 *Halsbury's Laws* (4th edn) para 1285 applies. Assuming that it is one where a new obligation is created by the Act, he says that it is also one where a specified means of enforcement is provided, so that there cannot be enforcement in any other manner.

In elaboration of these submissions Mr Drabble has pointed to the following features of the material provisions. First, they provide for a wide range of nuisances to be dealt with summarily, a local authority's powers to deal with them being expressed to be without prejudice to the exercise of any other powers vested in them by or under the Act (see s 92(1)). Secondly, s 92 does not itself impose any duty to abate a nuisance; in the normal case it is only where an abatement notice has been served under s 93 that the duty arises. Thirdly, in the normal case it is only when there has been default in complying with the notice that an offence is committed under s 94(2). Fourthly, because it can never be known until the hearing before the magistrates whether an offence has in fact been committed, it is highly unlikely that Parliament would have intended that the availability of a civil cause of action, if there was to be one, should depend on such an unpredictable event. Fifthly, the power to impose a fine is only one of several methods of enforcement for which provision is made. Under s 94(2) the magistrates have power to make a nuisance order (to which teeth are given by the further fine under s 95(1)) and such an order may prohibit the use of a building which is unfit for human habitation. Under s 95(2) a local authority may themselves abate a nuisance where a nuisance order has not been complied with.

In summary, Mr Drabble submits that Pt III of the 1936 Act is a self-contained code dealing with the abatement of statutory nuisances, and that there is no ground for construing it so as to incorporate the creation of a civil cause of action. He adds that, since this is not a case where the only method of enforcement provided by the Act is prosecution for the criminal offence of failure to perform the statutory obligation, the principles stated by Lord Diplock in *Lonrho Ltd v Shell Petroleum Co Ltd (No 2)* [1981] 2 All ER 456, [1982] AC 173 do not come into play.

In my judgment, the submissions made by Mr Drabble are correct. In answering them, Miss Tagliavini has relied primarily on a passage in the judgment of Shaw LJ in *McCall v Abelesz* [1976] 1 All ER 727 at 735, [1976] QB 585 at 600 where, after agreeing that the formulation of general rules as to when a penal statute may give rise by implication to a civil remedy for the benefit of a person harmed by an offence created by it is a dubious exercise, he said:

'The numerous authorities which have been cited in this regard do, however, suggest that the following conditions must be satisfied before such a remedy will be held to be so conferred: (1) the offence created must consist of a failure to perform a defined duty which the statute imposes on the potential offender; (2) the duty must be imposed for the benefit of a class of persons which includes the person harmed; and (3) the contemplated beneficiaries of the performance of the duty would, unless a correlative remedy is implied by the statute, be without any, or any effective, remedy

a
for the harm they may suffer from the failure to perform that duty, that is to say from the commission of the offence created by the statute.'

Miss Tagliavini has relied especially on the third of those conditions. She says, correctly, that, except for the £1,400 compensation awarded to Mr and Mrs Issa in the magistrates' court, the plaintiffs have no other effective remedy in this case. In particular, for the reasons stated by Lawton LJ in *Quick v Taff-Ely BC* [1985] 3

b
All ER 321 at 327, [1986] QB 809 at 821, the implied covenant, under what was then s 6 of the Housing Act 1957, that the landlord will keep the premises in a condition fit for human habitation does not apply. Moreover, says Miss Tagliavini, that covenant would have enured only for the benefit of Mr and Mrs Issa, as tenants of the premises, and not the plaintiffs themselves.

c
While I feel the force of Miss Tagliavini's submissions, there are, I think, two decisive answers to them. In the first place, the effect of Pt III of the 1936 Act must be judged at the date of its enactment, before the inflationary times with which we have since become familiar, when the landlord's implied covenant would have applied to these premises and to many like them. Secondly, and perhaps more significantly, I repeat that we are not dealing with the normal case.

d
In the normal case where a local authority is proceeding against someone who has caused, suffered or permitted a statutory nuisance to occur, those who suffer loss or damage as a result will already have a cause of action at common law. In the circumstances it is improbable, to say the least, that Parliament intended to create a further or alternative cause of action.

e
For these reasons I do not think that Miss Tagliavini's reliance on the third of Shaw LJ's conditions enables her to avoid the impact of Mr Drabble's submissions. Furthermore, she has been unable, in my view, to satisfy the second of those conditions. She was forced to say that the statutory duty here was imposed for the benefit of the class of persons aggrieved by the particular statutory nuisance. That is too nebulous a class either to come within Shaw LJ's

f
second condition or, indeed, within Lord Diplock's first exception to the general rule.

I conclude that the question of law should be answered in the negative. I would therefore allow this appeal, discharge the assistant recorder's awards of damages and interest and dismiss the plaintiffs' actions.

g
SAVILLE LJ. I agree.

BROOKE LJ. I agree.

It was an important part of Miss Tagliavini's submissions that Parliament must
h
have intended the early sections of Pt III of the Public Health Act 1936 to create a civil remedy for her clients because otherwise they would be without any remedy at all for the injury they have suffered and for which the assistant recorder awarded them a total of £10,000 in compensation.

In order to analyse the strength of this submission, it is necessary to put oneself
j
in the draftsman's chair at the time the 1936 Bill was enacted. At that time the plaintiffs' father, as the tenant of the flat, would undoubtedly have had a cause of action against his local authority landlord if his health had suffered as a direct result of the landlord's failure to comply with its statutory obligation to keep the flat fit for human habitation. The history of this statutory implied covenant, which was first included in s 12 of the Housing of the Working Classes Act 1885, is very clearly set out in Pt IV of the Law Commission's recent report, *Landlord*

and Tenant: Responsibility for State and Condition of Property (Law Com No 238
(1996)) p 32, para 4.7ff. The 1885 Bill was introduced by the then Prime Minister,
the Marquess of Salisbury, in ringing terms in order to complement by statute the
common law rule which compelled the lessor of a furnished house to enter into
a contract that his house was healthy to inhabit. The new implied statutory
obligation was always limited to lettings of premises below a defined annual
rental level, but the Law Commission has reminded us of the fact that, when the
relevant rent limits were doubled in 1909, the president of the Local Government
Board observed that as a result, 'with the exception of London, nearly all the
working classes of the Kingdom will be included'. In 1936 the relevant provision
was to be found in s 2(1) of the Housing Act 1936, itself a consolidation Act, which
re-enacted the implied condition that a house let for human habitation at a rent
lower than the prescribed level was at the commencement of the tenancy in all
respects reasonably fit for human habitation, and an implied undertaking by the
landlord that his house would be kept in that condition during the tenancy. For
the right of a tenant to recover damages for injury to health caused by a breach
of that covenant, see *Summers v Salford Corp* [1943] 1 All ER 68, [1943] AC 283.

When the 1936 Act was enacted, the present plaintiffs would not have had a
right to rely on the breach of the landlord's covenant to their father in order to
found a right of action of their own. As the Law Commission observed in 1970
in its report, *Civil Liability of Vendors and Lessors for Defective Premises* (Law Com
No 40) p 19, para 56:

'At common law a landlord was under no liability to the tenant's family or
visitors for injury suffered by reason of the condition of the premises. It was
considered that the letting transferred to the tenant all rights of control over
the premises and third parties must look to the occupier for any remedy at
law.'

I do not, however, consider it possible that Parliament must be taken to have
intended to create a wide-ranging civil remedy simply to assist a small minority
of people who did not already have a right of action in respect of the wide-ranging
types of nuisance mentioned in s 92 of the 1936 Act.

So far as the remedies available to a tenant's family are concerned, later history
shows that the Bill attached to the Law Commission's 1970 report was enacted in
substantially the same form as the Defective Premises Act 1972, and s 4(1) of that
Act does give members of a tenant's family a clear right of recourse against the
landlord if their health has been foreseeably damaged by a breach of the
landlord's new statutory duty to take such care as is reasonable in all the
circumstances to see that the premises are reasonably safe from the risk of
personal injury caused by a relevant defect. Section 4(3), however, restricts the
meaning of the words 'relevant defect' to defects in the state of the premises
arising from or continuing because of a failure by the landlord to carry out his
obligation to the tenant for the maintenance or repair of the premises. Successive
decisions of this court have shown how this remedy is now a completely dead
letter if the deplorable, unhealthy state of the premises, which has rendered them
unfit for human habitation, cannot be connected with an express or implied
breach of covenant by the landlord.

In the present case, the reason why the Hackney London Borough Council was
fined £500 and ordered to pay £1,400 compensation and over £2,000 costs was
because the family's flat was severely affected with condensation and associated
mould growth, which spread to the bedrooms. In *Quick v Taff-Ely BC* [1985] 3

a All ER 321 at 323, [1986] QB 809 at 815 Dillon LJ said that, because of fungus, mould growth and dampness, the tenant's council house was virtually unfit for human habitation in the winter when the condensation was at its worst. In *McNerny v Lambeth London Borough* (1988) 21 HLR 188 at 190 Dillon LJ observed that the scale of the dampness which had to be endured in that case led to constant colds and minor ailments being suffered by the plaintiff and her children b who had to live in those unhealthy conditions. In *Habinteg Housing Association v James* (1994) 27 HLR 299 a female tenant endured six years of misery caused by cockroaches, which Peter Gibson LJ (at 306) described as a quite appalling infestation for which she was in no way responsible. In none of these cases has the tenant or her family had any civil remedy for the injuries to their health or to their property which they have had to endure through living in unfit conditions.

c The reason for this apparent lacuna in the law was pointed out by this court 11 years ago in *Quick's* case. Parliament has not increased the relevant rental values relating to the implied covenant that the premises should be fit for human habitation since 1957, so that that implied covenant (which is now still to be found in s 8(1) of the Landlord and Tenant Act 1985) and the consequential value d to a tenant's family of s 4(1) of the 1972 Act are both completely dead letters. There remains, of course, in appropriate cases, the statutory implied covenant in s 11 of the 1985 Act, but this covenant is of no assistance to the tenant or to the tenant's family in the present class of case, which is not concerned with a failure to keep in repair the structure and exterior of the flat or the other items mentioned in that section. Unless and until Parliament is willing to revive, in new e tenancies at first, the covenant that premises of this type should be fit for human habitation, as the Law Commission has recommended in the report (Law Com No 238) it published in March 1996, people in the position of the present plaintiffs will remain wholly without remedy in the civil courts against their landlords, however grievously their health may have suffered because they are living in damp, unfit conditions.

f There is of course a limited remedy open to them because the courts have identified a power to make a compensation order if the statutory nuisance is still in existence or likely to recur at the time of the court hearing and the court imposes a fine. But in *Herbert v Lambeth London Borough* (1991) 24 HLR 299 at 304–305 Woolf LJ pointed out the limitations of this remedy, and it may be that the g effect of the recent decision of the Divisional Court in *R v Crown Court at Liverpool, ex p Cooke* [1996] 4 All ER 589 is to curtail this remedy still further. In that case Leggatt LJ, with whom Sir Iain Glidewell agreed, said (at 595):

h 'The power to make a compensation order under s 35 of the 1973 Act is, of course, not peculiar to statutory nuisance. So the power, and the monetary limit to which it is subject, were not themselves tailored to the requirements of statutory nuisance. It also seems unlikely that the legislature paid regard specifically to the period in respect of which compensation would be payable. By s 35 the court may make a compensation order "for any personal injury, loss or damage resulting from" the offence. The offence is of allowing j a statutory nuisance to exist at the complainants' premises at the date of the hearing. I see no warrant for construing s 82 (or s 35) so as to entitle the court to take account of the whole period for which the nuisance is alleged to have existed. That is not the subject of the complaint, which therefore gives no notice to the person responsible of the length of the period for which the nuisance is alleged to have existed.'

The present case throws up in vivid relief the injustice that may be caused because children whose health is damaged through living in damp, mouldy conditions have no right to claim compensation against local authority landlords for the injury they have suffered. But the courts must not try to provide a remedy by straining the law and misapplying legal principle.

In the *Habinteg* case (1994) 27 HLR 299 at 306 Staughton LJ started his brief judgment by saying that he was not satisfied that the dismissal of the tenant's claim was the right result which the law ought to reach and that the tenant ought to have some compensation for the misery she had suffered because of the cockroaches. He ended his judgment in these terms:

> 'It may be that the [1936] Act, or its successor, provides some means for securing that these matters are put right promptly, but it does not seem to have worked in this case. We are told that the Law Commission has been considering such a problem. It is to be hoped that they will recommend a solution. What is more, it is to be hoped that if they do, Parliament will carry it out. Judges and lawyers are sometimes reproached when the law does not produce the right result. There are occasions when the reproach should be directed elsewhere.'

This case demonstrates that recourse to the 1936 Act could bring about the abatement of a statutory nuisance eventually, and could ensure a modest award of compensation: Pt III of the Environmental Protection Act 1990 now provides the vehicle for these remedies. But it also demonstrates yet again that there continues to exist a class of case where a serious wrong continues to be without a remedy in the civil courts. Parliament has now had the Law Commission's report for over six months. The resolution of this injustice lies in decisions being taken about the allocation and distribution of public sector finance to the health service and to local government which are for ministers and Parliament and not for judges to take in our constitutional scheme of things.

For the reasons given by Nourse LJ, I agree that, although the Issa children have no other remedy in the civil courts, Miss Tagliavini's ingenious attempt to create a civil remedy out of Pt III of the 1936 Act, although in the finest traditions of the English Bar, is fundamentally unsound as a matter of legal principle, and that this appeal should be allowed.

Appeal allowed.

L I Zysman Esq   Barrister.

a # Re Oasis Merchandising Services Ltd (in liq)
Ward v Aitken and others

COURT OF APPEAL, CIVIL DIVISION

b PETER GIBSON, OTTON AND HUTCHISON LJJ

22, 23 JULY, 9 OCTOBER 1996

Maintenance of action – Champerty – Statutory exemption – Action by liquidator against directors for wrongful trading – Assignment of fruits of litigation to third party in return for funding of action – Damages recovered to be split between liquidator and
c *third party – Whether assignment of fruits of litigation within liquidator's statutory powers – Whether assignment within liquidator's power to sell any of company's property – Whether assignment within liquidator's power to do all such other things as may be necessary for winding up company's affairs and distributing its assets – Whether assignment unlawful as being champertous – Insolvency Act 1986, s 214,*
d *Sch 4, paras 6, 13.*

The liquidator of an insolvent company wished to bring a wrongful trading action against the directors under s 214[a] of the Insolvency Act 1986 seeking a contribution to the company's assets on the grounds that, as directors, they had permitted the company to continue trading when they knew or ought to have
e concluded that there was no reasonable prospect that it would avoid going into insolvent liquidation. Since the company had no assets and the creditors were unwilling to fund the action, the liquidator entered into an agreement with the sixth respondent (LWL), a company which provided specialist litigation support services for liquidators, whereby, in return for LWL financing the action, he sold
f and assigned to them all the fruits of the proposed action on the basis that LWL was to be reimbursed for its expenditure on the liquidation out of any moneys recovered and that the excess was to be divided in varying percentages for different tranches of excess, with the liquidator's percentage rising from 10% to a maximum of 50%. The agreement between the liquidator and LWL further provided that the action would be brought in the liquidator's name but under the
g direction of LWL. The liquidator obtained the consent of the liquidation committee and the Companies Court before entering into the agreement. On the directors' application, the action was stayed by the judge and the order of the Companies Court to enter into the agreement was set aside. LWL appealed, contending that although the agreement was admittedly champertous, it was
h nevertheless lawful because the sale of the fruits of the s 214 action fell within the liquidator's power under para 6 of Sch 4 to the 1986 Act 'to sell any of the company's property', or alternatively it fell within the liquidator's power under para 13 of Sch 4 'to do all such other things as may be necessary for winding up the company's affairs and distributing its assets'.

j **Held** – A liquidator of an insolvent company had no power under paras 6 and 13 of Sch 4 to the 1986 Act to enter into a champertous agreement to assign to a third party the fruits of litigation, brought by the liquidator under s 214 against the directors for wrongful trading, in return for the third party financing the s 214

---

a   Section 214, so far as material, is set out at p 1013 *a*, post

action. The 'property' referred to in para 6 of Sch 4 was confined to the property
of the company at the commencement of the litigation, and property
representing the same; it did not include property which only arose after the
liquidation of the company, which was recoverable only by the liquidator
pursuant to his statutory powers and which was then held by him on the
statutory trust for distribution. The fruits of the s 214 action clearly fell into the
latter category. Moreover, the power under para 13 of Sch 4 was limited to doing
what was necessary for winding up the company's affairs and distributing its
assets and it had not been shown that the agreement was necessary in that regard;
in any event, the power did not give statutory authority to do that which
otherwise was unlawful under the general law. The appeal would therefore be
dismissed (see p 1018 *d* to *f*, p 1019 *d* to *f* and p 1022 *d j* to p 1023 *d*, post).

Re M C Bacon Ltd (No 2) [1990] BCLC 607 and Re Ayala Holdings Ltd (No 2) [1996]
1 BCLC 467 applied.

Re Movitor Pty Ltd, Movitor Pty Ltd (rec and mgr app) (in liq) v Sims (1995) 19 ACSR
440 distinguished.

Per curiam. As a matter of policy there is much to be said for allowing a
liquidator to sell the fruits of an action provided that it does not give the
purchaser the right to influence the course of, or to interfere with the liquidator's
conduct of, the proceedings. The liquidator as an officer of the court exercising
a statutory power in pursuing the proceedings must be free to behave accordingly
(see p 1022 *f g*, post).

Re Movitor Pty Ltd, Movitor Pty Ltd (rec and mgr app) (in liq) v Sims (1995) 19 ACSR
440 considered.

Notes

For liquidator's powers exercisable without sanction and litigation by liquidator,
see 7(3) *Halsbury's Laws* (4th edn) (1996 reissue) paras 2337, 2341.

For maintenance and champerty in relation to assignment of fruits of litigation,
see 9 *Halsbury's Laws* (4th edn) paras 400–404, and for cases on the subject, see 8(2)
Digest (2nd reissue) 30, 127, *218–219, 1022*.

For the Insolvency Act 1986, s 214, Sch 4, paras 6, 13, see 4 *Halsbury's Statutes*
(4th edn) (1987 reissue) 868, 1056.

Cases referred to in judgment

Ayala Holdings Ltd, Re (No 2) [1996] 1 BCLC 467.
Ayerst (Inspector of Taxes) v C & K (Construction) Ltd [1975] 2 All ER 537, [1976] AC
167, [1975] 3 WLR 16, HL.
Bacon (M C) Ltd, Re (No 2) [1990] BCLC 607, sub nom *Re M C Bacon Ltd* [1991] Ch
127, [1990] 3 WLR 646.
Bang & Olufsen UK Ltd v Ton Systeme Ltd [1993] CA Transcript 834.
Camdex International Ltd v Bank of Zambia [1996] 3 All ER 431, [1996] 3 WLR 759,
CA.
Cyona Distributors Ltd, Re [1967] 1 All ER 281, [1967] Ch 889, [1967] 2 WLR 369,
CA.
Glegg v Bromley [1912] 3 KB 474, [1911–13] All ER Rep 1138, CA.
Grovewood Holdings plc v James Capel & Co Ltd [1994] 4 All ER 417, [1995] Ch 80,
[1995] 2 WLR 70.
Guy v Churchill (1888) 40 Ch D 481.

a *London and Overseas (Sugar) Co Ltd v Punjab National Bank* [1993] CA Transcript 1352; *affg sub nom Re Esal (Commodities) Ltd, London and Overseas (Sugar) Co Ltd v Punjab National Bank* [1993] BCLC 872.

Magor and St Mellons RDC v Newport Corp [1950] 2 All ER 1226, CA; *affd* [1951] 2 All ER 839, [1952] AC 189, HL.

b *Movitor Pty Ltd, Re, Movitor Pty Ltd (rec and mgr app) (in liq) v Sims* (1995) 19 ACSR 440, Aust Fed Ct.

Park Gate Waggon Works Co, Re (1881) 17 Ch D 234, CA.

Ramsey v Hartley [1977] 2 All ER 673, [1977] 1 WLR 686, CA.

Robbie (N W) & Co Ltd v Witney Warehouse Co Ltd [1963] 3 All ER 613, [1963] 1 WLR 1324, CA.

c *Seear v Lawson* (1880) 15 Ch D 426, CA.

Trendtex Trading Corp v Crédit Suisse [1981] 3 All ER 520, [1982] AC 679, [1981] 3 WLR 766, HL.

Yagerphone Ltd, Re [1935] Ch 392, [1935] All ER Rep 803.

d **Cases also cited or referred to in skeleton arguments**

Leitch (William C) Bros Ltd, Re [1932] 2 Ch 71, [1932] All ER Rep 892.

Leitch (William C) Bros Ltd, Re (No 2) [1933] 1 Ch 261, [1932] All ER Rep 897.

Norglen Ltd (in liq) v Reeds Rains Prudential Ltd, Mayhew-Lewis v Westminster Scaffolding Group plc, Levy v ABN AMRO Bank NV [1996] 1 All ER 945, [1996] 1
e WLR 864, CA.

Produce Marketing Consortium Ltd, Re (No 2) [1989] BCLC 520.

Weddell v J A Pearce & Major (a firm) [1987] 3 All ER 624, [1988] Ch 26, [1987] 3 WLR 592.

f **Appeal**

By notice dated 26 June 1995, the sixth respondent, London Wall Litigation Claims Ltd, appealed from the decision of Robert Walker J ([1995] 2 BCLC 493) on 7 June 1995 whereby he (i) stayed the proceedings under s 214 of the Insolvency Act 1986 instituted by Barry John Ward, the liquidator of Oasis Merchandising Services Ltd, against the first to fifth respondents, Timothy
g Aitken, Michael Scorey, Jonathan Aitken Kidd, Jonathan Aitken and John Hemingway, and (ii) withdrew the approval granted by Mr Registrar Pimm on 16 October 1991 for an agreement between the liquidator and the sixth respondent by which the latter was to finance and share with the liquidator the proceeds of actions taken by him under s 214. The liquidator, having also been granted leave
h to appeal by the judge, and having served a notice of appeal dated 27 June 1995, thereafter took no further part in the appeal proceedings. The facts are set out in the judgment of the court.

Robert Wright QC (instructed by *Ingledew Brown Bennison & Garrett*) for LWL.

j *Elspeth Talbot Rice* (instructed by *Jay Benning Levine & Peltz*) for the first and second respondents.

Robin Dicker (instructed by *Ashurst Morris Crisp*) for the fourth and fifth respondents.

Neither the liquidator nor the third respondent appeared.

Cur adv vult

9 October 1996. The following judgment of the court was delivered.

a

PETER GIBSON LJ. In English law maintenance (the giving of assistance or encouragement to a litigant by a person with no interest in the litigation nor any other motive recognised by the law as justifying his interference) and champerty (maintenance of a plaintiff bringing an action in consideration of a share in the fruits of the action) are no longer crimes or torts. But the abolition of such *b* criminal and tortious liability in 1967 has left unaffected any rule of law that a contract involving maintenance or champerty is to be treated as contrary to public policy or otherwise illegal (s 14(2) of the Criminal Law Act 1967). This appeal raises the question of the validity of a prima facie champertous agreement, entered into by a liquidator in purported exercise of a statutory power of sale, to *c* assign to a purchaser the fruits of an action brought by the liquidator in exercise of a statutory power conferred on him alone in respect of alleged wrongful trading by directors.

It is an appeal by the sixth respondent, London Wall Litigation Claims Ltd (LWL), with the leave of Robert Walker J from his order of 7 June 1995. By that *d* order the judge on the application of the first, second, fourth and fifth respondents stayed proceedings brought under s 214 of the Insolvency Act 1986 (the s 214 action) by the liquidator of Oasis Merchandising Services Ltd (the company) against the first to fifth respondents, who had at some stage been directors, or are alleged to have been shadow directors, of the company. Before instituting those proceedings the liquidator had on 18 November 1991 entered *e* into an agreement (the agreement) with LWL whereby LWL would fund the s 214 action. On 16 October 1991 the Companies Court gave the liquidator authority to enter into the agreement. The judge set aside the order of Mr Registrar Pimm giving that authority. The liquidator was given leave to appeal but after serving a notice of appeal he has taken no part in the hearing before this *f* court.

The company was incorporated in 1985. It traded in video and audio cassettes and associated products. It went into administrative receivership on 9 November 1987 and, being insolvent, was compulsorily wound up on 17 January 1988. The liquidator came to the conclusion that there was a prima facie case against the *g* first to fifth respondents for wrongful trading. On 12 October 1992 he commenced the s 214 action by issuing an originating application against those respondents, claiming relief under s 214. The s 214 action is being contested by them. It is unnecessary to say anything further about the issues in it. LWL on its own application was joined as the sixth respondent shortly before the hearing *h* before the judge.

Section 214 allows the liquidator of a company in the course of the winding up to bring proceedings against a person who is a present or former director (including a shadow director) of that company if it appears to the liquidator in the course of the winding up that sub-s (2) applies. It applies in relation to a person if *j* (i) the company has gone into insolvent liquidation, (ii) at some time before the commencement of the winding up that person knew or ought to have concluded that there was no reasonable prospect that the company would avoid going into insolvent liquidation, and (iii) that person was a director of the company at that time. The relief which may be granted is in this form:

a
'... the court, on the application of the liquidator, may declare that that person is to be liable to make such contribution (if any) to the company's assets as the court thinks proper.' (Section 214(1)).

Section 215(2), (3) and (4) provides that where the court makes a declaration under s 214(1) it may give certain further directions, including, where it makes a declaration in relation to a creditor, that any debt owed by the company to the *b* creditor and interest thereon be postponed.

The company had no assets which could be utilised to fund wrongful trading proceedings because on 12 September 1986 the company created a debenture in favour of Beaverbrook Investment plc, which as a secured creditor has been entitled to realise the entire assets of the company. Nor are the creditors of the *c* company, none of whom is owed more than £30,000, able or willing to fund such proceedings.

The liquidator obtained the consent of the liquidation committee as well as of the Companies Court before entering into the agreement five weeks after the commencement of proceedings. LWL is not a creditor of the company. Its main business is described in its accounts as 'the provision of specialist litigation *d* support service for liquidators'. The agreement recited that due to the statutory basis of the s 214 action it had to be brought by the liquidator in his name and not by the company, that the liquidator was unwilling to incur liability for the costs and expenses of pursuing the proceedings against the first to fifth respondents and that LWL had agreed to finance the proceedings. Recital (G) was in this form:

e
'The liquidator considers it desirable that he himself and/or [the company] by him should sell and assign to LWL all the "Fruits" of the Section 214 Action and (as provided in ... Clauses 2 and 3 below) his or [the company's] rights in respect of the Fruits of any other action or actions upon the terms hereof and in this Agreement or the Schedules hereto the said "Fruits" shall *f* mean any sum or sums of money (including any amount or amounts which shall have been received in respect of interest costs charges disbursements and expenses) received by the Liquidator as Plaintiff or as Liquidator of [the company] or by [the company] (i) under and by virtue of final judgment in or compromise or settlement of ... the Section 214 Action or (ii) in any way received from all or any of the [first to fifth respondents] (whether directly or *g* indirectly) or from any other defendant or defendants or from any third person or persons on their behalf in settlement of any such claim or claims against all or any of them and whether before or after any proceedings shall have been issued or commenced.'

h By cl 2 of the agreement:

'In consideration of the undertakings by LWL herein contained to the Liquidator [the company] acting by the Liquidator and the Liquidator himself in respect of his rights in respect of ... the Fruits of the Section 214 Action hereby sells and assigns to LWL absolutely all of the said rights of *j* himself and [the company] respectively: (i) in the Section 214 Action to be brought by the Liquidator on behalf of [the company] against the [first to fifth respondents] or any one or more of them ...'

That assignment was expressed to be an equitable assignment of the fruits.

By cl 4(a) the liquidator was to institute, carry on and prosecute the s 214 action and to do all such lawful acts and things as LWL might require for the purpose of

instituting carrying on and prosecuting the s 214 action. Clause 4(b) required him
to retain named solicitors to conduct the s 214 action. By cl 5 the liquidator was
to conduct the s 214 action and in particular any settlement negotiations in
accordance with the requirements and directions of LWL and in making such
requirements and directions LWL was to be entitled to have regard to its own
best interests as it should think fit. By cl 6 the liquidator was to compromise or
settle the action and take out of court any moneys which had been paid into court
as LWL advised and upon such terms as LWL considered fit. This clause was
subject to the following proviso:

'Provided further that notwithstanding the foregoing the Liquidator shall
be entitled to compromise settle or withdraw from [the s 214 action] and to
decline to commence any proceedings or to take any such monies out of
Court without the agreement of LWL if the Leading Counsel having the
conduct of the relevant case and approved or chosen by LWL shall have
advised that any such compromise settlement or withdrawal or taking of
monies out of Court should be made in the best interests of the Liquidator
and/or [the company] and before giving any such advice Counsel shall be
instructed to assume that [the company] has adequate financial resources of
its own with which to finance [the s 214 action] without recourse to LWL
and to ignore the financial effect of this Agreement.'

Clauses 7 and 8 contained detailed undertakings by LWL to finance litigation.
Much of the remainder of the agreement was concerned with the division
between the company and LWL of the fruits of the litigation. As the judge said
([1995] 2 BCLC 493 at 496):

'The general effects of these provisions ... is in substance for [LWL] to be
reimbursed for its expenditure on the litigation and ... for the excess to be
divided in varying percentages for different tranches of excess, with the
liquidator's percentage rising from 10% to a maximum of 50% on any excess
of £500,000. As a matter of form, however, this is expressed as additional
consideration for the purchase by [LWL] of all the fruits.'

By a further agreement dated 19 May 1992 the sole shareholder of LWL was to
pay £100,000 into a deposit account to be charged by the liquidator to secure any
order for costs which might be made in favour of the first to fifth respondents
against the liquidator.

The form of the agreement was no doubt governed by the fact that a claim
under s 214 is incapable of outright legal assignment because it can only be made
and pursued by a liquidator. It also reflects the natural desire of LWL to retain as
much control as possible over the litigation which it is to fund.

The basis of the application for a stay was that the agreement was champertous
and the s 214 action being funded by LWL thereunder was an abuse of process.
The judge described the issue before him as whether the agreement was, in
relation to the s 214 action, contrary to public policy on the ground of champerty
(at 496). He considered a number of authorities on trustees in bankruptcy and
liquidators assigning rights of action or rights in the fruits of an action and pointed
out that there are three routes by which one person may seek to dispose of, and
another person may seek to acquire, the prospect of benefiting from current or
future litigation against a third party (at 498). The first is the transfer of property
carrying with it the right to prosecute any cause of action closely related to that
property, such as the assignment of a debt. Such a transfer and any action

a brought by the transferee to enforce that right are not champertous (see, e g, *Camdex International Ltd v Bank of Zambia* [1996] 3 All ER 431, [1996] 3 WLR 759). The second is the assignment of a bare cause of action or bare right to litigate. Such assignments offend public policy (see, e g, *Trendtex Trading Corp v Crédit Suisse* [1981] 3 All ER 520, [1982] AC 679). The third is the assignment of the damages or other monetary compensation that may be awarded in an action in

b which judgment has not yet been given. Such an assignment, being an agreement to assign future property (damages if and when awarded), operates in equity and if supported by consideration will be valid and no question of unlawful maintenance or champerty will arise, at any rate when the assignee has no right to influence the course of the proceedings (see *Glegg v Bromley* [1912] 3 KB 474, [1911–13] All ER Rep 1138).

c   It was common ground before the judge, as it is before us, that the agreement is one for the assignment of the fruits of litigation, falling within the third category, rather than a transfer of property carrying a right of litigation or a legal or equitable assignment of a cause of action. It was not disputed by the liquidator or LWL that the agreement was champertous. But it was contended by them

d that the power conferred on the liquidator by para 6 of Sch 4 to the 1986 Act 'to sell any of the company's property' gave statutory authority to the sale of the fruits of the s 214 action and so made valid what otherwise would be void for champerty.

The first, second, fourth and fifth respondents contended that the fruits of a s 214 claim were not 'the company's property' within the meaning of para 6 of

e Sch 4, and that construction was upheld by the judge. He also said that this view was supported by the fact that proceedings under s 214 had a public or penal element and that in such litigation the court was entitled to expect to have the assistance of the liquidator, aware as he would be of his statutory responsibilities, and that even a partial loss of control by the liquidator of the litigation was

f objectionable. The judge accordingly granted a stay and of the court's own motion corrected the authority given by Mr Registrar Pimm to the liquidator to enter into the agreement.

LWL now appeals. Mr Robert Wright QC on its behalf again accepts that the agreement is champertous, but submits that there are two strands of public policy involved. One is the rule which prohibits an outsider with no commercial

g interest in the litigation, apart from obtaining a share of the proceeds, from financing the litigation for that share. The other is the rule that a liquidator should be able to obtain financial assistance under agreements which would otherwise be champertous to enable moneys to be recovered for the benefit of creditors. He submits that the agreement is lawful because it was a sale of the

h company's property within para 6 of Sch 4. Alternatively, he submits that the agreement is lawful because entering it was an act necessary for winding up the company's affairs and distributing its assets and so it was an act which the liquidator had power to undertake under para 13 of Sch 4.

There is a long line of authorities to the effect that where a trustee in

j bankruptcy or a liquidator wishes to exercise a power of sale to assign a cause of action for valuable consideration, the trustee or liquidator can enter into an agreement which otherwise would be void for maintenance or champerty. Thus in *Seear v Lawson* (1880) 15 Ch D 426 this court held that a trustee in bankruptcy could make an outright assignment of a cause of action against the grantee of property conveyed by the bankrupt. As Jessel MR said (at 433):

'The proper office of a trustee is to realize the property for the sake of
distributing the proceeds among the creditors. Why should we hold as a
matter of policy that it is necessary for him to sue in his own name? He may
have no funds, or he may be disinclined to run the risk of having to pay costs,
or he may consider it undesirable to delay the winding-up of the bankruptcy
till the end of the litigation. Considering these things, it seems to me to be à
priori probable that he would be entitled to sell it, but I prefer to rest my
decision upon the plain words of the statute.'

He held that a chose in action vested in the bankrupt before his bankruptcy fell
within the words 'all the property' of the bankrupt which the trustee was
empowered to sell.

In *Re Park Gate Waggon Works Co* (1881) 17 Ch D 234 a liquidator was similarly
held by this court to be entitled to assign outright a cause of action against a
director for misfeasance. In *Guy v Churchill* (1888) 40 Ch D 481 Chitty J considered
an assignment by a trustee in bankruptcy of a chose in action on terms that the
trustee and the assignee would share the fruits of the litigation. He said (at 488):

'The policy of the statute seems to be to give power to the trustee ... to
make arrangements in reference to *choses in action* which are considered
beneficial to the creditors. It would be a strange and inconsistent result to
say that although the right of action may be sold out and out it cannot be
disposed of on the terms that some part of the fruit of the action if successful
shall come back to the bankrupt's estate for division among his creditors.'

That decision was applied by this court in *Ramsey v Hartley* [1977] 2 All ER 673,
[1977] 1 WLR 686, where it was held that the statutory power of sale could be
exercised by a trustee in bankruptcy assigning to the bankrupt himself a chose in
action in return for a share of the fruits of the litigation.

Similarly in *Bang & Olufsen UK Ltd v Ton Systeme Ltd* [1993] CA Transcript 834
this court held that a liquidator can assign a cause of action in return for a share
of the fruits of the action, there being no valid distinction on this point between
the law of bankruptcy and the insolvent company legislation.

In *Grovewood Holdings plc v James Capel & Co Ltd* [1994] 4 All ER 417 at 422,
[1995] Ch 80 at 86 Lightman J aptly summarised the state of the law in this way:

'Accordingly, the authorities establish beyond question that both a trustee
in bankruptcy and a liquidator are given power to sell a cause of action on
terms that the assignees by way of consideration will pay over a share of the
recoveries. This statutory power necessarily precludes any challenge on
grounds of maintenance or champerty to such an agreement.'

Grovewood was a case where the sale by a liquidator to an outsider, who was to
fund an action in negligence against the company's stockbroker and adviser, was
not of the cause of action but of a beneficial interest in the fruits of the action.
Lightman J held that such a transaction was a 'sale' of the company's property
within para 6 of Sch 4. It is not suggested in this court that an assignment for
valuable consideration such as was effected by the agreement was not a sale for
the purposes of para 6. Lightman J went on to hold that para 6 conferred no
exemption from the law of champerty on a sale of fruits of litigation (as opposed
to the sale of a bare cause of action) when the sale included provision for the
purchaser to finance the litigation, and that accordingly the proceedings were
champertous and an abuse of process and would be stayed.

a   In the present case, Robert Walker J in obiter comments said that he had considerable difficulty with that part of Lightman J's judgment on which the *Grovewood* case was decided. Mr Dicker for the fourth and fifth respondents disclaimed any reliance on this part of Lightman J's judgment and accordingly we have heard no argument on the point. We will confine ourselves to saying that we see considerable force in Robert Walker J's comments and that we, in

b   particular, agree with him when he says that it is a question of construing the statutory power of sale ([1995] 2 BCLC 493 at 504). That seems to us to be the primary question in the present case.

It is to be noted at the outset that the present case is dissimilar to all the other cases to which we have referred, none of those cases relating to the assignment of the fruits of litigation when an essential part of the cause of action (viz that it

c   should appear to the liquidator in the course of the winding up that s 214(2) applied) did not arise until after the liquidation or bankruptcy commenced.

The starting point must be para 6, allowing, as it does, the liquidator to sell 'any of the company's property'. The reference to the property of the company imports the extended meaning given to 'property' by s 436, viz:

d   '"property" includes money, goods, things in action, land and every description of property wherever situated and also obligations and every description of interest, whether present or future or vested or contingent, arising out of, or incidental to, property ...'

e   Under the provisions relating to the insolvency of individuals, a bankrupt's estate is defined in a way that recognises that there is a distinction between, on the one hand, property belonging to or vested in the bankrupt at the commencement of the bankruptcy and, on the other hand, property which by virtue of a provision of the 1986 Act is comprised in that estate or treated as falling within such property belonging to or vested in the bankrupt at the

f   commencement of the bankruptcy (s 283(1) of the 1986 Act). By s 307 of the 1986 Act the trustee may by notice claim for the bankrupt's estate any property which has been acquired by or has devolved upon the bankrupt since the commencement of the bankruptcy, and by s 351 references to property comprised in the bankrupt's estate include any property which would be such property if a notice in respect of it were given under s 307. By para 9 of Sch 5 the

g   trustee in bankruptcy has power to sell any part of the property for the time being comprised in the bankrupt's estate.

In contrast, the provisions relating to company insolvency do not define the property of a company which liquidators can sell (save to the extent, already noted, that 'property' is given an extended meaning in s 436). By s 143 the

h   liquidator's functions in a compulsory winding up are to secure that the assets of the company are got in, realised and distributed. He is required to take into his custody or under his control 'all the property and things in action' to which the company is or appears to be entitled (s 144(1)), but in addition to and quite separately from that duty the liquidator is given certain powers to apply to the

j   court, and if the application is successful there will be an increase in the distributable assets, even though the company as such was never entitled to make that application. The statutory provisions do not expressly state that such after-acquired assets are 'the property of the company'.

The effect of the commencement of the liquidation of a company is that all assets then held by the company become subject to a statutory trust for unsecured creditors and, if there is a surplus, for contributories (see *Ayerst*

(Inspector of Taxes) v C & K (Construction) Ltd [1975] 2 All ER 537, [1976] AC 167). A secured creditor and his security fall outside the statutory trust to the extent that the creditor relies on his security. However he can value or realise the security and prove for the balance as an unsecured creditor or he can surrender his security and prove for the whole debt as an unsecured creditor.

The phrase 'the property of the company' is to be found not only in para 6 of Sch 4, but also in provisions relating to the powers of an administrator or administrative receiver, each of whom has the like power to sell 'the property of the company' (para 2 of Sch 1). That must have the same meaning as in para 6 of Sch 4. It would be very surprising if an administrator or an administrative receiver (who could continue to act after a liquidator was appointed) was empowered to sell the fruits of a future action under s 213 or s 214 by the liquidator. If such fruits fall within 'the property of a company', it is hard to see why they are not caught by a debenture holder's fixed and floating charge over all present and future assets of a company. But Mr Wright does not contend for such a result.

Considerations such as these lead us to consider whether a distinction should not be drawn between assets which are the property of the company at the time of the commencement of the liquidation (and the property representing the same), including rights of action which arose and might have been pursued by the company itself prior to the liquidation, and assets which only arise after the liquidation of the company and are recoverable only by the liquidator pursuant to statutory powers conferred on him. The scheme of the 1986 Act suggests that only the former falls within 'the property of the company' which an administrator or administrative receiver or liquidator can sell. Thus a right of action against directors for misfeasance which the liquidator (amongst others) can enforce under s 212 of the 1986 Act and the fruits of such an action are property of the company capable of being charged by a debenture, because the right of action arose and was available to the company prior to the winding up. But with this can be contrasted the right of action by a liquidator, and the fruits of such an action, for fraudulent preference or fraudulent or wrongful trading, which are not the property of the company and are not caught by a debenture (see Gough *Company Charges* (2nd edn, 1996) pp 122–123).

Such a distinction is supported by a number of authorities. First, in *Re Yagerphone Ltd* [1935] Ch 392, [1935] All ER Rep 803 Bennett J held that a debenture charging all the present and future assets of a company did not cover money recovered by the liquidators from fraudulently preferred creditors, because it never became part of the general assets of the company, but when received by the liquidators was impressed in their hands with a trust for those creditors amongst whom they had to distribute the assets of the company. Russell LJ in *N W Robbie & Co Ltd v Witney Warehouse Co Ltd* [1963] 3 All ER 613 at 622, [1963] 1 WLR 1324 at 1334 explained the decision in this way: 'a statutory right in and only in the liquidator to make such a [fraudulent preference] claim could never have been property of the company subject to the charge.'

In *Re M C Bacon Ltd (No 2)* [1990] BCLC 607, [1991] Ch 127 Millett J was concerned with the question whether costs of certain proceedings instituted by the liquidator were expenses in realising or getting in the assets of the company and, as such, entitled to priority under r 4.218(1)(a) of the Insolvency Rules 1986, SI 1986/1925. The proceedings were (1) to challenge the validity of a future charge as a voidable preference and (2) to make the bank liable under s 214. Millett J in answering the question in the negative referred to each of the limbs of a the proceedings and said that the proceedings were not brought by or on behalf of the company nor were they brought in order to recover assets belonging to the company at the date of the winding up. He pointed out that neither claim could have been made by the company itself (see [1990] BCLC 607 at 611, [1991] Ch 127 at 136). After referring with approval to the *Yagerphone* case, he said that a claim to set aside a voidable preference was not a claim to realise or get in any asset of

b the company. He continued ([1990] BCLC 607 at 613, [1991] Ch 127 at 138):

'In my judgment, the same reasoning applies with even greater force to a claim brought under s 214 of the 1986 Act, which can be brought only by a liquidator not an administrator and in the absence of an insolvent liquidation cannot be brought at all. In any case, I do not see how an application for such

c an order under the section can properly be described as an attempt to realise or get in an asset of the company. This must, in my view, mean an existing asset and, until the order has been made and complied with, there is no such asset.'

d Mr Wright accepts that Millett J correctly recognised that a claim under s 214 is not an asset of the company, but submits that the decision does not affect the question whether the proceeds of a claim under s 214 are included in 'the property of the company' for the purposes of para 6 of Sch 4. Robert Walker J ([1995] 2 BCLC 493 at 501) thought that the reasoning of Millett J was general in its application and followed it. We respectfully agree, supporting as it does the

e distinction which we would draw between the property of the company at the commencement of the litigation (and property representing the same) and property which is subsequently acquired by the liquidator through the exercise of rights conferred on him alone by statute and which is to be held on the statutory trust for distribution by the liquidator.

f A similar distinction is drawn in *Re Ayala Holdings Ltd (No 2)* [1996] 1 BCLC 467. In that case Knox J was concerned with the effectiveness of an assignment by the liquidator to a creditor of all rights to and choses in action relating to or in any way arising out of or in connection with an action against a secured creditor. The rights purportedly assigned included the right to assert that certain dispositions of the company's property after the commencement of the winding up were void

g under s 127 of the 1986 Act and that certain charges on the company's property were void under s 395 of the Companies Act 1985 as against the liquidator for non-registration. The assignee argued that the assigned rights were property of the company which a liquidator can sell under para 6 of Sch 4. Knox J posed the question: what does para 6 mean when it uses the expression 'property of the

h company'? He continued (at 480–481):

'In my judgment [the assignee's] argument overlooks one important distinction between property of the company, on the one hand, and the rights and powers of a liquidator, on the other. The property of a company includes rights of action against third parties vested in a company at the

j commencement of the winding up and to that extent the principles in *Ramsey v Hartley* undoubtedly apply and such rights can, as I see it, be sold by a liquidator pursuant to para 6 of Sch 4. What is to be distinguished in my view are the statutory privileges and liberties conferred upon liquidators as such and indeed upon trustees in bankruptcy who are officers of the court and act under the court's direction.'

Knox J went on to cite two passages from Millett J's judgment in the *M C Bacon* case and continued (at 483):

> 'Those passages, in my view, underline the fundamental distinction between assets of a company and rights conferred upon a liquidator in relation to the conduct of the liquidation. The former are assignable by sale under para 6 of Sch 4, the latter are not because they are an incident of the office of liquidator. This conclusion is, in my view, supported by the special status of the liquidator in company law.'

Mr Wright points out that the *Ayala Holdings* case was concerned with the question whether a liquidator can abdicate his duties by assignment and that s 214 was not in issue. But, as Robert Walker J observed (at 501), if a claim under s 127, which relates to the avoidance of any dispositions of 'the company's property' after the commencement of the winding up, and which therefore is likely to affect assets belonging to the company before the commencement of the winding up, cannot be assigned, Knox J's general distinction between the company's property and rights conferred upon the liquidator is even more strongly applicable to s 214.

It is also relevant to note the authorities on the predecessors to s 213 of the 1986 Act relating to fraudulent trading, though it should be borne in mind that the relief that could be granted under s 75 of the Companies Act 1928, s 275 of the Companies Act 1929 and s 332 of the Companies Act 1948 on the application of the official receiver, liquidator, a creditor or a contributory was a declaration that the guilty party should be personally responsible for all or any of the debts or other liabilities of the company as the court might direct. Under s 213, like s 214, the court may declare on the application of the liquidator alone that any guilty party is liable to make such contributions to the assets of the company as the court thinks proper. The effect of the earlier fraudulent trading provisions was that recoveries ordered to be made in respect of fraudulent trading were to swell the assets of the company to be distributed in accordance with the statutory scheme (see *Re Esal (Commodities) Ltd, London and Overseas (Sugar) Co Ltd v Punjab National Bank* [1993] BCLC 872; *affd* [1993] CA Transcript 1352, in which obiter dicta to the contrary of Lord Denning MR and Danckwerts LJ in *Re Cyona Distributors Ltd* [1967] 1 All ER 281, [1967] Ch 889 were disapproved). In *Re Esal (Commodities) Ltd* [1993] BCLC 872 at 883 Lindsay J said that he saw sums recovered under s 332 of the 1948 Act in a way corresponding to that whereby the recoveries of a liquidator from a fraudulent preference were held by Bennett J in the *Yagerphone* case [1935] Ch 392, [1935] All ER Rep 803 to be impressed with a trust for those creditors to whom distributions were to be made in the liquidation. In our judgment, the wording of s 213 even more clearly requires the same result, only the liquidator now being able to bring fraudulent trading proceedings and the recoveries being contributions to the assets of the company held on the statutory trust.

Mr Wright placed heavy reliance on a recent decision in the Australian Federal Court, *Re Movitor Pty Ltd, Movitor Pty Ltd (rec and mgr app) (in liq) v Sims* (1995) 19 ACSR 440. In that case the liquidator of a company sought directions from the court as to whether he could enter into a funding arrangement (involving both maintenance and champerty) with an insurer in respect of proposed proceedings by the liquidator against former directors of the company for insolvent trading. Drummond J held that the liquidator could do so in exercise of a statutory power to sell all or any part of 'the property of the company' in aid of performing his duty of realising the company assets. He said (at 444–445):

'The provision by strangers to the litigation of funds to insolvency administrators for the purpose of enabling them to pursue worthwhile claims on behalf of the entity under administration when, without that assistance, good claims might not be able to be prosecuted, will often serve a good public purpose. The policy of the legislature ... will frequently be frustrated because the insolvency administrator will often not have access to the financial resources necessary to pursue, for the benefit of the administration, claims which have reasonable prospects of success.'

After considering various authorities, to many of which we have already referred, he said that to do that which Parliament has authorised, either expressly or by necessary implication, cannot involve the doing of anything that is unlawful. He continued (at 449):

'Whether he sells a bare right of action or the fruits of the action, the only authority a liquidator has to make any such sale is this statutory power. It has long been accepted that a trustee in bankruptcy can lawfully sell a bare right of action owned by the insolvent to a stranger with no interest in it, although that would involve maintenance or champerty, but for the fact that he sells under the statutory authority. A liquidator has the same power. In my opinion, there is no reason why this statutory authority should not make lawful any other sale of the insolvent company's property by a liquidator, including the sale of a share in the proceeds of an action belonging to the company to a person with no interest in the litigation on terms that that person is to have control of the litigation, although that would involve champerty but for the transaction being made under that authority. This will be the position, provided only that the subject matter of the sale is "property of the company" within the statutory power.'

He referred to Millett J's remarks in *Re M C Bacon Ltd (No 2)* [1990] BCLC 607 at 613, [1991] Ch 127 at 138, which we have already cited, and continued (at 450):

'But given the difference between the insolvent trading provisions of s 214 of the English legislation and those of ss. 588M and 588W of the Corporations Law, this decision provides no authority, in my opinion, for contending that the property of the company does not include the expected fruits of an action brought under ss. 588M or under 588W. The right of the liquidator to recover damages created by each of these sections is described as a right to recover from the director and the holding company an amount equal to the loss or damage suffered as a result of the company's insolvent trading in which the director and the holding company were implicated "as a debt due to the company". That 'debt' arises once the conditions of liability have been fulfilled, something that must occur prior to commencement of any action for recovery under either section. Such a "debt" can properly be regarded as part of the property of the company which the liquidator is empowered to sell. Even if the rights to compensation created by ss. 588M and 588W are not regarded as true debts but rights sui generis, *Magor and St Mellons Rural District Council v Newport Corp* ([1950] 2 All ER 1226 at 1230–1231) is authority for holding that they are still well capable of falling within the definition of "property of a company" in the relevant provisions of the Corporations Law.'

We see the force of the policy argument expounded by Drummond J, but the
actual decision is, in our judgment, readily distinguishable. Indeed that judge *a*
himself distinguished what Millett J said on s 214 because that provision was
different from the Australian provisions. Both s 588M and s 588W of the
Corporations Law allowed the liquidator to recover 'as a debt due to the
company' an amount equal to the loss or damage resulting from insolvency. The
debt arose once the conditions of liability were fulfilled. That is not the language *b*
of s 214. We would add that we were referred by Mr Dicker to Gough *Company
Charges* (2nd edn, 1996) pp 122–123, in which the author, an Australian solicitor,
draws attention to the fact that in Australia recoveries made by the liquidator
under the Corporations Law for insolvent trading cannot form part of the assets
charged by a fixed and floating charge over all present and future assets of the
company and that there is a specific provision that moneys so recovered are not *c*
available to pay a secured debt of the company unless all the company's
unsecured debts have been paid in full. For completeness, we should say that the
Magor and St Mellons case, relating as it does to the question whether the right of
a council to a financial adjustment was property within the meaning of s 100 of
the Local Government Act 1888, does not appear to us to provide relevant *d*
assistance.

Like Robert Walker J we therefore conclude that, on its true construction, 'the
property of the company' in para 6 of Sch 4 does not include the fruits of litigation
brought by the liquidator under s 214. The judge also found that his conclusion
was strongly supported by the consideration that the liquidator pursuing an
application under s 213 or s 214 was not conducting ordinary civil litigation but *e*
litigation with a public or penal element and any loss of control by the liquidator
of that litigation was objectionable. For our part, we regard that as relevant not
to the question whether the fruits of such litigation are 'property of the company'
within para 6 of Sch 4 but to the propriety of the liquidator's act in entering into
the agreement and the correctness of the Companies Court in authorising that *f*
act. As a matter of policy we think that there is much to be said for allowing a
liquidator to sell the fruits of an action for the reasons given by Drummond J,
provided that it does not give the purchaser the right to influence the course of,
or to interfere with the liquidator's conduct of, the proceedings. The liquidator
as an officer of the court exercising a statutory power in pursuing the proceedings
must be free to behave accordingly. We are far from happy with the right of *g*
interference given by LWL by the agreement, which, as it now stands, does
enable LWL to dictate how the liquidator is to conduct the action (see, in
particular, cl 5). Indeed, despite Mr Wright's argument to the contrary, it seems
to us to enable LWL to prevent the liquidator from exercising his statutory power
under s 168(3) of the 1986 Act to apply to the court for directions in relation to *h*
this litigation, though we should record Mr Wright's offer on behalf of LWL that
the agreement should take effect as if the liquidator retained that power. The
proviso to cl 6 on which Mr Wright placed reliance is by its terms limited in its
application. It is to be noted that the rights of the insurer under the funding
agreement in the *Movitor* case were considerably less than those of LWL under
the agreement. *j*

Mr Wright relied in the alternative on the power contained in para 13 of Sch 4
enabling the liquidator 'to do all such other things as may be necessary for
winding up the company's affairs and distributing its assets'. We are not
persuaded that that power is wide enough to cover the present circumstances. It
is limited to what is *necessary* for winding up the company's affairs and

a   distributing its assets. Let us assume, without deciding, that where a liquidator considers it desirable to exercise a power to apply to the court for relief under s 214, that is for winding up the company's affairs. The liquidator's statement in his affidavit of 11 July 1991, viz that unless he was able to conclude the agreement and thereby fund the action the wrongful trading proceedings could not be brought, must now be viewed against the fact that the liquidator has negotiated

b   a contingency agreement with a large and highly reputable firm of solicitors for the pursuit of his claims, as appears from a letter dated 30 April 1996 from those solicitors to the solicitors of the fourth and fifth respondents. Whilst that would appear not to cover all the expenses of the litigation, it does suggest that the liquidator no longer regards the agreement as the only way of funding the s 214 action.

c   But in any event, we cannot accept that general words such as are to be found in para 13 of Sch 4 (in contrast to the specific power of sale in para 6 of Sch 4) must be taken to give statutory authority to do that which otherwise is unlawful under the general law. In our judgment, that power does not give the liquidator carte blanche to do an illegal act such as entering a champertous agreement.

d   For these reasons which owe much to the judge's lucid judgment and to Mr Dicker's admirable argument, we would dismiss this appeal.

Appeal dismissed. Leave to appeal to the House of Lords refused.

Paul Magrath Esq   Barrister.

Practice Direction

a

SUPREME COURT TAXING OFFICE

Costs – Taxation – Practice – Bill of costs – Fees payable

b

The Supreme Court Fees (Amendment) Order 1996, SI 1996/3191, increased the fees payable on taxation with effect from 15 January 1997. The main changes are: (i) On the lodging of a bill of costs for taxation: £3·75 for every £100, or part of £100, of the full amount of the bill as lodged. (ii) On a Solicitors Act 1974 taxation where a bill for taxation is lodged by the client (or party chargeable) the lodgment fee is limited to £50 unless the taxing officer orders that the full amount of the fee *c* be payable (there is no discretion to order anything in between). It should be noted that in solicitor and own client taxations the fee is applicable to every bill lodged. If the application for taxation is by the solicitor the full lodgment fee is payable. (iii) On the taxation of a bill of costs: £7·50 for every £100 or part of £100, of the amount allowed less any amount paid on lodging the bill. *d* (iv) Where a bill lodged on or after 15 January 1997 is withdrawn no refund of any fee already paid will be made. (v) There is no longer any power to reduce or remit fees in cases of hardship, nor is there any power in the taxing officer to require payment of any part of the taxing fee in advance.

The Lord Chancellor's Department has stated:

e

'The taxing fee payable on bills of costs lodged prior to 15 January 1997 is calculated on the basis of the fee order in effect at the time of lodgment, i.e. the fee is calculated at 5p for every £1 or part thereof. A fee will still be payable if a bill lodged prior to 15 January is withdrawn prior to taxation.'

The practice of the Supreme Court Taxing Office in such cases will be to continue *f* to have regard to para 2.2 of the practice direction (No 2 of 1992) (see [1993] 1 All ER 263 at 268, [1993] 1 WLR 12 at 17).

Calderbank offers

Parties need to be aware that a lodgment fee will have been paid when *g* proceedings for taxation were commenced. Therefore in making *Calderbank* offers (see *Calderbank v Calderbank* [1975] 3 All ER 333, [1976] Fam 93) the offer should be clear as to whether and to what extent any taxing fee is included. Similar remarks apply to interest and value added tax.

h

P T Hurst
3 February 1997   Chief Master.

End of Volume 1